International Journal on Advances in Intelligent Systems

2016 vol. 9 nr. 3&4

Printed from e-media with permission by:

Curran Associates, Inc.
57 Morehouse Lane
Red Hook, NY 12571

Some format issues inherent in the e-media version may also appear in this print version.

Printed by Curran Associates, Inc. (2018)

International Academy, Research, and Industry Association (IARIA)
412 Derby Way
Wilmington, DE 19810

Phone: (408) 893-6407
Fax: (408) 527-6351

petre@iaria.org

Additional copies of this publication are available from:

Curran Associates, Inc.
57 Morehouse Lane
Red Hook, NY 12571 USA
Phone: 845-758-0400
Fax: 845-758-2633
Email: curran@proceedings.com
Web: www.proceedings.com

The *International Journal on Advances in Intelligent Systems* is Published by IARIA.
ISSN: 1942-2679
journals site: http://www.iariajournals.org
contact: petre@iaria.org

Sponsored by IARIA
www.iaria.org

International Journal on Advances in Intelligent Systems
Volume 9, Number 3 & 4, 2016

International Journal on Advances in Intelligent Systems
Volume 9, Numbers 3 & 4, 2016

CONTENTS

Online Social Networking Software as Ad-Hoc Project Management Software in Capstone Project Courses

Brian Thoms
Computer Science and Information Technology
California State University, Channel Islands
Camarillo, CA, USA
brian.thoms@csuci.edu

Evren Eryilmaz
Information & Technology Management
Bloomsburg University
Bloomsburg, PA, USA
eeryilma@bloomu.edu

Abstract— **In this paper, we explore the use of online social networking (OSN) software as ad-hoc project management (PM) software. Through the adaptation of specialized OSN software, project teams can facilitate group collaboration as they work towards completing project milestones. This study aims to showcase the importance of sustained engagement throughout the lifecycle of the project, across both meta-level engagement with the external community and micro-level engagement within and among the project team members. More specifically, this work identifies how OSN technologies cultivate online community which can be shown to augment project motivation and participation resulting in project success. Under the lens of an existing theoretical model, one which highlights individual collaboration within online community spaces, we measure perceptions of the customized OSN software before and after its implementation. A content analysis highlights how successful project teams maximized features of the system, which is supported by a social network analysis (SNA), which highlights levels of individual engagement across the project lifecycle as they relate to online interaction and project results. Survey data identifies individual perceptions across various aspects of the system as it fosters social interaction and build online community, represented in terms of social capital.**

Keywords*- Social Networking Analysis; Computer Supported Collaborative Work; Collaborative Writing; Project Management; Capstone Project.*

I. Introduction

This research builds atop preliminary research highlighting how online social networking (OSN) software can facilitate success in project teams [1]. More specifically, this study measures the adoption of OSN software across information technology (IT) capstone courses.

When the New Year rang in on January 1, 2016 the estimated human population on earth was around 7.45 billion [2]. Of this population, 324 million currently live in the U.S., where it is estimated that 87% of the population have access to the Internet and 73% are using social technologies to collaborate and communicate online [3]. For digital natives, or individuals having grown up with internet technologies, it is estimated that 86% of digital natives participate in some form of OSN, with some estimates as high as 98% [4] [5] [6] [7].

Within academic environments, OSN software has found tremendous success, as grade schools, high-schools and colleges incorporate various types of social media into the classroom. In [8], Thoms et al. introduced a shift in modality away from traditional learning management systems, or LMS, towards more student-centric OSN software to support classroom activities. In this paradigm, OSN software provides users with a common set of tools that focus on course engagement through higher levels of peer-to-peer interactions. This research was extended in [9] to show how OSN software can yield greater levels of interaction and overall course satisfaction when compared against LMS software.

This research suggests that OSN software is uniquely suited to facilitate capstone courses, by providing an environment that supports intra-group, or project team communication via wiki and messaging and inter-group, or course communication including blogs and discussion boards. Grounded in theories of constructivism, engagement and social presence, the software design was measured using a content analysis, social network analysis (SNA) and survey data. Results showcase the beneficial nature of OSN software as a means for fostering project-level activities as individuals work towards the completion of their final IT artifact. In the process, OSN software also fosters engagement and interaction.

The rest of this paper is structured as follows. In Section II we introduce background for project-based communities of practice and identify the role capstone courses play in higher education. Section III establishes a theoretical framework that considers constructivism, engagement theory and social presence theory as integral components of OSN software used within the academic space. Section IV focuses on the OSN system design. Section V highlights the research methodology. Section VI details the results across two interventions. Section VII provides a comprehensive discussion and analysis of the results section. Section VIII identifies the limitations of this study. Section IX presents the conclusion followed by references in Section X.

II. Background

A. *Project-based Communities of Practice*

As identified in [10], college courses can be classified as niche communities of practice, which facilitate, among other things, shared understanding and identify among participants. In more successful communities of practice, sustained engagement and collaboration exist whereby knowledge-building becomes an intrinsic function of the community itself [11]. Although not all college courses mirror these ideals, capstone project courses strive to.

B. Capstone Courses

This paper focuses primarily on capstone project courses, which are typically milestone courses for college students and required for graduation. A popular mechanism adopted by many colleges and universities is requiring students to complete a year-long or semester-long capstone project in their junior or senior year of study in hopes of better preparing these students for similar activities they would encounter in the workforce. More so, as identified in [12], capstone courses aim to provide students with little, to no industry exposure, with a valuable experience prior to completing their degree.

Capstone project-based courses are also highly regarded and recommended as a core component of effective undergraduate education [13] [14]. Consequently, the inclusion of these projects into the undergraduate experience has been largely influenced by expectations from industry that graduates exhibit high-levels of problem solving, oral and written communication, teamwork and project management skills [15] [16]. These projects become especially important for students who are unable to attain industry experience prior to graduating, thus making project-based courses a bare minimum qualification for graduating students.

Often times, IT capstone courses are team-based, where groups of students work towards some end-goal. Where capstone projects are collaborative in nature, students are afforded greater opportunities to develop team-based skills and learn pivotal techniques in cooperation as individuals coordinate around a central IT artifact. Essentially, team-based projects help to prepare students to work effectively in teams [17]. The underlying mechanisms of team-based capstone projects in IT education and team-based projects in professional settings are similar because both methods involve expressing and discussing ideas in order to construct mutually acceptable explanations. Lainez et al. [18] suggest that capstone projects deliver skills that consider various business processes, product development, artifact design, implementation and also involve teamwork and problem solving. Problem solving, as identified further in Ayas and Zeniuk [19] can be instrumental in building healthy communities of practitioners.

Students value these experiences as well and capstone projects offer students a chance to begin developing a working portfolio prior to graduation. Dunlap [20] discovered that engaging students in learning and problem-solving activities reflects the true nature and requirements of workplace communities and help students feel better prepared to work effectively in their profession; a viewpoint supported by students as well [15]. Furthermore, Clarke [21] identified that industry-aligned projects increased student confidence and allowed students to explore areas of the IT field not covered in the academic curriculum.

Ultimately, within IT capstone courses, students are presented with opportunities to consolidate their understandings of "systems analysis, software development lifecycles, specific software design support tools, entity relationship modelling, entity life histories, database design, web site design, or web server programming" [22]. Furthermore, when students engage in experiential learning, they become active participants in the learning process, constructing their own internal knowledge through both personal and environmental experiences [22, 23]. Lynch et al. [24] found that IT capstone projects provide students the opportunity to build, not only technical skills of the discipline, but the social aspects of systems development as well.

III. THEORY

Human computer interaction (HCI) is an interdisciplinary field that encompasses concepts from numerous fields including computer and behavioral science. The theoretical model adopted in this research is one first proposed [25] and extended in [7] [8] and considers three primary constructs for fostering interaction within collaborative environments. The first construct focuses attention on the individual and their perceptions of their role within the project space. The second construct is engagement theory, which represents how individuals work collaboratively within the project space. A third construct, social presence theory, represents the project space as a thriving community.

A. Constructivism

Constructivism grounds a community to the individual and considers the interactions and experiences of the individual as crucial components of cooperation and goal achievement [26] [27]. Such interactions and experiences also consider a participant's engagement with certain technologies. Largely linked to the work of Piaget [28], who first theorized that learning can be based on the interaction and experiences of the learner within a specific context, constructivism provides a holistic view of individual learning and how individuals interact within larger groups. Additionally, Squires [29] states that constructivism focuses on individual control, with individuals making decisions that match their own needs. Thus, within a project space, individuals should be able to control how they interact with other team members and in a manner they feel most comfortable. Using the simplistic functionality of social software, instead of more complex PM software, individuals are provided with more flexibility and control.

B. Engagement Theory

In many capstone projects, teamwork is required, which requires communication and cooperation. Engagement theory states that individuals must be meaningfully engaged in project activities through interaction with others, which can be facilitated and enabled through specialized software [30]. Project software is not known for their exciting and group-oriented features, but OSN software is. OSN software provides environments that embrace interaction. Therefore by leveraging the popularity of OSN software, we hope to create an environment that promotes dialogue among team members.

Dalsgaard [31], whose research is supported in Waycott et al. [32] argues that social software can be used to support the constructivist approach set forth in the previous section. Social software engenders a cooperative approach to learning, where individuals work towards establishing a cohesive unit. In this respect, social software can refer to any loosely connected application where individuals are able to communicate with one another, and track discussions across the internet [33]. Consequently, the development of OSN software must consider the individual's point of view in such a manner that they are presented with a certain level of control and autonomy within the larger community. Once again, social software supports these philosophies and makes participants the locus of control within a larger self-governing environment.

C. *Social Presence Theory*

We introduce Social Presence Theory to understand the manifestation of our OSN as a dynamic and vibrant collaborative project space. Social Presence Theory considers the degree to which an individual's perception of the online community, affects his or her participation in the community [34] [35]. When individuals believe that others are interacting and exchanging information, individuals may be more inclined to engage themselves or not. As discussed in Garrison et al. [36], alternative methods for enhancing social presence must be explored to help substitute for the lack of visual cues individuals receive in face-to-face settings. Research by Richardson and Swan [37] identified that a student's perceived level of social presence directly relates to their perceived learning. From the lens of social presence theory, we consider students' ideas as knowledge objects that are improved continually through collaboration by discussing inconsistencies and resolving doubts [38]. In fact, the essence of social presence is that collaboration can promote conscious development of cohesive ideas that no single individual could have developed alone. Thus, pedagogically, we can view students as active constructors of knowledge who capitalize on each other's reasoning to gradually refine ambiguous, figurative, and partial understandings of important concepts. This suggests that increasing levels of community can yield higher levels of learning. OSN technologies work well in this regard and have successfully helped enhance social presence through peer feedback [39] and individual profiles and avatars [40], both of which are implemented within the OSN designs we investigated. Additionally, Thoms et al. [41] discovered that OSN technologies can foster higher levels of course learning through openness and collaboration and can align very well with course learning objectives.

Together, these three theories provide a holistic model that considers course community, individual learning styles and how each can be influenced and enhanced with technology.

IV. System Design

A. *Project Management Software*

The field of project management (PM) is quite mature and with this maturity comes a seasoned array of PM software to support project-based activities. Intrinsically, PM software looks to provide project teams with the ability to manage project activities including scheduling and planning. Scheduling typically refers to resource management and accounting and planning typically centers on organizing different phases of the project. Wikipedia alone compares over 300 PM platforms, from desktop platforms such as Microsoft Project to web-based platforms such as Basecamp.

While PM software may be a necessity for large-scale projects, for small-scale and short-term projects, sophisticated and complex PM software can be time-consuming. Additionally, adopting and learning to use PM software can be a daunting feat for nascent users, especially when the duration of a project is less than a year. Therefore, this study introduces OSN software as ad-hoc PM software; one supported by underlying theories that mirror students' underlying learning experiences.

B. *OSN Software as PM Software*

Prior to Web 2.0 and the explosion of social software, Preece [42] highlighted the difficulty that social software designers have in controlling interaction. To date, OSN designers still struggle to develop software that is both easy to use and useful. In this research, we extend existing OSN software, Elgg v1.8.2, which has already shown success in supporting our theoretical constructs [7] [8] [25] [51]. Elgg was founded in 2004 and is an open source OSN engine offering individuals and organizations with many of the components required to implement an online social environment.

Elgg provides an extensible platform for constructing a project-based OSN due to its large number of developer plugins. Identifying planning and scheduling as important criteria for project management Elgg provides support for the following features:

- Individual profiles to allow users to customize their online profile.
- Communities and community profiles for unique and isolated project spaces.
- Instant Messenger for real-time communication when team members are working synchronously but in remote locations.
- Group and individual blogs for sharing information and providing project updates.
- Wikis for collaborative writing and documentation.
- Calendars and notifications to create events and reminders for project milestones.
- File uploads with version control to support project documentation.
- Discussion boards for asynchronous conversational threads on project topics and activities.

Figure 1 highlights the community home page, or what a project team sees upon logging in. Although the homepage can be customized with specific modules, by default, users are presented with active content from across the site, which can be filtered by user or date.

Figure I. OLC Landing Page

C. Collaborative Writing Software

A significant artifact within a project-based OSN centers on the analysis and design of project objectives. As a shared artifact, collaborative writing software functions as a mechanism to support information sharing and group knowledge construction. A specific subset of collaborative writing, wiki software utilizes Internet-based technologies to facilitate the collaborative writing process by keeping track of page creation and page edits. Wikis provide unique opportunities for obtaining and managing user-driven content and are also effective for facilitating virtual collaboration and tracking the evolution of user-driven content, which aids in coordination and synchronization of group information. Wikis also provide for a shared dialogue and centralize information among project collaborators. Additionally, wikis allow members to engage in group learning and share in knowledge construction within a virtual community [43]. These notions are important for project teams working towards shared goals and shared meaning.

When wiki technology was first introduced, prior to the Web 2.0 explosion, collaborative writing was limited to early HTML-style markup [44]. Current wiki-technologies provide collaborators with a wide range of tools and share commonalities with other OSN software [45]. Illustrated in Figure 3, today's wikis are no longer syntax-based, with difficult HTML-style markup notation. Today's wikis incorporate rich-text editors, allowing even novice web users to contribute, a notion that is particularly important for student users, many of whom have limited experience constructing wikis. Recent research by Xu [46] implemented wiki-technology in project-based computer science courses, highlighting how wiki technology helped to centralize and capture all project activities through wiki pages created by both the instructor and students. Additionally, Popescu [47] discovered that wikis also helped students to find interesting information; by reading other teams' wiki pages, students could check their progress, see how they compare with others teams, look for inspiration and models and discover different ideas and approaches. A limitation identified in He and Yang [48] is that a wiki should not be a tool that aims to supplant communication channels and works best when additional modes exist. This limitation is accounted for in our OSN since the wiki comprises only one component.

D. Project-based Wiki

Figure 2 illustrates a read-only version of the wiki. In this view, users can present their project charter to the larger community.

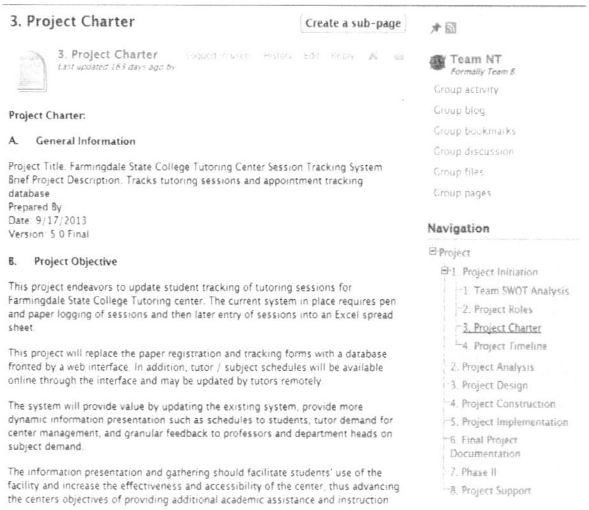

Figure II. OLC Wiki Page

Figure 3 illustrates wiki in edit-mode, which allows users access to edit the wiki page in a what-you-see-is-what-you-get (WYSIWYG) editor and also control who has access to the edit or view the wiki. In this view, editors can create content, link to existing content and control who has access to edit or view a document.

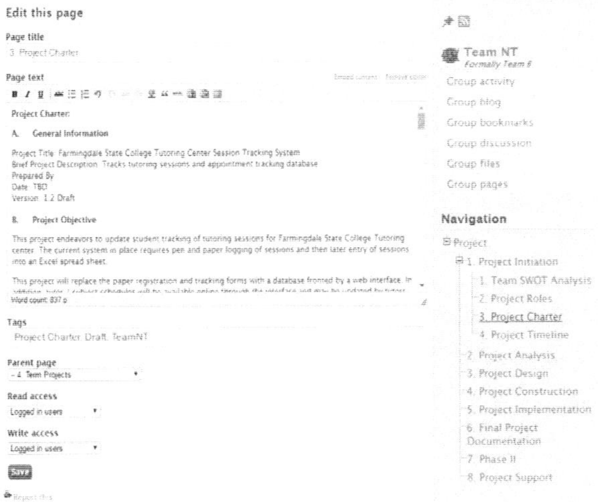

Figure III. OLC Wiki Page

V. RESEARCH METHODOLOGY

This research aims to measure the proposed design and is best categorized as a proof-of-concept case study. Our population of users consisted of 11 teams across two IT capstone courses. To measure how OSN software can be used as ad-hoc PM software, we measure how well the software facilitated team collaboration, peer-to-peer interaction, learning and course community. Each team worked together over a seventeen-week period and each team's goal was to construct a fully-functional IT artifact by the seventeenth week. The IT artifact comprised 40% of the project grade. Project documentation and weekly collaborative assignments constituted 30% and a course-wide discussion board also constituted 30%.

Project teams were comprised of three to four students and were formulated by the instructor prior to the start of the course. Due to a late-semester change, one project team consisted of two members.

In addition to the course-wide community, each team was assigned a designated OSN community, which consisted of file repository, blog and wiki space, with pre-defined templates for each of the project development phases. At the end of the semester, all teams were expected to present their final artifact to the class.

It was highly suggested that project teams utilize the wiki templates, as outlined by the instructor, but it was not required. As illustrated in Figure 3, predefined templates were constructed for each community space and included pages for: 1) Project Initiation, 2) Project Analysis, 3) Project 4) Design, 5) Project Construction, 6) Project Implementation, 7) Final Project Documentation, 8) Phase II and 9) Project Support. Students participating in the capstone course would already have taken a course on formal software methods and be familiar with the systems development lifecycle. The wiki aimed to realize knowledge acquired in this course.

Data was captured from each capstone course, over a period of six months.

VI. RESULTS

To explore how specialized OSN software can support project-based courses and enhance classroom learning, we collected data from multiple sources. Our first point of data collection is through survey research, which measures perceived levels of learning, community and interaction. To support survey findings, we perform a social network analysis and look at in-bound and out-bound interactions among OSN participants.

A. *Population & Demographics*

Demographic information was captured through pretest surveys conducted across two classes. Including the instructor, the total user population was 45. 15% of participants were female and 85% were male. 52% of participants were aged 18 to 25, 34% were aged 26 to 35, 12% were aged 36-50 and 2% were aged 50 and above. All participants were members of the IT capstone course, an upper-division course required for graduation.

B. *Content Generation*

Detailed in Table 1 is a breakdown of wiki contributions between Group 1 and Group 2. Group 1 consisted of 22 students, of which 16 played an active role in editing the project wiki resulting in 401 page edits across 114 unique pages. Group 2 consisted of 18 students, of which 16 played an active role in editing the project wiki resulting in 222 page edits across 108 unique pages.

TABLE I. WIKI CONTENT GENERATION

Metric / Results	Grp. 1	Grp. 2	Diff (%)
No. of Students	22	18	20%
Total Editors	16	16	-
Total Pages Created	114	108	5%
Total Pages Edited	401	222	58%
Average Page Edit	3.5	2.1	50%

C. *Survey Data Analysis*

Closed-ended pretest and posttest surveys were distributed to all participants resulting in 42 completed pretests and 35 completed posttest surveys. To ensure confidentiality, no personally identifiable information was collected.

1) *Perceptions on Interaction*

Cronbach Alpha scores for our survey constructs related to items associated with the OSN scored .83 indicating that survey items maintain an adequate level of internal consistency.

Detailed in Table 2 are factors relating to overall perceptions on interaction and collaboration. In pretest results 88% of individuals agreed or strongly agreed that high levels of interaction would be important. These numbers increased to 94% in posttest results. Additionally, 88% of individuals agreed or strongly agreed that learning through group collaboration would be important with 95% agreeing or strongly agreeing that exchanging feedback with others would be important. In posttest results, these numbers were 92% and 91% respectively. Regarding sense of community, 86% agreed or strongly agreed in pretest responses, while 85% agreed or strongly agreed in posttest responses.

2) OSN Perceptions on OSN

Detailed in Table 3 are factors relating to overall perceptions on interaction and collaboration. In pretest results 86% of individuals agreed or strongly agreed that interaction through an OSN would be important. These numbers decreased to 83% in posttest results. Additionally, 81% of individuals agreed or strongly agreed that an OSN would increase interaction. In posttest results, these numbers decreased to 77% for this item. Regarding learning, 71% agreed or strongly agreed that an OSN could support learning, while 68% agreed or strongly agreed in posttest responses. Regarding the OSNs ability to support community, 86% agreed or strongly agreed in pretest results, while 77% agreed or strongly agreed during posttest results.

3) Wiki Perceptions on Interaction

Detailed in Table 4 are constructs relating to the wiki and interaction. In pretest results 83% of individuals agreed or strongly agreed that they were interested in using the wiki, while posttest results found 77% of individuals agreeing with this statement. 81% of individuals agreed or strongly agreed that the wiki facilitated group cohesion with 81% also agreeing that it supported collaboration. These numbers were 83% and 83% in posttest responses. Regarding interaction, 77% agreed or strongly agreed that the wiki supported interaction, while 74% agreed or strongly agreed in posttest responses.

TABLE II. SURVEY RESPONSES (INTERACTION)

Survey Item	SA	A	N	D	SD	AVG	STDEV
(pre) High levels of interaction seem important.	50%	38%	7%	2%	2%	4.31	0.90
(post) High levels of interaction were important.	63%	31%	3%	3%	-	4.54	0.70
(pre) Learning through collaboration seems important.	38%	50%	7%	2%	2%	4.19	0.86
(post) Learning through collaboration was important.	63%	29%	3%	3%	35	4.46	0.92
(pre) Exchanging feedback seems important.	50%	45%	-	2%	2%	4.38	0.82
(post) Exchanging feedback was important.	57%	34%	6%	-	3%	4.43	0.85
(pre) A sense of community seems important.	43%	43%	10	2%	2%	4.21	0.90
(post) A sense of community was important.	54%	31%	11	-	3%	4.34	0.91

TABLE III. SURVEY RESPONSES (OSN DESIGN)

Survey Item	SA	A	N	D	SD	AVG	STDEV
(pre) Interaction through an OSN seems important.	36%	50%	7%	2%	5%	4.10	0.98
(post) Interaction through an OSN was important.	49%	34%	11%	6%	-	4.26	0.89
(pre) OSN will increase interaction.	43%	38%	12%	2%	5%	4.12	1.04
(post) OSN increased interaction.	37%	40%	14%	6%	3%	4.03	1.01
(pre) OSN will increase learning.	31%	40%	19%	5%	5%	3.88	1.06
(post) OSN increased learning.	37%	31%	23%	6%	3%	3.94	1.06

TABLE IV. SURVEY RESPONSES (WIKI AS A TECHNOLOGY)

Survey Item	SA	A	N	D	SD	AVG	STDEV
(pre) I am interested in using a wiki in this course.	34%	49%	12%	2%	2%	4.10	0.89
(post) I was interested in using a wiki in this course.	31%	46%	20%	3%	-	4.06	0.80
(pre) A Wiki will facilitate group cohesion.	33%	48%	12%	2%	5%	4.02	1.00
(post) A Wiki facilitated group cohesion.	29%	54%	14%	3%	-		0.74
(pre) A wiki will facilitate group collaboration.	32%	49%	12%	2%	5%	4.00	1.00
(post) A wiki facilitated group collaboration.	34%	49%	14%	-	3%	4.11	0.87
(pre) A wiki will facilitate group interaction.	33%	43%	17%	5%	2%	4.00	0.96
(post) A wiki facilitated group interaction.	31%	43%	20%	3%	3%	3.97	0.95

TABLE V. SURVEY RESPONSES (WIKI AS AD-HOC PROJECT MANAGEMENT SOFTWARE)

Survey Item	SA	A	N	D	SD	AVG	STDEV
(pre) A wiki will help facilitate project management.	33%	50%	12%	2%	2%	4.10	0.88
(post) A wiki facilitated project management.	37%	49%	11%	3%	-	4.20	0.76
(pre) A wiki will help organize project information.	40%	43%	13%	3%	3%	4.15	0.92
(post) A wiki organized project information.	37%	54%	9%	-	-	4.29	0.62
(pre) A wiki will facilitate content creation.	29%	50%	14%	2%	5%	3.95	0.99
(post) A wiki facilitated content creation.	34%	51%	14%	-	-	4.20	0.68
(pre) A wiki for project portfolios is an excellent idea.	39%	41%	15%	2%	2%	4.12	0.93
(post) A wiki for project portfolios was an excellent idea.	37%	49%	14%	-	-	4.23	0.69

4) Wiki Perceptions on Project Management

Detailed in Table 5 are factors relating to the wikis ability to facilitate project management. In pretest results 83% of individuals agreed or strongly agreed that a wiki could help facilitate project management. Levels of agreement rose to 86% in posttest responses. Similarly, pretest results show that 83% of individuals agreed or strongly agreed that a wiki could help organize project information, which rose to 91% in posttest responses. Additionally, 79% of individuals agreed or strongly agreed that the wiki would foster content creation and posttest results showed that 85% of individuals agreed or strongly agreed. Finally, 80% of individuals agreed or strongly agreed that the wiki would be an excellent way to showcase the capstone project. Levels of agreement rose to 86% in posttest results.

D. *Social Network Analysis (SNA)*

1) SNA Background

Social network analysis (SNA) is used to identify and measure interactions within an associated social structure. More specifically, an SNA utilizes numerous statistical measures for analyzing activity within a social structure and often times results in a visualized graph of the network as shown in Figure 4 and Figure 5. The ability to view social graph structure and community evolution can be a crucial measure of a learning design and can serve as an early indicator of its success [49].

2) SNA Design

In this study, SNA graphs were constructed in Microsoft Excel, with the 2014 NodeXL Template extension. NodeXL is a free and open source extension, which provides a range of basic network analysis and visualization features [50]. Using NodeXL, Figure 4 and Figure 5 were constructed using the Fruchterman-Reingold algorithm, which positions team members, or nodes, in a manner so that all edges are of more or less equal length and there are as few crossing edges as possible. Arrows, represent weighted interactions and larger arrows indicate a greater number of interactions between members. Bi-directional arrows occur when there is interactivity between students, measured in-degree and out-degree values. A higher average value for in-degree and out-degree indicates that those students more frequently interacted with one another.

3) OSN Sociograms

Illustrated in Figure 4 and Figure 5 are sociograms for two capstone courses utilizing the OSN software for PM-activities. Discussed in more detail in the Discussion, team members are identified by their group letter and group project grade. For example, B3(95) represents the third member of Group B and their final project grade was 95 out of 100.

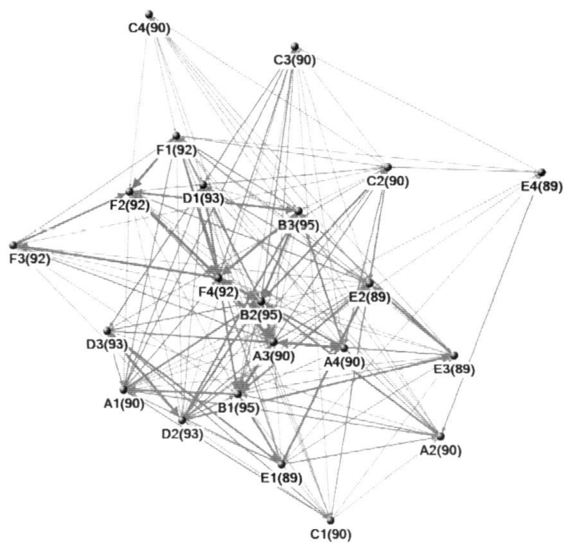

Figure IV. Group 1 Sociogram

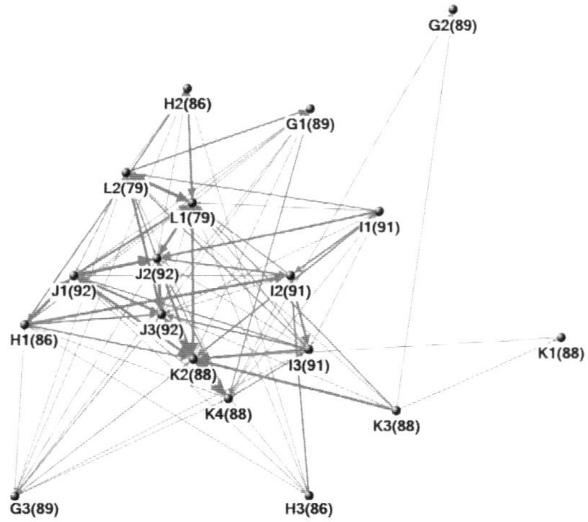

Figure V. Group 2 Sociogram

1) SNA Metrics

Identified in Table 6 are the SNA metrics calculated for Group 1 and Group 2. Overall, Group 1 experienced higher levels of overall interaction with 416 interactions compared to Group 2, which experienced modest levels of interaction with 189 interactions. The number of unique edges, which represents unique interactions between any two students was 115 for Group 1 and 60 for Group 2.

TABLE VI. SNA METRICS

Metric / Results	**Group 1**	**Group 2**	**Class Diff (%)**
Vertices	22	18	20%
Edges	416	189	75%
Unique Edges	115	60	63%
Min Degree	2	0	200%
Max Degree	15	12	22%
Avg. In-Degree	9.1	5.9	43%
Avg. Out-Degree	9.1	5.9	43%
Avg. Betweenness Centrality	7.81	9.2	16%
Density	.43	.35	21%
Avg. Grade	92	88	4.4%

Average in-degree and out-degree refers to the average number of interactions pointing in and out of a single node. For Group 1, average in-degree / out-degree was 9.1 with a standard deviation of 3.29 for in-degree and 1.93 for out-degree. For Group 2, average in-degree / out-degree was 5.9 with a standard deviation of 3.91 for in-degree and 2.68 for out-degree.

Betweenness centrality is an indicator of a node's centrality in a network and is calculated using the number of shortest paths from all vertices to all others that pass through a node. For Group 1, average betweenness centrality was 7.81 with a standard deviation of 5.16. For Group 2, betweenness centrality was 9.2 with a standard deviation of 8.77. Density, which is the count of the number of connections divided by the total number of possible connections, was .43 for Group 1 and .35 for Group 2. Finally, the average final group grade was 92 for Group 1 and 88 for Group 2.

VII. DISCUSSION

The overarching goals of this study is to present OSN software as a viable option for capstone courses, one that allows users to participate in course-level and team-level activities. To explore these claims, OSN software was introduced to two IT capstone courses, where we measured its ability to foster peer-to-peer interactions and support project success.

A. *OSN Promotes Teamwork*

An important role of the OSN was to facilitate the workflow of project teams. To measure this, we consider a couple of factors. First, we focus attention on survey responses relating to the wiki's ability to enhance group cohesion, collaboration and interaction. Pretest results showed a majority of individuals believed that the wiki could facilitate cohesion (82%), collaboration (82%) and interaction (75%). More so, however, it was very encouraging to discover high levels of agreement in the posttest that the wiki actually contributed to higher levels of cohesion (78%), collaboration (83%) and interaction (74%). Engagement theory is concerned with meaningful engagement. This amounts to finding the right tools for the right projects. Wiki software is geared towards collaboration and interaction where individuals bear witness to the evolution of a project's analysis and design. Wiki software also reinforces the notion that projects can be both user-centric and group-oriented, thus facilitating individual ownership and motivation.

Referring back to the sociograms in Figure 4 and Figure 5, the proximity of nodes reflects that these nodes interacted with one another more frequently. In other words, the closer a set of nodes are to one another, the more cohesive that group of nodes are as a single unit. In dynamic environments, bonds tend to strengthen as a network becomes denser. As one would expect within capstone projects, where students are working collaboratively towards project milestones, the network graph will likely organize in a manner where project members are relatively close to one another. In Figures 4 and Figure 5, this is the case, with the exception of a couple peripheral nodes (i.e. C1 and G2). This outcome would be expected in any organizational network where individuals, while functioning as part of the larger community, are still responsible for working within their own respective project teams in order to accomplish project milestones. Taken together, the quantitative results at hand indicate that students utilized the OSN to set achievable project goals, resolve misunderstandings about design decisions, and negotiate deliverables, similar to the way team-based IT projects function in the real world. In this way, collaborating students used one another as a resource for learning, while also working to complete their project milestones.

B. OSN and Wiki as Support for Project Success

An objective of this study was to investigate the role of OSN software in promoting project success. An important measure of project success stems from a group's ability to establish the parameters of success through analysis of business requirements and the design and construction of the IT artifact. Through an analysis of survey responses and grading of each team's final IT artifact, it was evident that the OSN helped contribute, in part, to each team's project success. In pretest survey responses, it was encouraging to discover that the majority of individuals believed that the OSN wiki would facilitate project management (83%), project information organization (85%) and content generation (83%). More so, it was encouraging to discover higher levels of agreement in posttest responses, where individuals perceived that the OSN wiki did, in fact, contribute to higher levels of project management (86%), project information organization (91%) and content creation (85%). Each of these factors is an important dimension of project management that promotes a shared understanding of technical requirements, which helps to mitigate expensive and time consuming rework. This concept can apply to both short-term and long-term real-world IT projects.

We acknowledge that survey results paint a limited picture, which is why we also dive into the interactions that took place across the OSN. Average project grades indicate a stronger performance by teams within Group 1 (92%) compared to teams within Group 2 (88%). We attribute this, in part, to the patterns of interaction that took place within the OSN and the levels of social capital that existed across both networks. More dense and active networks, such as with Group 1, tend to result in more communication and collaboration, which, in turn, can contribute to higher quality output. This is discussed in more detail in the next section.

C. OSN Software Builds Social Capital

Within IT capstone courses, and academic courses in general, OSN software provides opportunities for greater levels of social capital. Simply defined, social capital is the common social resource that facilitates information exchange, knowledge sharing, and knowledge construction through continuous interaction [51]. Social Presence Theory, which focuses on the degree to which an individual's perception of the online community, in its entirety, affects his or her participation in that community.

Analyzing the levels of community in Group 1 and Group 2, our first point of measurement refocuses attention back to the survey responses and, specifically, those constructs relating to the OSN software's ability to enhance interaction and community. Pretest results were encouraging and showed that individuals were positive from the start that community would be important (86%) and that an OSN could be an important resource for facilitating this community (86%). These perceptions continued throughout the lifecycle of the intervention and posttest results showed high levels of agreement that a sense of community did play an important role (85%) and that the OSN was an important factor for facilitating interaction (86%). Similarly, pretest results indicated that high levels of interaction would be important (88%) and that exchanging feedback with their peers would be important (95%). Again, posttest results supported these perceptions, revealing high levels of agreement across these constructs (94% and 91% respectively). The fact that the OSN is an open environment allowed team members to review the progress of their classmates and pose questions and receive responses in an open dialogue was likely a large contributor to these results. In environments where identity and affiliation play a role in shared outcomes, tools that support sharing and encourage interaction can enhance overall levels of trust and contribute positively to these shared goals [52].

A secondary factor for analyzing community support brings attention back to Figure 4 and Figure 5, which represent the peer-to-peer interactions within the OSN. The sociograms clearly identify Group 1 as a more tight-knit group that Group 2. While Group 1 consisted of 20% more students, an important indicator for social capital can be determined by network density. Group 1 maintained a density factor of .43, which means that around 43% of all individuals communicated with one another on a regular basis. Group 2, on the other hand, had a density of .35, or roughly 21% lower than Group 1. Within a smaller group, one might expect a greater level of activity among all nodes, but this was not the case. To make sense of this, it is important to reflect back on the notion that social capital considers individual's perception that the community is an active and vibrant space. Fewer interactions result in lower levels of perception across constructs related to these factors. Consequently, in the end, a lack of connectivity among participants resulted in a lower quality product as discussed in the previous section.

D. OSN as Support in Technical Learning

One final consideration should be discussed and centers on the introduction of OSN software within an academic setting and specifically for the purposes of learning and collaboration. While the merits of an OSN as a mechanism for project success and/or enhancing levels of academic community are debatable, the introduction of specialized social software, such as those integrated within an OSN, into team capstone courses provides a number of tangible and intangible benefits not measured completely in this research.

Social software is pervasive across today's dynamic business environments. Therefore students should be exposed to their applications outside of peer-networks such as Facebook and Snapchat and prior to their entering the workforce. Capstone courses are often a final course prior to graduating making them an optimal platform for their introduction. As a matter of consequence, establishing an online community of practice where students can engage in information sharing and knowledge construction through online social networking technologies introduced in this study, students may be better prepared for similar types of communication and interaction when they enter the IT workforce. Additionally, although we focus on academic communities in this study, research has found numerous similarities between computer supported learning and working teams that make knowledge gained in one setting applicable to another setting, making this research applicable to other domains [54].

VIII. Limitations and Next Steps

It is important to acknowledge the limitations in this research. One limitation considers grouping pretest and posttest results from Group 1 and Group 2. Rather than present the results per class, it was decided that a high-level view of student perceptions would provide better insight to the capabilities of an OSN as a tool to foster project management. A more in-depth analysis of Group 1 and Group 2, which focuses specifically on the differences between each course, may also prove interesting. Additionally, a primary goal of this research has been to showcase OSN software as a proof-of-concept for enhancing collaboration among project-based teams, which we believe was successful across a number of dimensions. As such, we currently do not compare our results against capstone students utilizing more formal PM software, nor do we compare LMS software as a viable option for PM software. Both limitations present opportunities for future research in this space.

IX. Conclusion

In this paper, we investigate the adoption of OSN software as a system for managing IT capstone projects. OSN software provides unique affordances across ad-hoc, short-term project teams and provides individuals with a user-centric environment capable of managing the project lifecycle, while also facilitating high-level discourse with the larger course community. Through the analysis of survey data and supported through a social network analysis, our findings show the powerful and positive impact OSN software has on supporting project success by facilitating peer-to-peer interaction and enhancing levels of collaboration.

X. References

[1] B. Thoms, E. Eryilmaz, "Online Learning Community Software to Support Success in Project Teams," *The Fifth International Conference on Advanced Collaborative Networks, Systems and Applications*, Oct. 2015.

[2] Worldometers, "World Population Meter," Retrieved online at http://www.worldometers.info/world-population/ on September 15, 2016.

[3] Internet Live Stats, "Internet Users By Country," Retrieved online at http://www.internetlivestats.com/internet-users-by-country/ on February 01, 2016.

[4] StatisticBrain, "Social networking statistics," Retrieved July 29, 2013, from: www.statisticbrain.com/social-networking-statistics.

[5] J. Jenks, "The digital world of millennials," *eMarketer*.

[6] D. Williamson, "Social network marketing: ad spending and usage, social network marketing," *eMarketer*. Retrieved June 02, 2008, from http://www.emarketer.com/Report.aspx?code=emarketer_2000478.

[7] D. Oblinger and D. Oblinger, "Is it age or IT: first steps toward understanding the Net Generation," *EDUCAUSE*, 2005.

[8] B. Thoms, N. Garrett and T. Ryan, "Online learning communities in the New 'U'. *Intl. Journal of Networking and Virtual Organisations*, 6(5), 2009.

[9] B. Thoms and E. Eryilmaz, "How media choice affects learner interactions in distance learning classes," *Computers & Education*, v75, 2014.

[10] J. Lave and E. Wenger, *Situated Learning: Legitimate Peripheral Participation*. Cambridge University Press, 1991.

[11] EC Adams and C. Freeman, "Communities of practice: bridging technology and knowledge," *Journal of Knowledge Management*, 4(1), pp. 38-44, 2000.

[12] K. Lynch, A. Goold and J. Blain, "Students' pedagogical preferences in the delivery of IT capstone courses," *Issues in Informing Science and Information Technology*, 1, 431-442, 2004.

[13] M. Shaw and JE Tomayko, "Models for undergraduate project courses in software engineering." In *Lecture Notes in Computer Science*, 536(1), 1991, pp 33-71.

[14] S. Fincher, M. Petre and M. Clark, *Computer science project work: principles and pragmatics*. London: Springer-Verlag, 2001.

[15] K. Gruenther, R. Bailey, J. Wilson, C. Plucker and H. Hashmi, "The influence of prior industry experience and multidisciplinary teamwork on student design learning in a capstone design course," *Design Studies*, v30(6), 2009, pp. 721-736.

[16] A. Goold and P. Horan, "Foundation software engineering practices for capstone projects and beyond," *Proceedings. 15th Conference on Software Engineering Education and Training*, 2002, pp.140-146.

[17] H. Topi, JS Valacich, RT Wright, K Kaiser, JF Nunamaker Jr, JC Sipior and GJ de Vreede, "IS 2010: Curriculum Guidelines for Undergraduate Degree Programs in Information Systems," *Communications of the Association for Information Systems* (26:1), 2010, pp. 359-428.

[18] M. Lainez, Y. Deville, A. Dessy, C. Dejemeppe, J. Mairy and S. Van Cauwelaert, "A project-based introduction to agile software development." In L. Alves, P. Ribeiro, and R. Machado, *Project-Based Learning: An Environment to Prepare IT Students for an Industry Career*. IGI Global, 2014, pp. 230-249.

[19] K. Ayas and N. Zeniuk, "Project-based learning: building communities of reflective practitioners," *Management Learning*, 32(1), 2001.

[20] JC Dunlap, "Problem-based learning and self-efficacy: how a capstone course prepares students for a profession," *Educational Technology Research and Development*, 53(1), 2005, pp. 65-85

[21] N. Clarke, "Evaluating student teams developing unique industry projects." *Proceedings of the 7th Australian Conference on Computing Education* (ACE2005), 2005, pp. 21-30, Newcastle, Australia.

[22] I. Newman, M. Daniels and X. Faulkner, "Open ended group projects: a 'tool' for more effective teaching." *Proceedings of the Fifth Australasian Conference on Computing Education*, Adelaide, Australia, 2003, pp. 95-103.

[23] D. Kolb, *Experiential learning - experience as the source of learning and development*. New York: Prentice Hall, 1984.

[24] K. Lynch, A. Heinze and E. Scott, "Information technology team projects in higher education: an international viewpoint," *Journal of Information Technology Education*, 6, 2007, pp. 181-198.

[25] B. Thoms, N. Garrett, M. Soffer and T. Ryan, "Resurrecting graduate conversation through an online learning community," *IADIS Multi Conference on Computer Science and Information Systems*, Lisbon, Portugal, 2007.

[26] C. Johnson, "A survey of current research on online communities of practice," *Internet and Higher Education*, 4(1), 2001, pp. 45-60.

[27] R. Palloff and K. Pratt, *Building learning communities in cyberspace: effective strategies for the online classroom*, San Francisco, California: Jossey-Bass, 1999.

[28] J. Piaget, *The Origins of Intelligence in Children*, New York, NY: Intl. University Press, 1952.

[29] D. Squires, "Educational software and learning: subversive use and volatile design," *Proceedings of the 32nd Annual Hawaii international Conference on System Sciences*, IEEE, 1999.

[30] G. Kearsley and B. Schneiderman, "Engagement theory: a framework for technology-based learning and teaching," Retrieved June 26, 2013, from http://home.sprynet.com/~gkearsley/engage.htm

[31] C. Dalsgaard, "Social software: e-learning beyond learning management systems," Retrieved June 26, 2013, from http://www.eurodl.org/materials/contrib/2006/Christian_Dalsgaard.htm

[32] J. Waycott, J., Sheard, C. Thompson and R. Clerehan, "Making students' work visible on the social web: a blessing or a curse?," *Computers & Education*, 68(1), 2013, pp. 86-95.

[33] M. Teeper, The rise of social software. *netWorker*, 7(1), 2003, pp. 18–23.

[34] C. Tu and M. McIsaac, "The relationship of social presence and interaction in online classes," *The American Journal of Distance Education*, 16(1), 2002.

[35] JA Short, E. Williams and B. Christie, *The Social Psychology of Telecommunications*. John Wiley & Sons, 1976.

[36] R. Garrison, T. Anderson and W. Archer, "Critical inquiry in a text-based environment: computer conferencing in higher education," *The Internet and Higher Education*, 2(3), 1999, pp. 87-105.

[37] JC Richardson and K. Swan, "Examining social presence in online courses in relation to student's perceived learning and satisfaction," *Journal of Asynchronous Learning Networks*, 7(1), 2003, pp. 68-88.

[38] L. Lipponen, K. Hakkarainen and S. Paavola, "Practices and Orientations of CSCL," In JW Strijbos, PA Kirschner and RL Martens, *What We Know About CSCL and Implementing It in Higher Education*. Springer Netherlands, 2004, pp. 31-50.

[39] A. Ma, "Computer supported collaborative learning and social creativity: a case study of fashion design," *Journal of Information, Information Technology, and Organizations*, 3(1), 2008, pp. 17-39.

[40] VN Vasileiou and F. Paraskeva, "Teaching role-playing instruction in Second Life: an exploratory study," *Journal of Information, Information Technology, and Organizations*, 5(1), 2010.

[41] B. Thoms, "A dynamic social feedback system to support learning and social interaction in higher education," *IEEE Transactions on Learning Technologies*, Issue: 99, 2011.

[42] J. Preece, "Sociability and usability in online communities: determining and measuring success," *Behavior and Information Technology*, 20(5), 2001, pp. 347-356.

[43] Elgg, "Elgg Statistics," Retrieved online from https://elgg.org/powering.php on February 01, 2016.

[44] B. Leuf and W. Cunningham, *The Wiki Way: Quick Collaboration on the Web*. Boston: Addison-Wesley Longman Publishing Co, 2001.

[45] M. Boulos, I. Maramba and S. Wheeler, "Wikis, blogs and podcasts: a new generation of web-based tools for virtual collaborative clinical practice and education," *BMC Medical Education*, 6(41), 2006, pp. 1472–1480.

[46] L. Xu, "Project the wiki way: using wiki for computer science course project management," *Journal of Computing Sciences in Colleges*, 22(6), 2007, pp. 109-116.

[47] E. Popescu, "Using wikis to support project-based learning: a case study," Proceedings of the 14th IEEE International *Conference on Advanced Learning Technologies*, Athens, Greece, 2014.

[48] W. He and L. Yang, "Is wiki a good tool facilitating team collaboration in undergraduate education?" *Proceedings of the 19th Pacific Asia Conference on Information Systems* (PACIS 2015), Marina Bay Sands, Singapore, 2015.

[49] L. Freeman, *The development of social network analysis*. Vancouver: Empirical Press, 2004.

[50] D. Hansen, B. Shneiderman and M. Smith, *Analyzing Social Media Networks with NodeXL: Insights from a Connected World*. Burlington: Morgan Kaufmann, 2011.

[51] B. Daniel, R. Schwier and G. McCalla, "Social capital in virtual learning communities and distributed communities of practice," *Canadian Journal of Learning and Technology*, 29(3), 2003, pp. 113–139.

[52] B. Thoms, N. Garrett N, JC Herrera and T. Ryan, "Understanding the Roles of Knowledge Sharing and Trust in Online Learning Communities," *Proceedings of the 41st Annual Hawaii International Conference on System Sciences*, January, 2008.

[53] A. Majchrzak, A. Malhotra and R. John, "Perceived individual collaboration know-how development through information technology–enabled contextualization: evidence from distributed teams," *Information Systems Research* 16(1), 2005, pp. 9-27.

[54] PA Kirschner and G. Erkens, "Toward a framework for CSCL research," *Educational Psychologist*, 48(1), 2013, pp. 1-8.

Transport Reduction in a Production Grid

Leo van Moergestel, Erik Puik and Daniël Telgen
Department of Computer science
HU Utrecht University of Applied Sciences
Utrecht, the Netherlands
Email: leo.vanmoergestel@hu.nl
John-Jules Meyer
Intelligent systems group Utrecht University
Utrecht, the Netherlands
Email: J.J.C.Meyer@uu.nl

Abstract—**In a production environment where different products are being made in parallel, the path planning for every product can be different. The model proposed in this paper is based on a production environment where the production machines are placed in a grid. A software entity, called product agent, is responsible for the manufacturing of a single product. The product agent will plan a path along the production machines needed for that specific product. In this paper, an optimization is proposed that will reduce the amount of transport between the production machines. The effect of two factors that influence the possibilities for reductions is shown in a simulation, using the proposed optimization scheme. These two factors are the redundancy of production steps in the grid and the number of steps where the order of execution is irrelevant. This paper presents for certain classes of production situations a method to reduce the number of transport hops between the production machines.**

Keywords-Multiagent-based manufacturing; production path planning.

I. Introduction

The production industry has had several revolutions. The first revolution was the use of steam power to facilitate production. The second revolution was the introduction of production lines based on the use of electrical energy and resulting in mass production. The rise of computer technology resulted in the third revolution. Many production tasks were automated, programmable logic controllers (PLC), distributed control systems (DCS) and robots were introduced on the production floor. The latest revolution is the integration of information technology in the production process as a whole. This has been described by the term industry 4.0 or cyber physical systems. The effect is that the requirements for manufacturing are rapidly changing due to newly arrived technologies like 3D-printing and end-user involvement using Internet technology.

At the Utrecht University of Applied Sciences, research is done on agile manufacturing. The aim is to achieve low-cost production of small quantities or even single user-specified products. This means that hardware, as well as software should be developed to make this possible. The work in this paper is based on a paper presented at the Intelli 2015 conference [1] and other previous work. The hardware that has been developed are cheap reconfigurable devices, called equiplets. Equiplets consist of a basic platform on which specific front-ends can be attached. When a front-end is attached to an equiplet, it will be capable to perform one or several specific production steps [2].

The software that is used in the production environment, is based on multiagent technology [3]. An agent is an autonomous software entity, having responsibilities and playing a role in the whole manufacturing software infrastructure. Two specific agent roles are the basis of the manufacturing system. The role and responsibility to have a single product made is assigned to a product agent. The role to control an equiplet and to offer production steps is assigned to an equiplet agent [4].

This paper will focus on the product agents and specifically the planning part of its role in the manufacturing. The main goal in this production process is to minimize the flow cost of products among the machines. Section II will show an overview of the roles and responsibilities of the product agent. This will also reveal the manufacturing concept used in our research. In Section III the definition of terms used in the paper are introduced and explained. After the introduction of the terms, the path planning approach is the topic of Section IV. To test this approach, the implementation has been tested in a simulated environment. The results of these simulations are given in Section V on results and discussion. In Section VI, related work is discussed among other work that is related to this new manufacturing paradigm. A conclusion and bibliography will end the paper.

II. Agent-based manufacturing

In the previous section, the concepts of product agent and equiplet agent have been introduced. The manufacturing concept will now be discussed. Industry 4.0 is also characterised as a cyber physical system. In this section these two parts will be explained starting with the physical aspect.

Figure 1. An equiplet

A. *Physical aspect*

As stated in the introduction, the actual production is done by so-called equiplets. The equiplets are placed in a grid topology for reasons that will be explained at the end of this section. Each equiplet offers one or more production steps and by combining a certain set of production steps, a product can be made. The set of production steps that can be performed, depends on the type of front-end that is attached to the equiplet. This way every equiplet acts as a reconfigurable manufacturing system (RMS) [5]. In Figure 1 an equiplet is shown. This equiplet is a pick-and-place machine based on a delta-robot mechanism. Agent technology opens the possibilities to let a grid of these equiplets operate and manufacture different kinds of products in parallel, provided that the required production steps are available [4].

B. *Cyber aspect*

Equiplets are represented by an equiplet agent. Every product requires a given set of production steps and the equiplets in the grid should implement these steps to make it possible to manufacture a specific product. Every product has its own software entity or product agent that is responsible for the manufacturing of a single product. By letting this product agent interact with the equiplet agents the actual manufacturing will take place. In the grid, more than one product agent can be active at any moment, so different products can be made in parallel.

For a product to be made, a sequence of production steps has to be done. More complex products need a tree of sequences, where every sequence ends in a half-product or part, needed for the end product. As a software representative of the equiplet, the equiplet agent advertises its capabilities as production steps on a blackboard that is available in a multiagent system where also the product agents live. A product agent is responsible for the manufacturing of a single product and knows what to do, the equiplet agents know how to do it. A product agent selects a set of equiplets based on the production steps it needs and tries to match these steps with the steps advertised by the equiplets. This selection of equiplets is called the planning and scheduling phase. The planning and scheduling of a product is an atomic action, done by the product agent in cooperation with the equiplet agents and takes several steps [6]. The planning and scheduling is atomic to prevent problems that arise if more product agents want to schedule steps on equiplets at the same time. If one agent is planning and scheduling, other newly arriving product agents have to wait until the agents finishes the allocation of equiplets. Let us assume that a single sequence of steps is needed.

1) From the list of production steps, the product agent builds a set of equiplets offering these steps;
2) The product agent will ask the equiplets involved about the feasibility and duration of the steps; Actually the equiplet agent will run a simulation of the step required using the parameters given, to check the feasibility and duration of the step.
3) Next the product agent will generate a path along equiplets;
4) The product agent will schedule the product path using first-fit (take the first opportunity in time for a production step) and a scheduling scheme known as earliest deadline first (EDF) [6];
5) If the schedule fails, the product agent reports this to the user and proposes a later production time if possible.

For more complex products, consisting of a tree of sequences, the product agent spawns child agents that are each responsible for a single sequence. A child agent has the same functionality as the parent agent, but is only responsible for a subset op production steps. The parent agent is in control of its children and acts as a supervisor. It is also responsible for the last single sequence of the product. In Figure 2, the first two half products are made using step sequences $< \sigma_1, \sigma_2 >$ and $< \sigma_3, \sigma_4 >$. These sequences are taken care of by child agents, while the parent agent will complete the product by performing the step sequence $< \sigma_4, \sigma_7, \sigma_2, \sigma_1 >$. It means that every single product agent, child or parent, has only a single sequence of steps to perform by itself.

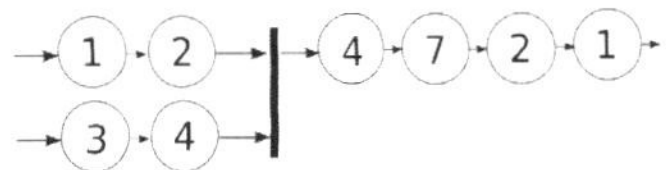

Figure 2. Manufacturing of a product consisting of two half-products

Some important features of the manufacturing model are:

- Every product agent is responsible for only one product to be made;
- The requests for products arrive at random;

- Every product will have its own path along the equiplets during manufacturing;
- The product agent will guide the product along the equiplets.

In the final implementation, a webinterface helps the end-user to design his/her specific product [2]. At the moment all features are selected, a product agent will be created. Because every product can have a different walk along the equiplets, the equiplets are in a grid arrangement that turns out to be more efficient than a line arrangement as used in batch processing [7].

III. Step path and product path

This section will define the concepts step path and product path. In Subsection III-A, step path classes will be introduced and in Subsection III-B special cases of step paths are discussed.

Consider a situation where a product is built by 11 production steps. Let us assume that we have 3 equiplets A, B and C. Equiplet agent A offers production step set $E_A = \{1, 2, 3, 4, 8\}$, $E_B = \{5, 6, 7\}$ and $E_C = \{9, 10, 11\}$. The product agent representing our 11-steps product will choose equiplet A first to perform steps 1, 2, 3 and 4. Next equiplet B is used to perform steps 5, 6 and 7. Then, we need again equiplet A for step 8 and finally equiplet C for the last tree steps 9, 10 and 11. This so called *step path* is visualized in Figure 3.

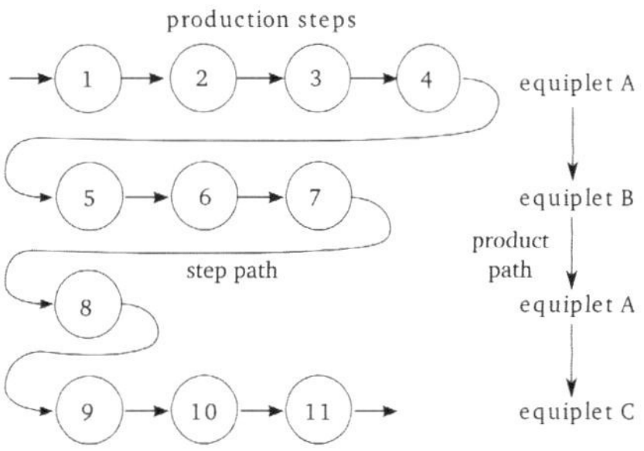

Figure 3. Step path and product path

Definition 1 (Step path). *A step path is a path along a sequence of production steps that a product agent has to follow to complete a product.*

In the example that is visualised in Figure 3 where the step path is shown, another path emerges. This is the path along the equiplest involved. In case of the example, it is a path from equiplet A to equiplet B, from equiplet B to A and finally from equiplet A to equiplet C. This type of path will be referred to as *product path*.

Definition 2 (Product path). *A product path is a path along a sequence of equiplets that a product agent has to follow to complete a product.*

A. Step path classes

In the previous example of our 11-step product (Figure 3) the production steps are in line so our path is a single thread. Figure 4 shows the two possibilities that are considered in this paper: a single line and a tree structure where two half-fabricates are combined.

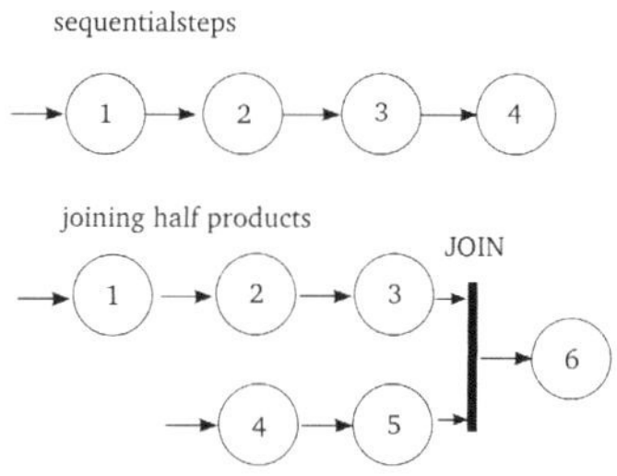

Figure 4. Two combinations of sequential production steps

When these product paths as shown in Figure 4 are written in sets (using: {...}) and tuples (using: < ... >) this results in:

- Single path, with tuple notation for a fixed order of steps: $< \sigma_1, \sigma_2, \sigma_3, \sigma_4 >$
- Joining half products: $< \{< \sigma_1, \sigma_2, \sigma_3 >, < \sigma_4, \sigma_5 >\}, \sigma_6 >$

B. Special cases of step paths

In some situations, the order of steps is irrelevant. This results in several possibilities for the step paths. Only one path of these possibilities should be chosen and the number of possibilities is $n!$ in case we have n steps with irrelevant order. This situation can be seen in Figure 5.

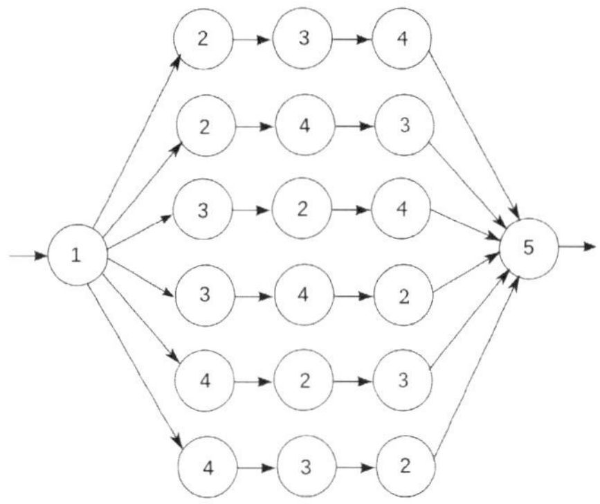

Figure 5. A set of steps with irrelevant order

In formula, this means that the set-notation is used for the steps with irrelevant order:

$$< \sigma_1, \{\sigma_2, \sigma_3, \sigma_4\}, \sigma_5 > \quad (1)$$

Parallelism can be achieved if the product has a tree structure as in Figure 6. On the left side of this figure, four incoming arrows, each denoting the start of a production path can be seen. Each path will construct a subpart for the final product and because these paths are independent, these subparts can be made in parallel. At every join in the figure these sub-parts are combined to be input to the next step or steps.

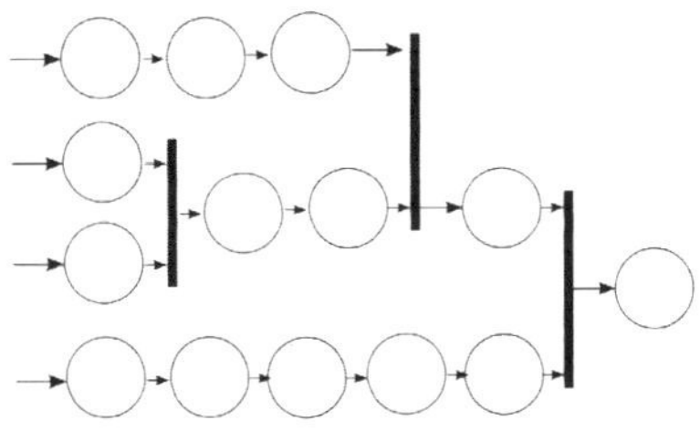

Figure 6. A tree of steps

In the situation of a tree structure a collection of product agents for a single product will be used. The start situation will be one agent, but this agent will spawn child-agents for the separate tuples. The parent agent is in control of its children and acts as a supervisor. It is also responsible for the last single sequence of the product. In Figure 6, we start at the right-hand side and walk backwards to the beginning of the production on the left. At every join child-agents will be created. The parent will wait for its children to complete their subpart. This will be done for every join and will be repeated until the start of the tree structure. When all agents succeed in planning and scheduling, the production will start. At every join the child agents are absorbed by the waiting agent, taking over the collected information and continuing the path until the end is reached as a single agent.

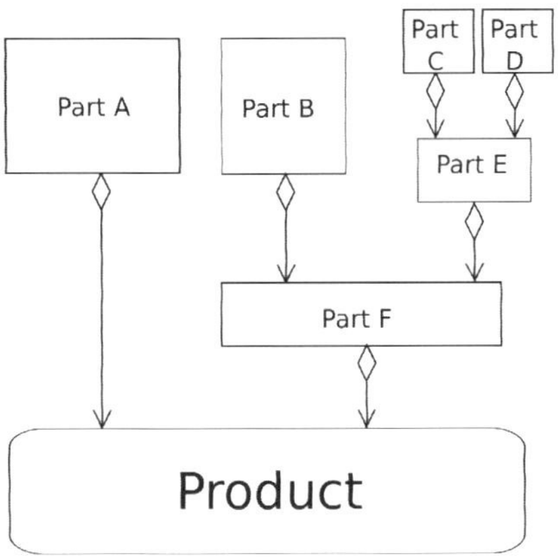

Figure 7. Product consisting of subparts

This situation arises many times, because most products consist of subparts (Figure 7). The product agent at the root of the tree will finally collect all information from its children. The effect of this decomposition of complex products is that every product agent only has to deal with a single tuple of production steps. The relationship between these product agents is the fact that they are working on the same product.

IV. Path planning

A product agent should plan a path along the equiplets. This path will depend on the product steps to be done and the equiplets involved. In this section, a graph-based model of the production is presented followed by matrix-based representations. These matrix-based representations will be used in the optimization system that is the main subject of this paper.

A. Graph representation

The production system can be represented using special classes of graphs, such as a bipartite graph and a tripartite graph.

Definition 3 (Bipartite graph). *A bipartite graph is defined as a triple $G = (V_1, V_2; E)$ where V_1 and V_2 are two disjoint finite sets of vertices and $E = \{(i_k, j_k) : i_k \in V_1, j_k \in V_2; k = 1...d\}$ is a set of edges. Let $|V_1| = m$ and $|V_2| = m$.*

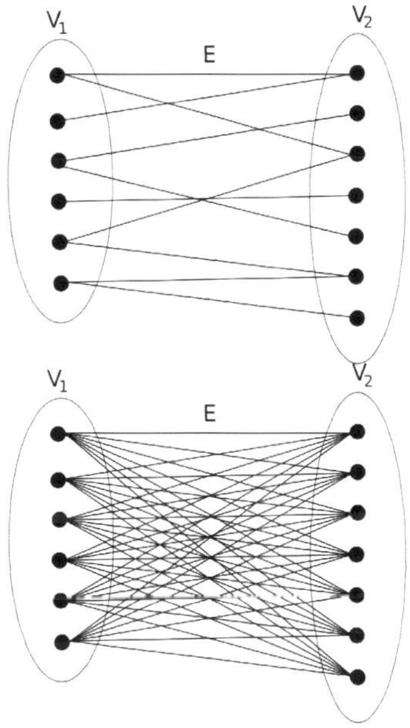

Figure 8. Bipartitegraph and complete bipatitegraph

If all vertices of V_1 have edges to all vertices of V_2 the graph is called a complete bipartite graph. If $|V_1| = m$ and $|V_2| = n$ this is denoted by $K(m, n)$.

Definition 4 (Product set). *Let V_1 and V_2 be two sets. The product set of V_1 and V_2 is the set of all ordered pairs (i, j) such that $i \in V_1$ and $j \in V_2$. This is written as $V_1 \times V_2$*

By definition of the product set, it means that a bipartite graph is complete if $E = V_1 \times V_2$. The product set is also called Cartesian product.

Definition 5 (Tripartite graph). *A tripartite graph is defined as a quintuple $G = (V_1, V_2, V_3; E_1, E_2)$ where V_1 and V_2 and V_3 are three disjoint sets of vertices and $E_1 = \{(i_k, j_k) : i_k \in V_1, j_k \in V_2; k = 1...d_1\}$ and $E_2 = \{(j_n, h_n) : j_n \in V_2, h_n \in V_3; n = 1...d_2\}$ are two sets of edges. Let $|V_1| = m$ and $|V_2| = m$.*

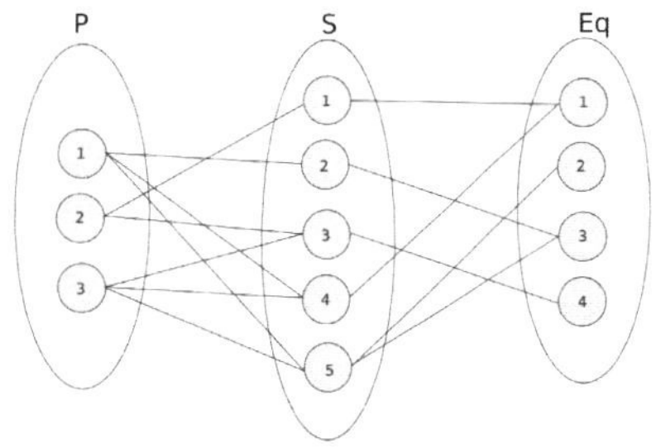

Figure 9. A tripartite graph as it occurs in the production system

In Figure 9 the situation is shown for the agile production system. On the left side the products to be made are in set P. In the middle, the set S of steps is displayed and on the right the set Eq of equiplets. Edges show the connection between the products and the steps as well as the steps and the equiplets. The step path for product P_1 is:

$$< \sigma_5, \sigma_2, \sigma_4 >$$

There are four equiplets, where Equiplet 1 offers steps σ_1 and σ_4, Equiplet 2 offers step σ_5, Equiplet 3 offers steps σ_2 and σ_5 and Equiplet 4 offers step σ_3.

B. Step matrix

Consider a grid G of N equiplets, together offering M production steps, this grid can be described by a matrix. This matrix is called *step matrix*.The step matrix G_{step} shows the mapping of equiplets to production steps.

$$G_{step} = \begin{pmatrix} a_{11} & a_{12} & \cdots & a_{1N} \\ a_{21} & a_{22} & \cdots & a_{2N} \\ \vdots & \vdots & \ddots & \vdots \\ a_{M1} & a_{M2} & \cdots & a_{MN} \end{pmatrix} \tag{2}$$

In this matrix, $a_{ij} = 1$ if equiplet E_i offers step σ_j, otherwise $a_{ij} = 0$.

C. Optimization

A step path is a sequence of production steps. For instance, consider a product to be built with three production steps, this product has step path:

$$< \sigma_5, \sigma_2, \sigma_4 > \tag{3}$$

Let us assume a simple grid with four equiplets E_1, E_2, E_3 and E_4, each offering a set of steps. The steps offered by an equiplet are denoted between parentheses as in $E_1(\sigma_1, \sigma_4)$. This grid can be described by this set of equiplets:

$$\{E_1(\sigma_1, \sigma_4), E_2(\sigma_5), E_3(\sigma_2, \sigma_5), E_4(\sigma_3)\} \tag{4}$$

This situation can also be described by the step matrix G_{step}.

$$\begin{array}{ccccc} & E_1 & E_2 & E_3 & E_4 \\ \sigma_1 & 1 & 0 & 0 & 0 \\ \sigma_2 & 0 & 0 & 1 & 0 \\ \sigma_3 & 0 & 0 & 0 & 1 \\ \sigma_4 & 1 & 0 & 0 & 0 \\ \sigma_5 & 0 & 1 & 1 & 0 \end{array} \tag{5}$$

A product agent will make a selection of these equiplets based on the production step or steps that must be performed to construct the product. Next, the product agent will ask the equiplet if the steps offered are feasible given the parameters for the steps. The positive response from the equiplet agent contains an estimated time to complete a given step. This information about the duration of a step will be used in the scheduling phase. When a negative response is received by the product agent it will discard the equiplet. Several solutions to map the steps to equiplets may exist. A sufficient solution for the given situation with a minimum of transitions is:

$$< E_3(\sigma_5), E_3(\sigma_2), E_1(\sigma_4) > \tag{6}$$

To find an efficient solution, we try to minimise the transitions or hops between different equiplets. This is done by using a so called production matrix G_p. This production matrix can be derived from the step matrix by selecting the rows of the production steps in the same order as in the tuple that describes the step path $< \sigma_5, \sigma_2, \sigma_4 >$.

$$\begin{array}{ccccc} & E_1 & E_2 & E_3 & E_4 \\ \sigma_5 & 0 & 1 & 1 & 0 \\ \sigma_2 & 0 & 0 & 1 & 0 \\ \sigma_4 & 1 & 0 & 0 & 0 \end{array} \tag{7}$$

The production matrix can be reduced by eliminating the columns that contain only zeros. This means that the equiplet on top of this column is not involved in the production of this specific product. In this case the column under E_4 will be removed. This results in a matrix (8) where for every σ_i in this step path a row of a production matrix is created:

$$\begin{array}{cccc} & E_1 & E_2 & E_3 \\ \sigma_5 & 0 & 1 & 1 \\ \sigma_2 & 0 & 0 & 1 \\ \sigma_4 & 1 & 0 & 0 \end{array} \tag{8}$$

The rows have the same order as the sequence of steps. Matrix element α_{ij} gives the relation between equiplet E_j and production step σ_x at row i. If the step σ_x at row i is supported by equiplet E_j then $\alpha_{ij} = 1$. Not supported steps result in $\alpha_{ij} = 0$.

Optimization should result in a new matrix, that will be called the path matrix, where α_{ij} has a slightly different meaning and can be different from 1 or 0, giving the product agent a clue for its choice. The product agent will choose the equiplet corresponding with the highest value of α_{ij}. The optimization is minimizing the transitions for a product from equiplet to equiplet. The optimizing algorithm will search for columns j with sequences of $\alpha_{ij} = 1$ and increment the values in a given sequence by the length of the sequence minus one. This will be done for all columns starting with $\alpha_{ij} = 1$. The matrix of the example has a column under E_3 with a length of 2, with the result that the values of this sequence will be incremented by 1. The production matrix transforms to the path matrix (9):

$$\begin{array}{cccc} & E_1 & E_2 & E_3 \\ \sigma_5 & 0 & 1 & 2 \\ \sigma_2 & 0 & 0 & 2 \\ \sigma_4 & 1 & 0 & 0 \end{array} \tag{9}$$

A value higher than 1 means that more steps can be done in sequence on the same equiplet. Based on this matrix, the product agent will choose equiplet E_3 for steps σ_5 and σ_2. The path matrix can be cleaned up by changing values that will not be used in the path to zero.

$$\begin{array}{cccc} & E_1 & E_2 & E_3 \\ \sigma_5 & 0 & 0 & 2 \\ \sigma_2 & 0 & 0 & 2 \\ \sigma_4 & 1 & 0 & 0 \end{array} \tag{10}$$

The optimization algorithm works stepwise and can be completely automatised. First the best starting point is searched for. This will reveal the best equiplet(s) to start with. Let us assume that we have n steps in the step path. This results in a production matrix of n rows. Suppose that the algorithm reveals a maximum set of k steps to be completed by one equiplet as a start. This means that after completing this sequence of k steps, $n - k$ rows, representing $n - k$ steps, should still be done. We reached this point of $n - k$ steps to be done, with the minimum of movements of the product between equiplets. The algorithm is applied to the remaining part (the $n - k$ rows) of the production matrix, without taking into account the previous k rows. We reach a new situation where the number of rows is again reduced. This is repeated until the number of remaining rows is 0. Because of the fact that after every iteration we reach a situation with the minimum of movements of the product between equiplets, the final situation, where the number of rows to be done is 0, will also be reached with the minimum of movements.

D. Region with irrelevant order of steps

Now, consider the situation where there exists a region in the production matrix where the order of steps is irrelevant. This region will be referred to as a region with irrelevant step order. If this irrelevant step order region concerns the whole production matrix, there are no borders with a region where the order is fixed as discussed before. We will discuss this situation first and next a situation where the irrelevant step order region is embedded in two regions with fixed order.

When there are no borders with other regions, the used approach is the following: generate a vector v from the matrix where we sum all separate columns. This means for element v_j of vector v, assuming a matrix with N rows:

$$v_j = \sum_{i=1}^{i=N} \alpha_{ij} \tag{11}$$

From this vector the highest value will be chosen as a start. The irrelevant region will decrease by v_j and a new vector will be generated for the remaining smaller region until all steps needed are taken into account.

When there are borders, a slightly different approach will be used. At the border at the top of the irrelevant step order region, there should be a sequence of at least one step resulting from the fixed step order region. In this case a search will be done to find the best match with this already available sequence from the previous region. The same approach holds for the region at the bottom. A special case in this situation could be a sequence that has the size of the special region. Such a sequence will be called a tunnel and special care should be taken. If there are no matches at the upper or lower border, first matching sequences should be investigated. Matching sequences will not introduce a hop and if these matching sequences at top of border do not cover the whole special region, the tunnel can eventually be used introducing two hops, but if the matching sequences on top and bottom together cover the region only one hop is needed.

Two caveats should be mentioned here. If the boundary with a fixed region has more than one maximum (that should be equal of course), these possibilities should be investigated for the best fit. This means we have to look for the maximum in the fixed region that can be extended to the longest sequence by adding a member of the vector v. The number of maxima (not the maxima itself) will give a clue about where to start, at the top or the bottom border. This will be shown in an example.

Another caveat has to do with overlapping sequences in irrelevant step order region. Consider the situation for a irrelevant region depicted in the matrix (12):

$$\begin{array}{cccc} & E_1 & E_2 & E_3 \\ \sigma_a & 1 & 0 & 0 \\ \sigma_b & 1 & 1 & 0 \\ \sigma_c & 0 & 1 & 1 \\ \sigma_d & 0 & 0 & 1 \end{array} \tag{12}$$

Generating the vector v will result in $(2, 2, 2)$. However, the choice to be made depends on the next vector that would result from this choice. If the middle maximum is chosen, the resulting vector v is $(1, 0, 1)$ resulting in a total of two transitions or hops. If the selection was for the first maximum the resulting v would be $(0, 1, 2)$, while choosing the last maximum v would be $(2, 1, 0)$. Both of the latter situations result in only one hop.

As an extra example of the approach discussed so far, consider the situation shown in Figure 10. At the top are two maxima having a value of 3, resulting from the evaluation of the previous fixed order region. The bottom has only one maximum, also resulting from the evaluation of the following fixed order region. The vector for the irrelevant order region is:

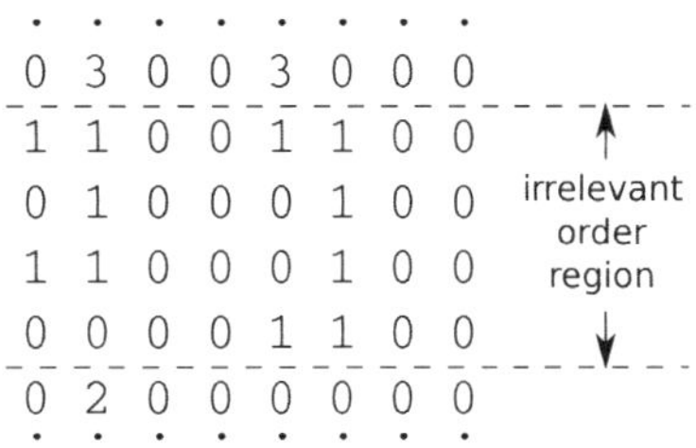

Figure 10. Border situations

$(2,3,0,0,2,4,0,0)$. Because the bottom border has the least number of maxima, we start there to fit with the vector values. If we started at the top, we could choose the first fit, but then we would loose the fitting possibility at the bottom. If the fitting at the bottom is performed, only one row is left to be handled, having vector $(0,0,0,0,1,1,0,0)$. This vector fits with one of the maxima at the top border resulting in matrix (13), having only one hop.

$$\begin{array}{cccccccc} . & . & . & . & . & . & . & . \\ 0 & 0 & 0 & 0 & 4 & 0 & 0 & 0 \\ 0 & 0 & 0 & 0 & 4 & 0 & 0 & 0 \\ 0 & 5 & 0 & 0 & 0 & 0 & 0 & 0 \\ 0 & 5 & 0 & 0 & 0 & 0 & 0 & 0 \\ 0 & 5 & 0 & 0 & 0 & 0 & 0 & 0 \\ 0 & 5 & 0 & 0 & 0 & 0 & 0 & 0 \\ . & . & . & . & . & . & . & . \end{array} \qquad (13)$$

E. Alternative paths

Having a path with a minimum of hops is nice, but in some cases it might by handy to have some alternatives at hand. To generate alternatives with the same number of hops, two possibilities can be used. When these possibilities are combined, a total number of four optimum paths can be calculated. However, it is not guaranteed that these paths are different. By using simple examples these approaches will be demonstrated. Consider the matrix (14), having no special region.

$$\begin{array}{cccccccc} 0 & 1 & 0 & 1 & 0 & 1 & 0 & 0 \\ 0 & 1 & 0 & 0 & 1 & 1 & 0 & 0 \\ 0 & 1 & 0 & 0 & 1 & 1 & 0 & 0 \\ 0 & 0 & 0 & 1 & 1 & 0 & 0 & 1 \\ 0 & 0 & 0 & 1 & 1 & 0 & 0 & 1 \\ 0 & 0 & 0 & 1 & 1 & 0 & 0 & 1 \\ 1 & 0 & 0 & 1 & 0 & 0 & 1 & 0 \\ 1 & 0 & 0 & 0 & 0 & 0 & 1 & 0 \end{array} \qquad (14)$$

If we apply the optimization algorithm starting from top to bottom and choosing the maximum most on the left, it will result in matrix (15):

$$\begin{array}{cccccccc} 0 & 3 & 0 & 0 & 0 & 0 & 0 & 0 \\ 0 & 3 & 0 & 0 & 0 & 0 & 0 & 0 \\ 0 & 3 & 0 & 0 & 0 & 0 & 0 & 0 \\ 0 & 0 & 0 & 4 & 0 & 0 & 0 & 0 \\ 0 & 0 & 0 & 4 & 0 & 0 & 0 & 0 \\ 0 & 0 & 0 & 4 & 0 & 0 & 0 & 0 \\ 0 & 0 & 0 & 4 & 0 & 0 & 0 & 0 \\ 1 & 0 & 0 & 0 & 0 & 0 & 0 & 0 \end{array} \qquad (15)$$

An alternative can be found by starting at the bottom, but again choosing the maximum most to the left. Now we get matrix (16):

$$\begin{array}{cccccccc} 0 & 1 & 0 & 0 & 0 & 0 & 0 & 0 \\ 0 & 0 & 0 & 0 & 5 & 0 & 0 & 0 \\ 0 & 0 & 0 & 0 & 5 & 0 & 0 & 0 \\ 0 & 0 & 0 & 0 & 5 & 0 & 0 & 0 \\ 0 & 0 & 0 & 0 & 5 & 0 & 0 & 0 \\ 0 & 0 & 0 & 0 & 5 & 0 & 0 & 0 \\ 2 & 0 & 0 & 0 & 0 & 0 & 0 & 0 \\ 2 & 0 & 0 & 0 & 0 & 0 & 0 & 0 \end{array} \qquad (16)$$

Possibility number three can be found by again starting at the top, but now choosing the maximum most to the right. The result is shown in matrixx (17):

$$\begin{array}{cccccccc} 0 & 0 & 0 & 0 & 0 & 3 & 0 & 0 \\ 0 & 0 & 0 & 0 & 0 & 3 & 0 & 0 \\ 0 & 0 & 0 & 0 & 0 & 3 & 0 & 0 \\ 0 & 0 & 0 & 4 & 0 & 0 & 0 & 0 \\ 0 & 0 & 0 & 4 & 0 & 0 & 0 & 0 \\ 0 & 0 & 0 & 4 & 0 & 0 & 0 & 0 \\ 0 & 0 & 0 & 4 & 0 & 0 & 0 & 0 \\ 0 & 0 & 0 & 0 & 0 & 0 & 1 & 0 \end{array} \qquad (17)$$

The fourth possibility can be found by starting at the bottom and selecting the maximum most on the right, resulting in matrix (18):

$$\begin{array}{cccccccc} 0 & 0 & 0 & 0 & 0 & 1 & 0 & 0 \\ 0 & 0 & 0 & 0 & 5 & 0 & 0 & 0 \\ 0 & 0 & 0 & 0 & 5 & 0 & 0 & 0 \\ 0 & 0 & 0 & 0 & 5 & 0 & 0 & 0 \\ 0 & 0 & 0 & 0 & 5 & 0 & 0 & 0 \\ 0 & 0 & 0 & 0 & 5 & 0 & 0 & 0 \\ 0 & 0 & 0 & 0 & 0 & 0 & 2 & 0 \\ 0 & 0 & 0 & 0 & 0 & 0 & 2 & 0 \end{array} \qquad (18)$$

An interesting aspect is looking at the percentage or number of equiplets that overlap. By this is meant the number of equiplets that are used in two alternatives. Table I shows this overlap for the four different solutions found. This overlap is very dependant on the initial matrix given, but from this example it becomes clear that the smallest overlap and perhaps the one of the best alternatives to our first solution is solution four where both strategies (starting top/bottom, choosing right/left) are changed.

Two remarks should be made at this point. First, when there are more than two maxima to choose from, only the maxima most on the left or most on the right will be chosen in the

TABLE I. percentage of overlap

	1	2	3	4
1	100	25	50	0
2	25	100	0	48
3	50	0	100	25
4	0	48	25	100

approach presented here. The idea of generating alternatives is to find another path with an equal numbers of hops, not to find all alternative paths with an equal number of hops. The algorithm should be fast and simple, as it is now. An alternative path should be considered if the scheduling constraints, like deadline or load of a certain equiplet give rise to looking for an alternative solution.

The second remark is that it is clear that alternatives in this situation (with a fixed sequence of steps), are only possible if steps are available at multiple equiplets. However, in case of a production grid, it is a good design strategy if equiplets are duplicated or that a certain step is available at more than one equiplet. This will prevent the existence of a single point of failure and will make the grid production platform more reliable.

V. Test results discussion

In this section, a description of the software implementation, the results, the time it takes to run the optimisation and discussion are presented.

A. *Software implementation*

To implement the optimisation algorithm, several command line tools running under Linux were developed. These tools were written in C, resulting in fast and compact applications. The reason for choosing Linux was based on the fact that the equiplet software and the agent platform for production, is also Linux-based.

a) Generate production matrix: The first tool developed was a tool to generate a production matrix. The parameters used are the dimension of the matrix and the number of one's per row. An output example with 5 rows, 8 columns and 4 one's per column looks like:

```
0 0 0 1 1 0 1 1
0 0 1 0 1 1 0 0
0 0 1 0 1 0 0 1
0 0 1 0 0 0 1 0
0 0 1 0 0 0 0 1
```

Because of the use of random numbers for determining the position of one's, many different matrices can be generated, given the same parameters for the dimensions.

b) Analyse the matrix: The first step to get to an optimum path is generated by the tool *analyse*. Given the previous matrix, *analyse* will count the sequences of one's in a column and adjust the numbers accordingly, resulting in:

```
0 0 0 1 3 0 1 1
0 0 4 0 3 1 0 0
0 0 4 0 3 0 0 1
0 0 4 0 0 0 1 0
0 0 4 0 0 0 0 1
```

c) cleanup: The result of *analyse* should be adjusted to get an optimum path. The tool *cleaunup* is used to adapt the matrices generated by analyse It will start from the beginning of a matrix and remove all irrelevant options, turning them to zero's. Another thing that will be done is adjusting the value for overlapping paths. If the highest value for a column is not unique, it will choose the one most to the left, this is the first one found.

```
0 0 0 0 3 0 0 0
0 0 0 0 3 0 0 0
0 0 0 0 3 0 0 0
0 0 0 2 0 0 0 0
0 0 0 2 0 0 0 0
```

d) Handle special region: The tool *special* is used to adapt the matrices generated by *analyse* and *cleanup*. The first thing that will be done is counting the total of one's in the special region per column. Next it will look for the best fit with the upper part, as well as a fit with the lower part. An adjustment will be made to the fitting parts found so far. Finally *special* will fill up the missing area with the best choice available and continue until the special region is completed

e) Tools for generating alternatives: To generate alternatives and still using the previous tools that work from top to bottim and left to right, two other simple tools have been developed. The tool *mirror* will generate a matrix that has a mirrored sequence of columns. For our example production matrix this looks like:

```
1 1 0 1 1 0 0 0
0 0 1 1 0 1 0 0
1 0 0 1 0 1 0 0
0 1 0 0 0 1 0 0
1 0 0 0 0 1 0 0
```

Using *mirror* twice will result in the original matrix again. The tool *upsidedown* will generate a matrix where the sequence of rows is inverted. For our example matrix this will look like:

```
0 0 1 0 0 0 0 1
0 0 1 0 0 0 1 0
0 0 1 0 1 0 0 1
0 0 1 0 1 1 0 0
0 0 0 1 1 0 1 1
```

Of course *mirror* and *upsidedown* can be combined resulting in matrix:

```
1 0 0 0 0 1 0 0
0 1 0 0 0 1 0 0
1 0 0 1 0 1 0 0
0 0 1 1 0 1 0 0
1 1 0 1 1 0 0 0
```

Using these two tools, the previous mentioned tools can still be used without any adaptation. The matrices are changed and the result can be put in the right order again.

B. Results

To test the optimising approaches discussed in the previous section, test sets have been generated. All these sets consist of 8 matrices. Thus, 8 equiplets are assumed and the production requires 32 steps. First the effect of redundancy is investigated. This is done by using test sets where at every row, there are 1, 2, 3 or 4 choices for equiplets to perform a certain step. The results of using the optimization approach are shown in Figure 11. In this figure, a slight decrease in the number of hops is shown. This is expected due to the fact that higher redundancy gives rise to longer sequences of steps on the same equiplet, thus reducing the number of hops.

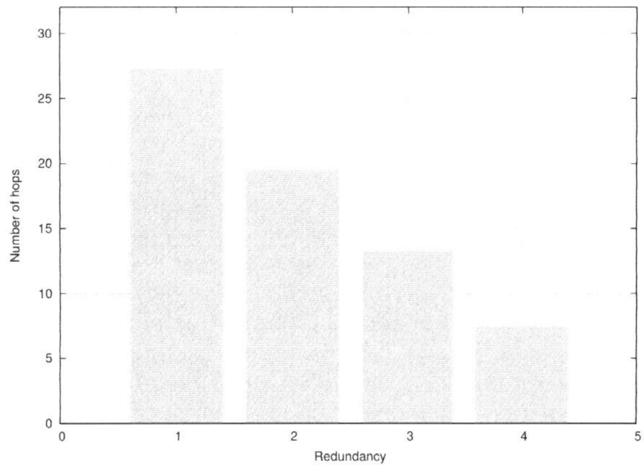

Figure 11. The effect of redundancy

Next, the effect of the size of the region where the order is irrelevant is investigated. This is done by using the same test sets that have been used to see what the effect of redundancy is. The size of the region where the order of steps is irrelevant, changes from 0 (no special region) until 32 (the whole matrix is a special region) in steps of 4. The special region is always placed in the middle of the matrix. The results for the test sets where the redundancy is only 1, are shown in Figure 12. In the subsequent Figures 13, 14 and 15 the results are shown for test sets having a redundancy of 2, 3 and 4. In all figures a decrease of the number of hops can be seen. This is also a result that is expected, because a region where the order of steps is irrelevant opens more possibilities to generate longer sequences of steps on the same equiplet.

C. Speed

This section will give an impression of the speed of the optimisation. The simulation where the optimisation was used, was run on a standard desktop system with an Intel(R) Core(TM)2 Duo CPU with a 2.33GHz clock and a 4096 KB cache. The system had 4GB of memory. The operating system was Linux (Ubunto 14.04 LTS). The command *time* was used to measure the execution time of the simulation containing the optimisation. The results for a manufacturing environment with 8 equiplets and 32 production steps were:

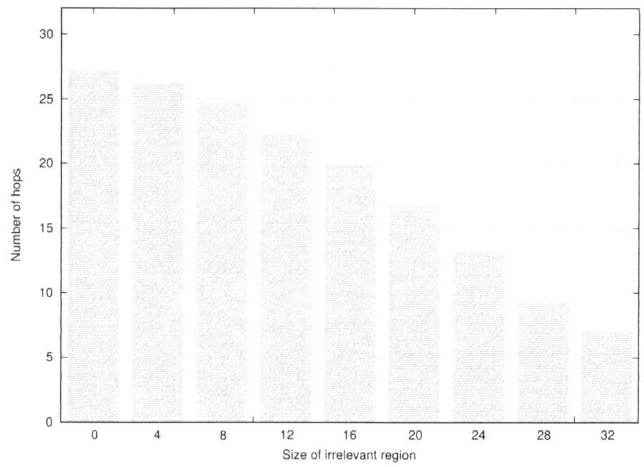

Figure 12. The effect of the size of the irrelevant step region

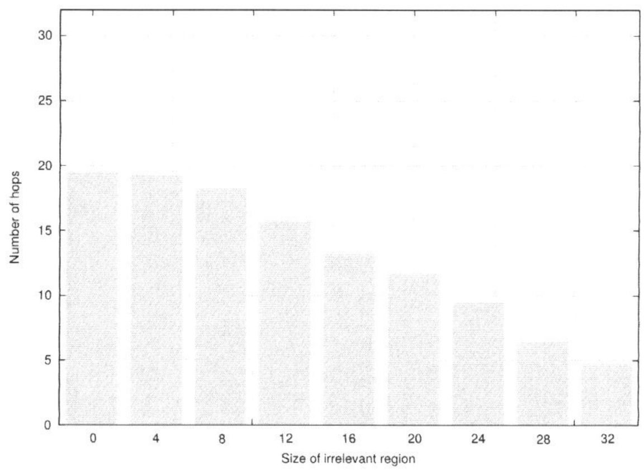

Figure 13. The effect of the size of the irrelevant step region

```
real 0m0.225s
user 0m0.003s
sys 0m0.007s
```

This shows that the actual computing time is actually very short in comparison to the transport time, where the time for a hop might be in the order of seconds.

D. Discussion

The test sets were used to test the optimising approach presented in the previous section and this approach turns out to work in the given situations. Important is to emphasize that reduction in transition or hops is an important optimization for the grid production paradigm. In [7], a transport system for the grid is described. This transport system is based on the use of automated guided vehicles (AVG). It turned out that the transport system becomes the bottleneck in a manufacturing grid if the production steps are relatively short, which is in

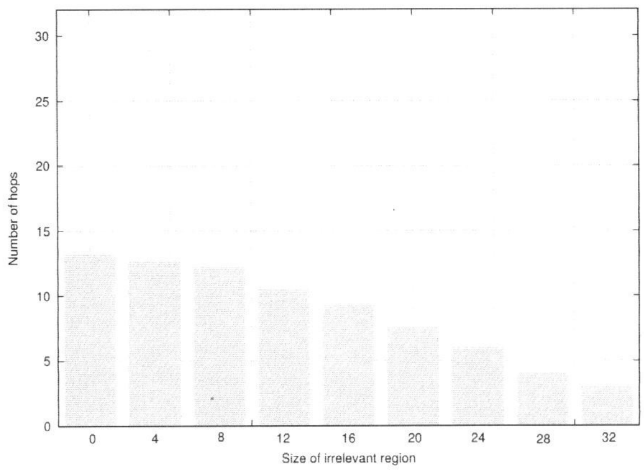

Figure 14. The effect of the size of the irrelevant step region

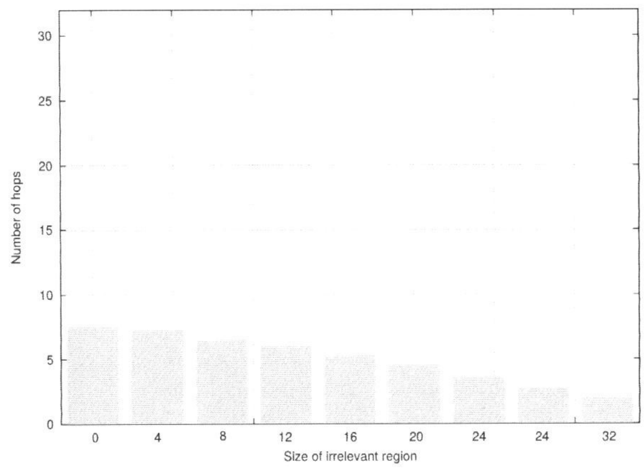

Figure 15. The effect of the size of the irrelevant step region

our system mostly the case. The optimization proposed here, will reduce the amount of AVG traffic and therefore alleviates the problem described in [7].

The optimization used and described in this paper was developed with the grid-based agile manufacturing environment in mind. The same approach can also be used in situations where workers are available, who can do one or more specific tasks needed in a certain project and where cooperation is required to reach the final goal of the project.

VI. Related work

This section will start with an overview on agent-based manufacturing. Especially the planning part will be given attention. Next, related problems in production planning, operations research and optimisation will be presented.

Important work in field of agent-based manufacturing has already been done. Paolucci and Sacile [8] give an extensive overview of what has been done. Their work focuses on simulation as well as production scheduling and control [9]. The main purpose to use agents in [8] is agile production and making complex production tasks possible by using a multiagent system. Agents are also proposed to deliver a flexible and scalable alternative for manufacturing execution systems (MES) [10] for small production companies. The roles of the agents in this overview are quite diverse. In simulations agents play the role of active entities in the production. In production scheduling and control agents support or replace human operators. Agent technology is used in parts or subsystems of the manufacturing process. The planning is mostly based on the type of planning that is used in MES. This type of planning is normally based on batch production. We based the manufacturing process as a whole on agent technology. In our case, a co-design of hardware and software was the basis. The planning will be done on a single product basis and not on batch production.

Bussmann and Jennings [11][12] used an approach that compares in some aspects to our approach. The system they describe introduced three types of agents, a workpiece agent, a machine agent and a switch agent. Some characteristics of their solutions are:

- The production system is a production line that is built for a certain product. This design is based on redundant production machinery and focuses on production availability and a minimum of downtime in the production process. Our system is a grid and is capable to produce many different products in parallel;
- The roles of the agents in this approach are different from our approach. The workpiece agent sends an invitation to bid for its current task to all machine agents. The machine agents issue bids to the workpiece agent. The workpiece agent chooses the best bid or tries again. This is what is known as the contract net protocol. In our system the negotiating is between the product agents, thus not disrupting the machine agents;
- They use a special infrastructure for the logistic subsystem, controlled by so called switch agents. Even though the practical implementation is akin to their solution, in our solution the service offered by the logistic subsystems can be considered as production steps offered by an equiplet and should be based on a more flexible transport mechanism.

So there are however important differences to our approach. The solution presented by Bussmann and Jennings has the characteristics of a production pipeline and is very useful as such, however it is not meant to be an agile multi-parallel production system as presented here. Their system uses redundancy to overcome the the problem that arises in pipeline-based production when one of the production systems fails or becomes unavailable. The planning is based on batch processing.

Other authors focus on using agent technology as a solution to a specific problem in a production environment. In [13] a multi-agent monitoring is presented. This work focusses on monitoring a manufacturing plant. The approach we use monitors the production of every single product. The work of Xiang and Lee [14] presents a scheduling multiagent-based solution using swarm intelligence. This work uses negotiating between job-agents and machine-agents for equal distribution of tasks among machines. The implementation and a simulation of the performance is discussed. We did not focus on a specific part of the production but we developed a complete production paradigm based on agent technology in combination with a production grid. This model is based on two types of agents and focuses on agile multiparallel production. The role of the product agent is much more important than in the other agent-based solutions discussed here. In our model, the product agent can also play an important role in the life-cycle of the product [15]. The design and implementation of the production platforms and the idea to build a production grid can be found in Puik [16].

The problem presented here is also related to the famous travelling salesman problem (TSP) [17]. However, there are important differences. In our case we try to reduce the number of hops, not to find the shortest path. This has to do with the fact that in our manufacturing model the transport of products in the grid should be reduced to prevent the situation of congestion and to reduce the production time for a certain product. In our system the order of production machines to be visited by a certain product is sometimes fixed and sometimes irrelevant, making it a problem that differs from TSP.

A transport related problem in manufacturing is known as the job shop scheduling problem [18]. This problem plays an important role in standard production cell-based systems. In that case the production time and availability of production cells is the basis for the problem to be solved.

VII. Conclusion

In this paper, a path planning optimization approach has been proposed an tested. The optimization turned to work out as expected and results in a reduce of traffic among the production machines. The optimization might be useful in other situations as well, especially in situations of production systems where the transport becomes a bottleneck. In future research, other step classes can be included like the situation where the order of sequences (tuples) of steps is irrelevant.

References

[1] L. v. Moergestel, J.-J. Meyer, E. Puik, and D. Telgen, "Optimizing product paths in a production grid," The Fourth International Conference on Intelligent Systems and Applications (Intelli 2015), St. Julians, Malta, 2015, pp. 150–156.

[2] L. v. Moergestel, J.-J. Meyer, E. Puik, and D. Telgen, "Implementation of manufacturing as a service: A pull-driven agent-based manufacturing grid," Proceedings of the 11th International Conference on ICT in Education, Research and Industrial Applications (ICTERI 2015), Lviv, Ukraine, 2015, pp. 172–187.

[3] M. Wooldridge, An Introduction to MultiAgent Systems, Second Edition. Sussex, UK: Wiley, 2009.

[4] L. v. Moergestel, J.-J. Meyer, E. Puik, and D. Telgen, "Decentralized autonomous-agent-based infrastructure for agile multiparallel manufacturing," Proceedings of the International Symposium on Autonomous Distributed Systems (ISADS 2011) Kobe, Japan, 2011, pp. 281–288.

[5] Z. M. Bi, S. Y. T. Lang, W. Shen, and L. Wang, "Reconfigurable manufacturing systems: the state of the art," International Journal of Production Research, vol. 46, no. 4, 2008, pp. 599–620.

[6] L. v. Moergestel, J.-J. Meyer, E. Puik, and D. Telgen, "Production scheduling in an agile agent-based production grid," Proceedings of the Intelligent Agent Technology (IAT 2012), Macau, 2012, pp. 293–298.

[7] L. v. Moergestel, J.-J. Meyer, E. Puik, D. Telgen, M. Kuijl, B. Alblas, and J. Koelewijn, "A simulation model for transport in a grid-based manufacturing system," The Third International Conference on Intelligent Systems and Applications (Intelli 2014), Seville, Spain, 2014, pp. 1–7.

[8] M. Paolucci and R. Sacile, Agent-based manufacturing and control systems : new agile manufacturing solutions for achieving peak performance. Boca Raton, Fla.: CRC Press, 2005.

[9] E. Montaldo, R. Sacile, M. Coccoli, M. Paolucci, and A. Boccalatte, "Agent-based enhanced workflow in manufacturing information systems: the makeit approach," J. Computing Inf. Technol., vol. 10, no. 4, 2002, pp. 303–316.

[10] J. Kletti, Manufacturing Execution System - MES. Berlin Heidelberg: Springer-Verlag, 2007.

[11] S. Bussmann, N. Jennings, and M. Wooldridge, Multiagent Systems for Manufacturing Control. Berlin Heidelberg: Springer-Verlag, 2004.

[12] N. Jennings and S. Bussmann, "Agent-based control system," IEEE Control Systems Magazine, vol. 23, no. 3, 2003, pp. 61–74.

[13] D. Ouelhadj, C. Hanachi, and B. Bouzouia, "Multi-agent architecture for distributed monitoring in flexible manufacturing systems (fms)," International Conference on Robotics and Automation, ICRA, 2000, pp. 2416–2421.

[14] W. Xiang and H. Lee, "Ant colony intelligence in multi-agent dynamic manafacturing scheduling," Engineering Applications of Artificial Intelligence, vol. 16, no. 4, 2008, pp. 335–348.

[15] L. v. Moergestel, J.-J. Meyer, E. Puik, and D. Telgen, "Embedded autonomous agents in products supporting repair and recycling," Proceedings of the International Symposium on Autonomous Distributed Systems (ISADS 2013) Mexico City, 2013, pp. 67–74.

[16] E. Puik and L. v. Moergestel, "Agile multi-parallel micro manufacturing using a grid of equiplets," Proceedings of the International Precision Assembly Seminar (IPAS 2010), 2010, pp. 271–282.

[17] W. Cook, In Pursuit of the Traveling Salesman: Mathematics at the Limits of Computation. Princeton University Press, 2012.

[18] S. Mirshekarian and D. Sormaz, "Correlation of job-shop scheduling problem features with scheduling efficiency," Expert Systems with Applications, vol. 62, 2016, p. 131147.

A Simple Data Cube Representation for Efficient Computing and Updating

Viet Phan-Luong

Aix-Marseille Université
Laboratoire d'Informatique Fondamentale de Marseille
LIF - UMR CNRS 7279
Marseille, France
Email: viet.phanluong@lif.univ-mrs.fr

Abstract—**This paper presents a simple approach to represent data cubes that allows efficient computing, querying and updating. The representation is based on (i) a recursive construction of the power set of the scheme of the fact table and (ii) a prefix tree structure for the compact storage of cuboids. The experimental results on large real datasets show that the approach is efficient in run time, storage space, and for incremental update.**

Keywords–Data warehouse; Data mining; Data cube; Data cube update.

I. Introduction

In data warehouse, a data cube built on a fact table with n dimensions and m measures can be seen as the result of the set of the Structured Query Language (SQL) group-by queries over the power set of dimensions, with aggregate functions over the measures. The result of each SQL group-by query is an aggregate view, called a cuboid, over the fact table. The concept of data cube, provided in the online analytical processing (OLAP) approach, offers important interests to business intelligence as it provides aggregate views of data over multiple combinations of dimensions that help managers to make appropriate decision in their business.

Though the concept of data cube is simple, there are many important issues in computation. In fact, in a data warehouse, the fact table has generally a big volume. This implies the cost in time and in storage space, when computing the cuboids. As the number of cuboids in a data cube is exponential with respect to the number of dimensions of the fact table, the cost to compute the entire data cube is considerable.

To improve the query response time on data cube, in OLAP, the data cube is usually precomputed and stored on disks. However, the storage space of all the data cube is exponential to the number of dimensions of the fact table. For efficiency, it is necessary to reduce the storage space. By reduction, the data cube is represented in a compact form that is stored on disks. We must access this form to compute the response to queries on data cube. There exists the trade-off between the storage space reduction and the query response time. The reduction of the storage space could increase the query response time. The research in OLAP focuses on the important efforts to make methods more efficient in computation and representation of data cubes. The compact representation of data cubes should offer efficient query computation.

In the life cycle of a data warehouse, the fact table can incrementally grow with new fact tuples. In consequence, the data cube must be updated. The update can be done by updating the stored representation based on the new data or by re-computing the entire representation of the data cube based on the updated fact table. On updating all cuboids, we can have the same problems as on re-computing all cuboids. However, it is interesting to know between the two possibilities, in what conditions, which one is more efficient than the other.

Further more, because of the big volume of the fact table and the exponential number of cuboids, we can have a tremendous number of aggregated tuples in the data cube. As consequence, the apprehension on such a number of aggregated tuples to make a good decision on business is a very important issue.

The above issues are among the important topics of research in data warehouse. There exist many approaches to compute and to represent the data cube. The work [1] presents a new approach to represent the data cube that is efficient in storage space and in computing. By this approach, the storage space of the data cube representation is reduced. However, we can have an efficient method to get all cuboids of the entire data cube from the reduced representation.

This work is an extension of [1]. The extension consists in: (i) development and improvement of the content and (ii) the study of data cube update based on the proposed representation.

The paper is organized as follows. Section II presents the related work and the contributions of this work. Section III introduces the concepts of the prime and next-prime schemes and cuboids. Section IV presents the structure of the integrated binary search prefix tree used to store cuboids. Section V is the core of the approach. It shows how to compute the data cube representation and how to restore the entire data cube from the reduced representation. Section VI presents an efficient algorithm for updating the data cube representation. Section VII reports the experimentation results. Finally, conclusion and further work are in Section VIII.

II. Related Work

To tackle the issues of the tremendous number of aggregated tuples of a data cube due to the big volume of the fact table and the exponential number of cuboids [2][3][4][5], many different approaches were proposed. In [6], instead of computing the complete data cube, an I/O-efficient technique based upon a multiresolution wavelet decomposition is used to build an approximate and space-efficient representation of the data cube. To answer an OLAP query, instead of computing the exact response, an approximate response is computed on this representation.

Iceberg data cube [7][8][9][10] is another approach to build incomplete data cube. In this approach, instead of computing all aggregated tuples, only those with support (or occurrence frequency) greater than certain thresholds are computed for the data cube. For efficient computation, the pruning technique in the search space is enforced based on anti-monotone constraints. This approach does not allow to answer all OLAP queries, because the data cube is partially computed.

To be able to answer all OLAP queries, many researchers focused the efforts to find the methods to represent the entire data cube with efficient computation and storage space. To reduce the time computing and the storage space, several interesting data structures were created. Dwarf data structure [11][12] is a special directed acyclic graph that allows not only the reduction of redundancies of tuple prefixes as the prefix tree structure, but also the reduction of tuple suffixes by coalescing the same tuple suffixes, using pointers. In addition Dwarf is a hierarchical structure that allows to store tuples and their subtuples on the same path of the graph, using the special key value ALL. Using Dwarf data structure for data storage, the exponential size of data cube is reduced dramatically. However, this structure is not relational and then cannot be directly apply in OLAP based on relational database tools (ROLAP).

In ROLAP, data cube is represented in relational tables. To be able to rapidly answer data cube queries, aggregate tables can be precomputed and stored on disks. To optimize the storage space, the aggregated tuples that can be deduced from already stored tuples are not stored, but represented by references to stored tuples. The reduction of the redundancies between tuples in cuboids is based on equivalence relations defined on aggregate functions [13][14] or on the concept of closed itemsets in frequent itemset mining [15][16].

The computation of all cuboids is usually organized on the complete lattice of subschemes of the dimension scheme of the fact table, in such a way the run time and the storage space can be optimized by reducing redundancies [3][13][14][17][18]. The computation can traverse the complete lattice in a top-down or bottom-up manner [9][19][20]. For grouping tuples to create cuboids, the sort operation can be used to reorganize tuples: tuples are grouped over the prefix of their scheme and the aggregate functions are applied to the measures. By grouping tuples, the fact table can be horizontally partitioned, each partition can be fixed in memory, and the cube computation can be modularized.

The top-down methods [19][20] walk the paths from the top to the bottom in the complete lattice, beginning with the node corresponding to the largest subscheme (the dimension scheme of the fact table, for the first processed path). To optimize the data cube construction, the cuboids over the subschemes on a path from the top to the bottom in the complete lattice can be built in only one lecture of the fact table. For this, an aggregate filter (accumulator), initialized with an empty tuple and a non aggregated mark, is used for each subscheme on the path. Each filter contains, at each time, only one tuple over the subscheme (associated with the filter) and the current aggregate value of the measure (or a non aggregated mark). Before processing, the tuples of the fact table are sorted over the largest scheme of the path. When reading the new tuple of the fact table, if over a subscheme of the currently processed path, the new tuple has the same value as the tuple in the filter, then only the aggregate value of the measure is updated. Otherwise, the current content of the filter is flushed out to the file of the corresponding cuboids on disk, and before the new tuple passes into the filter, the subtuple of the current content, over the next subscheme of the currently processed path (from the top to the bottom), is processed as the new tuple of the next subscheme filter. The same process is recursively applied to the subsequent subscheme filters.

To optimize the storage space of a cuboid, only aggregated subtuples with aggregate value of measure are directly stored on disk. Subtuples with non-aggregated mark are not stored but represented by references to the (sub)tuples where the non aggregated tuples are originated. Consequently, to answer a data cube query, by this representation, we may need to access to many different stored cuboids.

The bottom-up methods [13][14][17][20] walk the paths from the bottom to the top in the complete lattice, beginning with the empty node (corresponding to the cuboid with no dimension, for the first processed path). For each path, let T_0 be the scheme at the bottom node and T_n the scheme at of the top node of the path (not necessary the bottom and the top of the lattice, as each node is visited only once). These methods begin by sorting the fact table over T_0 and by this, the fact table is partitioned into groups over T_0. To optimize storage space, for each one of these groups, the following depth-first recursive process is applied.

If the group is single (having only one tuple), then the only element of the group is represented by a reference to the corresponding tuple in the fact table, and there is no further process: the recursive cuboid construction is pruned.

Otherwise, an aggregated tuple is created in the cuboid over T_0 and the group is sorted over the next larger scheme T_1 on the path. The group is then partitioned into subgroups over T_1. For each subgroup over T_1, the creation of a real tuple or a reference is similar to what we have done for a group over T_0.

When the recursive process is pruned at a node $T_i, 0 \leq i \leq n$, or reaches to T_n, it resumes with the next group of the partition over T_0, until all groups of the partition are processed. The construction resumes with the next path, until all paths of the complete lattice are processed, and all cuboids are built.

Note that in the above optimized bottom-up method, in all cuboids, if references exist, they refer directly to tuples in the fact table, not to tuples in other cuboids. This method, named Totally-Redundant-Segment BottomUpCube (TRS-BUC), is reported in [20] as a method that dominates or nearly dominates its competitors in all aspects of the data cube problem: fast computation of a fully materialized cube in compressed form, incrementally updateable, and quick query response time.

For updating a data cube with new tuples coming into the fact table, we can find in [20] the implementation of three update methods. (i) Merge method: build the data cube of the new tuples and then merge it with the current data cube. (ii) Direct method: update each cuboid of the current data cube with the new tuples. (iii) Reconstruction method: reconstruct the entire data cube of the fact table updated with the new tuples. These methods are experimented on different approaches to incrementally build the data cube, where the size of new dataset grows gradually from 1% to 10% of the size of the current fact table.

In the above approaches, the traversal of the complete lattice of the cuboids and the reduction of tuple redundancy by references imply the dependencies between cuboids. This can impact on the query response time and/or on the data cube update. Moreover, the representation of the entire data cube is computed for a specific measure and a specific aggregate function. When we need to have aggregate views on other measures and/or on other aggregate functions, we need to rebuild the data cube. To improve the query response time or the update time, indexes can be created for cuboids. Because of the tremendous number of aggregated tuples in the exponential number of cuboids, the time consuming for index creation may much longer than the time for building the data cube.

A. Contributions

This paper is an extension of the paper [1] that presents a simple and efficient approach to compute and to represent the entire data cubes. The extension consists in: (i) development and improvement of the contents (points 1 to 4 in what follows), and (ii) the implement of data cube update (point 5).

The efficient representation of data cube is not only a compact representation of all cuboids of the data cube, but also an efficient method to get the entire cuboids from the compact representation. The representation also allows to efficiently update the data cube when new data come into the fact table.

The main ideas and contributions of the proposed approach are:

1) Among the cuboids of a data cube, there are ones that can be easily and rapidly get from the others, with no important computing time. We call these others the prime and next-prime cuboids.
2) The prime and next-prime cuboids are computed and stored on disk using a prefix tree structure for compact representation. To improve the efficiency of search through the prefix tree, this work integrates the binary search tree into the prefix tree.
3) To compute the prime and next-prime cuboids, this work proposes a running scheme in which the computation of the current cuboids can be speeded up by using the cuboids that are previously computed.
4) Based on the prime and next-prime cuboids that are stored on disks, an efficient algorithm is proposed to retrieve all other cuboids that are not stored.
5) To update the data cube, we need only to update the prime and next-prime cuboids. An efficient algorithm for updating data cube is presented and experimented.

To compute the aggregates, this approach does not need to sort the fact table or any part of it beforehand. To optimize the computation and the storage space, the approach is not based on the complete lattice of subschemes of the dimension scheme and does not use sophisticated techniques to implement direct or indirect references of tuples in cuboids. Hence, there are no dependencies between the cuboids in the representation that can impact on query response time or on data cube update. Moreover, in contrast to the existing approaches in which the compact data cube is computed for a specific measure and a specific aggregate function and, to improve the query response time, the index can be created for data in the cuboids later, this approach prepares the data cube for any measure and any aggregate function by creating the cube of indexes.

III. PRIME AND NEXT-PRIME CUBOIDS

This section defines the main concepts of the present approach to compute and to represent data cubes.

A. A structure of the power set

A data cube over a dimension scheme S is the set of cuboids built over all subsets of S, that is the power set of S. As in most of existing work, attributes are encoded in integer, let us consider $S = \{1, 2, ..., n\}$, $n \geq 1$. The power set of S can be recursively defined as follows.

1) The power set of $S_0 = \emptyset$ (the empty set) is $P_0 = \{\emptyset\}$.
2) For $n \geq 1$, the power set of $S_n = \{1, 2, ..., n\}$ can be recursively defined as follows:

$$P_n = P_{n-1} \cup \{X \cup \{n\} \mid X \in P_{n-1}\} \quad (1)$$

P_n is the union of P_{n-1} (the power set of S_{n-1}) and the set of which each element is got by adding n to each element of P_{n-1}.
Let us call P_{n-1} the *first-half power set* of S_n and the second operand of P_n the *last-half power set* of S_n.

As the number of subsets in P_{n-1} is 2^{n-1}, the number of subsets in the first-half power set of S_n is 2^{n-1}. As each subset in the last-half power set of S_n is obtained by adding element n to a unique subset of the first-half power set of S_n, the number of subsets in the last-half power set of S_n is also 2^{n-1}. Every subset in the first-half power set does not contain n, but every subset in the last-half power set does contain n. Moreover, the subsets in the last-half power set can be divided in two groups: one contains the subsets having element 1 and the other contains the subsets without element 1.

Example 1: For $n = 3$, $S_3 = \{1, 2, 3\}$, we have:

$P_0 = \{\emptyset\}$; $P_1 = \{\emptyset, \{1\}\}$; $P_2 = \{\emptyset, \{1\}, \{2\}, \{1, 2\}\}$;
$P_3 = \{\emptyset, \{1\}, \{2\}, \{1, 2\}, \{3\}, \{1, 3\}, \{2, 3\}, \{1, 2, 3\}\}$.
The first-half power set of S_3 is:
$\{\emptyset, \{1\}, \{2\}, \{1, 2\}\}$.
And the last-half power set of S_3 is:
$\{\{3\}, \{1, 3\}, \{2, 3\}, \{1, 2, 3\}\}$.

B. Last-half data cube and first-half data cube

Consider a fact table R (a relational data table) over a dimension scheme $S_n = \{1, 2, ..., n\}$. In view of the first-half and the last-half power set, suppose that $X = \{x_1, ..., x_i\}$ is an element of the first-half power set of S_n ($\{x_1, ..., x_i\} \subseteq S_n$). Let Y be the smallest element of the last-half power set of S_n that contains X. Then, $Y = X \cup \{n\}$. If the cuboid over Y is already computed in the attribute order $x_1, ..., x_i, n$, then the cuboid over $X = x_1, ..., x_i$ can be computed by a simple sequential reading of the cuboid over Y to get data for the cuboid over X. So, we define the following concepts.

– We call a scheme in the last-half power set a *prime scheme* and a cuboid over a prime scheme a *prime cuboid*. Note that all prime schemes contain the last attribute n and any scheme that contains attribute n is a prime scheme.

– For efficient computing, the prime cuboids can be computed by pairs. Such a pair is composed of two prime cuboids. The scheme of the first one has attribute 1 and the scheme of the second one is obtained from the scheme of the first one by deleting attribute 1. We call the second prime cuboid the *next-prime cuboid*.

– The set of all cuboids over the prime (or next-prime) schemes is called the *last-half data cube*. The set of all remaining cuboids is called the *first-half data cube*. In this approach, the last-half data cube is computed and stored on disks. Cuboids in the first-half data cube are computed as queries based on the last-half data cube.

IV. INTEGRATED BINARY SEARCH PREFIX TREE

The prefix tree structure offers a compact storage for tuples: the common prefix of tuples is stored once. So, there is no redundancy in storage. Despite the compact structure of the prefix tree, if the same prefix has a large set of different suffixes, then the time for searching the set of suffixes can be important. To improve the search time when building the prefix tree, this work proposes to integrate the binary search tree into the prefix structure. The integrated structure, called the *binary search prefix tree (BSPT)*, is used to store tuples of cuboids. With this structure, tuples with the same prefix are stored as follows:

– The prefix is stored once.

– The suffixes of those tuples are organized in siblings and stored in a binary search tree.

Precisely, in C language, the structure is defined by :

```
typedef struct bsptree Bsptree; // Binary search prefix tree
struct bsptree{ Elt data;          // data at a node
                Ltid *ltid;        // list of RowIds
                Bsptree *son, *lsib, *rsib; };
```

where son, $lsib$, and $rsib$ represent respectively the son, the left and the right siblings of nodes. The field $ltid$ is reserved for the list of tuple identifiers ($RowId$) associated with nodes. For efficient memory use, $ltid$ is stored only at the last node of each path in the BSPT.

With this representation, each binary search tree contains all siblings of a node in the normal prefix tree.

Example 2:

Consider Table I that represents a fact table R1 over the dimension scheme $ABCD$ and a measure M. Fig. 1 represents the BSPT of the tuples over the scheme $ABCD$ of the fact table R1, where we suppose that with the same letter x, if $i < j$ then $xi < xj$, e.g., $a1 < a2 < a3$. In this figure, the continuous lines represent the son links and the dashed lines represent the lsib or rsib links.

In each binary search tree of Fig. 1, if we do the depth-first search in in-order, we can get tuples in increasing order as follows:

TABLE I. FACT TABLE R1

RowId	A	B	C	D	M
1	a2	b1	c2	d2	m1
2	a3	b2	c2	d2	m2
3	a1	b1	c1	d1	m1
4	a1	b1	c2	d1	m3
5	a3	b3	c2	d3	m2

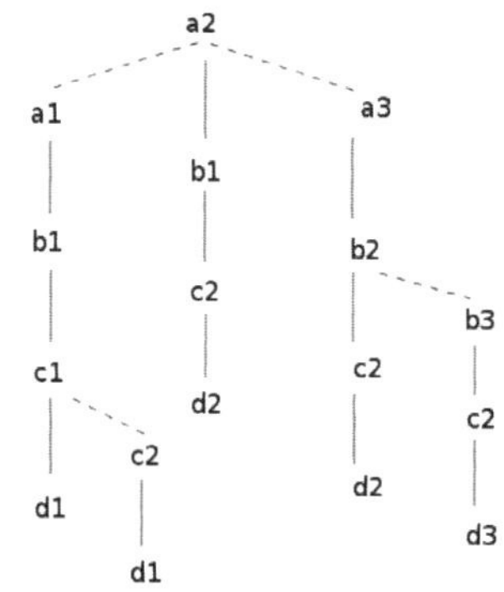

Figure 1. A binary search prefix tree

(a1, b1, c1, d1)
(a1, b1, c2, d1)
(a2, b1, c2, d2)
(a2, b2, c2, d2)
(a2, b3, c2, d3)

The BSPT is saved to disk with the following format:

$level : suffix : ltid$

where

– level is the length of the prefix part that the path has in common with its left neighbor,

– suffix is tuple (a list of dimension values) and,

– ltid is a list of tuple identifiers (RowId).

Cuboids are built using the BSPT structure. The list of RowIds associated with the last node of each path allows the aggregate of measures. For example, with the fact table in Table I, the cuboid over $ABCD$ is saved on disk as the following.

$0 : a1\ b1\ c1\ d1 : 3$

$2 : c2\ d1 : 4$

$0 : a2\ b1\ c2\ d2 : 1$

$0 : a3\ b2\ c2\ d2 : 2$

$1 : b3\ c2\ d3 : 5$

A. Insertion of tuples in a BSPT

The following algorithm, named *Tuple2Ptree*, defines the method to insert tuples into a BSPT, while maintaining the BSPT structure.

Algorithm Tuple2Ptree: Insert a tuple into a BSPT.

Input: A BSPT represented by node P, a tuple $ldata$ and its list of RowIds lti.

Output: The tree P updated with $ldata$ and lti.

Method:

If P is null then
create P with P->data = head(ldata);
P->son = P->lsib = P->rsib = NULL;
if queue(ldata) is null then P->ltid =lti;
else P->son = Tuple2Pree(P->son, queue(ldata), lti);
Else if P->data > head(ldata) then
P->lsib=Tuple2Ptree(P->lsib, ldata,lti);
else if P->data < head(ldata) then
P->rsib=Tuple2Ptree(P->rsib, ldata,lti);
else if queue(ldata) is null then
P->ltid = append(P->ltid, lti);
else P->son = Tuple2Ptree(P->son, queue(ldata), lti);
return P;

In the Tuple2Ptree algorithm, $head(ldata)$ returns the first element of $ldata$, $queue(ldata)$ returns the queue of $ldata$ after removing $head(ldata)$, and $append(P\text{->}ltid, lti)$ adds the list lti to the list of RowIds associated with node P.

B. Grouping tuples using binary prefix tree

To create the BSPT of a table of tuples where each one has a list of RowIds lti, we use an algorithm named *Table2Ptree*. This algorithm allows to group the tuples over the dimension scheme of the table, hence allows to create the corresponding cuboid. As nodes corresponding to each attribute of tuples are organized in binary search tree structures, we can get the cuboid with groups of tuples ordered in the increasing order.

Algorithm Table2Ptree: Build a BSPT for a relational table.

Input: A table R in which each tuple has a list of tids lti.

Output: The BSPT P for R

Method:

Create an empty BSPT P;
For each tuple ldata in R with its list of tids lti do
P = Tuple2Ptree(P, ldata, lti);
done;
Return P;

V. THE LAST-HALF DATA CUBE REPRESENTATION

This section presents a method to build the last-half data cube. It also shows how the data cube is represented by the last-half data cube and how the entire data cube can be restored from this representation.

A. Computing the last-half data cube

Let $S = \{1, 2, ..., n\}$ be the set of all dimensions of the fact table. To compute all prime and next-prime cuboids of the last-half data cube, we process as follows:

– Based on the fact table, we begin by computing the first pair of prime and next-prime cuboids, one over S and the other over $S - \{1\}$.

– In the sequence, based on the previously computed pairs of prime and next-prime cuboids we compute the other pairs of prime and next-prime cuboids. To control the computation, we use:

(i) A list to keep track of the generated prime schemes. This list is called the *running scheme* and denoted by RS and,

(ii) A current scheme, denoted by cS, that is set to a prime scheme that is currently considered in RS. From the current scheme, the further pairs of prime and next-prime cuboids are generated, based on the cuboid over the current scheme.

Through the computation of the last-half data cube, after the generation of the first pair of prime and next-prime cuboids, the dimension scheme S is the first prime scheme added into RS and cS is initialized to S. Then, for each dimension d, $d \neq 1$ and $d \neq n$, the prime scheme $cS - \{d\}$ is generated. If $cS - \{d\}$ is not yet in RS, then it is appended to RS and we compute the pair of prime and next-prime cuboids, one over $cS - \{d\}$ and the other over $cS - \{1, d\}$, based on the cuboids over cS. When all dimensions $d \in cS, d \neq 1, d \neq n$ are considered, cS is set to the next scheme in RS for generating new pairs of prime and next-prime cuboids. The process ends when all prime schemes of size $k > 2$ in RS are treated.

We associate each prime scheme X in RS with information that allows to retrieve the pairs of prime cuboids over X and $X - \{1\}$. This is not only necessary when computing the last-half data cube, but also when restoring the entire data cube.

More formally, we use the following algorithm, named $LastHalfCube$, for computing the last-half data cube.

Algorithm LastHalfCube

Input: A fact table R over scheme S of n dimensions.

Output: The last-half data cube of R and the running scheme RS.

Method:

0) Initialize the list RS to emptyset;
1) Append S to the RS;
2) Generate two prime and next-prime cuboids over S and S - {1}, respectively, using algorithm Table2Tree and R;
3) Set cS to the first scheme in RS; // cS: current scheme
4) While cS has more than 2 attributes do
5) For each dimension d in cS, d ≠ 1 and d ≠ n, do
6) Build a subscheme scS by deleting d from cS;
7) If scS is not yet in RS then append scS to RS and let Cubo be the already computed cuboid over cS;
8) Using Table2Ptree and Cubo to generate two cuboids over scS and scS - {1}, respectively;
9) done;
10) Set cS to the next scheme in RS;
11) done;
12) Return RS;

Example 3: An example of running scheme.

Table II shows the simplified execution of the LastHalfCube algorithm on a fact table R over the dimension scheme $S = \{1, 2, 3, 4, 5\}$. In this table, only the prime and the next-prime (NPrime) schemes of the cuboids computed by the algorithm are reported. The prime schemes appended to the Running Scheme RS during the execution of LastHalfCube are in the columns named Prime/RS. The first prime schemes are in the first column Prime/RS, the next ones are in the second column Prime/RS, and the final ones are in the third column Prime/RS. The final state of RS is $\{12345, 1345, 1245, 1235, 145, 135, 125, 15\}$. In Table II, the schemes marked with x (e.g., 145x) are those already added to RS and are not re-appended to RS.

TABLE II. GENERATION OF THE RUNNING SCHEME OVER $S = \{1, 2, 3, 4, 5\}$.

Prime RS	NPrime	Prime RS	NPrime	Prime RS	NPrime
12345	2345				
1 345	345				
		1 45	45		
				15	5
		1 35	35		
				15x	
12 45	2 45				
		1 45x			
		1 25	25		
				15x	
123 5	23 5				
		1 35x			
		1 25x			

Proof of correctness and soundness. To prove the correctness and soundness of the LastHalfCube algorithm, we only need to show that for a fact table R over a scheme S of n dimensions, $S = \{1, 2, ..., n\}$, the LastHalfCube algorithm generates RS with 2^{n-2} subschemes containing 1 and n as the first and the last attributes. For this, we can see that all subschemes appended to RS have 1 as the first attribute and n as the last attribute. So, we can forget 1 and n from all those subschemes. Therefore, we can consider that the first subscheme added to RS is $2, ..., n-1$. Over $2, ..., n-1$, we have only one subscheme of size $n-2$ ($C_{n-2}^{n-2} = 1$). In the loop For at point 5 of the LastHalfCube algorithm, alternatively each attribute from 2 to $n-1$ is deleted to generate a subscheme of size $n-3$. By doing this, we can consider as, in each iteration, we build a subscheme over $n-3$ different attributes selected among $n-2$ attributes. So, we build C_{n-2}^{n-3} subschemes. So on, until the subscheme $\{1, n\}$ (corresponding to the empty scheme after forgetting 1 and n) is added to RS. We have:

$$C_{n-2}^{n-2} + C_{n-2}^{n-3} + ... + C_{n-2}^{0} = 2^{n-2}$$

For each of these 2^{n-1} prime schemes, the LastHalfCube algorithm also computes the corresponding next-prime scheme. By adding the 2^{n-2} corresponding next-prime schemes, we have 2^{n-1} different subschemes. Thus, the LastHalfCube algorithm computes 2^{n-1} prime and next-prime schemes (and cuboids).

B. Data Cube representation

For a fact table R over a dimension scheme $S = \{1, 2, ..., n\}$ with measures $M_1, ..., M_k$, the data cube of R is represented by (RS, LH, F), where

1) RS is the running scheme, i.e., the list of all prime schemes over S. Each prime scheme has an identifier number that allows to locate the files corresponding to the prime and next-prime cuboids in the last-half data cube.

2) LH: The last-half data cube of which the cuboids are precomputed and stored on disks using the format to store the BSPT.

3) F: A relational table over $RowId, M_1, ..., M_k$ that represents the measures associated with each tuple of R.

Clearly, such a representation reduces about 50% space of the entire data cube, as it represents the last-half data cube in the BSPT format.

C. Computing the first-half data cube

In this subsection, we show how the cuboids of the first-half data cube are computed based on the last-half data cube.

Let $S = \{1, 2, ..., n\}$ be the dimension scheme of the data cube and $X = \{x_{i1}, ..., x_{ik}\}$ be the scheme of a cuboid in the first-half data cube that we need to retrieve. The size of X is k ($k < n$, $n \notin X$); n is the size of S and also the last attribute of S.

Let C be the stored cuboid over $X \cup \{n\}$ (C is in the last-half data cube). C is a prime cuboid if X contains attribute 1, a next prime cuboid, if not. Remind from Section IV that a tuple of a prime or next-prime cuboid is stored on disk in the BSPT format:

$level : suffix : ltid$

By BSPT structure, the tuples of C that have the same prefix over X are already regrouped together when C is stored on disk. For each such a group, we take the prefix and the collection of all tuple identifiers (RowId) in the lists of identifiers associated with these tuples to create a record (an aggregated tuple) of the cuboid over X. More formally, to build the cuboid over X, we use the following algorithm named *Aggregate-Projection*.

Algorithm Aggregate-Projection

Input: The representation (RS, LH, F) of a data cube over a dimension scheme $S = \{1, 2, ..., n\}$ and a scheme X of size k, such that $n \notin X$.

Output: The cuboid over X of the data cube represented by (RS, LH, F).

Method:

Let C be the prime cuboid over $X \cup \{n\}$;
// C is precomputed and stored in LH.

Let $level : suffix, t(n) : ltid$ be the 1st record in C;
// $t(n)$: the tuple value at attribute n. As the 1st record in C,
// we have $level = 0$ and $suffix$ is a tuple of size k.

Set $t_c = suffix; ltid_c = ltid$;
// ($t_c : ltid_c$): the record currently built for the cuboid over X

For each new record $level_w : suffix_w, t_w(n) : ltid_w$ sequentially read in C do

If $level_w \geq k$, then append $ltid_w$ to the end of $ltid_c$;
// case the new tuple of C has the same prefix as
// the tuple currently built.

Else

Write $t_c : ltid_c$ to disk as an aggregated tuple of the cuboid over X;

Update the elements of the tuple t_c, from rang $level_w + 1$ to rang k, with the corresponding attribute values of the tuple $suffix_w$ and

Re-initialize lti_c to $ltid_w$;

done.

D. Querying data cubes

In contrast to existing approaches, the present approach does not compute the representation of the data cube for a specific measure, neither for a specific aggregate function, but it computes the representation that is ready for the computation on any measure and any aggregate function. The last-half data cube is in fact the collection of index tables of tuples of the cuboids in the last-half data cube. We can get the cuboid over a scheme X with a specific measure M and a specific aggregate function g, based on the representation in Subsection V-B, by slightly modifying the Aggregate-Projection algorithm. The modified algorithm is named *Aggregate-Query*.

Algorithm Aggregate-Query

Input: The representation (RS, LH, F) of a data cube over a dimension scheme $S = \{1, 2, ..., n\}$ and a scheme X of size $k \leq n$, a measure M and an aggregate function g.

Output: The cuboid over X computed for g and M.

Method:

If $n \in X$ *then*
  Let C *be the prime cuboid* $\in LH$, *over* X;
  For each record $(level : suffix : ltid) \in C$ *do,*
    Let t *be the tuple built on* $level$ *and* $suffix$;
    Let Ω *be the set of values of the measure* M *computed on* $ltid$ *and the relational table* F;
    Apply g *to* Ω; *print* $(t : g(\Omega))$;
  done;
Else,
  Let C *be the prime cuboid over* $X \cup \{n\}$;
  Let $(level : suffix, t(n) : ltid)$ *be the 1st record in* C;
  Set $t_c = suffix; ltid_c = ltid$;
  For each new record $(level_w : suffix_w, t_w(n) : ltid_w)$ *sequentially read in* C *do*
    If $level_w \geq k$ *then append* $ltid_w$ *to the end of* $ltid_c$;
    Else,
      Let Ω *be the set of values of the measure* M *computed on* $ltid_c$ *and the relational table* F;
      Apply g *to* Ω; *print* $(t_c : g(\Omega))$;
      Update the elements of the tuple t_c, *from rang* $level_w + 1$ *to rang* k, *with the corresponding attribute values of the tuple* $suffix_w$ *and Re-initialize* lti_c *to* $ltid_w$;
  done.

VI. UPDATING DATA CUBES

For updating a data cube with new tuples coming into the fact table, we can have three data cube update methods. (i) The Merge method builds the data cube of the new tuples and then merge it with the current data cube. (ii) The Direct method updates each cuboid of the current data cube with the new tuples. (iii) The Reconstruction method reconstructs the entire data cube of the fact table updated with the new tuples.

In the present approach, a data cube is represented by its last-half. When new data coming into the fact table, to update the data cube, we need only to update its last-half. The three methods of data cube update can be applied to the representation by the last-half data cube. In particular, the Merge method and the Direct method can be more efficient with the last-half data cube representation: we must only merge or access to a half number of cuboids of the data cube. Moreover, as we do not walk the complete lattice of the cuboids in the data cube, we can update each cuboid independently.

The present work has implemented the update by the Direct method. For this, the cuboids of the current last-half data cube are restored from disk to main memory, in the binary search prefix tree structure. For each such a restored tree, the projection of new data on the scheme of the cuboid stored in the tree is inserted into the tree. Precisely, we use the following algorithm, named *LastHalfCubeUpdate*, to update the last-half cube.

Algorithm LastHalfCubeUpdate: Update the last-half data cube with new data tuples.

Input: The representation (RS, LH, F) of a data cube, where RS is the running scheme, LH the last-half data cube, F the current fact table, and a new fact table NF.

Output: The updated representation $(RS, LH', F \cup NF)$ where LH' is the last-half data cube of the updated fact table $F \cup NF$.

Method:

For each Sch *in the running scheme* RS *do*

1) From the last-half cube LH, *restore the prime cuboid associated with* Sch *in a BSPT;*

2) For each tuple t *of the new fact table* NF, *insert the restriction of* t *on* Sch *(i.e.,* $t[Sch]$*) into the BSPT of the prime cuboid using the Tuple2Ptree algorithm;*

3) Save the BSPT to disk;

4) From the last-half cube LH, *restore the next-prime cuboid associated with* $Sch - \{1\}$ *in a BSPT;*

5) For each tuple t *of the new fact table NF, insert the restriction of* t *on* $Sch - \{1\}$ *(i.e.,* $t[Sch - \{1\}]$*) into the BSPT of the next-prime cuboid using the Tuple2Ptree algorithm;*

6) Save the BSPT to disk;

done.

VII. EXPERIMENTAL RESULTS

The present approach to represent and to compute data cubes is implemented in C and experimented on a laptop with 8 GB memory, Intel Core i5-3320 CPU @ 2.60 GHz x 4, 188 Go Disk, running Ubuntu 12.04 LTS. To get some ideas about the efficiency of the present approach, we recall here some experimental results in [20] as references. The experiments in [20] were run on a Pentium 4 (2.8 GHz) PC with 512 MB memory under Windows XP.

For greater efficiency, in the experiments of [20], the dimensions of the datasets are arranged in the decreasing order of the attribute domain cardinality. The same arrangement is done in our experiments. Moreover, as most algorithms studied in [20] compute condensed cuboids, computing query in data cube needs additional cost. So, the results are reported in two parts: computing the condensed data cube and querying data cube. The former is reported with the construction time and storage space and the latter the average query response time.

The work [20] has experimented many existing and well known methods for computing and representing data cube as Partitioned-Cube (PC), Partially-Redundant-Segment-PC (PRS-PC), Partially-Redundant-Tuple-PC (PRT-PC), BottomUpCube (BUC), Bottom-Up-Base-Single-Tuple

(BU-BST), and Totally-Redundant-Segment BottomUpCube (TRS-BUC). The results were reported on real and synthetic datasets. For the present work, we report only the experimental results on two real datasets CovType [22] and SEP85L [23]. By reporting these results, we do not want to really compare the present approach to TRS-BUC or others, as we do not have sufficient conditions to implement and to run these methods on the same system and machine. Moreover, in those methods, the data cubes are computed for a specific measure and a specific aggregate function, whereas in the present approach, the data cube are prepared for any measure and any aggregate function. In fact, for each tuple in a cuboid, the present approach computes all RowIds of the fact table that are associated with the tuple. Hence, we cannot compare the present approach with those methods, on the run time and the storage space.

Apart CovType and SEP85L, the present approach is also experimented on two other datasets that are not used in [20]. These datasets are STCO-MR2010_AL_MO [24] and *OnlineRetail*[25][26].

CovType is a dataset of forest cover-types. It has ten dimensions and 581,012 tuples. The dimensions and their cardinality are: Horizontal-Distance-To-Fire-Points (5,827), Horizontal-Distance-To-Roadways (5,785), Elevation (1,978), Vertical-Distance-To-Hydrology (700), Horizontal-Distance-To-Hydrology (551), Aspect (361), Hillshade-3pm (255), Hillshade-9am (207), Hillshade-Noon (185), and Slope (67).

SEP85L is a weather dataset. It has nine dimensions and 1,015,367 tuples. The dimensions and their cardinality are: Station-Id (7,037), Longitude (352), Solar-Altitude (179), Latitude (152), Present-Weather (101), Day (30), Weather-Change-Code (10), Hour (8), and Brightness (2).

STCO-MR2010_AL_MO is a census dataset on population of Alabama through Missouri in 2010, with 640586 tuples over ten integer and categorical attributes. After transforming categorical attributes (STNAME and CTYNAME), the dataset is arranged in decreasing order of cardinality of its attributes as follows: RESPOP (9953), CTYNAME (1049), COUNTY (189), IMPRACE (31), STATE (26), STNAME (26), AGEGRP (7), SEX (2), ORIGIN (2), SUMLEV (1).

OnlineRetail is a data set that contains the transactions occurring between 01/12/2010 and 09/12/2011 for a UK-based and registered non-store online retail. This dataset has incomplete data, integer and categorical attributes. After verifying, transforming categorical attributes into integer attributes, for the experiments, we retain 393127 complete data tuples and the following ten dimensions ordered in their cardinality as follows: CustomerID (4331), StockCode (3610), UnitPrice (368), Quantity (298), Minute (60), Country (37), Day (31), Hour (15), Month(12), and Year (2).

Table III presents the experimental results approximately got from the graphs in [20], where "avg QRT" denotes the average query response time and "Construction time" denotes the time to construct the (condensed) data cube. However, [20] did not specify whether the construction time includes the time to read/write data to files.

Table IV reports the results of the present work on CovType and SEP85L, where the term "run time" means the time from the start of the program to the time the last-half (or first-half) data cube is completely constructed, including the time to read/write input/output files.

TABLE III. EXPERIMENTAL RESULTS IN [20]

CovType

Algorithms	Storage space	Construction time	avg QRT
PC	#12.5 Gb	1900 sec	
PRT-PC	#7.2 Gb	1400 sec	
PRS-PC	#2.2 Gb	1200 sec	3.5 sec
BUC	#12.5 Gb	2900 sec	2 sec
BU-BST	#2.3 Gb	350 sec	
BU-BST+	#1.2 Gb	400 sec	1.3 sec
TRS-BUC	#0.4 Gb	300 sec	0.7 sec

SEP85L

Algorithms	Storage space	Construction time	avg QRT
PC	#5.1 Gb	1300 sec	
PRT-PC	#3.3 Gb	1150 sec	
PRS-PC	#1.4 Gb	1100 sec	1.9 sec
BUC	#5.1 Gb	1600 sec	1.1 sec
BU-BST	#3.6 Gb	1200 sec	
BU-BST+	#2.1 Gb	1300 sec	0.98 sec
TRS-BUC	#1.2 Gb	1150 sec	0.5 sec

TABLE IV. EXPERIMENTAL RESULTS OF THIS WORK ON CovType AND SEP85L

CovType

	Storage space	Run time	avg QRT
Last-Half Cube	7 Gb	1018 sec	
First-Half Cube	6,2 Gb	435 sec	
Data Cube	13,2 Gb	1453 sec	0.43 sec

SEP85L

	Storage space	Run time	avg QRT
Last-Half Cube	2.8 Gb	444 sec	
First-Half Cube	2.6 Gb	172 sec	
Data Cube	5.4 Gb	616 sec	0.34 sec

As we do not compute the condensed cuboids, but only compute the last-half data cube and use it to represent the data cube, we can consider that the last-half data cube corresponds somehow to the (condensed) representations of data cube in the other approaches, and computing the first-half data cube corresponds to querying data cube. In this view, the average query response time corresponds to the average run time for computing a cuboid based on the precomputed and stored cuboids. That is, the average query response time for SEP85L is 172s/512 = 0.34 second and for CovType 435s/1024 = 0.43 second, because the cuboids in the last-half data cube are precomputed and stored, only querying on the first-half data cube needs computing.

Though the compactness of the data cube representation by the present approach is not comparable to the compactness offered by TRS-BUC, it is in the range of other existing methods. However, note that while the existing methods store aggregated tuples (or references) with the values of a specific aggregate function of a specific measure, the present approach stores aggregated tuples with lists of RowIds that allow to access to all measures of the fact table. It is similar for the run time to build the last-half data cube of CovType. However, the run time to build the entire (not only the last-half) data cube of SEP85L seems to be better than all other existing methods. On the average query response time, it seems that the present approach offers a competitive solution, because querying data cube is a repetitive operation and improving the average query response time is one of the important goals of research on data cube.

TABLE V. EXPERIMENTAL RESULTS OF THIS WORK ON STCO-MR2010_AL_MO AND OnlineRetail

STCO-MR2010_AL_MO	Storage space	Run time	avg QRT
Last-Half Cube	3.4 Gb	740 sec	
First-Half Cube	3.2 Gb	209 sec	
Data Cube	6.6 Gb	949 sec	0.20 sec

OnlineRetail	Storage space	Run time	avg QRT
Last-Half Cube	3 Gb	426 sec	
First-Half Cube	2.4 Gb	185 sec	
Data Cube	5.4 Gb	611 sec	0.18 sec

Table V reports the results of the present work on the datasets STCO-MR2010_AL_MO and OnlineRetail, where the term "run time" has the same meaning as in Table IV.

Tables VI and VII report the run time of the present approach for computing the cuboids with the aggregate functions COUNT and SUM, respectively, on the four datasets CovType, SEP85L, STCO-MR2010_AL_MO and OnlineRetail. Each value in these tables is the total time in seconds for computing all cuboids in the corresponding part of the data cube. For example, in the line COUNT Last-Half, we have the total time for computing 256 cuboids of the last-half data cube of SEP85L for the COUNT function is 172 seconds. The total time includes the computation time and the input/output time for reading data and rewriting the results to disk. In addition, COUNT Avg Time (or SUM Avg Time) is the average time for building a cuboid for the aggregate function COUNT (or SUM, respectively), based on the representation (RS, LH, F). For example, the average time for building a cuboid for the aggregate function COUNT on the dataset SEP85L is 326/512 = 0.64 second.

TABLE VI. RESULTS ON AGGREGATE-QUERY FOR COUNT

	CovType	SEP85L	STCO-M	OnlineR
COUNT Last-Half	467 sec	172 sec	195 sec	193 sec
COUNT First-Half	442 sec	154 sec	180 sec	176 sec
COUNT Data Cube	889 sec	326 sec	375 sec	369 sec
COUNT Avg Time	0.87 sec	0.64 sec	0.37 sec	0.36 sec

TABLE VII. RESULTS ON AGGREGATE-QUERY FOR SUM

	CovType	SEP85L	STCO-M	OnlineR
SUM Last-Half	481 sec	195 sec	217 sec	201 sec
SUM First-Half	444 sec	180 sec	204 sec	185 sec
SUM Data Cube	925 sec	375 sec	421 sec	386 sec
SUM Avg Time	0.9 sec	0.73 sec	0.41 sec	0.38 sec

For experimenting the data cube update, this work uses the same four datasets. Each original dataset is divided into two parts. The first part is used to create the last-half data cube and the second part is used to update the last-half data cube created on the first part. After the update, we have the same last-half data cube as we have created the last-half data cube with the entire original dataset. By this way, we can compare the time for incremental updating and the time for rebuilding the last-half data cube with the entire updated dataset. The ratio of the size of the second part to the size of the first part varies in $\{5\%, 11\%, 25\%, 43\%, 66\%\}$ (size in number of tuples). The experimental results are reported in Tables VIII and IX, where Update Time includes the time for restoring the current last-half data cube in main memory, the time for updating it, and the time for writing the updated last-half cube to disk. In addition, the lines Tot-Tuples, 1st Part, and 2nd Part represent respectively the numbers of tuples in the original dataset, in the first part, and in the second part.

TABLE VIII. INCREMENTAL DATA CUBE UPDATING TIME

	CovType	SEP85L	STCO-M	OnlineR
Tot-Tuples	581012	1015367	640586	393127
Ratio 5%				
1st Part	551959	964596	608553	373469
2nd Part	29053	50771	32032	19658
Update Time	864 sec	331 sec	414 sec	348 sec
Ratio 11%				
1st Part	522909	913831	576528	353814
2nd Part	58103	101536	64507	39313
Update Time	928 sec	372 sec	332 sec	369 sec
Ratio 25%				
1st Part	464809	812301	512478	314504
2nd Part	116203	203066	128107	78623
Update Time	962 sec	417 sec	582 sec	392 sec
Ratio 43%				
1st Part	406709	710771	448428	275194
2nd Part	174303	304596	192157	117933
Update Time	996 sec	470 sec	691 sec	417 sec
Ratio 66%				
1st Part	348609	609241	384378	235884
2nd Part	232403	406126	256207	157243
Update Time	1042 sec	515 sec	797 sec	441 sec

Table IX represents the time saved by incremental update, in comparison with the time to rebuild entirely the last-half data cube of the updated fact table. In Table IX,

– Rebuild Time is the time for rebuilding entirely the last-half data cube of the updated fact table,

– $x\%$-Updt-Time is the time for incremental update of the last-half data cube where $x\%$ is the ratio of the size of the second part to the size of the first part and,

– Time Saving is the difference between Rebuild Time and $x\%$-Updt-Time.

All the times includes the computation time and the input/output time, in seconds. Table IX shows that when the ratio of the size of the new fact table to the size of the current fact table varies from 5% to 25%, the incremental update is more interesting. Afterward, it would be better to rebuild entirely the last-half data cube of the updated fact table.

VIII. CONCLUSION AND FURTHER WORK

This work is an extension of [1] that represents a data cube by its last-half: the set of cuboids called prime (or next-prime) cuboids. All other cuboids are computed by a simple operation, called the aggregate-projection, based the last-half data cube. The representation is reduced because only a half of the data cube is stored using the binary search prefix tree (BSPT) structure. Such a structure offers not only a compact representation but also an efficient search method. Building a cuboid in the last-half data cube is reduced to building a BSPT. The BSPT allows efficient group-by operation without previous sort operation on tuples in the fact table or in cuboids.

TABLE IX. TIME SAVING BY DATA CUBE UPDATE

	CovType	SEP85L	STCO-M	OnlineR
ReBuild Time	1018 sec	444 sec	740 sec	426 sec
5%-Updt-Time	864 sec	331 sec	414 sec	348 sec
Time Saving	154 sec	113 sec	326 sec	78 sec
11%-Updt-Time	928 sec	372 sec	332 sec	369 sec
Time Saving	90 sec	72 sec	408 sec	57 sec
25%-Updt-Time	962 sec	417 sec	582 sec	392 sec
Time Saving	56 sec	27 sec	158 sec	34 sec
43%-Updt-Time	996 sec	470 sec	691 sec	417 sec
Time Saving	22 sec	-26 sec	49 sec	9 sec
66%-Updt-Time	1042 sec	515 sec	797 sec	441 sec
Time Saving	-24 sec	-71 sec	-57 sec	-15 sec

Each cuboid in the representation is in fact an index table in which tuples have a list of RowIds referencing to tuples in the fact table. The experimental results show that the average time for computing the a cuboid with the aggregate functions COUNT and SUM based on this representation is among the average time of the efficient methods. Moreover, based on this representation, we can compute the cuboids for any aggregate function and any measure, without rebuilding the representation when we change the measure or the aggregate function.

The experimental results of the incremental update on the four real datasets, using the Direct method, show that the time saving, with respect to the Reconstruction method, is interesting when the ratio of the size of the new fact table to the size of the current fact table varies from 5% to 25%. When the ratio is greater than 40%, it would be better to rebuild entirely the last-half data cube of the updated fact table.

On the above experimental results, we can conclude that the approach is interesting not only in computing time, storage space, and representation, but also interesting for querying and incremental update. As we can efficiently access to all aggregated tuples in the data cube, it is interesting to study the application of this representation in data mining, in particular, for classification or detection of anomalies.

REFERENCES

[1] V. Phan-Luong, "A Simple and Efficient Method for Computing Data Cubes," in Proceedings of the 4th International Conference on Communications, Computation, Networks and Technologies (INNOV), November 15-20, 2015, Barcelona, Spain, pp. 50-55.

[2] S. Agarwal et al., "On the computation of multidimensional aggregates," in Proceedings of the 22nd International Conference on Very Large Data Bases (VLDB), 1996, Mumbai (Bombay), India, pp. 506-521.

[3] V. Harinarayan, A. Rajaraman, and J. Ullman, "Implementing data cubes efficiently," in Proceedings of the 1996 ACM SIGMOD, Montreal, Canada, pp. 205-216.

[4] S. Chaudhuri and U. Dayal, "An Overview of Data Warehousing and OLAP Technology," SIGMOD Record Vol. 26, Issue 1, 1997, pp. 65-74.

[5] Y. Zhao, P. Deshpande, and J. F. Naughton, "An array-based algorithm for simultaneous multidimensional aggregates," in Proceedings of the 1997 ACM SIGMOD International Conference on Management of Data, Tucson, Arizona, USA, pp. 159-170.

[6] J. S. Vitter, M. Wang, and B. R. Iyer, "Data cube approximation and histograms via wavelets," in Proceedings of the 7th International Conference on Information and Knowledge Management (CIKM), 1998, Bethesda, Maryland, USA, pp. 96-104.

[7] K. S. Beyer, R. Ramakrishnan, "Bottom-up computation of sparse and iceberg cubes," in Proceedings of the 5th ACM International Workshop on Data Warehousing and OLAP, (SIGMOD), 1999, Philadelphia, Pennsylvania, USA, pp. 359-370.

[8] J. Han, J. Pei, G. Dong, and K. Wang, "Efficient Computation of Iceberg Cubes with Complex Measures," in Proceedings of the 2001 ACM SIGMOD International Conference on Management of Data, Santa Barbara, California, USA, pp. 1-12.

[9] D. Xin, J. Han, X. Li, and B. W. Wah, "Star-cubing: computing iceberg cubes by top-down and bottom-up integration," in Proceedings of the 29th International Conference on Very Large Data Bases (VLDB), 2003, Berlin, Germany, pp. 476-487.

[10] Z. Shao, J. Han, and D. Xin, "Mm-cubing: computing iceberg cubes by factorizing the lattice space", in Proceedings of the International Conference on Scientific and Statistical Database Management (SSDBM), 2004, pp. 213-222.

[11] Y. Sismanis, A. Deligiannakis, N. Roussopoulos, and Y. Kotidis, "Dwarf: shrinking the petacube," Proceedings of the 2002 ACM SIGMOD International Conference on Management of Data, Madison, Wisconsin, pp. 464-475.

[12] Y. Sismanis and N. Roussopoulos, "The polynomial complexity of fully materialized coalesced cubes," in Proceedings of the 30th International Conference on Very Large Data Bases (VLDB), 2004, Toronto, Canada, pp. 540-551.

[13] L. Lakshmanan, J. Pei, and J. Han, "Quotient cube: How to summarize the semantics of a data cube," in Proceedings of the 28th International Conference on Very Large Data Bases (VLDB), 2002, Hong Kong, China, pp. 778-789.

[14] L. Lakshmanan, J. Pei, and Y. Zhao, "QC-Trees: An Efficient Summary Structure for Semantic OLAP," Proceedings of the 2003 ACM SIGMOD International Conference on Management of Data, pp. 64-75.

[15] A. Casali, R. Cicchetti, and L. Lakhal, "Extracting semantics from data cubes using cube transversals and closures," in Proceedings of the 9th ACM SIGKDD International Conference on Knowledge Discovery and Data Mining (KDD), 2003, Washington, D.C., pp. 69-78.

[16] A. Casali, S. Nedjar, R. Cicchetti, L. Lakhal, and N. Novelli, "Lossless Reduction of Datacubes using Partitions," International Journal of Data Warehousing and Mining (IJDWM), 2009, Vol. 5, Issue 1, pp. 18-35.

[17] W. Wang, H. Lu, J. Feng, and J. X. Yu, "Condensed cube: an efficient approach to reducing data cube size," in Proceedings of the International Conference on Data Engineering (ICDE), 2002, pp. 155-165.

[18] Y. Feng, D. Agrawal, A. E. Abbadi, and A. Metwally, "Range cube: efficient cube computation by exploiting data correlation," in Proceedings of the International Conference on Data Engineering (ICDE), 2004, pp. 658-670.

[19] K. A. Ross and D. Srivastava, "Fast computation of sparse data cubes," in Proceedings of the 23rd International Conference on Very Large Data Bases (VLDB), 1997, pp. 116-125.

[20] K. Morfonios and Y. Ioannidis, "Supporting the Data Cube Lifecycle: The Power of ROLAP," The VLDB Journal, July 2008, Vol. 17, No. 4, Springer-Verlag New York, Inc., pp. 729-764.

[21] J. Gray et al., "Data Cube: A Relational Aggregation Operator Generalizing Group-by, Cross-Tab, and Sub-Totals," in Data Mining and Knowledge Discovery, 1997, Vol. 1, Issue 1, pp. 29-53, Kluwer Academic Publishers, The Netherlands.

[22] J. A. Blackard, "The forest covertype dataset," ftp://ftp. ics.uci. edu/pub/machine-learning-databases/covtype, [retrieved: April, 2015].

[23] C. Hahn, S. Warren, and J. London, "Edited synoptic cloud re- ports from ships and land stations over the globe," http://cdiac.esd.ornl.gov/cdiac/ndps/ndp026b.html, [retrieved: April, 2015].

[24] "2010 Census Modified Race Data Summary File for Counties Alabama through Missouri," http://www.census.gov/popest/research/modified/STCO-MR2010_AL_MO.csv, [retrieved: September, 2016].

[25] "Online Retail Data Set," UCI Machine Learning Repository, https://archive.ics.uci.edu/ml/datasets/Online+Retail, [retrieved: September, 2016].

[26] D. Chen, S. Liang Sain, and K. Guo, "Data mining for the online retail industry: A case study of RFM model-based customer segmentation using data mining," Journal of Database Marketing and Customer Strategy Management, 2012, Vol. 19, No. 3, pp. 197-208.

An Approach to Analyzing the Retirement Satisfaction among Men and Women Based on Artificial Neural Networks and Decision Trees

Ehsan Ardjmand
Department of Management, College of Business
Frostburg State University, Frostburg, USA
Email: eardjmand@frostburg.edu

Gary R. Weckman, Diana Schwerha
Department of Industrial and Systems Engineering
Ohio University
Athens, Ohio USA
Email: weckmang@ohio.edu, schwerha@ohio.edu

Andrew P. Snow
School of Information and Telecommunication Systems
Ohio University
Athens, Ohio USA
Email: snowa@ohio.edu

Abstract— **In this article, we will analyze the effect of different retirement satisfaction predictors on each other and the retirement satisfaction level among men and women. The following factors will be used as predicators of retirement satisfaction: health; wealth; smoking and drinking habits; education; faith; income; impact of health on activities of daily living; frequency of activities; and the number of people in a household. A set of 858 retired men and 1179 retired women from a 2012 Health and Retirement Study database have been chosen and analyzed. A neural network was trained for each gender in order to predict retirement satisfaction; it also generated a decision tree that symbolizes the retirement satisfaction and its predictors. The results demonstrate that health, age, smoking habits, income, and wealth are the most significant predictors for both genders, while for men, education also plays an important role in retirement satisfaction.**

Keywords- Retirement Satisfaction; Artificial Neural Networks; Multi-Layer Perceptron; Decision Tree

I. INTRODUCTION

This paper investigates the impact that various factors collected from a retirement survey and their predictive capability on retirement satisfaction through artificial neural networks and decision trees. This analysis was first reported in [1], and this paper expands on and extends some of those preliminary findings.

As the population of retired people is growing, retirement satisfaction has become a significant issue in aging and retirement research. It is predicted that around 24 percent of the United States' work force in 2018 will be at least 55 years old [2]. In addition to positive changes in lifestyle, retirement—as a major alteration in life for the elderly—can be the source of many negative experiences, such as loneliness, anxiety, and sometimes even psychological disorders [3].

There is a large body of research on factors which may have an effect on retirement satisfaction—among which health and wealth, as the two most important predictors, have been shown to have a positive correlation with this kind of satisfaction [4-9]. A positive psychological condition is also shown to have a positive correlation with retirement satisfaction [7].

Sexuality is also another analyzed factor in literature. Although there are many studies focusing only on men or women in terms of retirement satisfaction, the studies show that there is no significant difference among men and women in retirement satisfaction [7, 10-16].

Voluntary retirement, engagement in social activities, higher educational level, and having a spousal partner also can have a positive effect on retirement satisfaction [9, 13, 16-22].

Although the retirement satisfaction factors have been analyzed extensively in literature, the inter-relational effect of these factors remains an unchallenged problem. For example, we know that wealth and health have a positive correlation with retirement satisfaction [6], but how will a high level of wealth and a low level of health affect retirement satisfaction simultaneously? Additionally, what level of each factor is the threshold at which retirement satisfaction may be altered?

In this paper, using the data of 858 retired men and 1179 retired women from the 2012 Health and Retirement Study database, we predict the retirement satisfaction level as a dependent variable and the health, wealth, smoking and drinking habits, education, faith, income, impact of health on instrumental and regular activities of daily living (ADL)s, frequency of activities, and number of people in a household as independent variables by using a multi-layer perceptron neural network. We then try to illustrate the effect of different levels of independent variables on retirement satisfaction simultaneously by using a decision tree for both men and women.

In Section II, we explain the method and data we use for analysis. In Section III, a discussion on decision trees including the TREPAN Software. Section IV continues with the retirement satisfaction model followed with Section V containing the sensitivity analysis. Sections VI discuss the results of analyzing retirement satisfaction as an outcome of predictor variables are presented for both men and women. In Section VIi, the overall conclusion is stated.

II. DATA AND METHODOLOGY

The data for this research came from the 2012 Health and Retirement Study (HRS), which was launched in 1992.

A. *Health and Retirement Study*

The data for this research came from the 2012 Health and Retirement Study (HRS), which was launched in 1992. The total number of randomly considered retired people chosen from HRS for this study was 2037, which consisted of 858 men and 1179 women. Notice that only the respondents with no missing values in both dependent and independent variables were considered in this study.

The dependent variable is considered to be retirement satisfaction. If a person is reported to be retired in 2012 he/she is asked the G136 question, "All in all, would you say that your retirement has turned out to be very satisfying, moderately satisfying, or not at all satisfying?" The answer to this question is supposed to capture the retirement satisfaction level for retirees.

The independent variables in this research are the age (in months); years of education; belief in a higher power; self-report of health (based on a 5-point scale in which 1 shows excellent health and 5 shows very poor health); a binary variable which shows if the health limits the ability to work or not; level of difficulty in pursuing the ADLs (based on a 6-point scale in which 0 shows no difficulty and 5 shows someone is unable to perform ADL); mental health (based on a 9-point scale in which 0 is excellent and 8 is very poor); a set of binary variables that show if the person has blood pressure, diabetes, cancer, lung disease, heart problem and/or arthritis; frequency of vigorous, moderate, and light activity; a binary variable that shows if the person smokes or not; the number of alcoholic drinks consumed per week; wealth; income; and the number of people living in a household.

B. *Methodology*

In this research for modeling retirement satisfaction and other independent variables, we use a multi-layer feed forward neural network. For illustrating this relationship in a symbolic structure, we will use a decision tree technique proposed by Craven [23].

1) *Artificial Neural Networks (ANN)*

ANNs are mathematical models that mimic the human brain. Besides being considered a "black-box" model, ANNs also have the limitation of requiring a large amount of training and cross-validation data, i.e., typically three times more training samples than network weights [24]. Since their resurgence in the 1980s, ANNs have been applied to a variety of problem domains such as speech recognition [25] and generation [26], symbolic learning [27], robotic design [28], medical diagnostics [29], game playing [30], healthcare systems [31], stock market [32] and ecological modeling [33, 34]. Theoretically, it is possible to prove that a three-layered NN can estimate the value of a function with desirable accuracy [35, 36]. Since the relationship of retirement satisfaction and other independent variables is not necessarily linear and can be considered highly complex, feed forward neural networks can be a useful tool for predicting the value of retirement satisfaction.

There are many types of ANN topologies that have been comprehensively documented [37], and they range in their use and complexity. One of the most widely used ANNs is the feed forward neural network (FNN) [38]. For example, Figure 1 shows the general structure of a FNN. The network shown is fully connected, since each layer is connected via previous layers. The first hidden layer's neurons are connected to the second hidden layer's, and the second hidden layer's neurons are connected with all of the output layer's neurons.

There are two main paradigms of ANN training--supervised and unsupervised learning. The primary difference between the two learning schemes is that in supervised learning, known outputs, or--"targets"--are used to adjust the network's weights. In unsupervised learning, there is not a known output, and the method functions as a clustering algorithm.

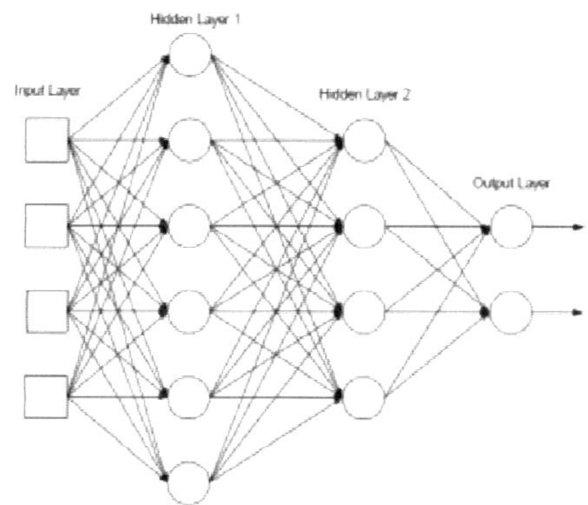

Figure 1. Feed Forward Neural Network.

III. DECISION TREES AND TREPAN

One of the main drawbacks of neural networks is the lack of explanation capability [39]. In order to represent the knowledge about retirement satisfaction learned by a neural network, we use decision trees. Decision trees classify data through recursive partitioning of the dataset into mutually exclusive subsets, which best explain the variation in the dependent variable under observation [40, 41]. A decision tree model consists of logical tests, which result in possible classifying consequences. Decision trees have been used to aid decision makers in many real-world problems [42, 43].

TREPAN is a novel rule-extraction algorithm that utilizes the behavior of a trained ANN [44]. Given a trained ANN, TREPAN extracts decision trees that provide a close approximation to the function represented by the network when there are issues of accurately calculating tree partitions, which are caused by limited sample sizes.

TREPAN uses a concept of recursive partitioning similar to other decision tree algorithms; however, in contrast to the depth-first growth used by other decision tree algorithms,

TREPAN expands using the "best first" principle. For conventional induction algorithms, the amount of training data decreases as a decision tree grows. Thus, there is less data at the bottom of the tree able to determine class labels accurately (see Figure 2).

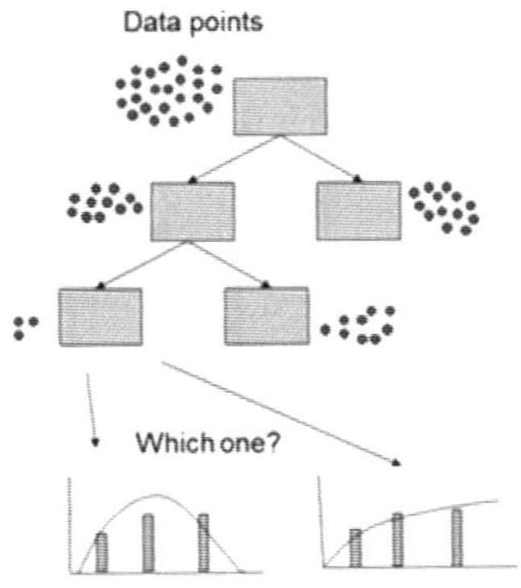

Figure 2. Determination of class labels as decision tree grows

In contrast, TREPAN uses an "oracle" to answer queries that determine decision tree splits better when sample instances are limited as shown in Figure 3. One important aspect of this feature is the user-determined parameter called minimum sample. TREPAN ensures that splits are determined with a minimum number of sample instances. If the number of instances at a particular node, *m*, is less than the minimum sample allowed, TREPAN will make membership queries equal to the minimum sample from the ANN oracle in order to artificially create sample instances to meet the minimum sample requirement.

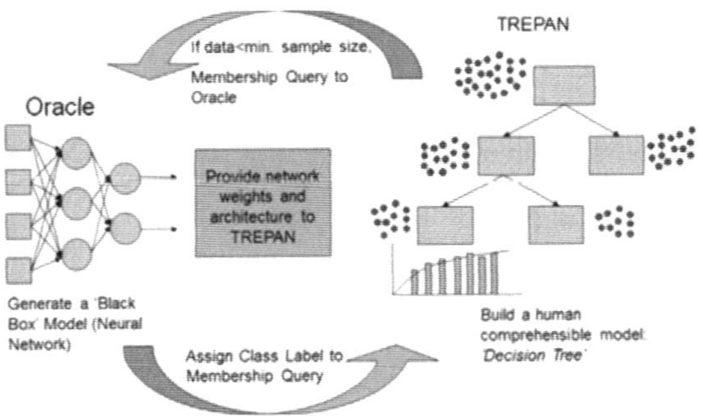

Figure 3. TREPAN Oracle

TREPAN uses an entropy-based criterion called "information gain" to determine the best position in which to partition the dataset. TREPAN uses M-of-N expressions as it splits upon the dataset. In this case, N rules are created. The algorithm also determines a value for M, which represents the minimum conditions that must be met, which in turn dictates the preceding node or final classification. This approach allows multiple features to be present in one node. To prevent testing of all the possible M-of-N combinations, TREPAN makes use of the heuristic "beam search" process. This process begins by selecting the best binary split at a given node based upon information gain. Additional splitting conditions are determined based on the initial rule's "complement" [48].

When sample instances are sparse, TREPAN interacts with an ANN oracle by means of membership queries. The goal of a membership query is to determine a new instance among a group of instances. To create appropriate sample instances, distributions of attribute values are created that conform to the decision tree constraints [45]. Once the ranges are determined, random pulls are made from the attributes' distribution in order for the oracle to accurately estimate the classification output label.

Stopping criteria TREPAN uses a 'local stopping criteria' while the tree is being grown. A node's 'impurity' is calculated based off the training samples available. Based on the characteristic of a node being evaluated, the local stopping criteria will determine if a node is acceptable to grow further, or if it should be terminated. TREPAN also uses a 'global stopping criteria'. Unlike the local criterion that evaluates terminal nodes during induction, the global stopping criterion considers the entire tree's size. Before induction, users determine a maximum tree size, which enables users to make trade-offs between the size and comprehensibility. Thus, if the maximum tree size is reached, the tree forming induction algorithm is finalized.

Pruning After the decision tree is fully grown, a 'naïve pruning' process is implemented. This process aims to detect sub-trees that have similar predicting accuracies for class-instances found in terminal nodes. The pruning process is performed using a recursive, post-order traversal of the tree, to simplify the final tree. The changes made to the tree during this process do not affect the predictive power of the decision tree because nodes or sub trees that do not contribute to the overall efficiency are removed or reduced. Thus, the goal of this operation is to reduce the size of the tree by replacing portions of the tree's splits with a single terminal node that is able to obtain the same level of accuracy of the full tree.

In addition to TREPAN algorithm Craven has also developed two of its important variations which are investigated further in this article. The single test TREPAN algorithm is similar to TREPAN in all respects except that as its name suggests it uses single feature tests at the internal nodes. Disjunctive TREPAN uses disjunctive "OR" tests at the internal nodes of the tree instead of the m-of-n tests. A more detailed explanation of the TREPAN algorithm can be found in Craven's dissertation [23].

Classification performance metrics assessing classifier performance is a very important aspect of comparing different classifiers. The classification accuracy or error rate is the percentage of correct predictions made by the model, which can be represented as a confusion matrix as shown in Table I. A confusion matrix is a matrix plot of predicted versus actual classes with all correct classifications depicted along the diagonal of the matrix. It gives the number of correctly classified instances, incorrectly classified instances, and overall classification accuracy. Consider a two-class (i.e., binary) classification problem where four possible outcomes are obtainable. In this case, true positives (TP), true negatives (TN), false positives (FP) and false negatives (FN) are all obtainable classifications. Based on these possible states, the overall classification accuracy is derived from equation (1).

$$\text{Accuracy (\%)} = (TP+TN) / (TP+FN+FP+TN) \times 100 \quad (1)$$

Table I: Example of confusion matrix

Class	*Predicted Class (Yes)*	*Predicted Class (No)*
Actual class (Yes)	TP	FN
Actual class (No)	FP	TN

IV. Retirement Satisfaction Model

For this study, we train a feed forward neural network with two hidden layers. There are 15 processing units in the first layer and 10 processing units in the second hidden layer, as well as tangent hyperbolic and linear transfer functions for the hidden and output layers, respectively, that use back propagation algorithms in NeuroSolutions 6.20 software. The output of the network, i.e., retirement satisfaction - is a continuous number. In order to convert the output of the network into the categorical scale of retirement satisfaction, we divide the output into three categories of $(-\infty,1.66]$, $(1.66,2.33]$, and $(2.33,+\infty]$, which are equivalent to not satisfying, moderately satisfying, and very satisfying. Notice that in the data we use the numbers 1, 2, and 3 to represent satisfying, moderately satisfying, and very satisfying, respectively.

V. Sensitivity Analysis

Another approach used in extracting knowledge from ANNs is Sensitivity Analysis, which attempts to model the interaction of various input factors [46]. Sensitivity analysis is a method used to extract cause and affect relationships between input and output variables. A given input is increased or decreased in small increments, typically by one, two, or three standard deviations, with all other variables fixed at their mean values, permitting the individual contributions of each variable to be assessed. The user can then identify interrelationships between input and output variables with this information.

Sensitivity analysis also provides feedback as to which input variables are the most significant relative to other input variables. Based on this analysis, insignificant variables could be removed from the ANN, which would reduce the size, complexity, and training times. However, this would remove the impact and relationships that the input variable has to the output and other input variables.

VI. Results

The final artificial feed forward neural network models had the following performance measurements for both Men (see Table II) and Women (see Table III). The table illustrates the model's ability for the train, cross-validation and testing datasets. The various measurements listed are root mean square error (RMSE), normalized root mean square error (NRMSE), mean absolute error (MAE), min and max absolute error (Min Abs Error and Max Abs Error) along with the final coefficient of correlation (r).

Table II: Model for Men Retirement Satisfaction Dataset

Performance	*Training*	*Cross-validation*	*Test*
RMSE	0.5878	0.6040	0.3455
NRMSE	0.2939	0.3020	0.5579
MAE	0.4833	0.4863	0.4833
Min Abs Error	0.0008	0.0024	0.0008
Max Abs Error	1.9318	1.7192	1.9318
r	0.6675	0.5556	0.6675

Table III: Model for Women Retirement Satisfaction Dataset

Performance	*Training*	*Cross-validation*	*Test*
RMSE	0.6424	0.6646	0.6993
NRMSE	0.3212	0.3323	0.3497
MAE	0.5352	0.5332	0.5855
Min Abs Error	0.0005	0.0028	0.0007
Max Abs Error	1.7948	1.8924	1.7753
r	0.6462	0.5990	0.5287

The numerical output from the neural network was converted into the categorical scale of retirement satisfaction, as mentioned earlier. The resulting confusion matrices were calculated along with their respective overall accuracies for the training and test datasets. Tables IV-VII demonstrates the ability of the TREPAN model to predict Retirement Satisfaction levels for both Men and Women using the single test algorithm.

Table IV: Men training set output based on single test algorithm

	Target	1	2	3	Total
Predicted	1	57	24	7	88
	2	57	123	60	240
	3	10	34	142	186
	Total	124	181	209	514

*Training Set Correctness: 322/514 = 0.626

Table V: Men test set output based on single test algorithm

	Target	1	2	3	Total
Predicted	1	14	5	1	20
	2	23	37	24	84
	3	5	11	52	68
	Total	42	53	77	172

*Test Set Correctness: 103/172 = 0.599

Table VI: Women training set output based on single test algorithm

	Target	1	2	3	Total
Predicted	1	153	32	20	205
	2	63	84	73	220
	3	16	89	176	281
	Total	232	205	269	706

*Training Set Correctness: 413/706 = 0.585

Table VII: Women test set output based on single test algorithm

	Target	1	2	3	Total
Predicted	1	49	26	11	86
	2	30	36	39	105
	3	7	35	62	104
	Total	86	97	112	295

*Test Set Correctness: 147/295 = 0.498

The decision tree model which created the logical tests resulting into the classifications shown in the tables above, where displayed as decision tree branches. Figure 4 and Figure 5 show the decision tree obtained for men and women regarding the relationships of the independent variables and retirement satisfaction. Notice that every rectangular shape in the decision tree shows a condition that, if met, the right branch should be followed. The left branch is for the case in which the condition is rejected. The oval shapes show the consecutive retirement satisfaction level in each branch.

As it is depicted in Figures 4 and 5, not all of the variables are involved in predicting retirement satisfaction. The reason is partially because of the low correlation of some independent variables and retirement satisfaction, as well as the overwhelming impact of these important variables on the latter that makes the other factors neutral. Another reason is the structure of the decision tree itself. By generating a decision tree, we are trying to extract the knowledge of the neural network, and the generated tree is formed in a way to represent the most possible knowledge in the form of rules according to the neural network, which can cause us to ignore some of the inputs.

In addition, more complex decision trees were created using the TREPAN and Disjunctive algorithms in order to see if the accuracy could be improved. Tables VIII-XI and Figures 6 and 7 display the capability and results of modeling created only for the Men's retirement satisfaction.

Notice that the overall accuracies of the various algorithms are similar but the Disjunctive algorithm has the highest overall test results. However, the disjunctive decision tree is a little harder to interpret the results as compared to the single test output.

Table VIII: Men training set output based on TREPAN algorithm

	Target	1	2	3	Total
Predicted	1	52	28	7	87
	2	61	108	40	209
	3	11	45	162	218
	Total	124	181	209	514

*Training Set Correctness: 322/514 = 0.626

Table IX: Men test set output based on TREPAN algorithm

	Target	1	2	3	Total
Predicted	1	18	6	3	27
	2	19	29	22	70
	3	5	18	52	75
	Total	42	53	77	172

*Test Set Correctness: 99/172 = 0.576

Table X: Men training set output based on Disjunctive algorithm

	Target	1	2	3	Total
Predicted	1	55	28	8	91
	2	61	116	53	230
	3	8	37	148	193
	Total	124	181	209	514

*Training Set Correctness: 319/514 = 0.621

Table XI: Men test set output based on Disjunctive algorithm

	Target	1	2	3	Total
Predicted	1	13	6	2	21
	2	25	34	13	72
	3	4	13	62	79
	Total	42	53	77	172

*Test Set Correctness: 109/172 = 0.634

In addition to the decision trees, sensitivity of the mean was performed on both the Men's and Women's neural network models (see Figure 8 and 9). The top 4 most sensitive variables for Men, as shown in Figure 8, is Mental health, Age, Wealth and Years of education. Whereas, for Women, the top 4 most sensitive variables, as shown in Figure 9, is Mental health, Self report of health, Age and Years of education.

The sensitivity of a single predictive variable can also be displayed as compared to Retirement Satisfaction. Figure 10 illustrates the behavior of the predictive variable 'Mental health' over the range of input values. Notice that in this case, for Men, as their mental health degrades (scale implies 0 is excellent and 8 is very poor) that the overall Retirement Satisfaction will typically drop from an average of 2.5 to 1.5.

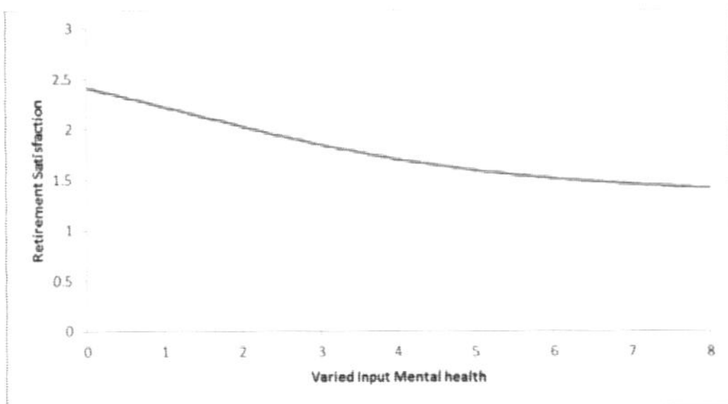

Figure 10. Mental health impact on retirement satisfaction for Men

Another illustration of how a predictive variable can impact retirement satisfaction is the 'Age' of the individual. Figure 11 displays the relationship, for Men, between 'Age' (months) and 'Retirement Satisfaction'. Notice that as the age of an individual increases so does retirement satisfaction.

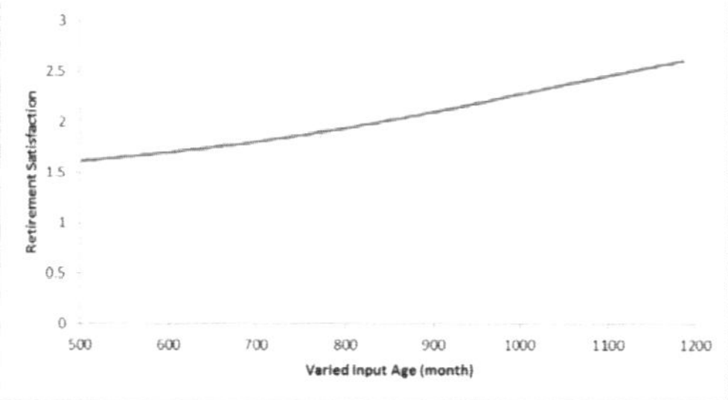

Figure 11. Age (months) impact on retirement satisfaction for Men

A. Comparison with Literature

All of the extracted rules in decision trees are consistent with the results in literature. Age has a positive correlation with retirement satisfaction [3]. This effect can be seen by following branches that point to older ages and comparing them to the other branches in Figures 4 and 5. High levels of mental and physical health correspond to higher retirement satisfaction [3, 4, 6-8]. Higher levels of wealth and income also correspond to higher retirement satisfaction [3, 5-7]. Years of education have a positive correlation with retirement satisfaction [20].

B. New Findings

In addition to the result comparisons to previous literature, some new patterns can be deduced from the decision tree. Compared to women, the years spent in education for men is an important factor. In Figure 4, one of the parameters that affect the retirement satisfaction in men is education level. However, in Figure 5 the education level is not a condition in defining the retirement satisfaction, which shows that for women, it is not an important parameter.

Since for men the wealth appears in higher levels of the decision tree, it follows that, compared to women, wealth for men is a more important factor. Following the same logic, we can see that compared to men, mental health is a stronger predictor for women. In addition, for women with poor health, wealth is not a predictor at all. Despite this, for men with poor overall health, age cannot predict the retirement satisfaction.

Among all the health conditions analyzed, only diabetes plays a significant role in explaining retirement satisfaction. In both decision trees, i.e., men's and women's – having diabetes can cause lower retirement satisfaction, except where the income level is rather high. Although poor conditions of physical and mental health for both men and women can cause low retirement satisfaction, a high amount of wealth and income can ameliorate this situation.

VII. Conclusion

In this paper, using the 2012 data of the Health and Retirement Study for 858 retired men and 1179 retired women, we trained a feed forward neural network to predict the retirement satisfaction, considering health, wealth, smoking and drinking habits, education, faith, income, impact of health on ADLs, frequency of activities, and the number of people in a household as independent variables. The knowledge of neural networks was represented in the form of a decision tree.

The results show a very high consistency with previous findings in literature. Additionally, some new knowledge regarding retirement satisfaction was also revealed in the form of rules in the decision tree. It was shown that, compared to women, years of education is more important to men in regards to retirement satisfaction. Under the condition of poor health, age is an important predictor of retirement satisfaction for women. Among all the health-related diseases, diabetes plays the most important role in terms of predicting retirement satisfaction. Additionally, a poor health condition can be negated by higher income or wealth.

To the best of our knowledge, the use of decision trees in retirement satisfaction is introduced for the very first time in this article. The results show that this technique can be a very powerful method for revealing hidden relationships between the various predictors of retirement satisfaction.

References

[1] E. Ardjmand, G. R. Weckman, D. Schwerha, and A. P. Snow, "Analyzing the Retirement Satisfaction Predictors among Men and Women Using a Multi-Layer Feed Forward Neural Network and Decision Trees," *ALLDATA 2016*, p. 111, 2016.

[2] D. Schwerha, C. Ritter, S. Robinson, R. W. Griffeth, and D. Fried, "Integrating ergonomic factors into the decision to retire," *Human Resource Management Review*, vol. 21, pp. 220-227, 2011.

[3] F. J. Floyd, S. N. Haynes, E. R. Doll, D. Winemiller, C. Lemsky, T. M. Burgy, *et al.*, "Assessing retirement satisfaction and perceptions of retirement experiences," *Psychology and aging*, vol. 7, p. 609, 1992.

[4] K. A. Bender, "An analysis of well-being in retirement: The role of pensions, health, and 'voluntariness' of retirement," *The Journal of Socio-Economics*, vol. 41, pp. 424-433, 2012.

[5] L. T. Dorfman, "Health conditions and perceived quality of life in retirement," *Health & Social Work*, vol. 20, pp. 192-199, 1995.

[6] C. W. Panis, "Annuities and retirement well-being," *Pension design and structure: New lessons from behavioral finance*, pp. 259-74, 2004.

[7] C. A. Price and S. Balaswamy, "Beyond health and wealth: Predictors of women's retirement satisfaction," *The International Journal of Aging and Human Development*, vol. 68, pp. 195-214, 2009.

[8] M. Reis and D. P. Gold, "Retirement, personality, and life satisfaction: A review and two models," *Journal of applied Gerontology*, vol. 12, pp. 261-282, 1993.

[9] N. Schmitt, J. K. White, B. W. Coyle, and J. Rauschenberger, "Retirement and life satisfaction," *Academy of Management Journal*, vol. 22, pp. 282-291, 1979.

[10] T. M. Calasanti, "Gender and life satisfaction in retirement: An assessment of the male model," *The Journals of Gerontology Series B: Psychological Sciences and Social Sciences,* vol. 51, pp. S18-S29, 1996.

[11] E. Fouquereau, A. Fernandez, and E. Mullet, "Evaluation of determinants of retirement satisfaction among workers and retired people," *Social Behavior and Personality: an international journal,* vol. 29, pp. 777-785, 2001.

[12] K. Hanson and S. Wapner, "Transition to retirement: Gender differences," *The International Journal of Aging and Human Development,* vol. 39, pp. 189-208, 1994.

[13] C. A. Price and E. Joo, "Exploring the relationship between marital status and women's retirement satisfaction," *The International Journal of Aging and Human Development,* vol. 61, pp. 37-55, 2005.

[14] K. Seccombe and G. R. Lee, "Gender differences in retirement satisfaction and its antecedents," *Research on Aging,* vol. 8, pp. 426-440, 1986.

[15] K. F. Slevin and C. Wingrove, "Women in retirement: A review and critique of empirical research since 1976," *Sociological Inquiry,* vol. 65, pp. 1-21, 1995.

[16] M. Szinovacz, "Preferred retirement timing and retirement satisfaction in women," *The International Journal of Aging and Human Development,* vol. 24, pp. 301-317, 1987.

[17] E. Bonsang and T. J. Klein, "Retirement and subjective well-being," *Journal of Economic Behavior & Organization,* vol. 83, pp. 311-329, 2012.

[18] B. A. Butrica and S. G. Schaner, "Satisfaction and engagement in retirement," 2005.

[19] L. T. Dorfman and M. M. Moffett, "Retirement satisfaction in married and widowed rural women," *The Gerontologist,* vol. 27, pp. 215-221, 1987.

[20] E. Fouquereau, A. Fernandez, A. M. Fonseca, M. C. Paul, and V. Uotinen, "Perceptions of and satisfaction with retirement: a comparison of six European union countries," *Psychology and Aging,* vol. 20, p. 524, 2005.

[21] Y. Kremer, "Predictors of retirement satisfaction: A path model," *The International Journal of aging and Human Development,* vol. 20, pp. 113-121, 1985.

[22] C. Kupperbusch, R. W. Levenson, and R. Ebling, "Predicting husbands' and wives' retirement satisfaction from the emotional qualities of marital interaction," *Journal of Social and Personal Relationships,* vol. 20, pp. 335-354, 2003.

[23] M. W. Craven, "Extracting comprehensible models from trained neural networks," University of Wisconsin–Madison, 1996.

[24] M. M. Nelson and W. T. Illingworth, *A practical guide to neural nets* vol. 1: Addison-Wesley Reading, MA, 1991.

[25] A. Waibel, "Modular construction of time-delay neural networks for speech recognition," *Neural computation,* vol. 1, pp. 39-46, 1989.

[26] T. J. Sejnowski and C. R. Rosenberg, *NETtalk: A parallel network that learns to read aloud*: MIT Press, 1988.

[27] J. W. Shavlik, R. J. Mooney, and G. G. Towell, "Symbolic and neural learning algorithms: An experimental comparison," *Machine learning,* vol. 6, pp. 111-143, 1991.

[28] G.-T. Hsu and R. Simmons, "Learning footfall evaluation for a walking robot," in *Proceedings of the Eigth International Workshop on Machine Learning*, 2014, pp. 303-307.

[29] M. Jabri, S. Pickard, P. Leong, Z. Chi, B. Flower, and Y. Xie, "ANN based classification for heart defibrillators," *Advances in neural information processing systems,* pp. 637-637, 1993.

[30] G. Tesauro, "Practical issues in temporal difference learning," in *Reinforcement Learning*, ed: Springer, 1992, pp. 33-53.

[31] G. G. Towell and J. W. Shavlik, "Extracting refined rules from knowledge-based neural networks," *Machine learning,* vol. 13, pp. 71-101, 1993.

[32] G. R. Weckman, R. W. Dravenstott, W. A. Young II, E. Ardjmand, D. F. Millie, and A. P. Snow, "A Prescriptive Stock Market Investment Strategy for the Restaurant Industry using an Artificial Neural Network Methodology," *International Journal of Business Analytics (IJBAN),* vol. 3, pp. 1-21, 2016.

[33] D. F. Millie, G. R. Weckman, W. A. Young, J. E. Ivey, D. P. Fries, E. Ardjmand, *et al.*, "Coastal 'Big Data'and nature-inspired computation: Prediction potentials, uncertainties, and knowledge derivation of neural networks for an algal metric," *Estuarine, Coastal and Shelf Science,* vol. 125, pp. 57-67, 2013.

[34] D. F. Millie, G. R. Weckman, G. L. Fahnenstiel, H. J. Carrick, E. Ardjmand, W. A. Young, *et al.*, "Using artificial intelligence for CyanoHAB niche modeling: discovery and visualization of Microcystis–environmental associations within western Lake Erie," *Canadian Journal of Fisheries and Aquatic Sciences,* vol. 71, pp. 1642-1654, 2014.

[35] K.-I. Funahashi, "On the approximate realization of continuous mappings by neural networks," *Neural networks,* vol. 2, pp. 183-192, 1989.

[36] K. Hornik, M. Stinchcombe, and H. White, "Multilayer feedforward networks are universal approximators," *Neural networks,* vol. 2, pp. 359-366, 1989.

[37] S. S. Haykin, *Neural Networks: A Comprehensive Foundation*: Prentice Hall, 1999.

[38] M. Amin-Naseri, E. Ardjmand, and G. Weckman, "Training the feedforward neural network using Unconscious search," in *Neural Networks (IJCNN), The 2013 International Joint Conference on*, 2013, pp. 1-7.

[39] E. Ardjmand, D. F. Millie, I. Ghalehkhondabi, W. A. Young II, and G. R. Weckman, "A State-Based Sensitivity Analysis for Distinguishing the Global Importance of Predictor Variables in Artificial Neural Networks," *Advances in Artificial Neural Systems,* vol. 2016, 2016.

[40] G. Liepins, R. Goeltz, and R. Rush, "Machine learning techniques for natural-resource data-analysis," *Ai Applications in Natural Resource Management,* vol. 4, pp. 9-18, 1990.

[41] D. Biggs, B. De Ville, and E. Suen, "A method of choosing multiway partitions for classification and decision trees," *Journal of Applied Statistics,* vol. 18, pp. 49-62, 1991.

[42] W. Leech, "A rule-based process control method with feedback," *ISA transactions,* vol. 26, pp. 73-78, 1986.

[43] P. Langley and H. A. Simon, "Applications of machine learning and rule induction," *Communications of the ACM,* vol. 38, pp. 54-64, 1995.

[44] M. Craven and J. W. Shavlik, "Using sampling and queries to extract rules from trained neural networks," in *ICML,* 1994, pp. 37-45.

[45] K. Krawiec, R. Słowiński, and I. Szczęśniak, "Pedagogical Method for Extraction of Symbolic Knowledge," in

International Conference on Rough Sets and current Trends in Computing, 1998, pp. 436-443.

[46] A. Saltelli, S. Tarantola, F. Campolongo, and M. Ratto, *Sensitivity analysis in practice: a guide to assessing scientific models*: John Wiley & Sons, 2004.

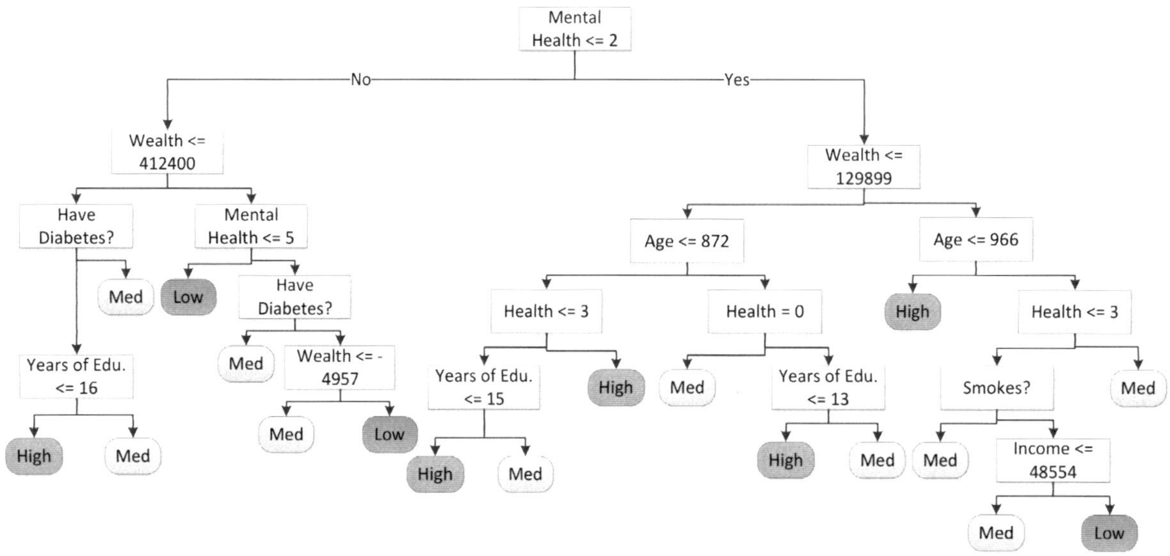

Figure 4. Decision Tree of Retirement Satisfaction for Men.

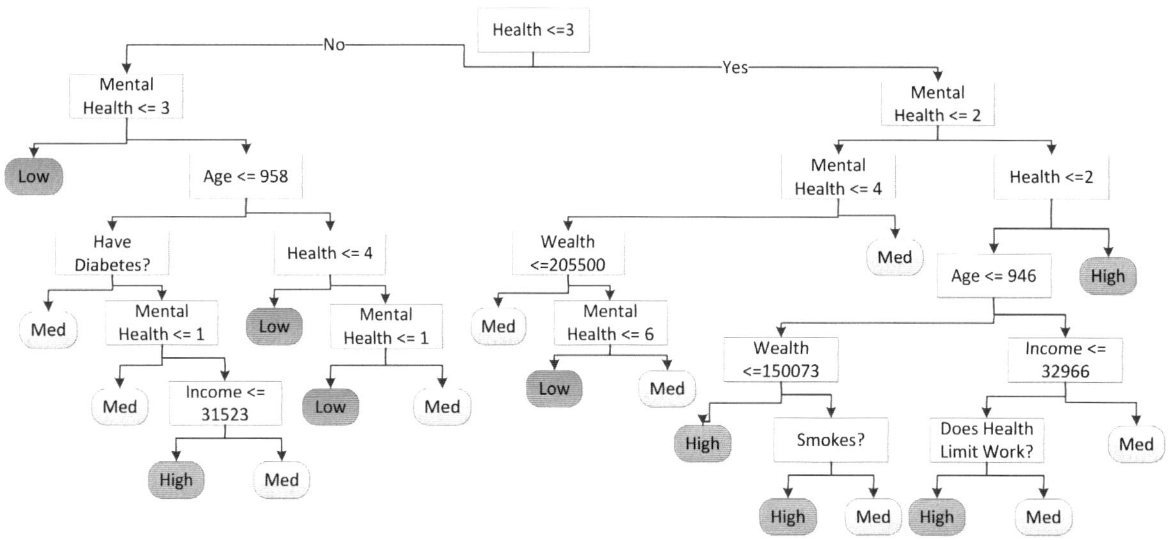

Figure 5. Decision Tree of Retirement Satisfaction for Women.

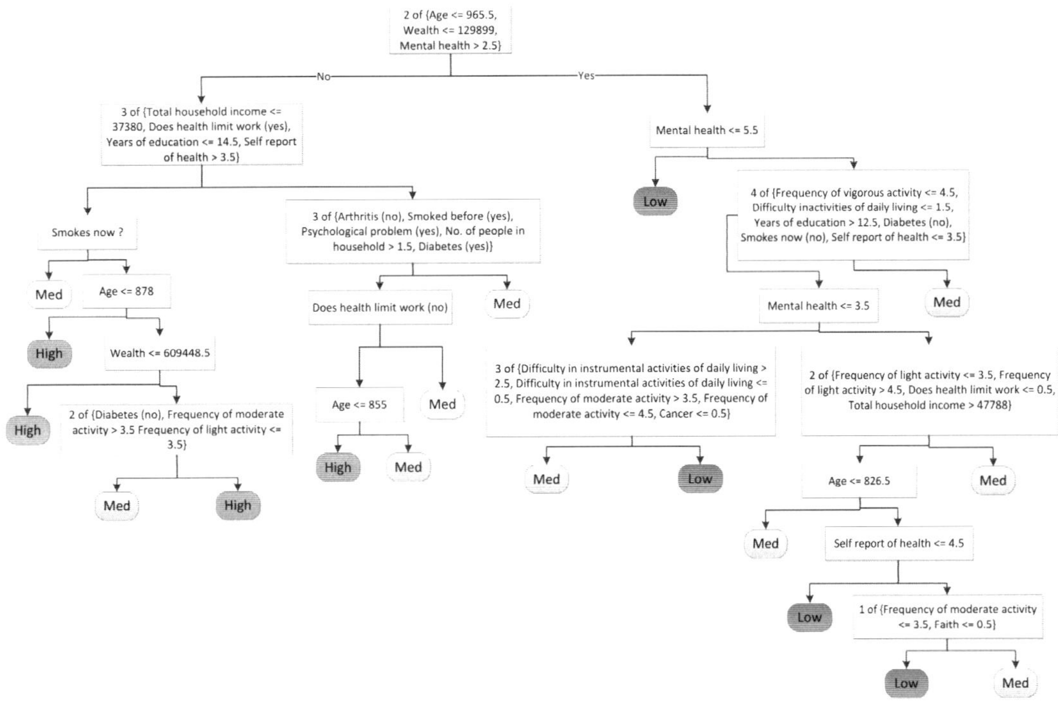

Figure 6. Decision Tree of Retirement Satisfaction for Men (Trepan)

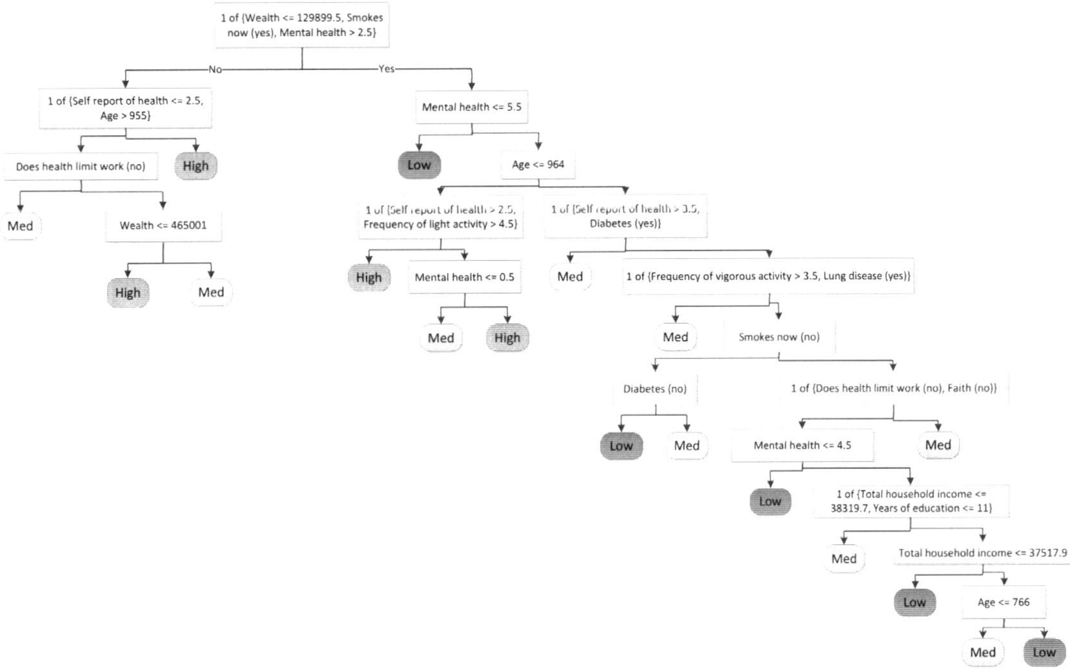

Figure 7. Decision Tree of Retirement Satisfaction for Men (disjunctive)

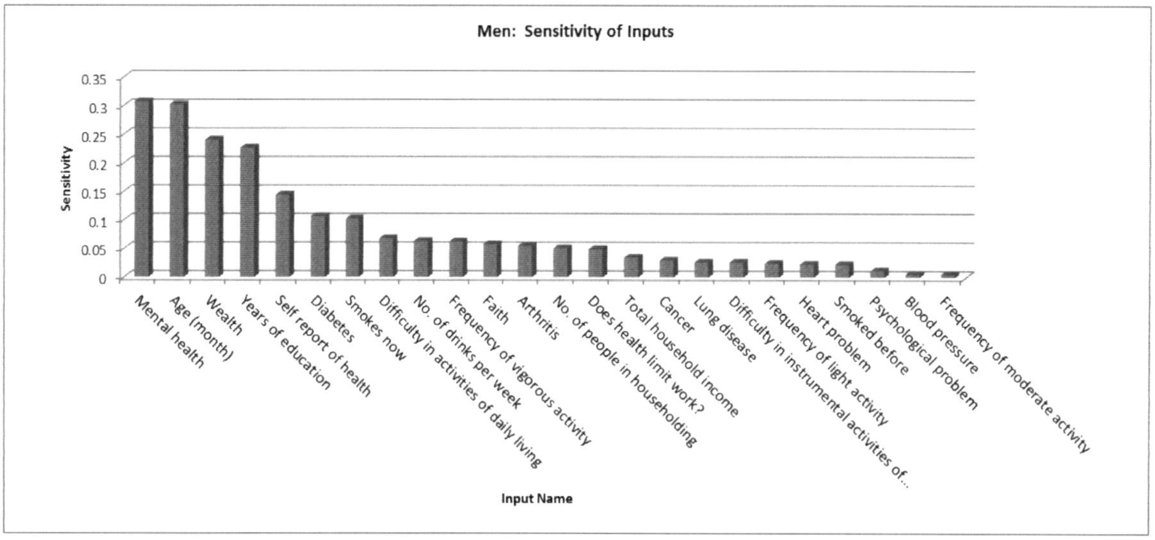

Figure 8. Sensitivity of input predictors on the Retirement Satisfaction for Men (sorted)

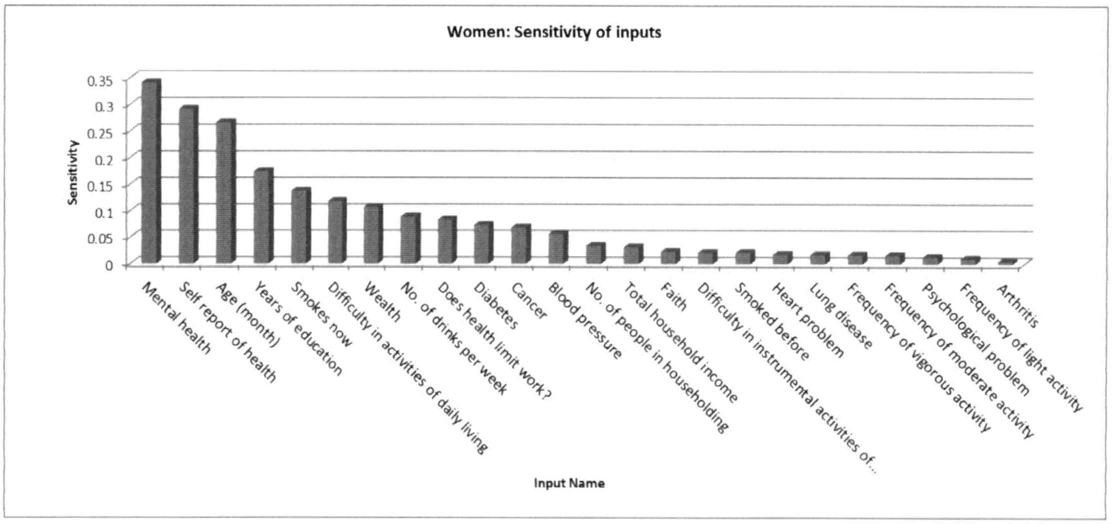

Figure 9. Sensitivity of input predictors on the Retirement Satisfaction for Women (sorted)

Automotive User Experience Design Patterns: An Approach and Pattern Examples

Alexander G. Mirnig, Tim Kaiser, Artur Lupp, Nicole Perterer,
Alexander Meschtscherjakov, Thomas Grah, Manfred Tscheligi
Christian Doppler Laboratory for "Contextual Interfaces"
Center for Human-Computer Interaction, University of Salzburg
Salzburg, Austria
Email: {firstname.lastname}@sbg.ac.at

Abstract— **Patterns are a methodology for capturing best practices and solutions to reoccurring problems in certain fields or disciplines. Applied to automotive interaction design they can combine empirical data, industry knowledge, and experts experience for state-of-the-art design solutions. In this paper, we present the patterns approach and its application to the automotive interaction domain, together with a newly generated set of eight in-vehicle user experience (UX) design patterns that describe answers to problems in automotive interaction design and engineering. These patterns are part of an ongoing project with the aim of providing a comprehensive, user experience focused, collection of design solutions for contemporary and future automotive designs. We present the pattern approach in general, the specific automotive approach and methodology, the patterns themselves, and finally discuss the benefits, drawbacks, and future work regarding patterns in the automotive domain.**

Keywords—design patterns; pattern identification and extraction; pattern reuse.

I. INTRODUCTION

This paper is an extended version of a full paper presented at PATTERNS 2016 [1]. The term 'pattern' has a wide range of meanings, both in everyday and academic language. Generally speaking, the term can be said to refer to a set of attributes that are common among a specific set of objects. In the context of this paper, however, it refers to a knowledge capturing and transfer method, first developed in the 19th century for the architecture domain [2]. One key idea behind this method was that the solutions gained via said method should be reusable to solve similar and recurring problems; hence the term 'patterns'.

The use of this method is well established in contemporary Human-Computer Interaction (HCI) and is considered advantageous for various reasons. First, patterns are a method to capture proven design solutions to reoccurring problems. Second, the use of patterns improves the design process (regarding both, time and effort spent) to a considerable degree [3][4]. Moreover, scientific research in HCI also strongly relies on communicating scientific findings to the industry. By translating these findings so that they convey relevant and useful information to designers and developers, patterns can help facilitate the design process by reducing time and effort that has to be put into it. Designing for a positive User Experience (UX) has become an increasingly important topic in academia and industry [5][6][7]. User Experience can be defined as *"the users sensory, emotional and reflective response to the interaction with a system in a context"* [8]. The car industry in particular has become a fast-paced global market that can draw substantial benefits from a modular and flexible documentation of best practices.

Automotive interface and interaction design is a complex and constantly evolving area. Driven by scientific findings and industrial progress, the number of interfaces and interaction devices, together with ways to interact with them, increases. The automotive domain, and the driver interaction space in particular, is a challenging environment to design in, given its emphasis on safety, minimizing distraction, and generally restrictive nature. There are no one-size-fits-all solutions for driver space design, and the challenge of providing contemporary solutions, which combine technological state of the art as well as driver and traffic needs, can be difficult. Due to the rapid progress in technology that is currently observable in the automotive domain, virtually every new day presents a new set of problems and challenges for designing novel interaction solutions.

Based on this consideration, we are in the process of creating a set of Contextual User Experience patterns for driver space design in the automotive domain, of which we present the eight most recent ones in this paper. In the following section, we will give an overview on the state of the art on Contextual UX patterns in general, and introduce our specific approach in Section III. In Section IV, we show each of the eight patterns and discuss these in Section V. We conclude the paper with a summary in Section VI.

II. RELATED WORK

In the original publication [1], we presented the eight automotive design patterns but outlined the pattern approach only very briefly and with no proper discussion. This extension aims to lend more context to the automotive patterns via a more extensive related work embedding, show our approach in greater detail, and discuss the initial pattern set, lessons learned, and remaining challenges. In this section, we will first introduce the original pattern approach and then talk about the relevance of patterns for User Experience design and research. After that, we introduce a number of existing pattern approaches in Human-Computer Interaction, which our approach draws from. We conclude this section with a brief overview of knowledge transfer and design information sources in the automotive domain.

A. Patterns

Patterns were first introduced by Christopher Alexander [2][9] as a way to capture and document solutions to recurring problems in the architecture domain. His work was adopted and expanded upon in several disciplines and, as a result, patterns have evolved towards a more widely applied means to capture problem solutions. HCI is among these disciplines and the pattern approach has been adopted in order to provide best practices and state of the art knowledge in this multi-disciplinary field [10][11]. Pattern approaches vary between disciplines, and, while attempts have been made, there is no widely accepted uniform cross-discipline pattern approach yet [12].

Köhne [13], who based his work on Quibeldey-Cirkel [14], presents a pattern finding process in several steps. The first step in this process is the so-called pattern mining, which consists of finding a solution and deciding whether or not it is adequate to solve a certain problem, after which it is written down, according to a predefined pattern structure. During the next step, the so-called *shepherding*, a domain expert (the *shepherd*) provides feedback regarding writing, formatting, and contents of the initial pattern to the pattern writer, who then iterates the pattern based on this feedback. This version is then discussed in a collaborative setting together with other pattern writers, after which the writer prepares the last non-public version of the pattern. This version is then put into a public online pattern repository, in which it is peer-reviewed. After any final edits to the patterns themselves have been made and the collection is deemed to be of good quality, it is published as a document and fully made available to the public.

Pattern mining is usually done by looking at actually implemented design solutions. But practical knowledge is not the only potential source for patterns - they can also be gained from scientific research. Martin et al. [15] mined patterns from ethnographical study results and then tried to generalize the observed phenomena and provide and/or apply them to other domains.

B. User Experience and the Need for Consolidated Solutions

In HCI, User Experience (UX) design is considered to be an important topic with relevance in both academic and industrial aspects [16][6]. In its most general meaning, User Experience research and design is a shift from a system-centered to a user-centered paradigm, in which the expected effects on the user are the focus of implementation and design decisions. However, putting this paradigm shift into practice is not a simple process and there are a vast number of UX approaches in academically oriented HCI studies alone. Reference to industry norms and standards can be helpful in such cases and mediate between the academic and practical sides of a multidisciplinary area such as HCI. For example, according to the ISO DIS 9241-210 standard, User Experience can be defined as "a person's perceptions and responses resulting from the use and/or anticipated use of a product, system or service." [17]. This specifies the concept of UX somewhat but more can be done. There is a need for a way to consolidate the information and recommendations from academia, standards, guidelines, and practical experience into realizable solutions.

C. Contextual User Experience Patterns

Recently, specific domains in HCI, such as UX research, employed patterns to collect and structure their knowledge based on empirical findings [4][11][18]. This is illustrated, e.g., by Martin et al. [19] and Crabtree [20] who use patterns for organizing and presenting ethnographic material. In 2010, Blackwell and Fincher [7] suggest adopting the idea of patterns and UX in the form of Patterns of User Experience (PUX). Such patterns should help HCI professionals to understand what kind of experiences people have with information structures.

In the same year, Obrist et al. [4] developed 30 UX patterns for audiovisual networked applications based on a wide range of collected empirical data, which was further categorized into main UX problem areas. An extension of these UX patterns, are the so-called Contextual User Experience (CUX) patterns. Accordingly, patterns are used to describe the knowledge on how to influence the users experience in a positive way by taking context parameters during the interaction with a system into account. Within their work, the authors provide a detailed description of how to structure CUX patterns in the car context. Three years later, Krischkowsky et al. [18] presented a step-by-step guidance for HCI researchers for generating patterns form HCI study insights. In particular, they intended to support User Experience (UX) researchers in converting their gathered knowledge from empirical studies into patterns. The structural foundation for the intended patterns is the so-called Contextual User Experience (CUX) patterns format, as mentioned before.

Following in the footsteps of Obrist et al. [11], we decided to pursue a three pronged approach towards driver space design and cover three major UX factors via appropriate design patterns.These factors are:

- *Mental Workload Caused by Distraction* [21]: Safety is paramount in an automotive environment, and distraction is one of the major contributing factors to accidents on the road [22][23]. Especially in UX, where functionalities and interface complexities are ever increasing, this is one of the most important factors to consider regarding driver safety.
- *Perceived Safety* [24]: The increased safety gained by designing for decreased mental workload and less distraction needs to be communicated to the driver. The difference between objective and perceived safety can be relatively large. For many situations, it has to be evaluated if car interfaces should increase or decrease perceived safety.

- *Joy of Use* [25][26]: Cars have more and more become instruments that are not simply means of transportation but are also used for entertainment. Thus, it becomes important that car interfaces can be used not only without frustration, but also in a way that makes using them a joyful experience.

We choose to focus on each of these factors for specific reasons. Mental Workload Caused by Distraction was chosen because it has been identified as one of the most safety-critical factors in traffic safety and because in-vehicle interactive systems bear particular inherent distraction potential. Perceived Safety was chosen because the communication of safety measures to the driver, which are not only limited to reducing in-vehicle distraction, needs to be ensured for successful interaction, thus complementing the first UX factor. Lastly, Joy of Use was chosen to make sure the eventual solutions are still suitable for a consumer-driven market, which the automotive domain is. We consider it important to keep in mind that the safest car is of little use if nobody has any intention to buy it.

D. Norms and Guidelines in Automotive Design and Engineering

The importance of norms and standards for the automotive domain has been stressed by Green in 2012 [27]. He argues that it should be required to include references to norms and standards when conducting experiments in the automotive domain, such as [28] or [29], in order to improve replicability and applicability of driver interface research.

There are several norms, standards, and guidelines that can supplement existing domain knowledge and aid automotive designers and engineers to follow basic human factors and usability rules. On one hand, there are norms and guidelines for the the general design of interactive systems. An example is the ISO 9241-110 [30], which provides general dialogue design principles and is part of the ISO 9241 standards family, which is a multi-part standard from the International Organization for Standardization covering different aspects of ergonomics of human computer interaction. On the other hand, there are guidelines for automotive designs often provided by automobile stakeholders, such as the AAM principles on Automotive User Interface (AUI) design [31], the JAMA guideline for in-vehicle display systems [32], the EU recommendation on safe and efficient in-vehicle information and communication systems [33], or the ISO 15005 norm on ergonomic aspects of dialogue management principles in road vehicles [34]. These often contain rather high level recommendations, which leaves a broad range of interpretation space for a designer. Yet, there are also very specific standards, such as the ISO 15008 [35], in which recommendations for alphanumerical character dimensions are given.

III. The Automotive Pattern Finding Process

The pattern finding process for car user experience patterns is described in detail by Mirnig et al. [36] and shall be reproduced here briefly and concisely; an illustrated overview can be found in Figure 1. In general, the process proceeds with the following five steps:

1) Problem finding and knowledge transfer workshop: The pattern finding process begins with an initial workshop, in which a small number (2-4 each) of both HCI researchers and automotive engineers and/or design experts participate. In this initial workshop, the focus is on knowledge transfer between the areas of academic HCI and automotive industry. The engineers are introduced to the pattern approach and the granularity of problems pattern solutions can be applied to. In a following discussion, the HCI researchers gather common and reoccurring problems, which the engineers face in their work. This happens in a top-down discussion, where overall issues or problem sources are defined first and are then broken down and refined during the course of the discussion. At the end of the workshop, the identified problems are compiled in a list and rated on 3-point priority scale (high, medium, and low priority).

2) Initial pattern mining: The initial pattern mining is done by HCI researchers, who are each assigned a number of problems with high to medium priority ratings. The number of patterns per researcher varies, depending on the number of researchers available, time constraints (if any), and number of high priority problems. In general, three to five problems (keeping in mind that one problem might result in more than one pattern) is a good number to aim for and keeps the workload for the individual at a manageable level. Naturally, the researchers should be competent regarding the academic aspect of the problems they are assigned. In the case of the UX automotive pattern collection, this meant that all of them should be familiar with UX and interface design, with specialization in the automotive domain being an additional plus, although not absolutely necessary. The first step is deciding whether or not the problem is a low or high level problem and whether or not its level of granularity is such that it requires one or several patterns. Each researcher then mines publications, demos, prototype presentations, and other available sources for solutions to the problem in question. These solutions can be partial, so that the researcher then combines all partial solution into one full solution for the eventual pattern. The pattern is written according to the structure outlined in the previous section and is then handed to another researcher for a first internal iteration. After this, the initial pattern or pattern draft is complete.

3) First iteration workshop: The initial patterns are presented to a group of automotive engineers in another workshop. Ideally, this workshop consists of some of the participants from the initial knowledge transfer workshop as well as participants who were not involved previously, in order to have a varied amount of viewpoints. The patterns are then read thoroughly by each participant and rated via a rating sheet based on the rating system developed by Wurhofer et al. [37]. Each pattern subcategory (Name, solution, etc.) is rated individually on a 5-point scale. When a pattern receives a rating of around or lower than 3 in any given subcategory, then it is marked for iteration. The workshop concludes with a discussion, in which the overall quality and

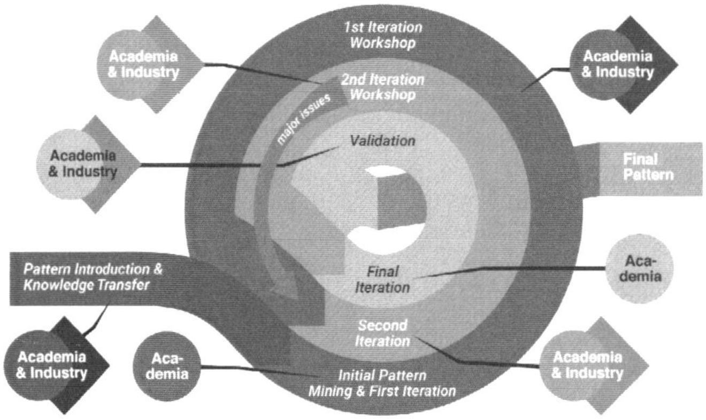

Figure 1. Overview of the Pattern Finding and Iteration Process.

cohesiveness of the pattern collection is discussed and any particular problematic patterns are identified.

4) Second iteration and workshop: After the workshop, the patterns undergo a second round of iterations, based on the ratings and feedback from the workshop. This time, they are iterated by at least one HCI researcher and at least one automotive engineer, in order to improve and ensure their practical relevance. The automotive engineer puts particular focus on supplementing the pattern with additional implementation examples (if available) and industry best practices. Like in the initial pattern writing, each pattern is cross-iterated by another researcher or engineer for typos, minor errors, structure, etc., before the second iteration is complete. The aim of the second iteration is content completion, i.e., the pattern solutions should be complete and fully described – all further iterations should only serve to improve structure, readability, and understandability. Once this iteration is completed, a second pattern workshop is conducted. The workshop proceeds like the first workshop, with the same rating system and discussion structure. In order to provide a fresh and unbiased view on the patterns and potentially identify new issues, the second workshop should, if possible, have some participants who were not part of the first workshop.

5) Final Iteration and Validation: After the workshop, the patterns are once again reworked based on the issues identified in the workshop. These should mostly be minor issues, although it is possible that major issues are found, which need to be dealt with. In that case, the pattern in question needs a content rework and is then put back in the loop for another content iteration workshop. Since it is usually not very efficient to schedule a workshop for only a handful of problematic patterns, these patterns are put aside temporarily. They are taken up again when a new batch of patterns is created and the appropriate iteration phase (and workshop) is reached. Once the patterns are reworked, the collection is provided to the industry experts for rating. Each pattern is rated individually, using the same rating system as before, and there is no need to do this in a workshop setting. In case a pattern receives a rating of around 3 or below at this stage, it is reworked and re-rated. It should be noted that this rarely, if ever, happens, since problematic patterns are usually identified before this stage. Once the patterns are all validated, the pattern collection is considered complete.

The resulting refined pattern structure consists of 9 parts: *Name* (a description of the solution of the pattern), *Intent* (a short abstract to allow quick judgment whether the pattern can be applied in a certain context), *Topics* (problem scope and addressed automotive user experience factor), *Problem* (a short but more detailed description of the problem which should be solved by the pattern), *Scenario* (an example application context of the pattern), *Solution* (the proposed solution), *Examples* (concrete examples of best practices), *Keywords* (other topics related to the pattern), and *Sources* (origin of the pattern).

IV. PATTERN COLLECTION

We developed a list of design problems together with designers and engineers working in the automotive industry and applied the aforementioned pattern generation approach, involving the industry stakeholders at several stages in the process. The following is one part of a resulting collection of patterns, which combines scientific and industry know-how into concrete problem solutions for UX-centered driver space design problems in the automotive domain. These patterns were edited regarding formatting and keywords as well as sources were removed for this publication. They are otherwise content-identical to the internally developed versions.

A. Pattern 1: Menu Depth and Number of Options

Intent: This pattern is about reducing distraction caused by navigating visual menus as a secondary task.

Topics: Workload caused by distraction, driver, haptic, input

Problem: While driving, navigation of in-vehicle user interface menus causes distraction. Given the safety implications of visual distraction, it is important to minimize visual demand of these menus.

Scenario: Drivers interact with visual menus to access information, communication and entertainment systems. Navigating menus with high visual demand severely distracts the driver and can thus lead to road deviations and crashes. Visual demand of menus is determined by a depth/breadth-trade-off. The deeper a menu, the less menu options per page there should be. A National Highway Traffic Safety Agency (NHTSA) guideline based on current research recommends that a driver should be able to complete a task in a series of 1.5 second glances with a cumulative time spent glancing away from the roadway of not more than 12 seconds [38].

Solution: Designing menus with limited depth allow drivers to complete secondary tasks in a relatively short time period. With the help of an empirically derived formula provided by Burnett et al. [39], it is possible to calculate different menu structures that comply with design guidelines:

$$T = D(0.87 + 1.24 * log(B)$$

where T = *time to complete the task*, D = *depth of menu* where B = *number of menu options*. Table I shows acceptable menu structures that comply with maximum task completion time according to the NHTSA guideline, as calculated using this formula.

TABLE I
MENU DEPTH AND NUMBER OF OPTIONS FOLLOWING NHTSA GUIDELINES

Menu Depth	Menu Breadth
3	12
4	5
5	3
6	2

Examples: see Figures 2 and 3.

B. Pattern 2: Display Touch Field Size

Intent: This pattern is about determining the optimal touch screen target size.

Topics: Workload caused by distraction, driver, touch screen, visual, haptic, input

Problem: Navigating in-vehicle displays while driving causes distraction, leading to road deviations and possibly to crashes. Thus, visual demand of touch screen menus has to be minimized while preserving maximum usability.

Scenario: Because they are easy to use and to understand, touch-screen interfaces are more and more used for operating in-vehicle systems. Drivers use them to control entertainment and navigation features provided by these systems as a

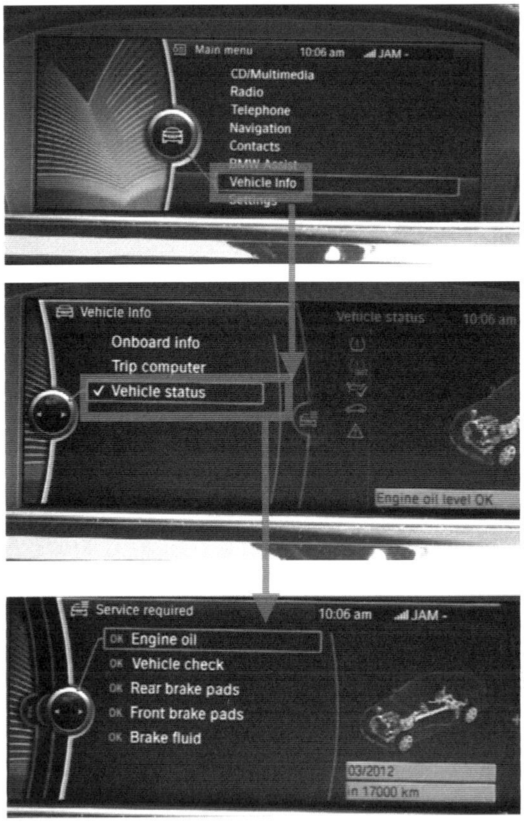

Figure 2. BMW iDrive - accessing vital information requires only three navigation steps.

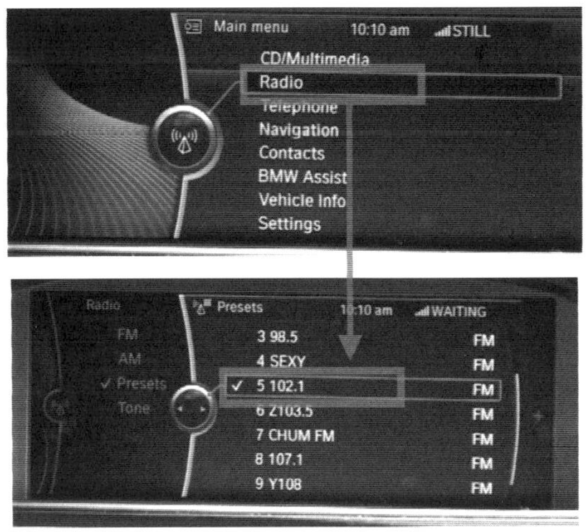

Figure 3. BMW iDrive - changing the radio station requires only two steps.

secondary task. The key factor for navigating these displays easily is the size of the touch target like a menu button [40]. Subjective usability ratings, as well as objective measures like task completion time and error rate heavily depend on this factor.

Solution: Touch targets need to be large enough in order to minimize task completion time and error rate. Design guidelines suggest a minimum contact surface area of 80 mm [38]. However, in a recent driving simulation study that focused on touch target size for in-vehicle information systems, the authors determined that a touch key size of at least 17.5x17.5 mm minimizes navigation error rate, lane deviations, driving speed variation and glance time while maximizing subjective usability ratings [41]. While touch screen size and overall visual complexity of the menu always have to be taken in consideration, the recommended touch key size may serve as a starting point for menu design.

Examples: See Figure 4.

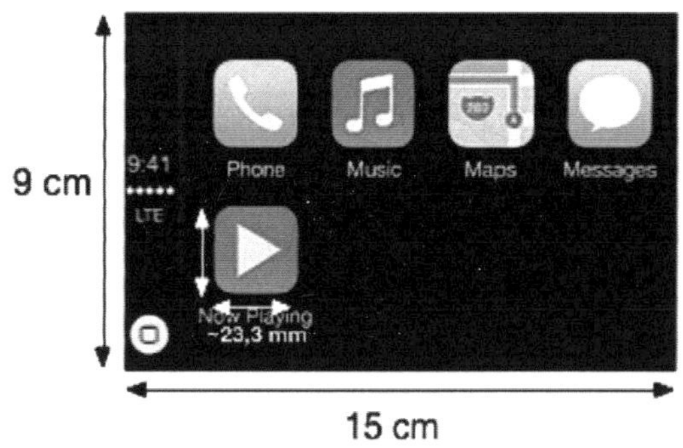

Figure 4. Apple Car Play menu.

C. Pattern 3: Auditory Information and Warnings

Intent: This pattern is about designing auditory information and warnings that are quick to capture and easy to comprehend.

Topics: Perceived safety, driver, acoustic, output

Problem: When using only visual warnings, driver distraction can occur. Still, drowsiness and inattentiveness increase the risk of traffic accidents. Thus, it is still necessary to direct the drivers attention to potential dangers by different means.

Scenario: Well-designed auditory warning systems can serve this purpose. Perceptibilty of auditory warnings depends on loudness, background noise and complexity. Also, the driver needs to know which actions have to be taken to react appropriately.

Solution: Different warning techniques are appropriate for different situations. According to Bliss and Acton [42], verbal speech notifications and auditory icons (sounds with real-world representations, e.g., the sound of a car engine) are equally efficient when it comes to response accuracy and reaction time. Auditory warnings also have to convey enough information to be accurately understood. Due to driving comfort reasons, warnings of low urgency should not be annoying and can even be quite pleasant, while high-urgency warnings are bound to be annoying [43].

Examples: Table II shows auditory warnings for some common situations of varying urgency. Empirical work on the perceived urgency of speech based warnings has been done [44].

D. Pattern 4: Choosing the Best Modality for Warning Displays

Intent: This pattern is about choosing the right warning display modality for different situations, combining different modalities if adequate.

Topics: Perceived safety, driver, multimodal, output

Scenario: In-vehicle information system (IVIS) information needs to be delivered effectively while minimizing the interference with driving. Display modality has a significant impact on the performance of in-vehicle information systems. Visual, auditory and tactile displays all have their advantages and disadvantages [45]: Visual warnings can be inspected at the drivers own pace and can be viewed multiple times. However, they cause visual distraction from the driving task and can be overlooked. Auditory warnings can be picked up without causing visual distraction, but they require the drivers full attention when they are displayed. Tactile warnings are highly noticeable, not influenced by noise and have no visual demand, but they are limited to a few types of information, such as simple alerts. In order to maximize IVIS efficiency, designers have to choose carefully between the different modalities.

Solution: When choosing between auditory and visual presentation, Table III offers decision guidelines based on current empirical research for a variety of cases. Some of these cases will probably benefit if combined with another display modality.

Examples: Figure 5 shows combined auditory and visual warnings. See [46] for a live demonstration.

E. Pattern 5: IVIS System Response Time

Intent: This pattern addresses the role of system response time while operating in-vehicle information systems by touch interfaces or hardware keys and its influence on driver distraction and comfort.

Topics: Workload caused by distraction, joy of use, driver, keys, visual, haptic, input

Problem: While getting more and more complex, many modern in-vehicle information systems possess significant delays when using them because of the sheer amount of information that they have to process. The influence of system response time - the delay of a systems response after user input until it is ready to take new commands - has

TABLE II
RECOMMENDED WARNINGS FOR COMMON SITUATIONS OF VARYING URGENCY

Urgency	Speech Based Warnings	Auditory Icons	Appropriate Situation
Informational (low)	Signal words that convey low urgency: "Notice", "Information"	Pouring water, steam, released air	Low petrol and oil levels, low tire pressure
Warning (moderate)	Signal words that convey medium urgency: Warning, Caution	Shutting car door, Roaringmotor sound, squeaking sound	Car door opened, speed limit exceeded, hand brake on
Critical (high)	Signal words that convey high urgency: Danger	Car horn, car crash, alarm siren	Blind spot overtaking, car drifting off road, collision possible

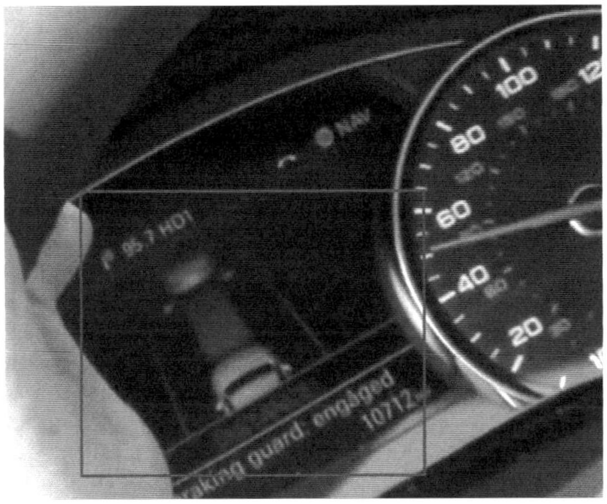

Figure 5. Audi A8 Distance Warning through a combination of auditory and visual warning displays.

been discussed as a potential source of driver distraction and annoyance [47].

Scenario: Drivers use in-vehicle information systems for a wide variety of functions. While navigating their menus, the IVIS processes large amounts of information, which may lead to long and uncertain loading times.

Solution: Keep system response time below 250 ms. According to current design guidelines [38], control feedback should be given within 250 ms after the input. A study by Utesch and Vollrath [48] showed that longer feedback delays (500 or 1000 ms) did not impair driving performance but caused significant annoyance in drivers. Keep system response times constant. It has also been shown in this study that delays that vary in their length distract the driver, while constant delays cause less off-road glances. It can be concluded that feedback delays should be kept constant so that waiting times for system response are predictable. For longer delays, use additional feedback modalities. According to guidelines of the European Commission [49], if system responses take longer than 250 ms, the system should inform the driver that it has recognized the input. If longer delays (500 ms and above) are inevitable, Utesch and Vollrath [48] recommend using acoustic or tactile feedback to indicate system readiness, as this will reduce off-road glances.

Examples:

1. Demonstration of a 2015 Audi MMI System, showing constant and short system response times [50].
2. Demonstration of a BMW 5 Series iDrive, showing long but constant delays [51].
3. Demonstration of an Apple CarPlay IVIS in the Ferrari FF showing long and variable delays. This might cause distraction and annoyance [52].

F. Pattern 6: In-Vehicle Display Icon Size

Intent: This pattern addresses recommended IVIS icon sizes.

Topics: Joy of use, driver, icons, visual

Problem: IVIS displays transport various pieces of information, some of which require quick and accurate recognition. However, as in-vehicle displays have to convey more and more information, available space on in-vehicle displays becomes sparse.

Scenario: Icons are a way of presenting information in a spatially condensed, yet clearly understandable way. When relying on icons, the driver needs to be able to quickly grasp and process information, which in turn requires that icons can be easily recognized.

Solution: According to Zwaga [64], icons perform better than text displays only if they are well designed. According to FHWA guidelines [65], choosing the adequate size for an icon can be determined with the following set of formulæ. See Figure 6 for an illustration of visual angle, distance and symbol height (where Symbol Height = the height of the symbol; Distance = distance from viewers eyepoint to the display; Visual Angle = angle in degrees. Height and Distance use the same unit of measure).

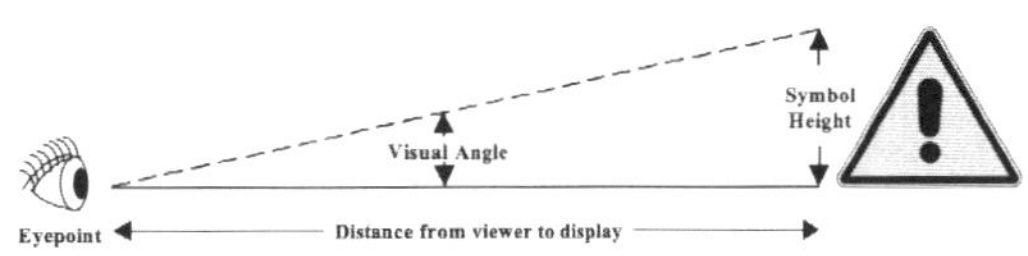

Figure 6. Relationship between Viewing Distance, Symbol Height and Visual Angle.

1. If viewer distance and Symbol Height are known,

TABLE III

RECOMMENDED WARNINGS FOR COMMON SITUATIONS OF VARYING URGENCY

Case	Primary Modality	Reason	Combine with...
High priority messages	Auditory [53][54]	Visual warnings alone are likely to be overlooked	Tactile [55] for decreased reaction times
Complex secondary task	Auditory [56][57][58]	Further distraction due to increased glance duration	Visual [59] for reduced reaction times and less navigation errors
Driving task is highly demanding, e.g., high driving speed	Auditory [56][57][58]	Divided visual attention poses a security risk	
Displaying instructions, commands, warnings or alarms	Auditory [60]	Speech is more suitable for this information type	Tactile [61]
Auditory message cannot be kept short and precise	Visual [62]	Auditory messages that are too long cause severe distraction	
Driver performs auditory tasks	Visual [44]	Auditory perception is partially or completely blocked	Tactile [63] for reduced lane deviations and annoyance, increased pleasantness

the following formulæ will calculate the distance.

$$arctan(\frac{Symbolheight}{Distance}) \quad (1)$$

or

$$\frac{3438\frac{Height}{Distance}}{60} \quad (2)$$

2. If distance and visual angle are known.

$$Distance[tan(VisualAngle)] \quad (3)$$

3. If visual angle and symbol height are known, the following formulæ will calculate the distance.

$$\frac{Symbolheight}{tan(VisualAngle)} \quad (4)$$

Examples: See Figure 7.

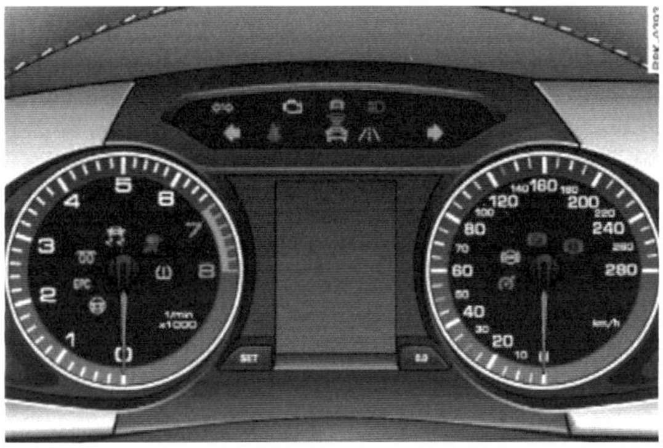

Figure 7. Audi A4 2008 Dashboard Icons, taken from the users manual [66].

G. Pattern 7: Visual Display Colour Choices

Intent: This pattern is about choosing adequate colours for visual displays.

Topics: Joy of use, driver, colors, visual

Problem: IVIS displays transport various pieces of information, some of which require quick and accurate recognition. However, as in-vehicle displays have to convey more and more information, they still need to be processed quickly.

Scenario: IVIS displays have to display information in a clear and efficient way. One way to achieve this is picking adequate colors for displays, so that reading and recognizing symbols can be accomplished without delay.

Solution: According to NHTSA guidelines, visual display colors should comply to a number of standards.

- Avoid using red/green and blue/yellow combinations so that color blind drivers can process the display easily.
- According to a survey conducted by Lee and Park [67], senior people prefer combinations with distinctive brightness contrasts between foreground and background color because of their better legibility.
- Displays that are too colorful distract the driver in various ways. Excluding black and white, a maximum of five different colours should be used.
- Use different colours for different priorities, e.g., red for critical alerts, amber for warnings, white for information.

Visual displays are easier to process if high color contrasts are used. A driving simulation study showed that inefficiently designed car displays strongly increase reaction times in driving tasks. They also increase reading errors [68]. Table IV shows color contrasts that guarantee high legibility.

TABLE IV

RECOMMENDED COLOR CONTRASTS FOR IVIS DISPLAYS

Black/yellow	Black/yellow
Black/white	Black/white
Black/orange	Black/orange
Blue/white	Blue/white
Green/white	Green/white
Red/white	Red/white

Examples: See Figure 8. This dashboard relies on white-on-black and orange-on-black contrasts which are highly visible. Orange is the only color used (beside black and white).

Figure 8. Dashboard with color contrasts that are highly visible.

Figure 9. BMW iDrive screen, showing blue-on-white contrasts with an orange highlight.

H. *Pattern 8: Physical Buttons versus Touch Screen Interfaces*

Intent: This pattern addresses the question whether touch screens or physical buttons should be used.

Topics: Workload caused by distraction, driver, touch screen, visual, haptic, input

Problem: Current touch-screen devices provide no tactile feedback concerning control orientation, location, separation from one another. While driving, they can not be operated with eyes on the road, which in turn leads to long off-road glances. NHSTA guidelines [38] suggest that touch interfaces should not be operated while driving. On the other hand, touch screen devices provide much more flexibility, which is needed to operate modern, feature-rich in-vehicle information systems.

Scenario: Drivers use in-vehicle information systems for a wide variety of functions. Ways to navigate through the increasing number of functions are getting more and more complex. Touch screen interfaces are getting more and more popular, but navigating them while driving is highly distracting.

Solution:

1) While driving, limit the amount of time spent to interact with touch devices. NHTSA recommends a maximum of six touches for every 12 seconds period [69]. Physical buttons do not require such strict regulations as their functionality is limited and they are not as visually distracting. Thus, functions that must be available to the driver while the car is moving should be represented by physical buttons or clearly identifiable, big touch buttons. Recommended limitations are as follows
   - For touch devices **without** haptic feedback, limit touch screen interactions to six touches for every 12 seconds.
   - For touch devices **with** haptic feedback, limit touch screen interactions only to certain functions.
   - No restrictions apply to physical buttons while driving.
   - No restrictions apply while standing.
2) Equip touch devices with haptic feedback. According to Harrison and Hudson [70], touch screens lead to a high number of off-road searching glances and require long periods of operation time. They also found that this could be mitigated by provide touch screens with haptic feedback, which is confirmed by other studies [71]. Studies suggest that this kind of feedback greatly increases performance and reduces operation time. If haptic feedback is used, touch devices still should to be limited to the functionality provided by traditional physical buttons.
3) Also, consider alternative input methods that do not require visual attention (e.g., voice interaction).

Examples: See Figure 10.

Figure 10. VW Passat dashboard which combines few physical buttons with a well-readable touch display.

V. DISCUSSION

A. Patterns in Use

The approach presented in this paper covers the pattern generation process from its initial problem finding stages up until the final validation of the eventual patterns. However, one thing the approach does not cover is something, which could be considered one of the more important metrics of the quality of a pattern - the successful application of a pattern. The evaluation phases all rely on the informed, but still subjective, judgments of industry experts. It can be assumed that these judgments are reliable due to the expertise of those making them. Still, an improved pattern approach would include an actual application or re-application of a pattern's described solution and another evaluation of the pattern, based on that implementation's success.

B. The Rule of One-Two-Three

A solution described in a pattern is expected to satisfy certain conditions. One of these is that the solution should be a *proven* one, meaning that it has worked or successfully been implemented in more than just one instance. A commonly applied rule in pattern writing is the so-called *Rule of Three* [72], which – when summed up roughly – considers a solution as proven if it has been successfully implemented at least three times. But is rather unusual to find the exact same information in two or more independent publications. In addition, the beyond state of the art nature of a good number of our solutions made it difficult to find an appropriate number of full solution implementations with adequate documentation. However, the combination of all sources yielded a substantial enough body to lend a certain degree of support to the viability and reproducibility of the described solutions. The fact remains, however, that many of the solutions described in our patterns do not satisfy the Rule of Three in a strict sense.

C. Experts vs. Novices

In our approach, we opted for more concise and shorter patterns in order to meet our industry partner's needs. The idea was to provide an eventual "patterns handbook", which could be consulted on-demand and at any time during their work. In doing so, we omitted deeper scenario descriptions, optional references and source material, and kept the number of illustrative examples to a minimum. This restructuring brought the desired increase in efficiency, but we expect that it is not without its drawbacks. In this case, our patterns are very likely to be less useful for novices than for experts, since they contain only the most essential information, in order to implement the described solution, which negates this one important benefit of patterns. Thus, we recommend for anyone who intends to adopt the pattern approach to decide whether or not increased efficiency or a broader pattern audience are more important, as it is unlikely that both goals can be realized at once.

D. Academia and Industry Access

Lastly, we should note that the approach we pursue is a rather particular one, with input taken from not only working implementations but also other sources, and integrated with industry stakeholders – both to enrich the pattern content and to better fit the eventual patterns to the stakeholders' needs. Pursuing such an approach requires sufficient available resources as well as access to both academic and industry experts, which is not always possible. Thus, the approach we pursue and briefly outlined in this paper is likely not suitable for everyone. The resulting patterns, however, should be.

VI. CONCLUSION

In this paper, we presented a collection of patterns, which deals with recurring questions of automotive design as reported by designers working in that area. By relying on design guidelines as well as empirical research, the collection tries to bridge the gap between regulations, standards, scientific findings, and industry knowledge. These patterns are intended to be of direct practical use for automotive designers. The pattern structure and length, which we described in earlier work [36], has been further adapted to fit automotive industry stakeholder needs, resulting in patterns with an increased emphasis on brevity and conciseness.

The automotive User Experience patterns proposed in this paper constitute a small part of a constantly growing collection of design knowledge. The speed of innovations, the complexity, and the range of functions of car interfaces is increasing constantly. In addition, even if there are more and more connections between single car interfaces, innovations do not necessarily occur in parallel. Thus, an equally dynamic approach to document best practices in design is required. As stated before, pattern collections are less holistic than guidelines and never really finished. New problems arise, new solutions to old problems are found, and sometimes proven solutions are found to not work as well as initially thought. This makes patterns arguably less suitable for traditional publishing as paper volumes, since these can, once printed, not be updated, save for issuing a new edition and print run. A database solution would be the obvious answer. A good example for such an online pattern resource is the Portland Pattern Repository Wiki [73]. Unlike a paper volume, however, such a database requires constant maintenance, dedicated moderation in case of crowdsourced editing and commenting functions and, of course, the initial infrastructure and server capacity.

Thus, the final pattern collection is still envisioned as a printed document, with the possibility of a later database conversion. While it is less dynamic than the more resource intensive database variant, this pattern collection shows how a pattern approach to car UX design can meet the demands of at least contemporary and near-future automotive design and the collection will continue to grow into a substantial body of car UX design knowledge. The goal of the first "complete" version of the pattern collection is expected to encompass 50 patterns, which cover some of the more important UX factors for driver space design [10].

ACKNOWLEDGMENTS

The financial support by the Austrian Federal Ministry of Science, Research and Economy and the National Foundation for Research, Technology and Development and AUDIO MOBIL Elektronik GmbH is gratefully acknowledged (Christian Doppler Laboratory for "Contextual Interfaces").

REFERENCES

[1] T. Kaiser, A. G. Mirnig, N. Perterer, A. Meschtscherjakov, and M. Tscheligi, "Car user experience patterns: A pattern collection in progress," in PATTERNS 2016, The Eighth International Conference on Pervasive Patterns and Applications. IARIA, 2016, pp. 9–16.

[2] C. Alexander, The Timeless Way of Building. New York, USA: Oxford University Press, 1979.

[3] A. Dearden and J. Finlay, "Pattern languages in hci: A critical review," Human-Computer Interaction, 2006, pp. 49–102, Sheffield Hallam University. [retrieved: 02, 2016] URL: http://research.cs.vt.edu/ns/cs5724papers/dearden-patterns-hci09.pdf.

[4] M. Obrist, D. Wurhofer, E. Beck, A. Karahasanovic, and M. Tscheligi, "User experience (ux) patterns for audio-visual networked applications: Inspirations for design," in Proceedings of the 6th Nordic Conference on Human-Computer Interaction: Extending Boundaries, ser. NordiCHI '10. New York, NY, USA: ACM, 2010, pp. 343–352. [retrieved: 02, 2016] URL: http://doi.acm.org/10.1145/1868914.1868955

[5] J. O. Borchers, J. C. Thomas, A. Sutcliffe, J. Coplien, and R. N. Griffiths, "Patterns: What's in it for hci?" in Extended Abstracts of the CHI 2001 Conference on Human Factors in Computing Systems. ACM, 2001.

[6] M. Hassenzahl and N. Tractinsky, "User experience-a research agenda," Behaviour & information technology, vol. 25, no. 2. Taylor & Francis, 2006, pp. 91–97.

[7] A. F. Blackwell and S. Fincher, "PUX: Patterns of User Experience," Interactions, vol. 17, no. 2. New York, NY, USA: ACM, 2010, pp. 27–31.

[8] M. Tscheligi, "User experience design for vehicles," in Christian doppler laboratory: contextual interfaces. Tutorial for conference AUI. ACM, 2012.

[9] C. Alexander, S. Ishikawa, and M. Silverstein, A Pattern Language: Towns, Buildings, Construction. New York, USA: Oxford University Press, 1997.

[10] A. G. Mirnig, A. Meschtscherjakov, N. Perterer, A. Krischkowsky, D. Wurhofer, E. Beck, A. Laminger, and M. Tscheligi, "User experience patterns from scientific and industry knowledge: An inclusive pattern approach," International Journal On Advances in Life Sciences, vol. 7, no. 3 and 4. IARIA, 2015, pp. 200–215. [retrieved: 02, 2016] URL: https://www.thinkmind.org/index.php?view=article&articleid=patterns_2015_2_30_70011.

[11] M. Obrist, D. Wurhofer, E. Beck, and M. Tscheligi, "Cux patterns approach: Towards contextual user experience patterns," in Proceedings of the 2nd International Conferences on Pervasive Patterns and Applications, PATTERNS, vol. 10. IARIA, 2010. [retrieved: 02, 2016] URL: http://www.thinkmind.org/index.php?view=article&articleid=patterns_2010_3_20_70079

[12] A. G. Mirnig and M. Tscheligi, "Introducing a general multi-purpose pattern framework: Towards a universal pattern approach," International Journal On Advances in Intelligent Systems, vol. 8, no. 1 and 2. IARIA, 2015, pp. 40–56. [retrieved: 02, 2016] URL: http://www.thinkmind.org/index.php?view=article&articleid=intsys_v8_n12_2015_4.

[13] S. Köhne, A Didactical Aproach towards Blended Learning: Conception and Application of Educational Patterns. Orig. title: Didaktischer Ansatz für das Blended Learning: Konzeption und Anwendung von Educational Patterns. Hohenheim, Germany: University of Hohenheim, 1995.

[14] K. Quibeldey-Cirkel, Design Patterns in Object Oriented Software Engineering. Orig. title: Entwurfsmuster: Design Patterns in der objektorientierten Softwaretechnik. Berlin, Germany: Springer, 1999.

[15] D. Martin, T. Rodden, M. Mark Rouncefield, I. Sommerville, and S. Viller, "Finding patterns in the fieldwork," in Proceedings of the Seventh European Conference on Computer Supported Cooperative Work. Kluwer Academic Publishers, 2001, pp. 39–58.

[16] J. O. Borchers, "A pattern approach to interaction design," AI & SOCIETY, vol. 15, no. 4, 2001, pp. 359–376.

[17] I. O. for Standardization, "Iso dis 9241-210. ergonomics of human system interaction - part 210: Human-centred design for interactive systems," Tech. rep., Switzerland, 2010.

[18] A. Krischkowsky, D. Wurhofer, N. Perterer, and M. Tscheligi, "Developing patterns step-by-step: A pattern generation guidance for hci researchers," in PATTERNS 2013, The Fifth International Conferences on Pervasive Patterns and Applications. IARIA, 2013, pp. 66–72. [retrieved: 02, 2016] URL: http://www.thinkmind.org/index.php?view=article\&articleid=patterns_2013_3_30_70053

[19] D. Martin, T. Rodden, M. Rouncefield, I. Sommerville, and S. Viller, "Finding patterns in the fieldwork," in Proceedings of the Seventh European Conference on Computer Supported Cooperative Work. Kluwer Academic Publishers, 2001, pp. 39–58.

[20] A. Crabtree, T. Hemmings, and T. Rodden, "Pattern-based support for interactive design in domestic settings," in Proceedings of the 4th Conference on Designing Interactive Systems: Processes, Practices, Methods, and Techniques, ser. DIS '02. New York, NY, USA: ACM, 2002, pp. 265–276. [retrieved: 02, 2016] URL: http://doi.acm.org/10.1145/778712.778749

[21] K. Young, M. Regan, and M. Hammer, "Driver distraction: A review of the literature," Distracted driving. Australasian College of Road Safety, 2007, pp. 379–405.

[22] M. A. Recarte and L. M. Nunes, "Mental workload while driving: effects on visual search, discrimination, and decision making," Journal of experimental psychology: Applied, vol. 9, no. 2. American Psychological Association, 2003, p. 119.

[23] J. Engström, E. Johansson, and J. Östlund, "Effects of visual and cognitive load in real and simulated motorway driving," Transportation Research Part F: Traffic Psychology and Behaviour, vol. 8, no. 2. Elsevier, 2005, pp. 97–120.

[24] R. Buchner, D. Wurhofer, A. Weiss, and M. Tscheligi, "Robots in time: How user experience in human-robot interaction changes over time," in Social Robotics. Springer, 2013, pp. 138–147.

[25] R. Buchner, P. M. Kluckner, A. Weiss, and M. Tscheligi, "Assisting maintainers in the semiconductor factory: Iterative co-design of a mobile interface and a situated display," in Proceedings of the 12th International Conference on Mobile and Ubiquitous Multimedia. ACM, 2013, p. 46.

[26] G. Stollnberger, A. Weiss, and M. Tscheligi, ""the harder it gets" exploring the interdependency of input modalities and task complexity in human-robot collaboration," in RO-MAN, 2013 IEEE. IEEE, 2013, pp. 264–269.

[27] P. Green, "Using standards to improve the replicability and applicability of driver interface research," in Proceedings of the 4th International Conference on Automotive User Interfaces and Interactive Vehicular Applications, ser. AutomotiveUI '12. New York, NY, USA: ACM, 2012, pp. 15–22.

[28] S. International, "Operational definitions of driving performance measures and statistics," Tech. rep., 2015.

[29] N. H. T. S. Administration, "Visual-manual nhtsa driver distraction guidelines for in-vehicle electronic devices," Tech. rep., 2010.

[30] I. O. for Standardization, "Iso dis 9241-110. ergonomics of human system interaction - part 110: Dialogue principles," Tech. rep., Switzerland, 2006.

[31] A. of Automobile Manufacturers, "Statement of principles, criteria and verification procedures on driver interactions with advanced in-vehicle information and communication systems," Tech. rep., 2006.

[32] J. A. M. Association, "Guidelines for in-vehicle display systems," Tech. rep., 2004.

[33] C. of the European Communities, "European statement of principles on human-machine interface," Tech. rep., 2006.

[34] I. O. for Standardization, "Iso dis 15005. road vehicles - ergonomic aspects of transport information and control systems - dialogue management principles and compliance procedures (draft)," Tech. rep., Switzerland, 2006.

[35] ——, "Iso dis 15008. road vehicles - ergonomic aspects of transport information and control systems - specifications and test procedures for in-vehicle visual presentation (draft)," Tech. rep., Switzerland, 2006.

[36] A. G. Mirnig et al., "Generating patterns combining scientific and industry knowledge: An inclusive pattern approach," in PATTERNS 2015, The Seventh International Conference on Pervasive Patterns and Applications. IARIA, 2014, pp. 38–45.

[37] D. Wurhofer, M. Obrist, E. Beck, and M. Tscheligi, "A quality criteria framework for pattern validation," International Journal On Advances in Software, vol. 3, no. 1 and 2. IARIA, 2010, pp. 252–264.
[38] A. Stevens, A. Quimby, A. Board, T. Kersloot, and P. Burns, NHTSA Design Guidelines for Safety of In-Vehicle Information Systems. National Highway Traffic Safety Administration, 2002.
[39] G. E. Burnett, G. Lawson, R. Donkor, and Y. Kuriyagawa, "Menu hierarchies for in-vehicle user-interfaces: Modelling the depth vs. breadth trade-off," Displays, vol. 34, no. 4. Elsevier, 2013, pp. 241–249.
[40] M. Pfauth and J. Priest, "Person-computer interface using touch screen devices," Proceedings of the Human Factors Society 25th Annual Meeting, no. 1, 1981, pp. 500–504.
[41] H. Kim, S. Kwon, J. Heo, H. Lee, and M. K. Chung, "The effect of touch-key size on the usability of in-vehicle information systems and driving safety during simulated driving," Applied ergonomics, vol. 45, no. 3. Elsevier, 2014, pp. 379–388.
[42] J. P. Bliss and S. A. Acton, "Alarm mistrust in automobiles: how collision alarm reliability affects driving," Applied ergonomics, vol. 34, no. 6. Elsevier, 2003, pp. 499–509.
[43] A. Guillaume, L. Pellieux, V. Chastres, and C. Drake, "Judging the urgency of nonvocal auditory warning signals: perceptual and cognitive processes," Journal of experimental psychology: Applied, vol. 9, no. 3. American Psychological Association, 2003, p. 196.
[44] J. Edworthy and E. Hellier, Complex Nonverbal Auditory Signals and Speech Warnings. Lawrence Erlbaum Associates Publishers, 2006, pp. 199–220.
[45] Y. Cao and M. Theune, "The use of modality in in-vehicle information presentation: A brief overview," in Proceedings of the 2nd International Workshop on Multimodal Interfaces for Automotive Applications (MIAA), in conjunction with IUI. ACM, 2010, pp. 1–5. [retrieved: 02, 2016] URL: https://www.ec-moan.org/~theune/PUBS/miaa2010-cao.pdf
[46] "Collision warning systems at the test track," 2012, [retrieved: 02, 2016] URL: https://www.youtube.com/watch?v=rYckJqp4XTc#t=45.
[47] P. Burns and T. Lansdown, "E-distraction: the challenges for safe and usable internet services in vehicles," in Internet Forum on the Safety Impact of Driver Distraction When Using In-Vehicle Technologies, 2000. [retrieved: 02, 2016] URL: http://www-nrd.nhtsa.dot.gov/departments/Human%20Factors/driver-distraction/PDF/29.PDF
[48] F. Utesch and M. Vollrath, "Do slow computersystems impair driving safety?" in European Conference on Human Centred Design for Intelligent Transport Systems, 2nd, 2010, Berlin, Germany. Humanist Publications, 2010.
[49] T. F. HMI, "European statement of principles on human machine interface for in-vehicle information and communication systems," Tech. rep., Commission of the European Communities, Tech. Rep., 1998.
[50] "2015 Audi MMI Infotainment Review in the 2015 Audi A3 Sedan," 2014, [retrieved: 02, 2016] URL: https://www.youtube.com/watch?v=xadb1vSXw7Q.
[51] "BMW 5 Series Connected-Drive (iDrive) Full Demo - including Head-Up Display," 2013, [retrieved: 02, 2016] URL: https://www.youtube.com/watch?v=Ulcgm-GN_M.
[52] "Apple CarPlay Demo," 2014, [retrieved: 02, 2016] URL: https://www.youtube.com/watch?v=TQz64rhefqY.
[53] C. Kaufmann, R. Risser, A. Geven, and R. Sefelin, "Effects of simultaneous multi-modal warnings and traffic information on driver behaviour," in Proceedings of European Conference on Human Centred Design for Intelligent Transport Systems. Humanist Publications, 2008, pp. 33–42.
[54] B. Seppelt and C. Wickens, "In-vehicle tasks: Effects of modality, driving relevance, and redundancy," Tech. Rep., 2003. [retrieved: 02, 2016] URL: http://www.aviation.illinois.edu/avimain/papers/research/pub_pdfs/techreports/03-16.pdf
[55] C. Ho, H. Z. Tan, and C. Spence, "Using spatial vibrotactile cues to direct visual attention in driving scenes," Transportation Research Part F: Traffic Psychology and Behaviour, vol. 8, no. 6. Elsevier, 2005, pp. 397–412.
[56] J. B. Hurwitz and D. J. Wheatley, "Using driver performance measures to estimate workload," in Proceedings of the Human Factors and Ergonomics Society Annual Meeting, vol. 46, no. 22. Sage Publications, 2002, pp. 1804–1808.
[57] S. G. Klauer, T. A. Dingus, V. L. Neale, J. D. Sudweeks, and D. J. Ramsey, "The impact of driver inattention on near-crash/crash risk: An analysis using the 100-car naturalistic driving study data," Tech. Rep., 2006.
[58] R. Srinivasan and P. P. Jovanis, "Effect of selected in-vehicle route guidance systems on driver reaction times," Human Factors: The Journal of the Human Factors and Ergonomics Society, vol. 39, no. 2. Sage Publications, 1997, pp. 200–215.
[59] Y.-C. Liu, "Comparative study of the effects of auditory, visual and multimodality displays on drivers' performance in advanced traveller information systems," Ergonomics, vol. 44, no. 4. Taylor & Francis, 2001, pp. 425–442.
[60] K. Stanney, S. Samman, L. Reeves, K. Hale, W. Buff, C. Bowers, B. Goldiez, D. Nicholson, and S. Lackey, "A paradigm shift in interactive computing: Deriving multimodal design principles from behavioral and neurological foundations," International Journal of Human-Computer Interaction, vol. 17, no. 2. Taylor & Francis, 2004, pp. 229–257.
[61] J. B. Van Erp and H. A. Van Veen, "Vibrotactile in-vehicle navigation system," Transportation Research Part F: Traffic Psychology and Behaviour, vol. 7, no. 4. Elsevier, 2004, pp. 247–256.
[62] Y. Cao, S. Castronovo, A. Mahr, and C. Müller, "On timing and modality choice with local danger warnings for drivers," in Proceedings of the 1st International Conference on Automotive User Interfaces and Interactive Vehicular Applications. ACM, 2009, pp. 75–78.
[63] D. Kern, P. Marshall, E. Hornecker, Y. Rogers, and A. Schmidt, "Enhancing navigation information with tactile output embedded into the steering wheel," in Pervasive Computing. Springer, 2009, pp. 42–58.
[64] H. Zwaga and T. Boersema, "Evaluation of a set of graphic symbols," Applied Ergonomics, vol. 14, no. 1. Elsevier, 1983, pp. 43–54.
[65] J. L. Campbell, J. Richman, C. Carney, and J. Lee, "In-vehicle display icons and other information elements. volume i: Guidelines, technical report," Tech. Rep., 2004.
[66] Audi A4 2008 Owner's Manual, http://www.alkivar.com/AUDI/Audi_A4_2008_Owner_s_Manual.pdf [retrieved: 02, 2016].
[67] M. Lee and J. Park, "Senior users color cognition and color sensitivity features in visual information on web-interface," in Universal Access in Human-Computer Interaction. Aging and Assistive Environments. Springer, 2014, pp. 129–137.
[68] E. S. Wilschut, G. Rinkenauer, K. A. Brookhuis, and M. Falkenstein, "performance in a lane-change task is vulnerable to increased secondary task complexity." TNO Publications, p. 5.
[69] Authors unknown, "Visual-manual nhtsa driver distraction guidelines for in-vehicle electronic devices," Washington, DC: National Highway Traffic Safety Administration (NHTSA), Department of Transportation (DOT), 2012.
[70] C. Harrison and S. E. Hudson, "Providing dynamically changeable physical buttons on a visual display," in Proceedings of the SIGCHI Conference on Human Factors in Computing Systems. ACM, 2009, pp. 299–308.
[71] H. Richter, R. Ecker, C. Deisler, and A. Butz, "Haptouch and the 2+ 1 state model: potentials of haptic feedback on touch based in-vehicle information systems," in Proceedings of the 2nd international conference on automotive user interfaces and interactive vehicular applications. ACM, 2010, pp. 72–79.
[72] A. Osmani, Learning JavaScript Design Patterns: A JavaScript and jQuery Developer's Guide. O'Reilly Media, 2012.
[73] C. . C. (C2), "The portland pattern repository wiki," Online, 2016. [retrieved: 02, 2016] URL: http://c2.com/cgi/wiki

Components for a SOA with ESB, BPM, and BRM

Decision Framework and architectural Details

Arne Koschel, Andreas Hausotter
University of Applied Sciences and Arts Hannover
Faculty IV - Business and Computer Science
Ricklinger Stadtweg 120, 30459 Hannover, Germany
Arne.Koschel@hs-hannover.de,
Andreas.Hausotter@hs-hannover.de

Malte Zuch, Johannes Busch, Juri Seewald
University of Applied Sciences and Arts Hannover
Faculty IV - Business and Computer Science
Ricklinger Stadtweg 120, 30459 Hannover, Germany
Malte.Zuch@hs-hannover.de, Johannes.Busch@stud.hs-hannover.de, Juri.Seewald@stud.hs-hannover.de

Abstract - **To keep their competitive edge, enterprises need to change their operational processes in a flexible and agile manner. A Service-oriented Architecture (SOA) may help to meet these needs. One key feature of a SOA is the externalization of business process logic. However, the logic process is often complex, hard to understand and difficult to adapt. This issue is due to a mingling of process and decision logic. In order to ensure flexibility and agility, decision logic should be moved to a separate service. In previous work, we provided a decision framework, which recommends an approach to actually realize such a "rule service" conceptually. We apply our framework in particular to the German insurance domain utilizing a standardized insurance process scenario. The paper presents the resulting SOA architecture, which has an Enterprise Service Bus (ESB), a Business Process Management (BPM) / Workflow Management System (WfMS), and a Business Rules Management System (BRMS) / rules engine as key components. As a key contribution here, we provide several internal architectural and implementation details including deployment and runtime views of our architecture.**

Keywords - Business Process Management (BPM); Business Rules Management (BRM); Business Rules Management System (BRMS); Enterprise Service Bus (ESB); Service-oriented Architecture (SOA).

I. INTRODUCTION

A. *Motivation*

Workflow Management Systems support companies in the management and execution of business processes [25]. Nowadays, the latest challenges for insurance companies such as the dynamic business environment and compliance with legal requirements highlight the need for business agility [2][24]. Business agility requires individual, quick, and flexible composition and adoption of business processes [9][10]. This can be done in the context of Business Process Management (BPM). As a result of the composition and adaption, the number of decisions may rise within the processes. Hence, the complexity of the business processes can lead to a lack of business agility [10]. Business rules provide an opportunity to reduce the complexity of the processes, whilst the complex decision logic is encapsulated. The necessary changes with respect to agility often relate to the complex decision logic and not to the process or business logic. Thus, the separation of decision logic and process logic on the modeling and implementation level is a useful approach to reduce complexity.

Comprehensive service-oriented approaches have the potential to create business agility [27]. Thus, a service-oriented architecture (SOA) can help to address challenges like the dynamic business environment. The service-oriented integration of BPM and Business Rules Management (BRM) provides potential to change business processes in an agile manner [11].

The results of interviews with experts of the insurance service sector emphasized that issue to choose an adequate approach to automate the execution of business rules within service-oriented architectures with respect to a missing decision support. Considering the dynamic business environment in the insurance services sector, the topics of the presented work are of potential value for several insurance companies (at least) in Germany [2][24].

B. *Contribution*

Our previous work [11] presents a decision framework, which recommends an approach to realize a "rule service" conceptually. It serves as the groundwork for the key contributions of this article, which are:

- The application of the decision framework to scenarios particularly suitable to the German insurance domain, but easily transferable to similar environments. Thus, while we do not claim to provide too much novelty from an overall generic SOA/BPM/BRM perspective, we do contribute a valuable case study including detailed design decisions. Thus, our work provides value, which is especially applicable to the German insurance domain in general.
- A resulting SOA, which has as key technical components an ESB, a BPM system/WfMS, a business activity monitoring (BAM), and a BRM system.
- The detailed design of our SOA includes four steps: (1) initial design, (2) design decisions, (3) product evaluation for key components of the architecture, and (4) a resulting final architecture.

- Moreover, our SOA is applied to a standardized insurance process application scenario ("Goodwill Process") working within the overall architecture from the German "Versicherungs-anwendungsarchitektur (VAA) [28]". The VAA is a set of standardized insurance processes, the "insurance application architecture".
- This paper significantly extends our work from [1]. In particular, we provide here much more conceptual and technical depth as key additional contributions. This includes more internal architectural and implementation details, for example, a runtime view and a deployment view of our architecture.

Our work takes place within the context of the current research activities of the "Competence Center – Information Technology and Management" (CC ITM) [5]. The CC ITM is a cooperation between IT departments from German insurance companies and our faculty. The aim of this cooperation is knowledge transfer and the combination of scientific research with practical experiences.

The remainder of the paper is structured as follows: In Section II we present prior and related work. In the following, we first show the application scenario in Section III, then our initial architecture in Section IV, implementing design decisions in Section V, an evaluation of products in Section VI, and eventually the resulting target architecture of the system in Section VII. Section VIII finalizes the article with a conclusion and an outlook to future work.

II. PRIOR AND RELATED WORK

The concept of a complex software architecture is always influenced by several factors. For handling the variability of decisions between those factors, a quantitative evaluation method can reduce complexity. In a previous work of the CC ITM, different concepts and technologies were discussed with such a quantitative evaluation method [18][16]. Therefore, different factors have been specified to build up a decision framework for identifying suitable business rule execution approaches. Further on, potential application scenarios have been identified by the CC ITM and the collaboration partners.

As a result, the standardized insurance process application scenario ("Goodwill Process") was selected. The scenario, introduced in Section III (cf. [34][18] for an extended version), is inspired by a common insurance application architecture ("GAA") used by the German insurance industry [28].

The basis of this work is specified by our partners from the insurance domain as well as the usage of the GAA. Within this specific domain, we contribute a valuable case study including detailed design decisions. Thus, our work provides novelty and value, which is especially applicable to the German insurance domain in general although might well be transferable to domains with similar requirements as well.

The required elements, which are to be implemented with a rule-based approach, were determined within this scenario. In this regard, we identified the business rule set "goodwill adjustment". An extraction process for business rules identification from business process models is mentioned in [20]. This process is useful, because business rules are often not explicitly included in the process models. A decision guideline for distinguishing between business process and business rule is presented in [22]. Requirements concerning business rules technologies are defined in [2][24]. The variables for determining suitable solutions for business rule implementation are illustrated in [23]. As a result of the literature review, the decision guideline, the requirements and the variables provide a contribution to the decision framework. Since no previous research allows a simple choosing of an adequate business rules execution approach this decision framework is the first to extend the current state of research through the linking of factors, indicators and business rules execution approaches. The determination of the specific business rules execution approach depends on the elements, which are to be implemented with a rule-based approach.

Concerning our project, the software architecture has to fit the demands of the insurance business. Requirements such as privacy and security protection of customer data excluded peer-to-peer (P2P) solutions despite the advantage of the high availability P2P solutions could offer. Thus, solutions with discrete data storage options and a higher reliability concerning requests were considered. Especially, the service-oriented approach with an agile business rules solution was identified as most fitting for the insurance sector. The combination of high cohesion and loose coupling increases the flexibility and maintainability of complex and highly distributed software architectures [12]. In particular, an ESB can fulfill the requirements of highly distributed SOAs [6].

The physical integration instead of a logical one was identified as the most fitting solution in [16], regarding the general SOA approach of the CC ITM project. Further on, reliable messaging and security aspects of a physical ESB are also supporting the general demands of the insurance business in terms of security. Because of the whole software architecture consisting of distributed software components, a cloud solution was determined as a potential extension for the current BPM solution [16]. The paper [7] highlights the benefits of migrating BPM solutions into the cloud, to fulfill the increasing future demand of adaptive solutions in a dynamic business environment.

As a result of all these findings, the following Section III presents our application scenario from the German insurance domain. With this standard scenario, we will analyze its underlying SOA-, BPM-, BAM-, and BRM based architecture.

III. APPLICATION SCENARIO

A special application scenario has been applied to evaluate the prototypical implementation, which we have been described in [11]. This scenario is depicted in Figure 1. The scenario is a sub-process of the overall process "claim processing". This overall process implements a standardized insurance companies use case, namely "handle a goodwill request" from the German "Versicherungsanwendungsarchitektur [28]".

A goodwill payment is a compensation voluntarily granted by the insurance company without any obligation. The company checks whether compensation should be provided and - if so - determines its amount. The triggering event is the repudiation of cover. Its goal is to preserve the business relationship with the partner (customer). The task "Set goodwill adjustment" determines the goodwill amount and is a typical case for a business rule in the German insurance domain.

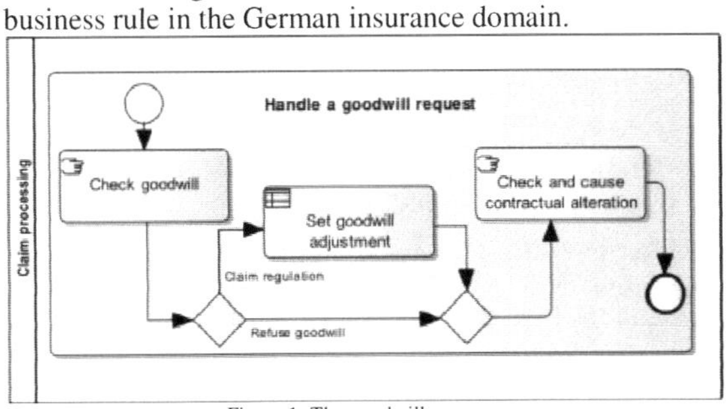

Figure 1: The goodwill process.

Within a process it makes sense to introduce certain tasks as business rules to gain flexibility or better maintainability. For example, some conditions at a certain decision point can change significantly more often than the overall business process. So, a flexibly changeable rule might offer more agility. These different requirements in flexibility directly influence the technically decisions about the actual rule realization/implementation.

IV. INITIAL ARCHITECTURE OF THE SYSTEM

To address these different requirements in flexibility regarding the implementation of business rules, we presented a decision framework in our prior work [11]. This paper compared different technical approaches for business rule execution (inference machine, database, configuration file and business applications) based on certain factors and indicators. By applying this decision framework, we decided to use a dedicated BRM inference machine for rule execution [11][16]. This approach has been identified as the most flexible one, especially with respect to the implementation of complex rules and larger rule sets. Next we will show the initial architecture of the system and will discuss its individual architectural components in detail. This architecture will process the described standard "Goodwill process" from Section III.

The architecture of the system for the "Goodwill Process" was composed from the following components (cf. Figure 2):

- The **WfM-Engine** (workflow management engine) was and still is the core of the whole architecture. It manages the business process, verifies the execution order of activities and routes the information flow between client and back-end. It contains a logical ESB to orchestrate different services. As concrete WfM-Engine, we use the product "Infinity Process Platform" (IPP) provided by SunGuard [13].
- The **BAMS** (business activity monitoring system) composes stored procedures and triggers. It is placed in an Oracle database and monitors the executions of activities used by the business processes. The BAMS is similar to complex event processing systems but uses a special form of logging. The monitoring allows the evaluation of business rule executions to improve the processes. It was designed by the CC ITM project.
- The **Client** component provides the functionality of the system to the user. It is currently a command console and menu based application, which allows the activation and execution of processes in the system. Currently, this client component is developed by the CC ITM and supports only the goodwill-scenario in a console-based user interface.
- The **Applications** provide the automatic execution of an activity or a single task. When they are invoked by the WfM-Engine, they execute the business logic that underlies the corresponding activity and report their result to the engine. Because the WfM-Engine only supports Enterprise JavaBeans (EJB) 2.x- and Web service calls, all applications are implemented as EJB 2.1 Beans.

Other components in Figure 2 are just supporting management and development background tools, which do not require a more detailed explanation here. The overall design decision and the composition of all its components to fulfill the requirements in flexibility and maintainability is described next.

V. DESIGN DECISIONS

The general big-picture of a software project is always the sum of every single design decision. The single decisions have to be chosen carefully. Therefore, a quantitative evaluation will help to support the decision-making.

A. *Business activity monitoring system and business rules management system*

To further improve the SOA aspect of the design, the introduction of a BRMS was considered. The BRMS would be responsible for managing the business logic and would also reduce some workload of the WfMS. Moreover, the BRMS would "user friendly" support modifications of business rules.

Overall, the BRMS is another "active rule" system, technical similar to the BAMS but with a different application-oriented purpose within our architecture. Regarding the responsibilities of these two systems, the introduction of a redundant component makes sense; the

BAMS has to monitor the whole WfMS architecture, while the BRMS only takes care of domain specific rules. This means, there will be two similar components for completely different tasks, combining both responsibilities would intermingle rules concerning different domains - a perilous path to take.

B. Enterprise service bus

The logical ESB, provided by the WfMS in use (IPP), was very restrictive in terms of supported applications and is not adaptable to offer security and transport protocols. Therefore, the advantages and disadvantages of a "homemade" physical ESB were compared with the advantages of the already existing logical ESB.

As presented in Table I, the advantages of using a physical ESB are significant and are outweighing the disadvantages.

Replacing the logical ESB with a physical one results in a more flexible architecture supporting the approach of loose couplings within the SOA. Therefore, the CC ITM team evaluated several solutions. For the concrete evaluation of the advantages and disadvantages of the different products, we will next discuss this evaluation with a quantitative approach.

VI. EVALUATION OF PRODUCTS

To find the best fitting set of products, a list of requirements was created and research was conducted on available alternatives. The evaluation process and its results are presented in this section.

Table I: ADVANTAGES AND DISADVANTAGES OF A LOGICAL AND PHYSICAL ESB FOR THE ARCHITECTURE.

	Advantages	Disadvantages
Logical	Already provided by the WfM-Engine	Dependence on the IPP WfM-Engine
	Responsibility for availability, security and reliability of the ESB outsourced to a third party company	Not expandable/modable for security, transport protocols and new interfaces
Physical	Lose coupling from IPP	More implementation work
	Less dependence on proprietary software components	
	More control and knowledge in self-programmed software components	Integration difficult or impossible due to the lack of knowledge
	More flexible software for security mechanisms, transport mechanisms and more interfaces	
	Future replacement of WfM-Engine easier (for example Stardust)	

A. ESB products

There are a lot of ESB solutions available today, analyzed in different publications. In this project, a long-list of possible ESB solutions was derived based on the publications [26][30][8][29][21][19]. These were the solutions:

Table II: THE LONG LIST OF ESB SOLUTIONS.

Apache Server Mix
Mule ESB
BEA System Aqualogic Service Bus
IBM WebSphere
Cape Clear
Oracle ESB
Fuse ESB
OpenESB
Talend Open Studio for ESB

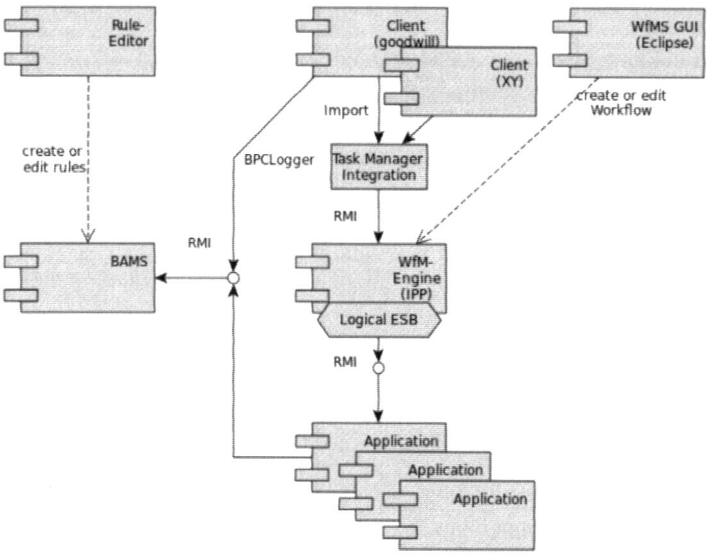

Figure 2: Initial architecture of the CC ITM project.

Because of some sources not being up-to-date, an additional study had to be undertaken by the project team in order to map the long list to the current situation on the market. It was discovered that some of the ESBs are included in different solutions now, because the manufacturers were acquired by other companies. For example, Fuse ESB currently belongs to JBoss Solutions from Red Hat Inc. [31].

In the next step, the long list was transformed into a short list. The conclusion drawn in [26][30][8][29][21][19] account for the choices made at this stage. Furthermore, special project requirements were used to extend the short list, such as the solution must:

- be open source and state-of-the-art
- work with both Windows and Linux operating systems respectively
- have an active support community
- provide an Enterprise JavaBeans connector for integration with existing components

The resulting short list is:

Table III: SHORT LIST OF ESB SOLUTIONS & EVALUATION (MAX. 100%).

Red Hat JBoss ESB	83.99%
Mule ESB	75.29%
OpenESB	83.98%
Talend ESB	89.87%

A full installation of each of the ESBs in the short list was not undertaken. Instead, the results of the comparative analysis in [3] were used, which describe detailed testing of solutions on different platforms, amongst which are Mule ESB, JBoss ESB and OpenESB. Talend ESB was evaluated in an interview [17] with an employee of Talend, using the criteria from [3]. These criteria belong to three categories, such as ergonomics, processing and environment.

For the evaluation of the ESB solutions, a value benefit analysis was performed. For this purpose, metrics and ratings for the criteria, and weightings for the categories have been defined [3]. Based on these specifications and the evaluation of the respective ESB product, the score has been calculated, which reflects the degree of fulfilment relative to 100% [3][17].

The combined results from both sources are also depicted in Table III. However, these numbers alone do not constitute the best solution, since possible problems of this result must be considered. Talend ESB was evaluated in 2013. The others were compared six years in before, so additional features might have been added in this period of time. Thus, despite it not having the best score, JBoss ESB was chosen by the team, because of its good documentation, wide usage and ability to run on JBoss Application Server 5.1, which was successfully used in the project before.

The compatibility of the ESB to the existing application server led to a low-effort integration into the architecture. After the ESB had been deployed on the server, it was necessary to ensure that the applications are not called by the logical ESB of the workflow engine directly any longer. Instead, the logical ESB will access the JBoss ESB which will call the applications. Referring to this, the JBoss ESB must provide an Enterprise JavaBeans service for the workflow engine. Therefore, the FacadeBean was created and the definition of the business process was altered, so that this Bean is accessed by the workflow engine when needed. These changes to the architecture are depicted in the final architecture diagram in Figure 7.

B. *Business rule execution approaches (BREA)*

In order to choose a business rules execution approach, a requirements analysis was undertaken, both for general business rules execution approach requirements and special requirements determined by the project. The former is defined in the Business Rules Manifesto from the Business Rules Group [4] and includes portability and user friendliness of the rule editor. The project requires the business rules execution approach to be:

- open source
- compatible with Linux and Windows operating systems respectively
- integrable with the existing JBoss ESB
- capable of processing complex business rules
- well documented, supported and constantly updated

In 2012, the team conducted a research on BRMS available on the market and created a list of suitable solutions. In order to assess the features of systems, an evaluation of BRMS was undertaken based on a criteria catalog developed by the project team based on a "Basel III" scenario [15][33]. The evaluation resulted in the BRMS short list in Table IV. The "Basel III" scenario asks for two typical indicators used by the underlying insurance business:

- liquidity coverage factor (LCR)
- net stable funding ration (NSFR)

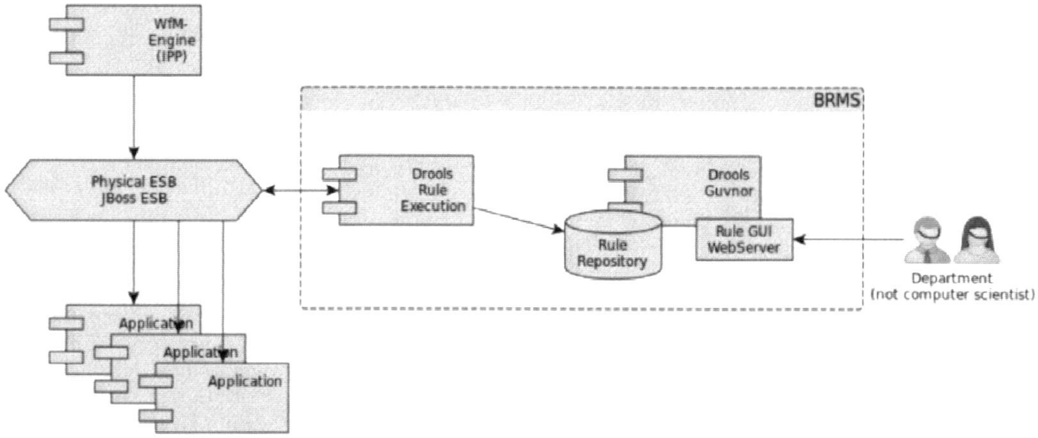

Figure 3: BRMS architecture with JBoss Drools and Guvnor.

In [15], the criteria are divided into nine groups: usability, ease of learning, run-time environment, performance, compatibility, functionality, safety and security, development and debugging, documentation. For each criterion, a score from one (worst case) to four (best case) was assigned to each product. The weighting of criteria was customized with respect to the specifics of the project. The evaluation results [14] are also presented in Table IV, although, those results cannot be used for judging about absolute quality of products. Nevertheless, due to restrictions of the project, an open source solution had to be chosen and therefore, JBoss Drools has been used in the prototype architecture.

JBoss Drools provides a complete system for business rules management, including a rule repository and a web server with a special site for rule management in Drools Guvnor. The BRMS architecture in the project is depicted in Figure 3.

Table IV: LIST OF BRMS SOLUTIONS& BRMS EVALUATION RESULTS (MAX. 100%).

Visual Rules	85.07%
JBoss Drools	61.09%
WebSphere ILOG JRules	77.19%

With this quantitative evaluation, we are able to identify the best fitting set of products to fulfill the requirements. The final system architecture build with those products is described next.

VII. TARGET ARCHITECTURE OF THE SYSTEM

There are several changes and optimizations between the basic and the target architecture of the system. Certain parts of the initial architecture have not been changed: Goodwill client, the connection between the client, the WfM-Engine and the BAMS are still as in the initial architecture. The original and modified parts are shown in Figure 7.

The first change of the initial architecture was the replacement of the logical ESB. For this purpose, JBoss ESB as a physical ESB was chosen as described before. Different applications will be called from the physical ESB instead of the logical one. Nevertheless, the logical ESB cannot be replaced completely, because it is an integrated part of the WfM-Engine. Also, it supports only EJBs and Web services connectors. Therefore, a connection between the logical ESB and physical ESB was developed. A simple Facade Bean represents this connection. It is called as an EJB from the logical enterprise service bus. All WfM-Engine calls will be channeled through the Facade Bean to different applications. Furthermore, the application calls in the process definition (XPDL file) were changed to leverage the physical ESB. To connect the applications to the JBoss ESB so called Services need to be described. The translation between the logical ESB and the Services is done by the Facade Bean. Moreover, the monitoring of these application calls is now handled by the JBoss ESB, for this purpose a connection between the JBoss ESB and the BAM-System was introduced.

The second change to the initial architecture was the integration of the BRMS. As stated before, the chosen BRMS is JBoss Drools. Its integration was realized through the connection between JBoss Drools and JBoss ESB. Furthermore, the BRMS was integrated into the process definition. Easily enough, a definition of a rule call is similar to an application call.

Management of the rule base is implemented by JBoss Drools Guvnor. Rules can be created or edited via a rule management website. Moreover, a rule storage (rule repository) is part of Guvnor.

The actual architecture is supported by decisions based on quantitative evaluation methods as well as on the expertise within the CC ITM team. We assume, a combination of quantitative methods and qualitative experience should offer an architectural design, able to challenge and be challenged by future demands.

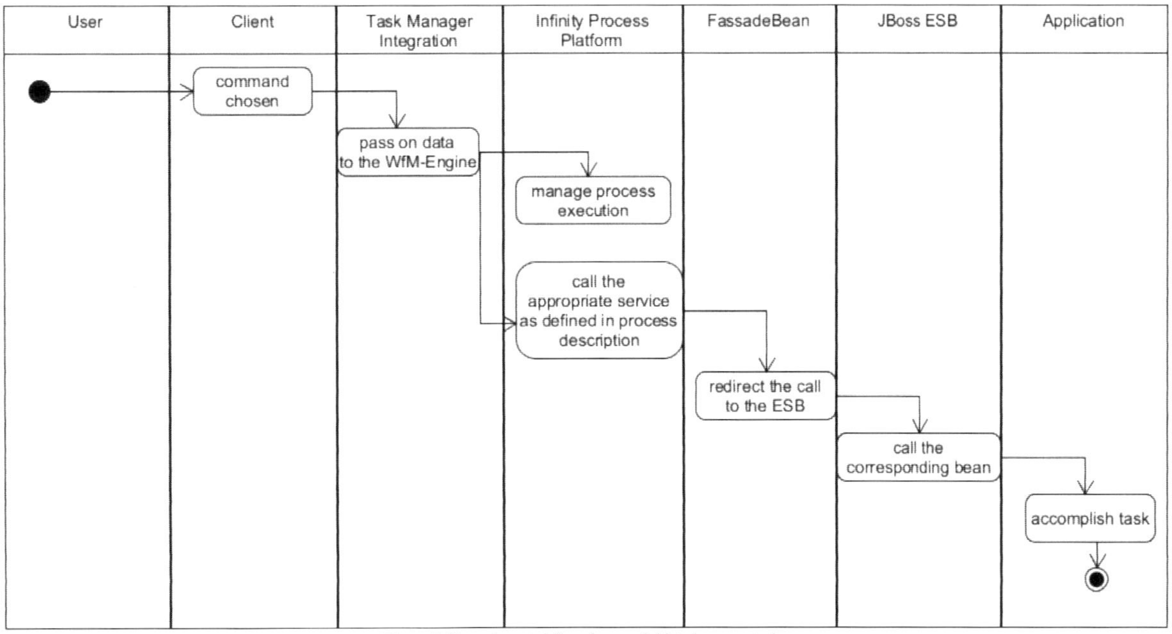

Figure 4: General control flow for user-initiated process tasks.

A. *Runtime View*

This section describes the dynamic view of the system's process [12]. The central process is "handle a goodwill request". It is a complex process that consists of many steps (service calls). Thus, the diagram of the process is not given here, but a short version is given in Figure 1. The general control flow for each step in the process initiated by the user is shown in Figure 4.

As mentioned before, the flow starts at the (command-line) client, passes the Task Manager and workflow engine. All service calls are mapped by the *FassadeBean* onto ESB service calls. Finally, the actual business logic is executed (service, application, etc.). All the most important user-initiated tasks follow this very similar pattern of calling the required activities and services to fulfil the desired task of the user. Following, the example use case "Select event of claim" (German: "Schadenfall auswählen") will be used to show the sequence of events in the system, based on the control flow from Figure 5.

The use case "Select event of claim" is the first step of the process. To initiate this use case, the user has to choose the specific option ("task 31: Select event of claim") on the (goodwill) console client and provide the id of the damage event. This information is transferred to the task manager integration component, to be more precise, to the component *CommandManager*. This component is responsible for providing this data to the workflow engine, using defined *TaskHandlingCommands*.

Simplified, the WfM-Engine (IPP) then receives the data and moves on to the next step in the process described in the specification, thus starting the use case "Select event of claim".

This use case requires interactions with further components (eventually services) of the system, defined in the process specification (XPDL file) as a call of a method in the *FassadeBean*. As already described in the previous section, the *FassadeBean* is a component (stateless session bean) that was built to enable the communication between the logical ESB of the WfM-Engine and the physical ESB (JBoss), because the engine does not support direct calls to an ESB.

So in this case, the purpose of the *FassadeBean* is to build the corresponding ESB call (JBoss Message objects, etc.) and provide it with the call information (especially the damage event id, process id, etc.) needed for the application scenario.

Simplified, the ESB calls the component (service) that is responsible for the business logic which is required for the service *damage case processing (DCP)*. Inside *DCP*, *damageManager* works the concrete method (*damageProcess*) to accomplish the task and returns the specific value object. Initially, this value object is required by the workflow engine and is returned by the *FassadeBean*.

Futhermore, the *damageManager* inside *DCP* calls the BPCLogger from BAMS, so that the execution of the task is monitored. For automated steps, the WfM-Engine calls the respective functions following the same control path via *FacadeBean* and ESB.

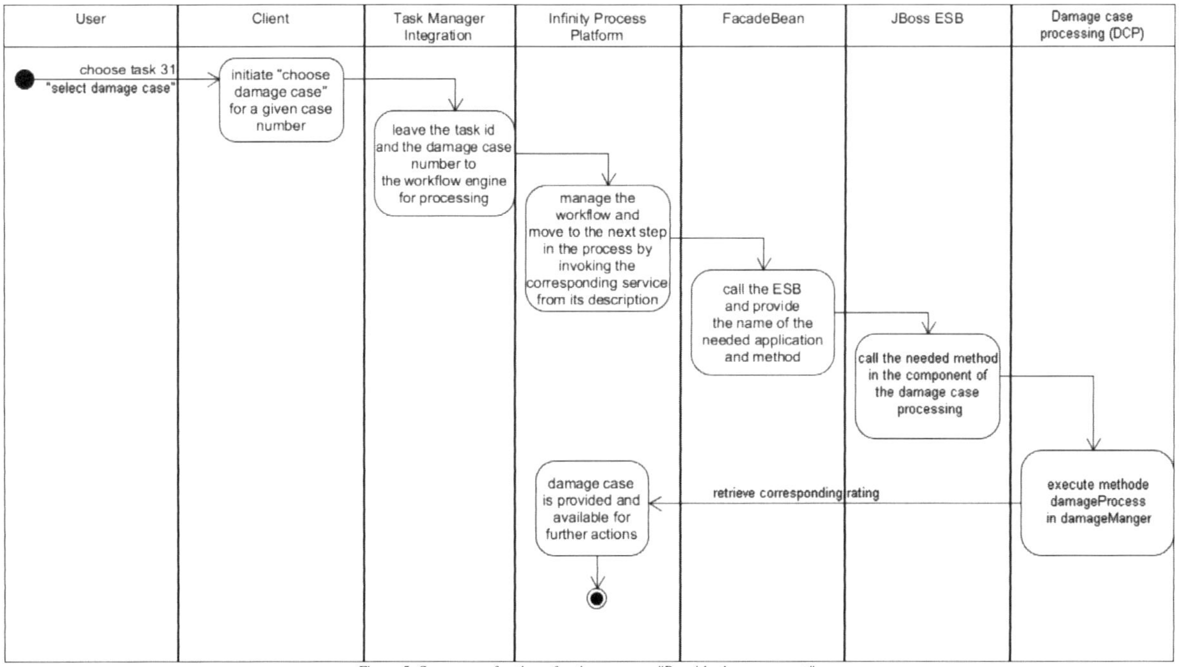

Figure 5: Sequence of actions for the use case "Provide damage event".

The Client gets updates about the status of the initiated task via the so called worklist through the task integration manager (*CommandMananger*). The update is shown on the console if needed.

The worklist itself is managed by the workflow engine. The information about the execution of tasks and processes is logged with BAMS and can be viewed in the audit trail database. Also, the WfM-Engine provides a web interface that can also be used for the same purpose. Whether a task has succeeded or not, is shown there. This web interface is also used for testing new created use cases. More information on testing is available in the corresponding programmer's guides of CC ITM.

After this presentation of the general runtime view, the following section will show the deployment view of the system.

B. Deployment View

As practical evaluation example, which provides even more technical depth, this section describes the technical implementation of a prototype of our implemented architecture [12]. For this purpose, we utilize the concept of a deployment view, which shows the actually implemented components, utilized technologies, technical communication protocols, and the deployment of all components to different nodes within a distributed system.

The deployment view of our architecture is depicted in Figure 6. The components that belong to the system are divided into the user client, the application server and the BAMS. Within this project, JBoss AS 5.1.0.GA is used as an application server. This application server also hosts the IPP 4.7.2 by executing the carnot.ear, as well as JBoss Enterprise Service Bus 4.1.2 and JBoss Drools 5.3. The hardware of the server, where the facade, workflow engine, ESB, Drools and the application scenario is deployed, realises the following hardware requirements:

- 1.5 GHz CPU
- 1 GByte RAM
- 70 GByte HDD

The usage of JBoss Drools / ESB is characterized by relatively low hardware demands. This allows to use a minimal and efficient hardware setup which already fulfils the demand in reactivity and processing speeds of the implementation of business rules and the execution of business processes. The BAMS component is deployed on an additional device. The device runs an Oracle Database Express Edition that realises the Business Activity Monitoring System. The hardware consists of:

- 1.5 GHz CPU
- 4 GByte RAM
- 40 GByte HDD

The BAMS is deployed on a separate device, because within the insurance business, there could occur high loads for the logging / monitoring. This high loads should not be able to affect the processing speed of the application server and its execution of business processes. So deploying the monitoring onto a separate device supports overall stability and reactivity of the overall system.

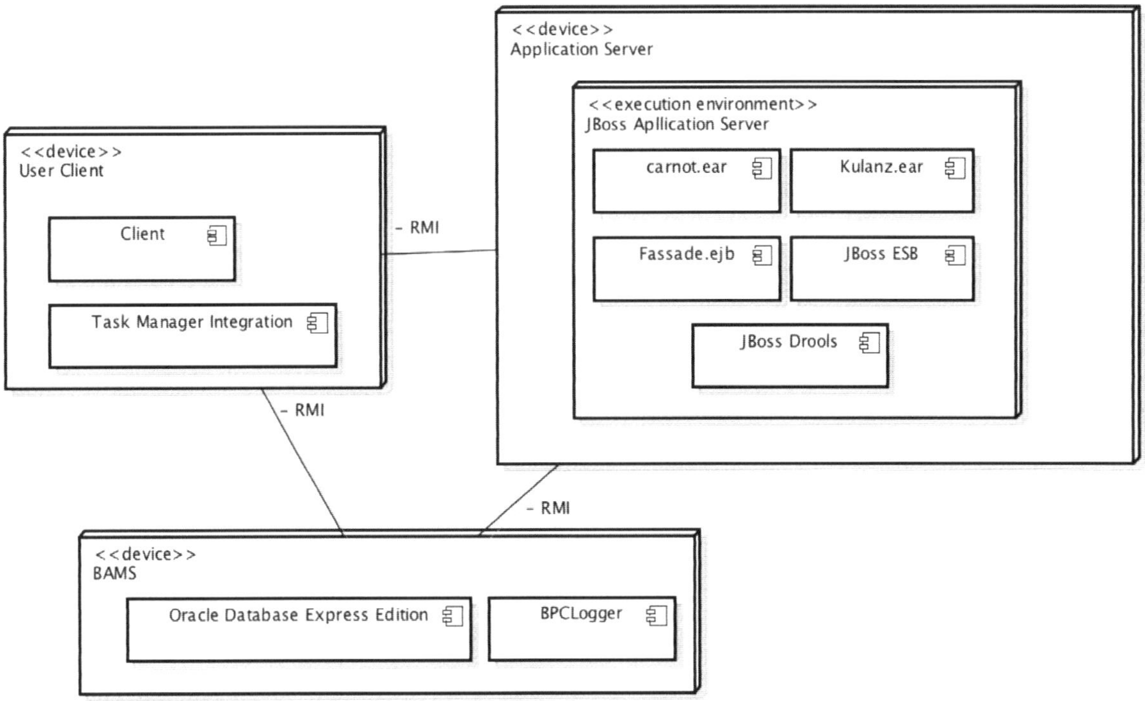

Figure 6: Deployment view of the system.

VIII. CONCLUSION AND FUTURE WORK

The presented overall architecture of the system consists out of four main components. This approach allows to process various client request and handle those in an efficient way, regarding complex business rules within the insurance business. As final summary, those for main components are characterized by the following:

- BAMS (business activity monitoring system):
  Used for flexible monitoring / logging, similar to complex event processing
- WfM (workflow management engine):
  The central component of the whole system, used for managing and executing all business processes.
- ESB (enterprise service bus):
  The (physical) ESB offers with loose couplings a high flexibility to handle interaction between various services within the insurance business scenario.
- BRMS (business rule management system):
  Especially the insurance business is characterized by specific rules. Those rules have to respect special (finance) laws and regulations. Therefore, the rule management have to be the most reliable and stable component of the system. The selected solution must fulfill high demand in trustiness and maintainability.

A. *Conclusion*

To manage the application landscape of businesses, for example, companies operating in the insurance services business, the combination of technologies such as SOA, business process management and business rules management is a promising approach. In order to ensure the optimum of agility and flexibility, the decision logic should be shifted to a separate SOA service.

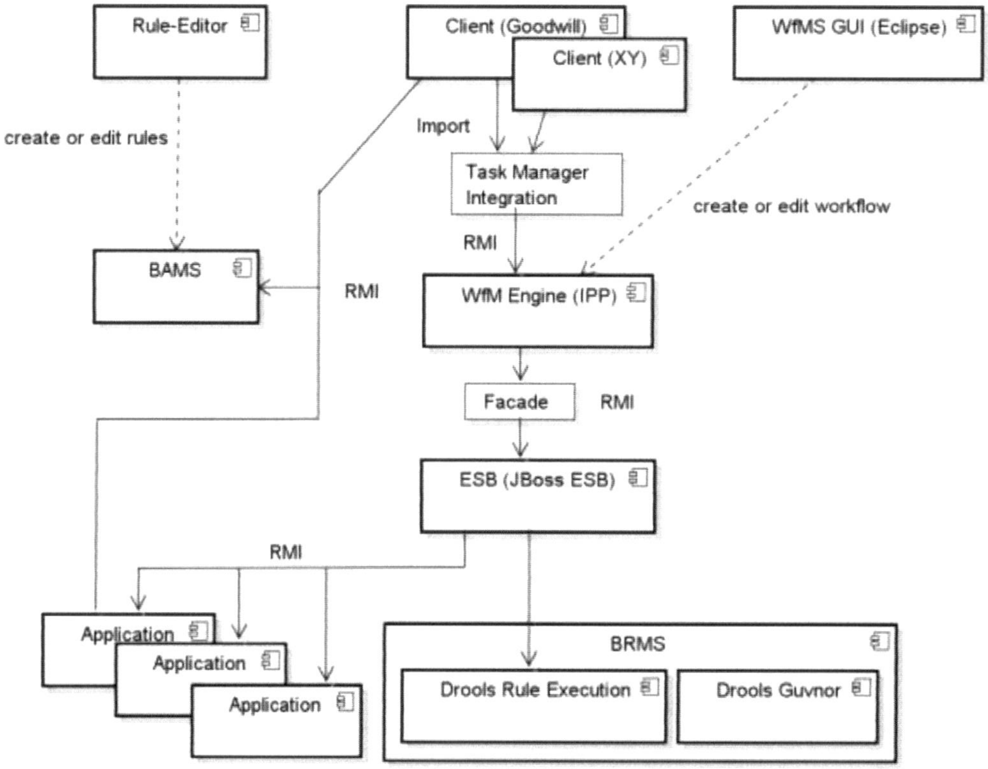

Figure 7: Final architecture of the overall system.

In our previous work, we presented a decision framework, which recommends an approach to realize such a "rule service".

As a key contribution of this article our decision framework is applied to a standardized insurance business process, namely "Handle a Goodwill Request". Starting from the initial design, making design and infrastructure decisions, we obtain an enhanced service-oriented target architecture with technical components such as ESB, BPM system, BAM, and BRM system.

Moreover, as a significant addition to our work from [1], we show in the present article much more details of the internal architecture an implementation. For example, we present the inner working dynamics of our architecture utilizing a runtime view of our architectural components as well as a deployment view of those components.

Thus, while we do not claim too much novelty for the general SOA/BPM/BRM case, we do provide a technically detailed SOA/BPM/BRM case study. This is in particular valuable for the German insurance industry [28] in general, but might well be transferable to domains with similar requirements as well.

B. *Future Work*

Based on these intermediate results, our subsequent research activities will focus on a detailed performance evaluation which may require a redesign of the target architecture. This evaluation is taking place within our current research project "QoS measurements for combined BRM, BPM and SOA environments in the insurance domain". As the insurance industry is receptive to cloud computing concepts and technologies - for example, product design and risk assessment frequently utilize cloud-based Software as a Service (SAAS) components - moving components of the target architecture towards the cloud might be a promising approach. Those components then might become generally usable, cloud-based services.

Therefore, the investigation of cloud computing solutions is another main activity of our research group. This includes conceptual and technical feasibility studies as well as security investigations and more. In our future work, we may also aim to address the aspect of "Threats to Validity" in some more depth.

Actually, the enhanced architecture contains some proprietary components, such as the BAM system. As businesses prefer to use standard infrastructure components, we intend to replace all proprietary components.

For this purpose, we (also) look at open source CEP tools. Another, but marginal issue is the optimization of the usability of the rule editor.

Last but not least our work on business rules management continues to take place within in our research.

REFERENCES

[1] A. Hausotter, A. Koschel, M. Zuch, J. Busch, A. Hödicke, R. Pump, J. Seewald, L. Varonina, "Applied SOA with ESB, BPM, and BRM – Architecture Enhancement by Using a Decision Framework," IARIA SERVICE COMPUTATION 2016: The Eighth International Conferences on Advanced Service Computing, Rome, Italy, 2016, pp 20-27.

[2] J. Boyer and H. Mili, "Agile Business Rule Development: Process, Architecture, and JRules Examples," Springer, Berlin, Germany, 2011.

[3] A. Buchholz, R. Hohloch, and T. Rathgeber, "Vergleich von Open Source ESBs (Comparison of Open Source ESBs)," Institut für Architektur von Anwendungssystemen, Univerität Stuttgart, Stuttgart, Germany, Fachstudie Nr. 81, 2007.

[4] Business Rules Group. (2003, November 1). "The Business Rules Manifesto," Version 2.0, edited by R.G. Ross) [Online]. Available: http://www.businessrulesgroup.org/brmanifesto.htm [retrieved: 02, 2016].

[5] Competence Center Information Technology and Management (CC ITM) [Online]. Available: http://f4.hs-hannover.de/forschung/kompetenzzentren/cc-itm/index.html [retrieved: 02, 2016].

[6] D. E. Chappell, "Enterprise Service Bus - Theory in Practice, O'Reilly," 2004.

[7] L. Chen, "Integrating Cloud Computing Services Using Enterprise Service Bus (ESB)," College of Business, Black Hills State University, 2012 [Online]. Available: http://sciedu.ca/journal/index.php/bmr/article/ view/674/387 [retrieved: 02, 2016].

[8] S. Desmet, B. Volckaert, S. Van Assche, D. Van Der Weken, B. Dhoedt, and F. De Turck, "Throughput Evaluation of Different Enterprise Service Bus Approaches," in Software Engineering Research and Practice (SERP), Las Vegas, Nev., 2007, pp. 378-384.

[9] M. Dohring, L. Karg, E. Godehardt, and B. Zimmermann, "The Convergence of Workflows, Business Rules and Complex Events," in 12th Intl. Conference on Enterprise Information Systems (ICEIS), 2010, pp. 338-343.

[10] T. van Eijndhoven, M. E. Iacob, and M. L. Ponisio, "Achieving Business Process Flexibility with Business Rules," in 12th Intl. IEEE Enterprise Distributed Object Computing Conference (EDOC), 2008, pp. 95-104.

[11] C. Gath, A. Hödicke, S. Marth, J. Siedentopf, A. Hausotter, and A. Koschel, "Always Stay Agile! – Towards Serviceoriented Integration of Business Process and Business Rules Management," in 6th Intl. Conf. on Advanced Service Computing (Service Computation), IARIA, Venice, Italy, 2014, pp. 40-43.

[12] M. Gharbi, A. Koschel, A. Rausch, and G. Starke, "Basiswissen für Softwarearchitekten (Fundamental Knowledge for Software Architects)," 2nd ed, dpunkt, Heidelberg, Germany, 2014.

[13] M. Gille, "The Benefits of Implementing Workflow," [Online]. Available: https://www.sungard.com/~/media/fs/wealth-retirement/ resources/event-docs/Omni-Summit-Presentations/Implementing%20Workflow.ashx [retrieved: 02, 2016].

[14] M. Diekmann, C. Gath, J. Harms, V. Jartsev, B. Kleine, and J. Siedentopf, "Business Rules Management - Evaluierung von Technologien und Werkzeugen für das Business Rules Management (Business Rules Management – Evaluation of Technologies and Tools for Business Rules Management)," CC ITM, Technical Report, 2012.

[15] J. Harms and B. Kleine, "Fragenkatalog Business Rules Management (Questionnaire: Business Rules Management)," CC ITM, Technical Report, 2012.

[16] A. Hödicke, "Concept and Prototypical Implementation of a Serviceoriented Software Architecture for a WfM- and BRM-System," M.S. thesis, Dept. Computer Science, Hochschule Hannover University of Applied Sciences and Arts, Hanover, Germany, 2013.

[17] A. Hödicke, "Evaluation of Talend ESB," CC ITM, Technical Report, 2013.

[18] A. Hausotter, C. Kleiner, A. Koschel, D. Zhang, and H. Gehrken, "Always Stay Flexible! WfMS-independent Business Process Controlling in SOA," in: IEEE EDOCW 2011: Workshops Proc. of the 15th IEEE Intl. Enterprise Distributed Object Computing Conference, IEEE: Helsinki, Finland, 2011, pp. 184-193.

[19] T. Krussman, A. Koschel, M. Murphy, A. Trenaman, and I. Astrova, "High Availability: Evaluating Open Source Enterprise Service Buses," in Proc. ITI 2009 31st Intl. Conf. on Information Technology Interfaces, Cavtat/Dubrovnik, Croatia, 2009, pp. 615-620.

[20] O. Levina, O. Holschke, and J. Rake-Revelant, "Extracting Business Logic from Business Process Models," in 2nd IEEE Int. Conference on Information Management and Engineering (ICIME), 2010, pp. 289-293.

[21] L. MacVittie (2006, March 10). "Review: ESB Suites," Network Computing, CMP Media LLC [Online] Available: http://www.networkcomputing.com/wireless-infrastructure/review-esb-suites/d/d-id/1216317 [retrieved: 01, 2016].

[22] M. Zur Muehlen, M. Indulska, and K. Kittel, "Towards Integrated Modeling of Business Processes and Business Rules," in 19th Australasian Conference on Information Systems (ACIS), 2008, pp. 690-697.

[23] M. L. Nelson, R. L. Rariden, and R. Sen, "A Lifecycle Approach towards Business Rules Management," in 41st Hawaii Intl. Conf. on System Sciences (HICCS), 2008, pp. 113-123.

[24] M. Schacher and P. Grassle, "Agile Enterprises with Business Rules: The Business Rules Approach," Springer, Berlin, Germany, 2006.

[25] T. Schal, "Workflow Management Systems for Process Organisations," Springer, Berlin, Germany, 1996.

[26] Z. Siddiqui, A.H. Abdullah, and M.K. Khan, "Qualified Analysis b/w ESB(s) Using Analytical Hierarchy Process (AHP) Method," in Intelligent Systems, Modelling and Simulation (ISMS), Kuala Lumpur, Malaysia, 2011, pp. 100-104.

[27] G. Starke and S. Tilkov (editors), "SOA Expertenwissen (SOA Expert Knowledge)," dpunkt, Heidelberg, Germany, 2007.

[28] GDV (Gesamtverband der Deutschen Versicherungswirtschaft e.V. – General Association of the German Insurance Industry), "Die Anwendungsarchitektur der Versicherungswirtschaft: Das Objektorientierte Fachliche Referenzmodell (The application architecture of the German insurance business – The functional object-oriented reference model," http://www.gdv-online.de/vaa/vaafehtml/dokument/ofrm.pdf, VAA Final Edition. Version 2.0., 2001 [retrieved: 02, 2016].

[29] K. Vollmer and M. Gilpin, "The Forrester WaveTM: Enterprise Service Bus, Q2 2006," Forrester Research, Cambridge, Mass., 2006.

[30] R. Woolley, "Enterprise Service Bus (ESB) Product Evaluation Comparisons," Utah Department of Technology Services, Salt Lake City, Utah, 2006.

[31] Red Hat Inc., "Red Hat JBoss Fuse: Overview," [Online]. Available: http://www.jboss.org/products/fuse/overview/ [retrieved: 02, 2016].

[32] Bank für Internationalen Zahlungsausgleich, "Basel III: Mindestliquiditätsquote und Instrumente zur Überwachung des Liquiditätsrisikos (Basel III: Minimal liquidity rate and instruments to supervise the liquidity risk," Basler Ausschuss für Bankenaufsicht, 2013, pp. 2. [Online]. Available: http://www.bis.org/publ/bcbs238de.pdf [retrieved: 02, 2016].

[33] Bank für Internationalen Zahlungsausgleich, "Basel III: Strukturelle Liquiditätsquote (Basel III: Structural liquidity rate)," Basler Ausschuss für Bankenaufsicht, 2014, pp. 1. [Online]. Available: http://www.bis.org/publ/bcbs271de.pdf [retrieved: 02, 2016].

[34] T. Bergemann, A. Hausotter, and A. Koschel, "Keeping Workflow Enabled Enterprises Flexible: WfMS Abstraction and Advanced Task Management," in 4th Int. Conference on Grid and Pervasive Computing Conference (GPC), 2009, pp. 19-26.

Using a Physics Engine in ACT-R to Aid Decision Making

Using A Physics Engine and Simulation for Physical Prediction in a Cognitive Architecture

David Pentecost[1], Charlotte Sennersten[2], Robert Ollington[1], Craig A. Lindley[2], Byeong Kang[1]
Information and Communications Technology[1]
Decision Sciences Program[2]
University of Tasmania[1]
CSIRO Data 61[2]
Hobart, Tasmania
[1]Australia
email: davidp12@utas.edu.au
email: charlotte.sennersten@csiro.au
email: robert.ollington@utas.edu.au
email: craig.lindley@csiro.au
email: byeong.kang@utas.edu.au

Abstract—**Advanced Cognitive Technologies can use cognitive architectures as a basis for higher level reasoning in Artificial Intelligence (AI). Adaptive Control of Thought – Rational (ACT-R) is one such cognitive architecture that attempts to simulate aspects of human thought and reasoning. The research reported in this paper has developed an enhancement to Adaptive Control of Thought – Rational (ACT-R) that will allow greater understanding of the environment the AI is situated in. Former research has shown that humans perform simple mental simulations to predict the outcomes of events when faced with complex physical problems. The method has been demonstrated by application in an autonomous squash player for which, predictive version of ACT-R achieves significantly improved performance compared with the non-predictive version.**

Keywords- Cognitive Architectures; ACT-R; 3D Simulation.

I. INTRODUCTION

This paper is an extended version of the paper "Predictive ACT-R (PACT-R)" published in "COGNITIVE 2016 : The Eighth International Conference on Advanced Cognitive Technologies and Applications" [1].

A challenge to robots in the real world is dealing with complex fast changing environments with fast paced decisions where there is little time for deliberation. This means that we need systems that can rapidly perceive, act and reason.

How could a cognitive robot – that is, a robot endowed with deliberative problem-solving – track and interact with fast moving objects in a complex environment? How could a robot interact or perform actions in a dynamic situation?

What do you do if you are asked to catch a ball that has been thrown in the air? You make a quick estimate of its trajectory, predict where you need to be to intercept it, and then move to that location. What about if it is going to bounce off a surface? Although there is now a little uncertainty, if you do not know the properties of the ball and surface, it is, nevertheless, not much more difficult to make a good enough prediction and correct for any errors after the bounce. What about if the ball bounces several times before you reach it? Now, you are more likely to start looking at the likely chain of events that will occur to predict the outcomes.

Artificial Intelligence (AI) in robotics commonly uses either an algorithmic approach, that is, a custom solution to a specific problem [2], or subsumption-like architectures that react to the world as it is perceived [3]. Reinforcement learning offers another approach, which allows agents to solve problems without expert supervision by interacting with their surrounding environment to learn cause and effect relationships. Reinforcement learning allows a robot to discover a behaviour through a trial and error approach without requiring explicit instructions for the solution [4].

The algorithmic approach is effective for well-understood problems with little variation, but it is not so good at responding to the unexpected. Subsumption follows a 'stimulus and response' model. It is good at dealing with immediate problems, like avoiding obstacles, but can be lacking when it comes to a multi-stage mission that may require evaluation and decision-making over several alternative sequences of actions. Cognitive architectures have been proposed as an alternative that could be more suitable for accomplishing missions that require sequences of decisions, rather than more purely reactive associations between sensor inputs and motor outputs.

The American Physiological Association defines cognition as, "Processes of knowing, including attending, remembering, and reasoning; also the content of the processes, such as concepts and memories." Cognitive architectures are based on theories of how the human mind reasons to solve problems. They are used to create AIs based on, or inspired by, human cognitive processes that work through problems in a systematic way [5]. They are based on a Computational Theory of Mind, which holds that the mind works like a computer, using logic and symbolic information to work through and solve problems. Symbolic information is, in a programming context, a textual/verbal approach to representing knowledge in a way that is abstracted from sensory data, since the relationships between words and their referents are conventional. This abstraction supports potentially complex symbolic reasoning processes, but omits much detailed information about objects and phenomena that the symbols refer to in a given context.

Hence cognitive architectures, like other approaches to AI, have their own limitations. For example, they are similar to expert systems [6][7][8] in using facts and production rules that require a human expert to create. They are strong at symbolic reasoning with logic, but the ontological status of symbols within human cognition is unclear [9], and the biological foundations of human cognition are very different from the nature of expert systems and formal logics [10]. Expert systems and formal logics are technologies, i.e., inventions of human cognition, rather than its basis. They may, nevertheless, be useful and even powerful representations of some human capabilities that are based upon much lower level biological mechanisms.

An aspect of human cognition that is not captured in most cognitive architectures is *simulation*. Imagination, and the use of imagined visualisations, constitutes a conscious result of simulation within human cognition. An example of the use of simulation in an artificial cognitive system is the Intuitive Physics Engine (IPE), which uses simulation to understand scenes [7]. IPE uses a fast approximate simulation to make a prediction of the outcome of a physical event or action, like the toppling of a stack of blocks.

In synthesizing a world, simulation provides a cognitive system with the richness of a sensed world, with far more detail than that, which can easily be captured in higher level symbolic world descriptions alone and at a potentially much faster speed than the perception of external processes bound to the physical process speed. Simulating a 3D world and aspects of its physics involves using mathematical models of world structure, kinematics, dynamics and object interactions in, which complex behaviours can be synthesized from a relatively small set of structural and physical equations. The quantisation of space and time in a simulation can be represented, e.g., to double floating point precision, resulting in an extremely large space of possible simulated world states and histories. The level of abstraction involved in declarative or symbolic representations is usually much higher than a simulated world state description, since it is expressed at a level suitable to verbalised decision processes, meaning that many simulation states can be compatible with a single declarative representation. That is, a declarative statement can provide a succinct and abstracted representation of a large set of world state denotations. For example, the first order predicate '*is_above*(A,B)' can apply to any object in a simulation that is above another object. But to represent all of those possible individual denotations (every possible situation and variation of positions in, which one object is above another) declaratively would be practically impossible. The declarative level of decision processing can be linked to the simulation state, e.g., via spatiotemporal operators linked to the simulation structure, such as testing for the relative 3D positions and sizes of objects A and B as a basis for assigning a truth value to the statement '*is_above*(A,B)'. Hence there is a useful balance between what can be represented and reasoned about most effectively using declarative representations, and the large number of potential states having small differences representable by a simulation. These are complementary modelling methods. To explore these concepts, this paper describes an experiment designed and implemented to further test the theory that simulation is a powerful component of cognition. The motivating research question was: "How can simulation and prediction improve decision quality in a cognitive architecture?" In the experiment designed to address this question, a predictive module was added to a cognitive architecture, and the performance of the predictive and non-predictive versions of the architecture were tested for controlling automated players of a virtual game. The predictive module used a 3D physics simulation engine to model the environment of an embodied AI, so that it could function in a dynamic situation without explicit coding of decision rules for all possible interactions in the environment. The simulation engine mathematically models interactions with the environment so that the cognitive module can handle physical events and actions with a reduced and simplified rule set.

An existing cognitive architecture, Adaptive Control of Thought – Rational ((ACT-R) [12][13][14]), was chosen for the research and extended with a novel predictive module. Two virtual robots were implemented to play a competitive game of squash (Figure 1). Squash is a racket and ball sport played in an enclosed room between two players. It was chosen because it provides both a physics challenge (tracking and hitting the ball), and a cognitive challenge (playing a good tactical game to out-manoeuver an opponent).

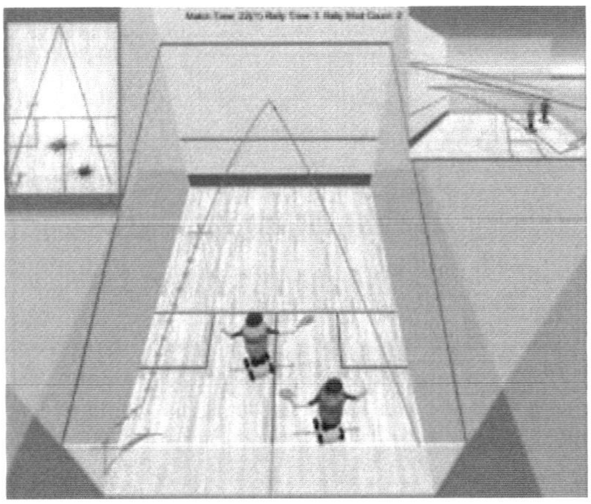

Figure 1. Squash Simulation showing AI controlled players. Predicited ball path is shown as grey track. Vertical lines are where the AI player can intercept the ball.

Section II of this paper gives some background to cognitive and non-cognitive architectures. In Section III a description of the research undertaken and methodology used is given. Section IV describes the AI modelling and how prediction was incorporated. Section V discusses the results obtained.

II. AI Architectures for Robotics

Cognitive architectures are based on theories of how the human mind reasons to solve problems. These are AI systems based on human cognitive processes that work through problems in a systematic way [5]. They are based on the Computational Theory of Mind [15], that proposes that the mind works like a computer running a program, using logic and symbolic information to work through and solve problems.

The cognitivist approach is a top down approach that follows a rule-based manipulation of symbols, and uses patterns of symbols, as designed by humans, to represent the world [16]. A key characteristic is that the mapping of perceived objects to their associated symbols is either defined by humans, or learned in a way that can be viewed and interpreted by humans. Decisions about, which actions to perform are derived by processing of the internal symbolic representations of the world. In contrast, the connectionist approach is a bottom up approach that proposes that intelligence is an emergent property of connected cells/nodes and networks; "Neurons wire together if they fire together" [17]. Within the cognitivist approach we will here focus on the cognitive architecture called ACT-R. ACT-R is a cognitive theory [14] that has been simulated in software as a production rule based, symbolic data model that includes elements of the connectionist view as sub symbolic data. It is usually referred to as a hybrid architecture.

Using cognitive architectures for robotics is described by Laird et al. in the adaptation of Soar (a similar cognitive architecture to ACT-R) for robot control [18]. For the robotic control task, Soar was extended to include mental imagery, episodic and semantic memory, reinforcement learning, and continuous model learning. Soar and ACT-R share features including procedural memory encoded as production rules, and semantic memory implemented as declarative associations. A number of architectures similar to Soar and ACT-R are reviewed in [19].

Most current operational robots do not use cognitive architectures. Instead, traditional robotic research and control has focused on software that solves problems having well formulated solutions; this can be referred to as the *algorithmic approach* [2]. These systems are particularly suited to well-defined tasks and domains. However, there is a need for higher level cognitive abilities to deal with less well defined problems. Unknowns are a challenge for robots where the problem is not fully specified. The strength of human cognition is the ability to solve unknowns in new or changing contexts. It is in these situations that cognitive architectures, which are based on theories of human cognition, offer potential capabilities for solving problems in uncertain situations.

The subsumption architecture is another alternative to cognitive architectures for robot control. The subsumption architecture approaches intelligence from a different perspective. Rather than rules that lay out a series of steps to accomplish a task, it uses a very sparse rule set that responds to sensor values to generate control outputs [20][21][22]. Brooks describes subsumption as a layered finite state machine where low-level functions, like "avoid obstacles", are subsumed into higher-level functions, like "wander" and "explore". Each successive layer gives increasing levels of competence. Lower levels pre-empt the higher levels, such that a robot can explore, but will avoid obstacles when necessary.

Key aspects of subsumption are: that it contains no high level declarative representations of knowledge; no declarative symbolic processing; no expert systems or rule matching; and it does not contain a problem-solving or learning module [2]. It responds to the world by reacting directly to sensor inputs, in order to generate corresponding control outputs.

Subsumption is based on the concept that the environment stands for itself, i.e., the architecture reacts directly to environmental features, without a mediating representation. It is a functional architecture without being, or using, a declarative model of the external world. This approach can be complementary to the cognitive architecture approach. The concept behind subsumption is a stimulus response model that is ideal for modelling low level instinctive behaviours, which can easily be incorporated into other cognitive architectures.

A robotic AI might be created completely within a single cognitive architecture, using rules that control every aspect of the decision-making process. But monolithic architectures are not always ideal for every style of decision-making. Society of Mind [24] is a theory that argues against the idea of a single unified architecture or solution that can account for intelligent behaviour. It proposes that intelligence arises from many simple specialised functions working together [23][24]. Hence Society of Mind theory argues for a modular approach to implementing intelligence. Implementing simulation as an extension to a cognitive architecture, but using an external 3D engine to model the environment, follows this concept.

ACT-R is a hybrid cognitive architecture consisting of both symbolic and sub-symbolic components [25]. It is a goal-orientated architecture. The symbolic data consists of facts and production rules. The sub-symbolic data is metadata about facts and production rules that influences, which facts are recalled and, which production rules are chosen to fire when multiple facts and rules fit the current situation. The sub-symbolic data can be seen as a hidden layer controlling the selection of rules not unlike the weights in the hidden layers of a neural network. This is a hybrid of symbolic and connectionist models of cognition [14].

ACT-R consists of multiple cognitive modules that implement either internal or external functionality. For example, a memory module would be an internal cognitive system that could hold declarative knowledge (facts and figures). A vision module would be an external system giving a representation of the external world to the architecture. Central to the Cognitive Architecture is the Procedural module for selection of rules, Figure 2.

The Procedural Module is a pattern matching system, it looks for combinations of values held in buffers. The buffers represent the current state of the cognitive modules that form the architecture. The contents of a buffer are a set of key name and value pairs. The combination of the content of all the buffers represents the architecture's current state. The patterns that the procedural module looks for are specified in production rules. A production rule is an if-then statement, i.e., that *if* some condition (pattern) is satisfied *then* an action is fired. The *if* part of a production rule looks for particular values in one or more cognitive module buffers; for example, it might specify that the visual module buffer contains data that a blue box is visible in the upper right corner of the view while the goal module is indicating that it should be looking for an object. If these conditions are met, then that rule is a potential candidate to be fired.

At its simplest the Procedural Module will randomly choose a rule to fire from amongst those that match the current conditions. However, the sub symbolic system can influence rule selection. Sub symbolic data can be seen as a weighting system for rule selection and these weights are either fixed or can be learnt through reinforcement learning.

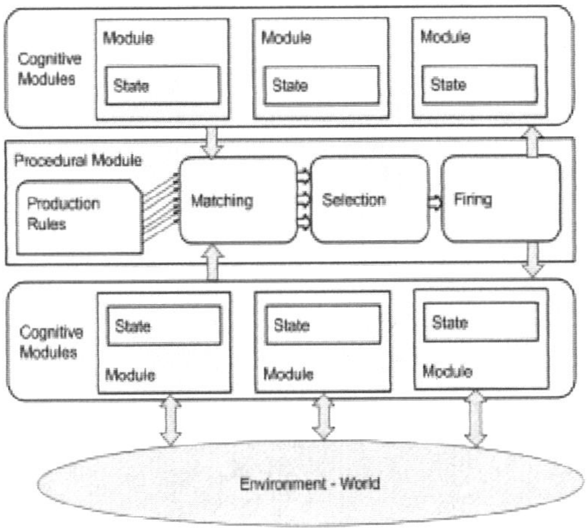

Figure 2. Basic structure of an ACT-R Cognitive Architecture

III. METHODOLOGY

This section describes the research design, and the implementation of the prediction and simulation extensions to ACT-R to constitute the Predictive-ACT-R (PACT-R) architecture.

A. Research Design

The research consisted of developing and implementing three elements: 1) the PACT-R cognitive module that implemented the simulation-based prediction system; 2) a virtual environment for testing; and 3) three AI models to test the system. The models are so called behavioural and functional scripts in the language of ACT-R. An ACT-R cognitive module was developed that mapped a symbolic representation of a simulated environment into the ACT-R framework. This module gave the required PACT-R functionality for interpreting and acting within the environment, as well as providing simple predictive capabilities using simulation.

The use of prediction and simulation in PACT-R was evaluated by comparing the performance of three AI models that each implemented different levels of prediction. The aim was to compare not only their performance, but also how easy/simple it was to model and use a predictive AI.

B. Implementation

The first of the three elements mentioned above, PACT-R cognitive module that implemented the simulation-based prediction system, gave the testing models (scripts) access to predictions about physical events, as well as a mechanism to take actions. The module was implemented in the Lisp programming language that ACT-R is implemented in, and added to the ACT-R code base.

Two predictive elements were added. The predictive module always provided a prediction of the ball's flight path for the purpose of intercepting and hitting the ball. A further predictive element was added that allowed the AI model to evaluate its own possible actions within a simulation to determine the likely outcome of those actions. Essentially, the model could ask very simple "what if?" questions about how its own actions might play out in the future.

The second element was a simulation of the game of squash implemented in the Unity™ game engine. The physics simulation element of PACT-R was also implemented in Unity™ to simplify implementation. The Lisp and Unity elements of PACT-R were connected using a UDP connection.

Squash is a racquet sport played in a closed room between two players. The ball is free to bounce around the walls, and a player is free to hit the ball against any wall as long as it reaches the front wall before a second bounce on the floor. The opponent also must reach the ball and play a shot before the second bounce. This requires fast paced decisions within a one to two second period. To play squash our cognitive model must make decisions within a frequent turn based action cycle.

The game of squash has been described as physical chess, since it is both physically demanding and highly tactical. The physical challenge is a result of the continuous explosive acceleration needed to react to, and retrieve, an opponent's shot.

The tactical element of the game plays out in the shot selection and how this can be used to apply pressure to the opponent. When deciding when and where to hit the ball the player is faced with many choices. Do they take the ball early before it reaches a wall? Do they wait and give themselves more time to play a better shot, knowing that this also gives their opponent more time to move to a stronger court position? Is a shot to the front of the court the right shot? It puts the opponent under more physical pressure, but if they reach it, with a bit of time to spare, it opens up a lot of attacking shots.

Squash is also a game of angles, much like a real-time game of snooker. Judging and playing the angles is an important part of the game. Using squash as the test scenario provides the known rule set for the game and existing tactical knowledge for implementing the AI models.

One important aspect of squash, that was not included in the implementation, was player fatigue. Players get tired and shot selections can be made to tire an opponent rather than simply winning the current rally. A tired player will move more slowly and tend to make weaker shots. This factor was excluded from the experimentation to reduce the number variables to the minimum needed.

In the following discussion, the games engine that hosts the squash simulation will be clearly distinguished from the physics engine that makes predictions. Due to time constraints, these shared a common code base, although it would have been more correct if the prediction physics used a rapid approximation of the environment. The game engine physics allows a deterministic perfect prediction that would be unobtainable in a real-world scenario. In the real world, there is uncertainty due to inaccuracies in both perception and motion. To compensate for this, the prediction physics were degraded by introducing randomness into the motion (2% to speed and direction) and by using a very low resolution interpretation of shot outcomes (only 3 interpretations of outcome; favourable, unfavourable and neutral).

The final element modelled squash-playing AIs as test scripts. Three evaluation test scripts were developed for testing and cross-comparison (see Figures 6 and 8 for two of these).

The following sections describe the high-level design of PACT-R and continues with specific implementation details.

1) Using Simulation and Prediction within a Cognitive Architecture

The research investigated the use of a physics engine to provide prediction for a cognitive architecture. The concept requires a physics engine that can model and simulate the environment of a robot controlled by a cognitive AI. The simulation provides a symbolic representation of the environment to a cognitive architecture. This gives the cognitive model (the production rules) the information it needs to understand and act within its environment.

One way of using this information could have been to explicitly encode rules that check for certain conditions, for example, whether an object is in a certain position, or is moving in a particular direction; or for the relationships between objects in the environment, for example, whether an object is to the left of another object [26][27]. From this, the rules can encode appropriate actions for the robot to take. This approach was the basis of the heuristic test model describe below.

We researched and explored an alternative approach that broke down the decision-making process into two phases. The first phase determined a set of possible actions that fit the current situation, implemented as a script in ACT-R. The actions, such as a low-hard-straight shot or a high-cross-court-lob, were passed sequentially to the physics simulation to predict their likely outcome. The second phase then picked the best of these as the action to be taken. Figure 3 shows a high-level diagram of this approach. The action with the best predicted outcome is the one that is fired.

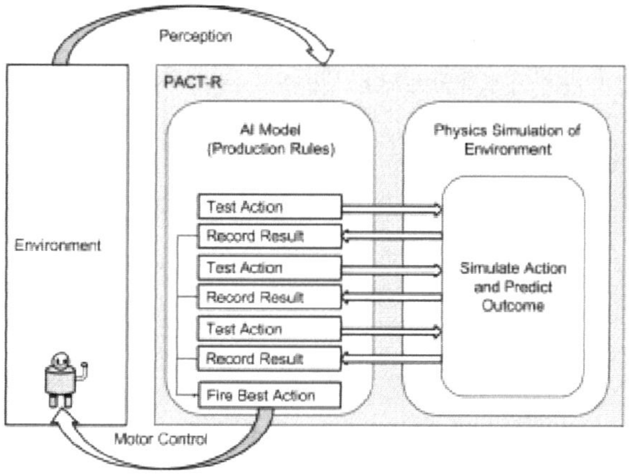

Figure 3. Overview of PACT-R. The simulated world is modelled in a physics engine. The cognitive model (a set of production rules) tests possible actions in the physics engine to determine how they play out before selecting an action to execute.

Below we proceed to break this overview down to describe the low-level implementation within the ACT-R cognitive environment.

2) PACT-R Module Implementation in ACT-R

The prediction system is implemented as an ACT-R module that both controls a robot and does a simulation of the robot's environment, for interpreting what is happening in that environment. The module is, logically, a single system, but in the implementation, it is broken into two functional parts, one residing in the ACT-R framework, and the other inside the Unity™ game engine, which includes a physics engine and also hosts the virtual world the robots exist in (Figure 4).

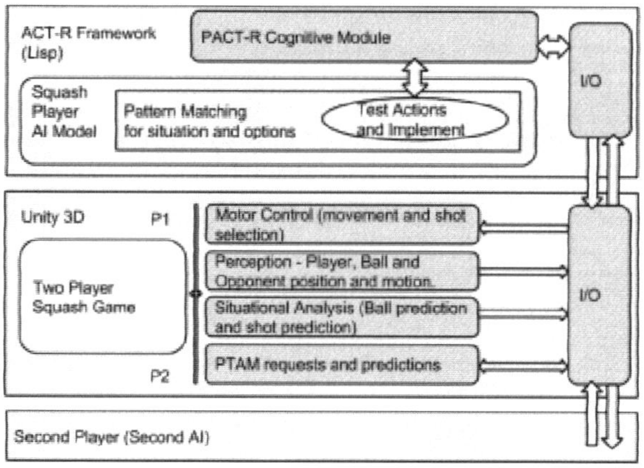

Figure 4. PACT-R (in red) within ACT-R and Unity. PACT-R adds a cognitive module to ACT-R that allows testing of actions as well as an interface to the external world (simulated in Unity)

The ACT-R component of the system maintains the current simulation and prediction state for use by the AI models, while the Unity™ component of the system contains a customised physics engine that can simulate both the squash ball's path, and the outcome of shots played by the robot. The two components of the module connect via a Universal Datagram Protocol (UDP) link, a standard part of the Internet Protocol (IP).

For PACT-R, the cognitive module represents implicit knowledge (of the sort that a squash player learns over many years) and the simulation. Implicit knowledge encodes the 'how' of movement and ball striking, while the simulation provides a basis for deciding 'what' and 'where'.

The PACT-R enhancement to ACT-R is implemented as an additional ACT-R cognitive module, Figure 4, that provides two buffers, one that commands are sent to, and the other that gives the model access to a simplified view of the environment (situation). The module communicates with the simulation engine, in Unity3d, to request predictions through the command buffer and to receive the predicted outcomes through the situation buffer.

IV. AI MODELLING AND PREDICTION

This section presents the outline of the AI models at a conceptual level, rather than dealing with the details of modelling them in ACT-R. Then, the implementation of the prediction module in ACT-R is presented, together with its interactions with the AI models, followed by a description of the evaluation and analysis framework for these models.

A. Prediction Models

The simulated task, playing squash, that the AI must perform is dynamic; the ball is in continuous motion and can follow complex paths as it interacts with the walls and floor. Likewise, the AI's robotic avatar is moving, as is the opponent.

ACT-R is designed to look for and respond to patterns in information in its buffers. The buffers hold information representing both the external world and the AI model's internal state. ACT-R can work with values and do simple comparisons, but doing complex calculations and mathematical evaluations is not its forte (although it is possible to call Lisp functions if required). It is the role of the modules, particularly those that deal with the external world, to abstract the situation into a simple symbolic representation that the AI model can reason about, by searching for patterns and relationships.

For a complex dynamic situation, this may present a problem, since an AI model requires deliberation (i.e., "thinking") time. That is, it needs time to recognise a pattern and fire a production for the situation the pattern represents. To solve a problem, it may have to fire a sequence of productions. For a dynamic situation, by the time a pattern has been recognised and acted upon, the situation may have already changed to something different.

The simulation-based module described here abstracts away the details of the environment into a simple set of relationships and events representing the elements in the scene. This abstraction is highly domain specific; in the implemented PACT-R, the abstraction focuses on the specifics of the game of squash.

For squash, PACT-R identifies three actors: *self, opponent* and *ball*. The module provides the AI model with information about the approximate locations of these actors within the squash court and information about what is happening, is about to happen, or what might happen. Real coordinates and vectors of motion are absent from the information. The aim was to focus on the tactical evaluation so the spatial relationships were evaluated in the PACT-R module and presented to the model in a very simple form.

For this research, a baseline capability of the prediction module included a prediction about the immediate known ball flight path that the AI model could use to intercept the ball, at an appropriate court position, to play a shot. This prediction was made following the opponent's shot when the ball's position and velocity could be determined. The ball's path was simulated in the physics engine, which tracked where the ball would travel as it bounced against the walls and floor. The path was calculated until it was determined that the ball would have bounced on the floor for a second time. This projected ball path was then used in the prediction module to determine locations where the player could intercept and hit the ball, based on their own movement ability.

The intercept positions were placed in the prediction module buffer used by the AI model, which allowed the models to intercept the ball without any further processing. The intercept position could have been under AI control, but this would have introduced more complexity to the modelling and introduced more independent variables to the test, making it difficult to determine cause and effect. For this reason, AI control and reasoning was limited only to the shot selection strategy.

To know where the ball and the player were within the squash court, the squash court was broken into strategic zones and all positions were given as zone numbers. The squash strategy implemented in the models was also based on zones, with a limited selection of shots available for each zone. The AI models selected a shot from those available in the zone where the ball was intercepted. The zones and shots are based on squash training drills commonly used to teach players basic strategy.

B. Evaluation and Analysis

Three AI models were developed and evaluated. The first model was a *basic random shot selection model* that functioned as the base line to determine whether shot selection by the other models was better than random chance.

The second model was a *heuristic model* that had an explicit shot selection rule-set derived from the human developer's experience of playing squash. This model's purpose was to provide an alternative method to the prediction model.

The third model used the *predictive* features of PACT-R to test shots for their likely outcome.

To evaluate the performance of the three models, a large amount of automatic data gathering and logging was conducted from the virtual environment. This data provided both comparative performance of the models, and an insight into how they won or lost.

For each test session the only variables were the shot selection strategies of the two competing AI models. Test sessions consisted of two AI models (out of three) loaded into the ACT-R environment, playing against each other over a series of rallies. Squash starts with a serve from one player to another. The two players then alternate shots until one is unable to retrieve or return the shot, and therefore loses. In squash this is called a rally. Data recorded included shot selection and state during the rally, and the final results of each rally. This was repeated for a fixed time (from three to eight hours) to generate a large sample set of data.

For a test run (a rally), the serve was alternated so there was no bias or advantage to either model. Player 1 always started on the forehand side (right), and player 2 on the backhand. The players were ambidextrous with no advantage to either side (unlike human squash players). The two robotic players were identical in their capabilities.

V. Results and Discussion

The three models discussed here all follow the same base strategy. They must choose from three or four shots available for the zone where the ball is to be hit. The basic model did not use any additional logic to choose a shot. The other two models tried to choose a shot that would force the opponent to have to travel the furthest to reach the ball in order to play their next shot.

A. *Basic Random Shot Selection Model*

The first AI model developed was a random shot selection model. This created a setup with three or four equally possible shots for each court zone for ACT-R to choose with its production rules. With no additional conditions in the rules, other than the court zone, a shot would be chosen at random from those available.

This model acted as a baseline control. It was also the only model used during development and balancing of the simulation and physics engine.

B. *Heuristic Selection Model*

The second model was a heuristic model that used ACT-R production rules that implemented a simple squash strategy that tried to choose shots that would be directed to an area of the court where the opponent was not present. For example, if the opponent was deep in the court (i.e., close to the front wall of the court), it would favour a short shot, and if the opponent was on the forehand side, it would favour a backhand shot. Shot selection rules for each zone were implemented using this simple strategy. In real squash, this approach is a good starting point for any human player.

Figure 5 is a flow chart representation of part of the heuristic model, although it only shows one shot selection choice, rather than the many that were required to model shots for all court zones. It should be noted that for ACT-R production rules, matching and firing does not proceed in a step-by-step fashion like a flow chart. The flow chart representation is used to show the logic, rather than the functioning of the models.

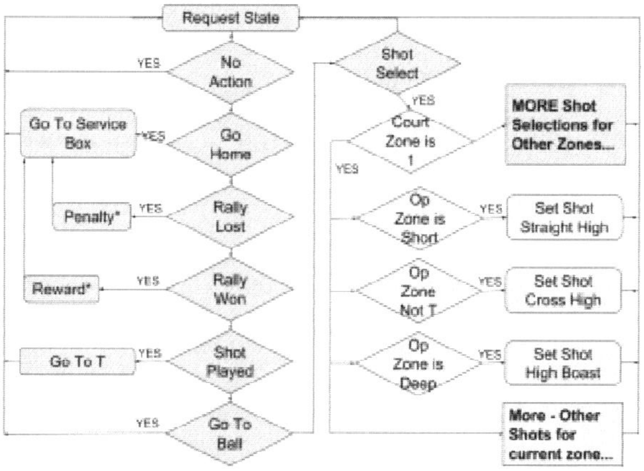

Figure 5. Heuristic AI flow chart. The left hand side shows supporting rules for general play. The right hand side shows one set of rules for shot selection in one of the twelve tactitical zones that the squash court was divided into.

Each diamond and rectangle pair in Figure 5 corresponds to a production rule. The heuristic model consisted of 45 production rules for shot selection, plus another 5 to implement the functionality required for starting and ending a rally, and for returning to a central court position when not returning a shot.

Figure 6 shows just one of the 45 rules required to select a shot for a zone. Each rule defines the conditions under, which it can fire and the action to be taken. In Figure 6 this rule tests where the ball will be intercepted and where the opponent is. This rule says that if the ball is wide (left or right side of court) AND in the mid court (from front to back) AND the opponent is at the front of the court THEN play the ball to the back of the court.

```
(p take-shot-z22-z23-StHi-OpSh
    =goal>
      ISA playing-mode
      state    2        ; play mode
    ?command>
      state free
    =predictive>    ; PACT-R module
      ISA predictive-state ; correct chunk type
      special 5     ; shot selection mode
      > intercept-zone-width 1 ; position wide
      intercept-zone-depth 2 ; position mid
      > op-zone-depth 2  ; op at front of court
    ==>
    +command>
      ISA command-packet
      req-cmd     4          ; Set Shot to play
      :req-param  51         ; Long High Straight
  )
```

Figure 6. Heuristic AI shot example rule (script). This is one rule from the right hand side of Figure 5. The key elements of the rule are in bold.

C. *Predictive Selection Model*

The third AI model was the predictive model. The random and heuristic models both had access to a prediction of the ball's path that they could use to determine where to go to hit the ball, and consequently, what shots they should be playing, based on where the shot was to be taken.

The predictive model went a step further in predicting the outcome of shots the AI model might take. This was done by allowing the AI model to choose a possible shot before passing that information to the prediction module for simulating and predicting its consequences. The module would simulate how the shot would play out to predict where the opponent would be when the shot was played, and how much difficulty they would have in then retrieving it and playing a counter shot. The prediction was based on the same strategy as the heuristic model, trying to find a shot that was as far from the opponent as possible.

The prediction system has one advantage over the heuristic model: as it is calculating the path of the shot under test, it sometimes found situations that it could not solve for the opponent to intercept with the ball. In essence, it had found winning shots that the opponent could not return. This result was passed back to the AI, which allowed the predictive model to find and choose these occasional winning shots.

Figure 7 shows the prediction model as a flowchart, and a sample rule. Unlike the heuristic model's 45 rules, this model only requires 26 rules for shot selection. Each rule defines a shot to be tested for a particular zone of the court.

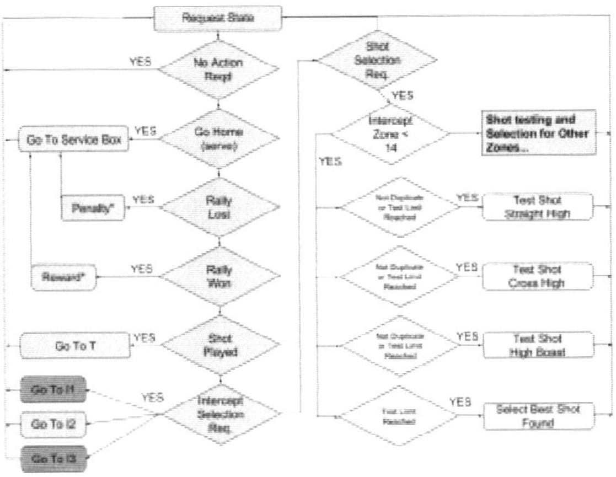

Figure 7. Predictive AI shot selection flow chart. The left side shows supporting rules for general play. The right hand side shows rules for testing shots from one strategic zone.

Figure 8 shows one of the rules for testing shots in the Predictive model. Each such rule sends a shot to be tested to the prediction engine. There were several such rules for each strategic zone. During the shot selection period, while the player was moving to intercept the ball, these would be randomly chosen and fired. The number of predictive tests that could be made was limited to four. The PACT-R cognitive module kept track of the best rule tested so far, and when all applicable rules have been tested another rule would retrieve the best shot and set it as the selected shot.

```
(p take-shot-z22-z23-StHi
    =goal>
      ISA playing-mode
      state    2              ; in play mode
    ?command>
      state free
    =predictive>              ; PACT-R module
      ISA predictive-state ; correct chuck type
      special 5            ; in prediction mode
      < prediction-count 4 ; more testing allowed
      - registered-shot 51 ; not already tested
      > intercept-zone-width 1 ; court pos wide
      intercept-zone-depth 2   ; and mid depth
    ==>
    +command>
      ISA command-packet
      req-cmd      5         ; Test Shot (predict)
      :req-param   51        ; Long High Straight
)
```

Figure 8. Predictive AI shot selection sample rule. This is one of 26 rules that selects a shot to be tested by the physics prediction engine.

The predictive system works by allowing the AI model to test shots that are available to play. This allowed the prediction system to usually come up with the best shot available within the limits of the prediction resolution. Figure 9 shows the progression of the shot testing as the cyan player moves to intercept the shot. The grey track shows the ball's current path in the top right frame. In subsequent frames blue tracks appear that represent possible shots. In the final frame the cyan player has played the best shot found, which is another straight shot down the left hand side (shown in grey again).

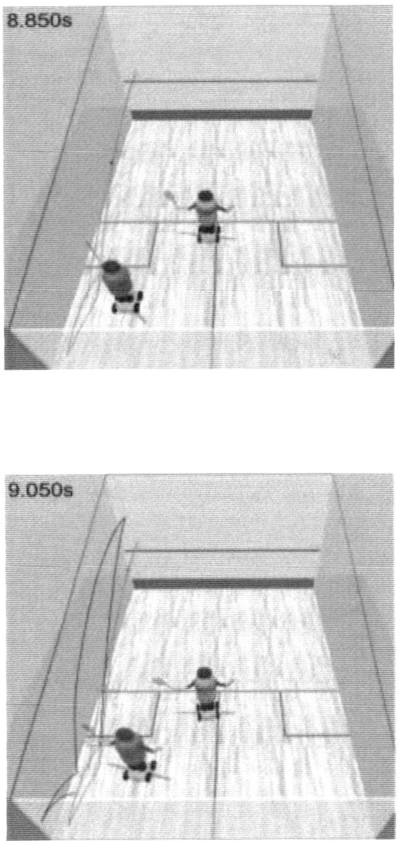

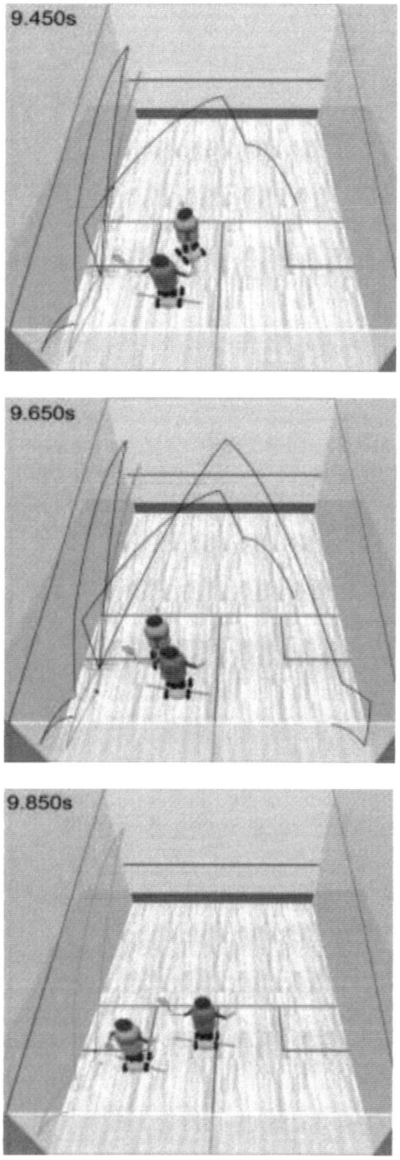

Figure 9. Time lapse of predictive shot selection showing test predictions for cyan robot (center of screen in first frame). Each image shows a new shot being considered (blue tracks). The last frame shows a single track for the final selected shot, in this example this was the first shot tested (second frame).

This sequence of shots takes place over a period 800ms. Figure 10 shows an abbreviated trace of the ACT-R rules firing for the sequence in Figure 9. Prediction tests are 200 ms apart, which is determined by ACT-R's default time for rule selection and firing. The first shot tested scored the highest and is selected as the shot to play in the FINAL-SHOT-SELECTION rule fired at the end of the trace.

```
9.050 PRODUCTION-FIRED TEST-SHOT-Z22-Z23-STHI
   Testing shot 51 0
   better predicted value 2 for 51
9.200 SET-BUFFER-CHUNK SPATIAL SPATIAL-STATE45
9.200 SET-BUFFER-CHUNK SITUATIONAL-STATE45
9.250 PRODUCTION-FIRED TEST-SHOT-Z22-Z23-BODF
   Testing shot 23 1
   predicted value 1 for 23
9.400 SET-BUFFER-CHUNK SPATIAL SPATIAL-STATE46
9.400 SET-BUFFER-CHUNK SITUATIONAL-STATE46
9.450 PRODUCTION-FIRED TEST-SHOT-Z22-Z23-CRHI
   Testing shot 52 2
   predicted value 1 for 52
9.600 SET-BUFFER-CHUNK SPATIAL SPATIAL-STATE47
9.600 SET-BUFFER-CHUNK SITUATIONAL-STATE47
...
9.850 PRODUCTION-FIRED FINAL-SHOT-SELECTION
```

Figure 10. ACT-R trace of a test and prediction sequence of rules being fired. This section shows three shots being tested at time 9.050, 9.250 and 9.450 seconds. The rule for retrieving and firing the best tested shot occurs at 9.850, the trace above skips over the period from 9.600 to 9.850 for brevity.

D. Declarative Memory Predictive Model

The research described so far exclusively used production rules to provide both declarative and procedural knowledge. A model based on a declarative memory model was also tested and evaluated after the primary research described in this paper was completed. This model was a reimplementation of the predictive model that replaced explicit rules with declarative knowledge that matched a situation to possible shot selection, as shown in Figure 11. This produces a more concise model since memory declarations are significantly smaller than rules.

This model suffered from performance issues due to the memory recall time imposed by ACT-R. The model could not submit a declarative memory request, retrieve the result and act on it a timely enough fashion to compete against the other models. In ACT-R, memory retrieval has additional time penalties, compared to production rule firing, which aims to emulate human recall performance. Detailed results were not gathered for this method.

```
(chunk-type zone-shot z s)
 (add-dm
   ;; Deep, back of court
   (z12-StHi ISA zone-shot z 12 s 51)
   (z11-StHi ISA zone-shot z 11 s 51)
   (z13-StHi ISA zone-shot z 13 s 51)
   (z12-CrHi ISA zone-shot z 12 s 52)
   (z11-CrHi ISA zone-shot z 11 s 52)
   (z13-CrHi ISA zone-shot z 13 s 52)
   (z12-BoDf ISA zone-shot z 12 s 23)
   (z11-BoDf ISA zone-shot z 11 s 23)
   (z13-BoDf ISA zone-shot z 13 s 23))

(p find-another-shot
  =retrieval>
    ISA      zone-shot
    s        =sh
    z        =zn
  ==>
  +retrieval>
    ISA      zone-shot
    z        =iz
  - s        =sh
```

```
    +situational>
      ISA command-packet
      req-cmd    5      ; Test Shot
      :req-param  =sh
  )
```

Figure 11. Declarative memory and retrieval production rule. The rule has been simplified for illustration. The =retrival> section retrieves the previous memory recall. +retrival> makes the next request. +situational> takes the previous retrieval and passes it to the predictive system for simulation and testing.

E. *Performance*

The three models that were developed could all play a game of squash since they all encoded some level of squash strategy into shots available in any situation. They differed in the method used to choose the shot from the subset available. Figure 12 shows the player to player performance of all three models. When playing identical models against each other, the results are even, as would be expected. Both heuristic and predictive models won over the basic random selection model, indicating that these models are performing better than chance.

Predicting the outcome of actions before selecting one was better at choosing a winning shot than the heuristic approach. The predictive model won significantly more rallies than the heuristic model. Out of 540 rallies played during a six hour test the predictive model won 312 of them to 228 by the heuristic model. The binomial test p-value for this is 0.0003, showing that this is unlikely to be due to random chance.

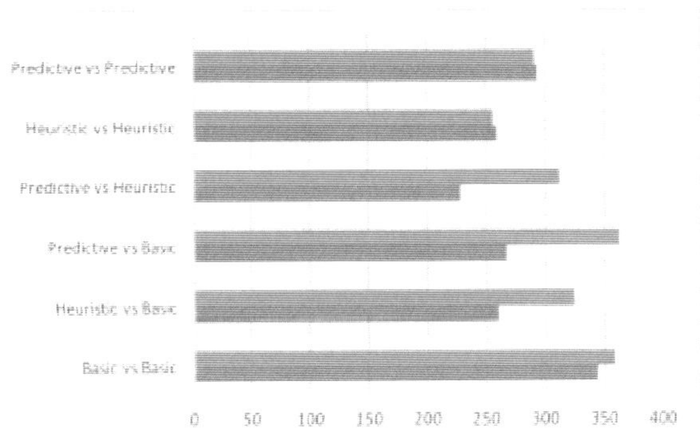

Figure 12. Head to head scores for all models. Each pair of bars is the scores of two tested AI models playing against each other over a six hour period.

When developing the models, there was a clear advantage to the basic and predictive models over the heuristic model in the reduced number of rules required to implement the shot selection strategy. The basic and predictive models required 25 and 26 rules, respectively. The heuristic model required 45 rules to implement a simple shot selection strategy.

The question the original research asked was "How can simulation and prediction improve decision quality in a cognitive architecture?" The answer to this is not straightforward. The results show that, within the limitations of the experiment, a predictive model – with an ability to use simulation to test its own actions to determine and evaluate their possible outcome – held a clear advantage over a model that used heuristics to test relationships between objects in a simulated scenario.

It is not, perhaps, surprising that an approach that provides predictions of the future, however imperfect, would have an advantage over reasoning about a situation based only on where objects are and how they were moving in the moment. The results of the investigation indicated that prediction provided a more effective appraisal of the value of an action, without requiring detailed rules.

There is a caveat here though: the evaluation of the heuristic model was an evaluation of its specific rule set, and it could have been developed further. Its rule set was not very complicated, and it is entirely possible that with a larger rule set and more detailed situational knowledge, it could have out-performed the predictive model. Indeed, both the heuristic and predictive models could have been developed further, to leapfrog each other in a virtual arms race. It is impossible to conclude that a predictive model would or could always outperform a purely heuristic model.

However, there was another aspect to the modelling. The predictive model only required 26 rules versus the 45 rules of the heuristic model. Not only were there less rules, they were simpler. Each rule simply stated a possible shot to test, and required no expert knowledge of how, or when, that shot might be used. In comparison, developing the heuristic rules required an understanding of squash strategy, and each rule had to be carefully considered as to how it would play out.

While both models could have been extended, the effort required to do so would have been considerably different. The heuristic model would require a lot of expert knowledge. The predictive model would have required only fixing some design issues and, perhaps, increasing the fidelity of the predictions. Of course, the predictive model does require a simulation engine that can predict outcomes of actions, however imperfectly. Developing the simulation does not require expert knowledge of squash either, but it does require being able to model the physics of the scenario. This is not an inconsiderable task and, even in the simple scenario used in this research, more time was spent developing the simulation than was required for the creation of the AI rule set.

VI. Future Work

The research described above only looked at a highly discrete problem, and the solution was very domain specific. The PACT-R cognitive model gave a scene description and predictions in a very squash-centric way. Continuing this methodology of creating a custom model and simulation for every scenario is time consuming, and it would be desirable to accelerate the process by finding a more generic way of describing physical relationships and actions within an environment.

It is unlikely that any solution could be truly generic. Such a solution would have to be able to model and simulate a large and arbitrary amount of the real world. Rather, a practical improved implementation of PACT-R would provide a generic framework that could be extended and adapted for specific scenarios.

PACT-R was intended for eventual use in robotics and embodied AI. However, taking this system into the real world presents the considerable challenge of perceiving and simulating at least a small part of the real world. For constrained situations this might not be so difficult. For example, in real-world squash, if you can detect and track the ball, it is then relatively easy to predict where it will go in the rectangular room that squash is played in. The bigger challenge would be predicting the outcome of shots, since this is not as clear-cut in the real world as it was in the simulation. The simulated shots were simplified, and the virtual robots were able to play them more consistently and accurately than any real human or robot would be able to. In a broader context the simulation could only be a probabilistic approximation of the real world and exploring what fidelity is needed to be functional is an area of possible future research.

The research also highlighted some issues when working with ACT-R that could be an interesting topic of future work. ACT-R's reinforcement learning mechanism did not work for this task since it would reinforce a single solution where a true squash player would always be choosing from a set of solutions. A flexible model would allow multiple solutions to a problem and some degree of random selection between them. In squash, as in many sports, there is an optimum decision based purely on the current circumstances, but it is not always the best choice to make if the opponent can predict the decision. Occasionally selecting a sub optimal solution can be an effective long term strategy. This is not something that is readily supported by ACT-R's reinforcement learning mechanisms.

In modelling within ACT-R pattern values, in rules, are tested with a basic set of comparative operators (>, <, =, etc.) While this is suitable for a lot of modelling, when implementing a squash strategy, it would have been convenient to have been able to model in fuzzy logic, where instead of yes/no answers, cold/cool/warm/hot answers were possible. The matching would bias the rule selection, rather than simply excluding or including specific rules. Giving ACT-R a fuzzy logic matching system would allow it to work better in situations where there is not a simple black or white answer.

ACT-R also has a declarative memory system (long term memory). This was tested after the main research was completed, but the results were poor due to the time penalty imposed by memory retrieval in ACT-R. There are additional issues related to the learning mechanism used in the memory system. That mechanism is based on a principle of spreading activation, where recently used memories are more likely to be recalled, and memories that share similar content are also more likely to be recalled (this is the spreading activation). This is not an appropriate mechanism for squash, since all shots and outcomes need to be considered equally. Despite these issues, the use of long term memory would seem to be a desirable feature, particularly as a key part of any cognitive system is learning. Sub symbolic learning is only one mechanism, episodic memory (stored in LTM) is another approach that should be considered in future versions.

If declarative memory had been used, how could it have been used, and what sort of learning mechanisms could have been applied? Could reinforcement learning be used with memories? Could there be negative and positive memories, a sort of 'positive memories' that are easily recalled, and 'negative memories' that are suppressed? These considerations may be crucial for applying simulation-based prediction in different robotic applications.

PACT-R respected ACT-R's timing for processing rules. This is based on human performance. Using this made testing and evaluation easier and more consistent. However, an artificial intelligence implemented on a computer does not need to be constrained by the limitations of human cognitive processing speeds. Likewise, the testing of actions in PACT-R was performed in a serial fashion. It would be possible to test multiple actions concurrently using common multiprocessing capabilities. These aspects remain to be tested and evaluated in a future version.

One possible negative aspect of PACT-R was that the cognitive decision process was partially outsourced to an external process. The cognitive rules choose a set of actions but the physics simulation made the final choice. This subverts the intent of a cognitive architecture like ACT-R where the cognitive model is expected to decide actions. Are there alternative approaches that could leverage the power of simulation to inform the model rather than bypass it?

The results obtained in this research suggest that using a physics engine within a cognitive architecture can simplify the cognitive modelling required in the decision making process although there were limits to the approach taken. Addressing those limitations in future research may lead to AIs based on cognitive architectures that are better suited to use in robotics.

REFERENCES

[1] D. Pentecost, C. Sennersten, R. Ollington, C. A. Lindley, and B. Kang, "Predictive ACT-R (PACT-R) Using A Physics Engine and Simulation for Physical Prediction in a Cognitive Architecture," in *COGNITIVE 2016 : The Eighth International Conference on Advanced Cognitive Technologies and Applications*, 2016, no. c, pp. 22–31.

[2] U. Kurup and C. Lebiere, "What can cognitive architectures do for robotics?," *Biol. Inspired Cogn. Archit.*, vol. 2, pp. 88–99, 2012.

[3] H. Q. Chong, A. H. Tan, and G. W. Ng, "Integrated cognitive architectures: A survey," *Artif. Intell. Rev.*, vol. 28, no. 2, pp. 103–130, 2007.

[4] J. Kober, J. A. Bagnell, and J. Peters, "Reinforcement learning in robotics: A survey," *Int. J. Rob. Res.*, vol. 32, no. 11, pp. 1238–1274, 2013.

[5] W. DUCH, R. J. R. J. OENTARYO, and M. Pasquier, "Cognitive Architectures: Where do we go from here?," *Proc. 2008 Conf. Artif. Gen. Intell. 2008 Proc. First AGI Conf.*, vol. 171, no. OCtOBER, pp. 122–136, 2008.

[6] P. Jackson, *Introduction to expert systems*. Addison-Wesley Pub. Co.,Reading, MA, 1986.

[7] J. C. Giarratano and G. Riley, *Expert Systems: Principles and Programming*. PWS Publishing Co., 1998.

[8] A. Ajith, "Rule-based Expert Systems HEURISTICS," *Handb. Meas. Syst. Des.*, vol. 1, no. g, pp. 909–919, 2005.

[9] C. A. Lindley, "Synthetic Intelligence: Beyond Artificial Intelligence and Robotics," in *Integral Biomathics*, Springer,

2012, pp. 195–204.

[10] C. A. Lindley, "Neurobiological Computation and Synthetic Intelligence," in *Computing Nature*, 2013, pp. 71–85.

[11] P. W. Battaglia, J. B. Hamrick, and J. B. Tenenbaum, "Simulation as an engine of physical scene understanding.," *Proc. Natl. Acad. Sci. U. S. A.*, vol. 110, no. 45, pp. 18327–32, 2013.

[12] J. R. Anderson, J. M. Fincham, Y. Qin, and A. Stocco, "A central circuit of the mind," *Trends Cogn. Sci.*, vol. 12, no. March, pp. 136–143, 2008.

[13] J. R. Anderson and C. D. Schunn, "Implications of the ACT-R learning theory: No magic bullets," *Adv. Instr. Psychol. (Vol. 5)*, vol. 5, pp. 1–34, 2000.

[14] J. R. Anderson, *How Can the Human MindOccur in the Physical Universe?* Oxford University Press, 2007.

[15] H. Putnam, "Brains and Behavior," *American Association for the Advancement of Science*, vol. Section L. 1961.

[16] S. Profanter, "Cognitive architectures," *HaupteSeminar Hum. Robot Interact.*, p. 27, 2012.

[17] S. Löwel and W. Singer, "Selection of Intrinsic Horizontal Connections in the Visual Cortex by Correlated Neuronal Activity," *Science (80-.).*, vol. 255, no. 5041, pp. 209–212, 1992.

[18] J. Laird, K. Kinkade, S. Mohan, and J. Xu, "Cognitive Robotics Using the Soar Cognitive Architecture," *8th Int. Work. Cogn. Robot.*, pp. 46–54, 2012.

[19] D. Vernon, G. Metta, and G. Sandini, "A survey of artificial cognitive systems: Implications for the autonomous development of mental capabilities in computational agents," *IEEE Trans. Evol. Comput.*, vol. 11, no. 2, pp. 151–180, 2007.

[20] R. Brooks, "A robust layered control system for a mobile robot," *IEEE J. Robot. Autom.*, vol. 2, no. 1, pp. 14–23, 1986.

[21] R. a. Brooks, "Elephants don't play chess," *Rob. Auton. Syst.*, vol. 6, no. 1–2, pp. 3–15, 1990.

[22] R. A. Brooks, C. Breazeal, M. Marjanovi, B. Scassellati, and M. M. Williamson, "The Cog Project : Building a Humanoid Robot," in *Computation for metaphors, analogy, and agents*, Springer Berlin Heidelberg, 1999, pp. 52–87.

[23] M. Minsky, R. Kurzweil, and S. Mann, "Society of mind," *Artificial Intelligence*, vol. 48, no. 3. pp. 371–396, 1991.

[24] P. Singh, "Examing the Society Of Mind," *Comput. Informatics*, vol. 22, pp. 1001–1023, 2003.

[25] T. Liadal, "ACT-R A cognitive architecture," *Univ. des Saarlandes*, pp. 1–16, 2007.

[26] M. Lochner, C. Sennersten, A. Morshed, and C. Lindley, "Modelling Spatial Understanding : Using Knowledge Representation to Enable Spatial Awareness in a Robotics Platform," vol. 7, no. c, pp. 26–31, 2014.

[27] C. Sennersten, A. Morshed, M. Lochner, and C. Lindley, "Towards a Cloud-Based Architecture for 3D Object Comprehension in Cognitive Robotics," no. CCI, pp. 220–225, 2014.

Astrophysical-oriented Computational multi-Architectural Framework: Design and Implementation

Dzmitry Razmyslovich
Institute for Computer Engineering (ZITI),
University of Heidelberg,
Mannheim, Germany
Email: dzmitry.razmyslovich@ziti.uni-heidelberg.de

Guillermo Marcus
NVIDIA Corporation,
Berlin, Germany
Email: gmarcus@nvidia.com

Abstract—**In this paper, we present the design details and the implementation aspects of the framework for simplifying software development in the astrophysical simulations branch - Astrophysical-oriented Computational multi-Architectural Framework (ACAF). This paper covers the design decisions involved in reaching the necessary level of abstraction as well as establishing the essential set of objects and functions covering some aspects of application development for astrophysical problems. The implementation details explain the programming mechanisms used and the key objects and interfaces of the framework. The usage example demonstrates the concept of separating the different programming aspects between the different parts of the source code. The benchmarking results reveal the execution time overhead of the program written using the framework being just 1.6% for small particle systems and approximating to 0% for bigger particle systems. At the same time, the execution with different cluster configurations displays that the program performance scales almost according to the number of cluster nodes in use. These prove the efficiency and usability of the framework implementation.**

Keywords–Astrophysics; Heterogeneous; Framework; Cluster; GPGPU.

I. INTRODUCTION

Astrophysical simulation tasks have usually high computational density, therefore it is common to use hardware accelerators for solving them. Also, the astrophysical simulations have a huge amount of data to calculate, which makes it reasonable to use computer clusters. But the data dependencies of the simulation algorithms limit the usage of big clusters because of high data communication rate. Therefore, the astrophysical simulations tasks are normally solved using heterogeneous clusters [1][2][3][4]. According to TOP500, the top-rated heterogeneous clusters use Graphics Processing Units (GPU) or Field Programmable Gate Arrays (FPGA) as computational accelerators.

The most important computational astrophysical problems include N-Body simulations, Smoothed Particle Hydrodynamics (SPH), Particle-Mesh and Radiative Transfer. All of them are usually approximated for the calculation purposes with respective particle physics problems. Where particle physics is a branch of physics which deals with existence and interactions of particles, that refer to some matter or radiation. Therefore, computational astrophysics data represents a collection of particles - a particle system. Each particle contains a number of parameters like position in 3D space, speed, direction, mass, etc. A collection of certain values for all parameters of all particles is named a state of a particle system. At the same time, the computational tasks embrace numerical solving of a number of equations, which evaluate the state of a particle system [5].

This means, astrophysicists should deal a lot with developing simulation programs capable to run on heterogeneous clusters. This requires certain expertise in the following subjects:

- astrophysics, since the problem consists of simulating the astrophysical objects;
- network programming for cluster utilizing;
- parallel programming and hardware accelerators programming including the usage of specific interfaces and languages;
- micro-electronics for designing FPGA boards.

This takes much time and demands professional expertise from astrophysicists, which restricts scientists to perform calculation experiments on clusters easily and distracts them from the main goal. So, the aim of our research is to **simplify software development for astrophysical simulations implementation reducing programming knowledge requirement**. The solution we suggest is the ACAF. ACAF stands for **A**strophysical-oriented **C**omputational multi-**A**rchitectural **F**ramework. The ACAF is a toolkit for development of astrophysical simulation applications. The target data to be processed with the ACAF is a set of states of a particle system.

Technically, developing of a distributed multi-architectural application could be divided into a set of the following aspects:

- balance loading;
- data communication between nodes;
- data communication between the devices inside of each node;
- computational interfaces for different architectures;
- programming languages for different interfaces (like Open Multi-Processing (OpenMP) for Central Processing Unit (CPU); Open Computing Language (OpenCL), Compute Unified Device Architecture (CUDA), Open Accelerators (OpenACC) for GPU and Very High Speed Integrated Circuit (VHSIC) Hardware Description Language (VHDL) for FPGAs).

All these aspects should be taken into account in order to develop an application and all of them should be examined for the current system in order to reach high computational performance. Hence, it makes sense to have the ACAF, which facilitates astrophysical research by providing the user with a set of objects and functions fulfilling the following requirements:

- the structure of an object and the semantics of a function should be plain and similar to the objects often used by scientists in other programming environments and in theoretical problem descriptions;
- the objects and functions should cover most of the heterogeneous programming aspects;
- there should be a possibility to extend the tools in use as well as to provide the alternative implementations of existing tools;
- the design of the framework should clearly split the algorithmic (mathematical, physical) part from the heterogeneous programming techniques;
- the definition of the distribution of data and computation over the cluster nodes should be user-friendly;
- the programming language for the framework implementation should be flexible enough to fulfill the previous requirements, the language should have as less run-time expenses (such as using Virtual Machines and etc) as possible, ideally the language should be similar to the one used by scientists at the current moment;
- finally, it would be an additional advantage to preserve a possibility to reuse the existing computational libraries.

The rest of the paper is divided into 7 sections. Section II highlights the currently existing standards, frameworks and languages for the software development targeted heterogeneous systems. Section III consists of 3 subsections, each of them presenting some design motivations and solutions we have used to reach the goal. Sections IV and V uncover some implementation details of the framework. In Section VI, the usage example of the current framework implementation is given. Section VII describes the benchmarking performed to evaluate the result framework. Finally, Section VIII concludes the paper with an outlook to the most important advantages of the ACAF.

II. Current State of Art

This section covers mostly used and important frameworks, libraries, languages and standards, which can optimize or simplify development of the specific astrophysical cluster applications.

A. Standards

This section gives an overview of the currently used programming standards and standard APIs for generic parallel heterogeneous programming. All the standards were designed for generic problems and therefore contain and require the implementation details, which are irrelevant or obvious for the astrophysical simulation applications. Nonetheless, studying the existing standards helps to identify the relevant level of abstraction and the relevant set of functions and structures.

- MPI [6] is a standardized message-passing system designed to function on a wide variety of parallel computers. MPI is widely used on many computer clusters for parallel computations on several machines. MPI can also be used for parallel computations on a single node by running multiple instances of the program. MPI provides the user with functions to efficiently exchange data in the parallel systems.
  MPI has nothing to do with the code parallelization: the program can be implemented with or without accelerators usage, with or without parallelizing and optimizing execution code. MPI offers an interface-independent network communication, which enables the possibility to eliminate the usage of any particular network protocols. Moreover, MPI provides not only plain data copy functions, but also a lot of collective data functions, like data reduction, data gathering. Using of MPI the user can abstract the network communication in the efficient way.
  Another advantage of MPI is the existence of a number of extensions, which often can enhance the network communication even further, such as enabling InfiniBand usage, parallel files handling (including HDF5 files) etc. The most interesting extension in terms of heterogeneous clusters programming is MVAPICH2.
- MVAPICH2 [7] is a novel MPI design, which integrates CUDA-enabled GPU data movements transparently into MPI calls. This means that the user can often eliminate additional steps for transferring data firstly to the host memory and then to GPU memory and backward. Since MVAPICH2 involves not only an efficient encapsulation of the function calls, but also utilization of the motherboard and GPU chips capabilities, the final effect can reasonably improve the performance.
  Hence, the user should still guarantee the correct lifetime management of GPU memory. The user should manually trigger the execution of the GPU code. And if the calculations should be done simultaneously on GPU and CPU or several GPU, MVAPICH2 can only be utilized by dividing the calculation on different devices of the same host into separate MPI processes. Another limitation of MVAPICH2 lies in supporting only CUDA-enabled GPUs.
  So, MPI and MVAPICH2 are important libraries for developing programs for heterogeneous clusters, but these libraries cover only a single aspect - communication between nodes and devices. Moreover, the libraries actually just abstract and simplify the network protocol usage. At the same time, the user should take care of allocation, distribution of the data, code execution, synchronization and so on. Therefore, these libraries cannot be seen as a solution for the problem we have identified. Still, while they can be used for efficient implementing of the framework in our research.
- CUDA stands for Compute Unified Device Architecture and is a parallel computing platform and an API model created by Nvidia. CUDA is currently used only for Nvidia GPUs. CUDA API model enables the user to utilize GPU for general-purpose computations on a single node.
  The program written with CUDA API consists usually of 2 parts:
  - a kernel code, which is going to be executed on

the GPU. Usually, the kernel code represents the actual mathematical calculations, since the mathematical part is the target of the accelerators usage approach. The kernel code is written in a variety of the C language - CUDA C.
  - a host code, which performs initialization, GPU memory management (including allocation, transferring and deallocation), kernel uploading and execution.

The user of CUDA API should control all aspects of the program lifetime. Having several GPU on the same node implies explicitly controlling each device and the corresponding memory space. Performing additional parallel calculations on CPU should be implemented as a standalone solution, because CUDA has nothing to do with CPU programming.
This means that CUDA is a utility for general-purpose GPU programming. It provides a possibility to efficiently develop general-purpose programs for Nvidia GPU devices. But being a generic tool implies that CUDA offers the user as much programming aspects as possible and requires as many implementation details as it is actually necessary. So, CUDA should be a part of the solution in our research. Still, it has not been designed to abstract the aspects we need to be covered.

- OpenMP [8] is a standard API for shared-memory programming in C/C++/Fortran languages, which enables easy and efficient development of the parallelized code using compiler directives. OpenMP parallelizes the program by distributing the execution of some code in the threads pool. OpenMP API is system independent, while the compiler is responsible for the correct system-dependent implementation.
In order to run some piece of code in parallel, the user should mark this code with an OpenMP pragma, it could be either a for loop, iterations of which will be distributed, or a number of sections each of which will run in a single thread. The necessary initialization calls and actual multi-threaded calls will be placed by the compiler preprocessor. Additionally, the user can specify which data should be local for a thread, which data should be shared between threads (also, some other basic data operations are available such as scattering, gathering and reduction).
Using OpenMP pragma instructions, it becomes very easy to parallelize the code for multi-threaded execution. Often, if a loop has no data dependencies between iterations, it is enough just to place a single pragma before loop and recompile the program. Conversely, the parallelization of a complex code requires certain mastering in OpenMP programming, but it is usually much easier to use OpenMP for pure calculations rather than to use the thread management system-dependent calls.
The current widely supported version 3.1 (Microsoft Visual Studio 2008-2015 support only version 2.0) is designed to execute the parallel parts of the code using only CPUs. This limits the actual profit of using OpenMP as a solution for the identified problem. But there are several extensions of OpenMP, which enable also accelerators usage. These extensions will be described in the following subsections.
- OpenACC is a standard for the programming of computational accelerators originally proposed by Nvidia (currently only CUDA-enabled GPU are supported). OpenACC uses the similar API as OpenMP and is also based on the preprocessor pragmas. Additionally to the standard OpenMP pragmas, OpenACC offers the instructions to control data allocation, data flow, accelerator kernels and accelerator parallel blocks. Using OpenACC in case of independent loop iterations the programming of computational accelerators can be done by adding a single pragma to the code. If no accelerators are present in the machine, CPU will be used for executing the code. In 2013, OpenACC was merged into the general OpenMP standard - OpenMP version 4.0. OpenACC as well as OpenMP 4.0 are currently supported by a limited number of compilers.
- OpenHMPP (HMPP for Hybrid Multicore Parallel Programming) is a programming standard for heterogeneous computing based on HMPP API developed by CAPS Enterprise. This API also uses preprocessor compiler directives for marking the code to run it on the hardware accelerator. The basic idea of OpenHMPP lies in defining a codelet - a pure calculation function which is intended to be performed by the hardware accelerator. Additionally, the user should define the data transfer points and codelet call points. At the current moment OpenHMPP is supported only by 2 compilers: CAPS Enterprise compilers and PathScale ENZO compiler suite.
Unfortunately, OpenMP and its extensions do not solve the problem as well. OpenMP API model definitely reduces the requirements in parallel programming skills abstracting the numerous function calls in easy-readable pragmas. Still, this model does not hide a lot of implementation details, which are out-of-interests for scientific programmers: device data allocation, data transferring, runtime synchronization, etc. On the other side, the API hides the device selection possibilities, which may be necessary for the advanced programmers. Additionally, this API does not cover at all any kind of network communications and is designed solely for a single node. This means that for heterogeneous computing clusters the user should manually manage MPI (or other) calls mixing them with OpenMP (OpenACC or OpenHMPP) pragmas to run the application on all the nodes, which furthermore complicates the final code.
- OpenCL [9] is an open standard for general purpose parallel programming across different heterogeneous processing platforms: CPU, GPU and others. The OpenCL programming model is quite similar to CUDA, but implies the usage aspects of different accelerators. As well as for CUDA, OpenCL program consists of 2 parts:
  - a kernel code, which is going to be executed on accelerators written in OpenCL C language.
  - a host code, which performs initialization, memory management (including allocation, transferring and deallocation), kernel compila-

tion, uploading and execution.

And as well as for CUDA, using OpenCL requires the user to control all aspects of the program lifetime. But in contrast to CUDA, OpenCL provides a possibility to run the kernel code on different GPU and other different accelerators such as DSPs (Digital Signal Processors), FPGAs (Field-Programmable Gate Arrays) etc. Also, OpenCL offers a simplified memory model for multi-accelerator contexts.

Nevertheless, OpenCL is designed for single machine implementations. There were some projects (such as CLara [10], the project is stalled at OpenCL 1.0), which implement a proxy for the remote devices providing an access to them over the network. This implies that the host code of a proxy is not able to provide some logic, to store some temporary buffers, to optimize the network data exchange. Rather, the project implies working with remote devices in the same way as with local devices, which can lead to the unnecessarily frequent and time-expensive data transfers. This limits the utilization of OpenCL for heterogeneous clusters programming. Still, the OpenCL use is possible in conjunction with MPI or other communication interface.

Moreover, OpenCL is a standard for parallel programming of computational accelerators. This means that OpenCL is not supposed to simplify the accelerators programming (still it fulfills this task for some platforms). Instead, it provides a standard way to incorporate the accelerators power into the end-user applications. Therefore, OpenCL could be an important part of the solution for our problem.

- SyCL [11] is a new C++ single-source heterogeneous programming model for OpenCL. SyCL takes an advantage of C++11 features such as lambda functions and templates. SyCL provides high level programming abstraction for OpenCL 1.2 and OpenCL 2.2. This means that SyCL simplifies the integration of OpenCL into the programming code, making the heterogeneous programming available without learning some specific language extensions (such as the OpenCL C language or the CUDA C language). Moreover, SyCL tends to be included in the upcoming C++17 Parallel STL standard. Still, being an enhancement of OpenCL standard, SyCL does not introduce any network interoperability restricting the heterogeneous programming model to a single machine.

B. *Libraries, Frameworks and Languages*

This section covers numerous libraries and frameworks used or possible to be used for solving the code complexity problem of heterogeneous applications. [12]

- Cactus [13] is an open-source modular environment, which enables parallel computation across different architectures. Modules in Cactus are called "thorns". A thorn encapsulates all user-defined code. The user has a choice either to combine the solution of the problem configuring one or several existing thorns or write a new thorn. Thorns are able to communicate with each other using the predefined API functions. A thorn consists of at least a folder and 4 administrative files written in Cactus Configuration Language: interface.ccl, param.ccl, schedule.ccl, configuration.ccl. Each of these files describes some particular properties of the configuration:
  - interface.ccl is similar to a C++ class definition providing the key implementation features of the thorn;
  - param.ccl tips which data is necessary for running the thorn and which data is provided by the thorn;
  - schedule.ccl defines under which circumstances the thorn is executed;
  - configuration.ccl specifies which milestones are required to run the thorn and which milestone provides the thorn. In the built configuration, each milestone can be provided not more than once, while the code base can have several thorns providing the same milestone. The example milestones are: LAPACK, OpenCL, IOUtil.

  The rest of the thorn implementation should be organized into the files written with the following languages: Fortran90, C, C++, CUDA C, OpenCL C. The thorn implementation should include the functions defined in interface.ccl. The files will be compiled and linked together during the building of particular configuration. In functions and kernels, the user should explicitly utilize the predefined Cactus macros and instructions, which are to be replaced with the necessary language constructions before compiling the program. Cactus code has a built-in support of MPI. The latest version of Cactus includes the thorns for utilizing accelerators with the help of CUDA and OpenCL. Having these thorns, the user is able to program the accelerators calling the simplified interface functions for copying data and executing kernels. The network communication and the data transfer with accelerators can also be implicitly managed by Cactus using the distributed data types.

  Nevertheless, having the distributed data types does not solve the problem completely, because implementing a new thorn is quite a complicated task. The user has no ability to combine different devices into the same solution, since the thorns are always synchronized. Cactus is only designed to solve time iterative problems.

- Charm++ [14] is a message-driven parallel language implemented as a C++ library. The usual Charm++ program consists of a set of objects called "chares". A chare is an atomic function, which performs some calculations. Chares communicate with each other using messages. The task of the programmer in Charm++ context lies in dividing the problem into work pieces, which can be executed with virtual processors. And the Charm++ library schedules these work pieces among the available processing units.

  A chare implementation should be written in C++ language. It represents several classes, which inherit some Charm++ classes. A typical chare has at least 2 classes: the main chare class, which initializes the environment and sets the necessary variables, and

a worker class, which contains calculation routines. Since the source code of chares is written in C++ language, it is possible to use any 3rd party libraries including the accelerating libraries such as CUDA, OpenCL etc. But using these libraries anyway involves the manual management of all the aspects of accelerators programming.
Another possibility to utilize GPU lies in using an additional Charm++ library - Charm++ GPU Manager. This library provides the user with simplified functions to interact with CUDA-enabled GPUs. The user should define a work request for GPU Manager providing a CUDA kernel, input and output arguments to be transferred to the GPU. The GPU Manager ensures the overlapping of transfers and executions on the GPU and runs a GPU kernel asynchronously.
Even with the help of the GPU Manager, writing GPU-enabled programs with Charm++ remains a complex task. Charm++ is a message-driven platform, therefore the user should program the chares keeping in mind all the possible input and output messages. The user should control all the aspects of GPU programming. With a help of GPU Manager, the user can save on some function calls. Still, he should fully control the workflow.

- Chapel [15] is a parallel programming language. Chapel provides the user with a high-level parallel programming model which supports data parallelism, task parallelism and nested parallelism. Being designed as a new standalone language, Chapel allows to use a high level of parallelism abstraction. This results in a compactly written code, which is at the same time highly optimized, since the compiler controls all the aspects. Chapel was initially designed for multicore Cray machines. But thanks to the high level of abstraction, Chapel was extended to support also the heterogeneous systems.
At the same time, being a standalone language, Chapel has limited possibilities for extending the functionality and for interoperating with other languages. Since Chapel is an open source project, everybody can change the compiler grammar for having new commands. Additionally, Chapel provides interoperability with the C language, which consists of implementing special binary bindings. Also, Chapel is able to generate a C interface and compile the source code into the shared library, so the code written in Chapel can be called from other C programs.
Hence, Chapel is a powerful language, which allows the user to write parallel programs with several lines of code. Since the compiler is responsible for all the aspects of deploying a parallel program: data transferring, load balancing, device's execution calls etc, it becomes difficult to control the workflow of the program. Moreover all the optimizations and extensions should be done on the language grammar level, which involves even higher expertise in parallel computing.

- Flash Code [16], [17] is a modular Fortran90 framework targeted to computer clusters. It uses MPI to distribute calculations over the cluster nodes and inside the node over CPU cores. The Flash Code was initially developed for simulating thermonuclear flashes. But due to the modularity of the system, a lot of other modules were implemented, which led to wider application range. The current version of Flash Code has a huge delivered code base: ca. 3500 Fortran files.
The Flash Code was designed much earlier than heterogeneous clusters became widely-used. Therefore, the framework has no built-in support for any hardware accelerators and relies on particular modules to optimize the calculations as much as possible. Flash Code has different module types. Each module type is responsible for one or another system aspect being usually quite atomic (solvers, grids, etc). This means that a module can be implemented using any accelerating techniques and libraries. Moreover, a module can be implemented as a standalone dynamic library with the necessary Fortran90 bindings to the Flash code.
But the modularity of the framework implies the unnecessary data transferring in case of heterogeneous systems. The framework cannot consider the device memory, therefore, data should always be loaded into the device on the entry of the module and unloaded on the exit, even if the next module needs it to be in the device memory. Moreover, the constant variables and arrays should be transferred to the device at each iteration. These disadvantages can impair the performance gap achieved by using heterogeneous systems.
Moreover, the modularity of the Flash Code does not incorporate the abstraction of the parallel programming. So, writing a new module requires the proficiency in parallel programming, including: hardware accelerators utilization; MPI usage; data distribution and synchronization techniques; etc.

- Some other frameworks and languages. AMUSE [18] is a Python framework designed to couple existing libraries for performing astrophysical simulations involving different physical domains and scales. The framework uses MPI to involve cluster nodes. Conversely, the utilization of any hardware accelerators should be a part of libraries coupled in a particular configuration.
Swarm [19] is a CUDA library for parallel n-body integrations with a focus on simulations of planetary systems. The Swarm framework targets single machines with Nvidia GPUs as hardware accelerators. The framework provides the user with a possibility to extend the calculations algorithm. But the final system is not scalable and cannot utilize the power of a cluster. So, the framework is only designed to solve some specific problems.
The Enzo [20] project is a adaptive mesh refinement simulation code developed by a community. The code is modular and can be extended by users. Enzo does not support network communication. Still, it contains several modules developed to utilize Nvidia GPUs using CUDA.
Among other languages, which are not so widely used, we should mention: Julia [21] language, X10 [22]

language, Fortress language. All these languages were initially designed for CPU clusters. Some of them provide ports or extensions for hardware accelerators. These ports and extensions usually have no abstraction for the accelerator memory space communications.
Finally, some other widely-used, but very domain-specific libraries are: WaLBerla [23], RooFit [24], MLFit [25].

III. ACAF Design and Structure

A. 3 Concepts Design

The design of the ACAF should be both user-friendly for astrophysicists and easily extendable for computer scientists. Therefore, we have designed the ACAF basing on 3 concepts (see Figure 1).

Figure 1. The 3-concepts design.

1) The **computational concept** describes the principal algorithm used for calculating. In other words, the computational concept is a mathematical, physical and astrophysical background of the problem solution and the environment necessary to execute the solution of the problem on some particular device. This concept bases on a set of efficient high-parallel multi-architectural algorithms. So that each algorithm had an efficient implementation for each architecture and device in use. And all implementations for the same algorithm could work together on different platforms.
2) The **data concept** describes logical and physical representation of the data used in a solution, as well as the distribution of this data. This concept lies both in a set of data-structures providing an efficient way of managing the data of the astrophysical objects; and a set of functions for manipulating these structures.
3) The **communication concept** describes data transfers and synchronization points between computing units. The concept lies in efficient data-distribution mechanisms, which guarantee the presence of the necessary data in the required memory space and in the required order. This means that the communication concept is responsible for transferring data from one memory space to another and for transforming it according to the user-defined, architecture-defined or device-defined rules.

Design of the computational concept is a technical problem lying in the space of a properly implemented set of programming interfaces to access the necessary functions on the necessary platforms.

Conversely, the design of the data concept and the communication concept can be coupled into a special distributed database. Here and further, we understand under the database its basic definition: a database is an organized collection of data. This database should provide the user with an interface for managing data. Besides, it should manipulate the data according to the requirements and properties of computational units and algorithms. Hence, the database should fulfill the following requirements:

- operating with a set of structures efficient for representing astrophysical data: tuples, trees (oct-trees, k-d trees), arrays;
- operating with huge amount of data;
- the native support of hardware accelerators like GPUs and FPGAs;
- the data should be efficiently distributed between both cluster nodes and the calculating devices inside of each node;
- the database should be programmatically scalable: the user should be able to extend the number of features in use - architectures; devices; data-structures; data manipulation schemes and functions; communication protocols;
- the database should store the data according to the function, device and platform requirements.

This means that this special database can be seen as a partitioned global address space (PGAS), which is already addressed in several existing solutions like Chapel and X10. But in our approach, we incorporate into the database not only partitioning of the address space, also other properties specified above.

Hence in this work, we address only the communication and data concepts - **the design and implementation of a distributed database**. The computational concept is designed to contain only the algorithms and functions, necessary to present the capabilities of the database.

B. Database Design

The target data for the ACAF database is a set of states of some particle system. According to the definition of a particle system (see Section I), there is no need for our database to store various data of various types. All parameters of a particle are some physical properties of it. So in computer representation, the parameters are usually either integer, float or double (integral) values. Hence in our database, only these types of data are considered. A state of some particle system can be represented in some computer memory space as an array of structures, where members of a structure are particle parameters, e.g., integral data types. Therefore, the ACAF database is targeted to store only arrays of integral data elements.

As soon as a particle system usually includes some millions of particles, it is common and necessary to use computer clusters and accelerators to simulate its states. So, the aim of the ACAF is to simplify implementing the simulations tasks targeted to be run on heterogeneous computer clusters utilizing as much computational power as possible. The efficient utilization of any computational device (e.g., processing unit) becomes possible only when all the parameters necessary for computation reside in the cheapest memory space in terms of access latency. The efficient use of low-level memory spaces (processor registers and near by caches of the unit) is a part of both compiler implementation and the operating system scheduler. At the same time, the programmer's task is to ensure the presence of data in the nearest high-level memory space (usually device Random-access memory (RAM)). Moreover, it is necessary to store data in high-level memory spaces in the format acceptable with computational algorithms. Hence, raw arrays are preserved in our database. This provides the direct access to the parameters of a particle.

The ability of the ACAF database to distribute data between cluster nodes and devices enables the scalability of data amount. So, the amount of data to be processed is only limited to the mutual storage capabilities of cluster nodes and devices.

Distributing data between cluster nodes and devices implies division and synchronization of data according to the particular implementation of the computational concept. At the same time, data synchronization in heterogeneous computer clusters implies interoperability of different programming technologies used on different computational devices. Since the ACAF database is targeted to utilize GPUs, CPUs, FPGAs and a network, the technologies we have used include:

- OpenCL and pthreads for CPUs;
- OpenCL and CUDA for GPUs;
- OpenCL for FPGAs;
- MPI for a network.

Interoperability of the technologies mentioned above means the following functionality of the ACAF database: copying and/or converting of memory buffers from one technology into another; synchronizing the memory buffer content distributed between different technologies.

Basing on this information, we have extracted the important constructing blocks of the ACAF database design. These blocks are described in the following subsections. And the full block diagram is shown in Figure 2.

a) Configuration: One of the input data the user should provide to the database is the configuration of the heterogeneous cluster utilization. The database is to be able to discover automatically the available and supportable hardware and technologies during the initialization phase. But only the user can define how to utilize the hardware. Particularly, the user should specify:

- which network communication interface should be used, if any;
- which technology should be associated to one or another device;
- which amount of items should be distributed to the devices;
- some other miscellaneous device-dependent and technology-dependent parameters necessary for the execution.

The configuration is the same for all the running instances of the project in the cluster.

b) Context: The configuration defines the context for the database and the framework. The context consists of the device/technology pairs and the network interface. The device is a certain C++ object uniquely identifying a certain hardware device on the particular machine. The technology is an interface, which declares the necessary functions to execute the instructions on the supported devices. Only the supported devices can be coupled with a particular technology. The technology defines by itself the full set of the supported devices. Finally, the network interface declares the function set to perform network communication.

In contrast to the configuration, the context represents the actual set of devices available in the current system, as well as the actual device/technology coupling which is possible in the current framework version and setup.

c) Distribution: The context together with the configuration defines the distribution - a collection of the device/-size and network node/size pairs. So, the distribution keeps information on the quantity of logical items to be stored on a certain device. At the same time, the network node sizes are automatically calculated and broadcasted over the predefined network interface. The correlation of the logical items count and the actual physical memory allocation is not a part of the distribution. The user can define several different distributions within the same configuration and use them for different aims.

d) Storage Objects: On the other hand, the context as well defines the storage objects - the instances of the storage interface, which declares the functional schema of operating with some physical memory space. Each storage object corresponds to some memory space (physical or virtual) and some programming interface for accessing this memory space. For example, the storage object can represent GPU memory space using OpenCL memory access functions, the main (RAM) memory space using the C++ memory functions or some remote network location accessible through the predefined network interface.

This means that the storage objects work with the low-level memory interactions. The storage objects do not know anything about the content of a particular memory block. The objects operate with byte-sized memory buffers.

e) Input and Output Data Definition: Another input the user provides is the definition of the input and output data of the algorithm. This definition describes the format of the data, the access, communication and synchronization schema, as well as the correspondence of the logical items count and the actual internal data items count.

f) Content Objects: Hence, the data description defines the content objects - the logic how to work with memory. Particularly, a content object determines the following properties of the data:

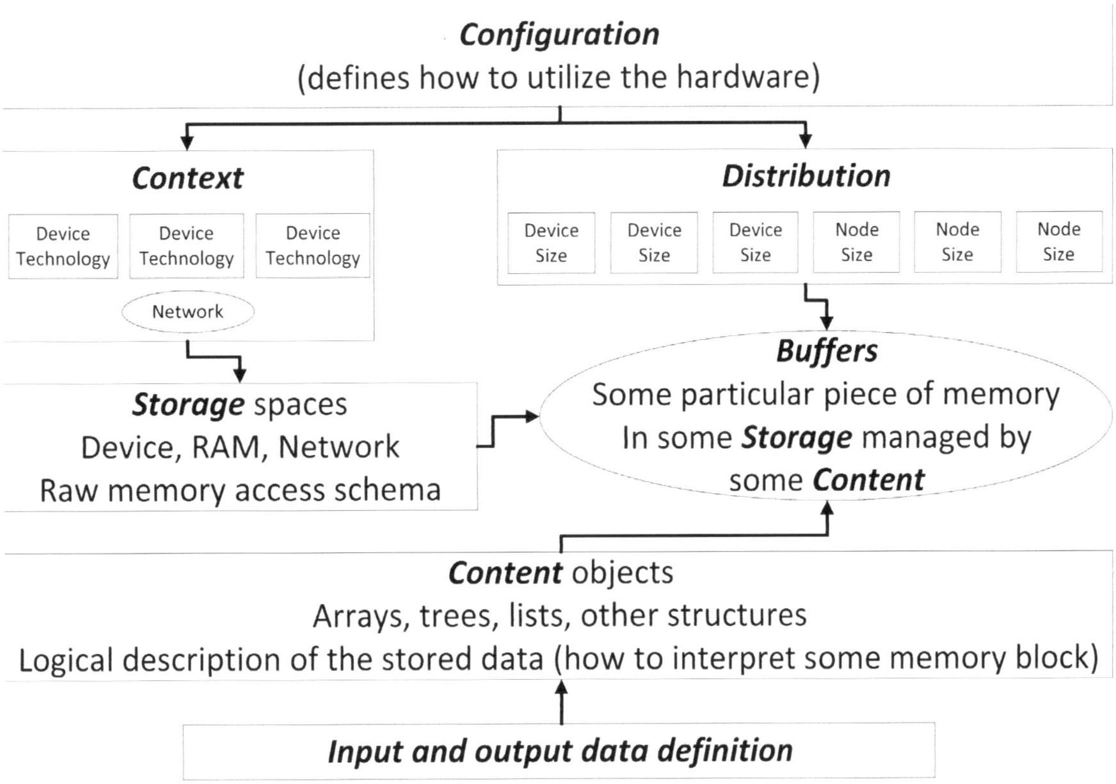

Figure 2. Diagram of ACAF database design.

- the type of the whole data collection;
- the types of the elements;
- the arrangement of the elements in the collection;
- the policy for reading the elements from a memory block;
- the policy for writing the elements;
- the possible directions and mechanisms of transferring the data;
- the correlation between the logical sizes defined by the distribution and the actual physical sizes of data.

g) Buffers: Finally, the content objects, the storage objects and a distribution define altogether the memory buffers. A memory buffer represents a range in certain memory space allocated by the storage object with the data arranged according to the content object. The size of the data is determined by the distribution with regard to the content factor. At the same time, a memory buffer object itself only contains the reference to the memory region, the size of this region and the storage object, which manages this region.

C. Design of Framework

In order to implement and test the abilities of the proposed database design, it is necessary to develop the computational concept of the heterogeneous programming problem. The computational concept is the mathematical representation of an astrophysical simulation. This means that this concept can be described with an algorithm, which evolves the state of the particle system and is able to operate on the data stored in the memory buffers of the database.

The mathematical background of an astrophysical simulation is a part of any astrophysical research, because this part represents the mathematical approximation of physical laws. The physical laws are a subject of the research:

- which laws are involved;
- which influence has a certain law, which of them are important and which of them can be ignored;
- how the laws work together;
- how a particular law should be approximated in order to be precise enough.

This means that the computational concept alone requires good programming skills from the astrophysicists, because the precision of the simulation depends on the particular implementation of the mathematical algorithm. The main difficulty in implementing the mathematical algorithm for a heterogeneous cluster lies in the necessity to implement the same algorithm several times for different technologies, which use different technology-dependent programming languages.

Consequently, it becomes reasonable to have some technology-independent programming language, which can be used for implementing the mathematical algorithm and can be afterward translated into the technology-dependent binaries. But as it was already mentioned, in this work we concentrate on the database implementation. Therefore, the proposed language is left for the future work. Still in this section, we provide the architectural design of the whole framework, including the computational concept.

The design of the framework is schematically presented in Figure 3 together with the elements of the database design (see Section III-B). Such design includes all the elements necessary to run an astrophysical simulation on a heterogeneous cluster.

a) Algorithm: Hence, for performing a simulation, the computational algorithm should be also provided by the user. The algorithm represents the mathematical approximations of the physical laws, which are aimed to evolve the state of the particle system.

b) Implementations: The computational algorithm together with the context object defines a set of the technology-dependent and device-targeted implementations. Each implementation of this set represents a particular set of instructions, which can be executed on the target device. This means that each implementation is bound to the technology used in the current context for the device.

IV. Implementation Design

In order to guarantee the correctness of the framework implementation and foresee the possible problems, we have firstly translated the proposed component-based framework design (see Figure 3) into the implementation design using the UML diagram. The detailed description of the classes including some implementation details is provided in Section V. This section gives the overview of the key mechanisms and techniques used in the implementation described in the following subsections.

A. Device Detection Mechanism

As it was described in Subsection III-B the first input data the framework expects from the user is the configuration. It provides the information how to utilize the hardware presented in the cluster. But such a hardware-related specification can be quite complex due to the big variety of components presented in the cluster and different possibilities to use these components.

Therefore, in order to simplify and minimize the data necessary for the framework from the user, it was decided to implement the device detection mechanism. The idea of this mechanisms lies in detecting the available computational devices on each node and finding out which technologies can be used for programming these devices. Finally, the detection mechanism is to foresee some extending possibility for future devices and technologies.

Taking all these requirements into account, the mechanism is divided into 2 logical parts - a collection of independent *Architecture* subclasses and a collection of independent *Technology* subclasses. Each *Architecture* subclass and each *Technology* subclass has a descriptive unique string identifier available for the user (this identifier is not the C++ subclass name).

Each *Architecture* subclass represents a device type (CPU, GPU, FPGA and etc.) and provides an ability to enumerate all the devices in the current system of this type. The particular enumeration technique depends on the implementation of the subclass and the type of the device. In the current framework, there are 2 subclasses implemented:

- CPUArchitecture enumerates CPU in the system. Since we have targeted the current implementation to work with Linux-based clusters, the CPUArchitecture class relies on the information provided in */proc/cpuinfo* file. The class parses the file on the initialization step and instantiates the *Device* objects.
- GPUArchitecture enumerates CPU in the system. This class scans the whole PCI bus of the system in order to find the devices of the VGA type, which are in fact GPUs. For each of these devices a *Device* object is instantiated.

Each *Technology* subclass represents a programming interface to interact with the devices. So, the framework requires that each subclass marks the devices supported by this interface. The marking process can be done in one of the following ways:

- The subclass checks the devices enumerated on the previous step by *Architecture* subclasses and for each device makes some tests in order to clarify the compatibility.
- The subclass scans the system for the available devices supported by this technology. (Usually, the interfaces provide the functions, which directly list the devices.) And then the subclass matches the devices enumerated by *Architecture* subclasses and the devices listed by the technology.

The described device detection mechanism is a part of the framework initialization. This means that when the framework is successfully initialized, it has a list of device objects, where each object corresponds to a certain *Architecture* subclass and is supported by some *Technology* subclasses (none is also possible).

B. Configuration File

Having the device detection mechanism is not enough to make the correct decision how to utilize the devices of the cluster. Notwithstanding the fact that some heuristic-based decision is still possible, the user should be able to influence the utilization schema. Therefore, it is necessary to have a configuration file to specify the following parameters:

1) which of the supported technologies should be selected for the context for each device available in the system;
2) the fallback behavior in case of the unsuccessful association between devices and technologies;
3) the desired network interface, if any;
4) one or several distributions, where each distribution describes a partitioning of the logical units between the devices and the nodes of the cluster.

Taking into account the device information available after the framework initialization, it becomes possible to simplify

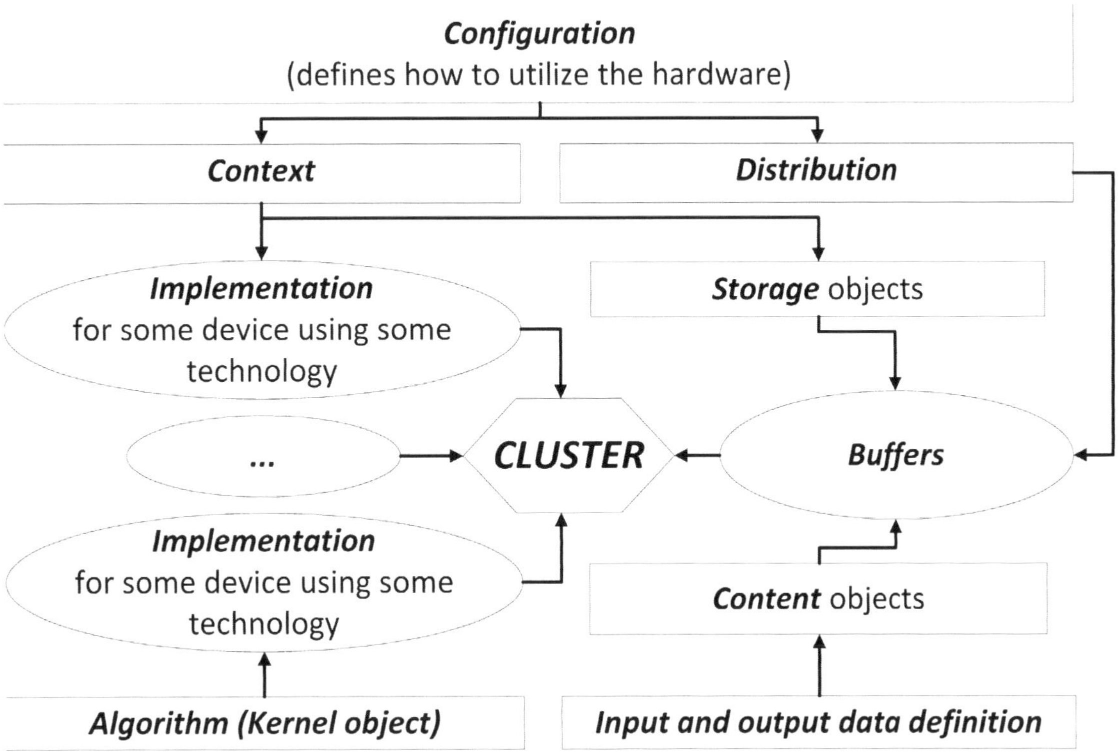

Figure 3. Diagram of the Astrophysical-oriented Computational multi-Architectural Framework design.

the specification of the device-technology association by requesting the user to provide the association using the following possibilities (in the order of the processing priority):

1) the technology name or the keyword "none" and an array of the full device names (as it was acquired by some *Architecture* subclass);
2) the architecture name and the technology name or the keyword "none".

In order to simplify the usage and the implementation of the configuration file specification it was decided to use the libconfig[26] format for the file. The file has the following structure:

- the top-level section "context", which includes the device-technology association specified above, including the optional parameter "skip", which indicates if the unsuccessfully associated devices are to be skipped;
- the top-level optional parameter "network", which specifies the network interface to be used;
- the top-level section "distribution", which contains one or several named subsections;
- each named distribution subsection consists of device-specific blocks: the full device name or the architecture name, size and block vectors.

C. Context, Database and Distribution Initialization

Using the automatically listed devices set and the user-provided configuration file, the context object can be initialized. The context initialization is based on parsing the configuration file and traversing the devices list, which was previously generated by the device detection mechanism. The result of the context initialization is a device-technology map. Only the devices listed in the map will be used later for the calculation. Another part of the context initialization is configuring the network interface according to the specification in the configuration file.

Using the initialized context, the database object can be initialized. The database initialization lies in the instantiation of the storage objects, responsible for device- and network-targeted transactions. The device-targeted storage objects are instantiated by the associated technology. And the network-targeted storage objects are instantiated by the network interface. Each storage object is an instance of some *Storage* subclass (for different targets there are also other intermediate interfaces in the class hierarchy such as *DeviceStorage*, *LocalStorage*, *NetworkStorage*). Each storage object is fully responsible for providing the communication schema with its target. The result of the database initialization is a set of storage objects.

Finally, the initialized context and database make it possible to instantiate the distribution objects. A distribution object describes a certain partitioning of an astrophysical simulation problem between the different computational devices of the cluster. The partitioning is based on logical units. The distribution objects are composed using the initialized context and the user-provided configuration file. The initialized context lists the devices, which will be used for the computation, while a particular subsection of the distribution section in the configuration file specifies the association of the devices to some size vector measured in the logical units. The logical units in the distribution object can represent either the actual particles count or some relative count, which can be converted to the particles count in the user-code using some factor.

The distribution initialization is divided into 2 steps:

1) at the first step, each network node initializes its local distribution for its own devices;
2) at the second step, the network nodes synchronize the sizes in order to gather the full distribution information.

D. Content Objects And Buffers Instantiation

As it was described in Subsection III-B, the user also provides the information about the input and output data of the algorithm. This information is provided by instantiating the objects of some *Content* subclass. Each *Content* subclass provides a certain typical logical access schema. This schema includes the following characteristics:

- the data container type - one-dimensional array, multi-dimensional array, oct-tree and so on;
- the unit type - some scalar values (such as mass, temperature), some vector values (position, velocity, acceleration) or something else;
- the ownership of the data in the multi-storage context - which copy has the correct values for a certain range in case of the data being duplicated in several memory spaces;
- the synchronization mechanism in the multi-storage context - how the data should be transferred in case of the data being duplicated and kept up-to-date.

Another part of the content object instantiation is the memory allocation for storing the parts of data. Therefore, each content instantiation includes the units distribution object as a parameter. The units distribution object is generated from the regular distribution object using some factor. Having the units distribution, the content object is able to request the database to allocate the necessary amount of memory in the storage associated with the device. The result of this allocation is returned as an instance of a certain *Buffer* subclass. This instance includes internally the buffer physical size, the pointer to the managing storage object, the address of the actual buffer (an address form depends on the buffer type) and other storage-specific parameters.

E. The Definition of The Computational Concept

As it was described in Subsection III-C, the computational concept represents the mathematical algorithm of the particle system evaluation based on physical laws of the particles interaction. In the framework context, this mathematical algorithm is represented as a collection of *Kernel* class instances. Each instance is parametrized with a collection of technology-targeted implementations and execution parameters.

The technology-targeted implementations are created using the device-technology association available in the context and the technology-specific programming code. For the current implementation of the framework, the user should provide all the technology-specific programming code snippets for the technologies in use. The code will be compiled and prepared for each device associated with the technology, the resulting executable binary is represented by an object of some *Implementation* subclass. This object encapsulates all the parameters necessary to run the code on a certain device. All the device-targeted instances of *Implementation* subclasses for the particular mathematical computation are incorporated and managed by a single *Kernel* object.

The execution parameters can be either scalar values or content objects. The scalar values are byte-copied to the target device memory space. And for each specified content object, the buffer allocated in the device memory is used.

F. Simulation Execution Principles

Taking all the described mechanisms into account, the user should perform the following steps for executing a simulation using the framework:

1) provide a configuration file using libconfig[26] syntax;
2) create the necessary content objects for all non-scalar distributed algorithm parameters;
3) write technology-specific execution code for all the technologies in use;
4) create the necessary kernel objects;
5) write the main execution logic using content objects and kernel objects in C++ language.

The last step usually consists of a time evolving loop. For each iteration of this loop, some kernels are executed and some content objects are synchronized. Alternatively, some output data can be generated. But since the loop is written in C++ language it can include as many different instructions as necessary.

G. Considered Limitations

The proposed design considers the following limitations in the functionality and utilization of the framework:

- The design targets exclusively the data-parallel problems. Therefore, the implemented framework cannot be directly utilized for the task-parallel problems. This limitation is grounded from the properties of the astrophysical simulation problems described in Section I. Moreover, the heterogeneous cluster computing is usually effective only for the data-parallel problems.
- The design and implementation of the framework targets x86-64 systems running a Linux Operating System. This limitation is formed by the statistics of TOP500 supercomputers, which shows that as of November 2015 90.6% of the supercomputers are x86-64 machines and 98.8% of the supercomputers run a Linux Operating System [27].

- The design of the framework preserves the separation of the computational resources by their type (*Architecture* subclasses) and the utilization schema (*Technology* subclasses). This separation forces the user to consider the specifics of the devices and to write the separate code for different devices in the current implementation. On the other hand, this limitation enables the user to finely tune the computation code for each device according to the utilization schema and enhances the extendability of the framework in terms of the supported device types and utilization schemes.

V. Classes Description

The suggested database is implemented as a part of the framework - the ACAF. The implementation is done in C++ language and is organized as a collection of classes. Some of them are template classes. We concentrate on the key classes used in the ACAF in this section.

A. Device

The *Device* class is one of the central classes in the framework implementation. An instance of this class represents a device in the current system. The class has the following private member fields:

- the vendor name as a string field and the vendor identifier as a variant architecture-dependent field;
- the device name as a string field and the device identifier as a variant architecture-dependent field;
- the pointer to the instance of the *Architecture* subclass, which has created this device object;
- the map of supported technologies and technology-specific identifiers of the device;
- the set of some architecture-defined, technology-defined or custom device properties.

Functionally, the *Device* class is simple and does not perform any tasks. All modification operations of the device are not public and can be called only by the friend classes. A single exception is adding of custom properties.

B. Architecture

The *Architecture* class is a common interface for all different computational device architectures. Under the device architecture we understand the design architecture of the device processing unit, which can be used for the computational purposes (e.g., CPU, GPU, FPGA etc.). The interface declares the common member functions and member fields for all the architecture subclasses. The main function of any *Architecture* subclass lies in enumerating the devices of some specific type. The framework relies on the unambiguous correspondence of the devices and the supported architectures: there is no such device, which can belong to more than one architecture.

Additionally, the *Architecture* class defines the static mechanism guarantying that each subclass is instantiated only once in the scope of one running process. This mechanism is based on the statical singleton instantiation of the *Architecture* subclasses during the framework library loading. All instances are stored in the static name-object map. Only the instances in the map will be taken into account by the framework.

To support some other computational architectures as the predefined ones, the user should implement another subclass of the *Architecture* class. The new subclass should provide the framework with the actual implementations of 2 pure virtual methods of the interface:

- *getName* - returns the name of the architecture;
- *rescan* - rescans the entire system in order to detect all available devices of the current architecture type; and stores the appropriate *Device* instances in the member variable.

The current framework implementation includes 2 subclasses of the *Architecture* class: *CPUArchitecture* and *GPUArchitecture*.

C. Technology

The *Technology* class is a common interface for all computational technologies. The interface declares the common member functions and member fields for all the computational technology subclasses. Any *Technology* subclass implements the following interface functions:

- *getName* - returns the name of the technology;
- *rescan* - scans the entire system to identify the devices supported by the technology and matches the devices, which were previously listed by some *Architecture* subclass. The matched instances are marked as supported with the technology. The particular matching mechanism depends on the technology type and the implementation: some technology can enumerate the devices directly, the other check the devices listed by the architectures to fulfill some criteria;
- *getStorage* - for each supported device the subclass should provide an instance of some *Storage* subclass, which is able to manage the device memory space;
- *implement* - for each supported device the subclass should provide an instance of some *Technology::Implementation* subclass, which is able to execute some programming code or some binary on the device. Usually, each *Technology* subclass provides also an implementation of the appropriate *Technology::Implementation* subclass.

The *Technology* class guarantees the singleton instantiation of the subclasses during the framework loading in the same way as the *Architecture* class.

Extending of the supported computational technologies can be done by implementing another subclass of the *Technology* class. The new subclass should provide the framework with the actual implementations of the 4 pure virtual methods mentioned above.

The current framework implementation includes 3 subclasses of the *Technology* class: *PthreadTechnology*, *OpenCLTechnology* and *CUDATechnology*.

D. Network

The *Network* class is a common interface for different network interfaces. The interface declares the common member functions and member fields for all the network subclasses. The main function of any *Network* subclass lies in defining the communication between the different nodes of the network.

The *Network* object is a singleton for each running instance of the program. This means that only one instance of a particular *Network* subclass can exist in the scope of a single running process.

To support some other network interfaces as the predefined ones, the user should implement another subclass of the *Network* class. The new subclass should provide the framework with the actual implementations of the 10 pure virtual methods of the interface:

- *getNodesCount* -returns the total number of the nodes in the network;
- *getMyNodeIdx* - returns the current node identifier;
- *allgather* - gathers the whole buffer from all the nodes;
- *alltoall* - gathers the whole buffer from all the nodes and redistributes it again between all the nodes;
- *send_bcast* - sends a broadcasting message to all the nodes in the same network as the current node;
- *recv_bcast* - receives a broadcasting message from the node;
- *send* - sends the content of some buffer to the remote buffer;
- *recv* - receives the content of the remote buffer in some local buffer;
- *init* - initializes the instance of the class;
- *instantiate* - for each node in the network creates an instance of some *NetworkStorage* subclass and adds it to the database.

The current framework implementation includes 1 subclass of the *Network* class: *MPINetwork*.

E. Context

The *Context* class represents a map of device-technology pairs. Each pair describes the utilization schema of the device presented in the system. The context is a singleton object for each running instance of the program. The context is initialized using the global *ACAF::config* based configuration. The *Context* class also hosts an instance of the *Database* class. When the initialization of the context is finished, the member database will be also initialized.

F. Storage

The *Storage* class is the interface for all the framework entities, which represent the engines for writing and reading the data to/from some memory space. All actual storage entities should inherit this class directly or indirectly in order to be correctly processed by the other framework entities. The interface class contains the declarations of the basic functions and also the trivial implementations for some of them. The interface class holds a collection of all owned memory buffers as a map of buffer-content pairs. All created buffers represent some pieces of memory with no connection to the particular format of the stored data (*Content* class). The most important methods of the class include:

- *init* - initializes the current instance of the class. The basic implementation adds the current instance to the database set of storage objects. All subclasses should call the parent init function in order to make sure that all the parts of the class are correctly initialized.
- *create* - creates a new buffer object for the specified content object and the necessary physical buffer size. Every *Storage* subclass creates an instance of some particular buffer class, which fits the aims and the functionality of the class.
- *find* - for the specified content finds the buffers owned by this storage object.
- *isSame* - checks if the current instance represents the same memory space as the instance passed over the arguments.

Usually, the actual storage objects do not inherit the *Storage* class directly, but inherit special subclasses, designed to simplify the implementation. Still, the user is able to extend the framework according to the research needs and implement the new storage types inheriting either the *Storage* class itself or some of its subclasses.

Storage::Buffer is an inner class of the *Storage* class. It declares the main interface for the buffer objects. A buffer object is a wrapper for some region in some memory space. The *Storage::Buffer* class declares the general functions for all the buffer subclasses. It is supposed that the actual memory space wrapped with the particular buffer object is used only by the "parent" storage class and its subclasses. Therefore, the *Storage::Buffer* class does not declare any memory access functions. The interface has one pure virtual function - *isSame*, which checks if the current buffer object wraps the same memory region as the object passed over the arguments.

G. Content

The *Content* class is a base interface for all the classes, which represent the data layout for some physical memory block. Each final implementation of the *Content* interface stores the full set of the buffers. This corresponds to the whole data range processed in the application. The interface declares some common functions for all the content objects:

- *fill* - fills the whole data range with some constant value;
- *random* - fills the whole data range with some random values;
- *synchronize* - synchronizes the content of the buffers in the current node with the other network nodes;
- *isSame* - checks if the current content object represents the same data as the one passed over the function arguments.

Each *Content* object is bound to some *Context* instance, since it defines which devices and network nodes are taken into account. It is supposed that *Content* objects should only be instantiated by some *Database* instance. But the user is able to implement any other classes, which correspond to the *Content* class concept, extending the possibilities of the framework. The current framework implementation provides 2 contents: a local array and a synced array.

H. Database

The *Database* class represents the central storage for all the data-related objects in the framework environment. Primary the database holds the following objects:

- a set of the *Storage* objects, where each object refers to some memory space (see Subsection V-F);

- a map of the named *Content* objects, where each object represents some data layout schema used in the user application (see Subsection V-G).

And if the storage objects are created by some other entities of the framework and just added to the appropriate *Database* instance, the *Content* objects are directly instantiated by the *Database* instance. For this purposes, the class defines a template function *create*, which takes a particular subclass of the *Content* class as a template argument. Also, the *create* function needs a name for the content and an instance of the *UnitsDistribution* class to initialize the newly created content object and to add it to the named map.

I. Kernel

The *Kernel* class represents a function running distributively with all its implementations for the available devices and all the necessary function arguments. The *Kernel* class is an end-user class. This means that the framework user is able to instantiate as many objects as necessary. The class provides the following manipulation functions:

- *add* - creates and adds an implementation of the kernel. The actual creation of the implementation object is forwarded further to the specified technology instance. The creation of the implementation object is done separately for each device assigned to the specified technology. Only the devices in the context of the kernel are taken into account.
- *set* - adds a value or a *Content* object to the list of the arguments of the kernel. A scalar argument value is passed to each implementation as it is. And the *Content* object is passed to each implementation in the form of the buffer corresponding to the device, where the implementation is executed.
- *start* - triggers the concurrent execution of all the available implementations of the kernel.

The order of the described functions reflects the usual work flow with a kernel object:

1) The user creates a named kernel object.
2) The user adds several implementations of the kernel for different technologies.
3) The user sets the necessary execution parameters of the kernel.
4) The user starts the kernel execution.

J. Extending the ACAF

The user has an opportunity to extend the functionality of the ACAF by implementing the other ancestor classes of the following entities:

- *Architecture* - to support other device types;
- *Technology* - to support other programming technologies;
- *Network* - to support other network protocols;
- *Content* - to support other logical data organizations.

VI. USAGE EXAMPLE

A running example of ACAF usage is represented with several parts: the configuration, the mathematical algorithm implementation and the environmental host code. The provided example represents the code necessary for running distributed NBody simulation on a cluster using MPI for network communication, pthread technology for CPU code and OpenCL technology for GPU code. Any changes in the resource utilization can be made by modifying the configuration file without any need to recompile the program.

A. Configuration File

A configuration file contains the network protocol, the *context* specification and possible distribution descriptions (see Figure 4).

```
network="MPI";
context: { skip = true; CPU = "pthread"; GPU = "OpenCL"; };
distribution: {
  default = (
    { architecture = "GPU"; size = [1024]; block = [256]; },
    { architecture = "CPU"; size = [256]; block = [4]; }
  );
};
```

Figure 4. The configuration example.

As it was described in Subsection III-B, the example configuration file provides the framework with the hardware utilization schema. Particularly, line-by-line the example file defines the following:

1) The "network" parameter defines that MPI should be used for the network communication within the cluster network. The calculation will be distributed over all the active nodes of the cluster. Eliminating this parameter will lead to the single-node computation.
2) The "context" parameter provides the textual context definition. All the CPU devices will be utilized by the pthread technology; all the GPU devices will be utilized by the OpenCL technology; all the other devices or the devices of the previous type not supported by these technologies will be skipped without producing any errors. Changing the "skip" parameter to value "false" will lead to the errors if there are any CPUs or GPUs not-supported by the assigned technologies.
3) The "distribution" section defines one entity with the name "default", which prescribes the following partitioning of the problem:
   a) Each GPU device processes 1024 items per iteration, calculating 256 items per work group.
   b) Each CPU device processes 256 items per iteration, calculating 4 items per thread job.

B. Algorithm Code (OpenCL and pthread)

According to the technologies specified in the configuration file and the host code initialization routine, the mathematical algorithm should be implemented for one or several technologies. In our example, the algorithm is implemented for OpenCL (see Figure 5) and pthread (see Figure 6) technologies, using respectively OpenCL C language and C++ language. The code of OpenCL implementation is represented as a separate file, while pthread implementation code is a part of the environmental host code and passed to ACAF as a pointer to the function.

```
#pragma OPENCL EXTENSION cl_khr_fp64 : enable
#pragma OPENCL EXTENSION cl_amd_fp64 : enable

#define SOFTENING 0.001

__kernel void force ( uint4 acaf_total,
  __global double  * mass, __global double4 * position,
  __global double4 * velocity, double time_step )
{
  __local double4 shared_position[ITEMS_PER_GROUP];
  size_t lid = get_local_id(0);

  shared_position[lid] = position[get_global_id(0)];
  double4 this_acc;
  this_acc.x = this_acc.y = this_acc.z = this_acc.w = .0;
  for ( size_t i = 0; i < acaf_total.x; ++i )
  {
    double4 dist = shared_position[lid] - position[i];
    this_acc += mass[i] * dist / powr(length(dist) + SOFTENING, 3.);
  }

  size_t gid = get_global_id(0);
  velocity[gid] += this_acc * time_step;
  position[gid] += velocity[gid] * time_step;
}
```

Figure 5. The OpenCL algorithm example.

```
#define SOFTENING 0.001

status force (
  const acaf::uint4 & jid, const acaf::uint4 & jtotal,
  const acaf::variant_vector & args
)
{
  double * mass = reinterpret_cast<double *>(*(args[0].get<void *>()));
  double4 * position = reinterpret_cast<double4 *>(*(args[1].get<void *>()));
  double4 * velocity = reinterpret_cast<double4 *>(*(args[2].get<void *>()));
  double time_step = *(args[3].get<double>());

  double4 this_pos = position[jid[0]];
  double4 this_acc (0.);
  for (size_t i = 0; i < jtotal[0]; ++i)
  {
    double4 dist = this_pos - position[i];
    this_acc += mass[i] * dist / pow(dist.length() + SOFTENING, 3.);
  }

  velocity[jid[0]] += this_acc * time_step;
  position[jid[0]] += velocity[jid[0]] * time_step;

  return error::Success;
}
```

Figure 6. The pthread algorithm example.

C. *Environmental Host Code*

Finally, the environmental host code represents the main function with initialization instructions, content creations, kernel instantiations and kernel running calls written in C++ programming language with the usage of the classes described in Section IV (see Figure 7).

This main function implementation provides the basic necessary code to initialize correctly the environment, to instantiate the entities, to perform the particle system evolving loop and to clean up the objects.

```
int main(int argc, char ** argv)
{
  MPI_Init(&argc, &argv);
  status s = error::Success;
  do
  {
    s = acaf::initialize(argc, argv);
    if (s.fail()) break;

    Handle < DataBase > db = Context::getContext()->getDB();
    LinearParticles distr(Context::getContext(), acaf_string("default"));
    Handle<Content> mass, pos, velo;

    {
      acaf::pair<Handle<Content>, status> tmp;
      tmp = db->create< SyncedArray<double, 1> >("mass", distr.units(1));
      if (tmp.second.fail()) cout << tmp.second;
      mass = tmp.first;
      mass->fill(acaf::variant(1.));
      tmp = db->create< SyncedArray<double4, 1> >("position", distr.units(1));
      if (tmp.second.fail()) cout << tmp.second;
      pos = tmp.first;
      pos->random(
        acaf::variant(double4({-1., -1., -1., 0.})),
        acaf::variant(double4({2., 2., 2., 0.}))
      );
      tmp = db->create< LocalArray<double4, 1> >("velocity", distr.units(1));
      if (tmp.second.fail()) cout << tmp.second;
      velo = tmp.first;
      velo->fill(acaf::variant(double4(0.)));
    }

    Kernel force("force", Context::getContext());

    double current_time = 0.;
    double end_time = 1.;
    double time_step = 0.01;

    s = force.add("OpenCL", "gravity.cl", "-cl-mad-enable", true);
    if (s.fail()) cout << s << endl;
    s = force.add("pthread", &::force);
    if (s.fail()) cout << s << endl;
    s = force.set(0, mass);
    if (s.fail()) cout << "Adding mass failed:" << s << endl;
    s = force.set(1, "position");
    if (s.fail()) cout << "Adding position failed:" << s << endl;
    force.set(2, "velocity");
    if (s.fail()) cout << "Adding velocity failed:" << s << endl;
    force.set(3, variant(time_step));
    if (s.fail()) cout << "Adding timestep failed:" << s << endl;

    while (current_time < end_time)
    {
      fos << "Current time: " << current_time << std::endl;
      s = force.start(distr.units(1));
      if (s.fail()) break;
      pos->synchronize();

      current_time += time_step;
    }
  } while (false);

  acaf::finalize();
  MPI_Finalize();

  if (s.fail())
    printf("An error %d (%s) occurred. Failed!\n", s.code(), s.name());
  else
    printf("Success!\n");

  return s.code();
}
```

Figure 7. The main function example.

- The initialization step includes 2 function calls: *MPI_Init* and *acaf::initialize*. According to the MPI user manual, the *MPI_Init* should always be the first function call of the application. Therefore, it is impossible to integrate it as a part of the framework initialization.
- The instantiation of the entities includes: the distribution creation using the configuration file; the contents creation and initialization (the masses are set to 1; the positions are randomized in the range between $(-1, -1, -1)$ and $(1, 1, 1)$; the velocities are set to $(0, 0, 0)$); the kernel creation and adding the available implementations and arguments.
- The particle system evolving loop consists of synchronous execution of the kernel, synchronizing the positions and proceeding to the next time frame.
- Finally, the clean up of the environment also includes 2 function calls symmetric to the initialization: *MPI_Finalize* and *acaf::finalize*.

VII. BENCHMARKING

To evaluate the framework using some measurable metrics, benchmarking with different parameters was performed. Benchmarking includes executing the usage example with different number of particles, different configurations (with or without some devices, with or without network utilization). The execution times for all different runs are combined in Figures 8, 9 and 10.

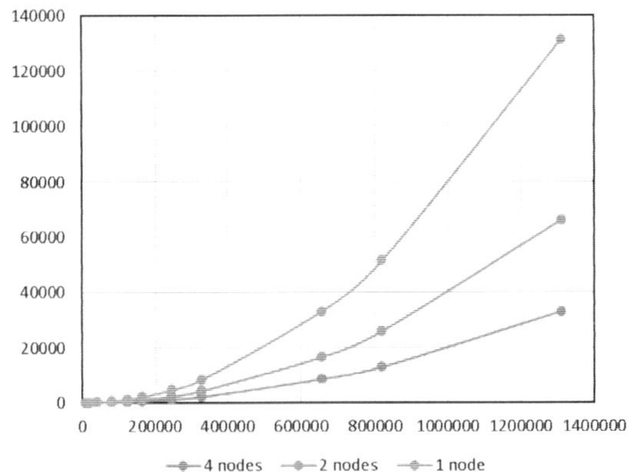

Figure 8. The full comparison chart of running the code on a different number of nodes.

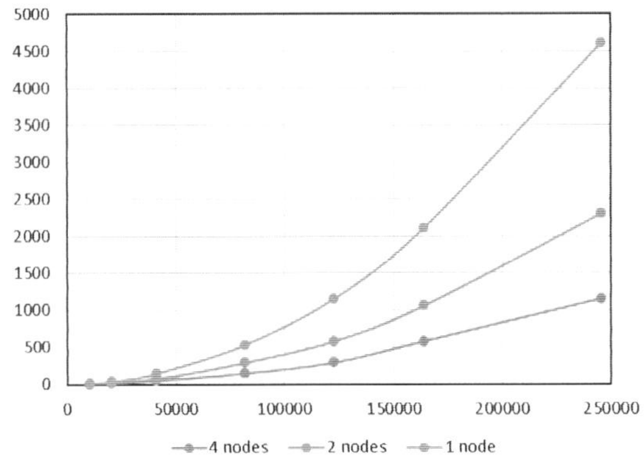

Figure 9. The lower range comparison chart of running the code on a different number of nodes.

The comparison charts show that the most efficient way to run the computation on the heterogeneous cluster using the ACAF is a distributed computation performed on GPU only. The deeper analysis of the execution times of the simulation within the different numbers of nodes shows:

- the average ratio of the execution times between 2 nodes configuration and 1 node configuration is 1.971x;
- the average ratio of the execution times between 4 nodes configuration and 2 nodes configuration is 1.97x;
- the average ratio of the execution times between 4 nodes configuration and 1 node configuration is 3.882x.

These ratios are quite near the ideal ratios 2, 2 and 4. This proofs the efficiency of the distribution mechanisms based in the design and implemented in the framework. The average ratios mentioned above consider only the distribution-effective

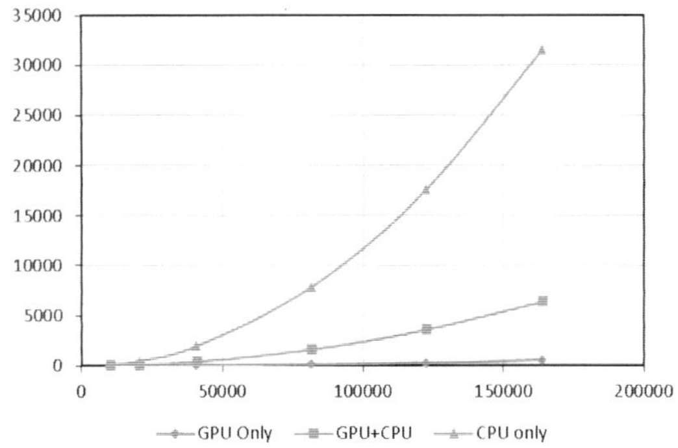

Figure 10. The comparison chart of running the code with different hardware configurations.

execution times, particularly, the cases with at least 81920 particles. For the lower amount of particles, the network transferring overhead drops the whole performance of the computation.

The comparison of different device configurations (GPU only, CPU and GPU, CPU only) shows that the GPU computation is 40x times faster, than CPU computation. This speed-up factor also explains that combining CPU and GPU computations makes no sense for the lower number of particles being 10x times slower as the GPU computation and 4x faster as the CPU computation.

Additionally, the comparison of the framework performance against the bare code performance was done. This comparison shows what is the overhead of using the framework. The bare simulation code consists of the network-distributed computations performed on GPU using the same OpenCL kernel. Figure 11 represents the percent overhead of the execution time of the usage example to the execution time of the bare implementation scaled over the particles number in the example system.

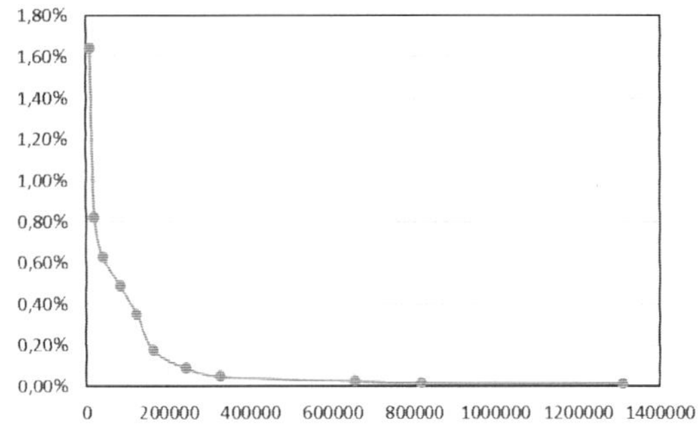

Figure 11. The comparison chart of the ACAF-based implementation to the bare implementation.

According to this chart, we can state that the time overhead of using ACAF approximates 0 for the bigger particle systems and is equal to 4 seconds for the case of 1310720 particles.

The tests were carried out on the following test platform: the 7-nodes cluster with 4 processing nodes, each of them has the NVIDIA GeForce GTX 285 GPU with 2GB of RAM, the Intel Xeon E5504 CPU and 6GB of RAM. The nodes run Linux OS. For each test the calculation was equally distributed over all 4 processing nodes.

VIII. Conclusion and Future Work

In this paper, we presented the design details, the implementation aspects and some benchmarking results for the **A**strophysical-oriented **C**omputational multi-**A**rchitectural **F**ramework. The ACAF is targeted to simplify the software development for astrophysical simulations implementation by providing the user with the set of objects and functions covering some aspects of application developing.

In the current work, we focused on the communication and the data concepts of software development problem designing the special distributed database. The database is aimed to process particle systems with float and/or double (integral) parameters. The database aims to store data in high-level memory spaces in the format acceptable with computational algorithms.

The current database implementation utilizes pthreads, OpenCL and CUDA technologies to run the calculation on CPU and GPU devices and MPI interface to distribute and exchange data over the network. The implementation uses 2 types of content: local array and synced array. Extending of the database functionality can be easily done by implementing the certain program interfaces.

We can conclude that the current ACAF implementation facilitates the development of network-enabled heterogeneous NBody force simulation program. With the help of ACAF, the user is able to write an application without the expertise neither in the network programming nor in the parallel programming of some devices (CPU, GPU). ACAF requires the user to do the following tasks:

- Write the configuration file, which specifies the devices and nodes to be used and defines the distribution of the data.
- Implement the mathematical, physical part of the program.
- Write the environmental code, which does the initialization, data definition, data initialization, kernel instantiation and defines the main particle system evaluation loop.

The following advantages can be mentioned as a result of comparing the final framework design and its implementation with the other approaches mentioned in Section II-B and the bare simulation code implementation :

1) The design of the framework prescribes the clear separation of the data mechanisms from the computational code and the environmental code. The data operations are managed by the data-relevant entities of the framework: *Database*, *Storage*, *Content*. This enables a possibility to encapsulate the necessary complex data operations: distribution of the data, its transferring, its synchronizing and etc.
2) The data operations are also separated logically according to the type of the operation: data allocating and transferring is managed by *Storage* classes, data interpretation and logic operations on the data are managed by *Content* classes, while the *Database* class guarantees the correct functionality and provides some misc functions. Such splitting helps to extend only the necessary framework parts.
3) The framework also splits the simulation implementation into several logical parts, which makes the coding task transparent:
   - the configuration file specifies the devices and nodes to be used and defines the distribution of the data;
   - the kernel implementations represent mathematical and physical parts of the code;
   - the environmental code does the initialization, data definition, data initialization, kernel instantiation and defines the main particle system evaluation loop.
4) The framework is designed as a C++ framework. This means that the user and the framework developer have an access to a big range of different powerful system calls and a variety of computational libraries and tools. So, the user has a choice either to reimplement the algorithm using the framework tools or to reuse the existing solution. Moreover, the availability of the system calls provides an option of performance-targeted tuning of the final application.
5) The framework encapsulates the device-specific operations using the *Architecture* and *Technology* classes. The encapsulation of the operations implies that the final user should not know and use some device-specific functions, libraries and tools. The framework classes separate also the functional aspects of the work with some device: *Architecture* class enables the devices of some specific type to be recognized and used by the framework; *Technology* class focuses on the device utilization schema. This separation facilitates the extension possibilities of the framework: the developer is able to target one of the aspects.
6) The framework also encapsulates the network-distributed communications and computations. This encapsulation enables the final users to avoid the network-related operations and to switch easily between the single-node configuration and the multi-nodes configuration.

Meanwhile, the current implementation of the framework has the following limitations and disadvantages:

1) The framework requires the knowledge and usage of the technology-targeted computational languages to utilize the computational devices, like OpenCL C and CUDA C for utilizing GPU. The computational kernel used by the framework to execute the actual calculations, should be implemented by the user for each technology combined in the current computational context. To avoid the necessity of having the individual kernel implementations for each technology, it is mandatory to design and implement some common parallel programming language, which can be further translated into the technology-specific languages. Still, it is crucial to preserve an ability to

use the native technology-specific programming languages in order to be able to finely tune a particular computational code.

2) Additionally to the technology-targeted programming languages requirement, the reentrance of the user-defined computational code is necessary, which complicates the implementation of the kernel for different devices. At the same time, the wrongly implemented kernel executed simultaneously on different data can lead to hard-recognizable incorrect results.
3) In comparison to the other approaches described in Subsection II-B, the proposed framework design still requires a lot of coding work to be done. The amount of coding can be reduced by implementing the Domain-Specific Language as a layer over the framework functionality.
4) The framework targets exclusively the data-parallel problems, particularly, the particle problems. The framework does not fit for the task-parallel problems. Utilizing the framework for some other data-parallel problems rather than the particle problems may require an implementation of some other *Content* subclasses.
5) There is no possibility to provide immediately some user-driven testing of the framework, since the main advantage of many other approaches (like Flash Code framework, see Subsection II-B) is availability of many different ready-to-use modules, the combination of which leads to the necessary solution. This means that the implemented framework misses the set of built-in modules/functions/classes, which will serve the same purpose.
6) Also the chosen programming language C++ is not an optimal one, because the most of the astrophysicists work at the current moment with Fortran90. This means that the actual using of the framework will imply the change of the working programming language.

The future work on the framework can be performed by extending it with the following features:

- The tree-structure content classes, which can be directly utilized for advanced SPH and NBody simulations. Such classes will significantly enhance the usability of the framework. The usage of the octree structures in the particle problems is the effective method in case of a big number of particles.
- The current implementation of the pthread technology provides an ability to implement a kernel within a pointer to the function of the particular semantic. Such usage schema is not optimal for the big projects with many different kernels. Therefore, it makes sense to have the dynamic calls to the functions for the pthread technology. The most reasonable way to implement the dynamic calling to the functions consists of using the third-party library "dyncall". The library also encapsulates the dynamic function semantic additionally to encapsulating the dynamic calls. This means that the arguments to the function will be passed directly without wrapping them into the *acaf::variant_vector* collection.
- The actual error handling mechanism relies on the initialization order of the error codes. This means that the particular integer error codes are dynamic and can differ within several runs of the same code on different machines. Such inconstant error codes complicate the integration of the framework into the complex applications, since the client application cannot process the errors by the integer codes. Therefore, the error handling should be revised to make the integer error codes more persistent.
- The current content classes provide only the full data range synchronization. This limitation prevents the framework usage for the very big data on the cluster with poor local storage capacities, when the full range of all the necessary data cannot be stored at once in the local memory. In this case, the computation of a single iteration is usually split into several steps. To support such processing schema, the framework needs the content classes for the partially synchronized arrays.
- Another useful feature for the framework is the support of astrophysical-native file formats: Hierarchical Data Format version 5 (HDF5), Flexible Image Transport System (FITS), etc. Such support will make it possible to initialize the data and report the results in the necessary formats without an additional effort from the user.
- Finally, the most valuable modification of the framework lies in designing and implementing of the Domain Specific Language, which is to encapsulate the current numerous framework function calls into the language commands. This modification will make the usage of the framework even more transparent and will significantly decrease the amount of the necessary coding work. Still, the language should preserve an ability to switch to the direct framework calls and to provide the kernel implementation in the technology-native programming languages.

REFERENCES

[1] D. Razmyslovich, G. Marcus, and R. Männer, "Towards an astrophysical-oriented computational multi-architectural framework," in COMPUTATION TOOLS 2016 : The Seventh International Conference on Computational Logics, Algebras, Programming, Tools, and Benchmarking. IARIA, 2016, pp. 19 – 26.

[2] N. Nakasato, G. Ogiya, Y. Miki, M. Mori, and K. Nomoto, "Astrophysical Particle Simulations on Heterogeneous CPU-GPU Systems," Jun. 2012. [Online]. Available: http://arxiv.org/abs/1206.1199

[3] R. Spurzem et al., "Astrophysical particle simulations with large custom GPU clusters on three continents," Computer Science - Research and Development, vol. 26, no. 3-4, Apr. 2011, pp. 145–151. [Online]. Available: http://www.springerlink.com/index/10.1007/s00450-011-0173-1

[4] T. Hamada and K. Nitadori, "190 TFlops Astrophysical N-body Simulation on a Cluster of GPUs," in 2010 ACM/IEEE International Conference for High Performance Computing, Networking, Storage and Analysis, no. November. IEEE, Nov. 2010, pp. 1–9.

[5] S. Braibant, G. Giacomelli, and M. Spurio, Particles and fundamental interactions: an introduction to particle physics, 2nd ed. Springer, 2011.

[6] W. Gropp, E. Lusk, and A. Skjellum, Using MPI (2Nd Ed.): Portable Parallel Programming with the Message-passing Interface. Cambridge, MA, USA: MIT Press, 1999.

[7] H. Wang, S. Potluri, M. Luo, A. Singh, S. Sur, and D. Panda, "Mvapich2-gpu: optimized gpu to gpu communication for infiniband clusters," Computer Science - Research and Development, vol. 26, no. 3-4, 2011, pp. 257–266. [Online]. Available: http://dx.doi.org/10.1007/s00450-011-0171-3

[8] L. Dagum and R. Menon, "Openmp: An industry-standard api for shared-memory programming," IEEE Comput. Sci. Eng., vol. 5, no. 1, Jan. 1998, pp. 46–55. [Online]. Available: http://dx.doi.org/10.1109/99.660313

[9] Khronos Group - OpenCL. [Online]. Available: http://www.khronos.org/opencl [retrieved: Nov., 2016]

[10] CLara. [Online]. Available: https://www.alpha-tierchen.de/ bkoenig/clara/ [retrieved: Nov., 2016]

[11] Khronos Group - SyCL. [Online]. Available: http://www.khronos.org/sycl [retrieved: Nov., 2016]

[12] A. Dubey et al., "A survey of high level frameworks in block-structured adaptive mesh refinement packages," Journal of Parallel and Distributed Computing, 2014.

[13] T. Goodale et al., "The Cactus framework and toolkit: Design and applications," in Vector and Parallel Processing – VECPAR'2002, 5th International Conference, Lecture Notes in Computer Science. Berlin: Springer, 2003. [Online]. Available: http://edoc.mpg.de/3341

[14] P. Jetley, L. Wesolowski, F. Gioachin, L. V. Kalé, and T. R. Quinn, "Scaling hierarchical n-body simulations on gpu clusters." in SC. IEEE, 2010, pp. 1–11. [Online]. Available: http://dblp.uni-trier.de/db/conf/sc/sc2010.html

[15] B. Chamberlain, "Chapel (cray inc. hpcs language)." in Encyclopedia of Parallel Computing, D. A. Padua, Ed. Springer, 2011, pp. 249–256. [Online]. Available: http://dblp.uni-trier.de/db/reference/parallel/parallel2011.html

[16] A. Dubey et al., "The software development process of flash, a multiphysics simulation code." in SE-CSE@ICSE, J. Carver, Ed. IEEE, 2013, pp. 1–8. [Online]. Available: http://dblp.uni-trier.de/db/conf/icse/secse2013.html

[17] B. Fryxell et al., "FLASH: An adaptive mesh hydrodynamics code for modeling astrophysical thermonuclear flashes," Astrophys. J. Supp., vol. 131, Nov. 2000, pp. 273–334. [Online]. Available: http://dx.doi.org/10.1086/317361

[18] S. Zwart, "The astronomical multipurpose software environment and the ecology of star clusters." in CCGRID. IEEE Computer Society, 2013, p. 202. [Online]. Available: http://dblp.uni-trier.de/db/conf/ccgrid/ccgrid2013.html

[19] S. Dindar et al., "Swarm-ng: a cuda library for parallel n-body integrations with focus on simulations of planetary systems," CoRR, vol. abs/1208.1157, 2012. [Online]. Available: http://dblp.uni-trier.de/db/journals/corr/corr1208.html

[20] The Enzo project. [Online]. Available: http://enzo-project.org/ [retrieved: Nov., 2016]

[21] J. Bezanson, A. Edelman, S. Karpinski, and V. B. Shah, "Julia: A fresh approach to numerical computing," CoRR, vol. abs/1411.1607, 2014. [Online]. Available: http://arxiv.org/abs/1411.1607

[22] P. Charles et al., "X10: An object-oriented approach to non-uniform cluster computing," SIGPLAN Not., vol. 40, no. 10, Oct. 2005, pp. 519–538. [Online]. Available: http://doi.acm.org/10.1145/1103845.1094852

[23] C. Feichtinger, S. Donath, H. Köstler, J. Götz, and U. Rüde, "WaLBerla: HPC software design for computational engineering simulations," Journal of Computational Science, vol. 2, no. 2, May 2011, pp. 105–112. [Online]. Available: http://dx.doi.org/10.1016/j.jocs.2011.01.004

[24] I. Antcheva et al., "{ROOT} - a c++ framework for petabyte data storage, statistical analysis and visualization," Computer Physics Communications, vol. 180, no. 12, 2009, pp. 2499 – 2512, 40 {YEARS} {OF} CPC: A celebratory issue focused on quality software for high performance, grid and novel computing architectures. [Online]. Available: http://www.sciencedirect.com/science/article/pii/S0010465509002550

[25] A. Lazzaro, S. Jarp, J. Leduc, A. Nowak, and L. Valsan, "Report on the parallelization of the MLfit benchmark using OpenMP and MPI," CERN, Geneva, Tech. Rep. CERN-OPEN-2014-030, Jul 2012. [Online]. Available: https://cds.cern.ch/record/1696947

[26] libconfig – C/C++ configuration file library. [Online]. Available: http://www.hyperrealm.com/libconfig/ [retrieved: Nov., 2016]

[27] TOP500. [Online]. Available: https://en.wikipedia.org/wiki/TOP500 [retrieved: Nov., 2016]

Adaptive Parameter-Dependent Output Feedback Controllers Synthesis Through LMI-Based Optimization

Graziano Chesi

Department of Electrical and Electronic Engineering
The University of Hong Kong
Pokfulam Road, Hong Kong
Hong Kong SAR
Email: chesi@eee.hku.hk

***Abstract*—A fundamental problem in engineering consists of designing adaptive output feedback controllers for stabilizing plants affected by parameters. This paper addresses this problem by proposing a novel approach for designing fixed-order fixed-degree adaptive parameter-dependent output feedback controllers. The proposed approach requires the solution of convex optimization problems with linear matrix inequalities, and provides a sufficient condition based on the construction of a function that quantifies a stability margin of the closed-loop system depending on the controller. This condition is nonconservative under some mild assumptions by increasing the size of the linear matrix inequalities.**

***Index Terms*—Adaptive Controller; Parameter-dependent; Stability; Linear matrix inequality.**

I. Introduction

A fundamental problem in engineering consists of stabilizing a plant. This is generally achieved by designing a stabilizing output feedback controller, i.e., a controller that elaborates the output of the plant in order to provide an input for the plant that makes the closed-loop system is stable. The design of such a controller is based on the model of the plant, and several techniques can be used.

Real plants are often affected by parameters. These can happen due to various reasons. One reason is that such parameters can represent quantities that the user can modify, such as the gain of an amplifier, in order to achieve a different performance. Another reason is that such parameters can represent quantities that are unknown or subject to changes, such as the mass, resistance, temperature, etc.

Whenever the plant is affected by parameters, the output feedback controller should be able to ensure stability for all admissible values of the parameters. For this, the controller should be dependent on the parameters in general, i.e., should be able to adapt to different plants corresponding to different values of the parameters. Such a controller would be, hence, adaptive, in particular parameter-dependent.

This paper addresses this problem, specifically, the design of adaptive output feedback controllers for stabilizing plants affected by time-invariant parameters. A preliminary conference version of this paper appeared as reported in [1].

It turns out that this is a difficult problem. Indeed, several conditions do exist in the literature for establishing stability of systems affected by parameters, in particular conditions based on convex optimization constrained by Linear Matrix Inequalities (LMIs); see for instance [2] [3] [4] [5] [6] [7] [8] [9]. However, such conditions lead to nonconvex optimization whenever a controller is searched for, due to the product of the Lyapunov function and the controller that generates Bilinear Matrix Inequalities (BMIs). See also [10] [11] for related studies. Also, several non-LMI strategies are available for the design of stabilizing feedback controllers for plants that are not affected by parameters, however, for plants affected by parameters, such strategies cannot be easily used in general.

In order to deal with this problem, a novel approach is proposed in this paper, which allows one to design a fixed-order fixed-degree adaptive parameter-dependent output feedback controller by solving convex optimization problems with LMIs. The proposed approach requires the solution of convex optimization problems with LMIs, and provides a sufficient condition based on the construction of a function that quantifies a stability margin of the closed-loop system depending on the controller. This function is searched for by exploiting polynomials that can be written as Sums Of Squares (SOS) of polynomials. The sufficient condition provided in this paper is nonconservative under some mild assumptions by increasing the size of the LMIs. Some numerical examples illustrate the proposed approach. This paper extends the technique for the design of robust static output feedback controllers proposed in our previous work [12].

The paper is organized as follows. Section II introduces the preliminaries. Section III discusses the motivation. Section IV describes the proposed approach. Section V present some illustrative examples. Lastly, Section VI concludes the paper with some final remarks.

II. Preliminaries

This section provides the preliminaries. Specifically, Section II-A introduces the problem formulation, and Section II-B reviews the class of SOS polynomials.

A. Problem Formulation

The notation adopted in this paper is as follows:

- $\mathbb{N}$: set of nonnegative integer numbers;
- $\mathbb{R}$: set of real numbers;
- $\mathbb{C}$: set of complex numbers;
- I: $n \times n$ identity matrix (of size specified by the context);
- A': transpose of matrix A;
- $adj(A)$: adjoint of matrix A;
- $\det(A)$: determinant of matrix A;
- $spec(A)$: set of eigenvalues of matrix A;
- $A > 0$: symmetric positive definite matrix A;
- $A \geq 0$: symmetric positive semidefinite matrix A;
- $\deg(a(x))$: degree of polynomial $a(x)$;
- s.t.: subject to.

Let us consider the plant

$$\left\{ \begin{array}{rcl} \dot{x}(t) & = & A_{pla}(p)x_{pla}(t) + B_{pla}(p)u(t) \\ y(t) & = & C_{pla}(p)x_{pla}(t) + D_{pla}(p)u(t) \end{array} \right. \quad (1)$$

where $t \in \mathbb{R}$ is the time, $x_{pla}(t) \in \mathbb{R}^{n_{pla}}$ is the state, $u(t) \in \mathbb{R}^{n_u}$ is the input, $y(t) \in \mathbb{R}^{n_y}$ is the output, $p \in \mathbb{R}^q$ is the vector of time-invariant parameters, and the matrices $A_{pla}(p)$, $B_{pla}(p)$, $C_{pla}(p)$ and $D_{pla}(p)$ are given matrix polynomials.

It is supposed that the vector of parameters is constrained into a semi-algebraic set, in particular

$$p \in \mathcal{P} \quad (2)$$

where

$$\mathcal{P} = \{p \in \mathbb{R}^q : \ a_i(p) \geq 0, \ i = 1 \ldots, n_a\} \quad (3)$$

and $a_i(p)$, $i = 1, \ldots, n_a$, are polynomials.

The plant (1) is controlled by the parameter-dependent output feedback controller

$$\left\{ \begin{array}{rcl} \dot{x_{con}}(t) & = & A_{con}(p)x_{con}(t) + B_{con}(p)y(t) \\ u(t) & = & C_{con}(p)x_{con}(t) + D_{con}(p)y(t) \end{array} \right. \quad (4)$$

where $x_{con}(t) \in \mathbb{R}^{n_{con}}$ is the state of chosen order $n_{con} \in \mathbb{N}$, and the matrices $A_{con}(p)$, $B_{con}(p)$, $C_{con}(p)$ and $D_{con}(p)$ are matrix polynomials to determine of chosen degree. For computation purpose, these matrix polynomials are expressed as

$$\left\{ \begin{array}{rcl} A_{con}(p) & = & \Phi_A(p,v) \\ B_{con}(p) & = & \Phi_B(p,v) \\ C_{con}(p) & = & \Phi_C(p,v) \\ D_{con}(p) & = & \Phi_D(p,v) \end{array} \right. \quad (5)$$

where $v \in \mathbb{R}^w$ is a vector of design variables, and $\Phi_A(p,v)$, $\Phi_B(p,v)$, $\Phi_C(p,v)$ and $\Phi_D(p,v)$ are matrix polynomials in p and v. The vector of design variables is searched for in the semi-algebraic set

$$\mathcal{V} = \{v \in \mathbb{R}^w : \ b_i(v) \geq 0, \ i = 1 \ldots, n_b\} \quad (6)$$

where $b_i(v)$, $i = 1, \ldots, n_b$, are polynomials. We denote the set of controllers (4) obtainable for $v \in \mathcal{V}$ as $\mathcal{C}$, i.e.,

$$\mathcal{C} = \{\langle \Phi_A(p,v), \Phi_B(p,v), \Phi_C(p,v), \Phi_D(p,v)\rangle : \ v \in \mathcal{V}\}. \quad (7)$$

The problem addressed in this paper is as follows.

Problem 1: Find a fixed-order fixed-degree output feedback controller (4) in the set $\mathcal{C}$ such that the closed-loop system (1)–(4) is well-posed and asymptotically stable for all parameters $p \in \mathcal{P}$.

□

Let us observe that Problem 1 contains several specific problems of interest, in particular the design of:

1) fixed-order (such as static) output feedback controllers for parameter-free systems, i.e., with no dependence on p;
2) common fixed-order (such as static) output feedback controllers for systems affected by parameters;
3) parameter-dependent (such as linearly) fixed-order (such as static) output feedback controllers for systems affected by parameters.

B. SOS Polynomials

Here we briefly review SOS polynomials; see for instance [13] and references therein for details. Let us start by introducing the following definition.

Definition 1: A polynomial $h(v)$ is said to be *SOS* if there exist polynomials $h_i(v)$, $i = 1, \ldots, k$, such that

$$h(v) = \sum_{i=1}^{k} h_i(v)^2. \quad (8)$$

□

A necessary and sufficient condition for establishing whether a polynomial is SOS can be given in terms of feasibility of an LMI. Specifically, let $d \in \mathbb{N}$ be such that

$$\deg(h(v)) \leq 2d. \quad (9)$$

Let $v^{\{d\}} \in \mathbb{R}^{\sigma(w,d)}$ be a vector whose entries are the monomials of degree not greater than d in x, e.g., according to

$$v^{\{d\}} = \left(1, v_1, \ldots, v_w, v_1^2, v_1 v_2, \ldots, v_w^d\right)' \quad (10)$$

where $\sigma(w,d)$ is the total number of such monomials given by

$$\sigma(w,d) = \frac{(w+d)!}{w!d!}. \tag{11}$$

Then, $h(v)$ can be expressed as

$$h(v) = v^{\{d\}'}\left(H + L(\alpha)\right)v^{\{d\}} \tag{12}$$

where $H \in \mathbb{R}^{\sigma(w,d)\times\sigma(w,d)}$ is a symmetric matrix such that

$$h(v) = v^{\{d\}'}Hv^{\{d\}}, \tag{13}$$

$L : \mathbb{R}^{\omega(w,d)} \to \mathbb{R}^{\sigma(w,d)\times\sigma(w,d)}$ is a linear parametrization of the linear subspace

$$\mathcal{L}(w,d) = \{L = L' : \ w^{\{d\}'}Lw^{\{d\}} = 0\}, \tag{14}$$

and $\alpha \in \mathbb{R}^{\omega(w,d)}$ is a free vector, where $\omega(w,d)$ is the dimension of $\mathcal{L}(w,d)$ given by

$$\omega(w,d) = \frac{1}{2}\sigma(w,d)(\sigma(w,d)+1) - \sigma(w,2d). \tag{15}$$

The representation (12) is known as Gram matrix method and square matricial representation (SMR). This representation allows one to establish whether a polynomial is SOS via an LMI feasibility test, which amounts to solving a convex optimization problem. Indeed, $h(v)$ is SOS if and only if there exists α satisfying the LMI

$$H + L(\alpha) \geq 0. \tag{16}$$

III. Motivation

This section explains the motivation for the proposed study. Specifically, Section III-A presents an example where the set of controllers that solve Problem 1 is nonconvex, and Section III-B presents an example where Problem 1 can be solved with a parameter-dependent controller but cannot be solved with a common controller.

A. Example 1

Hereafter, we present an example that highlights the difficulty of solving Problem 1, in particular showing that the set of controllers that solve this problem can be nonconvex.

Indeed, let us consider the plant (1) with

$$\left\{\begin{array}{lcl} A_{pla}(p) & = & \begin{pmatrix} 0.4 & -0.5p-0.5 & -2 \\ 4 & 0.3 & 0.7p-3.5 \\ 0.8p+2.2 & 3 & -1.3 \end{pmatrix} \\ B_{pla}(p) & = & \begin{pmatrix} 0 & -0.6 \\ -0.5 & 0.3 \\ 0 & -0.9 \end{pmatrix} \\ C_{pla}(p) & = & \begin{pmatrix} 1 & 1 & -1.6 \end{pmatrix} \\ D_{pla}(p) & = & \begin{pmatrix} 0 & 0 \end{pmatrix} \end{array}\right.$$

where the parameter p is constrained into the set

$$\mathcal{P} = [-1, 1].$$

This plant is controlled in closed-loop by the feedback controller (4) chosen of the form

$$\left\{\begin{array}{rcl} u(t) & = & D_{con}(p)y(t) \\ \deg(D_{con}(p)) & = & 0, \end{array}\right.$$

i.e., a common static output feedback controller. This controller is expressed as in (5) with

$$\Phi_D(p,v) = v$$

where $v \in \mathbb{R}^2$ is the vector of design variables constrained into the set

$$\mathcal{V} = [-3,3]^2.$$

Figure 1 shows the set of controllers v that solve Problem 1 found by brute force. As it can be seen, this set is nonconvex in this case.

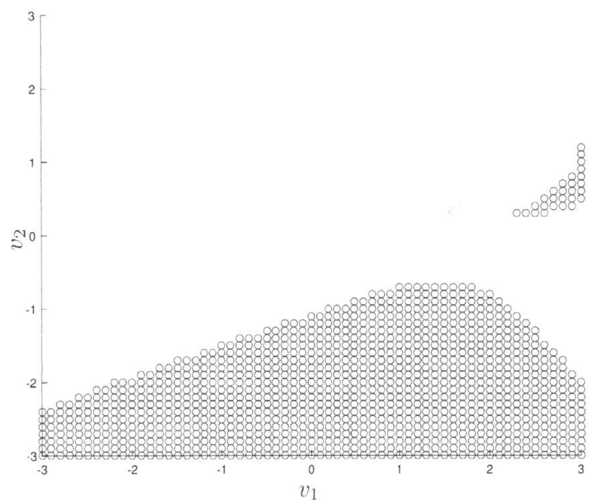

Fig. 1. Example 1. Set of controllers v that solve Problem 1 found by brute force. As it can be seen, the set is nonconvex in this case.

B. Example 2

Hereafter, we present an example that motivates the search for controllers that depend on the parameters for solving Problem 1, in particular showing that there exists such a controller but there does not exist any common controller that solves Problem 1.

Indeed, let us consider the plant (1) with

$$\left\{\begin{array}{lcl} A_{pla}(p) & = & \begin{pmatrix} -1 & 0 & -p+1 \\ 0 & -1 & 1 \\ p+1 & 0 & 0 \end{pmatrix} \\ B_{pla}(p) & = & \begin{pmatrix} 0 \\ 1 \\ 1 \end{pmatrix} \\ C_{pla}(p) & = & \begin{pmatrix} 1 & p & 0 \end{pmatrix} \\ D_{pla}(p) & = & 0 \end{array}\right.$$

where the parameter p is constrained into the set

$$\mathcal{P} = [-2, 2].$$

This plant is controlled in closed-loop by the feedback controller (4) chosen of the form

$$\begin{cases} u(t) &= D_{con}(p)y(t) \\ \deg(D_{con}(p)) &\leq 1, \end{cases}$$

i.e., a parameter-dependent static output feedback controller of degree not greater than 1 in the parameter. This controller is expressed as in (5) with

$$\Phi_D(p, v) = v_1 + v_2 p$$

where $v \in \mathbb{R}^2$ is the vector of design variables constrained into the set

$$\mathcal{V} = [-2, 2]^2.$$

Figure 2 shows the set of controllers v that solve Problem 1 found by brute force. As it can be seen, there exist parameter-dependent controllers but there do not exist common controllers that solve Problem 1 in this case.

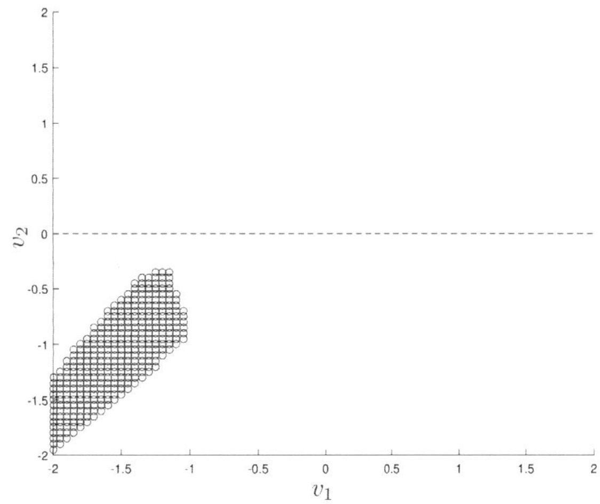

Fig. 2. Example 2. Set of controllers v that solve Problem 1 found by brute force. The dashed line denotes the region of common controllers. As it can be seen, there exist parameter-dependent controllers but there do not exist common controllers that solve Problem 1 in this case.

IV. Proposed Approach

This section provides the proposed approach. Specifically, Section IV-A derives the equation of the closed-loop system, Section IV-B investigates the well-posedness, Section IV-C tackles the asymptotical stability, Section IV-D derives the optimization problem used to determine a sought solution, Section IV-E explains how to determine such a solution, Section IV-F investigates the non-conservatism of the proposed approach, and Section IV-G reports some remarks.

A. Closed-Loop System

The first step of the proposed approach is to express the closed-loop system (1)–(4) as

$$\dot{x}(t) = A(p, v)x(t) \tag{17}$$

where $x \in \mathbb{R}^n$ is the state

$$x(t) = \begin{pmatrix} x_{pla}(t) \\ x_{con}(t) \end{pmatrix} \tag{18}$$

of dimension

$$n = n_{pla} + n_{con}, \tag{19}$$

and $A(p, v)$ is a matrix rational function in p and v. In particular, the expression of $A(p, v)$ is given by

$$A(p, v) = \begin{pmatrix} A_1(p, v) & A_2(p, v) \\ A_3(p, v) & A_4(p, v) \end{pmatrix} \tag{20}$$

where

$$\begin{cases} A_1(p, v) &= B_{pla}(p)E(p, v)^{-1}\Phi_D(p, v)C_{pla}(p) \\ & \quad +A_{pla}(p) \\ A_2(p, v) &= B_{pla}(p)E(p, v)^{-1}\Phi_C(p, v) \\ A_3(p, v) &= \Phi_B(p, v)\left(D_{pla}(p)E(p, v)^{-1}\Phi_D(p, v)\right. \\ & \quad \left.+I\right)C_{pla}(p) \\ A_4(p, v) &= \Phi_B(p, v)D_{pla}(p)E(p, v)^{-1}\Phi_C(p, v) \\ & \quad +\Phi_A(p, v) \end{cases} \tag{21}$$

and

$$E(p, v) = I - \Phi_D(p, v)D_{pla}(p). \tag{22}$$

The matrix rational function $A(p, v)$ can be expressed as

$$A(p, v) = \frac{A_{num}(p, v)}{A_{den}(p, v)} \tag{23}$$

where $A_{num}(p, v)$ is a matrix polynomial and $A_{den}(p, v)$ is a polynomial in p and v. Let us observe that $A_{num}(p, v)$ and $A_{den}(p, v)$ are non-unique since they are defined up to a scaling function. Hereafter, we adopt the following expressions for $A_{num}(p, v)$ and $A_{den}(p, v)$:

$$\begin{cases} A_{num}(p, v) &= adj(E(p, v)) \\ A_{den}(p, v) &= \det(E(p, v)). \end{cases} \tag{24}$$

B. Well-Posedness

The second step of the proposed approach addresses the well-posedness of the closed-loop system (1)–(4). Let us start by formally defining this concept as follows.

Definition 2: The closed-loop system (1)–(4) is said to be *well-posed* for all parameters $p \in \mathcal{P}$ for some controller v if the matrix $A(p, v)$ in (17) does exist for all $p \in \mathcal{P}$.

□

Let us observe that the matrix $A(p,v)$ in (17) does exist for all parameters $p \in \mathcal{P}$ for some controller v whenever

$$E(p,v) \text{ is non-singular } \forall p \in \mathcal{P}. \tag{25}$$

In this paper we impose well-posedness of the closed-loop system (1)–(4) by requiring that

$$|A_{den}(p,v)| > \rho_{wep} \quad \forall p \in \mathcal{P} \tag{26}$$

where $\rho_{wep} \geq 0$ is an arbitrary chosen threshold.

C. Asymptotical Stability

The third step of the proposed approach consists of ensuring asymptotical stability of the closed-loop system (1)–(4). Let us start by formally defining this concept as follows.

Definition 3: The closed-loop system (1)–(4) is said to be *asymptotically stable* for all parameters $p \in \mathcal{P}$ for some controller v if

$$\Re(\lambda) < 0 \quad \forall \lambda \in spec(A(p,v)) \ \forall p \in \mathcal{P}. \tag{27}$$

□

In this paper we impose asymptotical stability of the closed-loop system (1)–(4) by requiring that

$$\Re(\lambda) < -\rho_{sta} \quad \forall \lambda \in spec(A(p,v)) \ \forall p \in \mathcal{P} \tag{28}$$

where $\rho_{sta} \geq 0$ is an arbitrary chosen threshold.

In order to impose this constraint, let $\theta \in \Theta$ be an auxiliary variable, where

$$\Theta = \{-1, 1\}, \tag{29}$$

and let us define the characteristic polynomial of $\theta A_{num}(p,v)$ as

$$c(\lambda, p, v) = \det\left(\lambda I - \theta\left(A_{num}(p,v) + \rho_{sta} A_{den}(p,v) I\right)\right) \tag{30}$$

where $\lambda \in \mathbb{R}$ is an auxiliary variable. Let us express this characteristic polynomial as

$$c(\lambda, p, v) = \sum_{i=0}^{n} \tilde{c}_i(p,v)\lambda^i \tag{31}$$

where $\tilde{c}_i(p,v)$, $i = 1, \ldots, n$, are polynomials in p and v. Let us build the table

$$\begin{array}{ccc} r_{1,1}(p,v) & r_{1,2}(p,v) & \ldots \\ r_{2,1}(p,v) & r_{2,2}(p,v) & \ldots \\ \vdots & \vdots & \ddots \end{array} \tag{32}$$

where the generic entry in position (i,j), $i = 3, \ldots, n+1$ and $j = 1, 2, \ldots$, is given by

$$\begin{array}{rcl} r_{i,j}(p,v) & = & r_{i-1,j}(p,v) r_{i-2,j+1}(p,v) \\ & & -r_{i-2,j}(p,v) r_{i-1,j+1}(p,v) \end{array} \tag{33}$$

by using the initialization

$$\left\{ \begin{array}{rcl} r_{1,j}(p,v) & = & \tilde{c}_{n+1-2j}(p,v) \\ r_{2,j}(p,v) & = & \tilde{c}_{n-2j}(p,v). \end{array} \right. \tag{34}$$

Let us observe that the entries of the built table are polynomials in p and v.

The closed-loop system (1)–(4) is asymptotically stable for all parameters $p \in \mathcal{P}$ for some controller v if and only if

$$\left\{ \begin{array}{rcl} r_{i,1}(p,v) & > & 0 \ \forall i = 2, \ldots, n+1 \ \forall p \in \mathcal{P} \\ \theta A_{den}(p,v) & > & 0. \end{array} \right. \tag{35}$$

D. Optimization Problem

The fourth step of the proposed approach consists of introducing an optimization problem that will be used to determine a controller that solves Problem 1, if any.

Let us start by defining the polynomials $f_i(p,v)$, $i = 1, \ldots, n+1$, in p and v as

$$\left\{ \begin{array}{rcl} f_1(p,v) & = & \theta A_{den}(p,v) - \rho_{wep} \\ f_i(p,v) & = & r_{i,1}(p,v) \ \forall i = 2, \ldots, n+1. \end{array} \right. \tag{36}$$

Let $\xi(v)$, $\beta_{i,j}(p,v)$, $\gamma_{i,k}(p,v)$ and $\delta_k(v)$ be auxiliary polynomial variables, $i = 1, \ldots, n+1$, $j = 1, \ldots, n_a$ and $k = 1, \ldots, n_b$, and let us define

$$\left\{ \begin{array}{rcl} g_i(p,v) & = & f_i(p,v) - \xi(v) - \sum_{j=1}^{n_a} a_j(p)\beta_{i,j}(p,v) \\ & & -\sum_{k=1}^{n_b} b_k(v)\gamma_{i,k}(p,v) \\ h(v) & = & \rho_{pos} - \xi(v) - \sum_{k=1}^{n_b} b_k(v)\delta_k(v) \end{array} \right. \tag{37}$$

where $\rho_{pos} > 0$ is a chosen threshold whose role will be clarified in the sequel. Let us define the integral of $\xi(v)$ over $\mathcal{V}$ as

$$\Xi = \int_{\mathcal{V}} \xi(v)dv. \tag{38}$$

Let us observe that Ξ is a linear function of the coefficients of $\xi(v)$.

Let us define the optimization problem

$$\begin{array}{l} \Xi^* = \sup\limits_{\xi, \beta_{i,j}, \gamma_{i,k}, \delta_k} \Xi \\ \text{s.t.} \left\{ \begin{array}{l} g_i(p,v),\ h(v) \ \text{ are SOS} \\ \beta_{i,j}(p,v),\ \gamma_{i,k}(p,v),\ \delta_k(v) \ \text{ are SOS} \\ \forall i = 1, \ldots, n+1 \\ \forall j = 1, \ldots, n_a \\ \forall k = 1, \ldots, n_b. \end{array} \right. \end{array} \tag{39}$$

The optimization problem (39) is convex. Indeed, the cost function is linear in the decision variables, which are the coefficients of the polynomials $\xi(v)$, $\beta_{i,j}(p,v)$, $\gamma_{i,k}(p,v)$ and $\delta_k(v)$. Moreover, the constraints impose that some polynomials, which depend affine linearly on the decision variables, are SOS. From Section II-B it follows that these constraints are equivalent to LMIs in the decision variables and auxiliary variables. Therefore, the optimization problem (39) is convex since the cost function is convex and since the feasible set is convex.

Let us observe that the polynomial $\xi(v)$ quantifies a stability margin of the closed-loop system depending on the controller. This polynomial generalizes the concept of robust stabilizability function introduced in [12] for the design of robust static output feedback controllers.

E. Determining The Controller

The fifth step of the proposed approach consists of determining a controller that solves Problem 1, if any, from the solution of the optimization problem (39).

Specifically, let $h^*(v)$ and $\xi^*(v)$ be the optimal values of the polynomials $h(v)$ and $\xi(v)$ in the optimization problem (39). Let us define the set

$$\mathcal{H} = \{v \in \mathbb{R}^w : \ h^*(v) = 0, \ \xi^*(v) = \rho_{pos}, \ v \in \mathcal{V}\}. \quad (40)$$

The following theorem explains how Problem 1 can be solved with the proposed approached.

Theorem 1: All vectors v in the set $\mathcal{H}$, if any, define a controller (4) with matrices given by (5) that solves Problem 1.

Proof. See Appendix 1. □

Theorem 1 provides a sufficient condition for the solution of Problem 1. As it will be explained in the next section, this condition is nonconservative provided that some assumptions hold. The condition of Theorem 1 is based on the set $\mathcal{H}$, which is determined once that the optimization problem (39) has been solved.

How to determine the set $\mathcal{H}$? This can be done according to the following two steps:

1) search for the zeros of $h^*(v)$;
2) keep the zeros of $h^*(v)$ that satisfy $\xi^*(v) = \rho_{pos}$ and $v \in \mathcal{V}$.

The first step can be addressed via linear algebra operations once that the optimization problem (39) has been solved. A possibility consists of using the method proposed in [14] for solving systems of polynomial equations as explained hereafter:

1) once that the optimization problem (39) has been solved, one obtains from the LMI solver a positive semidefinite Gram matrix of $h^*(v)$, i.e., a matrix $H^* \geq 0$ such that
$$h^*(v) = v^{\{d\}'} H^* v^{\{d\}} \quad (41)$$
where $v^{\{d\}}$ is a vector of monomials in v;
2) since $H^* \geq 0$, one has that $h^*(v) = 0$ if and only if
$$v^{\{d\}} \in \ker(H^*). \quad (42)$$
Hence, the problem of finding the zeros of $h^*(v)$ is equivalent to the problem of finding vectors of monomials in $\ker(H^*)$;
3) the problem of finding vectors of monomials in $\ker(H^*)$ can be addressed by pivoting operations that reduce the problem to finding the roots of a polynomial in a single variable whenever the dimension of $\ker(H^*)$ is smaller than a certain value as shown in [14].

The second step is trivial since the number of zeros of $h^*(v)$ is finite for non-degenerate cases (one just keep the zeros that satisfy $\xi^*(v) = \rho_{pos}$ and $v \in \mathcal{V}$ through individual tests).

F. Non-Conservatism

The previous section has provided a sufficient condition for the solution of Problem 1 through Theorem 1. As it will be explained in the next section, this condition may be nonconservative. Let us start by introducing the following assumption.

Assumption 1: The sets $\mathcal{P}$ and $\mathcal{V}$ are compact. Moreover, the polynomials $a_i(p)$, $i = 1,\ldots,n_a$, in (3) and $b_i(v)$, $i = 1,\ldots,n_b$, in (6) have even degree, and their highest degree forms have no common root except zero.

□

The following theorem explains that the sufficient condition provided by Theorem 1 is nonconservative whenever Assumption 1 holds.

Theorem 2: Suppose that there exists a controller (4) with matrices given by (5) for some $v \in \mathcal{V}$ that solves Problem 1. Also, suppose that Assumption 1 holds. Then, the set $\mathcal{H}$ is nonempty for some $\theta \in \Theta$ for any sufficiently small threshold $\rho_{pos} > 0$.

Proof. See Appendix 2. □

It is worth observing that Assumption 1 introduces mild assumptions on Problem 1. Indeed, it is reasonable to assume that the sets $\mathcal{P}$ and $\mathcal{V}$ are compact, since the allowed values for parameters and controllers are bounded in practice, and since having $\mathcal{P}$ and $\mathcal{V}$ closed rather than open does not make differences in general. Also, one can assume without loss of generality that the polynomials $a_i(p)$, $i = 1,\ldots,n_a$, in (3) and $b_i(v)$, $i = 1, \ldots, n_b$, in (6) have even degree, because, if not, one could multiply the polynomials with odd degree times linear functions that are positive over $\mathcal{P}$ and $\mathcal{V}$ in order to fill this requirement without modifying $\mathcal{P}$ and $\mathcal{V}$. Lastly, the assumption that the highest degree forms of these polynomials have no common root except zero is automatically satisfied in many cases of interests. For instance, ellipsoids can be described by polynomials such as

$$a_1(p) = p'M_2p + M_1'p + M_0 \tag{43}$$

where $M_0 \in \mathbb{R}$, $M_1 \in \mathbb{R}^q$ and $M_2 \in \mathbb{R}^{q\times q}$, with $M_2 > 0$, and the highest degree form is $p'M_2p$ whose only possible root is the origin. Moreover, interval sets can be described by polynomials such as

$$a_i(p) = (m_{i,-} - p_i)(p_i - m_{i,+}) \quad \forall i = 1, \ldots, q \tag{44}$$

where $m_{i,-}, m_{i,+} \in \mathbb{R}$, with $m_{i,-} \le m_{i,+}$, and the highest degree forms are $-p_i^2$ whose only possible common root is the origin.

G. Remarks

The first remarks concerns the well-posedness of the closed-loop system (1)–(4). Let us observe that, whenever the plant (1) is strictly proper (i.e., $D_{pla}(p) = 0$) or the controller (4) is strictly proper (i.e., $D_{con}(p) = 0$), well-posedness is automatically satisfied, and (26) holds for any $\rho_{wep} \in [0, 1)$. This means that the polynomial $f_1(p, v)$ in (36) does not need to be introduced, and one can simply redefine (36) as

$$f_{i-1}(p, v) = r_{i,1}(p, v) \quad \forall i = 2, \ldots, n + 1. \tag{45}$$

The second remark concerns the polynomials $f_i(p, v)$ in (36). The polynomials $f_i(p, v)$ that are known to be positive over $\mathcal{P} \times \mathcal{V}$ (such as positive constants) do not need to be introduced, since the proposed approach aims to collect in the set $\mathcal{H}$ vectors v such that the polynomials $f_i(p, v)$ are positive for all parameters $p \in \mathcal{P}$. This also implies that, if there exists a polynomial $f_i(p, v)$ that is known to be non-positive for all parameters $p \in \mathcal{P}$ (such as non-positive constants), then Problem 1 has no solution.

The third remark concerns the threshold ρ_{pos} introduced in the polynomial $h(v)$ in (37). This threshold has to be chosen as a positive number, and it is introduced in order to ensure that the vectors v in the set $\mathcal{H}$ satisfy $\xi^*(v) > 0$ (since $\xi^*(v) = \rho_{pos}$). As said in the statement of Theorem 2, non-conservatism is ensured whenever ρ_{pos} is a sufficiently small positive number. Hence, one can simply choose ρ_{pos} as the smallest positive number allowed by the used computer.

V. Examples

In this section we present some illustrative examples of the proposed results. The computations are done in Matlab using the toolbox SeDuMi [15]. The threshold ρ_{wep} is not introduced since the considered plants are strict, and the other thresholds are chosen as $\rho_{sta} = 0$ and $\rho_{pos} = 0.1$. The degrees of the polynomials $\beta_{i,j}(p, v)$, $\gamma_{i,k}(p, v)$ and $\delta_k(v)$ are chosen as the largest degrees ensuring that the polynomials $g_{i,j}(p, v)$ and $h(v)$ have their minimum degrees.

A. Example 1 (continued)

Let us continue Example 1. Let us start by observing that the plant (1) is unstable for some values of the parameter, for instance

$$p = 0 \quad \Rightarrow \quad spec(A_{pla}(p)) = \{-1.049, 0.224 \pm j4.066\}.$$

This fact is also shown by Figure 3, which shows the eigenvalues of the plant for some values of the parameters in $\mathcal{P}$.

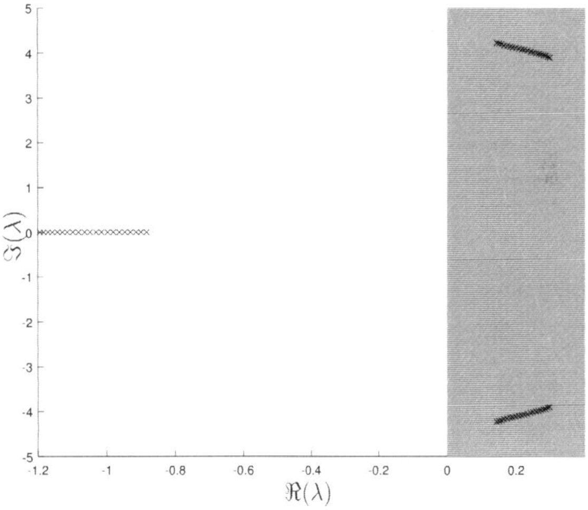

Fig. 3. Example 1. Eigenvalues λ of the plant (1) for some values of the parameters in $\mathcal{P}$. The dashed area denotes the region of unstable eigenvalues.

Let us describe the sets $\mathcal{P}$ and $\mathcal{V}$ as in (3) and (6) with

$$\begin{cases} a_1(p) &= 1 - p^2 \\ b_i(v) &= 9 - v_i^2 \quad \forall i = 1, 2. \end{cases}$$

Let us solve the optimization problem (39) by using a polynomial variable $\xi(v)$ of degree not greater than 2. We find

$$\begin{cases} \Xi^* &= -703.772 \\ \xi^*(v) &= -1.389v_1^2 + 0.977v_1v_2 + 5.686v_1 - 1.482v_2^2 \\ & \quad -7.230v_2 - 10.936. \end{cases}$$

Next, we determine the set $\mathcal{H}$ as explained in Section IV-E, finding

$$\mathcal{H} = \left\{ \begin{pmatrix} 1.345 \\ -1.995 \end{pmatrix} \right\}.$$

Therefore, from Theorem 1 we conclude that the controller obtained from the vector v in $\mathcal{H}$, i.e.,

$$D_{con}(p) = \begin{pmatrix} 1.345 \\ -1.995 \end{pmatrix}$$

solves Problem 1. This fact is also shown by Figure 4, which shows the eigenvalues of the closed-loop system (1)–(4) obtained with the found controller for some values of the parameters in $\mathcal{P}$.

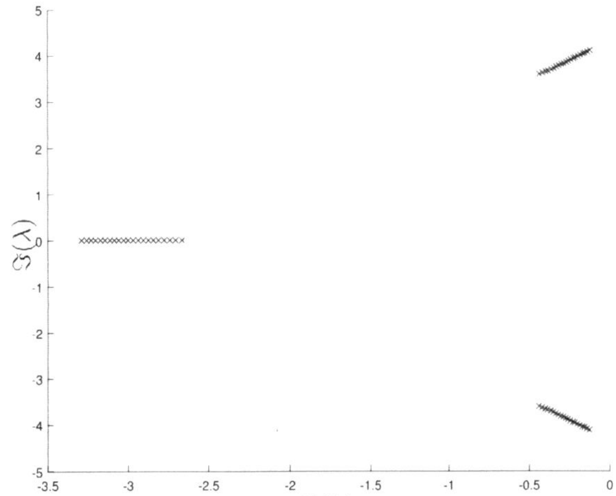

Fig. 4. Example 1. Eigenvalues λ of the closed-loop system (1)–(4) for some values of the parameters in $\mathcal{P}$.

B. Example 2 (continued)

Let us continue Example 2. Let us start by observing that the plant (1) is unstable for some values of the parameter, for instance

$$p = 0 \quad \Rightarrow \quad spec(A_{pla}(p)) = \{-1.618, -1, 0.618\}.$$

This fact is also shown by Figure 5, which shows the eigenvalues of the plant for some values of the parameters in $\mathcal{P}$.

Let us describe the sets $\mathcal{P}$ and $\mathcal{V}$ as in (3) and (6) with

$$\begin{cases} a_1(p) &= 4 - p^2 \\ b_i(v) &= 4 - v_i^2 \quad \forall i = 1, 2. \end{cases}$$

Let us solve the optimization problem (39) by using a polynomial variable $\xi(v)$ of degree not greater than 3. We find

$$\begin{cases} \Xi^* &= -160.105 \\ \xi^*(v) &= 0.149v_1^3 - 0.912v_1^2 v_2 - 1.288v_1^2 \\ & \quad -0.598v_1 v_2^2 - 0.676v_1 v_2 - 1.501v_1 \\ & \quad +0.377v_2^3 - 2.822v_2^2 - 6.242v_2 - 4.527. \end{cases}$$

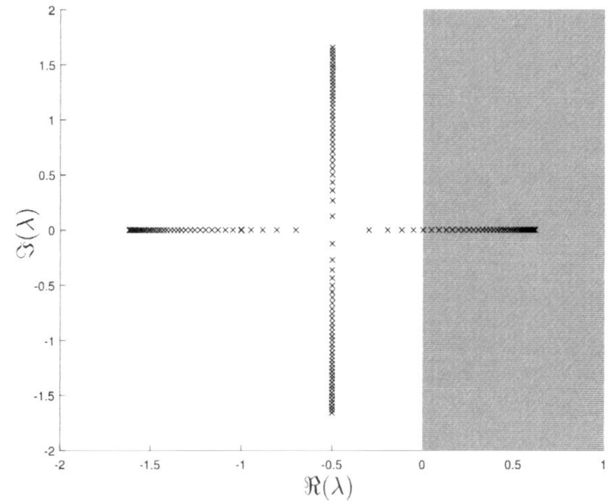

Fig. 5. Example 2. Eigenvalues λ of the plant (1) for some values of the parameters in $\mathcal{P}$. The dashed area denotes the region of unstable eigenvalues.

Next, we determine the set $\mathcal{H}$ as explained in Section IV-E, finding

$$\mathcal{H} = \left\{ \begin{pmatrix} -2.000 \\ -1.663 \end{pmatrix} \right\}.$$

Therefore, from Theorem 1 we conclude that the controller obtained from the vector v in $\mathcal{H}$, i.e.,

$$D_{con}(p) = -2 - 1.663p$$

solves Problem 1. This fact is also shown by Figure 6, which shows the eigenvalues of the closed-loop system (1)–(4) obtained with the found controller for some values of the parameters in $\mathcal{P}$.

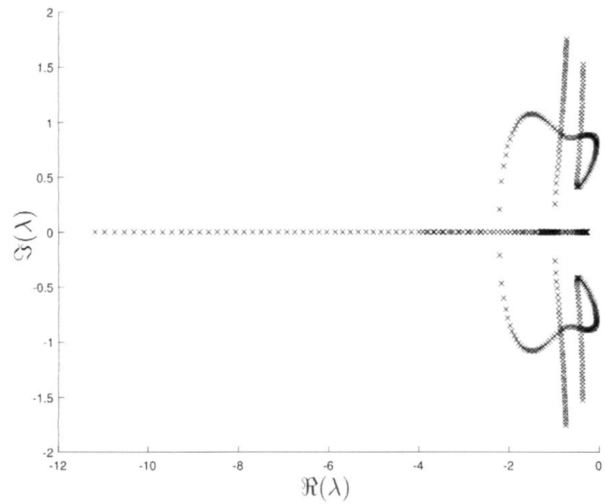

Fig. 6. Example 2. Eigenvalues λ of the closed-loop system (1)–(4) for some values of the parameters in $\mathcal{P}$.

VI. Conclusions

This paper has addressed the design of adaptive output feedback controllers for stabilizing plants affected by time-invariant parameters in the time-invariant case, which is a fundamental problem in engineering. A novel approach has been proposed for designing fixed-order fixed-degree adaptive parameter-dependent output feedback controllers. The proposed approach requires the solution of convex optimization problems with LMIs, and provides a sufficient condition based on the construction of a function that quantifies a stability margin of the closed-loop system depending on the controller. This condition is nonconservative under some mild assumptions by increasing the size of the LMIs. Future work can consider various directions. For instance, one could extend the proposed approach to the case of discrete-time systems. Also, the proposed approach could be generalized in order to deal with time-varying parameters.

Appendix 1

Proof of Theorem 1. Let $g_i^*(p,v)$ be the optimal value of $g_i(p,v)$ in the optimization problem (39). One has that $g_i^*(p,v)$ is a SOS polynomial. It follows that, for all $i = 1,\ldots,n+1$,

$$\begin{aligned} 0 &\leq g_i^*(p,v) \\ &= f_i(p,v) - \xi^*(v) - \sum_{j=1}^{n_a} a_j(p)\beta_{i,j}^*(p,v) \\ &\quad - \sum_{k=1}^{n_b} b_k(v)\gamma_{i,k}^*(p,v) \end{aligned}$$

where $\xi^*(v)$, $\beta_{i,j}^*(p,v)$ and $\gamma_{i,k}^*(p,v)$ are the optimal values of $\xi(v)$, $\beta_{i,j}(p,v)$ and $\gamma_{i,k}(p,v)$ in the optimization problem (39). One has that $\beta_{i,j}^*(p,v)$ and $\gamma_{i,k}^*(p,v)$ are SOS polynomials. Suppose $v^* \in \mathcal{H}$. Then, $h^*(v^*) = 0$, $\rho_{pos} = \xi^*(v^*)$ and $v^* \in \mathcal{V}$. Let $p^* \in \mathcal{P}$. One has $a_j(p^*) \geq 0$ and $b_k(v^*) \geq 0$. It follows that, for all $i = 1,\ldots,n+1$,

$$\begin{aligned} 0 &\leq f_i(p^*,v^*) - \xi^*(v^*) - \sum_{j=1}^{n_a} a_j(p^*)\beta_{i,j}^*(p^*,v^*) \\ &\quad - \sum_{k=1}^{n_b} b_k(v^*)\gamma_{i,k}^*(p^*,v^*) \\ &\leq f_i(p^*,v^*) - \rho_{pos}. \end{aligned}$$

Since $\rho_{pos} > 0$ one has

$$f_i(p^*,v^*) > 0 \quad \forall i = 1,\ldots,n+1.$$

From Sections IV-B–IV-C this implies that the controller v^* ensures that the closed-loop system (1)–(4) is well-posed and asymptotically stable for all parameters $p \in \mathcal{P}$. Therefore, v^* solves Problem 1.

Appendix 2

Proof of Theorem 2. Suppose that there exists a controller $\bar{v} \in \mathcal{V}$ that solves Problem 1. From Sections IV-B–IV-C this implies that

$$f_i(p,\bar{v}) > 0 \quad \forall i = 1,\ldots,n+1 \ \forall p \in \mathcal{P}$$

for some $\theta \in \Theta$. Let us define the function

$$\bar{f}(v) = \inf_{\substack{p\in\mathcal{P} \\ i=1,\ldots,n+1}} f_i(p,v).$$

It follows that

$$\bar{f}(\bar{v}) > 0.$$

Suppose that Assumption 1 holds. It follows that $\mathcal{V}$ is compact. Hence, there exists a polynomial $\xi(v)$ that approximates arbitrary well $\bar{f}(v)$ over $\mathcal{V}$, in particular such that

$$\left\{ \begin{array}{lcl} \bar{f}(v) & \geq & \xi(v) \ \forall v \in \mathcal{V} \\ \rho_{pos} & \geq & \xi(v) \ \forall v \in \mathcal{V} \\ \xi(\bar{v}) & > & 0. \end{array} \right.$$

Since $\mathcal{P}$ is compact, and since the polynomials $a_i(p)$, $i = 1,\ldots,n_a$, in (3) and $b_i(v)$, $i = 1,\ldots,n_b$, in (6) have even degree, and their highest degree forms have no common root except zero, it follows from [16] that there exist polynomials $\beta_{i,j}(p,v)$, $\gamma_{i,k}(p,v)$ and $\delta_k(v)$ such that the constraints of the optimization problem (39) hold. Since the objective of this optimization problem is to maximize the integral of $\xi(v)$ over $\mathcal{V}$, it follows that there exists $\rho_{pos} > 0$ such that

$$\xi^*(v^*) = \rho_{pos}$$

for some $v^* \in \mathcal{V}$, where $\xi^*(v)$ is the optimal value of $\xi(v)$ in this optimization problem. Since $h^*(v)$ is a SOS polynomial, one has

$$\begin{aligned} 0 &\leq h^*(v^*) \\ &= \rho_{pos} - \xi^*(v^*) - \sum_{k=1}^{n_b} b_k(v^*)\delta_k^*(v^*) \\ &= -\sum_{k=1}^{n_b} b_k(v^*)\delta_k^*(v^*) \end{aligned}$$

where $\delta_k^*(v)$ is the optimal value of $\delta_k(v)$ in the optimization problem (39). Since $\delta_k^*(v)$ is a SOS polynomial, one concludes that

$$0 \leq h^*(v^*) \leq 0,$$

which implies that $h^*(v^*) = 0$. Therefore, $v^* \in \mathcal{H}$, and the set $\mathcal{H}$ is nonempty for the considered value of $\theta \in \Theta$.

References

[1] G. Chesi, "On the synthesis of adaptive parameter-dependent output feedback controllers through LMI-based optimization," in *International Conference on Adaptive and Self-Adaptive Systems and Applications*, Rome, Italy, 2016, pp. 1–2.

[2] A. T. Neto, "Parameter dependent Lyapunov functions for a class of uncertain linear systems: an LMI approach," in *IEEE Conference on Decision and Control*, Phoenix, Arizona, 1999, pp. 2341–2346.

[3] P.-A. Bliman, "A convex approach to robust stability for linear systems with uncertain scalar parameters," *SIAM Journal on Control and Optimization*, vol. 42, no. 6, pp. 2016–2042, 2004.
[4] G. Chesi, A. Garulli, A. Tesi, and A. Vicino, "Polynomially parameter-dependent Lyapunov functions for robust stability of polytopic systems: an LMI approach," *IEEE Transactions on Automatic Control*, vol. 50, no. 3, pp. 365–370, 2005.
[5] E. N. Goncalves, R. M. Palhares, R. H. C. Takahashi, and R. C. Mesquita, "New approach to robust D-stability analysis of linear time-invariant systems with polytope-bounded uncertainty," *IEEE Transactions on Automatic Control*, vol. 51, no. 10, pp. 1709–1714, 2006.
[6] D. Peaucelle, Y. Ebihara, D. Arzelier, and T. Hagiwara, "General polynomial parameter-dependent Lyapunov functions for polytopic uncertain systems," in *International Symposium on Mathematical Theory of Networks and Systems*, Kyoto, Japan, 2006, pp. 2238–2242.
[7] C. W. Scherer, "LMI relaxations in robust control," *European Journal of Control*, vol. 12, no. 1, pp. 3–29, 2006.
[8] M. Sato and D. Peaucelle, "Robust stability/performance analysis for linear time-invariant polynomially parameter dependent systems using polynomially parameter-dependent Lyapunov functions," in *IEEE Conference on Decision and Control*, San Diego, CA, 2006, pp. 5807–5813.
[9] R. C. L. F. Oliveira and P. L. D. Peres, "Parameter-dependent LMIs in robust analysis: Characterization of homogeneous polynomially parameter-dependent solutions via LMI relaxations," *IEEE Transactions on Automatic Control*, vol. 52, no. 7, pp. 1334–1340, 2007.
[10] H. L. S. Almeida, A. Bhaya, D. M. Falcao, and E. Kaszkurewicz, "A team algorithm for robust stability analysis and control design of uncertain time-varying linear systems using piecewise quadratic Lyapunov functions," *International Journal of Robust and Nonlinear Control*, vol. 11, pp. 357–371, 2001.
[11] F. Wang and V. Balakrishnan, "Improved stability analysis and gain-scheduled controller synthesis for parameter-dependent systems," *IEEE Transactions on Automatic Control*, vol. 47, no. 5, pp. 720–734, 2002.
[12] G. Chesi, "Robust static output feedback controllers via robust stabilizability functions," *IEEE Transactions on Automatic Control*, vol. 59, no. 6, pp. 1618–1623, 2014.
[13] G. Chesi, "LMI techniques for optimization over polynomials in control: a survey," *IEEE Transactions on Automatic Control*, vol. 55, no. 11, pp. 2500–2510, 2010.
[14] G. Chesi, A. Garulli, A. Tesi, and A. Vicino, "Characterizing the solution set of polynomial systems in terms of homogeneous forms: an LMI approach," *International Journal of Robust and Nonlinear Control*, vol. 13, no. 13, pp. 1239–1257, 2003.
[15] J. F. Sturm, "Using SeDuMi 1.02, a MATLAB toolbox for optimization over symmetric cones," *Optimization Methods and Software*, vol. 11-12, pp. 625–653, 1999.
[16] M. Putinar, "Positive polynomials on compact semi-algebraic sets," *Indian Univeristy Mathematics Journal*, vol. 42, no. 3, pp. 969–984, 1993.

International Journal on Advances in Intelligent Systems, vol 9 no 3 & 4, year 2016, http://www.iariajournals.org/intelligent_systems/

Using Neural Networks to Predict the Functionality of Reconfigurable Nano-material Networks

Klaus Greff†, Ruud van Damme*, Jan Koutník†, Hajo Broersma*, Julia Mikhal*,
Celestine Lawrence*, Wilfred van der Wiel*, and Jürgen Schmidhuber†
†IDSIA, USI-SUPSI, Galleria 2, 6928 Manno-Lugano, Switzerland
Email: {klaus,hkou,juergen}@idsia.ch
*Faculty of EEMCS, CTIT Institute for ICT Research, and MESA+ Institute for Nanotechnology
University of Twente, The Netherlands
Email: {r.m.j.vandamme,h.j.broersma,c.p.lawrence,w.g.vanderwiel}@utwente.nl

***Abstract*—This paper demonstrates how neural networks can be applied to model and predict the functional behaviour of disordered nano-particle and nano-tube networks. In recently published experimental work, nano-particle and nano-tube networks show promising functionality for future reconfigurable devices, without a predefined design. The nano-material has been treated as a black-box, and the principle of evolution-in-materio, involving genetic algorithms, has been used to find appropriate configuration voltages to enable the target functionality. In order to support future experiments and the development of useful devices based on disordered nano-materials, we developed simulation tools for predicting candidate functionalities. One of these tools is based on a physical model, but the one described and analysed in this paper is based on an artificial neural network model. The advantage of this newly presented approach is that, after training the neural network to match either the real material or its physical model, it can be configured using gradient descent instead of a black-box optimisation, speeding up the search for functionality. The neural networks do not simulate the physical properties, but rather approximate the nano-material's transfer functions. The functions found using this new technique were verified back on the nano-material's physical model and on a real material network. It can be concluded from the reported experiments with these neural network models that they model the simulated nano-material quite accurately. The differentiable, neural network-based material model is used to find logic gates, as a proof of principle. This shows that the new approach has great potential for partly replacing costly and time-consuming experiments with the real nano-material. Therefore, this approach has a high relevance for future computing, either as an alternative to digital computing or as an alternative way of producing multi-functional reconfigurable devices.**

Keywords–nano-material network; neural network; simulation; unconventional computation; evolution-in-nanomaterio.

I. Introduction and Motivation

This paper is an extended version of the preliminary work reported in [1] that was presented by the first author at the FUTURE COMPUTING 2016 meeting in Rome. It demonstrates parts of the research that has been carried out within the framework of the FP7-project NASCENCE: NAnoSCale Engineering for Novel Computation using Evolution [2]. More details on the conceptual ideas and outcomes of this project can be found in [3], including many references to recently published work within the framework of the project. In the NASCENCE project, that was funded by the European Community, disordered networks of gold nano-particles have been successfully used to produce reconfigurable logic, with a very high degree of stability and reproducibility [4]. More recently, similar results have been obtained within the NASCENCE project with networks consisting of composite materials based on nano-tubes [5]. These breakthroughs present a proof of principle that indicates very promising prospects for using such nano-materials to perform more complicated computational tasks. But there are still many challenges that have to be addressed, and the production of and experimentation with these nano-material networks is very costly and time-consuming. An example network that has been used in the experimental work of [4] is shown as an atomic-force microscopy (AFM) image in Figure 1. We apologise for the rather bad visibility that is in fact quite typical for AFM images with such a high resolution (the small dots represent nano-particles of about 20 nm in diameter).

Figure 1. AFM image of one of the fabricated nano-particle networks in [4]

In order to predict candidate computational tasks of such networks, but avoiding the waste of scarce and expensive resources involved in experimentally exploring these nano-particle networks, we developed simulation tools for examining and predicting the capabilities of these nano-material systems. One of the considered simulation tools [6] is an extension of existing tools for simulating nano-particle interactions, like SPICE [7] or SIMON [8]. The latter tools are all based on Monte-Carlo simulations, using a physical model, and they have been validated for known designed systems from literature consisting of very small numbers of particles. Although these methods can, in principle, handle arbitrary systems of any size, their scalability and use for networks consisting of hundreds of nano-particles is a serious issue. Moreover, nano-particle networks like the ones used in [4] to date cannot be produced according to a predefined specific design.

To illustrate this, an example of one of the fabricated nano-particle networks that was used in the experimental work of [4] is shown as an AFM image in Figure 1. The AFM image clearly demonstrates the disordered nature of the fabricated nano-particle networks. Therefore, due to their disordered nature, it is not possible to use a physical model to accurately describe and predict the properties of such nano-material systems.

In the earlier mentioned conference paper [1], an alternative approach has been introduced and analysed, with little detail due to the page limit. We provide more details of the approach and results here. This novel approach is based on training artificial Neural Networks in order to model and investigate the nano-particle networks. Neural Networks (NNs; [9] [10] [11]) have proven to be powerful function approximators and have, especially recently, been applied to a wide variety of domains with great success [12] [13] [14]. Being essentially treated as black-boxes themselves, NNs do not facilitate a better understanding of the underlying quantum-mechanical processes that take place in the nano-material. For that purpose, physical models are more appropriate. But, in contrast to physical models, NNs provide differentiable models and thus offer interesting possibilities to explore the computational capabilities of the nano-material. In the sequel, NNs will be used, in particular, to search for configurations of input voltages such that the nano-material computes different Boolean logic functions, such as AND, OR, NOR, NAND, and XOR.

To enable the exploration of the computational capabilities of the nano-material by an NN, the NN needs to be trained first with data collected from the measurements on the nano-material. Since a physical model and an associated validated simulation tool for the nano-particle networks have already been developed [6], such training data can be obtained from the simulated nano-material. This also provides an opportunity for predicting functionalities in small nano-particle networks that have not been fabricated yet. This in turn can inform electrical engineers on the minimum requirements necessary for obtaining such functionalities, without the burden of costly and time-consuming fabrication and experimentation. As soon as the NN has been trained, searching for arbitrary target functions is very fast, and can happen without any access to the nano-material or its physical model.

The rest of the paper is organised as follows. Section II provides some technical details on the gold nano-particle networks that have been used in the experimental work of [4]. This section also describes the choices that have been made and that form the basis for the physical-model based simulation tool of [6], combining a genetic algorithm with Monte-Carlo simulations for charge transport. Section III presents simulation results obtained with these tools for an example network. Section IV shows how an NN was trained for modelling

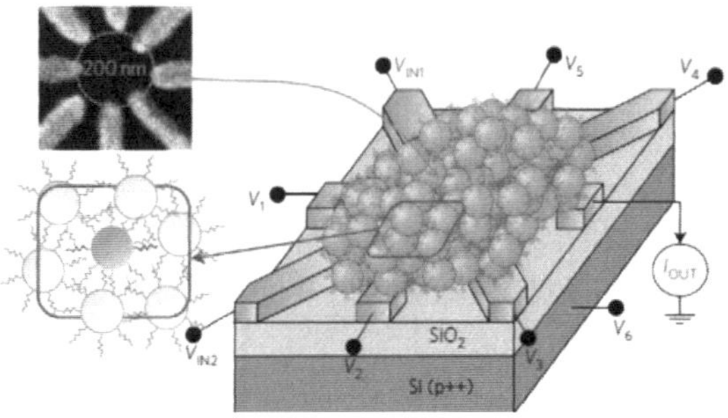

Figure 2. Illustration of a disordered network of gold nano-particles

the example network, using data collected from the physical-model based simulation tool. An analysis of the results is presented in Section V. Section VI is a newly added section that contains results of experiments that were performed after the FUTURE COMPUTING 2016 meeting. In these experiments a real material sample was used for collecting data to train an NN-model and predict functionalities, that were also validated afterwards using the real material. We finish the paper with a short section with some conclusions as well as an outlook to future work in Section VII.

II. NANO-PARTICLE NETWORKS AND THEIR SIMULATION

In collaboration with the NanoElectronics group at the MESA+ institute of the University of Twente, networks consisting of commercially available nano-particles of size 5-20 nm consisting of gold, and junctions of alkanedithiol of length 1-3 nm have been produced. The alkanedithiols stick to the metal and can form junctions (tunnel barriers) between particles. Figure 2 shows an illustration of such a network. The central circular region is about 200 nm in diameter. Recall that an AFM image of a real network has been shown in Figure 1. In a later stage, other organic molecules have been tried as well, but this is not relevant for the physical model or the simulation tool, only for the setting of the parameter values.

The networks investigated in the experimental work of [4] are relatively large (in the order of a hundred particles) and disordered. An artist's impression of such a network is given in Figure 3. More details on the production process and the electrical characterisation of these networks can be found in [4].

Under energetically favourable circumstances, the transport of electrons in such nano-particle networks is governed by the Coulomb blockade effect [15]: transport is blocked, except at almost discrete energy levels; there exactly one electron can jump. The dynamics of such a system is governed by stochastic processes: electrons on particles can tunnel through junctions with a certain probability. For such systems, there are basically two simulation methods to one's disposal: Monte-Carlo Methods and the Master Equation Method [16] [17]. Since the number of particles is large, the Monte-Carlo Method

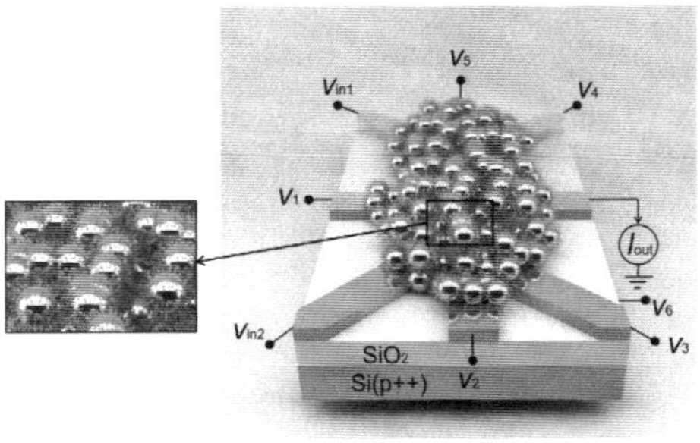

Figure 3. Artist's impression of a disordered nano-particle network

is the best candidate. This method simulates the tunnelling times of electrons stochastically. To get meaningful results, one needs to run the algorithm in the order of a million times. Doing so, the stochastic process gives averaged values of the charges, currents, voltages, etc. The approach for obtaining functionality is based on these physical effects combined with genetic algorithms for finding suitable settings of certain control voltages on configuration leads, as explained in more detail on the example network in the next section. This section concludes with a short explanation of the basic principles of evolution-in-materio and genetic algorithms.

Evolution-in-materio (EIM) is a term coined by Miller and Downing [18] that refers to the manipulation of physical systems using a form of computer-controlled artificial evolution [18]–[22]. It is a type of unconstrained evolution in which, through the application of physical signals, various intrinsic properties of a material can be heightened or configured so that a useful computational function is achieved.

The central idea of EIM is that the application of some physical signals to a material (configuration variables) can cause it to alter how it responds to an applied physical input signal and how it generates a measurable physical output (see Figure 4) [18].

Physical outputs from the material are converted to output data and a numerical fitness score is assigned based on how close the output is to a desired response. This fitness is assigned to the member of the population that supplied the configuration variables. Ideally, the material would be able to be reset before the application of new configuration instructions. This is likely to be important as without the ability to reset the material, it may retain a memory from past configurations. This could lead to the same configuration having different fitness values depending on the history of interactions with the material.

Mappings need to be devised which convert problem domain data into suitable signals to apply to the material. An input-mapping needs to be devised to map problem domain inputs to physical input signals. An output-mapping is required to convert measured variables from the material into a numerical value which can be used to solve a computational problem. Finally, a configuration-mapping is required to convert numerical values held on a computer into physical variables that are used to

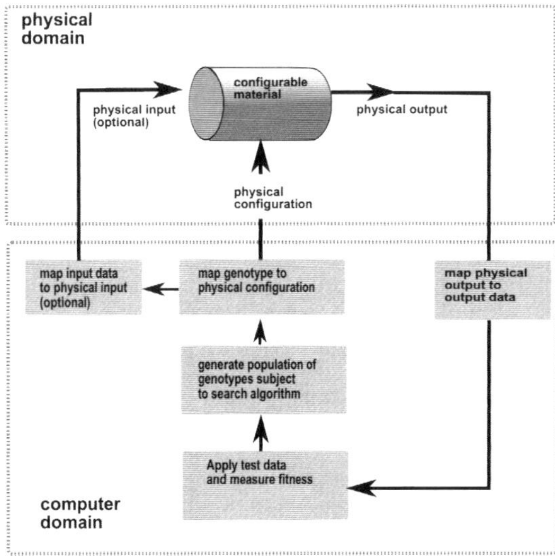

Figure 4. Concept of evolution-in-materio [18]

"program or configure" the material.

EIM is a bottom-up approach where the intrinsic underlying physics of materials is exploited as a computational medium. In contrast to a traditional design process where a computational substrate, e.g., silicon, is precisely engineered, EIM uses a bottom-up approach to manipulate materials with the aim of producing computation. Yoshihito discussed a closely related concept of "material processors" which he describes as material systems that can process information by using the properties of the material [23]. Zauner describes a related term which he refers to as "informed matter" [24]. It is interesting that inspection of much earlier research publications reveals that ideas similar to EIM, albeit without computers, were conceived in the late 1950s (particularly by Gordon Pask, see [25], [26]).

One of the key ingredients in EIM is the use of genetic algorithms, a form of computer-controlled artificial evolution. The main elements of a genetic algorithm are shown in Algorithm 1.

In evolutionary computing, the term genotype (or chromosome) is used to refer to the string of numbers that defines a solution to a search problem. The individual elements of the genotype are commonly referred to as genes. To solve a computational problem requires an assessment of how well a particular genotype represents a solution to the computational search problem. This is called a fitness function. The "survival-of-the-fittest" principle of Darwinian evolution is implemented by using a form of fitness-based selection that is more likely to choose solutions for the next generation that are fitter rather than poorer. Mutation is an operation that changes a genotype by making random alterations to some genes, with a certain probability. Recombination is a process of generating one or more new genotypes by recombining genes from two or more genotypes. Sometimes, genotypes from one generation are

Algorithm 1 Genetic Algorithm

1: Generate an initial population of size p. Set the number of generations g to 0
2: **repeat**
3: Calculate the fitness of each member of the population
4: Select a number of parents according to the quality of their fitness
5: Recombine some, if not all, of the parents to create offspring genotypes
6: Mutate some parents and offspring
7: Form a new population from the mutated parents and the offspring
8: Optional: promote a number of unaltered parents from Step 4 to the new population
9: Increment the number of generations $g \leftarrow g + 1$
10: **until** (g equals the number of generations required) **or** (the fitness is acceptable)

promoted directly to the next generation; this is referred to as elitism (see the optional step in Algorithm 1).

III. An Illustrative Example

As an example which is still relatively small and manageable, but shows interesting features, the described methods have been explored on the symmetric 4×4-grid consisting of the components shown in Figure 5.

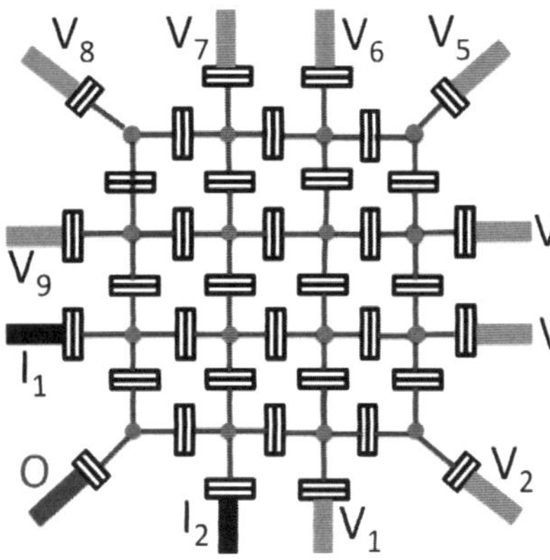

Figure 5. A symmetric 4×4-grid of 16 nano-particles with leads

In Figure 5, the 16 green dots represent the nano-particles; in between are the tunnelling junctions, with fixed C and R values. The two input leads and the single output lead are depicted as I_1 and I_2 and O, respectively. Voltages are applied to the configuration leads V_1-V_9, according to a genetic algorithm, and also to a back gate; this back gate is connected through tunnel barriers (a silicon oxide layer) to all nano-particles (for convenience we have not shown the back gate in the figure).

The fitness of the sets of configuration voltages is determined by how close the output for the four input combinations of the Boolean truth table is to the desired logic. More details can be found in [6].

1) Evolved Boolean Logic: Applying the developed simulation tool to the small network of Figure 5, it was possible to evolve all basic Boolean logic gates, using different computed (simulated and optimised) settings of the values of the free variables (the configuration leads voltages and the back gate voltage). The solutions for four of the cases, namely AND, NAND, OR and XOR, are illustrated as contour plots in Figure 6. The four plots are functions of the two input signals; the voltages of both inputs range from 0 to 10 mV, horizontally as well as vertically; the colour scheme ranges from blue for small values to red for high values of the output.

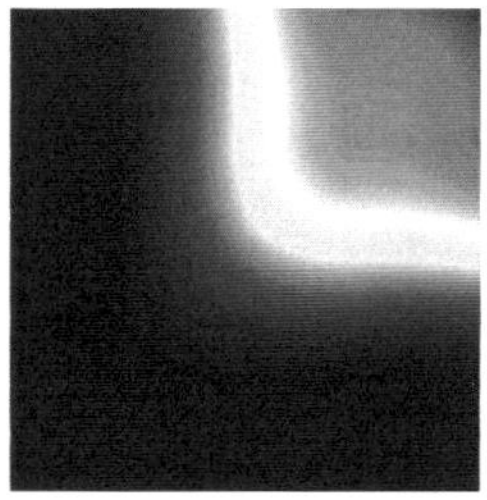

(a) simulated AND

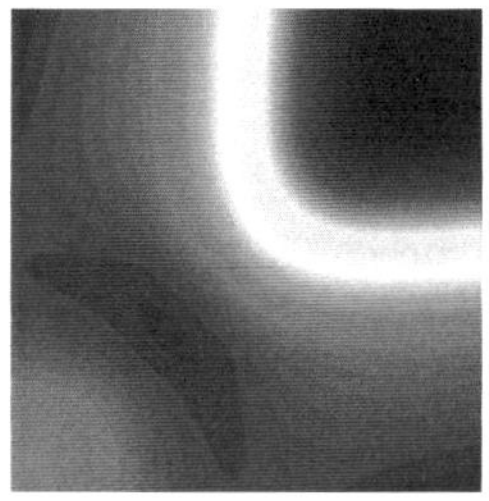

(b) simulated NAND

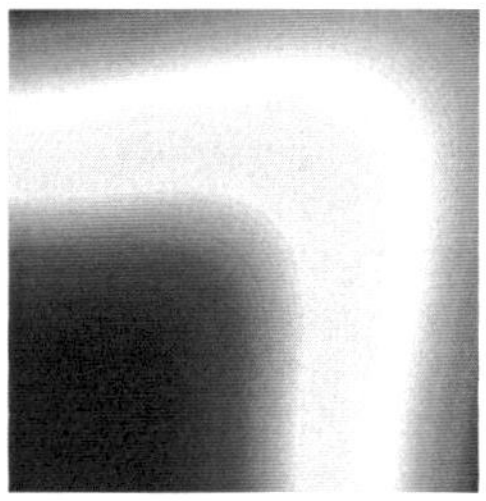

(c) simulated OR

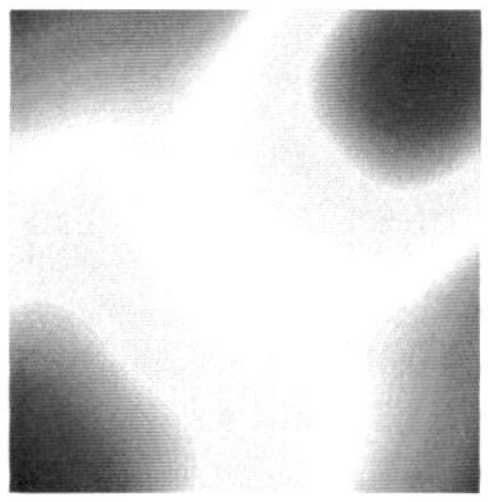

(d) simulated XOR

Figure 6. Contour plots of simulated evolved logic in the 4×4-grid

2) Discussion: From an electrical engineering point of view, the simulation results are very interesting, for several reasons. First of all, the example of Figure 5 can be configured into any of the basic Boolean logic gates, using only 16 nano-particles of size 5-20 nm. If one would like to design and build the same functionality with transistors, one would require at least 10 transistors. Secondly, in the designed circuit one would have to rewire the input and apply it at different places, whereas in the nano-particle network each of the input signals is applied at exactly one place. Even with current transistor sizes below 20 nm, the designed circuit would require the same or more space, and would dissipate substantially more energy.

It is interesting to note, that in the experiments with the real material samples [4], all basic Boolean gates were also evolved within an area with a diameter of around 200 nm, but with only six control voltages. However, currently these samples consist of 100-150 particles that are self-assembled into a disordered network.

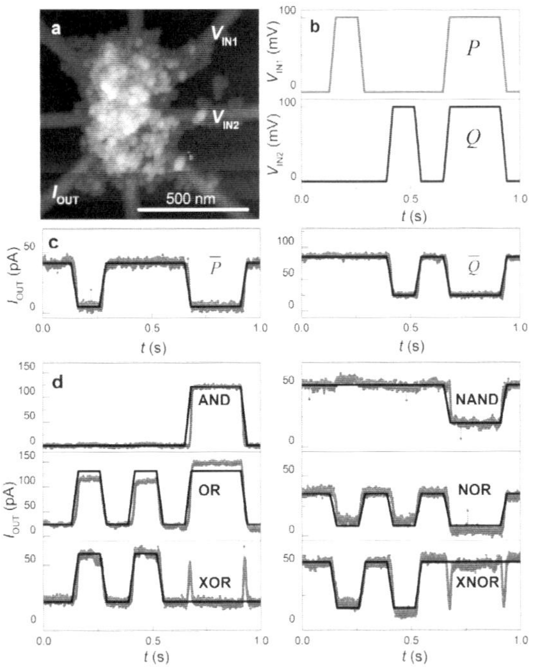

Figure 7. AFM image of an NP-network (**a**), the input voltages in mV applied to V_{IN1} and V_{IN2} (**b**) and the different logic outputs in pA read from I_{OUT} (**c** and **d**) [4]

In Figure 7(a) we see the same AFM image as before of one of the real networks that was used for the experiments in [4], where the two input electrodes and the output electrode are denoted by V_{IN1}, V_{IN2} and I_{OUT}, respectively. Time-dependent signals in the order of a hundred mV were applied to the input electrodes as illustrated in Figure 7(b), and a time-dependent current in the order of a hundred pA was read from the output electrode. The other five electrodes and the back gate have been used to apply different sets of static configuration voltages. Using a genetic algorithm, suitable sets of configuration voltages have been found to produce the output functions of Figure 7(c,d). Red symbols are experimental data, solid black curves are expected output signals (matched to the amplitudes of the experimental data). We observe two clear negators (inverters) for the input functions P and Q in Figure 7(c), and we observe a variety of Boolean logic gates in Figure 7(d), including the universal NAND and NOR gate. Supplementary work in [4] reveals that all these gates show a great stability and reproducibility. For the exclusive gates (XOR, XNOR) spike-like features are observed at the rising and falling edges of the (1,1) input, as might have been expected for a finite slope in the input signals. More details can be found in [4].

The remarkable thing here is not that we can produce logic gates using the electrical and physical properties of charge transport in neighbouring nano-particles. What is remarkable, is that we can do this with one and the same sample of a disordered nano-particle network in a circular region of about 200 nm in diameter, and by using only six configuration voltages. This shows the great potential for the approach. Note that a similar designed reconfigurable device based on today's transistor technology would require about the same space, and it would also require rewiring of the input signals to multiple inputs.

The experimental results as well as the simulations show the great potential for the approach, both in the bottom-up and top-down design regime. This could have a huge impact on future computing, either as an alternative approach to digital computing or as an alternative way to produce reconfigurable multi-functional devices, e.g., to support further down-scaling of digital components. Currently, we are not aware of any production techniques for constructing samples that come anywhere close to the 4×4-grid structure of Figure 5.

To obtain more insight in the underlying currents and physical phenomena, and with the long term goal to fully understand what is going on in terms of electron jumps and currents through these nano-particle networks, in [6] visualisation tools have been developed to analyse the processes that are taking place over time. In Figure 8, some pictures visualising the currents through the network are presented, in this case, as an example, when the network was configured as an AND. The amplitude of the currents is proportional to the area of the red arrows in the figure. The currents are all averaged over time. The tool also enables the calculation of variances, and it can show fast animations of the electron jumps as well. It is still an open problem to deduce an explanation for the patterns and jumps that cause the 4×4-grid to behave as a logic AND (or one of the other basic Boolean logic gates).

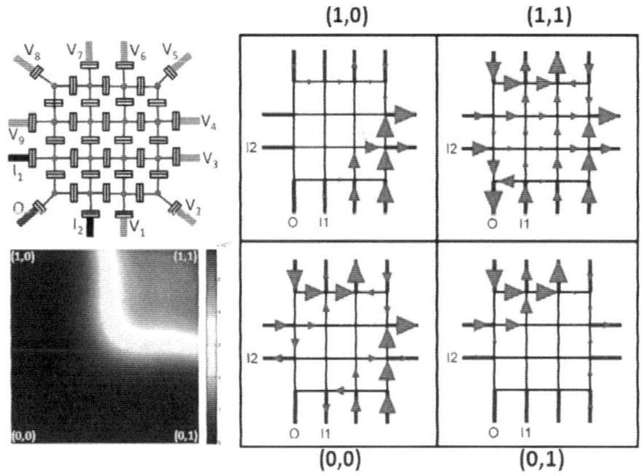

Figure 8. Averaged current patterns for simulated AND in the 4×4-grid

Figure 8 gives an impression of how complicated the traffic of electrons in such networks can get, and can hopefully in the future lead to more insight as to why they behave as logic. The plots do not explain anything as yet. We are currently trying to find macroscopic laws from the numerics, like real (first order) phase transitions, but so far without success. We have made similar pictures for the other Boolean logic functions, but they are not relevant for this paper. Therefore, we omitted them until we are in a better position to explain the relationship between the flow pattern and the observed logic.

In the next two sections, the use of artificial NNs to simulate the nano-material will be explained, as well as how to use the data collected from the above physical-model based simulations to explore the functionalities in the example of the 4×4-grid.

IV. Neural Networks

The key idea of this paper is to show how to use an NN-model for approximating the mapping from the input voltages to the output current, by training the NN on many randomly chosen examples. By using this approach, the aim is that the NN becomes a differentiable model of the potentially complex structures and processes that take place inside the nano-material. While the example that we use throughout will only treat the search for Boolean logic functions performed by the nano-particle network, the future goal is to use the NN-models in a more general sense to assess:

- **Complexity** of the nano-material: based on the training process, one can estimate whether the material contains learnable, interesting structures, only noise (if the training process cannot minimise the error), or simple structures (if the training of the NN-model turns out to be trivial).
- **Predictability**: if the trained NN becomes a good model of the nano-material, then it can further be used to predict outputs of the nano-material for any given inputs, and for searching for target functionalities.
- **Function**: the NN-model can be used as a substitute for the real nano-material. One can search for functionality in the NN-model first instead of performing measurements in the real nano-material. This can be particularly useful if the nano-material has, e.g., a limited lifespan or in case the experiments in the lab are very costly and time-consuming.

An example of a specific NN that turned out to be suitable for our experiments is illustrated in Figure 9.

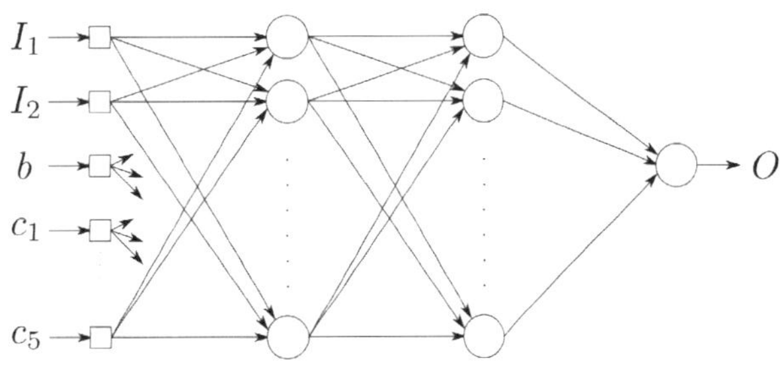

Figure 9. Illustration of an NN with two hidden layers

The NN of Figure 9 is used in the sequel for approximating the mapping from the input and configuration voltages to the output current, by training them using many randomly chosen examples, generated with the physical-model based simulation tool. By solving that task for a specific nano-particle network, the trained NN becomes a differentiable model for the complex quantum-mechanic interactions within the material sample. The voltages on the configuration leads and the input electrodes are scaled to have zero mean and unit variance, and serve as inputs to the NN. Referring to the 4×4-grid of Figure 5, in Figure 9, I_1 and I_2 denote the two input leads, b denotes the back gate, and $c_1, c_2, \ldots, c_5$ denote the other leads, in a symmetric fashion, so c_1 represents V_1 and V_9, and so on, whereas O denotes the output lead. A simplified illustration of the 4×4-grid is presented in Figure 10. The training objective is to minimise the Mean Squared Error (MSE) on the (also standardised) current of the output.

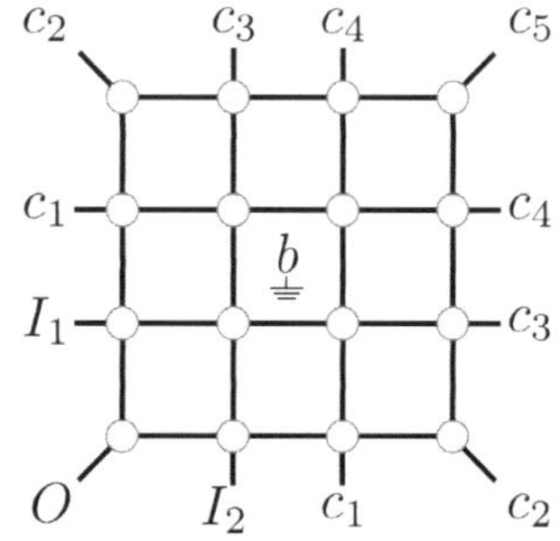

Figure 10. Simulated 4×4 nano-particle grid used for data generation

Deep feed-forward NNs have proven to be powerful function approximators, and especially recently they have been applied very successfully in a wide range of domains. They consist of a sequence of layers, where each layer computes an affine projection of its inputs followed by a pointwise non-linear function ψ:

$$\mathbf{h} = \psi(\mathbf{W}\mathbf{x} + \mathbf{b}),$$

where $\theta = \{\mathbf{W}, \mathbf{b}\}$ are the parameters of the layer.

By stacking these layers, one can build non-linear functions of varying expressiveness that are differentiable. In theory, these networks can approximate any function to arbitrary precision given enough layers and hidden units, and they also work very well in practice. This motivates the choice to use such deep feed-forward NNs to model the input-output characteristics of the nano-particle networks that were described earlier.

Figure 11 illustrates the different phases in the use of NN-simulations to search for functionality in the nano-material, starting with the training of the NN-model from data obtained from the real material or its physical model, then querying the trained NN-model for configurations that should provide a target functionality, and finally checking whether this functionality is indeed observed in the real nano-material or physical model.

For the purpose of training, the NNs are presented with pairs of input and output combinations taken from the real material or the physical model. The inputs are passed in, propagated through the NN, and the resulting output of the NN-model

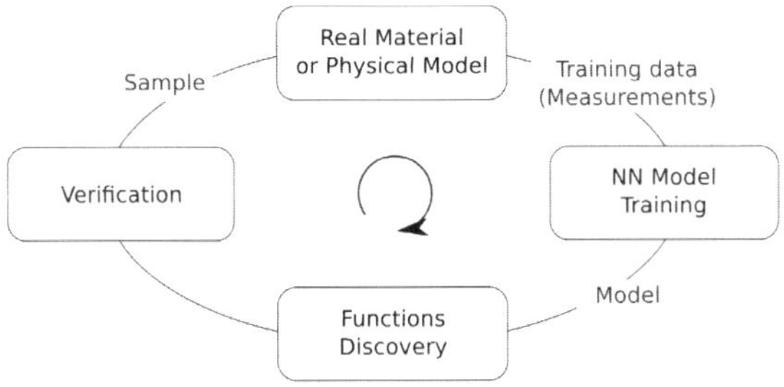

Figure 11. Closing the loop between the real nano-material or its physical model and the NN-simulation

is compared to the output of the real material or physical model. The difference between the output of the NN-model and the desired output (error) is propagated back through the NN-model in order to calculate the error gradient with respect to the particular network parameters θ. The full training is done by Stochastic Gradient Descend (SGD), meaning that the above is repeated over and over again while adjusting the parameters of the NN-model a little bit at each step. For efficiency reasons the gradients are calculated for batches of input and output combinations, hence a stochastic approximation of the full gradient is obtained.

Being essentially black boxes themselves, NNs do not directly facilitate a better understanding of the underlying quantum-mechanical processes, but they offer interesting possibilities to explore the computational capabilities of the nano-material. The trained NN is a differentiable approximate model of the nano-material: it maps inputs to outputs in roughly the same way as the real nano-material. This property can be used to run the model "backwards": find inputs that produce certain desired outputs by using a backpropagation algorithm to perform gradient descent, this time not on the weights but on the inputs. Here, it was required to go even further and use backpropagation to search for functions; in particular, the aim is to find settings of the configuration leads such that various combinations of the input leads (logic pairs) produce corresponding desired (logic) outputs. For this purpose, the NN must first be sufficiently well trained, which depends on data collected from the nano-material or the physical model. Afterwards, searching for arbitrary functions is very fast and can happen independently of the nano-material or the physical model.

A. Clustering and Visualisation

Some structure in the data can be difficult to recover by modelling it with an NN. To deal with these cases, we also employ two standard techniques from datamining: visualisation and clustering. Visualisation harnesses the powerful human pattern recognition abilities to discover structure that would otherwise remain hidden. Clustering, on the other hand, is an unsupervised learning method that tries to automatically partition the data into subsets (clusters) that are similar within, but dissimilar in-between clusters. The most commonly used clustering method is the K-Means method, which minimises the following function:

$$f(\mathbf{X}, \mathbf{S}, \theta) = \sum_{k=1}^{K} \sum_{\mathbf{x} \in S_k} \|\mathbf{x} - \mu_k\|^2 ,$$

where $\mathbf{X} = \{\mathbf{x}_1, \ldots, \mathbf{x}_N\}$ is the data, $\mathbf{S}$ is the partitioning of the data, and $\theta = \{\mu_1, \ldots, \mu_K\}$ are the cluster centres. This minimisation is done by initially setting the cluster centres randomly and then alternating between the two steps: 1) reassigning the points to the cluster with the closest centre and 2) moving all μ_i to the centre of their cluster i.

B. Closing the Loop

The configurations of the nano-material or its physical model that were searched for in the NN-model should then be confronted back with the source of the original data – the real material or the physical model. The purpose of such experiments is to close the loop, as illustrated in Figure 11, between the real materials, their simulations and the data mining models. This serves as a verification of whether the NN-models are sufficiently suitable models for representing the properties of the real material.

V. Results of Simulations on 4×4 Grid

In this section, the results of the NN-modelling of the 4×4 grids of Figure 10 are presented. The main subsections describe the way the data was collected and processed (Subsection V-A), and the way the NN-model was obtained and analysed (Subsection V-B). It should be emphasised again that this means we developed an alternative NN-model based on the data obtained from a physical model of a nano-particle network, not on data obtained from a real nano-particle network. In Section VI, we present similar results based on data obtained from a real nano-tube network.

A. Data Description

The experiments that are described here are on a simulated 4×4 grid (see Figure 10). The goal is to see 1) how well we can model the nano-material with a neural network and 2) to see whether we can use a trained NN to find logic functions. The simulated material consists of 16 gold nano-particles arranged in a 4×4 grid. It has a total of 13 electrodes (12 leads on the periphery and one backgate) attached to it. Two of these leads were used as inputs (I_1, I_2), one as output (O) and the other 10 as configuration leads. The goal of the measurements was to explore the functions that the nano-grid with 2 inputs can compute while varying the voltages at the configuration leads. Only symmetric functions (with $f(a,b) = f(b,a)$) were considered. So, in order to keep things simple, the 10 configuration leads were restricted to be symmetric, thus leading to 6 degrees of freedom for configuring the function. The nano-material was formally treated as a function $f_\theta(I_1, I_2)$

parameterised by $\theta = \{c_1, c_2, c_3, c_4, c_5, b\}$. To model the whole space of functions it can embody, a deep feed-forward NN was trained in order to predict the output current from the two inputs and 6 configuration voltages. Roughly one million samples were collected from simulations, where each sample corresponds to a run with these 8 voltages set at random, and one resulting output current that has been reached after a settling period. Figure 12 shows the distribution of the target samples in the collected data.

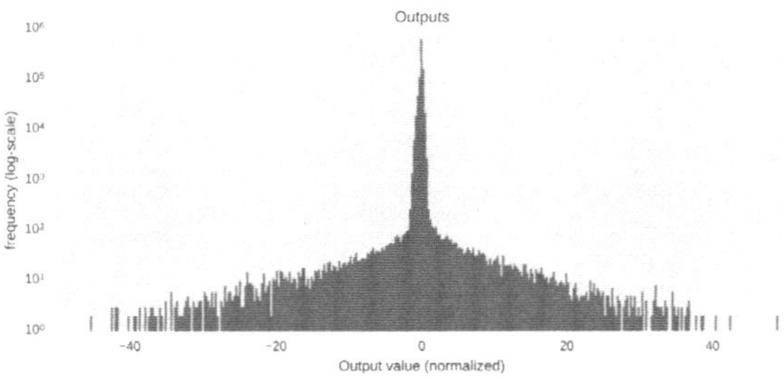

(a)

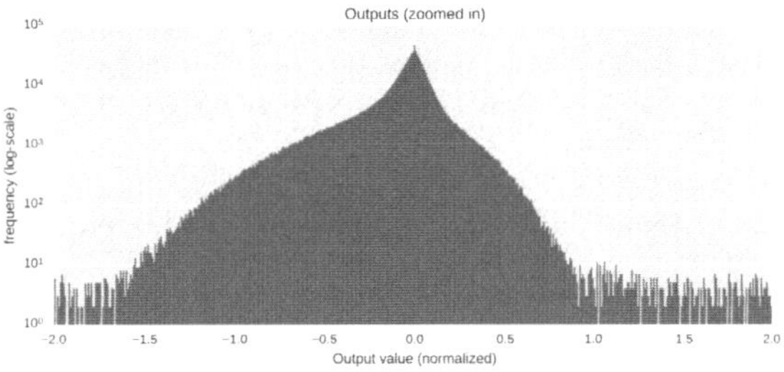

(b)

Figure 12. Initial distribution (a) and zooming in (b) of the training targets as contained in the data generated from the simulation

Figure 12(a) shows the initial distribution of the training targets as contained in the data generated from the simulation. It is clear that the data to be modelled forms a narrow peak around zero. The tails contain only widely distributed values close to zero. Zooming in the data as illustrated in Figure 12(b) provides a better insight into the interesting simulation outputs. From the data samples collected, 90% of these samples were used for training the NN-model and the rest for validation. For completeness, the visualisation of the parameter sweep across the two inputs is depicted in Figure 13.

The scatter plot of Figure 13 shows the outputs as a function of the varying input voltages, while the remaining leads are supplied with random voltages.

B. Analysis

The voltages on the configuration leads and the inputs are scaled to have zero mean and unit variance and serve as inputs to the NN-network, as depicted in Figure 9. The training objective is to minimise the mean squared error (MSE) on the standardised output voltage. The optimisation is done

Figure 13. Scatter plot of the outputs

using minibatch stochastic gradient descent with Nesterov-style momentum. Training is stopped once the MSE on the validation set did not decrease for 5 epochs, or after a maximum of 100 epochs.

The hyperparameters of the networks were optimised by random search over 40 runs [27]–[29]. The following parameters were sampled at random:

- learning rate η log-uniform from $[10^{-4}, 10^{-1}]$
- number of hidden layers from $\{1, 2, 5, 10\}$
- number of units in each layer from $\{8, 16, 32, 64, 128\}$
- activation function from {ReLU, tanh, sigmoid}.

The best performing network had 2 hidden layers with 128 rectified linear units each and was trained with a learning rate of $\eta \approx 1.6 \cdot 10^{-2}$. This is the network we use for the rest of the analysis.

1) Using the Model: The trained neural network model was used to find the logic functions by backpropagation of the error all the way to the inputs, i.e., following the error gradient for the inputs performs the gradient descent towards the input configurations that represent the example logic functions.

The dataset contains samples (input vectors) that have different values for the input leads, but share the same (random) values for the configuration leads along with the desired output values (perceptual aliasing). Gradient descent is then used to minimise the mean square error by adjusting the values for the configuration leads, but their values are kept the same for all examples. Formally, given the NN-model $\hat{f}$ of the nano-material, we define an error over our N input/output pairs

$((I_1^{(i)}, I_2^{(i)}, O^{(i)}))$:

$$E = \sum_{i=1}^{N} \frac{1}{2}(\hat{f}(I_1^{(i)}, I_2^{(i)}, \theta) - O^{(i)})^2$$

The gradient is then calculated using backpropagation:

$$\frac{\partial E}{\partial \theta} = (\hat{f}(I_1^{(i)}, I_2^{(i)}, \theta) - O^{(i)})\frac{\partial \hat{f}}{\partial \theta}$$

2) Global Optimisation: One problem with the method described above, is that it only performs a local search, which means that the solution it converges to might correspond to a bad local minimum (unlike when using evolutionary methods to configure the materials or the material models). In order to mitigate this problem, it was decided to first sample 10,000 random starting points (settings of the configuration leads), and perform just 10 iterations of the described local search on them. Only the starting point that leads to the lowest error is then optimised further for another 5,000 epochs, in order to obtain the final solution. In this way, we reduce the risk of getting stuck in a poor local minimum. Each search comprises 420K evaluations of the neural network, for a total of about a minute on a modern CPU.

3) Removing Outliers: After training several NNs on the simulation data, we discovered that more than half of the total prediction error stems from less than 0.1% of the data. These samples which account for most of the error also turn out to be outliers in terms of their output values, as can be seen in Figure 14.

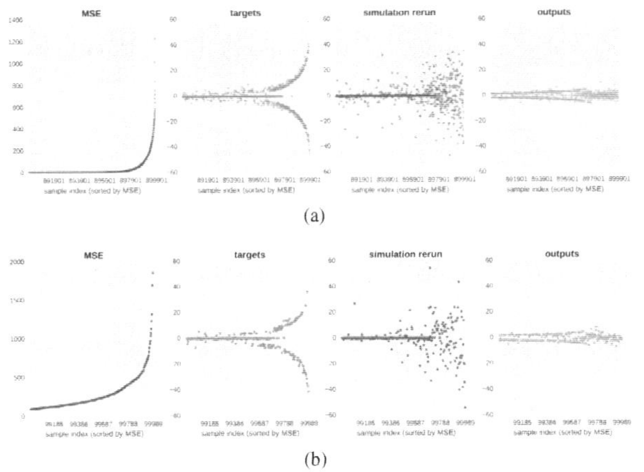

Figure 14. (a) Training and (b) validation errors of the worst 10% of the data

Figure 14 shows in (a) the training and in (b) the validation errors of the worst 10% of the data. We can see that as the mean square error (between the targets and outputs) goes up, it becomes hard to predict the data. After re-running the simulation, the targets become different due to the stochastic behaviour of the simulation, which is confirmed by non-predictability of such data using the NN-model.

Figure 15 provides more insight into the distribution of the most and least predictable data fragments.

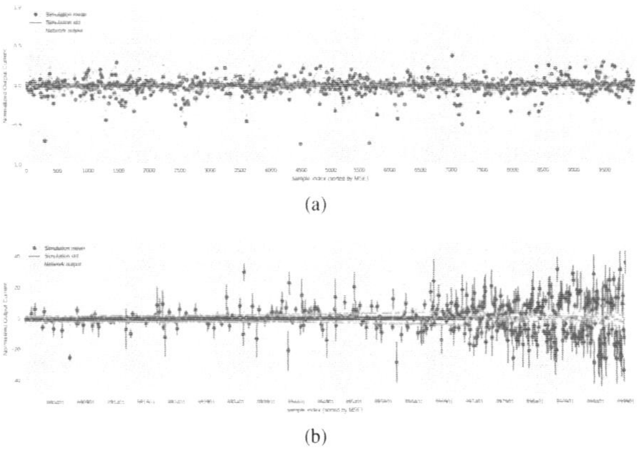

Figure 15. Most and least predictable data

The plots of Figure 15 show in (a) the first 10 k and in (b) the last 10 k data sorted according to the MSE. The simulation was executed multiple times. Vertical lines at each position depicts the distribution of the outputs for the given input configuration (the mean and the standard deviation). We can see that as the distributions get wider, the NN-model tends to have a harder time to predict the simulation outputs. The gradient for training the NN-network is thus dominated by the few unpredictable samples, leading the model to ignore the bulk of the data. For these reasons, it was decided to remove those outliers entirely from the dataset. After that the NN-network performed much better in modelling the material, as can be seen from Figure 16.

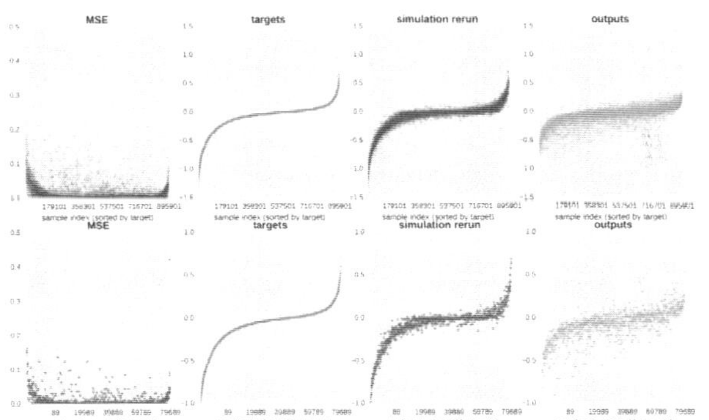

Figure 16. Experimental results after cleaning the data

Figure 16 shows the experimental results after cleaning the data. The 0.05% of the data (which covers the unpredictable subset) was removed in (a) from the training sets, and in (b) from the validation sets. We can see that re-running the simulations provides similar targets, hence the NN has no longer problems with predicting the simulation output. All results from here on have been obtained from the "cleaned" data.

C. Logic Gates Search by Gradient Descent

The overall aim was to find configurations for the simulated 4×4 nano-grid that turns it into a multi-functional reconfigurable device for computing some well-known Boolean logic functions, just like the physical-model based simulation did: AND, OR, XOR, NAND, NOR, XNOR. For this goal, we first had to decide which values of (x_0, x_1) to map (False, True) to. The obvious choice is $(0, 1)$, but values of $(0.2, 0.8)$, for example, would also still be acceptable. To circumvent the problem of choosing these values, the same gradient descent method was used to adjust the values for True and False for the inputs as well.

In particular, the following was done for each function:

1) generate eight random numbers, while assuring that $x_1 > x_0$
2) using these values, create a set of four input/output pairs (see Table I)
3) perform gradient descent on these 8 values, while maintaining $x_1 > x_0$

The scheme by which the four input/output pairs are created from the eight random values $x_0, x_1, \ldots, x_7$ for any of the logic functions, is explained in Table I, in this case for the logic OR. Note that this depends on $x_0 < x_1$.

TABLE I. THE SCHEME FOR CREATING THE FOUR INPUT/OUTPUT PAIRS (FOR THE LOGIC OR)

I_1	I_2	c_1	c_2	c_3	c_4	c_5	b	*out*
x_0	x_0	x_2	x_3	x_4	x_5	x_6	x_7	OR(F, F)
x_0	x_1	x_2	x_3	x_4	x_5	x_6	x_7	OR(F, T)
x_1	x_0	x_2	x_3	x_4	x_5	x_6	x_7	OR(T, F)
x_1	x_1	x_2	x_3	x_4	x_5	x_6	x_7	OR(T, T)

First, a global search for a good start point was performed and then the resulting vector was optimised further. The results can be seen in Figure 17. There, the resulting configurations for five logic functions are illustrated (one logic function per row). The leftmost column shows the desired output for the logic function, while the second column presents the actual response of the trained NN-model. In the rightmost column, the corresponding configurations are visualised. Using these back in the simulations based on the physical model, we obtain the outputs as presented in the third column.

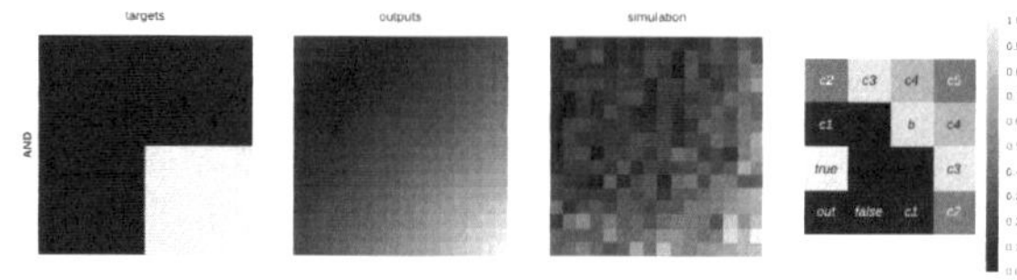

(a) AND

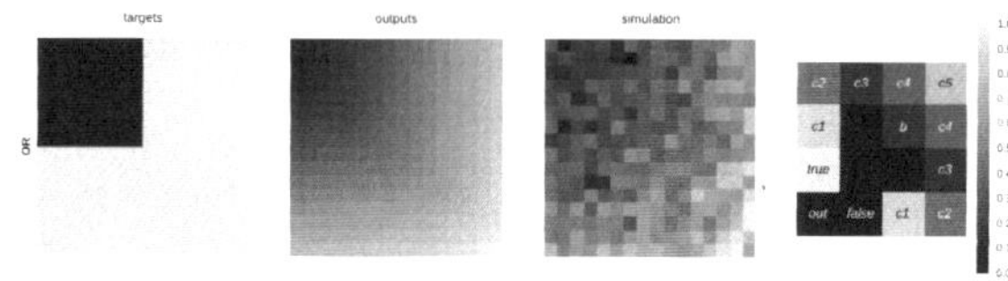

(b) OR

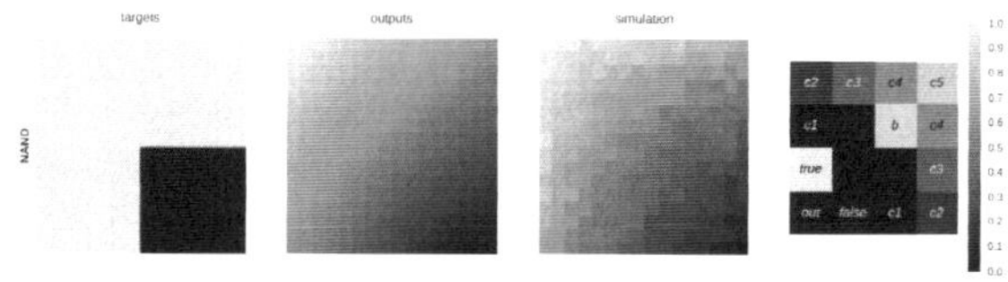

(c) NAND

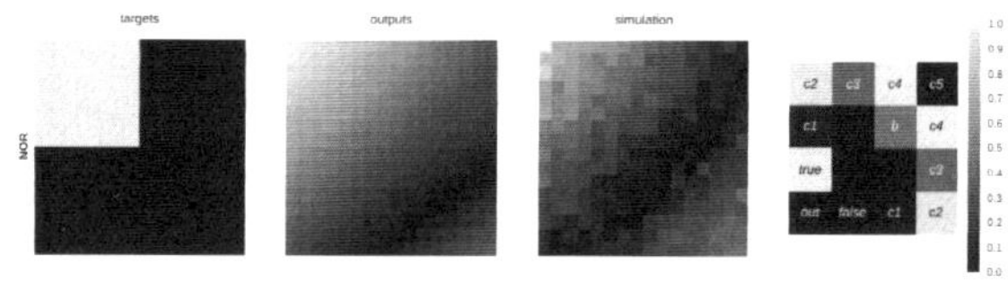

(d) NOR

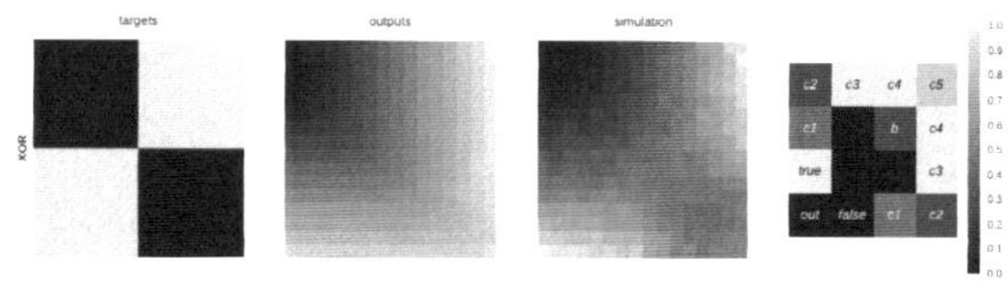

(e) XOR

Figure 17. Gates found using the NN-model, with configuration voltages (rightmost column), NN-model output (second column), desired logic (leftmost column), and the regenerated outputs of the physical material model (third column)

D. Results

From the plots in Figure 17, it can be seen that most of the target Boolean functions can be performed by the nano-material (according to the NN-model). Note that, what is most important is the response of the model in the corners, since we do not really care about values in between True and False. The smooth plots are just there to show how the model is behaving, and to give an impression on how robust the solutions are. For AND, OR, NAND, NOR and XOR, the values in the corners match the desired outputs quite well. In contrast, the search for the XNOR function failed to produce equally satisfactory results, indicating that this function might be difficult to perform for the nano-material under the given setup.

E. Verification in the Physical Model

The configurations found to represent the gates in the NN-model were then used to simulate the physical material model in order to see how well the model represents the original material model. The third column in Figure 17 shows the responses of the physical material model. Comparing these visualisations to the second column in Figure 17, one can see that the configurations found using the NN-model were successfully used to configure the original physical Monte Carlo-based model, and they produce similar outputs. We can observe noise, superimposed on the physical simulation outputs caused by the stochasticity of the simulation, whereas the NN-outputs are smooth because the NN is a deterministic model. The main result is that, even including the noise, the measurements of the physical model constitute the same logic functions as those found in the NN-model. To conclude, the NN-model can be trained to simulate the physical model, and the configurations found using the NN-model can be used to produce the same desired behaviour of the physical material model.

VI. Results of Simulations on SWCNT-sample

Very recently, we conducted similar experiments with real material samples composed of thin films of composites of single-walled carbon nano-tubes (SWCNTs). Instead of depositing nano-particles on an electrode array, the material deposited was a mixture of SWCNTs randomly mixed in an insulating material. The insulating material was either PMMA/PBMA (Polymethy/butyl methacralate) [30]. SWCNTs are mixed with PMMA or PBMA and dissolved in anisole (methoxybenzene). About 20 μL of material is then drop-dispensed onto the electrode array. This is dried at 100°C for 30 min to leave a film over the electrodes. SWCNTs are conducting or semi-conducting and the role of the PMMA/PBMA is to introduce insulating regions within the nano-tube network, to create non-linear current versus voltage characteristics.

Once these nano-tube networks have been fabricated, the approach and methodology are exactly the same as already described in earlier sections, except that we did not use a physical model for gathering training date: First, input-output data combinations were collected by more or less random measurements on the real material. Then, these combinations were used to train an NN-model. Finally, the NN-model was used to predict suitable settings of the configuration variables for the material to act as a Boolean logic gate, and these settings were validated by trying them on the real material. We complete this paper by giving a short description of one of the experiments and its results for one particular material sample.

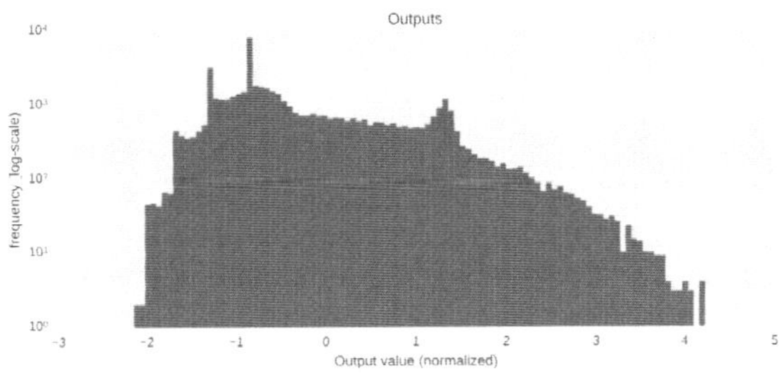

Figure 18. Distribution of the training targets obtained from the SWCNT-sample

In this experiment, roughly 55 k combinations of input-output date were collected from the SWCNT-sample. Two out of a total of eight electrodes were used as the two inputs for the logic function, one was used to read out an output, and the remaining six were used to configure the material. The output was sampled at 100 kHz, and averaged and rescaled between 0 and 1. The distribution of the output values is depicted in Figure 18.

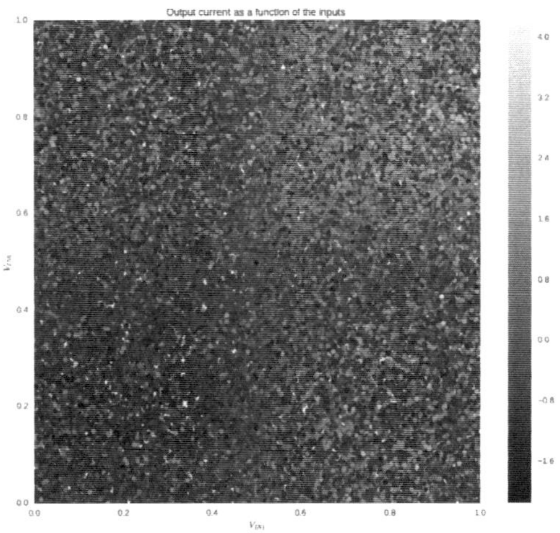

Figure 19. Scatter plot of a sweep across the two selected input electrodes

The scatter plot in Figure 19 shows a sweep across the two input electrodes while configuring the other six configuration electrodes with random voltages. One can clearly observe the variability of outputs provided by the SWCNT-sample.

A new NN-model with more hidden layers was used for the simulations. It consisted of a feed-forward network with 5 hidden layers, each layer having 120 units; the applied output function was ELU [31]. This NN-model was trained with the ADAM [32] optimiser for 50 epochs. Figure 20 shows how well the NN-model was able to match the training data.

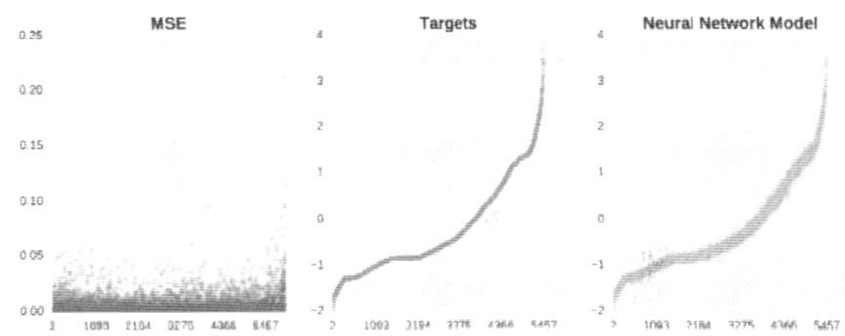

Figure 20. NN-model outputs compared to the outputs of the SWCNT-sample on the validation set

As in the nano-particle network example, suitable configuration voltages for different logic gates were searched in the trained NN-model, using gradient descent. The found configurations were then verified on the same SWCNT-sample that was used for the training data collection, hence closing the modelling loop. The results are visually summarised in Figure 21.

As in our earlier nano-particle network example, the resulting configurations for five logic functions are illustrated (one logic function per row). The leftmost column shows the desired output for the logic function, while the second column presents the actual response of the trained NN-model. In the rightmost

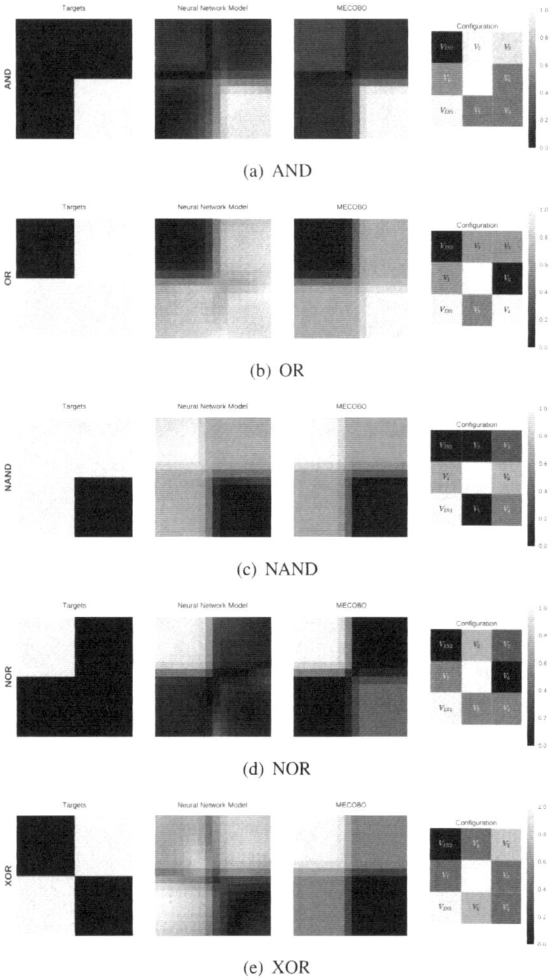

Figure 21. Gates found using the NN-model, with configuration voltages (rightmost column), NN-model output (second column), desired logic (leftmost column), and the regenerated outputs of the SWCNT-sample (third column)

column, the corresponding configurations are visualised. Using these back on the SWCNT-sample, we obtained the outputs as presented in the third column. Except for the XOR function, we see quite a good match between the predicted configurations from the NN-model and the actual performance of the SWCNT-sample provided with these configurations.

VII. Conclusion

This paper has demonstrated how an artificial Neural Network model can be applied to look for configuration voltage settings that enable different standard Boolean logic functions in the same piece of material consisting of a disordered nano-particle or nano-tube network. The training of the Neural Network was based on generated random data from a physical-model based simulation tool in case of the nano-particle networks, and on real data in case of the nano-tube networks. The results are promising and can inform the electrical engineers about possible functional capabilities of these material systems, without the need of fabricating and doing costly and time-consuming trial-and-error experiments on real nano-material networks. Of course, it is obvious that such experiments are unavoidable if it comes to actually testing real networks for the predicted functionalities. In fact, the capability of reconfigurable Boolean logic in small samples of nano-material networks has meanwhile been confirmed experimentally. It is likely, that this proof of concept will be the starting point for exciting new research, and open up the opportunity for a totally new approach to developing multi-functional stand-alone devices.

Next steps in this direction first of all involve the simulation of more real material samples, especially for larger nano-material networks and for more complex functions. For this, also new experiments are needed, in order to produce and collect sufficiently many input-output combinations to enable proper training of the Neural Network. This also requires new fabrication techniques, involving larger nano-material networks on micro-electrode arrays with more contact electrodes interfacing with the material, and with a more sophisticated back gate. The requirements can be predicted by simulations, in particular if one wants to turn to more complicated functionalities, like computational tasks that are difficult to perform with digital computers. Secondly, it would be worthwhile to apply the same modelling and simulation approach to other materials that show interesting physical properties and behaviour, like networks of quantum dots, sheets of graphene, and mixtures of such materials. Note that the same approach was very recently applied to samples of biological material consisting of slime moulds for discovering Boolean gates [33]. Thirdly, a natural next step would be to integrate the Neural Network modelling approach with the evolutionary search technique. These are amongst the future research plans we want to pursue.

Acknowledgment

We acknowledge financial support from the European Community's Seventh Framework Programme (FP7/2007-2013) under grant agreement No. 317662. We also thank the other partners in the NASCENCE project for producing the nano-material samples, and for their help in collecting the data.

References

[1] K. Greff, R. M. J. van Damme, J. Koutník, H. J. Broersma, J. Mikhal, C. P. Lawrence, J. Schmidhuber, and W. G. van der Wiel. Unconventional computing using evolution-in-nanomaterio: Neural networks meet nanoparticle networks. *FUTURE COMPUTING 2016*, pages 15–20, 2016.

[2] Hajo Broersma, Faustino Gomez, Julian Miller, Mike Petty, and Gunnar Tufte. Nascence project: Nanoscale engineering for novel computation using evolution. *International Journal of Unconventional Computing*, 8(4):313–317, 2012.

[3] H. J. Broersma, J. F. Miller, and S. Nichele. Computational matter: Evolving computational functions in nanoscale materials. In A. Adamatzky, editor, *Advances in Unconventional Computing Volume 2: Prototypes, Models and Algorithms*, pages 397–428. 2016.

[4] S. K. Bose *et al.* Evolution of a designless nanoparticle network into reconfigurable boolean logic. *Nature Nanotechnology*, 10(12):1048–1052, 2015.

[5] M. K. Massey *et al.* Evolution of Electronic Circuits using Carbon Nanotube Composites. *Scientific Reports*, 6, 2016. Article number 32197.

[6] R. M. J. van Damme, H. J. Broersma, J. Mikhal, C. P. Lawrence, and W. G. van der Wiel. A simulation tool for evolving functionalities in disordered nanoparticle networks. *EPSyM, IEEE WCCI 2016*, 2016.

[7] L.W. Nagel and D.O. Pederson. Simulation program with integrated circuit emphasis. Memorandum ERL-M382, University of California, Berkeley, April 1973.

[8] Christoph Wasshuber, Hans Kosina, and Siegfried Selberherr. A simulator for single-electron tunnel devices and circuits. *IEEE Transactions on Computer-Aided Design of Integrated Circuits and Systems*, 16:937–944, 1997.

[9] W. McCulloch and W. Pitts. A logical calculus of the ideas immanent in nervous activity. *Bulletin of Mathematical Biophysics*, 7:115–133, 1943.

[10] Frank Rosenblatt. The perceptron: a probabilistic model for information storage and organization in the brain. *Psychological review*, 65(6):386, 1958.

[11] P. J. Werbos. Applications of advances in nonlinear sensitivity analysis. In *Proceedings of the 10th IFIP Conference, 31.8 - 4.9, NYC*, pages 762–770, 1981.

[12] D. C. Ciresan, U. Meier, J. Masci, and J. Schmidhuber. A committee of neural networks for traffic sign classification. In *International Joint Conference on Neural Networks (IJCNN)*, pages 1918–1921, 2011.

[13] D. C. Ciresan, U. Meier, and J. Schmidhuber. Multi-column deep neural networks for image classification. In *IEEE Conference on Computer Vision and Pattern Recognition CVPR 2012*, 2012. Long preprint arXiv:1202.2745v1 [cs.CV].

[14] Hasim Sak, Andrew W. Senior, and Françoise Beaufays. Long short-term memory based recurrent neural network architectures for large vocabulary speech recognition. *CoRR*, abs/1402.1128, 2014. [retrieved: Feb, 2016].

[15] A.N. Korotkov. *Coulomb Blockade and Digital Single-Electron Devices*, pages 157–189. Blackwell, Oxford, 1997.

[16] Christoph Wasshuber. *Computational Single-Electronics*. Springer-Verlag, 2001.

[17] Christoph Wasshuber. Single-Electronics – How it works. How it's used. How it's simulated. In *Proceedings of the International Symposium on Quality Electronic Design*, pages 502–507, 2012.

[18] Julian F Miller and Keith Downing. Evolution in materio: Looking beyond the silicon box. *Proceedings of NASA/DoD Evolvable Hardware Workshop*, pages 167–176, July 2002.

[19] Simon Harding and Julian Francis Miller. Evolution in materio. In Robert A. Meyers, editor, *Encyclopedia of Complexity and Systems Science*, pages 3220–3233. Springer, 2009.

[20] Simon L. Harding and Julian F. Miller. Evolution in materio: Evolving logic gates in liquid crystal. *International Journal of Unconventional Computing*, 3(4):243–257, 2007.

[21] Simon L. Harding, Julian F. Miller, and Edward A. Rietman. Evolution in materio: Exploiting the physics of materials for computation. *International Journal of Unconventional Computing*, 4(2):155–194, 2008.

[22] Julian F. Miller, Simon L. Harding, and Gunnar Tufte. Evolution-in-materio: evolving computation in materials. *Evolutionary Intelligence*, 7:49–67, 2014.

[23] A. Yoshihito. Information processing using intelligent materials - information-processing architectures for material processors. *Intelligent Materials Systems and Structures*, 5:418–423, 1994.

[24] Klaus-Peter Zauner. From prescriptive programming of solid-state devices to orchestrated self-organisation of informed matter. In Jean-Pierre Banâtre, Pascal Fradet, Jean-Louis Giavitto, and Olivier Michel, editors, *Unconventional Programming Paradigms: International Workshop UPP 2004*, volume 3566, pages 47–55. Springer, 2004.

[25] P. Cariani. To evolve an ear: epistemological implications of Gordon Pask's electrochemical devices. *Systems Research*, 3:19–33, 1993.

[26] G. Pask. Physical analogues to the growth of a concept. In *Mechanisation of Thought Processes*, number 10 in National Physical Laboratory Symposium, pages 877–922. Her Majesty's Stationery Office, London, UK, 1958.

[27] R. L. Anderson. Recent advances in finding best operating conditions. *Journal of the American Statistical Association*, 48(264):789–798, December 1953.

[28] Francisco J. Solis and Roger J.-B. Wets. Minimization by random search techniques. *Mathematics of Operations Research*, 6(1):19–30, February 1981.

[29] James Bergstra and Yoshua Bengio. Random search for hyper-parameter optimization. *The Journal of Machine Learning Research*, 13(1):281–305, 2012.

[30] M. Mohid, J.F. Miller, S.L. Harding, G. Tufte, M.K. Massey, and M.C Petty. Evolution-in-materio: Solving computational problems using carbon nanotube-polymer composites. *Soft Computing*, xx:xx–xx, 2016. In press.

[31] Djork-Arné Clevert, Thomas Unterthiner, and Sepp Hochreiter. Fast and accurate deep network learning by exponential linear units (elus). *arXiv preprint arXiv:1511.07289*, 2015.

[32] Diederik Kingma and Jimmy Ba. Adam: A method for stochastic optimization. *arXiv preprint arXiv:1412.6980*, 2014.

[33] S. Harding, J. Koutník, K. Greff, J. Schmidhuber, and A. Adamatzky. Discovering boolean gates in slime mould. *ArXiv paper, submitted*, 2016. arXiv:1607.02168 [retrieved: November, 2016].

Metacognitive Support of Mathematical Abstraction Processes: Why and How - A Basic Reasoning

Hans M. Dietz

Institute of Mathematics
University of Paderborn
D 33098 Paderborn, Germany
Email: dietz@upb.de

***Abstract*—A significant and distinctive feature of human beings is the ability of performing abstraction operations, e.g., when forming categories of objects or even consciouly creating abstract objects as it is typical in mathematics. Although the possible range of corresponding abilities is certainly predetermined by individual genetic factors, a high-level abstraction performance will typically be achieved gradually by an intensive long-run practice in solving abstraction prone problems. On the other hand, mathematical abstraction is often considered to be a serious obstacle in mathematics education. As metacognition has turned out to be helpful in overcoming some other obstacles in the students' process of knowledge acquisition, one may ask whether metacognition may also serve as a remedy against the abstraction obstacle and, in particular, whether it may help to accelerate the acquisition of abstraction abilities. The paper provides some inital reasoning w.r.t. this possibility, proposes some basic principles of abstraction that could be taught on a metacognitive level, and presents a concept of a corresponding teaching experiment. Hopefully, it will provide more effective teaching as well as a better understanding of cognitive processes underlying mathematical abstraction.**

***Index Terms*—Abstraction; Mathematical Abstraction; Mathematics Education; Mathematical Reading; Metacognition.**

I. Introduction

The present article is a substantially enlarged and extended version of the authors recent paper "Metacognitive Support of Mathematical Abstraction Processes" [1] presented at the 2016 IARIA Cognitive conference in Rome.

Basic mathematics courses belong to the greatest challenges for first year university students from many disciplines. The author's long run experience in conducting such courses at the University of Paderborn indicates that one main reason for that is the lack of appropriate study and working techniques. For many students, the major obstacle in understanding mathematics is the lacking aptitude to understand its language. As a remedy, a system of in-teaching *metacognitive* support instruments named "CAT" was introduced [2]. CAT provides instructions that help to improve the studying and working routines. But more than that, its core focus is on enhancing the ability to read and understand mathematical texts properly [3][4]. Accompanying empirical studies [5][6] showed that improvements could be achieved by using CAT's metacognitive instruction tools.

Even with this, one often sees refusal or even fear of the perceived *abstractness* of mathematics. Moreover, many of the beginning students are quite unfamiliar with any kind of abstractness. Hence, coping with mathematics becomes particularly hard for them. This raises the question how to facilitate the "access to abstraction" for them.

It is impossible to rise this question without referring to the aspect of time, because good abstraction abilities are typically achieved "by doing", i.e., by solving problems that require – or at least promote – a certain level of abstraction. Even mathematicians develop their abstraction skills within a lengthy process of education and mathematical work. However, in basic courses for non-mathematicians, there is not enough time to re-run along this path. As an alternative, the present paper proposes to support some basic aspects of abstraction on a *metacognitive* level, by explicitly "teaching abstraction principles", with the objective to accelerate the process of acquiring abstraction skills.

In order to derive such rules, several aspects of abstraction are discussed. A generally adopted hypothesis is that abstraction operations are organized hierarchically. Piaget [7] has described that, and how, this hierarchy is run through in children's development of mathematical thinking. The hierarchical nature of abstraction was also emphasized by Dubinsky [8] [9] and Arnon et al. [10]. In contrast to the forementioned ones, the approach pursued here aims to additionally support the construction of several layers of abstraction by *explicit metacognitive instruction*. Although this work is still in an early stage it can be hoped that it shall yield not only better teaching instruments but a better understanding of the underlying cognitive processes as well. In particular, the hope for better teaching instruments is supported by the empirical findings from [5] [6] regarding CAT's instructions, which are essentially metacognitive.

As compared to [1], the novel contribution of the present paper covers both a broader and deeper embedding of the paper's subject in the corresponding research history – including new insights from quite recent work –, and a more thorough and lucid exposition of relevant concepts, including new examples for metacognitive support.

The paper is organized as follows: In Section II, the need of abstraction in economics education is highlighted. The nature of abstraction and its "economics" is discussed in Sections III, and IV. Section V deals with perceived abstraction aversity. The role of metacognition is discussed in Section VI. The following section deals with operational aspects of abstraction. Section VIII gives an outlook of a forthcoming teaching project and possible applications of the results.

II. Is Abstraction Educationally Needed?

It is often believed that abstraction is a matter of "pure mathematics" rather than of its applications. However, practically this is not true. Here are some fundamental reasons for that: In many applications, at least a basic understanding of the (abstract) language of mathematics is required. Further, abstraction is a core feature of building mathematical models for more or less "real" problems. Modeling requires a "translation" of representations of "real" objects, their attributes, and relations into the language of mathematics. And last but not least, precise reasoning often relies on the abstract logical structure rather than on the domain specific content of arguments. By these and other reasons, the ability to cope with abstraction is closely related to a high professional performance in several domains, as can be seen, e.g., from Greuel et al. [11].

Moreover, in economics, there is a particular demand of "abstraction" at least along four different lines. First, fundamental economic phenomena are explained with the help of abstract mathematical concepts. Look, e.g., at a preference relation as described here:

$$\underline{x} \preceq \underline{y} \quad :\Longleftrightarrow \quad 2x_1 + 3x_2 \leq 2y_1 + 3y_2. \tag{1}$$

The students must be able to read, understand, and handle symbolic expressions like this. Note that the context of considering such relations typically involves some set theory. From the economic point of view, set theory provides the appropriate language to describe, e.g., sets of possible economic decisions. Thus, the students should master this language to a certain minimal extent. However, the author's teaching experience says that even quite basic concepts of set theory are perceived as being rather abstract by many students.

Second, modern economics is interested in qualitative results that are valid under quite general assumptions. Accordingly, these results rely on abstract qualitative properties of the underlying models. For example, one can say a lot about the behavior of an enterprise that produces one good for a polypolistic market, given only that its internal cost function is *neoclassic*, regardless of its concrete form [3]. Hence the qualitative nature of the problems is in the foreground, while purely numerical calculations are of less significance.

Third, economics is concerned with complex systems and their equilibria. The study of such systems is often decomposed into studies of subsystems, the internal parameters of which are determined via optimization, given some exogenous parameters. But it has to be understood that these exogeneous parameters become endogenous when entering a higher level of consideration. That is, frequently there is no point in fixing numerical values, rather one has to develop kind of functional thinking.

And fourth, by employing modern and sophisticated results of mathematics, economics adopt the abstraction level of mathematics itself. This confirms that Devlin's [12] statement "The main benefit of learning and doing mathematics is not the specific content; rather it's the fact that it develops the ability to reason precisely and analytically about formally defined abstract structures" holds true for modern economics, as well as for other sciences.

III. What is Abstraction?

So far, "abstraction" was used in quite general way. For the purposes of this paper, some specific aspects of interest shall be described and put in the general context.

A. General Aspects

Everybody knows somehow and from somewhere "what is abstraction", as this word became present in a lot of domains. A common feature of many conceptions of "abstraction" refers to the latin word *abstrahere* in the philosophical sense of omitting unessential details of an object in the process of inductive thinking, resulting in a new – or simpler – entity, as it was described first by Aristotle. Until today, the term "abstraction" has conquered its place in various scientific disciplines: philosophy, psychology, linguistics, cognitive science, mathematics, computer science, education, and others – and beyond that as well in common understanding. Accordingly, the amount of varying interpretations as well as the number of publications on this subject is extremely large and indicates that "abstraction" is a rather rich and complex notion. It is neither possible nor the purpose of this paper to give a full account to all essential aspects of this notion. Rather it shall concentrate on some aspects that may be essential both from the cognitive point of view and for teaching mathematics.

B. Abstraction as Mental Processes

Henceforth, the term "abstraction" shall be used in the narrower sense to denote *individual mental processes*. Typically, these processes result in *abstract objects* or, more precisely, in new – and simpler – mental representations of previously present mental objects or their relations, respectively, or even in the creation of new mental objects. Clearly, there is a duality of abstraction processes and their results. Viewing abstraction as a process has a long history, as "... there is evidence in Aristotle's psychological and biological writings which suggests that abstraction is a component of the inductive process by which we reach universal concepts" (Smith [13]). An intrinsic feature of abstraction is that it can lead to a re-structured organization of mental knowledge structures (Hershkowitz et al. [14]). In a wider sense, "abstraction" will also be understood as individual mental processes of understanding and exploiting already existing abstract objects and concepts. It is obvious that these processes are of particular significance for learning mathematics and, thus, should be promoted.

Some Comments

The author is aware of the deficiencies of these explanations – after all, the given notion of abstraction refers to "mental processes" and "mental representations", or more specifically, to the change of the latter by means of the first. That is, these terms might need an explanation, too. Again, they are used frequently with varying senses. Given that both – processes, and representations – are present within our living organism, in the end they must be accomplished on a neuro-bio-physiological level, exist in distributed electric potentials, specific chemical substances or particular molecular structures and their changes. That is, the possibly most subtle explanation of cognitive functions may start from neuro-bio-physiological details.

However, the possibility to investigate these details with sufficiently high resolution has but developed within the last few years; knowledge about these basic mechanisms keeps on growing rapidly. On the other hand, reasoning about cognitive activities has a very long tradition, without having hands on that level. The key to this seeming puzzle is that research and reasoning on the subject "human thinking" used more or less abstract models of this subject, and more or less specific languages to describe these models as well.

With respect to research on cognitive systems these models can be understood, as C. Eliasmith [15] poses it, by different kinds of *metaphors*. He systematizes four mainstream metaphoric approaches known as *symbolicism*, *connectionism*, *dynamicism*, and the *Bayesian approach*. While symbolicism, roughly spoken, supposes that cognitive systems work similar like computers and process something like symbolic rules, as prominently stated by Fodor [16], connectionism sees brain functions better represented by abstract "neural" networks (Rumelhart and McClelland [17]). The dynamicism approach tries to tie brain functions closer to the continous flow of different input signals that have to be responded to within very short periods of time; it is related to systems and control theory. The Bayesian approach is prominently represented by Anderson [18] and the recent work of Tenenbaum, Griffiths, and others [19][20]. Eliasmith [15] points out that all of these metaphors are appropriate to explain *some* aspects of cognition, but perhaps neither of them is apt to explain *all*.

To sum up: Dependent on the respective purpose, it can suffice to use a metaphoric level of description. Abstraction (as performed by the mind) can perhaps be understood by abstract models of the mind's operation. For the purposes aimed at here, this exposition shall rely on verbal terms as used in mathematics education, education sciences, and in part in cognitive psychology. The view towards abstraction as a process of changing or creating mental representations in a particular manner seems to be widely accepted, even if not always a definition of abstraction is provided (see, e.g., Gentner [21]).

The role of abstraction in cognition

Although "... human cognition is certainly embodied, its embodiment is not what gives human cognition its advantage over that of other species. Its advantage depends on its ability to achieve abstraction in content and control" (Anderson et al. [22]). Indeed, much speaks for the view that abstraction is a *fundamental working principle of the brain*, that drives already early stages of mental development. Schulz et al. [23] come to the suggestion "... that children's ability to learn robust, abstract principles does not depend on extensive prior experience but can occur rapidly, on-line, and in tandem with inferences about specific relations. ... Researchers have proposed that such rapid learning is possible because children's inferences are constrained by more abstract theories ...". Skorstad et al. [24] stressed that "Current work in concept-formation suggests that abstraction does indeed take place during concept learning..." H. Ballard pointedly summarizes "brain computation as hierarchical abstraction" [25]. Shepard [26] argues "Possibly, behind the diverse behaviors of humans and animals, as behind the various motions of planets and stars, we may discern the operation of universal laws. "

In this line, the author conjectures that it is universal laws, too, that allow for abstraction and even drive it. Abstraction makes many cognitive operations feasible – by reducing the demand of ressources, energy consumption, and operational complexity. Hence the hypothesis that any particular abstractions occur as the result of optimization processes driven by universal laws.

Localization

It seems obvious that abstraction plays a prominent role in those brain domains that are responsible for conscious thinking and human language processing, but it is also quite reasonable to assume that abstraction mechanisms already work in more basic layers of the brain's functional architecture, in particular, when processing sensomotoric informations. Here, one of the most basic operations is visual pattern recognition, possibly followed by identifying simultaneously occuring similar patterns. The occurence of patterns – or patterns of patterns – is processed further by higher cognitive layers, associating these patterns with objects or events. The same can be said with respect to the parallel processing of other kinds of sensomotoric input. A particular task of even higher layers is to define or understand, respectively, categories of perceived objects, like "animal", "cat" vs. "dog", etc. This task is highly abstractive as it requires to detect essential common features and to neglect non-essential features of the objects; note that whether some features are "essential" or not depends on the underlying cognitive goal.

A further abstraction step is performed by creating category labels, and yet another by handling category labels instead of a variety of objects itself. From there, a much higher level of abstraction is achieved by including structural relations between categories or labels, respectively.

Some more words about the connection between abstraction and understanding, creating, or handling categories, as this connection is particularly strong: "The earliest theories of category representation (e.g., rule based and prototype) tended to view category knowledge as consisting of abstract information that summarizes the central tendency across examples. Rule-based theories and models hypothesize that category representations consist of one or more rules or definitions that can be be learned from experience ..." (Levering & Kurtz [27]). It appears to be obvious that *rules* themselves are abstract in its nature, even if they are physically represented. Gentner has pointed out that the human smartness is connected with the ability to create *relational* categories [21]. Relational properties have to be extracted from structured representations of objects, their attributes, and relations. The way this goes in comparison and analogy is described in terms of structure-mapping by Gentner et al. [28][29]. It seems to be natural that a similar description might be given w.r.t. abstraction as a particular form of structure-mapping.

Summarizing, it appears that abstraction processes are organized within a complex architecture that mirrors the functional brain architecture itself.

C. Mathematical Abstraction

Thinking about mathematical abstraction, too, goes back to Aristotle who, in "... the context of mathematics, ... uses the term 'abstraction' (aphairesis) to refer to the act of ignoring or disregarding matter and change from perceptible objects in order to isolate their specifically mathematical characteristics as distinct objects of thought" (Smith [13]). When talking about mathematical abstraction a slightly broader view shall be used; "mathematical abstraction" will refer to abstraction processes connected with "understanding mathematics" or "doing mathematics", respectively. This means that the objects of cognition themselves are representations of mathematical objects or relations.

Formally, mathematical abstraction is often understood as a (non-injective) mapping a, say, with $a(x)$ beeing an *abstraction* of x and, vice versa, each x with $f(x) = y$ being an *instantiation* of y. An early source of viewing it that way is Rinkens [30]; more recently, this view is taken up in abstract diagrammatic reasoning (Stapleton [31]).

Here, we have to be more specific w.r.t. the teaching objectives. It will be distinguished between *receptive*, *applicative* and *creative* abstraction. *Receptive* abstraction refers to individual brain activities that provide "understanding" of abstract concepts that have been defined beforehand by other individuals. To the opposite, *creative* abstraction is concerned with the construction of new mental representations without external inspiration. *Applied* abstraction means to employ abstract objects and relations, regardless whether these have been created by other individuals or not. Accordingly, enhancing receptive abstraction is the primary concern of teaching, where active and creative abstraction play an important role in problem solving, which comes into the focus in the advanced stages of teaching.

Although being complex, there are some particular aspects of abstraction that can be isolated. The following activities will be considered as basic aspects of abstraction:

- *encapsulation:*
  i.e., to see a number of objects as a whole entitiy, e.g., to see
  $$e^{\frac{4x^2}{23x+17}} \quad \text{as} \quad e^{\boxed{\text{something}}} \tag{2}$$
- *symbolization:*
  i.e., introducing abstract referents (indices) for patterns like expressions, relations, statements etc.; e.g.,
  $$e^{\frac{4x^2}{23x+17}} = e^{\boxed{a}}, \tag{3}$$
- *analogization:*
  i.e., identifying common features in different objects or domains and creating a new object out of them, e.g., identifying the common property of squares, rectangles, rhombus, etc., as being a quadrangle:
  COMMON(square, rectangle, rhombus, ...) = quadrangle
- *class formation:*
  i.e., encapsulation of a number of analogized objects, e.g., forming the class (or set) of quadrangles.

The following activities work upon a certain stock of pre-established abstract objects:

- *structural synthesis:*
  e.g., grouping separate objects x and y to a pair (x, y) being considered as a new object
- *object embedding:*
  i.e., seeing a particular object as an element of an appropriate category (set) in order to use category properties rather than individual properties, e.g., as here:
  $$e^{\frac{4x^2}{23x+17}} = e^{\varphi(x)} \tag{4}$$
  In the example, the left hand superscript expression is interpreted as evaluation of some differentiable function φ; hence, results for the whole class can be applied (e.g., the chain rule of differentiation).
- *switching embedding levels:*
  i.e., embedding/outbedding in nested structures; e.g., the changes of focus between a set and its elements.

Further abstraction operations work on structures on collections of objects rather than on objects itself:

- *structural alignment*
  in the sense of a simultaneous encapsulation of objects

and their connecting structures, typically followed by a symbolization.

Example: The expression

$$\begin{pmatrix} 1 & 7 \\ 3 & 5 \end{pmatrix} \cdot \begin{pmatrix} 2 & 8 \\ 9 & 4 \end{pmatrix} \tag{5}$$

(with the dot denoting usual matrix multiplication) could be seen as

$$\boxed{\textit{something}} \circ \boxed{\textit{something'}}$$

or even more briefly as

$$a \circ b,$$

say, with a, b denoting some objects of some category and $\circ$ denoting some operation, all of them still to be specified;

- *structure-object interchange:*

  that is, rendering *structures*, i.e., relations between different objects, to encapsulated *objects* of consideration
- *recursion:*

  i.e., establishing recursive structures within problems or within problem solving strategies; e.g., when trying to simplify the expression

$$A \cap (B \cup (A \cap (B \cup (A \cap (B \cup (A \cap B)))))). \tag{6}$$

This enumeration is by no means complete, but may suffice for the purpose of this paper.

IV. The Economics of Abstraction

As already mentioned, a significant feature of creative abstraction is to omit "unessential" details of the object under consideration. However, what is "unessential" can vary heavily with the underlying cognitive task. This can be observed in a variety of domains and is particularly true in mathematics. For example, the set of the real numbers, equipped with the usual addition and multiplication, represents different abstract objects at the same time, e.g., a vector space, a ring, a field, etc. Which property is "essential" clearly depends on the problem under consideration. Typically, the choice of the appropriate abstraction will ease the solution of a problem – the problem can be solved with less mental effort, within less time, with deeper insight in its nature, etc. Sometimes, it is even impossible to solve a given problem without appropriate abstraction. So far, this phenomenon is clearly a social experience of the mathematical community, but on the other hand, it can be re-experienced by each individual that deals with mathematical problems.

Hence the author's hypothesis: *A latent aversion against abstraction can be reduced by the individual experience of "economic benefits" when using abstraction.*

V. Abstraction Aversity

As mentioned, mathematics education is perceived as being difficult by many students. Often it is claimed that this is due to the abstractness of mathematics. This does reflect an attitude of restraint up to rejection towards abstractness. This may seem a little bit puzzling as without the hierarchically abstractive organization of brain functions there would be no human life. However, many of the brain abstractions remain unconscious or, at least, are not subject to conscious attention. That is, the conscious mind seems to reject activities that are quite basic for its very existence. However, there is evidence of such phenomena. E.g., Medin and Ross write "We have repeatedly demonstrated the limitations of people as abstract, deductive reasoners and noted with chagrin the difficulty of producing transfer of training or generalized problem-solving skills" [32].

While this statement refers to abstraction-related *actions*, there is also rejection of abstraction before any action takes place. Here is an example from the author's teaching practice. From time to time, the author uses to check whether the students captured a given matter – by directly asking them in the lecture. Often, the students have questions. In many cases, the author can answer explaining the subject

- either by a concrete numerical example
- or by using symbolic notation (variables).

The students can choose between these possibilities by a "ballot", i.e., by by raising their hands in favor of one of these two possibilities. In an auditory of about 500-600 people, the number of hands cannot be counted exactly; however, it is possible to obtain reasonably good estimates. In almost all cases

- about 80% of the votes prefer the numerical example
- only 20% prefer a more abstract explanation.

This observation matches a statement of Österholm, saying that the presence of symbols renders mathematical texts more difficult [33].

VI. What can Metacognition do?

When arguing that metacognition might help to accelerate the acquisition of abstraction abilities, there should be some justification. After all, the possible use of metacognition in education is not undisputed. Also, the relation of metacognition to abstraction should be considered. A pessimistic view is offered by Hajek: "... the formation of a new abstraction seems *never* to be the outcome of a conscious process, nor something at which the mind can deliberately aim, but always a discovery of something which *already* guides its operation" [34]. However, the author's experience with the metacognitive support system CAT allows for some optimism, as shall be seen below.

A. Some educational experience

As alredy mentioned, coping with mathematics belongs undoubtedly to the major challenges for many first-year university students. The author's long run experience in teaching basic mathematics courses for large numbers of future economists at the University of Paderborn indicated that one severe reason for the difficulties with mathematics is the lack of adequate techniques – for studying in general, and for coping with mathematics in particular.

As a remedy, the author started in 2010 to teach not only mathematical subjects itself, but as well appropriate strategies that allow to succcessfully deal with these subjects. These strategies, summarized by the logo "CAT", are rule based and of metacognitive type. The rules, referred to as *Checklists*, *Ampel* (german for traffic lights) and *Toolbox*, do not only address issues of a proper organization of the study process, but rather the organization of concept understanding, self assessment, and problem solving. As it is impossible to account to all details here, the reader is referred to [2][3][4] for a detailed description.

A distinctive feature of CAT is that teaching and exercising working methods became integrated part of the regular mathematics course. Already long before 2010, there had been several attempts to support the students – e.g., by offering them optional tutorials dealing with such methods. But these offers failed to be effective as most of the students did not take advantage of them. By introducing CAT in the regular course, all students can optionally benefit from this offer; they can learn what these methods aim at, how they work, judge them, and decide whether to employ them in their own work.

"Reading Mathematics"

CAT's major concern is to enable the students to read and understand mathematical texts and expressions properly – from the level of single signs, symbols, or words up to the level of valid mathematical concepts. The way to go is described by the Checklist "Reading" along five steps. This checklist is to be used together with the student's *vocabulary* – a written (and, hopefully, mental) list that keeps track of all new definitions and symbols. The five steps of the checklist are described in Table I.

TABLE I. The Checklist 'Reading'

S1: *Spell*
(Make sure to know the precise meaning/role of each single symbol, sign, or word.)
S2: *Read out*
(Try to read out the full phrase as a spoken sentence.)
S3: *Animate*
(Provide examples, and non-examples, respectively.)
S4: *Visualize*
(Provide a graphical visualization, if appropriate.)
S5: *Talk*
(Give an explaining talk to others, including questions and discussion.)

Basically, the first two steps of the Checklist "Reading" provide nothing but the lexical fundamentals of a concept. Consider, e.g., the phrase

$$M := \{\, n \in \mathbb{N} \mid \exists m \in \mathbb{N} : n = 2m \,\}. \tag{7}$$

In reasonably good course notes, all necessary ingredients are provided before this phrase occurs; here, we assume that the symbols " := ", "{...|...}", "∈", "ℕ", "∃", and ":" have been introduced beforehand. Clearly, the concept of sets has to be understood before, too. Note that a student who arrives at the above phrase when reading the course notes can easily perform the steps S1 and S2 of the Checklist "Reading", as all mentioned pre-defined ingredients can be imported from the vocabulary. After doing so, the student might arrive at a sentence like this:

(V1) *M is defined as the set of all natural numbers n with the property that there exists a natural number m such that n equals $2m$.*

One might think that such a – reasonably fluent – verbalization should reveal its meaning easily, hence the student should generate at a brief description like

(V2) *M is defined as the set of all even natural numbers.*

However, this is by far not true, as became evident from written exams, see, e.g., Dietz & Rohde [35]. In an appropriate task, about 50% of the students were able to provide a reasonable "read out" analogous to (V1), but only 10% could give a meaningful explanation like (V2) using their own words. That is, a fluent statement like (V1) does by far not guarantee a deeper concept understanding. Hence, (V1) has still to be followed by the steps S3, S4 and S5 of the Checklist "Reading" in order to arrive at a valid mental concept. Note that the mentioned results of the 2012 exams clearly indicate that many students, although they had been taught these steps, did not yet perform them in a satisfactory manner.

To henceforth support the students better in going through these steps, the instrument of a *Concept Base* was introduced – a kind of form sheet that augments the vocabulary entries of a concept – key word, definition, denomination, "read out", syntax – by compliant extensions like examples, non-examples (from S3), visualizations (from S4), useful statements, and applications (from the ongoing progress in the course). [4] gives an detailed account on how to perform these steps, in particular, how to obtain examples and visualizations.

Empirical findings

It should be stressed again that the mentioned rules are metacognitive in nature. Initially, these rules had been explained and exemplified within the lectures solely, based on the author's belief in their immediate persuasiveness. However, it turned out that this was not enough in order to change long-term working habits. Therefore, after 2010 the implementation and improvement of CAT was accompanied by several empirical studies.

An initial qualitative study [5] gave rise to the persuasion that metacognitive support, particularly for "reading mathematics", can be effective. From 2012 on, a quantitative pre-study and a three-stage main study were conducted. Several results are reported in [36] and [6]. The pre-study from 2012 showed clearly that, at that time, many students did not apply the CAT methods. Several reasons for that could be found:

- Essentially, the students missed support by the tutors.
- They did often not understand how the methods apply.
- Many students widely underestimated their own need and possible benefit of these methods.

As a consequence, all components of the teaching process – including tutorials, homework exercises, mentoring – have successively been aligned in order to "live" CAT. The investigations of the subsequent stages of the main study show that these measures led to a considerable increase in the acceptance of CAT. From [6] and from some yet unpublished data of the main study one can see the following: Recently, the Checklist Reading, Vocabulary, Toolbox, and Concept Base are ranked to be helpful by large majorities of the students (between 63% and 84%) and – except for the Concept Base – these tools are regularly used by the majority of students. Moreover, most of the students do use concept bases at least sometimes. Interestingly, many students esteem the helpfulness of these instruments even higher (Table II).

TABLE II. Rating of the helpfulness of CAT's instruments

Instrument of CAT	Percentage of students rating it "very helpful"
Checklist Reading	19.9
Vocabulary	38.5
Concept Base	16.4
Toolbox	32.2

As to the effects of CAT on the study success: At the described level of exploitation, CAT turns out to be definitively helpful for students with medium academic performance. In this group of students, the use frequency of CAT is positively correlated with the success rate of the final exam and negatively correlated with the grades (1='very good', 5 = 'insufficient'). Besides that, there are verbal comments of students like "... put more effort on rendering concept bases, as these are really important for own learning" (authors translation from german "mehr Aufwand auf die Erstellung von Konzeptbasen legen, da diese wirklich wichtig zum eigenen Lernen sind").

Admittedly, the utilization of CAT by the students did not yet reach the desired degree; in particular, the author believes that a more intense use of concept bases could promote deeper understanding a lot. The data from [6] suggest that many students do overestimate the time effort needed for utilizing concept bases. This problem might be overcome in the future by providing better information for the students. Further, both utilization and efficacy of the Ampel need to be substantially improved. But summarizing the results obtained so far, the metacognitive support has shown its potential to provide effective help for many students.

As to abstraction

In the same spirit, it appears that at least some aspects of conscious abstraction are amenable to meta-instructions. Goldstone & Sakamoto state that "If abstracting deep principles that cut across different domains is frequently valuable (see Anderson, Reder, & Simon, 1996 and Barnett & Ceci, 2002 for defenses of this assumption), then it is likewise valuable to find ways to promote this abstraction" [37].

B. "Value added" by metacognition

The metacognitive rules provided by CAT, although exemplified in the context of a mathematics course, are by far not bound to mathematics. Rather it appears that the provided working techniques could easily apply in other domains as well, with minor and obvious modifications. (This was at least one of the basic intentions when initiating CAT.) There is episodic evidence that some students applied Concept Bases in other courses, too. However, so far the long run effects of introducing CAT have not yet been investigated.

C. Metacognition as abstraction

It should be noted that metacognition itself is highly abstractive in its nature, because the rules of working and thinking become objects of interest rather than the proper subjects of the work and thinking. Of course, one may argue that metacognition is part of the brain's task management, which seems to be undeniable. However, in the author's opinion it seems to be more natural to consider task priorization, task ressource allocation, and time management as belonging to task management, whereas rules are abstract in nature.

VII. Operational Aspects of Abstraction

For the purposes of the project, we have to confine ourselves to selected aspects of abstraction. The selection takes into account:

- the needs of abstraction within the course
- the degree of operationability
- the degree of observability.

Recall that we want to support problem understanding and solving processes with the help of *metacognitive* abstraction rules. These can be understood as rules that guide and structure the *working process* rather than providing particular abstraction results. From this point of view, the focus will be on such aspects of abstraction that appear to be in reach of such metacognitive rules. Examples of such aspects are

- encapsulation/analogization/symbolization
- structuring
- recursion techniques and
- qualitative reasoning.

To illustrate the idea of abstraction meta-rules suppose that the student's problem under consideration is given by some text, formula or so, henceforth called the *document*. The first of the forementioned abstraction aspects is closely related to the visual input. Hence, the following meta-rules are suggested:

(R1) *Provide a clear* visual *organization of the document.*

(R2) *Identify large substructures.*
(If appropriate, *put them into containers* or *symbolize* them, respectively.)

(R3) *Identify similar patterns.*
(If appropriate, *symbolize* them.)

(R4) *Identify repetition indicators w.r.t. tasks or structures, respectively.*
(Try to use *one* solution for all repeated tasks and *one* principle to work with repeated structures.)

For example, consider this task for students:

Task 1: *Determine the operating minimum, given the following cost functions:* 1) $K_1(x) := 4x^2 + 15\,x + 42, x \geq 0$, 2) $K_2(x) := 242x^2 + 72x + 117, x \geq 0$, ... 5) $K_5(x) := 25x^2 + 5x + 242, x \geq 0$.

Obviously, there are at least three different levels of abstraction on which this task could be fulfilled. We call the least one *level*

(A0) Without any experience in abstraction-aided working, the students would tend to solve each of the problems 1 to 5 individually, using only numerical computations. This would imply to perform the corresponding ansatzes and solving techniques altogether five times, and probably some of the students would try to facilitate the computation somehow "on the way".

We claim that by respecting the above rules progress to a higher abstraction level could be promoted. Indeed, a better visual organization of the task according to rule (R1) might already change the document as follows:

Task 1: *Determine the operating minimum, given the following cost functions:*

1. $K_1(x) := \;\; 4\,x^2 + 15\,x + \;\; 42,\; x \geq 0$
2. $K_2(x) := 242\,x^2 + 72\,x + 117,\; x \geq 0$

... ...

5. $K_5(x) := \;\; 25\,x^2 + \;\; 5\,x + 242,\; x \geq 0.$

From here, looking both at the five *repetitions* as proposed by rule (R4) and at *similar patterns* as proposed by rule (R3), the students might more easily see the uniform structure

$$K_{\square}(x) := \square\, x^2 + \square\, x + \square,\; x \geq 0, \tag{8}$$

where the gray boxes symbolize containers with different contents. According to (R4), we recommend to find a unified solution from here. Thus, it is appropriate to follow (R3) and to symbolize the contents of the boxes as

$$K_{\square}(x) := a\; x^2 + b\; x + c\; x \geq 0. \tag{9}$$

Thus, the next *abstraction level* is attained:

(A1) The problem is solved in a *symbolic* rather than numeric way.

Using the symbolic approach, Task 1 can be solved *at once*, yielding a result in terms of the parameters a, b and c. Then, the desired five numerical results can easily be obtained by just plugging in the appropriate numbers.

Note that working on level (A1) rather than on level (A0) is quite obviously advantageous; it pays in time savings, less error sensitivity, qualitative insights, and also aesthetics. All these advantages can be experienced by the students themselves and they might also stimulate them to try such an approach again, when solving other problems. Analogous meta-rules can be formulated for structuring and recursion techniques, although there we shall need and exploit additional syntactical guidelines.

Let us look at another example. Suppose we are in a context where matrix multiplication was just introduced, defined in terms of abstract formulae and illustrated by numerical examples. No further rules of matrix multiplication have been given yet. Now the students are given the following task:

Task 2: *Decide whether these two terms describe one and the same matrix:*

$$\left(\begin{pmatrix} 1 & 7 \\ 3 & 5 \end{pmatrix} \cdot \begin{pmatrix} 2 & 8 \\ 9 & 4 \end{pmatrix}\right) \cdot \begin{pmatrix} 6 & -1 \\ 0 & 11 \end{pmatrix}$$

and

$$\begin{pmatrix} 1 & 7 \\ 3 & 5 \end{pmatrix} \cdot \left(\begin{pmatrix} 2 & 8 \\ 9 & 4 \end{pmatrix} \cdot \begin{pmatrix} 6 & -1 \\ 0 & 11 \end{pmatrix}\right).$$

It seems to be quite natural to answer this question directly by simply calculating both double matrix products and obtaining two equal results, namely

$$\begin{pmatrix} 390 & 331 \\ 306 & 433 \end{pmatrix}.$$

The situation changes if the same task is to be performed again – either several times with different numbers or just once, but with "uneasy" numbers – like in this (artificial) example:

Task 2': *Decide whether these two terms describe one and the same matrix:*

$$\left(\begin{pmatrix} 4263 & 7377 \\ 3521 & 5769 \end{pmatrix} \cdot \begin{pmatrix} 74650 & 70294 \\ 19032 & 54280 \end{pmatrix}\right) \cdot \begin{pmatrix} 6279 & 5017 \\ 3592 & 2156 \end{pmatrix}$$

and

...

Probably, some students might try again to apply numerical calculations, using some calculators. Nevertheless, it becomes plausible that the more effort an immediate calculation requires, the bigger the incentive to look for a simpler, more elegant, and typically more abstract solution. Some students might see, along the lines described before, as structure like that:

> **Task 2':** *Decide whether these two terms describe one and the same matrix:*
>
> $$(A \circ B) \circ C$$
>
> *and*
>
> $$A \circ (B \circ C).$$

So, the idea that associativity does also hold in matrix multiplication, which was just introduced, might occur – at least more easily than before.

At this point it should be stressed again that the initial progress in dealing with both forementioned tasks is heavily supported by our brain's ability to identify structural properties of the sensomotoric input, here more specifically: of the *visual* input. Processing any text-based mathematical task starts with processing its text. At a very raw level, even before reading the symbols and making sense of them, one can view such a text just like a picture. By doing so, one can detect structures like clusters, straight lines or axes, or even nesting of patterns. In our examples, the ideas governing abstraction are closely connected with such properties.

Turning back to Task 2', it remains to prove that this idea is really true – with A, B, C being matrices and "$\circ$" representing matrix multiplication " $\cdot$ ". It turns out that the attempt to do so reveals the possibility to obtain further neat abstractions on different levels.

To begin with, one has to understand that the following identity has to be proved:

$$(A \cdot B) \cdot C = A \cdot (B \cdot C) \tag{10}$$

or briefly

$$D^L = D^R \tag{11}$$

with $D^L := (A \cdot B) \cdot C$ and $D^R := A \cdot (B \cdot C)$. Note that this idea involves a – more or less conscious – combined encapsulation/symbolization operation.

The superficially "easiest" version to prove (10) is bound to matrix dimension (2,2) by writing

$$A = \begin{pmatrix} a & b \\ c & d \end{pmatrix}, B = \begin{pmatrix} f & g \\ h & j \end{pmatrix}, C = \begin{pmatrix} k & l \\ m & n \end{pmatrix},$$

say, and performing the necessary calculations symbolically. So one finds that

$$D^L_{11} = (af + bh)k + (ag + bj)m = D^R_{11};$$

analogously one shows that it holds

$$D^L_{ij} = D^R_{ij}$$

for *all* relevant pairs (i, j) of indices. Thus (11) is established. Again the solution is found by passing to abstraction level (A1). Its advantage is being valid for *all* (2,2) - matrices, irrespective of concrete numeric values.

Nevertheless, one may argue that this solution is still too laborious. Suppose one agrees upon this point of view. Then, it is time to look for another approach that might be more effective – i.e., more economic. Again, it turns out that this objective is attained via abstraction: The solution is promoted by CAT's Toolbox concept mentioned above. The first tools to be placed in the Toolbox when trying to prove anything are the necessary *definitions*. As assumed, the product of two matrices A and B of dimensions (L, M) and (M, N), respectively, was defined symbolically, namely to be the (L, N) matrix H with entries

$$H_{ij} = \sum_{m=1}^{M} a_{im} b_{mj} \tag{12}$$

$(i = 1, ..., L; j = 1, ..., N)$; one uses the notation $H =: A \cdot B$.

Now, in order to prove (10) by referring to this definition, one has to show that

$$\sum_{n=1}^{N} \sum_{m=1}^{M} a_{lm} b_{mn} c_{np} = \sum_{m=1}^{M} \sum_{n=1}^{N} a_{lm} b_{mn} c_{np} \tag{13}$$

holds for any matrices A, B and C of dimensions (L, M), (M, N) and (N, P), with $L, M, N, P \in \mathbb{N}$, respectively, and for all $l \in \{1, ..., L\}, P \in \{1, ..., P\}$, respectively. Note that it is quite straightforward to prove (13) by just exploiting the rules for addition and multiplication of real numbers. But, according to the author's experience, many students don't understand that (13) proves (10) right away. The reason for that lies in the fact that connecting (10), (13), and (12) involves a nested structural embedding; in particular, one and the same symbol – H – has to be identified subsequently with $A \cdot B$, $(AB) \cdot C$, $B \cdot C$, and $A(B \cdot C)$. That is, a targeted training of such operations might be quite desirable.

To summarize: Starting from abstraction level (A1) in connection with the desire for a higher working economy and guided by metacognitive instructions like Toolbox and abstraction rules, a higher degree of sophistication is attained. This higher degree of sophistication can be understood as a price that has to be paid in order to answer an initially simple question – but this price pays multiply, not only as proving (13) is that straightforward, but even more as, in the end, this solution of the initial task becomes quite easy and, moreover, provides a deeper conceptual insight into the matrix calculus.

Qualitative reasoning

Now what about *qualitative reasoning*? This refers to abstraction level

(A2) This level of abstraction is achieved when referring to more general – and thus more abstract – classes of objects when solving a given problem.

Here, there are two main directions of interest: First, the mathematical generalization; the second direction might be called "economic generalization".

Mathematical generalization: Here, the more general classes of objects are defined *within* mathematics.

Consider, e.g., the following task:

Task 3: *Determine*

$$\min_D f \quad \left(= \min_{x \in D} f(x)\right) \tag{14}$$

for a given differentiable function f on some interval D. As long as f is described by a computable expression as, e.g., in Task 1 or in (9), it can be assumed that most of the students would try to run a standard approach by solving $f'(x) = 0$ for x and reasoning about the solution(s) that have been found (if so), possibly by additionally inspecting the boundary points of D.

However, a more abstract point of view is taken if they try to figure out whether f obeys some useful *qualitative* properties. E.g., if it can easily be seen that f is *increasing*, there is no point in trying to solve $f'(x) = 0$; instead it is known in advance that if $\min f$ exists it is attained in the left boundary of D. Similarly, if one knows that f is *convex* than one also knows that each local minimum of f is automatically global – saving energy, e.g., when reasoning about the number and types of solutions of $f'(x) = 0$.

Note that this kind of viewing the problem requires the readiness to invest some more abstract thoughts before starting to really tackle the problem; however, in many cases this investment will pay. In addition, the initial investment will not be that expensive, because the students do have some quite easy tests for mononocity and convexity at hand.

Economic generalization:

In modern economics one considers classes of functions named "cost functions", "production functions", "utility functions", etc., often in combination with qualitative attributes like being "neoclassic". Intrinsically, these classes and attributes, respectively, can be defined in terms of mathematical properties. At the same time, they obey a strong economic significance. To be able to reason in terms of these notions – and thus on the second abstraction level – is quite valuable for ongoing economists.

Returning to Task 1, the students might enter level (A2) by observing that *each K is a neoclassic cost function*. Thus, the operating minimum – as the minimum average variable costs - is nothing but the limit of the average variable costs as $x \downarrow 0$. Now it is quite easy to obtain the same results as above.

Clearly, to step here from level (A1) is quite complex and requires a solid theoretical background. It is clear that to work on this level cannot – and shall not – be trained before this solid theoretical background was laid out. But provided this was done, a corresponding meta-rule could be

(R5) *Try to work in economic categories rather than with numeric examples.*

To follow this rule, the students need a very clear overview over the mathematical tools at their disposal. This overview is supported by the toolbox concept as described in [3].

VIII. The Project

The forementioned meta-rules can only brought to life by an intense training that shows how to use them and how they can help to re-structure ones own work in order to gain more progress within the same time. We intend to test and to improve corresponding training measures within a voluntary project group. These measures should

- positively change the students' attitude towards abstraction
- increase the aceptance of (at least passive) abstraction
- enhance the ability of active abstraction
- enrich the regular teaching process.

The project group shall be constituted by random choice from a set of voluntary applicants, hence there shall be an untreated control group as well. The only incentive for participating shall be the perspective of being able to cope better with mathematics, but no examen credits shall be promised.

As to the program: Before and after the series of proper training units we shall perform guideline based interviews as well as observed and videotaped working sessions. Through appropriately designed tasks, it shall be observed whether the students become more apt to understand and use abstract approaches than before. The training sessions shall focus on the different aspects of abstraction, as mentioned above. Tasks 1 – 3 might serve as a possible examples: First, before the training starts, the students are asked to solve a task of this kind by their own. Their approaches and solutions are observed and video documented. After that, we introduce the meta-rules and explain how they work in these and other examples. It will be important to address the benefits of using abstract approaches as well. The students will be given a series of example tasks, with the help of which they can exercise their ability in pracising the meta-rules. At the end of the training sessions, the students shall be given another set of tasks, and again their approaches and solutions are documented. Ideally, there shall be a tendency to work on a (slightly) higher abstraction level as at the beginning of the training. It can be expected that this effect will be the more significant the more the students can gain positive own experience.

IX. Conclusion

In large and heterogeneous basic mathematics courses students need support to manage mathematical abstraction. The paper described some particular aspects of mathematical abstraction that, so the author's hypothesis, can be trained with the help of metacognitive rules. As a justification of this hypothesis it is shown that metacognitive rules already have proved to be helpful in another context, i.e., in supporting "reading mathematics" and problem solving. In addition, some examples of metacognitive rules that address abstraction are provided. Further a framework for an appropriate field study in order to investigate the possible effects of a metacognitive-rule based training of mathematical abstraction was presented.

Although performing such a field study as well as adjusting the training instruments is subject to future work, the present discussion might be inspiring for those that intend to deal with mathematical abstraction as a human cognitive ability, in particular by supporting abstraction in mathematics education.

REFERENCES

[1] H. M. Dietz, "Metacognitive support of mathematical abstraction processes," *COGNITIVE 2016: The Eighth International Conference on Advanced Cognitive Technologies and Applications*, pp. 62–65, 2016, ISBN: 978-1-61208-462-6.

[2] ——, "CAT – a Model for In-teaching Methodical Support for Novices. (in german; original title: CAT – Ein Modell für lehrintegrierte studienmethodische Unterstützung von Studienanfängern," in *Biehler, R. et al. (Eds.), Teaching and Learning Mathematics in the Transition Phase (in german; original title: Lehren und Lernen von Mathematik in der Studieneingangsphase)*. Springer, 2015, pp. 131–147.

[3] ——, *Mathematics for Economists · The ECOMath Handbook. (in german, original title: Mathematik fuer Wirtschaftswissenschaftler · Das ECOMath Handbuch)*. Springer Gabler, Heidelberg et. al., 2012.

[4] ——, *Semiotics in Reading Maths*, in Kadunz, G. (ed.), Semiotic Perspectives of Learning Mathematics (in german, original title: Semiotische Perspektiven auf das Lernen von Mathematik), Springer, Heidelberg, 2015, part IV, chapter 1, pp. 185–203.

[5] H. M. Dietz and J. Rohde, "Methodological study support for first semester students in service mathematics." *Beiträge zum Mathematikunterricht*, 2012, (In german; german title: Studienmethodische Unterstützung für Erstsemester im Mathematikservice.).

[6] F. Feudel and H. M. Dietz, "Teaching study skills in mathematics service courses - how to cope with students' refusal?" *Teaching Mathematics and its Applications*, 2016, (submitted).

[7] J. Piaget, *El nacimiento de la inteligencia en el nino*. Critica, Barcelona, 1975 (1985).

[8] E. Dubinsky, *Reflective Abstraction in Advanced Mathematical Thinking*, chapter 7 in: Tall, D. (Ed.), Advanced Mathematical Thinking, Kluwer, Dordrecht, 1991, pp. 195-126.

[9] D. Tall, Ed., *Advanced Mathematical Thinking*. Kluwer, Dordrecht et al., 1991.

[10] I. Arnon, *et al. APOS Theory. A Framework for Research and Curriculum Development in Mathematics Education*. Springer, New York et al., 2014.

[11] G.-M. Greuel, R. Remmert, and G. Rupprecht, Eds., *Mathematics - Driving Force of Business (in german, original title: Mathematik - Motor der Wirtschaft)*. Springer, Jan. 2008.

[12] K. Devlin, *Introduction to Mathematical Thinking*. Devlin, Petaluma, 2012.

[13] A. J. Smith, *Aristotle on Abstraction. Ph.D. Thesis*. The Johns Hopkins University, Baltimore, 2010.

[14] B. Hershkowitz, B. Schwarz, and T. Dreyfus, *Abstraction in context: Epistemic actions*, in: N. Seel (Ed.), Encyclopedia of the Sciences of Learning Vol. 32, No.2, New York: Springer, 2012, pp. 195-222.

[15] C. Eliasmith, *How to build a brain: a neural architecture for biological cognition*. Oxford Univ. Press, 2013.

[16] J. Fodor, Ed., *The Language of Thought*. Crowell, New York, 1975.

[17] D. Rumelhart and J. McClelland, *Parallel distributed processing: Explorations in the microstructure of cognition*. MIT Press/Bradford Books, Cambridge M.A., 1986, vol. Number 1.

[18] J. Anderson, *The adaptive character of thought*. Routledge, New York, 1990.

[19] J. Tenenbaum and T. Griffiths, "Generalization, similarity, and Bayesian inference," *Behavioral and Brain Sciences*, vol. 24, pp. 629–641, 2001.

[20] T. Griffiths and J. Tenenbaum, "Optimal predictions in everyday cognition," *Psychological Science*, vol. 17, pp. 767–773, 2006.

[21] D. Gentner, "Why we are so smart," *Rumelhart Prize Talk, 2016 Annual Meeting of the Cognitive Science, Philadelphia*, August 12, 2016.

[22] J. Anderson, D. Bothell, M. Byrne, S. Douglass, C. Lebiere, and Y. Qin, "An integrated theory of the mind," *Psychological Review*, vol. 111, No. 4, 2004.

[23] L. Schulz, N. Goodman, J. Tenenbaum, and A. Jenkins, "Going beyond the evidence: Abstract laws and preschoolers? Responses to anomalous data." *Cognition*, vol. 109 (2), pp. 211–223, 2008.

[24] J. Skorstad, D. Gentner, and D. Medin, "Abstraction processes during concept learning: A structural view." in *Proceedings of the Tenth Annual Conference of the Cognitive Science Society*. Cognitive Science Society, 1988, pp. 419–425.

[25] D. H. Ballard, *Brain Computation as Hierarchical Abstraction*. MIT Press, Cambridge, Jan. 2015.

[26] R. N. Shepard, "Toward a universal law of generalization for psychological science," *Science, New Series*, vol. 237, No. 4820, pp. 1317 – 1323, 1987.

[27] K. Levering and K. Kurtz, *Generalization in Higher Order Cognition*. Taylor & Francis Group, New York and Hove, 2010, pp. 175 – 197.

[28] A. D. Markman and D. Gentner, "Structure mapping in the comparison process," *American Journal of Psychology*, vol. 113 (4), pp. 501– 538, 2000.

[29] D. Gentner, "Structure-mapping: A theoretical framework for analogy," *Cognitive Science*, vol. 7, pp. 155 – 170, 1983.

[30] H. D. Rinkens, *Abstraktion und Struktur. Grundbegriffe der Mathematikdidaktik (in German)*. Henn Verlag, Ratingen, 1973.

[31] G. Stapleton, "Reaoning with constraint diagrams," 2004, Ph.D. thesis, University of Brighton.

[32] D. L. Medin and B. H. Ross, *The Specific Character of Abstract Thought: Categorization, Problem Solving, and Induction*, in Sternberg R.J. (Ed.), *Advances in the Psychology of Human Intelligence* Vol. 5, Lawrence Erlbaum, Hillsdale, 1989, pp. 189-223.

[33] M. Österholm, "Characterizing reading comprehension of mathematical texts." *Educational Studies in Mathematics*, vol. 63, pp. 325–346, 2006.

[34] F. Hajek, *New Studies in Philosophy, Politics, Economics, and the History of Ideas*. Routledge & Kegan Paul, London, 1978.

[35] H. M. Dietz and J. Rohde, "Adventures in Reading Maths," in *Petersburg Department of V.A. Steklov Institute of Mathematics of the Russian Academy of Science (Ed.): Philosophy, Mathematics, Linguistics: Aspects of Interaction (PhML 2012). Proceedings of the International Scientific Conference St. Petersburg, May 22-25*, 2012, pp. 61–68.

[36] F. Feudel, "Studienmethodische Förderung in der Mathematik für Wirtschaftswissenschaftler - Chancen und Schwierigkeiten." *Beiträge zum Mathematikunterricht*, 2015.

[37] R. L. Goldstone and Y. Sakamoto, "The transfer of abstract principles governing complex adaptive systems," *Cognitive Psychology*, vol. 46, pp. 414 – 466, 2003.

International Journal on Advances in Intelligent Systems, vol 9 no 3 & 4, year 2016, http://www.iariajournals.org/intelligent_systems/

On the Integration of Lifecycles and Processes for the Management of Structured and Unstructured Content

A Practical Perspective on Content Management Systems Integration Architecture

Hans-Werner Sehring
Namics
Hamburg, Germany
e-mail: hans-werner.sehring@namics.com

Abstract—**In practice, content management systems are in widespread use for the management of web sites, to implement intranet solutions, for provisioning content to mobile applications, and for the publication of a range of documents created from diverse content. Such content is typically structured in a media agnostic way in order to support multi-channel publication. An emerging class of multimedia databases is digital asset management systems that specialize in the management of unstructured content. Despite the market for content management products aiming at integrated solutions that cover most content management aspects, there is a trend to augment content management systems with systems that offer dedicated functionality for specific content management tasks. In practice, there is particular interest in systems incorporating both a content management system and a digital asset management system. Both kinds of systems have a notion of content lifecycles and processes for their management. Therefore, particular attention has to be paid to the alignment of those across system boundaries. There are various ways of integrating content management systems to accomplish this. All integration forms exhibit individual strengths and weaknesses, achieved with differing implementation effort. The choice of the adequate integration architecture, therefore, depends on many factors and considerations that are discussed in this paper.**

Keywords-content lifecycle; content management; content management processes; content management system; content syndication; digital asset management; multimedia asset management; multimedia database; software architecture; solution architecture; systems integration.

I. INTRODUCTION

This article discusses a range of integration forms for systems specialized in the management of structured and unstructured content. The requirements and technical constraints are taken from real-world experience with practical projects. The presentation of the discussion is an extended form of that given in the conference paper [1], augmented with some additional thoughts on loose system integration by document interchange.

Content Management Systems (CMSs) are in widespread use today for the maintenance of web sites or documents by content producers and editors. Typical CMSs aim to manage both structured content (often in the form of hierarchies or graphs of content objects) and unstructured content, namely binary data that is shipped as some media file of a certain standard format (like, e.g., images and videos in different formats, text files documenting some process step, or content marshaled for content transmission).

In practice, CMSs host elaborate processes that deal with structured content while offering only very basic functionality for unstructured content. CMS customers have an increasing demand for additional functionality for the treatment of binary multimedia content [2].

Consequently, there is a current trend to augment CMS installations with a multimedia database of the newly emerged class of *Digital Asset Management systems* (DAMs).

Both CMSs and DAMs provide a complete feature set for the management and distribution of content, the major difference being the kind of content they specialize in. Since both CMSs and DAMs are designed to manage content and publish it on the web, their integration therefore is not obvious. In fact, depending on the particular requirements of a web site, different integration forms may be suitable, each providing its own advantages and drawbacks.

In this paper, we discuss integration approaches for systems consisting of a CMS and a DAM. All approaches considered are derived from actual scenarios found in commercial projects. They all assume the CMS to deliver web pages and the DAM to contribute embedded multimedia documents [3]. The integration approaches differ in the point within the content lifecycle at which the DAM contributes.

The remainder of this paper is organized as follows: In Section II, we discuss the characteristics and functionality of CMSs and DAMs. In Section III, we review the lifecycle of content and digital assets, respectively, in typical CMS and DAM implementations. The core of this paper consists firstly of the discussion of two sets of approaches to systems integration that work on content and on document level, with each approach operating at different times in the content and asset lifecycle. Secondly, it consists of an evaluation of implementations of all approaches concerning required adaptations to the CMS or the DAM. Section IV presents integration approaches that rely on tight coupling of systems on content level. According implementation considerations of these approaches are discussed in Section V. Approaches using a looser coupling based on document exchange are presented in Section VI. The necessary system properties are discussed in Section VII. The paper concludes with a summary and outlook in Section VIII.

II. Contributing Systems and Their Functionality

With CMSs and DAMs there are two classes of systems that deal with the editing of content and shipping of content.

Both contain editing facilities including workflows and quality assurance processes. Both offer rendering and playout functionality, usually targeted at specific usage scenarios. These scenarios differ between software products (performance, editing of unique documents vs. management of uniform mass content, etc.).

As the names indicate, the systems differ in the kind of entities they deal with. CMSs focus on the management of structured content and on publication of documents that are created from compositions of pieces of content. DAMs deal with unstructured content that is managed, transformed, and published on a binary level, and that is augmented with descriptive data (metadata).

Consequently, CMSs and DAMs address similar use cases, but they put a different focus on the functionalities as discussed in the subsequent subsections.

A. Content Management Systems

CMSs provide their service as follows (see also [4]).

1) Content creation: CMSs offer tools for manual creation of content by editors and for the automated import of content from external sources, be it from files, from feeds, or by means of content syndication. On creation, typically some initialization tasks can be performed. E.g., some properties of content might be given default values, or substructures are automatically created and linked.

2) Content editing: Part of a CMS is an editor tool that is used to manipulate content, to control its lifecycle (see Section III), and to preview renderings of content. Content manipulations include adding value to content, the maintenance of description data, and the addition of layout hints and other channel-specific settings, e.g., URLs for the publication of content in the form of world wide web resources. Editing tools can be form-based with a separate preview. In this case editors work on "raw" content. They can preview documents as they are created from content for selected publication channels. Alternatively, editors can work in-document, in which case the editor manipulates documents, and manipulations are mapped to the corresponding content. Often there are workflows to control the editing processes. For example, workflows can observe mandatory content properties and they can steer translation processes in the case of multilingual content.

3) Quality assurance: Quality assurance for content consists of approval and publication, although in some CMS products these two activities are one. Approval marks content as being suitable for publication. Publication finally makes it available to the target audience – in the form of rendered documents. Quality assurance is realized by assigning editing, approval, and publication tasks to different roles. This way, the person who created content cannot publish it directly. Instead, someone else reviews the content. Making publication a separate step serves two purposes: Firstly, a series of editing steps will be bundled to form one new publication. Secondly, publication is the point in time where the integrity of the overall product, e.g., the web site, should be checked. From the perspective of an approver (reviewer), it is acceptable to consider incomplete document sets. A reviewer, e.g., checks one article, but will not necessarily approve linked articles. At the time of actual publication, though, a CMS should check completeness and consistency of the publication, e.g., ensuring that every link has exactly one target and that this target is published. Quality assurance should be embedded in the CMSs workflows.

4) Rendering: Rendering is the process of creating documents from content. Structured content typically is rendered by mapping content structures to document layouts. Typically, *view templates* define the overall layout and the placement of content. Content objects are often rendered in a type-specific way. E.g., numbers are printed as strings using the locales number format (e.g., "10.000,00"). The ability to manipulate binary content is limited compared to that of a DAM with matching capabilities. CMSs offer general functionality on media content suited for a particular publication channel, e.g., for the web. This particular case includes rendering of images for adaptive design, e.g., to resize them for specific channels or to apply device-specific format conversions.

5) Playout: The shipping of rendered documents, called delivery or playout, is not necessarily a core functionality of a CMS. But since playout usually is tightly coupled with rendering, most CMS products include a playout component. Some CMSs target high performance output, e.g., supporting horizontal scaling or caching of content and documents. Sometimes playout components are integrated with Content Delivery Networks (CDNs). In the course of this paper we do not consider topics like user-generated content where content is also created at the playout side.

B. Digital Asset Management Systems

DAMs offer a varying set of functionality for the management of binary documents and metadata. Binary multimedia documents can be of various kind, e.g., image, video, text. Certain accordingly specialized DAMs are sometimes referred to as *Multimedia Asset Management* systems (MAMs). In the course of this paper we consider general DAM functionality only. A DAM's functionality includes the following [5].

1) Asset Creation: Assets are created in a DAM as content is in a CMS, manually or in automated processes. Manual creation is typically accomplished by means of an external authoring tool like an image processing or video transcoding system. Its output is uploaded to the DAM.

2) Asset Editing: Consequently, editing is typically restricted to the maintenance of structured information (descriptive data, e.g., defining time code information in moving image, legal information, provenance information, etc. [6]). Binary manipulations are performed by authoring tools. Editing may take place in workflows [7].

3) Quality assurance: DAMs have an approval process like the one of CMSs. Workflows for quality assurance can typically be customized. Legal rights are important for many DAM applications. Media can only be used if the according rights are available. In these cases quality assurance often includes temporal constraints depending on the licensing of rights-protected multimedia documents.

4) Rendering: The rendering of digital assets consists of format conversions, media manipulations, and generating multimedia documents from multiple assets. Transcoding particular video formats for different browsers or mobile platforms is a typical conversion task. Manipulations include image manipulation, e.g., scaling of images for adaptive design, inserting logos in photos, watermarking of documents, etc. An example for document generation is the assembly of a video from moving image and sound for multilanguage videos. Whole hypermedia documents can theoretically be created this way. Another example is the addition of descriptive data to multimedia assets as meta data, e.g., Exif data. In business applications, text documents for, e.g., contracts may be generated in a personalized way based on customer data and a current transaction.

5) Playout: DAMs typically can deliver assets, at least by shipping online to the web or offline by creating files, e.g., for print. Some DAMs offer more sophisticated playout functionality, e.g., reliable delivery, at-most-once delivery, exactly-once-delivery, or digital rights management. DAMs specialized in video management offer a playout based on QoS parameters. In particular, they measure network latency during video transmission to be able to sacrifice image quality in favor of synchronicity if needed [8].

III. CONTENT AND DIGITAL ASSET LIFECYCLES

Both content objects managed by a CMS and assets managed by a DAM have a lifecycle. In most of the CMS and DAM software products, these lifecycles are explicitly represented by states of the objects. Fig. 1 illustrates the states and possible state changes as described below.

The content object lifecycle starts with content objects being *created*. This can happen manually by direct instantiation, automatically by having dependent objects created by software, e.g., parts of compound objects, or by importing external content, e.g., from files or news feeds.

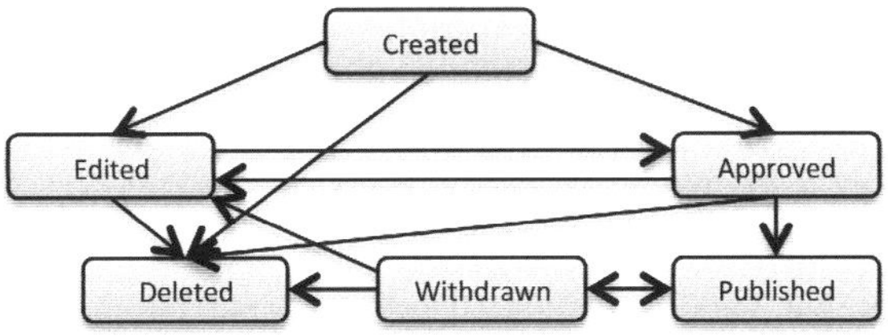

Figure 1. Lifecycle states of content objects.

Subsequent editing adds value to content. Changes affect the actual content or descriptive information that is also stored in content objects. In particular, editing may include linking content objects to each other in order to create multimedia documents from the resulting object graphs. Typically it depends on the content's model whether a reference is maintained by the link source or by the target, and thus, which object is marked as *edited*. This stated is maintained explicitly in order to mark content as requiring quality assurance.

Quality assurance for content is reflected in a dedicated approval step that marks content as being suitable for publication. Such content is, depending on the CMS product, either directly available for rendering and shipping or it constitutes a candidate for a final publication step. In the course of this paper we consider a dedicated publication step. The *approved* state allows implementing a review process as presented in II.A.3).

Note that due to the approval state, edited content cannot directly be *published*.

An approved object that is edited becomes unapproved (edited state). This requires content changes to be subject to review. Typically CMSs support versioning of content and this way allow an approved version to be online and a newer version to be edited.

In most states, a content object can be *deleted*. Only for published content this is not possible because deletion might break links from other (still published) documents. Therefore, in some CMSs content needs to be unpublished or *withdrawn* before. This gives the system the chance to check the modified publication for existing links.

Assets, being a different form of content, have a similar lifecycle. They are initially created inside a DAM, be it by import from external sources or by original authoring and storing the results inside the DAM.

Editing assets is no primary use case of a DAM [9], but the maintenance of descriptive information is a regular task.

DAMs support quality assurance by an approval process similar to that found in CMSs.

In addition to the publication functionality of a CMS, a DAM may prepare a multimedia document for playout by actually storing a rendered variant. E.g., modified images may actually be stored inside the DAM's repository.

All lifecycle states of content of CMSs and DAMs may differ for content variants, e.g., language-dependent content, or there may be additional states. E.g., when translating a text, all variants in other languages might change state to a state *requires translation* not shown above.

IV. TIME OF ASSET INTEGRATION AT CONTENT LEVEL

Even if the management of structured and that of unstructured content are separated utilizing a CMS and a DAM, respectively, content and assets will finally be combined in published documents.

There are various integration scenarios to relate content and assets within workflows leading to the generation of integrated presentations.

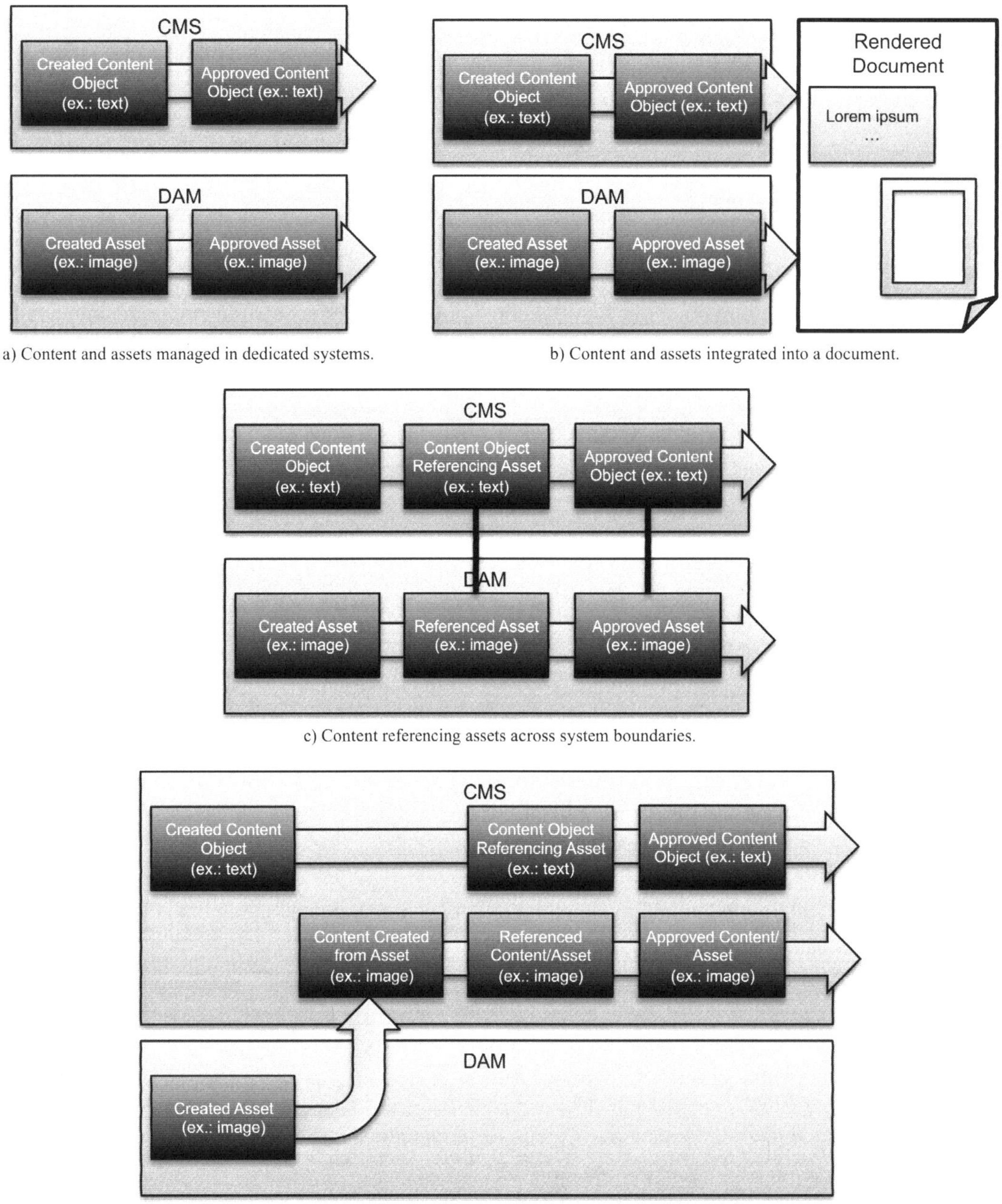

a) Content and assets managed in dedicated systems.

b) Content and assets integrated into a document.

c) Content referencing assets across system boundaries.

d) Assets copied from a DAM into a CMS.

Figure 2. Example content and asset lifecycle relationships.

For the integration scenarios we only consider the case of a CMS being used to prepare content and to define how to render documents. This is the particular strength of a CMS that cannot be substituted by a DAM. Therefore, the CMS will always be in lead when considering the overall document publication process.

We analyze integration approaches that integrate content and assets at different points in their lifecycles. For these approaches the actual integration of assets into content is discussed on content and document level.

For a specific system, the integration approach should be chosen out of the given alternatives based on the requirements that the overall system needs to fulfill and based on the implementation effort. Implementation effort arises since CMSs and DAMs are typically not prepared to have their content align to external content's lifecycle.

Each integration form has its specific advantages and disadvantages and addresses a different set of requirements.

The subsections of this section each discuss advantages and disadvantages of one approach on the content level.

The subsequent Section V discusses the implementation effort of each integrated solution working at content level.

Sections VI and VII lead the according discussion for document level approaches.

As indicated above, the approaches differ in the point in time at which an asset is integrated into the CMS. The points in time considered here are:

- Document playout time: the point in time at which a document is transferred to a publication channel, e.g., delivered to a network on request.
- Document rendering time: the point in time at which a document is created from CMS content and assets.
- Content publication time: the point in time at which content (that may contain references to assets) is published. This means, it is marked as being available to rendering.
- Content approval time: the point in time at which the quality of content is assured. Here, the approval of content of a CMS is considered since the CMS drives the overall document creation workflow. The time of asset approval is not considered for the processes.
- Content editing time: in particular, the time when assets are related to content.
- Asset creation time: the time when a new asset shows up in a DAM. It is important because from that point in time on the asset might be related to content in order to be used in a document later on.

Integration approaches with actions triggered at these lifecycle states are discussed in the following subsections.

To illustrate the approaches we use a schematic view on systems and processes as presented in Fig. 2.

Fig. 2(a) shows a CMS and a DAM. The darker boxes on their inside show content objects in certain lifecycle states. The content in the CMS could be textual content, e.g., an article consisting of a headline and the text. The asset in the DAM may be an image.

The light broad arrows in the boxes representing the systems depict the lifecycle of the objects managed by the respective system. In the CMS there is a newly created content object that then becomes approved. A similar flow is shown for an asset in the DAM.

To the right of Fig. 2(b) a document is shown. The lifecycle arrows that are leaving the system boxes indicate that content is rendered into the document according to a chosen layout before playout. The "Lorem ipsum" box shall represent a paragraph of text that is created from the textual content coming from the CMS. The bordered rectangle represents an image created from an image asset from the DAM. Note that this example does not conform to the state diagram in Fig. 1; content as well as assets typically have to be published before playout. This additional step is omitted here in order to simplify the figure.

Fig. 2(c) shows the setting of a reference as a special case of editing: content is given a reference to an asset, depicted by the solid lines crossing system boundaries. In this case it is an external reference to an asset existing inside a DAM. The reference is kept over lifecycle steps (here: approval of both content and the related asset).

Fig. 2(d) illustrates the case that an asset is copied into the CMS. The curved arrow indicates that a new content object is created in the CMS as a copy of an asset residing in the DAM. Typical CMSs can hold multimedia content, so this copy can be created directly. The CMS cannot in general offer the same functionality like the DAM, though.

The operations on content shown in Fig. 2 are the basis for all integration scenarios discussed in the remainder of this paper.

A. *Integrating Assets at Playout Time*

The integration at playout time takes place outside the cooperating systems and happens in the scope of the produced documents only. CMS and DAM do not exchange content. The CMS renders documents that contain references to the DAM's playout channel. E.g., on the web, the CMS generates an HTML page with HTTP references to images managed by the DAM.

This integration form makes full use of the DAM's functionality with respect to rendering and playout. Documents are created from both content and assets at the latest point in time possible. This way, it is the loosest integration form that happens at the point of document assembly, possibly in a client, e.g., a web browser. The equivalent in an information system is the presentation layer.

In the case of web content management this scenario requires the DAM to be exposed to the Internet in order to be able to deliver the assets for inclusion into documents.

Though this frontend integration makes this approach the most volatile one, it is often preferred in practice due to its comparably low implementation costs and due to the fact that all of the DAM's functionality is being used.

A CMS's editor tool allows content objects to be related to each other. Such relationships are required either to be able to link documents or to define content structures that lead to documents composed of various content objects, e.g., by means of aggregation.

Fig. 3 uses the example of an image related to text. This integration scenario – as well as all the other ones discussed in the course of this paper except for the integration at creation time – requires an extension of the CMS's editor tool using a search function in the accompanying DAM. At the same time the search functionality of the DAM is required to be exposed to the CMS. This way, CMS users can pick assets from the accompanying DAM in order to relate the entities.

In the example of Fig. 3, a reference to an image was made while editing textual content. The text containing the reference to the image was approved. In parallel, the asset holding the image was approved in the DAM.

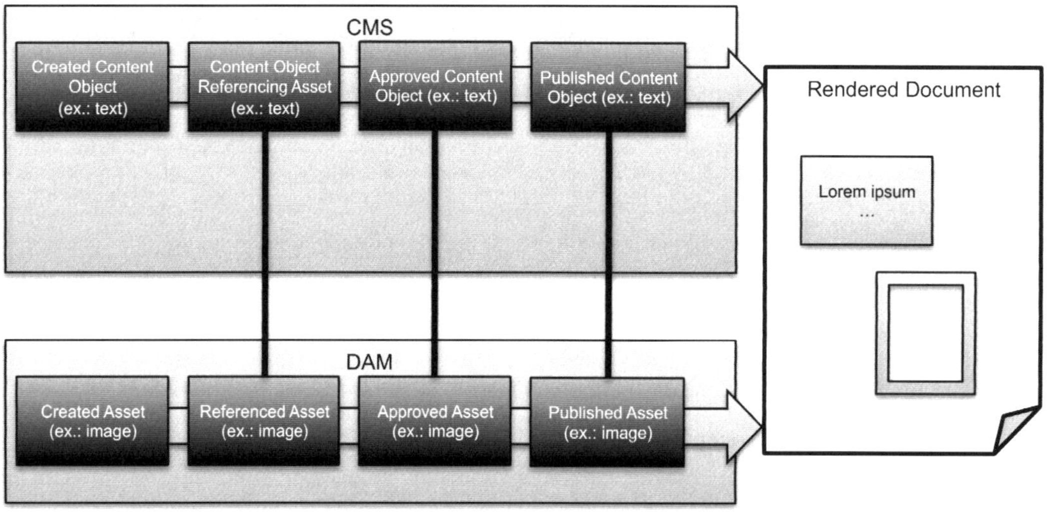

Figure 3. Example asset integration at playout time.

For integration at playout time, the CMS stores proxy content (as asset references) only at editing time. Such proxy content represents an asset from the DAM. It is created when an asset reference is defined using the editor tool.

The external references from proxy content to the asset it represents require the DAM to provide stable external assets IDs or addresses.

The CMS renders proxy content objects as references to the according assets residing inside the DAM that delivers them directly into the documents.

There is no general way to prevent possible runtime errors due to assets that have been deleted or ones that have otherwise become inaccessible. Since the lifecycles of content objects and assets are decoupled, assets might, e.g., be deleted while still being referenced by content objects and thus being required in a multimedia document.

The situation can gradually be bettered by deeper systems integration. The DAM may send notifications on assets becoming unavailable to the CMS that registers for such events with the DAM. But it is unclear what actions the CMS should take. Depending on publication strategies, all content referencing such an asset may become inaccessible, as well as (transitively) all content referring to such content. In other cases, it might be possible to remove such references but leave the rest of the content intact.

Based on notifications, content may be disapproved and unpublished. In general, the automatic execution of these operations without quality assurance can lead to unwanted effects. Therefore, such propagation of lifecycle events has to be introduced in an application-specific way.

B. *Integrating Assets at Render Time*

The integration at playout time takes place in the documents' layout only. The next earlier point in time is rendering where the documents are created from content.

Rendering is the latest point in time at which assets are copied into the CMS. Right before published content is rendered as documents, referenced assets are copied into the CMS. Proxies are replaced by actual asset content.

Fig. 4 illustrates this. Both content objects in the CMS and assets reach the publish state independently of each other. When content rendering starts, a content object holding the asset content is created (shown as "Published Content/Asset"). The document is rendered from CMS content only.

Like most of the integration scenarios, as discussed in the previous subsection, this one requires: (1) an extension of the CMS's editor tool with a search in the accompanying DAM, (2) capabilities to manage asset references in order to relate assets to content (e.g., using proxy content objects), and (3) means to deal with the fact that asset and content lifecycles cannot be synchronized in a generic way.

During rendering, references to assets are resolved in the CMS. Assets are transferred to the CMS and stored at least in the public stage. The benefit of this step is increased independence from the asset lifecycle from this point on: asset deletion no longer leads to inconsistent publications out of the CMS. Nevertheless, disapproval of an asset does not automatically lead to withdrawal of corresponding and referring content, partially decreasing the effectiveness of the DAM's quality assurance.

The problem with unavailable assets exists as in the preceding case. Yet it does not occur at playout time, but instead at rendering time. This makes no difference in most contemporary CMSs. In offline CMSs that render documents in advance, this can be beneficial, though.

As at playout time, gradual improvement can be reached by receiving events concerning an asset's lifecycle after creation of proxy content in the CMS. A referenced asset might become unavailable for publication later on due to disapproval or deletion from the DAM. The according events should therefore be handled by the CMS. References may have to be removed as described for playout time, and copied assets may have to be removed from the CMS.

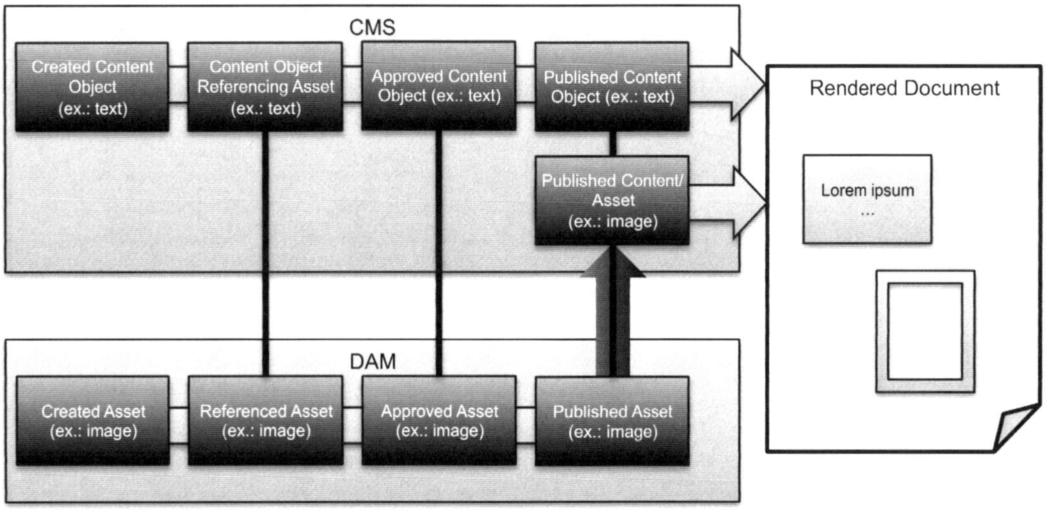

Figure 4. Example asset integration at rendering time.

C. *Integration Assets at Publication Time*

This integration scenario is much like the preceding ones, only that it integrates assets even earlier in the asset/content lifecycle, namely during publishing as the process of making content available to rendering and playout (Fig. 5).

Typically, content is published in a transitive way. E.g., when an article is published, all related images need to be published in the same step as well, or otherwise the publication of the article will fail. The quality assurance process needs to have set the approval state accordingly.

This integration scenario is based on an extension of the CMS's publishing process in a way that assets are retrieved from the DAM and stored as content in the CMS during the process (based on proxy content objects created at editing time), at least in the public stage. This scenario is based on the assumption that it is insufficient to apply quality assurance to the proxies alone because of asynchronous asset modifications in the DAM. Instead, the assets' approval state is checked as part of the publishing process of the CMS.

In contrast to the preceding scenarios, the CMS is leveraged from having to consider unavailable assets at playout time in this scenario. Still, the decoupled lifecycles of asset and corresponding content need to be dealt with. To this end, there either needs to be a synchronization of asset and content state based on notifications as discussed before, or the CMS neglects the approval state in the DAM and maintains the state on the basis of content objects only.

In this integration scenario, as opposed to the preceding ones, the CMS's publication, rendering, and playout capabilities are used for digital assets. Section V.B discusses the resulting implications. The DAM's playout functionality (see Section II.B) will not be utilized.

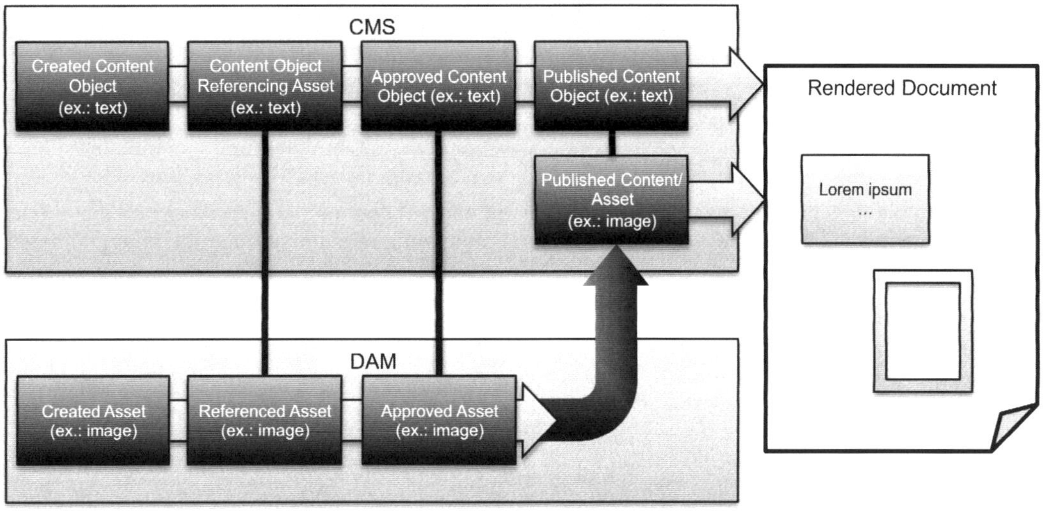

Figure 5. Example asset integration at publication time.

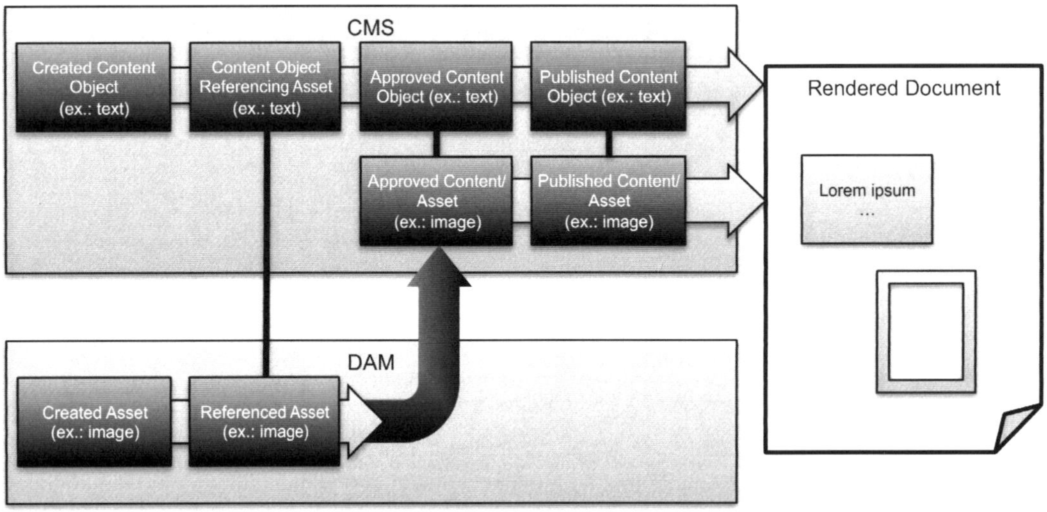

Figure 6. Example asset integration at approval time.

D. Integration Assets at Approval Time

Quality assurance of multimedia assets can be transferred to the CMS by integrating at approval time.

As Fig. 6 indicates, the approval state is not maintained by the DAM, but only in the CMS. The management of the approval states manifests itself by copying assets into the CMS.

To this end, the approval process of the CMS needs to be extended. Usually this process just consists of recording the information that the quality of some content was approved. It has to be extended by the creation of content as copies of assets and the establishment of event handlers.

Later disapproval of assets needs to be recognized by the CMS in order to adjust the state of asset copies. This can be achieved by event propagation as in the other scenarios.

E. Integration Assets at Editing Time

Assets can be added to the CMS at editing time, e.g., when a reference to an asset is added to some content. This requires an extension of the CMS's editor with (a) search in the accompanying DAM like in the cases above and (b) on-the-fly content creation from assets selected from the search result by an editor.

Fig. 7 shows the rather short lifecycle of an asset in the DAM for this scenario. Assets are created in the DAM. When they are first used in content, they are copied into the CMS.

In contrast to the scenarios from the preceding sections, Fig. 7 also shows that no external references from content to assets are required in this scenario. On first use, assets are copied, not only referenced.

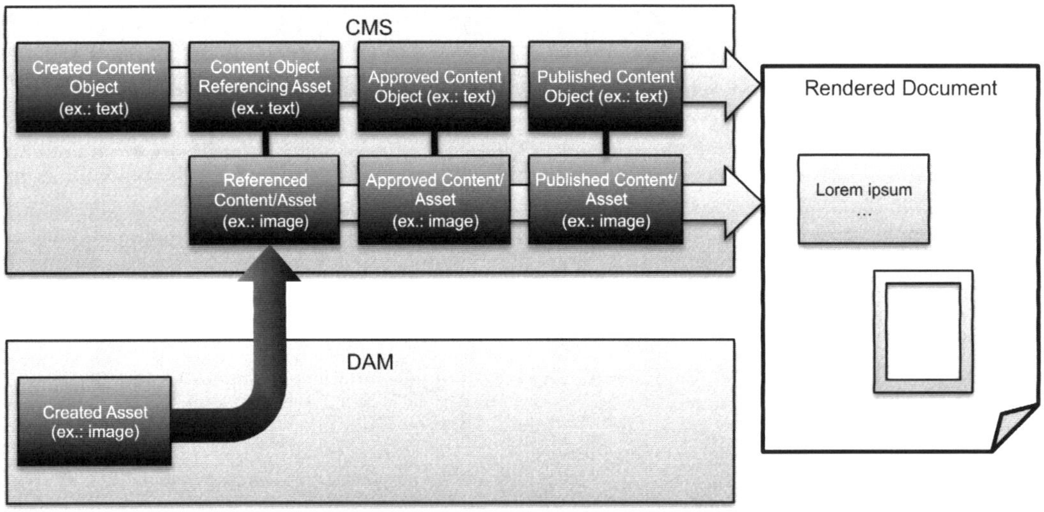

Figure 7. Example asset integration at editing time.

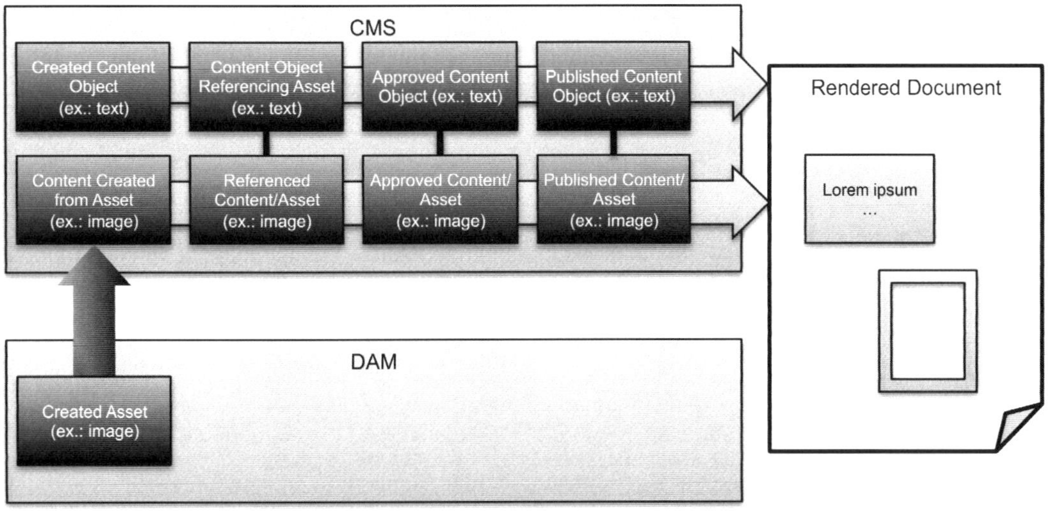

Figure 8. Example asset integration at creation time.

In this scenario the DAM does not manage the assets' approval state. In general the CMS is responsible for the whole content in this state since assets already have been transformed into CMS content.

If assets are integrated in the CMS before approval time they need to be monitored for subsequent changes, though. Assets may be edited before approval, and changes have also to be applied to the copies in the CMS. To this end, there needs to be synchronization once content has been created from an asset. This synchronization may be eager (on every asset change) or lazy (on demand, e.g., at playout time).

With integration at approval time and before, rendering and playout are performed by the CMS (s.a.).

Integration at editing time also transfers the quality assurance of assets to the CMS.

F. *Integrating Assets at Asset Creation Time*

The earliest possible integration of assets is at the time of their creation: assets are added to the CMS as soon as they are created in the DAM. Fig. 8 illustrates this.

For this to happen, the DAM needs to notify the CMS about new assets being created. The CMS then copies such assets into its own repository.

This scenario only makes sense if the DAM is also used in processes other than document production through a CMS – otherwise there would be no need for a DAM at all. When assets still have an independent lifecycle inside the DAM then the integration requires continuous synchronization. This synchronization is performed eagerly in order to provide assets as content for selection within CMS. There is no need for an extended editor that allows searching the DAM since copies of the assets can directly be found in the content base.

In this scenario, nearly all DAM functionality is neglected in favor of the corresponding CMS functions. As in the above scenarios quality assurance is controlled by the CMS, and rendering and playout are carried out solely by it.

V. Required System Adaptations for Asset Integration at Content Level

In order to implement the integration of a CMS with a DAM in one of the forms presented in the preceding section, some extensions or adaptations to the software products are required. Table I gives an overview of required adaptations and attributes them to the integration scenarios.

For the analysis of the implementation measures we do not need to distinguish between approval and playout time.

Selected product features and implementation aspects are discussed in the subsections of this section: functionality that is required in the participating systems in Section V.A and features of typical products that will not be employed in Section V.B.

A. *Added Functionality*

The scenarios that rely on continuous synchronization of assets and corresponding content objects are typically implemented through notifications by events, e.g., the event of an asset having been modified. In these scenarios the DAM needs to be an event source and the CMS an event subscriber. The DAM will produce events and transmit them to subscribers. The CMS registers for such events and interpret them based on the assets state change.

For CMS products that cannot be extended with custom code for the event handling, there needs to be an external software component that listens to such events and then triggers some actions inside the CMS. In this case the CMS needs to provide an externally usable API for the required operations.

In order to relate events to content created from assets, the DAM has to provide stable IDs or addresses (like, e.g., URLs) of assets. This is particularly important due to the fact that assets are long-lived. If the actual DAM does not provide such IDs or addresses, artificial IDs need to be maintained explicitly as part of the metadata.

TABLE I. CHANGES TO SOFTWARE PRODUCTS DEPENDING ON ASSET INTEGRATION TIME

Aspects	**Form of Integration**				
	Creation time	*Editing time*	*Approval/public. time*	*Render time*	*Playout time/never*
Changes to CMS	• subscribe to and listen to events (from DAM) or expose public API; create content on asset creation or modification	• media selection dialog changed to query DAM • on-the-fly content creation upon asset utilization (linking) • subscribe to and listen to events (from DAM) or expose public API; modify content on asset modification	• media selection dialog changed to query DAM • surrogate objects for assets • on-the-fly content creation on public stage upon asset (proxy) approval • check of asset's approval state upon asset proxy approval	• media selection dialog changed to query DAM • surrogate objects for assets • on-the-fly content creation on public stage upon asset (proxy) rendering	• media selection dialog changed to query DAM • surrogate objects for assets
Changes to DAM	• event source for CMS • stable external IDs (to relate assets in events)	• query interface for CMS • event source for CMS • stable external IDs (to relate assets in events)	• stable IDs/addresses • query interface for CMS • interface to query approval state from CMS	• stable IDs/addresses • query interface for CMS • event source for CMS	• stable IDs/addresses • query interface for CMS
Unused CMS functionality	•	•	• quality assurance (approval)	• quality assurance • rendering (assets)	• quality assurance • rendering (assets) • playout (assets)
Unused DAM functionality	• rendering • playout	• rendering • playout	• rendering • playout	• playout	

Most events are related to specific revisions of assets. For those events, subscribers need IDs that reference asset revisions, not assets in general. For an example of IDs fulfilling this requirement see the CMIS object IDs [10].

As described in the preceding section, some integration scenarios rely on an asset selection dialog integrated into the CMS's editing tool. Usually, such a dialog exists, but is used to select multimedia content from the CMS itself. This dialog has to be extended in a way that allows picking assets from the DAM that have not previously been imported into the CMS. Such a dialog must furthermore be backed by functionality to create content (if not already existing) from the chosen asset, either with a copy of the content or with a link to the asset.

In order for the asset selection to work, the DAM has to offer search functionality to the CMS (editor). The search result contains, depending on the scenario, the asset data or the asset ID or address.

B. *Unused Functionality of the Software Products*

There exists functionality that is provided both by a CMS and a DAM. In an integrated system, the corresponding redundant functions of one the systems may not be used. From an architectural point of view, this makes no change. But certain strengths and weaknesses of the products might not be considered in an optimal way in particular integration scenarios.

In those integration scenarios where the CMS handles references to assets in the DAM only, the quality assurance measures, usually some approval process, of the CMS are not in effect for assets. Approving a content object just makes a statement about a version of the corresponding asset at approval time, but assets may change without the handles inside the CMS being altered.

The aforementioned event-based synchronization can be used to monitor the approval state of assets and to adjust the approval state of the corresponding content objects. But considering the whole asset lifecycle there are situations that cannot be handled. The most drastic example is a valid asset that is (rightfully) referenced by published content. If now the asset is deleted then the CMS notices the state change. But it cannot decide whether to keep the image reference (thus rendering documents with missing images), whether to remove the images reference from all content objects (thus automatically altering the content; an operation that is usually unwanted in CMSs), or whether to disapprove all content objects containing the image reference (an operation that has to be applied recursively and can thus have unexpected effects).

The same questions arise for already rendered documents. It depends whether they should be kept, since they were correct at the time of rendering, or whether they should be dismissed, since they are outdated.

If integration of a CMS and a DAM takes place in a way that assets are copied to the CMS before playout time, the rendering and possibly playout functionality of the DAM will not be utilized. This is a major drawback of those integration scenarios since these are about the most powerful contributions of a DAM.

A CMS typically offers very limited rendering functionality for multimedia content, if any (see Section II.A). In the subsequent Section VI, we discuss integration approaches that allow to use more of a DAM's rendering functionality.

Playout with QoS parameters is usually not provided by a CMS, but by some DAMs. Unfortunately, playout by the DAM cannot be used with integration by the time of rendering or earlier.

Depending on the point in the asset lifecycle at which assets are integrated into a CMS, the rendering and possibly playout functionality of the CMS is not used for content originating from assets. As pointed out above, the corresponding functions of a DAM are typically more powerful that those of the CMS (see Section II.B). But there are some things to consider in specific scenarios.

The rendering of assets often is influenced by context-specific parameters of the publication channel at hand. For adaptive web design, for example, images are scaled to the actual screen size of the device posing a request, videos are transcoded to suitable formats, etc. In addition, some CMS installations allow editors to define the image formats used in particular situations, e.g., renderings in certain contexts. This cannot be achieved as easily when the DAM has the duty of rendering assets.

With respect to playout a CMS does not provide the media-specific functionality found in a DAM, in particular there is no quality-controlled adaptive playout. On the other hand, the CMS uses a playout infrastructure consisting of sophisticated caching, inclusion of content delivery networks, etc. This infrastructure has partly to be made available to them DAM.

VI. Asset Integration at the Binary Level

From an editing viewpoint the integration at the time of asset creation or editing time often is the most beneficial. In these cases assets are directly available to the content editor and can be managed alongside with the structured content. Editors work with the CMS only, and can thus directly preview content renderings, have only one workflow to follow, etc.

But, as discussed above, central DAM functionality is lost concerning rendering and layout. The benefits of the introduction of a DAM are neglected to some degree. If the CMS is the only client of the DAM, then they are lost completely.

To allow more of a DAM's rendering functionality to come into play in such an integration scenario, a variation of the corresponding integration approach can be pursued.

In the preceding section we assumed the systems to pass "raw" content to the other, limiting the DAM to a multimedia database. Alternatively the synchronization of asset content can be considered a logical playout step from the DAM with the CMS being the receiver of rendered documents.

Though this variant does not help for playout (QoS parameters, etc.), it allows the integrated system participating in the DAM's functionality to render multimedia content (see Section II.B).

Fig. 9 shows an example illustration of asset integration performed this way. Here, an asset is inserted when a reference to it is made from content.

When an editor choses an asset (using an extended selection dialog querying the DAM as discussed above), it is copied to the CMS similar to the case described by Section IV.E. In the example used here, an approved version of the asset is considered and thus has to exist.

But instead of requesting the asset's media content through some interface, the DAM's rendering facilities are used to create a multimedia document (typically in some binary format) from the asset. The document is then imported into the CMS as part of a newly created content object representing the asset.

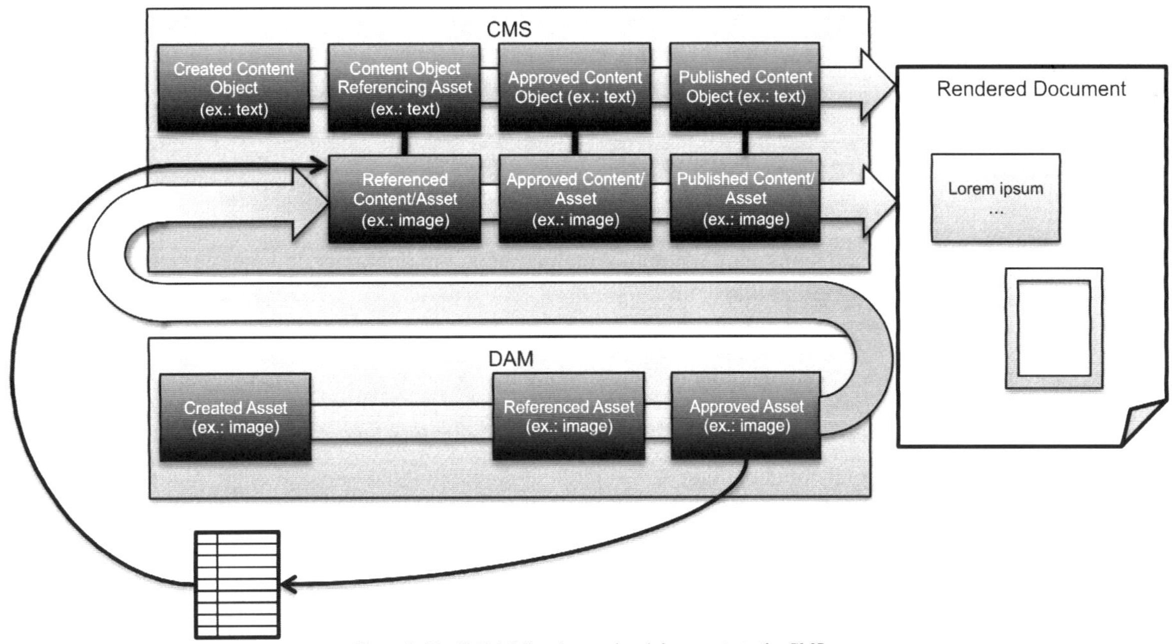

Figure 9. The DAM delivering rendered documents to the CMS

This way, the DAM's rendering capabilities can be used while still creating a copy inside the CMS for the editor.

In the following subsections we discuss aspects of this variation of the integration.

A. *Time of Asset Integration*

The integration of assets in to the CMS can happen at different points in time of the content's and assets' lifecycle. Fig. 9 uses the example of content editing time and approved assets.

The considerations of a choice of the point in time at which to integrate are the same as in the case of direct content access (Section III).

Additionally, the lifecycle state of the asset can vary. Some DAMs require the asset to be in approved or published state in order to be rendered and shipped. Even if the software product does not enforce this behavior, it might be a design choice to handle assets this way. In this case the editor might not receive a copy of the asset that was chosen, but an older revision that went through quality assurance.

B. *Rendering of Multimedia Documents*

The main benefit achieved by the approach of exchanging multimedia documents is the employment of the DAM for the rendering of assets.

Nevertheless, the CMS typically manipulates binary content once more. It does so because it was built following the assumption that binary content was created manually and that it is not optimized for a particular layout.

Such additional media manipulations performed by the CMS have two advantages: It allows editors to direct renditions by a CMS. An example is attributes in the descriptive data that are interpreted during rendering to parameterize the rendering process. Furthermore, the CMS can provide adaptive renderings based on a client's context, e.g., to adapt images to screen resolution.

Particular attention has to be put on the interplay of the DAM's and the CMS's media manipulation functionality. A graphic, for example, would be stored in raw format inside the DAM. It provides a rendered version to the CMS, e.g., in a predefined format and resolution. During the shipping of the content from within the CMS this will in turn prepare the graphics data by scaling it for the usage at hand (full screen version, smaller embedded version, high resolution print version). The concatenation of the manipulation functions may lead to quality losses compared with a one-step rendering through the DAM's rendering functions.

In cases where there is no interference between the DAM's and the CMS's rendering of assets, the concatenation allows combining the quality of renditions provided by a DAM at rendering time with the adaptations possible in the CMS at playout time.

If there are losses in quality caused by chained transformations, additional manipulations by the CMS are not advisable. In that case, only one of the systems should perform these.

If the DAM provides rendered media documents then the according functionality of the CMS is not used. In this scenario there should at least be renderings for different defined contexts to not completely loose the ability of playout time adaptations. The dynamic rendering is replaced by choosing among variants for which documents are rendered in advance. To this end, the DAM needs to be configured to produce the variants required for the documents that are produced by the CMS.

In the opposite case the DAM provides assets in original (maximum) quality to the CMS and leaves manipulations to it. The typically better rendering capabilities of the DAM are neglected.

The typical tradeoff regarding this design choice is the often better quality of renderings provided by a DAM and the advanced functions if offers on binary documents opposed to the adaptivity possible with the CMS as the playout system.

C. *Asset Description Data*

A copy of an asset in the CMS does not only consist of the media data, but also reflects the description data or metadata. Such data is managed in the DAM to describe the media, the entities it represents, regulations of its use, etc.

During rendering, most or all of the description data is not contained in the rendered multimedia document. It is only used internally for management purposes. Therefore, data has to be transmitted to the CMS using a different channel.

In Fig. 9 the table icon in the lower left represents this channel. It represents an externalization of metadata, e.g., as a database or a file.

A DAM does typically not produce such a record or file. The export of the data has to be added to the DAM product. A matching importer needs to be set up for the CMS.

The file has to be generated in way that it can be associated with the media document (e.g., by file name or by contained data that identifies the document). Particular care has to be taken when documents are created with high frequency, so that there is more than one version of the document and the data.

VII. Required System Adaptations for Asset Integration at Binary Level

All the implementation measures listed in Section V are also required in scenarios in which the DAM delivers rendered media documents to the CMS. They are related to the synchronization of the lifecycle states of assets in the DAM and their surrogates managed in the CMS. These measures are, therefore, needed in these scenarios as well.

Consequently, all properties from Table I are also valid here. For the exchange of documents some additional means are required. These are discussed in this section.

Table II shows the cumulated requirements to the CMS and DAM configuration.

A. *Added Functionality*

Central to the approach of exchanging rendered documents is the DAM acting on request of the CMS. To this end, the DAM needs to be equipped with a service accessible by the CMS. The interface of this service allows to request rendered multimedia documents plus metadata.

TABLE II. CHANGES TO SOFTWARE PRODUCTS DEPENDING ON ASSET INTEGRATION TIME AT BINARY LEVEL

Aspects	Form of Integration				
	Creation time	*Editing time*	*Approval/public. time*	*Render time*	*Playout time/never*
Changes to CMS	• subscribe to and listen to events (from DAM) or expose public API; create content on asset creation or modification • import documents produced by the DAM • import asset metadata exported by the DAM	• media selection dialog changed to query DAM • on-the-fly content creation upon asset utilization (linking) • subscribe to and listen to events (from DAM) or expose public API; modify content on asset modification • import documents produced by the DAM • import asset metadata exported by the DAM	• media selection dialog changed to query DAM • surrogate objects for assets • on-the-fly content creation on public stage upon asset (proxy) approval • check of asset's approval state upon asset proxy approval • import documents produced by the DAM • import asset metadata exported by the DAM	• media selection dialog changed to query DAM • surrogate objects for assets • on-the-fly content creation on public stage upon asset (proxy) rendering • import documents produced by the DAM • import asset metadata exported by the DAM	• media selection dialog changed to query DAM • surrogate objects for assets
Changes to DAM	• event source for CMS • stable external IDs (to relate assets in events) • render documents on requests posed by the CMS • export metadata and relate it to rendered document	• query interface for CMS • event source for CMS • stable external IDs (to relate assets in events) • render documents on requests posed by the CMS • export metadata and relate it to rendered document	• stable IDs/addresses • query interface for CMS • interface to query approval state from CMS • render documents on requests posed by the CMS • export metadata and relate it to rendered document	• stable IDs/addresses • query interface for CMS • event source for CMS • render documents on requests posed by the CMS • export metadata and relate it to rendered document	• stable IDs/addresses • query interface for CMS
Unused CMS functionality	• rendering (assets) depending on rendering quality	• rendering (assets) depending on rendering quality	• quality assurance • rendering (assets) depending on rendering quality	• quality assurance • rendering (assets) depending on rendering quality	• quality assurance • rendering (assets) depending on rendering quality • playout (assets)
Unused DAM functionality	• playout	• playout	• playout	• playout	

If there are render variants, e.g., different image resolutions, the rendering service should accept parameters to describe the requested render variant. The interface also needs to define the format of the result.

In practice, there are possible variations of the way the DAM transmits the result to the CMS. Fig. 9 indicates that the document is passed directly to the CMS as the result of the rendering service the DAM provides, while metadata is written to a file. Such a file needs to be accessible by both the DAM and the CMS.

Alternatively, the metadata might be shipped together with the document using some specific format defining how to marshal the tuple *(document, metadata)*.

As yet another alternative, the document might be written to a common storage location as the metadata records are. Then the CMS reads the document from this common storage.

Synchronicity is the main consideration to choose among the alternatives. Exchanging files typically leads to asynchronous provision of the document. While this frees the DAM from real-time delivery, asynchronous operation is not possible in all cases. E.g., at render time the CMS needs to receive the document and metadata in time.

On the side of the CMS there needs to be an importer that creates a content object from the DAM's export. This importer works on the result of the render request. If it is executed synchronously, the importer has the obligation to create CMS content instantly.

In a quite loose coupling the CMS importer observes the shared memory location to wait for the exported rendered assets. E.g., it may do so by watching a directory in a shared file system.

This loose coupling also adds a buffer and a level of fault tolerance to the systems' coupling, since the documents and data records are persisted for the time of the request. When the document import lags behind the document creation – a typical case – then the shared storage serves as a kind of persistent buffer. It also makes the system robust against temporal failures leading to restarts of the CMS.

When more than one CMS instance waits for files and processes the imports, the queue of documents serves as a queue to distribute the load among the instances.

B. *Unused Functionality of the Software Products*

The main advantage of integration that is based on document exchange lies in the additional functionality of the software products used in comparison to the case of direct content access. In all cases, the rendering functions of the DAM are used.

Whether the rendering capabilities of a CMS are employed for media data depends on the quality losses of chained document rendering (see above). Often there will be a tradeoff between rendering quality and extra effort on the one hand, and the ability to render documents specific to the context of a request on the other. Therefore, the rendering functionality for binary content of a CMS may be unused.

The playout functionality of a DAM is used only when integrating assets at playout time.

VIII. Summary and Outlook

The paper closes with a summary and an outlook.

A. *Summary*

This paper presents various forms of integration of a CMS and a DAM. If the CMS is in lead regarding the overall content management process – the basic assumption of the work presented here – then the main difference between the integration forms is the point in the content and asset lifecycle at which an asset is introduced in the CMS.

With the CMS in lead there is, however, no way to utilize the playout capabilities of a DAM except for the integration at playout time. However, integration this late in the lifecycle does not allow assuring the overall quality using the means of the CMS.

Consequently, there is no optimal integration form. The choice of the right integration point depends on the application to build.

All integration forms exhibit individual strengths and weaknesses, achieved with differing implementation effort.

The choice of a suitable integration form, therefore, depends on different factors and considerations discussed in this paper.

B. *Outlook*

This article describes insights gained from practical projects. In the future, additional research will round up these insights in a systematic way.

For integrated solutions – like a CMS combined with a DAM in this case – we would like to see a repository of typical requirement/solution patterns. This way, the experiences made can be preserved and solutions can be reapplied.

The discussion in this paper shows that many decisions rely on the particular properties of the software products used. The solution scenarios should, therefore, be refined to consider actual software products with their individual capabilities to be of increased value in practical applications. This may lead to additional integration scenarios.

Furthermore, some decisions have to be made on the basis of more specific requirements: the integration approach in general, but also implementation details like, e.g., the way how to handle concurrent asset modifications in the DAM and in the CMS. A comprehensive catalog containing more refined use cases and blueprints for typical solutions is required in practice.

The medium on which documents are transmitted is not considered in this paper. The Internet is the main distribution channel in many cases. There are dedicated networks, e.g., for mobile applications [11]. These may require specific considerations.

Future work will try to extend the considerations to more general integration scenarios in the field. A quite prominent example is product information management fulfilled by, e.g., a CMS in cooperation with catalog management or a CMS combined with a shop solution.

Acknowledgment

The author thanks his employer, Namics, for the opportunity to follow his scientific ambitions by publishing some of his thoughts. In particular since these relate to and extend commercial activities.

Fruitful discussions with numerous colleagues (current and former), business partners, and customers led to the insights presented in this paper. Thanks go to all of them.

My thanks also go to the anonymous reviewers for the constructive hints that helped to improve this paper.

References

[1] H.-W. Sehring, "An Overview Over Content Management System Integration Approaches: An Architecture Perspective on Current Practice," in Proceedings of The Eighth International Conference on Creative Content Technologies (CONTENT) 2016, March 2016, pp. 30-35.

[2] Ovum, Making the case for digital asset management in retail: Using technology to manage digital assets effectively. Whitepaper, August 2015.

[3] A. Saarkar, Digital Asset Management. Whitepaper, Cognizant Technology Solutions, 2001.

[4] S. King, "Web content management," in Computer Technology Review. Los Angeles, vol. 22, issue 11, p. 9, 2002.

[5] D. Austerberry, Digital Asset Management: How to Realise the Value of Video and Image Libraries. Amsterdam, Boston: Focal Press, an imprint of Elsevier Ltd., 2004.

[6] Y.-M. Kim et al., "Enterprise Digital Asset Management System Pilot: Lessons Learned," in Information Technology and Libraries, John Webb, Ed. vol. 26, no. 4, 2007.

[7] T. Blanke, "Digital Asset Ecosystems: Rethinking crowds and cloud," Chandos Publishing, 2014.

[8] H. Thimm and W. Klas, "Playout Management in Multimedia Database Systems," in Multimedia Database Systems, K. C. Nwosu, B. Thuraisingham, and P. B. Berra, Eds. Springer US, pp. 318-376, 1996.

[9] C. D. Humphrey, T. T. Tollefson, and J. D. Kriet, "Digital Asset Management," in Facial Plastic Surgery Clinics of North America, vol. 18, no. 2, pp. 335-340, 2010.

[10] Content Management Interoperability Services (CMIS) Version 1.1. 23 May 2013. OASIS Standard. [online]. Available from: http://docs.oasis-open.org/cmis/CMIS/v1.1/os/CMIS-v1.1-os.html

[11] H. Koumaras, D. Negrou, F. Liberal, J. Arauz, and A. Kourtis, "ADAMANTIUM project: Enhancing IMS with a PQoS-aware Multimedia Content Management System," in Journal of Control Engineering and Applied Informatics (CEAI), vol. 10, no. 2, pp. 24-32, 2008.

Mobile Text Messaging Quality Assessment

Janusz H. Klink
Telecommunications and Teleinformatics Department
Wroclaw University of Science and Technology
Wroclaw, Poland
e-mail: janusz.klink@pwr.edu.pl

Abstract— **Telecommunication services are expected to be of good quality and offered for a reasonable price. Operators, competing strongly for customers, always present their products in the best light, and underline the highest service quality, which is often measured in incomparable circumstances, using different procedures and measurement methods. The paper presents the efforts of European standards institutions, regulators and operators in the scope of improving the provision of telecommunication services and ensuring quality. The author presents the main parameters that influence the quality of Short Message Service, which represents a wide range of text messaging services and shows the method and environment for measuring end-to-end delivery time. The measurement scenarios performed in both the real network and also a laboratory environment are presented. The results of measurements, performed in the real networks of four operators in Poland, show that the message delivery time fluctuates during the course of the day and also depends on the operator. Generally however, the short text service is of good quality and is highly assessed by users. The author also presents also the quality of experience model for text messaging.**

Keywords- mobile text messaging; SMS; QoS; QoE; quality assessment.

I. INTRODUCTION

In the last few decades, mobile telephony has reached a deeper level of penetration worldwide than cars, radio or TV. From over 700 million registered users in 2000, the mobile cellular industry has grown considerably and exceeded 7 billion subscriptions in 2015. With the increased number of mobile subscribers over the world, Short Message Service (SMS), has gained a huge popularity among the users (around 8 trillion messages a year) and is also described in numerous scientific papers [1-4]. Moreover, after voice, messaging is the biggest revenue-generating mobile service on the telecommunication market [5]. Although, in some countries SMS has peaked, and the traffic volumes are in decline, there are still more countries where overall SMS traffic and its use-per-subscriber is still growing. A significant growth in mobile subscribers is observed in the Middle East, Asia, Africa and Latin America, thus the dominance of SMS in the immediate future is unthreatened. According to [5] SMS will be one of the major worldwide communication tools for the next decade, despite the progressive extension of user equipment utility. The increase in the processing power of mobile devices has made them significantly more multi-functional and allows Internet browsing, emailing, multimedia and instant messaging. Despite the rapid growth of the so called Over-The-Top (OTT) messaging apps and Voice over IP (VoIP) services, SMS is still generating more than half of the total mobile messaging revenue (Fig. 1) [6].

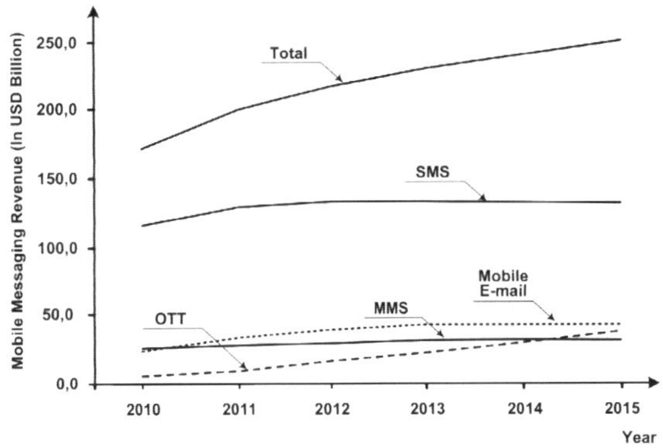

Figure 1. Mobile messaging revenue in recent years

Such large revenues mean that SMS will remain an important service for mobile operators for many years. While Instant Messaging (IM) and SMS are both text messaging services, there are differences that encourage different user behavior. IM is a two-way communication with many quick responses, whereas SMS is an individually paid-for message that is used to just send information. While there are low to zero costs for the user when using IM, travelers stick to using SMS as it is cheaper than purchasing a mobile data package or subscribing for a data roaming plan in order to send a few messages. SMS is common to all phones and almost all users [6] while IM usually requires smartphones with dedicated apps and specific knowledge of how to use it, which can be a barrier for some sections (older) of society. Moreover, the market for IM is fragmented by different services that cannot communicate with each other. Users also choose IM apps based on their geographical location. While WeChat and Line are clearly the leaders in China and Japan respectively, WhatsApp is also far bigger in East and South-East Asia than the USA.

One of the major factors that allow service providers to keep their customers is the price, which is diminishing year by year, the next factors being common availability, simplicity, and good quality. Service quality is becoming an increasingly more important factor to users at the moment of choosing a network operator or service provider [2-8]. Thus, many operators' efforts are concentrated on the efficient mechanisms for handling the message traffic [9]. On the other hand, a service-oriented management is focused on service quality rather than network performance [10]. An effective evaluation of service quality can help a service provider to increase customer satisfaction which plays a key role in influencing a user's decision on staying with or changing a provider. Soldani and al. [11] claim that over 80% of customer defections (churning) are due to frustration over the product or service and the inability of the provider/operator to deal with this effectively. Moreover, this is a chain reaction, where one frustrated customer will tell other people about his bad experience. An operator cannot assess the level of its service quality based on checking customer complaints, but should have a more active attitude as statistics have shown that for every person who calls with a problem, there are another 29 who will never call. On the other hand, about 90% of customers will not complain before defecting. This churn directly affects the profitability and image of the operator or service provider. Thus, the way to avoid such situation is to devise a strategy to manage and improve the Quality of Experience (QoE) [12].

The QoE based research mechanism for control and management of resources is also getting more attention in literature [13-15]. The SMS quality evaluation is also important in terms of the professional deployment of the service [16]. It is of great importance to the many local governments (e.g., in Poland) that implement SMS to notify inhabitants and all people about emergency states [17]. There has been a noticeable increase in text messaging applications in healthcare, as a part of mobile Health (mHealth) programs, for behavior modification, disease management and surveillance, prevention and public health education, data collection, etc. [18, 19]. On the other hand, growing competition among service providers and network operators forces these entities to provide high quality services. The question of how to describe this quality and what parameters should be used, is asked not only by operators but also by regulators of the telecommunications market in the European Union [20]. One of the factors motivating telecommunications industry operators to act in this direction are regulations undertaken both at the European level [21, 22], and in individual Member States [23, 24]. A particular example of this can be seen in the case of Poland, where on the Electronic Communications Office's initiative (2012), a Memorandum on Cooperation for Improving the Quality of Services in the Telecommunications Market has been signed. The first stage of works was finalized in the form of an official report [25], which was published by the Electronic Communications Office in February 2014. Despite long discussions, the current edition of this report does not define any QoS requirements for SMS, but there is a hope for a gradual expansion of the scope of this document. Although, SMS is not a real-time service, it is often perceived as such (a near-real-time) service [26] by a huge amount of users. Therefore, two factors seem to be important from the QoS point of view, these are: delivery rate and time of delivery. Nowadays, the delivery rate is mainly at a high level, reaching, in the case of many operators, values around 95% [17]. However, these factors are correlated with each other, because the delivery rate also depends, among other things, on the delivery threshold time after which the message is considered as lost. Therefore, delivery time seems to be a key performance indicator (KPI), which is much more crucial for the service quality perceived by the users. They want the information to be delivered in acceptable time. But what does it mean? In the era of information and communication technologies with more and more bandwidth and rich service offerings, user demands concerning the service are also growing. Today SMS is more often treated as an almost instantaneous communication medium for rapid exchange of information, and even a form of text dialogue between people [26]. The arrival delays could be a serious problem for time sensitive content such as customer account changes, last-minute tickets, product availability notifications etc. Online booking services and airlines, for example, already use SMS to notify travelers of the status of flights [27, 28]. A relatively short time of message delivery is one of the main factors describing SMS quality affecting its application and popularity among users. In Section II the author presents the basics of SMS functionality and the main parameters and statistics describing the quality of the service, according to the ETSI standards [29]. Section III describes the main prerequisites concerning service quality assessment in the real network. Sections IV and V present the method and tools used during measurements in the real network, taking into account connections inside one network and between different networks, respectively. The message delivery time distributions are also presented and discussed. In Section VI the author proposes, on the basis of measurements results, the Quality of Experience model for SMS. Section VII presents the conclusions and the plans for the future work.

II. Short Message Service Quality

SMS, belonging to the so-called "non-real-time" class, is a "store-and-forward" type of service [30]. Communication between two users is done via at least one server, acting as an intermediary unit. A user's equipment transmits a message to the server, which optionally sends it to the next server and so forth. The end server, after receiving the message, informs the recipient's equipment of receiving a message and, finally, the user can read the message. SMS was originally designed for the transmission of text information, where the length of a single data unit cannot exceed 140 bytes and, according to ETSI standards [31], remains constant regardless of the number of characters transmitted in a single message. Depending on the alphabet used, the maximum message length may vary between 70 and 160 characters. When the information is longer, then it is divided and encapsulated into several 140-byte data units, and sent as separate messages.

According to ITU-T recommendations the quality study presented in this paper only takes into account the information that does not exceed the size of a single data unit [32]. The test scenarios for concatenated message sending are for further study. On the other hand, ETSI standards give very detailed information regarding SMS quality parameters and their computation.

The most important parameters are:

- SMS Successful Ratio - the ratio of correctly sent messages, expressed by the probability of correct message sending and its delivery to a service center,
- Completion Rate for SMS - indicator of properly delivered messages, expressed by the percentage of messages successfully sent and delivered to a recipient,
- End-to-End Delivery Time for SMS - time to deliver a message from end to end, expressed as the time measured from the moment of sending a message by a sender to a service center until it is received by a recipient.

Monitoring of the parameters, mentioned above, is crucial for the operator, who has to watch over the process of service delivery at every stage of its implementation. It gives the knowledge of network performance, which in turn impacts the quality of service [33]. The measurements can be done based on the following scenarios:

- using all real traffic in the network (in a specific period of time),
- using a sample of real traffic,
- making the test calls,
- a combination of the above.

Message loss and message integrity are valid concerns, however, they are handled by lower layer network mechanisms and protocol, which are outside the scope of this paper. From the user's point of view, it is very important that messages are delivered to the recipient as soon as possible and in an unchanged form. From this perspective, it can be seen that the parameter which probably has the strongest impact on the SMS quality, perceived by the user, is the End-to-End Delivery Time.

According to the ETSI standard [29], the following statistics should be provided separately:

- the mean value in seconds for sending and receiving short messages,
- the time in seconds within which the fastest 95% of short messages are sent and received,
- the number of observations performed.

It should be noted that, concerning the mobile environment, the values of QoS parameters, can be affected not only by congestion in the SMS system or signalling channels but also by network or service non-accessibility in the claimed area of coverage. In that case, operators may wish to distinguish the effects of coverage and access congestion. From the user's point of view there is no need to do it, because all these phenomena have an impact on the end-user perception.

III. Measurements Set-Up

The most representative for the network are statistics calculated from measurements on real traffic performed in a long period of time and in the whole network. This is obviously the most expensive case and it is therefore valuable to limit the measurements to the needed number and representative population of Network Termination Points (NTPs) or Service Access Points (SAPs). When sampling or test calls are used, it should be ensured that the results reflect the service quality perceived by customers. In general, the choice of adequate origin and destination NTPs for the measurements may be based on the national/international numbering plan, on traffic patterns/distribution or on geographic coverage. Measurements should be scheduled so as to reflect traffic variations over the hours of a day, the days of the week and even the months of the year [29]. Network specific characteristics and user behaviour, depending on the kind of networks under study, i.e., fixed, mobile or a combination of them, need to be taken into account. SMS quality assessment using an intrusive method (based on test messages sending) has the advantage to precisely analyse the service quality over defined configurations because it is an end to end analysis and correlates well with user perception. The main drawback of such a kind of method is that it provides a limited view of the quality of service provided by the operator or service provider, in general. This is due to a restriction of the measurements to the analysed test configuration or specific network area. It is obviously impossible to do such kinds of measurements everywhere in the network and it is therefore important to specify the number of measurement locations, so that the measurement points can be spread according to the size of the examined network. In practice, the drive tests are used to determine the quality of service that is experienced by users in main meeting places and communication paths. As a rule of thumb, the number of samples (tests) within a measurement campaign correlates with the reliability of results. In general, the higher the number of collected data samples, the more precise and trustworthy the results are. The number of observations for message delivery times depends, like the number of observations for any quantitative variables, on the variability of measured data. Therefore there is a need to perform some pilot tests or take into consideration the results of former measurements in the network in order to get some initial data. The number of observations can be calculated by formula (1):

$$n = \frac{z^2_{1-\frac{\alpha}{2}}}{a^2}\left(\frac{s}{mean(x)}\right)^2 \tag{1}$$

where:

$z^2_{1-\alpha/2}$ – the 1-α/2-percentile of the standard normal distribution,

s – the expected standard deviation of the call set up time (from former measurements),

mean(x) – the expected mean value of the measured value (from former measurements).

a – the relative accuracy.

The results are presented in Table I.

TABLE I. NUMBER OF OBSERVATIONS NEEDED

s/mean(x)	No. of observations
< 0.1	100
0.1 to 0.3	1 000
> 0.3 to 0.5	2 500
> 0.5 to 0.7	5 000
> 0.7 to 0.9	7 500
> 0.9	10 000

where:

$z^2_{1-\alpha/2}$ = 1.96 for a confidence level of 95%,

a = 2%,

Taking into account the number of tests to be performed and the usually limited time of measurement, particular attention should be paid to the scheduling of SMS tests. This means that a subsequent SM towards the same destination can affect the result of a previous SMS test if the second SM is sent before stating the result of the first one [31]. So, to avoid such a situation, a proper time interval between the sending of messages should be kept. An alternative way to increase the number of tests is by sending the SMs towards different destinations. In such a way, the queuing per destination mechanism is bypassed.

IV. IN-NET MEASUREMENTS PERFORMED IN THE REAL ENVIRONMENT

This Section presents the method, measurement environment, results, and evaluation of SMS quality provided by leading mobile operators functioning in Poland, i.e., Orange, Play, Plus and T-Mobile.

A. Method and the Measurement Environment

Data was collected from more than 120 000 tests (individual observations) performed during one week in Wroclaw - one of the biggest cities in Poland (650 000 inhabitants). The test environment (Fig. 2) consists of measuring robots (one per operator), each covering a Personal Computer with a 3G modem and specially designed application that manages the measurement and data collection process. Each robot plays both roles: sender and receiver. Initially, the first one sends a previously prepared text message to the Short Message Service Center (SMSC) located in the operator network, inserting its own number (i.e., both: the sender and receiver belong to the same network) in the destination address field. The time of the message sending is written down into a special record of a log file on the robot's hard disk. The SMSC then sends the message further, i.e., to the receiver, which in this situation is the same robot that sent the message before. Next, the receiving part of the robot is informed of the incoming message and then it also records the current time in the log file. In this way, the file collects a number of records with the times of sending and receiving the particular messages. In the next step the robot sends the message to another robot that is connected to the other operator's network. All previous actions are repeated and then the next operator's network is chosen as the destination in a round-robin scheme. The robot software allows the setting of the frequency of message sending in an order, based on message delivery time observed, in order to avoid traffic congestion (Fig. 3).

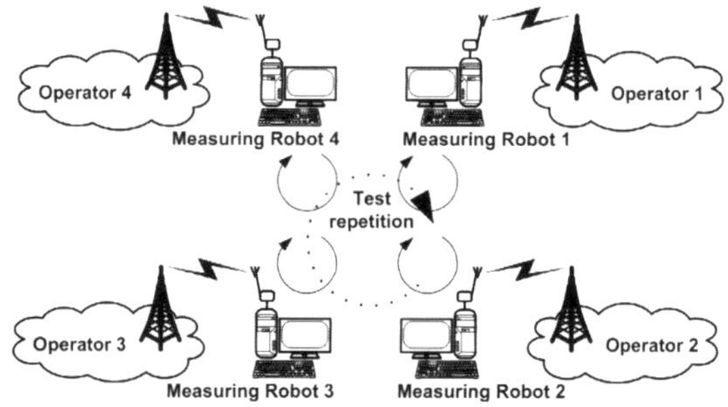

Figure 2. The test environment for the SMS parameter measurement in real mobile networks

It should be noted that such a solution causes the risk of substantially reducing the number of tests when the delivery time increases enormously. In order to eliminate such phenomenon, it is possible to limit the maximum acceptable delivery time and, if it is overrun, the expected message may be recognized as lost. Then the sending of the next message can start. In this phase of the measurements such a time limit was not used so that the robots were able to capture all delivery time cases.

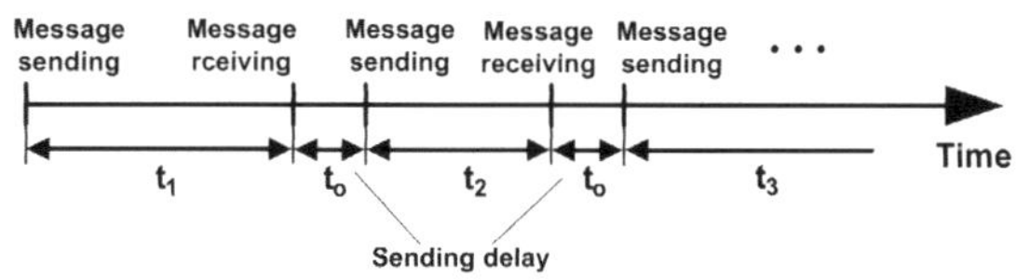

Figure 3. Sequential message sending scenario

B. Message Delivery Time Distributions

The measurements performed in real networks, as mentioned before, allowed the message delivery time distributions in each network to be determined (Figs. 4-7). After analysis of the distributions it can be stated that very long delivery times occur in the case of some operators (e.g., Play), which may be irritating to some customers. From a statistical point of view, however, they are not of considerable importance (it concerns about 10^{-4} cases). Moreover, it is negligible especially in the case of discarding 5% of the highest values before further analysis. The majority of the captured message delivery times do not exceed 10 seconds which means that SMS users should be satisfied. Moreover, almost 99% of the messages were delivered in a time of no higher than 6 seconds in the case of three operators. Only in the Play network the message delivery time distribution was different. The question is: are the captured message delivery times satisfactory in the case of real time text messaging applications? More detailed analysis will be shown in the Section IV, where the scores of subjective measurements will be taken into account.

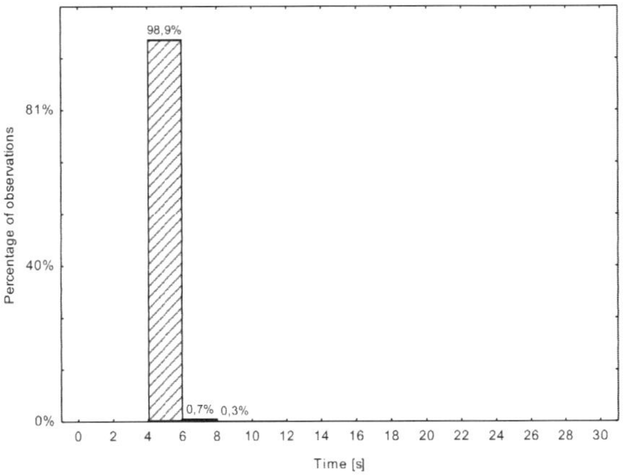

Figure 4. Message delivery time distribution in the Orange network

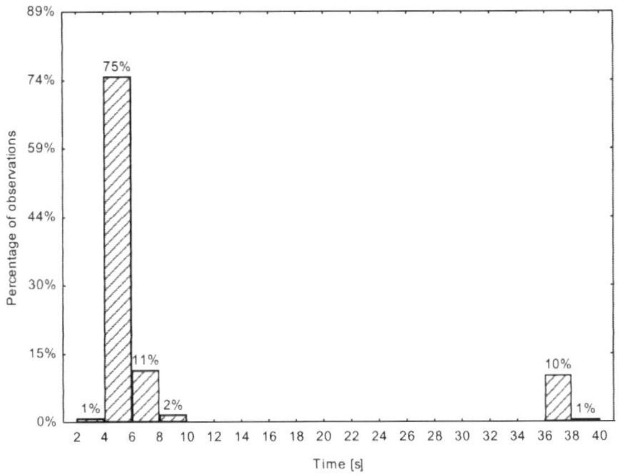

Figure 5. Message delivery time distribution in the Play network

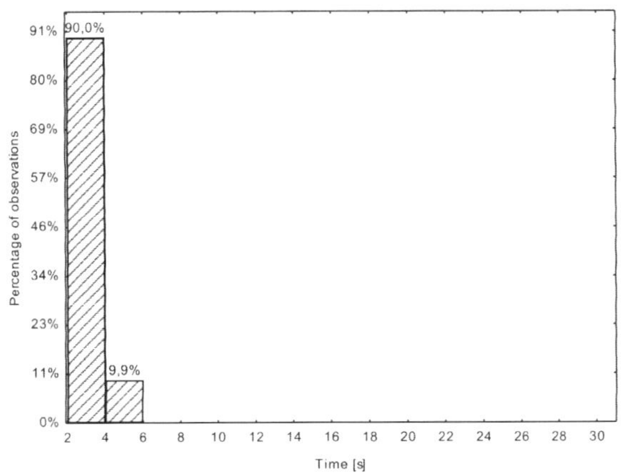

Figure 6. Message delivery time distribution in the Plus network

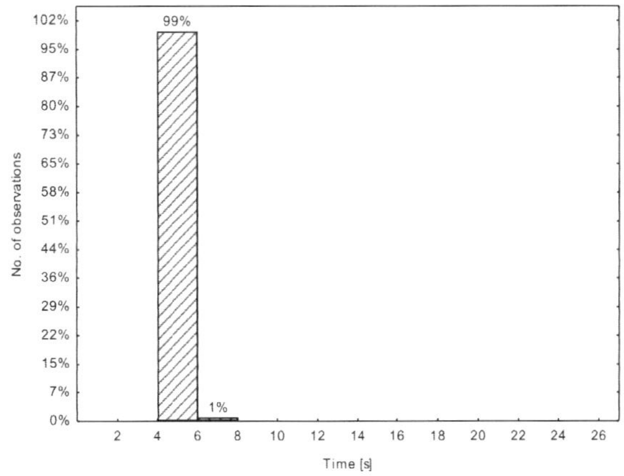

Figure 7. Message delivery time distribution in the T-Mobile network

C. Message Delivery Time as a Function of the Time of Day

Analysis of the results showed that message delivery time, as expected, is not stable and is diversified depending on the operator (see Table II).

It can be noted that the lowest mean value of the message delivery time (3.6 s) occurred in the case of operator No. 3.

TABLE II. COMPARISON OF MESSAGE DELIVERY TIMES

No.	Operator (number)	Delivery time [s]				
		Mean	Min.	Max.	Std. dev.	Median
1	Orange (OR)	4.66	2.8	26.1	0.47	4.6
2	Play (PY)	15.79	3.1	**10815**	**256.4**	4.5
3	Plus (PS)	**3.6**	3.3	65.7	0.68	3.5
4	T-Mobile (TM)	4.96	3.1	23.7	0.39	4.9

A slightly worse score can be seen in networks 1 and 4. The longest delivery times, as well as standard deviation, was offered by operator No. 2. Such rough analysis can lead us to the conclusion that the SMS does not work properly and many of users may be dissatisfied with the service. On the other hand, when we take into account the median, which is by definition the value located in the middle of the population, it can be noted that it is comparable with the appropriate parameters of the other operators. Moreover, the median value seems to be a better parameter describing the service quality experienced by the users in the case of high standard deviation of QoS parameters. As mentioned before, ETSI proposes to describe the message delivery time by presenting the time within which the fastest 95% of short messages are sent and received [29]. According to the above, the distributions of message delivery times as a function of the time of day are presented in Figs. 8-11. The black points represent median values, whereas the dashed boxes show the ranges of delivery time after discarding 5% of the lowest and highest values, respectively. In other words, they represent 90% of the population. Moreover, the top level of each dashed box

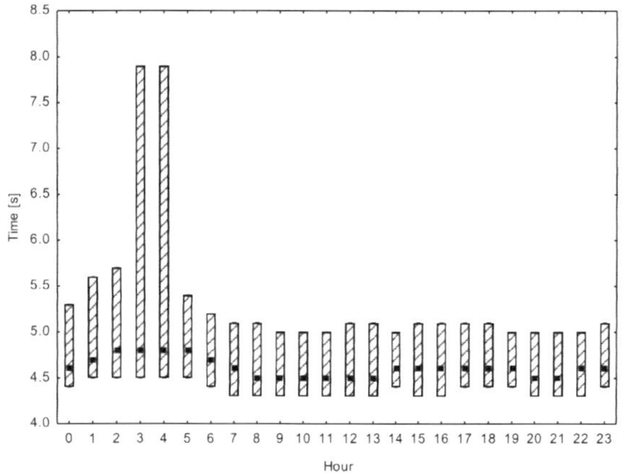

Figure 8. Short message delivery time in the Orange network as a function of the time of day

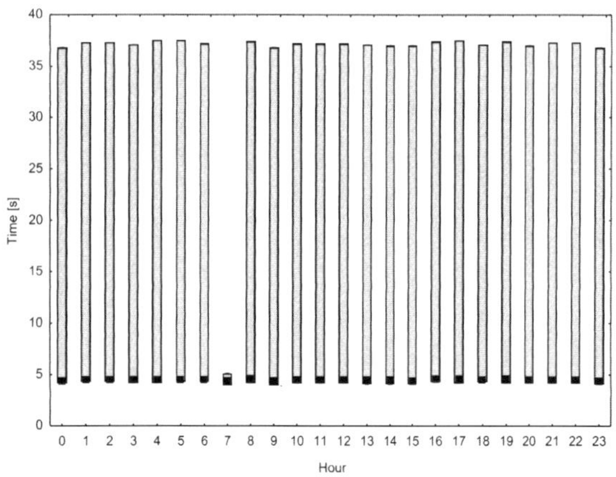

Figure 9. Short message delivery time in the Play network as a function of the time of day

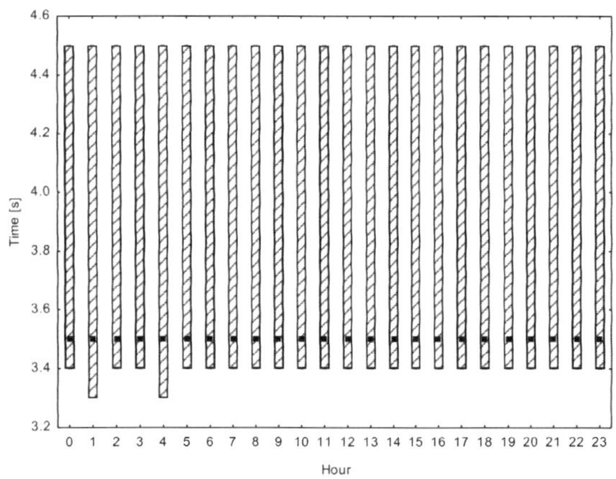

Figure 10. Short message delivery time in the Plus network as a function of the time of day

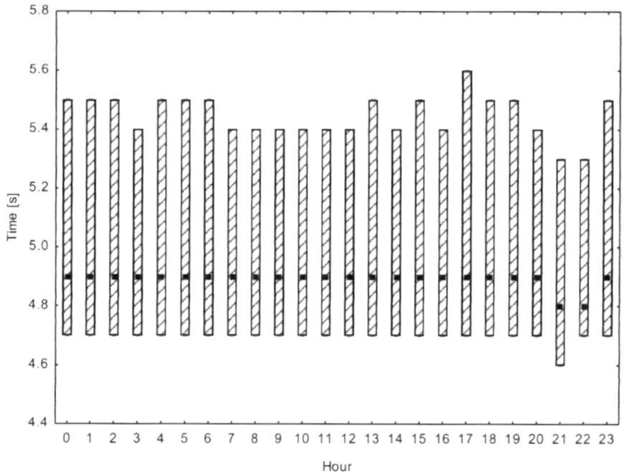

Figure 11. Short message delivery time in the T-Mobile network as a function of the time of day

denotes the highest limit of delivery time for 95% of messages sent in the relevant hour [29]. As presented in Fig. 4, fluctuations of the message delivery time experienced by almost all SMS users of the Orange network, do not exceed the value of 6 seconds. The highest deviation is observed at around 3 and 5 o'clock in the morning. The results of the observations performed in the Play network show the values of delivery time deviation that are almost at the same level, except for one hour (7 a.m.), during the whole day. However, compared to the Orange network, the range of deviations, observed in the individual time intervals, is much wider here. Moreover, it can be seen that users of the Play network experience relatively high fluctuations of message delivery times not only in specific hours but during the whole day. It should be noted that the median values and deviations of the message delivery times, presented in Figs. 8- 11, are valid for 90% of observations and may slightly differ from the values shown in Table I, which takes into account all the captured data. Although the median (or even the mean) values of the message delivery times and their deviations can be used to compare the different operator's network performances or QoS parameters, they do not answer the question concerning the quality assessed by the users. For this reason, the relation between objectively measured QoS parameters and the quality of experience (QoE), which is subjective, should be determined.

V. INTER-NET MEASUREMENTS PERFORMED IN THE REAL ENVIRONMENT

In this section, the author presents the second part of the measurements performed in the real network. This is an extension of the previous investigations and not only covers separate measurements performed in networks of different operators (In-Net) but also takes into account relations between networks (Inter-Net) as well. Although the operators remained the same, the author changed the location of the measurements from an urban to rural area of the same part of Poland (Lower Silesia district).

A. Method and the Measurement Environment

Each "inter-operator" relation is described by 1440 measurements, i.e., one measurement per minute (60 samples per hour), which results in more than 23 000 measurements in total. The test environment consists of measuring robots (one for the operator), analogous to the ones presented in Fig. 2. However, the measurement scenario was extended to inter-network investigations. In order to compare Inter-Net relations, the author, as a first step, performed the In-Net investigations for each network separately. The author does not analyse delivery times as a function of the time of day but shows how the examined networks fulfil ETSI requirements [29, 30]. One of the main parameters, as mentioned before, is the time in seconds within which the fastest 95% of short messages are sent and received. Therefore, the cumulative distribution function (CDF) of the message end-to-end delivery times is determined for each operator.

Figure 12 shows that at least 95% of messages in the examined (rural) area of the Orange network are delivered in a time of no longer than 16 s. That is more than twice as long as in the urban area tested before (see Fig. 4). Moreover, as presented in Fig. 13, these times are of higher deviation and most of the messages are delivered between the 10th and 12th second. Significantly longer delivery times were observed in the Play network, where 95% of messages were delivered to their destination in a time exceeding 30 seconds (Fig. 14).

It is interesting that most of the messages reach the receiving station, as in the Orange network, in comparable time, i.e., in less than 10 seconds. Twelve seconds are needed to deliver 84% of the messages. However, very long delivery times are observed here more often than in the case of measurements in the urban area. As presented in Fig. 15, over 7% of messages are delivered in a time exceeding 30 seconds.

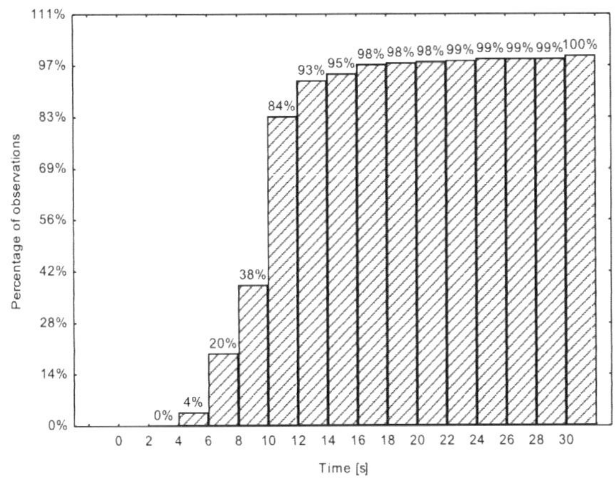

Figure 12. Cumulative Distribution Function of end-to-end message delivery time in the Orange network

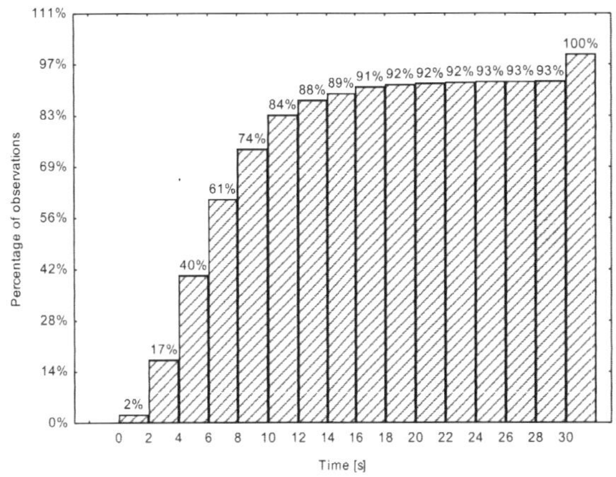

Figure 14. Cumulative Distribution Function of end-to-end message delivery time in the Play network

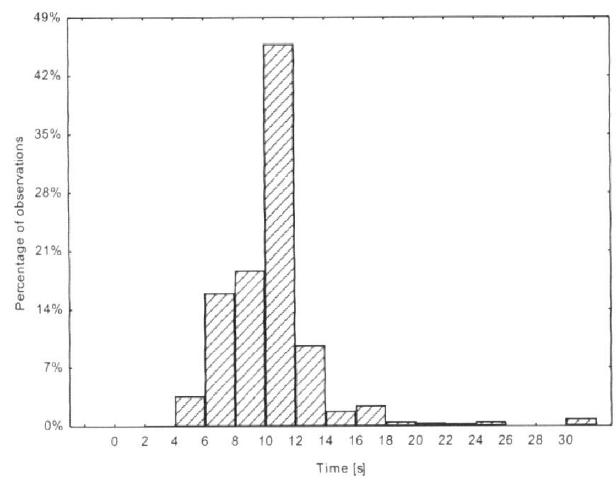

Figure 13. Probability Density Function of end-to-end message delivery time in the Orange network

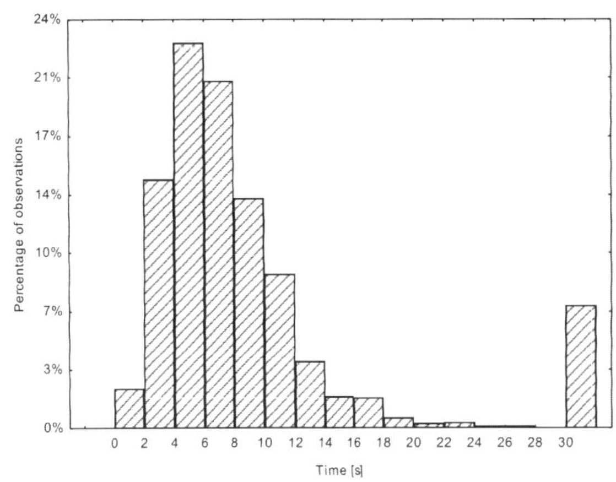

Figure 15. Probability Density Function of end-to-end message delivery time in the Play network

The fact that the vast majority of messages in the Play network are delivered in a relatively short time can positively influence user perception of the service. On the other hand, a fairly large amount of messages are delivered in a time of longer than 30 s, which means that 95% of them are delivered in the longest time when compared with the other examined networks.

The Plus and T-Mobile networks behave in similar way to the Orange network, which means that 95% of messages are delivered in a time of less than 20 seconds (in the case of the last two it is 18 s) and the observed delivery times are of a standard deviation that is significantly lower than in the Play network (Fig. 16-Fig. 19).

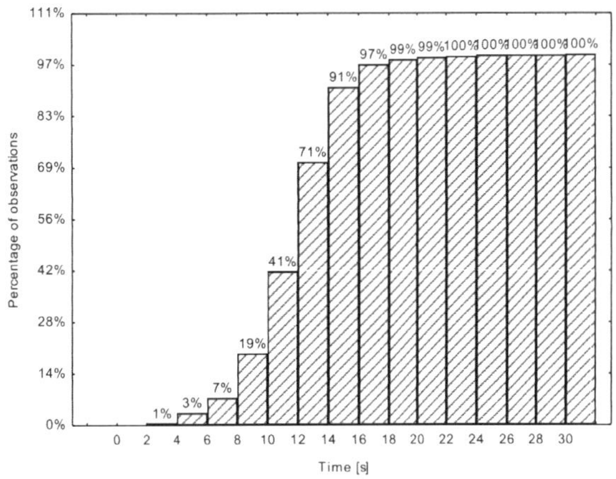

Figure 16. Cumulative Distribution Function of end-to-end message delivery time in the Plus network

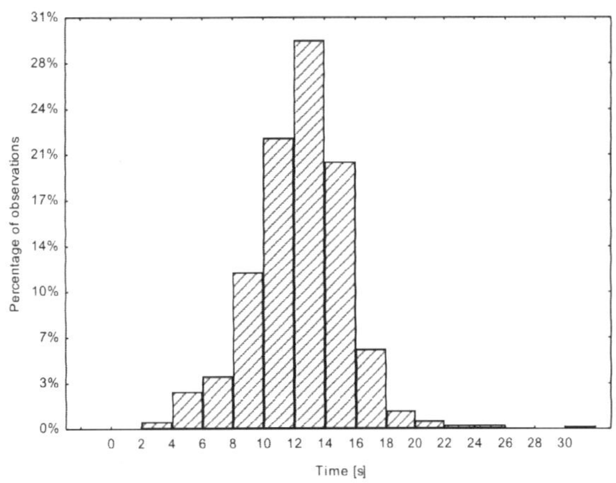

Figure 17. Probability Density Function of end-to-end message delivery time in the Plus network

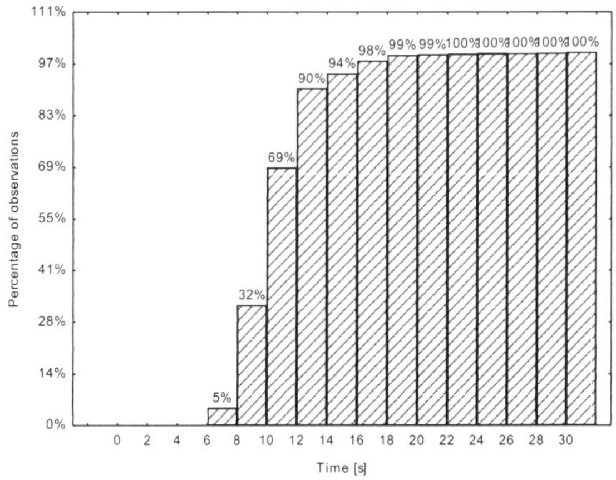

Figure 18. Cumulative Distribution Function of end-to-end message delivery time in the T-Mobile network

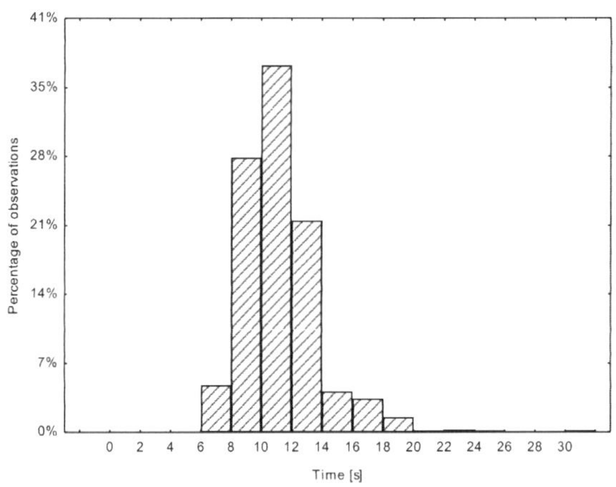

Figure 19. Probability Density Function of end-to-end message delivery time in the T-Mobile network

Analysis of the message delivery process shows that the mean value of message delivery times, in the case of messages exchanged between users belonging to different operator networks, is usually higher than in the case of transmitting them inside an individual network. Exceptions to this rule are seen in the Play and Orange networks where In-Net measurements show comparable or even higher mean values of message delivery times (Tables III and IV). In almost every network the maximum values of message delivery times significantly exceed the mean values (even 20 times or more). Additionally, high values of standard deviation of delivery times are observed for almost all the operators. An exception to the rule is the Plus network, where these times are low and rather stable, i.e., of low standard deviation. It concerns both, In-Net and Inter-Net measurements as well.

TABLE III. COMPARISON OF MESSAGE DELIVERY TIMES INSIDE NETWORKS

Operator		Delivery time [s]					
		Mean	Min.	Max.	Std. dev.	Median	Skew
Orange	(OR)	11.5	3	312	10.2	11	20.5
Play	(PY)	41.1	1	**2170**	**201.3**	7	7.7
Plus	(PS)	13	3	74	3.8	13	5.6
T-Mobile	(TM)	11.8	7	59	2.9	11	4.7

TABLE IV. COMPARISON OF MESSAGE DELIVERY TIMES BETWEEN NETWORKS

Operator		Delivery time [s]					
		Mean	Min.	Max.	Std. dev.	Median	Skew
OR	PY	18.4	3	563	42.6	11	8.1
OR	PS	19.6	1	1046	75.4	9	9.9
OR	TM	11.2	4	244	8.9	10	17.1
PY	OR	107.3	1	3268	414.5	8	5
PY	PS	37.5	1	2154	200.4	6	7.7
PY	TM	41.5	1	2186	209.8	7	7.2
PS	OR	14	5	128	5	14	11.4
PS	PY	15.4	6	196	9.7	15	10.5
PS	TM	13.9	5	74	3.4	14	3.5
TM	OR	13	7	46	2.7	13	2
TM	PY	127	7	4293	539.4	13	5.7
TM	PS	13.3	6	202	11.1	11	8.1

For all the In-Net and Inter-Net relations a median value of message delivery time was determined. As presented in Tables III and IV, in most cases and due to asymmetry of its probability distributions, these values significantly differ from the mean values. Analysis of the data shows non-zero (positive) skewness, which denotes that most of the delivery times measured are lower than the calculated mean value. It suggests that the median value should not be treated as the main performance indicator, describing quality of the service.

In general, the median is better suited for skewed distributions, like in our cases, to derive a central tendency since it is much more robust and sensible. If the median is not equal to the mean, it is an indicator for statistical outliers, i.e., a small number of extreme measurement data values that significantly influence the mean value [34]. From a statistical point of view it is understandable, but from a practical point of view the median value additionally gives us information about the so called common user perception of the service quality. Even if the mean value of message delivery time is high, a median value could be quite moderate, which denotes that the vast majority of the users are satisfied with the service quality.

As mentioned before, from a practical point of view, the message delivery time is the most relevant statistic for at least 95% of messages [29]. The results are presented in Table V.

More detailed analysis of the longest delivery times for 95% of the fastest messages, with the participation of the stations connected to the Play network, showed that these times are as follows:

- 75 s – for messages inside the Play network,
- 560 s – for messages sent from the Play to Orange network,
- 240 s – for messages sent from the T-Mobile to Play network.

TABLE V. COMPARISON OF MESSAGE DELIVERY TIMES FOR 95% OF THE FASTEST MESSAGES

Originating network	Destination network / Max. delivery times for the fastest 95% of messages [s]			
OR	**OR**	**PY**	**PS**	**TM**
	16	28	18	16
PY	**OR**	**PY**	**PS**	**TM**
	>30 (560)	**>30 (75)**	18	16
PS	**OR**	**PY**	**PS**	**TM**
	20	20	18	18
TM	**OR**	**PY**	**PS**	**TM**
	18	**>30 (240)**	20	18

Such long delivery times are usually acceptable for general-purpose use, but may be critical or even unacceptable for professional applications and near-real-time communication.

VI. QOE MODEL

This paragraph presents the method and test-bed for assessing the quality experienced by users (QoE) of text messaging services. When identifying QoE metrics in general, there are as many different expectations as there are users, but most of these expectations can be grouped under two main categories: *reliability* and *quality* [11]. The main KPIs, in the service reliability dimension, are:

- availability (anywhere),
- accessibility (anytime),
- access time (setup time),
- continuity (service retainability).

The quality category can be described by the second group of KPIs as follows:

- quality of session,
- bitrate,
- active session throughput,
- system responsiveness,
- packet loss,
- end-to-end delay and delay variation.

Depending on the type of service, the value of each of these metrics translates to a different level of impact on the actual QoE. Some can be totally irrelevant in one case while being the most important in another. The most important KPIs for SMS users seem to be end-to-end delay and its variation.

The concept of the measurement environment is based on the server emulating the service provider and also several test positions representing user terminal equipments (Fig. 20). Each position consists of a Personal Computer (PC) with a special application emulating the mobile phone. A group of testers (40 selected users) send and receive short messages (1200 in total). In the experiment all test messages have the same format and content.

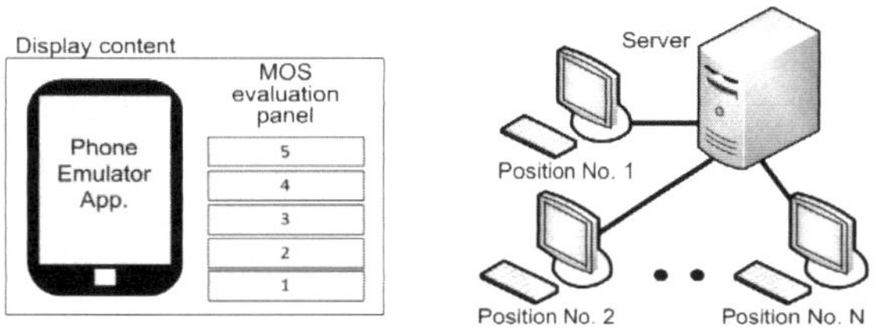

Figure 20. The laboratory test environment for the evaluation of text messaging Quality of Experience

The users send a number of messages which are passed through the server to the destination addresses after a period of time. This may be controlled during the test. After receiving the message, users assess the service quality by evaluating the end-to-end delivery time and choosing the appropriate marks from the MOS evaluation panel, where MOS stands for Mean Opinion Score, expressed in a 5-level scale (0 – the worst case and 5 – the best one, respectively). All the test parameters and user marks are stored on the server and saved for further analysis. Several dozen users took part in the experiment and more than 1.2 thousand tests were performed. The results of the tests allowed a QoE model to be built (2), which indicates a relationship between end-to-end message delivery time and service quality perceived by the users. Statistical analysis shows a significant correlation (almost 80%) between message delivery times and the users' evaluation grades. Next, regression analysis was performed and, using ordinary least squares (OLS) estimation, the approximate relation between message delivery time and users' grades (in MOS scale) was determined:

$$\mathrm{MOS} = -0.1 \cdot T + 4.97 \tag{2}$$

where: T - message delivery time.

Due to the fact the distribution of the data was not normal (checked by the Shapiro-Wilk test [35]), the author made a validation of the model, using the Mann–Whitney–Wilcoxon (MWW) test [36]. The test can even be applied on unknown distributions, contrary to the t-test, which can only be applied on normal distributions [37]. This test showed a good estimation of the users' quality perception, under assumption of 95% confidence interval (significance level $p<0.05$).

As was mentioned before, the mean value of the QoS parameter may not always be the best indicator of the network performance or the quality perceived by users. Therefore, the author presented the SMS QoE model, which shows the relation between the message delivery times and the median values of user ratings (Fig. 21). Thus, the author proposed a new name for the scale, i.e., Median Opinion Score (MedOS). The black points represent the median value, whereas the upper level of the dashed boxes determines the scores given by the 95% of users experiencing the specific message delivery times. Four levels of quality, acceptable by users, were defined, i.e., excellent quality (EQ), good quality (GQ), fair quality (FQ) and poor quality (PQ), respectively.

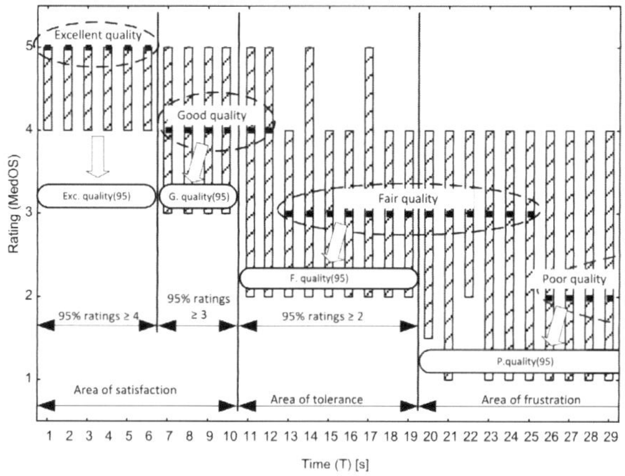

Figure 21. The quality experienced by the users majority (MedOS scale)

Next, four ranges of the message delivery times were assigned to the proper quality levels (EQ, GQ, FQ or PQ) on the basis of median values of user scores, given for those times (see the dashed ellipses in Fig. 21). According to ETSI [29], the quality levels should take into account the best 95% of samples (here messages). The Excellent Quality level, denoted by EQ(95), is reached when the median of user scores is equal to 5, and 95% of the samples have ratings equal or higher than 4.

TABLE VI. SHORT MESSAGE DELIVERY TIME DISTRIBUTION FOR 95% OF CAPTURED SAMPLES – IN-NET URBAN AREA

Operator	Percentage (*P*) [%]			WAQF
	EQ	GQ	FQ	
OR	100	0	0	5
PY	80	13.7	6.3	4.74
PS	100	0	0	5
TM	100	0	0	5

The same procedure is applied to the other quality levels (there were no scores falling into the poor quality range). In this way, the relations between the message delivery times (QoS) and proper quality levels (QoE) were determined. Table VI presents, according to the MedOS scale, the measurement results obtained from the four examined real networks. Next, the Weighted Average Quality Factor (WAQF) was calculated using (3).

$$WAQF = (P_{EQ} \cdot 5 + P_{GQ} \cdot 4 + P_{FQ} \cdot 3 + P_{PQ} \cdot 2)/100 \quad (3)$$

The measurements in the rural area revealed that quite a significant percentage of messages that were delivered in very long times, recognized as unacceptable in near-real-time communication (see Tables VII and VIII).

TABLE VII. SHORT MESSAGE DELIVERY TIME DISTRIBUTION FOR 95% OF CAPTURED SAMPLES – IN-NET, RURAL AREA

Operator	Percentage (*P*) [%]				WAQF
	EQ	GQ	FQ	PQ	
OR	4	34	60	2	2.23
PY	40	34	18	8	3.73
PS	3	16	80	1	1.64
TM	0	32	67	1	2

TABLE VIII. SHORT MESSAGE DELIVERY TIME DISTRIBUTION FOR 95% OF CAPTURED SAMPLES – INTER_NET, RURAL AREA

Relation	Percentage (*P*) [%]				WAQF
	EQ	GQ	FQ	PQ	
OR-PY	1	48	45	7	2,59
OR-PS	2	68	26	4	3,19
OR-TM	2	52	45	1	2,68
PY-OR	39	30	19	12	3,61
PY-PS	54	30	11	5	4,14
PY-TM	41	38	17	4	3,85
PS-OR	1	11	87	1	1,41
PS-PY	1	9	88	2	1,36
PS-TM	2	11	86	1	1,45
TM-OR	0	14	85	1	1,46
TM-PY	0	21	60	19	1,85
TM_PS	1	39	55	5	2,29

In this case the WAQF differs considerably from the In-Net results obtained in the urban area, which were higher. On the other hand, there was no significant difference between In-Net and Inter-Net results observed in the rural area.

WAQF seems to be used as one of the parameters that allow a comparison of the SMS quality provisioned by different operators. However, it is necessary to be very careful when drawing general conclusions concerning QoE in the examined networks based on this factor due to the fact there is no simple relation between these measures. This should be a matter of further investigation.

More detailed statistical analysis seems to be good in such a case and the median value and the time within which the fastest 95% of short messages are sent and received [29] should at least be taken into account.

VII. CONCLUSION AND FUTURE WORK

Nowadays, the text messaging is one of the most popular means of communication and a high quality of the service is therefore crucial in today's competitive market. Operators should continuously monitor network performance parameters in order to detect and isolate the problems and different kinds of threats that can impact on the quality experienced by the end-users. Thus, it is very important to not only have knowledge about the values of objectively measured performance parameters, but also about their influence on the service quality subjectively perceived by users. The results presented in the article show that the SMS provisioned by the operators functioning in the examined area of the Polish telecommunication market is of very good quality and can be used, to some extent, as a medium which also supports other kinds of text communication, especially those that require short end-to-end delivery times and immediate user-to-user interactions. Obviously, message delivery time fluctuates during the course of the day and also depends on the operator, but generally brings great satisfaction to users. It should also be noted that such a relatively small amount of collected data does not allow to a general statement about the whole Polish network to be made. Such a generalization could be made after collecting data from a bigger and representative number of selected areas, which will be done in the next step of the investigations. The author plans to build a Service Quality Monitoring System, which will be prepared to measure SMS KPIs in a wider area using so called drive tests and a central management system that will control the measurement scenarios and data collection. All data will be centrally processed and presented on a web-page.

It should be underlined that although SMS cannot be treated as a real-time messaging service, it can in some cases be used as an alternative. The main strengths of SMS are worldwide availability and the fact that there are no special requirements for user equipment or any specific software applications. Further work will be devoted to developing the QoE model towards a more comprehensive investigation of the quality issues, regarding not only intra- but also inter-operator communication.

ACKNOWLEDGMENT

The author would like to thank Pawel Bardowski for his contribution to the test-bed set-up and his valuable remarks in the course of preparing this article. A special thanks to Zbigniew Salamacha for his work during the editorial process.

REFERENCES

[1] J. Klink and P. Bardowski, "The methodology of text messaging quality assessment," ComputationWorld 2016. The Eighth International Conferences on Advanced Service Computing. Service Computation 2016 IARIA, March 20 - 24, 2016.

[2] O. Turel, A. Serenko, and N. Bontis, „User acceptance of wireless short messaging services: Deconstructing perceived value," Information & Management 44, pp. 63–73, 2007, DOI: 10.1016/j.im.2006.10.005.

[3] Portio Research. *SMS: the language of 6 bilion people*. [Online]. Available from: http://www.openmarket.com/wp-content/uploads/2015/10/ OpenMarket-Portio-Research-SMS-the-language-of-6-billion-people.pdf.

[4] A. Perez, Short Message Service, in VoLTE and ViLTE: Voice and Conversational Video Services over the 4G Mobile Network, John Wiley & Sons, Inc., Hoboken, NJ, USA, 2016. doi: 10.1002/9781119318453.ch10.

[5] PortioResearch. *Worldwide A2P SMS Markets 2014-2017. Understanding and analysis of application-to-person text messaging markets worldwide*. [Online]. Available from: http://www.strikeiron.com/wp-content/uploads/2014/04/ worldwide-sms-markets-portio-strikeiron.pdf.

[6] Portio Research. Mobile Messaging Futures 2014-2018. [Online]. Available from: http://www.portioresearch.com.

[7] D. Seo, C. Ranganathan, and Y. Babad, "Two-level model of customer retention in the US mobile telecommunications

service market," Telecommunications Policy 32, 2008, pp. 182-196.

[8] R. Virvilaite, V. Saladiene, and D. Skindaras, "The Relationship between Price and Loyalty in Services Industry," Engineering Economics, Vol. 63, No. 4 (2009), pp. 96-104.

[9] J. Zheng and E. Regentova, „QoS-based Optimal Buffering for Short Message Transfer in GPRS/UMTS Networks," Vehicular Technology Conference, 2005, 2005 IEEE 61st (Volume:5), pp. 2721-2725, doi: 10.1109/VETECS. 2005.1543841.

[10] Y. Du, W. Zhou, B. Chen, and J. Song, "A QoE based Evaluation of service quality in wireless communication Network," International Conference on New Trends in Information and Service Science, 2009, pp. 552-557, doi: 10.1109/NISS.2009.163.

[11] D. Soldani, M. Li, and R. Cuny, "QoS and QoE Management in UMTS Cellular Systems," Wiley, New York 2006.

[12] H. A. Tran and A. Mellouk, "QoE Model Driven for Network Services," Wired/Wireless Internet Communication, 8th International Conference, Lulea, Sweden, June 2010.

[13] H. Yamada, N. Fukumoto, M. Isomura, S. Uemura, and M. Hayashi, "A QoE based service control scheme for RACF in IP-based FMC networks," E-Commerce Technology and the 4th IEEE International Conference on Enterprise Computing, E-Commerce, and E-Services, 23-26 July 2007, Page(s):611 – 618.

[14] B. De Vleeschauwer, F. De Turck, B. Dhoedt, P. Demeester, M. Wijnants, and W. Lamotte, "End-to-end QoE Optimization Through Overlay Network Deployment," International Conference on Information Networking, 2008, 23-25 Jan. 2008 Page(s):1 – 5.

[15] J. M. Monteiro and M. S. Nunes, "A Subjective Quality Estimation Tool for the Evaluation of Video Communication Systems," Computers and Communications, 2007. ISCC 2007. 12th IEEE Symposium on 1-4 July 2007 Page(s): MW - 75 - MW – 80, 2007.

[16] A. Waadt, G. Bruck, P. Jung, M. Kowalzik, and T. Trapp, "QoS Monitoring for Professional Short-Message-Services in Mobile Networks," 2nd International Symposium on Wireless Communication Systems, Siena 2005. doi: 10.1109/ISWCS.2005.1547692.

[17] X. Meng, P. Zerfos, V. Samanta, S. H. Y. Wong, and S. Lu, "Analysis of the Reliability of a Nationwide Short Message Service," 26th IEEE International Conference on Computer Communications, INFOCOM 2007, doi: 10.1109/INFCOM.2007.211.

[18] L. Schilling, G. Bennett, S. Bull, A. Kempe, M. P. Wretling, and E. Staton, "Text Messaging in Healthcare Research Toolkit," School of Medicine, Center for Research in Implementation Science and Prevention, Unoiv. Of Colorado, October 2013. [Online]. Available from: http://archive.careinnovations.org/programs-grants/texting/.

[19] P. Mechael, H. Batavia, N. Kaonga, S. Searle, A. Kwan, A. Goldberger, L. Fu, and J. Ossman, "Barriers and gaps affecting mHealth in low and middle countries: policy white paper," Colombia, USA. Centre for Global Health and Economic Development Earth Institute, Colombia University, 2010. [Online]. Available from: http://www.mhealthknowledge.org/resources/barriers-and-gaps-affecting-mhealth-low-and-middle-income-countries.

[20] BEREC Guidelines for QoS in the scope of Net Neutrality, Ref.: X/2012/060 – 27/07/2012. [Online]. Available from: http://www.beuc.eu/ publications/2012-00510-01-e.pdf.

[21] Directive 2009/140/EC of the European Parliament and of the Council. Official Journal EU L.337/37, 25 November 2009.

[22] Directive 2009/136/EC of the European Parliament and of the Council. Official Journal EU L.337/11, 25 November 2009.

[23] The Telecommunication Law, Journal of Laws of the Republic of Poland No. 171, item 1800 with subsequent ammendments, 16 July 2004,.

[24] Regulatory Strategy of the President of the Office of Electronic Communications until 2015. [Online]. Available from: https://www.uke.gov.pl/strategia-regulacyjna-do-roku-2015-8802.

[25] Memorandum on cooperation with the aim of telecommunication service quality improvement report, February 2014. [Online]. Available from: http://www.uke.gov.pl/files/? id_plik=14759.

[26] T. L. Lai, „Service Quality and Perceived Value's Impact on Satisfaction, Intention and Usage of Short Message Service (SMS)," Information Systems Frontiers 2004, Volume 6, Issue 4, pp 353-368.

[27] A. Dickinger, P. Haghirian, J. Murphy, and A. Scharl, "An Investigation and Conceptual Model of SMS Marketing," Proceedings of the 37th Hawaii International Conference on System Sciences, 2004.

[28] F. Newell and K. N. Lemon, "Wireless Rules - New Marketing Strategies for Customer Relationship Management," New York: McGraw-Hill, 2001.

[29] ETSI EG 202 057-2 V1.3.2, User related QoS parameter definitions and measurements. Part 2: Voice telephony, Group 3 fax, modem data services and SMS, 2011.

[30] ETSI TS 102 250-2 V2.2.1, QoS aspects for popular services in mobile networks; Part 2: Definition of Quality of Service parameters and their computation, 2011.

[31] ETSI TR 102 529 V1.1.1, SMS Testing Guidelines. Measurement Methodologies and Quality Aspects, 2009.

[32] ITU-T E.804, Quality of telecommunication services: concepts, models, objectives and dependability planning – Terms and definitions related to the quality of telecommunication services. QoS aspects for popular services in mobile networks, February 2014.

[33] ITU-T E.800, Quality of telecommunication services: concepts, models, objectives and dependability planning (...). Definitions of terms related to quality of service, 2008.

[34] B. Staehle, A. Bizenhoefer, D. Schlosser, and B. Boder, "Quantifying the Influence of Network Conditions on the Service Quality Experienced by a Thin Client User," Measuring, Modelling and Evaluation of Computer and Communication Systems (MMB), 2008 14th GI/ITG Conference, pp. 1-15.

[35] N. Razali and Y. B. Wah, "Power comparisons of Shapiro–Wilk, Kolmogorov–Smirnov, Lilliefors and Anderson–Darling tests," Journal of Statistical Modeling and Analytics 2 (1): 21–33, 2012.

[36] M. P. Fay and M. A. Proschan, "Wilcoxon–Mann–Whitney or t-test? On assumptions for hypothesis tests and multiple interpretations of decision rules," Statistics Surveys 4: pp. 1–39, 2010. DOI:10.1214/09-SS051.

[37] J. A. Rice, "Mathematical Statistics and Data Analysis," Third Edition, Duxbury Advanced, 2006.

Taming the Complexity of Elasticity, Scalability and Transferability in Cloud Computing

Cloud-Native Applications for SMEs

Peter-Christian Quint, Nane Kratzke
Lübeck University of Applied Sciences, Center of Excellence CoSA
Lübeck, Germany
email: {peter-christian.quint, nane.kratzke}@fh-luebeck.de

Abstract—**Cloud computing enables companies getting computational and storage resources on demand. Especially when using features like elasticity and scaling, cloud computing can be a very powerful technology to run, e.g., a web service without worries about failure by overload or about wasting money by paid use of unneeded resources. For using these features, developers can use or implement cloud-native applications (CNA), containerized software running on an elastic platform. Nevertheless, a CNA can be complex at planning, installation and configuration, maintenance and searching for failures. Small and medium-sized enterprises (SMEs) are mostly limited by their personnel and financial restrictions. So, using these offered services can facilitate a very fast realization of the software project. However, by using these (proprietary) services it is often difficult to migrate between cloud vendors. This paper introduces C^4S, an open source system for SMEs to deploy and operate their container application with features like elasticity, auto-scaling and load balancing. The system also supports transferability features for migrating containers between different Infrastructure as a Service (IaaS) platforms. Thus, C^4S is a solution for SMEs to use the benefits of cloud computing with IaaS migration features to reduce vendor lock-in.**

Keywords–Cloud-Native Application; Elastic Platform; Microservice; SME; Vendor Lock-In; Container Cluster; Cloud Computing; Elasticity; Scalability; Transferability

I. INTRODUCTION

Note: This paper presents our research prototype C^4S (Container Cluster in Cloud Computing System), which was previously presented in [1]. This extended paper includes further information about our target user group, CNAs as basic technology and more details about C^4S.

Infrastructure as a service (IaaS) enables companies to get resources like computational power, storage and network connectivity on demand. IaaS can be obtained on public or private clouds. Public clouds are provided by third parties for general public use. Type representatives are Amazon's Elastic Compute Cloud (EC2) and Google Compute Engine (GCE). Private Clouds are intended for the exclusive use by a single organization [3]. They are mostly installed on the respective company's own infrastructure. OpenStack is a cloud platform for providing (not exclusively) private clouds. One big benefit using cloud computing is the elastic scaling. Elasticity means the possibility to match available resources with the current demands as closely as possible [4]. Scalability is the ability of the system to accommodate larger loads by adding resources or accommodate weakening loads by removing resources [4]. With auto-scaling, resources can be added automatically when they are needed and removed when they are not in use [5]. The resources are allocated on demand and the customer only has to pay for requested resources. The system described in this paper will support several, public and private, cloud environments. Features like elastic scaling and transferability will also be available. We define transferability as the possibility to migrate some or all containers between different cloud platforms. This is needed to avoid vendor lock-in by the cloud providers, which is a major obstacle for small and medium-sized enterprises (SMEs) in cloud computing [6]. Only a few research projects deal with the specific needs of SMEs in cloud computing [7].

In the last few years, container technologies like Docker became more and more common. Docker is an open source and lightweight virtualization solution to provide an application deployment without having the overhead of virtual machines [8]. With Docker, applications can be easily deployed on several machine types. This makes launching containers from the same application (image) possible, e.g., on a personal computer or a datacenter server.

Container clusters like Kubernetes (arose from Google Borg) [9] and Mesos [10] can deploy a huge number of containers on private and public clouds. A big benefit of cluster technologies is the horizontal scalability of the containers, the fast development and the contained software defined network, which is often necessary for distributed container applications. Container and container cluster software are mostly open source and free to use.

C^4S is designed to (automatically) deploy and operate container cluster applications without vendor lock-in. Moreover, the system will be able to monitor the cloud platform, the container cluster and the containers themselves. Beside bare reporting, the system will offer methods to keep the application running in most failure states. Altogether, the ***C^4S*** can make container cluster cloud computing technologies usable for SMEs without large and highly specialized IT departments. ***C^4S*** is especially designed as a cloud solution for SMEs.

This paper is **structured** as follows: Section II deals with the target group of the upcoming ***C^4S*** cloud management system. The technical background in form of cloud-native applications

TABLE I. SME definition of the European Union [2]

Enterprise category	Headcount: annual work unit	Annual turnover	or	Annual balance sheet total
Medium-sized	<250	≤ EUR 50 million		≤ EUR 43 million
Small	<50	≤ EUR 10 million		≤ EUR 10 million
Micro	<10	≤ EUR 2 million		≤ EUR 2 million

and elastic platforms is explained in Section III. The C^4S prototype is introduced in Section IV, followed by the major requirements of the system and the reasons for their selection in Section V. The architecture of the research prototype is presented in Section VI, the usage scenarios in Section VII and followed by a report about the current development status in Section VIII. The intended validation of concept is delineated in Section IX. Related work is described in Section X. Finally, the conclusion follows in Section XI.

II. CLOUD COMPUTING AND SMES

SMEs are mostly financially and personnel-wise restricted (see the European definition of SME [11]) and the management of container cluster applications with features like transferability and elasticity is complex. Thus, it can be hard to handle this complexity for a small (maybe only one person size) IT department. In the beginning, using services like IaaS might be very simple but the use of advanced cloud technologies like clusters, containers and cloud benefits like auto-scaling and load balancing can quickly grow into complex technical solutions. The cloud provider supplied services (e.g., auto-scaling) might pose another issue due to often having non-standardized service APIs. This is often resulting in inherent vendor lock-in [12]. However, there are products and services to manage multi-provider-clouds like the T-System Cloud Broker [13]. These management solutions also have disadvantages, i.e. they are mostly commercial, proprietary solutions and also often inherently designed for very big companies. These kind of cloud broker services move the dependencies from the cloud provider to the system/service provider like T-Systems. Amazon EC2 Container Service works only with Amazon EC2-instances, which means there is still a vendor lock-in. Both solutions just shift vendor lock-in to another company or another level of IaaS provisioning. Creating an open source system for easy deployment and managing of cloud applications in a container cluster would support SMEs using these technologies which reduces worries about vendor lock-in.

Our research is about avoiding vendor lock-in in cloud computing. Although our upcoming system is usable for all type of companies, we have placed the emphasis on a solution for SMEs because of their huge potential when using cloud technologies. The majority of companies located in Europe can also be defined as SME and we surmise that our solution for SMEs can rather easily adapt for the use in large companies than otherwise.

There are several definitions about SMEs. The Statistical Office of the European Union (Eurostat) defines SMEs by three

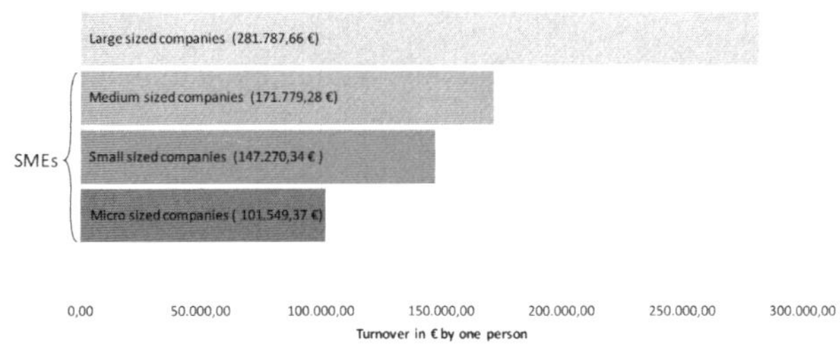

Figure 1. Average turnover by employee in ICT companies, separated by company type (data from 2013) [15]

thresholds criteria: Staff headcount and either annual turnover or annual balance sheet total (see Table I and [2], [14]). 99.76% of all companies in the information and communication sector (ICT) are SMEs (958,663 in total, data from 2013) [15]. Regardless of this, the turnover per employee is significantly depending on the size of the company (see Figure 1). We suspect that the economy of scale is partly a reason for this: Mass production can reduce the cost of a single part [16]. In the case of ICT SMEs, this might be reasoned by small IT-facilities and limitated hardware performance.

However, cloud computing can help SMEs to bridge the disadvantages. A large scale of computational resources is not limited to large companies any more. So, instead of buying a server to calculate something in a week, a single person can also use cloud computing to rent more powerful virtual machines which can do this job in a day or even faster. Worries about investment risks can be avoided by using cloud computing. Resources can be requested on demand. This pay on demand model combined with auto-scaling functionality can prevent unnecessary costs [17] when, e.g., a new web service does not have the intended success. On the other hand, if the new service is widely used, there is no danger of service-crash because of inadequate resources. E.g., Animoto, a small video creation service company, scaled from 50 servers up to 3,500 in three days [18] as a result of a viral growth. For most companies, especially SMEs this is probably not possible in this manner by using own infrastructure. However, there is a lack of standardization in cloud computing. Different cloud providers offer different cloud services. Because of non-existing or supported standardized APIs, also nearly similar services provided by different vendors are often not swappable. Oftentimes, this makes a migration to another provider expensive and time-consuming [19] and is economically not useful/possible, especially for SMEs with financial and personal limitations.

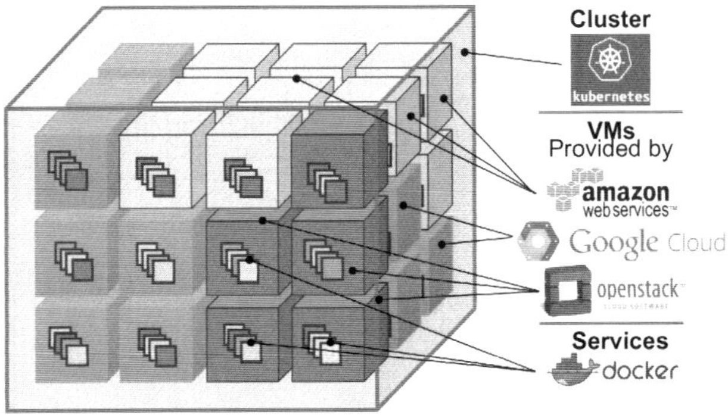

Figure 2. The elastic platform can be a cluster consisting of VMs. These VMs can be offered by different cloud providers.

III. CLOUD-NATIVE APPLICATIONS (CNA)

Migrating to the cloud also provides requirements for the application architecture. Although, it is possible to use a single virtual machine to run an, e.g., monolithic and not distributed application in a cloud environment, the most useful features of cloud computing, like elasticity and scaling, cannot be used or only with big restrictions. In order to apply these features, the application has to be designed to run on distributed systems. Our solution restricts the usable software architecture on CNAs only. This might be a hard limitation but enables running applications in an auto-scaling, fault-tolerant and highly available way with the possibility to migrate to any cloud infrastructure anytime.

A. Definition of Cloud-Native Application

As its name implies, cloud-native applications are designed for working in cloud computing environments. In research, the term "cloud-native" was firstly used in 2012 by F. Leymann and his research group (the corresponding conference papers: [21], [22]). In general, there is no completely accepted definition of the term "cloud-native". This paper follows the understanding proposed by [20]:

A cloud-native application is a distributed, elastic and horizontally scalable system composed of (micro)services which isolates state in a minimum of stateful components. The application and each self-contained deployment unit of that application is designed according to cloud-focused design patterns and operated on a self-service elastic platform.

B. Components of a CNA

To create CNAs according to the proposed definition, the following technologies may be used:

Microservices. From legacy, applications have been often designed according to a monolithic software architecture. That means, a program is designed as a monolithic block. This block contains all or the most parts of the application. In contrast, in the microservice architectures, the application is spliced into (micro)services. Each service should be *small and focused on doing one thing well* [23]. This has a lot benefits in elastic cloud computing. The development and maintenance is simplified in a way that the services can be developed in small teams which operate independently and are specialized in a particular area. Each service can be updated without touching other application parts. Another big feature is the scalability of the single services. Instead of creating more and more instances of the whole monolith, only the required services have to be increased. Of course, microservices also bring new complexity to the application design. It is important to define what the individual service should contain. In practice, microservices are often not fully self-sufficient but expanding and updating a service should not require the need to adjust all other services.

The microservice architecture is used by well-known companies such as Netflix, Twitter, Dropbox and Amazon.

Elastic Platform. An elastic platform includes one or several container clusters and is used for the automatic deployment of the cloud-native application. The elastic platform uses resources in form of virtual machines. These resources are offered by private and/or public cloud provider.

However, these virtual machines used as nodes in the cluster must not necessarily be running on the same cloud infrastructure (see Figure 2). Popular open-source container clusters are Kubernetes, Apache Mesos and Docker Swarm.

Reference Model. The NIST-Definition of cloud-computing [3] defines three service models and four deployment models. These models are very common and useful for a lot of tasks. However, they are not fine-grained enough to describe the technology layers of a CNA suitable in an engineering point of view. For our research we use the cloud-native reference model (ClouNS) described in [20]. As shown in Figure 3, ClouNS consists of six layers covering four view points. The node centric view point covers the architectural layers 1-3. The layer 1 is the physical host. In cloud computing this part is mostly controlled by the IaaS provider and not visible for the user. The second and third layer corresponds to the IaaS model of the NIST definition. Usually, the IaaS provider offers a set of virtual machine types and operating system images to the user which can select a fitting configuration. However, the virtual machines are mostly connected to an internal network and useable over the internet. The Layer 3 also provides a standardized way of self-contained deployment units (e.g. the Docker engine). The cluster centric view point covers Layer 4. This describes the elastic platform and has often three sublayers. The cluster scheduler connects several (up to over one hundred thousand) nodes (Layer 3) to a logical unit. This enables a cluster of (Layer 3) nodes from different IaaS providers and makes an interoperable cloud and also the migration from one cloud platform to another possible. The use of a scheduler can avoid vendor lock-in. The overlay

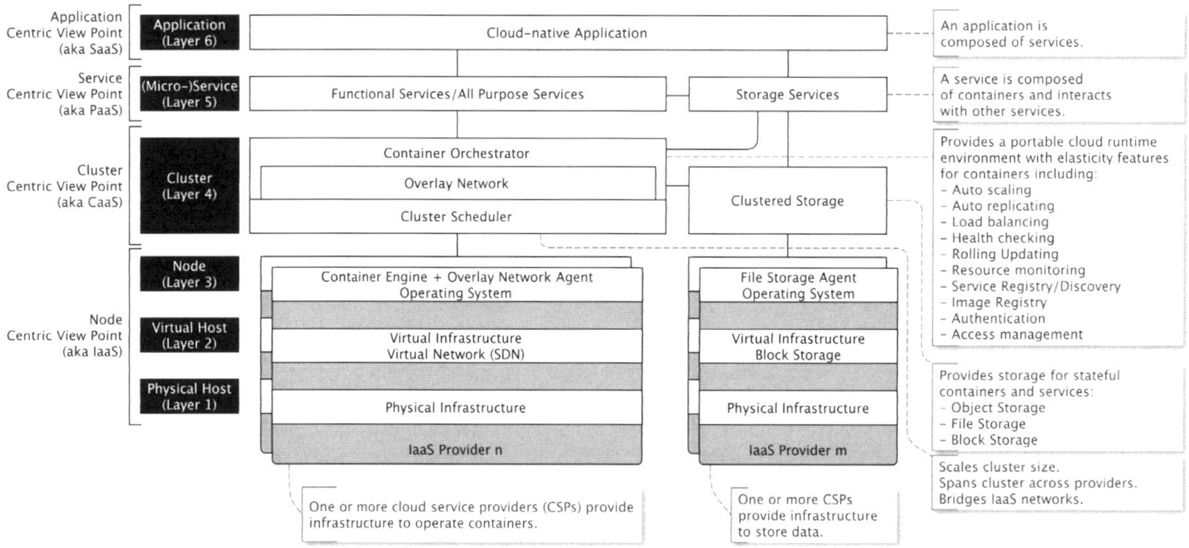

Figure 3. Cloud-native Application Reference Model (ClouNS), taken from [20]

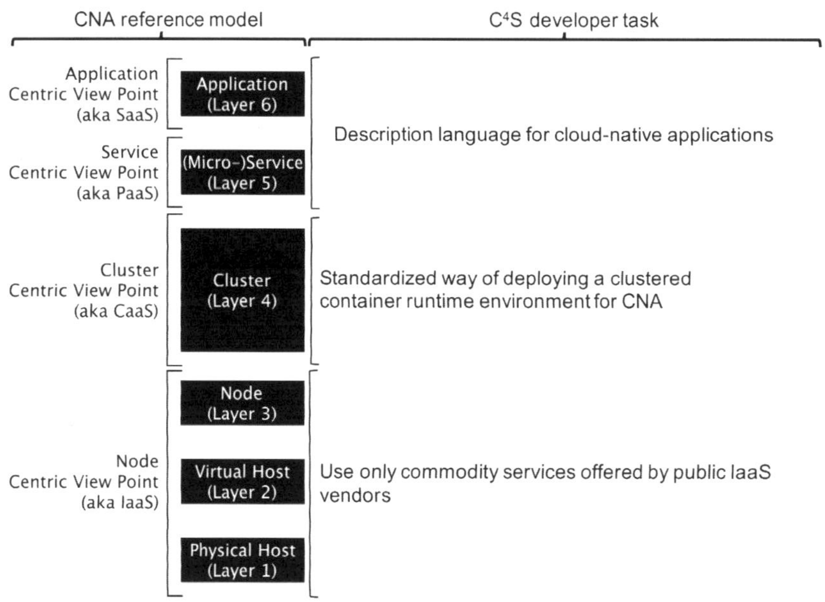

Figure 4. Developer task

network enables the communication between the containers in the cluster. Popular implementations are Flannel and Weave. Some overlay network solutions (like Weave) also enable an encrypted communication which facilitates interoperable working cluster with a high security. The orchestrator arranges the containers on different machines and enables (depending of the used cluster software) load balancing, container scaling and increases the fault tolerance by distributing container instances of the single images on several nodes. The service centric view point covers Layer 5. A (micro)service can also consist of a composition of containers. These containers are stored in the cluster (Level 4) and cannot be assigned to the specific (Layer 3 and under) machines. The application centric view point covers Layer 6, the application. If a Layer 5 service can be used over a human machine interface, it can also be a Layer 6 application. Usually, Layer 6 applications are a combination of Layer 5 services and often corresponding the SaaS model. This reference model is used to classify the single technologies of our cloud-native system and simplifies the description of our system architecture.

IV. RESEARCH PROTOTYPE C^4S

C^4S is our upcoming prototype to deploy and control CNAs.

The system is designed to handle the high complexity of a container cluster with benefits like elasticity, auto-scaling and transferability. Feature requirements and the technical specifications are explained below and illustrated in Table II. As shown in Figure 4, a solution to define secure, transferable and elastic services of typical complexity will be provided by designing and developing a generic cloud service description language. Thus, these services are deployable to any IaaS cloud infrastructure. This work promotes the implementation of easy-to-handle, elastic and transferable CNAs. The basic idea of our approach is to limit the use of cloud provided services to the basic - using computational and storage resources in the form of virtual machines. All other offered services increase the risk of vendor lock-in. Therefore, we use already available container und cluster technologies to provide features like auto-scaling, elasticity, load balancing and fault tolerance.

Next to avoiding proprietary services, we avoid vendor lock-in by the possibility of a fast, easy and always executable cloud platform migration. As illustrated in Figure 2, a cluster consists of several nodes. These nodes do not necessarily run on the same platform. This allows creating an interoperable cloud system. Of course, this technology has a high degree of complexity. Because of the limited (personal and financial) resources of most of the small companies, little (in extreme one man sized) IT departments must also be able to handle this complexity. Therefore, we focus on the usability of the interfaces and a high degree of automation. For a future validation of our approach we are developing the prototype system C^4S. We will show the feasibility of a system which avoids vendor lock-in, supports cloud features like scaling and load balancing and can hide the inherent complexity for the use of SMEs. We assume, that the requirements (described in the next Section V) of the prototype are also included in a future system designed for the productive use.

V. MAJOR REQUIREMENTS OF C^4S

C^4S is a system designed for an easy access to cloud computing benefits without having dependencies like IaaS vendor lock-in. To fulfill this goal the following technical and practical conditions are required.

A. Cloud-Native Applications

The basic feature of C^4S is to deploy a distributed cloud-native (container) application on cloud environments. Therefore, the user can easily configure the needed containers, the interfaces and the cloud environments. According to this configuration, the system can automatically deploy the application. The system will also monitor the application and inform the user if a failure is detected. According to the error, the system will try to fix it automatically to minimize the downtime. The user has an overview over the running application and can also get information about every single container. After the initial deployment, changes of the container composition are still possible. So, application parts (e.g., container types) can be replaced, e.g., to keep the application up to date.

B. Elastic Platform

The elastic platform (Layer 4 in the ClouNS model), technically a container cluster, is used for the automatic deployment of the cloud-native application. The elastic platform uses resources in form of virtual machines (Layer 2). These resources (Layer 2/3) can be obtained by private and/or public IaaS platforms. These virtual machines, used as nodes in the cluster, must not necessarily be running on the same cloud infrastructure. So, this architecture enables the use of a multiple-providers environment. Also, a provider migration is always possible. According to the configuration, the system can create virtual machines automatically and integrate them to the cluster. Another included benefit is the possibility of terminating and correspondingly down scaling of the elastic platform in the scope of functions. In the practical use, the elastic platform can be composed of open-source container cluster systems such as Kubernetes, Apache Mesos and Docker Swam.

C. Elasticity, Load Balancing and Auto-Scaling

As described in Section I, cloud computing enables features like elasticity, scalability and load balancing. C^4S enables the user to handle the inherent complexity of these features in an easy way. C^4S will have auto-scaling features. Thus, it is necessary to differentiate between scaling the services (Layer 5) and the cluster (Layer 4).

Service scaling: C^4S will be able to detect overload of the payload services. In this case, C^4S scales the services with deploying more container instances on the elastic platform.

Platform scaling: The system also detects if the cluster has only a few free resources left to orchestrate the container. In

TABLE II. Relation of the CNA reference model [20] and the functionality of C^4S.

(According to [20])			
View Point Classification	**Layer Classification**		**Features of C^4S**
Application Centric View Point	Application	Layer 6	Description Language for defining Deploying and controlling Monitoring Scaling
Service Centric View Point	(Micro-) Service	Layer 5	
Cluster Centric View Point	Cluster	Layer 4	Deploying and controlling Load Balancing Monitoring Scaling
Node Centric View Point	Node	Layer 3	Creating and Terminating
	Virtual Node	Layer 2	Monitoring
	Physical Host	Layer 1	(Task of the provider only)

this case, the system automatically requests new virtual machines provided by the IaaS vendors. After the new resources are available they will be used to extend the cluster. Of course, downscaling the container application and the elastic platform is also supported. So, the cost for unneeded machines can be reduced. Downtime (or other system failures) because of overload can be prevented or shortened.

Load balancing is depending on the used cluster software. At first C^4S will support Kubernetes. This software is designed to orchestrate containers, so it provides load balancing functionality.

D. Prevent Dependencies

To avoid vendor lock-in by the cloud provider, the system can install a multi-cloud container cluster with transferability features. All or some containers can migrate from one cloud provider to another on demand. Accordingly, the user can select the using IaaS platform(s) and is able to change this choice anytime. To prevent dependencies by used software and services, the C^4S will be published under MIT license. It is recommended that all third-party parts like the cluster software are also open source. Thus, the consuming companies can adapt the source code to their special needs and are able to avoid dependencies to the C^4S themselves. The system has to be designed in a generic way for several IaaS platforms (see Figure 5, fourth block). Beside the cloud platforms, the users should not be limited by the choice of the container cluster. The modular architecture enables later extensions for missing cluster connectivity (see Figure 5, third block).

E. Optimization for SMEs

The inherent complexity of this architecture has to be useable by SMEs with only a few (in extreme one person size) IT-staff. To hide the complexity, the user should be able to set all necessary parameters easily. Therefore, especially the graphical user interface will be developed under consideration of usability aspects. To handle the complexity, C^4S needs a high degree of automation. This includes features like auto-scaling the services (Layer 5-6) and auto-scaling the elastic platform (Layer 4 and involved Layer 3). Scaling the services depends on the resource consumption of the individual container type. The system creates or terminates container instances in the cluster automatically. Auto-scaling of the cluster is done by creating or terminating virtual machines (Layer 2). So, C^4S requests and obtains new VMs and integrates them as nodes (Layer 3) automatically into the elastic platform (Layer 4). In the reverse direction, unused resources should be set free to save money. Therefore, the system can request a termination of machines automatically. Hence, they are not available as nodes for the elastic container platform any more.

VI. SYSTEM ARCHITECTURE OF C^4S

The architecture, as illustrated in Figure 5, is divided into four blocks. The core of C^4S are the monitoring, the deployment and the storage engine. The user can manage the deployment and get the monitoring events over two interfaces. The other two parts are the elastic platform and the IaaS environments.

A. Interfaces

For deploying, managing and controlling the cloud-native application and the elastic platform, the user can use two different types of interfaces:

The **Command Line Interface** (CLI) can be used to get monitoring information about the cloud-native (container) application, the elastic platform and the host-machines (VMs running on an IaaS platform). The user can manage actions like the initial start of the application and cluster deploying. Therefore, the configurations have to be set manually and the

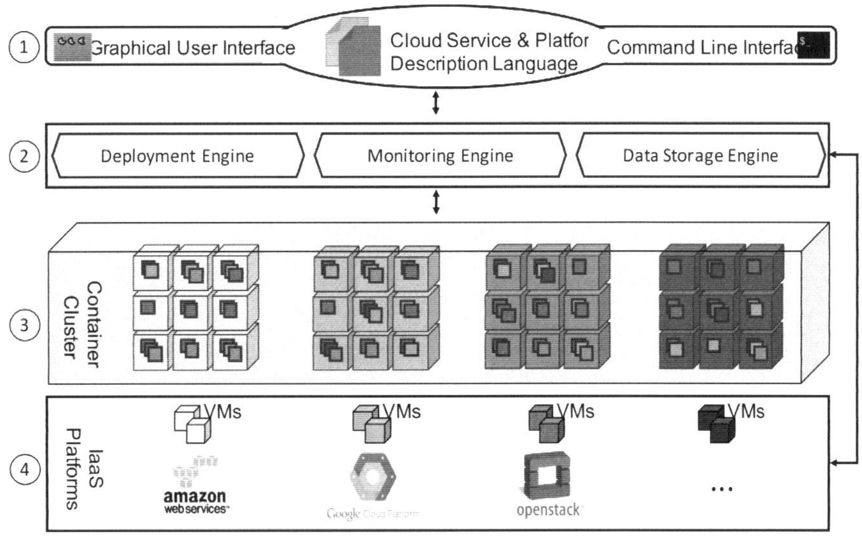

Figure 5. Architecture overview

Cloud Service Description Language has to be used for defining the cloud-application. Configuring the elastic platform has to be done with the use of the **Cloud Platform Description Language**.

The web-based **Graphical User Interface** (GUI) can be used for a more visual and simpler interaction with ***C*⁴*S***. The GUI provides graphical overviews for observing the used IaaS infrastructure, the cloud-native application and the elastic platform. Next to loading and storing the configuration (defined with the Cloud Platform Description Language and the Cloud Service Description Language), the user can use web forms to set the parameters. ***C*⁴*S*** automatically converts the set values into the required language format. In later developing processes several useful workflows will be integrated. So, this will help the user, e.g., to select the optimal host machine type for the individual purposes or processing a cloud provider migration.

After installing ***C*⁴*S***, the cloud-native application and the platform do only have to be configured over the interfaces. Creating and deleting virtual machines, installing the elastic platform and deploying the application on the platform will be automatically done by the system without manual interaction.

B. Engines

C*⁴*S contains several engines. As shown in Figure 6, these engines are interacting to realize features like auto-scaling the platform and the services.

The **Monitoring Engine** is an important part of the system. ***C*⁴*S*** will support several monitoring systems. So, the system has to monitor the **services** and also the **elastic platform** (clustered virtual machines provided by the IaaS platform). The system will proactively collect data and information from all services, the cluster software and the host systems of the platform. In case of the platform monitoring, the system analyzes, e.g., CPU performance, memory usage, free disk size and other performance data. This makes it possible to detect failure states, usage and load problems (like less free resources by high load of the cluster). The monitoring engine is also able to get statistics about the services. So, the health status of every container type can be analyzed. If the monitoring engine detects events such as under- or overload, the deployment engine will be notified.

The **Deployment Engine** is responsible for deploying the elastic platform and the services on it. Therefore, the engine can request the creation or termination of virtual machines running on a cloud platform. The new assigned VMs will be attached to the elastic platform to enlarge it. The engine can send a request to terminate a VM to the IaaS platform. The termination of VMs decreases the cluster. Thus, this can **reduce the cost** because only necessary machines are in use and the customer does not have to pay the IaaS provider for unused resources. In combination with the monitoring engine, the deployment engine is used for **platform auto-scaling** and makes the system more **fault tolerant**, too. So, if a few machines break down because of errors on the infrastructure of the cloud provider, the system automatically creates virtual machines on another provider to prevent or compensate downtime of the application. The workload of the containers can trigger to create or free more of them. The engine is also responsible for deploying the cloud-native application (in form of a service-composition) on the cluster. So, new services or service updates (switching the running service implementation) can be deployed with the deployment engine.

The **Data Storage Engine** is compatible with several block

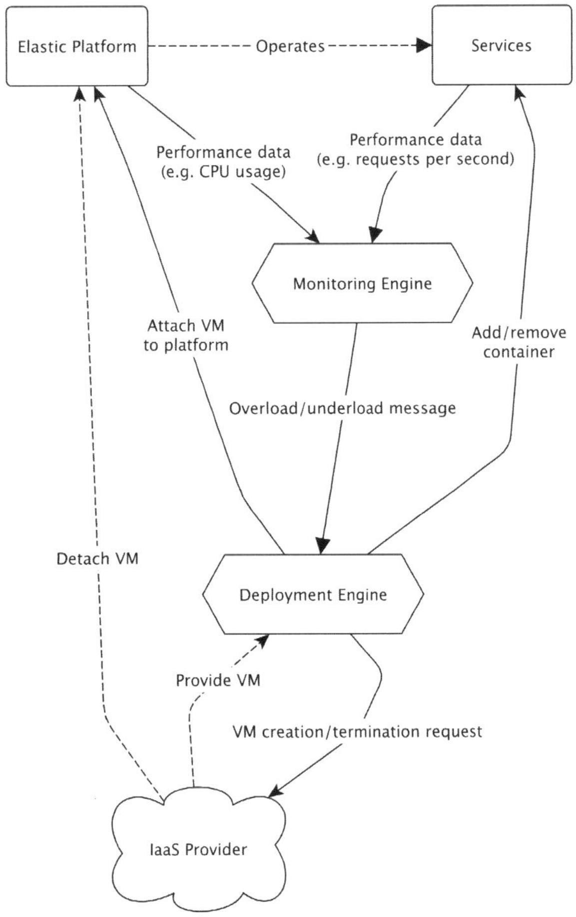

Figure 6. Data flow diagram of the deployment and the monitoring engine

and object storage systems to avoid vendor lock-in. The engine enables scalability and security features for data storage (not illustrated).

C. Elastic Platform

According to the configuration, the elastic platform will be installed automatically. The first versions of C^4S will support Kubernetes. However, the system is designed generically to enable future extensions. So, several container cluster will be supported in later versions. The deployment engine can enlarge or decrease the cluster by creating or terminating cluster nodes. The deployment of the containers (cloud-native application) will also be controlled by the deployment engine. Next to scaling the container application and the cluster itself, other features like load balancing are included.

D. IaaS Platforms

According to the configuration, the required computing and storage resources (in form of virtual machines) will be requested automatically from the private and/or public IaaS platform(s). Therefore, C^4S includes the "ecp-deployer", published at [24]. Currently, AWS and OpenStack Mitaka is directly supported. However, the deployer is designed to load plugins for supporting new platforms or new versions of them in a simple manner. This is also well documented to enable an uncomplicated extension-development.

VII. WORKFLOWS

C^4S is designed for **deploying and controlling cloud-native applications** and the **elastic platform**. Like shown in Figure 7, this can be done in the following logical steps:

- **1.** The user can use the command line interface and also the graphical interface to deploy and control the application. First of all, the elastic platform and the application have to be described.
- **1a.** For defining the container-composition (image type, hierarchy, connection, etc.), C^4S uses a cloud service description language. Using the CLI, this can be done manually. Alternative, if using the GUI, the set parameters will be parsed automatically into the correct format.
- **1b.** Next to the parameters of the IaaS providers, the machine types, the credentials, the platform type (e.g. Kubernetes or Apache Mesos) also scaling limitations, load balancing setting and so on, have to be configured. Therefore, the cloud platform description language has to be used. Similarly to step 1a., this can be done in a comfortable way using the GUI or using the CLI directly.
- **2a.** According to the settings, the system gets resources by the IaaS provider/cloud-platform in form of virtual machines.
- **2b.** The created virtual machines will be automatically included as nodes to the elastic platform.
- **3.** Now, C^4S starts deploying the applications (e.g. Docker container-composition) on the cluster. After that, the initial deploying of the cloud-native application is finished.
- **n.** (Without illustration:) According to the description, C^4S is able to create/terminate virtual machines to scale the cluster itself.

To **avoid vendor lock-in**, it is important for C^4S to support several elastic platforms (e.g. Kubernets or Apache Mesos) and IaaS provider. Nevertheless, C^4S is designed to **migrate between different cloud provider** in an uninterruptible process. The user only has to set the configuration of the target provider (named "Provider B" in Figure 8) and command the system to start the migration. According to Figure 8, C^4S will automatically process the following steps:

1. In general, the container type should be deployed on several different nodes for failure protection and for an uninterruptible migration.

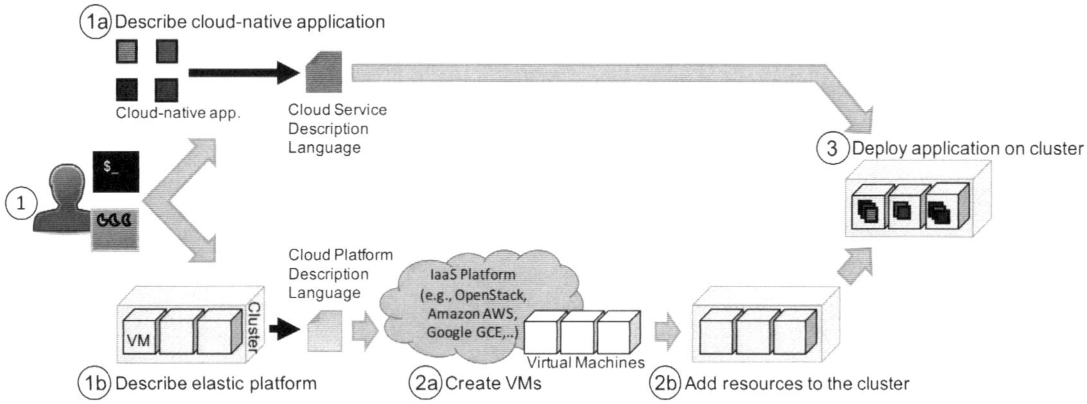

Figure 7. Deploying workflow

2. At first, C^4S allocates virtual machines provided by the target vendor to enlarge the elastic platform.
3. After the system terminates a "Provider A" virtual machine, the cluster decreases and containers are missing. The elastic platform detects that containers are missing and starts deploying them anew. In this way, the system terminates all machines from the original provider successively.
4. In the end, no virtual machine of the initial used provider is in use any more. The migration is completed and in accordance with the normal activities of the elastic platform, load balancing and scaling processes will be done on demand.

VIII. COMPLETED RESEARCH AND CURRENT STATUS

Our system is designed for CNAs. This includes the use of container virtualization (e.g., Docker, Rkt). Container based operating system virtualization can be used for scalable and high performance tasks [25]. For using more than one container, container cluster can be used to operate in in a highly available and scalable way. The cluster itself also contains a software-designed network (SDN). C^4S is based on this technology. As internal part of C^4S, it is important to know if the network performance impact using these technologies is acceptable or not. Therefore, we developed ppbench [26], a tool for benchmarking network performance according to the use of container technology, the use of a cluster/SDN, the message size, the machine type and the programming language. It could be determined that the performance impact depends on all factors. Therefore, it is not possible to make basic disclosures about what is generally the best programming language or the ideal message size or if the use of a SDN has an acceptable impact on the network performance in general. However, with ppbench, reasonable combinations of these parameters can be determined in the context of a CNA design. The biggest insights from the benchmark tests are: the selection of the programming language has a big effect on the performance and the impact of a SDN depends on the machine type - using high-core machines can make the impact of the SDN negligible. All our findings about performance impacts using container and container clusters are published in [26], [27], [28], [29].

A Container Cluster should run on homogeneous machine types to provide fine-grained resource allocation capabilities [10]. Our solution for a migratable and/or interoperable cloud system requires an elastic platform consisting of nodes (virtual machines) provided by multiple providers. Accordingly, the choice of machine types of different providers is not trivial. We developed EasyCompare, an automatic benchmark suite for selecting most similar virtual machines provided by different cloud service providers. We used our tool to compare VMs provided by the two public cloud service providers Amazon Web Services and Google Compute Engine. In our benchmark experiments we compared 195 machine pairs and could only identify three machines pairs with a high similarity. All other machine pairs (over 98.5% of all possible combinations) are not or only useable with restrictions as cluster nodes. Although the selection of suitable machines is limited, the recommended pairs consist of "n1-standard" (GCE) and "m3" (AWS) machines. These machine types are universally useable and not limited to special tasks. They are also cost effective and not the most expansive machine types. Especially for SME, the limited selection options can have the advantage of a fast and simple decision. Particularly with regard to the performance, we generally recommend the machine-pairs with the highest amount of cores. We have published more details about EasyCompare and the benchmark results in [30], [26].

This first release of the **elastic container platform deployer** is accessible under [24]. The tool enables creating, deleting and changing an elastic platform consisting of many nodes which can be provided by different IaaS platforms/vendors in an easy manner. We have chosen Kubernetes as cluster software for the first version. Nevertheless, the deployer still supports OpenStack, Amazon AWS and Google GCE.

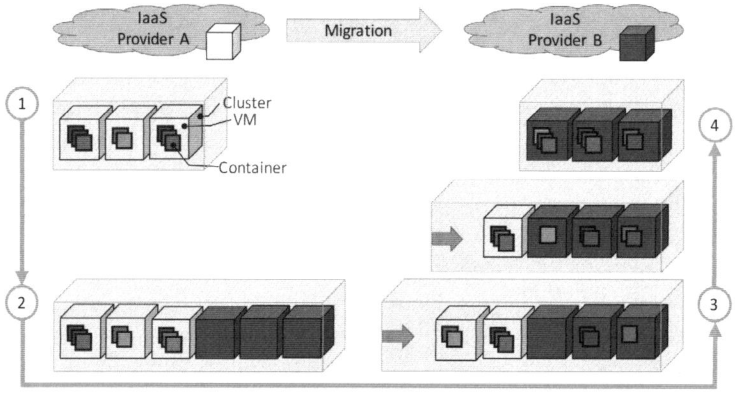

Figure 8. Migration workflow

TABLE III. Functional range of the planned releases

Version	Features
0.1	Kubernetes on OpenStack, Amazon AWS and Google GCE
0.2	Storage extension
0.3	Auto-scaling features
0.4	Deployment language
1.0	Stable version

We will continuously release new versions of C^4S after finishing significant parts. The rough planning, shown in Table III, did not include smaller releases which contain bugfixes, the GUI and enhancements to other cloud platforms or cluster software. We plan to release a stable version of C^4S by the end of 2017.

IX. Intended Validation of Concept

It will be shown that SMEs can manage a container cluster over (multi) cloud platforms. At first it will be demonstrated that building a system which fits all the required features is possible. Therefore, a working, open source C^4S prototype which conforms the requirements set in Section V will be developed. The system has to be implemented in a modular and extendable way. As a cluster platform, C^4S will support Kubernetes first, other cluster environments will follow. Presenting interchangeability and the open source type of C^4S will show that dependencies by the used software can be prevented. To avoid vendor lock-in by the cloud provider, the prototype must be able to install a multi-cloud container cluster. First, the system will be compatible with the IaaS cloud platform type representatives Amazon EC2, Google GCE and OpenStack. To support other platforms, appropriate drivers can be implemented. Transferability features like moving all containers from one cloud platform to another will be implemented. Terminating all containers and virtual machines on one provider and creating them on another at the same time, without changes in features like elasticity and auto-scaling, will proof that C^4S is preventing vendor lock-in. The software will also manage container application deployment. It will deploy a container cluster, create and terminate containers and is usable for deploying applications. Also, workloads will be created to test the auto-scaling features. With enforced failure states, the robustness of the system will be demonstrated. It will be shown that the system is able to keep the applications running even when containers and virtual machines get disconnected. In the second part of the proof of concept, a company will employ the software. Thus, the expense for a small business using the container cluster manager will be evaluated. Finally, a proof of concept will be realized by several business companies. These companies will use the C^4S system on their own for testing a productive application deployment with real workload. Load balancing, elasticity, auto-scaling and transferability features will be applied in production. This way it will be shown that SMEs can handle the complexity of a container cluster application running on multiple cloud platforms without vendor lock-in or dispensing with features like auto-scaling.

X. Related Work

Currently, technologies related to our workspace like container, cluster and cloud computing are still under hyped development. A lot of these technologies are still in productive use, also as a technical baseof very successful IT companies like Netflix, Amazon and others. Because of the hype and also the productive use by big companies, technologies, e.g., Docker are rising their opportunities and scope very fast. However, till now we couldn't find a solution which fits all requirements and features set in Section V, but there are several solutions with overlapping features and/or usage scenarios available.

A. *IaaS Management and Transferability*

Container migration from one cloud provider to another is an important feature of C^4S.

Vendor lock-in is caused, i.e., by a lack of standards [19]. Currently the proprietary EC2 is the de facto standard specification for managing cloud infrastructure. However, open standards like OCCI and CIMI are important to reduce vendor lock-in situations [31]. C^4S includes a special IaaS driver for each supported cloud provider. Other research approaches in cloud migration can be reviewed under [32]. There are several solutions like Apache Libcloud, KOALA [33], Scalr, Apache jclouds and deltacloud and T-Systems Cloud Broker for managing and deploying virtual machines on IaaS platforms. Except for the T-Systems Cloud Broker, the solutions are open source but have mostly payable services, reduced functionality or limited virtual machine quantities. These systems support features like creating, stopping and scaling virtual machines on IaaS cloud platforms. Some of them like the T-Systems Cloud Broker, Scalr and Apache jclouds are designed for cross-platform IaaS deployment. In contrast to the C^4S requirements, the presented cloud managers are limited to IaaS managing and do not offer container deploying services. Some of them do not prevent vendor lock-in by cloud providers or create new dependencies by itself (e.g., T-System Cloud Broker, KOALA are limited to Amazon AWS API compatible services).

B. Application Deployment

Peinl et al. [34] have defined requirements for a container application deployment system. These strongly coincide with the requirements for the C^4S system, which have been discussed in Section V. The research group also gives an overview about container cluster managing. For easy deploying a container application with monitoring, scaling and controlling benefits, there exist several commercial solutions like the Amazon EC2 Container Service, Microsoft Azure Container Service and Giant Swarm. Limited to the providers own IaaS infrastructure, these solutions are not designed for multi-cloud platform usages, especially between public clouds (a requirement of C^4S). Open source cluster managers like Apache Mesos and Kubernetes are designed to run workloads across tens of thousands of machines. The benefits and issues using cluster technologies are a very high reliability, availability and scalability [10] [9]. However, they are not designed to create and terminate virtual machines (like AWS instances), but to deploy applications on given resources. So, they cannot prevent cloud provider dependencies on their own, but provide essential ingredients to do so. Another cluster management tool for increasing the efficiency of datacenter servers is called Quasar which was developed by the Stanford University and designed for maximizing resource utilization. The system performs coordinated resource allocation. Several techniques analyze performance interferences, scaling (up and out) and resource heterogeneity [35].

XI. CONCLUSION AND OUTLOOK

In Europe, 98% of all companies are small and medium-sized. With cloud computing, SME can have access to computational resources which were limited to large companies in the past. Cloud features like elasticity and scaling can make the use of cloud resources more economical and effective. However, nowadays these features are only offered as non-standardized services by IaaS vendors. Using these services leads to a dependence on the cloud provider. Our approach is to use the base computational and storage resources only. All other offered services increase the risk of vendor lock-in. Therefore, we use already available container und cluster technologies to provide features like auto-scaling, elasticity, load balancing and fault tolerance. This is done by developing a prototype system called C^4S. The system is designed to operate CNAs with the above named features in a vendor lock-in free manner. It supports multi-IaaS-provider environments and is designed to realize cloud-provider migrations. The system is also implemented in a modular and generic way to allow an easy adaptation to different cloud platforms and container cluster software. The used technologies like the container and the storage cluster have an inherent complexity. Especially for SMEs with a small (in extreme one person sized) IT department it is important to hide this complexity. Hence, C^4S provides a high degree of automation.

Although C^4S is just under development, several functionalities have been already implemented. The system can create virtual machines provided by Amazon Web Services, Google Compute Engine and OpenStack and utilize them as nodes for the elastic platform (currently we have chosen Kubernetes as cluster type representative for the first deployer release). Decreasing the cluster by terminating virtual machines is possible, too. The next step is the creation of a deployment language for dedicated containers to run on a Kubernetes container cluster, finding solutions for container cluster scaling problems and handling stateful tasks like file storage. The system will be implemented in a modular and generic way to allow an adaptation for different cloud platforms and container cluster software. With C^4S, SMEs will be able to deploy and operate their container applications on an elastic, auto-scaling and load balancing multi-cloud cluster with transferability features to prevent vendor lock-in.

ACKNOWLEDGMENT

This research is funded by German Federal Ministry of Education and Research (Project Cloud TRANSIT, 03FH021PX4). The authors thank the University of Lübeck (Institute of Telematics) and fat IT solution GmbH (Kiel) for their support of Cloud TRANSIT.

REFERENCES

[1] P.-C. Quint and N. Kratzke, "Overcome Vendor Lock-In by Integrating Already Available Container Technologies - Towards Transferability in Cloud Computing for SMEs," in 7th. Int. Conf. on Cloud Computing, GRIDS and Virtualization (CLOUD COMPUTING 2016), 2016, pp. 38–41.

[2] European Commission, "Commission recommendation (2003/361/ec) of 6 may 2003 concerning the definition of micro, small and medium-sized enterprises," 2003. [Online]. Available: http://www.eur-lex.europa.eu/LexUriServ/site/en/oj/2003/l_124/l_12420030520en00360041.pdf

[3] P. Mell and T. Grance, "The nist definition of cloud computing," 2011.

[4] M. Armbrust, A. Fox, R. Griffith, A. D. Joseph, R. Katz, A. Konwinski, G. Lee, D. Patterson, A. Rabkin, I. Stoica et al., "A view of cloud computing," Communications of the ACM, vol. 53, no. 4, 2010, pp. 50–58.

[5] M. Mao and M. Humphrey, "Auto-scaling to minimize cost and meet application deadlines in cloud workflows," in Proceedings of 2011 International Conference for High Performance Computing, Networking, Storage and Analysis. ACM, 2011, p. 49.

[6] N. Kratzke, "Lightweight virtualization cluster - howto overcome cloud vendor lock-in," Journal of Computer and Communication (JCC), vol. 2, no. 12, oct 2014.

[7] R. Sahandi, A. Alkhalil, and J. Opara-Martins, "Cloud computing from smes perspective: A survey-based investigation," Journal of Information Technology Management, vol. 24, no. 1, 2013, pp. 1–12.

[8] J. Turnbull, The Docker Book: Containerization is the new virtualization. James Turnbull, 2014.

[9] A. Verma, L. Pedrosa, M. Korupolu, D. Oppenheimer, E. Tune, and J. Wilkes, "Large-scale cluster management at google with borg," in Proceedings of the Tenth European Conference on Computer Systems. ACM, 2015, p. 18.

[10] B. Hindman, A. Konwinski, M. Zaharia, A. Ghodsi, A. D. Joseph, R. Katz, S. Shenker, and I. Stoica, "Mesos: A platform for fine-grained resource sharing in the data center," in Proceedings of the 8th USENIX Conference on Networked Systems Design and Implementation, ser. NSDI'11. Berkeley, CA, USA: USENIX Association, 2011, pp. 295–308. [Online]. Available: http://dl.acm.org/citation.cfm?id=1972457.1972488

[11] Definition recommendation of micro, small and medium-sized enterprises by the european communities. Last access 12th Nov. 2016. [Online]. Available: http://eur-lex.europa.eu/legal-content/EN/TXT/?uri=uriserv:OJ.L_.2003.124.01.0036.01.ENG

[12] N. Kratzke, "A lightweight virtualization cluster reference architecture derived from open source paas platforms," Open J. Mob. Comput. Cloud Comput, vol. 1, 2014, pp. 17–30.

[13] "Cloud Brokerage - A single portal for all IaaS providers," T-Systems, Tech. Rep., 2014, whitepaper. [Online]. Available: https://www.t-systems.com/whitepaper/77588/dl-wp-cloud-brokerage-tech.pdf

[14] European Union, "User guide to the sme definition," 2015. [Online]. Available: http://ec.europa.eu/DocsRoom/documents/15582

[15] Eurostat, "Annual enterprise statistics by size class for special aggregates of activities (NACE Rev. 2)[Code: sbs_sc_sca_r2]," 2016.

[16] B. J. Pine, Mass customization: the new frontier in business competition. Harvard Business Press, 1993.

[17] M. Armbrust, A. Fox, R. Griffith, A. D. Joseph, R. H. Katz, A. Konwinski, G. Lee, D. A. Patterson, A. Rabkin, I. Stoica et al., "Above the clouds: A berkeley view of cloud computing," 2009.

[18] J. Bezos, "Amazon. com ceo jeff bezos on animoto," Startup School, 2008.

[19] J. Opara-Martins, R. Sahandi, and F. Tian, "Critical review of vendor lock-in and its impact on adoption of cloud computing," in Information Society (i-Society), 2014 International Conference on. IEEE, 2014, pp. 92–97.

[20] N. Kratzke and R. Peinl, "ClouNS - A Reference Model for Cloud-Native Applications," in Proceedings of 20th. International Conference on Enterprise Distributed Object Computing Workshops (EDOCW 2016), 2016.

[21] V. Andrikopoulos, C. Fehling, and F. Leymann, "Designing for cap - the effect of design decisions on the cap properties of cloud-native applications," in Proceedings of the 2nd International Conference on Cloud Computing and Services Science, 2012, pp. 365–374.

[22] S. Garcia-Gomez, M. Escriche-Vicente, P. Arozarena-Llopis, F. Lelli, Y. Taher, C. Momm, A. Spriestersbach, J. Vogel, A. Giessmann, F. Junker et al., "4caast: Comprehensive management of cloud services through a paas," in Proceedings of the 2012 IEEE 10th International Symposium on Parallel and Distributed Processing with Applications. IEEE Computer Society, 2012, pp. 494–499.

[23] S. Newman, Building Microservices. " O'Reilly Media, Inc.", 2015.

[24] ecp_deploy. Last access 30th Nov. 2016. [Online]. Available: https://rubygems.org/gems/ecp_deploy

[25] S. Soltesz, H. Pötzl, M. E. Fiuczynski, A. Bavier, and L. Peterson, "Container-based operating system virtualization: A scalable, high-performance alternative to hypervisors," SIGOPS Oper. Syst. Rev., vol. 41, no. 3, Mar. 2007, pp. 275–287.

[26] N. Kratzke and P.-C. Quint, "How to Operate Container Clusters more Efficiently? Some Insights Concerning Containers, Software-Defined-Networks, and their sometimes Counterintuitive Impact on Network Performance," International Journal On Advances in Networks and Services, vol. 8, no. 3&4, 2015.

[27] N. Kratzke and P.-C. Quint, "ppbench - A Visualizing Network Benchmark for Microservices," in Proceedings of 6th. International Conference on Cloud Computing and Service Sciences (CLOSER 2016), 2016.

[28] N. Kratzke and P.-C. Quint, "Investigation of Impacts on Network Performance in the Advance of a Microservice Design," in Cloud Computing and Services Science Selected Papers, ser. Communications in Computer and Information Science (CCIS), M. Helfert, D. Ferguson, V. M. Munoz, and J. Cardoso, Eds. Springer, 2016.

[29] N. Kratzke, "About microservices, containers and their underestimated impact on network performance," Proceedings of CLOUD COMPUTING, vol. 2015, 2015.

[30] N. Kratzke and P.-C. Quint, "About Automatic Benchmarking of IaaS Cloud Service Providers for a World of Container Clusters," Journal of Cloud Computing Research, vol. 1, no. 1, 2015, pp. 16–34. [Online]. Available: http://jccr.uscip.us/PublishedIssues.aspx

[31] C. Pahl, L. Zhang, and F. Fowley, "Interoperability standards for cloud architecture," in 3rd International Conference on Cloud Computing and Services Science, (CLOSER 2013), 2013, pp. 8–10.

[32] P. Jamshidi, A. Ahmad, and C. Pahl, "Cloud migration research: a systematic review," Cloud Computing, IEEE Transactions on, vol. 1, no. 2, 2013, pp. 142–157.

[33] C. Baun, M. Kunze, and V. Mauch, "The koala cloud manager: Cloud service management the easy way," in Cloud Computing (CLOUD), 2011 IEEE International Conference on. IEEE, 2011, pp. 744–745.

[34] R. Peinl and F. Holzschuher, "The docker ecosystem needs consolidation," in 5Th Intl. Conf. on Cloud Computing and Services Science (CLOSER 2015), 2015, pp. 535–542.

[35] C. Delimitrou and C. Kozyrakis, "Quasar: Resource-efficient and qos-aware cluster management," ACM SIGPLAN Notices, vol. 49, no. 4, 2014, pp. 127–144.

International Journal on Advances in Intelligent Systems, vol 9 no 3 & 4, year 2016, http://www.iariajournals.org/intelligent_systems/

VASCO - Digging the Dead Man's Chest of Value Streams

René Berndt, Nelson Silva, Christian Caldera,
Ulrich Krispel, Eva Eggeling
Fraunhofer Austria Research GmbH
Visual Computing
Email: {rene.berndt, nelson.silva, christian.caldera
ulrich.krispel, eva.eggeling}@fraunhofer.at

Alexander Sunk, Gerhard Reisinger, Wilfried Sihn
Fraunhofer Austria Research GmbH
Production and Logistics Management
Email: {alexander.sunk, gerhard.reisinger, wilfried.sihn}
@fraunhofer.at

Dieter W. Fellner
Institute of Computer Graphics and Knowledge Visualization (CGV), TU Graz, Austria
GRIS, TU Darmstadt & Fraunhofer IGD, Darmstadt, Germany
Email: d.fellner@igd.fraunhofer.de

***Abstract*—*Value stream mapping* is a lean management method for analyzing and optimizing a series of events for production or services. Even today the first step in value stream analysis – the acquisition of the *current state map* – is still created using pen & paper by physically visiting the production line. We capture a digital representation of how manufacturing processes look like in reality. The manufacturing processes can be represented and efficiently analyzed for future production planning as a *future state map* by using a meta description together with a dependency graph. With VASCO we present a tool, which contributes to all parts of value stream analysis - from data acquisition, over analyzing, planning, comparison up to simulation of alternative *future state maps*. We call this a holistic approach for *Value stream mapping* including detailed analysis of lead time, productivity, space, distance, material disposal, energy and carbon dioxide equivalents – depending in a change of calculated direct product costs.**

Keywords*–*Value stream mapping; lean management; content authoring.

I. Introduction

Value Stream Mapping (VSM) is an abstract lean manufacturing technique for optimizing the material and information flows from production up to the delivery of products to the customers. Usually this is done by drawing current and future state maps by hand, allowing the optimization of production by identifying bottlenecks and wastes. With VASCO [1] we introduce a tool, which supports the complete work flow from acquisition, to analysis of the current state, up to planning the future state.

Figure 1 shows a typical hand-drawn board template for data acquisition at the "shop-floor". The concepts of VSM are usually represented by a set of standard symbols, which got various properties attached. Typical properties, e.g., for a VSM process (which represents a production step like welding or assembly) include information about the process time, scrap rate, workers involved in the production, but can also contain data about published enhancements of traditional VSM, e.g., space usage for production and logistics, transport distance and transport time [2].

The history of designing process maps and flowcharts to represent the flows of materials and information in a factory can be traced at least back to 1915, where in a book by Charles

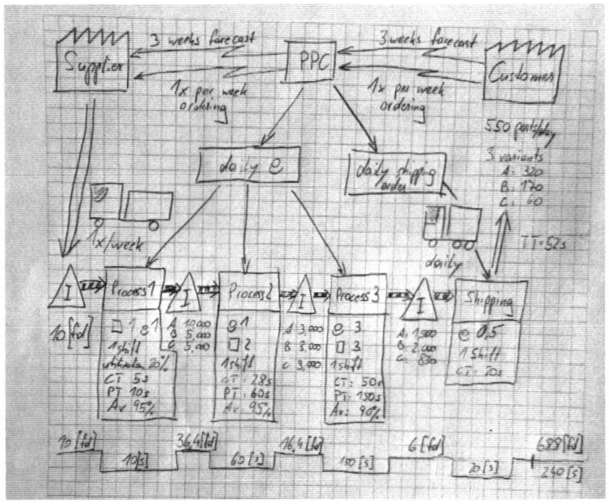

Figure 1. Typical hand-drawn VSM diagram created during a shop floor acquisition in a production facility.

E. Knoeppel entitled "Installing Efficiency Methods" we can find interesting graphical representations about the processes and routing in a manufacturing plant [3].

Nowadays, value stream mapping with traditional pen & paper method faces new challenges in practical utilization. Relevant problems or limitations for the approach presented here are: (1) indicators that are not aligned with a lean approach; (2) Processes measurements – problems/difficulties in measuring data in processes – cases where time data and quantity measurements are impractical due to layout problems, product complexity, or process type; (3) obsolescence of the current state map. The authors mentioned, that these problems and limitations can be addressed by use of ICT in data collection in production and using standards in measurement procedures. Thus, reproducibility and repeatability evaluation of CSM and alternative FSMs will be possible in the sense of supporting management in decision making. Furthermore, it is mentioned that VSM supports management when improving production conditions regarding Eco-design by identifying and eliminating environmental wastes [4].

Hence, it is necessary to have company wide standards for drawing, data collection and analyzing current state maps. Therefore, VASCO was established to close this gap for standardized analysis of CSM as well as enabling the planning of successful FSMs of value streams in a digital manner. As a result, a better decision making on shop floor level is supported when applying VASCO continuously.

The next section will give an overview of the related work and programs which inspired the creation of VASCO. Section 3 shows the main functionality of VASCO, how VSM diagrams are modeled within the system and how the automatic calculations are handled. Following, section 4 describes the underlying model based approach to calculate VSM-KPIs by entering resource consumption as input parameters. In section 5, a use case is presented to show VASCO in action and trying to close the gap from a practical point of view. Section 6 shows how VASCO can be used within dynamic simulation studies to enhance traditional "static simulation" of VSM. The last section concludes our work and will give an outlook on further research.

II. Related Work

VSM was originally developed as a method within the Toyota Production System [5][6] and introduced as a distinct methodology by Rother & Shook [7]. VSM is a simple, yet very effective, method to gain a holistic overview of the conditions of the value streams within a production environment. Based on the analysis of the current state maps, flow-oriented future state maps are planned and implemented [7], [8], [9].

A value stream includes all activities, i.e., value adding, non-value adding and supporting activities that are necessary to create a product (or to render a service) and to make it available to the customer. This includes the operational processes, the flow of material between the processes, all control and steering activities and also the flow of information [10]. In order to assess possible improvement potential, VSM considers, in particular, the entire process time (sum of time of all production steps) compared with the overall lead time (time from the customer ordering to the moment of delivery). The greater the distinction between operating time and lead time the higher the improvement potential [8].

Several organizations and researchers described sustainability indicators in their works but, however, there is no universal standard published yet. Further development of sustainability reporting in the production practice can be identified [11]. This made it important to define criteria that help to develop strategies for the evaluation and improvement of sustainability [12]. Paju et al. list a compilation of indicators, which can be used in a Sustainable Manufacturing Mapping [10]. In the following widely used indicators, like used, i.e., in the GRI standard [13], are explained. The following indicators are necessary to evaluate:

(a) **Disposal** due to waste of the resource 'material': Here, the legal EU definition of waste *'(...) means any substance or object which the holder discards or intends or is required to discard'* [14]. Material waste means all non-productive output (NPO) including solid and fluid waste [15]. An established categorization for produced waste is taken from the 'DIRECTIVE 2008/98/EC OF THE EUROPEAN PARLIAMENT AND OF THE COUNCIL' [14], which orders the 'R' strategies reuse, recycle, recovery and disposal descending by importance. The reduction of waste therefore begins with prevention, followed by reuse or recycle and (thermal) recovery [16]. The efficiency of a manufacturing system is defined with the ratio of output in comparison with the input. Despeisse et al. explain that a system which utilizes the generated waste internally and sees it as a resource is more efficient than a system that does not so. Additional approaches such as redesign and re-manufacture [17] are not considered in this paper, since they are not applied in VSM.

(b) **Solvents**: Depending on the manufacturing process solvents are used in paints or adhesives. In the literature solvents are used as sustainability indicators [13].

(c) **Water**: often used for cooling, heating or cleaning in a production process [11]. E-VSM primarily focuses on water [18].

(d) **Energy and CDE/carbon footprint**: Since non-renewable energy has a direct impact on greenhouse gas, energy must be seen as an important indicator for sustainability [17]. Common energy and material forms in production which are used as sustainability indicators are electricity, natural gas and compressed air [10]. Furthere diesel or district heating can be included [19] more diesel or district heating can be included [19]. Several approaches exist in order to measure and improve energy and CDE indicators:

(i) Usually, the energy efficiency as quotient of net production value and primary energy consumption with the unit EUR/MWh, is used as a characteristic value and the system of the production is seen as a black box [11].

(ii) Modeling approaches in the traditional factory design with the objective of energy and resource efficiency [20]; [21].

(iii) The specification DIN EN ISO 50001 as amended, supports companies to establish an energy management system as well as during operation of the processes in order to achieve an improvement in energy efficiency, the use of energy and the energy consumption.

(iv) various approaches for CO2 assessment over the entire product life cycle, while the phase manufacturing (production) is usually represented as a single object in the entire modeling [22]. Analogous to accounting, the resource deployments are considered overall and calculated to the finished products [23].

(v) In the method carbon footprint analysis, the total greenhouse gas (GHG) emissions are estimated in terms of carbon equivalence (i.e. as tons of carbon dioxide equivalent [tCO2e] or grams of CO2 equivalent per kilowatt hour of generation [gCO2eq/kWh] from a specific product [24].

(vi) In Value Stream Mapping, different approaches are known to set the focus on environmental sustainability in order to obtain economic improvements as well. The method Energy Value Stream Mapping [8] with focus on energy saving examines each manufacturing step in energy intensity and energy waste, both in operating and start-up and shut-down phases. The work of Erlach is practical and supports direct implementation of energy savings by guidelines [25]. But only the resources and energy media Electricity, gas and compressed air are examined. An overall CO2 assessment is not supported.

(vii) 'Multi-Layer-Stream Mapping' (MSM) evaluates all processes in the value stream by efficiency-data, by comparing the value-adding to the total energy- and resource use. The aim is to get 100% efficiency at all stages of production. A visual indication of the waste supports the user communicating the saving potential. This indication is not only applicable to resource inputs with environmental impact, but the CO2 assessment is not supported [19].

(viii) the approach to assess energy value-streams in production and logistics in respect of time- and energy-consumption (EVSM) focuses on aligning use of energy to value adding and non-value adding shares in operating times with scope of periphery 1-3 in a detailed way. The views of Hopf, Haag and Lourenco are combined in this approach [26].

(ix) SVSM is able to rate the waste-generation in value stream using a model which is integrated in VSM-Tool VASCO [27]. In summary, core ideas of the presented approaches are implemented in the model of VASCO. This allows management to identify possible improvement potentials and quantify them. Hence, a goal-oriented prioritization of measures to improve the value stream is supported.

Value stream simulation can be used in lean manufacturing to support the optimization of production [28]. It allows an early stage insight into productivity, effectiveness and service level without the need of creating detailed and time consuming simulation models. This means that a simulation in lean management workshops can now be done by lean experts instead of relying in simulation experts. Traditionally VSM is a pen & paper tool that captures the state of the system at the state it was drawn. Component based modeling divides the simulation into a set of simulation blocks [29]. These blocks can be used to create value stream maps that are generic and reusable. In our application VASCO, we also support several reusable blocks that allow the user to easily create value stream diagrams that are reusable in a standardized way. By utilizing standard simulation building blocks one can easily know the state of the system under different circumstances allowing for better decision making. Another important aspect of using value stream maps and specially in a digital form, is that the production and delivery processes are optimized from the customers' point of view [7].

In the seminal work of Wei Xia and Jiwen Sun [30] on simulation guided value stream and lean improvement, the authors give a good description of a typical value stream mapping application. This typical application is then enhanced by the usage of event simulation in the manufacturing process. The authors discuss how that greatly contributes to a better perception of the entire value stream mapping (VSM) and simulation processes. In the work of [31] a simulation model is used to evaluate the performance of an automotive manufacturing system as a function of demand. Prakash and Chen [32] developed a simulation model of a flexible manufacturing system, and investigated its performance. In the work of Welgama et al. [33] two cell designs were analyzed, for a manufacturing facility taking in consideration operator and material handling utilization factors. Kyukab et al.[34] used simulation to identify parameters to improve system performance at a motor production facility. Bischak [35] describes simulation in performance evaluation of a textile manufacturing module with moving workers. Park, Matson and Miller [36] describe a simulation approach used to verify that the daily throughput requirements can be met at a new assembly plant, and it is used to determine the maximum throughput of the facility, and to characterize how the component buffers behave in terms of quantity fluctuations and identified possible system bottlenecks. Shang et al. [37] uses a combination of simulation and optimization to evaluate the design of a cellular manufacturing system. In the work of Persson [38] the author investigates the impact of a varying level of system structure detail, when modeling a manufacturing system. Suri et al. [39] used simulation to validate analytic models and predict the system performance for a single material handling device case. In addition to using simulation to directly analyze and predict system performance, simulation has been used to validate analytic models [39]. There is not much work reported regarding manufacturing and simulation based methodology [40]. Additional and detailed examples of VSM simulation are needed in different types of actual production settings.

VSM is also seen as a tool to show the outcomes in a shorter period of time at minimal costs. The lean consultants can now represent and capture the current state of the process at a certain state and time and start projecting the future proposed state of the value stream. Based on lean concepts the two states can be simulated and key measurements are assessed. These simulation results can easily demonstrate the improvements [41]. In manufacturing, there are three types of operations that are undertaken to represent a type of waste that might occur: non-value adding, necessary but non-value adding and value-adding operations [42]. The first type is pure waste with unnecessary actions that should be completely eliminated. The second type involves actions that are necessary but might be wasteful. The third type are value-adding operations representing processes that convert raw materials into finished products.

The capture of information to a digital form is often not sufficient. From the point of view of using a digital tool to capture the state of a process, there are several applications that can be used and are available. However, in their paper, Shararah et al. [29] introduce the Value Stream Map Simulator using ExtendSim (VSMSx) as a powerful tool designed to facilitate the implementation of lean manufacturing by simulating the value stream map through standardized simulation building blocks. The company Siemens created as part of their Product Life-cycle Management - PLM product line, an optional extension library called Plant Simulation Value Stream Mapping (VSM) Library [43]. The company immediately reported productivity increases by as much as 20 percent and improvements of 60 percent related with the reduction of inventories and cycle time. Other benefits such as investment risk reduction (through early feasibility analysis capabilities), better line planning and allocation and significant increases in the resource utilization were also highlighted. The capability of being able to define what-if scenarios without disturbing existing production systems during the planning process is pointed as one of the most important features of any value stream mapping planning tool. Plant simulation is also referred as an important feature of such systems, because it facilitates the comprehension of complex production systems and processes. Resource utilization, material flows and supply chains maybe therefore optimized. The question of "Why perform value stream mapping in Plant Simulation?" is also debated in this technical report. Factors such as the reduction of cost for data collection by reducing the number of objects describing the processes (by utilizing pre-defined logic blocks) or the reduction in analysis effort through automated analysis modules have an important role in deciding to use

VSM. In order highlight the dynamic effects (which remain hidden in the static paper based mapping of the value chain), a digital representation (through computer simulation) of the value stream is required.

According to Nash & Poling [44], the value stream mapping has some disadvantages associated with it. It points to the fact that originally, VSM did not include any significant monetary measure for value. It is the stakeholders responsibility to determine determine which activity can be marked as value as well as which activity can be marked as waste. The task of decision-finding may take a lot of valuable time.

Another important challenge arises from the fact that there is the need to not only capture data and information about the processes and the information flows involved, but also it is beneficial to have a digital representation of how these processes look like in reality [45], in fact ultimately we would like to achieve what is sometimes called "The Digital Twin Concept Model" [46]. Similarly, in our approach we are taking the steps necessary to provide this type of vision. When we analyze the current arrangement of an assembly line and we capture this information on a VSM diagram (current state). At a later stage we do not want to come back to the production area to visual re-check the arrangement of machines, workers, to discover how are the parts actually delivered and stored or to know what are the space constrains to be able to describe and demonstrate how the actual work of the existent implemented processes is being performed. To have a better view of what should be improved when preparing the future state VSM, it is desirable that the new digital tool for the creation of VSMs can allow the users to capture and then to find annotations in the form of pictures, videos or 3D representations of the past, current and future reality of the production sites. Therefore, every time a user is handling a VSM diagram, he will be able at any step of the process to access these digital catalog of the different processes, that are now linked to the VSM digital representation.

A field research on available standard software tools showed a lack in possibility of detailed analysis. While some tools just provide basic drawing aids for creating value stream maps (e.g. Microsoft Visio [47]), other tools like iGrafx [48], Plant Simulation [49] or SmartDraw [50] also support lead time calculations and basic simulation. None of them considers the availability of data in production lines, which is a big deal nowadays in order to cope with all the complexity and achieve transparency. Nevertheless, detailed analysis and transparency of value streams are needed to reveal improvement potentials.

To address the challenges in mastering the increasing complexity in the VSM data models, we are developing a highly customizable tool for authoring and managing value streams. The next section gives an insight on the key features of VASCO.

III. VASCO MAIN FUNCTIONALITES

VASCO is implemented as a Microsoft Visio Plugin. This allows to reuse the drawing and connecting shapes functionality already provided by Visio. A VASCO value stream diagram can be combined with other shapes and features included by Visio or other 3rd-party AddIns. One important aspect in the design of the VASCO focuses on the user experience. Figure 2(a) shows the ribbon toolbar for VASCO. All available control elements are optimized for the fast creation of VSM diagrams,

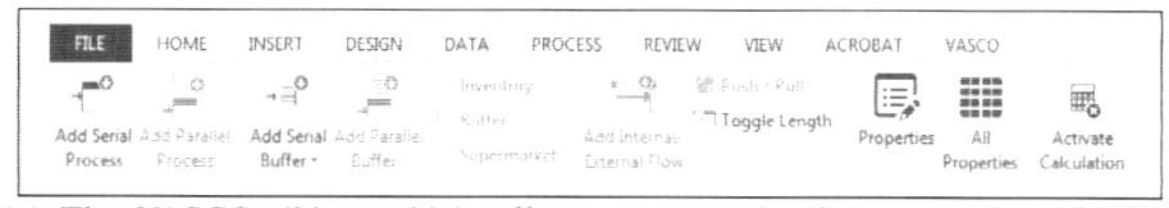

(a) The VASCO ribbon which offers a support for fast generation of VSM diagrams.

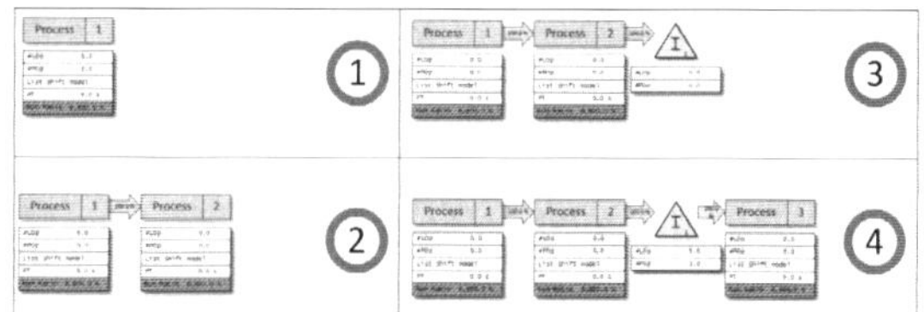

(b) Drawing a simple VSM.

Figure 2. With minimum user interaction the drawing process in Figure 2(b) can be achieved with our VASCO toolbar shown in Figure 2(a)

especially adding and positioning process or buffer symbol. Typical repeating tasks are automated like the adding of serial process/buffer symbols, where VASCO already connects the two symbols using an internal flow connector. The inserted process/buffer stays selected, so that the user can immediately use the commands "Add serial process"/"Add serial buffer" multiple times. Figure 2(b) shows how to create a VSM diagram. From (1) to (4) using only mouse clicks - or if you are on a touch device, then only 4 touch events are needed, which is much faster then a hand-made drawing. Therefore, the usual manual steps of transforming the hand-made drawings into digital documents is now completely obsolete when using VASCO.

A. *Definition of VASCO symbols*

As seen in figure 3 a value stream consists of a variety of standardized shapes and information. VASCO adds properties and the calculation logic to the VSM shapes to the main VSM symbols:

Figure 3. The standard VSM symbols (from left to right): Supplier, Customer, Process, Buffer, External flow, Internal flow.

- The **supplier** is the manufacturer which ships the goods into the factory.
- The **customer** is a company, merchant or another entity who orders goods and requires them to be shipped regularly. The customer determines the demand and the resulting takt time, which is a key value driving almost all calculations within a value stream.
- The **process** is a step, which adds value to goods by altering or modifying it.
- The **buffer** is an intermediate step where the factory goods are stored. This storage might be an input for the next process, a general depot for delivering goods to the customer or from the supplier.
- The **external flow** connects a supplier or a customer with a buffer or a process.

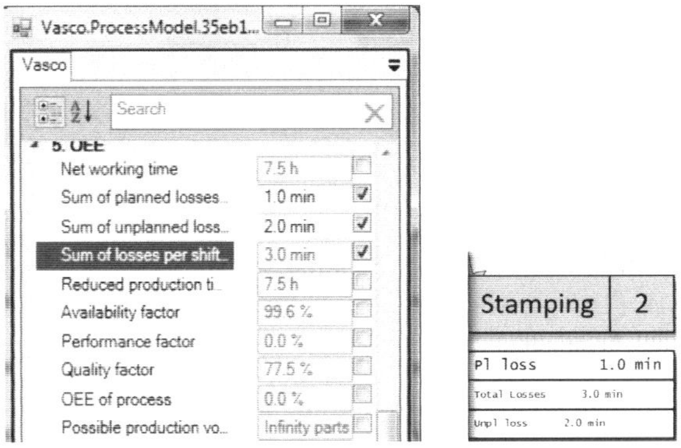

(a) The complete property model of the stamping process.

(b) Selected attributes of the property model displayed below the process symbol. 4(a).

Figure 4. The properties of the stamping process and how the process is displayed on the VASCO sheet.

- The **internal flow** connects buffers and processes with each other. The main difference between an external and an internal flow is that a internal flow might connect a process with multiple buffers or processes. This means that the internal flow is augmented with a property called material spreading which defines how many percent of material spreads from one process or buffer to their successors.

A valid *value stream graph* consists of one supplier at the start, one or more customers at the end, one or multiple processes, and zero or multiple buffers. Each of the processes and buffers are connected with internal flows and two external flows connecting the supplier and customer with the network.

B. Intelligent Symbols

One of the significant features of VASCO is that all symbols defined in Section III-A, are fully customizable by a configuration file. This configuration file defines which properties are added to the symbol. These properties can be classified into two major categories: manual input values or calculated values. The manual values are entered by the user, whereas the calculated values depend on a formula consisting of manually entered or other calculated values. The formula definition is also part of the configuration file and can be modified even at run-time.

For example, let's have a process which drills a hole into a plate. This process has two manual input values. The value adding time which is the time period when the drill actually drills the hole and the setup time. The setup time is the time period needed for positioning the drill and the time the assembly line needs to bring the plate into position. With these two values in the process it is possible to add a third value, the process time which automatically calculates the sum of the setup time and the value adding time. This automatic calculated value can be displayed on a databox in the process shape (see Figure 4). If a value of these properties changes, all dependent values are updated immediately (see Figure 4(a)).

One special case of calculated values is when the values not only depend on the local process, like in the example above, but also in other places from other symbols, like the following processes. These special calculations are called graph calculations. The graph calculations are also defined in the configuration file, but require a complete value stream graph in order to perform their calculations. For this, VASCO has two different modes. The first mode, is the design mode. In this mode the user can add processes, buffers and connect them with each other. The calculations which are only local are calculated in this mode. The second mode, is the calculation mode, where all graph calculations calculate their value. In this mode it is not possible to add, remove or connect symbols with each other.

To get a better picture about the calculation mode consider a customer who requires 100 items. We have 3 processes which are connected in series. Each process has a scrap rate of 10%. Now each of the processes has to accommodate the scrap rate of the following processes and produce more goods. That in the end the customer gets his 100 items. Therefore, in our example the first process requires 139 items. This example can become arbitrarily complex with parallel processes and the material spreading in internal flows. In the calculation mode all values are live updated and displayed. So if the customer requests that the factory delivers more items, it is then immediately visible how many more raw material the first process requires. This is also the reason why it is not allowed to edit the path, remove or add further processes during the calculation mode, as all values would be invalid with a unfinished value stream graph.

When a user adds a new intelligent symbol to a diagram, e.g., a buffer, this symbol becomes now automatically the current selected symbol. This allows the automation of the possible next choices for symbols that can be added to the diagram (connected to the current symbol). In this way, when the user looks to the application main toolbar, only symbols that are possible to be connected to the previous symbol, are available for a next drop in the diagram. When the user intent is to connect two symbols, e.g., the user wants to connect a buffer with a process, the user pre-selects these two symbols. After this step, the application automatically highlights the possible connections that can be added between the selected symbols. The users reported that these methods significantly improve the productivity and the usability of our application interface. These and other improvements will be the target of future studies, where we will access the overall usability of the tool and compare it with other existent VSM applications.

C. Key Performance Indicators (KPI) and Data Lines

As referred in the related work section, an important aspect in the analysis of VSM diagrams is the extraction and automatic calculation of *Key Performance Indicators* (KPI).

Key performance indicators can be calculated locally, e.g., for a single process (e.g. OEE rate) or buffer (e.g. local lead time) - but also for the value stream (e.g. total lead time) as a graph-based calculation. These values are calculated automatically and are visualized in several data lines below the drawn value stream.

When discussing with the main key holders (manufacturing and production consultants or VSM and processes simulation owners) involved in the event of capturing processes and information flows (as well as many other related information captured now in a digital form), one of the most desired features is the capability of calculating improved business metrics.

Figure 5. The Comments plugin allows to annotate VSM symbol with photos and videos taken from the camera of a tablet.

VASCO KPIs		
Flow rate / Flussrate	1.39	[%]
Lead time / Durchlaufzeit	36.51	[fd]
Processtime / Prozesszeit	3.38	[min]
Total number of employees / Anzahl Mitarbeiter ges.	6	[#/day]
Production / Produktion	5	[#/day]
Logistics / Logistik	1	[#/day]
Employee productivity / Mitarbeiterproduktivität	75	[parts/pers.]

Figure 6. The Key Performance Indicator giving an overview of the operating numbers in the factory.

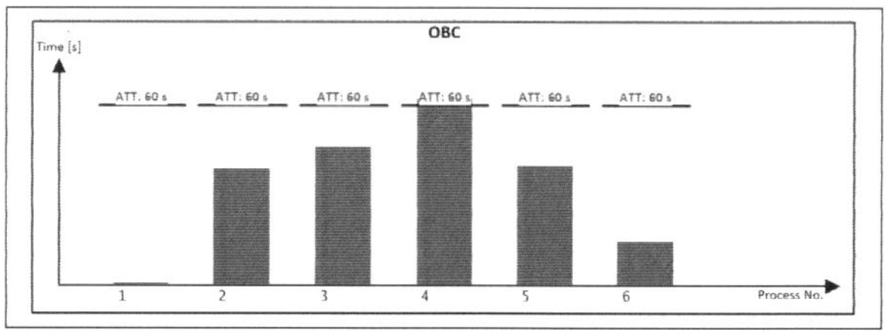

Figure 7. OBC showing the process time in relation to the takt time.

These metrics allow the evaluation of factors that are critical to the success of an organization. In our tool we calculate and present metrics that are related with human resources, costs, performance and workload balancing management. These are essential to the reduction of costs and to the improvement of performance of processes and persons.

We present results to the users in a concise way through resume maps in each step of the calculations procedures. This is a realistic and simple way to digitally represent the past, current and future reality inside all manufacturing sites.

D. *Extensibility*

One key-feature of VASCO is extensibility. While self being an Microsoft Visio addin, it can be customized by plugins itself. The basic version of VASCO is already shipped with three plugins, extending the basic functionality of the tool:

- **Comment-Plugin** VASCO was designed to make the acquisition and calculation of a new value stream easier and to replace the pen & paper acquisition. With the pen & paper method it is always possible to add different comments to the different symbols. In order to give the VASCO user a similar feature during the acquisition a comment plugin was created. This comment plugin enhances every symbols on a VASCO page with a comment tab (see Figure 5). When we observed during the data acquisition process that users sometimes only copied key figures from a machine into this comment tab, we further enhanced the comment-plugin with a snapshot ability. With this snapshot ability the user doesn't need to copy the values himself. The user only has to take a snapshot with the tablet. It is also possible to record a video with the comment plugin. This can be done to record different views of the machine or to record the voice of the person who does the acquisition so that there is not even the need to write textual facts in the comments box.
- **KPI-Plugin** The KPI-Plugin adds an additional visual features (see Figure 6) to the Visio page. This shape displays the key performance indicators of the factory in a clear fashion. Once a VASCO graph is complete and VASCO itself is in calculation mode, the values are calculated and automatically updated when a value in the graph changes.
- **OBC-Plugin** The operator balance chart (OBC) visualizes the total amount of work of each process compared to the takt time. An OBC supports the critical task of redistributing work elements among operators. This is essential for minimizing the number of operators needed by making the amount of work for each operator very nearly equal to, but slightly less than, takt time [51]. Figure 7 shows the OBC chart of the given example.

IV. Model-based, Process-oriented Calculation of Resource Consumption

This section describes the 'ideal-typical re-utilization cycle'. It is the basis for evaluation of sustainability indicators in value streams. In each process of the value stream an ideal-typical re-utilization cycle is underlain virtually. Each ideal-typical re-utilization cycles includes the mentioned categories to handle waste: reuse, recycle, recovery and disposal. However, usually additional material is required in production which is not used for producing finished products. This creates waste of material resources. Waste of material resources is assigned to each ideal-typical re-utilization cycle of a process. Waste occurs depending on process technology. This waste can be reused, recycled, recovered or brought to the disposal site. But before immersing into the ideal-typical re-utilization cycle and the calculation of sustainability indicators, the connection of the elements of a value stream as process chains need to be discussed. A series of processes combined with parallel material flows lead to highly dependent elements (processes, buffers, transports) of the value stream.

A. *Cumulated Scrap Rate*

With a serial sequence of processes of a value stream and the occurring scrap rates at processes, each upstream process has to produce more to finally provide the required amount to the customer. Contrary to the direction of material flow the cumulated scrap rate increases for each process of the value stream accordingly. As a result, the calculation of cumulated scrap rate for each process in a serial sequence is:

$$S_{cum}(i) = 1 - \prod_{i=n}^{1}(1 - s_i) \quad (1)$$

- s_{cum} – cumulated scrap rate along a value stream [%]
- s_i – scrap rate of a process i [%]

Starting from the actual customer demand D_{net}, the customer demand per process (i) results in:

$$D_{net.p}(i) = \frac{D_{net}}{1 - s_{cum}(i)}$$

- $D_{net.p}(i)$ – increased net demand per process due to cumulated scrap rate at process i [parts per time period]
- D_{net} – net demand of customer [parts per time period]
- s_{cum} – cumulated scrap rate [%]

This formula is essential for the calculation of total waste along a value stream. Another effect of the cumulated scrap rate is not considered in this paper, but should be mentioned because of practical relevance in Value Stream Mapping: The cumulated scrap rate causes an increase of the required net demand per process upstream the considered value stream. Therefore, the customer tact time is not assumed to be constant for each process. Strictly speaking, the specific tact time of each process has to be reduced due to an increased required net demand while keeping available net working time constant.

B. Calculation of waste at single processes

The waste of material resources for each process in the value stream is, as described above, associated with the ideal-typical re-utilization cycle. This waste can generally occur in three ways; see Formulas 3, 4 and 5.

$$W_{nok} = (D_{net.p} - D_{net}) \cdot d_n$$

- W_{nok} – waste due to cumulated scrap rate [kg per time period]
- $D_{net.p}$ – increased net demand of customer [parts per time period]
- D_{net} – net demand of customer [parts per time period]
- d_n – net weight of input resource [kg per part]

W_{nok} is the waste because of not fulfilling quality requirements such as damaged or improperly manufactured parts. The gross material input is d_g. Due to the chosen manufacturing process additional resource input W_{ok} is often necessary and calculated as follows:

$$W_{ok} = D_{net.p} \cdot (d_g - d_n)$$

- W_{ok} – waste due to material input difference [kg per time period]
- $D_{net.p}$ – increased net demand of customer [parts per time period]
- d_g – gross weight of input resource [kg per part]
- d_n – net weight of input resource [kg per part]

The net material input is d_n, e.g., the material input differences between gross and net is sprue in injection moulding or paint sludge in the painting processes. As a third category, waste because of set-ups $W_b(i)$ is introduced. This waste is usually produced in batch production or discontinuous shift models. The above proportions of all waste depend on the considered time period. The waste proportion because of set-up is usually not in the same observation period as the required amount of the customer D_{net}. For this reason, the following proportionality is presented:

$$\frac{W_r(i)}{D_{net.p}(i)} \propto \frac{W_b(i)}{b(i)}$$

- W_r – waste due to set-ups [kg per time period]
- $D_{net.p}$ – increased net demand per process due to cumulated scrap rate [parts per time period]
- W_b – waste per batch [kg per batch]
- b – batch size [parts per batch]

W_b presents the average waste per batch; b is referred to as batch size. The sum of waste per observation period, e.g., shift, is calculated as follows:

$$W = W_{nok} + W_{ok} + W_{set-up}$$

- W – total waste [kg per time period]
- W_{nok} – waste due to cumulated scrap rate [kg per time period]
- W_{ok} – waste due to material input difference [kg per time period]
- W_{set-up} – waste due to set-ups [kg per time period]

To convert the waste per unit the calculated waste per observation period must be divided by the observation period. Thus, the waste per part w(i) for each process i is:

$$w(i) = \frac{d_g(i)}{1 - s_{cum}(i)} - d_n(i) + \frac{W_b(i)}{b(i)}$$

- $w(i)$ – total waste per ok part [kg per ok part]
- d_g – gross weight of input resource [kg per part]
- s_{cum} – cumulated scrap rate [%]
- d_n – net weight of input resource [kg per part]
- W_b – waste per batch [kg per batch]
- b – batch size [parts per batch]

The waste per unit can be calculated for each process and each resource which is used. This waste of material resources is supplied to the ideal-typical utilization process and rated. Simplifying the mathematical model, only the primary resource is considered, which excludes process water, solvents or packaging.

C. Ideal-typical re-utilization cycles for each process

In this chapter, the ideal-typical re-utilization cycle gets introduced. The three types of waste of each process get assigned to the introduced categories reuse, recycle, recovery and disposal. In all categories but disposal, material gets used somehow else again, whereas disposals get transported to landfill. Each process of a value stream gets layers for the re-utilization categories (see Figure 8). One specific re-utilization cycle then consists of five transport activities, three buffers and the re-utilization process itself to become an ideal-typical re-utilization cycle. This ideal-typical re-utilization cycle is applicable for all kinds of production/assembling processes. An example to illustrate is an injection moulding process. Due to set-ups, sprue and scrap rate waste is created to produce

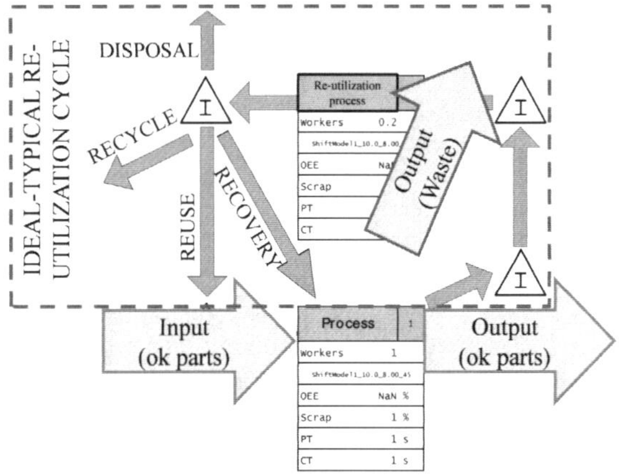

Figure 8. Principle of an ideal-typical re-utilization cycle.

customer demand; 80% of total waste is recycled to produce other products (e.g. a linoleum covered floor) and 20% is disposal so we have two layers. The machine operator puts all types of waste into one or more containers, which get transported by forklift to a silo for shredding. After shredding, the ready-to-recycle material waits in bags on a pallet. All efforts like space, transport distance and time for re-utilization can be assessed similar to classic VSM approach. Furthermore, one can separate between several resource types in value stream to distinguish types of disposals. On the one hand, this modeling of resource flows at processes seems not replicable when drawing value streams with paper and pen, but on the other hand it is suitable to be represented in a VSM software tool. Figure 8 shows system boundaries and layers of an ideal-typical re-utilization cycle of a process in a value stream.

D. Calculation of sustainability indicators and disposals data line

Applying ideal-typical re-utilization cycles at processes of a value stream enables the calculation of sustainability indicators such as disposals by the presented model. This model can then be applied to calculate waste and disposal for all resource types in the same way. Practical examples next to primary input resources are solvents, drinking water, process water and packaging materials. Finally, all criteria needed for sustainability and/or customer reporting can be calculated in the same way with the presented model. When calculating total lead time of a value stream, all waiting times in buffers are added; same when calculating total process time with adding up all process times in processes. These two values are represented in the time data line at the very end of a value stream. We use the same approach for the disposals data line. All types of resource disposals are summed up to calculate the total disposals value. As an example to illustrate, a specific value stream consists of four serial processes and the process technologies are injection moulding, painting, assembling and sequencing. Types of disposals of primary input resources are therefore synthetics, coating and parts from bill-of-material in unit kilogram per part. Other resources may be solvents and process water at coating process as well as cardboard and synthetics of packaging material at assembly process. All categories of disposals can be summed up apart from each other and/or altogether to represent the disposals of a whole value stream. The final disposals data line of a value stream is shown in Figure 10; sustainability indicators are calculated per part to be comparable.

E. Data Model and Calculations

This section describes the data model used in VASCO and discusses some implementation aspects.

1) Graph Structure: Naturally, the elements of a drawn value stream map correspond to a graph structure. Generally, a graph $G = (N, E)$ consists of a set of *nodes* (or vertices) N together with a binary relation E on the set [52], each two nodes whose relation evaluates to true are called *connected*, and such relations are called *edges*. If the edges have an associated direction, the graph is called a directed graph.

Our design rationale for a consistent data model for a VSM map is a graph that represents all aspects of the map. Therefore, each concept of a VSM (e.g. a process or a flow) is represented by a node $n \in N$ in the graph, relations between VSM concepts are represented by a directed edge $e \in E$ between the corresponding nodes. Each node, or concept, contains a set of named properties. Each property is associated to a value, which can either be **fixed**, i.e., the value is entered as a numerical value, or **calculated**, therefore, it depends on the values of other properties, in some cases even from other nodes. Edges in this data model do not contain properties. We call this data model the *concept graph*.

2) Evaluation of Calculated Values: Naturally, the dependencies of calculated values impose an ordering on the evaluation of such values. One could implement such an ordering by assigning priority values to properties under the assumption that all dependencies will be correctly handled if the nodes are evaluated in priority order, however, all nodes would have to be re-evaluated if a value changes, which is

- slow, as many values will be recalculated even if they do not depend on a changed value which is a problem especially for larger graph, i.e., a scaling problem
- error-prone, as the implementation has to make sure that the assumption holds, i.e., changing one formula may require to change priority values of many other formulas

Furthermore, while such constraints can be maintained without much effort for some calculations, e.g., one value of a concept depends on another value of the same concept, there may exist more complicated dependencies, e.g., one value depends on another value of all concepts of type process.

Our solution to this problem is to represent the dependencies of calculated values in an additional graph structure, the *dependency graph*, which allows to re-evaluate just the dependent values if a value is altered. An example can be seen in Figure 9: the main VSM structure is encoded using the blue rounded rectangle concept nodes (e.g. Buffer) and black dashed edges. The nodes of the second graph consist of properties of VSM concept nodes, represented by green elliptic nodes, the dependencies of calculated values are represented by blue dotted edges. Dependencies are encoded as influences, i.e., each value points to all values that depend on it in their calculation.

First experiments implemented this second graph structure, the *dependency graph*, explicitly. However, this approach did

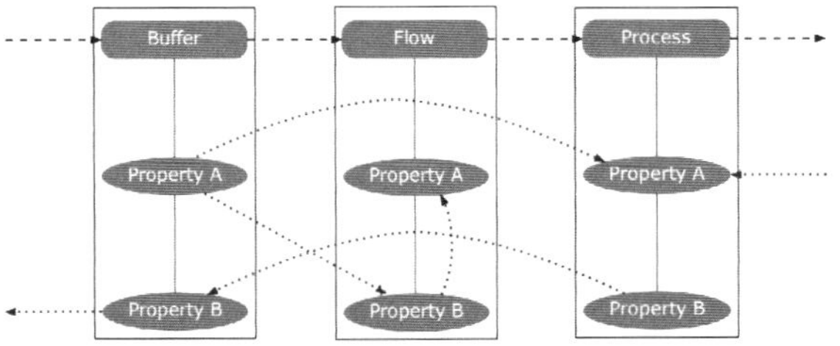

Figure 9. The data model of VASCO captures the structure of the VSM graph.

not scale well as all structural changes to the VSM graph also need to be propagated to the dependency graph. Therefore, we propose a meta representation for any calculated value in the system that separates dependencies from calculations

- an *identifier* function that identifies all *dependent* nodes of a given concept graph, and
- a *evaluation* function that performs the actual calculation reading the values from identified nodes and returns the calculated value.

These two methods help for an efficient evaluation, as there are situations where the dependency information depends on a concrete concept graph structure (e.g. dependency on all concepts of type flow). In these cases, the dependencies and consequently the calculation will change if the concept graph structure changes.

Using the identifier function, the dependency graph can be built straightforward: For each calculated value, its dependencies are determined using the identifier function, each dependency is mapped to an influence edge in the dependency graph. In our implementation, the dependency graph is rebuilt on each structural change of the concept graph. We call the complete dependency of a value, i.e., all dependent values, and their dependencies and so on, the *influence hierarchy*.

If the user changes a fixed value using the VASCO GUI, the influence hierarchy is identified via a graph traversal (e.g. breadth-first search or depth-first search) of the directed dependency graph, starting at the changed value. Thus, the traversal also yields the correct ordering for evaluation, and all values are re-calculated by calling the evaluation function for each node of the traversal.

V. Use Case: Assessment of Disposal and CO2 in Value Stream

The following use case is based on a simplified example from the automotive supplier industry, which has been extensively modeled and evaluated in practice. To reduce complexity here, a simple serial value stream is selected. The described process chain is represented by 'thermoforming', 'injection moulding', 'welding', 'assembly' and 'shipping' (see Figure 10). It should be noted, that the process steps, their sequence and frequency as well as the present conditions of process parameters are fictitious. The contemplated automotive supplier manufactures modules for various OEM, the production of side interior door panels has been selected as the product family.

A. Input of related resource consumption in VASCO

By opening the properties of the process shapes, the user is able to input relevant resource consumption to calculate the **disposal** and **CDE-value** per part. Due to the use of resources and the three types of waste, for each process the share of disposal can be calculated. Here the disposal is 0.25 kg per part, which is entered into the input mask (see Fig. 11 Input of Disposal). Measures to reduce disposal share may be, for example (a) allocating the waste to one of the other types reuse, recycle or recovery or (b) reducing the total waste by investing into new processes or design changes.

Next, the resource consumption to calculate the CDE-value per part are entered. In this use case these are direct input of energy resources as 'energy intensities', which can be measured at the process (equals '2. Energy direct' Fig. 4). At the selected process thermoforming, 3 kWh electric energy input per part is entered into the text field 'Electricity'. Furthermore, energy input values of the infrastructure (indirect), for example lightning, heating/cooling and compressed-air, can be entered. In practice, this is done by measuring these values directly at the process. Indirect energy input values are measured, e.g., at the circuit breaker panel and assigned to processes and buffers by allocation dependent on space. As a result, additional calculations apart from VASCO are needed, which are very extensively in practice. The situation is similar to the elements 'buffer' and 'transport'. Furthermore, the traditional aspect of VSM should not get lost, so certain simplifications have to be made when input indirect energy consumption, e.g., for lightning, etc. Nevertheless, the significance to management is still given.

Therefore, it is required for buffers to collect and enter all energy input values in VASCO. For transports, only direct energy inputs are gathered; the indirect energy input value of the needed space cannot be assigned to a specific product family. To avoid inaccuracies, it is recommended to assign the indirect proportion of transport to the inventory space. In Fig. 5 the input mask for transports and stocks is displayed. Here the user enters the total energy consumption for current (0.0230 kWh per part), gas (0.01 kWh per part) and compressed air (here: none).

The ideal-typical re-utilization cycle, which has been defined in section 3.3, is assessed by analogy with the previously presented elements in VASCO value flow (see Fig. 14). First, for each recycling category (here: Reuse), the energy-input-values in kWh are entered in the period of customer requirements (for example, per shift or working day). Following VASCO calculates the energy inputs per manufactured good part and also the Carbon Dioxide Equivalent (CDE). The conversion is explained in the following chapter.

B. Entering the conversion factors for CO2 assessment as CDE-value

VASCO has a tab 'CDE' in the general VASCO properties in which, among other cost rates, shift patterns and transports can be defined. These unique requirements apply to the entire value stream, so that the energy inputs for electricity, gas, compressed air and other resource inputs, such as solvents, can be entered.

The values entered here are location-specific conversion factors, which for example depend on the energy mix of the electricity supplier or the chemical composition of the solvent. Here, the CDE conversion factors for current (0.43 kg CO2 per kWh), gas (0.18 kg CO2 per kWh), compressed air (0.2 kg CO2 per kWh) and solvents (1.22 kg CO2 per kWh) are

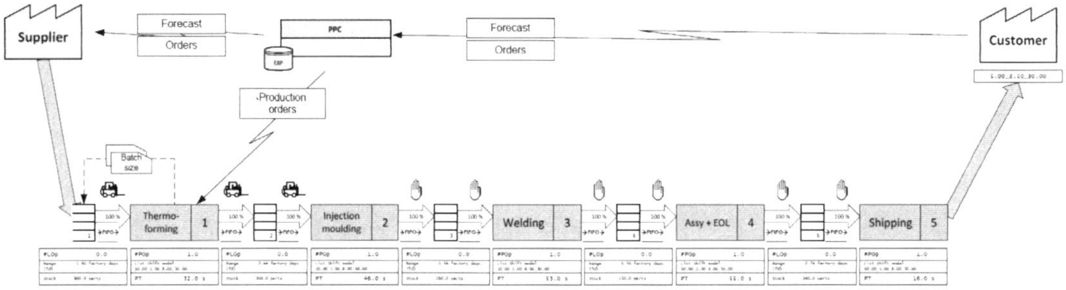

Figure 10. Input of resource consumption to calculate disposal per part

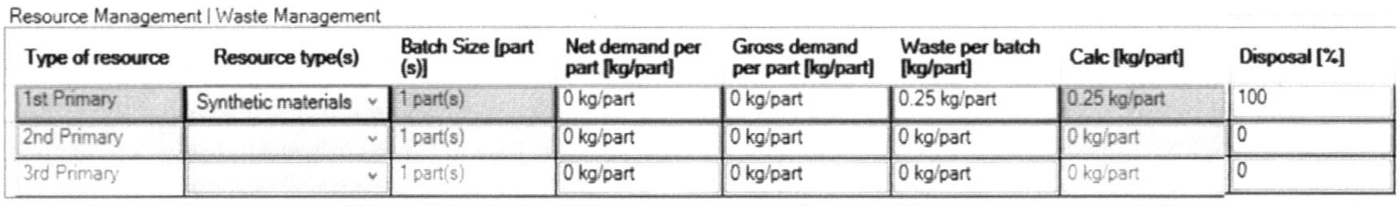
Resource Management | Waste Management

Type of resource	Resource type(s)	Batch Size [part (s)]	Net demand per part [kg/part]	Gross demand per part [kg/part]	Waste per batch [kg/part]	Calc [kg/part]	Disposal [%]
1st Primary	Synthetic materials	1 part(s)	0 kg/part	0 kg/part	0.25 kg/part	0.25 kg/part	100
2nd Primary		1 part(s)	0 kg/part	0 kg/part	0 kg/part	0 kg/part	0
3rd Primary		1 part(s)	0 kg/part	0 kg/part	0 kg/part	0 kg/part	0

Figure 11. Input of resource consumption to calculate disposal per part

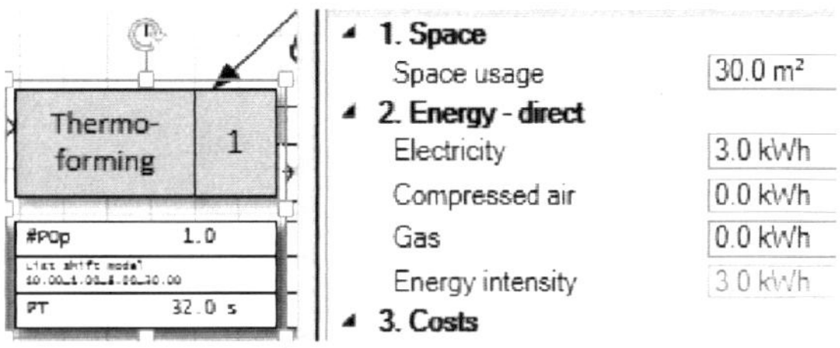

Figure 12. Input of the direct energy consumption of a process in VASCO

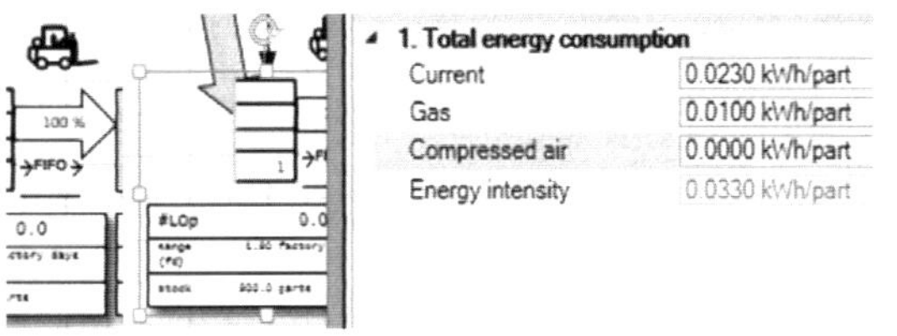

Figure 13. Input of the energy consumption at the VSM elements 'transport' and 'buffer' in VASCO

values according to the energy contracts of production site entered by the user in VASCO.

C. Displaying the CO2 assessment in value stream

The CO2 assessment of production is done through accumulation of direct and indirect energy inputs over the entire value stream that is, for all processes, transports and stocks / buffers and subsequent conversion to the equivalent CO2-value (CDE) per produced part. It should be noted that total energy consumption is calculated by number of good parts (here: D_{net} - cp. Cumulated scrap rate) produced and shipped to the customer.

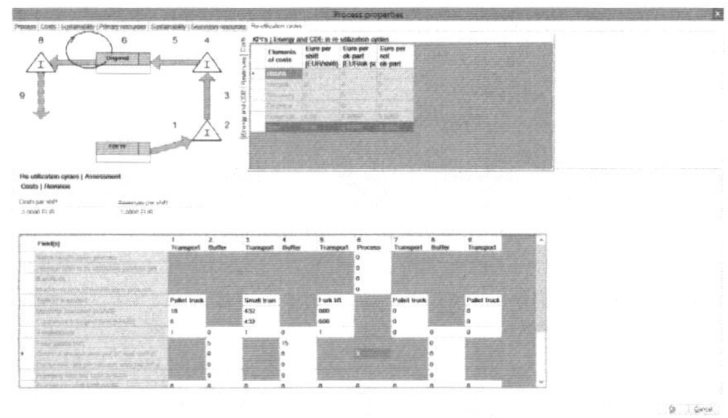

Figure 14. Energy consumption and CDE assessment in ideal-typical re-utilization cycle (here: Reuse) in VASCO

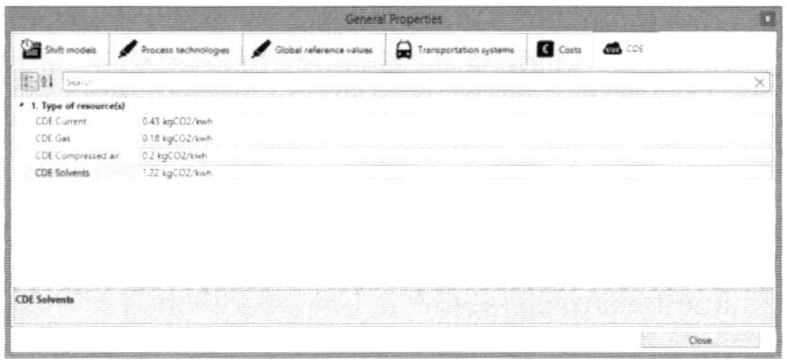

Figure 15. Input for the CDE conversion factors in VASCO

D. Visual representation of the value stream in VASCO

The following figure (Fig. 17) shows the holistically analyzed value stream with focus on time, disposal and CDE-value. This visual representation of the value stream deposited with meaningful and generally accepted indicators makes it possible to search specifically for potential improvements in resource use and derive the best possible improvement measures. In addition, further possible measures can be evaluated in a secure laboratory situation to support investment decisions

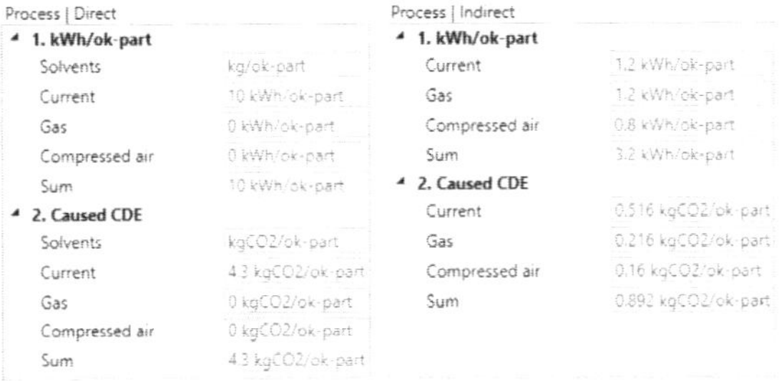

Figure 16. KPI overview with focus on CDE-value per good part (accumulated over whole value stream)

on a resilient basis. The upper data line is the traditional time line indicating the ranges of each stock / buffer compared to the total time of the processes. The middle data line displays the disposals in kg per good part (here: ok-p.) that occur at every process. The values at the right show the sum of disposals of every process, while T-DISP is the total disposal including packaging. In this use case, these are 0.25 kg per part, while no disposal for packaging occurs. The lower data line represents the CO2 assessment along the value stream. The upper stairs correspond to the direct energy consumption in kWh/part, the lower stairs are the sum of direct and indirect (structural) energy consumption per part (here: good part which leaves the process). The arrows in opposition to the direction of material flow are for the energy consumption in the ideal-typical re-utilization cycle. In this example use case 5.2486 kg CO2 per good part (here: ok-p.) are emitted as carbon dioxide equivalent (for electricity, natural gas, compressed air and solvents) into the atmosphere.

VI. The Role of Simulation

The ultimate goal of lean manufacturing is to reduce waste in human resources, inventories and time to market [30]. This allows a company to be more responsive to customer demands, while producing high quality products in an efficient and economical way [53].

Value Stream Mapping (VSM) is one important principle in lean manufacturing, because it provides understanding on how product and information flows affect each other. Traditionally VSM only provided a static picture of a process, but not in our VASCO VSM tool. VASCO VSM allows the user to see where value is added into the value stream, and calculations can be performed automatically. Through the adding of additional simulation capabilities, we can now evaluate behavioral issues of processes.

With lean manufacturing and VSM, the company can easily recognize and eliminate sources of waste. It is visible how each operation contributes to the whole, so that change decisions can be made when bottlenecks exist. It provides the ability to visualize information and product flows, and it allows the study of where, when, and how waste occurs. The implementation of lean principles involves applying concepts like Kanban, layout planning, visual control, and takt time calculations [54]. There are several reasons why waste usually occurs, and they are well described in the literature [55]. These seven types of waste are: over production, unnecessary inventory, long waiting (e.g. including long inactivity and lead times), excessive transportation, defects (e.g. in materials, causes rework or quality problems), ineffective motion (e.g. process not well designed), and inappropriate processing (e.g. due to wrong set of tools, in procedures or in systems).

The integration between VSM and simulation improves processes in general, because it makes visible both the static and the behavioral characteristics of a process [30].

A. Simulated Guided VSM – Design Approach

Firstly, VSM is usually applied as part of the lean production tools portfolio. It highlights process inefficiencies, transaction and communication mismatches, and it also guides improvement areas.

Secondly, simulation is used to reduce uncertainty and create common and justifiable overviews. This is done by visualizing dynamic processes. It is a complementary tool for VSM because it provides the quantifiable evidence needed to justify a lean approach. A simulation model is developed to replicate the operation of the existing system, and also the improved future system which should modify or replace the current implemented system. This is done with the objective of incorporating better lean principles.

Usually, the approach [30] is to construct a comprehensive model for the manufacturing process. Distinct scenarios are derived to uncover an optimal future state of the process, according to the VSM analysis. Various simulation scenarios are then developed. The simulated results are acquired and investigated, and they are matched against real production data to verify the respective model accuracy.

Simulation is therefore a guiding tool to assist organizations with the decision to implement improved lean principles. This is achieved by quantifying first the benefits of applying VSM. Then, a road map is created to help illustrate how VSM can be used to design the future states. Lastly, the developed simulation scenarios mimic the real behavior of past and future manufacturing processes.

B. Considerations on Applying Simulation

Like stated before, VSM has been traditionally viewed as a paper-and-pencil exercise. Several paper drafts (digital format in VASCO), are developed to answer specific questions on efficiency and technical issues related to lean tool implementation [56].

However, sometimes the future state map cannot be designed just by having an idea of what to change. The prediction of inventory flows and levels, is not feasible only with static data. Most traditional VSM applications do not use simulation, because in the past these required a long preparation time and effort. The development of a useful simulation model tended to be a lengthy process, which required thoughtful validation (i.e. experiments and statistical data). Usually, this development was also not well aligned with the quicker cycle time needed for manufacturing.

Nowadays, simulation is sometimes seen as not worth of the additional time and money investment. When simulation models are developed and well validated, the company gets trusted statistical data which will be valuable for the optimization of future states. Nevertheless, in today's world, simulation is also used as a way to reduce uncertainty and to create a common view. It helps explore alternatives generated by different responses to VSM design questions. If simulation is

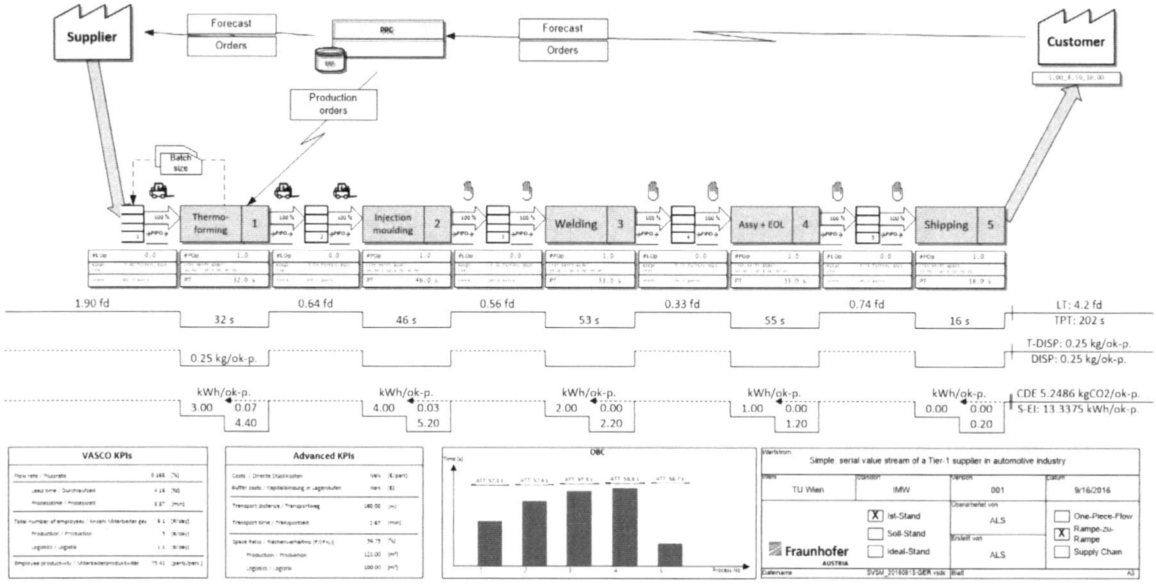

Figure 17. Representation of a holistically analyzed value stream in VASCO with data lines Lead Time, Disposal and CDE

integrated into a VSM tool, it can be flexible and robust to detail changes in VSM.

C. Creating a Common View Through Simulation Guided VSM Work-flows

According to previous work in this field [30], a key problem in getting everybody to a common view is related to the absence of visual depictions, i.e. the ability of being able to explain to others about the current state dynamics. After this challenge, comes the inability to communicate an action plan that can be understood by all stake-holders. To this end, VSM and an integrated simulation tool can definitely help in visually capturing and demonstrating current and future states that can accommodate changes.

A value stream is a collection of actions (both value-added and non-value-added) required to produce a product or product family, which uses the same resources, starting with raw material and ending with the customer [57]. The VSM is defined as "the simple process" of directly observing the flows of information and materials as they currently occur, visually summarizing them, and then envisioning a future state with much better performance [53]. The primary objective of the VSM is to identify all kinds of waste in the value stream and to take actions to eliminate these [56]. Researchers have created many lean tools to optimize individual operations. However, most of them fail in providing a clear visual representation of the material and information flows throughout the entire process [58]. The VSM creates a common base for the process, thus facilitates more thoughtful decisions to improve it [59]. This helps plan and link lean initiatives through a systematic data capture and analysis. The VSM has emerged as the preferred way to implement lean principles, inside facilities and at the supply chain level [60].

Sometimes, management decisions rely only on external results and expected benefits reported by VSM implementations external to the company. However, this is always an insufficient justification, and lacks the quantifiable evidence needed to convince to adopt lean principles [61].

VSM was literally drafted by answering specific questions on issues related to efficiency and on technical lean tool implementation [56]. In some cases, however, the future state map cannot be designed by solely using static data. For example, predicting the inventory flows and levels is impossible having only static data.

Developing a useful simulation model tended to be a time consuming task, not well aligned with the relatively quicker cycle times. However, simulation as a process simulation model, is often used to reduce uncertainty and create a consensus view. This is done by visualizing dynamic process views for a given future state. Additionally, it helps explore alternatives generated by different responses to those design questions. Simulation is capable of generating resource requirements and performance statistics whilst remaining flexible to specific organizational details.

Simulation has been considered as one of the most flexible analytic tools in the manufacturing system design and operation areas. It is used to handle uncertainty and create dynamic views of lead time and machine utilization. This enables quantification of results, and provides a possibility to compare the expected performance relative to that of the present one. Thus it can be used to assist organizations with the decision to implement the VSM, by quantifying benefits from applying lean principles in their specific situation. The majority research in this field describes the use of simulation to analyze existing or planned manufacturing systems.

Value stream mapping simulation is useful also for value stream mapping training. Each process has a defined cycle time. These cycle times are not the same, and because the work cells are interlinked, inventory builds up in between each cell. One can change many parameters, such as: cycle time, up time percentage, number of shifts, or the total available time, for each station. This is where the simulation comes into play, e.g., by simulating the first stations with a fast processing time, and the last station with slow times, we get as a result a "ton" of inventory in the middle (bottleneck). Parameters can also be entered based on group's discussion. The group can flip back and forth between the simulation and the VSM, to check how changes affect the simulated processes.

D. Value of Simulation and the Future State of VSM

Here, we refer again to the seminal work of Wei Xia and Jiwen Sun [30], where the authors give clear explanations on the value of having a simulation guided VSM work-flow. In both VSM and simulation, many "what-if" scenarios can be tested and a choice is made regarding the optimal one(s). These scenarios have distinctive key points, like the addition or subtraction of machines, and balancing of work shifts. The simulated results are used to understand accumulation of work-in-progress (WIP) before and after each process, e.g., to compare a machine efficiency or to properly account for variability. They are utilized to balance throughput, WIP and production lead time. The simulation model is a general tool for future shift, product mix and expansion decisions. Being able to achieve a higher production volume and fulfill the demand of the customer within shorter lead times is a great marketing advantage. Driven by these simulated results the company modifies the layout plan and the future state diagram.

The so called, simulation guided VSM [30], allows the management to distinguish between value added and non-value added activities. It has the potential to be a strategic decision making tool for process redesign and continuous improvement. With detailed information obtained from the simulation guided VSM, it is for example possible, to determine if cost savings or increased revenues can be made with additional capital investment.

For the operational staff, implementing simulation guided VSM can be more convenient, interactive, and straightforward than the traditional paper-and-pencil based VSM.

VSM is not always sufficient to describe the current state of a manufacturing process and design a desired future state. Simulation is then utilized to enhance but not replace the VSM by visualizing better dynamic features of the future state before implementation. Different simulation scenarios are developed by observing the actual processing times of activities in the manufacturing process and then characterizing their variation by statistical distributions.

Simulation also adds a fourth dimension, i.e. time, to the value stream map. After being simulated, the VSM is no longer just a snapshot. VSM is now a moving picture, which offers insights that may have been missed if only VSM alone had been used. Simulation of the VSM allows the lean team to quickly implement try changes, without interruptions in the production processes.

VSM is a valuable tool in lean manufacturing and in the continuous improvement effort. Simulation makes testing ideas easier, cheaper, and quicker, and gives an immediate assessment of the future proposed changes to the system. The VSM process provides the model and the data, making it easier to prepare and perform all the simulation work. Therefore, VSM and simulation complement each other very well.

E. Integration of VASCO VSM with Process Simulator

In VASCO, we developed an integration between the act of preparing VSM state diagrams, and a process simulation application called, ProModel - Process Simulator [62]. The main goal is to provide a simulation function from within our VSM tool VASCO. Besides the usual visualization and calculation of production processes, our partner manufacturing companies, also expected the development of a simulation function. This function should contribute to a significant increase in quality results of the production process analysis, Which allows to check important parameters, such as:

- Process capacities
- Buffer capacities
- Overall output in a certain period of time

We based our decision for the selection of the simulation tool (ProModel – Process Simulator), on the analysis of some of the following requirements:

- a discrete event simulation of manufacturing processes
- the user interface used to transfer data between VASCO VSM and the simulation tool, should be easy to use
- the tool should have a strong credibility in automotive industry, as well as in other industries
- require a minimum amount of integration and programming effort
- low costs involved in terms of licensing
- support MS–Visio and Excel import/export functionality
- integrate the VSM data directly into the simulation
- include batching/un-batching, shift models, routes and resources, order system and dispatching rules (FIFO, LIFO, percentage, conditional)
- clear and visually appealing results (include parameters like: throughput per day/shift, process utilization, waiting and blocking percentage and visualization capabilities, i.e. histograms and other charts)
- allow to compare multiple scenarios and allow for multiple runs with different distributions (accurate results)

We considered feedback from several partners which are experts in applied VSM and simulation of processes. The company ProModel helped, by providing development licenses for our integration development. Process Simulator proved to be efficient by fulfilling all the major requirements of our partners. Manual and automatic integration between VSM and the simulation was developed. The automatic integration allows users to transfer bi-directional data between VASCO VSM and the simulation tool. Nevertheless, the users are still able to manually edit and transfer all the VSM and simulation parameters if necessary. It was necessary to introduce in our tool minor modifications regarding the automatic exit representation of process scrap, as required by the simulation tool (Figure 18).

Many other parameters (e.g. buffer capacity analysis) will be available during the final integration version between VSM and Simulation.

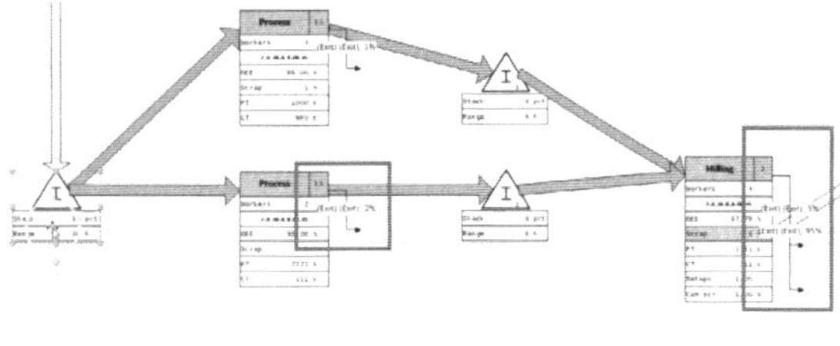

Figure 18. Simulation prototype: scrap-exit per process represented by new percentage arrows (inside red squares).

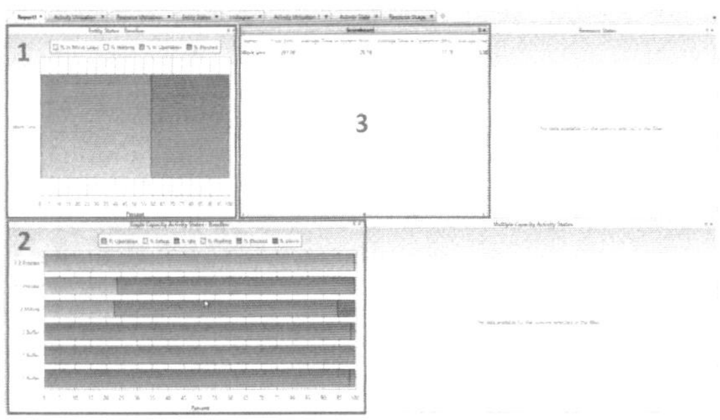

Figure 19. Example results (red squares) obtained from our VSM-Process Simulator integration. Histograms show expected capacities/through-puts of buffers and processes. In (1) we can observe the work unit results. In (2) the different processes and buffers percentages (operation, setup, idle, waiting, blocked, down). In (3) the total number of product produced and average times.

In this work we present preliminary results obtained in our simulation prototype tool. It is not yet a full implementation with Process Simulator (Figure 19).

The integration between VASCO VSM and Process Simulator has multiple benefits. Firstly, there is no need to manually exchange VSM parameter' values between a separated VSM tool and a simulation tool. These steps are now fully automatic and integrated in one tool. Secondly, users with different levels of expertise in the manufacturing site or on-training, can now experiment with both tools (VSM and simulation) in an integrated way, and try out different scenarios. Users can now test real changes very quickly and experiment while learning about VSM and lean manufacturing. Thirdly, multiple scenarios can be tested, leading to an optimal definition of the VSM future state.

VII. Future Work & Conclusion

With VASCO it is possible to use only one tool throughout the complete work-flow of value stream analysis. It dramatically simplifies the data acquisition at the shop-floor and offers a large tool set for analyzing and improving the production/logistic value chain.

Also the extraction of production metrics can be done at any stage of the work-flow creation, allowing the users to immediately have calculations feedback about the impact of their changes when designing future state maps. Lastly, by using our tool the users can capture information along the entire value stream analysis process, starting with visits to the production sites, where the users can capture images and videos of the working processes as side annotations, up to the creation of a new diagram based on previous processes work-flow states with comparisons between multiple state realities of the existent manufacturing processes, where the users can still access all the annotated information about old and current manufacturing processes. The integration of sustainability criteria within a VSM will significantly help manage and reduce the amount of waste, resulting from the manufacturing processes. This provides new metrics and KPI's that help to capture each company production reality in a digital way.

One minor extensibility limitation is that calculations are coded into the core system. While we are able to supply new functionality to the users using the plugin system, we plan to enable the definition of any type of calculation to the end user This definition should be flexible enough to handle all types of calculations, but simple enough without the need for complex programming tasks. This will be achieved by using a domain specific language (DSL) for calculations that contains important abstractions for the specification of VSM concepts.

Another important aspect is the integration of continuous improvement routines like CIP in VSM and VASCO, that will significantly help manage and reduce several types of waste (MUDA), resulting from the manufacturing processes. This will also provide new ways to improve metrics and KPIs of VSM

User experience is always a primal focus in all industrial applications. We are planning experiments where the users will perform fundamental tasks with our tool. With the help of an eye tracker equipment we will record data about the way users perform their tasks and about their individual preferences.

It is our intention to assess how our tool is used in reality by the final users and to study it's usability. We expect to be able to use this data to improve the overall experience of the users and as a way to boost the productivity of the users when working with our tool.

References

[1] R. Berndt, N. Silva, C. Caldera, U. Krispel, E. Eggeling, A. Sunk, T. Edtmayr, W. Sihn, and D. W. Fellner, "VASCO - Mastering the Shoals of Value Stream Mapping," CONTENT 2016, The Eighth International Conference on Creative Content Technologies, 2016, pp. 42–47.

[2] P. Kuhlang, T. Edtmayr, and W. Sihn, "Methodical approach to increase productivity and reduce lead time in assembly and production-logistic processes," CIRP Journal of Manufacturing Science and Technology, vol. 4, no. 1, 2011, pp. 24–32.

[3] C. E. Knoeppel, Installing efficiency methods. New York, The Engineering Magazine, 1915.

[4] A. J. D. Forno, F. A. Pereira, F. A. Forcellini, and L. M. Kipper, "Value Stream Mapping: a study about the problems and challenges found in the literature from the past 15 years about application of Lean tools," The International Journal of Advanced Manufacturing Technology, vol. 72, no. 5-8, Feb. 2014, pp. 779–790.

[5] T. Ohno, Toyota Production System: Beyond Large-Scale Production. Productivity Press, Mar. 1988.

[6] J. K. Liker, The Toyota Way: 14 Management Principles from the World's Greatest Manufacturer. Munich: McGraw-Hill, 2004.

[7] M. Rother and J. Shook, Learning to see: value stream mapping to add value and eliminate muda. Cambridge: Lean Enterprise Institute, 2003.

[8] K. Erlach, Wertstromdesign. Berlin, Heidelberg: Springer Berlin Heidelberg, 2010.

[9] T. Klevers, Wertstrom-Mapping und Wertstrom-Design. Verschwendung vermeiden - Wertschöpfung steigern, 1st ed. Landsberg am Lech: mi-Fachverlag, Jan. 2007.

[10] P. M., H. J., H. M., A. Heikkil, J. B., and L. S., Framework and Indicators for a Sustainable Manufacturing Mapping Methodology. Lyons, 2010.

[11] M. Mani, J. Madan, J. H. Lee, and K. W. Lyons, "Sustainability characterization for manufacturing processes," K. Gupta, Sustainability characterisation for manufacturing processes, Int. J. Prod. Res., Bd, vol. 52, 2014.

[12] C. Jasch, "environmental performance evaluation and indicators," J. Clean. Prod., Bd. 8, Nr, vol. 8, no. 1, Feb. 2014.

[13] G. R. Initiative, "Global reporting initiative," [Online] Available at: https://www.globalreporting.org/Pages/default.aspx (30, vol. 12., 2014.

[14] E. Commission, "Directive 2008/98/EC on waste (Waste Framework Directive)," [Online] Available at: http://ec.europa.eu/environment/waste/framework/ (06, vol. 11., 2014. [Online]. Available: http://ec.europa.eu/environment/waste/framework/

[15] M. Kurdve, S. Shahbazi, M. Wendin, and C. Bengtsson, "Waste flow mapping to improve sustainability of waste management: a case study approach," Wiktorsson, Waste flow mapping to improve sustainability of waste management: a case study approach, J. Clean. Prod., Bd, vol. 98, 2015.

[16] M. Despeisse and M. R. Oates, "Sustainable manufacturing tactics and cross-functional factory modeling," D. Ball, Sustainable manufacturing tactics and cross-functional factory modeling, J. Clean. Prod., Bd, vol. 42, 2013.

[17] W. Faulkner and F. Badurdeen, "Sustainable Value Stream Mapping (Sus-VSM): methodology to visualize and assess manufacturing sustainability performance," Badurdeen, Sustainable Value Stream Mapping (Sus-VSM): methodology to visualize and assess manufacturing sustainability performance, J. Clean. Prod., Bd, vol. 85, 2014.

[18] A. S. J. Torres and A. M. Gati, Environmental Value Stream Mapping (EVSM) as sustainability management tool. M, 2009.

[19] E. J. Loureno, A. J. Baptista, and J. P. Pereira, "Multi-Layer Stream Mapping as a Combined Approach for Industrial Processes Eco-efficiency Assessment," Re-engineering Manufacturing for Sustainability, vol. 98, 2013.

[20] H. Hopf, Methodik zur Fabriksystemmodellierung im Kontext von Energie- und Ressourceneffizienz. Wiesbaden: Springer Vieweg, 2016.

[21] H. Haag, Eine Methodik zur modellbasierten Planung und Bewertung der Energieeffizienz in der Produktion. Stuttgart: Fraunhofer Verlag, 2013.

[22] Y. Kishita, Y. Ohishi, M. Uwasu, M. Kuroda, and H. Takeda, Evaluating the life cycle CO2 emissions and costs of thermoelectric generators for passenger automobiles: a scenario analysis. Hara, Evaluating the life cycle CO2 emissions and costs of thermoelectric generators for passenger automobiles: a scenario analysis, J. Clean, 2016.

[23] R. Feiz, J. Ammenberg, L. Baas, M. Eklund, and A. Helgstrand, "Improving the CO2 performance of cement, part I: utilizing life-cycle assessment and key performance indicators to assess development within the cement industry," Marshall, Improving the CO2 performance of cement, part I: utilizing life-cycle assessment and key performance indicators to assess development within the cement industry, J. Clean. Prod., Bd, vol. 98, 2015.

[24] T. J. Roosen and D. J. Pons, Environmentally Lean Production. Pons, Environmentally Lean Production: J, 2013.

[25] E. K., "Energiewertstrom," Stuttgart, Springer Verlag, 2009.

[26] E. Mller and T. Stock, "A method to generate energy value-streams in production and logistics in respect of time- and energy-consumption," Schillig, A method to generate energy value-streams in production and logistics in respect of time- and energy-consumption, Prod. Eng., Bd, vol. 8, 2014.

[27] A. Sunk and T. Edtmayr, Ansatz zur Bewertung der Abfallentstehung im Wertstrom. Sihn, Ansatz zur Bewertung der Abfallentstehung im Wertstrom, in Industrial Engineering und Management, H, 2016.

[28] M. Stärz and T. Strigl, "Using value stream simulation to support lean manufacturing workshops," Proceedings of the Winter Simulation Conference, 2012.

[29] M. Shararah, K. El-Kilany, and A. El-Sayed, "Component based modeling and simulation of value stream mapping for lean production systems," Proc. of FAIM Conference, 2010, pp. 881–888.

[30] W. Xia and J. Sun, "Simulation guided value stream mapping and lean improvement: A case study of a tubular machining facility," Journal of Industrial Engineering and Management, vol. 6, no. 2, 2013, pp. 456–476.

[31] F. T. S. Chan, "Using simulation to predict system performance: a case study of an electrophoretic deposition plant," Integrated Manufacturing Systems, vol. 6, no. 5, 1995, pp. 27–38. [Online]. Available: http://dx.doi.org/10.1108/09576069510093451

[32] A. Prakash and M. Chen, "A simulation study of flexible manufacturing systems," Computers & Industrial Engineering, vol. 28, no. 1, 1995, pp. 191–199.

[33] P. S. Welgama and R. G. J. Mills, "Use of simulation in the design of a JIT system," International Journal of Operations & Production Management, vol. 15, no. 9, 1995, p. 245.

[34] K. Cho, I. Moon, and W. Yun, "System analysis of a multi-product, small-lot-sized production by simulation: A Korean motor factory case," Computers and Industrial Engineering, vol. 30, no. 3 SPEC. ISS., 1996, pp. 347–356.

[35] D. P. Bischak, "Performance of a manufacturing module with moving workers," IIE transactions, vol. 28, no. 9, 1996, pp. 723–734.

[36] Y. H. Park, J. E. Matson, and D. M. Miller, "Simulation and analysis of the mercedes-benz all activity vehicle (aav) production facility," in Simulation Conference Proceedings, 1998. Winter, vol. 2, Dec 1998, pp. 921–926 vol.2.

[37] J. S. Shang and P. R. Tadikamalla, "Multicriteria design and control of a cellular manufacturing system through simulation and optimization," International Journal of Production Research, vol. 36, no. 6, 1998, pp. 1515–1528.

[38] J. F. Persson, "The impact of different levels of detail in manufacturing systems simulation models," ROBOTICS AND COMPUTER-INTEGRATED MANUFACTURING, vol. 18, no. 3-4, 2002, pp. 319–325.

[39] R. Suri and R. R. Hildebrant, "Modelling flexible manufacturing systems using mean-value analysis," Journal of Manufacturing Systems, vol. 3, no. 1, 1984, pp. 27–38.

[40] Y.-H. Lian and H. Van Landeghem, "Analysing the effects of Lean manufacturing using a value stream mapping-based simulation generator," International Journal of Production Research, vol. 45, no. 13, 2007, pp. 3037–3058.

[41] M. Ravesh, "Confirming lean transformation outcomes by using simulation," Proceedings of the Asia Pacific Industrial Engineering & Management Systems Conference, 2012, pp. 1732–1736.

[42] Y. Monden, Toyota Production System: An Integrated Approach to Just-In-Time, 4th Edition. CRC Press, 2012.

[43] SIEMENS, "Tecnomatix plant simulation: Value stream mapping," SIEMENS, Tech. Rep., 2012.

[44] M. A. Nash and S. R. Poling, Mapping the Total Value Stream: A Comprehensive Guide for Production and Transactional Processes, 1st Edition. CRC Press, 2008.

[45] T. Rohrlack. A bentley solution paper for automobile manufacturers: The digital factory from concept to reality. [Online]. Available: http://ftp2.bentley.com/dist/collateral/whitepaper/DFWhitepaper.pdf [retrieved: January, 2016]

[46] M. Grieves. Digital twin: Manufacturing excellence through virtual factory replication. LLC. (2014)

[47] Microsoft Corporation, "Professional Flow Chart and Diagram Software — Microsoft Visio," www.visiotoolbox.com, 2016, [Online; retrieved: January, 2016].

[48] iGrafx, LLC, "iGrafx Flowcharter," http://www.igrafx.com/, 2016, [Online; retrieved: January, 2016].

[49] Cards PLM Solutions B.V., "Tecnomatix Plant Simulation," http://www.cardsplmsolutions.nl/en/plm-software/tecnomatix/plant-simulation-6, 2016, [Online; retrieved: January, 2016].

[50] SmartDraw, LLC, "SmartDraw Value Stream Mapping," http://www.smartdraw.com/value-stream-map/, 2016, [Online; retrieved: January, 2016].

[51] Lean Lexicon 5th Edition. Berlin, Heidelberg: Lean Enterprise Institute, Inc., 2010.

[52] R. J. Wilson, Introduction to Graph Theory. New York, NY, USA: John Wiley & Sons, Inc., 1986.

[53] J. P. Womack and D. T. Jones, Lean thinking: banish waste and create wealth in your corporation. Simon and Schuster, 2010.

[54] R. Barker, "The Design of Lean Manufacturing Systems Using Time-based Analysis," International Journal of Operations & Production Management, vol. 14, no. 11, 1994, pp. 86–96.

[55] W. G. Sullivan, T. N. McDonald, and E. M. Van Aken, "Equipment replacement decisions and lean manufacturing," in Robotics and Computer-Integrated Manufacturing, vol. 18, no. 3-4, 2002, pp. 255–265.

[56] M. Rother and J. Shook, "Learning to See: Value Stream Mapping to Create Value and Eliminate Muda," Lean Enterprise Institute Brookline, 2003, p. 102.

[57] P. Childerhouse and D. R. Towill, "Analysis of the factors affecting real-world value stream performance," International Journal of Production Research, vol. 40, no. 15, 2002, pp. 3499–3518.

[58] S. J. Pavnaskary, J. K. Gershensony, and A. B. Jambekarz, "Classification scheme for lean manufacturing tools," Int. J. Prod. Res, vol. 41, no. 13, 2003, pp. 3075–3090.

[59] T. Mcdonald, E. M. V. Aken, and A. F. Rentes, "Utilising Simulation to Enhance Value Stream Mapping : A Manufacturing Case Application Utilising Simulation to Enhance Value Stream Mapping : A Manufacturing Case Application," International Journal of Logistics Research and Applications, vol. 5, no. 2, 2002, pp. 213–232.

[60] P. Hines and N. Rich, "The seven value stream mapping tools," International Journal of Operations & Production Management, vol. 17, no. 1, 1997, pp. 46–64. [Online]. Available: http://www.emeraldinsight.com/doi/abs/10.1108/01443579710157989

[61] R. Detty and J. Yingling, "Quantifying benefits of conversion to lean manufacturing with discrete event simulation: A case study," International Journal of Production Research, vol. 38, no. 2, 2000, pp. 429–445.

[62] N. L. Coppini, L. C. Bekesas, E. A. Baptista, M. Vieira, and W. C. Lucato, "Value stream mapping simulation using ProModel software," in IEEE International Conference on Industrial Engineering and Engineering Management, 2011, pp. 575–579.

SpMV Runtime Improvements with Program Optimization Techniques on Different Abstraction Levels

Rudolf Berrendorf
Computer Science Department
Bonn-Rhein-Sieg University
Sankt Augustin, Germany
e-mail: rudolf.berrendorf@h-brs.de

Max Weierstall
Computer Science Department
Bonn-Rhein-Sieg University
Sankt Augustin, Germany
e-mail: max.weierstall@h-brs.de

Florian Mannuss
EXPEC Advanced Research Center
Saudi Arabian Oil Company
Dhahran, Saudi Arabia
e-mail: florian.mannuss@aramco.com

Abstract—**The multiplication of a sparse matrix with a dense vector is a performance critical computational kernel in many applications, especially in natural and engineering sciences. To speed up this operation, many optimization techniques have been developed in the past, mainly focusing on the data layout for the sparse matrix. Strongly related to the data layout is the program code for the multiplication. But even for a fixed data layout with an accommodated kernel, there are several alternatives for program optimizations. This paper discusses a spectrum of program optimization techniques on different abstraction layers for six different sparse matrix data format and kernels. At the one end of the spectrum, compiler options can be used that hide from the programmer all optimizations done by the compiler internally. On the other end of the spectrum, a multiplication kernel can be programmed that use highly sophisticated intrinsics on an assembler level that ask for a programmer with a deep understanding of processor architectures. These special instructions can be used to efficiently utilize hardware features in processors like vector units that have the potential to speed up sparse matrix computations. The paper compares the programming effort and required knowledge level for certain program optimizations in relation to the gained runtime improvements.**

Keywords–Sparse Matrix Vector multiply (SpMV); vector units; Single Instruction Multiple Data (SIMD); OpenMP; unrolling; intrinsics.

I. INTRODUCTION

This paper is an extended version of the conference paper [1]. Sparse matrices arise from the discretization of partial differential equations and are therefore widely used in many areas of natural and engineering sciences [2], especially in simulations. Examples of applications areas are mechanical deformation, fluid flow and electromagnetic wave propagation. An often used operation on such matrices is the multiplication of a sparse matrix with a dense vector (SpMV). This operation is often the most time consuming operation in iterative solvers (e.g., CG, GMRES [2]), which are among the most time consuming operations in many simulations. Therefore, much attention has been given to optimize this operation. As SpMV is a memory bandwidth bound operation and as sparse matrices can get very large, much attention has to be given to the management and access to the matrix data [3], [4]. One important point in an optimization discussion is the choice of an appropriate storage format for the sparse matrix. More than 50 storage formats have been published in the past, among them [5]–[10]. The choice of format depends mainly on the given matrix structure (e.g., diagonal, high / low matrix bandwidth, etc.) and the target architecture, e.g., multicore CPU, multiprocessor system, Graphics Processor Unit (GPU). For example, Compressed Sparse Row (CSR) [2] is a rather general storage format for sparse matrices that performs quite well on CPU-based systems and is used in many applications. Strongly related to a storage format is the way how the SpMV operation is actually implemented, i.e., how the data stored in the format is processed. This computational kernel is mainly a traversal over the data structures in a certain way given by the storage format. But even for a fixed storage format like CSR, there are quite different ways how to program the CSR kernel for the SpMV, with opportunities for program optimization on different abstraction levels. This paper deals with the spectrum of opportunities and discusses some alternatives, their programming effort, the required level of expertise and the achieved performance gain.

CPUs and memory systems are optimized for specific workloads in programs. Other than utilizing the memory hierarchy, instruction pipelining and vector units in processors can have a significant influence on a program's performance [11]. For instruction pipelining, large basic blocks are favorable in a program. All recent processors have also some implementation of vector registers and related vector instructions [12], [13] that can significantly speed up computations that exploit this architectural feature. Compilers can optimize code with large basic blocks with much room for optimizations and by vectorizing loops [14]–[18], as long as all data dependencies are respected [19]. A general problem with many SpMV implementations is, that the SpMV kernel is quite small, often only a single or a few lines of code surrounded by one or two loops, and therefore the basic block is rather small. Fig. 1 shows as an example a simplified and non-optimized basic version of a SpMV operation appropriate for the CSR format.

Some high level programming models, especially designed for parallel (and therefore resource intensive) computing, have

```
void SpMV_Basic(Vector &v, Vector &u) {
  // iterate over all rows of the matrix
  for(int i=0; i<nRows; i++) {
    // handle all non-zero elements in a row
    for(int j=rowStart[i]; j<rowStart[i+1]; j++) {
      u[i] += values[j] * v[columnIndex[j]];
    }
  }
}
```

Figure 1. Basic code version for the SpMV operation for the CSR data format (simplified).

some notations to give hints to a compiler concerning the vectorization of code. For example, OpenMP [20] as the de facto standard for shared memory parallelism has got in the recent version 4 some annotations to guide a compiler in using vector units in a processor. But vectorizing compilers and directives to give a compiler hints have a long history and existed already before OpenMP [21]. Such annotations can be used to speed up computational kernels like the SpMV to supply a compiler in a non-standardized way with additional semantic information, if necessary.

One way to optimize a program is to use certain optimization options of a compiler, e.g., a single meta option `-O3` enables already many individual compiler optimizations. Other than leaving all optimizations to a compiler, there are program optimization techniques known that allow to restructure a program to optimize certain operations (that a compiler may not detect). This restructuring of source code can be done by an expert programmer or by a sophisticated tool [16], [22], [23].

And, in a fourth way, if, for example, a compiler is not able to generate fast code because, for example, complex index expressions exist, a programmer may use vector intrinsics on a rather low abstraction level to program the hardware directly on a more or less assembler level [24]. For some high level language like C / C++, this can be accomplished by using compiler extensions called intrinsics that look like functions calls in the programming language and correspond to one or few assembler instructions.

In a summary, there are certain levels on which a time consuming operation may be speed up. In this paper, the question will be answered for the SpMV operation what the programming effort is that is needed for an optimization and what performance improvement one can get, if any.

The paper is structured as follows. Section II gives an overview on related work. After that, Section III discusses some program optimization techniques in more detail that are used for the investigations in this paper. Section IV describes the test environment for our evaluation. Section V shows and discusses performance results. The paper is summarized in Section VI.

II. Related Work

There are several dimensions of related work.

Compiler writers give hints in user guides [14], [25], [26] and technical notes [27] how to optimize programs and how to write programs in a way such that a compiler can apply optimizations. Further than that, there exist often optimization guides with a detailed description of hardware features that a programmer can use and should use to get performance [28]–[30].

In [31], Wende discusses the use of SIMD (Single Instruction Multiple Data [12]) functions, i.e., vector intrinsics, to improve the performance on Intel Xeon processors and Xeon Phi coprocessors [32] especially for branching and conditional functions calls. He found that for this special application scenario there are only rare situations with a performance improvement by using vector intrinsics. This was mostly the case if the ratio of arithmetic operations to control logic is low.

Dedicated to the SpMV operation, many papers were published describing performance related program optimizations of various types (e.g., register blocking) that were applied in [33]–[36].

There exist various reference implementation of storage formats for sparse matrices where a highly optimized SpMV code uses vector intrinsics. Among them are the formats / implementations CSR5 [6] / [37] and CSB [38] / [39]. As only an implementation exists that uses intrinsics, there is neither a comparism of programming effort in relation to runtime improvement nor an estimation of programming effort. But just to give the reader an estimate how complex such an optimization can be to optimize the SpMV operation for a certain platform, the reference implementation of yaSpMV [40] can be used. The (non-optimized) code for a CPU has 16 lines of C++ code while the highly optimized version for a GPU has approx. 700 lines of rather complex code.

Code optimization is often a multi-dimensional problem, as various architectural features likes register usage, vector units, caches, pipeling among others combined with implementation parameters of storage formats for sparse matrixes (e.g., slice sizes, blocking) influence each other. Different to a manual code optimization done by a programmer using to his knowledge a good combination of such parameters, auto tuning is a way to explore such a large parameter space automatically through extensive offline testing and eventually an additional and faster online testing finding experimentally a good combination of all parameters that fit to the given architecture and given sparse matrix. For the SpMV operation, there exist various implementations that use this technique, e.g. Poski [35], [41], CSX [42] and yaSpMV [40]. The programming effort to generate such an auto tuning framework is very high. The overhead to determine good hardware parameter values out of a large space of possible values can be high, but this is not important as such an exhaustive search has to be done once per system and offline. But also the online runtime overhead can be quite substantial that has to be done once when the non-zero structure of a sparse matrix is known. Often this is only profitable if many SpMV exectutions are done in the following with a fixed matrix structure and the tuning overhead can be compensated with an appropriate runtime improvement for the SpMV operation. Such research is more related to automate code optimization for certain hardware architectures rather than relating optimization techniques to each other.

Additional work was done to select good parameter values in a large parameter space for the SpMV using machine learning techniques. In [43] Lehnert et al. use linear regression, gradient boosting and k Nearest Neighbor techniques to decide at runtime, which matrix format / SpMV kernel should be used for a given matrix and, which thread mapping should be used, dependend on a few statistical parameters describing the matrix structure. In an offline training phase data is gathered in many program runs. While the runtime for these offline tests can be quite substantial (but need to be done only once), the overhead for the *online* decision is quite low (in the order of 10 % of a SpMV operation) for the linear regression / gradient boosting approach while the k Nearest Neighbor approach has a larger runtime overhead that can be in the order of tens to hundreds of SpMV operations. Additional work in using machine learning techniques to improve the SpMV execution was done by Sedaghati et al. [44], [45] using decision trees. Li [7] uses a probalistic approach for that.

III. Program Optimizations

Nowadays, processor and memory architectures are rather complex. Many architectural optimizations have been done in last decade's processor architectures that may improve the performance of programs significantly. Such architectural improvements include multi scalarity, out-of-order execution, pipelining, hardware prefetching and many others [12], [13]. For all enumerated hardware optimizations it is favorable to have large basic blocks (code without any branch).

A significant performance boost for many applications is the use of vector registers / units that are available in almost all recent processor architectures [28], [46], [47]. These vector architectures follow the well-known SIMD principle [48] that one instruction is applied to several operands at the same time. For a vector width of n data elements, this may result in a speedup of up to n. Recent processors eligible in High Performance Computing (HPC) have a vector register / unit width of up to 256 bits, corresponding to 4 double precision elements that are mostly used in scientific simulations, each 64 bits. Recent announcements show [49], [50] that the vector width will double in the near future with a nominal floating point performance increase of a factor of two. The SpMV operation is eligible to utilize vector units. How efficient such vector units can be utilized depends mainly on the chosen storage format and non-zero structure of the matrix. The CSR format is an example of such a format that can benefit from vector units. Vector units and instruction sets utilizing such units have evolved over time. Newer processor architectures of the Intel family have vector registers and units of size 256 bits and support the AVX (Advanced Vector Extensions) instruction set [51] (processor lines Sandy Bridge EP and Ivy Bridge EP) or the instruction set AVX2 (the most recent Haswell EP and Broadwell EP). Among other things, AVX2 enhances AVX with additional instructions for integer operations and fused multiply add that is of interest with SpMV operations.

The enlargement of basic blocks in a loop body and the use of vector registers are two techniques that can be used to speed up a SpMV operation. There are now certain levels of abstraction on which a programmer may influence these and other optimizations. In the following, in more detail opportunities are discussed a programmer may use to speed up the SpMV operations (and others).

A. *Compiler Flags*

A simple optimization strategy is to leave any optimization to a compiler. This is the strategy used most often by nearly all programmers. A programmer may specify on a rather coarse scope of one complete source file a general compiler optimization level (i.e., `-O0, -O1, -O2, -O3, -Ofast` as available with most compilers) leaving any detailed decisions and optimization strategies related to that optimization levels solely to the compiler according to the specified optimization level. Such flags are merely meta flags turning on/off a bunch of optimizations or a finer level specific to a compiler. All compiler understand the same meta flags, but the exact meaning of these flags (i.e., which specific optimizations are turned on) is open to a compiler.

An optimization level of `-O0` disables any optimization and is only useful for debugging and should not be used for productions runs. Specifying an optimization level of `-O1` enables basic optimizations that are often sufficient to generate efficient code for programs that have a not too complex program structure. A level of `-O2` instructs many compilers to enable more, advanced and more costly optimization techniques but that have no influence on the semantics of a program, i.e., no optimizations are applied that may change the meaning of a program as, for example, using a faster floating point arithmetic. A level of `-O3` often includes additional optimizations that allows the use of operations that may change (slightly) the meaning of a program; therefore this level has to be chosen with care. Even further is the optimization level `-fast` that enables optimizations that may change the semantic of a program using faster arithmetic or even speculative execution, generate processor specific code (that may not execute on processors of a previous generation), and do interprocedural and link-time optimizations that may take significantly more compile/link time as with other optimization levels.

Additionally, on a finer level special compiler options can be used to include certain optimization techniques or to utilize certain architectural features. An example for that is to allow the generation of code that utilizes the latest additions in the instruction set of a specific processor generation. For example, the compiler option `-march=haswell` of the GNU compiler g++ [25] allows the generation of advanced instructions only available on Intel Haswell processors. Alternatives would be for the previous generations of Intel processors `-march=ivybridge` or `-march=sandybridge`. The code may be no longer executable on processors of generations previous to the one specified. Other compilers have the same possibilities but with a different syntax of such an option. Without the specification of such an architectural option the compiler generates code with an instruction set that corresponds by default to a rather old processor family to allow the compiled program to run on many systems, even older ones.

The PGI compiler [26] offers an option to instruct the compiler to generate vector code utilizing vectors of a specific size. For example, the option `-tp=haswell -Mvect=simd:256` directs the compiler to generate code for Haswell processor, i.e., utilizing the Advanced Vector Extensions 2 (AVX2) instruction extensions, and to work with vectors of up to 256 bits.

Usually, compilers have flags to generate reports on various levels of details what they could optimize, what not, and in this case why. For example, the Intel compiler generates with the options `-qopt-report=5 -qopt-report-phase=vec` a very detailed report with information concerning the vectorization of code. An example for a report for a simple SpMV implementation with two nested loops is shown in Fig. 2. According

```
LOOP BEGIN at SparseMatrixCSR.cpp(568,3)
   remark #15542: loop was not vectorized: inner loop was already vectorized

   LOOP BEGIN at SparseMatrixCSR.cpp(573,5)
   <Peeled loop for vectorization>
   LOOP END

   LOOP BEGIN at SparseMatrixCSR.cpp(573,5)
      remark #15388: vectorization support: reference this has aligned access   [ SparseMatrixCSR.cpp(575,7) ]
      remark #15389: vectorization support: reference this has unaligned access   [ SparseMatrixCSR.cpp(575,7) ]
      remark #15381: vectorization support: unaligned access used inside loop body
      remark #15305: vectorization support: vector length 2
      remark #15399: vectorization support: unroll factor set to 4
      remark #15309: vectorization support: normalized vectorization overhead 0.533
      remark #15300: LOOP WAS VECTORIZED
      remark #15442: entire loop may be executed in remainder
      remark #15448: unmasked aligned unit stride loads: 1
      remark #15450: unmasked unaligned unit stride loads: 1
      remark #15458: masked indexed (or gather) loads: 1
      remark #15475: --- begin vector loop cost summary ---
      remark #15476: scalar loop cost: 14
      remark #15477: vector loop cost: 7.500
      remark #15478: estimated potential speedup: 1.810
      remark #15488: --- end vector loop cost summary ---
   LOOP END

   LOOP BEGIN at SparseMatrixCSR.cpp(573,5)
   <Remainder loop for vectorization>
   LOOP END
LOOP END
```

Figure 2. Example of a detailed Vectorization Report as given by the Intel Compiler.

to this report, the inner loop was vectorized and the outer loop not. The way how the information is presented makes clear that such a report should only be used by an experienced programmer who is aware of the meaning of the terms used in the report and the consequences that a programmer should take.

B. Loop Unrolling

The SpMV operation is an operation that often contributes to a large portion (e.g., 50 %) of the runtime of a simulation that itself can run for hours, days or even weeks. Therefore performance aware programmers are willing to spend time to speed up such computational kernels if a compiler would not be able to do so.

Unfortunately, the non-optimized SpMV has for many matrix storage formats a rather small loop body of the innermost loop (one or a few lines of code) as, for example, shown in Fig. 1. This means that all these hardware optimizations described in the introduction of this section cannot be utilized efficiently if a compiler cannot handle this by itself, i.e., enlarging the innermost loop body to a larger basic blocks.

A well-known technique called loop unrolling [16], [17] enlarges the basic block of a loop body. This can be favorable if the loop body is rather small (as for most formats with the SpMV operation) and therefore the instruction pipeline runs soon out of instructions. Additionally, with a larger basic block a compiler may have more opportunities to optimize, e.g., to keep reused index values in registers.

Loop unrolling can be realized manually by a programmer (which is often tedious and error-prone), by using appropriate directives / annotations in a code that instruct a compiler to

```
void SpMV_Unroll(Vector &v, Vector &u) {
  // iterate over all rows of the matrix
  for(int i=0; i<nRows; i++) {
    // handle all non-zero elements in a row
#pragma unroll(4)
    for(int j=rowStart[i]; j<rowStart[i+1]; j++) {
      u[i] += values[j] * v[columnIndex[j]];
    }
  }
}
```

Figure 3. Example of an explicitly unrolled loop using a directive.

unroll a loop by a certain factor, or internally by a compiler without a programmer's intervention. Explicit loop unrolling using directives will be used as one of the optimization techniques discussed later, which could be profitable if a compiler is not able to enlarge a basic block by himself. An example for an unrolled loop using such directives is given in Fig. 3.

C. Language Directives for Vectorization

Sometimes, a compiler may not be able to recognize that certain optimization techniques could be applied to a code sequence. For example, this may be the case because the compiler cannot know at compile time the value of certain variables, the alignment of variables or cannot exclude data dependencies because of complex index expressions. But, if a programmer can assure that, for example, a certain variable is always larger than 100 the compiler could optimize this program code. There exist program annotations for exactly these situations to tell a compiler some additional semantic

```
void SpMV_SIMD(Vector &v, Vector &u) {
  // iterate over all rows of the matrix
  for(int i=0; i<nRows; i++) {
    // handle all non-zero elements in a row
    double s = 0;
#pragma omp simd reduction(+:s)
    for(int j=rowStart[i]; j<rowStart[i+1]; j++) {
      u[i] += values[j] * v[columnIndex[j]];
    }
  u[i] = s;
  }
}
```

Figure 4. Example of the use of a OpenMP SIMD directive.

```
double haddSum( __m256d tmp) {
   // vecA := ( x2 , x1 )
   const __m128d vecA = _mm256_castpd256_pd128(tmp);
   // vecB := ( x4 , x3 )
   const __m128d vecB = _mm256_extractf128_pd(tmp,1);
   // vecC := ( x4+x3 , x2+x1 )
   const __m128d vecC = _mm_hadd_pd(vecA,vecB);
   // vecS := ( x4+x3+x2+x1 , x4+x3+x2+x1)
   const __m128d vecS = _mm_hadd_pd(vecC,vecC);
   // returns x4+x3+x2+x1 as double
   return mm_cvtsd_f64(vecS);
}
```

Figure 5. Example code for the use of compiler intrinsics.

information. Dependent on the programming language or compiler this may be done in different ways.

An example is OpenMP [20] where in the fourth version of this standard certain extensions were added that allow a programmer to specify (among parallelism, which is the main focus of OpenMP) that certain parts of a program should be vectorized by the compiler, including hints how to do that or assumptions that a compiler can rely on at that point of the program.

A small example for that is the piece of code shown in Fig. 4. Here, the pragma tells the compiler to vectorize the inner loop and to handle the variable `s` as a reduction variable with a special treatment (this is necessary due to the loop carried data dependence on `s`).

The `simd` directive requests an OpenMP compiler to vectorize that part of a program that is in the scope of this directive. For the `simd` directive there are additional clauses beside the shown **reduction** clause possible, mainly assuring certain program properties. Among them are:

- `aligned` specifies that the specified data objects are aligned to a certain byte boundary.
- `safelen` guaranties that n consecutive iterations can be executed in parallel / are independent.
- `linear` tells the compiler that the loop variable has a linear increase.

Similar compiler directives `simd` (vectorize code) and `ivdep` (ignore vector dependencies) outside of the OpenMP standard are known to several compilers with a similar meaning. We have seen no large differences in performance results for these alternatives.

As explained already before, a programmer can be guided for using such directives in an appropriate way by looking at a compiler report that tells whether a piece of code could be vectorized or not (see Fig. 2 for an example). If code could not be vectorized, the reason for that is also given. But this statement must be restricted as the output is often presented in a way that most times only an experienced programmer that understands how a compiler works internally can understand this information in all details.

To use the vector directives in our code, it was necessary with appropriate directives to assure the compiler that the vectors used were aligned (and which must be the case). Additionally, it was necessary (taken from the output of the vectorization report) to copy values of C++ member variables to block local variables. Otherwise, no vectorization of the code took place.

D. Vector Intrinsics

A compiler needs to generate special vector instructions to utilize the vector units in a processor. Sometimes a compiler may not be able to detect an appropriate situation because the data dependence analysis in the compiler cannot safely exclude any dependencies. Or a compiler generates sub-optimal code for that situation. In such situations, a programmer may himself "generate" vector instructions by using so called vector intrinsics.

Vector intrinsics [24] are available with some widely used compilers, e.g., GNU g++ [25], Intel compiler icpc [14]. With these intrinsics a programmer has more or less direct access to vector instructions of the underlying hardware. But please be aware that this functionality is on the level of assembler instructions where one has to manage vector registers and vector instructions directly. Also at most (or better exactly) 4 double values have to be handled in parallel for recent vector units. This means that the code has usually an additional loop that iterates in an appropriate way over blocks of 4 consecutive double values. Needless to say that such an intrinsic code looks quite different to an original code in a high-level programming language.

The example in Fig. 5 shows how to add 4 values using vector intrinsics (this is a small sub problem of a SpMV operation). `__m128d` and `__256d` are special vector types that must be used and `_mm...` are function calls that correspond to vector instructions. This small example makes it very clear that using intrinsic functionality makes a program hard to read / understand because hardware features are programmed embedded within a high level language like C or C++.

E. How to Choose the Right Program Optimization Strategy?

As already explained, performance aware programmers are willing to write rather complex code if an operation like the SpMV that contributes to a large portion of the runtime of a program can be speed up. The spectrum of optimization techniques shown above has consequences for programmers. The first approach (use a compiler switch) leaves any decision and optimization to the compiler. This is a possibility that is quite comfortable for a programmer and does not require any sophisticated skills from a programmer unless options are chosen that may influence the semantics of a program. If this approach produces the most efficient code, this should be the way to go.

The next possibility is to leave many things to the compiler but to give additional hints to the compiler using pragmas / directives at a finer granularity (e.g., with the scope of one loop). A compiler bases its decision concerning vectorizability (and many other optimizations) on data dependency information [19]. When a compiler cannot decide if a part of a program is optimizable / vectorizable, the opportunities that a hardware architecture gives to dispose cannot be utilized. But giving additional hints to a compiler, a programmer needs experience and expert knowledge how a compiler works and what information it may miss in certain parts of a program. If a programmer assures wrong properties (e.g., safe distance of iterations) a compiler may even generate wrong code. If a programmer uses such directives, the programming effort (additional lines of code) is rather small but the required level of expertise is high.

The last option is to allow a programmer direct access to the functionality a hardware provides. This allows to utilize the available functionality in an efficient way. Although this may look for a normal programmer scary, performance-aware programmers are used to such things. But this has severe consequences. One point is that the programming level is quite low and the resulting program is therefore hard to write and read (see the example in Fig.ř effig:Intrinsics). Additionally, programming is now getting platform specific, i.e., a program kernel developed and optimized for an Intel Haswell system is *not* executable on / not optimized for an older Ivy Bridge / Sandy Bridge system. This means that any company using such advanced features in their programs has to provide an expert that is aware of all architectural features of hardware generations in use and how to use them properly. Additionally, different code versions have to be maintained.

Comfortability to the programmer is one aspect of consideration. If this would be the only aspect it is clear that the approach that would be used is to leave everything to the compiler. Many simulations in natural science run for hours, days or even weeks. Often a large part of the runtime is executed in rather small parts of the program, computationally intense program kernels like the above mentioned SpMV operation. For such really performance critical parts of a program all possibilities are analyzed that may lead to a decrease in runtime, even on the intrinsic level. Therefore, the question at this point is whether and if yes how much can a program benefit from optimization techniques in the spectrum discussed above? Or is an optimizing compiler able to deliver the same (or even better) performance? And what is the programming effort in relation to a possible gain in performance?

The discussion and the following evaluation is done for a sequential program version. We have seen, that the results discussed in the following sections are transferable to parallel programming models like OpenMP [20] as well. But additional problems have to be handled as well, like processor locality, thread mapping and load balance. A comparism of using different parallel programming models for the SpMV on a GPU can be found, for example, in [52].

IV. Experimental Setup

To answer these questions raised above the rather small SpMV program kernel was used. As this kernel has only (dependent on the matrix storage format and the optimization technique) few lines of code, the influence of the optimization techniques could be clearly seen.

TABLE I. SYSTEMS USED.

system name	SB	HW
instruction set	AVX	AVX2
architecture	Sandy Bridge EP	Haswell EP
processor (Intel Xeon)	E5-2670	E5-2680 v3
cyle time in GHz (TurboBoost)	2,6	2,5

Sparse matrices can get in production runs very large (for example, up to 10^9 rows). They are stored is an appropriate storage format that takes advantage of the sparsity and the non-zero structure of a sparse matrix. A proper SpMV kernel code is needed that fits the storage format. We used our own implementation of the SpMV operation in C++ using storage formats of different code complexity. Beside the rather simple structured storage formats COO and CSR [2], we used also more sophisticated storage formats with more complex SpMV kernels, namely BRO-ELL [53], SELL-C-σ [5], VBL [54] and ESB [55]. An example for a basic implementation of the simple CSR format we use in our subsequent comparism was already shown in Fig. 1 (in a rather simplified and compact version).

We used four different versions for the optimizations for each format. As an information in parentheses the number of lines of code for the CSR format to realize that:

- *normal*: the unmodified version similar to the version in Fig. 1 (9 lines)
- *unroll*: the compiler was told with a directive to unroll a loop four times, similar to the version shown in Fig. 3 (12 lines)
- *simd*: the compiler was told with a directive to vectorize the code / to generate vector instructions similar to the version shown in Fig. 4 (16 lines)
- *intrinsics*: our own implementation using vector intrinsics (68 lines). The code often contains distinctions, which vector instruction set AVX or AVX2 should be used and different intrinsics must be used in some parts of the program, dependent on the instruction set.

To measure performance numbers we use systems of different generations of Intel processors (Intel Sandy Bridge and Haswell). Table I gives an overview of relevant system parameters and systems names. The older Sandy Bridge generation supports only the AVX instruction set, in newer Haswell systems additional features are available in the AVX2 instruction set.

As data sets we used sparse matrices with different properties that may influence the performance of a SpMV operation. For example, the distribution of non-zero values over the matrix and in a row may have an influence on the utilization of vector units and loop unrolling. In total, 111 matrices were used. The matrices are taken form the Florida Sparse Matrix collection [56] and from the Society of Petroleum Engineers (SPE) challenge [57].

We used two compilers in recent versions:

- *g++*: GNU g++ version 5.3.0 [25]
- *icpc*: Intel icpc version 16.0.2 [14]

TABLE II. PARAMETER SPACE IN THE EVALUATION.

parameter	count
processor families	2
compilers	2
matrix formats	6
test matrices	111
SpMV iterationsper run	100
optimization techniques	4

In the compiler options we always specified the target architecture to allow processor specific optimizations. In difference to the program version discussed in [1], additional code was added / changed to enable more compiler optimizations. These changes that were necessary to improve even further the runtime of the SpMV operation are partially discussed in the following chapter. It should be noted, that without these code optimizations that are now already incorporated into the basic version this version would perform substantially slower in certain cases.

To filter accidental effects that may happen on any system, each SpMV measurement was repeated 100 times and the median was taken as the measurement value.

Table II gives an overview over the parameter space in our evaluation. It follows that for our experimental setup $2 \times 2 \times 6 \times 111 \times 100 \times 4 = 106,560$ SpMV executions were executed.

V. Evaluation

Each optimization is discussed independently and afterwards an overall comparism is done. For generalizable statements, statistical result values over all 111 matrices are given. Additionally, absolute result values are given for one single matrix, the SPE matrix `spe5Ref_a`, which shows often a similar behavior compared to many other matrices. This matrix is used as a representative for more detailed analysis.

After a discussion of the influence of compiler options, the results for the three optimization techniques unrolling, vector directives and intrinsics are each presented in a common way:

1) a chart showing the percentage of test instances with a runtime improvement,
2) a chart with average speedup values over all matrices.

The charts differentiate between the matrix storage formats.

A. Influence of Compilers and Compiler Levels

Both compilers in use provide comfortable compiler switches to turn on certain global optimization levels: `-O0` up to `-O3`. The optimization level 0 should be used for debugging only and not for production runs. The Intel compiler provides further an additional level `-fast` and the GNU compiler the option `-Ofast` to additionally turn on processor specific optimizations as well as interprocedural optimizations and link time optimizations for the Intel compiler. But with this option the code eventually runs no longer on processors of previous generations while with the option `-O3` the code is still runnable on all recent systems. The default value for g++ is no optimization, the default for icpc is level 2.

To evaluate the influence of an optimization level, a basic SpMV kernel version was used for each sparse matrix storage format, but already modified in a way that a compiler can generate efficient code out of this (see remarks above). This

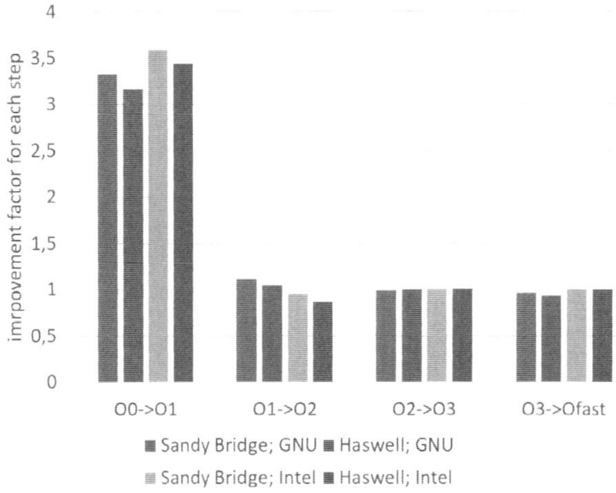

Figure 6. Average runtime improvements for each additional optimization level over all matrices.

leaves many opportunities for a compiler but places also challenges to the compiler to detect how the code looks like (in the sense of optimization potential) and what the best alternative for code generation is.

Table III shows as a representative example the detailed results for the matrix `spe5Ref_a` on the Sandy Bridge system and Haswell system. The results are transferable to the other matrices and are therefore general statements concerning our SpMV implementation. Both compiler show a significant performance increase going from `-O0` to `-O1`. Again the remark, that the level `-O0` should only used for debugging purposes and not used in any production version. The further transition to `-O2` shows some minor additional performance increase with the GNU compiler and s small perormance degradation with the Intel compiler. But all levels above `-O2` show no or only a small increase in performance. The compiler do already optimizations with `-O2` and even `-O1` that contribute to the best runtime performance. An older version of the Intel compiler that was used in [1] has shown a significant increase in performance on a Haswell system using the compiler option `-fast` that could be attributed to the fact that only with this option architectural features of the Haswell processor generation were utilized. The recent Intel compiler version utilizes the AVX2 units already with lower optimization levels. There are also a few cases where a lower optimization level (sometimes even the level `-O1`) produces a better result than a higher level. And in some of these cases, the difference was quite significant. This can be seen, for example, in Table III with the SELL-C-σ format. Here, compilers do aggressive optimizations that tend to be counter-productive in this cases.

While Table III shows absolute performance numbers for one example matrix and three matrix formats, Fig. 6 shows summarized statistics over all matrices and all 6 matrix formats. In this table, the average improvement factor over all matrices is shown going from one optimization level to the next. A factor higher than 1 means an average increase in performance, a factor lower than 1 means a performance drop. As already seen and discussed with the single example matrix, the transition to level `-O1` shows a huge increase

TABLE III. RUNTIMES IN MILLISECONDS FOR VARIOUS COMPILER OPTIMIZATION LEVELS FOR THE EXAMPLE MATRIX `spe5Ref_a` AND SELECTED FORMATS.

	Intel Sandy Bridge (SB)						Intel Haswell (HW)					
	g++			icpc			g++			icpc		
	CSR	BRO-ELL	SELL-C-σ	CSR	BRO-ELL	SELL-C-σ	CSR	BRO-ELL	SELL-C-σ	CSR	BRO-ELL	SELL-C-σ
-O0	213	737	372	223	769	388	190	603	337	193	624	357
-O1	63	171	121	58	208	118	55	115	107	53	132	105
-O2	57	156	118	53	190	126	61	106	106	53	126	139
-O3	57	156	118	52	191	126	60	105	105	52	126	139
-(O)fast	57	156	118	53	192	125	77	106	129	53	126	138

in performance, as expected. But interestingly, with these compiler versions there is in average no additional increase in performance for higher levels of optimization and even sometimes a small degradation (for example, in the last column of Table III again with the SELL-C-σ format).

Whether a compiler can detect in the source code opportunities for optimizations or fail on this can have a significant influence on the runtime of a program, especially when small parts of the source code (few lines of code of a SpMV kernel) contribute to a major part of the program's runtime. This can be seen with the results for the CSR format as given in Table III. In a previous paper [1] large differences in runtime were reported for the Intel compiler with the CSR SpMV kernel switching from optimization level `-O3` to `-fast`. In a deeper analysis of the compiler generated code it was later found that a rather simple overloaded and inlined array access operator `[]` in C++ that was defined to abstract from the concrete realization of the storage format in the code contributed to a significant drop of nearly 50 % in performance for all optimization levels other than `-fast` with the Intel compiler compared to the GNU compiler. The Intel compiler could not handle this piece of code (which is from a programmer's point of view rather simple) with all optimization levels other than `-fast` while the GNU compiler could handle this even for lower optimization levels. After replacing the overloaded operator `[]` with a pointer copy and a normal C++ `[]` operator also the Intel compiler could optimize this, which can be seen in the CSR results given in Table III. Fig. 7 shows the relevant modified code. It should be pointed out that this "optimization" that was necessary because otherwise a compiler could not optimize a code, breaks software abstraction that is very import in software development. With this solution the concrete storage format of a vector is no longer hidden by a class.

In all following discussions, an optimized code (see, for example, the discussion with overloaded array access operator) together with a optimization level `-O3` is used as the default option and the effect of the other optimization techniques are related to these results.

```
void SparseMatrixCSR::SpMV2(const Vector &v, Vector &u) {

  // Faster access to vector data, but loosing abstraction.
  // u[i] and v[i] with an overloaded [] operator
  // prevented compiler optimizations with certain compilers
  // Now copy the values-pointer of the vector class
  // to a local pointer variable.
  const double *const vValues = v.getValues();
  double *const uValues = u.getValues();

  // iterate over all rows of the matrix
  for(int i=0; i<nRows; i++) {
    // handle all non-zero elements in a row
    for(index_t j=rowStart[i]; j<rowStart[i+1]; j++) {
      uValues[i] += values[j] * vValues[columnIndex[j]];
    }
  }
}
```

Figure 7. Loosing software abstraction to handle compiler's disability to optimize code (simplified version shown).

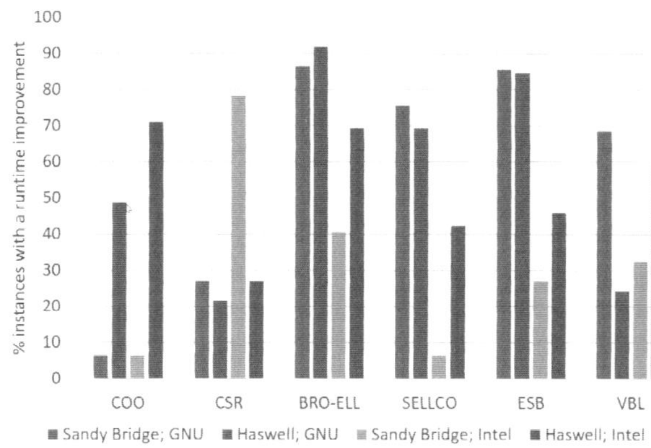

Figure 8. Percentage of Instances that showed a runtime improvement with loop unrooling.

B. Unrolling Loops

Different to leaving everything to the compiler with a single compiler option, loop unrolling is used here as the first explicit optimization. It is used to enlarge basic blocks as most SpMV kernels are rather small. This enables a compiler at the basic block level (i.e., without the need to understand complex loop structures) to optimize register usage, a better utilization of functional units and a reduction of the loop overhead for small loop bodies, as is in our case for all matrix formats. As already discussed, this can be used rather comfortable with directives specifying before a loop that this loop should be unrolled, specifying optionally an unroll factor as a parameter. We found out empirically that an unroll factor of 4 performed best.

Fig. 8 shows the percentage of instances that showed a runtime improvement, differentiated by matrix format. Figure 9 shows the average speedup that can be achieved using this technique. As can be seen in the figures, the influence of unrolling on the performance is minimal, all speedups are near to 1. This can be seen also looking at individual speedup results of the formats, which are not shown here. The conclusion is here that both compilers use already techniques that are able to enhance basic blocks for the reasons stated above, e.g. doing

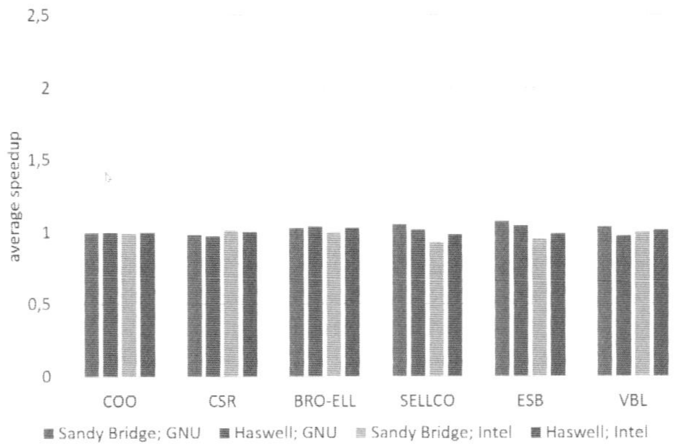

Figure 9. Average speedup with loop unrolling.

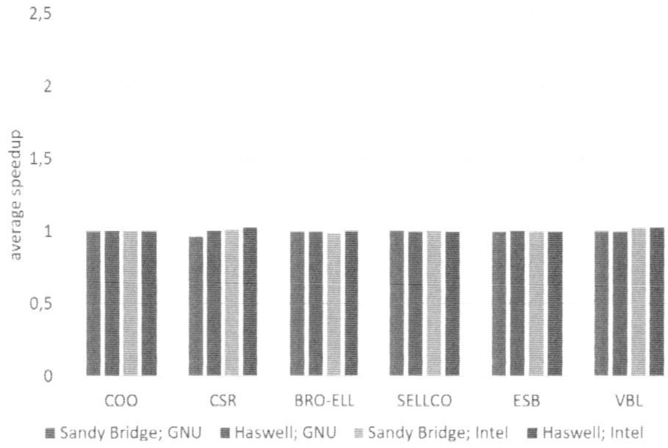

Figure 11. Average speedup with vector directives.

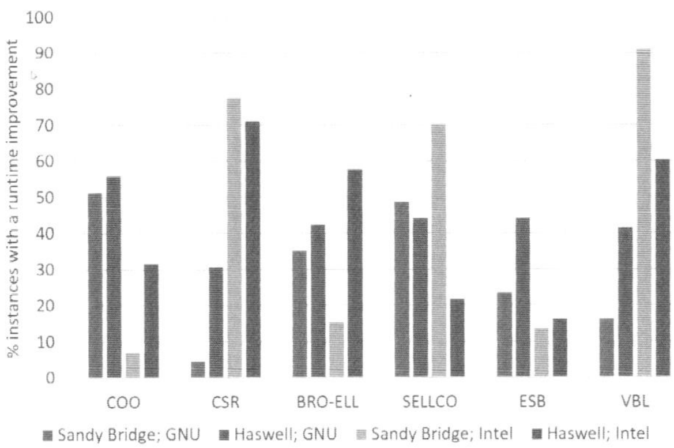

Figure 10. Percentage of Instances that showed a runtime improvement using vector directives.

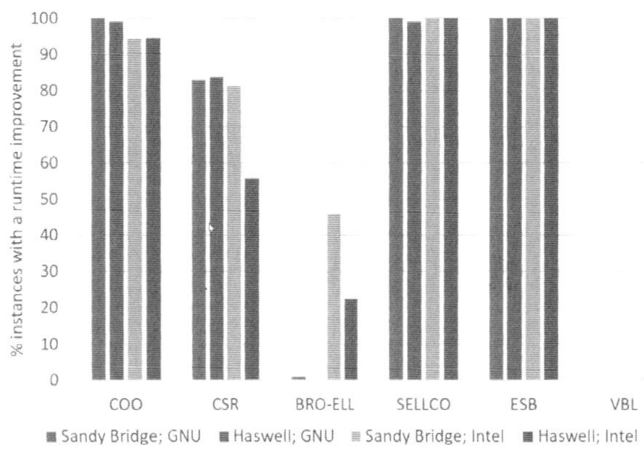

Figure 12. Percentage of Instances that showed a runtime improvement using intrinsics.

unrolling by their own.

C. Using Vector Directives

Vector directives are used to give a compiler additional information and hints. The question was here whether compilers are able to detect themselves opportunities for vectorization by just analyzing the source code or if additional hints are necessary.

As already stated in [1], just specifying a single vector directive is not sufficient to get good performance results. Sometimes this was even counterproductive as a compiler was asked to vectorize but without being able to understand how to do that efficiently. Analyzing all performance information that we gathered we found that several additional information was necessary for the compiler beside the vector directive. Quite important for the Intel compiler was to additionally tell the compiler through additional directives that vector data is aligned at certain byte boundaries (and which has to be assured through appropriate data allocations).

The results were obtained in using OpenMP `simd` directives to explicitly request a vectorization. We found no significant performance difference in using compiler specific vector directives that some compilers know.

Fig. 10 shows the percentage of problem instances that got a performance improvement. Fig. 11 shows the average speedup that was gained in using this directives. Similar to the results for unrolling, there is no real performance gain in using this technique. The compilers are already able to utilize vector units with the modified code, the normal optimization options and by specifying with an additional compiler option for what target architecture code should be generated.

D. Using Intrinsics

While the previous two code optimization techniques are rather high level techniques with few lines of additional code / directives, applying the intrinsic technique is totally different. Here a new program kernel has to be programmed on a rather low abstraction level and explicitly taking a vector length of 4 into account that the hardware units provide. The programming effort is much higher and a deep knowledge of the target processor architecture is essential. For the VBL format, we have not realized a solution with intrinsics and therefore no numbers are shown for that format.

Fig. 12 shows the percentage of problem instances that got a performance improvement. Fig. 13 shows the average speedup that was gained in using this directives, differentiated

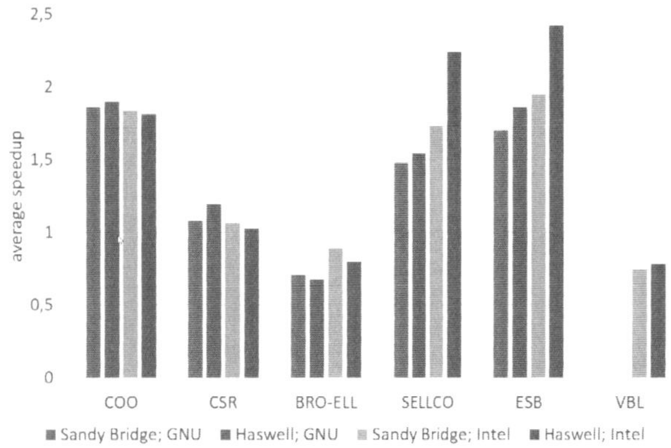

Figure 13. Average speedup with intrinsics.

between the formats. Here, the results are rather different compared to the previous two techniques discussed earlier that have shown no significant performance differences to the compiler's own optimization.

There are three classes of results. In the first class – the formats COO, SELL-C-σ and ESB – a huge performance gain exists when using intrinsics. This gain is up to a factor of nearly 2.5 compared to the pure compiler solution with a high optimization level. Here, an intrinsic programmer was able to find a (much) better performing solution than the compiler. The ESB SpMV intrinsic kernel is rather complex using internally an unrolling technique and utilizing special instructions from the advanced AVX2 instruction set. Also the COO intrinsic kernel is rather complex and uses special AVX2 instructions. Different to that, the SELL-C-σ intrinsic kernel is relative simple using intrinsics only in the innermost loop.

The second class is the format CSR showing no large differences in runtime for the intrinsic solution compared to the compiler generated code.

And in the third class are the formats BRO-ELL and VBL where a performance degradation can be seen for all or nearly all problem instances. Surprisingly (or not?) these are the intrinsic kernels that have the highest complexity / most lines of code (see later Table V for that). Here it may be that the programmer may just be overcharged by the complexity. A compiler applies a strong formal background on code generation and bases its decision on cost estimations. It seems that for very complex code this has advantages.

The performance behavior discussed is mostly invariant of the compiler used (with exceptions for the SELL-C-σ and ESB format).

E. *Evaluation Summary*

This section summarizes the performance results and relates that to the programming effort that was necessary to reach that. Table V shows the programming effort stated in the number of source lines that was necessary to realize the techniques for the different formats. For the unrolling technique one or a few lines of rather simple additional code was sufficient and no further specific knowledge was required from the programmer. For the vector directive solution, specifying the vector directive alone was not sufficient to get reasonable performance. Additionally, certain additional information was necessary to specify (alignment of vector data). But again, only a few additional lines of high-level code were sufficient and this additional code was not very complex. The programming effort for an intrinsic solution is on the other side very high, very complex and the solution looks rather different to all other solutions for that sparse matrix format. For example, the solution for the VBL format (where many complex code lines were produced but no performance gain was achieved with the intrinsics) has many highly adapted small kernels for a selection of different vertical, horizontal or rectangular block sizes, each programmed in a very different way.

Table IV summarizes the absolute run times for the various compiler levels and manual optimizations on the example matrix, differentiated between three of the six formats used.

The first technique used was compiler flags and the additional information on the target architecture to enable processor specific optimizations in the compiler. The additional effort and needed knowledge for using compiler flags is minimal and no code change is necessary. The results show that already with a small optimization level efficient code is generated for the SpMV operation. Using higher optimization levels did not show significant improvements and sometimes even a small performance degradation. Using just a compiler switch is the preferred method almost always to go for most programmers, unless a really compute intensive kernel should be optimized.

The explicit unrolling technique did not show any major change in runtime, neither in a positive nor in a negative direction. Here, the compilers did already a good job in the field if the programmer just specifies a coarse grain optimization level. The programming effort and necessary expertise to use loop unrolling is quite low.

Using the `simd` compiler directive to ask explicitly for vectorization is easy to use but requires a deeper knowledge, e.g., on data dependencies to avoid wrong code generation as the compiler relies on the given information. As explained above, such a directive alone was not sufficient and additional directives on data alignment must be given. Without the additional alignment information, vectorization was in certain cases prohibited or done in a wrong way, which could result even in a severe performance degradation. The performance results gained with this approach (including directives and alignment specification) for our SpMV kernels are very similar to just using a compiler optimization option. Therefore, the additional programming effort is not really necessary. But for other program codes this may be advantageous where a compiler could *not* handle the code itself without additional information.

To use intrinsics a deep understanding of a processor architecture and the available instruction set is necessary. Additionally, the algorithm may be quite different to the normal version when expressing it on an intrinsic level. The program code is totally different to the original code and quite hard to read and write, at least for a programmer who is not used to intrinsics. Additionally, for different processor families and even processors versions different code must be developed, which makes program maintenance hard and costly. But for half of the formats very high performance improvements could be reached with this approach. The SpMV kernels that did not perform as well as the pure compiler generated code were the

TABLE IV. RUNTIMES IN MILLISECONDS FOR VARIOUS COMPILER OPTIMIZATION LEVELS AND OPTIMIZATION TECHNIQUES FOR THE EXAMPLE MATRIX `spe5Ref_a` AND SELECTED FORMATS.

	Intel Sandy Bridge (SB)						Intel Haswell (HW)					
	g++			icpc			g++			icpc		
	CSR	BRO-ELL	SELL-C-σ	CSR	BRO-ELL	SELL-C-σ	CSR	BRO-ELL	SELL-C-σ	CSR	BRO-ELL	SELL-C-σ
-O0	213	737	372	223	769	388	190	603	337	193	624	357
-O1	63	171	121	58	208	118	55	115	107	53	132	105
-O2	57	156	118	53	190	126	61	106	106	53	126	139
-O3	57	156	118	52	191	126	60	105	105	52	126	139
-(O)fast	57	156	118	53	192	125	77	106	129	53	126	138
unrolling	56	152	66	52	187	82	63	101	77	52	118	127
directives	59	156	74	184	188	81	61	106	83	178	126	128
intrinsics	50	190	49	50	171	48	51	134	51	52	129	51

TABLE V. NUMBER OF CODE LINES TO REALIZE THE SPMV (INCLUDING CODE FOR A DIRECT VECTOR ACCESS AS EXPLAINED ABOVE).

	COO	CSR	BRO-ELL	SELL-C-σ	VBL	ESB
normal	5	9	45	16	23	37
unrolling	6	12	46	17	25	39
directives	12	16	47	17	31	42
intrinsics	76	68	303	72	738	170

most complex ones where the assumption is that the program complexity was too high for a human programmer (at least in a fixed amount of available time).

VI. Conclusions

SpMV is a time critical operation in many applications. Optimizing this operation is a challenge. One way to optimize the execution of a SpMV operation is to use the right storage format, mostly dependent on the non-zero structure of the matrix and the target architecture. But additionally to the format, there are various opportunities to tackle that problem on a program optimization level, then partially dependent on the compiler used.

In this paper, several optimization approaches were described and compared to each other concerning programming effort / required expert knowledge and achieved performance. This was done using implementations of six different storage formats for sparse matrix and related SpMV implementations.

It was shown that using a simple compiler switch turning on a certain optimization level in a compiler results in a good performance for the SpMV operation with minimal/no effort. Already the first level of optimization was sufficient to reach that performance. This could only be achieved *after* some code changes were done that prevented otherwise optimizations. An example was the overloaded array access operator where the performance of the Intel compiler generated code dropped to one halve, even with a high optimization level. Replacing the use of that operator with a direct access to an array structure inside a class increased the performance to a normal level in compensation to the fact that an important software abstraction was lost.

The explicit optimization techniques loop unrolling (with alignment specification) and vector directives have shown no performance differences to a pure compiler optimization. The programming effort for these techniques is rather low, the required expertise is very low for loop unrolling and higher when using vector directives as for a wrong specification a compiler may generate code that produces wrong results.

The fourth approach was using intrinsics on an assembler level. The performance results were ambiguous. Three of the six SpMV implementations got a huge performance boost of up to a factor of 2.5 in average compared to the pure compiler solution with a high optimization level. For one format there was no significant difference in performace. And for the two remaining formats there was a performance degradation. The latter formats have the most complex intrinsic realizations. The programming effort and required expertise level for intrinsics is by far the highest. The number of code lines necessary for an intrinsic realization was often near a factor of 10 compared to a native implementation, sometimes even more. And an intrinsic implementation needs to be enhanced or even completely rewritten for a new processor architecture.

In summary, most programmers should rely on the optimizations done by a compiler. Only for rare cases of very compute intensive program kernels like SpMV there should be thought about an intrinsic solution. As long as the complexity of this code does not get too high, a human programmer in a fixed amount of available development time can speed up such computations substantially, which can justify the effort.

Acknowledgements

Jan Ecker, Javed Razzaq and Simon Scholl at Bonn-Rhein-Sieg University helped us in many discussions. We would also like to thank the CMT team at Saudi Aramco EXPEC ARC for their support and input. Especially we want to thank Ali H. Dogru for making this research project possible.

References

[1] R. Berrendorf, M. Weierstall, and F. Mannuss, "Program optimization strategies to improve the performance of SpMV-operations," in Proc. 8th Intl. Conference on Future Computational Technologies and Applications (FUTURE COMPUTING 2016), 2016, pp. 34–40.

[2] Y. Saad, Iterative Methods for Sparse Linear Systems, 2nd ed. SIAM, 2003.

[3] A. Buluc, S. Williams, L. Oliker, and J. Demmel, "Reduced-bandwidth multithreaded algorithms for sparse matrix-vector multiplication," in Proc. Intl. Parallel and Distributed Processing Symposium (IPDPS'2011). IEEE, 2011, pp. 721–733.

[4] S. Williams, L. Oliker, R. Vuduc, J. Shalf, K. Yelick, and J. Demmel, "Optimization of sparse matrix-vector multiplication on emerging multicore platforms," in Proc. ACM/IEEE Supercomputing 2007 (SC'07). IEEE, 2007, pp. 1–12.

[5] M. Kreutzer, G. Hager, G. Wellein, H. Fehske, and A. R. Bishop, "A unified sparse matrix data format for efficient general sparse matrix-vector multiply on modern processors with wide SIMD units," SIAM Journal on Scientific Computing, vol. 26, no. 5, 2014, pp. C401–423.

[6] W. Liu and B. Vinter, "CSR5: An efficient storage format for cross-platform sparse matrix-vector multiplication," in Proc. 29th Intl. Conference on Supercomputing (ICS'15). ACM, 2015, pp. 339–350.

[7] K. Li, W. Yang, and K. Li, "Performance analysis and optimization for SpMV on GPU using probalistic modeling," IEEE Trans. Parallel and Distributed Systems, vol. 26, no. 1, Jan. 2015, pp. 196–205.

[8] W. Liu and B. Vinter, "Speculative segmented sum for sparse matrix-vector multiplication on heterogeneous processors," Parallel Computing, vol. 49, 2015, pp. 179–193.

[9] J. Wong, E. Kuhl, and E. Darve, "A new sparse matrix vector multiplication GPU algorithm designed for finite element problems," arXiv.org, vol. abs/1501.00324, 2015, pp. 1–35.

[10] J. Razzaq, R. Berrendorf, S. Hack, M. Weierstall, and F. Mannuss, "Fixed and variable sized block techniques for sparse matrix vector multiplication with general matrix structures," in Proc. Tenth Intl. Conference on Advanced Engineering Computing and Applications in Sciences (ADVCOMP 2016), 2016, to appear.

[11] J. Razzaq, R. Berrendorf, J. P. Ecker, S. E. Scholl, and F. Mannuss, "Performance characterization of current CPUs and accelerators using micro-benchmarks," Intl. Journal on Advances in Systems and Measurements, vol. 9, no. 1&2, 2016, pp. 77–90.

[12] J. L. Hennessy and D. A. Patterson, Computer Architecture: A Quantitative Approach, 5th ed. Morgan Kaufmann Publishers, Inc., 2012.

[13] D. A. Patterson and J. L. Hennessy, Computer Organization and Design – The Hardware Software Interface, 5th ed. Morgan Kaufmann, 2014.

[14] Intel C++ Compiler 16.0 User and Reference Guide, https://software.intel.com/en-us/intel-cplusplus-compiler-16.0-user-and-reference-guide ed., Intel Corporation, 2016, retrieved: August 2016.

[15] L. Project, The LLVM Compiler Infrastructure, http://llvm.org/, 2014, retrieved: August 2016.

[16] R. Allen and K. Kennedy, Optimizing Compilers for Modern Architectures. San Francisco: Morgan Kaufmann, 2002.

[17] K. D. Cooper and L. Torczon, Engineering a Compiler, 2nd ed. Burlington, MA: Morgan Kaufmann, 2012.

[18] S. S. Muchnick, Advanced Compiler Design and Implementation. San Francisco: Morgan Kaufmann, 1997.

[19] U. Banerjee, "An introduction to a formal theory of dependence analysis," The Journal of Supercomputing, vol. 2, 1988, pp. 133–149.

[20] OpenMP Application Program Interface, 4th ed., OpenMP Architecture Review Board, http://www.openmp.org/, Jul. 2015, retrieved: August 2016.

[21] Cray Research Inc., CF90 Commands and Directives Reference Manual, 1995, sR-3901 2.0.

[22] R. Eigenmann, J. Hoeflinger, G. Jaxon, Z. Li, and D. Padua, "Restructuring Fortran programs for Cedar," Concurrency - Practice and Experience, vol. 5, no. 7, Oct. 1993, pp. 553–573.

[23] K. A. Tomko and S. G. Abraham, "Data and program restructuring of irregular applications for cache-coherent multiprocessors," in Proc. ACM Int'l Conf. Supercomputing, Jul. 1994, pp. 214–225.

[24] Intel Intrinsics Guide, https://software.intel.com/sites/landingpage/IntrinsicsGuide/ ed., Intel, 2015, retrieved: August 2016.

[25] GCC, the GNU Compiler Collection, Free Software Foundation, retrieved: August 2016. [Online]. Available: https://gcc.gnu.org/

[26] PGI Compilers and Tools, https://www.pgroup.com/, retrieved: August 2016.

[27] M. Corden, Requirements for Vectorizable Loops, Intel, https://software.intel.com/en-us/articles/requirements-for-vectorizable-loops/, 2012, retrieved: August 2016.

[28] Intel® 64 and IA-32 Architectures Optimization Reference Manual, Intel, http://www.intel.com/content/dam/www/public/us/en/documents/manuals/64-ia-32-architectures-optimization-manual.pdf, Jun. 2016, retrieved: August 2016.

[29] Intel® 64 and IA-32 Architectures Software Developer's Manual. Volume 1: Basic Architecture, Intel, http://www.intel.com/content/dam/www/public/us/en/documents/manuals/64-ia-32-architectures-software-developer-manual-325462.pdf, Jun. 2016, retrieved: August 2016.

[30] Software Optimization Guide for AMD Family 15h Processors, AMD, http://support.amd.com/TechDocs/47414_15h_sw_opt_guide.pdf, 2042, retrieved: July 2016.

[31] F. Wende, "SIMD enabled functions on Intel Xeon Phi CPU and Intel Xeon Phi coprocessor," Konrad-Zuse Zentrum fr Informationstechnik Berlin, Tech. Rep. ZIB-Report 15-17, Feb. 2015.

[32] G. Chrysos, Intel® Xeon Phi™ Coprocessor – The Architecture, https://software.intel.com/en-us/articles/intel-xeon-phi-coprocessor-codename-knights-corner, 2012, retrieved: November 2014.

[33] G. Goumas, K. Kourtis, N. Anastopoulos, V. Karakasis, and N. Koziris, "Understanding the performance of sparse matrix-vector multiplication " in Proc. 16th Euromicro Intl. Conference on Parallel, Distributed and Network-based Processing (PDP'08), 2008, pp. 283–292.

[34] E. Saule, K. Kaya, and U. V. Catalyrek, "Performance evaluation of sparse matrix multiplication kernels on Intel Xeon Phi," in Proc. Intl. Conference on Parallel Processing and Applied Mathematics (PPAM 2013), 2013, pp. 559–570.

[35] R. W. Vuduc, "Automatic performance tuning of sparse matrix kernels," Ph.D. dissertation, University of California, Berkeley, 2003.

[36] R. Nishtala, R. W. Vuduc, J. W. Demmel, and K. A. Yelick, "Performance modeling and analysis of cache blocking in sparse matrix vector multiply," University of California at Berkeley, EECS Department, Tech. Rep. UCB/CSD-04-1335, 2004.

[37] CSR5 reference implementation, https://github.com/bhSPARSE/Benchmark_SpMV_using_CSR5.

[38] A. Buluc, J. T. Fineman, M. Frigo, J. R. Gilbert, and C. E. Leiserson, "Parallel sparse matrix-vector and matrix-transpose-vector multiplication using compressed sparse blocks," in Proc. 21th Annual Symp. on Parallelism in Algorithms and Architectures (SPAA'09), 2009, pp. 233–244.

[39] CSB reference implementation, http://gauss.cs.ucsb.edu/~aydin/csb/html/index.html.

[40] S. Yan, C. Li, Y. Zhang, and H. Zhou, "yaSpMV: yet another SpMV framework on GPUs," in Proc. 19th ACM SIGPLAN Symposium on Principles and Practice of Parallel Programming (PPoPP'14), 2014, pp. 107–118.

[41] pOSKI: parallel Optimized Sparse Kernel Interface, http://bebop.cs.berkeley.edu/poski/, retrieved: August 2016.

[42] V. Karakasis, T. Gkountouvas, K. Kourtis, G. Goumas, and N. Koziris, "An extended compression format for the optimization of sparse matrix-vector multiplication," IEEE Transactions on Parallel and Distributed Systems, vol. 24, no. 10, Oct. 2013, pp. 1930–1940.

[43] C. Lehnert, R. Berrendorf, J. P. Ecker, and F. Mannuss, "Performance prediction and ranking of spmv kernels on gpu architectures," in Proc. 22th Intl. European Conference on Parallel and Distributed Computing (Euro-Par 2016), 2016, p. to appear.

[44] N. Sedaghati, A. Ashari, L.-N. Pouchet, S. Parthasarathy, and P. Sadayappan, "Characterizing dataset dependence for sparse matrix-vector multiplication on GPUs," in Proc. 2nd Workshop on Parallel Programming for Analytics Applications (PPAA'15). ACM, 2015, pp. 17–24.

[45] N. Sedaghati, T. Mu, L.-N. Pouchet, , S. Parthasarathy, and P. Sadayappan, "Automatic selection of sparse matrix representation on GPUs," in Proc. 25th Intl. Conference on Supercomputing (ICS 2015). ACM, 2015.

[46] AMD64 Architecture Programmers Manual. Advanced Micro Devices, 2013, vol. 3: General-Purpose and System Instructions.

[47] ARM, ARM v8 Architecture Reference Manual, 2010.

[48] M. Flynn, "Some computer organizations and their effectiveness," IEEE Trans. Computers, vol. C-21, 1972, pp. 948–960.

[49] Skylake (microarchitecture), Wikipedia, http://en.wikipedia.org/wiki/Skylake_(microarchitecture), retrieved: August 2016.

[50] J. Jeffers, J. Reinders, and A. Sodani, Intel Xeon Phi Processor High Performance Programming, Knights Landing Edition. Cambridge: Morgan Kaufman Publishers, Inc., 2016.

[51] ISA Extensions, Intel, https://software.intel.com/en-us/isa-extensions/intel-avx, retrieved: May 2016.

[52] J. Ecker, R. Berrendorf, J. Razzaq, S. E. Scholl, and F. Mannuss, "Comparing different programming approaches for SpMV-operations on GPUs," in Proc. 11th International Conference on Parallel Processing and Applied Mathematics (PPAM 2015), vol. 9573. Springer International Publishing, 2016, pp. 537–547.

[53] W. Tang, W. Tan, R. Ray, Y. Wong, W. Chen, S. Kuo, R. Goh, S. Turner, and W. Wong, "Accelerating sparse matrix-vector multiplication on GPUs using bit-representation-optimized schemes," in Proc. Intl. Conference on High Performance Computing, Networking, Storage and Analysis (SC'13). ACM, 2013, article no. 26.

[54] A. Pinar and M. T. Heath, "Improving performance of sparse matrix-vector multiplication," in Proc. ACM/IEEE Conference on Supercomputing (SC'99). IEEE, Nov. 1999.

[55] X. Liu, E. Chow, M. Smelyanskiy, and P. Dubey, "Efficient sparse matrix-vector multiplication on x86-based many-code processors," in Proc. Intl. Conference on Supercomputing (ICS'13). ACM, 2013, pp. 273–282.

[56] T. A. Davis and Y. Hu, "The University of Florida Sparse Matrix Collection," ACM Trans. Math. Softw., vol. 38, no. 1, Nov. 2010, pp. 1:1–1:25.

[57] SPE Comparative Solution Project, Society of Petroleum Engineers, http://www.spe.org/web/csp/, retrieved: February, 2016.

Cost Considerations About Multi-Tenancy in Public Clouds

Uwe Hohenstein, Stefan Appel
Corporate Technology
Siemens AG, Corporate Technology, Otto-Hahn-Ring 6
D-81730 Munich, Germany
Email: {Uwe.Hohenstein,Stefan.Appel}@siemens.com

Abstract— **Multi-tenancy is often considered as the key element to economical Software-as-a-Service as it represents an architecture model where one software instance serves a set of multiple clients of different organizations – the so-called tenants. This reduces operational costs due to the decrease of the number of application instances and required resources. Since nearly every multi-tenant system requires a database, this paper focuses on database aspects of multi-tenancy and particularly stresses on cost aspects in public cloud environments. Starting with an investigation of the price schemes of cloud providers, this paper illustrates the broad variety of price factors and schemes. It is discussed in detail why this makes it difficult to set up vendor-independent strategies to achieve cost-efficient multi-tenancy and what challenges arise. Anyway, the paper derives certain, vendor-specific strategies, which require adapting multi-tenant architectures to fit the respective cloud providers' specifics.**

Keywords-multi-tenancy; databases; cost; SaaS.

I. INTRODUCTION

Software is more and more becoming an on-demand service drawn from the Internet, known as Software-as-a-Service (SaaS). SaaS is a delivery model that enables customers, the so-called *tenants*, to lease services without local installations and license costs. Tenants benefit from a "happy-go-lucky package": The SaaS vendor takes care of hardware and software installation, administration, and maintenance. Moreover, a tenant can use a service immediately due to a fast and automated provisioning.

Multi-tenancy is a software architecture principle allowing SaaS to make full use of the economy of scale: A shared infrastructure for several tenants saves operational cost due to an increased utilization of hardware resources and improved ease of maintenance. Thus, multi-tenancy is often considered as the key to SaaS.

Several authors discuss architectures according to what is shared by tenants: the topmost web frontend, middle tier application server, and underlying database. Concerning the database, a number of patterns exist, which support the implementation of multi-tenancy.

This paper extends the work presented in [1]. We report on industrial experiences when deploying multi-tenant SaaS in public clouds. Particularly, we focus on cost aspects of multi-tenancy for SaaS because we feel economical aspects not appropriately tackled so far in research. Indeed, economic concerns are important as SaaS providers need to operate with high profit to remain competitive. This is challenging due to diverging price schemes. Since nearly every multi-tenant system requires a database, we focus on database aspects of multi-tenancy. Even if various software engineering techniques propose NoSQL databases, relational systems are still often used in industrial applications, especially if being migrated to the Cloud. We elaborate on the huge differences of price schemes for relational database systems of public cloud providers and discuss the impact on multi-tenancy.

Compared to our previous work in [1], we here update the price schemes and take into account two further Cloud offerings. Comparing both papers thus illustrate how prices and price schemes evolve over time. Moreover, we applied a uniform and systematic analysis for all Cloud database offerings.

Section II presents some related work and motivates why further investigations about cost aspects are necessary. We introduce general cost aspects in Section III before discussing the price models of various well-known public cloud providers in two broad categories: Virtual databases in Section IV and virtual database servers in Section V. The particular offerings are from Amazon Web Services (AWS), HP Cloud, IBM, Microsoft Azure, and Oracle. We discuss in detail the impact of the price models on multi-tenancy strategies and the difficulties to optimize costs. In particular, we quantify the respective costs for implementing multi-tenancy by comparing a *1-DB-per-tenant* and a *1-global-DB* strategy. The first one provides a virtual database (DB) of its own for each tenant, thus achieving high data isolation. In the second variant, several tenants share a common database without physical data isolation. Since some offerings provide a virtual database server (instead of a single database), the same distinction can be made for DB servers. Further variants as discussed by [2] are irrelevant in this work. For Virtual Machines (VMs) with a database server, we investigate scale-out scenarios. Section VI summarizes some major findings. Finally, conclusions are drawn in Section VII.

II. STATE OF THE ART

The work in [3] considers performance isolation of tenants, scalability issues for tenants from different continents, security and data protection, configurability, and data isolation as the main challenges of multi-tenancy. These topics are well investigated. For instance, [4] discusses configurability of multi-tenant applications in case studies.

The possible variants of multi-tenancy have been described, among others, by [2][5][6]. Based on the number of tenants, the number of users per tenant, and the amount of data per tenant, [7] makes recommendations on the best multi-tenant variant to use.

Armbrust et al. [8] identify short-term billing as one of the novel features of cloud computing and [9] consider cost as one important research challenge for cloud computing. However, cost aspects do need seem to be a recent research topic since most work is about 5 years old. Moreover, existing work on economic issues around cloud computing mostly focus on cost comparisons between cloud and on-premises and lease-or-buy decisions [10]. For example, [11] provides a framework that can be used to compare the costs of using a cloud with an in-house IT infrastructure, and [12] presents a formal mathematical model for the total cost of ownership (TCO) identifying various cost factors. Other authors such as [9][13], focus on deploying scientific applications on Amazon, thereby pointing at major cost drivers. [14] performs the TPC-W benchmark for a Web application with a backend database and compares the costs for operating the web application on several major cloud providers. A comparison of various equivalent architectural solutions, however, using different components, such as queue and table storage, has been performed by [15]. The results show that the type of architecture can dramatically affect the operational cost.

Cost aspects in the context of multi-tenancy are tackled by [16][17]. They consider approaches to reduce resource consumption as a general cost driver, looking at the infrastructure, middleware and application tier, and what can be shared among tenants. Another approach, discussed by [18], reduces costs by putting values of utilization and performance models in genetic algorithms.

The authors of [19] develop a method for selecting the best database, in which a new tenant should be placed, while keeping the remaining database space as flexible as possible for placing further tenants. Their method reduces overall resource consumptions in multi-tenant environments. Cost factors taken into account are related to on-premises installations: hardware, power, lighting, air conditioning, etc.

Based on existing single-tenant applications, [20] stresses on another cost aspect for multi-tenant applications: maintenance efforts. The recurrence of maintenance tasks (e.g., patches or updates) raises operating cost as well.

The work in [21] recognizes a viable charging model being crucial for the profitability and sustainability for SaaS providers. Moreover, the costs for redesigning or developing software must not be ignored in SaaS pricing. Accordingly, [16] discusses a cost model for reengineering measures.

The challenges of calculating the costs each tenant generates for a SaaS application in a public cloud are discussed in [22]. This is indispensable to establish a profitable billing model for a SaaS application. The paper shows that only rudimentary support is available by cloud providers.

To sum up, the profitable aspects of multi-tenancy for SaaS providers are researched insufficiently. All the mentioned work is quite general and does mostly not take into account common public cloud platforms and their price schemes. Even best practices of cloud providers, for instance [17] and [23], do not support SaaS providers to reduce cost. As the next section illustrates, there is a strong need to investigate cost aspects for those platforms.

III. COST CONSIDERATIONS

Deploying multi-tenant applications in a public cloud causes expenses for the consumed resources, i.e., the pricing scheme of cloud providers comes into play. Unfortunately, the price schemes for cloud providers differ a lot and are based upon different factors such as the data volume, data transfer, etc. That is why we investigate the price schemes for databases of some major public cloud providers. The goal is to discuss variances in price schemes and how these affect multi-tenancy strategies for SaaS applications.

Please note it is *not* our intention to compare different cloud providers with regard to costs or features: For example, The Oracle cloud offers Oracle database servers, which are not provided by the Microsoft cloud, and vice versa. Hence, there is no common basis for a direct comparison of providers. This is also the reason why we keep the providers anonymous. Furthermore, the price schemes of cloud providers are quite diverging and incorporate different factors. We rather illustrate the variety of price schemes and service offerings leading to different strategies. Moreover, the prices are changing frequently, while the scheme usually remains stable. We here refer to the state as of August 2016. The price information can be found at their homepages.

We only consider resources that are available on-demand to fully benefit from the cloud. This excludes, e.g., reserved instances since those require long-term binding and thus impose a financial risk.

To structure the discussion, we distinguish between two major categories in Section IV and V, virtual databases and virtual database servers, respectively. While a virtual database server offers full control like operated on premises, particularly allowing one to create several databases within that server, a virtual database is just one database managed by the provider without further control.

IV. VIRTUAL DATABASES

In this section, we assume that each tenant demands a certain amount of database storage. We then compare the costs for storage that is provided using a dedicated database per tenant (1-DB-per-tenant) with a global database for all tenants (1-global-DB) to guide a decision. Please note the term "database" is used in the sense of something that can be authenticated individually.

A. *Offering 1*

Offering 1 is a database server available as Platform-as-a-Service (PaaS) in a public cloud. PaaS is one of three delivery models according to the NIST definition [24]: "The consumer does not manage or control the underlying cloud infrastructure including network, servers, operating systems, or storage, but has control over the deployed applications and possibly configuration settings for the application-hosting environment." That is, a database can be provisioned without any installation and administration. PaaS performs an automatic management (patches etc.) and internal replication of data. In particular, PaaS includes software licenses, which seems to be reasonable for multi-tenancy. There will be no elasticity without PaaS, since licenses must be ordered in time.

TABLE I. PRICE SCHEME FOR OFFERING I.

Consumption	*Price*	*Additional GB*
0 to 100 MB	$4.995 (fix price)	
100 MB to 1 GB	$9.99 (fix price)	
1 to 10 GB	$9.99 for 1st 1 GB	$3.996
10 to 50 GB	$45.96 for 1st 10 GB	$1.996
50 to 150 GB	$125.88 for 1st 50 GB	$0.999

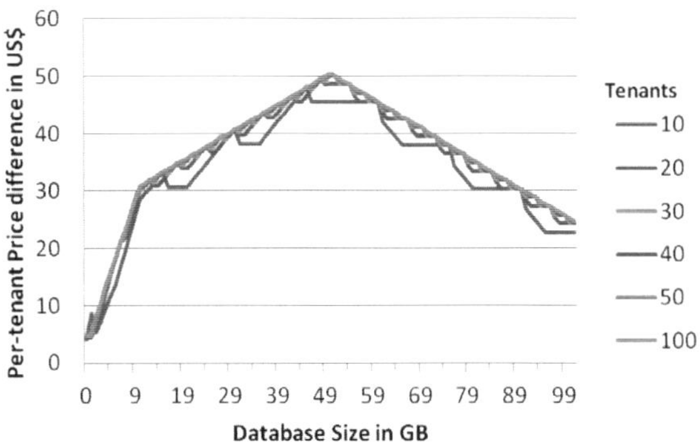

Figure 1. Price difference per tenant for Offering 1.

Table I presents the recent prices for a Microsoft SQL Server in the US East region. In addition, outgoing data is charged for each database individually with a decreasing rate. The first 5 GB are for free, each additional GB is charged with 8.7ct/GB and 8.3ct/GB above 10 TB, decreasing to 5ct/GB for more than 350TB. However, the cost reduction is insignificant unless there is extremely high outgoing transfer. There is only a 40ct benefit for 100GB of outgoing data.

The storage consumption is the main cost driver. Each database is paid for the amount of stored data. There is no cost difference between using one or several database servers for hosting the databases due to virtualization. We even could not detect any performance difference between placing databases on one virtual server or several ones. One has to pay for the consumed storage in every database independently of how many databases and servers are used.

At a first glance, the price scheme suggests the same costs for 1-DB-per-tenant and 1-global-DB (keeping all tenants). There seems to be no cost benefit for sharing one database amongst several tenants, since SaaS providers are charged for the total amount of used storage. However, there are indeed higher costs for individual tenant databases since

- sizes larger than 1 GB are rounded up to full GBs;
- smaller databases are more expensive per GB than larger ones due to a progressive reduction.

Since pricing occurs in increments of 1 GB, hundred tenants with each a 1.1 GB database are charged with 100*2 GB, i.e., 100 * $13.986 = $1398.60 a month. In contrast, one database with 100 * 1.1GB = 110 GB is charged with $185.82, i.e., a total difference of $1212.78 or a difference of $12.13 for each tenant (per-tenant difference).

Figure 1 compares the costs of both strategies for various numbers of tenants (10,20,...,100). The x-axis represents the database size, the y-axis the per-tenant difference in US$, i.e., the additional amount of money a SaaS provider has to pay for *each* tenant compared to a 1-global-DB strategy (note that the prices in Figure 1 must be multiplied by the number of tenants to obtain the total costs). The difference stays below $10 for tenant sizes up to 3 GB. The number of tenants is mostly irrelevant. This is why the lines are superposing; only the "10 tenants" line is noticeable. In the worst case, we have to pay $50 more for each tenant with a 1-DB-per-tenant strategy. A linear price drop occurs after 50 GB because even 1-DB-per-tenant uses larger and cheaper databases. Anyway, a 1-DB-per-tenant strategy can become quite expensive compared to a 1-global-DB strategy.

Please note the amount of *used* storage is charged. That is, an empty database is theoretically for free. However, even an empty database stores some administrative data so that the costs are effectively $4.995 per month (for < 100MB). Anyway, these are small starting costs for both a 1-DB-per-tenant and a 1-global-DB strategy.

There is no difference between provisioning a 10 GB and a 150 GB database from a cost point of view as the stored data counts. A 1-global-DB strategy, having the problem not to know how many tenants to serve, can start with 150 GB, thus avoiding the problem of later upgrading databases and possibly risking a downtime while having low upfront cost. Even for a 1-DB- per-tenant strategy, larger databases can be provisioned in order to be able to handle larger tenants without risk.

However, there is a limitation of 150 GB per database, which hinders putting a high amount of tenants with larger storage consumption in a single database. Reaching the limit requires splitting the database into two.

Along with this comes the challenge to determine a cost-efficient placement strategy. Assume an existing 90 GB database and that we need 40 and 30 GB more space for two further tenants: Putting 60 GB into the existing 90 GB database and 10 GB into a new one is the cheapest option with $225.75 + $45.96 = $271.71, more than $70 cheaper than using a new 40 GB and a new 30 GB database: $165.84 + $105.84 + $85.88 = $357.56. Even using a new 70 GB is more expensive with $311.70. An appropriate tenant placement strategy is to fill databases up to the 150 GB threshold, maybe minus some possible space for tenants' expansions, e.g., $286.58 = $205.80 (90+40 GB) + $85.88 (30 GB).

Please note this offering has been deprecated and replaced with Offering 2 by the cloud provider since our last analysis in [1].

B. *Offering 2*

This candidate offers three tiers (**B**asic, **S**tandard, **P**remium). Table II shows the Microsoft SQL Server prices in the US East region for various performance levels inside.

TABLE II. PRICE SCHEME FOR OFFERING 2.

Level	*Price/ month*	*DB size*	*Session limit*	*Max. concurrent logins & requests*	*Transaction rate / hour*
B	~$5	2	300	30	20,160
S0	~$15	250	600	60	31,320
S1	~$30	250	900	90	61,200
S2	~$75	250	1,200	120	165,600
S3	$150	250	2400	200	367,200
P1	~$465	500	2,400	200	457,200
P2	~$930	500	4,800	400	946,800
P4	~$1,860	500	9,600	800	1,778,400
P6	~$3,720	500	19,200	1,600	3,988,800
P11	~$7,001	1000	32,000	3,200	6,339,600

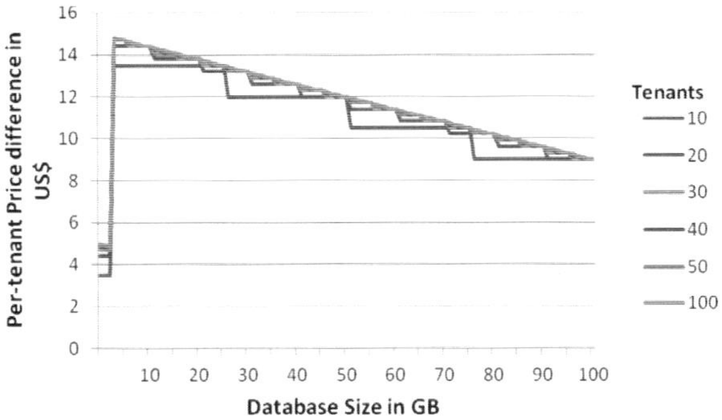

Figure 2. 1-DB-per-tenant vs. 1-global-DB for Offering 2.

Again, this is a PaaS offering for a virtual database. Each individual database is paid according to the price scheme. But in contrast to Offering 1, the *provisioning* of the tier is relevant, not the effective storage consumption.

Figure 2 compares per-tenant costs for the 1-DB-per-tenant and 1-global-DB strategies in the same way as in Figure 1. We here use S0 databases for 1-global-DB because S0 are the cheapest option: To store 50GB each for 20 tenants, we can use 4*S0 ($60), 2*P1 ($930) or 1*P11 ($7,001). But it is important to note that the global DB is then distributed over several databases. 1-DB-per-tenant uses B (<= 2 GB) and S0 (> 2 GB) depending on the required size. It becomes obvious that a global database with 2*P1 (with $930) is even more expensive than 1-DB-per-tenant with 20*S0 ($300).

One of the worst cases that could happen for 1-DB-per-tenant is to have 100 tenants with 2.2 GB (S0) each, resulting in $1500 per month since each tenant cannot be satisfied with the B tier. In contrast, 1 * 220 GB (S0) for 1-global-DB costs $15. That is a per tenant difference of $14.85.

However, it is unclear here whether an S0 level is sufficient for handling 100 tenants from a performance point of view.

A 1-DB-per-tenant strategy is about $5 more expensive if the size is lower than 2 GB, and about $15 otherwise. The difference is never higher than $14.77, and drops to $12 for 50 GB and to $9 for 100 GB.

For each database, we have to pay at least $5 a month for at most 2 GB and $15 for up to 250 GB. The costs occur even for an empty database. These upfront costs have to be paid for a 1-gobal-DB, too, starting with the first tenant.

Especially for a 1-global-DB approach, a new challenge arises: Each service level determines not only an upper limit for the database size but also for the number of allowed parallel sessions and the number of concurrent requests. Furthermore, there is an impact on the transaction rate (cf. Table II). We have to stay below these limits. Upgrading the category in case of reaching the limit happens online, i.e., without any downtime – in theory: if the database size limit is reached, no further insertions are possible until the upgrade has finished. According to our experiences, such a migration can take several minutes up to hours depending on the database size. If the allowed number of sessions is reached, no further clients can connect unless sessions are released by other users. And if the transaction rate is insufficient, the performance will degrade. Hence, a prediction of tenants' data and usage behavior is required. The number of sessions might become the restrictive factor for a 1-global-DB strategy. In the following, we discuss the impact of the number of users and required sessions on costs by means of sample calculations.

Keeping 100 tenants in 1*S0 offers 600 sessions, i.e., 6 sessions per tenant (which might be too small); the monthly costs are $15. We can scale-up to 1*P3 with 19,200 sessions, i.e., 192 per tenant, for a high price of $3720. To achieve the same number of sessions, we can also scale out to 32*S0 for $480 or use 64*B for $360 if each database is smaller than 2 GB. In contrast, a pure 1-DB-per-tenant strategy for 100 tenants costs $500 for B: This seems to be affordable, especially because of 30,000 available sessions. For the price of one P3, we also get 248*S0 databases with 148,000 sessions (6 times more than 1*P3) and a 3 times higher transaction rate of 7,752,480.

For serving 100 tenants with 20 parallel users each, we need 2000 sessions in total. We can achieve this by either 7*B (for $35), 4*S0 ($60), 3*S1 ($90), 1*P1 ($465), or 2*S2 ($500) with very different prices. A pure 1-DB-per-tenant for B is with $500 in the price area of the last two options, but supporting 300 sessions per tenant instead of 20.

Figure 3 illustrates the costs in US$ to achieve x sessions for 100 tenants. B1 represents a pure 1-DB-per-tenant strategy using B-level instances. The P levels are most expensive, even S2 is quite expensive. An obvious question is what the benefit of higher levels in the context of multi-tenancy is. Table III compares several configurations with same prices. There is no consistent behavior. However, several smaller machines seem to be superior to same priced larger ones with a few exceptions. One exception is row (c) where 1*P2 is a little better than 2*P1. More sessions can usually be achieved if n smaller tiers are used instead of one larger one for the same price.

Considering Table II again, we also notice that the session and transaction rates increase from tier to tier within each group less proportional than the prices. Exceptions for transaction rates are S1->S2 and P1->P2. It seems to be reasonable to scale out instead of scaling-up to obtain more sessions and transactions.

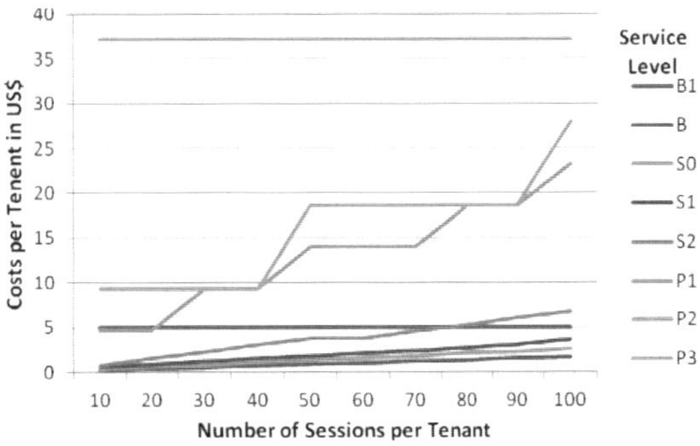

Figure 3. Costs to achieve x sessions per tenant for Offering 2.

TABLE III. COMPARISON OF CONFIGURATIONS.

	Configuration		*# sessions for*		*Transaction rate*	
	1 vs.	*2*	*1 vs.*	*2*	*1000/h (1 vs. 2)*	
a	5*S0	1*S2	3000	1200	156	154
b	2*S0	1*S1	1200	900	62	56
c	2*P1	1*P2	4800	4800	756	820
d	4*P2	1*P3	19200	19200	3283	2646
e	31*S0	1*P1	18600	2400	969	378

Another advantage is that upfront costs can be saved. A 1-global-DB strategy requires a high-level database with a high price already for the first tenant independent of the number of eventually stored tenants.

Indeed, it is difficult to derive a strategy for identifying a suitable configuration. Important questions arise:

- Is an upgrade possible in short time, without outage? This would allow for 1-global-DB to start small for few tenants and upgrade if performance suffers or the number of sessions increases. For 1-DB-per-tenant, we could start with B and upgrade to S0.
- Are only the session and transaction rates of a level relevant, or are there any other (invisible) performance metrics to consider? The documentation mentions only that the predictability, i.e., the consistency of response times, is increasing from B to Px, however being the same within a tier.

C. Offering 3

Offering 3 provides a MySQL database as PaaS. The regular prices are for virtualized databases on an hourly basis. The payment is based upon the following factors:

- The instance type, which limits the maximal database size and determines the RAM (cf. Table IV).
- The outgoing data transfer: the first GB is for free, we then pay 12ct/GB up to 10 TB, further GBs for 9ct up to 40 TB etc.

TABLE IV. PRICE SCHEME FOR OFFERING 3.

Instance Type	*RAM*	*Storage*	*Price/month*
XS	1 GB	15 GB	$73
S	2 GB	30 GB	$146
M	4 GB	60 GB	$292
L	8 GB	120 GB	$584
XL	16 GB	240 GB	$1,168
XXL	32 GB	480 GB	$2,336

In contrast to Offering 1, the provisioned storage is paid. The prices and the features increase with the instance type linearly, i.e., each next higher instance type doubles the RAM and maximal database size for a doubled price.

Comparing the strategies, we notice that 5 tenant databases à 15 GB (XS) are charged with $365. One global database à 75 GB is more expensive (!) with $584 since we are forced to provision a 120 GB (L) database. The difference per tenant is $43.80. However, using 15 GB (XS) increments for 1-global-DB, we can achieve the cheaper price.

Hence, we should use XS partitions in order not to pay for unused storage. Thus, an appropriate cost strategy for 1-global-DB is to fill XS databases one by one with tenants. However, this has architectural implications in order to connect each tenant to the right database instances. A 1-DB-per-tenant approach could also benefit that way. There is no need to use larger instances unless we do not want to spread tenant data across databases due to implementation effort. However, an implication is that additional administrative effort (e.g., for backup) becomes necessary, and even more, the application's code is affected by distributing and collecting data from several XS databases in case of customer data "fragmentation". This has an impact on the total cost (cf. [3]) but is beyond the scope of this paper.

A worst case scenario is storing 15 tenants with 100 MB each. 1-DB-per-tenant is charged with $1095 = (15*XS), while one global XS database costs $73 for 1.5 GB. That is a difference per tenant of $68.13.

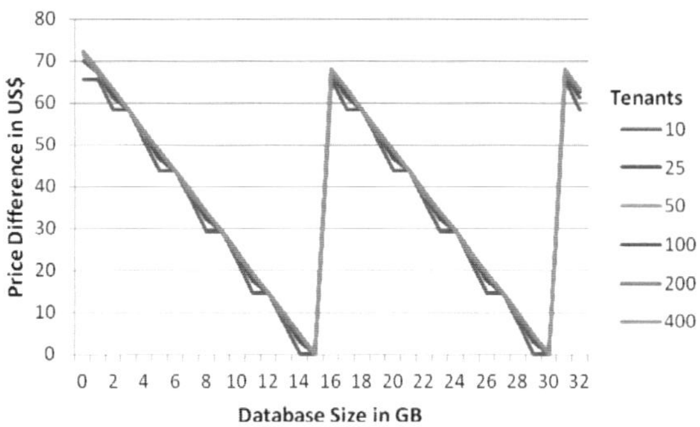

Figure 4. Price diff. of 1-DB-per-tenant vs. 1-global-DB for Offering 3.

Figure 4 illustrates that 1-DB-per-tenant, compared to 1-global-DB based upon XS databases, is more expensive for sizes much smaller than the storage threshold. Reaching the threshold, the difference diminishes. Hence, it is reasonable to use one database for each tenant if the storage size is near a threshold. In summary, we observe larger per-tenant differences depending on database sizes. The range where the difference stays below $20 is very small. Moreover, the variances for different numbers of tenants are small. Note, Figure 4 has a different scale compared to Figure 1 and 2, but the saw tool behavior is repetitive up to 100 tenants and beyond.

An incremental acquisition of XS databases even saves upfront costs. However, it is an open issue to be investigated whether larger instances provide a better performance. The time for upgrading from one instance type to another is not important here.

D. *Offering 4*

Three database types are available in this PaaS offering, each limiting the maximal amount of storage. Table V shows that each type also limits the allowed data transfer.

TABLE V. PRICE SCHEME FOR OFFERING 4.

Type	*Max database size*	*Data Transfer*	*Price/month*
5GB	5 GB	30 GB	$175
20GB	20 GB	120 GB	$900
50GB	50 GB	300 GB	$2,000

A comparison of the types gives some first insights: 20GB is 5 times more expensive than 5GB, but offers only 4 times more data transfer and storage. 50GB is 2.2 times more expensive than 20GB, but offers 2.5 times more data transfer and storage. And 50GB is 11 times more expensive than 5GB, but offers only 10 times more resources. Hence, 20GB has the worst price ratio, 5GB the best one. Obviously, using 5GB databases seems to be reasonable for either strategy unless we do not want to spread tenant data across databases.

Table VI compares a 1-DB-per-tenant configuration (the first line in each group) with others. For 200 tenants à 4GB, using 20GB databases is more expensive than 1-DB-per-tenant; the same holds for 100 tenants à 5GB.

TABLE VI. COMPARISON OF SAMPLE CONFIGURATIONS

Config	*#tenants*	*database size*	*Costs*	*Data transfer*	*Per-tenant costs*
100*5GB	100	1 GB	17,500	3000	175
2*50GB			4,000	600	40
5*20GB			4,500	600	45
20*5GB			3,500	600	35
200*5GB	200	4 GB	35,000	6000	175
16*50GB			32,000	4800	160
40*20GB			36,000	4800	180
100*5GB	100	5 GB	17,500	3000	175
10*50GB			20,000	3000	200
25*20GB			22,500	3000	225

Figure 5. Price Diff. of 1-DB-per-tenant vs. 1-global-DB for Offering 4.

Figure 5 summarizes the price-per-tenant differences if 5GB increments are used in both strategies. A 1-DB-per-tenant strategy is only reasonable if the database size is near a multiple of 5 GB, or if the required data transfer is high. The larger the distance is, the higher will be the per-tenant costs compared to a 1-global-DB. This saw tooth behavior is repeating. The number of tenants has again no real impact. The per-tenant costs can be even higher in this offering than for Offering 3.

Since the data transfer is limited by the instance type, a challenge arises for the 1-global-DB strategy: this can stop several or all tenants from accessing the database. Additional data transfer cannot be acquired even for extra charges.

A possible strategy for 1-global-DB is to start with 5GB and to add further ones later; this means less upfront costs. Moreover, 5GB is the cheapest category wrt. gains.

Please also note that downsizing is not possible. This causes further costs in case a tenant stops using the SaaS service.

V. VIRTUAL DATABASE SERVERS

As a major difference to the offerings in the previous section, in this category a virtual machine (VM) with a database *server* is provisioned and paid instead of a single database. The database server offers full control like operated on-premises. Several databases can be managed in that server, especially one dedicated database for each tenant with individual credentials. This directly implies that a 1-DB-per-tenant strategy is feasible. A strong isolation is thus given without any extra charge. As a consequence, the question is not about 1-global-DB vs. 1-DB-per-Tenant, but instead how many database servers with what equipment we have to apply for the expected number of tenants and users. To perform an evaluation, we assume that the number of tenants, the amount of data, and the access profiles are known. The question is what VM configuration is sufficient for a given number of tenants and amounts of data. This allows for a better comparison of equipments for given prices.

Unfortunately, the tenants are coming time after time. This means that the *upfront costs* for the cheapest database server are important, since these are the starting costs.

Moreover, we investigate how the costs evolve with the number of tenants. There are basically two strategies: The first *scale-up* strategy uses a cheap database server and sets up another database within this server for each new tenant until the overall performance decreases. Whenever the existing server reaches performance limits, the type of server is upgraded to a higher tier being better equipped; a high number of tenants/databases can be handled by a larger VM. However, this implies that such an upgrade must be possible within short time and without downtime in the meantime. Due to our experiences, this is not always the case. In the best case, the new VM is set up while the existing one is still running. However, the data has to be migrated from old to new, and depending on the amount of data this process could take some minutes. That is two VMs have to be paid during the transfer. A deeper empirical performance evaluation of candidates should be performed to clarify these issues. As an alternative, a larger machine with better equipment can be provisioned from the beginning, however, causing high upfront costs already for some few tenants.

If an upgrade could cause a downtime or other problems, one can apply a *scale-out* strategy which starts small with a single server and then extends the number of servers whenever the used servers get overloaded. Then, the expenses increase tenant by tenant. An incremental provisioning can help to avoid an upgrade and its consequences and also to reduce tenant-independent upfront investments, which occur already with the first tenant. Hence, the difference between n small DB servers and a less number of larger DB servers, having similar equipment, will be analyzed.

A. *Offering 5*

Offering 5 provides a virtual machine (VM) with a Microsoft SQL Server for various operating systems. The price model is quite complex covering several factors.

TABLE VII. PRICE SCHEME FOR OFFERING 5

Tier	*vCores*	*RAM*	*TempDisk*	*VM/month*	*DBS*	*#disks*
A0	1	768 MB	20 GB	$15	$298	1
A1	1	1.75 GB	70 GB	$67	$298	2
A2	2	3.5 GB	135 GB	$134	$298	4
A3	4	7 GB	285 GB	$268	$298	8
A4	8	14 GB	605 GB	$536	$595	16
A5	2	14 GB	135 GB	$246	$298	4
A6	4	28 GB	285 GB	$492	$298	8
A7	8	56 GB	605 GB	$983	$595	16
A8	8	56 GB	382 GB	$1,823	$595	16
A9	16	112 GB	382 GB	$3,646	$1190	16
D1	1	3.5 GB	50 GB	$127	$298	1
D2	2	7 GB	100 GB	$254	$298	2
D3	4	14 GB	200 GB	$509	$298	4
D4	8	28 GB	400 GB	$1,018	$595	8
D11	2	14 GB	100 GB	$600	$298	2
D12	4	28 GB	200 GB	$1,080	$298	4
D13	8	56 GB	400 GB	$1,943	$595	8
D14	16	112 GB	800 GB	$2,611	$1190	15

At first, a VM has to be chosen for hosting the database server. Table VII summarizes the prices for a Windows OS in the East US region. Each tier has a different number of virtual cores (vCores), RAM, and temporary disk space. A0-A7 covers the standard tier. A8 and A9 are network-optimized instances adding an InfiniBand network with remote direct memory access (RDMA) technology. The D-tier is compute-optimized with 60% faster CPUs, more memory, and a local SSD. An OS disk space of 127 GB is available and must be paid with ignorable 2.4ct per GB/month.

Furthermore, the database server (i.e., the software) is charged per minute (cf. column DBS in Table VII). The prices depend on the number of cores of the used VM: $298 for 1- to 4-core machines, $595 for 8 cores, and $1190 for 16 cores for a SQL Server Standard Edition in a month. The Enterprise Edition is more expensive, e.g., $4464 for a 16-core VM.

Additional costs occur for attached storage. There is a maximum of number of 1TB data disks (#disks in Table VII). The costs are 5ct/GB-month for the first 4000 TB of consumed storage in a page blob; the price decreases by 0.5ct per GB-month for more than 4000 TB. The gain by using one VM instead of several ones is thus extremely small. In general, the costs are dominated by other factors than disk space.

The question is what configuration is sufficient for a given number of tenants and amounts of data. Unfortunately, no performance hints are provided to ease the decision. Table VIII presents a brief evaluation of an SQL Server Standard Edition compares an A9 tier with several smaller machines summing up to the same price of about $4836.

TABLE VIII. CONFIGURATIONS COMPARABLE TO A9 VM.

configuration	*# vCores*	*RAM*
15,4 * A0	15.4	11.6
13,2 * A1	13.2	23.2
11,2 * A2	22.4	39.2
8,5 * A3	34.2	59.8
4,2 * A4	34.2	59.8
8.9 * A5	17.8	124.5
6 * A6	24.5	171.4
3 * A7	24.5	171.5
2 * A8	16	111.9
1 * A9	16	112

The configurations 8.5*A3 and 4.2*A4 obviously provide the highest number of vCores, more than twice compared to the reference 1*A9, while 6*A6 and 3*A7 offer the highest amount of RAM, again much more than 1*A9. That is, 1*A9 is not the best choice. Using A0s or A1s offers the least equipment because of the high portion of $298 for the database software for each instance, e.g., here are high minimal costs of at least $311 per month for each database server ($13 for the smallest Windows VM A0 Basic plus the database server). In general, it looks reasonable to avoid high-class VMs such as A9 and to use several middle-class VMs depending on whether favoring vCores or RAM. Moreover, a larger VM can be used for other purposes as well if being idle.

Similar considerations can be made to achieve a certain amount of RAM or number of vCores. For example, Table IX shows several options to achieve 112 GB RAM with very different prices and numbers of vCores. Analogously, there are many variants for 14 or 28 GB RAM, each yielding different vCores with prices ranging from $246 to $600 for 14GB RAM, and from $492 to $1089 for 28 GB RAM.

TABLE IX. CONFIGURATIONS TO ACHIEVE 112 GB RAM.

configuration	*# vCores*	*price (decreasing)*
8*D11	16	$4,800
8*A4	64	$4,288
8*D3	32	$4,072
2*D13	16	$3,886
1*A9	16	$3,646
2*A8	16	$3,646
1*D14	16	$2,611
8*A5	16	$1,968
2*A7	16	$1,966

Next, we investigate another scenario: We assume that a new tenant arrives each day. A scale-out strategy starts with an A0 instance, since this has the lowest price with $313, and to add further A0 instances whenever performance degrades. Let us assume that such a situation occurs with every new tenant, i.e., every tenant requires a new A0 VM. We compare this configuration with two others that immediately start with 1*A9 and 6*A6 respectively. Figure 6 shows the daily cost for each variant. After 15 days, we obtain the following cumulated costs:

a) 15*A0: $1271
b) 6*A6: $948
c) 1*A9: $2418

The cumulated costs for A9 are clear: that is exactly the price for half a month. In case of A0 VMs, we start with 1 VM for the first day, two VMs for the second day etc. In case of A6 VMs, we can use the first instance for the first 4 days (1 VM is comparable to 4*A0 wrt. vCores), and so on. Obviously, A6 VMs are a good choice. Using 6*A6 incrementally is cheaper than A0 VMs with the beginning of the third day. Already starting with a high-end A9 VM is about twice as expensive even after 15 days.

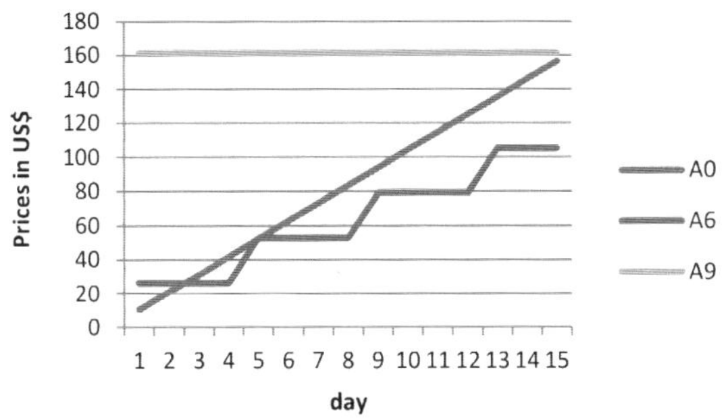

Figure 6. 15-day scale-out scenario for Offering 5.

B. *Offering 6*

Similar to Offering 5, this option again offers a VM running a database server, however, with some differences regarding pricing. Several database systems such as MySQL, Oracle, PostgreSQL, and SQL Server are supported in various database instance types.

TABLE X. PRICE SCHEME FOR OFFERING 6.

Category	*Instance type*	*Price / month*	*vCPU*	*RAM*
Standard	M	$478.15	1	3.75
	L	$594.95	2	7.5
	XL	$981.85	4	15
	XXL	$1960.05	8	30
Memory-optimized (MemOpt)	L	$744.60	2	15
	XL	$1489.20	4	30.5
	XXL	$2219.20	8	61
	4XL	$4409.20	16	122
	8XL	$8818.40	32	244

The prices depend on the chosen instance type, the type of database server, and the region. The prices for a SQL Server Standard Edition in the US East region are presented in Table X. The underlying VM and the SQL Server license are already included in the price. The instance type determines the number of virtual CPUs (vCPU) and the main memory. Please note that other database systems such as MySQL also support cheaper VMs in a micro edition.

An additional cost factor is the outgoing data transfer to the Internet: 1 GB-month is for free. The prices then start with 12ct/GB and decrease to 9ct/GB for data volumes exceeding 40TB. For instance, if we have 100 tenants with 512GB data transfer each (in total 50TB), using one database server for all tenants will be charged with $5836.80 (40 TB à 12ct/GB + 10 TB à 0ct/GB) while using 50 DB servers will end up with $6144 (100 * 512GB * 12ct/GB). Hence, the savings are $308, i.e., $3 for each tenant, for quite a high amount of data transfer.

Furthermore, the amount of data is charged according to two alternative classes of database storage:

(1) General purpose SSD for 11.5ct per GB-month with a range from 5 GB to 3 TB; 3 IOPS per GB are included (this is the base performance; 3,000 I/O requests per second are temporarily allowed).

(2) Provisioned IOPS for 12.5ct per GB-month and additional $0.10 per requested IOPS/month, with a range from 100 GB to 1 TB and 1,000 IOPS to 10,000 IOPS.

IOPS (IO per second) determines an upper limit for IO. IO itself is not charged.

The upfront costs for each database server are determined by the minimal settings: The smallest installation in terms of cost for a SQL Server is Standard Medium (M) with $478.15/month. Provisioned IOPS storage is available at a minimum of 100 GB and 1000 IOPS, i.e., $12.50 (100*12.5ct) plus $100 (1000 IOPS à 10ct) ending up with costs of at least $112.50 per server. Using alternate general purpose storage, we have to provision at least 5 GB for 57.5ct (5*11.5ct); but then only 15 IOPS are available (see (1) above). Hence, setting up a minimal SQL Server, e.g., for each tenant, comes with at least $478.73 using general purpose storage, while provisioned storage is much more expensive with $590.65.

Again, we have to decide how many servers of what type are reasonable for a multi-tenant environment. We use a Standard XXL VM as a reference and compare it with several smaller VMs of the same overall price in Table XI.

TABLE XI. CONFIGURATIONS COMPARABLE TO XXL VM

configuration	*# vCores*	*RAM*
4.1*M	15.4	4.1
3.3*L	24.7	6.6
2*XL	29.9	7.9
1*XXL	30	8

The provided equipment differs a lot. Here, both 1*XXL and 2*XL offer the best price/equipment ratio.

Next, we again perform the 15-day scale-out scenario in Figure 7 comparing a scale-out with M, XL, and XXL for 5GB general purpose storage. We here consider 4*M being equivalent to 1*XL and 8*M equivalent to 1*XXL. We obtain the following cumulated costs after 15 days:

a) 8*M Standard: $1913
b) 2*XL Standard: $1178
c) 1* XXL Standard: $1437

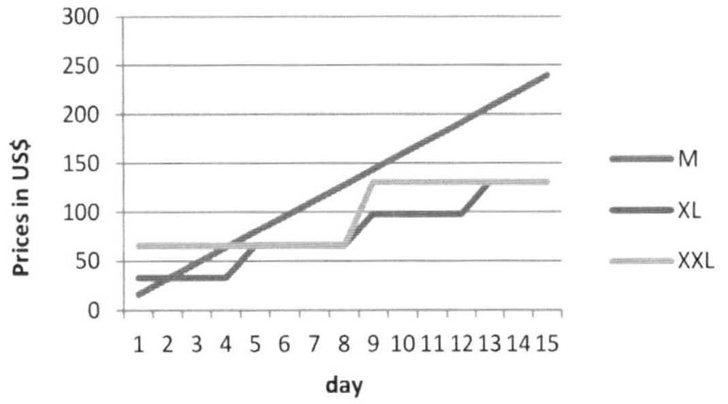

Figure 7. 15-day scale-out scenario for Offering 6.

Obviously, b) is the best option after 15 days, and starting with the third day it becomes cheaper than 8*M. XL benefits from an incremental provisioning compared to XXL. This also gives more flexibility for provisioning IOPS according to tenants' requirements.

A high-end server might be more appropriate since the network performance also increases with a higher instance class according to the documentation.

It is important to note that the *provisioned* numbers are relevant, not the effective usage. This means, the required storage for each tenant has to be estimated in order not to overpay for unused resources. The same holds for the IOPS rate. These costs occur already for the first tenant independently of consumed resources.

Another important question is what IOPS rate is sufficient since the IOPS rate is a limiting factor: Throttling of users can occur if the limit is reached. Obviously, keeping several tenants in one server requires higher IOPS rates. It is unclear what the advantage of provisioned storage is compared to general purpose storage. From a pure cost perspective, 6000 IOPS are charged with $600 for provisioned storage. To achieve 6000 IOPS with general purpose storage, we have to use 2TB (remind the factor in (a)), i.e., being much cheaper with $230 and already including storage cost. Since there is an upper database limit of 1 TB in any case, general purpose IOPS ends with 9,000 IOPS; provisioned storage can handle up to 6,000 IOPS.

C. *Offering 7*

This offering provides a DB2 server in two editions: Standard and Advanced (Enterprise Server Edition). Standard corresponds to the DB2 Workgroup Server Edition, while Advanced is based on the DB2 Advanced Enterprise Server Edition, thus offering some advanced features such as compression, database partitioning, materialized query tables, query parallelism, multi-dimensional clustering etc. in addition. Both editions are offered for different tiers, S to XXL, each determining the physical hardware with the number of cores, RAM, IOPS, and attached storage. The S-L tiers use SAN, while XL and XXL both use SSDs and RAID10 for the first and RAID1 for the second disk array. Standard/Advanced S/M/L all have a 1 Gbps network, in contrast to a 10 Gbps redundant network for XL/XXL. Table XII presents the monthly prices for the region US.

TABLE XII. PRICE SCHEME FOR OFFERING 7.

Tier	*Cores*	*RAM [GB]*	*IOPS*	*DB Size*	*Price/month [US$]*	
					Standard	*Advanced*
S	2 à 2 GHz	8	100GB, 500 IOPS	100 GB + 500 GB	1,000	1,250
M	4 à 2 GHz	16	100 GB, 1200 IOPS	100 + 1000 GB	1,700	2,200
L	8 à 2 GHz	32	100 GB, 1600 IOPS	100 GB + 2000 GB	3,000	4,000
XL	12 (2.4 GHz)	128	10 Gbps	6 * 1.2 TB + 2 * 800 GB	6,000	8,000
XXL	32 (2.7 GHz)	1024	10 Gbps	16 * 1.2 TB + 2 * 800 GB	-	16,000

TABLE XIII. CONFIGURATIONS COMPARABLE TO XL VM.

configuration	*# vCores*	*RAM*	*IOPS*	*DB Size*
6*S	12	48	3000	3600
3.5*M	14	56	4235	3882
2*L	16	64	3200	4200
1*XL	12	128	-	8973

Again, the major concern is how many instances of what type should be used. The decision between Standard and Advanced must be based upon functional requirements and is not mainly affected by multi-tenancy cost aspects.

Table XIII compares several standard edition configurations the prices of which are the same as 1*XL. Again, the equipment differs a lot. 1*XL is best except for the number of cores, where 2*L has the lead. 2*L seems to be quite balanced. IOPS numbers are not given for XL.

TABLE XIV. CONFIGURATIONS COMPARABLE TO L VM.

Configuration	*cores*	*RAM [GB]*	*DB Size*	*IOPS*	*Price [US$]*
4 * S	8	32	2,400 GB	2,000	4,000
2* M	8	32	2,200 GB	2,400	3,400
1 * L	8	32	2,100 GB	1,600	3,000

Table XIV compares several variants for the standard edition with 8 cores and 32 GB RAM each. The alternatives are nearly equally equipped except the storage that is slightly decreasing. But concerning IOPS, 2*M seems to be the best choice. The L instance suffers here. However, one L machine is much cheaper than several smaller instances. Taking XL into account, the prices double L obtaining 4 times of RAM and about 4 times of disk space. The same behavior is visible for the advanced edition. XL has 2*12 virtual cores due to hyper-threading with 2 threads per core, and thus 3 times more virtual cores.

Every tier doubles the equipment of the previous one for less money more or less. As a conclusion, it seems to be reasonable to start with low upfront cost, i.e., an S instance, until performance, database size, or IOPSs reach its limit. Then an upgrade to the next tier becomes necessary.

In a 15-day scale-out scenario we compare a scale-out with S, L, and XL. Figure 8 displays the result. We consider 6*S being equivalent to 1*XL. After 15 days, we obtain the following cumulated costs:

a) 6*S: 4000
b) 2*L: 2200
c) 1*XL: 5400

Obviously, b) is the best option after 15 days, and starting with the third day it becomes cheaper than 8*M.

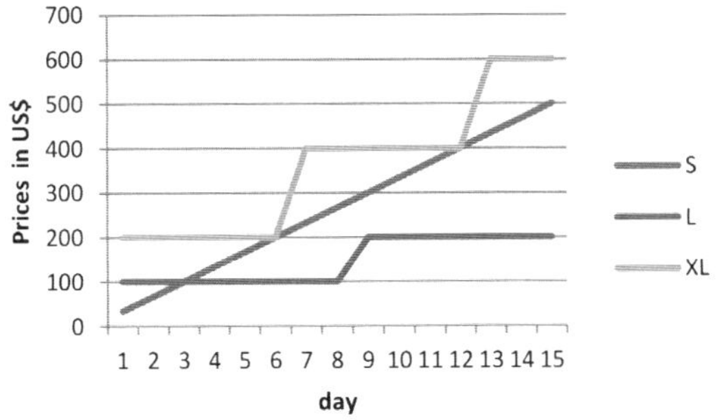

Figure 8. 15-day scale-out scenario for Offering 7.

D. Offering 8

This offering provides again a database server, in this case either Oracle 11gR2 or Oracle 12cR1. That is, a 1-DB-per-Tenant strategy is at no additional cost. Several choices have to be made:

- *Compute*: General purpose (GP) or High-memory (HM).
- *Editions*: Standard (SE), Enterprise (EE), High performance (HP), Extreme performance (XP). XP covers all the database enterprise management packs except RAC One Node, while HP has no Active Data Guard, in-memory feature, and RAC (Real Application Cluster).
- *Service level*: Virtual image or DBaaS (Database-as-a-Service). *Virtual Image* provides a compute environment with pre-installed VM images that include all software needed to run an Oracle server. All maintenance operations, including backup, patching and upgrades, are not automatically performed. *DBaaS* provides everything that the Virtual Image option offers, but also includes a pre-configured server through streamlined provisioning as well as automatic backup, patching and upgrades, and point-in-time recovery.
- *Virtual CPU* (vCPU): 1, 2, 4, 8, or 16. 1 vCPU corresponds to 1 physical Intel Xeon processor with hype-threading (or 2 virtual CPUs): 1 vCPU has 7.5 GB RAM for a GP instance and the RAM scales linearly up to 120 GB for 16 vCPU; a HM compute instance doubles the RAM compared to GP.

The choice of edition is only affected by functional requirements. Similarly, the decision for the service level depends on the desired level of comfort.

Table XV shows the monthly prices for an Oracle database server with its variants; it is important to note that these prices are per vCPU! Further costs occur for:

- compute: Each vCPU is charged with $75 per month (hourly metering);
- data transfer: 1 GB/month for free, then 12ct for each additional GB/month, increasing to 5ct for more than 150 TB;
- block storage: 5ct per GB/month;
- I/O requests: 5ct per 1,000,000 requests per month outbound.

TABLE XV. PRICE SCHEME FOR OFFERING 8 (FOR 1 VCPU).

Service level & compute / Edition	*DBaaS [US$]*		*Virtual Image [US$]*	
	GP	*HM*	*GP*	*HM*
SE	400	500	600	700
EE	1500	1600	3000	3100
HP	2000	2100	4000	4100
XP	3000	3100	5000	5100

For multi-tenancy considerations, the prices for data transfer, storage, and I/O requests can be neglected since they do not affect the per-tenant cost. There is gain for handing multiple tenants in one server in this respect.

Concerning the upfront cost, the smallest configuration is available for $475 (1 vCPU (SE, GP) for $75 + $400 for standard edition) plus storage, data transfer, and I/O requests.

One important observation is that a HM instance offers twice as much RAM as a GP, i.e., a standard edition with 1 vCPU HM compute is available for $500, while a standard edition with 2 vCPU GP is charged with $800, both offering the same 15 GB RAM. HM is thus a cheap option if RAM is important.

Quite obviously, the number of vCPUs is crucial for cost considerations, as the number is a multiplier for the cost of the DB server and the compute instance: 2 vCPUs double the prices for both and also RAM and cores. As a consequence, there is no cost difference between n * 1-vCPU machines and 1 * n-vCPU machine. Consequently, an incremental provisioning of 1-vCPU VMs for an increasing number of tenants is reasonable. That is, the 15-day scenario, comparing 1 vCPU wih 4 vCPU, yields some expected results presented in Figure 9. Using incrementally 1*vCPU is even on a per-day basc starting with the first day cheaper, which let the cumulated cost become after 15 days:

a) 1 vCPU: $1900
b) 4 vCPU: $2280

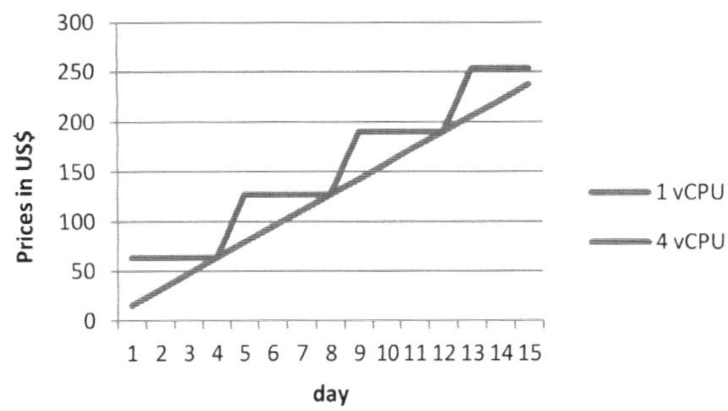

Figure 9. 15-day scale-out scenario for Offering 8.

However, one important question remains open: What is the advantage of a better n-vCPU instance, particularly compared to several smaller instances? Unfortunately, no specification beside the increase of RAM can be found in this respect. Further investigations are thus required.

VI. SUMMARY

Several differences have become apparent in the previous section and lead to several orthogonal facets:

- Database vs. database server: Sometimes, *databases* are paid (cf. Offerings 1-4); sometimes DB servers are provisioned (cf. Offering 5-8). The latter allows one to set up several databases within the database server, each database having specific credentials, i.e., tenant isolation comes for free. However, it becomes difficult to determine the right size of the VM, especially for avoiding upfront costs.
- Provision vs. consumption: Some offerings charge for *provisioned* storage (Offering 2-8), i.e., upfront costs occur even if small data is stored. Others (Offering 1) charge for storage *consumption* thus avoiding starting costs. However, the consumption approach is less prominent.
- Certain thresholds: Each offering has different tiers to choose from. Such a tier defines some thresholds. In most cases, each tier comes with an upper limit on the database size. Offerings 2 and 4 define certain limits on transaction rates, data transfer, or number of sessions, Offering 7 a limit on IOPS. Reaching such a limit could stop a SaaS application for serving tenants.
- For Offerings 3, 5, 6, 7, and 8, equipment such as RAM increases with each level, while this is not controllable and visible in Offerings 1, 2, and 4.
- Prices depend on the features such editions (Offering 7 and 8) or installation comfort (DBaaS in Offering 8). However, the decision is not affected by multi-tenancy considerations.

Moreover, we can distinguish between direct and indirect cost factors. *Direct* cost factors are immediately visible in the price scheme such as storage, IOPS, sessions, cores, or data transfer. We detected *indirect* cost factors, too. For example, it might be necessary to use and pay a larger virtual machine (VM) in order to achieve a certain transaction rate, e.g., Offering 2, or IOPS (Offering 7).

VII. CONCLUSION NAD FUTURE WORK

This paper took a deeper look into the price schemes of popular cloud database providers and investigated their cost impact on multi-tenancy. We thereby focused on storing tenants' data in relational databases. We showed that a cost-efficient database deployment for multi-tenancy heavily depends on providers due to very different price schemes.

The broad spectrum of price schemes makes it difficult to find an appropriate provider-independent cost-optimized configuration for multi-tenant applications. However, we could present some analyses for virtual databases by comparing the cost of a 1-DB-per-tenant and a 1-global-DB strategy and displaying the characteristics for different tenant sizes. The results also have a strong impact on the cloud provider selection. For example, if a strong isolation is requested, a provider with too high prices for a 1 DB-per-tenant strategy might not be qualified for a selection.

Furthermore, we investigated the category of virtual database servers. Here, we could derive some vendor-specific strategies what category of database servers is suited.

As a consequence, it is difficult to select *the* best provider from the cost perspective. But we think that our analysis helps architects of multi-tenant software to decide upon a cloud offering for the anticipated requirements. Besides architects, cloud providers can benefit from our analysis when it comes to adjust their service offerings.

This all affects portability of SaaS applications, too. It is not easy to define an economic provider-independent strategy for multi-tenancy. Furthermore, architectures must take into account several aspects. For example, monitoring consumption becomes necessary [22] because of thresholds such as a database upper limit of parallel sessions, IO limits, or any other type of throttling. This is indispensable to react in time if a threshold is reached because a service is in danger of being stopped [25].

Future work will tackle open questions, including practical investigations. One important question is about the provisioning time. This point is relevant in any strategy since additional databases have to be acquired. Similarly, upgrading a database level is important for saving upfront costs.

Finally, we intend to collect further challenges from an industrial perspective.

REFERENCES

[1] U. Hohenstein and S. Appel, "The Impact of Public Cloud Price Schemes on Multi-Tenancy", in 7th Int. Conf. on Cloud Computing, Grids and Virtualization, Rome (2016), pp. 22-29.

[2] F. Chong, G. Carraro, and R, Wolter, "Multi-Tenant Data Architecture," June 2006, http://msdn.microsoft.com/en-us /library/aa479086.aspx [retrieved: November 2016].

[3] C. Bezemer and A. Zaidman, "Challenges of Reengineering into Multitenant SaaS Applications," in: Technical Report of Delft Uni. of Technology, TUD-SERG-2010-012, 2010.

[4] R. Mietzner, F. Leymann, and M. Papazoglou, "Defining Composite Configurable SaaS Application Packages Using SCA, Variability Descriptors and Multi-Tenancy Patterns," in 3rd Int. Conf. on Internet and Web Applications and Services (ICIW), 2008, pp. 156-161.

[5] S. Walraven, E. Truyen, and W. Joosen, "A Middleware Layer for Flexible and Cost-Efficient Multi-Tenant Applications," in Proc. on Middleware, 2011 (LNCS 7049), pp. 370-389.

[6] R. Krebs, C. Momm, and S. Kounev, "Architectural Concerns in Multi-Tenant SaaS Applications," in CLOSER 2012, pp. 426-431.

[7] Z. Wang et al, "A Study and Performance Evaluation of the Multi-Tenant Data Tier Design Pattern for Service Oriented Computing," in IEEE Int. Conf. On eBusiness Engineering, (ICEBE) 2008, 94-101

[8] M. Armbrust et al., "A View of Cloud Computing," Communications of the ACM, 53(4), April 2010, pp. 50-58.

[9] A. Khajeh-Hosseini, I. Sommerville, and I. Sriram, "Research Challenges for Enterprise Cloud Computing," in Proc. 1st ACM Symposium on Cloud Computing, SOCC 2010, Indianapolis, pp. 450-457.

[10] E. Walker, "The Real Cost of a CPU Hour," Computer 2009, Vol. 42(4), pp. 35-41.

[11] M. Klems, J. Nimis, and S. Tai, "Do Clouds Compute? A Framework for Estimating the Value of Cloud Computing," in Designing E-Business Systems. Markets, Services, and Networks, Lecture Notes in Business Information Processing, Vol. 22, 2008, pp.110-123.

[12] B. Martens, M., Walterbusch, and F. Teuteberg, "Evaluating Cloud Computing Services from a Total Cost of Ownership Perspective," 45th Hawaii International Conference on System Sciences (HICSS-45), 2012, pp. 1564-1572.

[13] D. Kondo, B. Javadi, P. Malecot, F. Cappello, and D. Anderson, "Cost-Benefit Analysis of Cloud Computing versus Desktop Grids," in Proc. of the 2009 IEEE Int. Symp. on Parallel&Distributed Processing, May 2009, pp 1-12.

[14] D. Kossmann, T. Kraska, and S. Loesing, "An Evaluation of Alternative Architectures for Transaction in Processing in the Cloud," ACM SIGMOD 2010, pp. 579-590.

[15] U. Hohenstein, R. Krummenacher, L. Mittermeier, and S. Dippl, "Choosing the Right Cloud Architecture - A Cost Perspective," in Proc. on Cloud Computing and Services Science (CLOSER), 2012, pp. 334-344.

[16] C. Momm and R. Krebs, "A Qualitative Discussion of Different Approaches for Implementing Multi-Tenant SaaS Offerings," in Proc. Software Engineering 2011, pp. 139-150.

[17] C. Osipov, G. Goldszmidt, M. Taylor, and I. Poddar, "Develop and Deploy Multi-Tenant Web-Delivered Solutions Using IBM Middleware: Part 2: Approaches for Enabling Multi-Tenancy," in: IBM's technical library, 2009.

[18] D. Westermann and C. Momm, "Using Software Performance Curves for Dependable and Cost-Efficient Service Hosting," in Proc. on Quality of Service-Oriented Software Systems (QUASOSS), 2010, pp. 1-6.

[19] T. Kwok and A. Mohindra, "Resource Calculations With Constraints, and Placement of Tenants and Instances for Multi-Tenant SaaS Application," in Proc. Int. Conf. on Service-Oriented Computing, (ICSOC) 2008. LNCS, Vol. 5364, pp. 633-648.

[20] C. Bezemer, A. Zaidman, B. Platzbeecke, T. Hurkmans, and A. Hart, "Enabling Multitenancy: An Industrial Experience Report," in: Technical Report of Delft Uni. of Technology, TUD-SERG-2010-030, 2010.

[21] T. Dillon, C. Wu, and E. Chang, "Cloud Computing: Issues and Challenges," in Proc. 24th Int. Conf. on Advanced Information Networking and Applications, 2010, pp. 27-33.

[22] A. Schwanengel and U. Hohenstein, "Challenges with Tenant-Specific Cost Determination in Multi-Tenant Applications," in 4th Int. Conf. on Cloud Computing, Grids and Virtualization, Valencia (2013), pp. 36-42.

[23] Microsoft, "Developing Multitenant Applications on Windows Azure". http://msdn.microsoft.com/en-us/library/ff966499.aspx [retrieved: January 2016]

[24] P. Mell and T. Grance, "The NIST definition of cloud computing," National Institute of Standards and Technology, Sept. 2011. http://csrc.nist.gov/publications/nistpubs/800-145/SP800-145.pdf [retrieved: November 2016].

[25] A. Schwanengel, U. Hohenstein, and M. Jaeger, "Automated Load Adaptation for Cloud Environments in Regard of Cost Models," in Proc. on CLOSER, 2012, pp. 562-567.

[26] B. Berriman, G. Juve, E. Deelman, M. Regelson, and P. Plavchan, "The Application of Cloud Computing to Astronomy: A Study of Cost and Performance," Proc. of 6th IEEE Int. Conf. on e-Science, 2010, pp. 1-7.

[27] M. Lindner, F. Galán, and C. Chapman, "The Cloud Supply Chain: A Framework for Information, Monitoring, Accounting and Billing," in Proc. on ICST Cloud Computing, 2010, pp. 1-22.

A Study of Designing Service Model for Sightseeing Using BLE Beacons -To Provide Tourism Information of Traditional Cultural Sites -

Yuko Hiramatsu, Fumihiro Sato
Faculty of Economics
Chuo University
Hachioji-shi, Tokyo, Japan
Email: {susana_y, fsato}@tamacc.chuo-u.ac.jp

Atsushi Ito, Hiroyuki Hatano, Mie Sato, Yu Watanabe
Graduate School of Engineering,
Utsunomiya University
Utsunomiya-shi, Tochigi, Japan
Email: {at.ito, hatano, mie, yu}@is.utsunomiya-u.ac.jp

Akira Sasaki
GClue Inc.
Aizu-wakamatsu-shi,
Fukushima, Japan
Email: akira@gclue.jp

Abstract—**We have developed a new smartphone application for helping tourists using Bluetooth Low Energy (BLE) beacons. The application not only provides a guide for a specific location but also explains the traditional customs and history of the area. There are several smartphone applications for sightseeing and are usually designed to provide extensive information through photos, detailed explanation and users' comments. Such applications are convenient. However, a large amount of information is not always appealing to tourists. If tourists feel that they have to know many things about an area, is the travel attractive anymore? The promise of the unexpected is one of the things that make traveling attractive. Our trials in Nikko, one of the world heritage sites in Japan, demonstrate the effectiveness of the BLE beacon for sightseeing, especially for foreign visitors and young Japanese people, who walk around the area on foot. The application displays information near each beacon. Beacons on the route to the main shrine provide information regarding the local tradition and history of that area. However, the exact location of the beacons is unknown to the tourists before they visit the area. It might be a surprise like an Easter eggs for tourists. Shop owners install beacons in their shops and provide information regarding their products and menus. The people living the area help the tourists engage in local cultural activities, enhancing the tourists' experience of a traditional cultural city. In addition, we have created a quiz function focused on specific landscapes. This application is aimed at becoming a gateway to understanding traditional culture. Through trials, it was proved that our service model using smartphone and BLE beacons were very useful to support sightseeing.**

Keywords–Location-Based Service; BLE Beacon; Local information; Smartphone Application; World Heritage; Zeigarnik effect.

I. INTRODUCTION

The main purpose of this study is to develop a system to help the tourists engage in local cultural activities, enhancing the tourists' experience of a traditional cultural city. We introduce our remarkable points of our service model for tourist information and technology.

A. Services using Information and Communication Technology

Information and communication technology (ICT) is widely used for travel and tourism and has now made considerable information available. Tourists get information about maps, shops, accommodations, museums, events etc. However, the plethora of information available on the Web and SNS is not always appealing to tourists. We have to consider what information is appealing to tourists, when they should receive it and who the target users of this information should be. Before using big data in cloud by GPS signals for tourists, we should re-inspect and analyze the information contents.

We have been studying a service model for tourist using Bluetooth Low Energy (BLE) beacon [1]. In this paper, we investigated the information needs of tourists in Nikko and describe the result of experiments of provision of information using a BLE beacon system in detail.

This study was selected as one of the research themes of SCOPE [2] and was funded by the Ministry of Internal Affairs and Communications of Japan [3].

B. Psychology of Tourists

Many previous studies have investigated environmental psychology and tourism. Pearce and Stringer [4] studied the issue from the viewpoint of physiology, cognition and individual variation. It has been shown that among the factors that drive people to travel to new places, the expectation of experiencing the extraordinary plays a leading role [5]. The term 'extraordinary' here means experiences clearly different from the usual lifestyle. Thus, busy workers may crave relaxation, while bored young people may crave excitement. Therefore, separately identifying specialized target audiences and providing them with the unique information that matches their expectations is necessary.

C. Cultural Differences

Tourism involves encounters with people and places. Each place has its own characteristic culture, and these differences between cultures make travel interesting and exciting. However, some tourists do not recognize the cultural significance of traditional sites.

For example, Japan has ancient temples, many of which are located far from train stations. While this may at first appear to make visits inconvenient, traveling the route to the temple has traditionally been a central feature of the visit. There are often a series of wells en route to the main temple, at which visitors to the shrine purify themselves by washing their hands and their hearts, as well as smaller temples surrounding the main one. Tourists who are unaware of this tradition may not sense the full experience. Information on this is, however, difficult to find on the Web, and if it exists, it is often buried among the numerous photographs and comments left by visitors unfamiliar with the location.

The rest of this paper is structured as follows. Section 2 discusses related works. Section 3 sets out our proposal based on user research in Nikko. In Section 4, we propose a service proposal for young tourists and foreigners, and provide outline of system design. Section 5 provides the result of experiments and display the effect and usefulness of our service model and smartphone application including quizzes to give satisfaction to visitors of Nikko. At last, in section 6, we summarize this research and discuss future studies.

II. Related Works

A. Our Previous Work

Students go on school trips in Japan [6]. While such outdoor activities are valuable, students cannot fully grasp the artistic or cultural value and meaning of the objects or scenery by simply viewing them [7]. To address this problem, we developed a new learning model for outdoor study [8] [9].

Human beings do not always recognize what they see. For example, in the game of photo hunt, we may not be able to tell the difference between two similar photographs. However, once a particular object is noticed, our attention is focused on it. We exploited this concept by developing a quiz to be used as a trigger to draw attention to a particular object in the scenery that the students were viewing. The quizzes encouraged positive responses. We argue that such methods will be beneficial for other tourist groups as well.

B. Related Works

1) Application for sight seeing: Many sightseeing applications for smartphones already exist in Japan [10], which allow tourists to access information about restaurants, souvenir shops and local weather, as well as to download maps. Counting only local applications, 666 such applications were identified in a 2015 study. Although 96% of these were free, 91% were downloaded only 10,000 or fewer times [11]. The EU's TAG CLOUD project (Technologies lead to Adaptability and lifelong enGagement with culture throughout the CLOUD) used smartphone technology to provide information about traditional cultural sites [12] and to investigate ways of enabling cultural engagement using cloud-based technologies. While the TAG CLOUD uses a cloud-based service, our application was designed to work without requiring access to the cloud, since Internet connections may be limited in rural areas.

2) Beacon system: There are several types of indoor location services offered through Wi-Fi APs. However, using them is difficult since the location information using a Wi-Fi AP is not accurate enough. One reason for this is the low number of APs. Usually, there are not enough APs in a space such as a shopping mall.

Recently, iBeacon [13] has become popular for location-based services. The iBeacon function is provided in an iOS framework and is suitable for location-based services. From a technical viewpoint, iBeacon uses BLE that is a very low-power device working on batteries. On the contrary, Wi-Fi APs usually require AC power. Furthermore, iBeacon is cheaper than Wi-Fi APs. Therefore, installing BLE beacon in a target area is very simple.

Moreover, there are several iPhone users in Japan. 50.2% of the smartphone users in Japan have bought iPhones (January 2016) [14]. This is another reason that iBeacon is popular in the Japanese market.

BLE beacons are mainly used for indoor location-based services to indicate locations and display information. For example, they are set in shopping malls or museums. When smartphones receive signals from a beacon, product information or pictures are displayed on the screen. In addition, distributing coupons using beacons in a shop is possible. BLE Beacons are also used for control systems helping in maintaining bus records etc.

Therefore, there are many related papers about the indoor use of the BLE beacon [15][16][17][18]. For example, there is a service for migrating signage displays and the movement of its users. This system tracks specific movements of users and provides Web contents to them. To track a user, this system estimates the position of the user based on the Bluetooth signal strength [19].

As a novel approach, we have been using BLE beacons outdoor [1] [20]. We can transmit local information using beacons or push technology, which makes it is useful for tourists and shop owners to send local or seasonal information. The beacon system is useful for tourists from the viewpoint of power supply as well.

III. Service Proposal

We administered questionnaires to the visitors to Nikko [21], in order to know the focus points for our new system, on September 2014. A total of 606 questionnaires (534 in Japanese and 72 in English) were completed. Table I shows the results of the rotated matrix.

TABLE I. Rotated Matrix.

	Component		
	1	*2*	*3*
Nature/Landscape	.008	.810	.189
History/Culture	.017	.853	.053
Street	.478	.680	.049
Traditional performing arts	.473	.676	.122
Food	.644	.269	.157
Activity	.716	.173	.226
Shopping	.835	.154	.093
Night spot	.760	-.005	.209
Personal exchange	.647	.053	.294
Easy booking	.151	.037	.868
Quality & price of hotels	.307	.039	.771
Transportation	.116	.147	.639
Prices	.279	.346	.477

Extration Method:Principal Component Analysis
Rotation Method: Varimax with Kaiser Normalization
a. Rotation converged in 5 itertion

Cluster analysis was used to confirm this pattern. Respondents were asked to evaluate sightseeing activities in Nikko on a scale of one to five. As shown in Table I, the responses were clustered into three main groups:

- People who focus Food, Activity, shopping, Night spot, Personal exchange ⇒ A group who valued its own active experiences

- People who focus Nature/Landscape, History/Culture, Street, traditional performing arts ⇒ A group who valued nature, history, or traditional factors
- People who focus easy booking, Quality and prices of hotels, Transportation, Prices ⇒ A group who valued the quality of accommodation or the price of goods and services

We used these 3 components. Using Ward's method, which is an alternative approach for performing cluster analysis, the data was then classified into five clusters with these 3 components. As only three persons belonged to the 5th cluster, we classified the results into the following four clusters, as shown in Fig. 1.

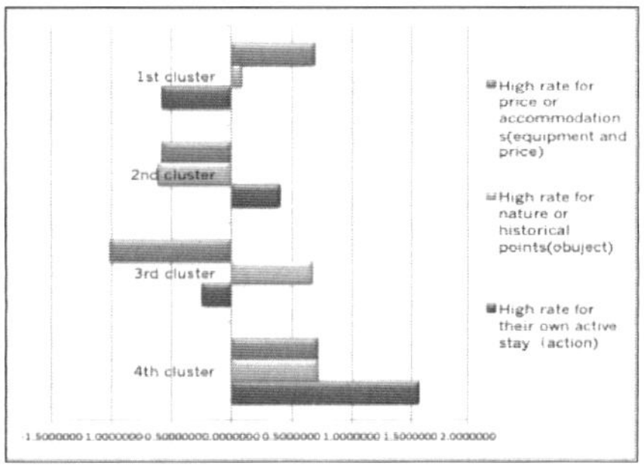

FIGURE 1. EVALUATION OF THE PREFERENCES OF THE FOUR CLUSTERS.

1) Tourists who do not wish to be active, or who are mainly concerned about prices and accommodation (n = 140).
2) Tourists who do not have any special interests, but who wish to stay active (n = 103).
3) Tourists interested in nature or history (n = 62).
4) Tourists who give a high rating to almost everything in Nikko or who particularly wish to stay active (n = 37).

Tourists in the 1st cluster would like to visit the famous hot springs in Nikko and are unlikely to be interested in extensive information about Nikko, since they visit Nikko primarily for rest. Tourists in the 4th cluster are active and have many interests, but are less numerous than those in the 1st cluster.

The age composition of the groups is shown in Fig. 2. Over 70% of those in the 4th cluster were under 30 years old.

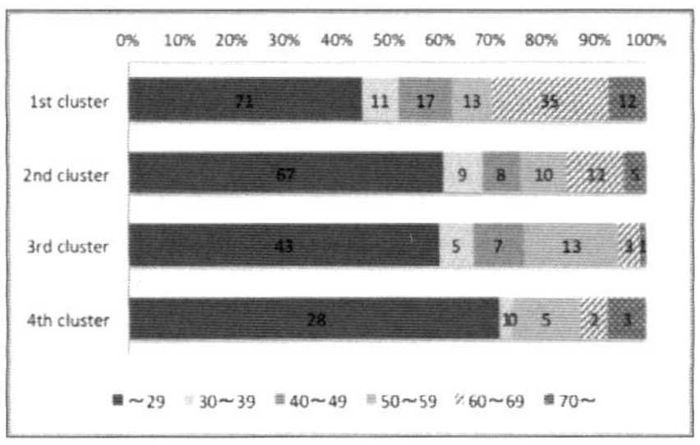

FIGURE 2. AGES OF TOURISTS IN THE FOUR CLUSTERS (%).

Young tourists tend to plan active trips to Nikko. Their characteristic tendencies are as follows:

- They come to Nikko by train and navigate Nikko by bus or on foot.
- They are smartphone users.
- They know little about traditional culture.
- They like to experience new things.

A key finding was that young people reported that they would like to have enjoyed Nikko more completely and that most of them were smartphone users. According to the survey of Ministry of Internal Affairs and Communications in Japan, 94.1% of 20's use smartphone in 2014 [22].

Responses from foreign tourists showed the same profile.

IV. SERVICE PROPOSAL FOR YOUNG TOURISTS AND FOREIGNERS

We explain our system and report the results of our trials and explain the role-played in Nikko.

A. Service Flow

Tourists who know little about the area and the history currently exchange comments using SNS. We therefore addressed the use of beacons to allow residents of the tourism area to recover information from such tourists. We designed our service system as shown in Fig. 3.

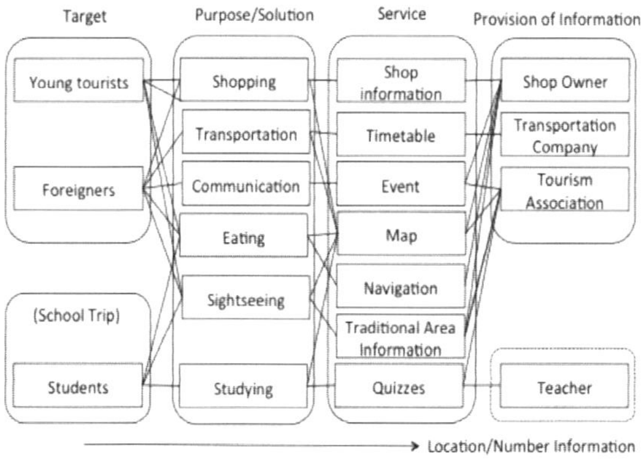

FIGURE 3. SERVICE FLOW.

Shop owners gave us information about the goods they stock, seasonal festivals and other information. Tourists could access this near the beacon, which was located in front or at the entrance of the shop. Bus timetables were furnished by the local bus operator and information about local attractions was supplied by the tourist association. This information was displayed on a map in the smartphone application (Fig. 4).

In addition, we devised several quizzes using the Zeigarnik effect [23], aimed at young students on school trips. This is a psychological effect. We, human beings remember better an unfinished event or an incomplete one. If students answer a quiz, they might keep thinking about it till they look at the object, the answer of the quiz near iBeacon.

Shop owners could then access customer traffic diagrams, and teachers could monitor the location of their students.

FIGURE 4. BUS TIMETABLE.

TABLE II. FUNCTIONS AND DEVICES IN A SMART PHONE.

Functions	*Devices in a smart phone*	*Relation between tourist information*
Communication	3G/LTE	Download Info.
	WiFi	Download Info./Find Location (Indoor)
	BT	Find Location (Indoor)
Location	GPS	Find Location (Outside)
Near Field Communication	NFC	Get Short Information
	RFID	
	BLE	
Motion Sensor	Accelerometer	Detect Steps
	Gyro	Detect Movement
	Compus	Detect Direction
Picture	Camera	Get picture/Get Short Information through 2D barcode

B. Comparison of Technologies that can be used for Sightseeing in Historic Areas

Current smart phones incorporate a range of sensors. Table II lists the functions of these devices and their potential use in tourist information services. Several of the devices can be used to collect information and identify the location of smartphone users.

However, foreign tourists rarely use roaming data communication services because of their high cost, so we also designed a service that did not require the use of 3G/LTE. As both GPS and the camera quickly deplete the battery, we designed our service to work without them. The use of AR was a potentially interesting alternative navigation method; however, it proved impossible to run this in the background. The final design of our application was as shown in Fig. 5. We assumed the following design constraints:

1) Information should be displayed using the BLE beacon. For near-field communication, NFC and RFID may also be used. NFC requires activating a tag, which is inconvenient for tourists. RFID works in a similar way to a BLE beacon, but no smartphone has the RFID function.
2) If 3G/LTE is not available, it must be possible to download applications and information using Wi-Fi. In the Nikko area, the City of Nikko provides a free Wi-Fi service at the railway station and in some shops, allowing tourists to download applications. Wi-Fi provides location data, in order to replace GPS.
3) The application should provide a full range of information including location, shopping information and bus timetables. Real-time information such as temporary changes to bus routes because of festivals or the blooming of cherry blossom should be downloadable using free Wi-Fi.

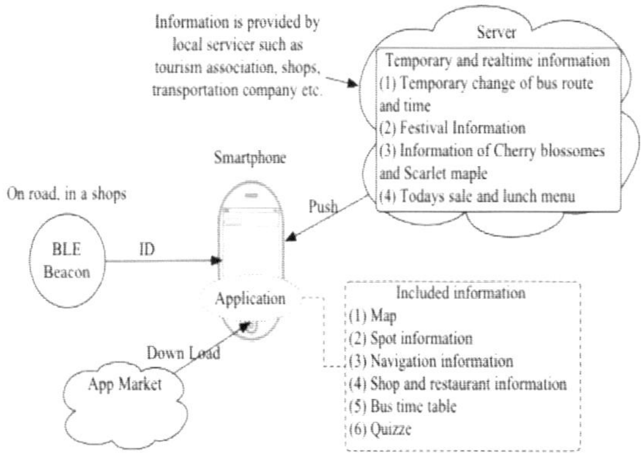

FIGURE 5. SYSTEM DIAGRAM.

C. Information on Nikko as a World Heritage Site

Using beacons, we sent location-specific information within a range between 2.3 and 10 m [24], which transformed an anonymous road into a zone immersed in Japanese culture. (Refer to Fig. 6)

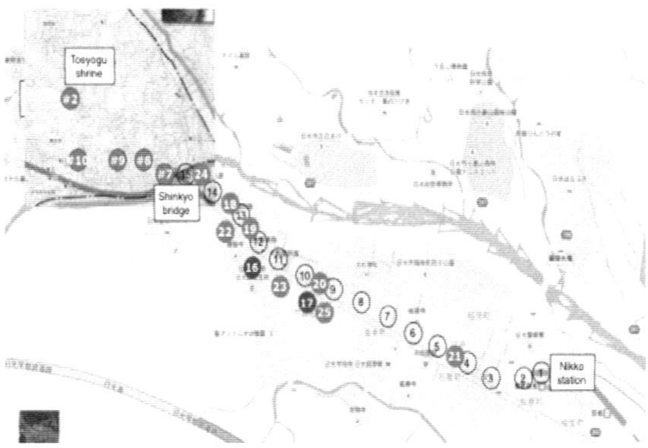

FIGURE 6. BEACON MAP AT NIKKO.

This reflects the traditional Japanese method of attending services of worship, in which the journey to and from the service are not the same. Before entering a temple or shrine, tourists purify themselves. After leaving the shrine, they eat or go shopping. This is an established Japanese cultural custom, which has long been taken for granted.

The erection of signboards is seldom permitted in Nikko, following the Convention Concerning the Protection of the World Cultural and Natural Heritage (UNESCO, 1972). Using beacons, we were able to show the information on a smartphone. We created a traditional road, ' SANDOU ' (it means a road approaching the main temple or shrine in Japanese), for the Nikko cultural heritage site. Using our beacon system, tourists could pause on the road, some to read information about the traditional temple there and others to find shops selling Japanese sweets, while young students answered a quiz. The road became a pilgrimage route to the shrine.

D. Designing the Application and Locating the Beacons

Many trials using BLE beacons have been reported in which location-specific and shopping information was provided in shopping malls and train stations. However, the BLE beacon has rarely been used for outdoor sightseeing.

Beacons send advertising messages at prefixed intervals using channels 37, 38 and 39. iBeacon, defined by Apple, sends advertising messages every 100 ms [13]. An important characteristic of BLE is its low power consumption. BLE requires only 1/10 to 1/100 the power of classic Bluetooth signalling, and a beacon may function for a year or more without a battery change.

To improve the visitor experience, we imposed the following requirements on the system:

- Reduce power consumption by avoiding the use of GPS.
- Provide sightseeing information related to the BLE beacon location.
- Have navigation operate in both foreground and background while displaying the distance from the station to the Shinkyo Bridge entrance to Toshogu (the main shrine).
- Display a timetable of main bus routes.

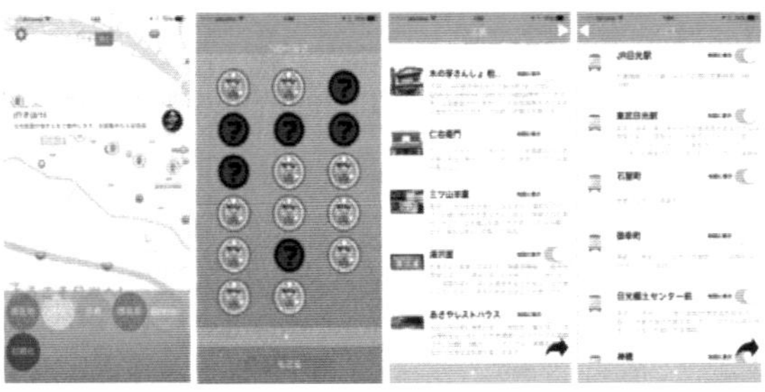

FIGURE 7. SCREENSHOTS OF OUR APPLICATION NAMED " NIKKO KAMEN NAVI ".

Figure 7 displays screenshots of the application named " NikkoNavi ". This application was implemented on iPhone (5 or later models).

Figure 8 explains the software components of this application. In the operating system (OS), BLE access function

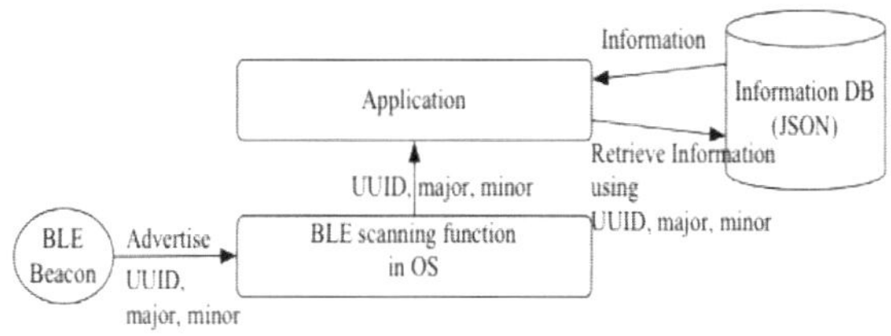

FIGURE 8. SOFTWARE DESIGN TO USE BLE BEACON.

always scans advertising message. If the OS catches an advertising message, the information of the advertising message is forwarded to the application. For example, Core Location framework of iOS (7 or later) provides three properties such as proximity UUID, major and minor.

Android 5.0 or later also provides similar function. If the information such as UUID, major and minor is received from a beacon, the application retrieves information that matches triples (UUID, major and minor). For example, if UUID=cb86bc31-05bd-40cc-903d-1c9bd13d966a, major=1, minor=1, the information relating to the beacon located in the Nikko Station is retrieved from DB and it is displayed on the screen of the smart phone. Each beacon provided information related to its location. For example, when the application received a signal from beacon #13, it displayed ' On the left, there is a slope. At the end of the slope, there is an old temple named Kannonji; 180 m to Shinkyo Bridge and 1,250 m to Nikko train station ' . The visitor could use this information to find a small, historic temple.

To ensure stable reception of signals between the Nikko station and Shinkyo Bridge, we calculated the distance between the beacons as follows. In order to receive a signal from a beacon in the background, a smartphone must receive the signal for one minute or longer. We set a beacon to send a one-directional message using a steel signboard.

V. EVALUATION

In this section, we discuss the effectiveness of our system.

A. First Trial: Discovery of Beacons

Six students and three faculty members participated in the first trial, conducted on November 9, 2014.

1) Discovery of Beacons: We tested the beacons under three scenarios:

Scenario 1: Walking from Nikko station to Shinkyo Bridge
Scenario 2: Taking a bus from Nikko station to Shinkyo Bridge
Scenario 3: Walking to the Nikko visitor centre from Shinkyo Bridge while visiting shops where a beacon was located

In Scenario 1, users located approximately 95% of the beacons while walking. The beacon system worked as expected.

In Scenario 2, the results were prima facie unstable. If the user sat in the back of a bus, the smartphone was located near the window, but if the user sat in a front seat, the smartphone was below the window. In the former case, the smartphone could easily capture signals from beacons, but in the latter case, the metal body of the bus blocked the signal. As the smartphone captured the beacon signal once a minute, the signals from some beacons were missed. Detailed testing of the relationship between the position at which the smartphone is held and the bus speed is a subject for future study.

In Scenario 3, about 80% of the beacons were found, although in one case, only 33% were found. This suggests that the beacon system works best when users have already decided which shops to visit.

2) User awareness of the beacons: We asked subjects to monitor their awareness of the vibration and sound emitted by the smartphone when a beacon was found. The results showed that if users were holding the smartphone in their hand, awareness of the beacon was high, at approximately 60%. However, if the phone was in the user ' s pocket, awareness fell to about 40%. Because it is dangerous to use a smartphone while walking on the road, different ways must be found to alert users to the beacon. In this regard, wearable devices such as smart watches might prove useful. This will be addressed in the next phase of our study.

3) Overall evaluation: We asked the participants to record their overall impression of sightseeing using the BLE beacon. The most common responses were ' useful ' and ' fun ' .

The map, in particular, contributed to a feeling of safety (2.77 in 3 grades) and the information about shops was appreciated (2.70 in 3 grades). Key comments on the ' SANDO ' (a Japanese road approaching the main shrine) included the following: ' I found a small spring on the road ' and ' The information on the little temple was good ' . The participants appreciated the information triggered by the beacon.

B. Second Trial: The Zeigarnik Effect

1) In order to evaluate the Zeigarnik Effect: Detailed navigation systems are commonly created for trips. Going further, we have deliberately created a function to provide incomplete experiences for students using the Zeigarnik effect.

The Zeigarnik effect carries the name of Bluma Zeigarnik, a Lithuanian-born psychologist. This effect explains that completed tasks are less recalled than uncompleted tasks.

Using the same beacons, we created quizzes about history and tradition of Nikko in order to make some uncompleted points memory and to evaluate d the results consequence of the Zeigarnik effect.

FIGURE 9. THE SCREENSHOTS OF QUIZZES.

We intended to design this tool for students undertaking a school trip. Figure 9 shows screenshots of our quiz function. The screens were designed using Japanese traditional patterns, and we used some traditional words inform the Edo periods (200-400 years ago). However, those words are used by elderly people now and young people just understand the meanings. We wanted students to experience an old atmosphere using this function on a smartphone that is a symbol of cutting-edge technology. This function was used as an entrance to find some secret of Nikko by attempting to solve quizzes containing traditional cultural information.

This was tested on September 26 and 27, 2015. Twenty-eight students participated in the test, of whom 23 completed ten quizzes on the road to Toshogu Shrine and a control group of five students walked the route without the application. The participants were first asked to complete quizzes about the area, whose answers could be found by observing objects at the site.

Before and after the walking using this application, the participants answered questionnaires as followings.

1) Before the test
   - Evaluations about factors for travel
   - Evaluations about Nikko (1)
2) Immediately after the test
   - About the evaluation of the application
   - Drawing a map from the Nikko station to the main shrine
3) After one month
   - Checking three points on a photograph
4) After two months
   - Evaluations about Nikko (2)

After the walk, the participants were first asked to complete a questionnaire and to draw a map of the area [25]. Drawing a map is said that memory is mainly visual [26]. The answers given by users of the application were more concrete than those of the control group. Application users were able to place an average of 9.18 objects on the map from the station to the shrine, whereas the controls identified an average of only 5.80. Application users could not only remember the answers to the quiz questions but could also recall the shops near the beacon sites where they had answered the quiz.

After a gap of a month, the participants completed another questionnaire and checked three points on a photograph from the route they had walked in Nikko. Heat maps were created on the basis of the responses. Four photographs of the route to the main shrine were used: two in the main shrine itself and two showing several characteristic points.

FIGURE 10. HEAT MAP ON THE WAY TO THE MAIN SHRINE.

Figure 10 shows a heat map of the route to the main shrine. The participants paid no heed to the architecture along the route. This is in contrast to the photographs in the shrine where the gaze of the participants was directed to lettering.

The red point is a restaurant sign with very big letters. Attention was also paid to written signs on the road. The street was recognized as the way to the main shrine. The yellow point shows that little attention was given to the BLE beacon in which no letters were present in the photograph.

FIGURE 11. HEAT MAP IN THE SHRINE (QUIZ USERS).

FIGURE 12. HEAT MAP IN THE SHRINE (NON QUIZ USERS).

Figure 11 shows that the participants paid heed to the architecture of the shrine, particularly to the upper part on the right side. This was in contrast with the approach route.

Figure 12 is the heat map by non-application users (n=19). That is the same photo as Fig. 9. Comparing Fig. 9 with Fig. 10, the upper part on the right side is significantly different.

The results confirmed that the use of the quizzes exploiting the Zeigarnik effect improves recall. Students remembered both the BLE beacon and the objects used in the quizzes.

The use of quizzes in the application helped users to recall the shops around the beacons immediately after the trial. In the future, we will expand the scope of our study to include ' SANDO ' on the route to the main Toshogu Shrine.

2) The Results of Data Analysis: We compared two same questionnaires, before and two months after to the trip in Nikko.

The evaluations of Nikko changed as described in Fig. 13. Before the trip, in accordance with tourist psychology [5],

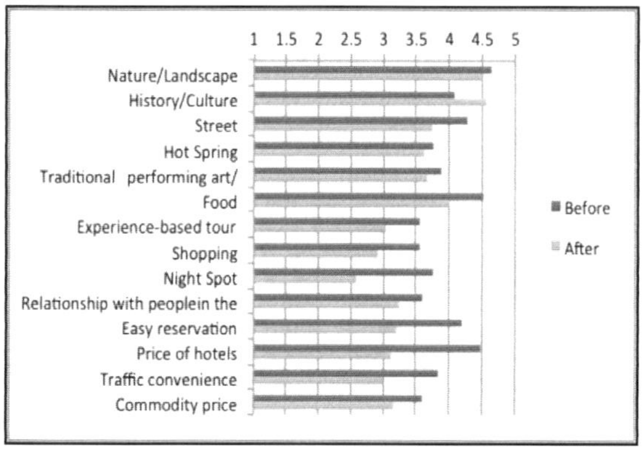

FIGURE 13. THE EVALUATION ABOUT NIKKO BEFORE AND AFTER THE TRIP (5 POINTS ' LIKERT SCALE).

the participants expected to gain some new experiences. After the experience, their expectations decreased, except for the subject of 'History/Culture', which was remarkable. Using our application, the participants evaluated the traveling experience higher after the trip than before the trip on this point.

In addition, we analyzed their answers to questionnaires regarding our application. The results of the cluster analysis are shown in Table III. Using Ward ' s method, the data were then classified into tree clusters. Cluster 1 tended to evaluate tangible factors of our application. Cluster 2 tended to evaluate general impression. Cluster 3 evaluated contents (quizzes) and the map that was being used for the quizzes ' rally. Each colored article reflected the highest numerical value in the tree clusters.

We compared two evaluations on the traveling parameters of each cluster (Refer to Table IV).

TABLE III. THE EVALUATIONS OF OUR APPLICATION (COMPRISING CLUSTER ELEMENTS).

	Cluster 1	*Cluster 2*	*Cluster 3*
Impression	3.29	4.57	3.25
Interface	4.00	4.14	3.25
Usability	3.00	3.71	3.25
Font size	4.14	4.00	4.00
Sound	4.43	3.29	3.25
Color	4.57	4.29	3.25
Expression	4.29	3.86	3.25
Contents(Quizzes)	3.14	4.14	4.25
Visibility of the Map	3.43	3.29	5.00

There are remarkable features in cluster 3. They evaluated six factors higher after the trip than before the trip. In the other two clusters, they evaluated only two or three factors higher. In cluster 3, particularly, they evaluated 'History/Culture' high; the numerical value increased by 1.5 points after the trip, in the five-points ' Likert scale. However, the 'interaction with the local people ' was lower than in the other two clusters.

After two months, the impressions of this application and evaluation of user interface faded out in cluster 1. However, according to the answers in cluster 3, the quizzes ' contents made the area more attractive than before.

TABLE IV. THE EVALUATIONS OF OUR APPLICATION (COMPRISING CLUSTER ELEMENTS).

	(A) Before the trip			(B) 2 months after the trip			Incremental difference (B-A)		
Cluster	1	2	3	1	2	3	1	2	3
Nature/Landscape	5.00	5.00	3.75	4.43	4.83	4.50	-0.57	-0.17	**0.75**
History/Culture	4.29	4.71	3.25	4.43	4.80	4.75	0.14	0.09	**1.50**
Street	4.43	4.29	4.50	4.00	3.83	4.00	-0.43	-0.45	-0.50
Hot Spring	4.14	3.71	3.50	3.57	3.50	3.25	-0.57	-0.21	-0.25
Traditional Performing Art /Specialty	3.86	4.00	3.75	3.71	3.83	4.00	-0.14	-0.17	**0.25**
Food	4.71	4.43	4.25	3.71	3.83	4.75	-1.00	-0.60	**0.50**
Experience-based tour	3.43	3.57	2.50	3.00	2.83	3.75	-0.43	-0.74	**1.25**
Shopping	4.14	3.14	3.50	3.00	3.17	3.75	-1.14	0.02	**0.25**
Night Spot	3.71	3.00	4.50	3.00	2.67	3.00	-0.71	-0.33	-1.50
Relationship with people in the area	2.83	3.29	3.00	3.71	3.33	3.00	**0.88**	**0.05**	0.00
Easy reservation	4.00	3.29	3.75	3.00	3.17	3.00	-1.00	-0.12	-0.75
Price of hotels	4.57	3.71	5.00	3.00	3.17	3.50	-1.57	-0.55	-1.50
Traffic convenience	4.71	4.43	4.50	3.29	3.50	1.75	-1.43	-0.93	-2.75
Commodity price	4.14	3.57	3.75	3.00	3.83	3.25	-1.14	0.26	-0.50

3) About the contents of quizzes using iBeacons: The previous section has shown that playing a quiz rally with our application remained in the memories of the participants. We would like to describe these quizzes in detail in this section.

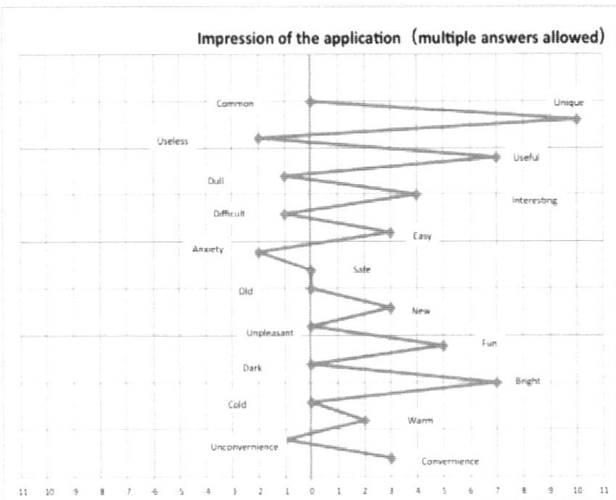

FIGURE 14. IMPRESSIONS OF QUIZZES FUNCTION.

Our quiz rally function of the application made the participants gain positive impressions (Fig. 14). They felt the application was unique, useful and smart. Their answers leaned toward the right side in the figure, which means they were favorable impressions.

There is a characteristic point in their answers. Two types of responses to the quizzes were observed; some quizzes were taken up by several participants, whereas others were not selected by any. Some users evaluated the quizzes as interesting, while others mentioned that they were difficult. However, the quizzes certainly attracted their attention. On the contrary, no one mentioned some quizzes.

The answers pertaining to the quizzes were very interesting.

The quizzes about just history were not highly evaluated. In contrast, participants highly evaluated quizzes on traditions and the local culture related to the actual daily life of the local people or in comparison to the other nation ' s customs and traditions. For example, they were interested in a quiz about height above sea level of their location. Participants were urged to compere with the places they have known in their ordinary lives. The answer showed them the place they were is as tall as the Tokyo Sky Tree, the highest tower in Japan. To compere with their already known place made them to feel how the location was high and were surprised. If the answer showed only the number of height above sea level, they would not be interested in the quiz so much. The explanation of the quiz told them that the holy places are established at higher place than usual lives.

They seemed to enjoy the cultural gap among them.

4) Additional Research: This quiz function was designed for school trips in Japan. Before the trip, students gained insights about the destination such as history, traditions and specific art monuments in the area and created some quizzes for the other classmates. They did not know what types of quizzes were being prepared by the other students. The students prepared for their outdoor excursion as an incomplete experience. Such an incomplete experience arouses human interest in the object.

Therefore, we conducted additional research on high-school students. Eleven students participated in our test on 5th of December 2015. Before the test, they had created several quizzes for our application, and they had already added them into our application.

They answered the same questionnaires as in our previous test (not all, but two questionnaires: the evaluation of our application and the evaluation of Nikko). The data from nine students was valid. Two of them lived near the Nikko area; thus, we did not use these data.

According to the results of the questionnaires, high-school students remembered objects in the area better than the previous participants did. Moreover, they answered that they were satisfied with our application more than previous participants were. In addition, most of them chose ' interesting ' as their impression of our application (eight out of nine high-school students). However, the data numbers were few to analyze with statistical significance. Therefore, we aim to continue our research on this subject.

C. The Results of the Research for Foreign and Japanese Tourists

We asked tourists to install our application named ' Nikko Kamen Navi ' at the Tobu Nikko Station on the 29th-30th August, 26th-27th September and 8th November 2015. Some users voluntarily answered the web questionnaire after using this application.

The total number of participants was 57:15 of them were English-speaking foreign visitors, and 42 were Japanese tourists. Both foreigners and Japanese tended to answer that our application was convenient, interesting and helpful. However, foreigners chose these words on a larger percentage than Japanese; A total of 47.62% (20 people) of the Japanese tourists and 73.33% (11 people) of the foreigners answered that this application was convenient.

Figure 10 shows a heat map of the route to the main shrine. Japanese students paid attention to the Japanese letters in that photo. They walked while looking at signboards on the way to the main shrine. However, those inscriptions were only in Japanese. There were no signboards for foreigners because the area belongs to the world heritage site, and it was difficult to place some new signboards. Foreigners had little information on the way to the main shrine. Therefore, providing them with basic information using such an application proved to be necessary.

VI. CONCLUSIONS

Smartphone sightseeing applications offer several types of information. However, tourists visit sites to see real places and experience the real environment, while the smartphone is only a tool to enhance the experience. Thus, the information provided to the target audience must be refined. Tourists are not primarily motivated by convenience; in fact, unfamiliar experiences or inconvenience may actually arouse their curiosity.

Traditional cultural locations have special historical or cultural significance. Introducing tourists to relevant cultural information about these locations helps to create a strong impression. Our application aims to provide such information. Owners of shops en route to the main shrine provided us with not only information concerning their shops but also local traditions and seasonal events, enriching the information available to tourists. A web questionnaire showed that tourists found the information about shops useful. In the survey, 89.2% of the respondents were under 30 years of age. Foreigners could access the information using the English pages.

Local information can be used to attract visitors to other cultural sites around the world, particularly in world heritage sites designated as special protection areas, where signboards are banned.

Japanese students studied the history and specific artworks of the area before their school trip. By creating quizzes for their classmates and tackling quizzes that the others had prepared, interest was sparked. This provided the basis for our use of the Zeigarnik effect, in which completed tasks are less well-remembered than uncompleted tasks. Thus, we deliberately created incomplete experiences.

From a technological viewpoint, we are planning to introduce two new functions. One will allow the beacon to function on a solar battery; the other is to enhance the positioning system. We can get the time information to reach the beacon points now (refer to Fig. 15). However, these data still cannot be used for ships on the way to the main shrine.

It is possible to develop a PDR assisted by BLE Beacon. We measured the change in the strength of the beacon signal around a beacon. Figure 16 shows that near the beacon, the strength of the signal increases. At this point, correcting the PDR error is possible if the PDR system has the data of exact position (longitude and latitude) or the signal contains its location data (longitude and latitude). We have developed a test application that can measure such data. We are planning to conduct some tests using this application.

Such improvements will be useful for shop owners in order to use tourist information. There are two different types of users of this application. If we hope to continuously use this application, we have to consider not only tourists but also local users, i.e., the shop owners. They will install this application and sometimes input seasonal information, advertisements or other announcements. It is important for the application to renew the seasonal information; thereby making the information more relevant and useful.

In addition, this system will be useful during times of disaster, letting people know the location of the nearest safe

GoogleMap

Details of Log

beacon_history_id	user_id	beacon_id	major	minor	locale	app_ver	save_at	create_at
3007	50	1	1	1	en	1.0.0 Ver1026	2015-10-26 17:10:43	2015-10-26 17:10:44
3129	50	4	1	4	ja	1.0.0 Ver1026	2015-11-01 15:30:29	2015-11-01 15:30:29
3130	50	20	1	23	ja	1.0.0 Ver1026	2015-11-01 15:30:30	2015-11-01 15:30:30
3131	50	18	1	21	ja	1.0.0 Ver1026	2015-11-01 15:30:31	2015-11-01 15:30:31
3132	50	19	1	22	ja	1.0.0 Ver1026	2015-11-01 15:30:32	2015-11-01 15:30:32

FIGURE 15. LOG DATA OF THE APPLICATION.

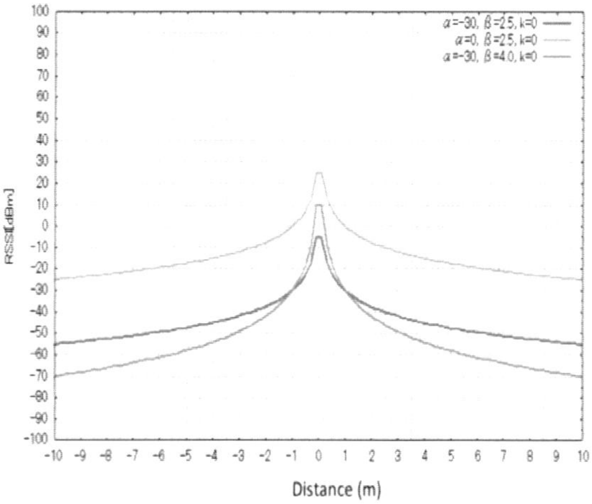

FIGURE 16. MODELS FOR PDR.

place via the map. Communication traffic often occurs after a disaster. Our application can be used without requiring Internet access.

We are planning a collaboration with the other world heritage site in Kyusyu, the south area in Japan. We will use our beacon technology and application to provide descriptions and explanations of the traditional places and customs. In some cases, someone will carry a beacon and participants are going to look for it. There are many methods to use beacons. It is easy to put beacons at some events, too.

Our main goal is to inform tourists about traditional cultures. Our system allows knowledge of the culture of a location to be transmitted to the next generation and to foreigners. Such travel information will inspire tourists and encourage them to treat the culture respectfully.

ACKNOWLEDGMENT

We would like to express special thanks to Mr. Funakoshi (Nikko Tourism Association), members of the ‘Study group on School Trip’, Mr. Takamura and Mr.Yoshida (Hatsuishi-kai: An association of Nikko shopping streets), Mr. Daisuke Yawaka and Mr. Takao Masuda (Chuo Univ.).

This research was performed as a SCOPE (Strategic Information and Communications R&D Promotion Programme) project funded by the Ministry of Internal Affairs and Communications (MIC) in Japan.

REFERENCES

[1] Y.Hiramatsu, F. Sato, A. Ito, H. Hatano, M. Sato, Y. Watanabe, and A. Sasaki, "A Service Model using Bluetooth Low Energy Beacons -To Provide Tourism Information of Traditional Cultural Sites -," SERVICE COMPUTATION 2016, pp. 14-19, March 2016.

[2] The Ministry of Internal Affairs and Communications, Strategic Information and Communications R&D Promotion Programme, [Online]. Available from: http://www.soumu.go.jp/main_sosiki/joho_tsusin/scope/, [Nov. 30, 2016].

[3] The Ministry of Internal Affairs and Communications of Japan [Online]. Available from: http://www.soumu.go.jp/english/index.html, [Nov. 30, 2016].

[4] P. L. Pearce and P. F. Stringer, "The effect of task interruption and closure on perceived duration," Annals of Tourism Research 18, pp. 136-154, 1991.

[5] T. Sasaki, "Psychology of Tourism," Kitahojishobou,Kyoto, pp. 51-59, 2007.

[6] Study Group on School Trip, The research Report about usage of ICT devices at junior high school and high school, [Online]. Available from: http://joyful-shu-gaku.com/, [Nov. 30, 2016].

[7] The research report about usage of ICT devices at junior high school and high school, Study Group on School Trip, [Online]. Available from: http://joyful-shu-gaku.com/, [Nov. 30, 2016].

[8] Y. Hiramatsu., A. Ito, and F. Sato, "The Site-specific Learning Model on Mobile Phones Using Zeigarnik Effect - Designing Collaboration Tool for Outdoor Studying," Poster Presentation at HCII (International Conference on Human-Computer Interaction), 2013.

[9] Y. Hiramatsu, A. Ito, M. Fujii, and F.Sato, "Development of the Learning System for Outdoor Study Using Zeigarnik Effect," HCII 2014, pp. 127-137, (table of contents Part 2), 2014.

[10] Magazine of Information Processing Society Japan, IPSJ-MGN531103.pdf, October 2012.

[11] Y. Kurata, M. Aoki, and H. Ai., "Outline of the Local Application Research in Japan (in Japanese)," Society of Tourism Informatics, Kanazawa, pp. 68-69, 2015.

[12] Tag Cloud, Technologies lead to Adaptability and lifelong engagement with culture throughout the CLOUD project, [Online]. Available from: http://www.tagcloudproject.eu, [Nov. 30, 2016].

[13] What is iBeacon? A Guide to Beacons, [Online]. Available from:http://www.ibeacon.com/what-is-ibeacon-a-guide-to-beacons/, [Nov. 30, 2016].

[14] Kantar Worldpanel ComTech, "Smartphone OS sales market share, " [Online]. Available from: http://www.kantarworldpanel.com/global/smartphone-os-market-share/intro

[15] R. Faragher, "An Analysis of the Accuracy of Bluetooth Low Energy for Indoor Positioning Applications," University of Cambridge, UK; R. Harle, University of Cambridge, UK [Online]. Available from: www.cl.cam.ac.uk/~rmf25/papers/BLE.pdf, [Nov. 30, 2016].

[16] R. Faragher, "Location Fingerprinting With Bluetooth Low Energy Beacons," IEEE Journal on Selected Areas in Communications,Volume:33 , Issue: 11, pp. 2418-2428, May 6, 2015.

[17] M. Radhakrishnan, A. Misra, R. Krishna Balan, and Y. Lee, "Smartphones and BLE Services: Empirical Insights," IEEE 12th International Conference on Mobile Ad Hoc and Sensor Systems (MASS), pp. 226-234, Oct. 2015.

[18] M. Hultgren and D. Papathanopoulos, "Evaluating the usage of Bluetooth Low Energy Beacons and Smartphones for Indoor Positioning Systems," University of Gothenburg Chalmers University of Technology, Department of Computer Science and Engineering Göteborg, Sweden, June 2014.

[19] Y. Niwa, S. Shiramatsu, T. Ozono and T. Shintani, "Realizing a Direction Estimation System for Notification using Bluetooth Beacons," IPSJ Interaction 2015, pp.537-541, 2015.

[20] A. Ito, H. Hatano, M. Fujii, M. Sato, Y. Watanabe, Y. Hiramatsu, F. Sato, and A. Sasaki, "A trial of navigation system using BLE beacon for sightseeing in traditional area of Nikko," IEEE International Conference on Vehicular Electronics and Safety (ICVES) 2015, pp. 170-175, Nov. 2015.

[21] Nikko City Official Homepage, "Tourist Information," [Online]. Available from:http://www.city.nikko.lg.jp.e.tj.hp.transer.com, [Nov. 30, 2016].

[22] The Ministry of Internal Affairs and Communications of Japan [Online]. Available from: http://www.soumu.go.jp/main_content/000357569.pdf, [Nov. 30, 2016].

[23] B. V. Zeigarnik, "On finished and unfinished tasks," In W. D. Ellis (Ed.), A sourcebook of Gestalt psychology, New York: Humanities Press, 1967.

[24] IMApp Indoor Mobile App, [Online]. Available from: http://www.ultravioletapp.it/folio/imapp/, [Nov. 30, 2016].

[25] P. W. Thorndyke and B. Hayes-Roth, "Individual differences in spatial knowledge acquired from maps and navigation," Cognitive Psychology 14, pp. 560-589, 1982.

[26] R. N. Haber and L. G. Standing, "Direct measures of short-term visual storage," Quarterly Journal of Experimental Phycology 21, pp. 43-54, 1969.

Smartphone functions in photo-elicitation sessions for teachers´continuing professional development

Antonio Bautista
Faculty of Educacion
Complutense University
Madrid. Spain
e-mail: bautista@edu.ucm.es

Laura Rayón
Faculty of Education
University of Alcala
Alcala de Henares. Spain
e-mail: laura.rayon@uah.es

Yolanda Muñoz
Faculty of Education
University of Alcala
Alcala de Henares. Spain
e-mail: yolanda.munozm@uah.es

Ana María De las Heras
Pedagogy Department
UDIMA
Madrid. Spain
e-mail: anamaria.delasheras@udima.es

***Abstract*- In this paper, we advance the results of a study on the use of smartphone functions supported by photo-elicitation processes in the permanent training of primary-school teachers. The study began in January 2015 and will end in December 2017. Three teachers participated from the primary schools Jaime Vera and Concepción Arenal in Madrid and La Paloma in Azuqueca de Henares (Guadalajara), Spain. The smartphone functions used for photo elicitation by these teachers to reflect on the dilemmas and difficulties in their practice include: taking photos of classroom situations that are judged difficult by teachers then viewing these photos. It includes recording an audio track of sessions reflecting on the content of the photos; playing back the recorded audio tracks to transcribe their content. Identifying the theories and beliefs from where participating teachers' decisions are based is another function and, finally, storing and get it back all this information in the cloud (Dropbox, Drive, at the rest). The main goal of this paper is to show how the different applications of smartphones enable teachers´ learning as well as their personal and social development through reflection processes of their practices.**

Keywords - teacher education; photo-elicitation; digital hybrids; smartphones.

I. INTRODUCTION

This article is an extended version of the paper we presented at eLmL 2016 entitled *The Role of Smartphones in Teacher Training Mediated Through Photo-Elicitation* [1]. We present the work we are carrying through about smartphones in education, related with continuing training of primary education teachers.

Why has our current line of research focussed on this digital tool and not others? Because, beginning in 2015, smartphones became the most common devices for accessing the Internet, compared to other resources such as the computer [2]. The implementation of mobile phone technology has risen in the last year, meaning it is now available in 96.7% of homes and has become the most common device for getting online, with a growth of 5.9% in its use for the Spanish citizens.

Furthermore, according to Fundación Telefónica's report "The Information Society in Spain" in 2015, Spanish Internet users display the highest adoption rate for mobile devices, with smartphones (82.8%) the most popular, followed by other devices such as tablets (58.9%) and e-readers (37.4%). These figures are higher than those in surrounding countries. Such is the impact of smartphones that, according to the report [3], 90% of users connect every or almost every day to the Internet using this device, and 75% do so several times a day.

The reasons used to explain this increase on its use usually include the features of these digital hybrids. The most essential factors proposed are connectivity and accessibility any time of day, as well as size reduction of these devices. Such features are contributing to the effect that, little by little, smartphones are becoming human digital prosthetic devices. The principal feature guaranteeing success of the smartphone is that they are multi-function devices. In only a few years they have evolved from telephones that only allowed users to call and send SMSs, to devices that can connect us to the Internet so that we can communicate with hundreds of people on social networks, take photos and record videos that are shared in real time with our contacts, offer the possibility of geolocalisation, commerce, entertainment and so on. The number of options has exploded with mobile applications that are often created by communities of people grouped around an interest. So "the mobile phone is becoming a tool of global communication: via the social networks and with the extension of Internet access we can communicate worldwide through text, image, sound or video. Such features offer us thousands of applications to make our daily lives easier: information of all kinds, access to content and entertainment, or maps that can find a route to a nearby destination. And all this in the palm of your hand" [4].

These features give smartphones the ability to have a high impact in people's personal lives. This is true especially in the areas of user communication and socialization. People have gradually modified the way they relate to each other daily by popularising the use of multiple languages of representation, such as audiovisual language. They have even contributed to decreasing face to face interaction in favour of interactions through multiple virtual spaces in real time [5], rapidly and fluidly [6].

> "The implementation and social penetration of a new communication technology that has become widely accepted alters and transforms people's communicative habits. Linked to that, changes occur in the information uses that individuals can make of the new medium. [...] The purposes of communication (communicating, informing, working or dealing with professional matters, entertaining oneself, having fun, training, etc.) converge in the new device." [7].

For these reasons, in recent years, smartphones have played a key role in communication between people through distinct web environments and, especially, in different applications. Smartphones have encouraged the use of multiple languages of representation where the image is becoming a normal medium that people use to communicate their experiences. Precisely this support for multiple languages or systems of representation is what gives smartphone the potential to have a positive impact in educational processes. In other words, smartphones enable the creation of teaching situations that offer both students and teachers the chance of participating and having experiences; those experiences will guide them towards learning as well as personal and social development.

First, we present the potential of smartphones to create new communication spaces through the multiple languages that users have at their disposal. Second, we analyze the role of smartphones in educational practice, making a review of the most significant work in relation to the topic. Further on, we explain the photo-elicitation as a process that uses photography to communicate life situations and experiences of people, followed by the objectives and method of research, results obtained so far and to finish the conclusions and future work.

II. Smartphones as Support for Multiple Languages or Systems of Representation

Texts, audio, photos and videos play an essential role in communication using smartphones. These resources offer many options: recording and editing using multiple applications for the creation of memes that combine image and text, or for producing images in movement, podcasts and video podcasts. The applications specialized in photography such as Flickr and Instagram that are used on these devices are important too.

Meanwhile, these multi-representational communication environments have been increasingly studied in the last decade. A number of terms have been coined, such as *multimedia* communication that focusses attention on the representation media used in human relationships. Jenkins coined the term *multichannel* to refer to the platforms and applications that allow interaction in different forms of representation [8]. In this respect, the use of different languages has increased. For example, the audiovisual messages, due to the combination of several of the smartphone features and the virtual space available, they allow to a single device to capture an image or video, edit it, publish and broadcast it in different places simultaneously (WhatsApp, Facebook, Instagram, YouTube, Flickr, blogs, Wikis and so on). These uses, as seen, lead to new forms of communication and socialisation and have an impact on our projection in virtual collective spaces. More recently we have noticed a big number of detailed studies of these communication spaces. There is a deluge of literature on the role that virtual space plays in interpersonal relationships. In this respect, the term *media ecology* was coined to emphasise the idea that the new technological devices and communicative channels create spaces that determine how people and society interact and act in different areas: medicine and health, administration, transport and so on [9]. These authors understand the relevance of the technological devices in our lives in the way that they interlink our public and private selves.

Based on these ideas, it is important to highlight the studies [10][11] that are centred on the interactions mediated by technology; in those studies take on special relevance the intentions and emotions emerging from the relationships maintained. So the expression *polymedia* spaces was coined, to designate integrated communication environments aimed to discover, and to understand the possibilities that the simultaneous use of diverse environments offer us with the multimodal language to relate through technology. Always taking into account users' social and emotional dimension. These studies focus on the personal experience of the use of smartphones. They identify the emotional implications that specific communication environments have for users. These environments can combine old practices such as voice calls with the transmission and exchange of productions such as images between users.

These are emotive components that, as we shall see below, are frequent and therefore need to be represented as part of the situations experienced in classrooms and schools. In this sense, images have gained prominence in showing people's subjective experience. In the same way that texts speak to us, images also speak to us of events, people and things, but furthermore, and more importantly, they are capable of generating meanings, the personal interpretations associated to such representations. In short, a picture does not show us the world but different ways of seeing the world. "Man aims to represent the world, not according to the laws of an important truth, but according to the laws that emerge from his own observation and daily experience" [12].

Roland Barthes highlighted the subjective and mainly emotional dimension that still images activate. He is a reference in the communication sphere because he focussed his reflections on the sensations and emotions that a photograph produces [13]. In this sense, the interest of photography does not reside so much in aesthetic beauty as in the composition of the elements that it shows us. Today Barthes' words remain relevant since in our use of smartphones, the individual's gaze becomes increasingly important through the productions that the latter shares on his or her networks compared to the institutional "viewpoint".

In this way, the user's voice gains prominence, increasing the visibility of multiple viewpoints and situations that were traditionally ignored by the established communications media – a question that has been subject to criticism [14]. Because a smartphone is such an everyday object, it can contribute to the cause of literacy that enables people's emancipation, making us all critical receivers and informers.

To achieve such a premise, we must mention the importance in this matter of an education that provides individuals with the technological competencies needed to intervene freely and critically in these virtual environments. Consequently, we point to the importance of a multimodal means of communication where, apart from making use of different media and digital environments, it is crucial that we have the skills needed for these new forms of communication that are important in the Information Society [15]. Since we work with teachers we would especially like to focus on them. Using a smartphone should be something more than just another object people can use to communicate with those around them. How these devices are used requires some reflection, so teaching staff can discover new roles for these devices in teaching while continually improving their work or, in other words, move forward in their professional development. This means that teachers must acquire technological competencies that enable more independent use, as proposed in "UNESCO's AMI curriculum for teachers", that opts for audiovisual and digital training that goes beyond the mere instrumental use of technological resources [16]. In this way teachers will become capable of making a critical use of the media in their lives and profession, and smartphones will be increasingly present in educational settings to make their initial and continuing training practice more dynamic.

III. Smartphones in Educational Practice

Before demanding that the smartphone play a role in teachers' professional development, they have been used by teachers in different teaching situations to help students in the educational processes aimed at their instruction and training in the diverse stages of primary, secondary and university education. These uses come under the heading of the so-called "M-learning" or electronic learning based on mobile devices with wireless connection (smartphone, iPad, PDA, etc.) as part of significant learning in formal and non-formal contexts throughout life [17] [18]. Meanwhile, mobile learning is being defended as a fundamental strategy to easily break the limitations of time and space through the use of free time and ubiquitous learning [19]. Regarding teaching material, of note is the use of mobile devices in the creation and communication of written texts and multimodal narrative stories in the teaching of second and third languages [20].

A milestone in the primary education stage was the "personalized intelligent mobile learning system (PIMS)", developed in 2008 to improve reading skills in students through news texts in English. The results show that reading skills in free time improve while there is a reduction in the cognitive overload during the reading process [21].

On the use of smartphones and other devices for improving communication in secondary education, the studies highlight the use of mobile phones to access content, as well as so students can receive immediate feedback on their learning that can provide them with a positive motivation for continuing the educational process [22]. Furthermore, in this educational stage, smartphones have begun to be used for reflexive learning and so that students become aware of the opportunities for accessing information that is within their reach throughout the day in multiple contexts [23]. In these studies, the learning activities using mobile devices helped students create conceptual maps, videos, photos, comparative tables, activities to complete and so on [24].

Higher education is where we can perhaps find a wider use of smartphones aimed at the induction training of future teachers, the students in Education faculties. They seek to train students so that they can implement the use of mobile devices in diverse subjects [25]. The functionality that university teachers make of smartphones is primarily focussed on using them as a support for virtual platforms or to enhance e-learning services in universities [26]. Furthermore, we see that the main progress in this field is based on teachers creating photographic and video digital narratives using mobile devices so they can include them in their future methodological strategies [27]. The conclusion of this study group on the use of mobile phones in teaching is that they can substantially help to improve the performance of students since they encourage information search and retrieval processes, without forgetting other fundamental aspects such as the fact that these devices are giving them a voice and the chance to participate in building knowledge in teaching and learning processes. In this sense changes are being generated in basic education.

Yet, in the field of teacher training, smartphones have been used mainly in induction training that is aimed at preparing future teachers in the use of this device for training purposes. The focus here is on teaching the different basic subjects, such as mathematics, social sciences, physical education and so on while, consequently, forgetting about the use of this device for their own continuing training or professional development as a teacher. In this way, with the work we describe in this article, we have begun a fresh line of research using smartphones in photo-elicitation situations aimed at encouraging teachers' reflection on their own practice.

IV. The Role of Smartphones in Teacher Training Mediated Through Photo-elicitation

We begin this section by explaining two conceptual elements. Both are essential to understand the functionality of the phones in teacher training. These are: the reflection on own practice, and photo-elicitation as a means of signification.

A. *Reflecting on teaching practice*

Extensive theorising exists on the value of professionals' critical reflection on their own practice in order to improve their work [28][29]. Teachers can be helped to improve their work once they are aware of their beliefs, theories, attitudes, values and so on. To do so, teachers must be "forced" to make these explicit. This occurs because they are questioned about what they do, and this is achieved by reflecting on his practice as a teacher. This reflection is included and is one of the three moments of a loop or cycle of Action Research [30]. Each is made up of a procedure consisting of the three following phases (see Figure 1):

1- Planning the teaching or specifying within a document the aims, cultural content, materials and so on that the teachers are going to work on or will need over a period of time.

2- Executing the plan and recording certain moments of it. The plan must be followed and information must be recorded on what occurred during the process. Because it is difficult to reflect on the action while it is taking place, reflection has to take place afterward. To avoid forgetting things or missing relevant details the action must be recorded.

What technological tools are needed to help teachers record their actions and reflect upon them? Those whose primary function is producing information; in other words, audio recorders and cameras that can be found on one of the current digital hybrid devices: smartphones. We propose that mainly teachers should follow this procedure, taking photos of those moments so that later, outside the classroom, they can verbally analyse the content. Therefore, we focus on the languages of verbal and photographic representation.

3- Analysing, questioning, discussing and reflecting on what happened. After having carried out the plan, one must reflect on the value of what took place; we encapsulate it using photo elicitation, for that reason it is also necessary to use the information reproduction functions that all digital hybrid devices contain. The result of this phase leads to new knowledge on the decisions taken, on the whys or wherefores of the latter and consequently new knowledge of the theories, beliefs and so on that underlie them.

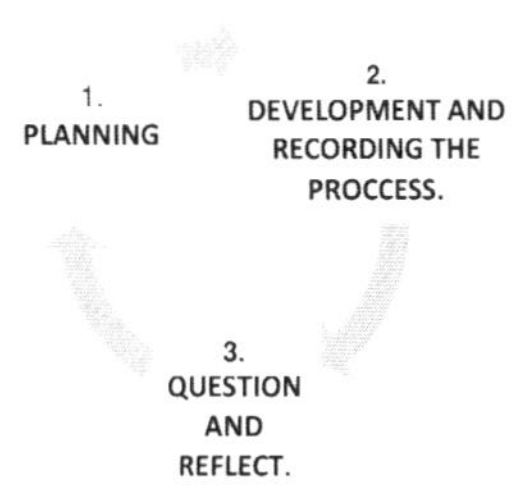

Figure 1. Action-research in the permanent teacher training adapted from Elliot [30].

This generated knowledge gradually enriches or improves the work plan for the following action inquiry loop and consequently enhances the teacher-tutor's training.

B. *On photo-elicitation as a means of reflection.*

Photo-elicitation consists of using photos to communicate people's life experiences. Eliciting means drawing something out of oneself, arousing an experience, establishing a bridge between the past and the present using a photo [31][32]. This is a form of narration where images are used to elicit the thoughts, interpretations and meanings that people place on the actions, objects or events represented in the photos. It aims to capture an image of reality that can be used to see aspects of the image "through the others' eyes", along with particular interpretations that other people have of that image.

This procedure has been used in diverse spheres of social and cultural intervention. For example: as a reflective procedure forming the basis for intervention plans based on the narrations of participating young people with HIV [33];

as a critical practice for social regeneration through community change [34][35][36]; and to promote health in a participative manner [37] .

In the teacher training sector, diverse experiences emphasise the value of photo-elicitation for narrating and building the teacher's experiential knowledge. For example, using this procedure, the nature and content of the pedagogical beliefs of sixteen adult educators was explored and compared to their past school experiences [38]. Likewise, it has been used to get teachers to talk about the needs generated when teaching students with autism spectrum disorders [39], and also in teacher induction training to capture classroom situations on camera to illustrate changes in their teaching practices [40]. These studies highlight the reflective nature of photo-elicitation to understand how teachers master new pedagogical approaches and apply them in their teaching practice in the classroom.

In short, the photo-elicitation consists of capturing an image so as to describe it later. Several procedures exist in the field of education: one is that directed by the teacher and the photos she or he takes; another, when students take the pictures, and finally, a mixed procedure where everybody takes photos. This means the photos are taken by users to be screened later so users can describe what they represent and explain what they have experienced.

In this sense, we consider that photo elicitation is a good procedure for understanding the tangible and intangible aspects of human beings' lives – in our case, the three primary school teachers who aim to improve their teaching practice. At the point of reflection within the action inquiry loops, photos taken by the participants are shown (in our case, only the teachers) on different teaching moments as a base document to question, query or wonder about some aspect of the content depicted (see Figure 2).

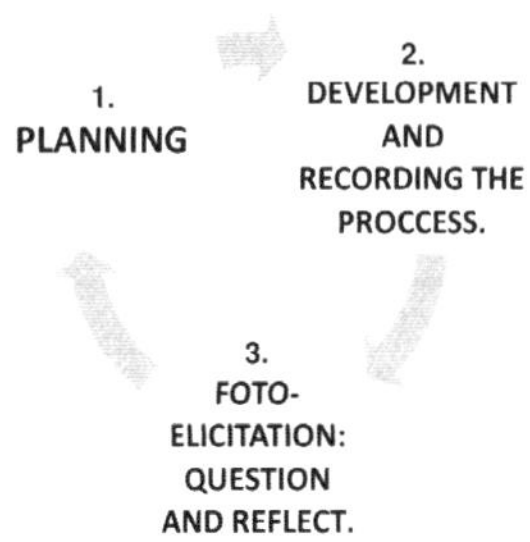

Figure 2. Place of Photo-elicitacion in the process of research-action.

This is how we have used one of the underused action inquiry procedures called observational and narrative, McKerman said: that an underdeveloped resource in the conduct of curriculum action inquiry is the use of the still photograph [41]. Likewise, two aspects that were not considered in prior studies make our research innovative and useful. The first is the incorporation or use of photo-elicitation into action-research loops, specifically in the reflection phase. The second is giving teachers a smartphone so that they can record and analyse the difficulties and dilemmas arising in the classroom and school.

Below we describe the aims and research method used to discover the positive aspects of photo-elicitation situations in action research processes and also the functions required of smartphones in these processes.

V. Aims and Research Method

This research has two objectives:

a) Identify the functions required on a smartphone in the training of primary teachers based on photo elicitation processes.

b) Know whether the photo-elicitation sessions help teachers change their teaching practice.

The data needed to achieve the above aims are being gathered through a supported discussion group in two session types we call photo elicitation and audio reflection.

Photo elicitation sessions. These are held every two weeks. During this time, the teachers take photos of events, tasks, dilemmas, conflicts, behaviours and so on that they consider most relevant and interesting in the life of their classroom and other spaces in the center. After each fourteen-day period, the above-mentioned meeting takes place. It lasts about 75 minutes with each teacher separately and takes place when they have some free time during the school day in their respective schools. To do so, the photos taken by each teacher are shown and the teacher, the research group members and student representatives comment on the reasons that led her or him to take each photo. Next, the other group members formulate questions or doubts on the content of the images and the reasons provided by the teacher and students, either on the decision taken at a specific classroom moment, or on the tasks undertaken by students, etcetera.

Audio reflection sessions. An audio recording is being made of the photo elicitation sessions with a two-fold research purpose. Firstly, to analyze each teacher's statements and respond to the questions posed in the first aim of the project, regarding the different uses of the smartphone. Secondly, to codify and create the information provided in the photo elicitation session to be used in the second aim.

The information analysis was conducted with the help of the NVivo 10 software application. We are using it specifically to incorporate each photograph shown or projected in the photo-elicitation sessions and relate it to the verbal content it evoked. Furthermore, it is being used to establish initial relationships between the text transcriptions of the interviews with participating teachers, using the *Links* function in NVivo 10. Lastly, we are applying the *Queries* and the *Nodes* functions in that software to define the coding. These queries are guided by the questions and aims of the study. For example, to discover the functions provided by, or required of, smartphones in the process of teacher training in general, and in the photo-elicitation sessions in particular, we conduct text searches for terms such as *advantages, positive impact, uses, utilisation, application, has the function of, helps to, enables or makes possible, save, search, retrieve, view* and so on.

To answer the first research objective, this first analysis has helped us to identify situations (codes) or moments of the photo-elicitation sessions where reference is made to the functionality of smartphones. When we talk about functions of smarphones we refer to the meaning of a Smartphone for teachers in different situations or experiences of use. What we intend with our analysis is to identify all those meanings or functions provided by these experiences of the three teachers. From our point of view, to know these functions we must identify and understand the experiences with these intelligent mobiles that caused them. We understand that the most direct way of knowing these human experiences is to narrate them, rather than to quantify them. This explains that, for us, each situation of photo-elicitation is equivalent to an open interview, that situations do not need a questionnaire, because the questions are oriented from the spontaneous manifestations of the teachers about images of moments in their classrooms.

In the next section we will explain the categories discovered to date in relation to the first aim of the study, focus of this article.

As stated in the summary above, the discussion group that conducted this reflection consists of the teacher who is the center of the training process, the members of the research team who were present during the prior photo elicitation session, and some students when they appear in the photos. The parents gave permission to use the photos where their children appeared as long as such use was confined to teaching and research purposes.

VI. RESULTS

In order to respond to the first aim, we are working on the content of the photo-elicitation sessions recorded in audio. But furthermore, the observations by many of the members of the research team are focussing on the use that teachers make of smartphones during action-research loops. The significance of these uses observed for each teacher is being compared and validated in formal and informal interviews conducted with them. We then group these results according to the meanings given by teachers and the representation systems used and commented on by them.

A). Global meanings provided on the hybrid nature of these devices, that are a product of the assessments teachers made in informal and formal interviews conducted at the end of each trimester:

"School teacher 2: The good thing about having a state-of-the-art phone is that you have everything together all the time.

Researcher: What do you mean "everything together"?

School teacher 2: Well, you can take a photo or record what they say, or record a video on how they are working in class or playing in the playground … Ah! And I can also write a note to explain a photo and send it on WhatsApp so it doesn't slip my mind to talk about it later." (Interview fragment, 11/3/2016).

"Researcher: How is taking photos and send them to going?

School teacher 3: Quite well. When I have taken photos I'm not worried about sending them because I can do so easily on WhatsApp once I'm home and more relaxed ... The truth is I forgot to send you the photos after the last session because I had a very busy week and I'll send them when things calm down. I have them stored on my phone and can send them straight off." (Interview fragment, 27/04/2016).

B) Specific functions assigned to and required from smartphones that are the result of observation carried out by researchers in their field work and the statements of participating teachers when asked about their experience with these devices:

- *On taking the photos*:

"Researcher: What were your decision-making processes for taking each of the photos in your classroom? What factors played a role?

School teacher 1: When making the decision to take a photo two types of factor came into play: external and internal:

- External: Events occurred in my environment that needed to be dealt with and solved because they affected classroom organisation. I decided to take a photo when I observed something unusual in the group. If I compiled enough photos it reduced the risk and uncertainty when dealing with these topics.

- Internal: Something clicks inside me and I know that something was happening that required more time and analysis than we currently had available in the classroom to try to solve it. And having this great opportunity, to take photos, I was able to relive these moments later and analyse them more carefully. I could break them down into smaller parts that would let me make more accurate decisions." (Interview fragment, 14/12/2015).

On the same question the researcher asked above, but asked in later trimesters:

"School teacher 1: I feel calmer when I can save the photos I take in class because I know I will later have time to think about them and about what is said in meetings. Uploading them to Dropbox so you can see them and help me out reassures me". (Interview fragment, 16/03/2016).

"School teacher 2: When there is something I am not clear about, or I have doubts about something that is happening at school or in my class concerning the relation with the 6th-year students, I can see it solves the problem when I take a photo and tell myself: there it is, saved on my phone so I won't forget it and I can send it by WhatsApp to the research group to view it the next time they come." (Interview fragment, 27/05/2016).

"Researcher: Can you comment on "What is it that makes you take a photo?"

School teacher 3: Those things that worry me, that don't go well in class .... Such as, for example, Leire's classmates' rejection of her, so I take the photo ... and as time has passed, well, I see it's working, because they (the students) are fine. This leads me to take the photo to comment on it later, because they are responding." (Interview fragment, 27/03/2016).

"Researcher: Can you comment on what these photo-elicitation sessions have most contributed to your work?

School teacher 1: These images have helped me to value my time far more as well as the importance of the photos themselves. Being able to view the images taken in class over and over again means I can make much more sensible and suitable decisions regarding the personal situation of each of my students". (Interview fragment, 14/12/2015).

School teacher 3: "I have realised that we do many things and are not aware of the day to day, and that they work ... The change in students, for example. I realised after the sessions with you that I have accomplished things – I have even gotten the families to change... And that makes me feel good, it reassures me". (Interview fragment, 27/06/2016).

Regarding the use of digital image projectors, only one of the three teachers, referred to in the article as teacher 1, preferred to observe the photographs through their projection on a wall screen. The reasons she stated were that in the classroom where the photo-elicitation sessions took place they had a digital projector anchored in the ceiling. Another reason is that she "had a habit of seeing the big picture whenever there was a group meeting, because it was easier and more comfortable to see and discuss its content".

- On the audio.

"Researcher: When I arrived during playtime, I saw you in the class wearing your earphones. Do you like to listen to music when you're alone?

School teacher 2: No, it wasn't music. Since I knew you were coming, I was listening to the recording I have on my mobile phone of what we talked about last time, about the photos of the playground conflict.

Researcher: Yes, I think that listening to the discussion again helps you to reflect on and draw conclusions from it.

School teacher 2: Yes, but I don't do it just for that, but also to hear myself, to improve my speaking, to avoid repeating certain words too often, to avoid using fillers, that I sometimes use without realising it.

Researcher: Do you always keep the audio recordings on your phone?

School teacher 2: Yes, mainly because in my phone I have them sorted by date, that helps me to find them easily." (Interview fragment, 27/05/2016).

- On the texts.

"Researcher: I see you've added captions to almost all the photos you have taken.

School teacher 1: I like to write notes on the photos so that I don't forget what they mean.

Researcher: In fact, the text helps to define an image's polysemy. Above all, it is necessary when you want to communicate accurately to others what that photo means to you.

School teacher 1: It even helps me personally, because I like to read the transcripts that were made of the conversations during the photo-elicitation sessions stored on Dropbox.

Researcher: To see why we act how we do in class?

School teacher 1: For many reasons. It's reassuring to read and then re-read slowly what we said. To find out how others see what I do and, strangely, to understand how I think and act without being aware of it. When I read that you are surprised or when you ask me questions, I understand better how sometimes I don't do things so logically or, rather, coherently, such as not being constant..." (Interview fragment, 16/03/2016).

"Researcher: Why do you take a notebook into the photo-elicitation sessions?

School teacher 3: Because when I take written notes, it helps me to communicate and express what each photo means, the feeling that a specific object, action or situation has for me. In the notebook I write down the feelings that the photo elicits... I realise that I make notes very fast, so fast that I almost can't stop to analyse what is happening in the day to day." (Interview fragment, 27/06/2016).

The above data confirm the positive assessment by teachers of the general functions of accessibility, multimodality, connectivity and so on, indicated in the review of studies we made in the earlier sections of this article. Yet, this reveals a number of specific functions that help to develop the photo-elicitation sessions in the action-research loops. As we will argue in the conclusions, all of the functions related to production, storage and retrieval of information are present in the representation of images, sound and text. Even so, the three teachers say there is a lack of applications that simplifies taking written notes and storing them on their mobile phone as easily as they take a photo or record an audio file. They compensate this handicap with alternative procedures such as writing a WhatsApp message.

VII. Conclusions and Future Work

1) Regarding the **first aim**, the functions that the three teachers required of a smartphone are:

A) It can be seen that the teachers assign a number of overall functions to these mobile devices, specifically those that refer to accessibility, their hybrid nature, connectivity and multi-functionality. Overall, operating as a sort of human digital prosthetic device, smartphones are enabling these teachers to store and retrieve information at any place or time. So from the point of view of the digital divide, any material aspect can be reduced by gaining access to digital devices and, through them, information.

B) Specific functions assigned to and required of smartphones:

B1. *Taking photos* of classroom situations that the teachers considered complex and conflictive, such as dilemmas, difficulties arising from the students and so on.

This is the most sought-after smartphone function in photo-elicitation sessions included in action-research loops.

B2. Saving photos on the smartphone or *storing them in the cloud* (Dropbox, Drive, etc.).

We observed that this function is used more or less depending on the teachers' "smartphone literacy". Specifically, School teacher 2 only knew how to store information (images and audio) on her phone and send them by WhatsApp to the group, as long as the files were not too large. She did not know how to store and retrieve information on cloud applications such as Drive or Dropbox. So a degree of technological literacy is needed at the start of photo-elicitation sessions.

B3. *Viewing those photos* in the photo elicitation sessions independent of the existence of a digital projector.

Independently of the existing technological equipment in the school (laptops, interactive digital whiteboards, digital projectors, etc.), teachers and members of the research team were always able to view the photos they had taken on the smartphone screen itself to analyse and discuss any difficult situation or specific dilemma arising in their classes.

B4. *Making audio recordings* of the sessions to reflect on the content of the projected photos, as well as the interviews conducted with participating teachers.

This is a function of smartphones that has provided help not just to teachers to be able to listen again to their statements in photo-elicitation sessions, but also to the research team, to conduct the analysis and create the experiential information provided by participating teachers.

B5. *Uploading the audio files in the cloud* (Dropbox, Drive, etc.).

In contrast to the photos, the audios were recorded by the research group. Firstly they were recorded on a Smartphone and later stored in each centre's Dropbox account, that all participants, teachers and researchers could access.

B6. *Playing the recorded and stored audio files* to transcribe their content and identify the theories and beliefs from where the decisions of the participating teachers are based.

As with the above function, this function was basically used by the research team. However, it is clear from in the information provided during the interviews that the teachers also used this function to listen to themselves again and, as School teacher 2 said, "to improve my speaking, to avoid repeating certain words too often, to avoid using fillers, that I sometimes use without realising it."

B7. *Storing the texts transcribed in the cloud* (Dropbox, Drive, etc.) for later analysis.

This function was only included by the research team because it was responsible for making the text transcripts of the audio recording content.

B8. *Reading the transcripts stored in the cloud.*

Similar to function B6 above, this function was used by the research team *to analyse* the theories, beliefs, attitudes and so on, from where the teachers' behaviours and decisions were based. Once this was established, teachers could be informed and become aware of such habits. At that point, teachers could reflect and assess whether they would change these practices or not, especially those that are not aligned with the ideas and educational principles they defend. But this function was also included by teachers, to carefully read the content of the transcripts and "understand how [they] think and act without being aware of it".

This second group of features, the specific ones assigned to or required of smartphones, enables us to tackle the functional dimension of the digital divide because they allow teachers to build knowledge using the stored information to reflect and discuss their teaching practices in classrooms and schools. So teachers, as well as being users of the information, are becoming producers of knowledge on their professional teaching practice.

2) Concerning the study's **second aim**, based on the results as of late June 2016, it can be stated that teachers are changing the way they design and approach teaching situations. This is because, according to the analysis of the transcriptions of the photo elicitation sessions, the teachers are becoming aware that they base their actions and decisions on five different aspects of their person:

-Theories: rational ideas or arguments, with a scientific basis.

-Beliefs: ideas or arguments with no scientific basis.

-Attitudes: forms or kinds of willingness to do or respond to something.

-Habits: routines they use in certain situations.

-Emotions: feelings about a situation that guide decisions.

The teachers have shown a disposition to change once they become aware that the above five components influence their motivations and decisions, both to improve the school tasks in the classroom and to address the personal difficulties of their students.

Finally, we should indicate that all of the smartphone functions that the teaching staff required in the discussion or photo elicitation processes (those that take place when viewing the image of a photo taken by the teacher and projected on-screen) were used to record moments in the classroom, to bring some quietness to the educational practice in order to slow down the analytical processes. These pauses made it possible to describe and interpret the content reported by the participating teachers, allowing them to reflect and comment on their theories, beliefs, attitudes, habits and emotions so that, once aware of them, the teachers uncovered those that are incongruous with their idea of education or unsuitable for working with that unique and unrepeatable group of students in a specific context.

In the future, we want to deepen the possibilities for smartphones to locate, select and project a part or element of a photograph. We think that the analysis of these details of an image can help teachers to evoke their theories and beliefs. Also, we want to use smartphones to store and play music during sessions photoelicitación. We think that both, the projection of detail and background music, can improve the evocation of the beliefs and emotions that have promoted the decisions taken in their classrooms.

We cannot conclude this article without referring to an ethical aspect of continuing professional development. The teachers come to these professional development sessions with very different training or skills in the use and application of smartphones in general, and in education in particular. This leads us to believe that certain minimum digital skills training on smartphones is needed in the future to enable teachers to store and access information and produce knowledge. It is basic training in a subject we have called *smartphone literacy*.

ACKNOWLEDGMENT

A project subsidised by the Ministry of Economy and Competitiveness of the Spanish Government, within the R&D&i State Plan, reference EDU2014-57103-R.

REFERENCES

[1] A. Bautista, L. Rayón, Y. Muñoz and A. M. de las Heras, "The role of smartphones in teacher training mediated through photo-elicitation," The Eighth International Conference on Mobile, hybrid, and On-line Learning (eLmL2016) IARIA, Apr. 2016, pp. 83-86. ISBN: 978-1161208-471-8.

[2] Instituto Nacional de Estadística. *INE: Encuesta sobre Equipamiento y Uso de Tecnologías de Información y Comunicación en los Hogares 2015.* [Online]. Available from: http://www.ine.es/dyngs/INEbase/es/ 2016.12.06

[3] Distendria: *Informe Mobile en España y en el Mundo 2015.* [Online]. Available from: http://www.ditrendia.es/ 2016.12.06

[4] N. Arroyo, Información en el móvil. Barcelona: Editorial UOC, 2011.

[5] N. Baym, Personal Connections in the Digital Age. Cambridge: Polity, 2010.

[6] M. Hand, "Persistent Traces, Potential Memories: Smartphones and the Negotiation of Visual, Locative, and Textual Data in Personal Life," Convergence: The International Journal of Research into New Media Technologies, vol. 22, nº 3, pp. 269-286, Aug. 2014, doi: 10.1177/1354856514546094.

[7] C. Costa Sánchez, "Ciberperiodismo en el Smartphone. Estudio de la Multimedialidad, Usabilidad, Hipertextualidad e Interactividad de las Aplicaciones de Medios Nativos Digitales para Smartphone," Estudios sobre el Mensaje Periodístico, vol. 18, pp. 243-251, Oct. 2012, doi:10.5209/rev_ESMP.2012.v18.40978.

[8] H. Jenkins, Convergence Culture: Where Old and New Media Collide. New York: NYU Press, 2006.

[9] M. Ito et al., Hanging Out, Messing Around and Geeking Out: Kids Living and Learning with New Media. Cambridge: MIT Press, 2010.

[10] M. Madianou and D. Miller, "Polymedia: Towards a New Theory of Digital Media in Interpersonal Communication," International Journal of Cultural Studies, vol. 16 nº 2, Aug. 2012, pp. 169-187, doi: 10.1177/1367877912452486.

[11] M. Madianou, "Smartphones as Polymedia," Journal of Computer-Mediated Communication, vol. 19 nº 3, pp. 667-680, Apr. 2014, doi: 10.1111/jcc4.12069.

[12] J. J. Fernández Ibáñez, Didáctica de la Imagen: Educación de la Sensibilidad Visual. Deusto: ICE, 1986.

[13] R. Barthes, La Cámara Lúcida. Notas sobre la Fotografía. Barcelona: Paidós, 1990.

[14] L. Másterman, Teaching the Media. Londón: Routledge, 1990.

[15] C. Bazalgette and D. Buckingham, "Literacy, Media and Multimodality: a Critical Response," Literacy, vol. 47, nº 2, pp.95-102, Jul. 2013, doi: 10.1111/j.1741-4369.2012.00666.x.

[16] VV.AA. Alfabetización Mediática e Informacional, AMI. Currículum para Profesores. París: UNESCO, 2011 [Online]. Available from: http://www.unesco.org/new/es/media-services/ 2016.12.06

[17] M. Sharples, "Disruptive Devices: Mobile Technology for Conversational Learning," International Journal of Continuing Engineering Education and Lifelong Learning, vol. 12, pp. 504-520, 2003, doi:10.1504/IJCEELL.2002.002148.

[18] T. White, A. Booker, C. Carter, and L. Martin, "Integrating digital and mathematical practices across contexts: A manifesto for mobile learning," International Journal of Learning and Media, vol. 3 nº3, pp. 7-13, Apr. 2011, doi: 10.1162/ijlm_a_00076

[19] C. M. Chen and Y. L. Li, "Personalised Context-Aware Ubiquitous Learning System for Supporting Effective English Vocabulary Learning" Interactive Learning Environments, vol. 18 nº 4, pp. 341-364, Jan. 2009, doi: 10.1080/10494820802602329.

[20] The New London Group, "A Pedagogy of Multiliteracies: Designing Social Future," Harvard Educational Review, vol. 66, nº 1, pp. 60-92, 1996.

[21] T. Y. Liu, "A Context-Aware Ubiquitous Learning Environment for Language Listening and Speaking," Journal of Computer Assisted Learning, vol. 25, nº 6, pp. 515–527, Sep. 2009, doi: 10.1111/j.1365-2729.2009.00329.x.

[22] N. Castro and I. Gómez, "Incorporación de los Códigos QR en la Educación Física," Retos, nº 29, pp: 114-119, 2016, [Online]. Available from: http://recyt.fecyt.es/index.php/retos/ index/ 2016.12.06

[23] B. Tabuenca, D. Verpoorten, S. Ternier, W. Westera and M. Specht, "Fostering reflective practice with mobile technologies. Workshop on awareness and reflection in technology-enhanced learning" ARTEL/EC-TEL, Sep. 2012, Saarbrücken (Germany) [Online]. Available from: http://hdl.handle.net/1820/4405/ 2016.12.06

[24] T. W. Greaves, J. Hayes, L. Wilson, M. Gielniak, and E. L. Peterson, Revolutionizing Education through Technology: the Project RED Roadmap for Transformation. Washington DC: International Society for Technology in Education, 2012.

[25] P. Henríquez, J. Organista, and G. Lavigne, "Nuevos Procesos de Interactividad e Interacción Social: Uso de Smartphones por Estudiantes y Docentes Universitarios," Revista Actualidades Investigativas en Educación, vol. 13, nº 3, pp. 1-21, Mar. 2013, [Online]. Available from: http://www.scielo.sa.cr/pdf/aie/v13n3/a12v13n3/ 2016.12.06

[26] A. Peña et al., "Tools and Strategies for Competences Assessment (TASCA)," Revista Internacional de Aprendizaie y Cibersociedad, vol. 17, nº 1, pp. 11-34, 2013, [Online] Available from: https://riunet.upv.es/handle/10251/46131/ 2016.12.06

[27] J. Herrington, J. Mantei, A. Herrington, I. W. Olney, and B. Ferry, "New technologies, new pedagogies: mobile technologies and new ways of teaching and learning,".Annual Conference of the Australasian Society for Computers in Learning in Tertiary Education (ASCILITE 2008). Melbourne, Australia: Deakin University, Dec. 2008, pp. 419-427, http://www.ascilite.org/conferences/melbourne08/procs/ 2016.12.08

[28] J. Gimeno, El Curriculum: Una Reflexión sobre la Práctica. Madrid: Morata, 1988.

[29] D. Schön, Educating the reflective Practitioner. San Francisco: Jossey-Bass Publishers, 1987.

[30] J. Elliott, La Investigación-Acción en Educación. Madrid: Morata, 1990.

[31] M. Clark-Ibañez, "Inter-City Children in Sharper Focus. Sociology of Childhood and Photo Elicitation Interviews," in Visual Research Methods, C. Stanczak, Ed. Los Ángeles, CA: Sage, pp. 167-196, 2007.

[32] D. Harper, "Talking about Pictures: A Case for Photo Elicitation," Visual Studies, vol. 17 nº 1, pp. 13-26, 2002, doi: 10.1080/14725860220137345

[33] C. Mitchell, N. DeLange, R. Moletsane, J. Stuart, and T. Buthelezi, "Giving a Face to HIV and AIDS: On the Uses of Photo-Voice by Teachers and Community Health Care Workers Working with Youth in Rural South Africa," Qualitative Research in Psychology, vol. 2, nº 3, pp. 257-270, Jul. 2008, doi: 10.1191/1478088705qp042oa.

[34] R. Purcell, "Images for Change: Community Development, Community Arts and Photography," Community Development Journal, vol. 44 nº1, pp. 111-122, Jan. 2009, doi: 10.1093/cdj/bsm031

[35] M. C. Desyllas, "Using Photovoice with Sex Workers: The Power of Art, Agency and Resistance," Qualitative Social Work, vol. 13 nº 4, pp. 477-501, Jul. 2014, doi: 10.1177/1473325013496596.

[36] R. Fortin, S. F. Jackson, J. Maher, and C. Moravac, "I WAS HERE: Young Mothers Who have Experienced Homelessness use Photovoice and Participatory Qualitative Analysis to Demonstrate Strengths and Assets," Global Health Promotion, vol. 22 nº1, pp. 8-20, Mar. 2015, doi: 10.1177/1757975914528960.

[37] C. C. Wang, W. K. Yi, Z. W. Tao, and K. Carovano, "Photovoice as a Participatory Health Promotion Strategy," Health Promotion International, vol. 13 nº1, pp. 75-86, Mar. 1998, doi: 10.1093/heapro/13.1.75.

[38] E. Taylor, "The Relationship between the Prior School Lives of Adult Educators and their Beliefs about Teaching Adults," International journal of lifelong education, vol. 22 nº1, pp. 59-77, Jan. 2013, doi: 10.1080/02601370304828.

[39] C. R. Carnahan, "Photovoice: Engaging Children with Autism and their Teachers," Teaching Exceptional Children, vol. 39 nº2, pp. 44-50, Nov. 2006.

[40] F. Wolfenden and A. Buckler, "Teacher Learning in Sudan: Building Dialogue around Teachers' Practices through Reflective Photography," in Photography in Educational Research: Critical Reflections from Diverse Contexts, S. Miles and A. Howes, Eds. Abingdon: Routledge, pp. 79–95, 2015.

[41] J. McKernan, Curriculum Action Research. London: Kogan Page, 1991.

Enhancing the WordNet Exploration and Visualization in Neo4J with a Tag Cloud Based Approach

Enrico G. Caldarola*†, Antonio Picariello*, Antonio M. Rinaldi*‡, Marco Sacco†
*Department of Electrical Engineering and Information Technologies
University of Naples Federico II, Napoli, Italy
†Institute of Industrial Technologies and Automation
National Research Council, Milano, Italy
‡IKNOS-LAB Intelligent and Knowledge Systems
University of Naples Federico II, LUPT
Email: enricogiacinto.caldarola@unina.it, antonio.picariello@unina.it, antoniomaria.rinaldi@unina.it, marco.sacco@itia.cnr.it

Abstract—**Visualization is the closer phase to the users within the data life cycles phases, so, there is no doubt that an effective, efficient and impressive representation of the analysed data may result as important as the analytic process itself. Starting from previous experiences in importing, querying and visualizing WordNet database within Neo4J and Cytoscape and extending a previous work by the authors, this work aims at improving the WordNet Graph visualization by exploiting the features and concepts behind tag clouds. The objective of this study is twofold: first, we argue that the proposed visualization style is able to put order in the messy and dense structure of nodes and edges of WordNet, showing as much as possible information from the lexical database and in a clearer way; secondly, we think that the tag cloud approach applied to the synonyms rings reinforces the human cognition in recognizing the different usages of words in a language like English. The ultimate goal of this work is, on the one hand, to facilitate the comprehension of WordNet itself and, on the other hand, to investigate techniques and approaches to get more insights from the visual representation and analytics of large graph databases.**

Keywords–WordNet; Big Data; Data and Information Visualization; Neo4J; Graph Database; NoSQL.

I. Introduction

In this paper we extend a previous work in visualizing and exploring the WordNet lexical database [1], by using one of the most spread tool in the graph databases management systems landscape, namely Neo4J. At the end of this section, the major contributions to this work with respect to the original one have been illustrated, while in the following paragraph a panorama of the main concepts related to Information Visualization will be provided.

A subtle difference exists between *data* and *information*. The first are raw, they simply exist and have no significance beyond its existence (in and of themselves) [2]. Data are just numbers, bits of information, which '*...have no way of speaking for themselves. We speak for them. We imbue them with meaning.*' [3]. On the contrary, information is data that have been given meaning by way of relational connection, by providing context for them. Even more subtle is the distinction between *Data Visualization* and *Information Visualization*. If the main goal of the first one is to communicate information clearly and efficiently to users, involving the creation and study of the visual representation of data – i.e., "information that has been abstracted in some schematic form, including attributes or variables for the units of information" [4] – the main task of the second one is the study of (interactive) visual representations of abstract data to reinforce human cognition. The abstract data may include both numerical and non-numerical data, such as text and geographic information. Beyond Information Visualization, an other outgrowth field is *Visual Analytics* that can be defined as 'the science of analytical reasoning facilitated by interactive visual interfaces.' [5]. Today, in many spheres of human activity, massive sets of data are collected and stored. As the volumes of data available to various stakeholders such as business people or scientists increase, their effective use becomes more challenging. Keeping up to date with the flood of data, using standard tools for data management and analysis, is fraught with difficulty. The field of visual analytics seeks to provide people with better and more effective ways to understand and analyse these large datasets, while also enabling them to act upon their findings immediately, in real-time [6]. Thus, the challenges that the Big Data imperative [7], [8] imposes to data management severely impact on data visualization. The "bigness" of large data sets and their complexity in term of heterogeneity contribute to complicate the representation of data, making the drawing algorithms quite complex. Just to make an example, let us consider the popular social network Facebook, in which the nodes represent people and the links represent interpersonal connections; we note that nodes may be accompanied by information such as age, gender, and identity, and links may also have different types, such as colleague relationships, classmate relationships, and family relationships. These kind of techniques can be useful in enhanced recommender systems [9]. The effective representation of all the information at the same time is really challenging. The most common solution is to use visual cues, such as color, shape, or transparency to encode different attributes. In this regard, tag clouds are a popular method for representing variables of interest (such as popularity, frequency of occurrence of a term, and so on) in the visual appearance of the keywords themselves using text properties such as font size, weight, or color [10]. The objective of the study presented in this work aims at providing a visualization style able to put order in the messy and dense structure of nodes and edges of WordNet exploiting the features of the *Labeled Property Graph Data Model*, showing as much as possible information from the lexical database and in a clearer way. At the same time, we think that the tag cloud approach applied to the synonyms rings reinforces the human cognition in recognizing the different usages of words in a language like English and that can help the comprehension of WordNet itself and, on the other hand, the research of techniques and approaches to get more insights from the visual representation and analytics of large graph databases. As mentioned at the beginning, most of the content in this paper starts from a previous work of the authors [1], this one being an extension of the first one. In particular, this paper provides a more complete state-of-the-art section, an essential description of Neo4J Graph Management System and a description of the procedure to import WordNet in Neo4j more rich in details than that in [1]. Since the study conducted in this paper consists in the visual representation of WordNet as a large graph in Neo4j [11] and Cytoscape [12], a particular attention is paid to *Graph Visualization*, referring to other well-known works in the literature for a complete review of the techniques and theories in Information Visualization [13][14][15][16]. The reminder of the paper is organized as follows. After a review of the main works existing in the literature about graph visualization in Section II, Section III describes the WordNet meta-model and clarifies the ground concepts related to WordNet landscape Section IV describes how WordNet has been imported in Neo4J and its visualization in Cytoscape. Section V goes to the hearth of this work *rationale* by illustrating the way a tags cloud approach is used to effectively draw the graph of WordNet synonyms rings in Cytoscape. Finally, Section VI draws the conclusion summarizing the major findings and outlining future investigations.

II. RELATED WORKS

In the most common sense of the term, a graph is an ordered pair $G=(V,E)$ comprising a set V of vertices or nodes together with a set E of edges or lines, which are 2-element subsets of V (i.e., an edge is related with two vertices, and the relation is represented as an unordered pair of the vertices with respect to the particular edge). Graphs are traditional and powerful tools for visually representing sets of data and the relations among them by drawing a dot or circle for every vertex, and an arc between two vertices if they are connected by an edge. If the graph is directed, the direction is indicated by drawing an arrow. A graph drawing should not be confused with the graph itself (the abstract, non-visual structure) as there are several ways to structure the graph drawing. All that matters is which vertices are connected to which others by how many edges and not the exact layout. In practice it is often difficult to decide if two drawings represent the same graph. Depending on the problem domain some layouts may be better suited and easier to understand than others. The pioneering work of W. T. Tutte [17] was very influential in the subject of graph drawing, in particular he introduced the use of linear algebraic methods to obtain graph drawings. The basic graph layout problem is very simple: given a set of nodes with a set of edges, it only needs to calculate the positions of the nodes and draw each edge as curve. Despite the simplicity of the problem, to make graphical layouts understandable and useful is very hard. Basically, there are generally accepted aesthetic rules to draw a graph [18], which include: distribute nodes and edges evenly, avoid edge crossing, display isomorphic substructures in the same manner, minimize the bends along the edges. However, since it is quite impossible to meet all rules at the same time, some of them conflict with each other or they are very computationally expensive, practical graphical layouts are usually the results of compromise among the aesthetics. Another issue about graph layout is predictability. Due to the task of graph visualization, it is important and necessary to make the results of layout algorithm predictable [19], which means two different results of running the same algorithm with the same or similar data inputs should also look the same or alike. There exists different graph visualization layouts in literature, such as: the Tree Layout, the Space Division Layout, the Matrix Layout and the Spring Layout[20], to mention a few.

Below is a brief overview of graph layouts and visualization techniques grouped by categories.

A. Node-link layouts

To this category belong the following layouts:

1) Tree Layout: it uses links between nodes to indicate the parent-child relationships. A very satisfactory solution for node-link layout comes from Reingold et al. [21]. Their classical algorithm is simple, fast, predictable, and produces aesthetically pleasing trees on the plane. However, it makes use of screen space in a very inefficient way. In order to overcome this limitation, some compact tree layout algorithms have been developed to obtain more dense tree, while keeping the classical tree looks [22]. Eades [23] proposes another node-link layout called radial layout that recursively positions children of a sub-tree into a circular wedge shape according to their depths in the tree. Generally, radial views, including its variations [24], share a common characteristic: the focus node is always placed at the center of the layout, and the other nodes radiate outward on separated circles. Balloon layout [25] is similar to radial layout and are formed where siblings of subtrees are placed in circles around their father node. This can be obtained by projecting cone tree onto the plane.

2) Tree Plus Layout: since large graphs are much more difficult to handle than trees, tree visualization is often used to help users understand graph structures. A straightforward way to visualize graphs is to directly layout spanning trees for them. Munzner [26] finds a particular set of graphs called quasi-hierarchical graphs, which are very suitable to be visualized as minimum spanning trees. However, for most graphs, all links are important. It could be very hard to choose a representative spanning tree. Arbitrary spanning trees can also possibly deliver misleading information.

3) Spring Layout: this layout, also known as *Force-Directed* layout, is another popular strategy for general graph layouts. In spring layout, graphs are modelled as physical systems of rings or springs. The attractive idea about spring layout is that the physical analogy can be very naturally extended to include additional aesthetic information by adjusting the forces between nodes. As one of the first few practical algorithms for drawing general graphs, spring layout is proposed by Eades in 1984 [27]. Since then, his method is revisited and improved in different ways [20], [28]. Mathematically, Spring layout is based on a cost (energy) function, which maps different layouts of the same graph to different non-negative numbers. Through approaching the minimum energy, the layout results reaches better and better aesthetically pleasing results. The main differences between different spring approaches are in the choice of energy functions and the methods for their minimization.

B. Space Division Layout

In this case, the parent-child relationship is indicated by attaching child node(s) to the parent node. Since the parent-child and sibling relationships are both expressed by adjacency, the layout should have a clear orientation cue to differentiate these two relationships.

1) Space Nested Layout: nested layouts, such as Treemaps [29], draw the hierarchical structure in the nested way. They place child nodes within their parent node.

C. 3D Layout

In this case, the extra dimension can give more space and it would be easier to display large structures. Moreover, due to the general human familiarity with 3D in the real world, there are some attempts to map hierarchical data to 3D objects we are familiar with.

D. Matrix Layout

Graphs can be presented by their connectivity matrixes. Each row and each column corresponds to a node. The glyph at the interaction of (i, j) encodes the edge from node i to node j. Edge attributes are encoded as visual characteristics of the glyphs, such as color, shape, and size. The major benefit of adjacency matrices is the scalability.

In this work the Spring layout will be used as it represents one of the most spread strategy in graph visualization and shows aesthetically pleasing results.

Specifically concerning the visualization of WordNet, there are not many works in the literature. In [30], the authors make an attempt to visualize the WordNet structure from the vantage point of a particular word in the database, this in order to overcome the down-side of the large coverage of WordNet, i.e., the difficulty to get a good overview of particular parts of the lexical database. An attempt to apply design paradigms to generate visualizations that maximize the usability and utility of WordNet is made in [31], whereas, in [32] a radial, space-filling layout of hyponymy (IS-A relation) is presented with interactive techniques of zoom, filter, and details-on-demand for the task of document visualization, exploiting the WordNet lexical database. The visualization approach used in this work uses the Spring layout to draw the graph-based representation of WordNet in Cytoscape and a tag cloud-based strategy to represent the synonim rings from WordNet. Moreover, as a general rule the principled representation methodology we agree on is the *Visual Information Seeking Mantra* presented by Scheiderman in [33]. It can be summarized as follows: "overview first, zoom and filter, then details-on-demand".

III. Neo4J WordNet Case Study

The case study presented in this paper consists in the *reification* of the WordNet database inside the Neo4J GraphDB. In the following subsections a description of wordNet and Neo4J is provided.

A. Neo4J

Neo4J is a scalable, native graph database purpose-built to leverage data and its relationships. It is developed by Neo Technology, Inc and its developers describe it as an ACID-compliant transactional database with native graph storage and processing. Neo4j is one of the most popular graph database according to db-engines.com. In Neo4j, everything can be modelled by the *Labeled Property Graph Data Model*, which is based on connected entities (the nodes) which can hold any number of attributes (key-value-pairs). Nodes can be tagged with labels representing their different roles in your domain. In addition to contextualizing node and relationship properties, labels may also serve to attach metadataindex or constraint informationto certain nodes. Relationships provide directed, named semantically relevant connections between two node-entities. A relationship always has a direction, a type, a start node, and an end node. Like nodes, relationships can have any properties. In most cases, relationships have quantitative properties, such as weights, costs, distances, ratings, time intervals, or strengths. As relationships are stored efficiently, two nodes can share any number or type of relationships without sacrificing performance. Note that although they are directed, relationships can always be navigated regardless of direction. One of the most appreciated feature of Neo4J Graph Management System is Cypher, a declarative, SQL-inspired language for describing patterns in graphs visually using an iconic, acscii-art language [34]. It allows to state what we want to select, insert, update or delete from our graph data without requiring us to describe exactly how to do it.

B. WordNet

WordNet [35][36] is a large lexical database of English. Nouns, verbs, adjectives and adverbs are grouped into sets of cognitive synonyms (synsets), each expressing a distinct concept. Synsets are interlinked by means of conceptual-semantic and lexical relations. In this context, we have defined and implemented a meta-model for the WordNet reification using a conceptualization as much as possible close to the way in which the concepts are organized and expressed in human language [37]. We consider concepts and words as nodes in Neo4J, whereas semantic, linguistic and semantic-linguistic relations become Noeo4J links between nodes. For example, the hyponymy property can relate two concept nodes (nouns to nouns or verbs to verbs); on the other hand a semantic property links concept nodes to concepts and a syntactic one relates word nodes to word nodes. Concept and word nodes are considered with *DatatypeProperties*, which relate individuals with a predefined data type. Each word is related to the represented concept by the ObjectProperty *hasConcept* while a concept is related to words that represent it using the ObjectProperty *hasWord*. These are the only properties able to relate words with concepts and vice versa; all the other properties relate words to words and concepts to concepts. Concepts, words and properties are arranged in a class hierarchy, resulting from the syntactic category for concepts and words and from the semantic or lexical type for the properties. The subclasses have been derived from the related categories. There are some union classes useful to define properties domain and codomain. We define some attributes for Concept and Word respectively: Concept *hasName* that represents the concept name; *Description* that gives a short description of concept. On the other hand Word has Name as attribute that is the word name. All elements have an ID within the WordNet offset number or a user defined ID. The semantic and lexical properties are arranged in a hierarchy. In Table I some of the considered properties and their domain and range of definition are shown.

Figures 1(a) and 1(b) show that the two main classes are: Concept, in which all the objects have defined as individuals and Word which represents all the terms in the ontology.

The subclasses have been derived from the related categories. There are some union classes useful to define properties domain and co-domain. We define some attributes for Concept and Word respectively: Concept *hasName* that represents the concept name; *Description* that gives a short description of concept. On the other hand Word has Name as attribute that is the word name. All elements have an ID within the WordNet offset number or a user defined ID. The semantic and lexical properties are arranged in a hierarchy (see figure 2(a) and 2(b)). In Table I some of the considered properties and their domain and range of definition are shown.

TABLE I. PROPERTIES

Property	Domain	Range
hasWord	Concept	Word
hasConcept	Word	Concept
hypernym	NounsAnd VerbsConcept	NounsAnd VerbsConcept
holonym	NounConcept	NounConcept
entailment	VerbWord	VerbWord
similar	AdjectiveConcept	AdjectiveConcept

The use of domain and codomain reduces the property range application. For example, the hyponymy property is defined on the sets of nouns and verbs; if it is applied on the set of nouns, it has the set of nouns as range, otherwise, if it is applied to the set of verbs, it has the set of verbs as range. In Table II there are some of defined constraints and we specify on which classes they have been applied w.r.t. the considered properties; the table shows the matching range too.

TABLE II. MODEL CONSTRAINTS

Costraint	Class	Property	Constraint range
AllValuesFrom	NounConcept	hyponym	NounConcept
AllValuesFrom	AdjectiveConcept	attribute	NounConcept
AllValuesFrom	NounWord	synonym	NounWord
AllValuesFrom	AdverbWord	synonym	AdverbWord
AllValuesFrom	VerbWord	also_see	VerbWord

Sometimes the existence of a property between two or more individuals entails the existence of other properties. For example, being the concept dog a hyponym of animal, we can assert that animal is a hypernymy of dog. We represent this characteristics in OWL, by means of property features shown in Table III.

TABLE III. PROPERTY FEATURES

Property	Features
hasWord	*inverse* of hasConcept
hasConcept	*inverse* of hasWord
hyponym	*inverse* of hypernym; *transitivity*
hypernym	*inverse* of hyponym; *transitivity*
cause	*transitivity*
verbGroup	*symmetry* and *transitivity*

IV. IMPORTING WORDNET IN NEO4J AND VISUALIZING IT IN CYTOSCAPE

The WordNet lexical database has been imported in Neo4J [38] and afterward visualized in Cytoscape according to a procedure similar to that described in a previous work by the authors [39]. The whole process is illustrated in Figure 3 and it involves three phases and three components: the *importing from WordNet* module, the *serializer* module and the *importing within Neo4J* module. The first phase has been implemented using a Java-based script that access the WordNet database through JWI (MIT Java Wordnet Interface) API [40][41] and passes all the information related to synsets, words, semantic relations and lexical relations to the serializer module, producing appropriate serialized data, following a proper schema that will be described in the following. This one, the main actor of the second phase, serializes the wordnet database into five csv files, suitable to be efficiently and effectively imported into Neo4J database. The last component, which is related to the third phase of the process, is responsible for importing the previously serialized information into Neo4J database. The importing from WordNet takes place via five different sub-operations which respectively retrieve: the information related to synsets, the semantic relations among synsets, the words, the lexical relations among words and finally the links between the semantic and the lexical world, i.e., how a word is related to its concepts (or its meaning) and *viceversa*.

The intentional schema of each serialized data is shown as follow:

1) The synset file contains the following fields:
    a) *Id*: the univoque indentifier for the synset;
    b) *SID*: the Synset ID as reported in the WordNet database;
    c) *POS*: the synset's part of speech;
    d) *Gloss*: the synset's gloss, which express its meaning.
2) The semantic relations file contains the following fields:
    a) *Prop*: the semantic relation linking the source and the destination synsets;
    b) *Src*: the source synset;
    c) *Dest*: the destination synset;
3) The words file contains the following fields:
    a) *Id*: the univoque indentifier for the word;
    b) *WID*: the Word ID as reported in the WordNet database;
    c) *POS*: the word's part of speech;
    d) *Lemma*: lexical represenntation of the word;
    e) *SID*: the synset Id whose the word is related.
4) The lexical relations file contains the following fields:
    a) *Prop*: the lexical relation linking the source and the destination words;
    b) *Src*: the source word;
    c) *Dest*: the destination word;
5) The lexical-semantic relations file contains the following fields:
    a) *Word Id*: the word id of the word that is linked to the synset on the right via the *hasConcept* relation;

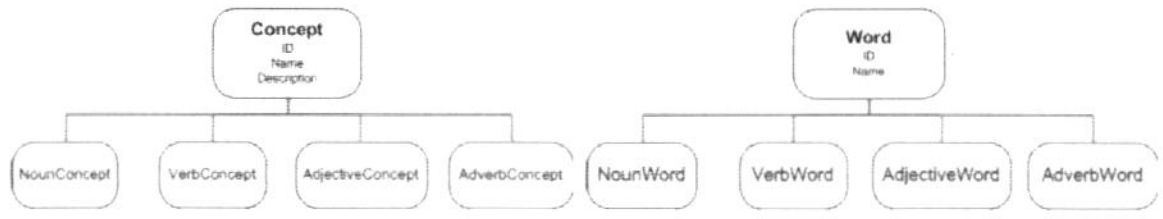

(a) Concept (b) Word

Figure 1. Concept and Word

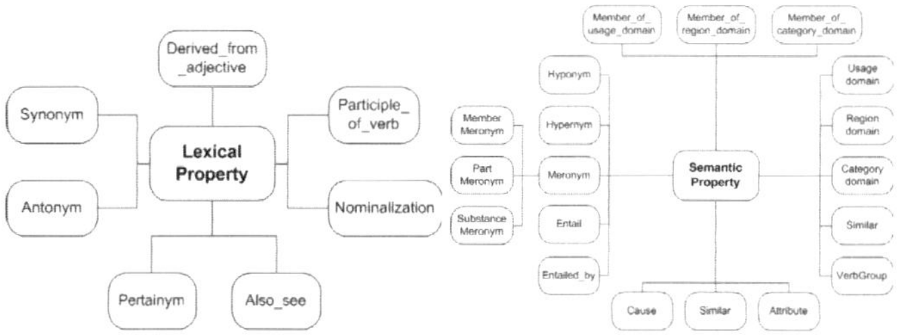

(a) Lexical Properties (b) Semantic Properties

Figure 2. Linguistic properties

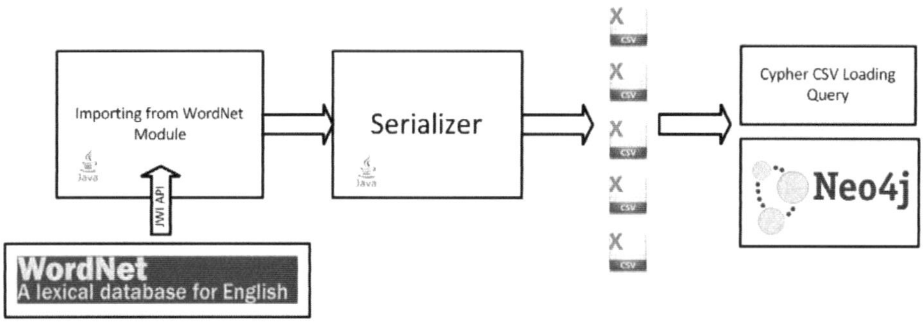

Figure 3. WordNet importing schema

b) *Synset Id*: the synset id of the synset that is linked to the word on the left via the *hasWord* relation;;

In order to import all the information contained in the serialized data and translate them into a graph data structure, the meta-model described in the previous section has been used: each synset and word has been converted into a node of the graph with label respectively: *Concept* and *Word*. Each semantic relation has become an edge between two concept nodes with the *type* property expressing the specific semantic relation holding between the concepts. Each lexical relation has been converted into an edge between two word nodes with a type property expressing the specific lexical relation between the word nodes. Finally, the word nodes have been connected to their related concept nodes through the *hasConcept* relation.

The Cypher query code used to import all the serialized information stored into csv lines is shown as follows:

```
USING PERIODIC COMMIT 1000
LOAD CSV WITH HEADERS FROM "PATH_TO_THE_FIRST_FILE"
AS csvLine

CREATE (c: Concept {
id: toInt(csvLine.id),
sid: csvLine.SID, POS:
csvLine.POS,
gloss: csvLine.gloss })

CREATE CONSTRAINT ON (c: Concept)
ASSERT c.id IS UNIQUE

USING PERIODIC COMMIT 1000
LOAD CSV WITH HEADERS FROM "PATH_TO_THE_SECOND_FILE"
AS csvLine
MATCH (src:Concept { id: toInt(csvLine.Src)}),
(dest:Concept { id: toInt(csvLine.Dest)})

CREATE (src)-[:semantic_property
{ type: csvLine.Prop }]->(dest)

USING PERIODIC COMMIT 1000
LOAD CSV WITH HEADERS FROM "PATH_TO_THE_THIRD_FILE"
AS csvLine

CREATE (w: Word {
id: toInt(csvLine.id),
wid: csvLine.WID,
POS: csvLine.POS,
lemma: csvLine.lemma,
sid: toInt(csvLine.SID) })

CREATE CONSTRAINT ON (w: Word)
ASSERT w.id IS UNIQUE

USING PERIODIC COMMIT 1000
LOAD CSV WITH HEADERS FROM "PATH_TO_THE_FOURTH_FILE"
AS csvLine

MATCH (src:Word { id: toInt(csvLine.Src)}),
(dest:Word { id: toInt(csvLine.Dest)})

CREATE (src)-[:lexical_property
{ type: csvLine.Prop }]->(dest)
```

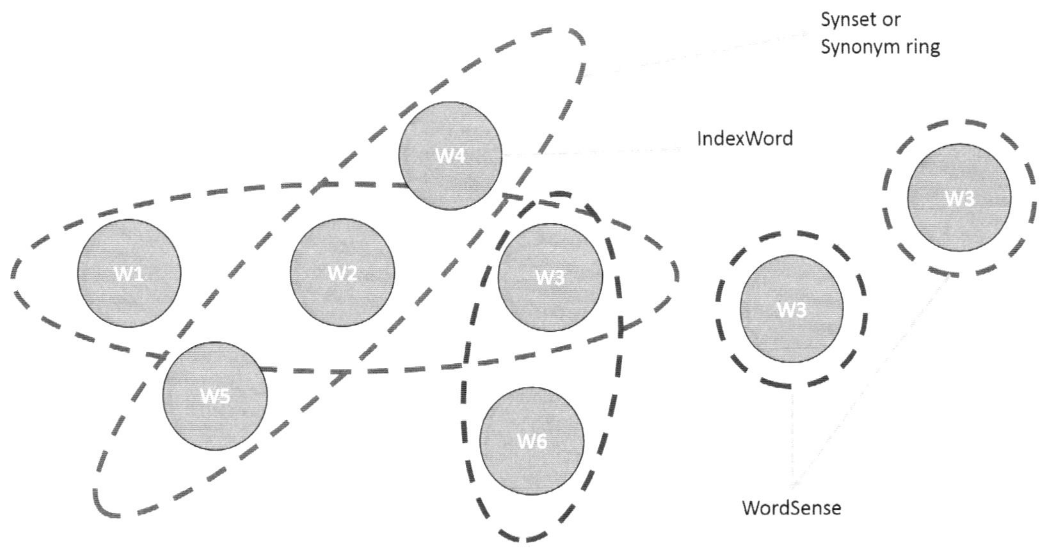

Figure 4. WordNet synsets, index words and word senses.

```
USING PERIODIC COMMIT 1000
LOAD CSV WITH HEADERS FROM "PATH_TO_THE_FIFTH_FILE"
AS csvLine

MATCH (src:Word { id: toInt(csvLine.Word)}),
(dest:Concept { id: toInt(csvLine.SID)})
CREATE (src)-[:hasConcept]->(dest)
```

Having applied the importing procedure described above, this work focuses on the visualization of WordNet and the most expensive part of the work has consisted in defining a Cytoscape custom style to represent the *synonyms rings* as tag clouds in an effective and clear way. This surely represents the novelty of this approach. We preferred to load WordNet objects from JWI APIs and serialize them in custom csv files, which were then imported throughout Cypher macros, instead of using already existing WordNet RDF serialization [42], because, this way, we could add some useful information in the csv lines like the *word frequency*, the *polysemy*, and so forth, for the sake of the successive representation in Cytoscape. And that is also why we prefer to create a custom tool to import the WordNet database in Neo4J instead of using already existing tools. Before diving into the procedure details, it is worth to clarify the distinction and provide some useful definitions coming from JWI APIS about *synsets*, *synsets (or synonyms) rings*, *index words* and *word senses*. Figure 4 try to put light on this. As discussed in the previous section, a synset is a concept, i.e., an entity of the real world (both physical or abstract) meaning something whose meaning can be argued by reading the *gloss* definition provided by WordNet. Its meaning can be also understood by analysing the semantic relations linking it to other synsets or by the synset (or synonyms) ring. This one is a set of words (hereafter mentioned as index words) generally used in a specific language (such as English) to refer to that concept. The term synset itself is used to refer to set of synonyms meaning a specific concept. On the contrary, an index word is just a term, i.e., a *sign* without meaning; so that, only when we link it to a specific concept we obtain a word sense, i.e., a word provided with a meaning. An index word has got different meanings according to the context in which it is used and because of a general characteristic of languages: the *polysemy*. For example, the term *home* has nine different meanings if it is used as noun, and so, it belongs to nine different synsets. In fact, the WordNet answer when we search for *home* is the following:

1. (430) home, place — (where you live at a particular time; "deliver the package to my home"; "he doesn't have a home to go to"; "your place or mine?")
2. (350) dwelling, home, domicile, abode, habitation, dwelling house — (housing that someone is living in; "he built a modest dwelling near the pond"; "they raise money to provide homes for the homeless")
3. (116) home — (the country or state or city where you live; "Canadian tariffs enabled United States lumber companies to raise prices at home"; "his home is New Jersey")
4. (43) home — (an environment offering affection and security; "home is where the heart is"; "he grew up in a good Christian home"; "there's no place like home")
5. (38) home, nursing home, rest home — (an institution where people are cared for; "a home for the elderly")
6. (36) base, home — (the place where you are stationed and from which missions start and end)
7. (7) family, household, house, home, menage — (a social unit living together; "he moved his family to Virginia"; "It was a good Christian household"; "I waited until the whole house was asleep"; "the teacher asked how many people made up his home")
8. (7) home plate, home base, home, plate — ((baseball) base consisting of a rubber slab where the batter stands; it must be touched by a base runner in order to score; "he ruled that the runner failed to touch home")
9. (3) home — (place where something began and flourished; "the United States is the home of basketball")

In addition to synsets glosses, WordNet gives us some useful statistic information about the usage of the term *home* in each synset. The position of the term in each synonyms ring tell us how usual is the use of the term to signify that concept. The position of the term in each synset is a measure of the usage frequency of the term for each concept: higher the position, higher the frequency. Moreover, by counting the number of synsets which a term belongs to, it is possible to obtain its polysemy (e.g., the number of possible meanings of *home*). JWI is able to tell us all this information about synset and word senses. In particular, for each synset we have collected the following fields in the csv files:

1) *Id*: the univoque indentifier for the synset;
2) *SID*: the Synset ID as reported in the WordNet

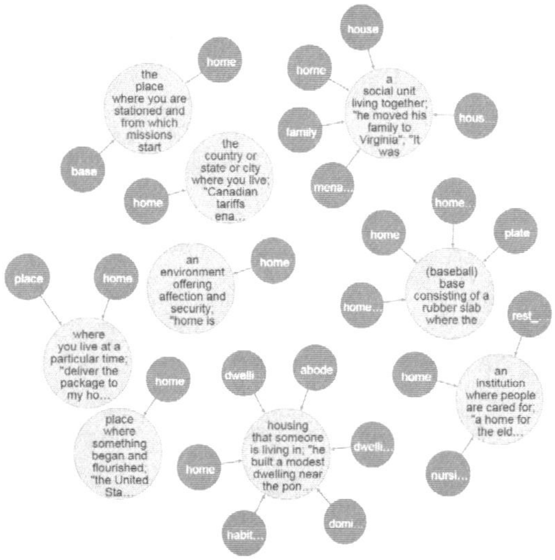

Figure 5. WordNet synset rings containing the 'home' word

database;

3) *POS*: the synset's part of speech (POS);
4) *Gloss*: the synset's gloss which express its meaning;
5) *Level*: the hieararchical level of synset in the whole WordNet hierarchy.

For word senses we have collected the following fields:

1) *Id*: the univoque indentifier for the word sense;
2) *POS*: the word's part of speech (POS);
3) *polysemy*: the word polysemy;
4) *frequency*: the word frequency of the word sense as previously explicated.

A third csv file stores the semantic links existing between synset by reporting the IDs of the source and target synset and the type of semantic link existing between them, such as hypernym, hyponym, meronym, etc.

In addition to the previous files, a final file lists the links between each word sense and each synset. This file is very simple, it just contains a line for each pair (Word Sense, Synset) in WordNet. Other minor and not significant fields have been added for the sake of the visualization in Cytoscape, such as *label* (a human readable label for the nodes) and *dimension* (used to suggest a plausible diameter for the Synset node representation according to its depth in the WordNet hierarchy). The code to convert WordNet synsets into csv tables is available at https://github.com/eureko/WordNetToCSVFiles/.

In order to import all the information contained in the csv files and translate them into a graph data structure inside Neo4J [11], the meta-model described in Section II has been used. Each synset and word sense have been converted into a node of the graph with label respectively: *Synset* and *WordSense*. Each semantic relation has become an edge between two synset nodes with the *type* property expressing the specific semantic relation holding between the concepts. Finally, the word sense nodes have been connected to their related concepts nodes through a specific relation. This allows to effectively represent synonyms ring through the Neo4J web visualizer. For example, Figure 5 shows the results of the following Cypher query:

```
match (a: WordSense {POS: 'NOUN'})-[r]->(c: Synset)
        where (c)<-[]-(: WordSense {label: 'home'})
                return a,r,c
```

The figure reports nine synset rings for the term *home*. The filled circles represents the synset and contain the synset gloss definition, while the white circles around contain the word terms used to signify such synset.

V. The Tag Cloud-Based Representation of WorNet Synonyms Rings

The work described in this paper has encountered challenges that are quite close to the typical Big Data scenario. In fact, this version of WordNet graph (v. 2.1) includes 117597 synsets rings containing 207106 word senses conveyed by 155327 index words, 283837 semantic relations (cfr., Section III) linking synsets each other and 207016 semantic-lexical links between index words and synsets. With these big numbers, the manipulation, the querying and the visualization of the graph become quite challenging. The visualization of the entire structure of WordNet in terms of all synsets, words, semantic and lexical relations in a way that is elegant and intelligible at the same time, is a *chimera*, due to the performance issues of the visualization tools, in particular when sophisticated drawing algorithms are used, and to the strongly connected nature of information to be represented, which often results in a messy and dense structure of nodes and edges. Just to have an idea, Figure 6 shows a representation of an excerpt of WordNet (5000 semantic relations over 3404 synsets) obtained from *Cytoscape* v.3 graph visualization tool. The Neo4j running instance has been accessed via a specific plug-in, namely cyNeo4j, that converts the query results into Cytoscape table format and then create a view according to a custom style and a selected layout like the *Force-directed graph drawing algorithm* before mentioned. The resulting figure is more considerable for global analysis, or for its look and feel, than for actual information that you can retrieve from it. Nevertheless, thanks to the force-directed algorithm, it is possible to observe agglomerates of nodes and edges, which correspond to specific semantic categories and can help users in zooming the desired semantic area.

Thus, it is necessary to simplify the representation of the network by following some functional and esthetic criteria. In this regard, we have selected some simple representation criteria, listed as follows:

1) the efficiency of the visualization, i.e., avoid the information redundancy and the proliferation of useless signs and graphics as much as possible;
2) the effectiveness of the visualization, i.e., grant that the graphical representation of the network covers the whole informative content of the WordNet graph-based implementation;
3) the clearness of visualization, i.e., use light colors, such as gray, light blue, dark green, etc. with a proper level of brightness and with an appreciable contrast.

Furthermore, the adoption of tag cloud based representation for the synonyms rings brought us to use the statistical linguistics measures of *polisemy* and *frequency* of a term as visual cues in drawing the word signs attached to a certain synset.

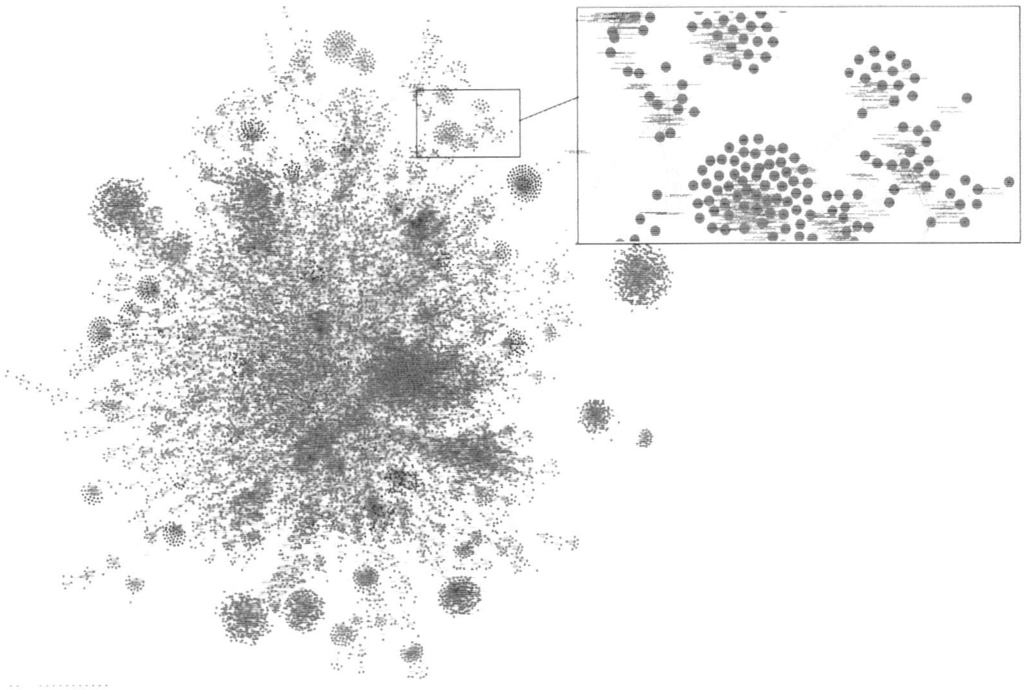

Figure 6. Large scale representation of 5000 relations and 3404 synsets in WordNet

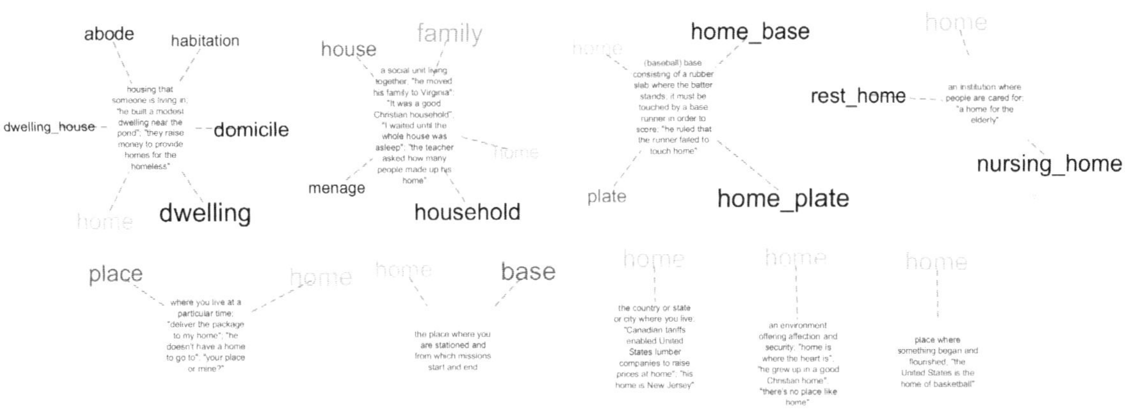

Figure 7. WordNet synset rings containing the 'home' word with the customized style in Cytoscape

Technically, higher the frequency of the word sense, larger is the font used to represent such word in the corresponding synonym ring, as well as, higher is the polysemy of a word in the whole WordNet, lighter is the shade of gray used to tag such word. All the word senses are connected to the corresponding synset through a blank gray line and each synset is represented through a short text containing its gloss. Semantic relations between synsets are represented through a transparent green arc showing a label that report the type of the semantic link (e.g., hypernym, hyponim, meronym, etc.). Figure 7 shows the application of the style rules described above to the same cypher query from *home* mentioned in the previous section. For each sense of the term *home*, the figure shows the tag cloud based representation. Some considerations arise from the figure above. The lighter gray used for the term 'home' is due to its high polysemy (9). This color is intentionally weak to demonstrate how vague is the term alone without a context making it meaningful. Things get worse, for

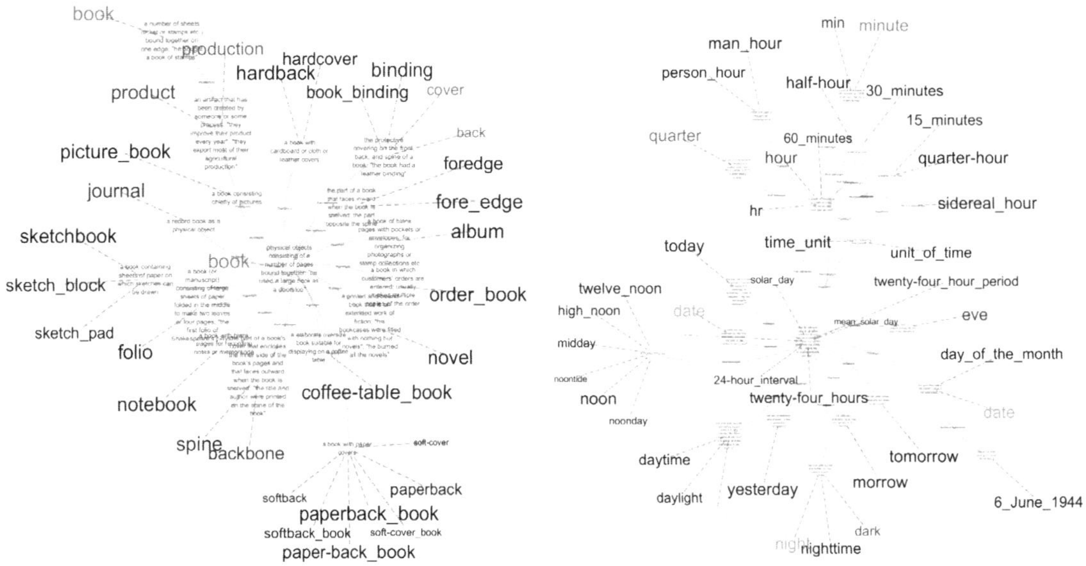

(a) Something about *book*.

(b) Something about *time*.

Figure 8. WordNet excerpts in Cytoscape with custom style.

example, with terms like *head* or *line* with a polysemy equal to 33 and 29, respectively. On the contrary, the term *home_plate* is large in size and as a strong gray shade because of its low polysemy (1) and high frequency when used in the context of baseball.

Figures 8(a) and 8(b) show more representations of WordNet excerpts to fully demonstrating the customized style resulting from this work. The figure are obtained through the following Cypher query where 'keyword' is substituted with *book* and *time*:

```
MATCH (a: WordSense {label: '<keyword>'})-[r]->
        (b: Synset)-[t: semantic_property]->
                (f: Synset)<-[s]-(c: WordSense)
        return a,r,b,t,f,s,c
```

The figures above also highlights the semantic relations existing between synsets showing a more complete representation of WordNet with the new visualization style described in this work.

VI. Conclusion and Future Work

Starting from previous experiences in importing, querying and visualizing WordNet in Neo4J and Cytoscape, a tag cloud based approach has been proposed in this paper as a new solution to make more effective and intelligible the representation of the WordNet graph. The results shown in this work are twofold: first, the new visualization style is able to put order in the messy and dense structure of nodes and edges of WordNet, showing as much as possible information from the lexical database and in a clearer way; secondly, the tag cloud approach is able to reinforce the human cognition in recognizing the different usages of words in English, w.r.t. the concepts they are related to. In fact, the proposed solution not only shows the synsets and the semantic relations holding between them, but also gives clues about the frequency of use of the synonyms for each synset. Future investigation may surely go in the direction of improving the criteria to simplify the WordNet representation with an evaluation for the visualization methods also validated by usability tests in which the user can express a consensus whether the representation is friendly or not, and the information inside WordNet is easily accessible or not. Finally, according to other studies, which aim at improving the tag cloud with semantics [43] and adding multimedia information to the knowledge representation model [44], we will investigate on the use of semantic properties and more efficient metrics to measure the relatedness among WordNet terms [45], also applying other visual features to combine these information [46] and improve the quality of WordNet visualization. Moreover, the process of ontology integration using general and domain specific ontologies [47], [48] needs the investigation of more efficient visualization tool to improve the understanding of very large knowledge base content and structure.

References

[1] E. G. Caldarola, A. Picariello, and A. M. Rinaldi, "Wordnet exploration and visualization in neo4j, a tag cloud based approach," in Proceedings of the Eighth International Conference on Information, Process, and Knowledge Management. IARIA, 2016, pp. 94–99.

[2] G. Bellinger, D. Castro, and A. Mills, "Data, information, knowledge, and wisdom," 2004.

[3] N. Silver, The signal and the noise: Why so many predictions fail-but some don't. Penguin, 2012.

[4] M. Friendly, "Milestones in the history of data visualization: A case study in statistical historiography," in Classificationthe Ubiquitous Challenge. Springer, 2005, pp. 34–52.

[5] J. J. Thomas and K. A. Cook, Illuminating the Path: The R&D Agenda for Visual Analytics National Visualization and Analytics Center. National Visualization and Analytics Center - U.S. Department of Homeland Security, 2005.

[6] D. A. Keim, J. Kohlhammer, G. Ellis, and F. Mansmann, Mastering the information age-solving problems with visual analytics. Florian Mansmann, 2010.

[7] E. G. Caldarola, A. Picariello, and D. Castelluccia, "Modern enterprises in the bubble: Why big data matters," ACM SIGSOFT Software Engineering Notes, vol. 40, no. 1, 2015, pp. 1–4.

[8] E. G. Caldarola, M. Sacco, and W. Terkaj, "Big data: The current wave front of the tsunami," ACS Applied Computer Science, vol. 10, no. 4, 2014, pp. 7–18.

[9] V. Moscato, A. Picariello, and A. M. Rinaldi, "A recommendation strategy based on user behavior in digital ecosystems," in Proceedings of the International Conference on Management of Emergent Digital EcoSystems. ACM, 2010, pp. 25–32.

[10] S. Bateman, C. Gutwin, and M. Nacenta, "Seeing things in the clouds: the effect of visual features on tag cloud selections," in Proceedings of the nineteenth ACM conference on Hypertext and hypermedia. ACM, 2008, pp. 193–202.

[11] Neo Technology Inc. Neo4j: The world's leading graph database. [Online]. Available: http://neo4j.com (2016)

[12] M. E. Smoot, K. Ono, J. Ruscheinski, P.-L. Wang, and T. Ideker, "Cytoscape 2.8: new features for data integration and network visualization," Bioinformatics, vol. 27, no. 3, 2011, pp. 431–432.

[13] R. Spence, Information visualization. Springer, 2001, vol. 1.

[14] R. Mazza, Introduction to information visualization. Springer Science & Business Media, 2009.

[15] U. M. Fayyad, A. Wierse, and G. G. Grinstein, Information visualization in data mining and knowledge discovery. Morgan Kaufmann, 2002.

[16] C. Ware, Information visualization: perception for design. Elsevier, 2012.

[17] W. T. Tutte, "How to draw a graph," Proc. London Math. Soc, vol. 13, no. 3, 1963, pp. 743–768.

[18] H. Purchase, "Which aesthetic has the greatest effect on human understanding?" in Graph Drawing. Springer, 1997, pp. 248–261.

[19] I. Herman, M. Delest, and G. Melancon, "Tree visualisation and navigation clues for information visualisation," Computer Graphics Forum, vol. 17, no. 2, 1998, pp. 153–165.

[20] T. M. Fruchterman and E. M. Reingold, "Graph drawing by force-directed placement," Softw., Pract. Exper., vol. 21, no. 11, 1991, pp. 1129–1164.

[21] E. M. Reingold and J. S. Tilford, "Tidier drawings of trees," Software Engineering, IEEE Transactions on, no. 2, 1981, pp. 223–228.

[22] L. Beaudoin, M.-A. Parent, and L. C. Vroomen, "Cheops: A compact explorer for complex hierarchies," in Visualization'96. Proceedings. IEEE, 1996, pp. 87–92.

[23] W. Huang, S.-H. Hong, and P. Eades, "Effects of sociogram drawing conventions and edge crossings in social network visualization." J. Graph Algorithms Appl., vol. 11, no. 2, 2007, pp. 397–429.

[24] G. J. Wills, "Nicheworksinteractive visualization of very large graphs," in Graph Drawing. Springer, 1997, pp. 403–414.

[25] J. Carriere and R. Kazman, "Research report. interacting with huge hierarchies: beyond cone trees," in Information Visualization, 1995. Proceedings. IEEE, 1995, pp. 74–81.

[26] T. Munzner, "H3: Laying out large directed graphs in 3d hyperbolic space," in Information Visualization, 1997. Proceedings., IEEE Symposium on. IEEE, 1997, pp. 2–10.

[27] P. Eades, "A heuristics for graph drawing," Congressus numerantium, vol. 42, 1984, pp. 146–160.

[28] E. R. Gansner and S. C. North, "Improved force-directed layouts," in Graph Drawing. Springer, 1998, pp. 364–373.

[29] B. Johnson and B. Shneiderman, "Tree-maps: A space-filling approach to the visualization of hierarchical information structures," in Visualization, 1991. Visualization'91, Proceedings., IEEE Conference on. IEEE, 1991, pp. 284–291.

[30] J. Kamps and M. Marx, "Visualizing wordnet structure," Proc. of the 1st International Conference on Global WordNet, 2002, pp. 182–186.

[31] C. Collins, "Wordnet explorer: applying visualization principles to lexical semantics," Computational Linguistics Group, Department of Computer Science, University of Toronto, Toronto, Ontario, Canada, 2006.

[32] ——, "Docuburst: Radial space-filling visualization of document content," Knowledge Media Design Institute, University of Toronto, Technical Report KMDI-TR-2007-1, 2007.

[33] B. B. Bederson and B. Shneiderman, The craft of information visualization: readings and reflections. Morgan Kaufmann, 2003.

[34] Neo Technology Inc. Neo4j: Cypher query language. [Online]. Available: https://neo4j.com/developer/cypher/ (2016)

[35] C. Fellbaum, "Wordnet," The Encyclopedia of Applied Linguistics, 1998.

[36] G. A. Miller, "Wordnet: a lexical database for english," Communications of the ACM, vol. 38, no. 11, 1995, pp. 39–41.

[37] A. M. Rinaldi, "A content-based approach for document representation and retrieval," in Proceedings of the eighth ACM symposium on Document engineering. ACM, 2008, pp. 106–109.

[38] J. Webber, "A programmatic introduction to neo4j," in Proceedings of the 3rd annual conference on Systems, Programming, and Applications: Software for Humanity. ACM, 2012, pp. 217–218.

[39] E. Caldarola, A. Picariello, and A. M. Rinaldi, "Big graph-based data visualization experiences - the wordnet case study," in Proceedings of the 7th International Joint Conference on Knowledge Discovery, Knowledge Engineering and Knowledge Management, 2015, pp. 104–115.

[40] M. A. Finlayson, MIT Java Wordnet Interface (JWI) User's Guide, Version 2.2.x, 2013.

[41] ——, "Java libraries for accessing the princeton wordnet: Comparison and evaluation," in Proceedings of the 7th Global Wordnet Conference, Tartu, Estonia, 2014.

[42] Wordnet RDF. [Online]. Available: http://wordnet-rdf.princeton.edu/ (2016)

[43] A. M. Rinaldi, "Improving tag clouds with ontologies and semantics," in IEEE International Workshop on Text-Based Information Retrieval (TIR'12) in conjunction with DEXA12. IEEE, 2012.

[44] ——, "A multimedia ontology model based on linguistic properties and audio-visual features," Information Sciences, vol. 277, 2014, pp. 234–246.

[45] ——, "An ontology-driven approach for semantic information retrieval on the web," ACM Transactions on Internet Technology (TOIT), vol. 9, no. 3, 2009, p. 10.

[46] ——, "Using multimedia ontologies for automatic image annotation and classification," in 2014 IEEE International Congress on Big Data. IEEE, 2014, pp. 242–249.

[47] A. Cataldo and A. M. Rinaldi, "An ontological approach to represent knowledge in territorial planning science," Computers, Environment and Urban Systems, vol. 34, no. 2, 2010, pp. 117–132.

[48] E. G. Caldarola, A. Picariello, and A. M. Rinaldi, "An approach to ontology integration for ontology reuse in knowledge based digital ecosystems," in Proceedings of the 7th International Conference on Management of Computational and Collective intElligence in Digital EcoSystems, ser. MEDES '15. New York, NY, USA: ACM, 2015, pp. 1–8. [Online]. Available: http://doi.acm.org/10.1145/2857218.2857219

You Might Have Forgotten This Learning Content! How the Smart Learning Recommender Predicts Appropriate Learning Objects

Christopher Krauss *, Rakesh Chandru ‡, Agathe Merceron †, Truong-Sinh An †, Miggi Zwicklbauer * and Stefan Arbanowski *

*Fraunhofer Insitute for Open Communication Systems
Kaiserin-Augusta-Allee 31, 10589 Berlin, Germany
Emails: christopher.krauss@fokus.fraunhofer.de, miggi.zwicklbauer@fokus.fraunhofer.de, stefan.arbanowski@fokus.fraunhofer.de

†Beuth Hochschule fuer Technik Berlin
Luxemburger Str. 10, 13353 Berlin, Germany
Emails: merceron@beuth-hochschule.de, sinhan@beuth-hochschule.de

‡DILAX Intelcom GmbH
Alt-Moabit 96b, 10559 Berlin, Germany
Email: rakesh.chandru@dilax.com
(Rakesh Chandru contributed to this paper as employee of Fraunhofer FOKUS)

Abstract—**In digital learning environments, analysis of students' interactions with the learning objects provides important information about students' behavior. This can lead to a better understanding of the learning process and thus, optimizes teaching and learning. The aim of the ongoing research project "Smart Learning" is to introduce a novel mobile Learning Companion App in order to support a blended-learning approach in the training of Energy Consultants at the Chamber of Crafts Berlin, university lecturers as well as company internal summer schools. Thereby, students can keep track of their individual predicted knowledge level on different learning objects at every point in time and get personalized learning recommendations based on the expected learning progress. Moreover, teachers make use of learning analytics in order to get an overview of students' progress and so, be aware of possible weaknesses. The relevance of learning items change significantly over the period of a course – students may start with a low knowledge level, learn specific topics and afterwards slowly forget the lessons learned. Thus, learning environments require a new prediction paradigm for recommender systems: The relevance score of an item depends on different contextual factors. Especially forgetting plays a crucial role as people tend to forget lessons learned. Information stored in individual's memory is either erased or cannot be retrieved due to several reasons. This process is influenced by different parameters: external ones, such as the item's media type, difficulty level and so on, as well as the individual's memory strength. This paper introduces the main ideas of the overall system, its architecture, app design and mathematical concepts as well as a novel approach to include the effect of forgetting in a time-dependent recommender system that is specialized in the area of Technology Enhanced Learning.**

Keywords–Smart Learning; Forgetting; Learning Companion; Recommendation Engine; Learning Analytics

I. INTRODUCTION

Career advancement requires employees to continuously update their skills and, in many cases, to document their up-to-date knowledge with a certificate. In Germany, the Chamber of Crafts (Handwerkskammer) provides numerous vocational trainings that lead to the obtainment of a certificate. Trainees are full-time professionals. Until now most of the trainings are fully face-to-face. The aim of the project "Smart Learning in Vocational Training" [1] is to introduce a blended-learning approach in the training of Energy Consultants. Learning material is currently structured and developed using different digital media: texts, animations, screencasts, videos. During lecture phases trainees learn hands-on with a professional. To prepare and to review face-to-face learning, they can access online what they need, when they need it, with the help of a novel mobile web application called the Learning Companion App (LCA).

LCA provides trainees with access to learning materials and stores user interactions according to an opt-in procedure. In that respect, it is similar to a Learning Management System (LMS) that can also run on desktops or mobile devices. However, LCA makes use of a set of server-side software components. The full system integrates a recommendation engine and a learning analytics module [2]. Based on the stored interactions and making use of the recommendation engine, LCA shows trainees their progress and recommends them learning material after calculating their current learning need. This feature of actively guiding learners through the material by means of recommendations distinguishes LCA from common LMS. A learning analytics module is being developed for instructors/instructional designers. As LMSs do, LCA differentiates between users according to their role.

Instructors can use LCA to access dashboards that give them an overview of learners' progress. Thus, before face-to-face meetings, for example, instructors can review the advancement of trainees and adapt their teaching. Other dashboards show the progress of learners when completing self-estimation of learning objectives before and after completing a learning unit. These dashboards, also accessible through LCA, are useful for instructional designers to judge and, possibly, review the quality of the individual course elements, named Learning Objects (LO).

This paper is organized as follows: Section II introduces related work on recommendation techniques and analytics for education. Section III explains the overall architecture of the currently implemented components and Section IV focuses especially on the Learning Companion App and the underlying techniques. Afterwards the learning analytics and recommender modules are introduced and followed by a detailed explanation of the Smart Learning Recommender. Especially the forgetting effect in Section VIII shows a novel approach in Technology Enhanced Learning. We conducted two studies resulting in a mathematical formula that represents an approximation of human forgetfulness. However, it is still a challenge to compare the overall system with existing ones in academia. These issues are discussed in section IX. The paper concludes with a short summary and an outlook on planned further evaluations.

II. Related Work

Many modern web services, such as movie portals and e-commerce services, but also online learning courses, offer a vast amount of content items. Users quite often lose the overview and get buried in details. A recommendation engine aims at identifying the most relevant items for a specific user that fit the individual needs and thus, makes the interaction on that web service more efficient.

A. Recommender Systems in Technology Enhanced Learning

Olga C. Santos [3] discusses different barriers in Technology Enhanced Learning (TEL) and describes six factors that influence this domain. The factors are motivation, platform usage, collaboration with class mates, accessibility considerations when contributing, learning style adaptations and previous knowledge. The results show a decrease of the need to consume all available learning objects, when getting learning recommendations.

Learning and recommending learning objects in a digital environment, such as in mobile, hybrid and online learning, is "an effort that takes more time and interactions compared to a commercial transaction. Learners rarely achieve a final end state after a fixed time. Instead of buying a product and then owning it, learners achieve different levels of competences that have various levels in different domains" [4]. The learner shall find appropriate content for the preparation of a lesson in order to: 1) Be motivated, 2) Recall existing knowledge and 3) Illustrate, visualize and represent new concepts and information [4]. Moreover, recommender systems in On-line Learning can also be used for actual teaching as well as for knowledge evaluation and assessment.

Manouselis et al. [4] argued that more than the half of all published recommender systems in the area of Intelligent Learning Technologies were still at a prototyping or concept level and only 10 have been evaluated in trials with real participants. Most of these systems are designed to predict items in a closed system using the two-dimensional Collaborative Filtering user-item-matrix, such as "CourseRank" [5] of the Standford University, "Altered Vista" [6] that uses Association Rules of frequently used learning objects in courses or "RACOFI" [7], a rule-applying collaborative filtering system "that assists on-line users in the rating and recommendation of audio (Learning) Objects". However, these recommenders only work on a flat item hierarchy and without time or extended context data. Nevertheless, it seems to be very important to include the intrinsic and extrinsic motivation of students, in terms of "pedagogical aspects like prior knowledge, learning goals or study time" [4].

B. Context-Sensitive Learning Recommendations

In order to improve the online learning environment, Hayriye Tugba Ozturk [8] proposes a method of sequential analysis of discussions among students and teachers in a Learning Management System (LMS). A similar kind of research is carried out by Angel F. Agudo-Peregrina [9], where the interactions in the learning management system is analyzed, based on an agent (student-student, student-teacher, student-content), frequency of use (access to learning resources, creation of class interactions and so on) and participation mode (active or passive) for predicting students' academic performance.

The "APOSDLE" recommender service [10] uses an extended user profile as input for appropriate content recommendations and a web tool for ontology evaluation for identifying semantic similarities. The "Multi-Attribute Recommendation Service" [11], in turn, uses ratings on different attributes and criteria for the same learning object in order to calculate proper recommendations. Moreover, Huang et al. [12] uses a Markov chain model to calculate sequences of learning objects and recommend learning paths, and the "Learning Object Sequencing" [13] uses a novel sequencing rule algorithm by processing topical ontologies. The "Moodle Recommender System" [14] shows the significant role of learning paths and completion rates of learning objects that are of interest for recommender systems to assist other learners. Our Smart Learning Recommender engine follows a similar approach by taking the context, in terms of various factors, as well as item sequences and hierarchies into account.

C. Time-dependent Recommenders

Drachsler et al. [15] underline the significance of the attribute that represents time taken to complete learning objects. Pelanek et al. [16] evaluated the closed correlation between multidimensional student skills and the timing of problem solving that "may be useful for automatic problem selection and recommendation in intelligent tutoring systems and for providing feedback to students, teachers, or authors of educational materials". However, most research on time-dependent recommendation engines have been done in the area of movie predictions: Liang Xiang [17] demonstrates four different time factors that affects recommending videos. They are the change in interest of a whole society over the time, changes in users' rating habits, changes in items' popularities and changes in users' attitudes towards some type of items. In a study conducted by Liang He [18], neighborhood group and user preferences are computed for different time intervals. In

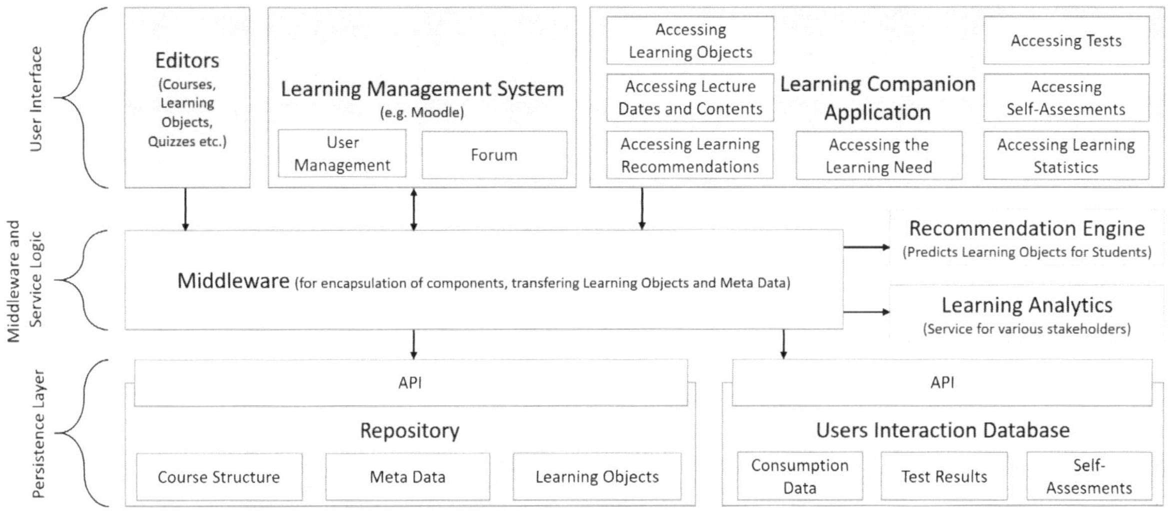

Figure 1. Architecture of the Smart Learning Infrastructure

each interval, rating data is analyzed to find users with similar interests. The predictions are computed using ratings and weights provided for each interval. This approach improves the prediction accuracy for time based collaborative filtering. The recommender system designed by Pooyan Adibi [19] tries to find each user's interest in different groups of items and computes the predictions of rating the user will give in near future. It was observed that the designed system has lower prediction errors when considering the rating time – not only in normal scenario, but also for cold start users. These studies show that the inclusion of forgetting in recommender systems improves the prediction accuracy. Zhang et al. [20] describe an approach to consider changes in users' interests when recommending the items for the users. A novel K-nearest neighbor algorithm [21] finds time-based neighborhoods of a user. Even though these movie recommenders inspire the development of our Smart Learning Recommender, they mostly analyze and predict the users' interests in items instead of considering the users' knowledge [22]. Learning environments, in turn, represent a significantly different prediction paradigm: students have to learn all relevant objects to pass the final exam, no matter whether they are interested in it or not.

Unfortunately, it seems that, in the area of mobile and online learning, no recommender system covers the time aspect of changing knowledge levels – even though it seems to have great impact. LCA continuously tracks the learning behavior of individual users over the whole course period, forecasts their learning need on specific LOs at every point in time and recommends appropriate learning objects.

D. Dashboards and Graphical User Representations

Santos [23] proposes "a graphical representation that will help to compare the recommenders' performance in eLearning scenarios". While this was originally designed for life-long learning, we reused this idea to give the student insights in his learning progress within a course and to visualize different context factors in order to show the current status of his learning need on a specific content.

Learning dashboards to support teachers in different teaching contexts have been proposed by different authors. All dashboards provide some form of visual summary of the use of learning materials by learners [24] [25] [26]. The visual summary proposed by Elkina, Fortenbacher and Merceron [25] is particularly interesting: All interactive exercises and questions in the course have been tagged with learning objectives. Based on students performance, the learning dashboard provides instructors with an overview of all learning objectives, represented by a bar each. The proportion of green, yellow and red in the bar reflects the proportion of learning progress in the class; the grey portion of the bar shows students with too little activity to enable a classification of their performance. As argued by Martinez-Maldonado et al. [27], it is essential to establish a dialogue with future users of dashboards while designing them. Adopting such a user-centered approach and re-using analyses developed in the LeMo tool [25], dashboards are being developed that adapt elements of the overview proposed to the bigger variety of learning objects present in LCA.

III. Architecture

One focus of the Smart Learning project is to provide a reusable generic infrastructure for various users with different client devices, for different courses covering several topics – not restricted to institutions like Chamber of Crafts, but also usable by universities and adult education centers. While users are still managed in the LMS, learning objects are stored only once in a repository and can be shared by and accessed from various learning management systems.

Figure 1 illustrates the architecture and the interworking of the core components. Each component is encapsulated and only connected to the middleware, which, in turn, exchanges contents and metadata in standardized formats via standardized interfaces. Components and standards are described in turn.

Figure 2. Learning Companion Application: Presentation of the course structure on a smartphone (left picture) and the learning need overview on a tablet (right picture)

The Learning Companion App plays a key role for the infrastructure. It is the entry point for students to access courses, learning objects and lecture dates as well as to get recommendations for the next best contents to be learnt and tracks all relevant user interactions. It is a responsive web application capable of being displayed on regular modern desktop web environments, but especially on smartphones and tablets to enable mobile learning. The application gives everywhere and everytime access to all learning objects offered in the taken courses. Presently, it recommends the top-five most relevant learning objects for the current situation, right after the login process. However, students can access the whole course in a chronological or didactic order, or according to their own personalized setting. Students can optimize their schedule by filtering the important items that fit in the available time period – for instance when waiting for the bus or going to class. Each learning object item is represented by a tile and shows, besides its title, its predicted relevance for the student on a 0 - 100% scale, so that a student can identify and compare the importance of different items at a glance. Different buttons allow access to the content itself, sub-items, exercises, discussion forums or a more detailed version of the learning need representation and the predicted relevance of that item. Figure 2 shows two screens: the course structure on a smartphone and the detailed learning need representation on a tablet. Teachers, in turn, use LCA to get access to the Learning Analytics module that gives an overview of students' progress in the course.

The LMS is used to register and manage all users and offers discussion forums. In order to allow a consistent interaction with all components, the students (and teachers) credentials of the existing Learning Management Systems are required to authenticate at the Learning Companion App. This kind of single-sign-on approach is implemented in the middleware.

The repository acts as a digital asset store, which holds course structures, learning objects and their metadata. At the lowest level, a learning object is a simple HTML document, a video, a screencast, a progress evaluation quiz and so on, all with at least one learning objective. Low-level LOs are stored as IMS Learning Tools Interoperability (LTI) [28] to integrate them with different LMSs. Moreover, questions and tests are specified according to the IMS Question and Test Interoperability (QTI) specification [29]. Low level learning objects can be bundled into bigger learning objects, and this iteration can be repeated. In the current energy consultant course, low-level LOs are combined in learning units, learning units in sections and a set of sections make up the course. That way, low level LOs can be reused in several courses. A manifest file is created to bundle the LOs together. A player that is presently stored in the repository renders the learning units and QTI specified tests. Further, the player generates automatically self-assessment questions using the learning objectives of a learning unit. The metadata associated with a low level LO contains, among others, its learning objectives, average study time defined by instructors and prerequisite LOs. These data are stored using the IMS Learning Resource Meta-data (LOM) specification [30]. When LOs are combined, the metadata of the whole is generated automatically from the parts. A course structure is stored following the IMS Common Cartridge standard [31].

Different editors have been implemented as easy to use web applications for instructional designers. A LOM-Editor allows to specify the metadata of any existing LO and to store the corresponding file in the repository. A QTI-editor allows creating questions, to bundle them into tests following the QTI specification and to store them in the repository; presently seven types of questions are available: single selection, multiple selection, extended text, text entry, numeric, matrix and order. Finally, a LO-Editor allows bundling LOs into bigger ones and generating the metadata file automatically. Users interactions with any LO are stored according to the opt-in procedure chosen by the user. Interactions are persisted using

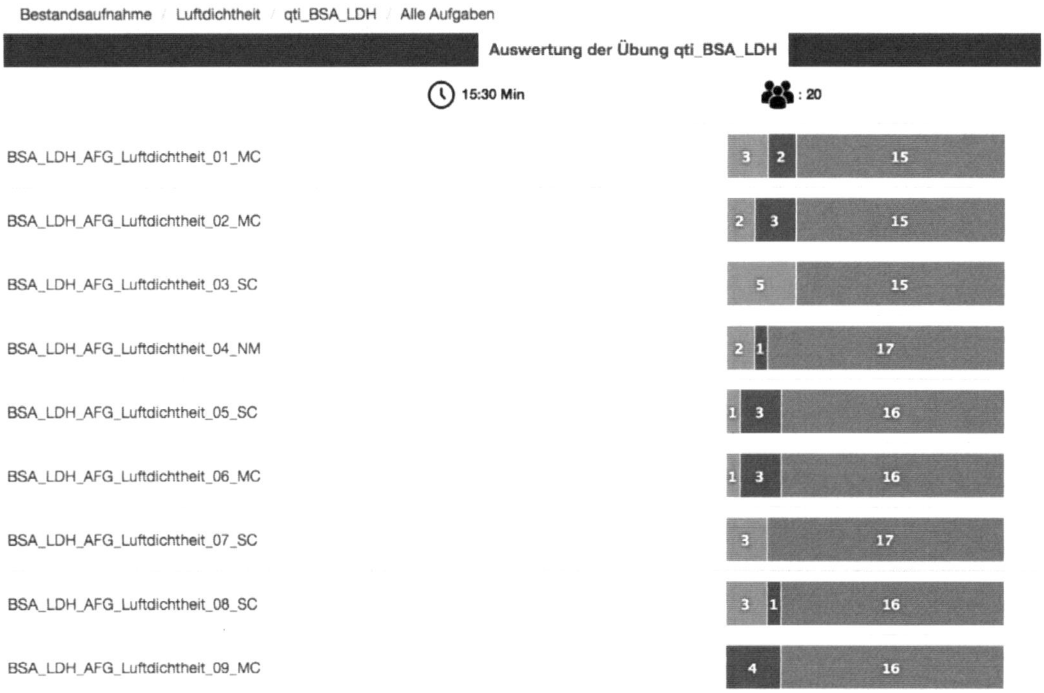

Figure 3. Learning Analytics Module

the xAPI specification [32] in the free learning record store called learning locker.

The recommendation engine and the learning analytics service load the needed interaction data in regular intervals in order to determine students performance. The Smart Learning Recommender (SLR) aims at identifying the most suitable learning object for the requesting student based on the calculated knowledge level and learning need for that item. The learning analytics service, in contrast, is designed for other stakeholders. Teachers can observe the overall progress and performance of students and figure out weaknesses in learning and understanding.

IV. Personal Tracking via the Learning Companion App

A key role in connecting the users' interaction in LCA with the learning analytics service or recommendations engine is attributed to the formal and informal activity statements reflecting the collected user data. In recent years, the Experience API [32] with its xAPI statements supporting long-term data mining continuously moves in the academic focus. A typical statement consists of the three properties: "Actor", "Verb" and "Object". An xAPI statement can also carry the optional properties "Context" and "Results" containing more information for new insights like in the following statements:

- "StudentA (Actor) completed (Verb) Question1 (Object) in the context of Quiz1 in Course1 and the result is success with 2 attempts based on the raw score of 80 with a max score of 100 and a scale of 0.8"
- "StudentB stopped VideoY started at position 00:01:30 in the context of LearningUnit2 of Course1 resulting in duration of 00:01:42".

The player mentioned in the preceding section as well as LCA triggers xAPI statements.

A. *Learning Analytics as Feedback for the Teachers*

As mentioned in the introduction, the main dashboard should allow instructors to get an overview of learners' progress and receive details on demand [33]. It offers details on the selected learning object. We follow the approach of the LeMo-Tool [25] in associating a bar to each object with the colors green, yellow and red, see the work of An et al. [34] for more detailed explanations. Taking the example of a test made of several questions, green represents how often the test has been completely solved, yellow how often it has been partially solved and red how many students have not solved it at all. Following a similar scheme, details on each question show the number of correct answers in green, partially correct in yellow, wrong answers in red and missing answers in grey; see Figure 3. Further details according to the question's type can be obtained. Filters allow to choose particular time periods for the dashboard.

B. *Recommendations for Students*

Recommendation engines in a closed domain, like in intelligent learning, are following a special paradigm: At the end of a course, where only a closed user group interacts with a finite amount of items, in this case learning objects, most students provide feedback on almost all items. However, common prediction techniques do not cover that the user's need for learning particular items changes significantly over time – inversely proportional to the user's knowledge level on these learning objects. In this work a time-dependent context-sensitive representation of a user-model is introduced. This helps users to be aware of their learning level and get appropriate learning recommendations as well as teachers to get a direct feedback on the learning behavior. In our Smart Learning Recommender (SLR) – first introduced in [35] – we relate each student with each available learning object in the taken course and aggregate all xAPI statements with time information. We do that to predict the user's knowledge level on all content items and, in turn, recommend relevant learning objects in order to compensate predicted weaknesses. The remainder of the paper focuses on this novel recommender approach.

V. Learning Need and Relevance Function

Learning recommendation is all about identifying the learning need of a user u for an item i at a specific time t. The user-item-pair is presented by a relevance score $rscore_{u,i}$ having the value from 0 to 1, where 0 indicates the lowest relevance and 1 indicates the highest possible relevance. The relevance score defines a time and context dependent value and is expressed as a time dependent function:

$$rscore_{u,i,t} = rf_{u,i}(t) \tag{1}$$

The relevance function $rf_{u,i}(t)$ of user u for item i is derived from several sub-functions $rf_{u,i,x}(t)$ of individual factors $x_1, ..., x_n$, as a function of time t, each representing another context.

The factor itself is based on real user-item value pairs $rscore_{u,i,t,x}$. Since the real learning need changes continuously over time, the factor can be abstracted as continuous function, as well. We identified the following different factor types and considered formulas per user, item and time. Figures 4 to 9 show the spectrum of relevance scores as functions of the main factor parameters.

1) Interaction with a learning object: This factor indicates how much of the available material $availableContent_i$ for a learning object i was accessed by a student u at a specific moment in time t:

$$rscore_{u,i,t,x1} = 1 - \frac{accessedContent_{u,i,t}}{availableContent_i} \tag{2}$$

This can be the percentage of a watched video or audio item as well as how much the student scrolled through a text. We cannot guarantee that student really studied that content, but is our first indication for predicting the knowledge level.

Figure 4. Relevance values for interactions

2) Processing time of a learning object: This factor indicates how long the student learned a learning object. It is 0 when the student needed exactly the intended time and between 0 and 1 if he needs more or less time than defined in the metadata.

$$rscore_{u,i,t,x2} = \left| 1 - \sqrt{\frac{timeNeededForLearning_{u,i,t}}{timeIntendedForLearning_i}} \right| \tag{3}$$

In an initial phase, we work with an upper bound for the time that is needed for learning: The square root lessens the effect when a student did not exactly learn the intended time. If the user needed more than 4 times of the time, the learning need is 1. In combination with the percentage of interaction, the processing time allows a good approximation whether a student really worked through that content.

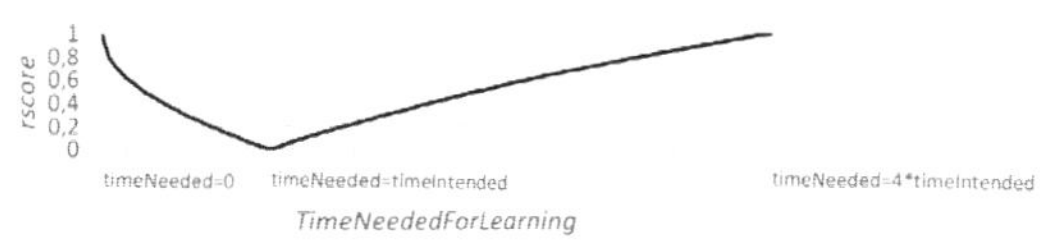

Figure 5. Relevance values for processing time

3) Self-assessments for this learning object: A student can explicitly define his knowledge level in particular points in time on a 1 to 5 stars scale:

$$rscore_{u,i,t,x3} = 1 - \frac{currentKnowledgeLevel_{u,i,t}}{highestKnowledgeLevel} \tag{4}$$

We ask for this feedback in various situations, even when students have just read the title of a learning object. They can adjust the self-assessment at any time.

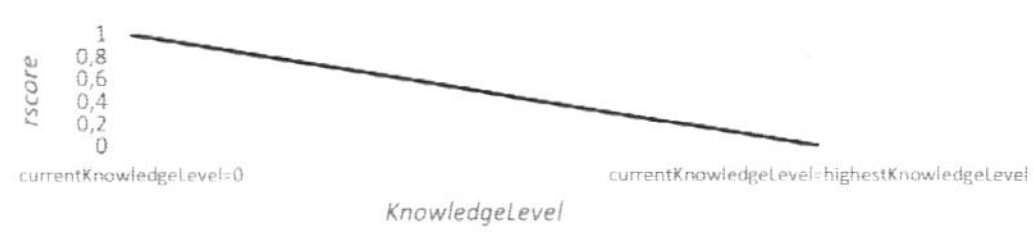

Figure 6. Relevance values for self-assessments

4) Performance in exercises: The percentage of wrong answered questions represents the relevance of the exercise factor:

$$rscore_{u,i,t,x4} = 1 - \frac{rightAnswers_{u,i,t}}{allAnswers_i} \tag{5}$$

Equation (5) is the same as $\frac{wrongAnswers_{u,i,t}}{allAnswers_i}$. Left out answers will be treated as wrong answers, so that the relevance score is only 0, when a student correctly answered all questions.

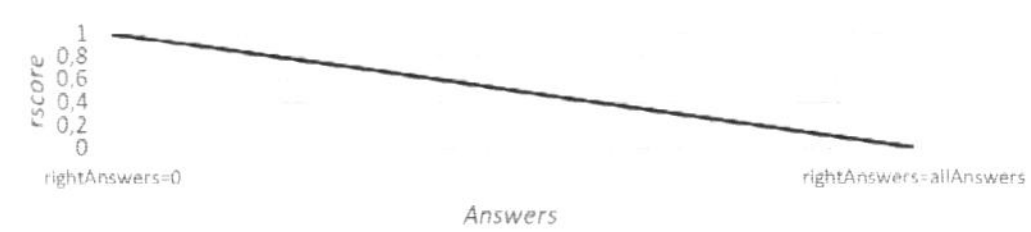

Figure 7. Relevance values for exercises

5) Fulfilled pre-requisites: The more a student learned the underlying learning objects, the higher the relevance score of the subsequent items:

$$rscore_{u,i,t,x5} = \frac{fulfilledPreRequisites_{u,i,t}}{allPreRequisites_i} \tag{6}$$

This factor is not directly affected by the users' interaction. It depends on the learning of prerequisite items. Thus, a learning object gets more relevant when a users understood the required basics. In case there is no pre-requisite for a learning object, the relevance score is 1.

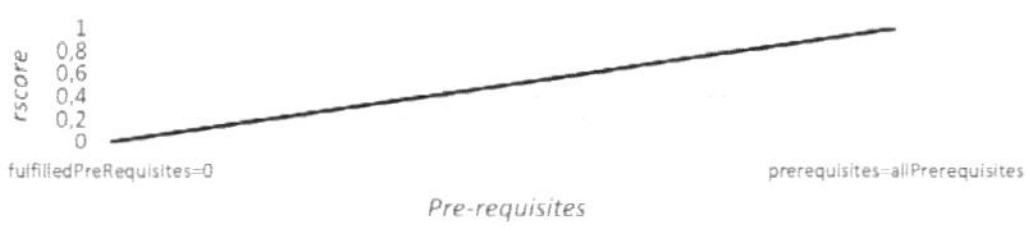

Figure 8. Relevance values for fulfilled prerequisites

6) The lecture times factor indicates the timely relevance of a learning object for face-to-face lectures. The closer the lecture at time $timeOfLecture$, the higher the relevance score:

$$rscore_{u,i,t,x6} =$$
$$1 - \left(prepPhaseFactor * \frac{timeOfLecture_i - t}{courseDuration}\right)^2 \quad (7)$$

The $courseDuration$ (time of course ending minus time of course start) must be higher then 0 and the $timeOfLecture$ must be within the $courseDuration$. The $prepPhaseFactor$ needs to be defined by the teacher and defines the duration of both: the preparation as well as the wrap up phase of a lecture, where the contents concerned are more relevant. For instance, for $prepPhaseFactor = 1$ the preparation phase is exactly the course duration, for $prepPhaseFactor = 2$ it is half the course duration, for $prepPhaseFactor = 4$ the preparation phase is one quarter of the course duration and so on. The higher the number, the later the begin of the preparation phase and, thus, the later the recommendation of this learning object. In case the current time t does not fall in the preparation or wrap-up phase, the relevance score is set to 0.

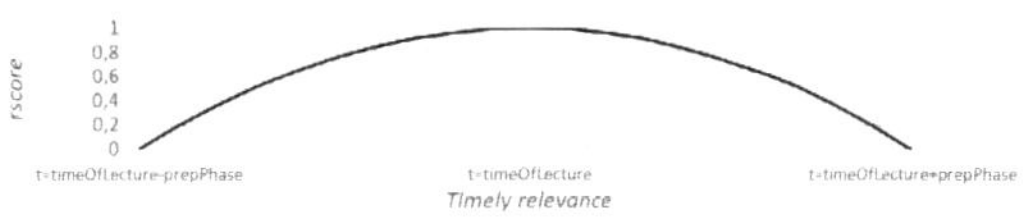

Figure 9. Relevance values for lecture times

7) Exam relevance: Learning objects that are more relevant for exams show a higher relevance score than optional contents – expressed by a constant value defined in the learning object metadata.
8) Collaborative learning needs: The relevance functions of similar users on this learning object are taken into account in order to offset underestimations and bad learning plannings for the current user. In an initial phase, the mean average learning need of all other students (but without their collaborative learning need to avoid recursion loops) for this learning object represent this factor. The plan is to replace this mean learning need by a weighted average factor of nearest-neighbors, who show the most similar learning curves.
9) Forgetting effect: After learning an object, the gained knowledge will decrease over time. This factor has been analyzed with real students in order to model an appropriate forgetting factor. Details on this factor are described in the following section.

Each factor's relevance score represents an aspect of the learning need. It is restricted to the range of $[0, 1]$ and will be further evaluated and adjusted in the future. At the end, all single-factor functions are weighted. The weighted average of all factors describes the total learning need of the learning object for that user and is calculated as

$$rf_{u,i}(t) = \frac{\sum_{x=1}^{n}(w_x * rf_{u,i,x}(t))}{\sum_{x=1}^{n} w_x} \quad (8)$$

Here w_x is the weight of a single factor x in $\{x_1, ..., x_n\}$ and n is the number of factors – currently, $n = 9$. At the beginning, the weights are predefined by experts, such as teachers.

VI. Forgetting Factor

The study on human forgetting began in early 19th century. Hermann Ebbinghaus [36] gave the first and still representative equation for the forgetting curve. He noticed that forgetting is high during the initial period after learning and gradually decreases over time. An experiment was conducted by Harry P. Bahrick [37] to test the recall and recognition of 50 English-Spanish word pairs over a period of 8 years. The results showed that the recall and recognition percentage of words is greater in larger intersession intervals, indicating the influence of spacing on forgetting. In recent years, some recommender systems re-used the equation from Ebbinghaus to improve predictions for the e-commerce and entertainment domain [38] [39].

Some research highlights positive aspects of forgetting, especially forgetting in the area of big data. For instance, "forgetting" or "trashing" might be a necessary instrument when storing or processing information of huge data sets in order to handle less data in total and improve the overall performance [40]. However, this section focuses on human forgetting of learning contents that must be avoided to pass the final exam.

A. *Parameters of Forgetting*

The decay theory [41] states that a person's memory of a learned content fades away over time, when it is not used. That is why forgetting represents a special relevance factor function $rf_{u,i,forgetting}(t)$ in the Smart Learning Recommender. Apart from time, we identified the following parameters that influence forgetting:

- Media type: The type of learning objects plays a vital role in remembering (cf. [3] [42]). In our approach, the media types are text, exercise, audio, graphics/image, video and multimedia.
- Difficulty level: The learning content represents different difficulty levels [42]. A common way of categorizing difficulty level is easy, medium and hard. It can be set based on the amount of content, detail level of information and so on. Forgetting will increase from difficulty level easy to hard.
- Prior knowledge: Learner's prior knowledge about the course helps to easily understand the course as

compared to a learner who is new to the course. Hence, with prior knowledge, the learner remembers more [3] [42].

- Learner's interest towards the content: If the learner is not interested in a subject, forgetting tends to be at a higher rate compared to the subject of interest [42].
- Learner's memory strength: Every person in the world is different from each other, so their memory. A learner with higher memory strength can remember more, compared to a learner with lower memory strength.
- Repetition: During repetitions, students learn the offered items again. Repetition is very helpful in strengthening the memory of learned content [36] [43].
- Repetition spacing: Constant repetitions at regular intervals will help to retain learned content. However, when the time spacing between initial learning and repetition is large, the percentage of increase in memory of the content is also high compared to the percentage increase with short repetition interval [43].
- Re-remembrance due to retention tests: Most research does not take the effect of retention tests for the re-remembrance into account: When people are asked about a topic, the questions in the retention test can act as a retrieval cue and allow the learner to correlate the words in the question to the previously learned content – thereby, remembering the forgotten concept as a side-effect.
- Retention test spacing: Similar to the repetition spacing, the gap in time between two successive retention tests can also have an influence on the re-remembrance. The more spacing, the smaller the effect of re-remembrance.

We conducted an experiment with a group of eight people to confirm and study the effect of the parameters that could influence forgetting. The duration was eight to ten weeks and involved people from different fields like information technology, medicine and business administration. The eight people learn a learning object at the beginning of the experiment. In regular intervals, we performed retention tests to observe the learner's knowledge. 5-8 questions from a group of 10-12 questions that represent the key information of the given topic are randomly picked and posed at the person to test the percentage of forgetting. The assumption: the progress of wrongly answered questions (in percent) over time represent the progress of forgetting. In the experiment, the parameter values are varied, to get a clue about its effect on forgetting. We presented different media types, in terms of texts and videos with different complexity levels. In some cases, the learning objects needed to be learned again at specific points in time to evaluate the repetition effect. Figure 10 shows an excerpt from the survey results with the forgetting progress of videos that have been watched only once and show different lengths and complexity levels.

B. Mathematical Description

Based on the experiment, a mathematical model for forgetting is derived, given by Equation (9). We analyzed the progress of forgetting during the study (e.g., in Figure 10)

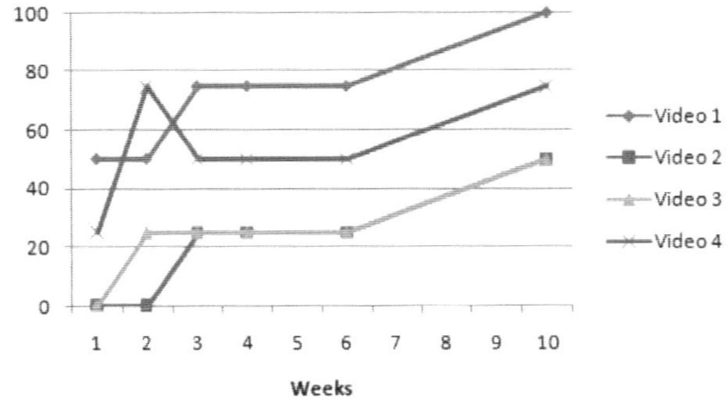

Figure 10. Survey results for forgetting of videos with different complexity levels that have only been watched at the beginning of the experiment. The y-axis represent the percentage of wrong or not answered questions per retention test. Thereby each 12,5% stand for one of eight answered questions.

and searched for a mathematical abstraction that represents the forgetting best:

$$rf_{u,i,forgetting}(t) = factorEffect(t) + \alpha \quad (9)$$

The model includes two main parameters: the $factorEffect$ with respect to learning times and media metadata as well as a personalized parameter α that customizes the forgetting equation for the learner and thus, represents the individual forgetting process. The value of forgetting is restricted between 0 and 1 as well as all the other factors. The $factorEffect(t)$ corresponds to the following exponential function:

$$factorEffect(t) = 1 - e^{-(timeFactor(t) - E_{rep} - E_{ret} + E_m + E_d)} \quad (10)$$

Thereby, the e-function shows the most similar progress compared to the participants forgetting in the survey and a set of parameters represent the exponent. Where E_{rep} is the repetition effect, E_{ret} is the retention test effect, E_m is the media type effect and E_d represents the difficulty level. If the learner does not repeat to learn a learning object or does not answer retention tests, these parameters are set to 0.

The values for E_m are in the range $[0, 0.1]$. For example, media types which increases the retention by the highest possible value would be assigned 0. In our case, videos and animations are assigned 0.04 and text with 0.1. The difficulty level E_d can vary between 0 and 0.1, as well, where easy is assigned 0 and hard with 0.1. The $timeFactor$ represents the forgetting – only with respect to time:

$$timeFactor(t) = \frac{t - T_f}{T_c} * \sqrt{\frac{T_c}{T_s}} \quad (11)$$

Where $t - T_f$ corresponds to the difference between current time t and the first access time of the learning content T_f in days. T_c is the total course duration. T_s represents the speed of forgetting (if no other parameter affects forgetting), that is set in an initial version to 30 days for a course duration T_c of 180 days, and can be adjusted by the teacher if needed. As forgetting starts as soon as one starts learning an object, the relevance score is set to 0 before the first access of the content.

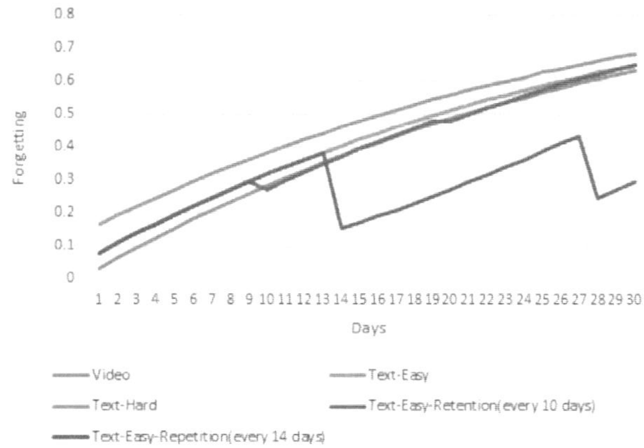

Figure 11. Mathematical model for predicted forgetting of different media types and with retention tests and repitions on a 0 to 1 scale.

It can be observed from the Formula (11) that there will be an increase in the value of $timeFactor(t)$ with longer course durations.

The equations for the effect of repetition and re-remembrance due to retention tests are given by Equations (12) and (13).

$$E_{ret} = n_{ret} * \frac{T_c - T_{d,ret}}{T_c} * K_{ret} \quad (12)$$

Where T_c is the total course duration expressed in days and $T_{d,ret}$ is the number of days after the last retention test. n_{ret} is the retention test count. The constant K_{ret} at the end of the equation indicates the weight by which the forgetting is reduced. The ideal value for the constant is 0.01, based on the observations from the experiment.

$$E_{rep} = timeFactor * \frac{T_c - T_{d,rep}}{T_c} * K_{rep} \quad (13)$$

E_{rep} includes the *timeFactor* that was initially given by Formula (11), $T_{d,rep}$ is the number of days elapsed after last repetition. The constant K_{rep} at the end of the equation indicates the weight by which the forgetting is reduced. In our experiment the ideal value for this constant is 0.75.

Factors like memory strength and the learner's interest towards the content are specific to each learner. These factors make the forgetting curve unique for each learner, but need further evaluations. The adapting constant α requires the conduction of retention tests. If there is no retention test planned, the adapting constant is set to 0. The value α personalizes the forgetting curve by taking the learner's performance in the retention into account. It is given by the following formula:

$$\alpha = \frac{predictedScore - actualScore}{2} \quad (14)$$

It represents the deviation between the regular forgetting curve – given by the factor effect in Formula (10) – and the real forgetting progress of a single person – determined by retention tests. Figure 11 shows the curves for forgetting under different settings of the factors, but without the inclusion of personalization parameter.

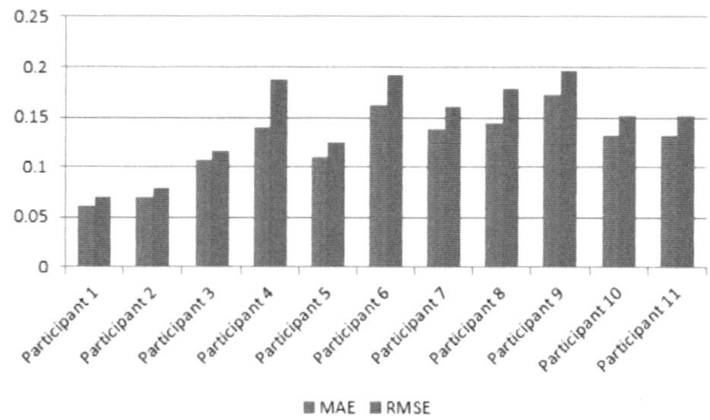

Figure 12. Error values for different participants

C. *Preliminary Evaluation of the Forgetting Effect*

Since this work shows a novel approach on forgetting and only a few data sets were published (e.g., [44]), which do not match all requirements of this approach, we generated our own data. We conducted a similar experiment as at the beginning in order to evaluate the correctness of our thesis. In our evaluation, 11 participants learned a previously unknown learning object just once. Over a period of eight to ten weeks, they had to answer retention tests in regular intervals. Each questionnaire consisted of four to eight questions and every single question was just asked once. The evaluation resulted in the analysis of the prediction accuracy using Mean Absolute Error (MAE) and Root Mean Square Error (RMSE). See Figure 12 for error values of different participants.

The results are compared with those from the equation of Hermann Ebbinghaus [36]. Table I shows the average values of MAE and RMSE for the results from this study and from the Ebbinghaus equation for forgetting. It can be noticed that the average MAE and average RMSE are nearly 3 times lower in the model developed in the current study compared to the existing model from Ebbinghaus. This indicates a higher prediction accuracy of the model developed for forgetting in the current study, but still requires further experiments. We incorporate the forgetting factor as well as the other factors for a learning object and thus, predict its overall learning need for the given user.

VII. Multi-level Learning Recommendations

After aggregating the factor values for each single learning object, the overall recommendation engine compares the learning need values of the requesting student for all contents in the course. The model of the SLR can be created offline: The relevance functions are computed in regular intervals by processing all existing user-item-time-triplets. When a user requests recommendations, the relevance scores for all items, in turn, are calculated online by considering the current time value for t. Afterwards, the items are sorted by their learning

TABLE I. Error values for forgetting models

Equation	MAE	RMSE
by Hermann Ebbinghaus	0.3518	0.3896
SLR Forgetting	0.1245	0.1461

need value. The result is a list of learning objects beginning with the highest relevance scores that represents the most important topics for the student that need to be learned at that time.

Figure 13 shows how the learning need of an item is presented graphically to a learner. It shows an example of a learning object in a 21 weeks long course and with a lecture on this topic in week 6; the student learned the content in weeks 4, 6, 7, 15, 18 and 19. The personal knowledge level defines how successful a student is in learning an item and is inversely proportional to the learning need of the student towards the learning object. The knowledge level $kl(t)$ can be computed from the relevance function $rf(t)$ as

$$kl(t) = 1 - rf(t) \tag{15}$$

Using this visualization, students have a chance to understand how the system calculates the prediction and might change factor weights to adjust new recommendations.

Moreover, learning objects are stored in a multi-level hierarchy to topically structure a course – top-level items represent a container with a set of sub-level items. A leaf item (a learning object without children) contains the minimum information set that is at least required to understand the given (sub-)topic. The user may provide item feedback, in terms of self-assessments, exercises, interactions and processing time, on all hierarchy levels. This differentiation allows a representation of diverging knowledge levels for top- and sub-level items – e.g., a student might have a good high-level understanding of a topic, but misses some details on specific sub-level contents or vice versa. In case the user has not provided the same type of feedback on the item's parent before, it is implicitly transferred from the child to the parent object. So, the parent may implicitly represent the average of all child learning objects.

The engine needs to avoid recommending the same topic with different detail levels within the predicted list. An algorithm iterates over the generated Top-N list, beginning with the most relevant learning object. An item will be eliminated from the list, in case a related child or parent learning object that describes the same topic shows a higher score. As a result, students will get recommendations for all topics of a course in a predicted order, but only on an appropriate detail level.

VIII. Challenges and Experimental Design

The introduced three-dimensional user-item-matrix (containing user-item-time-triplets) also leverages common collaborative filtering approaches. The calculation and weighting of nearest neighbors will be done by also considering the time aspect. Therefore, the deviation of two user-item-pairs will not only be based on the subtraction of two constants any more – as for common collaborative filtering approaches. It will be based on the correlation of the corresponding relevance functions of two learners. The assumption: the higher the correlation coefficient of two learning need functions of different students on the same item, the more similar their knowledge and their learning behavior. If one learning need function decreases from 1 to 0 over time, just because the student has learned this content perfectly, and the learning need function of another user shows the same progress, the correlation coefficient is high. If, in contrast, one function goes down and the other one goes up, the coefficient will indicate an anti-proportional progress and is very low. The Pearson Correlation Coefficient, for instance, requires a linear trend function. Thus, the main progress, in terms of the starting point and the end point values can be used for a reduced linear learning need function. Taking the correlation information into account, the system can identify similar learners, because of similar learning trends and similar knowledge levels. Moreover, it can be used to classify and cluster general learning types (e.g., slow or fast ones), all with similar learning trends. The ideal composition of different learning types in one learning group will then need intensive calibration. Algorithms covering time-dependent item-based as well as neighborhood-based classification and rating prediction are going to be evaluated. Another big challenge of this approach comes from predictions of the future learning need by extrapolating specific factor functions, for instance the forgetting effect. In the planned experiments, different algorithms, weights and settings are going to be further analyzed.

Since this work shows a novel approach for time-dependent learning object recommendations, the need for an evaluation based on an academic data set is very high. Unfortunately, only a few data sets are published (e.g., [45] or [46]) and no data set matches all requirements of this approach. We need the information for at least one factor function (as introduced in Section V), such as learning object interactions or performance in exercises, in order to conduct basic experiments. It is essential that there is a set of learning objects not only learned by different students, but also by the same student at multiple points in time. The change of the relevance of a learning object for a specific user over time represents the key aspect of the approach. Moreover, we need detailed feedback for each user interaction as well as on the learning object itself. At least, the challenge data set from KDD Cup 2010 on Educational Data Mining [44] matches some requirements. It is divided into 5 different packages (e.g., "Algebra I" and "Bridge to Algebra" from 2005 and 2008) with between 575 and 6,043 students per package. It contains a detailed description of the students' performances when solving mathematical problems and thus, represents typical learning behavior. One evaluation approach would be to subdivide the KDD item data into different context factors – each influencing the total learning need. However, the KDD data set contains a lot information on the interaction with learning objects as well as the processing time and results in exercises, but data on other essential factors as well as structured metadata on the hierarchy and topical sequences of learning objects are missing.

That is why new studies with learners are going to be conducted at the Chamber of Crafts Berlin in two consecutive 5 month courses – each with the same newly generated learning objects and metadata, but different students in each course. At the beginning of each course, the participants are asked to answer surveys with demographic information and their motivation. We require this information to set their interaction with our system in a context and afterwards draw conclusions (such as "digital natives enjoyed the system", "technical beginners did not understand it" or the like) and adapt the system. During the course, participants will get access to the learning objects exclusively via a provided Learning Companion Application to keep track of their learning behavior. Moreover, they can give feedback at any time, how helpful a specific recommendation was and whether the learning need shows a proper presentation of their real knowledge. This data is important for accuracy

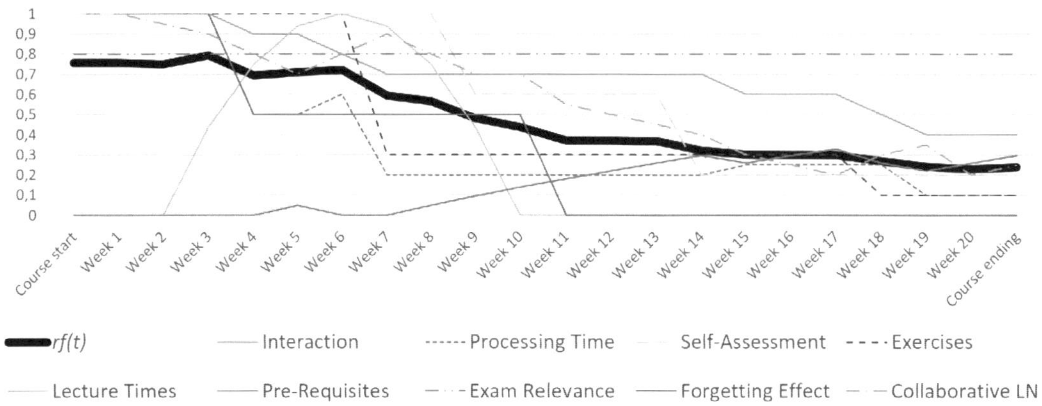

Figure 13. Example of a learning need function with individual factors

measurements as well as the analysis and adjustment of factor weights. At the end, the participants are asked to answer a second survey summarizing their overall perception of the system. We will relate the final exam grade with the tracked learning behavior data, but due to local data protection regulations, it is optional only.

Moreover, we are adapting this system to additional studies: at the Technical University of Berlin (a programming-oriented course called "Advanced Web Technologies") as well as an institute-internal summer school with the same contents as for the Technical University. The first one will have approximately 40 student participants with a mandatory exam at the end. As the target groups are different for all three experiments, we hope to get more generic feedback, that allows us to optimize the system for a broad range of future participants. The studies help to increase the performance of the system with each experimental iteration. We plan to publish the mined information as an anonymized open source data set.

IX. Conclusion

We introduced a novel Learning Companion App, which allows learners to access standardized learning objects everywhere and at any time. Each user interaction will be persisted and processed in order to predict the individual knowledge level of students, recommend the most important learning contents for a user and allows to analyze the overall performance in the course with the learning analytics service.

The Smart Learning Recommender aims at assisting students during blended-learning courses; in lectures; during the preparation of these lectures, the wrap-up and exam learning phase. Thereby, the engine shows an extended user model: the item feedback of each user is subdivided into different context factors. In contrast to rule-based recommendation engines and classification machine learning algorithms, it also respects the changing knowledge level on specific learning objects in a continuous time interval. Moreover, the system respects the overall course structure, in terms of the best topical sequence and thematic hierarchies consisting of topics and sub-topics. Due to the lack of an appropriate academic data set, studies with real learners will evaluate typical learning behaviors, how the SLR performs with different settings and how users accept learning recommendations. An analysis of the students' knowledge level at several points in time will result in an accurate representation of the different factors and their weights.

The inclusion of human forgetting in recommending learning items is a whole new approach in the field of TEL. The equation developed for forgetting in this study, serves as a preliminary model for computing the forgetting curve for a learner. The results from the assessment of the model have shown an improvement of the prediction accuracy. But there is still a lot of work for improving this model and the results are based on an initial experiment, with a small group of people. There is a need to evaluate this model on a large scale. In addition, other parameters like size and structure of the content, effect of successive repetitions, meaningfulness of the content, other media types and inter-dependencies of different parameters will be further studied.

As a next step, studies with trainees enrolled in this 5 months training at the Chamber of Crafts will be conducted with two consecutive courses in order to improve the system iteratively; the first one begins in September 2016 and the second in March 2017. Moreover, a University course as well as a summer school is planned. These studies evaluate real world learning behavior: how LCA performs and how users accept digital learning media and individual learning recommendations. Teachers will adapt their traditional courses to a LCA supported blended-learning approach with the help of the information provided by the learning analytics module. This component will be developed further to include analyses appropriate for instructional designers.

Acknowledgment

The authors would like to thank the whole Smart Learning team for their great work and many constructive ideas. Special thanks go to Christian Fuhrhop, who proofread this paper and made a lot of practical suggestions.

The Smart Learning project is sponsored by the German Federal Ministry of Education and Research (Bundesministerium fuer Bildung und Forschung – BMBF) under the project funding number 01PD14002A.

References

[1] C. Krauss, A. Merceron, T.-S. An, M. Zwicklbauer, and S. Arbanowski, "The smart learning approach - a mobile learning companion application," In Proceedings of The Eighth International IARIA Conference on Mobile, Hybrid, and On-line Learning (eLmL 2016), Venice, Italy, Volume: 8, April 2016, pp. 13–16.

[2] M. Zwicklbauer, C. Krauss, M. Merceron, Scharp, and J. Kania, "Smart learning: the digital learning companion for vocational training [org. title: Smart learning: Der digitale lernbegleiter fr die berufliche bildung]," Proceedings of DeLFI 2015, Gesellschaft fr Informatik Publisher, Munich, 2015, pp. 227–232.

[3] O. C. Santos and J. G. Boticario, "Recommendation strategies for promoting elearning performance factors for all," Proceedings of the 6th Workshop on Intelligent Techniques for Web Personalization & Recommender Systems, 2008, pp. 89–98.

[4] N. Manouselis, H. Drachsler, R. Vuorikari, H. Hummel, and R. Koper, "Recommender systems in technology enhanced learning," in Recommender systems handbook. Springer, 2011, pp. 387–415.

[5] G. Koutrika, B. Bercovitz, F. Kaliszan, H. Liou, and H. Garcia-Molina, "Courserank: A closed-community social system through the magnifying glass." in ICWSM, 2009.

[6] M. M. Recker and D. A. Wiley, "A non-authoritative educational metadata ontology for filtering and recommending learning objects," Interactive learning environments, vol. 9, no. 3, 2001, pp. 255–271.

[7] H. Boley, "Racofi: A rule-applying collaborative filtering system. in 2003 ieee," in WIC International Conference on Web Intelligence/Intelligent Agent Technology, 2003, pp. 430–434.

[8] H. T. Ozturk, D. Deryakulu, H. Ozcinar, and D. Atal, "Advancing learning analytics in online learning environments through the method of sequential analysis," in Multimedia Computing and Systems (ICMCS), 2014 International Conference on. IEEE, 2014, pp. 512–516.

[9] Á. F. Agudo-Peregrina, Á. Hernández-García, and S. Iglesias-Pradas, "Predicting academic performance with learning analytics in virtual learning environments: A comparative study of three interaction classifications," in Computers in Education (SIIE), 2012 International Symposium on. IEEE, 2012, pp. 1–6.

[10] H. Stern, R. Kaiser, P. Hofmair, P. Kraker, S. N. Lindstaedt, and P. Scheir, "Content recommendation in aposdle using the associative network." J. UCS, vol. 16, no. 16, 2010, pp. 2214–2231.

[11] N. Manouselis, R. Vuorikari, and F. Van Assche, "Simulated analysis of maut collaborative filtering for learning object recommendation," in Proceedings of the 1st Workshop on Social Information Retrieval for Technology Enhanced Learning, 2007, pp. 27–35.

[12] Y.-M. Huang, T.-C. Huang, K.-T. Wang, and W.-Y. Hwang, "A markov-based recommendation model for exploring the transfer of learning on the web," Journal of Educational Technology & Society, vol. 12, no. 2, 2009, pp. 144–162.

[13] L.-p. Shen and R.-m. Shen, "Learning content recommendation service based-on simple sequencing specification," in Advances in Web-Based Learning–ICWL 2004. Springer, 2004, pp. 363–370.

[14] J. Janssen, C. Tattersall, W. Waterink, B. Van den Berg, R. Van Es, C. Bolman, and R. Koper, "Self-organising navigational support in lifelong learning: how predecessors can lead the way," Computers & Education, vol. 49, no. 3, 2007, pp. 781–793.

[15] H. Drachsler, H. Hummel, B. Van den Berg, J. Eshuis, W. Waterink, R. Nadolski, A. Berlanga, N. Boers, and R. Koper, "Effects of the isis recommender system for navigation support in self-organised learning networks," Journal of Educational Technology & Society, vol. 12, no. 3, 2009, pp. 115–126.

[16] R. Pelanek and P. Jarusek, "Student modeling based on problem solving times," International Journal of Artificial Intelligence in Education, vol. 25, no. 4, 2015, pp. 493–519. [Online]. Available: http://dx.doi.org/10.1007/s40593-015-0048-x

[17] L. Xiang and Q. Yang, "Time-dependent models in collaborative filtering based recommender system," WI-IAT '09., vol. 1, 2009, pp. 450–457.

[18] L. He and F. Wu, "A time-context-based collaborative filtering algorithm," in Granular Computing, 2009, GRC'09. IEEE International Conference on. IEEE, 2009, pp. 209–213.

[19] P. Adibi and B. T. Ladani, "A collaborative filtering recommender system based on user's time pattern activity," 2013 5th IKT Conference, 2013, pp. 252–257.

[20] Y. Zhang and Y. Liu, "A collaborative filtering algorithm based on time period partition," in Intelligent Information Technology and Security Informatics (IITSI), 2010 Third International Symposium on. IEEE, 2010, pp. 777–780.

[21] Y. Liu, Z. Xu, B. Shi, and B. Zhang, "Time-based k-nearest neighbor collaborative filtering," in Computer and Information Technology (CIT), 2012 IEEE 12th International Conference on. IEEE, 2012, pp. 1061–1065.

[22] C. Krauss, L. George, and S. Arbanowski, "TV predictor: personalized program recommendations to be displayed on smarttvs," in BigMine'13. ACM, 2013, pp. 63–70.

[23] O. C. Santos, "A recommender system to provide adaptive and inclusive standard-based support along the elearning life cycle," in Proceedings of the 2008 ACM conference on Recommender systems. ACM, 2008, pp. 319–322.

[24] K. Verbert, S. Govaerts, E. Duval, J. L. Santos, F. Van Assche, G. Parra, and J. Klerkx, "Learning dashboards: an overview and future research opportunities," Personal and Ubiquitous Computing, vol. 18, no. 6, 2014, pp. 1499–1514.

[25] M. Elkina, A. Fortenbacher, and A. Merceron, "The learning analytics application lemo–rationals and first results," International Journal of Computing, vol. 12, no. 3, 2013, pp. 226–234.

[26] A. Dollár and P. S. Steif, "Web-based statics course with learning dashboard for instructors," Proceedings of computers and advanced technology in education (CATE 2012), 2012.

[27] R. Martinez-Maldonado, A. Pardo, N. Mirriahi, K. Yacef, J. Kay, and A. Clayphan, "The latux workflow: Designing and deploying awareness tools in technology-enabled learning settings," in Proceedings of the Fifth International Conference on Learning Analytics And Knowledge. ACM, 2015, pp. 1–10.

[28] IMS-LTI - Learning Tools Interoperability Specification, IMS Global Learning Consortium, 2015 Std.

[29] IMS QTI - IMS Question & Test Interoperability Specification, IMS Global Learning Consortium, 2005 Std.

[30] IMS LOM - Learning Resource Meta-data Specification, IMS Global Learning Consortium, 2006 Std.

[31] IMS CC - IMS Common Cartridge Specification, IMS Global Learning Consortium, 2015 Std.

[32] J. M. Kevan and P. R. Ryan, "Experience api: Flexible, decentralized and activity-centric data collection," Technology, Knowledge and Learning, vol. 21, no. 1, 2016, pp. 143–149.

[33] B. Shneiderman, "The eyes have it: A task by data type taxonomy for information visualizations," in Visual Languages, 1996. Proceedings., IEEE Symposium on. IEEE, 1996, pp. 336–343.

[34] T.-S. An, F. Dubois, E. Manthey, and A. Merceron, "Digitale infrastruktur und learning analytics im co-design," In Proceedings of the Workshop learning Analytics, co-located with the 14th e-Learning Conference of the German Society for Computer Science, Potsdam, Germany, 11th September 2016. To appear., pp. 8–17.

[35] C. Krauss, "Smart learning: Time-dependent context-aware learning object recommendations," in Proceedings of the 29th International Florida AI Research Society Conference (FLAIRS-29), AAAI, Key Largo, 2016, pp. 501 – 503.

[36] H. Ebbinghaus, "Memory: A contribution to experimental psychology, translated by henry a ruger and clara e bussenius," 1913.

[37] H. P. Bahrick and E. Phelps, "Retention of spanish vocabulary over 8 years," Journal of Experimental Psychology: Learning, Memory, and Cognition, vol. 13, 1987, pp. 344–349.

[38] Y. Hong and L. Zhuanyun, "A collaborative filtering recommendation algorithm based on forgetting curve," Journal of Nanjing University, vol. 46, no. 5, 2010, pp. 520–527.

[39] H. Yu and Z. Li, "A collaborative filtering method based on the forgetting curve," in 2010 International WISM Conference, vol. 1. IEEE, 2010, pp. 183–187.

[40] V. Ermolayev, R. Akerkar, V. Terziyan, and M. Cochez, "Towards

evolving knowledge ecosystems for big data understanding," Big data computing, 2013, pp. 3–55.

[41] J. Brown, "Some tests of the decay theory of immediate memory," Quarterly Journal of Experimental Psychology, vol. 10, no. 1, 1958, pp. 12–21.

[42] W. Thalheimer, "How much do people forget?" Work-Learning Research, Inc. Somerville, MA, USA, 2010.

[43] P. I. Pavlik Jr. and J. R. Anderson, "Practice and forgetting effects on vocabulary memory: An activation-based model of the spacing effect," Cognitive Science, vol. 29, no. 4, 2005, pp. 559–586.

[44] J. Stamper, A. Niculescu-Mizil, S. Ritter, G. Gordon, and K. Koedinger, "Algebra i 2008-2009," Challenge data set from KDD Cup 2010 Educational Data Mining Challenge., 2010.

[45] P. Cortez and A. M. G. Silva, "Using data mining to predict secondary school student performance," Proceedings of 5th FUture BUsiness TEChnology Conference (FUBUTEC 2008), 2008.

[46] R. Wang, F. Chen, Z. Chen, T. Li, G. Harari, S. Tignor, X. Zhou, D. Ben-Zeev, and A. T. Campbell, "Studentlife: assessing mental health, academic performance and behavioral trends of college students using smartphones," in Proceedings of the 2014 ACM International Joint Conference on Pervasive and Ubiquitous Computing. ACM, 2014, pp. 3–14.

Integration of Knowledge Resources and Advanced Association Processing for Geosciences and Archaeology

Claus-Peter Rückemann
Westfälische Wilhelms-Universität Münster (WWU),
Leibniz Universität Hannover,
North-German Supercomputing Alliance (HLRN), Germany
Email: ruckema@uni-muenster.de

Abstract—**This paper presents the main research results on a major task for knowledge discovery: The integration of knowledge resources and advanced association processing. The research includes the integration of references to many types of objects and elements, e.g., adding conceptual knowledge via references to a universal classification. Creating sustainable multi-disciplinary knowledge resources and enabling advanced features for processing of associations is one of the major goals of long-term knowledge development and discovery, especially allowing the use of advanced association processing and computation facilities. Research has shown that discovery in geosciences and archaeology widely benefits from a multi-disciplinary approach. The paper also presents respective association processing results exploiting the integration of such geoscientific and archaeological knowledge resources components. The practical application scenario is based on content from a natural sciences and archaeology research and studies campaign at the ancient city of Kameiros, Greece. The created resources are providing content, structures, and features for exploiting computation facilities, especially a multitude of reference types. The focus is to integrate multi-disciplinary knowledge resources and association processing, which allows to extend and exploit long-term content discovery on a data-centric base and gain new insights.**

Keywords–Knowledge Discovery; Association Processing; Scientific Knowledge Resources; Universal Decimal Classification; Advanced Computing.

I. INTRODUCTION

This extended research presents the main results on a major task for knowledge discovery: The integration of knowledge resources and advanced association processing. The research is based on the results from multi-disciplinary projects for the creation of objects and concordances, which are intended to be used for long-term knowledge creation knowledge processing, and advanced computing. The basic fundaments of the results were presented at the DigitalWorld / GEOProcessing 2016 conferences in Venice, Italy [1]. Previous research was conducted for creating knowledge resources and developing application components for supporting and providing advanced integrated systems for geoscientific, multi-disciplinary, and multi-lingual application scenarios. Existing data collections, unstructured and structured, combine a number of insufficient features and drawbacks, missing long-term aspects, support for multi-disciplinary conceptual knowledge, for classification, and for advanced and fuzzy methods like associations.

The purpose of the integration of the developed resources and components is to provide advanced knowledge object features, especially association processing features and computation in context with long-term multi-disciplinary and multi-lingual knowledge documentation and discovery. The new resources and application developments presented here are based on selected frameworks and resources, which have been created over the last two decades. The knowledge resources and Collaboration house framework [2] allowed for the implementation of multi-disciplinary, long-term knowledge resources and application components, for dynamical use as well as for complex and high end computation. The resulting components are used for universal and consistent documentation of knowledge and scientific research, and for consequent long-term purposes. These components are created using a universal classification [3], a flexible and portable all-purpose programming environment [4], and appropriate international standards [5]. In this case, for advanced association processing, new workflows had to be created and dynamically integrated into the framework components. Such implementation is possible if on the one hand the components' workflows allow a flexible integration of workflows, e.g., via scripting and compiled sources and on the other hand that structured knowledge resources can be extended for allowing a multitude of references types. The combination allows to create associations by making use of the available structures, processing, and computation facilities. For these purposes, the object and media knowledge resources and the framework components were basically extended to support a data-centric approach.

This data-centric approach includes the integration of references to many types of multi-disciplinary knowledge resources' objects and elements, e.g., adding conceptual knowledge via references to a universal classification. Therefore, the implementations and case study focus on spanning disciplines. In this case the major starting points are geosciences and archaeology and their referenced disciplines' context.

This paper is organised as follows. Section II presents the state of integration and frameworks with knowledge resources. Sections III and IV introduce the integration of workflows and reference types. Sections V and VI discuss the creation and processing of associations and how computational facilities can be exploited. Section VII presents and discusses an integration case study and implementation in context of geosciences and archaeology. Sections VIII and IX give an evaluation, present the main results and summarise the lessons learned, conclusions and future work.

II. State of Integration and Frameworks

The resources and implementations are based on the integration of three major components: An architecture framework, long-term, multi-disciplinary knowledge resources, and a mostly widely used universal classification framework. The architecture implemented for an economical long-term strategy is data-centric and based on development blocks. Figure 1 shows the three main columns: Application resources, knowledge resources, and originary resources. The central block in the "Collaboration house" framework architecture [6], is represented by the knowledge resources, scientific resources, object collections, containers, databases, and documentation (e.g., LX [7], collections, containers). These resources provide multi-disciplinary content, context, and references, including structured and unstructured data, factual and conceptual knowledge.

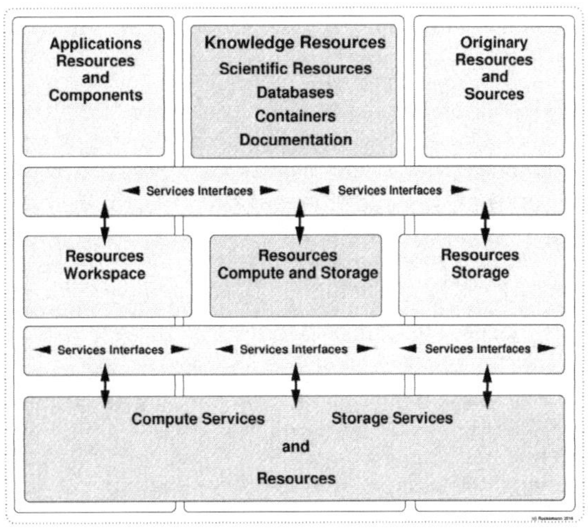

Figure 1. Architecture: The knowledge resources are the central component within the long-term architecture. Three major layers labelled (1), (2), (3).

The resources also refer to originary resources and sources (e.g., textual data, media data, photos, scientific data, literature). The knowledge resources are used as a universal component for compute and storage workflows. This feature can also be applied for supporting dynamical and ontology-based multi-agent, e.g., for production management as with the implementation supported by the European Framework Programme 7 (FP7) [8]. Application resources and components (Active Source, Active Map, local applications) are implementations for analysing, utilising, and processing data and making the information and knowledge accessible. The related information, all data, and algorithm objects presented are copyright the author of this paper, LX Foundation Scientific Resources [7], all rights reserved. The structure and the classification references based on the LX resources and UDC [9], especially mentioning the well structured editions [3] and the multi-lingual features [10], are essential means for the processing workflows and evaluation of the knowledge objects and containers. Both provide strong multi-disciplinary and multi-lingual support. The three blocks are supported by services' interfaces. The interfaces interact with the physical resources: In the local workspace, in the compute and storage resources where the knowledge resources are situated, and in the storage resources for the originary resources. The layers or 'levels' are labelled (1), (2), and (3) within the architecture. (1) is associated with the disciplines creating and using knowledge resources, application resources, and originary resources, 'realia'. (2) is associated with the tasks and contributions of services providers. (3) is associated with the computer and storage resources provided by resources providers. All of these components do allow for advanced scientific computing and data processing, as well as the access of compute and storage resources via services interfaces. The resources' needs depend on the application scenarios to be implemented for user groups. The framework allows to create any collaboration required for the development and operation of knowledge resources, required services, and High End Computing resources like compute and storage.

III. Integration of Workflows

The integration of association processing workflows with the workflows for creating arbitrary result matrices is most flexible and efficient and was based on the organisation and object features (Figure 2) in the knowledge resources. Object details and definitions have been discussed with computational views [11]. Workflow steps are labelled with lowercase letters. Layers are labelled with numbers, primary layers are underlined. The illustration shows that object information is gathered from the objects and references in collections and containers. Configurable algorithms like filters and mapping are then used to compute a result matrix. The result matrix is considered "intermediate" because any of such workflows can be used in combination with other workflows, workflow chains or further processing.

(a) Geoscientific Association Processing Workflow Request: A request for geoscientific knowledge resources is initiated from within a discovery workflow. Such request is created in level (2) within the architecture.
(b) Geoscientific Knowledge Resources: The respective resources are initialised for the workflow. The knowledge resources are located in level (1).
(c) Collections and containers: The collections and containers within the resources are provided.
(d) Association Processing Algorithms and Definitions: The algorithms and definitions for the association processing are called. The processing involves (1), (2), and (3), especially the last two.
(e) Association Processing Intermediate Result Matrix: An intermediate result matrix is created by the algorithms and definitions. The matrix creation involves (1), (2), and (3), especially (2).
(f) Geoscientific Association Processing Workflow Reply: Such reply is created in level (2) within the architecture.

Figure 3 illustrates selected knowledge resources' objects, focussing on references in collections and containers.

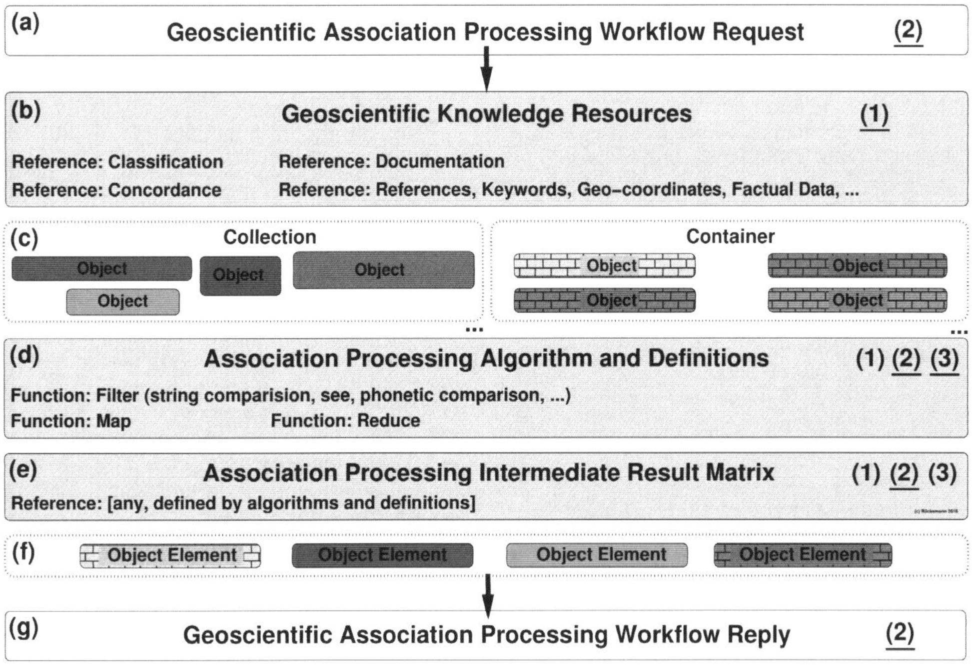

Figure 2. Geoscientific association processing workflow: Creation of intermediate result matrices from geoscientific resources and references (collections and containers) in reply to workflow requests. Workflow steps are labelled with lowercase letters. Layers are labelled with numbers, primary layers are underlined.

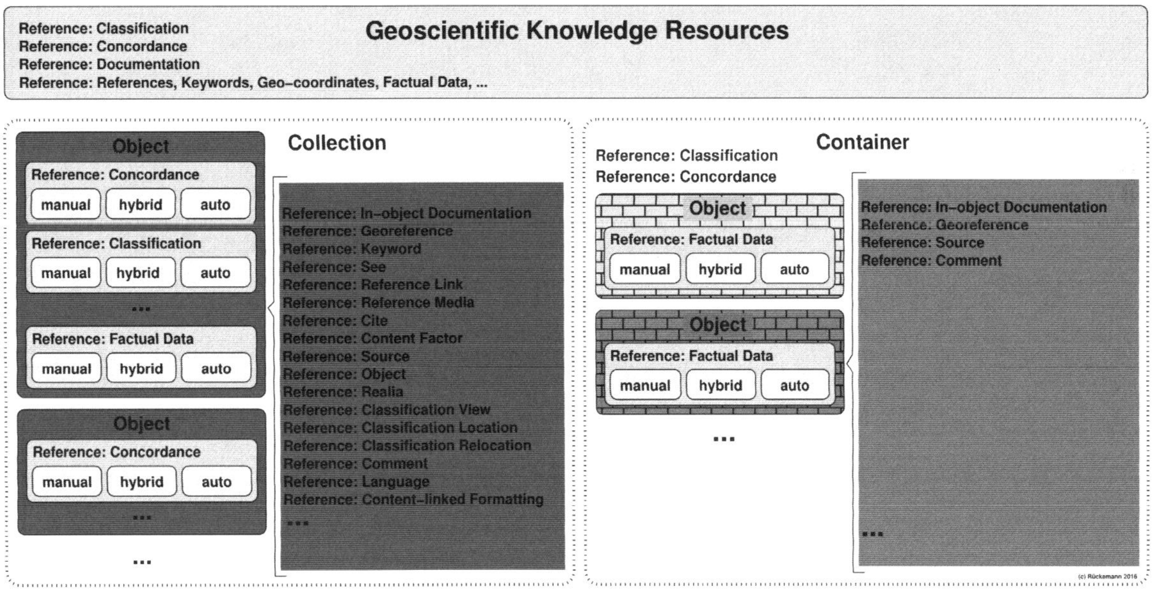

Figure 3. Geoscientific knowledge resources and objects: Selected knowledge resources' objects containing references for concordances and classifications in collections and containers. The excerpt illustrates a distinct handling of manually, hybrid, and automatically created data.

IV. Implementation of Reference Types

Objects can carry any type of references. Objects can be grouped, e.g., in collections or containers. When larger groups are created then also these groups can carry their references. These references may occur in any combination but in practice these references will be a subset or a complementary set to the objects' references. Objects can be created by manual, automated, and hybrid means. Therefore, any type of references of that kind may exist.

Tables I and II show excerpts of the references, which were added to be used within the knowledge resources for two types of object groups, namely collections and containers.

TABLE I. GEOSCIENTIFIC KNOWLEDGE RESOURCES' COLLECTION AND CONTAINER REFERENCES TYPES USED FOR PROCESSING (EXCERPT).

References Types	*Group and Implementation Example*	
Classification	O & C	UDC
Concordance	O & C	UCC
In-object documentation	O & C	Text
Factual data	O & C	Text, data
Georeference	O & C	Geocoordinates
Keyword	O & C	Text
See	O & C	Text
Reference link	O & C	URL
Reference media	O & C	Link
Citation	O & C	Cite, bib
Content Factor	O & C	CONTFACT
Source	O & C	Text
Object	O & C	Text, code
Realia	O & C	Text
View, conceptual	O & C	Classification view
Location, conceptual	O & C	Classification location
Relocation, conceptual	O & C	Classification relocation
Comment	O & C	Text
Language	O & C	EN, DE
Content-linked formatting	O & C	Markup, LaTeX

TABLE II. GEOSCIENTIFIC KNOWLEDGE RESOURCES' IMPLEMENTED EXTERNAL REFERENCES TYPES USED FOR PROCESSING (EXCERPT).

References Types	*Group and Implementation Example*	
Tag	E	Text, tags
Index Entry	E	Text, idx
Glossary Entry	E	Text, glo
List Entry	E	Text, lis

The reference types are organised in three major groups: Object collections (O), object containers (C), and external or externally created references (E).

This case study primarily addresses geoscientific and archaeological resources. The resources were extended for using a multitude of references types of creating associations (Tables II and I). Therefore, the resources especially contain georeferences, UDC classifications for any object, including complex conceptual knowledge, geoclassification, concordances like Universal Classified Classification (UCC) [12], and Content Factors [13] in order to describe [14] the content. Many reference types are part of the objects. Nevertheless, in practice, the organisation of references is more uniform within containers.

The reference types shown provide a lot of information regarding content and context, which could otherwise not be deducted from the object data itself. In addition, all reference types may exist in multiple views, multiple languages, and multiple context – any of which can be added in instances created by manual, automatic, and hybrid means.

V. Creation of Associations and Processing Means

As far as the algorithms implemented in components carry essential information for processing and computation, e.g., for creating new results and output, they should be documented with the knowledge resources themselves. As associations can be created by arbitrary workflows, it is most important to know, which components can carry which facilities and how to exploit, e.g., in a multi-disciplinary context like geosciences and archaeology. Important aspects for the quality of results of the association processing are geocoordinates, associations, conceptual knowledge, and supporting methodologies.

Geocoordinates' data is for example used to spatially select and associate objects. Geocoordinates can be part of

- knowledge objects,
- containers and container objects,
- references (e.g., knowledge resources' references or Google Maps references).

Conceptual knowledge data, e.g., used for the classification of objects of any kind, can be part of

- knowledge objects,
- containers and container objects,
- unstructured data, mostly used with automated processes with lower quality results.

Associations can especially result from rich content, from constellations of content and

- context in object collections,
- context in object containers,
- in-text references (comparisons, see, ...),
- internally,
- link-references (links to external resources),
- external resources,
- between all components.

Supporting methodologies and technologies, which can be exploited for the creation and processing of associations are

- string comparisons,
- transliterations,
- phonetics,
- statistics,
- metadata,
- Content Factor,
- object elements rhythm,
- dynamical data, ...

Associations were used for developing knowledge resources, optimising result matrices, e.g., within knowledge discovery workflows, creating concordances, creating references, improving knowledge objects and resources, gaining new knowledge. The combination allows various degrees of precision and fuzzyness as required for spanning multi-disciplinary and multi-lingual data. An optimisation can improve the quality of data, especially the quality of associations introduced for automated classification of unstructured data.

VI. Exploitation of Computation Facilities

Within the layers, there are three kinds of facilities, which are targets to be exploited by computation.

(1) **First block:** Knowledge resources.
Storage services and resources.
- Purpose: Data.
- Task/Method: Creation, development, maintenance processes.
- Implementation: Editing components, versioning tools, and high end text editors are used together with automation tools and scripting. The knowledge resources themselves are based on fully portable structures and markup.

(2) **Second block:** Services and interfaces.
Layer: Dedicated infrastructure.
- Purpose: Workflows.
- Task/Method: Scripting, workflow description.
- Implementation: Perl, Tcl, and C are used for an implementation.

(3) **Third block:** Processing.
Layer: Compute services and resources.
- Purpose: Individual and parallelised processes and tasks as well as dynamical and interactive processes.
- Task/Method: Batch system, configuration, dedicated resources.
- Implementation: Here, Portable Batch System (PBS), Torque, and Moab are used, formerly also IBM LoadLeveler and Condor. As far as required for a certain scenario also dynamical or interactive jobs can be executed.

The exploitation of computation facilities is mostly based on these three featured component groups and the described implementation. This realises the purposes of extracting data and information, utilising workflow scripts, and submitting dynamical and batch jobs.

VII. Integration and Association Case Study

The implementation has been done according to the described architecture and enabling the required association processing workflows based on the available components. Therefore, the major implementation tasks concentrated on the content related facilities, especially the geoscientific and archaeological knowledge resources, and the application components, which delivered an appropriate starting point for a case study. The respective features were created in the knowledge resources' objects, which were under continuous development over the last decades in the LX knowledge resources. The application components have been extended and configured to work with the required application scenario. This includes the dynamical components from the Geo Exploration and Information (GEXI) project, e.g., the actmap components, based on Perl and Tcl scripting, C and Fortran.

The implementation for the case study was integrated with the the base for this case study, the long-term knowledge resources (LX Foundation Scientific Resources), which were developed and used over several decades, including geoscientific and archaeological objects and containers. A case study example based on the created resources is presented with the following workflow.

A. *Volcano and Rhodos association discovery workflow*

The workflow starts with the target to find possible associations and links between "Vesuvius" and "Rhodos".

1) Entry nodes: Vesuvius – Rhodos (Rhodos/Rhodes etc.).
2) Criteria and definition set.
3) Filter association processing criteria.
4) Filter association processing.
5) Selection and generation of compute instructions.
6) Sorting.
7) Formatting.
8) Selection.
9) First level association - both nodes.
10) Second level association.
11) Common object 1 and 2 (level 1).
12) Common object 11 and 22 (level 2).

Steps 2) to 5) of the workflow analyse and implement the criteria and definitions for the request and prepare the appropriate compute instructions. Steps 6) to 8) handle the sorting, formatting, and the selection of the intermediate result matrix. Steps 9) and 10) generate a first level association and after that a second level association. The concluding steps 11) and 12) generate the common objects for levels 1 and 2.

B. *Resources and content*

As an example, an object excerpt for one of the entry nodes is shown in Figure 4, which shows a referenced Vesuvius collection object containing factual and conceptual knowledge.

```
Vesuvius [Volcanology, Geology, Archaeology]:
         (lat.) Mons Vesuvius.
         (ital.) Vesuvio.
         Volcano, Gulf of Naples, Italy.
         Complex volcano (compound volcano).
         Stratovolcano, large cone (Gran Cono).
         Volcano Type: Somma volcano,
         VNUM: 0101-02=,
         Summit Elevation: 1281\UD(m). ...
         Syn.: Vesaevus, Vesevus, Vesbius, Vesvius
         s. volcano, super volcano, compound volcano
         s. also Pompeji, Herculaneum, seismology
         compare La Soufrière, Mt. Scenery, Soufriere
         %%IML: UDC:[911.2+55]:[57+930.85]:[902]"63"(4+37+23+24)=12=14
         %%IML: GoogleMapsLocation: http://maps.google.de/maps?hl=de&gl=de&vpsrc
          =0&ie=UTF8&ll=40.821961,14.428868&spn=0.018804,0.028238&t=h&z=15
```

Figure 4. Workflow entry node: Knowledge resources collection object "Vesuvius" (LX resources, geoscientific collection, excerpt).

The object carries names and synonyms in different languages, dynamically usable geocoordinates, UDC classification and so on, including geoclassification (UDC:(37), Italia. Ancient Rome and Italy). The listing in Figure 5 shows an instance of a container entry excerpt from a volcanological features container.

```
CONTAINER_OBJECT_EN_ITEM: Vesuvius
CONTAINER_OBJECT_EN_PRINT: Vesuvius
CONTAINER_OBJECT_EN_COUNTRY: Italy
CONTAINER_OBJECT_EN_CONTINENT: Europe
CONTAINER_OBJECT_XX_LATITUDE: 40.821N
CONTAINER_OBJECT_XX_LONGITUDE: 14.426E
CONTAINER_OBJECT_XX_HEIGHT_M: 1281
CONTAINER_OBJECT_EN_TYPE: Complexvolcano
CONTAINER_OBJECT_XX_VNUM: 0101-02= ...
```

Figure 5. Processed instance of a simple knowledge resources container entry (LX resources, geoscientific container, excerpt).

The container component contains a large number of volcanic features and volcanoes, like Vesuvius, Thera, and Santorini. The excerpts have been processed with the appropriate `lx_object_volcanology` and `lx_container_volcanology` interfaces, selecting a number of items and for the container also items in English and German including a common formatting. The resources' access and processing can be done in any programming language, assuming that the interfaces are implemented. For example, combining scripting, filtering, and parallel programming can provide flexible approaches. The criteria and definitions are given by variables (Figure 6).

```
MATRIXLX
MATRIXRESLEV1
MATRIXRESLEV11
MATRIXRESLEV2
MATRIXRESLEV22
```

Figure 6. Criteria and definitions: Variables (LX Resources, excerpt).

The resource levels instruct the routines to execute two levels, one primary plain discovery each and a secondary in-depth discovery considering the primary results. The filter, selection, and processing instructions are handled by generators. The internal sequence is shown in Figure 7.

```
gen_matrix_pipe_level0_level1 "Vesuvius"
gen_pipe_reslevel1 | \
gen_grep_formatrix | \
gen_grep_forstrip
...
gen_matrix_pipe_level0_level1 "Rhod.s"
gen_pipe_reslevel11 | \
gen_grep_formatrix | \
gen_grep_forstrip
...
gen_matrix_pipe_level0_level2 "Kameiros"
gen_matrix_pipe_level2_level22 "Pozzolan"
gen_pipe_reslevel22 | \
gen_grep_formatrix | \
gen_grep_forstrip
```

Figure 7. Sequence of association routines for discovery workflow, dual-level (LX Resources, excerpt).

The sort, formatting, and selection are done with the function calls (`forstrip`). The "Vesuvius – Rhodos" association delivers "Kameiros", "Thera", "Santorini", and further intermediate result matrix elements from the secondary in-depth discovery.

C. *The Kameiros' material results*

The case study integrates the geoscientific and archaeological collection and container context and English entries. Figure 8 shows an excerpt of a referenced Kameiros object entry with UDC classification, media, and citation references, including geoclassification (UDC:(38), Ancient Greece).

```
Kameiros [Archaeology, Geophysics, Remote Sensing, Seafaring]:
         Greek city, Rhodos Island, Dodekanese, Greece.
         Modern location name Kámiros, Greece.
         ...
         Object:               Ancient architecture, stone, cement.
         Object-Keywords:      water tank, cement, lower area
         Object-Type:          Realia object.
         Object-Location:      Kameiros, Rhodos, Greece.
         Object-FindDate:      2011-10-27
         Object-Photo:         Claus-Peter Rückemann, ...
         %%SRC: 2013 CPR
         %%IML: media: YES 20130922 {LXC:DETAIL----} {UDC:(0.034)(38)770}
          LXDATASTORAGE://.../img_1342.jpg
         %%IML: UDC-Object:[902+903.2]+691.54+720.32+(38)+(4)
         ...
         %%IML: cite: YES 19980000 {LXK: concrete; pozzolan; Kameiros; Rhodos;
          Rhodes; Greece; Archaeology; Geosciences} {UDC:...} LXCITE://
          Koui:1998:Kamirian
         %%IML: cite: keyword: object: water storage tank
         %%IML: cite: keyword: material: concrete; Santorine earth mixed;
          natural cement; volcanic earth; lime
         %%IML: cite: keyword: location: Kameiros; Kamiros; Rhodos; Rhodes;
          Thera; Santorine; island of Yali; island of Nisyros
         ...
         %%IML: cite: YES 20120000 {LXK: cement; pozzolan; Kameiros; Rhodos;
          Rhodes; Greece; Archaeology; Geosciences} {UDC:...} LXCITE://
          Snellings:2012:Cementitious
         ...
         %%IML: cite: YES 20110000 {LXK: concrete; pozzolan; Kameiros; Rhodos;
          Rhodes; Greece; Archaeology; Geosciences} {UDC:...} LXCITE://
          Courland:2011:Concrete
         ...
         %%IML: cite: YES 20110000 {LXK: Archaeology; Geosciences; Vesuvius;
          Pompeji} {UDC:...} LXCITE://Hartge:2009:Vesuvius
         vgl. Rhodos, Iálissos, Lindos, Akandia
```

Figure 8. Association result matrix element, object "Kameiros" (LX resources, archaeological collection, excerpt).

The association processing "Vesuvius – Rhodos" revealed the reference to Vesuvius / (via Kameiros-associated citations) Pozzuoli / pozzolan. The excerpt also delivers a number of associated references on ancient concrete technology [15], cementitious materials [16], history of concrete [17], and evolution of concrete [18].

Looking for secondary documentation on eruptions being associated with Pozzuoli, e.g., the 1631 eruption of Vesuvius, delivers bibliographic sources like [19], which provides a lot of unique context information from an original source. This means there are several associations linking Vesuvius with Rhodos and one link is a technology, based on material from geoscientific context, documented in an archaeological site.

Figure 9 shows an excerpt of a referenced Thera object entry with UDC classified knowledge objects delivered from the association processing.

```
Thera    [Volcanology, Geology, Archaeology]:
         Volcano, \lxidx{Santorini}, Greece.
         Volcano Type: Somma volcano,
         Country: Italy,
         Subregion Name: Italy,
         VNUM: 0101-02=,
         VEI: VEI7,
         Volcano Status: Historical,
         Summit Elevation: 564\UD{m}.
         s. VEI
         %%IML: UDC:[911.2+55]:[57+930.85]:[902]"63"(4+38+23+24)=14
         %%IML: keyword: volcano, eruption, Santorini, Thera, crete, Minoan
          civilisation, culture, Mycenae, culture, fleet, volcanic ash, vanish,
          rise, historical city, catastrophe
```

Figure 9. Association result matrix element, object "Thera" (LX resources, excerpt).

The matrix element delivers additional information and references, e.g., to volcanic features containers via the volcano number (VNUM) and the Volcanic Explosivity Index (VEI).

In this means, the knowledge resources provide data and references for the association routines. Result matrices are computed from the association result matrix elements (example excerpts Figures 8 and 9), which have been deducted from the knowledge resources using the association routines.

The above sequence of association routines (Figure 7) was used for the creation of a result matrix (routines implemented in `lxgrep_in_depth`). The listing in Figure 10 shows an extended excerpt of the intermediate result matrix output for this case example.

```
MATRIXentry{Vesuvius}
MATRIXcitekeywords{location: Vesuvius, Italy}
MATRIXindex{pozzolan}
MATRIXindex{Campi Flegrei}
MATRIXindex{Pozzolana}
MATRIXindex{Pozzuoli}
MATRIXindex{Puteoli}
MATRIXkeywordcontext{keyword-Context: KYW :: 1634-1676 Polyhistor ...}
MATRIXkeywordcontext{keyword-Context: KYW EN :: earthquake, seismology, seismics
 , Fogel, Fogelius, volcano, Vesuvius}
MATRIXkeywordcontext{keyword-Context: KYW REF S. 62 :: Vesuvius; pyroklastischer
  Strom; Aschewolke; Pozzuolo; Dreißigjähriger Krieg}
MATRIXkeywordcontext{keyword-Context: KYW REF S. 63 :: Schwefel, Solfatara,
 Fumarole}
MATRIXkeywordcontext{keyword-Context: KYW :: terrae motus, terra motus, motus
 terrae, Erdbeben, Seismologie, Seismik, Erdbewegungen}
MATRIXkeywordcontext{keyword-Context: KYW :: Vulkanismus, Vulkanologie, Vesuv,
 Vesuvius, Vesuvium, Erdbeben, Beben}
MATRIXkeywordcontext{keyword-Context: TXT :: 1631/1632 16xx, terra motus,
 fogelius}
MATRIXkeywordcontext{keyword-Context: TXT :: Fogelius, Historici Pragmatici
 universal, Terrae motus, Physica}
MATRIXkeywordcontext{keyword-Context: TXT REF S. 175 :: Pozzuolo ...}
MATRIXkeywordcontext{keyword-Context: TXT REF S. 183 :: Pozzo di Somma}
MATRIXkeywordcontext{keyword-Context: TXT REF S. 73 :: Grotta del Cane}
MATRIXseealso{phlegra, Solfatara}
MATRIXseealso{Traß}
MATRIXsynonym{Puzzuolana}
MATRIXsynonym{Vesaevus, Vesevus, Vesbius, Vesvius}
...
MATRIXentry{pozzolan}
MATRIXindex{diatomaceous earth}
MATRIXindex{iron oxide}
MATRIXindex{Kameiros}
MATRIXindex{Kamiros}
MATRIXindex{Phlegraean Fields}
MATRIXindex{Pozzolana}
MATRIXindex{pozzolanic activity}
MATRIXindex{pozzolanic earths}
MATRIXindex{pozzolanic material}
MATRIXindex{Pozzuoli}
MATRIXindex{Puteoli}
MATRIXindex{Rhodes}
MATRIXindex{tuffs}
MATRIXindex{Vesuvius}
MATRIXseealso{Traß}
MATRIXsee{Puzzolane}
MATRIXsynonym{Puzzuolana}
...
MATRIXentry{Kameiros}
MATRIXcitekeywords{material: concrete; Santorine earth mixed; natural cement;
 volcanic earth; lime}
MATRIXcitekeywords{material: pozzolan}
MATRIXcitekeywords{material: Pozzuoli volcanic pumice}
MATRIXcitekeywords{material: stone called Santorini}
MATRIXcitekeywords{method: Ternary CaO-SiO2-Al2O3 diagram, major SCM groups}
MATRIXcitekeywords{object: water storage tank}
MATRIXcompare{Rhodos, Iálissos, Lindos, Akandia}
MATRIXindex{Pozzolana}
MATRIXindex{Pozzuoli}
MATRIXindex{Puteoli}
MATRIXindex{Puzzolana}
MATRIXindex{Vesuvius}
MATRIXobjectkeywords{Object-Keywords: water cistern, top area}
MATRIXobjectkeywords{Object-Keywords: water pipeline, clay, upper area}
MATRIXobjectkeywords{Object-Keywords: water tank, cement, lower area}
MATRIXseealso{Traß}
MATRIXsee{pozzolan}
MATRIXsee{Puzzolane}
MATRIXsee{Rhodos}
MATRIXsynonym{Puzzuolana}
MATRIXsynonym{Puzzuolane}
MATRIXtextintext{Kámiros, Greece}
MATRIXtextintext{Object: Ancient architecture, stone, cement}
MATRIXtextintext{Object-Location: Kameiros, Rhodos, Greece}
MATRIXtextintext{Pozzolan}
MATRIXtextintext{Puzzolane}
```

Figure 10. Intermediate result matrix output, groups (excerpt).

The example contains excerpts of three different element groups. The according object entries are "Vesuvius", "pozzolan", and "Kameiros".

The potential number of referenced objects in an intermediate result matrix depends on the references sources and the discovery algorithms. The number used for further steps depends on selection and filter criteria applied for the respective context. The potential elements and the number of elements in a group can vary depending on the resources and objects referred.

The groups result from association processing of knowledge resources' objects. The groups contain intermediate matrix element references referring to the objects integrated into the knowledge resources. Examples for this case are shown in Table III.

TABLE III. INTERMEDIATE MATRIX ELEMENT REFERENCES FROM ASSOCIATION PROCESSING OF KNOWLEDGE OBJECTS (EXCERPT).

Matrix Element	*Meaning*
`MATRIXentry`	Object entries in knowledge res.
`MATRIXcitekeywords`	Citation keywords
`MATRIXindex`	Index entries
`MATRIXkeywordcontext`	Context keywords
`MATRIXsee`	'see' references
`MATRIXseealso`	'see also' references
`MATRIXsynonym`	Synonym references
`MATRIXcompare`	'compare' references
`MATRIXobjectkeywords`	Object keywords
`MATRIXtextintext`	References of text in object text

The matrix elements allow various precise (e.g., see, see also) and fuzzy (e.g., keywords) references, which are used for association processing algorithms.

When we extend the discovery and integrate chronological and associated objects and locations from the resources then the result matrix also includes years with volcanic, geological, geophysical, and technological context. Possible sources are collections and containers.

The listing in Figure 11 shows a representation of additional result matrix elements associated for this case after these attributes were considered.

```
MATRIXtextintext{date: -300000 Vesuvius, volcanic activity, oldest deposits}
MATRIXtextintext{date: -001800 Vesuvius, volcanic activity, Avellino eruption}
MATRIXtextintext{date: -001680 Santorin, Aegean, volcanic eruption, Thera}
MATRIXtextintext{date: -000700 Vesuvius, volcanic activity}
MATRIXtextintext{date: -000227 Rhodos, seismic activity}
MATRIXtextintext{date:  000062 Vesuvius, seismic activity, earthquake, Pompeji
 destruction}
MATRIXtextintext{date:  000079 Vesuvius, volcanic activity, explosive eruption,
 ash cloud, tuff, Pompeji destruction, Herculaneum, Stabiae}
MATRIXtextintext{date:  000142 Rhodos, seismic activity}
MATRIXtextintext{date:  000202 Vesuvius, volcanic activity}
MATRIXtextintext{date:  000345 Rhodos, seismic activity}
MATRIXtextintext{date:  000472 Vesuvius, volcanic activity}
MATRIXtextintext{date:  000512 Vesuvius, volcanic activity}
MATRIXtextintext{date:  000515 Rhodos, seismic activity}
...
MATRIXtextintext{location: Kameiros, island Rhodes, Greece; Kamiros, Greece;
 Rhodos; Rhodes}
MATRIXtextintext{location: Thera; Santorine; island Yali; island Nisyros}
MATRIXtextintext{location: Vesuvius}
MATRIXtextintext{location: Solfatara, Vesuvius}
MATRIXtextintext{location: Pantheon, Rome}
MATRIXtextintext{location: Caesarea Maritima}
MATRIXtextintext{location: Hagia Sophia, Konstantinopel}
...
MATRIXtextintext{material: pozzolan}
MATRIXtextintext{material: volcanic tuff}
MATRIXtextintext{material: Opus caementitium}
MATRIXtextintext{material: pozzolanic activity}
MATRIXtextintext{material: pozzolanic earths}
MATRIXtextintext{material: pozzolanic material}
MATRIXtextintext{material: volcanic ashes}
MATRIXtextintext{material: diatomaceous earth}
```

Figure 11. Additional result matrix entries for intermediate result matrix associated with integrated resources (excerpt).

The example contains excerpts of additional entries resulting for the three according object entries "Vesuvius", "pozzolan", and "Kameiros" from the above example case. Two aspects are most interesting for the discovery:

1) The new content and context, e.g., the context of Pantheon, Caesarea Maritima, and the Hagia Sophia in the context of Kameiros, Rhodos.
2) The possibility of referencing classifications to groups of content and context, e.g., date, location, and material.

These groups contain additional matrix elements referring to the objects integrated into the knowledge resources. An excerpt of additional matrix entry references from objects is shown in Table IV.

TABLE IV. ADDITIONAL INTERMEDIATE MATRIX ELEMENT REFERENCES FROM ASSOCIATION PROCESSING (EXCERPT).

Matrix Element	*Meaning*
`MATRIXtextintext...date: ...`	Date reference
`MATRIXtextintext...location: ...`	Location reference
`MATRIXtextintext...material: ...`	Material reference

In this case, all the additional references result from texts integrated in object texts (`MATRIXtextintext`). The associated additional information from the object references contains chronological information, location information, and material information.

The overall result is a very rich matrix. With its elements, an advanced matrix links different content and context from many hundreds to many thousands of objects and sources. The listing depicts the content of the result matrix in a readable formatting and excerpts some elements.

The matrix also contains references to the source data within the knowledge resources (for examples on media and citation references see Figure 8) and also refers to many other structured and unstructured data, e.g.,

- terms,
- names,
- locations,
- georeferences,
- bibliographic data,
- citations,
- classification, and
- media data.

As has been shown, media data can be integrated and documented with the knowledge resources, e.g., either as objects or sub-objects. This documentation also allows dependencies between object.

D. The integrated Kameiros' media references results

Media objects contain own references, e.g., classification, citations, documentation, and keywords and can therefore contribute in many ways to new insight – besides their intrinsic media content. The following photo data (Figure 12) from the media references for "Kameiros" was delivered by the result matrix.

The photos have been taken in 2013 by the Knowledge in Motion (KiM) natural sciences and archaeology sections in the ancient city of Kameiros on Rhodos, Greece, during the Geo Exploration and Information (GEXI) Eastern Mediterranean research and studies campaign. Today, the location on the western coast of the island of Rhodes is named Kamíros.

Figure 12. Integrated media photo objects associated with the knowledge object "Kameiros", referring to pozzolane and Vesuvius (LX resources).

The data shows the respective photo objects integrated with the knowledge resources and usable with the association processing, which were resulting for the presented case study. The sort order of the photo object chain reflects the arrangements of the locations: On top level to bottom level of the excavated site (photo objects from left to right, from top to bottom).
In detail, the results show in this sort order

1) the top level water tank,
2) the top level water pipeline following downhill,
3) an excavated part of the water pipeline,
4) a lower level water tank,
5) a single element of the water pipeline system,
6) and a bottom level water tank.

Object chains can be created by their objects' attributes, e.g., in this case by classification, spatial position, and altitude.

The water tanks are coated with the 'pozzolan' cement material, part of which are still in place, e.g., in the bottom level water tank.

Each of the objects in the object chain contains classification references to the pozzolan material, therefore the objects provide the missing link: These references from ancient Kameiros are also associated with Vesuvius volcano and refer to the later Roman adoption of comparable cement 'pozzolan' technology. These Rhodian realia are widely associated with natural phenomena, therefore this is reflected for the objects by many references [20] to respective phenomena and other places, e.g., on Rhodes, like Epta Piges, Rodini Park, the Nymphaion of Rhodes, cisterns, as well as geological water level marks.

Continuation of the case study [21] has conceived the documentation available and planning the additional research and development and the data to be collected and added to the knowledge resources.

VIII. Evaluation

The integration of multi-disciplinary knowledge resources and association processing can provide large benefits for creating result matrices and content. The integration and implementation is consequently data-centric. The implementation is as well as far data-centric as possible: "The term data-centric refers to a focus, in which data is most relevant in context with a purpose. Data structuring, data shaping, and long-term aspects are important concerns. Data-centricity concentrates on data-based content and is beneficial for information and knowledge and for emphasizing their value. The value of knowledge depends on the 'currency' used for individual scenarios.

The value of an integration depends on the scenario and priorities. There is no general knowledge-based means available for defining the value of integration and implementation other than by the value of knowledge gained. Technical implementations need to consider distributed data, non-distributed data, and data locality and enable advanced data handling and analysis. Implementations should support separating data from technical implementations as far as possible." [22].

According to the definition this means, that data and technical implementations can be separated and the created knowledge resources and technical components comply to the above criteria.

The structure and the aggregation of references increase the flexibility of possible workflows. Increasing the quality of data in the described type of long-term knowledge resources – by including references – can increase the quality of result matrices from discovery processes.

The examined case showed that a technology and material, which have not been explicitely documented in context of a knowledge resources object, can be associated with the context of different objects. Here, the Greek origin of the "pozzolan" technology was associated, which was named after the later use in Roman times.

Association processing can support discovery processes even when references are not explicitely available in text and documentation, and would therefore be unexpected or unknown. Association processing can use multi-level discovery in order to gain additional information, which is not visible from an otherwise isolated documentation.

The developed structures and methods can be widely beneficial for knowledge development and discovery as well as for creating implementations for advanced discovery components. The methodology allows to extend and exploit long-term multi-disciplinary content documentation and discovery and gain new insights from otherwise not associated data.

IX. Conclusion

This paper presented the research on the integration of knowledge resources and advanced association processing and presented features and benefits for the processing of associations. Major results from the resources side as well as from the research on geosciences and archaeology were shown.

First, the research shows that knowledge resources and association processing can be integrated most efficiently and flexibly. The major reason is, that structured knowledge resources can be successfully extended for allowing a multitude of integrated references types, e.g., geoclassification and media. The structured resources can also carry references and associations to differently structured or unstructured resources. Besides structured resources, also scenarios based on unstructured resources can benefit from an integration.

Second, the implementation shows that integration is least invasive to the knowledge resources and to the workflows. For both, knowledge resources and implementations, an arbitrary individual development can be preserved. The required parts of the workflows can stay modular.

The elements from associations contained in the result matrix are not procurable when using only plain methods like simple string search or plain discovery. Furthermore, the integration of methods, e.g., association, classification, and phonetic algorithms, allows any degree of precision and fuzziness.

A layered concept can be deployed with the implementation of computation and storage facilities. From the structural and knowledge point of view, the extended features are least invasive to the described type of knowledge resources and procedures.

From the geoscientific and archaeological side the factual results are most notable because the methodology integrates multi-disciplinary and multi-lingual knowledge beyond conventional means and shows a large number of associations, which cross multiple disciplines and languages.

The association processing has shown to benefit from additional elements referring to objects added to intermediate result matrices. Different data and media can be included, e.g., by documentation and classification, which vastly extends the spectrum of possible applications and can foster new insight.

The flexibility of the knowledge processing benefits from the advanced organisation of the data, which enables various scalable computational means for implementing directed graphs to fuzzy links, for which High End Computing resources can be deployed.

Future work will be focussed on further developing the multi-disciplinary knowledge resources and creating advanced methods for describing the content and context of objects.

It will be interesting to see applications of an integration of knowledge resources and association processing as resulting from this research. Feedback on the used 'currency' and the value of knowledge and data from different scenarios will be welcome. The new method should carry facilities for supporting long-term knowledge development and analysis as well as for enabling automation and High End Computing.

ACKNOWLEDGEMENTS

We are grateful to the "Knowledge in Motion" (KiM) long-term project, Unabhängiges Deutsches Institut für Multi-disziplinäre Forschung (DIMF), for partially funding this implementation, case study, research and studies campaign, and publication under grant D2012F1P04497 and to its senior scientific members, especially to Dr. Friedrich Hülsmann, Gottfried Wilhelm Leibniz Bibliothek (GWLB) Hannover, to Dipl.-Biol. Birgit Gersbeck-Schierholz, Leibniz Universität Hannover, and to Dipl.-Ing. Martin Hofmeister, Hannover, for the contributions to the research on the development and application of classifications. and for fruitful discussion, inspiration, practical multi-disciplinary case studies, and the analysis of advanced concepts. We are grateful to Dipl.-Ing. Hans-Günther Müller, Cray, for his work on flexible practical solutions to architectural challenges and excellent technical support. We are grateful to all national and international partners in the Geo Exploration and Information cooperations for their constructive and trans-disciplinary support. We thank the Science and High Performance Supercomputing Centre (SHPSC) for long-term support of collaborative research since 1997, including the GEXI developments and case studies.

REFERENCES

[1] C.-P. Rückemann, "Advanced Association Processing and Computation Facilities for Geoscientific and Archaeological Knowledge Resources Components," in Proceedings of The Eighth International Conference on Advanced Geographic Information Systems, Applications, and Services (GEOProcessing 2016), April 24–28, 2016, Venice, Italy. XPS Press, 2016, Rückemann, C.-P. and Doytsher, Y. (eds.), pages 69–75, ISSN: 2308-393X, ISBN-13: 978-1-61208-469-5, ISBN-13: 978-1-61208-060-4 (CDROM), TMDL: geoprocessing_2016_4_20_30144, URL: http://www.thinkmind.org/download.php?articleid=geoprocessing_2016_4_20_30144 [accessed: 2016-06-05], URL: http://www.thinkmind.org/index.php?view=article&articleid=geoprocessing_2016_4_10_30144 [accessed: 2016-06-05].

[2] C.-P. Rückemann, "Integrated Computational and Conceptual Solutions for Complex Environmental Information Management," in The Fifth Symposium on Advanced Computation and Information in Natural and Applied Sciences, Proceedings of The 13th International Conference of Numerical Analysis and Applied Mathematics (ICNAAM), September 23–29, 2015, Rhodes, Greece, Proceedings of the American Institute of Physics (AIP), vol. 1738. AIP Press, 2016, Simos, T. E., Tsitouras, C. (eds.), ISBN-13: 978-0-7354-1392-4, ISSN: 0094-243X (American Institute of Physics Conference Proceedings, print), ISSN: 1551-7616 (online) (eISSN), DOI: 10.1063/1.4951833.

[3] "Multilingual Universal Decimal Classification Summary," 2012, UDC Consortium, 2012, Web resource, v. 1.1. The Hague: UDC Consortium (UDCC Publication No. 088), URL: http://www.udcc.org/udcsummary/php/index.php [accessed: 2016-01-10].

[4] "Tcl Developer Site," 2016, URL: http://dev.scriptics.com/ [accessed: 2016-01-10].

[5] "ISO 14000 - Environmental management," 2016, URL: http://www.iso.org/iso/iso14000 [accessed: 2016-01-10].

[6] C.-P. Rückemann, "Enabling Dynamical Use of Integrated Systems and Scientific Supercomputing Resources for Archaeological Information Systems," in Proceedings INFOCOMP 2012, Oct. 21–26, 2012, Venice, Italy, 2012, pp. 36–41, ISBN: 978-1-61208-226-4, URL: http://www.thinkmind.org/download.php?articleid=infocomp_2012_3_10_10012 [accessed: 2016-08-28].

[7] "LX-Project," 2016, URL: http://www.user.uni-hannover.de/cpr/x/rprojs/en/#LX [accessed: 2016-06-05].

[8] D. T. Meridou, U. Inden, C.-P. Rückemann, C. Z. Patrikakis, D.-T. I. Kaklamani, and I. S. Venieris, "Ontology-based, Multi-agent Support of Production Management," in The Fifth Symposium on Advanced Computation and Information in Natural and Applied Sciences, Proceedings of The 13th International Conference of Numerical Analysis and Applied Mathematics (ICNAAM), September 23–29, 2015, Rhodes, Greece, Proceedings of the American Institute of Physics (AIP), vol. 1738. AIP Press, 2016, Simos, T. E., Tsitouras, C. (eds.), ISBN-13: 978-0-7354-1392-4, ISSN: 0094-243X (American Institute of Physics Conference Proceedings, print), ISSN: 1551-7616 (online) (eISSN), DOI: 10.1063/1.4951834.

[9] UDC, Universal Decimal Classification. British Standards Institute (BSI), 2005, Complete Edition, ISBN: 0-580-45482-7, Vol. 1 and 2.

[10] "UDC Online," 2016, URL: http://www.udc-hub.com/ [accessed: 2016-01-10].

[11] C.-P. Rückemann, "From Multi-disciplinary Knowledge Objects to Universal Knowledge Dimensions: Creating Computational Views," International Journal On Advances in Intelligent Systems, vol. 7, no. 3&4, 2014, pp. 385–401, ISSN: 1942-2679, URL: http://www.iariajournals.org/intelligent_systems/intsys_v7_n34_2014_paged.pdf [accessed: 2016-08-28].

[12] C.-P. Rückemann, "Creation of Objects and Concordances for Knowledge Processing and Advanced Computing," in Proceedings of The Fifth International Conference on Advanced Communications and Computation (INFOCOMP 2015), June 21–26, 2015, Brussels, Belgium. XPS Press, 2015, pp. 91–98, ISSN: 2308-3484, ISBN-13: 978-1-61208-416-9, URL: http://www.thinkmind.org/download.php?articleid=infocomp_2015_4_30_60038 [accessed: 2016-08-28].

[13] C.-P. Rückemann, "Enhancement of Knowledge Resources and Discovery by Computation of Content Factors," in Proceedings of The Sixth International Conference on Advanced Communications and Computation (INFOCOMP 2016), May 22–26, 2016, Valencia, Spain. XPS Press, 2016, Rückemann, C.-P., Pankowska, M. (eds.), pages 24–31, ISSN: 2308-3484, ISBN-13: 978-1-61208-478-7, ISBN-13: 978-1-61208-061-1 (CDROM), TMDL: infocomp_2016_2_30_60047, URL: http://www.thinkmind.org/download.php?articleid=infocomp_2016_2_30_60047 [accessed: 2016-06-18], URL: http://www.thinkmind.org/index.php?view=article&articleid=infocomp_2016_2_30_60047 [accessed: 2016-06-18].

[14] F. Hülsmann, C.-P. Rückemann, M. Hofmeister, M. Lorenzen, O. Lau, and M. Tasche, "Application Scenarios for the Content Factor Method in Libraries, Natural Sciences and Archaeology, Statics, Architecture, Risk Coverage, Technology, and Material Sciences," KiM Strategy Summit, March 17, 2016, Knowledge in Motion, "Unabhängiges Deutsches Institut für Multi-disziplinäre Forschung (DIMF)", Hannover, Germany, 2016.

[15] M. Koui and C. Ftikos, "The ancient Kamirian water storage tank: A proof of concrete technology and durability for three millenniums," Materials and Structures, Nov. 1998, Vol. 31, Issue 9, 623–627, DOI: 10.1007/BF02480613, ISSN: 1359-5997 (print), ISSN: 1871-6873 (online), Kluwer Academic Publishers.

[16] R. Snellings, G. Mertens, and J. Elsen, "Supplementary Cementitious Materials," Reviews in Mineralogy & Geochemistry, vol. 74, 2012, pp. 211–278, ISSN: 1529-6466, DOI: 10.2138/rmg.2012.74.6.

[17] R. Courland, Concrete Planet: The Strange and Fascinating Story of the World's Most Common Man-Made Material. Prometheus Books, 2011, ISBN: 978-1-61614-482-1, 396 p.

[18] A. A. Camões and R. M. Ferreira, "Technological evolution of concrete: from ancient times to ultra high-performance concrete," Structures and Architecture, 2010, pp. 1571–1578, ISBN: 978-0-415-49249-2.

[19] R. Hartge, Vesuvius, ..., An Eye Witness Report of the Vesuvius Eruption 1631/1632 (in German: Vesuvius, Kulturgeschichtliche Betrachtungen zu den vulkanischen Kräften und Der aufgeschobene Weltuntergang? Ein Augenzeugenbericht vom Vesuv-Ausbruch 1631/1632). Verlag Die Blaue Eule, Essen, 2009, ISBN: 978-3-89924-233-1, 292 p.

[20] B. Gersbeck-Schierholz and C.-P. Rückemann, "From Past to Present: Information on Water, Wind, and Sun and Their Significance," KiM Sky Summit, Knowledge in Motion, September 25, 2016, Sky Summit Meeting, "Unabhängiges Deutsches Institut für Multi-disziplinäre Forschung (DIMF)", Hungaria, 2016.

[21] C.-P. Rückemann and B. Gersbeck-Schierholz, "Ancient Water Systems and Ageless Knowledge and Technologies," KiM Sky Summit, Knowledge in Motion, September 19, 2013, Sky Summit Meeting, "Unabhängiges Deutsches Institut für Multi-disziplinäre Forschung (DIMF)", Rhodos, Greece, 2013.

[22] C.-P. Rückemann, Z. Kovacheva, L. Schubert, I. Lishchuk, B. Gersbeck-Schierholz, and F. Hülsmann, Best Practice and Definitions of Data-centric and Big Data – Science, Society, Law, Industry, and Engineering. Post-Summit Results, Delegates' Summit: Best Practice and Definitions of Data-centric and Big Data – Science, Society, Law, Industry, and Engineering, September 19, 2016, The Sixth Symposium on Advanced Computation and Information in Natural and Applied Sciences (SACINAS), The 14th International Conference of Numerical Analysis and Applied Mathematics (ICNAAM), September 19–25, 2016, Rhodes, Greece, 2016, URL: http://www.user.uni-hannover.de/cpr/x/publ/2016/delegatessummit2016/rueckemann_icnaam2016_summit_summary.pdf [accessed: 2016-11-06].

Old Habits as a Resource for Design: On Learning and Un-learning Bodily Knowledge

Tone Bratteteig
Department of Informatics
University of Oslo
P.B. 1080, 0316 Oslo, Norway
tone@ifi.uio.no

Guri Verne
Department of Informatics
University of Oslo
P.B. 1080, 0316 Oslo, Norway
guribv@ifi.uio.no

Abstract—**There are many reasons why artifacts and systems are difficult to use in practice. In this paper, we investigate such difficulties as a basis for design for ease of use. Difficulties may stem from the artifact or system itself, or from the artifact or system in use in its real use context. Technology introduces new tasks, and both learning new tasks and unlearning old habits can be challenging. We discuss how users' previous knowledge and habits can be used to understand how and why an artefact is difficult to use. This understanding is useful for designing artefacts that are easy to use. We end the paper with presenting a conceptual framework for design for coherence and simplicity from the users' perspective, where users' habits and bodily knowledge act as resources for design.**

Keywords—usability; habits; automated behaviour; automation; participatory design.

I. INTRODUCTION

Usability is often defined as the ease of use and learnability of an artifact, sometimes narrowed down to specific users in a specified use context having specific achievement goals (e.g., ISO 9241). But what does "ease of use" mean more precisely? We have tried to find out what it is that makes some artifacts difficult to use for some users. This paper builds on an earlier paper [1] and expands the empirical material as well as the depth of discussion of possible reasons why some things turn out to be difficult to use. Our aim is that knowledge about how a piece of technology is difficult to use can be used as a basis for designing solutions that are easy to use.

Much of the research on artefacts that are easy – or difficult – to use is based on Nielsen [2], who lists five aspects of usability: learnability, efficiency, memorability, low error rate, and satisfaction. A more elaborate list is given by [3], who present eight aspects: consistency, universal design, feedback, closure of dialogs, reversal of action, control, error prevention, and memory load. Except for universal design, all the aspects are general and concern the design of the artifact seen as a stand-alone context-independent thing. Our research shows, however, that it is difficult to achieve a total independence of contextual design elements – it is impossible and even unwanted: "All products make some reference to either products extant during previous generations or products from different companies or product families." [4]. Such references are important to build on when trying to understand how to use the product. Even well-designed stand-alone artifacts can be difficult to use for users not sharing the contextual competence pre-supposed in the design. We have seen this in our and our colleagues' research, where we focus on elderly people and the technological support that is supposed to enable them to live independently in their homes longer [5].

The paper is structured as follows: Section II gives a review of literature about problems in using technologies. In Section III, we present two studies of use of technology: the use of public services like tax, and the use of common home artifacts like remote controls or mobile devices that need charging. Section IV summarizes the challenges we have identified in our research. In Section V we discuss the competencies users need to use an artifact, and how such competencies are experienced and embodied. Section VI summarizes what we have found to make things difficult to use. In Section VII, we turn to design for ease of use: we discuss how we can go from knowing about the difficulties people have using an artifact to design of an artifact that is easy for them to use. We divide the discussion in two parts, addressing first how designing with users can end up with design results that are easy to use, and lastly we discuss a more general approach to automation that addresses how the design itself creates user problems and how these can be resolved. Section VIII concludes the paper.

II. PROBLEMS WHEN USING TECHNOLOGY

A close study of people using IT artifacts reveals that they often find technology difficult to use (e.g., [6]). A classic study is Suchman's study of use of a Xerox copy machine [7][8] demonstrating how operating a copy machine was difficult due to the difference between the scripted "plan" in the copy machine and the users' (situated) understanding of copying. Another classic is Gasser's study of how people work around computer systems that do not fit the work they need to do, which shows that people carry out their jobs also with non-supporting artifacts [9]. Even when an IT system works well, it may not work well together with other systems [10][6]. Just using more than one system can create problems as they are often not designed as parts of a larger coherent system or network [11].

A different set of studies shows that an artifact can be used in different ways, e.g., Barley's classic study [12] of the introduction of a CT scanner into the radiology departments at two different hospitals. Although the same technology was introduced, the cooperation and social organisation of the radiology work developed differently. In one department the radiology work became more decentralised with delegated responsibility; in the other, responsibilities became unsettled and the relation between the radiologists and the technicians became less close. This study shows that the same artifact can be part of very different socio-technical practices.

For designers, it is particularly interesting to study the non-users of an artifact. They are, however, very difficult to get hold of (unless they can be located in a particular place, e.g., an organization). Orlikowski [13] and Star and Ruhleder [14] describe how people are not using a computer system with good reasons, indicating that contextual matters (like reward systems) may offer good reasons for not using a system – irrespective of the usability aspects of the system itself. If the system appears to hamper the career of its users by having them share things that are important for their own careers, they will not do that. Even a small uncertainty about how data can be used and by whom may result in not sharing those data [15].

As a way to get access to non-users of the public service web pages of the tax authorities, Verne [16] studied people calling the tax authorities' call centre. She found that even if tax rules are complicated most of the questions concern relatively simple tax issues and that the callers' problems are concerned with interpreting and applying the rules to their own life. Similarly, [17] studied single parents' use of mandatory online services for communicating with the public service and found that some single parents believe that the civil servants do not inform them of the benefits they are eligible to. This causes the single parents to interact with the case handlers through traditional channels such as the telephone or personal meetings. In this example, lack of trust in the relationship with the civil servants led to non-use of a mandatory online service.

Several studies of assistive technology in the homes of elderly people have been carried out, see e.g., [1][18]. Noting that much of the technology is not used, Greenhalgh et al. focus on the subjective opinions and experiences from the elderly's own technology use. They call for a different design approach in order to develop technology that supports the elderly in achieving what matters to them and enhances the quality of their life [19]. Many of the current solutions aimed at elderly users are imported from other application areas and not designed specifically for an elderly user group, e.g., touch screens [20].

We also see that the level of automation of some of the tasks seem to confuse people. Cummings [21] describes automation with reference to human control (decision-making) and information: at the lowest level of automation the computer offers no assistance and the human takes all decisions and actions. At the highest level of automation, the computer decides everything "and acts autonomously, ignoring the human" (p. 2). Fully automated systems may seem like a tempting solution to making systems easy to use but artefacts that act autonomously can pose problems even when they are not used in any active sense – in particular when errors occur [22][23][24].

We know a great deal about systems and artifacts that are not easy to use, but what is less clear is how to get from knowing what is difficult to designing a solution that is easy to use. In this paper, we have set out to do this: we analyse a set of studies of difficult-to-use-technologies in order to arrive at design ideas for easy-to-use solutions.

We report from a set of qualitative interpretive case studies [25] aimed at developing new knowledge on how to design technology [26] that will be experienced as useful and easy to use in practice. As we have been interested in finding out why and how artefacts are difficult to use, hence we have chosen a qualitative rather than quantitative approach to evaluate technologies. Studies of use in situ give a better basis for answering these questions than usability studies where a test person is given a set of pre-defined tasks to solve outside of the real use context.

III. Difficult-to-use

Investigating people's reasons for not using an artifact is very instructive for designers: there may be a range of logical and sensible reasons for not using an artifact or using it in "wrong" ways. In this section, we report from our studies of users and non-users of computer technology.

A. *Badly designed Systems and Artifacts*

Some artifacts are difficult to use because of the design. Verne's [22] study of citizens' calls to the tax information call centre showed that many callers had tried to use the online tax self-service without succeeding. Listening in to 474 telephone calls over a period of 22 months gave a basis for understanding the callers' problems. Examples of problems ranged from not finding their PIN-code to more specific questions like a woman receiving welfare benefits and had tax deducted from her pension, but being aware that welfare pension was tax-free she asked for help in correcting the tax deduction. From eight in-depth semi-structured interviews with call advisors and their managers we learned about their work practices and their experiences of the callers' issues. The call centre advisors often walk the callers through the self-service web site and commented to us that the online services were not user-friendly. To callers who do not know which numbers in their tax card they need to change, there is no difference between filling out a paper form and reporting online. But online tax self-services may introduce additional complexity for the citizens [22].

Tax in Norway is almost fully automated. Throughout the year, employers deduct tax from their employees' wage payments and forward to the tax collector. This deduction is specified in the tax card, which is produced by the Tax Administration based on last year's tax return form and information provided by the citizen if needed. The tax return form is produced semi-automatically by the Tax Administration based on input from employers, other public agencies and the citizen [27].

Because tax laws and regulations vary a lot between countries, examples from the tax area are often complicated. We therefore offer a similar but simpler case: online student registration for classes [28]. New students at the University of Oslo are assigned a personal online account when they register. At first this account contains no services or information; the student can only use it for paying the entrance fee to the university. When the fee is paid, the status of the student is changed to "active student" in the system, and services such as signing up for classes become available. Many students do not understand that more services become available after they have paid the fee, and report the non-availability of services and information as an error [28].

A second set of examples can illustrate our point further. The examples are taken from an evaluation study of IT technology for independent living in an apartment building adapted to elderly people [5], involving sensors, alarms and a tablet connected to the Internet. Our investigations started in 2012 and include a number of studies carried out by colleagues and students in our research group. The studies document that many of the technologies do not function well in everyday use. The tablet, for example, has a wall-mounted charger station designed to charge while showing the time (Fig. 1 upper). However, the slot for positioning the charger in the right position is narrow and difficult to see, and many users do not manage to mount it right and do not discover this until the battery is empty [29]. Also the very common stove alarm is difficult to use for people in wheel chairs or people who find it difficult to hold the turn-off-switch while stretching and bending over the stove to turn the alarm off (Fig. 1 lower).

These examples illustrate that artifacts and technology themselves can create problems for their users.

B. *The Artifact in Use*

Some artifacts are difficult to use because of the use context and the use situation. Verne's [22] study of callers found that many people call because they need help with matching the rules and regulations with events and circumstances in their life, not because tax regulations and rules are complicated. Her data includes several examples of simple tax rules that may represent problems when applied to a person's life situation.

* When citizens move, they are required to send a notification of address to the Population Register. A citizen called to ask if he needed to send a notification to the tax authorities when he changed his job. (The answer is no.)

*A newly retired citizen needed guidance on how her new status affected her personal economy and on which of her different types of incomes are subject to which taxes.

*A house owner who earned money from renting her house asked if renovating costs could be deducted from her tax. She rented the apartment to her son, and wondered how the rules were applied in this case.

In all three examples, the life situation or circumstances of the citizen triggered the phone call. In the first example, the caller's life situation was irrelevant to the tax regulation in question, but in the two others the life situation needed to be matched with the rules and regulations by a tax expert.

Again our second set of examples is everyday technologies used by elderly people in their homes. We found that these types of difficulties arise when people use technologies that they do not have previous experience with. One example is an active woman, approximately 85 years old, who uses a hearing aid. She is well organised, educated, and has had an active work life, and she uses everyday technologies like her TV effortlessly. Her occupational therapist has tried to teach her how to use an amplifier for her hearing aid: a wireless microphone that amplifies sounds and submits to her hearing aid.

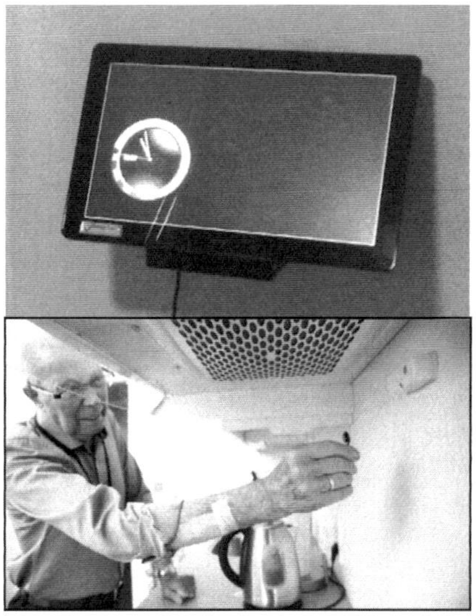

Figure 1. Welfare technology: Tablet charging (above), stove alarm (below).

The "accessory pen" is easy to use once fitted to the hearing aid: the manufacturer says that it is "zero hassle" because it is "completely simple to use, with one-click connection of receivers and fully automated settings" [30]. Using the pen involves pushing one small button in addition to charging it. However, the old woman finds the pen difficult to use. She does not remember how to use it from one therapist visit to the next. She wants to charge it before she uses it, but forgets. The occupational therapist (whose job it is to adapt support devices to individual users) has suggested that she instead can charge it after she has used it, and that she can keep it in the charger until the next time she needs it. But in the "old days", keeping devices in the charger could be dangerous, and the old woman therefore does not want to do this – even if the therapist assures her that with this equipment there is no danger. The old woman often finds her hearing aid amplifier not charged when she needs it.

A lady aged 70-something said that she was "not very experienced with technology" when we interviewed her about her use of technology. During the interview, she told us about her use of her TV with several remote controls, her iPad, and a variety of apps, including an app for buying online bus tickets and one for cloud storage of family pictures. She used FaceTime on her iPhone but considered

Skype to be too difficult. Skype was installed on her PC and she considered everything concerned with the PC to be too cumbersome. She avoided using it, but used her iPad and iPhone every day.

C. Other's Doings

Some technology problems are caused by factors outside the user's control, e.g., by actions or errors made by third parties. Some callers to the tax information call centre had a problem having their welfare support reduced because the welfare agency "tidied up their systems" and deducted 50 % of the benefits because of a missing tax card. The tax authorities receive many calls from people who have not received a tax card in the mail, but this is often their own doing (or rather: not doing). However, in one case the street address had been changed by the municipality, and since the caller had not moved she was not aware that she needed to send a notification of change of address.

A more complicated case was a young man who had received a bill for penalty tax for underreporting his income two years ago. His employer had gone bankrupt and his reported income was disputed. There was no employer who could confirm the callers' claims, and he had no documentation of his version of what had happened. In principle, he needed to document the non-event of not underreporting income. The advisor helped him by suggesting steps to take to retrieve documentation and proceed with his claims in his case with the tax authorities.

The smart home technologies in the apartment building for elderly people had automatic electricity saving. However, the first winter everybody experienced that the apartments were very cold, and the elderly people (who normally need higher indoor temperatures because they do not move much) had to get help from the janitor service to correct the temperature. It took a long time to find out that some of the basic calculations for the electricity system were wrong resulting in faulty temperature regulation in the individual apartments [23]. We (the authors) work in a smart building ourselves and have experienced similar difficulties when trying to identify the reasons for bad temperature regulation mechanisms. When using artifacts that are part of a larger complex system, the problems that a user experiences may very well be the result of other people's activities or errors.

IV. Different Challenges

Difficulties using artifacts can have several sources: the artifact itself, the artefact-in-context, and shared artifacts that others use and interact with. The users are often unable to distinguish between these sources.

Difficulties that stem from the artifact or system itself pose challenges for users, that are afraid to make errors or reluctant to use cumbersome technology. Such challenges can be met with various practical measures to stimulate and enhance use, such as moving the technology to a place where it is easier to reach, as in the case of the turn-off switch for the stove alarm, which is difficult to reach and the positioning of the tablet charger (see Fig. 1). Users can be trained in using online services, another practical measure towards the challenges posed by difficult technology (see e.g., [31]).

Difficulties that stem from the artifact-in-context or in-interaction pose a different set of challenges. Difficulties stemming from the artifact-in-context originate in challenges with relating the technology to the users' own life situation or circumstances. In order to do their own taxes in a competent way citizens need to learn and to understand the tax rules and regulations and understand how their life situation matches or not matches with concepts from the rules. Active use of an accessory hearing aid requires that the user establishes a new practice that fits into her life and that she can follow up without help from the occupational therapist. To address such challenges, a user may need external help to explain and interpret rule systems or technologies.

Difficulties that stem from others' actions and interactions are the hardest challenges to meet. It seems that errors that stem from other people's actions are particularly difficult to understand as they often surface in unexpected ways and need some kind of "debugging" to be comprehensible. This kind of debugging requires special competence and can be time-consuming. External help is often needed to disentangle difficulties that stem from complex interactions [27]. And often there is not one best solution [14].

We sum up the kinds of difficulties in Table I, and indicate what kinds of challenges they pose.

TABLE I. DIFFERENT KINDS OF DIFFICULTIES WITH ARTIFACTS AND SYSTEMS, AND THE CHALLENGES THEY POSE

What is difficult?	Kinds of difficulties		
	Artifact	*Context*	*Activities by others*
Examples:	Holding the turn-off switch. Positioning of the charger. Online tax self services	Personal economy when retiring. Tax deductions for renting out a house to family. Tax card when starting a new job	Bankrupcy by an employer. Welfare agency "tidies up their systems". Errors made by subcontractors.
Challenges:	Practical measures: moving a charger, teaching.	Matching artifact with own life situation or circumstances	Disentangling interactions and complexities

Even though the challenges that meet the users are different, the general feature is that users need experience from previous similar situations in order to be able to differentiate between approaches to resolving the difficulties. The competence for addressing problems can be gained in many ways.

V. Competence

Competence, as the ability to do something successfully or efficiently, is important for using technology. The examples in Section III show that competence can concern the design that makes the operation of the technology difficult (III.A) as well as the adaptation of the technology to the actual situation (III.B). In both cases, the users have to do fitting work [9] in order to use the technology

A. What we Know

A usability test of a video conferencing system showed that users who did not have the same technological experience as the designers (which in this case was an iPhone) did not understand the interaction mechanisms and had problems operating the system [32]. Langdon et al. [4] discuss this problem on a more general level, showing that "similarity of prior experience to the usage situation was the main determinant of performance, although there was also some evidence for a gradual, age-related capability decline." (p. 179). They conclude that in their test of driving a new car "there was … some clear evidence that experience may be more influential than age" (p. 189). Docampo [33] has identified four technology generations: electro-mechanical period, remote control era, use of displays, and use of layered menus, basically distinguishing between before and after 1960. The generations affect how people learn new technology and are visible as a discontinuity of errors and task timings between the generations.

Previous experience is a salient feature that builds self-efficacy [34]. According to self-efficacy theory for human agency, belief in one's own competence and mastery is important for succeeding. In their study of the effects of training programs in computer use for older adults, Wild et al. [35] found that after one year of consistent computer use the participants reported reduced levels of anxiety and increased self-confidence in their abilities to use computers. Participants with mild cognitive impairments were less likely to demonstrate increased efficacy and competence. This is in line with our own empirical findings. We interviewed an occupational therapist, who had the experience that elderly people with mild cognitive impairments were able to learn new practices, but they would need much training and follow-up from her.

Langdon et al. [4] suggest that *"prior experience with similar products and product features is a strong predictor of the usability of products over the wider range of capabilities. This similarity results from experience with same brand, or functionally and perceptually differing products, provided that key functional features and visual appearances are maintained. . … In particular, in the absence of prior experience of a product interaction interface, or with the appearance of product features, users of all age groups apparently resorted to a means-end or trial and error based approach that was slow, repetitive and error prone."* (p. 190). Hurtienne and Langdon [36] suggest a continuum of knowledge sources starting with 1) innate knowledge like reflexes and 2) sensorimotor experiences like speed, gravity (early childhood learning), 3) culture (everyday life), and 4) expertise acquired in a profession or hobby. Knowledge about tools crosses these "levels" of knowledge. They suggest that knowledge residing on the sensorimotor level of the continuum is basic to most people and is acquired early in life. Knowledge from culture or professional life differs.

B. How we Know

Langdon et al. found that previous experience provided guidance on how to carry out their tests: "Memories relating to the experience of products will be stored in the long term memory and the ability of the central executive to find the relevant knowledge will depend on the cues provided and the level of previous experience." [4:182]. They conclude that their older test-participants were not able to use the technology, which "is consistent with the idea that they had no previous experience to provide guidance on how to complete the trials, rather than being of lower cognitive capability as a result of ageing." [4:190].

Using technology is also a bodily experience. Höök [37] discusses bodily ways of knowing in her study of the challenges she experienced when learning the English style of horseback riding based on her background in riding Icelandic style. Competence in and experience from horseback riding resides in the body and is expressed by more or less automatic bodily reactions and responses to external events. She uses her experience from learning a new riding style as a basis for reflections on how to design for bodily experiences.

There are subtle differences in how the rider interacts with the horse within these riding schools. Communication with a horse is mainly bodily as the rider gives signals with her legs and hands, but also less explicitly with body posture and movements. The horses are trained to react differently to signals (from the legs, hands, body posture) from the rider. In the English riding style, the rider aims to not disturb the horse with her movements because the horse is trained to move independently based on previously given signals, for example to trot in a circle. The rider aims to sit in a "loose" way on the back of the horse. In the Icelandic style, the rider will need to push forward with her bodily movements and put tension into the horse to enable an unusual gait such as the tölt.

Höök [37] describes how she needed to practice again and again with constant feedback from the instructor to be able to learn the new movements, positioning and interactions. Even though she cognitively knew and understood how she was supposed to move and position her body, it was difficult to *do/perform* the new movements at the right time.

C. Learning and Un-learning

Learning new movements and ways of communication implies unlearning the old ways [37]. Unlearning bodily ways of knowing implies consciously and deliberately practicing *not* doing the usual activity and instead practice something new. Having learnt how and when to perform a new movement is different from practicing the old habits. Unlearning bodily knowledge requires conscious cognitive work before it becomes a habitual and automated practice.

Höök's movements for performing Icelandic horse riding were automated while the new riding style was not. The transition required that she spent conscious effort to unlearn the old and learn the new.

Automatic thoughts and behaviour occur without any need for conscious effort as "[m]ost of our thoughts and behaviors tend to be automatic or have automatic components, and for good reason. These processes are fast, allowing us to do things like drive to work without having to think about how to turn the steering wheel each time we get into a car" [38: 991]. Our conscious attention can be directed towards issues that need it more. Such "automaticity" is a result of practicing and repeating an activity over and over again, often coupled with an external event that will later trigger the automatic thought or behaviour. Automaticity occurs on low cognitive levels.

For our purposes in this paper, automaticity and habit plays the same role in describing repeated behaviour that does not require any conscious attention or deliberation. Habitual activities may be triggered by environmental and contextual cues [39]. If a situation requires flexibility and change, strong habits may often emerge as errors. Conscious change away from habitual behaviour is demanding, and people act according to old habits when they are distracted, under time pressure and with limited ability. Older adults were less able to modify habitual behaviour [39].

An example of deep automaticity may happen when using modern hearing aids, where the wearer can train his or her brain to filter out noise from the sound that s/he wants to hear in order to get the most out of the hearing aid. The brain needs some years to re-adjust, and middle-aged people will benefit from starting to use the hearing aids before it is strictly necessary. People who do not start using them until their 70ies may experience that their brains will be very slow in adjusting and they may experience the hearing aid as insufficient and unpleasant. The brain needs time to allow for automation that enables the filtering activity to take place outside of the conscious brain activity [40].

As an example of automation of symbolic interaction we will refer to a woman in her seventies, who told us about her technology use. Our informant is retired, and in periods of her life she has been seriously ill and received treatment. But now she is active in her community with activities and organisations and she is active in her home. She does not have a smartphone and often experience problems when writing sms-es. She asks her husband to finish her sms if she needs help. However, she is the one who masters the remote control for the TV. She says (with a smile) that she has to, because her husband rarely watches TV. Her son gave her a simplified remote control for her birthday, which she never uses – she took it to be a prank and has not taken it as a serious artifact. She has no problems using the usual TV remote control (Fig. 2).

Changes in rules and regulations as well as in the technology for doing taxes introduce new tasks for the citizens. In 2008 submitting the tax return form was made optional in that Norwegian citizens could just accept the figures that was already gathered by the tax authorities and presented in a pre-completed form. Accepting was done by a non-action: by *not* making changes in the pre-completed form. Hence, learning to differentiate and understand when to report changes has become a separate task. Many of the callers were not aware that they did not have to send in a paper form, and that they could report online [16]. In practice it can be difficult to differentiate between learning new tasks and unlearning old tasks, but we argue that analytically they create different kinds of challenges.

Figure 2. A retired woman just laughed about using her large-sized and simplified remote control for her TV set (normal remotes to the left).

Wu et al. [41] present a participatory design project with people with anterograde amnesia, aimed at developing a "memory aid" for and with them. They base their design on the fact that "amnestics rely heavily on external memory aids, such as a calendar or an action item list." (p. 217). Their design provides *a "tool [that] will assist amnestics when they feel lost or disoriented by providing information as to their whereabouts and their* intent *for being where they are. A person having amnesia will typically follow familiar routines in their daily life, such as the same route home, because deviating from this path will often result in disorientation. Our tool enables an amnestic to grow increasingly confident and* independent *in exploring new locations and situations – a feat that is very difficult in current practice."* [41, original emphasis].

The tool was based on the fact that amnestics' procedural memory to a large extent remains intact; therefore, it was possible to train new routines and skills for using the tool. "Interestingly, the overall similarity of products that has been experienced before does not have to be high to allow effective learning" [4].

Occupational therapists working with elderly people have told us that people often install electric water heaters in the homes of their old relatives in order to avoid that they start a fire if they forget the kettle on the stove. However, if the elderly person has a "bad day" and is particularly forgetful, s/he may put the water heater on the stove as a bodily habit, and this may cause fire.

VI. What is Difficult – Seen from the User

Looking closer at what is difficult suggests a distinction between learning and un-learning tasks. We found that the sources for the difficulties were the tasks to learn and the old tasks to unlearn: the two different processes are experienced in different ways both in cases where the artifact is difficult itself and when it is the fitting of the technology to the situation that appears to be difficult. We came across examples of actions and errors made by third parties, such as vendors, employers, other public agencies and other technologies. In these cases, the situation was experienced as unpredictable and confusing and not possible to explain by the user unless s/he had a deep knowledge of the complexity of the technology in its social environment.

We sum up our analysis of what is difficult in Table II, expanding Table I with rows from this more detailed analysis of the nature of the difficulties.

TABLE II. WHAT IS DIFFICULT SEEN FROM THE USER

What is difficult	Kinds of difficulties		
	Artifact	*Context*	*Activities by others*
New tasks to learn	Holding the turn-off switch. Positioning of the charger. Online tax services.	Personal economy after retiring. Charge device after use. Check pre-completed form	Check and act if something unusual
Old tasks to unlearn	Handling paper forms. Putting kettle on stove.	Charge device before use. *Not* pushing the horse. Changed tax rules.	Need trust to stop doing.
Basic knowledge for the task	Understand tax and web pages. Understand a water boiler.	When does the new apply?	Understanding the ecology of humans and technology
Challenges:	Practical measures: moving a charger, teaching.	Matching artifact with own life situation or circumstances. Differentiating between old and new.	Disentangling interactions and complexities.

All the elements in Table II point to existing competence or lack of competence presupposed by the artifact that may make the artifact difficult to use. But how do we go from knowing what is difficult-to-use to designing something that is easy-to-use?

VII. DESIGNING FOR EASE-OF-USE

The three different kinds of difficulties can be a basis for approaching design of easy-to-use technology solutions. In this section, we report from some design experiments with elderly people by colleagues and students [5][18][29][42][43] as well as our own design suggestions based on analysis of identified user problems [22].

Designing from the users' perspective starts with investigating their subjective experiences and competencies. Elderly users need much practice and repetition to establish new habits and unlearning old habits may be the hardest part. Unlearning may require trust to let old habits go to be sure that they are not necessary, e.g., for security. As unlearning old tasks is a challenge in itself, a design that builds on old, habitual tasks will be experienced as less challenging for the user. Enhancing and extending the old tasks instead of making them obsolete in a new design can be experienced as a simple design by the user.

Using everyday technologies like radios, mobile phones, water heaters or remote controls is normally easy and often automated and habituated. Many of our memories and competencies sit in our bodies as automatic movements or perception (e.g., music, smells) and can be carried out without conscious deliberation. A design that incorporates that the user can rely on his/her old habits can make the changing of old practices more likely and the design more robust. Robustness towards unintended and unexpected use is important for the user's ability to manage and carry on with the original task (see e.g., [44]).

Designing for new habits in old age is possible, as the example of the memory aid for the amnestic people above showed [41].

In the large project on evaluation of technologies for independent living, designing for ease-of-use has been explored in two ways: through design of artifacts that resemble familiar technologies [45], and by collaborative design with elderly people on designing or testing different technological solutions in order to identify what works with a minimum of new tasks to learn.

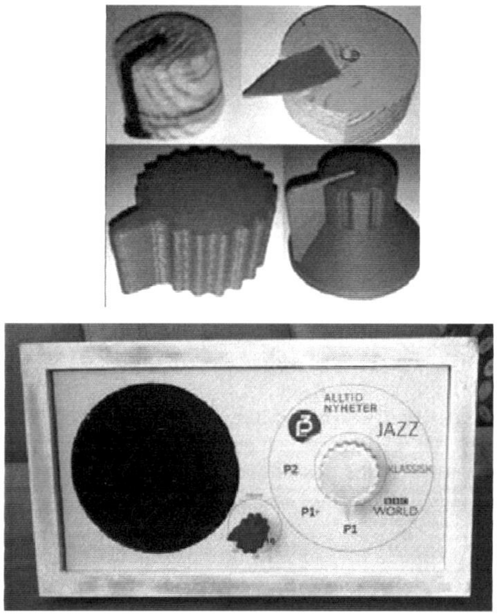

Figure 3. The prototypes for the knob (above) and the digital radio (below). Photo by Johnsen et al. [43].

An example of the first design approach is the design of a digital radio that was co-designed with in total 25 elderly people [43]. Johnsen et al. aimed to design interaction mechanisms that built on old and familiar bodily skills when designing a new way of operating a digital radio [ibid]. Using rotary controls for operating the radio – like in the old days – enabled them to make sense of the interface with their body even if they intellectually could not understand or remember how to turn on the radio. They easily recognized the button as a device for rotary movement. Several buttons were designed and tested for a good grip for old hands and recognizable positioning with different textures and shapes [43], see Fig. 3.

Figure 4. Testing several different induction chargers. Photo: Iversen [42].

The second design approach involved testing a large number of different solutions to the same problem. One example is a test of induction chargers carried out to identify problems and ease-of-use [29]. As a way to provide easy charging of phones, Iversen and Joshi [29] collected seven different off-the-shelf induction chargers and asked a group of elderly men to evaluate them (see Fig. 4). Trying out different technologies and experiencing how they offered different degrees and kinds of difficulties turned out to be instructive to the elderly users as well as to the designers. Furthermore, Joshi [45] built on knowledge about earlier habits, e.g., the fact that in "the old days" (i.e., when they were young adults) telephones had wires and were usually located in a specific place, on a particular table by the entrance door. Maybe it would be easier to charge the mobile phone if, instead, always putting the phone in "its place" was the thing to remember (see e.g., [46]).

Another example is from a participatory design process organized and facilitated by Stark [31]. A group of elderly visitors to an elderly activity centre found their online banking services to be difficult to use: the web site was seen as confusing, with too much irrelevant information and choices on the pages. One of them started a "data club" aimed at helping other elderly visitors with their Internet banking. Stark recruited some of the people frequently visiting the data club to join her in designing a new online banking solution. The design process consisted of seven meetings, and during these meetings the elderly participants suggested a design that was based on a very different logic from the current Internet banking solution. In the new "Easy Bank" banking solution the service mimics the tasks carried out by people going (in person) to the bank: they pay their bills or they want information about their bank account(s). Instead of presenting the bank customer with a virtual place where one can access a range of different bank services, the new "EasyBank" design presents the two most frequent activities: paying bills and getting information about the account, see Fig. 5.

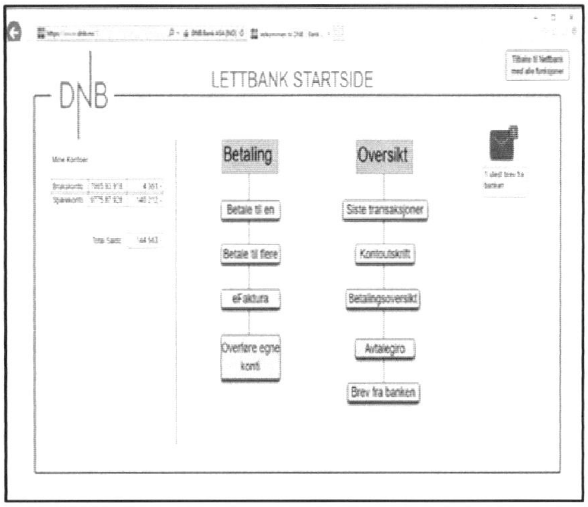

Figure 5. A suggestion for an "easy online banking" made by a group of elderly users [31].

Making online banking easy by referring to well-known and established banking habits may make it easier to adopt the new way of doing banking. It seems that the logic of the current banking solution is grounded in how the bank sees the world rather than what bank customers may be interested in doing in the bank. One can argue that making the Internet bank a virtual "bank place" where lots of services can be activated is a more open solution that may serve all bank customers, however, for most of the less frequent users of bank services paying bills and checking your account are what they do in the bank. Stark's new "Easy Bank" solution is an example of taking the non-expert user's point of view when designing the services, and then designing the service as it is seen from these users. At a more general level technology is often used to automate some tasks and hence enable more self-service or more available services.

Fig. 6 illustrates our view of how technology influences the tasks done by a human user. Fig. 6a illustrates a loosely defined set of tasks for a particular purpose (e.g., doing taxes) as seen from the human's perspective. Fig. 6b illustrates how technology takes over some of the tasks: they become automated. Fig. 6c shows the automated task area as seen from the human user's point of you: s/he encounters some left-over tasks that are not automated and some new tasks.

The tasks left for the human interacting with the technology may appear as fragmented and there may be no or little coherence between different subtasks. New tasks can be of a very different kind than the original set of tasks. Fig. 4d illustrates that in order to make the tasks left for the human user coherent and foreseeable, we should design a coherent set of tasks left for the user instead of letting the technology decide what is automated [22].

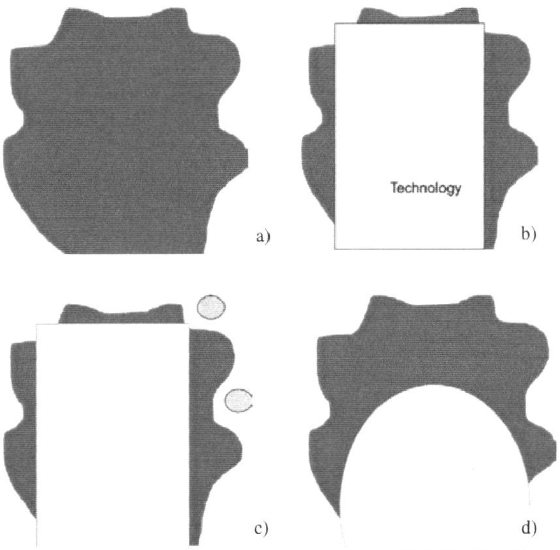

Figure 6. Automation removes some tasks from the user and introduce others. a) A set of tasks for a user - not clearly defined. b) Some of the tasks are made obsolete because of technology. c) Fragmented tasks left for the human user. d) A coherent set of tasks for a user.

Automation and service development usually takes its starting point from the needs and material basis of the service provider. Automation is based on what can be automated. The service provider's logic structures how services and functionality is presented for the users. Users will need to learn and understand the provider's logic to use the services in independent and autonomous ways. Looking for the users' logic will make possible design starting with the user's perspective.

Managing the boundaries between tasks made redundant by technology, tasks left for the user to do and emerging new tasks is a challenge in itself. Design from the user's perspective aims to present the tasks for the human interacting with technology as a coherent whole and with connected subtasks. This will enable the user to disentangle the problems s/he encounters.

Understanding *when* to deviate from old habits and do new tasks requires sorting things out, which should be supported by the design and by training and practicing (with or without helpers). Matching the artifact with the personal use situation and context represents a challenge [22][47], in particular if the artifact is complex (like tax). Showing ways of matching, e.g., by providing several examples, can help the user in the matching of her/his situation with the technology requirements: s/he may be lucky and find an example similar to her situation. FAQs and help texts can provide such examples in the artifact itself, while human helpers like call advisors and occupational therapists will have to assist if the matching is too difficult to be carried out by the user alone. Graphical illustrations and simulations can also help explain complex systems like the tax system.

Often very simple re-designs can contribute to explaining how the automated system works, and reduce the users' anxiety that something is wrong (and at the same time reduce the load on the service provider's call centre/help desk). In the registration service for new students (see Section III A), merely sending an email to new students when they open an account that more services will become available as soon as they pay their fee, will help. The students understand why there are no services/menu choices available and that it is not an error [28]. A citizen who changes her tax card online can receive an email saying that a change is registered, and when she can expect a new tax card to be operative. This will enable a citizen who does *not* receive such an email the next time she makes an online change to understand that her online changes were not registered. Instead of calling the tax authorities, she may be able to check into the matter herself.

A smooth transition between an old and a new system is demonstrated by Denman and Nachman [48], who worked with designing for one user: Professor Stephen Hawking. Hawking uses a specially built interface that enables him to write and speak with an artificial voice based on small muscular movements as input. His use of the interface was developed through many years, and his practices were deeply dependent on and rooted in his old system. Denman et al. found that making changes in the interface was challenging as "Stephen had a rhythm in his use of his system" and he knew some aspects of it by hearth in a way that speeded up his operations even though the operation was based on, e.g., choosing a word from an alphabetic list. Hawkings knew the list by hearth, and was faster using the old list than a new word-prediction engine that suggested appropriate words. Use of the old list involved more typing, which turned out to be faster as Hawking could type without having to read the words in the list as he knew it by heart. The new system was installed as optional and Hawking could switch between the old and new systems, leading him to get practice with the new word-prediction engine. After some time of switching between the old and the new system, Hawking could make better use of the new system and increasingly preferred it over the old one [49].

Starting to use technology that is new to oneself requires mental attention and a cognitive effort. Technology use often involves symbol manipulation and abstract thinking, which may be demanding. People act by force of habit in stressful situations and when they have reduced capabilities because of for example illness or old age [39]. In demanding life situations users need to spend their energies on their primary tasks, and there may not be spare capacity available for the attention needed to learn to use a technology new to them.

Elderly people use technology in many ways. However, our empiric material show that for elderly people, who are not interested in technology as a field of study and for its own sake may only embrace new technologies when they fit into their life. Using technology can contribute to continuity and control, health and well-being when the elderly people can use it their own way and for their own purposes [50].

VIII. CONCLUSION AND FUTURE WORK

Based on examples from our research on design with and for elderly people and on citizens doing taxes, we describe how artifacts and systems become difficult to use. We have reflected on how we can use knowledge about difficulties in a constructive way to suggest better designs. In the paper, we make an analytical distinction between types of difficulties according to where they appear: in the artifact / system itself or when used in its use situation / context. Our analysis also includes a discussion of the differences between learning new tasks and/or competences to benefit from the technology and un-learning old habits and practices. In addition, difficulties stemming from activities and errors made by others may occur, and in order to be able to disentangle the problem and sort out what can be done, the user needs to understand the larger ecology of the service system.

We suggest that habits and bodily knowledge can be used as resources for design to enable users to benefit from familiarity and coherence. Building on and extending old habits instead of making them obsolete in a new design can be experienced as very simple for the user – independent of any usability assessment based on criteria that are external to and irrelevant for the particular user in the particular situation. Our aim has been to present a conceptual framework for design for the user's subjective perspective.

Our conclusion is that "easy-to-use" is difficult to design, and that the notion of "ease-of-use" hides the complexity that comes when artifacts are used in real life contexts. Both the identification of what makes things difficult and what turns out to be easy to use challenge a notion of "usability" that looks at the artifact as a de-contextualized object. Easy to use is a characteristic of the relation between a user, her/his activity and the technology that supports that activity. It is thus both situational and personal. This makes it even more challenging to go from what is difficult to use to designing easy to use artifacts. What is difficult to use is not so easy to detect before the artifact is used hence designers can learn a lot from studying use practices. We therefore argue that usability might be a less useful measure for evaluating a design.

ACKNOWLEDGMENTS

The study of technologies for assisted living was part of a larger research project on "Autonomy and automation in an information society for all", which has involved several colleagues, and we especially thank Suhas Joshi, Anita Woll, Rune Rosseland and Sisse Finken for providing data that we build on in our discussion. Also a large number of student projects has been carried out, and we have included several of them in the empirical basis for this paper. We thank them for their contributions, and have referred to their reports in the reference list. Also the participants in the "BRIS" project have contributed to our discussions. We also want to thank the staff and elderly residents at the municipal apartment building and in the BRIS projects as well as the advisors and managers at the Tax Information Call Centre for their contributions to our research.

REFERENCES

[1] T. Bratteteig and G. Verne, "From Difficult Artifacts to Easy to Use Designs," ACHI, IARIA, 2016, pp. 185-191

[2] J. Nielsen, Usability Engineering, Morgan Kaufmann Publishers, 1994, ISBN 0-12-518406-9.

[3] B. Shneiderman and C. Plaisant, Designing the User Interface: Strategies for Effective Human-Computer Interaction, Addison-Wesley Publ. Co. Reading, MA, 2010.

[4] P. Langdon, T. Lewis, and J. Clarkson, "The effects of prior experience on the use of consumer products," Univ.Access Inf.Soc., vol. 6, 2007, pp. 179-191.

[5] S. G. Joshi and T. Bratteteig, "Designing for Prolonged Mastery. On involving old people in Participatory Design," Scandinavian Journal of Information Systems, 28(1), 2016.

[6] S. Bly, B. Schilit, D. W. McDonald, B. Rosario, and Y. Saint-Hilaire, "Broken expectations in the digital home," CHI 2006, Montréal, Quebec, Canada, Apr. 22-27, pp. 568-573

[7] L. Suchman, Plans and Situated Actions. The Problem of human-machine communication. Cambridge University Press, 1987.

[8] L. Suchman, Human-Machine Reconfigurations, Cambridge University Press, New York, 2007.

[9] L. Gasser, "The Integration of Computing and Routine Work," ACM Transactions on Office Automation, vol. 4, no. 3, 1986, pp. 205-225.

[10] J. Söderström, Jävla skitsystem (in Swedish: Stupid bloody system), Karneval 2011, ISBN 9789187207525, http://www.slideshare.net/Jonas_inUse/stupid-bloody-system, retrieved 03/2016.

[11] J. Grudin, "The case against user interface consistency," Communications of the ACM, vol. 32, no. 19. 1989, pp. 1164-1173.

[12] S. R. Barley, "Technology as an occasion for structuring: Evidence from observations of CT scanners and the social order of radiology departments," Administrative science quarterly, vol. 31, no. 1, 1986, pp. 78-108.

[13] W. Orlikowski, "Learning from Notes," CSCW'92, ACM, New York, 1992, pp. 362-369.

[14] S. L. Star and K. Ruhleder, "Steps Toward an Ecology of Infrastructure: Design and access for Large Information Spaces," Information systems research, vol. 7, no. 1, 1996, pp. 111-134.

[15] T. Bratteteig, "The Unbearable Lightness of Grouping: Problems of introducing computer support for cooperative work," Proceedings of NOKOBIT 1998, Oslo, 99-113.

[16] G. Verne, "Two faces of autonomy. Learning from non-users of an e-service," Systems, Signs and Actions, vol. 8, no. 1, 2014, pp. 6–24

[17] C. Ø. Madsen, Why do they keep calling? Single parents' Domestication of mandatroy e-government self-service channels, PhD dissertation, IT University of Copenhagen, 2015.

[18] S. G. Joshi and T. Bratteteig, "Assembling fragments into continuous design: On participatory design with old people," Nordic Contributions in IS Research, 6th Scandinavian Conference on Information Systems, SCIS 2015, Oulu, Finland, August 9-12, 2015, Proceedings

[19] T. Greenhalgh et al., "What matters to older people with assisted living needs? A phenomenological analysis of the use and non-use of telehealth and telecare." Social science & medicine, 93:86-94, 2013.

[20] A. Culén and T. Bratteteig, "Touch-Screens and Elderly users: A Perfect Match?" In Leslie Miller (ed.), ACHI 2013, IARIA, 2013, pp. 460-465.

[21] M. L. Cummings, "Automation Bias in Intelligent Time Critical Decision Support Systems," AIAA 3rd Intelligent Systems Technical Conference 2004, pp. 1-6.

[22] G. Verne, The winners are those who have used the old paper form. On citizens and automated public services, PhD Thesis, University of Oslo, 2015, http://urn.nb.no/URN:NBN:no-50321.

[23] J. C. Doksrød, Understanding the complexity of error detection in smart homes, Master thesis, Department of Informatics, University of Oslo, 2016

[24] L. Bainbridge, "Ironies of automation," Automatica vol. 19, no. 6, 1983, pp. 775-779. doi:10.1016/0005-1098(83)90046-8.

[25] C. Marshall and G.B. Rossman, Designing Qualitative Research, Sage, 2016.

[26] D. Randall, R. Harper, and M. Rouncefield, Fieldwork for Design. Theory and Practice. Springer Verlag, 2007.

[27] T. Bratteteig, G. Verne, "Conditions for Autonomy in the Information Society: Disentangling as a public service," Scandinavian Journal of Information Systems 24(2), 2012.

[28] M. Ekdal and S. Tomt, «Hæ? Hvorfor har ingen fortalt meg dette?» En analyse av IT-løsningene ved UiO i et tjenestedesignperspektiv, Master thesis, Department of Informatics, University of Oslo, 2016.

[29] T. R. Iversen and S.G. Joshi, "Exploring Spatial Interaction in Assistive Technology through prototyping," AHFE conference, Procedia Manufacturing, Elsevier Publishing Co., 2015.

[30] http://www.phonak.com/fi/b2c/fi/products/wireless-accessories/products/roger.html, retrieved 11/2016.

[31] K. H. Stark, «Du må vite hvor du skal lete» - Eldres bruk av nettbaserte tjenester, Master thesis, Department of Informatics, University of Oslo, 2016.

[32] T. H. Paulsrud, A discussion of Technological Frames applied at a Usability Test, Master thesis, Department of Informatics, University of Oslo, 2011.

[33] R. M. Docampo, Technology Generations handling complex User Interfaces, PhD dissertation, TU Eindhoven 2001, ISBN 90-386-0913-2.

[34] A. Bandura, "Self-efficacy mechanisms in human agency," American Psychologist vol. 37, no. 2, 1982, pp. 122-147.

[35] K. V. Wild et al., "Computer related self-efficacy and anxiety in older adults with and without mild cognitive impairment," Alzheimer's & dementia: the journal of the Alzheimer's Association, vol. 8, no. 6, 2012, pp. 544-552.

[36] J. Hurtienne and P. Langdon, "Prior Knowledge in Inclusive Design: The Older, the More Intuitive?" ACM Conference 2009.

[37] K. Höök, "Transferring Qualities from Horseback Riding to Design," NordiCHI, October 16-20 2010, pp. 226–235, ACM, ISBN: 978-1-60558-934-3.

[38] T. P. Wheatley and D. M. Wegner, "Automaticity in action," In: N. J. Smelser and P. B. Baltes, International encyclopedia of the social and behavioral sciences, London: Pergamon, 2001, pp. 991-993.

[39] W. Wood and D. Rünger, "Psychology of Habit," Annu. Rev. Psychol. 2016, 67:11.1–11.26

[40] S. Haugland, hearing aid specialist, personal communication 2015.

[41] M. Wu, B. Richards, and R Baecker, "Participatory Design with individuals who have Amnesia," The Participatory Design Conference ,Toronto 2004, pp. 214–223, ACM, ISBN: 1-58113-851-2/04/07.

[42] T. R. Iversen, Exploring tangible interaction: Alternative interfaces for assisting elderly users, Master Thesis, Department of Informatics, University of Oslo, 2015.

[43] E. Johnsen, M. Ofstad and S. Subaschandran, Care+: Can we make the interface of the radio easier for elderly users in the digital age?, Student report, Department of Informatics, University of Oslo, 2015.

[44] A. Woll, "Aging in Place: Dealing with Breakdown of Welfare Technology," Selected Papers of the Information Systems Research Seminar in Scandinavia, vol. 4, 2013, pp. 77- 90.

[45] S. G. Joshi, Prolonging interaction - Re-connecting old people with purposeful interaction, PhD. dissertation manuscript, University of Oslo, forthcoming, 2017.

[46] L. Palen and S. Aaløkke, 'Of Pill Boxes and Piano Benches: "Home-made" Methods for Managing Medication,' CSCW 2006, pp. 79-88.

[47] G. Bowker and S. L. Star, Sorting Things Out: Classification and Its Consequences. Massachussets Institute of Technology, Cambridge, Massachussets, 1999.

[48] P. Denman and L. Nachman, 'Designing for „a" user: Stephen Hawking's UI,' PDC, 2016, Aug 15 – 19, Aarhus, Denmark.

[49] P. Tawadrous, "UX Designer Pete Denman's Talents Led Him to Stephen Hawking. His Success Shattered Myths and Broke Down Barriers," Jobs@Intel Blog, http://blogs.intel.com/jobs/2016/07/12/ux-designer-pete-denman-and-stephen-hawking, 2016, retrieved 11/2016

[50] M. Loe, "Doing it my way: old women, technology and wellbeing." Sociol Health Illn 32 (2), 2010, pp. 319-334.

Iterative Evaluation of a Driver Assistant Client in ICT-Systems in the Context of Urban Logistics and Electric Vehicles

Johan Buchholz, Sebastian Apel, Christian Stolcis and Volkmar Schau

Chair of Software Technology
Friedrich Schiller University Jena, Germany
Email: {johan.buchholz, sebastian.apel, christian.stolcis, volkmar.schau}@uni-jena.de

Abstract—**Information and communication technology (ICT) systems for electric vehicles (EVs), which support planning, monitoring and analysing urban area logistics can become complex and difficult to use. In Smart City Logistik (SCL) project a driver assistant client (DAC) was developed to help to overcome fears, limited information and uncertainty in the context of urban logistics. To evaluate the users' needs and intentions an iterative and open approach was designed and consequently used. Triangulation helped to get the best possible insights out of each of three phases of development, and the findings were used to improve the DAC. A lot of uncertainty accompanied the beginning of the project, so qualitative information was gathered to understand how the drivers work routines look like and which attitudes towards new technologies prevailed. A more quantitative approach helped to collect a broad range of opinions on specific usability topics before a final simulated system setup contributes to ask a wide variety of users their experiences. This agile and iterative approach helped to identify important aspects while designing the DAC and compare different solutions, e.g., regarding necessary functionalities, menu-structure, font, button-size, and other parameters. The implementation of these findings enabled the project partners to develop a broadly accepted user interface and system that will be used in electric vehicles in urban logistics.**

Keywords–Survey; Usability; Electric Vehicles; Simulated Environment.

I. Introduction

Since the need of delivering goods increased massively in the past decade and will increase further in the next years [2], the use of electric vehicles (EVs) for last-mile delivery could help to reduce the air and sound pollution substantially, especially in inner cities[1]. In fact, most researchers agree that even well beyond 2020, the capacity of batteries will not fit future range demands [3]. This restriction affects mainly available EVs, which are designed for the transportation of goods. Therefore, many companies have qualms to use this new technology because of range limitations, low density of recharging stations, and long charging time [4]. Nevertheless, no matter which technological restrictions appear with EVs compared to traditional vehicles, for most companies it all comes down to the ability to plan the vehicle usage, including the certainty that the planned tour can be done. In fact, many companies interviewed during the Smart City Logistik (SCL) project, have already tours within the range of an EV, or at least can adopt tours with little effort.

The research project SCL pursues the goal to develop such a system, which provides relevant information on EV-specific restrictions and helps to overcome fears and to support the usage within urban logistics. As part of the German special federal research program for Information and Communication Technologies for Electric Mobility II (ICT II) [5], the SCL project supports the integration of EVs in fleets through the usage of information and communication technology (ICT).

One of the most important parts of such a holistic system is the assistance of the driver. In a complex socio-technical system where EVs are used within urban logistics, the driver needs to cope with additional information (such as range, battery status, etc.) to fulfil his primary task of delivering goods. To reduce stress and uncertainty resulting from these important additional parameters, a driver assistant client (DAC) focussing on the needs of drivers was developed, evaluated, and implemented as a prototype during the SCL project. Therefore, a concept for technology assessment was developed, combining existing methods from social and computer sciences for the specific project. In an agile managed project, we needed to focus on methods that provided flexibility and direct user feedback. The results help to achieve the goal, to develop and improve mockup and demonstrator along the users' needs. This general concept can be applied to other projects in the field of computer-human interaction, which are confronted with similar conditions and challenges regarding uncertainty and user expectancies.

In Section II existing work regarding the DAC, the prototype evaluation and other ICT-systems for EVs will be outlined briefly. A more detailed picture of the problem, the purpose of the DAC, and its main functionality will be given in Section III. Subsequently, the research design to improve the DAC in an iterative procedure and to assess the users' expectations will be outlined. It consists of three primary qualitative and quantitative surveys: In a first step, seven drivers were interviewed to get insights into their daily routines and attitudes towards supporting technology. This step is described in Section IV. The subsequent Section V shows how these findings were used to build the prototype. Later, 43 participants tested two different DAC prototypes and evaluated them with a focus on usability (Section VI). The third part of the evaluation includes the development of the functional demonstrator and is accompanied by a simulator-based test with participants from logistic companies and is described in Section VII.

[1]This paper is an extended version of a contribution to the international conference on advances in computer-human interactions (ACHI) 2016 in Venice, Italy [1].

II. State of the Art

Previous work on methods for software design shows a broad range of techniques that can be applied in different development stages. Cognitive walkthroughs, heuristic evaluation, formal usability inspections [6] offer interesting and valuable insights into a development process. More theoretical work focusses on the users' needs and expectancies as relevant factors for technology acceptance. Factors that influence the use of a socio-technical system cover the perceived usefulness, the attitude towards using a technology, and others [7], [8]. Other works in the field of DACs or EVs point out important factors that are relevant in the given context [9], but focus too much on the economic decisions of private households and cannot be adapted entirely to our project. Unfortunately, knowledge about important factors while using the DAC in a commercial context in EVs is rare. When it comes to a long-term research project in a field, where user acceptance is rather unknown, a flexible methodology that provides different forms of knowledge in various project stages is needed. Therefore, methods from social sciences were used. A qualitative research part is used to gather knowledge [10], and quantitative research helps to evaluate existing knowledge and design within a broader range of participants [11].

Apart from the very project, different projects investigate multiple aspects of the emerging technology of EVs and are funded within the German Information and Communication Technologies for Electric Mobility II (ICT EM II) program. The focus of ICT EM II is on new concepts for intelligent technology in EVs (Smart Car), combined with power supply (Smart Grid) and ideas for mobility (Smart Traffic) [12]. Projects like sMobility, iZEUS, Adaptive City Mobility (ACM), eTelematik and E-Wald focus on EV use in different kind of scenarios. However, all of them use ICT-systems to support different kind of EV-users. These projects indicate the broad range of driver assistance systems and mobile clients, as well as the need to evaluate them.

In a complex socio-technical system where EVs are used within different kinds of scenarios and the driver needs to cope with additional information (such as range, battery status, etc.) to fulfil his primary task, it is essential to reduce stress and uncertainty resulting from these important additional parameters. The used DAC has to fit the drivers needs, which have to be assessed thoroughly in each project.

III. The Driver Assistance Client

In the context of urban logistics, the driver has to cope with a lot of information, which often comes along with stress and the insecurity about the actual range of an EV. Since the range depends on a lot of parameters (e.g., battery capacity, driving speed, weather conditions, weight, etc.), the consideration of all those influencing parameters would be a complex process while driving. To reduce stress and eliminate insecurity, the DAC was developed. Basically, it works as a navigation system, providing optimised routes for EV, considering different range-affecting parameters of the vehicle while focussing on the planned tour. At the start of a tour, the driver can retrieve the tour on the DAC, which is already optimised and considers all parameters for the EV he is using. During the tour, the driver will be navigated to each point, gets information on possible changes to the tour, and all relevant information (e.g., traffic and weather conditions). As a result of this, the driver is relieved from thoughts about the range of the vehicle. Because the tour is always optimised and adapted to changes, the driver will be able to perform his tour and drive back carefree to the starting point.

Since the DAC should assist the driver while driving and reduce the added complexity, it needs to be easy-to-use in a vehicle. To find an optimal way to support the driver we elaborated an approach for the realisation of the DAC, wherein each iteration the acceptance and usability have been evaluated. The findings were used to improve further versions of the DAC.

IV. The Interview

In theoretical discourses on technology use, EV and driver assistance systems, different factors that influence the attitude, expectations, and acceptability towards these technologies in general public, are described [7, p. 188] [8, p. 447]. Beside these common factors, there may be particular ones among employees in logistics who use EV, which result from their specific situation (e.g., the employer-employee relationship leads to an involuntary use of the system). In the first place, the professional drivers need to perform their work task without unwanted disruptions by technological peculiarities and EV-specific uncertainties. To overcome the theoretical debate on barriers and drivers of technology acceptance, empirical evidence was gathered in qualitative interviews. Seven drivers from different companies were interviewed, using a semi-structured guide that was developed in advance. The interviewees were asked about their common work tasks, their attitude towards new technologies in general and EVs in detail, their expectations towards a DAC, some demographic items, and their employment biography. A content analysis of the interviews was conducted, and the deductive-inductive creation of categories [13] shed light on possible acceptance factors and requirements regarding a DAC in EV-based urban logistics. In theoretical debates, the general acceptance factors are described as perceived usefulness, perceived ease of use, the attitude towards using a technology [7, p. 188], and some models include the behavioural intention to use the system as well. These factors are influenced by moderators such as subjective norms, experience, the image of technology, job relevance, output quality, or the voluntariness of use [8, p. 447]. We found empiric evidence in the interviews regarding these items. Using the computer-assisted qualitative data analysis software f4analyse [14], we found out that the drivers tend to prefer a passive system. The system should give them useful information on important events during their tour, while not forcing them to act in a single, specified way. Other hints pointed in the direction of up-to-date maps, estimation and inclusion of time and range restrictions, the ease of use of and favoured support while implementing the system. These important factors for technology users were considered while developing the first versions of the DAC.

V. Building the Prototype

Taking into account the requirements that were identified in the interviews, as well as previous research, a first horizontal prototype was developed. Horizontal means in this case that the prototype has no real functionality, and was designed as a draft for the evaluation of the user interface. Figure 1 shows the tour overview and Figure 2 shows the information

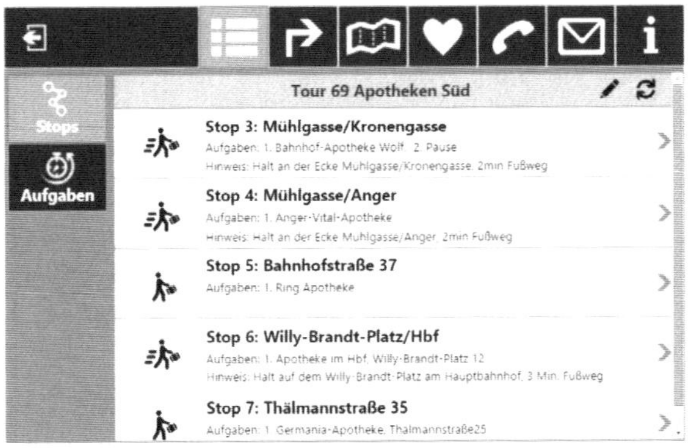

Figure 1. Tour overview of Prototype 1

Figure 3. Tour overview of Prototype 2

overview of the prototype. Both figures offer an impression of the main design. The main menu has been arranged on the top to allow switching directly between the main views such as tour information, navigation, map, vehicle status, direct call, messages and common information. To allow the navigation through different information, the submenu is arranged on the left side in each view. Since the DAC should be used on a mobile device with touch screen, big buttons were used, enriched with understandable and clear icons. After login the user directly views the tour overview with all relevant information on stops and clients. While driving, the user will mainly use the navigation view, which represents the route guidance.

During the development of the first prototype, some details of the design were questioned. So, a second prototype was build, which offers the same basic functionality, but has a slightly different user interface (UI) regarding the views. Figure 3 shows the tour overview for the second prototype. The main menu is also situated on the top of the screen and the submenu also on the left side, whereas the view of the content is divided into two parts, the item list and the content of the selected item. In Prototype 1, the list disappears when an item is selected, in Prototype 2 the item list remains visual, so the user can always see which item is currently selected.

Another difference compared to Prototype 1 is the overview of the main menu shown in Figure 4, which shows up directly

Figure 2. Navigation view of Prototype 1

after login. This UI provides an overview of all available functionalities. Creating two prototypes allowed to evaluate more options and the advantages and disadvantages from slightly different views. The evaluation itself and the results are described in the next section.

VI. PROTOTYPE EVALUATION

After developing the first two DAC-prototypes, possible users were asked for feedback in an online survey, targeting potential difficulties that may appear while using EVs in logistics. Before the users performed some basic tasks using the two prototypes, they were asked about different aspects of usability, using a standardised questionnaire focussing on the EN ISO 9241-110 norm [15], which was slightly adapted to the research context. For questions regarding the functions of the DAC, perceived ease of use, and intuitiveness, the users were asked to rank the particular characteristics of the prototypes on an ordinal 7-step-scale and to add qualitative information in free-text fields. Due to limitations in availability of interview partners at the partner companies who took part in the research project (and the resulting inefficiency to carry out the study on-site), an online questionnaire was developed using LimeSurvey [16], and an additional device with the DAC prototypes was brought to the partner companies. In each company, a contact person was instructed and responsible for conducting the evaluation. The access to the questionnaire was restricted by a 6-digit access code, which was handed out to the interviewees by the contact person in an envelope with some further instructions on the evaluation procedure. While the code itself was in a non-personalized envelope, it was possible to track the respondents' company and the order in which both prototypes were evaluated. The evaluation order was randomised based on the access code, which also made it possible to match the answers to the proper prototype. With this step, distortions as a result of answer patterns were prevented, and this procedure offered a high level of depersonalization. The online questionnaire was accessible for a period of 14 weeks, and the users were able to participate independently, at their individual best point in time. When participating, the users opened the envelope, accessed the online questionnaire and answered some fundamental questions before the first prototype was shown on the second screen. After performing some tasks, the users were asked to answer questions and rate the usability of the prototype,

Figure 4. Main menu of Prototype 2

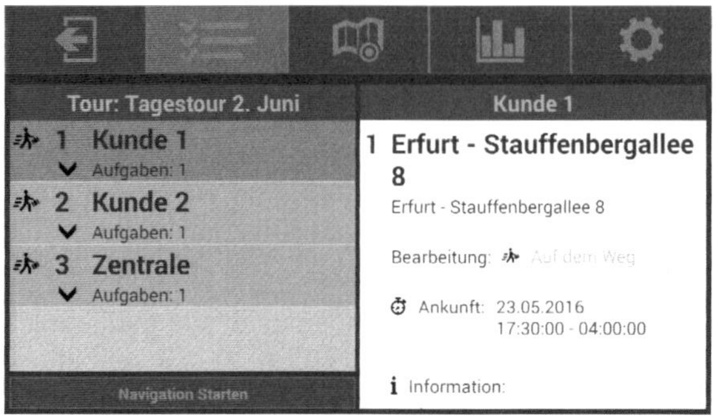

Figure 5. Tour overview of the demonstrator

before the same procedure started for the second prototype. The questionnaire concluded with free-text fields for ideas of improvement and some demographic questions.

With this approach, standardised and comparative information, as well as qualitative insights into the perceived usability of the two evaluated prototypes were gathered from 45 users. While two answers were excluded from the SPSS analysis due to reasonable doubt of sufficiency (e.g., when the evaluation of DAC was carried out in just a few seconds), the remaining 43 cases gave us some interesting insights on the usability of the evaluated prototypes.

First we examined the data and searched for feasible answer patterns between the first and second part of the questionnaire. It might be possible that the first evaluated mockup is rated below the second one in general (e.g., because of learning effects). Table I summarises the result of a sign test, addressing this question. The hypothesis is that the answers to the first and second part of our survey may differentiate simply due to the order of the questions. However, the null hypothesis (that the answers do not differentiate between the first and second block of questions) cannot be rejected in most cases. Regarding Table I, only the answers to question 13 tend to differentiate between the first and second part of the survey. This specific question used a double negative within its statement and the remarks in the free-text fields suggest that this confused at least some participants. As a consequence we decided to drop this question.

TABLE I. The result of the sign-test is used to check possible pattern of answers regarding the order of our evaluated mockups.

Statements (comparison of similar answers within the first and second part of this survey)	**Exact sig. (2-sided)**
1) The software offer required functionalities to handle tasks efficiently.	,115
2) The software is easy to use.	,388
3) The software facilitates a simple orientation through a uniform design.	,607
4) The used icons / terms reflect the underlying functionality.	,115
5) The size of the used buttons is appropriate.	,227
6) The size of the used icons is appropriate.	1,000
7) The size of the used fonts is appropriate.	,286
8) The software has a uniform concept for different kinds of interactions.	,143
9) The software requires little time to learn.	,344
10) The Software is easy to understand without any external support or user manual.	1,000
11) The software allows an easy switching between menus or masks.	,359
12) The software provides an excellent overview of their feature set.	,824
13) The software does not miss to inform about whether an entry was successful or not.	,070

In Table II, the median values to the closed statements are compared. Medians are used because of our input values, which can not be interpreted as a linear value due to the ordinal 7-step-scale. Regarding Prototype 1 and 2, the median values vary slightly only. The result tends to show a median around 4 to 6, while 4 is interpreted as a neutral rating and 5 to 6 as a positive rating. However, the used buttons within the prototypes were evaluated differently. The answers from the free-text fields complement our analysis.

As a conclusion we can summarize that in general, none of the two prototypes was evaluated better than the other. According to our analysis, Prototype 1 showed better results regarding the usability, while Prototype 2 achieved better results in clearness of design and intuitiveness. Based on these results, a set of adaptations was elaborated. Basically, it combines the positive characteristics of both prototypes. Finally, these adaptations were used to build a functional demonstrator of the DAC, which is described in the next section.

VII. THE FUNCTIONAL DEMONSTRATOR AND EVALUATION

The most important difference regarding the prototypes and the demonstrator is that the latter is fully functional. Compared to the indicated functionality of the prototypes, the demonstrator has been reduced, based on the results of the evaluation. The remaining main functionality covers the tour overview, turn by turn navigation, status overview and settings. Figure 5 shows the tour overview and on the upper border the main menu. The submenu has been removed completely, so that the available space could be used in a better way. Also, the navigation view has been improved by removing unimportant buttons, such as the zoom in and out buttons (see Figure 6). To save space and reduce complexity, the vehicle status and common information (e.g., weather, traffic, etc.) have been merged into the status overview, and the direct call and messages views have been removed.

After two iterations, the DAC has been implemented as a fully functional demonstrator based on the recommendations of

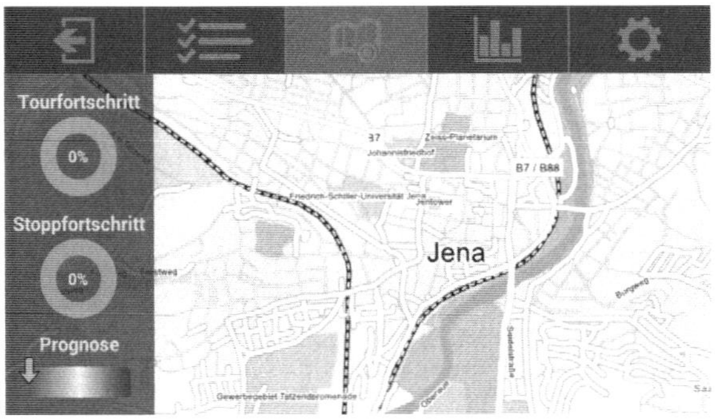

Figure 6. Navigation view of the demonstrator

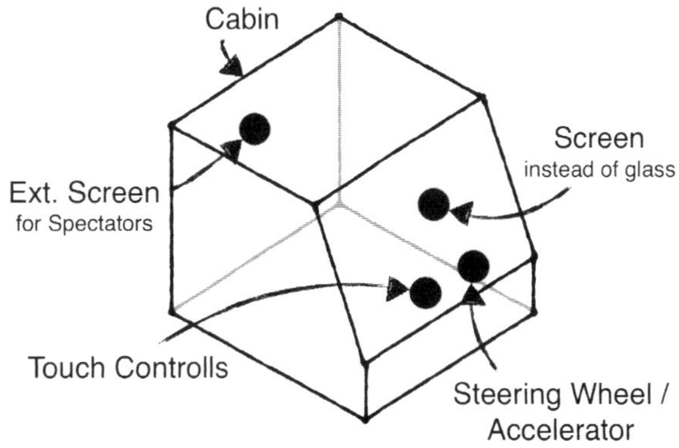

Figure 7. The Functional Demonstrator.

the participants during the evaluation. To ensure a high quality and a high usefulness, another iteration step concluded the project. In order to get further information on usability, the driver should use the DAC during his normal working day. To collect more data on possible insufficiencies, one final evaluation was carried out. This one focussed on drivers without particular EV-experience and was planned as a quantitative questionnaire.

Due to the fact that only a few drivers at the partner companies were able to participate while actually using EVs and the DAC, the significance of the results is restricted as a consequence. To overcome this problem, the demonstrator was evaluated by a higher number of professional drivers in Eltrilo [17], a simulator that was developed during the SCL project and is capable of simulating a real-world environment based on map data. Specific scenarios (e.g., transportation from a hub into town with multiple stops) can be simulated and be part of the evaluation.

Figure 7 presents the Eltrilo cabin schema. In front of the driver, a flat screen is the new virtual glass windshield in this setup. Besides the steering wheel, there are two additional small screens which form the cockpit. The cockpit touch screen allows switching cabin equipment (e.g., radio, air condition, lights) on or off. On the second screen, a navigation system and the cabin state (e.g., velocity is displayed). The driver assistance client is installed in the cockpit.

TABLE II. Table with median values according to closed questions within the mockup evaluation.

Statements	Median Prototyp 1	Median Prototyp 2
1) The software offer required functionalities to handle tasks efficiently.	4 (+/-)	4 (+/-)
2) The software is easy to use.	5 (+)	5 (+)
3) The software facilitates a simple orientation through a uniform design.	5 (+)	5 (+)
4) The used icons / terms reflect the underlying functionality.	5 (+)	5 (+)
5) The size of the used buttons is appropriate.	5 (+)	6 (++)
6) The size of the used icons is appropriate.	5 (+)	5 (+)
7) The size of the used fonts is appropriate.	4 (+/-)	4 (+/-)
8) The software has a uniform concept for different kinds of interactions.	5 (+)	5 (+)
9) The software requires little time to learn.	4 (+/-)	4 (+/-)
10) The Software is easy to understand without any external support or user manual.	4 (+/-)	4 (+/-)
11) The software allows an easy switching between menus or masks.	5 (+)	5 (+)
12) The software provides an excellent overview of their feature set.	5 (+)	5 (+)

This simulator setup represents all components as used in real scenarios. The environment itself is based on real map data and generated through the procedural mechanism. This environment simulates specific scenarios like transportation from the hub into town with multiple stops. The simulation environment can create entirely terrain with height profiles, different types of roads, houses and road signs based on various kind of input data (e.g., ASTER GDEM V2 for height profiles and Open Street Map (OSM) data for road and house information).

Getting this into practice requires functional components as shown in Fig. 8. Primarily, some virtual simulation environment are necessary (1) and combined with real components, e.g., the DAC (2) and server (3). Realistic simulation behaviour and position mapping is possible. The componentes are linked to the simulation through a simulated telematic unit[2] (4) by using a data interface. Finally, this setup needs the car simulation (5) itself, some consumption simulation (6) which produces consumption based on user input when interaction with the simulated car and in-car electronics (7), e.g., speedometer and switches for hardware elements like light and air condition. A more detailed overview of components and architectural drafts

[2]Hardware element to gather telemetric data in real scenarios.

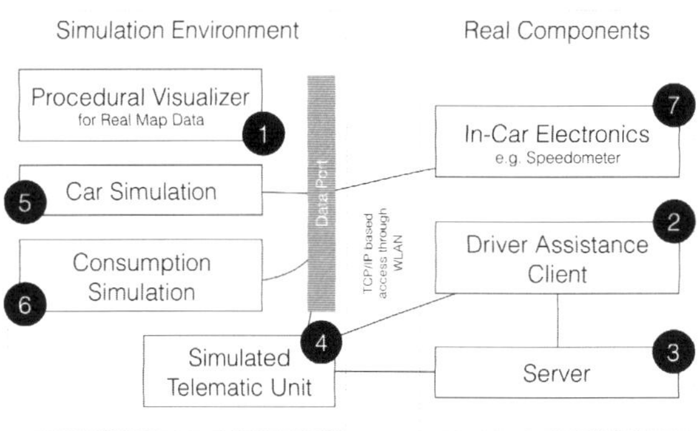

Figure 8. Components within the simulation environment.

TABLE III. Table with median, min and max values according to closed questions within the demonstrator evaluation.

Statement	Median	Min.	Max.
1) The software offer required functionalities to handle tasks efficiently.	5 (+)	1 (—)	7 (+++)
2) The software requires redundant input.	5 (+)	2 (–)	7 (+++)
3) The software provides enough information about input which is allowed and necessary.	5,5 (+)	1 (—)	6 (++)
4) The software provides situation based explanations, in the case of asking for, which is helpful.	5 (+)	1 (—)	7 (+++)
5) The software facilitates a simple orientation through a uniform design.	5 (+)	3 (-)	6 (++)
6) The software provides enough information about current running tasks.	5 (+)	2 (–)	7 (+++)
7) The software has a uniform concept for different kinds of interactions.	5 (+)	4 (+/-)	7 (+++)
8) The software requires little time to learn.	5,5 (+)	1 (—)	7 (+++)
9) The software requires that you have to remember a lot of details.	5 (+)	1 (—)	7 (+++)
10) The software is easy to understand without any external support or user manual.	5 (+)	1 (—)	7 (+++)
11) The software enforces an unnecessarily rigid compliance of processing steps.	4 (+/-)	2 (–)	5
12) The software allows an easy switching between menus or masks.	5 (+)	4 (+/-)	7 (+++)
13) The software enforces unnecessary interruptions of work.	5 (+)	1 (—)	7 (+++)
14) The software provides easy to understand error messages.	4 (+/-)	1 (—)	7 (+++)
15) The software requires at mistakes, on the whole, a slight correction effort.	4 (+/-)	1 (—)	5
16) The software provides accurate troubleshooting information.	4 (+/-)	1 (—)	5
17) The software can adapt well to my personal, individual nature of the work execution.	4,5 (+)	3 (-)	7 (+++)
18) The software is adaptable to varying tasks by myself, according to its possibilities.	5 (+)	4 (+/-)	7 (+++)

is published in [18] and [17].

In order to use Eltrilo, the DAC was installed into the simulator and connected to the live-system via a mobile network connection. In a first step, the participants received some detailed instructions on what they should do on their tour and how to use the DAC while performing their tasks in the simulator. During the simulation, some events affecting the tour were triggered, to simulate unpredictable changes of plans. In a second step, the participants were asked to answer a questionnaire on their experience in the demonstrator, as well regarding usability. The approach is similar and comparable to the investigation described in Section VI but bases on the improved demonstrator.

The simulator experiment was conducted in three different companies and ten drivers answered the questionnaire. Table III reflects the median, minimum and maximum values of the closed questions. The overall result tends to show a median around 4 to 5. Furthermore, the users were capable to use this system in combination with the DAC. All users were able to fulfil their virtual logistical task within a previously unknown scenario. Some users remark that the navigation system needs to react faster, has to give an improved overview on traffic information, and has to inform about exceptions and problems earlier. Regarding the functionality, some participants remarked that it is adequate, but has to become more stable. However, the last evaluation step doesn't replace the evaluation of experiences with the system in daily work routines. The results visualise a first trend and require more user feedback and experiences for further results.

VIII. Conclusion and Future Work

The development of a technological solution requires multiple iteration steps, a fact that is crucial for the evaluation and that is considered in the presented research design: opening up for qualitative information in the beginning of the project, where knowledge is limited and uncertainty about important acceptance factors is high, before focussing on the gathered knowledge and comparable evaluation questions with regard to existing norms and standards, is one way to assess technology development and to gain valuable information on user expectancy and experience. Due to the agile project management, the technology evaluation has to be open at any point in time for new information and changes, and needs to combine appropriate qualitative and quantitative research methods. This helps to achieve the best possible results, which can be implemented in further technology development.

This approach was used in the SCL project consequently. The first interview showed important aspects in the drivers' daily work routines that had to be considered while developing the DAC. The drivers prefer a passive system that gives hints and relevant, up-to-date information. The prototype evaluation revealed the positive aspects of two slightly different mockups that were implemented in the functional demonstrator. Two iterations resulted in a fully functional prototype of the DAC, which is broadly accepted by possible users. The third iteration step was done using a complex simulator environment, which used real map data and consumption simulations in combination with the other components used in SCL. The evaluation with ten participants showed that this system helps to fulfill the main task of the users in general and to reduce complexity. However, simulator stability has to be improved. In another step, feedback from the experiences while using the system in EVs in daily routines might complement the findings of this evaluation that accompanied the development of the SCL system.

Finally, these results will help developers while creating DACs in the context of EVs. As a next step, the evaluation can be carried out by a higher number of participants from different contexts (e.g., private users as well) to find additional use cases for the developed technological system. Additionally, it is required to expand this evaluation within a final study to get experimental data with working drivers. From a methodological perspective, a systematical analysis of methods for the evaluation of user expectancies can help to learn from different disciplines (e.g., computer sciences, social sciences) and to optimise the way, socio-technical systems are created and adapted to the users' needs.

Acknowledgements

We would like to thank all members of the SCL research team here at FSU Jena – there are too many to name them all in person. We would also like to extend our gratitude to our partners within the research consortium, end users, as well as research institutions and industrial developers. This project is supported by the German Federal Ministry for Economic Affairs and Energy in the IKT-II für Elektromobilität program under grant 01ME121(-33).

References

[1] C. Stolcis, J. Buchholz, and V. Schau, "Evaluation of a driver assistant client in the context of urban logistics," in ACHI 2016: The Ninth International Conference on Advances in Computer-Human Interactions,

A. L. Culén, L. Miller, I. Giannopulu, and B. Gersbeck-Schierholz, Eds. Venice, Italy: IARIA XPS Press, April 2016, pp. 235–239.

[2] European Commission, A roadmap for completing the single market for parcel delivery. Brussels: European Commission, 2013.

[3] K. Young, W. Caisheng, L. Y. Wang, and K. Strunz, Electric Vehicle Battery Technologies, 1st ed. New York: Springer Science+Business Media, 2015.

[4] Nationale Platform Elektromobilität, Ladeinfrastruktur für Elektrofahrzeuge in Deutschland. Statusbericht und Handlungsempfehlung 2015 (Recharging Infrastructure for Electric Vehicles in Germany. Status Report and Recommended Action. Nationale Platform Elektromobilität, 2015.

[5] Bundesministerium für Wirtschaft und Energie, "IKT für Elektromobilität (ICT for Electromobility) II," Internet, http://www.bmwi.de/BMWi/Redaktion/PDF/Publikationen/Technologie-und-Innovation/ikt-elektromobilitaet,property=pdf,bereich=bmwi2012,sprache=de,rwb=true.pdf, 2016.03.16, 2013.

[6] J. Nielsen, "Usability inspection methods," in Conference Companion on Human Factors in Computing Systems, ser. CHI '94. New York, NY, USA: ACM, 1994, pp. 413–414. [Online]. Available: http://doi.acm.org/10.1145/259963.260531

[7] V. Venkatesh and F. D. Davis, "A theoretical extension of the technology acceptance model: Four longitudinal field studies," Management Science, vol. 46, no. 2, 2000, pp. 186–204.

[8] V. Venkatesh, M. G. Morris, G. B. Davis, and F. D. Davis, "User acceptance of information technology: Toward a unified view," MIS Quarterly, vol. 27, no. 3, 2003, pp. 425–478.

[9] S. Arndt, Evaluierung der Akzeptanz von Fahrerassistenzsystemen. Modell zum Kaufverhalten von Endkunden. VS, Verl. für Sozialwissenschaften, 2011.

[10] J. Gläser and G. Laudel, Experteninterviews und qualitative Inhaltsanalyse. Wiesbaden: VS Verlag für Sozialwissenschaften, 2009.

[11] R. Schnell, P. B. Hill, and E. Esser, Methoden der empirischen Sozialforschung. München [u.a.]: Oldenbourg, 2008.

[12] Bundesregierung Deutschland, "IKT für Elektromobilität II," Internet, http://www.bmwi.de/BMWi/Redaktion/PDF/Publikationen/Technologie-und-Innovation/ikt-elektromobilitaet,property=pdf,bereich=bmwi2012,sprache=de,rwb=true.pdf, visited 2015-10-21, Mai 2013.

[13] U. Kuckartz, Qualitative Inhaltsanalyse. Methoden, Praxis, Computerunterstützung (Qualitative Content Analysis. Methods, Practice, Computer-assistance). Weilheim und Basel: Beltz Juventa, 2012.

[14] Dr. dresing and Pehl GmbH, f4analyse 1.0.0-rc4- Computer Assisted Qualitative Data Analysis Software (CAQDAS), Internet, https://www.audiotranskription.de/f4-analyse, 2016.03.16, Marburg.

[15] J. Prümper, "Isonorm 9241/110-s: Evaluation of software based upon international standard iso 9241, part 110 - manuscript questionnaire," Internet, http://people.f3.htw-berlin.de/Professoren/Pruemper/instrumente/ISONORM_9241_110-S_2010.pdf, 2016.03.16, Berlin, 2010.

[16] C. Schmitz and LimeSurvey Core Development Team, "Limesurvey - free open source survey tool," Internet, https://www.limesurvey.org/en/, 2016.03.16.

[17] V. Schau, S. Apel, K. Gebhardt, J. Kretzschmar, M. Mauch, and C. Stolcis, "Evaluating ict-systems for electric vehicles within simulated environments," in Proceedings for the 19th Gulf Engineering Forum Smart Solutions, Kuwait City, in press.

[18] V. Schau, S. Apel, K. Gebhardt, J. Kretzschmar, C. Stolcis, M. Mauch, and J. Buchholz, "Intelligent infrastructure for last-mile and short-distance freight transportation with electric vehicles in the domain of smart city logistic," in Proceedings of the International Conference on Vehicle Technology and Intelligent Transport Systems, April 2016, pp. 149–159.

Knowledge Graph based Recommendation Techniques for Email Remarketing

László Grad-Gyenge
TU Vienna
Vienna, Austria
laszlo.grad-gyenge@tuwien.ac.at

Hannes Werthner
TU Vienna
Vienna, Austria
hannes.werthner@tuwien.ac.at

Peter Filzmoser
TU Vienna
Vienna, Austria
peter.filzmoser@tuwien.ac.at

Abstract—**This paper presents the knowledge graph, a graph based information modelling technique. The method generalizes the concept of information sources and defines a hybridization technique at the information representation level. Depending on the amount of collaborative and content-based information available, the balance of the hybridization is also discussed. The principles of the defined calculation methods, as generalization and transitivity facilitate the paradigm of relatedness. To evaluate the efficiency of the knowledge graph, graph based recommendation calculation techniques are defined and evaluated in an email remarketing activity, a real-world recommendation scenario. The results show that the spreading activation based recommendation technique is capable to increase the performance of the remarketing task.**

Keywords–knowledge graph; recommender system; spreading activation; network science; email remarketing

I. Introduction

This paper presents the detailed results of our experiments on knowledge graph based recommendation techniques as introduced in our conference paper [1]. In this paper, our goal is to give a deeper insight into graph based methods and also to present the detailed evaluation results of our experiment.

Graph based recommender systems are a potential alternative to representation learning based recommendation techniques. Unlike the current trend of recommender systems finding latent factors in the "taste space", graph based methods focus more on distance like measures and relatedness [2] between the nodes in the knowledge graph. According to our past experiments, graph based methods have the potential to eliminate the cold start problem, to converge faster as rating estimators [3] and to act as the basis of relatedness based recommendation techniques.

The graph based information representation is general and flexible. It can act as a potential alternative to tensor based information modelling [4]. Recommendation techniques typically work with a previously and exactly defined information representation model. Compared to these methods, the knowledge base [3] models the information in a heterogeneous multigraph. The nodes of the graph are different entities playing role in the recommendation scenario. The edges of the graph are the various relations between the entities. An important aspect of our work is to model as much information as available in the knowledge base and develop methods capable to manage the heterogeneous information. Our basic philosophy is the more information we have, the higher is the possibility to avoid the cold start case.

Early recommender systems [5] can be treated as function estimators. Collaborative filtering estimates the rating values by calculating a weighted average on the existing rating values. Recommendation spreading [3] can be treated as the generalization of collaborative filtering for the graph based case. The advantage of the method is that it successfully alloys the information found in the rating values and the information found in the structure of the network. The most important feature of recommendation spreading is the faster calculation of the error on the rating estimation.

State of the art recommender systems are typically utilized in an information retrieval scenario. It means that instead of focusing on rating estimation, the task is to provide a list of recommended items to the user in question. The user rating on items relation can be generalized as the user interest on items, which relation type acts as the basis of the prominent, representation learning based recommendation learning techniques. On one hand, the application of state of the art techniques to generate rating estimation is quite atypical. On the other hand, state of the art methods usually derive the recommendations based on user preferences on items. Graph based methods have the potential to generalize the concept of information sources and to develop calculation methods based on the relatedness between the nodes instead of being constrained by the user preference based paradigm.

An important aspect of our work is that the information representation and the calculation methods are clearly separated. This methodology eliminates the unnecessary dependencies between the two tasks and also leads to a cleaner approach on the theoretical side.

On the representation side, an information representation method is defined to alloy the information sources of the traditional recommendation techniques as collaborative filtering, content-based filtering and some knowledge based cases. Our primary motivation to introduce this information representation method is to involve the content-based and knowledge based information sources in addition to the collaborative information in the cold start case. An important feature of the knowledge graph is that in a real-world application, before the production state, the graph contains only the content-based and the knowledge based information. If the recommendation calculation method is general and uses all the information available in the knowledge base, the recommendation system can be treated more content-based than collaborative. As the users start to interact with the system, the knowledge base will contain more collaborative information, the system acts more as a collaborative filtering technique. Thinking about the amount of information available in the aforementioned categories, the order of magnitude of collaborative information is typically higher than the order of magnitude of content-based information. To summarize it, working with general calculation method based on the knowledge graph, as the users interact with the system, the recommendations turn to be collaborative from content-based. In other words, based on the information representation method, the limes of the recommendation system is collaborative.

Looking at the calculation methods, graph based representation inherently provides the platform to involve novel calculation techniques to generate recommendations. In contrast to representation learning based techniques, graph based recommendation methods can be described as proximity calculation methods between the nodes of the graph. Various techniques can be involved to calculate the proximity measure. We think that a well elaborated proximity measure should incorporate also the topology of the graph and the length of the paths between the nodes. In other words, the parallel paths between two nodes should increase the value of the proximity measure. In addition, the results of network science can also be utilized, as network science provides several techniques to analyse a graph and methods to calculate the centrality of specific nodes.

Referring to our past results on the MovieLens 1M dataset [6], the knowledge graph based methods have the potential to significantly increase the coverage of the recommendation methods and also show faster convergence regarding the mean absolute error of the rating estimation [3]. Regarding top list recommendations, graph based methods show an increase in the quality regarding to precision, recall and NDCG [2]. In this paper we would like to focus on the performance of the graph based techniques on the email remarketing domain.

A state of the art application of recommender systems is web remarketing. The essence of remarketing is to present personalized offers to the user on media different to the origin of the offer. Remarketing is basically a post event activity, the users will be offered with items after their visit to the specific portal. Web remarketing is a prominent class of remarketing, where the promotion activity is to be done in on-line systems. Criteo [7], a prominent company in this field provides web based personalized offers based on the activity of a user.

In our experiment, the recommendation techniques are evaluated in the email remarketing system, PartnerMail [8]. Email remarketing is the remarketing activity utilizing newsletters as the media of the promotion task. The emails sent contain a list of promoted products, the products are selected by the evaluated recommendation methods. The personalization is based on the user activity collected in Booker [9], an electronic commerce portal selling books. The performance of spreading activation based methods, network science centrality measures and the human is compared. Our results show an increase in the performance of the newsletters regarding the click-through rates. We can also state that email based remarketing activity leads to a higher customer engagement based on the personalization, thus it delivers a business value.

This paper is organized as follows. Section II presents related work from the aspect of information representation and recommendation calculation techniques. This section also discusses hybridization techniques as an important, inherent feature of the knowledge graph. Section III presents the knowledge graph, our information representation technique. At first, short examples are provided about the information representation of the traditional methods and the hybridization technique of the knowledge graph. After that, the problem is reflected through an information rich example containing heterogeneous information sources. Then, the definition of the knowledge graph is provided. Finally, the balance of the collaborative and the content-based information is analysed from a more theoretical point of view. Section IV covers the calculation methods operating on the knowledge graph as collaborative filtering, spreading activation, recommendation spreading and the human expert. Having the methods defined, the paradigm of relatedness is discussed. Section V describes the dataset of the experiment. Section VI discusses the evaluation method. Section VII presents the results of the evaluation. Section VIII concludes the paper and defines the directions of the further research.

II. Related Work

As mentioned in Section I, the methodology of the information representation and the recommendation calculation is clearly separated in our work. Section II-A focuses on the evolution of recommendation techniques from the aspect of involved information sources. Section II-B discusses various calculation techniques operating on graphs. To emphasize the hybridization capability of the knowledge graph, Section II-C analyses various hybridization techniques of recommender systems.

A. Representation

In this section we show various information representation methods developed to model the increasing amount of information sources involved into the recommendation calculation process. Related work on this topic is organized to show the evolution of information sources foreshadowing the need of a more general information representation technique.

The information necessary to perform the traditional collaborative filtering method [10], i.e., the user preferences on the items are represented in a matrix, which is typically sparse. The rows of the matrix denote the users, the columns of the matrix denote the items. The values of the matrix represent the user preferences on items. Missing values in the matrix refer the unknown or non-obtained preference values. The user preference in this case is the user rating on the specific item. The representation of the matrix of collaborative filtering is discussed in Section III-A1.

Konstas et al. [11] work on music track recommendation utilizing a graph based recommendation technique. In order to increase the recommendation quality, Konstas et al. involve tags into the recommendation scenario. The graph based knowledge base assign a type to the nodes and the edges. The approach is based on "user", "music track" and "tag" node types and "average user play count", "user listened to", "user tagged" and "track is tagged" relation types. The knowledge graph is represented as a partitioned adjacency matrix. Each partition represents the appropriate relation type.

Contextual information is a very useful information source to enhance the quality of the recommendations. To involve the context into the recommendation process, a tensor based information representation technique is applied typically. Such approaches are conducted by, e.g., Hidasi et al. [12] and Adomavicius et al. [13]. Their representation approach is a three dimensional tensor, the dimensions of the tensor are "users", "items" and "context information". Looking at the mentioned approach, the tensor based representation technique can be treated as the clarification of the partitioned matrix based method.

Referring to homophily [14] and social confluence [15], the social network is a useful information source of recommendation techniques. The social network is typically represented in a graph, where the nodes of the graph represent the persons and the edges of the graph represent the social relationships. Kazienko et al. [16] introduce a multi-layered graph to represent the social network of the users in the recommendation scenario. Each layer of the graph contains homogeneous information, such as contact lists, tags, groups, favourites and opinions.

To examine the representation, there are examples of both the non-directed and the directed case. The application of the directed social relationships is more visible in the years of 2004-2006 in the trend of involving the trust network of Epinions [17] into the recommendation process [18], [19], [20]. To continue with the directed case, Guy et al. [21] improve the weighting scheme of collaborative filtering by deriving the weights also from the social ties. He et al. [22] combines user attribute values, item attribute values and social ties with a naïve Bayes approach. Yang et al. [23] apply Bayesian inference to social network in a distributed approach. Gu et al. [24] apply matrix factorization to predict user-event participation with the help of the social network.

The research results presented in this chapter show a trend of involvement of an increasing number of information sources. The evaluation of the methods show that additional information can significantly increase the recommendation quality. This collective finding motivated us to develop a generalized information representation method, so that additional information sources can be added to the knowledge base without the modification of the representation model. To cover the problem, a graph based information representation method has been elaborated, which is able to model the information need of the calculation methods mentioned in this section.

Recent works show a remarkable progress on the research of knowledge graph based recommendation techniques. Kouki et al. [25] define the knowledge graph as a bipartite graph of users and items allowing heterogeneous relations between the nodes of the graph. Hu et al. [26] utilize a heterogeneous social network to identify the leads. In their work, Hu et al. introduce label propagation and analyse various path configurations between the nodes of the graph. Catherine et al. [27] apply a probabilistic logic approach to the knowledge graph containing heterogeneous information. Burke et al. [28] present a heterogeneous network of information working with various two dimensional projections of the network.

Regarding to the current research on the knowledge graph, our intention is to define the representation method as clear and general. Our definition does not restrict the knowledge graph to be bipartite but assigns a type to each node and to each edge. Referring to the paradigm of relatedness as discussed in Section IV-B, by our definition, the paths between the nodes are not restricted by their type but are treated as relations in general. Our framework also provides a method to incorporate both the user and the item attributes. In addition, the defined calculation methods do not work with graph projections but are clearly graph oriented.

B. Methods

In this section, an overview of graph based recommendation calculation techniques evolved is provided. Our goal is to illustrate the potential of the graph based information representation, as there are already various calculation methods developed utilizing the information contained in the graph. At first, random walk based methods are presented. Conducting a random walk is a straightforward method to deliver recommendations utilizing reasonable computing capacities. After that, propagation based methods are discussed in the directed and also in the non-directed case. The advantage of the propagation methods compared to the random walk method is the elimination of the stochastic behaviour. The drawback of the propagation is the computation intense implementation. Then, network science related methods are presented to introduce the non-personalized recommendation methods. Finally, neural network methods are discussed to show the potential of networks consisting of non-linear calculation units.

In this paper, spreading activation based recommendation techniques are evaluated. The motivation behind is the following. In order to clearly see the performance of the graph based representation, our intention is to eliminate the stochastic behaviour. In addition, as our goal is to increase the coverage, non-directed methods are involved, as directed paths lead to a lower connectivity in the knowledge graph. Finally, spreading activation has the capability to take both the distance and the parallel paths in the graph into account.

1) Random Walk: Random walk methods treat the recommendation problem as a stochastic process on a Markov chain. To model a discrete time Markov chain with a graph based knowledge base, the states and the transition probabilities for the stochastic process are to be defined. Each node of the directed graph can be assigned to a state in the Markovian model. The transition probabilities from a specific state can be defined by normalizing the weight of each outgoing edge with the sum of the weights of the outgoing edges.

Jamali et al. [29] introduce the TrustWalker algorithm on the Epinions dataset. They define the recommender graph as the graph of the users, the edges of the graph are explicit trust statements between users. The approach is to estimate item ratings based on existing ratings of trusted or transitively trusted users. To increase the coverage of rated items, the method estimates the rating of a particular item based on the rating of similar items. The item similarity is defined with Pearson correlation. Their method is to conduct a random walk on the graph to find a trusted user. The walk is to be stopped based on a probability depending on the length of the path, the user to rate for and the item to rate. The random walk basically selects a suitable trusted user then it returns the rating of the trusted user on the item in question. If the specific item is not rated by the user, the method returns the rating of a similar item. Jamali et al. emphasize an important feature of the Trustwalker method, the ability to calculate a confidence value for the estimated rating value. They define the confidence as the variance of the rating estimation of several random walks. As a random walk is definitely a less resource exhaustive method than for example spreading activation, a straightforward method to increase its precision is to run multiple instances and return an aggregated value of the estimated ratings.

2) Trust Propagation: Trust propagation is a well researched area. Several publications appeared in this field. Guha et al [30] and Ziegler et al. [18] examine the propagation of trust and distrust. Hess et al. [31] propagate trust on a two layered recommendation graph. Golbeck [32] propagate trust on a film trust database. The idea behind trust propagation is to calculate recommendations based on trust relationships. A well known web portal in this area, Epinions [17] allows its users to rate items on the platform and explicitly express trust in other users. Trust in this case means trusting in other user's opinion, namely the rating. The basic idea behind trust propagation is to extend the direct trust relationship with a transitive method and generate the recommendations with the help of the extended trust metric. Applying graph related methods in trust calculations foreshadows the application of a more general, graph based knowledge base methods.

3) Spreading Activation: Spreading activation has been introduced by Quillian [33] and is a common method in the fields of associative networks [34], semantic networks and neural networks. The method is defined iterative, where the active nodes in the network activate their neighbouring nodes in each iteration step. The method defines a decay factor also for the node activations and for the spreading values. These decay factors has to be tuned depending on the application domain. The outcome of spreading activation is a list of graph node and activation pairs. By sorting the activated nodes on their activation in a descending order after the termination, we come to a prioritized list of the recommended items. An important property of the spreading activation algorithm is that it takes into account the topology of the paths from the source node to the recommended nodes by aggregating the spreading value of the paths in parallel.

Ziegler et al. [35] introduce the AppleSeed method on the Epinions dataset. The recommendation graph in this case is the trust network with users in its nodes and weighted trust statements in its edges. The goal of Ziegler et al. is to extend the local trust statements from neighbouring nodes to farer extent. An important feature of the AppleSeed Trust Metric is the avoidance of the dead ends. A typical problem of spreading activation methods is that nodes with zero outdegree have the opportunity to capture the spreading values by accumulation. To manage this problem, Ziegler et al. suggested backward trust propagation. When backward trust propagation is applied, a virtual edge is created from all nodes (except the source node) to the source node. The aim of these virtual edges is to trace back the activation to the source nodes. Based on the virutal edges, the dead end nodes spread their activation to the source and the accumulation of the activation can be avoided.

4) Network Science: Network science evolved methods and measures to analyse huge and complex networks [36]. Such networks are for example public transport networks, telecommunication networks, biological networks, sociological and semantic networks.

In order to measure the importance of the nodes of networks, network science developed various centrality measures. These measures represent the position or importance of a node in the network. Such measures are for example: degree centrality, closeness centrality, betweenness centrality and eigenvector centrality. Degree centrality counts the edges belonging to the node. Closeness centrality is the inverse of farness, which is the sum of the length of paths from the node to all other nodes. Betweenness centrality is the number of how many times a node lays on the shortest path between two nodes. Eigenvector centrality is proportional to the sum of the eigenvector centralities of its neighbours, it is a recursive definition and is calculated with the eigenvalue decomposition of the adjacency matrix of the network. PageRank [37], a well known measure for the nodes of large directed networks is basically a walk in the graph with random restart.

The mentioned centrality measures define a global measure for a network node. It means that the application of the standard centrality measures is not suitable for personalized recommendations. To illustrate the potential of network science methods, Fogarasi et al. define a personalized PageRank calculation method [38].

Jeong et al. [39] extend the traditional collaborative filtering method with network science measures. Their recommendation graph contains the social network of the users. Their dataset contains YouTube web page visiting data, which information is not incorporated into the network. In their approach, Jeong et al. extend the weighting scheme of the traditional collaborative filtering formula. The weights of the original formula are based on implicit similarity between the users, e.g., the Pearson correlation of the issued ratings on the common rated items. Jeong et al. modify this implicit similarity to a weighted sum of the implicit similarity and a network science centrality measure. In their experiment, they evaluate different weighting schemes and various centrality measures. Their results show that incorporating network science measures increase the precision of the recommendations, but also show that the recommendation quality becomes weak if higher weights are assigned to the network science measures. Jeong et al. also found that degree centrality based recommendation shows the highest performance. Referring to homophily [14] and social confluence [15], persons in a social network with high degree centrality have a high number of social network connections and can be treated as influencers.

In addition to the case introduced by Jeong et al., a potential application scenario of network science measures are the global recommendations. In the cold start case, when the actual recommendation technique is not capable to deliver recommendations, in order to provide items to the particular, a fallback method is necessary. The fallback method is inevitably non-personalized, it provides high coverage and a lower precision. Such non-personalized recommendation techniques are, e.g., recommending top selling items, most visited items or most mentioned items. Network science provides alternative methods to find top items in the set of recommendable items.

5) Neural Network: The common application areas of neural networks are function approximation, regression, time series prediction, classification novelty and anomaly detection. Neural networks are the general and flexible tools of artificial intelligence. According to Haykin [40], neural networks can be represented with directed graphs, which makes neural networks applicable in the field of graph based recommender systems. A possible application represents the nodes of the graph with artificial neurons and the edges of the graph with the synapses. This representation assumes that the knowledge base of the recommender system is a directed graph.

a) Calculations: The application of artificial neural networks is based on the calculation of the activations of the neurons. The activations are calculated with the network function. A typical network function is a simplified model of how natural neurons work. The network function basically calculates the activation of one neuron based on the neurons on its input. It can be calculated by applying the activation function to the weighted sum of the inputs of a neuron. To make calculations more general a bias is also added to the weighted sum. The network function is defined in Equation (1).

$$s_i(x) = \varphi(\sum_j w_{ij} s_j(x) + b_i) \quad (1)$$

where $s_i(x)$ denotes the network function of neuron i, w_{ij} denotes the weight of neuron j activating neuron i, b_i denotes the bias of neuron i and φ denotes the activation function, which in most cases is a nonlinear function.

The calculation of the value of the network function is an iterative process. In the initial step, depending on the application, certain neurons are activated. The iteration steps can be calculated either synchronously or asynchronously. The synchronous method updates the activation of all the neurons at once. The asynchronous method works with a predefined order or based on random selection. The iterative process is to be stopped after a certain limit of steps is reached or the change of the activations is under a specific threshold value.

b) Architecture, Hidden Nodes: A neural network consists of several information processing units, of the artificial neurons. These units are simple and in most cases nonlinear. To make these information processing units able to develop more sophisticated functions or transformations, they are combined into different architectures as also described by Bengio [41]. Several architectures of artificial neural networks contain hidden nodes typically organized in hidden layers, e.g., multi-layer feed-forward networks [42]. The application of hidden nodes is to develop a more suitable mapping between input and output nodes. In the case of a representation learning problem, the role of the hidden nodes is feature extraction.

c) Training: The most powerful feature of artificial neural networks is the ability to learn. Artificial neural networks achieve this task by training the synapse weights between the neurons of the neural network. There are several methods to train a neural network. These methods can be classified into three main categories, as supervised learning, unsupervised learning and reinforcement learning.

Supervised learning systems are trained based on sample input and the corresponding output values, which in the case of recommender systems could mean user-item pairs, e.g., the expressed explicit or implicit interest by the user on the specific item.

Unsupervised learning in artificial neural networks can be applied to develop internal representations of sample data without any feedback to the system. Although recommender systems are based on user interaction and we can take the benefit of user feedback data to train a neural network based recommender system, there are existing approaches to involve unsupervised learning into the training process of neural network based recommender systems. Unsupervised learning systems can also be applied to develop internal or sparse representation and can be used as data compression method as a part of another recommender system architecture.

Reinforcement learning methods are applied in scenarios, where the feedback is present after a certain operation steps. For reinforcement learning methods there is no immediate input-output training data available. When a feedback is specified to a reinforcement learning system, it adjusts its internal representation according to the feedback value. An important feature of reinforcement learning methods is that the outcome of the operation is based on decisions in the past. The training should affect also those components, which were responsible for past decisions.

A prominent example of supervised learning is the error back-propagation [43]. Error back-propagation is a common training technique of multi-layered neural networks. Its mechanism is to adjust the synapse weights based on the error in the output of the network. Error is propagated back in the layers of the network by the influence of the neurons on the final error.

An example of training synapse weights in the case of unsupervised learning is Hebbian learning. Hebbian learning [44] is based on the Hebbian theory in neuroscience. In a nutshell, the rule can be explained as the synaptic binding increases between two neurons if the neurons are activated together. Equation (2) presents the formula of the Hebbian learning.

$$\Delta w_{ij} = F(y_i, x_j) \quad (2)$$

where Δw_{ij} is the change of weight of neuron j activating neuron i, y_i is the postsynaptic signal of neuron i, x_j is the presynaptic signal of neuron j and F is the learning function, e.g., $F(x, y) = \eta(xy)$.

d) Hopfield Network: Originally, Hopfield networks [45] are intended to be used as associative memory and noisy pattern recognition methods. Hopfield networks are basically recurrent artificial neural networks. The Hopfield network is not a feed-forward and is not a layered neural network. The two important properties of Hopfield networks are: the synaptic weights are symmetric ($w_{ij} = w_{ji}, \forall i, j$) and no unit has connection with itself ($w_{ii} = 0, \forall i$), where w_{ij} denotes the synaptic influence of the neuron j to the input of neuron i. Equation (3) presents the network function applied in Hopfield networks.

$$s_i^{(H)}(x) = \begin{cases} 1 & : \sum_j w_{ij} s_j(x) \geq \theta_i \\ -1 & : \sum_j w_{ij} s_j(x) < \theta_i \end{cases} \quad (3)$$

where $s_i(x)$ is value of the network function of neuron i, w_{ij} is the weight of neuron j activating neuron i and θ_i.

A well known problem of Hopfield networks can be derived from its iterative training method. It is not guaranteed that Hopfield networks converge to the global optima.

To see a concrete example, Huang et al. [46] define a two layer artificial neural network. A layer is defined for the customers and a layer is defined for the items. The relations between the customers are calculated by demography similarity, the relations between the items are calculated by content similarity, the relations between the layers are defined by the purchase events. Huang et al. calculate the recommendations by applying the Hopfield Net algorithm. In their experiment, the network is not trained, the network is used only for calculation. Their evaluation results show increased recommendation quality.

e) Boltzmann Machine: A Boltzmann machine [47] is a stochastic recurrent neural network. Boltzmann machines consist of stochastic neurons. The neurons can be in either in the state 1 or 0. The Boltzmann machine defines symmetric synaptic connections between its neurons. The neurons of a Boltzmann machine are divided into two classes, as visible and hidden neurons. The visible neurons receive the training input, the hidden neurons develop the internal representation based on the training samples. The task of the hidden neurons is to explain the underlying constraints of the visible neurons. Boltzmann Machines are trained with the gradient descent method.

Salakhutdinov et al. [48] utilize the Restricted Boltzmann machine to generate recommendations. Salakhutdinov et al. create a separate Boltzmann machine for each user. The visible nodes represent recommendable items, the hidden nodes represent features developed by the Boltzmann machine. Salakhutdinov et al. apply a conditional multinomial distribution in their a pivot model, and enhance the pivot model by modelling the distribution of the hidden units with Gaussian distribution and finally introduce the Conditional Restricted Boltzmann Machine to incorporate additional information into their model. In the latter case, the model can be treated as a multilayer stochastic neural network. Salakhutdinov et al. define the calculation of recommendations as a prediction on a probabilistic graph model. To generate a prediction, they join all Restricted Boltzmann Machines to generate the estimation for each rating value. By joining the restricted Boltzmann machines developed on a per user basis, Salakhutdinov come to a large stochastic neural network, where the joint distributions are trained on an individual level. The final rating value is generated by calculating an estimated value of the estimated distribution on rating values. Referring to their results, Salakhutdinov et al. managed to reach an error rate 6% better than the score of Netflix's own system.

C. Hybridization

The basic motivation behind hybridization techniques is to alloy different recommendation methods in order to eliminate their drawbacks and to combine their strengths. A comprehensive study about various hybridization techniques is provided by Burke et al. [49]. In their work, Burke et al. define the classic hybridization techniques as weighted, switching, mixed, feature combination, cascade, feature augmentation and meta-level hybridization. Weighted hybridization combines the preference estimations of various techniques to produce recommendations. A state of the art example of the weighted hybridization is presented by Dooms et al. [50]. Dooms et al. claim that their recommender system is also tested against real-world requirements. Switching hybridization switches between the various methods based on the context. Mixed hybridization present the combination of recommendation lists of multiple methods to the user. Feature combination merges the features found in different datasets for a particular method. Cascading hybridization follows a sequential architecture of recommendation methods, where the output of a technique acts as the input of the next technique in the pipeline. Feature augmentation based hybridization is similar to the cascade method but the output of the preceding method are features and not recommendations. In the case of the meta-level hybridization, the trained model is shared between the methods.

To summarize the classic recommendation techniques, typically, the hybridization is conducted at the calculation level. The information shared between the methods are the recommendations themselves or the trained model of the particular method. The exception is the feature combination hybridization, where the information sources are alloyed at the information representation level. This is the point where our work is related to the results of Burke et al. Our goal is to provide a general information representation technique to alloy heterogeneous information sources, thus to define the hybridization at the information representation level. This is the reason why the methods operating on the alloyed information sources are inherently hybrid methods.

The knowledge graph is capable to incorporate heterogeneous information sources and to act as the background of hybridization at the representation level. Kouki et al. [25] utilize the knowledge graph to combine multiple different sources into a single unified model. Burke et al. [28] define a heterogeneous graph calculating the recommendations with the help of two dimensional projections of the graph. In contrast to the representation method of Kouki et al., we provide a more general definition of the knowledge graph and examine the performance of the calculation methods in this more general environment. Referring to the results of Burke et al., the information is modelled in a heterogeneous knowledge graph but in our case, the recommendation methods operate clearly on the graph.

III. Representation

This section discusses the information representation method. Our intention is to define a modelling technique, which (i) is general, (ii) is capable to model heterogeneous information sources, (iii) defines a hybridization at the representation level and (iv) has the potential to eliminate the cold start problem.

By definition, the generalization of the information representation should cover the major classic recommendation classes as collaborative filtering, content-based filtering and knowledge based approaches. The question is how the combination of the information sources is modelled in the knowledge graph. Section III-A covers this topic by discussing each classic case and also how the information representation technique alloys the different knowledge representation approaches.

An important consequence of working with generalized representation is the increase in the amount of information to be processed by the calculation methods. Referring to Section II-A, based on the experiments in the past, additional information sources typically increase the recommendation quality. Looking at the problem from the opposite point of view, the more information sources are modelled, the less the calculation methods are constrained by the lack of information. Based on an information rich knowledge base, the calculation methods have the possibility to select the useful information sources and avoid the misleading ones. Following this strategy, our intention is to represent as much information as possible, in order not to constrain the recommendation methods in achieving high coverage.

The increase in the amount of information managed by the knowledge graph also leads to a possible decrease in the number of cold start cases. Graph based calculation methods are indirectly or directly based on the existence of a path or paths between the user and the item in question. Increasing the amount of information sources leads to a more dense graph meaning a higher probability of the existence of a path between two specific nodes.

Generalizing the information sources means operating with heterogeneous information. In the beginning of our research [51] the question has been posed if is it even possible to deliver recommendations based on heterogeneous information sources. Our past results [3], [1] prove that combining heterogeneous information sources leads to an increase in the recommendation quality, as the error rate converges faster, the coverage is higher and top list recommendations are more relevant to the user than in the case of the benchmark methods.

A. Classic Methods & Hybridization

A widely known categorization of recommender systems also described by Jannach et al. [52] introduces three main categories of recommender systems: collaborative filtering, content-based filtering and knowledge-based methods, which categorization we refer to as the classic methods. Jannach et al. also describe various hybridization techniques. These techniques combine different recommendation methods to raise the efficiency of the individual methods. As the main advantage of the graph based representation is the capability to model various information representation scenarios, in order to demonstrate its potential, in this section we show how the information source of classic recommendation cases are to be represented in a graph and also provide an example of alloying the discussed representation cases.

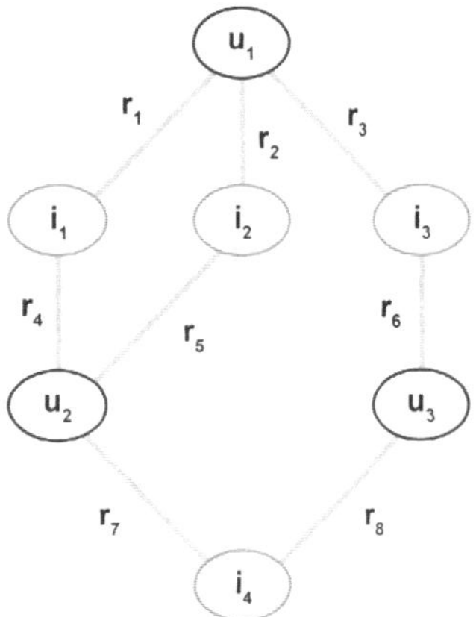

Figure 1. Collaborative Filtering Network

1) Collaborative Filtering: The idea behind collaborative filtering is to find people similar to the user the recommendations are generated for. The similarity is based on the rating values based on the commonly rated items. Having the similar users found, the next step is to calculate a rating estimation for the items rated only by the similar users but not rated by the user in question. The rating is a weighted average of the known rating values issued by the similar users. The weights are the similarities. An important property of collaborative filtering is that the method works with one type of relation between the entities, the rating relation. Despite its simplicity, collaborative filtering is proven to show high performance compared to other recommendation techniques. The weakness of the method is the information sparse case, when the knowledge base does not contain a sufficient number of user interactions to calculate the recommendations from.

Figure 1 presents a sample scenario of the graph based representation of the information necessary to produce recommendations utilizing the collaborative filtering technique. The graph contains users and items in its nodes and ratings in its relations. The nodes denoted with u represent the users. The nodes denoted with i represent the items. The relations denoted with r represent the ratings of the specific user on the specific rating.

In the sample scenario we would like to find recommended items for u_1. In our case u_1 expressed interest on i_1, i_2 and i_3. In the graph based case, the similar taste is represented in the graph by expressed interest on the same items. As u_1 is interested in i_1 and i_2 and u_2 is also interested in i_1 and i_2, the users can be treated similar. The degree of the similarity depends on the rating values assigned to r_1, r_2, r_4 and r_5. Similarly, u_1 is interested in i_3, u_3 is also interested in i_3, the users can also be treated similar. The degree of similarity in this case depends on the value assigned to r_3 and r_6. To calculate the rating estimation for u_1 on i_4, the r_7 and the r_8 is to be averaged. The weights are determined by the degree of similarity.

In the graph based case, this relation does not necessarily have to be a rating relation. In our research, we work with the more general concept of user interest, which covers, e.g., a purchase event, a rating event or a clicked on event. The concrete type of interest depends on the application domain.

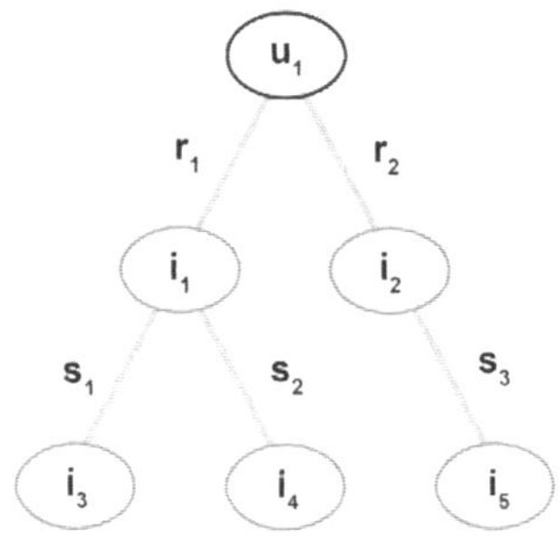

Figure 2. Content-based Filtering Network

2) Content-based Filtering: A general content-based filtering method operates with two types of relationships. In the first step, content-based filtering finds the items the particular user already expressed interest in. Then, in the second step, the methods recommends items, which are similar to the already known items. To accomplish this task, content-based filtering needs a similarity or distance measure between the items.

To simplify the explanation, the interest in our example is concreted as the user rating relation. Similarly to the collaborative filtering case, Figure 2 shows a sample scenario of a content-based filtering recommendation case. The graph contains users and items in its nodes and ratings and similarities in its relations. The nodes denoted with u represent the users. The nodes denoted with i represent the items. The relations denoted with r represent the ratings of the specific user on the specific item. The relations denoted with s represent the similarity of the items the relation starts and ends at.

To recommend items for u_1, the items the user already expressed interest in can be found by following the rating relations r_1 and r_2 and come to items i_1 and i_2. The similar items are to be found by the relations s_1, s_2 and s_3. Finally, the method recommends items i_1, i_2 and i_3. The preference order of the recommended items depends on the concrete rating and similarity values.

Looking at the scenario above, in order to generate recommendations, content-based filtering requires both user interaction and information about the items to recommend. Comparing content-based filtering to collaborative filtering, the latter method requires less user interaction in order to be able to deliver recommendations.

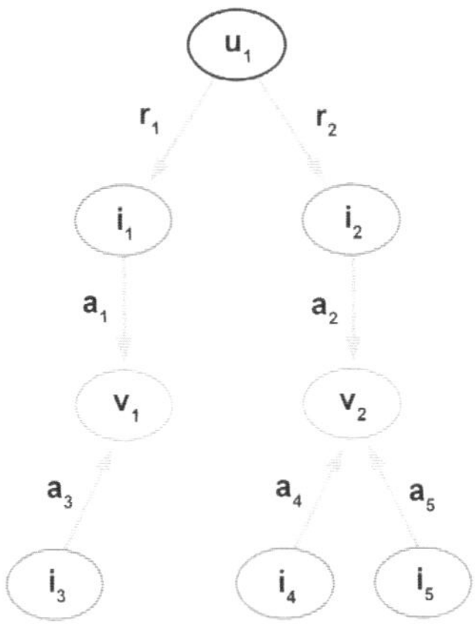

Figure 3. Knowledge-based Network

3) Knowledge-based Recommendation: The applications of quantitative decision support [53], reasoning [54] and decision tree [55] can also be treated as knowledge-based recommendation techniques. In order to conduct knowledge-based recommendation methods, available knowledge on the application domain should be present.

The application of knowledge-based techniques typically requires the users to specify their interest via interaction in order to avoid the cold-start problem. Neidhardt et al [56] requires the users to specify their travel destination interests by selecting multiple pictures representing the factors of travel destination representation. These methods typically also involve a user interface solution to acquire the required information. An illustrative example of user interaction is the constraint based recommendation [57], e.g., the approach of Felfernig et al. [58]. Regarding its methods, knowledge-based recommendation is a diverse and heterogeneous area. Although graphs are suitable to represent decision tree and rule based system based recommendation cases, we do not cover this direction. In our work we focus on representing user attributes, item attributes and domain knowledge.

Figure 3 illustrates a sample scenario of a knowledge-based recommendation method. The graph contains nodes representing users, items and attribute values. The node denoted with u represent the user. The nodes denoted with i represent the items. The nodes denoted with v represent the attribute values. Our representation technique assigns a node to each attribute value. We refer to these nodes as attribute nodes. Attribute value nodes represent the concrete values of attribute nodes. For example, in order to represent cloth sizes, the knowledge base should contain a node for size "S", "M" and "L", respectively. The relations denoted with r represent the ratings of the specific user on the specific item. The relations denoted with a represent that the specific item has a the specific attribute value.

In the sample scenario we would like to find recommended items for u_1. As the figure shows, u_1 expressed interest in i_1 and i_2. Items i_1 and i_3 share the attribute value v_1. Items i_2, i_4 and i_5 share the attribute value v_2. The preference order of the recommended items depends on the concrete rating values and also on the calculation method whether it takes into consideration the number of outgoing edges of attribute nodes.

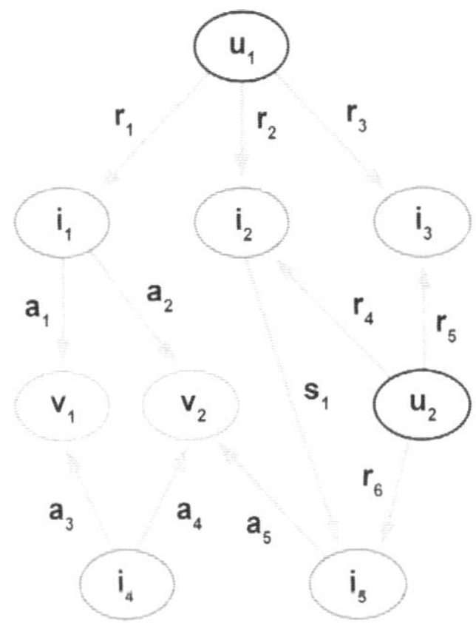

Figure 4. Hybrid Network

4) Hybridization: The primary goal of the hybridization techniques is to combine different recommendation methods to achieve better performance and to avoid the pitfalls, e.g., the cold-start effect. To accomplish this task, various hybridization techniques were evolved in the past decades of recommender systems research. To mention some techniques, the scoring of the source engines can be combined by for example weighting, switching or mixing. More advanced techniques are feature combination, cascading, feature augmentation or meta-level hybridization [49]. In our research, we work with a hybridization technique, which incorporates the existing information at the information representation level. We assume that more general calculation methods can be developed by moving the hybridization technique to the information representation level.

Figure 4 presents a sample network representing heterogeneous information. In this example we show how to merge the information types presented in the previous 3 sections. The graph contains nodes representing users, items and attribute values. The nodes denoted with u represent the users. The nodes denoted with i represent the items. The nodes denoted with v represent the attribute values. The edges denoted with r represent the ratings of the specific user on the specific item. The edges denoted with a represent that the specific item has a the specific attribute value. The edges denoted with s represent the similarity of the items the relation starts and ends at.

In the example, we would like to recommend items for u_1. The user expressed interest in items i_1, i_2 and i_3. Items i_1 and i_4 share the attribute values v_1 and v_2. Items i_1 and i_5 share the attribute value v_2. Users u_1 and u_2 share their interest on items i_2 and i_3. The similarity of i_2 and i_5 is represented with s_1.

The paths between u_1 and i_4 (r_1, a_1, a_3 and r_1, a_2, a_4) represent a knowledge-based recommendation case. The paths between u_1 and i_5 are more heterogeneous. The path r_1, a_2, a_5 represents a knowledge-based case. The path r_2, s_1 represents a content-based case. The paths r_2, r_4, r_6 and r_3, r_5, r_6 represent two collaborative filtering cases. The example shows a recommendation scenario based on heterogeneous information. Moreover, the graph incorporates the information types necessary to conduct classic recommendation techniques.

B. An Information Rich Example

The previous section covered the information sources of the classic methods. In this section we would like to present an imaginary scenario, the recommendation case of perfumes. The example presents a more complex case illustrating the possibilities of the graph based representation.

Due to personal reasons, Eve wants to try a new perfume in order to replace her current one, Orienta. She already did a research. The two possible candidates are Pinky and Fracca. Asking her boyfriend, Peter, he recommends Pinky. She also asks her friend, Irene but she has no experience with the mentioned fragrances. To help Eve, Irene asks her friends, Petra and Sarah. Petra recommends Pinky. Sarah prefers Fracca. As Eve wants to make a substantial decision, she further analyses the products to find out that Fracca is produced in Paris and Orienta is produced in Angers. To generalize it, these perfumes are produced in France. In addition to other components, Orienta contains Musk and Amber. Eve prefers Musk to Amber. Musk can also be found in Pinky and Amber can also be found in Fracca. [51]

Figure 5 visualizes the perfume scenario. The recommendation case contains various types of information. The dark blue edges represent the social network of the example. The social relationships can also be detailed, as the "in relation" and "friends" relation types show. The persons involved are Eve, Peter, Irene, Petra and Sarah. Referring to social influence, the relations between Eve and Irene and then Irene and Petra illustrate the transitivity of the social relations. Relations of type "like" and "dislike" illustrate the user-item interactions, which is an example of the collaborative case. The relations of type "component of", "produced in" and "located in" stand for the example of knowledge based recommendations. The "ARM" type stands for the association rule mining, illustrating that aggregated information can also be involved into the recommendation process. To conclude it, the example presents a combination of information sources of social networks, collaborative methods, knowledge-base methods and association rule mining.

C. Definition

Based on the issues discussed in the previous sections, this section presents the definition of the information representation method, as we refer to it, the knowledge graph. Depending on the application scenario, the definition is provided for both the directed and the undirected case. The knowledge graph is a labelled, weighted, restricted multi-graph.

1) The Directed Case: Equation (4) presents the definition of the directed knowledge graph.

$$\mathcal{K}_d = (T_n, T_e, N, E_d, t_n, t_{e_d}, r_{e_d}), \quad (4)$$

where N denotes the set of nodes existing in the graph. $E_d \subseteq \{(u, v)|u \in N \wedge v \in N \wedge u \neq v\}$ denotes the set of directed edges between the nodes. T_n denotes the set of node types. T_e denotes the set of edge types. The function $t_n \subset N \times T_n$ assigns a node type to each node. The function $t_{e_d} \subset E_d \times T_e$ assigns an edge type to each edge. The partial function $r_{e_d} \subset E_d \times \mathbb{R}$ assigns a rating value to some of the edges.

Equation (5) introduces the set of directed edges of type rating.

$$E_{d,\texttt{Rating}} = \{e \in E_d | t_{e_d}(e) = \texttt{Rating}\} \quad (5)$$

2) The Undirected Case: Equation (6) presents the definition of the undirected knowledge graph.

$$\mathcal{K}_u = (T_n, T_e, N, E_u, t_n, t_{e_u}, r_{e_u}), \quad (6)$$

where $E_u \subseteq \{\{u, v\}|u \in N \wedge v \in N \wedge u \neq v\}$ denotes the set of undirected edges between the nodes. The function $t_{e_u} \subset E_u \times T_e$ assigns an edge type to each edge. The partial function $r_{e_u} \subset E_u \times \mathbb{R}$ assigns a rating value to some of the edges.

Equation (7) introduces the set of directed edges of type rating.

$$E_{u,\texttt{Rating}} = \{e \in E_u | t_{e_u}(e) = \texttt{Rating}\} \quad (7)$$

3) Further Definitions: Equation (8) introduces the set of nodes of type `Person`. Equation (9) introduces the set of nodes of type `Item`.

$$N_{Person} = \{n \in N | t_n(n) = \texttt{Person}\} \quad (8)$$

$$N_{Item} = \{n \in N | t_n(n) = \texttt{Item}\} \quad (9)$$

At the moment, type assignments do not influence the final recommendation result and are introduced for completeness and further research.

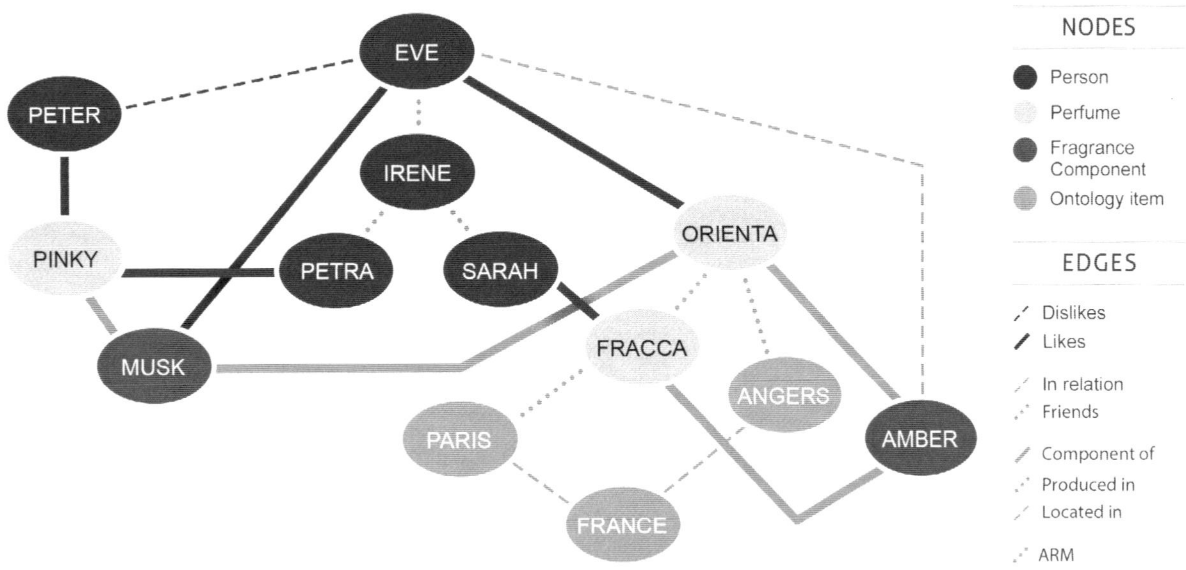

Figure 5. A Heterogeneous Recommendation Scenario

D. The Balance of the Hybridization

To summarize the previous sections, the knowledge graph is capable to represent the information necessary to conduct both collaborative filtering, content-based filtering and knowledge based recommendation. The hybridization of the information sources is conducted at the representation level.

Looking at the origin of the information, the information sources can be classified as static and user generated. Static information is defined as the content-based and the knowledge based information. This information is typically supplied by knowledge workers of the software system the recommender system is attached to. The user generated information is described as the information derived from the interaction of the users with the software system (in most cases the items).

TABLE I. Count of graph edges by type in the MovieLens dataset

Edge type	Count
PersonAgeCategory	6 040
PersonGender	6 040
PersonOccupation	6 040
PersonZipCodeRegion	6 040
ItemGenre	6 408
ItemYearOfPublishing	3 883
ItemRating	1 000 209

To illustrate the amount of information the calculation methods operate on, Table I presents the amount of edges by edge type in the MovieLens 1M dataset [6] represented in the knowledge graph as described in one of our previous papers [3]. The total number of static edges is 34 451. The total number of user generated edges is 1 000 209. The example shows that the magnitude of the amount of the user generated edges is significantly higher than the magnitude of the amount of the static edges, which case is typical in the case of real-world applications.

Referring to one of our principles, a properly defined calculation method should treat the information sources as general. The method should not distinguish the information source types at the algorithmic level. If the calculation method meets this condition, the behaviour of the method depends on the magnitude of the amount of information found in the knowledge graph. In the information sparse case, when the knowledge graph is sparse on user generated information and relatively rich on static information, the calculation method tends to be more content-based or knowledge-based. As the users start to interact with the system, the user generated content will be emphasized and the calculation methods will behave more like the collaborative methods.

The main advantage of the knowledge graph can be described from this aspect. If there is not enough user generated information available, the methods automatically focus on the static information. In the case of a vast of user interaction in the graph, the behaviour of the methods become more collaborative like.

IV. Methods

This section provides definition of the methods in the knowledge graph based case. The experiments conducted are organized to evaluate the spreading activation, network science based methods and the performance of the human expert. The methods collaborative filtering and recommendation spreading are also covered, in order to illustrate the paradigm of relatedness [2]. Some methods deliver personalized recommendations, some methods are non-personalized. The involvement of non-personalized methods is discussed in Section VI.

A. Definitions

1) Collaborative Filtering: Figure 6 illustrates the collaborative filtering method [59] in the graph based case.

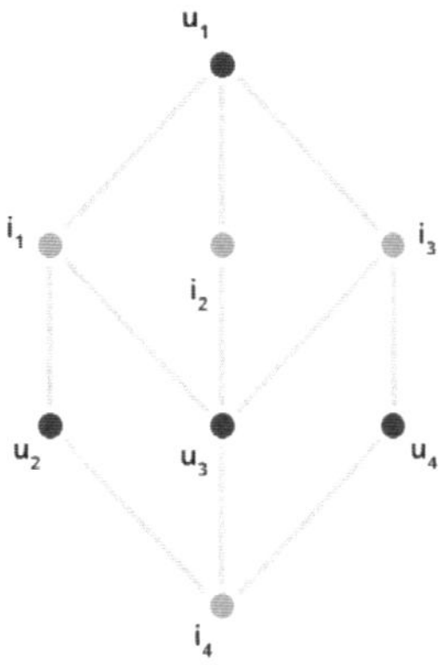

Figure 6. Collaborative Filtering

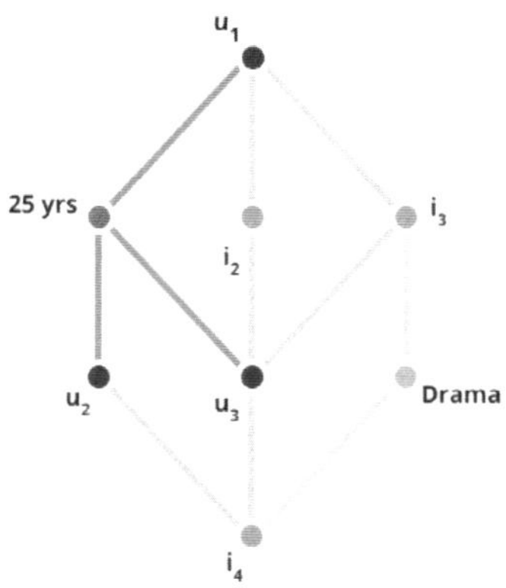

Figure 7. Spreading Activation

The graph contains users and items. Nodes denoted with u represent the users. Nodes denoted with i represent the items. Edges represent the user ratings on the items. As collaborative filtering derives its calculations based on rating values, only the edges of type `Rating` are necessary to calculate the rating estimation. These edges are denoted with grey colour.

In the graph based case, collaborative filtering can be calculated in two phases. In the first phase, the users having a common rated item with the user in question should be selected. In the second phase, the rating estimations are to be calculated for the items rated by the selected users but not by the user in question.

Equation (10) provides the definition of the rating estimation formula of the collaborative filtering method in the case of the undirected knowledge graph, $\mathcal{K}_u$. The rating estimation is provided for user u on item i.

$$\hat{r}_{u,i} = \bar{r}_u + \frac{\sum_{e \in E_{u,\mathtt{Rating}}, \{v,i\}=e, u \neq v} (r(e) - \bar{r_v}) s_{u,v}}{\sum_{e \in E_{u,\mathtt{Rating}}, \{v,i\}=e, u \neq v} s_{u,v}}, \quad (10)$$

where $\hat{r}_{u,i}$ denotes the estimated rating value for user $u, u \in N_{\mathtt{Person}}$ on item $i, i \in N_{\mathtt{Item}}$. $\bar{r}_u$ denotes the average of the already issued ratings by user u, $u \in N_{\mathtt{Person}}$. $s_{u,v}$ denotes the similarity between user u and v, $u \in N_{\mathtt{Person}}$, $v \in N_{\mathtt{Person}}$ and is defined as the Pearson similarity of the issued ratings by the users on the common rated items.

To summarize it, collaborative filtering is a rating estimation method. Its essence is to calculate a weighted average of the known rating values, where the weight of a specific rating is defined as the similarity of the issuer of the rating to the user in question. Another important feature of the collaborative filtering method is that it averages the rating values after subtracting the average of the ratings issued by the user from each rating value.

2) Spreading Activation: Figure 7 illustrates the spreading activation method [33]. The example graph contains users, user attributes, items and item attributes. Nodes denoted with u represent the users. Nodes denoted with i represent the items. The node with caption "25 yrs" illustrates a concrete user attribute value. The node with caption "Drama" illustrates a concrete item attribute value. Edges of colour gray represent the user ratings on the items. Edges of colour red represent that the specific user has the specific user attribute value. Edges of colour yellow represent that the specific item has the specific item attribute value. In contrast to collaborative filtering, spreading activation utilizes all edges in the knowledge graph regardless of their respective type.

As already mentioned in Section II-B3, spreading activation operates on a graph. To calculate recommendations with the method on the undirected knowledge graph ($\mathcal{K}_u$), an activation value is calculated for the nodes of the graph. Equation (11) defines the activation score function.

$$a_{(k)} \subset N \times \mathbf{R}, \quad (11)$$

where k denotes the iteration step.

In the initial step of the calculation, the activation of the node representing the user the recommendations are to be generated for is set to 1. The activation of all the other nodes is set to 0 as described in Equation (12).

$$a_{(0)}(n) = \begin{cases} 1 & : n = n_s \\ 0 & : n \neq n_s \end{cases} \quad (12)$$

where n_s denotes the node represents the user to generate the recommendations for. This node is to be referred as the source node.

Spreading activation is an iterative method. In each iteration step, a part of the activation is kept at the node, and another part of the activation is propagated to its neighbours. The former amount is determined by the `activation relax` (r_a) parameter. The latter amount is determined by the `spreading relax` (r_s) parameter. The propagated activation is divided among the neighbour nodes equally. Equation (13) defines the propagation of the activation.

$$a_{(k+1)}(n) = r_a a_{(k)}(n) + r_s \sum_{m \in M_n} \frac{a_{(k)}(m)}{z_m}, \quad (13)$$

where k denotes the iteration step, $k > 0$. M_n denotes the neighbour nodes of n, $M_n = \{m | \{m, n\} \in E_u\}$. z_m denotes the count of neighbours of m, $z_m = |\{p | \{m, p\} \in E_u\}|$.

The termination criteria is step based. If the iteration reaches the specified `step limit` (c), the propagation stops.

To summarize it, spreading activation basically calculates a proximity value in the graph. As the activation is relaxed with the length of the path between two nodes, the activation value of a node depends on its distance from the source node. As the parallel paths between two nodes result in the accumulation of the activation spreading to the node, spreading activation takes the structure of the graph also into consideration.

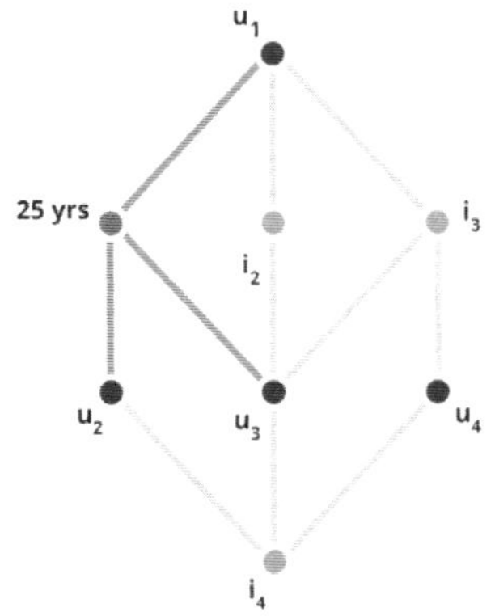

Figure 8. Recommendation Spreading

3) Recommendation Spreading: Figure 8 illustrates the recommendation spreading method introduced by Grad-Gyenge et al. [3]. The example graph contains users, user attributes and items. Nodes denoted with u represent the users. Nodes denoted with i represent the items. The node with caption "25 yrs" illustrates a concrete user attribute value. Edges of colour gray represent the user ratings on the items. Edges of colour red represent that the specific user has the specific user attribute value. In contrast to spreading activation, recommendation spreading utilizes all types of edges in the knowledge graph with one constraint. The last edge of the path leading to the recommended item should have the type `Rating`.

Recommendation spreading operates on the undirected knowledge graph ($\mathcal{K}_u$). The method is basically the generalization of the collaborative filtering for the graph based case. The method modifies the classic collaborative filtering formula by defining the weights of the averaged rating values based on the structure of the graph. Recommendation spreading is a spreading activation based method running the same iteration to propagate the activation values. During the iteration, the activation flown through each edge is summarized. Equation (14) defines the weights of the rating values.

$$A_e = \sum_{i \in [0, c-1], n \in e, n \in N_{\texttt{Person}}} r_s \frac{a_{(i)}(n)}{z_n}, \tag{14}$$

where e denotes the edge to summarize the flown through activations for, $e \in E_{u,\texttt{Rating}}$.

To estimate the rating values, recommendation spreading uses the sum of the flown through activations as the weight of the rating value of the corresponding edge. Equation (15) provides the formula of recommendation spreading.

$$\hat{r}_{u,i} = \bar{r}_u + \frac{\sum_{e \in E_{u,\texttt{Rating}}, \{v,i\}=e, u \neq v} (r(e) - \bar{r_v}) A_e}{\sum_{e \in E_{u,\texttt{Rating}}, \{v,i\}=e, u \neq v} A_e}. \tag{15}$$

4) Network Science: In the cold-start case, when personalized recommendation is not possible due to the lack of information about the user in question, non-personalized recommendation is necessary. Non-personalized recommendation can be conducted e.g, by presenting top selling or hand-picked items. Network science centrality measures provide a possible alternative to the mentioned methods.

Network science [36] developed several centrality measures to assign a number to the nodes of a graph representing the importance of each node based on its position. In our experiments, degree centrality, closeness centrality, betweenness centrality and eigenvector centrality based recommendations are analysed. The mentioned measures are introduced in Section II-B4.

To calculate non-personalized recommendations, the involved network science centrality measures are calculated on the directed knowledge graph ($\mathcal{K}_d$). The relevance order of the nodes is determined by the centrality score of the nodes.

5) Human Expert: Human expert based recommendations are also involved in the experiment, to act as the baseline method. As human expert based personalization is not feasible due to capacity and financial constraints, the method is managed as non-personalized. As described in Section VI, the evaluation of the methods is organized into campaigns. The human expert provided a list of recommended items, thus the same list of items is offered to all users in the same campaign. The recommended items are selected based on publicly available best seller lists, domain knowledge and market experience.

B. The Paradigm of Relatedness

Looking at Figure 6, Figure 8 and Figure 7, collaborative filtering, recommendation spreading and spreading activation can be compared from the aspect of constraints on the paths between the nodes representing the entities of the recommendation scenario. To illustrate the constraints on the paths, the edges of different types are denoted with different colours.

Collaborative filtering essentially operates only with relations of type `Rating`. In the case of recommendation spreading, the edges in the path between the users and the items are less constrained. There is no constraint on the type of the edges except for the last edge of the path, which edge has to be the type of `Rating`. Spreading activation defines no constraint on the type of the edges in the paths.

The reason behind the existence of these constraints can be found in the different purpose of the methods. The goal of collaborative filtering and recommendation spreading is to generate rating estimations. To generalize the concept "user ratings", we introduce the concept "user interest". User interest can be any explicit or implicit user interaction on the items. Looking at representation learning (e.g., SVD) based methods, these methods find the latent factors of the user interest space. In other words, these methods are based on and are constrained by the paradigm of user interest.

The goal of spreading activation is to assign preference scores to the nodes. To achieve this task, spreading activation operates on the generalized knowledge base, where different types of relations are represented at the same generalization level. Looking at the entities of the recommendation scenario represented as the nodes of the graph, we introduce the concept of relatedness, the relatedness of the entities of the recommendation scenario. The concept of relatedness incorporates two important features, the generalization and the transitivity. The generalization has already been discussed. To illustrate the transitivity of the relatedness with concrete examples, an item can be recommended because it is similar to an already bought item or because the friend of the user likes it. As spreading activation is general and is also transitive regarding its calculations, it is based on the paradigm of relatedness. To provide further explanation, Grad-Gyenge et al. [2] demonstrate the paradigm of relatedness on the MovieLens dataset [6].

V. Dataset

During the evaluation period, the portal offered 117 367 books to its visitors. The electronic commerce system is based on a relational database, thus its data is to be transferred and transformed into the knowledge graph. To fulfil this task, the portal is integrated with PartnerMail via its web based API. The PartnerMail API provides methods to manage the knowledge graph by inserting, updating and deleting the nodes and the relations of the graph. Based on the integration, the user data, item data and user interactions are transferred to the knowledge graph in real-time.

The database of Booker [9] contains users, books, user attributes, book attribues, user interactions and the book category tree. The attributes of the users are hometown and birth year. These attributes are specified by the user and are not mandatory fields. Book attributes are author, publisher, year of publishing, number of pages and price. These attributes are specified by the distributor of the books and are typically specified. The books are organized into a tree-like category structure by the knowledge workers of the portal. The portal also contains a wish-list feature. With the help of the wish-list, users can maintain a list of books intending to buy.

To model the available information in the knowledge graph, each user and each item is represented with a node. As also discussed in Section III-A2, a node is created for each attribute value. The nodes representing the users and the items are connected to these nodes representing attribute values with an edge of the appropriate type. In some cases, an item can have multiple attribute values. In this case, the item is connected to multiple attribute nodes. Such case is for example a book having multiple authors. The representation of the category tree is straightforward in the graph based case. A node is created for each category and each subcategory. The nodes are connected then with the edges of the appropriate type.

In order to cover also the user interactions, different kind of relations between the users and the books are stored in the knowledge base. The user interactions can be classified as expressing explicit or implicit interest. For example, if a user visits the web page containing the description of a book, an edge is inserted into the knowledge graph to represent the implicit interest. If a user puts items to their wish-list, the inserted edge represent an explicitly expressed interest.

The information is represented in the knowledge base as defined in Section III. Table II presents the node types introduced to store the entities of the recommendation scenario

TABLE II. Node Types and Occurrences.

Type	*Count*
`Person`	17 134
`HomeTown`	105
`BirthYear`	7
`Item`	117 367
`Author`	45 918
`Publisher`	6 351
`YearOfPublishing`	67
`NumberOfPages`	5
`PriceCategory`	5
`ItemCategory`	598

and also the occurrence counts of the nodes. Nodes of type `Person` represent the users of the system, as customers and persons signed up to the newsletter. Nodes of type `HomeTown` represent the hometown of the persons. A node is created for each hometown. Nodes of type `BirthYear` represent the birth year of the persons, e.g., `1978`. A node is created for each birth year. Nodes of type `Item` represent the books offered to the users, e.g., `Manga` and `Hieronymus Bosch`. Nodes of type `Author` represent the authors of the books, e.g., `Kurt Vonnegut` and `John Updike`. A book can have multiple authors. Nodes of type `Publisher` represent the publisher of the bookes, e.g., `Osiris Publishing` and `A & C Black`. Nodes of type `YearOfPublishing` represent the year of publishing of the books, e.g., `2007`. Based on the consultations with the experts of Booker, the number of pages of the books is organized into categories. The following categories are defined `0-60`, `61-100`, `101-200`, `201-500` and `501-1000`. Nodes of type `NumberOfPages` these categories. Similarly to page number categories, price categories are also defined as `0-1000`, `0-3000`, `1001-3000`, `3001-6000` and `6001-10000`. As the defined categories are overlapping, a book can belong to multiple categories, similarly like in the case of the author. Nodes of type `ItemCategory` represent the main and subcategories defined by the knowledge engineers of Booker. Such categories are for example `travel`, `art` and `religion`.

TABLE III. Edge Types and Occurrences.

Type	*Count*
`PersonBirthYear`	8
`PersonHomeTown`	175
`ItemAuthor`	127 613
`ItemCategory`	30 800
`ItemNumberOfPages`	112 524
`ItemPriceCategory`	212 473
`ItemPublisher`	116 746
`ItemYearOfPublishing`	96 653
`BoughtItem`	22 064
`OnWishList`	2 972
`ItemVisited`	4 590
`SubCategory`	486

Table III presents the edge types introduced to store the relations between the entities of the recommendation scenario and also the occurrence counts of the edges.

Relations of type `PersonBirthYear` between nodes of type `Person` and nodes of type `PersonBirthYear` connects the specific persons to their birth year. Relations of type `PersonHomeTown` between nodes of type `Person` and nodes of type `HomeTown` connects the specific persons to their hometown. Relations of type `ItemAuthor` between nodes of type `Item` and nodes of type `Author` connects the specific book to its author or authors. Relations of type `ItemCategory` between nodes of type `Item` and nodes of type `ItemCategory` connects the books to their appropriate category or categories. Relations of type `ItemNumberOfPages` between nodes of type `Item` and nodes of type `NumberOfPages` connects the items to their appropriate page category or categories. Relations of type `ItemPriceCategory` between nodes of type `Item` and nodes of type `PriceCategory` connects the items to their appropriate price category or categories. Relations of type `ItemPublisher` between nodes of type `Item` and nodes of type `Publisher` represent connects the books to their publisher. Relations of type `ItemYearOfPublishing` between nodes of type `Item` and nodes of type `YearOfPublishing` connects the books to their year of publishing. Relations of type `SubCategory` between nodes of type `ItemCategory` connects the subcategories to their higher level category. Relations of type `BoughtItem` between nodes of type `Person` and nodes of type `Item` represent the purchase interaction. Relations of type `OnWishList` between nodes of type `Person` and nodes of type `Item` represent the wish-list interaction. Relations of type `ItemVisited` between nodes of type `Person` and nodes of type `Item` represent the interaction the user visited the web page of the book.

To interpret the amount of edges presented in Table III, in can be read that the knowledge base is rich on item attributes but is sparse on person attributes. The reason for it is the different source of the information. The item attributes are presented by the publishing companies, while the user attributes are described by the users. The wish-lists are also densely populated. The number of edges of type `ItemAuthor` is higher than the number of nodes of type `Item`. The difference illustrates that certain books have multiple authors. The difference between the count of edges of type `ItemNumberOfPages` and `ItemPublisher` shows that the item attributes are not specified for all items. The higher number of `ItemPriceCategory` is caused by the overlapped `PriceCategory` intervals.

An important drawback of the dataset is the relatively low amount of edges of type `ItemVisited`. The reason of this problem can be found in the organization of the purchase work-flow on the portal. In order to increase the click-through rates, Booker requires the users to log-in only at the end of the purchase process. This is the reason why users typically anonymously browse the content of the portal and the user interest of this type can not be logged.

As already mentioned, the electronic commerce system forwards the information to the knowledge graph in real-time. During the experiment, the amount of nodes and edges in the knowledge graph constantly increased. The amount of nodes and edges presented in Table II and Table III were recorded on 23 January, 2015.

VI. EVALUATION

The evaluation of the methods is based on the email based remarketing activity of the web portal Booker. The essence of remarketing is to provide offers to the visitors of the electronic commerce portal after their visit. In our experiment, the offered items are selected by the recommendation techniques and are sent in personalized emails to the visitors. Depending on the actual method, the list of the items can be personalized or non-personalized. The emails are organized into several newsletter campaigns.

As already mentioned in Section V, the electronic commerce system constantly updates the knowledge graph. The recommendation techniques operate on this knowledge graph and are invoked at the point of time a list of recommended items is required from the email sending and personalizing software PartnerMail. During the evaluation period, the click-through events of the users are logged. The evaluation of the methods is essentially based on the click-through rates.

A. *Newsletters Sent*

The evaluation period has been conducted between 16 Jul, 2014 and 14 Jan, 2015. The newsletters are organized into 16 campaigns. To summarize the amount of evaluation cases, during the experiment, 241 062 emails have been sent of which 35 229 emails have been opened.

The campaigns can be classified as `Recommender system` based campaigns and `Human expert` based campaigns. In the case of a `Recommender system` based campaign, a personalized recommendation technique is invoked for each user. If the method is not able to generate a sufficient number of recommendations due to the cold-start case, a non-personalized technique is involved as a fall-back method. This technique ensures that an email can be sent to all contacts. In the case of the `Human expert` based case, the non-personalized, human expert based recommendation method is utilized.

TABLE IV. NEWSLETTER SEND DATES.

Type	*Date sent*
Recommender System	2014-07-16
Human Expert	2014-07-23
Recommender System	2014-07-26
Recommender System	2014-08-01
Human Expert	2014-08-06
Human Expert	2014-08-27
Recommender System	2014-08-29
Recommender System	2014-09-12
Human Expert	2014-09-22
Recommender System	2014-09-26
Human Expert	2014-10-02
Human Expert	2014-10-09
Recommender System	2014-10-15
Human Expert	2014-10-22
Recommender System	2014-10-31
Recommender System	2014-12-14

Table IV summarizes the newsletter campaigns. Column *type* presents the type of the campaign, column *Date sent* contains the send date. The date of the last campaign is 2014-12-14 and the end of the experiment is 2015-01-14. The additional month is involved in order to be able to measure the click-through events of the users.

B. *Methods*

As the knowledge graph does not contain user rating on items, some of the recommendation techniques described in Section IV could not be involved into the evaluation process. To generate personalized recommendations, the spreading activation, as described in Section IV-A2, is utilized. The fall-back methods in this case are the centrality measure based techniques, as defined in Section IV-A4. The human expert based method is described in Section IV-A5. In this case no fall-back method is necessary, as the method is non-personalized.

Based on our past results [3], we focused on the different settings of the `step limit` parameter setting both the `spreading relax` and the `activation relax` to a constant value, 0.5. Human expert and network science based methods require no further configuration.

In the assembling phase of a campaign, the concrete method configurations have to be specified. It means that in a campaign only the specified method or methods are evaluated.

C. Recommendation Lists

The methods described in Section IV assign a preference value to the nodes of the graph. To assemble a list of recommended items, the nodes are sorted in descending or by their preference value. Nodes with no preference value are not included in the list. The preference value is defined (i) as the rating estimation in the case of collaborative filtering and recommendation spreading, (ii) as the activation in the case of spreading activation and (iii) as the centrality value in the case of network science methods.

A relatively simple filtering technique is applied to the list of recommended items in order in increase user satisfaction. The rules are defined by the human expert and are summarized as (i) at most 2 books can be present from the same author, (ii) books are excluded from consecutive newsletters for two months and (iii) already purchased books are excluded. Having the list generated, the first n items are selected and presented to the user.

D. Evaluation Measures

User interaction is measured by various click-through events. These events are specific to email remarketing and basically model the work-flow of the purchase process. The following steps are modelled during the evaluation: sending a newsletter, opening a newsletter, clicking on an item in a newsletter, ordering an item and paying for the item. The states according to the process are identified as `Sent`, `Opened`, `Clicked`, `Ordered` and `Paid`.

In order to preserve the computational resources, the emails sent by PartnerMail do not embed the images into the content of the email but rather contain a reference to the images. A typical email client software does not download these referred images due to security and privacy concerns. The displaying of these images requires user interaction. The user can instruct the email client to download and display the images in the email. As the images are served by our server, PartnerMail records this event in the evaluation log.

The links in the emails contain a unique identifier and point to the PartnerMail server. If a user clicks on a link, the PartnerMail server logs the click-through event based on the unique identifier and forwards the user to the web page of the book on the Booker portal.

The books are to be ordered by the users on the web page of the specific book on the Booker portal. As the portal is integrated with PartnerMail, the order events are immediately forwarded to the knowledge graph. If the user cancels the current work-flow but returns later and finalizes the order, PartnerMail still records the appropriate click-through event.

Depending on the type of the payment method, the pay events can be separated from the order events. In the case of a credit card based payment, the payment immediately follows the order. In the case of the cash based payment, the customer orders the book and pays for it personally when physically picks up the books. In the latter case, a mentionable amount of work-flows do not reach the `paid` state, as it involves additional resources from the customer.

VII. Results

In this section, the results of the evaluation described in Section VI are presented. At first, a broad overview of the remarketing emails is provided in numbers. Then, the conversion rates are analysed for each recommendation technique. Finally, the performance of the method configurations is discussed.

TABLE V. Count of newsletters per state and recommendation technique

State	Spreading Activation	Network Science	Human Expert
Sent	**66 148**	**72 884**	102 030
Opened	11 700	9 206	14 323
Clicked	1 265	260	772
Ordered	24	0	17
Paid	**17**	0	**6**

Table V presents the number of remarketing emails sent during the evaluation period. The rows of the table represent the state of the emails as described in Section VI-D. The columns of the table represent the recommendation technique as described in Section VI-B. The values of the table are the count of emails in the particular state generated with the particular recommendation technique.

Our primary finding is the increase in the performance of the emails in the case of the `Spreading Activation`. Comparing the number of emails in the `Paid` state of the `Spreading Activation` to the `Human Expert`, the `Spreading Activation` shows a higher number of the `Paid` cases despite of having a lower amount of `Sent` cases. In this broad overview, `Network Science` based methods show a poor performance, as the number of `Paid` recommendations in this case is 0.

The high number of cold start cases can be determined by analysing the number of the fall-back method based recommendation cases. Also looking at our past results [3], comparing the number of sent `Spreading Activation` cases to the number of sent `Network Science` cases, a relatively high portion (52%) is identified. Also consulting with the experts of the electronic commerce system, the reason behind the high amount of cold start cases can be found in the dataset. Several users signed up only for the newsletter. In their case, the knowledge graph does not contain sufficient information to generate the recommendations, as spreading activation is not able to find a path between the user and any of the items.

To further analyse the performance of the methods, the subtables of Table VI present the conversion rates of each technique. The rows of the tables contain the source states. The columns of the tables contain the destination states. The values of the table contain the measured conversion rates of the states of the emails.

Conversion rate based comparison provides a more clean picture. Comparing the performance of the `Spreading`

TABLE VI. CONVERSION RATES OF THE RECOMMENDATION TECHNIQUES

(a) Spreading activation

	Opened	Clicked	Ordered	Paid
Sent	17.688%	1.912%	0.036%	0.026%
Opened		10.812%	0.205%	0.145%
Clicked			1.897%	1.344%
Ordered				70.833%

(b) Network Science

	Opened	Clicked	Ordered	Paid
Sent	12.631%	0.357%	0.000%	0.000%
Opened		2.824%	0.000%	0.000%
Clicked			0.000%	0.000%
Ordered				0.000%

(c) Human Expert

	Opened	Clicked	Ordered	Paid
Sent	14.038%	0.757%	0.017%	0.006%
Opened		5.390%	0.119%	0.042%
Clicked			2.202%	0.777%
Ordered				35.294%

Activation to performance of the Human Expert, 0.026% of the personalized emails resulted in a purchase event, while the ratio is 0.006% in the case of the Human Expert. Looking at the individual conversion rates, the Spreading Activation shows a higher performance in all cases, except the Clicked to Ordered conversion. To conclude it, personalized email remarketing has the potential to outperform the human expert based remarketing, thus the personalization has the potential to increase the business value.

Analysing the conversion rate from the Sent to the Opened state, the performance of the methods (17.688%, 12.631%, 14.038%) is different but the difference is significantly smaller than in the next conversion step. This is the step, where there users do not have the sufficient information to make the decisions based on the content of the emails. The conversion in this step is more based on the engagement of the users to the brand, the content has a low influence to this decision.

The Opened to Clicked conversion rate is influenced more by the content of the items. The state transition rates in this step (10.812%, 2.824%, 5.390%) better represent the performance of the methods, as the difference in the conversion rates is more visible. In this conversion, the Spreading Activation shows the highest performance, Human Expert shows approximately the half of its performance and Network Science delivers the lowest conversion rate.

The web page of a book provides the most detailed information about a recommended item, thus the Clicked to Ordered state transition is at most influenced by the information about the books. In this conversion step, the performance of the Network Science methods drops to 0 showing the low relevance of the items selected by this technique. The Collaborative Filtering shows a bit better performance than the Spreading Activation.

The last conversion step is the Ordered to the Paid transition. As the Network Science does not reach this conversion step, the performance of the Spreading Activation (70.833%) and the performance of the Human Expert (35.294%) is to be compared in this step. Similarly to the Opened to Clicked conversion, the performance of the Spreading Activation is two times the performance of the Human Expert. This conversion rate is the last step where the payment is to be performed. Regarding the decision making process, this conversion step does not involve information about the products from the user. The decision to perform at this point is emotion based driven by the finances.

To conclude the results, the spreading activation based recommendation technique outperforms the human expert in the conversion steps, where the human decision making is not analytical but is more emotional. In other words, spreading activation is to be applied in the recommendation cases, where a more emotional decision making is necessary.

TABLE VII. Conversion rates of the method configurations

Method Configuration	Opened	Clicked	Ordered	Paid
Spreading Activation 3	15.3982%	1.6581%	0.0000%	0.0000%
Spreading Activation 4	17.7506%	1.7468%	0.0483%	0.0345%
Spreading Activation 5	16.9413%	1.9600%	0.0068%	0.0000%
Spreading Activation 6	17.8073%	1.9073%	0.0404%	0.0180%
Spreading Activation 7	**21.0223%**	**2.4182%**	**0.0962%**	**0.1099%**
Betweenness Centrality	12.7597%	0.3514%	0.0000%	0.0000%
Closeness Centrality	12.5700%	0.3010%	0.0000%	0.0000%
Degree Centrality	**13.2988%**	0.3879%	0.0000%	0.0000%
Eigenvector Centrality	10.5723%	**0.4365%**	0.0000%	0.0000%

Table VII presents the performance of the method configurations. The rows represent the method configurations. In the case of Spreading Activation, the number following the name of the method indicates the value of the step limit parameter. Network science based methods are not configurable. The columns of the table present the destination states. The values of the column present the conversion rates from the Sent state to the state denoted in the column title of the cell.

Analysing the configurations of the Spreading Activation method, the step limit setting 7 leads to the highest conversion rate. The step limit settings 3 and 5 lead to a poor performance, as the recommendations based on this technique did not lead to a purchase event. The detailed results show that fine tuning the step limit parameter is important, as the performance of the methods strongly depends on this setting.

Analysing network science methods, involving degree centrality leads to the highest Sent to Opened conversion and eigenvector centrality leads to the highest Sent to Clicked conversion.

VIII. CONCLUSION AND FUTURE WORK

This paper presented the knowledge graph, an information representation technique capable to model heterogeneous information sources and also to alloy the information sources of the classic recommendation methods as collaborative filtering, content-based filtering and knowledge-based methods. The knowledge graph defines a hybridization method at the information representation level and also generalizes the concept of information sources, as discussed in Section III.

As our approach separates the information representation and the calculation methods, the methods are expected to manage the information in the knowledge graph as general. Looking at the static and the user generated information sources, the balance of the hybridization has been examined at the theoretical level in Section III-D. A principle of the information representation methods of the knowledge graph is the generalization of the information sources. The generalization at the representation level induced generalization and transitivity also at the calculation level as discussed in Section IV-B.

The evaluation of the methods has been conducted in a real-world experiment, as the conversion rates of an email remarketing scenario have been measured. In the experiment, spreading activation, network science and human expert based methods have been compared. The evaluation results show that the personalization of the emails have the potential to increase the performance of the email remarkating regarding to the conversion rates and the business value. Network science based methods proven to deliver low quality recommendations. A more theoretical result is the spreading activation based methods are intended to be used in an emotion based decision making scenario.

In the future, we plan to evaluate the methods in a web remarketing scenario. To achieve this, several optimization and GPU techniques should be involved in order to be able to generate the recommendations with a reasonable time need. On the theoretical side, we would like to alloy network science and representation learning based recommendation methods.

REFERENCES

[1] L. Grad-Gyenge and P. Filzmoser, "Recommendation Techniques on a Knowledge Graph for Email Remarketing," in *eKNOW 2016, The Eighth International Conference on Information, Process, and Knowledge Management*. eKNOW (2016): IARIA XPS Press, 2016, pp. 51–56.

[2] ——, "The Paradigm of Relatedness," in *AKTB 2016 : 8th Workshop on Applications of Knowledge-Based Technologies in Business*, 2016, pp. 13–20.

[3] L. Grad-Gyenge, P. Filzmoser, and H. Werthner, "Recommendations on a Knowledge Graph," in *MLRec 2015 : 1st International Workshop on Machine Learning Methods for Recommender Systems*, 2015, pp. 13–20.

[4] B. Hidasi and D. Tikk, "Fast ALS-Based Tensor Factorization for Context-Aware Recommendation from Implicit Feedback." in *ECML/PKDD (2)*, ser. Lecture Notes in Computer Science, P. A. Flach, T. D. Bie, and N. Cristianini, Eds., vol. 7524. Springer, 2012, pp. 67–82. [Online]. Available: http://dblp.uni-trier.de/db/conf/pkdd/pkdd2012-2.html#HidasiT12

[5] R. Agrawal, T. Imielinski, and A. N. Swami, "Mining Association Rules between Sets of Items in Large Databases." in *SIGMOD Conference*, P. Buneman and S. Jajodia, Eds. ACM Press, 1993, pp. 207–216.

[6] J. L. Herlocker, J. A. Konstan, A. Borchers, and J. Riedl, "An Algorithmic Framework for Performing Collaborative Filtering," in *Proceedings of the 22Nd Annual International ACM SIGIR Conference on Research and Development in Information Retrieval*, ser. SIGIR '99. New York, NY, USA: ACM, 1999, pp. 230–237. [Online]. Available: http://doi.acm.org/10.1145/312624.312682

[7] Criteo. (2016, Dec.) Criteo. [Online]. Available: http://www.criteo.com/

[8] CreoGroup. (2016, Dec.) PartnerMail. [Online]. Available: http://www.partnermail.eu/

[9] aLap. (2016, Dec.) Booker.hu Online Bookstore - Order a Book. [Online]. Available: http://www.booker.hu/

[10] D. Jannach, M. Zanker, A. Felfernig, and G. Friedrich, *Recommender Systems: An Introduction*. New York, NY, USA: Cambridge University Press, 2011. [Online]. Available: http://www.amazon.com/exec/obidos/redirect?tag=citeulike07-20&path=ASIN/0521493366

[11] I. Konstas, V. S. 0002, and J. M. Jose, "On social networks and collaborative recommendation." in *SIGIR*, J. Allan, J. A. Aslam, M. Sanderson, C. Zhai, and J. Zobel, Eds. ACM, 2009, pp. 195–202. [Online]. Available: http://dblp.uni-trier.de/db/conf/sigir/sigir2009.html#KonstasSJ09

[12] B. Hidasi and D. Tikk, "Fast ALS-Based Tensor Factorization for Context-aware Recommendation from Implicit Feedback," in *Proceedings of the 2012 European Conference on Machine Learning and Knowledge Discovery in Databases - Volume Part II*, ser. ECML PKDD'12. Berlin, Heidelberg: Springer-Verlag, 2012, pp. 67–82. [Online]. Available: http://dx.doi.org/10.1007/978-3-642-33486-3_5

[13] G. Adomavicius and A. Tuzhilin, "Context-Aware Recommender Systems," in *Recommender Systems Handbook*, F. Ricci, L. Rokach, B. Shapira, and P. B. Kantor, Eds. Springer, 2011, pp. 217–253. [Online]. Available: http://dblp.uni-trier.de/db/reference/rsh/rsh2011.html#AdomaviciusT11

[14] D. Easley and J. Kleinberg, "Homophily," in *Networks, Crowds, and Markets: Reasoning About a Highly Connected World*. Cambridge University Press, 2010. [Online]. Available: http://www.cs.cornell.edu/home/kleinber/networks-book;http://www.bibsonomy.org/bibtex/29b041bdba459fdc749a0b13de3d343d3/mstrohm

[15] J. Tang, S. Wu, and J. Sun, "Confluence: conformity influence in large social networks." in *KDD*, I. S. Dhillon, Y. Koren, R. Ghani, T. E. Senator, P. Bradley, R. Parekh, J. He, R. L. Grossman, and R. Ut hurusamy, Eds. ACM, 2013, pp. 347–355.

[16] P. Kazienko, K. Musial, and T. Kajdanowicz, "Multidimensional Social Network in the Social Recommender System," *CoRR*, vol. abs/1303.0093, 2013. [Online]. Available: http://dblp.uni-trier.de/db/journals/corr/corr1303.html#abs-1303-0093

[17] Epinions. (2016, Dec.) Epinions. [Online]. Available: http://www.epinions.com/

[18] C.-N. Ziegler and G. Lausen, "Propagation Models for Trust and Distrust in Social Networks," *Information Systems Frontiers*, vol. 7, no. 4-5, pp. 337–358, Dec. 2005. [Online]. Available: http://dx.doi.org/10.1007/s10796-005-4807-3

[19] P. Massa and P. Avesani, "Trust-Aware Collaborative Filtering for Recommender Systems." in *CoopIS/DOA/ODBASE (1)*, ser. Lecture Notes in Computer Science, R. Meersman and Z. Tari, Eds., vol. 3290. Springer, 2004, pp. 492–508. [Online]. Available: http://dblp.uni-trier.de/db/conf/coopis/coopis2004-1.html#MassaA04

[20] A. Jøsang, S. Marsh, and S. Pope, "Exploring Different Types of Trust Propagation." in *iTrust*, ser. Lecture Notes in Computer Science, K. Stølen, W. H. Winsborough, F. Martinelli, and F. Massacci, Eds., vol. 3986. Springer, 2006, pp. 179–192. [Online]. Available: http://dblp.uni-trier.de/db/conf/itrust/itrust2006.html#JosangMP06

[21] I. Guy, N. Zwerdling, D. Carmel, I. Ronen, E. Uziel, S. Yogev, and S. Ofek-Koifman, "Personalized recommendation of social software items based on social relations." in *RecSys*, L. D. Bergman, A. Tuzhilin, R. D. Burke, A. Felfernig, and L. Schmidt-Thieme, Eds. ACM, 2009, pp. 53–60. [Online]. Available: http://dblp.uni-trier.de/db/conf/recsys/recsys2009.html#GuyZCRUYO09

[22] J. He and W. W. Chu, "A Social Network-Based Recommender System (SNRS)," in *Data Mining for Social Network Data*, 2010, pp. 47–74.

[23] X. Yang, Y. Guo, and Y. Liu, "Bayesian-Inference-Based Recommendation in Online Social Networks." *IEEE Trans. Parallel Distrib. Syst.*, vol. 24, no. 4, pp. 642–651, 2013. [Online]. Available: http://dblp.uni-trier.de/db/journals/tpds/tpds24.html#YangGL13

[24] H. Gu, M. Gartrell, L. Zhang, Q. Lv, and D. Grunwald, "AnchorMF: Towards Effective Event Context Identification," in *Proceedings of the 22Nd ACM International Conference on Conference on Information & Knowledge Management*, ser. CIKM '13. New York, NY, USA: ACM, 2013, pp. 629–638. [Online]. Available: http://doi.acm.org/10.1145/2505515.2505548

[25] P. Kouki, S. Fakhraei, J. Foulds, M. Eirinaki, and L. Getoor, "HyPER: A Flexible and Extensible Probabilistic Framework for Hybrid Recommender Systems," in *Proceedings of the 9th ACM Conference on Recommender Systems*, ser. RecSys '15. New York, NY, USA: ACM, 2015, pp. 99–106. [Online]. Available: http://doi.acm.org/10.1145/2792838.2800175

[26] Q. Hu, S. Xie, J. Zhang, Q. Zhu, S. Guo, and P. S. Yu, "HeteroSales: Utilizing Heterogeneous Social Networks to Identify the Next Enterprise Customer," in *Proceedings of the 25th International Conference on World Wide Web*, ser. WWW '16. Republic and Canton of Geneva, Switzerland: International World Wide Web Conferences Steering Committee, 2016, pp. 41–50. [Online]. Available: http://dx.doi.org/10.1145/2872427.2883000

[27] R. Catherine and W. Cohen, "Personalized Recommendations Using Knowledge Graphs: A Probabilistic Logic Programming Approach," in *Proceedings of the 10th ACM Conference on Recommender Systems*, ser. RecSys '16. New York, NY, USA: ACM, 2016, pp. 325–332. [Online]. Available: http://doi.acm.org/10.1145/2959100.2959131

[28] R. Burke, F. Vahedian, and B. Mobasher, "Hybrid recommendation in heterogeneous networks," in *International Conference on User Modeling, Adaptation, and Personalization*. Springer, 2014, pp. 49–60.

[29] M. Jamali and M. Ester, "TrustWalker: a random walk model for combining trust-based and item-based recommendation." in *KDD*, J. F. E. IV, F. Fogelman-Soulié, P. A. Flach, and M. Zaki, Eds. ACM, 2009, pp. 397–406. [Online]. Available: http://dblp.uni-trier.de/db/conf/kdd/kdd2009.html#JamaliE09

[30] R. Guha and P. Raghavan, "Propagation of Trust and Distrust," *null*, pp. 403—412, 2004. [Online]. Available: http://citeseerx.ist.psu.edu/viewdoc/summary?doi=10.1.1.2.3157

[31] C. Hess, K. Stein, and C. Schlieder, "Trust-enhanced visibility for personalized document recommendations," in *SAC '06: Proceedings of the 2006 ACM symposium on Applied computing*. New York, NY, USA: ACM, 2006, pp. 1865–1869. [Online]. Available: http://portal.acm.org/citation.cfm?id=1141277.1141718

[32] J. Golbeck, "Semantic Web Interaction through Trust Network Recommender Systems," in *End User Semantic Web Interaction Workshop at the 4th International Semantic Web Conference*, 2005.

[33] M. R. Quillian, "Semantic memory," in *Semantic Information Processing*, M. Minsky, Ed. Cambridge, MA: MIT Press, 1968, pp. 227–270.

[34] N. V. Findler, Ed., *Associative Networks: The Representation and Use of Knowledge of Computers*. Academic Pr, 1979. [Online]. Available: http://www.amazon.com/Associative-Networks-Representation-Knowledge-Computers/dp/0122563808%3FSubscriptionId=13CT5CVB80YFWJEPWS02&tag=ws&linkCode=xm2&camp=2025&creative=165953&creativeASIN=0122563808

[35] C.-N. Ziegler and G. Lausen, "Spreading Activation Models for Trust Propagation," in *Proc. IEEE International Conference on e-technology, e-commerce, and e-service (EEE)*, Taipei, Taiwan, March 2004, pp. 83–97, best paper award for EEE2004.

[36] D. Easley and J. Kleinberg, *Networks, Crowds, and Markets: Reasoning About a Highly Connected World*. Cambridge University Press, 2010. [Online]. Available: http://www.cs.cornell.edu/home/kleinber/networks-book

[37] L. Page, S. Brin, R. Motwani, and T. Winograd, "The PageRank Citation Ranking: Bringing Order to the Web," Stanford University, Tech. Rep., 1999.

[38] D. Fogaras, B. Rácz, K. Csalogány, and T. Sarlós, "Towards scaling fully personalized pagerank: Algorithms, lower bounds, and experiments," *Internet Mathematics*, vol. 2, no. 3, pp. 333–358, 2005. [Online]. Available: http://scholar.google.de/scholar.bib?q=info:FrrSSl4mADMJ:scholar.google.com/&output=citation&hl=de&as_sdt=0&ct=citation&cd=1

[39] J. H. Jeong and J. W. Kim, "Personalized Recommendation Based on Collaborative Filtering with Social Network Analysis," in *International Conference on Information and Computer Applications*, ser. ICICA 2012, vol. 24. IACSIT Press, 2012, pp. 67–71.

[40] S. Haykin, "Neural Networks Viewed as Directed Graphs," in *Neural Networks: A Comprehensive Foundation*. Prentice Hall, 1999, pp. 702–718. [Online]. Available: http://www.bibsonomy.org/bibtex/2e13a49ec715f4e52f1dcca0d4c5c8b2c/chrmina

[41] Y. Bengio, "Learning Deep Architectures for AI." Tech. Rep. 1, 2009. [Online]. Available: http://dblp.uni-trier.de/db/journals/ftml/ftml2.html#Bengio09

[42] D. Svozil, V. Kvasnicka, and J. Pospichal, "Introduction to multi-layer feed-forward neural networks," *Chemometrics and Intelligent Laboratory Systems*, vol. 39, no. 1, pp. 43–62, 1997. [Online]. Available: http://www.sciencedirect.com/science/article/pii/S0169743997000610

[43] S. Haykin, "Back-Propagation Algorithm," in *Neural Networks: A Comprehensive Foundation*. Prentice Hall, 1999, pp. 183–195. [Online]. Available: http://www.bibsonomy.org/bibtex/2e13a49ec715f4e52f1dcca0d4c5c8b2c/chrmina

[44] ——, "Hebbian Learning," in *Neural Networks: A Comprehensive Foundation*. Prentice Hall, 1999, pp. 77–80. [Online]. Available: http://www.bibsonomy.org/bibtex/2e13a49ec715f4e52f1dcca0d4c5c8b2c/chrmina

[45] ——, "Hopfield Models," in *Neural Networks: A Comprehensive Foundation*. Prentice Hall, 1999, pp. 702–718. [Online]. Available: http://www.bibsonomy.org/bibtex/2e13a49ec715f4e52f1dcca0d4c5c8b2c/chrmina

[46] Z. Huang, W. Chung, T.-H. Ong, and H. Chen, "A Graph-based Recommender System for Digital Library," in *Proceedings of the 2Nd ACM/IEEE-CS Joint Conference on Digital Libraries*, ser. JCDL '02. New York, NY, USA: ACM, 2002, pp. 65–73. [Online]. Available: http://doi.acm.org/10.1145/544220.544231

[47] S. Haykin, "Boltzmann Machine," in *Neural Networks: A Comprehensive Foundation*. Prentice Hall, 1999, pp. 584–591. [Online]. Available: http://www.bibsonomy.org/bibtex/2e13a49ec715f4e52f1dcca0d4c5c8b2c/chrmina

[48] R. Salakhutdinov, A. Mnih, and G. E. Hinton, "Restricted Boltzmann machines for collaborative filtering." in *ICML*, ser. ACM International Conference Proceeding Series, Z. Ghahramani, Ed., vol. 227. ACM, 2007, pp. 791–798. [Online]. Available: http://dblp.uni-trier.de/db/conf/icml/icml2007.html#SalakhutdinovMH07;http://doi.acm.org/10.1145/1273496.1273596;http://www.bibsonomy.org/bibtex/2537c88cc0b98318ebbad1f76bfd0c451/dblp

[49] R. Burke, "Hybrid Recommender Systems: Survey and Experiments," *User Modeling and User-Adapted Interaction*, vol. 12, no. 4, pp. 331–370, Nov. 2002. [Online]. Available: http://dx.doi.org/10.1023/A:1021240730564

[50] S. Dooms, T. Pessemier, and L. Martens, "Online Optimization for User-specific Hybrid Recommender Systems," *Multimedia Tools Appl.*, vol. 74, no. 24, pp. 11 297–11 329, Dec. 2015. [Online]. Available: http://dx.doi.org/10.1007/s11042-014-2232-7

[51] L. Grad-Gyenge and H. Werthner, "Network Science @ Recommender Systems," in *Effective, Agile and Trusted eServices Co-Creation*. TUCS Lecture Notes 19 (2013): Turku Centre for Computer Science, 2013, pp. 67–77. [Online]. Available: http://publik.tuwien.ac.at/files/PubDat_219604.pdf

[52] D. Jannach, M. Zanker, A. Felfernig, and G. Friedrich, *Recommender Systems An Introduction*. Cambridge University Press, 2011.

[53] H. K. Bhargava, S. Sridhar, and C. Herrick, "Beyond Spreadsheets: Tools for Building Decision Support Systems," *Computer*, vol. 32, no. 3, pp. 31–39, Mar. 1999. [Online]. Available: http://dx.doi.org/10.1109/2.751326

[54] R. Reiter, "A Theory of Diagnosis from First Principles," *Artif. Intell.*, vol. 32, no. 1, pp. 57–95, Apr. 1987. [Online]. Available: http://dx.doi.org/10.1016/0004-3702(87)90062-2

[55] A. Gershman, A. Meisels, K.-H. Lüke, L. Rokach, A. Schclar, and A. Sturm, "A Decision Tree Based Recommender System." in *IICS*, ser. LNI, G. Eichler, P. G. Kropf, U. Lechner, P. Meesad, and H. Unger, Eds., vol. 165. GI, 2010, pp. 170–179. [Online]. Available: http://dblp.uni-trier.de/db/conf/iics/iics2010.html#GershmanMLRSS10

[56] J. Neidhardt, R. Schuster, L. Seyfang, and H. Werthner, "Eliciting the Users' Unknown Preferences," in *Proceedings of the 8th ACM Conference on Recommender Systems*, ser. RecSys '14. New York, NY, USA: ACM, 2014, pp. 309–312. [Online]. Available: http://doi.acm.org/10.1145/2645710.2645767

[57] A. Felfernig and R. Burke, "Constraint-based Recommender Systems: Technologies and Research Issues," in *Proceedings of the 10th International Conference on Electronic Commerce*, ser. ICEC '08. New York, NY, USA: ACM, 2008, pp. 3:1–3:10. [Online]. Available: http://doi.acm.org/10.1145/1409540.1409544

[58] A. Felfernig, "Koba4MS: Selling Complex Products and Services Using Knowledge-Based Recommender Technologies." in *CEC*. IEEE Computer Society, 2005, pp. 92–100. [Online]. Available: http://dblp.uni-trier.de/db/conf/wecwis/cec2005.html#Felfernig05;http://doi.ieeecomputersociety.org/10.1109/ICECT.2005.57;http://www.bibsonomy.org/bibtex/268088334dec36badb214253e5ec8812d/dblp

[59] P. Resnick, N. Iacovou, M. Suchak, P. Bergstrom, and J. Riedl, "GroupLens: An Open Architecture for Collaborative Filtering of Netnews," in *Proceedings of the 1994 ACM Conference on Computer Supported Cooperative Work*, ser. CSCW '94. New York, NY, USA: ACM, 1994, pp. 175–186. [Online]. Available: http://doi.acm.org/10.1145/192844.192905

Supporting the Development and Management of Learning Experiences in Location-Based Mobile Games

The EVANDE project

Dimitris Makris, Konstantinos Makris, Polyxeni Arapi, Stavros Christodoulakis
Laboratory of Distributed Multimedia Information Systems and Applications (TUC/MUSIC)
Technical University of Crete
Chania, Greece
e-mail: {dmakris, makris, xenia, stavros}@ced.tuc.gr

Iasmi Stathi, Eleni Spiridaki, Charalampos Fassoulas
Natural History Museum of Crete (NHMC)
University of Crete
Heraklion, Greece
e-mail: {iasmi, evande, fassoulas}@nhmc.uoc.gr

Abstract— **Mobile location-based games, exploiting the unique capabilities of mobile devices, such as camera, GPS and compass, can have high learning potential. On one hand, they present a very attractive form of learning for modern students, even very young ones, who have already developed their skills in computer games and are very familiar with the use of mobile devices. On the other hand, location-based games provide a unique opportunity for education since they connect an area with a story, and their activities may result in social, experiential and situated learning. These characteristics can make them a powerful tool in a number of applications, including education, nature and museum exploration, city sightseeing, natural disasters awareness and prevention training. In this paper, we present the design and implementation of PlayLearn, a platform for the development and management of learning experiences in mobile location-based games, consisting of: (a) an authoring tool, supporting the creation and management of games, scenario editing, user interface customization and organization of gaming activities, and (b) a mobile application, compatible with most state-of-the-art mobile devices and platforms, supporting the play of games created by the authoring tool. Our implementation supports the Experience API, allowing the activities that happen as part of gaming (learning) experiences to be recorded, tracked and shared in a Learning Record Store. PlayLearn is part of the EVANDE (Enhancing Volunteer Awareness and education against Natural Disasters through E-learning) project learning infrastructure used for the development of mobile games for the training of civil protection volunteers and local authorities' staff.**

Keywords- mobile educational games; location-based games; learning experiences; experiential learning.

I. Introduction

Location-based services on mobile phones have become very popular in recent years. These services have been developed to provide location-based information to the user. This information derived from the location-based-services can be used in entertainment and education to create games that use the geographical location of the user or other people as an essential part of the game [1]. A -so called- mobile location-based-game [2] is a type of pervasive game in which the game-play evolves and progresses via a player's location. Thus, mobile location-based games must provide some mechanism to allow the player to report their location. Frequently, this is performed by some kind of localization technology, e.g., by using satellite positioning through GPS. The difference between a video game and a location-based game focusing on the same story is that the later has a closer connection between game and reality.

In terms of the main objective, mobile location-based games may be categorized as games that are created for fun, for learning or for mixed objectives [3]. All these categories of games seem to have a higher learning potential. On the one hand, modern students, even very young ones, have already developed skills in computer games and are very familiar with the use of mobile devices, and educational mobile games can provide a very attractive form of learning for them. On the other hand, the location-based games provide a unique opportunity for education since they connect a geographic area or object with a story. The physical and cultural surroundings are an integral part of the game space, and the location of the gamers is a key aspect of the game-playing activity. By visiting the actual locations, the story becomes more authentic and therefore leads to better educational results. Essentially, the games of this kind allow the user to collect data from the real world and assign them to the game's map. De Souza et al. [4] have observed that these activities produce learning that is social, experiential and situated. The combination of informal learning and mobile outdoor games can be seen as a relevant arena for conducting novel learning activities that involve learners in different tasks including physical motion, problem solving, inquiry and collaboration [5].

Learning experiences are those events and activities from which we learn by experience and can identify, to a certain extent, what we have learned. Different Learners have different characteristics and preferences (e.g., learning style, educational level, background knowledge etc.) and these affect how these learning experiences might be organized in terms of their activities as well as the learning material that should support those activities to achieve specific goals [6].

Experiential learning, according to Kolb [7], can exist without a teacher and relates solely to the meaning-making process of the individual's direct experience. Knowledge is continuously gained through both personal and environmental experiences.

The Experience API (xAPI) is an eLearning software specification that allows learning content and systems to speak to each other in a manner that records and tracks all types of learning experiences [8]. The results of learning experiences are stored in a Learning Record Store (LRS), which may exist in a traditional Learning Management System (LMS), or on its own (installed or web-based). xAPI does not require a learning experience to take place in any particular medium (mobile, desktop, tablet), offline or online, or in any particular system. By collecting and analyzing xAPI for a specific learner, a picture of the learner's activities, achievements, competencies and interests can be created, drawing on experiences using multiple devices and multiple activities [9]. Exposing data through the xAPI provides a means for interoperability but also allows for innovation of learning content, experiences, and systems, something that is not easily afforded in the current learning model [10].

The use of xAPI with mobile devices is a powerful combination which can leverage learning, since it enables opportunities for capturing the activities from diverse learning experiences that take place exploiting the unique capabilities of the mobile platform for learning, such as the mobile phone's camera, GPS and compass. This may lead to new kinds of learning experiences and a much wider adoption of mobile-based performance support [10]. For instance, if a learning design was predicated on students taking pictures of examples of a particular phenomenon, and then sharing and discussing these with other students, the xAPI enables the various activities in this learning design to be recorded and tracked in an LRS in the form of activity streams. Later, the teacher could retrieve this information from the LRS, initiate a discussion with the students in the class, or even improve the learning design of the game according to the results to fit better the needs of the learners and learning context. These are only some of the many uses and benefits of adopting xAPI to track and share learning experiences.

In this paper, we present the design and implementation of PlayLearn, a platform for the management of learning experiences in location-based mobile games. The games supported follow a flexible model, allowing our framework to support a wide variety of games in various applications. The platform consists of: (a) an authoring tool (web application) supporting the creation and management of mobile location-based games, including scenario editing, user interface customization and organization of gaming activities, and (b) a player application (mobile application) for supporting the play of games created using the authoring tool. The player application is compatible with most state-of-the-art mobile devices/platforms, while both tools have been designed with flexibility and extensibility in mind. Moreover, our implementation supports the Experience API (xAPI), allowing the activities that happen as part of the gaming (learning) experiences to be recorded, tracked and shared in a Learning Record Store (LRS).

PlayLearn is part of EVANDE project learning infrastructure. EVANDE (Enhancing Volunteer Awareness and education against Natural Disasters through E-learning) [11] is a European project co-funded under the Union Civil Protection Mechanism. It aims to create a new learning tool to train civil protection volunteers and local authorities' staff on the topics of floods, forest fires, earthquakes and European civil protection policies through the identification of best practices and knowledge, the development an e-learning platform and tools to host e-learning courses, games and training activities, as well as the organization and implementation of local-based dissemination and training actions. Two piloting e-games based on mobile devices (e.g., tablets, mobile smart phones) are being developed within the framework of the European project. One of them is presented in detail in this paper.

The structure of the rest of this paper is as follows: Section II presents systems and research related to this work. Section III specifies the model for describing educational games. Section IV presents the architecture that has been designed and implemented, while Section V provides some more insight on the implementation of the platform. Section VI introduces EVANDE project and describes in detail how this framework and infrastructure is used for the creation and management of mobile games for the training of civil protection volunteers and local authorities' staff presenting one of the two main piloting game scenarios developed. Finally, Section VII summarizes and reviews the presented work and sketches some perspectives for future extensions.

II. Related Work

Various types of location-based games and platforms have extensively been reported by several authors, such as in [3] and [5]. In this section, we are focusing on those that are closer to our work.

Geocaching [12] is an outdoor activity where players try either to find hidden caches using GPS coordinates, or hide their own caches and register their location. Activities are supported by: (a) a desktop application enabling the searching, filtering and previewing of geocaches, as well as (b) a mobile application that in addition to the previous features provides basic navigational assistance. Geocaching applications support strictly basic treasure hunt outdoor activities without providing in depth game experience. On the contrary, PlayLearn provides a game authoring tool and a player application supporting different game types based on a great variety of activities that can be either bounded or not to specific locations. Using our tools, the user is able to create his own game, share it and play it with others. Furthermore, we provide the capability to organize location based events allowing the participants to have a real in depth gaming experience either by competing or cooperating.

WHAIWHAI [13] is an interactive story based on a gaming platform and developed to offer a way of exploring the less touristic and unknown city places. Players are supposed to walk the city, collect clues, answer enigmas and discover popular and traditional tales. Although games are customizable in terms of difficulty, time limit and number of players, WHAIWHAI is limited to exploration activities. On the contrary, PlayLearn provides tools and services for creating and playing various types of games, exploited under different contexts and targeting users of certain age groups.

Tourality [14] is a location-based game where the user's main goal is to visit several predefined spots of certain interest. In multiplayer mode, the game focuses on time, requiring the user to be faster than the others, maintain a high score and compete either by participating in a team or alone. Although Tourality enhances competitiveness and cooperation, it focuses strictly to these characteristics leaving aside any in depth educational activity that a game may provide. On the contrary, using PlayLearn a user is able to create different games consisted of a variety of educational activities based on specific user profiles. By doing so, the player of these games, apart from visiting a set of specific places, is able to browse educational material of different types (video, image, sound, text), answer riddles, perform metadata annotation tasks, search for hidden treasures, get rewards etc.

AnswerTree [15] is a collaborative mobile location-based educational game designed to teach 8-12 year old players about trees and wildlife. The game is designed around collecting virtual information cards about notable trees by answering questions. Collaboration is encouraged by the fact that solutions to these questions are obtainable through sharing knowledge with other cardholders. Apart from this, AnswerTree is a static game targeting users of specific profile, interests and goals. On the other hand, using PlayLearn users are able to achieve the same goals while having the opportunity to extend their game (either by creating their own educational activities or selecting from a broad set of preexisting ones), personalize the user interface and organize events.

ARIS [16] is a platform for creating and playing mobile games, tours and interactive stories and it is considered the most relevant work compared to ours. Its authoring tool is available as desktop application and provides the ability to specify the game location, create quests and upload multimedia files. Apart from these features, it does not provide any functionality for organizing gaming events focused on player profiles, and unlike PlayLearn's authoring application, the game creator cannot customize the user interface of the game. Another important limitation is that ARIS game player application is designed as a mobile application available only for iPhones. On the contrary, we provide a game player for the majority of mobile phone operating systems including iOS, Android and Windows. Additionally, PlayLearn's game player application is also available through the browser.

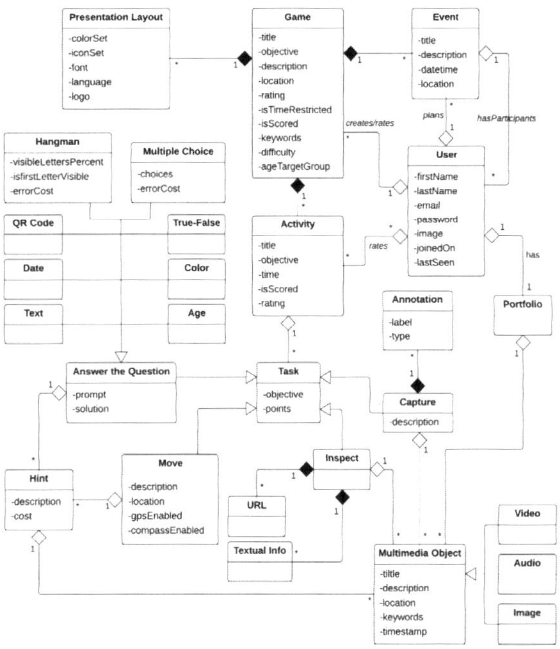

Figure 1. PlayLearn core model

III. MODEL

The model developed and supported by the PlayLearn platform for the creation of location-based educational games has been designed with flexibility and extensibility in mind, to be able to describe as many as possible different types of games. Figure 1 presents the core model entities in the form of a class diagram.

The *Users* of the system include both game creators and players, differentiating based on their role. The *Game* class represents the games which can be created, managed and played by *Users* using PlayLearn. A *Game* has a goal and consists of several descriptive and presentation metadata, while it is possible for the creator to adapt its *Presentation Layout* (e.g., color set, icon set, fonts, language, logo, etc). A *Game* consists of a sequence of *Activities* with certain objectives that have to be tackled by the player to support the game goal. *Activities* consist of *Tasks* which are considered as the actions to be performed in order to achieve the respective activities' objectives. There are currently four types of *Tasks*:

- *Move* is a type of Task in which the user needs to navigate in order to reach a specific destination.
- *Inspect* is a type of Task in which the user has to read a text document, apothegm or any other piece of information in textual form (*Textual Information*), or view an image/video and listen to a sound (*Multimedia Object*).
- *Answer the Question* is a type of task in which the user should provide an answer for a given question. The type of the question can be of many types, including *Multiple Choice, True – False, Text* (the player should provide his answer in plain text), *Hangman* (the player needs to find a hidden word), *QR Code* (the player scans a pattern code, after searching for it in a specified location range), etc.
- *Capture* is a type of task in which the user has to record a video, take a photo, or record a sound. It can

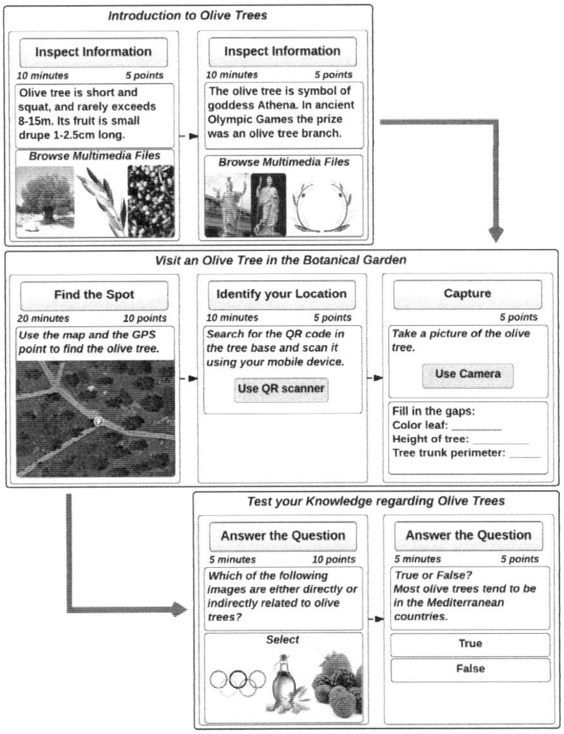

Figure 2. A simple game example for a visit to a Botanical garden to explore olive trees, consisting of three activities corresponding to the pre-visit, visit and post-visit phases

be extended to require the *Annotation* of the captured *Multimedia Object* with metadata.

The *Multimedia Object* class represents multimedia objects of type: video, image, text, and audio. Each type of Multimedia Object is depicted as a different class, holding its own descriptive attributes. The *Audio* class represents the multimedia objects of type sound. Optionally, it contains a GPS point specifying the location that has been recorded. The *Image* class represents the multimedia objects that are of type image. Optionally, it contains a GPS point with information about the location where it was captured, as well as other descriptive metadata. The *Video* class represents the multimedia objects that are of type video. Optionally, it contains a list of GPS points with information about the location where it was recorded, as well as any other information provided by the camera. The list of GPS points can be used to recreate the path that the user took for the duration of the capturing. Each User has a *Portfolio* that corresponds to a library with *Multimedia Objects*, which are used in games creation.

Games can be used for the organization of gaming *Events*, which can be created and shared by *Users* in order to promote gaming activities in certain locations. Each *Event* may refer to a specific game, location and date/time. Additionally, the list of the event participants can be either open or restricted to specific user groups. Since Games can be bounded to a specific place, such information along with game classification, target group, rating and difficulty can be used for game searching and filtering.

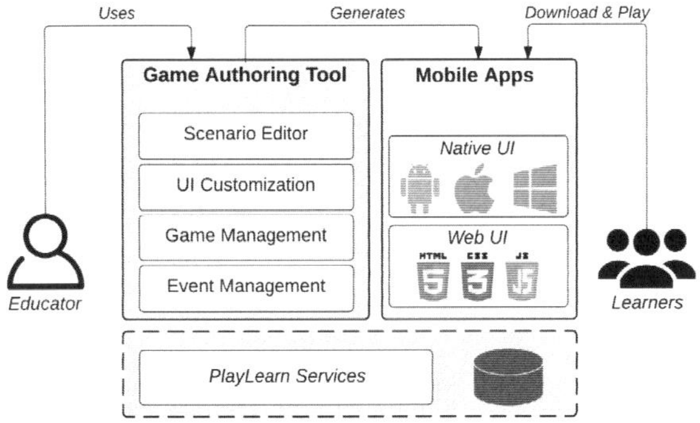

Figure 3. PlayLearn conceptual architecture

Figure 2 presents a simple game example for a visit of preliminary school pupils to a Botanical garden to explore olive trees, consisting of three activities corresponding to the pre-visit, visit and post-visit phases.

IV. ARCHITECTURE

Built as a web application, the system adopts the Rich Internet Application (RIA) principles, which promote the development of web applications as desktop applications performing business logic operations on the server side, as well as on the client side. The client side logic operates within the web browser running on a user's local computer, while the server side logic operates on the web server hosting the application.

Figure 3 presents the conceptual architecture of the PlayLearn platform. The main parts of this architecture are: (a) The Game Authoring Tool used by the Educator for the creation of games, providing functionality for game scenario design, game and event management, and UI customization, and (b) the Mobile Apps providing both Native UI to support mobile devices with different OS (Android, iOS, Windows) and a Web UI, which are used by the Learners to download and play the games created by the Authoring Tool during events organized by the Educators. The Game Authoring Tool and the Mobile Apps are supported by a number of services and repositories that are described in detail in the following paragraphs.

The overall system architecture is presented in Figure 4. For the development of the application we adopted several design patterns [17]. The use of well-established and documented design patterns speeds up the development process, since they provide reusable solutions to the most common software design problems [18][19]. The Model-View-Controller (MVC) design pattern [20][21] and the Observer pattern were used on the client side, and a multi-tier architecture was implemented on the server side, which are described in the following sections.

A. Server Side

The Server Side part of our platform adopts a multi-layered architectural pattern consisting of three basic layers

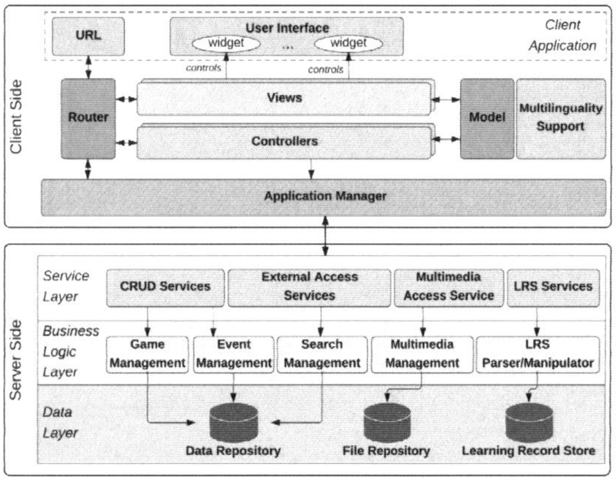

Figure 4. PlayLearn system architecture

(Figure 4): The *Service Layer*, the *Business Logic Layer* and the *Data Layer*. This increases the system's maintainability, reusability of the components, scalability, robustness, and security.

The *Service Layer* controls the communication between the client-side logic and the server-side logic, by exposing a set of services (operations) to the client-side components [22]. These services comprise the middle-ware concealing the application business logic from the client and have been built as RESTful [23][24]. The basic system services are:

- *CRUD Services*, facilitating the creation, retrieval, update and deletion of a game, an event associated with a game, a user etc.
- *External Access Services*, providing the means for the client side and external systems to use the data of the system.
- *Multimedia Access Services*, enabling access to the uploaded multimedia files and their respective thumbnails, and
- *LRS Services*, facilitating the creation of statements. A Learning Record Store (LRS) is a place to store learning records and is connected with the xAPI. As xAPI-enabled activities generate statements, they're sent to an LRS. The LRS is simply a repository for learning records that can be accessed by a Learning Management System (LMS) or a reporting tool.

The *Business Logic Layer*, also known as *Domain Layer*, contains the business logic of the application and separates it from the Data Layer and the Service Layer. In more detail:

- The *Game Management Module* is responsible for the game management, as well as for the activity and task (de)composition in our system.
- The *Event Management Module* is responsible for the event management.
- The *Search Management Module* handles the search and filter queries posed on our dataset and delivers the obtained results to the appropriate component of the Service Layer.
- The *Multimedia Management Module* is responsible for managing the persistence and serving of multimedia files, as well as for performing basic metadata extraction and thumbnail generation.
- The *LRS Parser/Manipulator Module* is responsible for the persistence and accessing of gaming results that have been collected and obtained during a gaming activity.

The *Data Layer* accommodates external systems which are used to index and persist both data and multimedia files. Such systems are:

- The *Data Repository*, storing all the data of the system,
- the *File Repository*, persisting the multimedia files and thumbnails, and
- the *Learning Record Store*, archiving the collected results of the gaming activities which have been already performed.

B. Client Side

The Client Side of the PlayLearn applications is responsible for the interaction with the user. It refers to both the authoring tool (web application) and the player application (mobile application). All the actions performed by an individual are handled by the client side logic which undertakes the presentation of the information as well as the communication with the server. In order to achieve a high level of decoupling between the components forming the client logic we adopted the Model View Controller (MVC) design pattern, as well as the Observer pattern. The usage of the MVC pattern introduces the separation of the responsibilities for the visual display and the event handling behavior into different entities, named respectively, View and Controller.

The *Model* refers to the business objects which are being used by our system. When the system needs to present information about a business object, the client side requests the respective information from the server side using the services that the later exposes. Similarly, when an update on the Model needs to be persisted, the client side sends the updated Model to the server side, triggering the indexing and storage of the business objects by the appropriate modules and external systems.

The *Views* are responsible for the presentation of information in the user interface. Each view controls a number of widgets on the application's graphical user interface. It consists of several handlers that are responsible for listening user actions, as well as HTML templates that define the presentation of the widgets.

The *Controllers* are the modules that respond to the user input and interact with the Views in order to perform any change on the user interface. Furthermore, they maintain the Model and change it appropriately. Every View has a dedicated Controller managing, handling and propagating any changes that are to be performed or have already been performed to the user interface. Moreover, there are several cases where a "composite" Controller manages a number of other Controllers in order to create complex widgets.

The Router is used for deep-linking URLs to controllers and views. It manages the URL of the client browsers, providing a different path to each distinct interface, without raising a browser event that will force a reload on the whole page. When the URL changes the Router analyzes the new path and handles the transition to the new View. This is performed using mappings between the different URLs supported in the system, the Controllers and the Views.

The *Multilinguality Support* module manages the translation of the user interface elements through the use of certain configuration files. The process is easily adaptable and the system can be extended to support any language with minimum effort. It is worth to mention that currently the graphical user interfaces of the system have been already translated in English and Greek.

V. IMPLEMENTATION

The PlayLearn platform has been successfully implemented as described in the previous sections. Its server side is based on Java and makes extensive use of the Spring Framework in order to tackle certain backend aspects like data access. For persistency storage, MongoDB is used. One of the reasons that led us to choose MongoDB is that most of our data does not conform to a rigid relational schema. Hence, we cannot bind it in the structure of a relational database and we need some more flexibility. Due to the fact that MongoDB allows us to store parts of our data in different forms with minor effort, our back end is considered compatible with the Learning Record Store and xAPI. Moreover, this makes our system capable of supporting interoperability with other external systems with minimum effort.

Regarding the client side, both the game authoring tool and the player application are based on the latest web-application standards, rely on the JavaScript programming language and make extensive use of the AngularJS framework. Moreover, they have been created in order to match different user requirements, and thus their user interfaces are implemented differently in order to match the goals of their stakeholders. Apart from JavaScript, the user interface layout has been built using HTML5 and CSS3. The player application has been packaged as a native mobile application with the use of Phonegap, making it compatible with all the major mobile platforms. This allows our application to run without the need of internet access, or loading its source each time that the user accesses it. Additionally, the use of Apache Cordova allowed us to provide more functionality by using various native platform features that are otherwise unavailable to web applications.

Figure 5 presents the graphical user interface of the game authoring tool. More specifically, it shows the use of the scenario editor while the user creates a new task of type "Capture" in order to populate an already existing activity of a game named "Explore Olive Trees". The left side of the user interface is used for presenting the game activity list, while the right side is used as the main working area for customizing activity tasks. The top bar is used for the main menu inspection, user interface customization (in terms of language and layout), as well as for changing personal settings. Figure 6 presents the graphical user interface of the

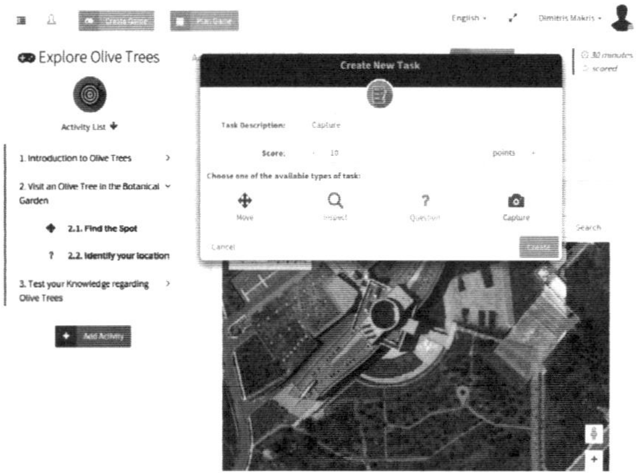

Figure 5. Game authoring tool (web application)

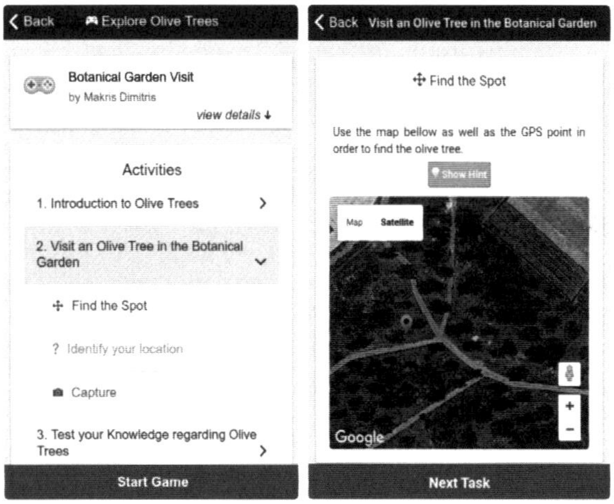

Figure 6. Player application (mobile application)

mobile application that was generated by the game authoring tool in Figure 5. The screenshot on the left side shows the preview that is presented to the user just before starting the game. It includes basic information such as the event, the game, the creator and the list of activities that need to be completed. On the other hand, the screenshot on the right has been taken during playing the game and shows an activity task of type "Move" requiring the user to use the map in order to navigate to a specific spot of interest.

VI. GAMES DEVELOPMENT IN EVANDE PROJECT

The Laboratory of Distributed Multimedia Information Systems and Applications at the Technical University of Crete (TUC/MUSIC), the developer of PlayLearn, is collaborating with the Natural History Museum of Crete (NHMC) in order to develop and run two piloting e-games based on mobile devices (e.g., tablets, mobile smart phones) within the framework of the European project EVANDE. EVANDE (Enhancing Volunteer Awareness and education against Natural Disasters through E-learning) [11] is a European project co-funded by the European Union Civil Protection Mechanism (Grant Agreement No. ECHO/SUB/2014/693261). EVANDE is targeting to the training of civil protection volunteers and local authorities' staff on the topics of floods, forest fires, earthquakes and European civil protection policies. Additionally, the EVANDE project aims at the exchange of experiences in order to strengthen the cross-border collaboration and effectiveness of civil protection policies and activities among the participating countries and the involved target groups.

The EVANDE project (2015-2016) is coordinated by the Natural History Museum of Crete-University of Crete, in Greece and involves also the following partners:

- Technical University of Crete - Laboratory of Distributed Multimedia Information Systems and Applications, GREECE
- Consorci De La Ribera, SPAIN
- Beigua European & Global Geopark, ITALY
- Earthquake Planning & Protection Organisation, GREECE
- Fondazione Hallgarten – Franhetti/Centro Studi e Formazione Villa Montesca, ITALY
- Centre for Educational Initiatives, BULGARIA

Several activities are developed by EVANDE project. Besides mobile games, these activities also include the publication of technical reports on natural hazards, the European civil protection policies and best practices and the organization of an international volunteers' meeting in Italy.

Among the main outcomes of the EVANDE project, the development of an e-learning platform [25] is also included, to train local authorities' staff and civil protection volunteers on floods, forest fires, earthquakes and European civil protection policies. The e-learning courses are free of charge and require only a simple registration.

A. Education and Public Awareness in Natural History Museum of Crete

The Natural History Museum of Crete (NHMC) (nhmc.uoc.gr) is a pioneer institute at national and European level in the study and management of the natural environment, in public awareness, education and sensibilisation of local people as well as visitors from abroad through its Centre of Environmental Training (NHMC-CET), in linking university activities with the Society and is also involved in the set-up of a network of Ecological Museums. In its permanent Exhibition Halls, of 3500 m2, in the city of Heraklion, Crete, the natural environment of the eastern Mediterranean area with special emphasis on Greece and Crete is displayed.

Combining its scientific and educational knowledge, NHMC pursues special interest in Integrated Learning Strategy Plan for the active diffusion of the knowledge accumulated to all sectors of the society. More specifically, Education and Learning in NHMC follow 5 strategic poles: a) Bridging NHMC with Formal and Informal Education: 36 educational workshops for school groups connect NHMC with school curricula and families, using Inquiry-based learning, theatrical games, creative manufacturing, observation exercises, field trips, ICT games etc.; b) Life Long Learning: in NHMC-CET, more than 4000 teachers and other professionals have been trained on Environmental and Pedagogical issues. All training courses have been Quality assured and Validated; c) Volunteering: members of the club "Friends of the NHMC" participate in several indoor and outdoor activities; d) Awareness of People with Special Needs: specialized workshops take place; e) Editions: educational packages for Eastern Mediterranean natural environment are produced.

Most of the educational and public awareness activities are carried out into NHMC permanent Exhibition Halls, where the NHMC Centre for Environmental Training (NHMC-CET) is also activated.

B. EVANDE mobile games

Promoting exploration with mobile location-based educational games is vital to be able to teach players knowledge about specific areas where a crisis can happen [26]. A location-based game provides a low-cost solution for promoting exploration, as it can easily be extended to any area. Due to their nature, mobile location-based games comprise a powerful learning tool in study and awareness of the nature, characteristics and evolution of physical phenomena and practicing on the field on best practices and strategies to prevent and respond on the most effective manner, benefiting the maximum from human and technical resources. For example, a vital part of understanding the risks of an earthquake or flood event is to have knowledge of one's local area. In an evacuation scenario, knowing where it is safe to go is important. Training on these issues is among the main topics covered by the EVANDE project.

The mobile games produced in the context of EVANDE project aim to test innovative methods for the training of civil protection volunteers and local authorities' staff, through the use of new technologies. In addition, they aim to enrich all the educational activities of the NHMC offered to schools, families, local and international visitors.

One of the game scenarios developed aims to simulate an earthquake drill. In this scenario, players (civil protection volunteers or local authorities' staff working in civil protection) are supposed to act as rescuers that have the task of saving a family trapped in the Exhibition Halls of the NHMC during an earthquake. They are given information about the escape map of the NHMC and the assembly outdoor points that are defined by the local civil protection emergency plans. They need to select their protective and rescuing equipment and take virtual decisions during the unexpected virtual incidents they face in their rescue operation. The aim of the unexpected incidents is to test the knowledge of players and encourage their critical thinking and team work. An indicative example of an unexpected incident that the e-game includes is the case of an injured person that interrupts the normal rescuing operation of the family. Once the players manage to rescue the people in need (the family and the injured person) they have to reach an outdoor assembly point to avoid the risk of tsunami that might appear during the virtual earthquake. The exact game scenario is presented in detail in Table I. As a result of this e-game scenario, players familiarize themselves with rescue operations and problems and gain knowledge on the real assembly points of their local emergency plans.

NHMC's facilitators will have the chance after the end of the e-game to reflect with players on civil protection guidelines and preparedness measures. Players can share with NHMC's staff their experience with rescue operations and define the existing challenges and the proposals for improvement of the drills or the local emergency plans. In addition, the conclusions of the piloting operation can be used for the planning of follow-up activities in the framework of the wider educational programs of the NHMC.

TABLE I. A GAME SCENARIO SIMULATING AN EARTHQUAKE DRILL

Game title	Rescuing a family and accompanying it to the assembly point defined by the evacuation plan/local emergency plan of Heraklion of the Municipality of Heraklion
Game goal	There is a strong earthquake happening during the visit of a family to "Ereunotopos" in the NHMC. As a result, a mother and a child are trapped in the night camping space of "Ereunotopos" due to the fall of the ceiling. The persons are still safe and sound however they can't walk, according to the information that the emergency base station has. The player needs to provide first aid to the family and accompany it to the assembly point outdoors, near to the NHMC.
Locations where the activities of the game will take place	**Point 1:** Base floor, entrance of the NHMC, virtual emergency base station **(Starting point)** **Point 2:** Stares connecting the outdoor yard (-1 floor) with the main street**Point 3:** Lift **Point 4:** Night camping space ("Ereunotopos"), Exhibition halls of the NHMC, where the family is. An injured person is also there. (-1 floor). **Point 5:** Emergency exit the outdoor yard (-1 floor) **Point 6:** Assembly point (outdoor space between the 3rd Elementary School and the Church of Agia Triada) **(Ending point)**
Time restriction/Time available to perform the game	No time restriction
Information about the score to be achieved by the winner	Players gain 1 point if they reply correctly to some questions.

Loca-tion	**Task type**	**Task description**	**Score**
ACTIVITY 1 Players' preparation (informing players about their tasks, the equipment they need to take, the NHMC emergency (evacuation) plan, the Evacuation Plan with Assembly points as defined by the Local Emergency Plan of the Municipality of Heraklion)			
Point 1	**Inspect**	You have to locate the mother with the child who are trapped in "Ereunotopos" (-1 floor), provide them with fist aid and accompany them to the most suitable assembly point of the Municipality of Heraklion. Before starting, you should get informed about the NHMC's emergency (evacuation) plan, the Evacuation Plan with Assembly points as defined by the Local Emergency Plan of the Municipality of Heraklion) and take your equipment from the base station.	
Point 1	**Inspect**	Emergency and Evacuation Plan with Assembly points (Local Emergency Plan of the Municipality of Heraklion). 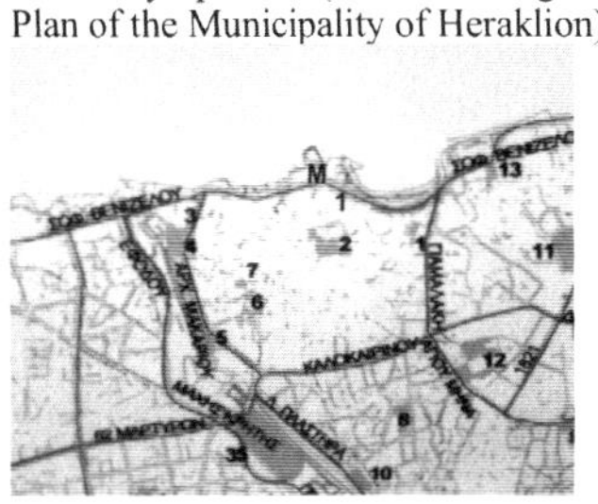	
Point 1	**Answer the question (multi choice)**	Choose the most suitable set of equipment: 1. Helmet, phosphoric jacket, torch, whistle, first aid box, wireless communication equipment, emergency and evacuations plan in printed version (CORRECT), 2. Combat boots, torch, gloves, first aid box, emergency and evacuations plan in printed version (WRONG)	1
Point 1	**Inspect**	You took your equipment and you are ready to start your mission! In the middle of your route you will find QR codes that you need to scan in order to confirm if your route is correct and in line with the emergency/evacuation plan.	
Point 1	**Move**	Move towards the -1 floor where "Ereunotopos" and the family are.	
ACTIVITY 2 Locating the trapped family, provision of first aid to the family, accompanying the family to the assembly point outdoors, exit from the "Ereunotopos"			
Point 2 or Point 3	**Answer the question (QR code)**	Did I choose the right way to move from one floor to the other? Scan the QR code. 1. If player is at stares - **Point 2** (CORRECT) *QR code text:* Yes. In the cases of the earthquakes we don't use the lift. There is danger to be trapped there. 2. If player is at the lift - **Point 3** (WRONG) *QR code text:* No. Your selection was wrong. There is danger to be trapped in the lift. Go to the stairs (**Point 2**).	1
Point 2	**Move**	Continue your route from the stairs (**Point 2**) to the night camping site in	

		"Ereunotopos", where the family is (**Point 4**, -1 floor).	
Point 4	**Answer the question (QR code)**	Find the QR code and scan it in order to confirm that you arrived at the right place. *QR code text:* You arrived at the right place.	
Point 4	**Inspect**	You just arrived but you see there is an injured person that can't walk.	
Point 4	**Answer the question (multi choice)**	What do you do in such case? Choose the correct answer. 1. I provide the first aids to the injured person and to the family and accompany all to the assembly station. (WRONG) 2. I inform the emergency base station about the injured person. I provide the first aids to the injured person but continue my route with the family in order to rescue them. (CORRECT)	1
Point 4	**Move**	Continue your route from "Ereunotopos" (**Point 4**) to the assembly place through the emergency exit door (**Point 5**).	
Point 5	**Answer the question (QR code)**	Find the QR code and scan it to confirm that you selected the right emergency exit door (**Point 5**). *QR code text:* You have selected the right emergency exit door.	
ACTIVITY 3 Choosing the safest assembly point according to the guidelines of the Institute of Geodynamics (after you exit from the NHCM) .			
Point 5	**Inspect**	The Institute of Geodynamics issued guidelines due to a possible tsunami caused by the earthquake. In case of tsunami, people must distance themselves from the coast, due to the difficulty in predicting the wave high.	
Point 5	**Answer the question (multi choice)**	Which Assembly Point is the most suitable according to the guidelines of the Institute of Geodynamics? 1. Playground of Bodosakeio School. (WRONG) 2. Outdoor space between the 3rd Elementary School and the Church of Agia Triada. (CORRECT)	1
Point 5	**Move**	Move to the Assembly Point of the outdoor space between the 3rd Elementary School and the Church of Agia Triada (**Point 6**) (*The GPS and an interactive map are used to help the player reach the destination*)	
Point 6	**Answer the question (QR code)**	Find the QR code and scan it in order to confirm that you reached the Assembly Point of the outdoor space between the 3rd Elementary School and the Church of Agia Triada. *QR code text:* You are at the right place. You reached the Assembly Point between the 3rd Elementary School and the Church of Agia Triada.	
Point 6	**Inspect**	The outdoor space between the 3rd Elementary School and the Church of Agia Triada is the best option between the two assembly points because is more distant from the coast. When there is a tsunami risk, you have to distance yourself from the coast, as much as possible.	
Point 6	**Inspect**	Congratulations! You completed your mission. Press next to see your score and end the game.	

VII. CONCLUSIONS

In this paper, we presented the design and implementation of PlayLearn, a platform for the development and management of learning experiences in location-based games. PlayLearn provides an authoring tool (web application) supporting the creation and management of mobile location-based games, including scenario editing, user interface customization and organization of gaming activities, and a player application (mobile application) supporting the play of games that have been created using our authoring tool. The PlayLearn's player application is compatible with most state-of-the-art mobile devices/platforms, while both tools have been designed with flexibility and extensibility in mind. The underlying model supports a great variety of basic building blocks that can be exploited by a user in order to create a great range of complex and structured location-based gaming experiences. The activities that happen as part of these gaming (learning) experiences are recorded, tracked and shared in a Learning Record Store (LRS) by supporting xAPI. Both applications have been evaluated for their usability through the use of pluralistic walkthroughs and extensive paper prototyping.

PlayLearn is part of the EVANDE project learning infrastructure used for the development of mobile games for the training of civil protection volunteers and local authorities' staff. The pilot testing of the mobile games developed during the EVANDE project can lead to their improvement for wider use in the future, ensuring the follow up of the project. More specifically, these e-games: a) could be combined with other civil protection educational tools developed by the NHMC within the frames of previous and running European civil protection projects, such as PATCH (ECHO 070401/2009/540426/SUB/A4) [27], RACCE (EU, Civil Protection Financial Instrument, 070401/2010/579066 /SUB/C4) [28], SEE (ECHO/SUB/2012/638511) [29], CPMODEL (ECHO/SUB/2014/693249) [30], EPRES (ECHO/SUB/2014/698447) [31], etc.) and b) could be integrated with several educational programmes and/or pathways implemented for school groups, families and individual visitors, such as "I am protected by the seismic danger", etc.

In terms of the technical infrastructure, our future plans also include the following: (a) direct connection with repositories persisting observational data like GBIF, BioCASE and Natural Europe [32], in order to easily enrich the educational content of a game, (b) direct connection with well known cultural heritage repositories like Europeana [33], and (c) enabling the creation of observations during the play of a game [34], as well as their further dissemination to related repositories.

ACKNOWLEDGMENT

The work presented in this paper is partially funded in the scope of the EVANDE (Enhancing Volunteer Awareness and education against Natural Disasters through E-learning) project co-funded under the Union Civil Protection Mechanism, Grant Agreement No. ECHO/SUB/2014/ 693261.

REFERENCES

[1] D. Makris, K. Makris, P. Arapi, and S. Christodoulakis, "PlayLearn: A Platform for the Development and Management of Learning Experiences in Location-Based Mobile Games," The Eighth International Conference on Mobile, Hybrid, and On-line Learning (eLmL 2016) IARIA, Apr. 2016, pp. 43-48, ISSN: 2308-4367, ISBN: 978-1-61208-471-8.

[2] Location-based game. [Online]. Available from: https//en.wikipedia.org/wiki/Location-based_game 2016.11.30

[3] N. Avouris and N. Yiannoutsou, "A review of mobile location-based games for learning across physical and virtual spaces," Journal of Universal Computer Science, 2012, vol. 18 (15), pp. 2120-2142, Aug. 2012, doi: 10.3217/jucs-018-15-2120.

[4] De. Souza, E. Silva, and G. C Delacruz, "Hybrid Reality Games Reframed Potential Uses in Educational Contexts," Games and Culture, Sage Publications, vol. 1 (3), pp. 231-251, Jul. 2006, doi: 10.1177/1555412006290443.

[5] D. Spikol and M. Milrad, "Physical activities and playful learning using mobile games," Research and Practice in Technology Enhanced Learning, vol. 3 (3), pp. 275–295, Nov. 2008, doi: 10.1142/S1793206808000562

[6] P. Arapi, N. Moumoutzis, M Mylonakis, and S. Christodoulakis, "A Framework and an Architecture for Supporting Interoperability Between Digital Libraries and eLearning Applications," Book chapter in "Digital Libraries: Research and Development: First International DELOS Conference, Pisa, Italy, February 13-14, 2007, Revised Selected Papers", Springer Berlin Heidelberg, vol. 4877, pp. 137-146, doi: 10.1007/978-3-540-77088-6_13.

[7] D. A. Kolb, Experiential learning. [Online]. Available from: https://en.wikipedia.org/wiki/Experiential_learning 2016.11.30

[8] J. Delano and A. Shahrazad, "Using the Experience API to Track Learning," Infoline (Numbered), vol. 1304, American Society for Training & Development, 2013.

[9] P. Durlach, J. Poltrack, K. Murray, and D. Regan, "Modernizing Education," MT2, vol. 18(5), 2013.

[10] K. Murray, P. Berking, J. Haag, and N. Hruska, "Mobile Learning and ADL's Experience API," Connections, vol. 12 (1), 2012, pp. 45–49.

[11] EVANDE - Enhancing Volunteer Awareness and education against Natural Disasters through E-learning. [Online]. Available from: http://www.evande.eu 2016.11.30

[12] Geocaching. [Online]. Available from: https://www.geocaching.com/ 2016.11.30

[13] WHAIWHAI. [Online]. Available from: http://www.whaiwhai.com/en/ 2016.11.30

[14] Tourality. [Online]. Available from: http://www.tourality.com/ 2016.11.30

[15] A. Moore, J. Goulding, E. Brown, and J. Swan, "AnswerTree – a Hyperplace-based Game for Collaborative Mobile Learning," The mLearn Conference, Oct. 2009.

[16] ARIS Games. [Online]. Available from: http://arisgames.org/ 2016.11.30

[17] E. Gamma, R. Helm, R. Johnson, and J. Vlissides, Design Patterns, Elements of Reusable Object-Oriented Software. Addison-Wesley, 1995.

[18] D. Alur, D. Malks, and J. Crupi, Core J2EE Patterns: Best Practices and Design Strategies (2nd Edition). Prentice Hall, 2 edition, 2003.

[19] M. Fowler, Patterns of Enterprise Application Architecture. Addison-Wesley, Boston, ersteauflage edition, 2003.

[20] T. Reenskaug, Models - Views - Controllers. Technical report, Technical Note, Xerox Parc, 1979.

[21] T. Reenskaug, The Model-View-Controller (MVC) Its Past and Present, 2003.

[22] G. Alonso, Web Services: Concepts, Architectures and Applications. Springer, 2004.

[23] C. Pautasso, O. Zimmermann, and F. Leymann, "RESTful Web Services vs. "Big" Web Services: Making the Right Architectural Decision," The 17th international conference on World Wide Web, ACM, Apr. 2008, pp. 805–814, doi: 10.1145/1367497.1367606.

[24] R. T. Fielding and R. N. Taylor, "Principled Design of the Modern Web Architecture," ACM Transactions on Internet Technology (TOIT), vol.2(2), pp. 115–150, May 2002, doi: 10.1145/514183.514185.

[25] EVANDE e-learning platform (Coursevo). [Online]. Available from: http://evande.coursevo.com 2016.11.30

[26] I. Di Loreto, S. Mora, and M. Divitini, "Collaborative Serious Games for Crisis Management: An Overview," The IEEE 21st International Workshop on Enabling Technologies: Infrastructure for Collaborative Enterprises (WETICE 2012), Jun. 2012, pp. 352-357, doi: 10.1109/WETICE.2012.25.

[27] PATCH – Prevention Analysis and Tools for Cultural Heritage. [Online]. Available from: http://www.montesca.it/patch/index.asp 2016.11.30

[28] RACCE - Raising earthquake Awareness & Coping Children's Emotions. [Online]. Available from: http://racce.nhmc.uoc.gr/ 2016.11.30

[29] SEE - Safeguarding Educational Environment. [Online]. Available from: http://www.montesca.eu/see/ 2016.11.30

[30] CPMODEL - Civil Protection Massive Open Developed E-Learning for strategies of Resilience. [Online]. Available from: http://www.cpmodel.eu/ 2016.11.30

[31] E-preS - Monitoring and Evaluation of Natural Hazard Preparedness at School Environment. [Online]. Available from: http://e-pres.di.uoa.gr/ 2016.11.30

[32] G. Skevakis, K. Makris, V. Kalokyri, P. Arapi, and S. Christodoulakis, "Metadata Management, Interoperability and Linked Data Publishing Support for Natural History Museums," International Journal on Digital Libraries (IJDL), vol. 14 (3), pp. 127–140, Aug. 2014, doi:10.1007/s00799-014-0114-2.

[33] K. Makris et al., "Federating Natural History Museums in Natural Europe," The 7th Metadata and Semantics Research Conference (MTSR 2013), Special track on Metadata & Semantics for Cultural Collections & Applications, Nov. 2013, pp. 361-372, doi: 10.1007/978-3-319-03437-9_35.

[34] C. Tsinaraki, G. Skevakis, I. Trochatou, and S. Christodoulakis, "MoM-NOCS: Management of Mobile Multimedia Nature Observations using Crowd Sourcing," The 11th International Conference on Advances in Mobile Computing & Multimedia (MoMM 2013), ACM, pp. 395-404, Dec. 2013, doi: 10.1145/2536853.2536887.

Computing Similarity between Users on Location-Based Social Networks

Soha Mohamed*†, Alia I. Abdelmoty*
*School of Computer Science & Informatics, Cardiff University, Wales, UK
Email: {AlySA, AbdelmotyAI}@cardiff.ac.uk
† Faculty of Computers and Information, Helwan University, Cairo, Egypt

***Abstract*—With the current trend of embedding location services within social networks, an ever growing amount of users' spatiotemporal tracks are being collected. These tracks can be used to generate user profiles to reflect users' interests in places. User-contributed annotations of places, as well as other place properties, add a layer of important semantics that if considered, can result in more refined representations of the users? profiles. In this paper, we study how such place-oriented profiles can be used to represent similarity between users of Location-Based Social Networks (LBSN). Spatial as well as semantic dimensions of the user-provided information are used within a folksonomy data model to represent relationships between users, places and tags. The model allows simple co-occurrence methods and similarity measures to be applied to build different views of personalized user profiles. Basic profiles capture direct user interactions, while enriched profiles offer an extended view of user's association with places and tags that takes into account relationships in the folksonomy. The main contribution of this work is the demonstration of how the different data dimensions captured on location-based social networks can be combined to represent useful views of user profiles and to compute similarity between users.**

***Index Terms*—GeoFolksonomy; User Profiles; Location-based Social Networks.**

I. Introduction

This work focuses on Location-Based Social Networks (LBSN) that collect information on users' interests in physical places in the real world. By "switching on" location on devices, we are giving away information on our whereabouts, our daily routines, activities, experiences, and interests. Thus, in comparison to other personal information, location data are possibly the most crucial type of data of relevance to privacy, as it pulls together our virtual and physical existences and thus raises critical questions about privacy in both worlds. This work proposes methods for constructing user profiles using different dimensions of the data captured from users on LBSN [1], and demonstrates how these profiles can be used to measure different aspects of similarity between users.

Studying user similarity from LBSN data is useful, as information available about users, their locations and activities are normally sparse. User similarities can be exploited to predict types of activities and places preferred by a user based on those of users with similar preferences. So far, previous works have studied data produced from LBSN from the point of view of enhancing the services provided by these networks, namely, for point of interest (POI) recommendations. There, the question of concern is to find places of interest to a user based on their history of visits to other places and their general interaction with the social network. Most works relied mainly on the spatial dimension of user data [2], with some works more recently exploring the relevance of the social and content data dimensions on these networks [3]. However, data dimensions are normally treated separately, or their outputs are combined in fused models.

In this paper, both semantic and spatial interactions of users are used to project distinct and complementary views of personalised user profiles. Thus, user's annotations on places they visit are compiled in semantic profiles, while collective user annotations on places are used to create specific profiles for places that encapsulate user's experiences in the place. Place profiles, in turn, are used to construct personalised user profiles. In comparison to previous works in the area of recommendations, LBSN data are treated as folksonomies of users, places and tags. User annotations in the form of tips, their interaction with places, in the form of check-ins, as well as general place properties, namely, place categories and tags, are analysed concurrently to extract relations between the three elements of the folksonomy. Simple co-occurrence methods and similarity measures are used to compute direct and enriched user profiles.

Similarity between users can then be computed using the different views of user profiles; using their direct interactions with the social network or extended with a holistic view of other users' interaction with the network in different regions of geographic space. Previous works attempting a similar approach used matrix factorization techniques to handle the multiple data dimensions, but did not consider the use of the range of content data as used in this paper. Sample realistic data from Foursquare are used to demonstrate the approach and evaluation results show its potential value.

The main contributions of this work can be summarized as follows: 1) Collecting users' direct feedback on venues from LBSNs. Users' interaction on LBSNs can be regarded as user feedback on geographic places they visited and interacted with. User's visits to places are recorded along with their comments and tags. 2) Modelling different levels of user profiles extracted from the heterogeneous user feedback in LBSNs. User-generated traces at venues in LBSNs include both spatial and implicit semantic content. The location traces are treated equally to the semantic traces inferred from their interaction with the place through tagging and tipping. Collective behaviour of users on the network are also used to understand the place characteristics and these in turn are further used in the modelling of user profiles. 3) Similarity between users on LBSN is approached in a uniform manner within the proposed framework, thus providing means of computing spatial, semantic or a combined view of user similarity on these networks. 4) Evaluation experiments are carried out using samples of realistic data sets for a representative number of users with different levels of usage of the LBSN.

The rest of the paper is organised as follows. Section II provides an overview of related work and approaches. In Section III, a geo-folksonomy data model for LBSN is introduced and in Section IV different types of user profiles are defined using this model. Section V describes the approaches to computing similarity between users and detailed evaluation experiments are reported in Section VI. The paper concludes in Section VII with an overview of future work.

II. Related Work

Works on modelling user data in LBSN mainly consider two problems; a) place (or point of interest) recommendation, and b) user similarity calculation. Different types of data are used by different approaches, namely, geographic content, social content as well as textual annotations made by users. Also, different methods are used in analysing the data, for example, distance estimations for geographic data modelling and topic modelling for annotation data analysis. In the area of POI recommendation, works range from generic approaches that uses the popularity of places [4] to recommendation methods that are based on user's individual preferences [5]. A useful survey of these approaches can be found in [6].

Based on check-in data gathered through Foursquare, Noulas and Mascolo [7] exploit factors such as the transition between types of places, mobility between venues and spatiotemporal characteristics of user check-in patterns to build a supervised model for predicting a user's next check-in. Ye, Lui and Lee [5] investigated the geographical influence with a power-law distribution. The hypothesis is that users tend to visit places within short distances of one another. Other works considered other distance distribution models [8]. Gao, Tang and Liu [9] considered a joint model of geo-social correlations for personalized POI recommendation, where the probability of a user checking in to a new POI is described as a function of correlations between user's friends and non-friends close to, and distant from a region of interest. Liu, Xiong and Papadimitriou [10] approached the problem of POI recommendations by proposing a geographical probabilistic factor model that combines the modelling of geographical preference and user mobility. Geographical influence is captured through the identification of latent regions of activity for all users of the LBSN reflecting activity areas for the entire population and mapping the individual user mobility over those regions. Their model is enhanced by assuming a Poisson distribution for the check-in count which better represents the skewed data (users visiting some places one time, while other places 100s of times). Whilst providing some useful insights for modelling the spatial dimension of the data, the above works do not consider the semantic dimension of the data.

Correlations between geographical distance and social connections were noted in [11] [3]. Techniques of personalized POI recommendation with geographical influence and social connections mainly study these two elements separately, and then combine their output together within a fused model. Social influence is usually modeled through friend-based collaborative filtering [12] [5] [13] with the assumption that a user tends to be friends with other users who are geographically close to him, or would want to visit similar places to those visited by his friends. Ying, Lu, Kuo, and Tseng [14] proposed to combine the social factor with individual preferences and location popularity within a regression-tree model to recommend POIs. The social factor corresponds to similar users; users with common check-ins to the user in question. In this paper, we also use this factor when extending user profiles to represent places of interest within the region of user activity.

More recently, the importance of content information for POI recommendation was recognised. Two types of content can be considered, attributes of places and user-contributed annotations. Place categories are normally used as an indication of user activity, thus a user visiting a French restaurant would be considered as interested in French food, etc. User annotations in the form of tips and comments are analysed collectively to extract general topics to characterise places or to extract collective sentiment indications about the place. Examples of works that considered place categories are [15] [16] [17] [18]. In [15] [16], Latent Dirichlet Allocation (LDA) model was used to represent places as a probability distribution over topics collected from tags and categories or comments made in a place and similarly aggregate all tips from places a user has visited to model a user's interest. Aggregation was necessary as terms associated with a single POI are usually short, incomplete and ambiguous. [17] on the other hand modelled topics from tweets and reviews from Twitter and Yelp, and assumed that the relations between user interests and location are derived from the topic distributions for both users and locations. In [18], a probabilistic approach is proposed that utilize geographical, social and categorical correlations among users and places to recommend new POIs from historical check-in data of all users. In this paper, we also model user's association to place through the place's relation to tags, but add the influence of other users relations in the place to the equation. Aiming at improving the effectiveness of location recommendation, Yang, et al [19] proposed a hybrid user POI preference model by combining the preference extracted from check-ins and text-based tips which were processed using sentiment analysis techniques. Sentiment analysis is an interesting type of semantics which we do not consider in this work, but can be incorporated in future work.

So far, most works on user similarity mainly focused on structured, e.g., geographic coordinates, or semi-structured, e.g., tags and place categories, data. Recently, Lee and Chung [20] presented a method for determining user similarity based on LBSN data. While the authors made use of check-in information, they concentrated on the hierarchy of location categories supplied by Foursquare in conjunction with the frequency of check-ins to determine a measure of similarity. Mckenzie, Adams, and Janowicz [16] suggest exploring unstructured user-contributed data, namely tips provided by users. A topic-modelling approach is used to represent users' interests in places. Venues (places in Foursquare) are described as a mixture of a given number of topics and topic signatures are computed as a distribution across venues. User similarity can then be measured by computing a dissimilarity metric between users' topic distribution. Their method of modelling venues is interesting, but it limits the representation of user profiles, where profiles are based on generated topics derived from collective user annotation on places. Thus, individualised association of users with the place is somewhat ignored. In contrast to the above approach, our model does not assume constraints on the number of topics represented by the tags, but combines the individual's association with both tags and place in the creation of user profiles.

Social links between users have also been widely utilized to improve the quality of location-based recommender systems, since the social friends are more likely to share common interests on POIs than strangers. Most current works derive the similarities between users from social links and put them into the traditional memory-based or model-based collaborative filtering techniques. For example, some literature [8], [13], [21]–[23] seamlessly integrated the similarities of users into the user-based collaborative filtering techniques, while others [19], [24], [25] employed the user similarities as the regularization terms or weights of latent factor models.

III. The Geo-Folksonomy Model

The location-based social networking platform Foursquare was used as our source of data. It holds a large number of crowdsourced venues (> 65 million places) from a user population estimated recently to around 55 million users. As the application defines it, a venue is a user-contributed "physical location, such as a place of business or personal residence." Foursquare allows users to check in to a specific venue, sharing their location with friends, as well as other online social networks, such as Facebook or Twitter. Built with a gamification strategy, users are rewarded for checking in to locations with badges, in-game points, and discounts from advertisers. This game-play encourages users to revisit the application, compete against their friends and contribute check-ins, photos and tips. Tips consist of user input on a specific venue, normally describing a recommendation, experience or activity performed in the place.

In this work, we use a folksonomy data model to represent user-place relationships and derive tag assignments from users' actions of check-ins and annotation of venues. In particular, tags are assigned to venues in our data model in two scenarios as follows.

1) A user's check-in results in the assignment of place categories associated with the place as tags annotated by this user. Thus, a check-in by user u in place r with the categories (represented as keywords) x, y and z, will be considered as an assertion of the form $(u, r, (x, y, z))$. This in turn will be transformed to a set of triples $\{(u, r, x), (u, r, y), (u, r, z)\}$ in the folksonomy.
2) A user's tip in the place also results in the assignment of place categories as tags, in addition to the set of keywords extracted from the tip. Thus, in the above example, a tip by u in r with the keywords $(t_1, \cdots, t_n)$, will be considered as an assertion of the form $(u, r, (x, y, z, t_1, \cdots, t_n))$, and is in turn transformed to individual triples between the user, place and tags in the folksonomy.

The process of extracting keywords from tips is done by tokenizing the tip into a set of words (terms) on white space and punctuation. Then we remove all words with non-latin characters and stop words. The output is a set of single words (term vector). Furthermore, we use Wordnet syntactic category and logical groupings for classifying the extracted terms. For example, Wordnet 'noun.act' category is used to filter action verbs and nouns to describe a user- or place- associated activity (ex. swimming, buying or eating).

The data capturing process results in the creation of a *geo-folksonomy*, which can be defined as a quadruple $\mathbb{F} := (U, T, R, Y)$, where U, T, R are finite sets of instances of users, tags and places respectively, and Y defines a relation, the tag assignment, between these sets, that is, $Y \subseteq U \times T \times R$, [26] [27].

A geo-folksonomy can be transformed into a tripartite undirected graph, which is denoted as folksonomy graph $\mathbb{G}_{\mathbb{F}}$. A geo-Folksonomy Graph $\mathbb{G}_{\mathbb{F}} = (V_{\mathbb{F}}, E_{\mathbb{F}})$ is an undirected weighted tripartite graph that models a given folksonomy $\mathbb{F}$, where: $V_{\mathbb{F}} = U \cup T \cup R$ is the set of nodes, $E_{\mathbb{F}} = \{\{u, t\}, \{t, r\}, \{u, r\} | (u, t, r) \in Y\}\}$ is the set of edges, and a weight w is associated with each edge $e \in E_{\mathbb{F}}$.

The weight associated with an edge $\{u, t\}, \{t, r\}$ and $\{u, r\}$ corresponds to the co-occurrence frequency of the corresponding nodes within the set of tag assignments Y. For example, $w(t, r) = |\{u \in U : (u, t, r) \in Y\}|$ corresponds to the number of users that assigned tag t to place r.

Figure 1 depicts the overall process of user profile creation. The process starts with data collection of check-ins and tip data from Foursquare, that are then processed to extract users, places and tags and their associated properties. The modelling stage includes the definition of relationships between the three entities and the application of folksonomy co-occurence methods to extract the different types of profiles. Place and tag similarity calculations are used to further extend the basic profiles to build different views of enriched user profiles.

IV. User Modelling Strategies

We propose an approach to modelling users in LBSN that represents a user's spatial, semantic and combined spatio-semantic association with place. A spatial user profile represents the user's interest in places, while a tag-based profile describes his association with concepts associated with places in the folksonomy model. A spatio-semantic profile describes the user specific interest in certain concepts associated with places in his profile. A user profile is built in stages. Starting with a basic profile that utilises direct check-in and annotation histories, a user profile is then extended by computing the

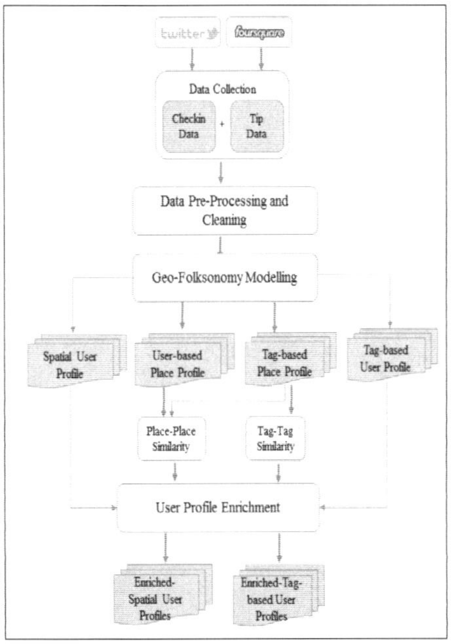

Fig. 1. The framework of the proposed system.

relationship between places and concepts derived from the collective behaviour of other users in the dataset. A basic profile represents actual interactions with places, while the extended profile describes "recommended" associations given overall interactions between users, places and concepts in the dataset. We are able to model such interactions separately in the extended profile by controlling the similarity function used to create the profile. For example, we can focus on modelling the types of places visited by the user or take into account visit behaviour of other users whose profiles overlap with the user, as discussed below.

A. Basic User Profiles

Definition 1: **Spatial User Profile** A spatial user profile $P_R(u)$ of a user u is deduced from the set of places that u visited or annotated directly.

$$P_R(u) = \{(r, w(u,r)) | (u,t,r) \in Y, \\ w(u,r) = |\{t \in T : (u,t,r) \in Y\}|\} \quad (1)$$

$w(u,r)$ is the number of tag assignments, where user u assigned some tag t to place r through the action of checking-in or annotation. Hence, the weight assigned to a place simply corresponds to the frequency of the user reference to the place either by checking in or by leaving a tip.

We further normalise the weights so that the sum of the weights assigned to the places in the spatial profile is equal to 1. We use $\overline{P_R}$ to explicitly refer to the spatial profile where the sum of all weights is equal to 1, with $\overline{w}(u,r) = \frac{|\{t \in T:(u,t,r) \in Y\}|}{\sum_{i=1}^{n}\sum_{j=1}^{m} |\{t_i \in T:(u,t_i,r_j) \in Y\}|}$, where n and m are the total number of tags and resources, respectively. More simply, $\overline{w}(u,r) = \frac{N(u,r)}{N_T(u)}$, where $N(u,r)$ is the number of tags used by u for resource r, while $N_T(u)$ is the total number of tags used by u for all places.

Correspondingly, we define the tag-based profile of a user; $P_T(u)$ as follows.

Definition 2: **Semantic User Profile** A semantic user profile $P_T(u)$ of a user u is deduced from the set of tag assignments linked with u.

$$P_T(u) = \{(t, w(u,t)) | (u,t,r) \in Y, \\ w(u,t) = |\{r \in R : (u,t,r) \in Y\}|\} \quad (2)$$

$w(u,t)$ is the number of tag assignments where user u assigned tag t to some place through the action of checking-in or annotation.

$\overline{P_T}$ refers to the semantic profile where the sum of all weights is equal to 1, with $\overline{w}(u,t) = \frac{N(u,t)}{N_R(u)}$, where $N(u,t)$ is the number of resources annotated by u with t and $N_R(u)$ is the total number of resources annotated by u.

Furthermore, we define a spatio-semantic profile of a user $P_{RT}(u)$, that is a personalised association between user, place and tag.

Definition 3: **Spatio-Semantic User Profile** Let $\mathbb{F}_u = (T_u, R_u, I_u)$ of a given user $u \in U$ be the restriction of $\mathbb{F}$ to u, such that, T_u and R_u are finite sets of tags and places respectively, that are referenced from tag assignments performed by u, and I_u defines a relation between these sets: $I_u := \{(t,r) \in T_u \times R_u | (u,t,r) \in Y\}$.

A spatio-semantic user profile $P_{RT}(u)$ of a user u is deduced from the set of tag assignments made for place r by u.

$$P_{RT}(u) = \{([r,t], w_u([r,t])) | (t,r) \in I_u, \\ w_u([r,t]) = |\{t \in T_u : (t,r) \in I_u\}|\} \quad (3)$$

where $w([r,t])$ is how often user u assigned tag t to place r.

$\overline{P_{RT}}$ is the spatio-semantic profile where the sum of all weights is equal to 1, with $w_u([r,t]) = \frac{N(u,[r,t])}{N_{RT}(u)}$, where $N(u,[r,t])$ is the number of times u annotate r with t, and $N_{RT}(u)$ is the total number of tags assigned by u for r. (Note that tag assignment by users for a place comes from both the explicit action of annotation as well as implicit action of checking-in as represented in the geo-folksonomy model).

B. Basic Place and Tag Profiles

So far, the basic user profile provides only a limited view of the user association with places and concepts derived directly from captured data. Basic profiles reduce the dimensionality of the folksonomy space by considering only 2 dimensions at a time; user-place and user-tag, leading to a loss of correlation information between all three elements.

Users profiles can be extended to represent possible latent relationships in the data. Thus a user profile can be used to present places (respectively tags) similar to those in the basic profile, where similarity between places (respectively tags) is measured through the collective actions of other users of check-ins and annotations.

To compute tag-tag similarity, profiles for tags are first defined through the places they are used to annotate. Thus, a *place-based tag profile* ($P_R(t)$) of a tag t is a weighted list of places r that are annotated by t. That is, $w(r,t)$ is determined by the number of users' check-ins and tips that resulted in assigning t to r in the geo-folksonomy. Similarity between tags is defined as the cosine similarity between their place-based tag profiles as follows.

$$CSim(t_1,t_2) = \frac{|P_R(t_1) \cap P_R(t_2)|}{\sqrt{|P_R(t_1)|.|P_R(t_2)|}} \quad (4)$$

On the other hand, similarity between places is defined by measuring the similarity of their tag-based and user-based profiles. Let $P_T(r)$ and $P_U(r)$ be the tag-based place profile and user-based place profile for place r (defined in a similar manner to user profiles above). Conceptually, a tag-based place profile is a description of the place by the tags assigned to it and a user-based place profile is an account of users' visits to the place.

Cosine similarity between tag-based place profiles ($CSim_{tag}(r_1,r_2)$) and between user-based place profiles ($CSim_{user}(r_1,r_2)$) define a tag-oriented ranking and user-oriented ranking, respectively. These similarity rankings can be aggregated using the so-called Borda method [28] to compute a generalised similarity score between two places.

$$PSim(r_1,r_2) = \gamma * CSim_{tag}(r_1,r_2) + (1-\gamma) * CSim_{user}(r_1,r_2) \quad (5)$$

where $0 \leq \gamma \leq 1$ is a parameter that determines the balance of importance given to similarity scores from $P_T(r)$ and $P_U(r)$. Conceptually, similarity between two places is a function of the overlap between their tag assignments only (for $\gamma = 0$), a measure of their common visitors only (for $\gamma = 1$), or both (for γ between 0 and 1).

C. Enriched User Profiles

We extend the basic user profiles by the information extracted from the computation of tag and place similarity above. The enriched user profiles will therefore present a modified view of how users are associated with places that reflect collective user behaviour on the LBSN.

Definition 4: **Enriched Spatial User Profile** An enriched spatial user profile $\acute{P}_R(u)$ of a user u is an extension of the basic profile by places with the highest degree of similarity to places in $\overline{P_R(u)}$. Let R_u be the set of all places in $\overline{P_R(u)}$ and w_i is the weight associated with place i in the profile.

$$\acute{P}_R(u) = \{< r_i, w_i > | \quad w_i = \left\{ \begin{array}{ll} w_i & ,\text{if } r_i \in R_u \\ w_i * Max(PSim(r_i,r_j)) & ,\forall(r_i \in \{R-R_u\} \wedge r_j \in R_u) \end{array} \right\} \quad (6)$$

We extend the profile by the 10 most similar places to every place in the user profile. The process of building the enriched spatial profile from place similarity with γ as an input is shown in Figure 2. The complexity of the enrichment algorithm is $O(N * M)$, where N is the number of users and M is the number of places in the user profile.

```
procedure SPATIALENRICHMENT(P_R(u),γ)
    for all place r_i in Spatial-Profile P_R(u) do
        Compute PSim(r_i, r ∈ P_R(u)) from Eq. (5).
        Find top-10 similar places((r_j, sim_j))
        for each < r_j, sim_j > in top similar places do
            w_j = w_i * sim_j
            add < r_j, w_j > to P_R(u)
        end for
    end for
    return Ṕ_R(u)
end procedure
```

Fig. 2. Algorithm for building the enriched user profile.

Definition 5: **Enriched Semantic User Profile** An enriched semantic user profile $\acute{P}_T(u)$ of a user u is an extension of the basic profile by tags with the highest degree of similarity to tags in $\overline{P_T(u)}$. Let T_u be the set of all tags in $\overline{P_T(u)}$ and w_i is the weight associated with tag i in the profile.

$$\acute{P}_T(u) = \{< t_i, w_i > | \quad w_i = \left\{ \begin{array}{ll} w_i & ,if t_i \in T_u \\ w_i * Max(Sim(t_i,t_j)) & ,\forall(t_i \in \{T-T_u\} \wedge T_j \in T_u) \end{array} \right\} \quad (7)$$

A similar algorithm to that of enriching place profiles is used for choosing the tags and weights.

Definition 6: **Enriched Spatio-Semantic User Profile** An enriched spatio-semantic user profile $\acute{P}_{RT}(u)$ of a user u is an extension of the basic profile by tags and places with the highest degree of similarity to tags in $\acute{P}_{RT}(u)$. Let T_u be the set of all tags in $\overline{P_T(u)}$, R_u be the set of all places in $\overline{P_R(u)}$ and w_{ij} is the weight associated with tag i and place j in the profile.

$$\acute{P}_{RT}(u) =< [r_i,t_j], w_u(r_i,t_j) > |w_u(r_i,t_j) = \left\{ \begin{array}{ll} w_u(r_i,t_j) & ,\text{if } r_i \in R_u and t_j \in T_u \\ w_u(r_i,t_j) * Max(PSim(r_i,r_k)) & ,t_j \in P_T(r_k) \wedge r_k \in \{R-R_u\} \\ 0 & otherwise \end{array} \right\} \quad (8)$$

The spatio-semantic profile is extended with the most similar places to the user profile and these are assigned a weight computed using the place similarity value for all tags in their place-tag profiles and 0 for tags that are not in their profile. Thus the user simply inherits relationships with all the tags and their associated weights from basic places that are deemed similar to those in his profile.

1) User Profile Example: Here an example is given of a sample user profile created from the dataset used in this work. 'user164' checked in 600 different venues, with associated 400 venue categories. Note that one venue can have more than one venue category. Figure 3 shows the top 20 tags in his semantic user profile. Figure 4 shows the filtered tags from his profile that represent human activity (approximately 5% of all tags), as derived by mapping to Wordnet *noun.act* category.

Figures 5 and 6 show the spatial profile and the enriched spatial profile for user 'user164', respectively. $\gamma = 0.5$ was used in the place similarity equation of the enriched profile.

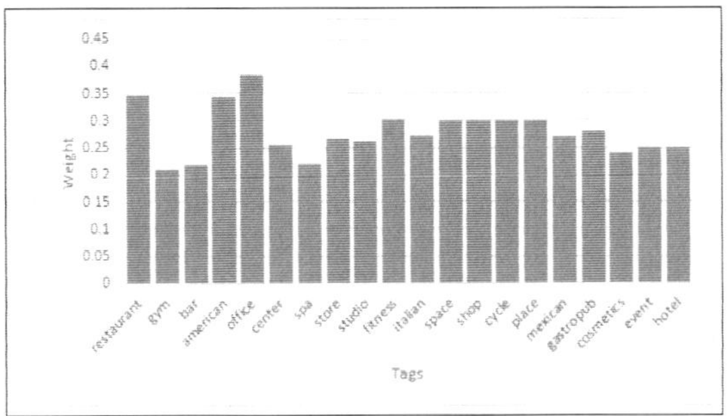

Fig. 3. Example Semantic user profile for user 'user164'.

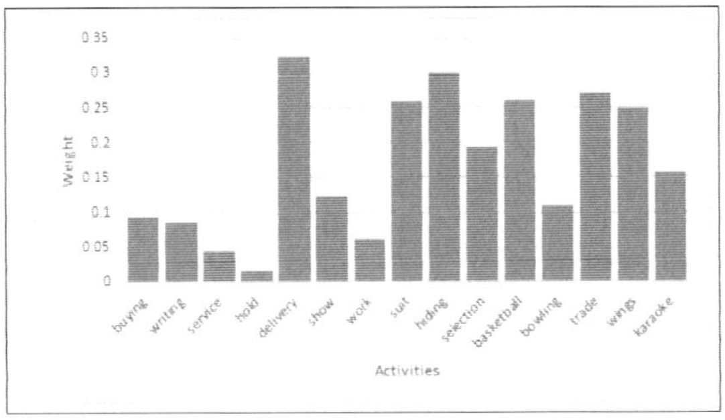

Fig. 4. Tags representing activities in the Semantic user profile of user 'user164'.

The size of the dots in the figures represents the weight (representing the degree of association) of the place in the profile. As shown in the figure, the level of association is more prominent for many more places in the enriched spatial profile.

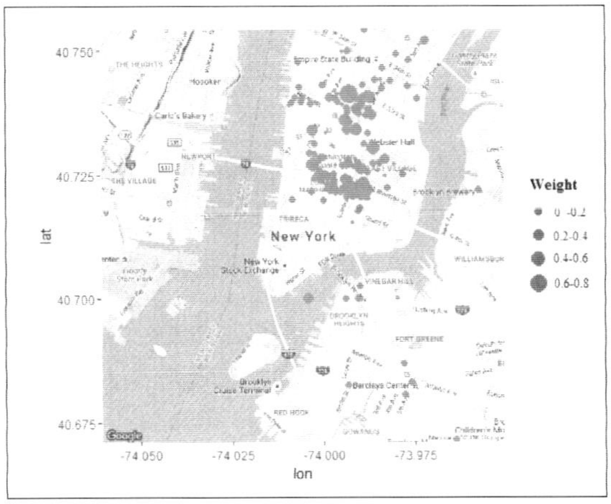

Fig. 5. Spatial user profile for user 'user164'.

V. Measuring User Similarity

Similarity between users can be measured on the basis of their spatial, semantic or spatio-semantic profiles. Spatial profiles gives a measure of user preferences in places. While the basic spatial profile will discover a map of common places that the users visited or annotated, the enriched spatial profile

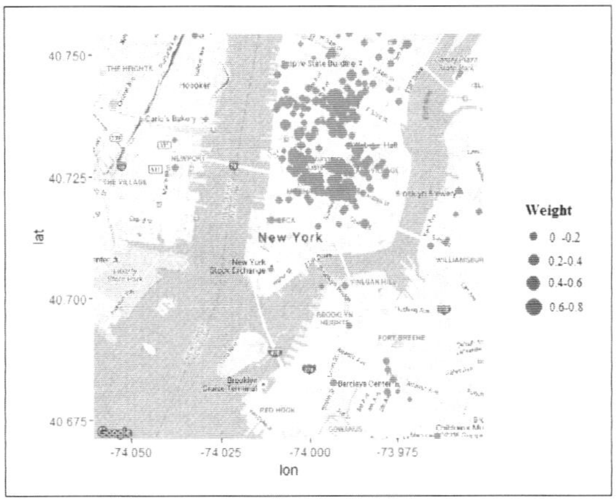

Fig. 6. Enriched spatial user profile for user 'user164' with $\gamma = 0.5$.

will produce an extended map of places that are likely to be of interest to both users. Similarity of spatial profiles can answer the question of which other users visiting habits to places are similar to mine?

Semantic profiles, on the other hand, is a conceptual measure of user interests. Semantic filters on the types of concepts, e.g., themes of user activity or place type, can be applied to the folksonomy to give a more focussed view of user interests. Similarity of semantic profiles can answer questions such as, which other users share the same sort of activities as I do?

Spatio-semantic user similarity is a measure of personalised interests in places, as well as their associated concepts. It gives a holistic view of user preferences in place and will answer questions of which other users are interested in this (specific) place and share the same experiences or interests in this place.

Cosine similarity between any of the above types of profiles can be used to compute the similarity between users. The application of this process can be constrained by region of interest, by considering only users who have a high degree of similarity between their basic spatial profiles.

Figure 7 shows a bar chart of similarity values between 'user164' and other users, using their basic spatial and enriched spatial profiles. The figure demonstrates the impact of enrichment on user similarity, where this user appears to become more similar to other users in his profile (e.g., with 'user134'), given an extended view of their interests in places and their associated concepts.

VI. Experiments and Results

A. Datasets

Data about venues, tips and users who left the tips can be collected directly from Foursquare. However, users' check-in data are normally private. Many Foursquare users tend to push their check-in activity through Twitter; thus allowing another means of tracing the check-in information.

Approximately (10 months) of check-in data in New York city were collected from Foursquare between April 2012 and February 2013. This data consists of 227,428 anonymized user check-ins, with venue ids, venue category, longitude and

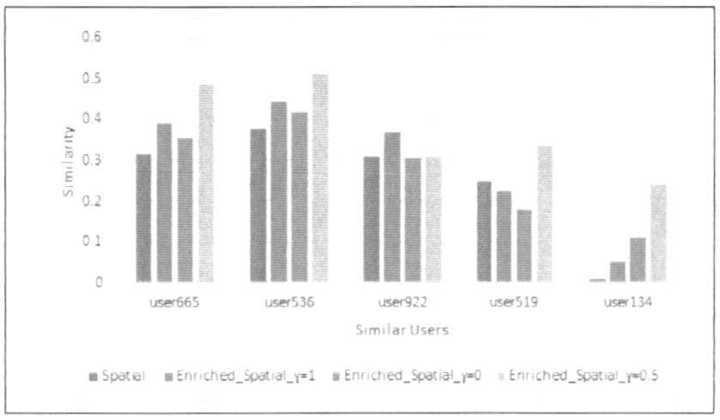

Fig. 7. Similarity between 'user164' and other users using their spatial and enriched spatial profiles.

latitude of venues and time stamps of check-ins. The data was then used to recursively extract venue-related tips (tip id, text and time stamp), and subsequently all venues for users related to the tips collected. 604,924 tips were collected for 167,786 users in 36,940 venues. Time stamps of the tip data range from January 2009 to June 2015. Figure 8 shows the number of places versus the number of users in the collected dataset. As the figure shows, about 94% of the users visited less than 10 places and about 3% of users visited 11 to 20 places and the remaining 3% visited 21 to 400 places.

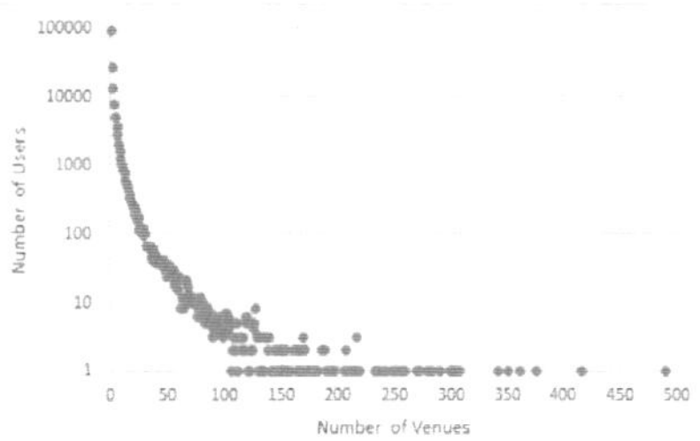

Fig. 8. Number of users versus the number of venues visited in the dataset.

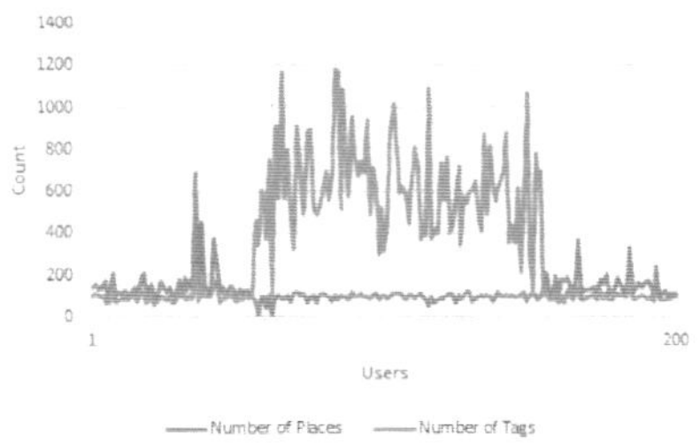

Fig. 9. Number of distinct places and tags for each user in the dataset.

Experiments were carried out using a sample of 400 users (200 users with a high frequency of check-ins and co-location rate and 200 users with a low frequency usage). Evaluation results for the profiles are presented for the high frequency users, but later a comparison between the two data sets is also given. Tables I, II shows summary statistics of the used sample datasets for both groups of users.

TABLE I. High Frequency Users' Dataset

Number of Venues	10,988
Total number of Checkins	50,584
Total Number of Tips	10,469
Total Number of Disitnct Tags	13,396
Number of users	200
Total Number categories	495
Total Number of Relationships	165,453

TABLE II. Low Frequency Users' Dataset

Number of Distinct Venues	4,411
Total number of Checkins	4,212
Total Number of Tips	2,900
Total Number of Tags	5,949
Number of users	200
Total Number categories	374
Total Number of Relationships	57,786

B. Evaluation of User Profiles

The evaluation experiment aims to measure the impact of using the full range of content captured on LBSN when building user profiles in comparison to using only partial views based on the check-in information. The experiment takes the form of place (and tag) top-N recommendation problem using the different constructed user profiles and seeks to establish how well the profiles reflect the user spatial and semantic characteristics when using the LBSN. The algorithm used for computing the top-N recommendations using spatial profiles is shown in Figure 10.

We use recall@N, precision@N and F1@N as our success measures, where N is a predefined number of places (or tags) to be recommended. Recall measures the ratio of correct recommendations to the number of true places (or tags) of a test check-in or tip record, whereas precision measures the ratio of correct to false recommendations made. Recall and precision are given by the following equations.

$$recall = \frac{TP}{TP + FN}$$
$$precision = \frac{TP}{TP + FP}$$

True positives (TP) is the number of correct place (or tags) recommended; false positives (FP) is the number of wrong recommendations and false negatives (FN) is the number of true place (or tags) which were not recommended. F1 is a

TABLE III. Descriptive statistics of Check-ins for User Categories

Check-ins	Low Frequency Users	High Frequency Users
Mean	26.685	123.455
Median	28	105.5
Mode	29	104
Standard Deviation	6.221682	65.91199
Sample Variance	38.70932	4344.39
Range	29	648
Minimum	9	42
Maximum	38	690
User Count	200	200

```
procedure SPATIO-SEMANTIC TOP-K RECOMMENDER(γ,TopK)
    for each u_i do
        SpatialEnrichment(P_R(u_i), γ)
    end for
    for all u_i, u_j do
        Fetch profiles P_R(u_i), P_R(u_j)
        Compute CSim(u_i, u_j) .
    end for
    for each u_i do
        Fetch most similar user u_j
        Sort < r_j, w_j > of P_R(u_j)
        Recommend TopK r_j that are not in P_R(u_i)
    end for
    return TopK < r_j, w_j >
end procedure
```

Fig. 10. Spatio-semantic Top-K recommendation algorithm.

combined measure of recall and precision and is given by

$$F1 = \frac{2 * precision * recall}{precision + recall}$$

The values of TP, FP and FN are determined by randomly splitting the users into two sets; the training set and the testing set. Multi-fold cross-validation was used to ensure a fair partitioning between test data and training data. Data were split 90% for training and 10% for testing, and the process was repeated 5 times to create 5 folds and the mean performance was reported.

1) Evaluation of Spatial Profiles: Results for the enriched user profiles using the proposed top-N recommendation method are presented. Different versions of the enriched spatial profiles, using different place similarity measures were created, a) using $\gamma = 0$ (to represent enrichment with place-tag similarity only), b) using $\gamma = 1$, (to represent enrichment with place-user similarity only), and c) using $\gamma = 0.5$ for an aggregated view of both effects. Hence, result sets are shown for the following user profiles. 1. Enriched-(Spatial + Tag) 2. Enriched-(Spatial+ User) 3. Enriched-(Spatial + All).

We compare the results of the top-N recommendation using the three different profiles with traditional Item-based Collaborative Filtering (IBCF) [29] and User-based collaborative Filtering (UCBF) [30] approaches, applied against the basic spatial user profile for recommending top-1, 2, 3, 4, 5, 10, 20, 30, 40, 50. Figures 11, 12 and 13 show the precision, recall and F1-measure for all approaches. As is shown in the figures, enriched user profiles demonstrate significantly better performance in comparison to the traditional approaches. In particular, the F1 measure for the combined profile (Spatial + All) outperforms the UBCF approach by 10% on average and the IBCF approach by 12% on average.

2) Evaluation of Semantic profiles: A similar experiment was carried out to evaluate the semantic user profiles. Again, the results were compared to the UBCF and IBCF approaches. Figures 14, 15 and 16 show the results of the top-10, 20, 30, 40, and 50 tag recommendations using the different

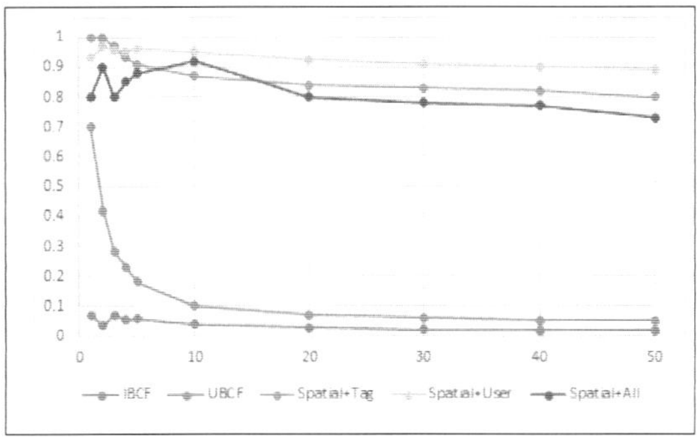

Fig. 11. Precision values for the top-N place recommendations.

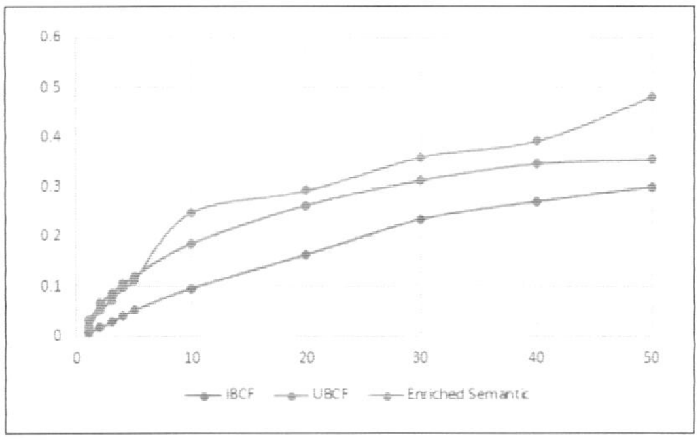

Fig. 12. Recall values for the top-N place recommendations

methods. As shown in Figure 14, the enriched semantic profile demonstrates significant improvements with respect to both the UBCF and IBCF approaches. Results demonstrates the quality of the enriched semantic user profiles, and thus confirm their utility for more accurate representations of user profiles.

C. Evaluation of User Similarity Approaches

1) Methodology: The measure of user similarity is evaluated as an Information Retrieval problem where we search for the most similar user to a particular user in question. Place categories are used as a basis of ground truth comparison and evaluation.

Table IV shows an example; where distinct categories for the top-10 most visited places are shown for two sample users (with similarity value of 0.65). Foursquare attaches more than

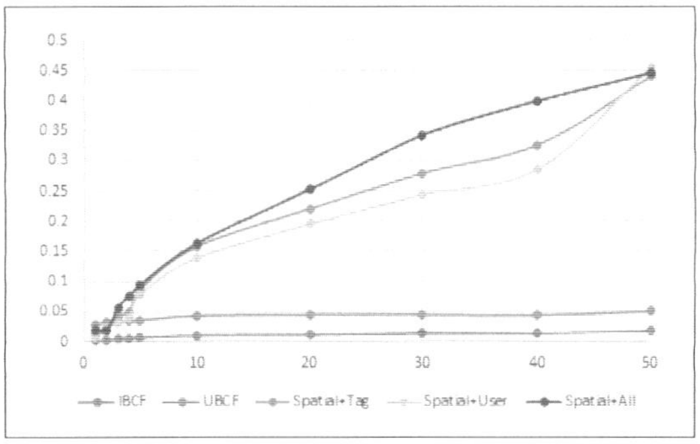

Fig. 13. F1 measure values for the top-N place recommendations

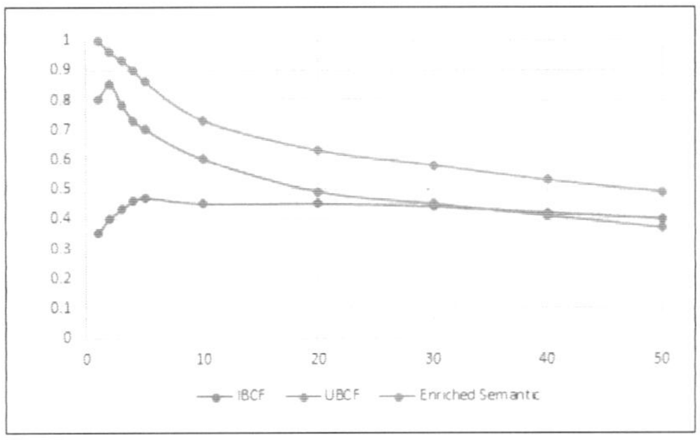

Fig. 14. Precision values for top-N tag recommendations.

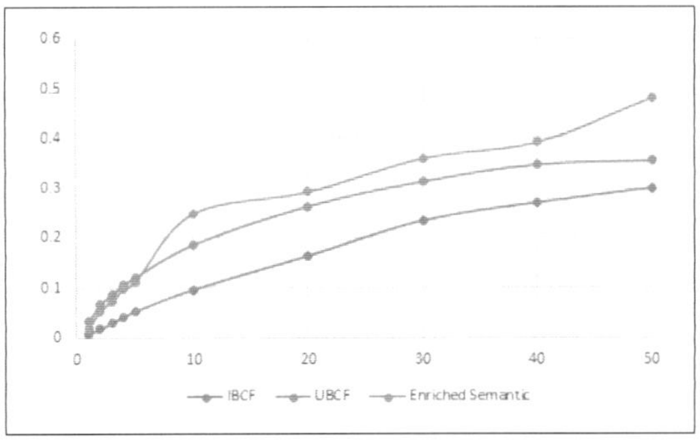

Fig. 15. Recall values for top-N tag recommendations.

one category to a place, and thus, there may be more than 10 categories for the top-10 places . The highlighted cells show the common categories between the two users.

Precision, recall and F-Measure are used as evaluation metrics in the same way they are used in the IR literature. These are defined below.

$$Precision = \frac{|f(u) \bigcap f(u_{sim})|}{f(u_{sim})} \quad (9)$$

$$Recall = \frac{|f(u) \bigcap f(u_{sim})|}{f(u)} \quad (10)$$

$$F1 = \frac{2 * precision * recall}{precision + recall} \quad (11)$$

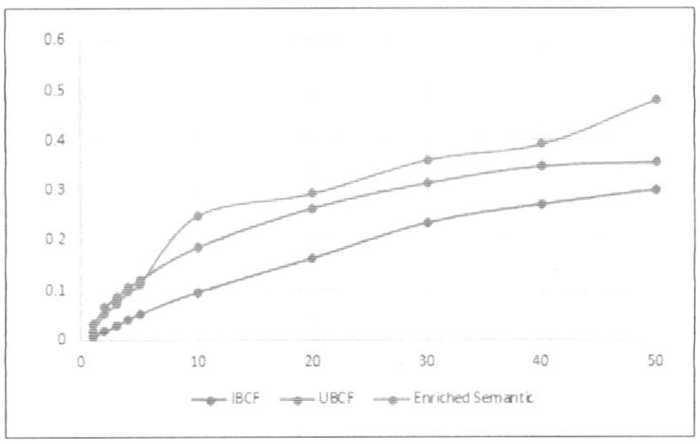

Fig. 16. F1 measure values for top-N tag recommendations.

TABLE IV. Distinct categories for top-10 most visited place for two users with similarity value of 0.65

User 1	*User 2*
"American Restaurant"	"BBQ Joint"
"Coffee Shop"	"Bagel Shop"
"Shoe Store"	"Train Station"
"Pizza Place"	"Leather Goods Store"
"Office"	"Deli / Bodega"
"Train Station"	"Seafood Restaurant"
"Gym / Fitness Centre"	"Hotel"
"BBQ Joint"	"Clothing Store"
"Deli / Bodega"	"Residential Building"
"Donut Shop"	"Bakery"
"Metro Station"	"Park"
"Leather Goods Store"	"Shoe Store"
	"American Restaurant"
	"Meeting Room"
	"Office"

where f(u) is the set of the distinct categories of the top-k places of user u, u_{sim} is the most similar user, and f(u_{sim}) is the set of distinct categories of the top-k places of the most similar user u_{sim}. Hence, precision represents the ratio of common categories between the two users in reference to those of the first user, while recall presents the same ration with respect to the second user. The F1 measure is the harmonic mean of precision and recall.

2) *Similarity of Spatial Profiles:* The evaluation experiment aims to measure the impact of using the full range of content captured on LBSN when building user profiles in comparison to using only partial views based on check-in information. We calculate the user similarity between the following user profiles:

1) Spatial User profile; ($user\_sim$)
2) Enriched Spatial with $CSim_{tag}$, $\gamma = 1$; ($user\_sim_{tag}$)
3) Enriched Spatial with $CSim_{user}$, $\gamma = 0$; ($user\_sim_{user}$)
4) Enriched Spatial with combined similarity, $\gamma = 0.5$); ($user\_sim_{combined}$)

Table V is a compilation of the precision, recall and F1-measure values for the various user similarities. For each profile, we fetch the frequent top-5, 10, 20, 30, 40, 50 venues and then evaluate their categories using the equations.

As can be shown in the table, similarity computation with the enriched spatial profiles produce a higher degree of precision, recall and F-measures in general, whilst the best results are for the enriched profiles with the combined place similarity. Results indicate that location tracks may not be the best basis for finding similar users and that a combined treatment of both the spatial and semantic dimensions can produce more accurate views of user profiles.

To further clarify the improvements in the evaluation metrics figures 17, 18 and 19 present the improvement in percentage of the metrics of the enriched profile over the basic spatial profile.

TABLE V. User Similarity Evaluation: Precision, Recall, F1-measure.

Precision				
Top-K Places	$user\_sim$	$user\_sim_{tag}$	$user\_sim_{user}$	$user\_sim_{combined}$
Top-5	0.29016885	0.2836818	**0.2936379**	0.27810863
Top-10	0.32131577	0.28528178	0.28525722	**0.35280818**
Top-20	0.3590904	0.35163218	0.35682544	**0.3996159**
Top-30	0.38940138	0.39706513	0.40721306	**0.42995644**
Top-40	0.41870615	0.43158174	0.45326504	**0.4587258**
Top-50	0.43747735	0.48375404	0.49606603	0.46999252
Recall				
Top-K Places	$user\_sim$	$user\_sim_{tag}$	$user\_sim_{user}$	$user\_sim_{combined}$
Top-5	0.2910496	0.26843706	0.28794414	**0.2881556**
Top-10	0.31549093	0.28207284	0.28236988	**0.36440614**
Top-20	0.35180694	0.16477493	0.35360697	**0.4058911**
Top-30	0.37913677	0.38837454	0.4045744	**0.44445464**
Top-40	0.39773872	0.41915244	0.44400847	**0.4669912**
Top-50	0.40748206	0.45438704	**0.48419788**	0.47782102
F1-measure				
Top-K Places	$user\_sim$	$user\_sim_{tag}$	$user\_sim_{user}$	$user\_sim_{combined}$
Top-5	0.29060855	0.27584896	**0.29076314**	0.28304298
Top-10	0.3183767	0.28366823	0.28380620	**0.35851338**
Top-20	0.35541135	0.35070109	0.35520891	**0.40272906**
Top-30	0.38420052	0.39267175	0.40588944	**0.43708534**
Top-40	0.40795319	0.42527629	0.44858900	**0.46282160**
Top-50	0.42194730	0.46861089	0.49006011	**0.4738744**

A positive value means an improvement in performance. As can be observed, the average gain in precision and recall is best demonstrated in the case of enriched profile with the combined spatial and semantic measures.

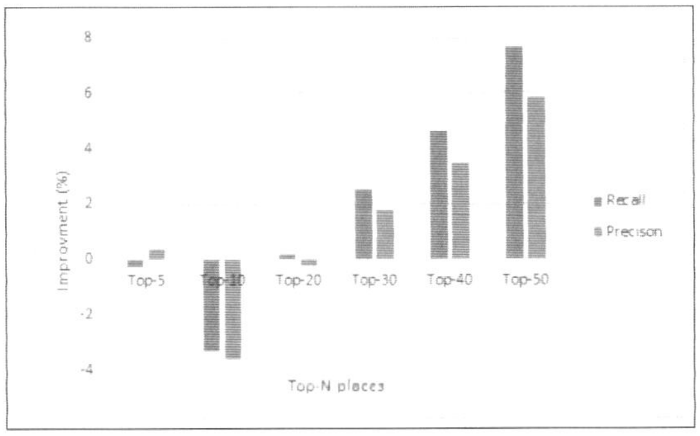

Fig. 17. $user\_sim_{user}$ versus user_sim

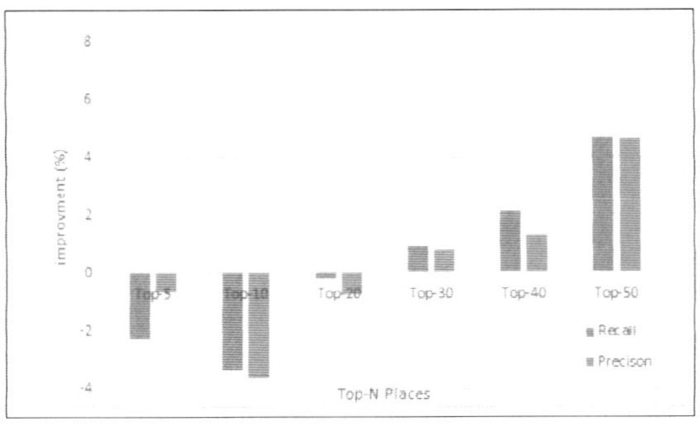

Fig. 18. $user\_sim_{tag}$ versus user_sim

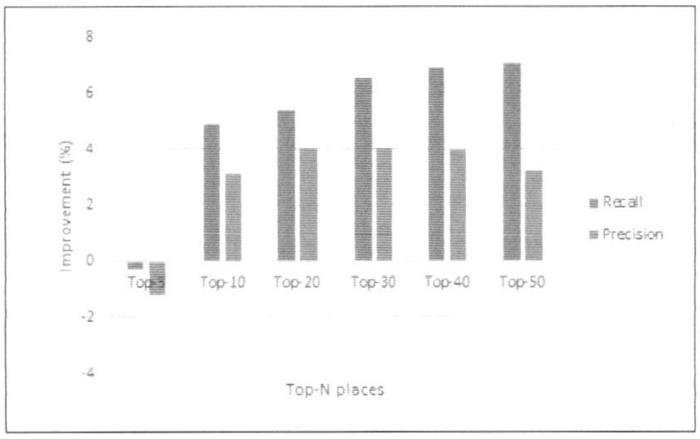

Fig. 19. $user\_sim_{combined}$ versus user_sim

To evaluate the overall performance of similarity methods, *the Mean Average Precision* (MAP) measure is employed. MAP is a commonly used summary measure of a ranked retrieval run. In our experiment, it stands for the mean of the precision score after each relevant user is retrieved for different top-N values, as in Equation (12).

$$MAP = \frac{\sum_1^N p@n}{N} \tag{12}$$

Figure 20 shows a comparative study of MAP between the different user similarities from different profiles baselines, and confirms the improved results for the enriched combined user similarity.

3) Similarity of Semantic Profiles: A similar experiment to the above is carried out for evaluating both the basic and enriched semantic profiles. Table VI shows the precision, recall and F1 measure values. As can be seen in the table, the enriched semantic similarity method performed better than the basic one. A compilation of an overall picture of the spatial

TABLE VI. Semantic Similarity Evaluation

	Precision		Recall		F1 measure	
	Semantic	*Enriched Semantic*	*Semantic*	*Enriched Semantic*	*Semantic*	*Enriched Semantic*
Top-5	0.304228	0.284233	0.302118	0.275948	**0.296848**	0.277169
Top-10	0.337925	0.283362	0.326494	0.279485	**0.319749**	0.279089
Top-20	0.389438	0.365204	0.344888	0.360197	0.348238	**0.35966**
Top-30	0.423739	0.410384	0.351962	0.405662	0.361898	**0.402931**
Top-40	0.456672	0.452301	0.369331	0.443004	0.382173	**0.441523**
Top-50	0.468839	0.49545	0.372371	0.474493	0.386104	**0.475632**

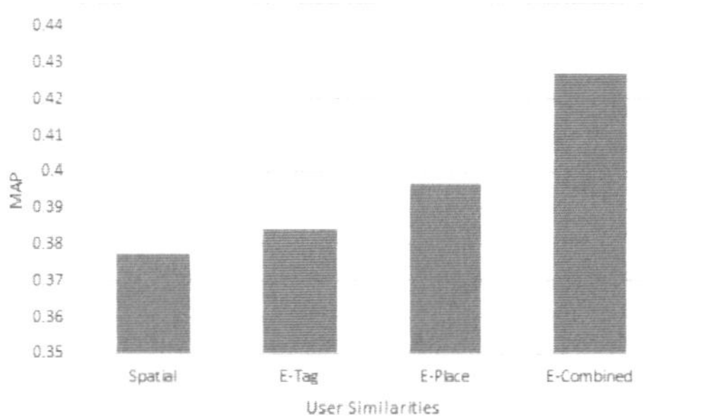

Fig. 20. Mean Average Precision (MAP) values for the different user similarities

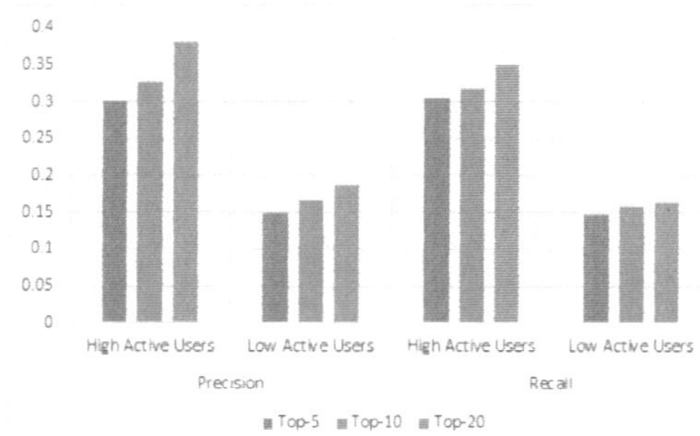

Fig. 22. Activity effect on combined user similarity

similarity against the semantic similarity methods is shown in Figure 21.

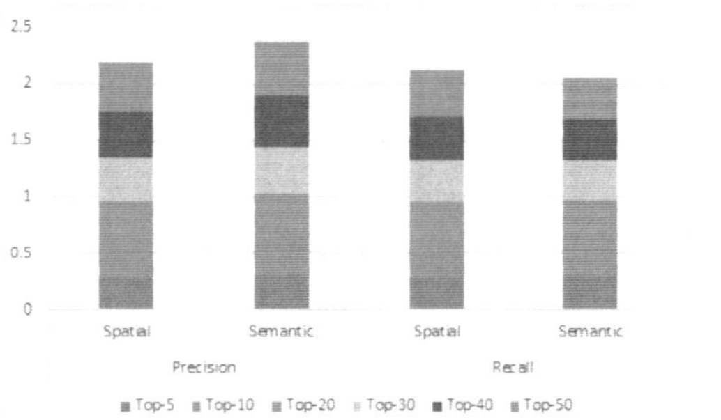

Fig. 21. Precision and Recall values for Spatial Versus Semantic User Similarity Evaluation

4) Influence of User Activity: Here a comparison is made between the similarity methods, given different levels of user activity on the LBSN. 200 users were chosen with high frequency of usage of the network and 200 others with a much reduced frequency as described in Table III.

Figure 22 summarises the results of the evaluation using the similarity method with $\gamma = 0.5$. As can be expected, the figure demonstrates how both the precision and recall values are higher in the case of frequent user.

VII. Conclusions

This paper considers the problem of user profiling on location-based social networks. Both the spatial (where) and the semantic (what) dimensions of user and place data are used to construct different views of a user's profile. A place is considered to be associated with a set of tags or labels that describe its associated place types, as well as summarise the users' annotations in the place. A folksonomy data model and analysis methods are used to represent and manipulate the data to construct user profiles and place profiles. It is shown how user profiles can be extended from a basic model that describes user's direct links with a place, to enriched profiles describing richer views of place data on the social network. The model is flexible and can be adjusted to focus on the spatial and semantic dimensions separately or in combination. Results demonstrate that the proposed methods produce user profiles that are more representative of user's spatial and semantic preferences. The framework is used a a basis for computing different methods of similarity between users. Experimental results were carried out on a representative set of users of a LBSN and demonstrate the efficacy of basing the similarity on profiles that combine both the semantic and spatial information in the data. To our knowledge, no other works have proposed similar treatments of the problem before. Future work will consider the temporal dimension of the data, which adds another layer of complexity as well as explore further inference of useful semantics from the data, e.g., representation of activities or experiences carried out in geographic places.

VIII. Acknowledgment

This work was performed using the computing facilities of the Advanced Research Computing @ Cardiff (ARCCA) Division, Cardiff University.

References

[1] S. Mohamed and A. Abdelmoty, "Uncovering user profiles in location-based social networks," in *GEOProcessing 2016: The Eighth International Conference on Advanced Geographic Information Systems, Applications, and Services*, 2016, pp. 14–21.

[2] Q. Li, Y. Zheng, X. Xie, Y. Chen, W. Liu, and W.-Y. Ma, "Mining user similarity based on location history," in *Proceedings of the 16th ACM SIGSPATIAL international conference on Advances in geographic information systems*. ACM, 2008, pp. 34–42.

[3] H. Gao, J. Tang, and H. Liu, "Exploring social-historical ties on location-based social networks." in *ICWSM*, 2012, pp. 114–121.

[4] X. Cao, G. Cong, and C. S. Jensen, "Mining significant semantic locations from gps data," *Proceedings of the VLDB Endowment*, vol. 3, no. 1-2, pp. 1009–1020, 2010.

[5] M. Ye, X. Liu, and W.-C. Lee, "Exploring social influence for recommendation-a probabilistic generative model approach," *arXiv preprint arXiv:1109.0758*, 2011.

[6] J. Bao, Y. Zheng, D. Wilkie, and M. Mokbel, "Recommendations in location-based social networks: a survey," *GeoInformatica*, vol. 19, no. 3, pp. 525–565, 2015.

[7] A. Noulas and C. Mascolo, "Exploiting foursquare and cellular data to infer user activity in urban environments," in *14th International Conference on Mobile Data Management*, vol. 1. IEEE, 2013, pp. 167–176.

[8] J.-D. Zhang and C.-Y. Chow, "igslr: personalized geo-social location recommendation: a kernel density estimation approach," in *Proceedings of the 21st ACM SIGSPATIAL International Conference on Advances in Geographic Information Systems*. ACM, 2013, pp. 334–343.

[9] H. Gao, J. Tang, and H. Liu, "gscorr: modeling geo-social correlations for new check-ins on location-based social networks," in *Proceedings of the 21st ACM international conference on Information and knowledge management*. ACM, 2012, pp. 1582–1586.

[10] B. Liu, H. Xiong, S. Papadimitriou, Y. Fu, and Z. Yao, "A general geographical probabilistic factor model for point of interest recommendation," *Knowledge and Data Engineering, IEEE Transactions on*, vol. 27, no. 5, pp. 1167–1179, 2015.

[11] E. Cho, S. A. Myers, and J. Leskovec, "Friendship and mobility: user movement in location-based social networks," in *Proceedings of the 17th ACM SIGKDD international conference on Knowledge discovery and data mining*. ACM, 2011, pp. 1082–1090.

[12] D. Zhou, B. Wang, S. M. Rahimi, and X. Wang, "A study of recommending locations on location-based social network by collaborative filtering," in *Advances in Artificial Intelligence*. Springer, 2012, pp. 255–266.

[13] H. Wang, M. Terrovitis, and N. Mamoulis, "Location recommendation in location-based social networks using user check-in data," in *Proceedings of the 21st ACM SIGSPATIAL International Conference on Advances in Geographic Information Systems*. ACM, 2013, pp. 374–383.

[14] J. J.-C. Ying, E. H.-C. Lu, W.-N. Kuo, and V. S. Tseng, "Urban point-of-interest recommendation by mining user check-in behaviors," in *Proceedings of the ACM SIGKDD International Workshop on Urban Computing*. ACM, 2012, pp. 63–70.

[15] B. Liu, Y. Fu, Z. Yao, and H. Xiong, "Learning geographical preferences for point-of-interest recommendation," in *Proceedings of the 19th ACM SIGKDD international conference on Knowledge discovery and data mining*. ACM, 2013, pp. 1043–1051.

[16] G. McKenzie, B. Adams, and K. Janowicz, "A thematic approach to user similarity built on geosocial check-ins," in *Geographic Information Science at the Heart of Europe*. Springer, 2013, pp. 39–53.

[17] B. Hu and M. Ester, "Spatial topic modeling in online social media for location recommendation," in *Proceedings of the 7th ACM conference on Recommender systems*. ACM, 2013, pp. 25–32.

[18] J.-D. Zhang and C.-Y. Chow, "Geosoca: Exploiting geographical, social and categorical correlations for point-of-interest recommendations," in *Proceedings of the 38th International ACM SIGIR Conference on Research and Development in Information Retrieval*. ACM, 2015, pp. 443–452.

[19] D. Yang, D. Zhang, Z. Yu, and Z. Wang, "A sentiment-enhanced personalized location recommendation system," in *Proceedings of the 24th ACM Conference on Hypertext and Social Media*. ACM, 2013, pp. 119–128.

[20] M.-J. Lee and C.-W. Chung, "A user similarity calculation based on the location for social network services," in *Database Systems for Advanced Applications*. Springer, 2011, pp. 38–52.

[21] G. Ference, M. Ye, and W.-C. Lee, "Location recommendation for out-of-town users in location-based social networks," in *Proceedings of the 22nd ACM international conference on Information & Knowledge Management*. ACM, 2013, pp. 721–726.

[22] M. Ye, P. Yin, W.-C. Lee, and D.-L. Lee, "Exploiting geographical influence for collaborative point-of-interest recommendation," in *Proceedings of the 34th international ACM SIGIR conference on Research and development in Information Retrieval*. ACM, 2011, pp. 325–334.

[23] J. J.-C. Ying, W.-N. Kuo, V. S. Tseng, and E. H.-C. Lu, "Mining user check-in behavior with a random walk for urban point-of-interest recommendations," *ACM Transactions on Intelligent Systems and Technology (TIST)*, vol. 5, no. 3, p. 40, 2014.

[24] C. Cheng, H. Yang, I. King, and M. R. Lyu, "Fused matrix factorization with geographical and social influence in location-based social networks." in *Aaai*, vol. 12, 2012, pp. 17–23.

[25] Y.-L. Zhao, L. Nie, X. Wang, and T.-S. Chua, "Personalized recommendations of locally interesting venues to tourists via cross-region community matching," *ACM Transactions on Intelligent Systems and Technology (TIST)*, vol. 5, no. 3, p. 50, 2014.

[26] F. Abel, "Contextualization, User Modeling and Personalization in the Social Web," PhD Thesis, Gottfried Wilhelm Leibniz University Hannover, April 2011.

[27] A. Hotho, R. Jäschke, C. Schmitz, and G. Stumme, "Information retrieval in folksonomies: Search and ranking," in *Semantic web: research and applications, proceedings*. Springer, 2006, pp. 411–426.

[28] C. Dwork, R. Kumar, M. Naor, and D. Sivakumar, "Rank aggregation methods for the web," in *Proceedings of the 10th international conference on World Wide Web*. ACM, 2001, pp. 613–622.

[29] B. Sarwar, G. Karypis, J. Konstan, and J. Riedl, "Item-based collaborative filtering recommendation algorithms," in *Proceedings of the 10th international conference on World Wide Web*. ACM, 2001, pp. 285–295.

[30] M. J. Pazzani, "A framework for collaborative, content-based and demographic filtering," *Artificial Intelligence Review*, vol. 13, no. 5-6, pp. 393–408, 1999.

The KOOLO app

A case study of self-tracking, visualization, and organizing personal moods

Maja van der Velden
Dept. of Informatics
University of Oslo
Oslo, Norway
majava@ifi.uio.no

Margaret Machniak Sommervold
Dept. of Informatics
University of Oslo
Oslo, Norway
margarma@ifi.uio.no

Abstract — **Self-tracking refers to the regular collection of data about oneself. Smartphones and wearables have made self-tracking a pervasive activity. This paper describes the design process of a self-tracking mood functionality, which is part of the KOOLO mobile application. The purpose of the KOOLO application is to support young patients, teenagers and young adults with long-term health challenges, in the transition from child-oriented to adult-oriented healthcare. We implemented a design approach, based on a participatory design process combined with a focus on the wellbeing of the whole person, not just the diagnosis. The result was a mood tracking functionality that collects qualitative mood data in the form of color-tagged photos. The visualization of the data resulted in both a quantification of the data as well as in an interactive mood map. The organization of the color-tagged photos, in the form of a timeline and map, enables the user access to the mood data in different ways.**

Keywords — lived body, lifeworld; m-health; participatory design; qualitative self; transition; visualization, young patients.

I. INTRODUCTION

This paper presents our design research on a mood tracking functionality for a mobile phone application for young patients, who are preparing themselves for the transition to adult health care [1]. It addresses the self-tracking of the expression of moods and emotional experiences, through visualization, in a mobile phone application called KOOLO. The main aim of KOOLO is to support young patients in the transition from child-oriented healthcare to adult-oriented healthcare. This research is part of the KULU research and design project, which focuses on the design and use of interactive technologies with and for young people (15-25 years old) with chronic health challenges. KULU is a Norwegian acronym for Cool Technologies for Youth with Long-term Health Challenges (http://www.kulu.no)

Self-tracking or self-monitoring refers to the practice of collecting data about oneself on a regular basis. It "seeks to make known something that is typically not a subject of reflection, with the aim of converting previously undetected bodily reactions and behavioral clues into traceable and perceptible information" [2, p. 69].

Through the use of mobile phones and wearables, digital self-tracking has become a popular way to gather data about a wide variety of features of one's life, e.g., food, activity, sleep, health, productivity, and mood. These "everyday processes are translated into information" [2, p. 80], which can be used in generating abstract graphs and figures left to the receiver's interpretation. Self-tracking can result in qualitative as well as in quantitative data. The latter is associated with the "quantified self", a term first coined in 2007 by Gary Wolf and Kevin Kelly, which they also described as "self-knowledge through numbers" [3].

In our research and design activities, the experiences of the young patients take up a central place. This is also expressed in one of the central concept in our research, the *lived body* [4]. This notion refers to a more holistic understanding of the body. One of our design participants expressed this as follows: "the doctor should be interested in me, all of me, not just my diagnosis" [5].

Self-tracking focuses on making the features of one's life and body visible. Can we self-track the *lived body*? This paper will present some preliminary findings resulting from a design process with young people with chronic health challenges.

The contribution of this paper is as follows. It locates the design of a mobile application for young patients in the larger discussion of self-tracking. It adds to the literature in designing interactive technologies from the perspective of young people with health challenges. We present our particular design approach, which enables patients to be met as co-designers and experts of their own life and facilitates patient contributions to the design of health IT. Secondly, it contributes to understanding the life of young patients. It shows how they value moods in their life and the importance of taking a holistic perspective when tracking moods. In addition, the paper contributes to the sparse literature on the visualization of qualitative self-tracking data, by presenting a design concept that visualizes the quantification of qualitative data. Lastly, it contributes to understanding the role of technology in the life of young people in general. Teenagers and young adults' technology preferences and use are often very different from those of the researchers. Designing with the future users of a technology increases the chance that the technology reflects the values and needs of that particular user group.

The remainder of the paper is organized as follows. In Section II, we will discuss self-tracking and the use of visualization. We found in the literature that the self-tracking of mood is considered beneficial for both mental and physical health, but quantitative self-tracking and its visualizations can lead to a undesirable objectification of the body. We found no examples of the visualization of qualitative self-tracking. We will therefore, in Section III, explore some concepts that support a holistic patient body perspective in our design process. We also will present SHARM (Situation-based learning; Having a say; Adaptability; Respect; Mutual learning), our methodological framework, based on Participatory Design, which we used in our design activities with the young patients. In Section IV, we present the design process, the methods used, the different stages in the development of the mood tracking functionality, and the final results. In Section V, we discuss the design process and its results and in the final section, we present our concluding remarks and outline future research.

II. SELF-TRACKING

Tracking or monitoring data of different aspects of one's life is an established and persuasive activity [6]. Digital technologies, in particular mobile ones, made it possible to automate large amounts of data collection through the use of build-in sensors, such as accelerometers, gyroscopes, magnetometers, and humidity, pressure, light, and proximity sensors. Wearables, which often extend the tracking functionality of smartphones, can have other sensors, such those that measure heart rate, blood pressure, blood sugar, etc. In addition to the automated sensor-based input, data can be collected through manual user input, for example food intake, period and ovulation, and changes in skin growths, etc.

Working in an environment with young adults, who all have a smartphone, we implemented a scoping survey among our students to understand the occurrence of self-tracking apps. We approached 50 students and received 45 responses (23 male and 22 female students). Twenty-five students used one or more apps (13 male and 12 female students). The most popular functionalities were tracking of activity, such as steps (19 respondents), pulse (10 respondents), sleep (7 respondents); food intake or calories (6 respondents) and menstruation (4 respondents). Non-users often had particular ideas about self-tracking apps: "Apps do not measure in an appropriate way, for example blood pressure" (f/22) or "I do not trust health apps. They can measure wrongly" (f/19). Two respondents pointed to possible negative side-effects of such apps. One used a fitness app, but not other health apps because "It is easy to get too much involved; this can result in a negative self-image (f/20). Another student mentioned "self-tracking apps can make you too self-centered (f/19).

A. *Typology of self-tracking*

Lupton has developed a typology of self-tracking: private, pushed, communal, imposed, and exploited self-tracking [7]. According to Lupton, the aim of *private* self-tracking is self-awareness and improvements in particular aspects of one's life, such as better sleep and better health or control over mood swings. Data collection is self-motivated and for personal reasons; they are not shared or shared with selected others. In contrast, *pushed* self-tracking is motivated by others. External encouragement for self-tracking, such as in the workplace or as part of a health care program, results in data that may benefit both the promotor of self-tracking and the individual doing the tracking. The collected data is often shared with particular others (health care professionals, employers, insurance companies, etc.).

A third category in Lupton's typology is *communal* self-tracking, in which the individualistic behavior of self-tracking is perceived as part of a larger community of trackers. Data are shared, via especially designed social media platforms, "to further one's own interests and goals". In contrast, *imposed* self-tracking is solely for the benefit of others, such as forced productivity self-tacking in the workplace and monitoring of location, alcohol, and drug use by authorities.

Exploited self-tracking is private, pushed, communal or imposed self-tracking, in which the data collection is used for the mainly commercial interests of a third party. The self-tracker may not always be aware of this exploitation.

One line of investigation in the self-tracking literature focuses on the body that is being tracked. In the context of the phenomenological distinction between the *objective body* and the *subjective, lived body*, Pritz mentions that self-tracking focuses on the objective body and thus replaces experiences of the subjective body, which cannot be trusted [8]. Wiederman [9], on the other hand, found no conflicts between the objective and subjective body, but argues that the body can never be reduced to calculations that produce data.

Ruckenstein [2] explores the concept of *data double*, first described as the result of surveillance data [10]; the process in which a person is first divided up in different data streams, as a result of monitoring, and then these data streams are put together in the form of a data profile that is stored on computers in different places. Ruckenstein describes the process of assembling self-tracking data as a re-assembly of the body; a new way of having access to the body, "giving a new kind of value to their personal realities and everyday doings" [p. 81-82]

B. *Quantified and qualified self-tracking*

The majority of self-tracking apps and technologies collect quantitative data. Aspects of one's life are measured in the form of time, speed, weight, location, inputs, states (e.g., mood or blood sugar level), number of events, etc. The "quantified self" is becoming a global phenomenon, with self-trackers meeting each other in cities around the world to compare data and discuss tracking technologies [11].

Qualitative self-tracking can be defined as "*using mobile technology to recurrently record qualities of experience or environment, as well as reflections upon them, with the intention of archiving aspects of personal life that would otherwise be lost, in a way susceptible to future review and revision of concerns, commitments and practices in light of such a review* [12].

Several researchers argue against maintaining a strict division between qualified and quantified self-tracking [7][13][14]. For example, Davis argues that the quantified self has a qualitative component, which is "key in mediating between raw numbers and identity meanings. If self-quantifiers are seeking self-knowledge through numbers, then narratives and subjective interpretations are the mechanisms by which data morphs into selves. Self-quantifiers do not just use data to learn about themselves, but rather, use data to construct the stories that they tell themselves about themselves."

C. Visualization of self-tracking data

The collection of data is often invisible, especially when sensors are used. Data visualization tools are then used to organize and present the data in a meaningful manner, often in the form of graphs, colors, and quantities (e.g., Figures 1 and 2).

Figure 1. Visualizing self-tracking data I (https://zapier.com/blog/best-fitness-tracking-apps/)

Figure 2. Visualizing self-tracking data II (http://www.healthviewx.com/solutions/patient-tracking/)

Personal analytics, personal visualization, and personal visual analytics [15][16], are some of the terms that are used to refer to this particular type of data visualization. According to Few, good data visualization "encodes information in a manner that our eyes can discern and our brains can understand" [17]. A good visualization:

- Clearly indicates how the values relate to one another, e.g., a part-to-whole relationship.
- Represents the quantities accurately.
- Makes it easy to compare the quantities.
- Makes it easy to see the ranked order of values.
- Makes obvious how people should use the information - what they should use it to accomplish - and encourages them to do this.

We did not find literature that discusses the visualization of qualitative self-tracking data.

In the context of self-tracking for people with health challenges, it is important to stress the reliability and accuracy of the self-tracking technologies collecting data for the visualizations. Among others, [18] and [19] report some inaccuracy in commercial wearables and smartphone applications measuring activity levels. While the authors argue that this is acceptable in cases of healthy users wanting to improve their physical health and lifestyle, these inaccuracies contribute to the limited use of mass-marketed self-tracking technologies in clinical studies and healthcare practices [20].

D. Tracking moods and emotions

Moods are often differentiated from acute emotional states, such as being angry, sad or happy. They last longer and are often not related to an immediate trigger: "mood state appears to be an integrative function of the organism's acute emotional experiences over time" [21]. In the field of IT health, e-health, and m-health (health IT), this differentiation disappears when describing or designing mood technology. This becomes for example clear in [22], which categorizes mood technologies into *Technology that measures mood*; *Technology that expresses user mood*; *Technology that adapts to user mood*; and *Technology that influences user mood.* Another categorization of mood technology is diagnosis-based versus general mood. For example, mood apps can address specific mood disorders, such as bipolar disorder [23], anxiety disorders [24], and depression [25], or have a more general approach, such as happy apps [26]. According to Matthews et al. [27], mood tracking, in the form of mood monitoring or mood charting, is widely used in mental health.

In a scoping study, Seko et al. [28] found that mobile phones are an appropriate way to engage youth in therapeutic activities and that "the ability of mobile phones to offer personal space is also considered to increase levels of perceived autonomy, control, and self-esteem in young users" which can strengthen their mental health. The participation and adherence rate to treatment was higher for mobile phone apps than on paper [27], [29], rating mood was seen as most useful [30]. Young people with chronic physical health challenges are more likely to have mood-related issues, ranging from emotional problems to mood disorders [31], [32]. Nevertheless, mobile phone applications still depend on additional therapy in order to be effective, they play a supportive role rather than being able to replace professional treatment.

Self-tracking of moods is also relevant in the context of physical health. Moods and emotions are central components of the *subjective well-being* (SWB) concept. In an extensive review of evidence indicating a positive relation between SWB and health and longevity, Diener and Chan [33] argue that moods and emotions are not only a result of people's life and health situation. The authors present research indicating that "positive moods such as joy, happiness, and energy [...] were associated with reduced risk of mortality in healthy populations, and predicted longevity, controlling for negative states" [p.3]. Despite the controversy surrounding causality explanations between positive SWB and better life expectancy among cancer patients, the authors argue "patients in the low range for SWB would experience better health if their SWB could be raised" [p.33]. Diener and Chan [33] also suggest adding SWB to public health goals and place the responsibility for increasing SWB at a societal level.

In *Making Emotions Count: The Self-Tracking of Feelings*, Pritz [8, p. 184] argues that the self-tracking of moods and emotions can be understood within two opposing views on the social regulation of feelings in modern Western societies: the view that supports the hypothesis of the domestication, disciplining, and instrumental objectification of emotion, and the view that supports the hypothesis of informalization of emotion. Self-tracking brings the two together, as "emotions are treated as phenomena that can be ordered, regulated and normalized" and at the same time "treated as "personal resources for self-knowledge and self-fulfillment".

III. Conceptual Framework

A conceptual framework consisting of three main components guided our research and design activities with teenagers and young adults with chronic health challenges :

a) The lived body

Our research participants made clear that they want to be met as young people, not as patients. Their wish to push their 'patientness', the quality of being a patient, to the background is also confirmed in the literature [34]–[36]. Young patients use the terms *normal* and *regular* to express how they want to be perceived and treated by the world around them [35], [36]. They acknowledge their illness, but want to have lives like their peers and they do not want their caregivers to see only their diagnosed bodies [5].

This particular positioning by the young patients can be explained with the notion of the *lived body*, the body as experienced by the self and as being-in-the-world, as described in phenomenology [37], [38]. The concept that encompasses both the lived body and its experiences in the world is the notion of lifeworld. Lifeworld can be described as "the world of lived experience or the beginning pace-flow from which we divide up our experiences into more abstract categories and names" [39]. Lifeworld theory describes five intertwined dimensions in which these experiences become meaningful: temporality, spatiality, intersubjectivity, embodiment, and mood [39]. Mood, in this context, is described as a "messenger of the meaning of our situation" or our being-in-the-world, "mood is complex and often more than words can say" [39].

b) Lifeworld-led care

Lifeworld-led care is a particular perspective on healthcare, which focuses on the wellbeing of the whole person, not just the illness or diagnosis [40], [41]. This perspective is both a deepening of the understanding of patient-centered care and a critique on the dehumanisation and depersonalization of care, not the least through the use of technology [41]. The aim of a lifeworld-led design approach is to let the young patients' *lived experiences* of everyday life, diagnosis, and technology use, guide the design of new technology that supports them in living their everyday life with their health challenges [41].

c) SHARM approach

In order to provide an enabling environment in which young patients can build forth on their lived experiences, KULU implements its design activities within a participatory methodology called SHARM, which is based on Participatory Design [42][43]. The participation of young people as co-designers of their own healthcare technologies enables a design space in which the young participants can position themselves in the way they perceive themselves and how they want to be perceived by others. The SHARM approach is based on five principles [44]: 1) *Situation-based action* locates the design activities in the lifeworld and relationships of the participants; 2) *Having a say* is about creating real opportunities for participants to share the decision-making power; 3) *Adaptability* is about applying tools and methods in the design activities that can easily adapt to the participants' changing physical or emotional state; 4) *Respect* is about treating the young participants as experts on their own life and body; and 5) *Mutual learning* refers to choosing methods and tools that enable the participants to lean as much from the researcher/designers as the researcher/designers do from the participants.

This framework was applied in a research and design project with the Youth Council of the Akershus University Hospital (AHUS), in Norway. The Youth Council had made a wish list of issues and technologies they wanted to use in the design project with KULU. The transition to adult healthcare was one of the main concerns of the Council and they wanted to explore how a mobile phone application (app) could support them in the transition process.

This paper reports in particular on the design of the mood tracker functionality for a multifunctional transition app. The design process consisted of four workshops and an online prototype evaluation. The workshops took place in two large meeting rooms and were attended on average by seven Youth Council members. In total, ten young patients participated, five male and five female participants, who were between 14 and 21 years old. They had a variety of chronic diagnoses. The project was evaluated and approved by the data authority for universities in Norway and the privacy officer of AHUS. All participants had given their consent to participate. Additional consent was sought from the legal guardians of the participants that were younger than 16 years old. Further details of the design process can be found in [44], which we describe the larger design context, with multiple design projects, in which the design research described in this paper took place.

IV. Results from the Design Process

A. Identifying functionality

During the first workshop, the functionality of the KOOLO transition app was explored with a brainstorming technique [45], resulting in two lists: *Cool-to-have* and *Must-have* [46]. The *Must-have* list consisted of functionalities that the app needs in order to be used, such as calendar for doctor appointments, alarm for taking medicines, checklists, and *recording of the general state* of the user (e.g., mood, energy level), but also attributes, such as *colors* and *privacy*. Color preferences were perceived as very personal and one of the participants proposed that colors could be used to personalize the app [47]. A password or pass code was suggested to keep the content of the app separate from other apps [46]. The *Cool-to-have* list mentioned aspects and functionalities that made the app extra attractive for young people, such as an 'Instagram'-like environment, music play-list (similar to 'Spotify'), and film and television program tips [46]. An analysis of the group discussion of all proposals resulted in the identification of three categories: to have an *overview* (medicines, appointments, routines); strengthen *autonomy* (recording the general state, checklists); and *entertainment* (music, tips).

Figure 3. Design proposals for registering the general state: 1) using a humor-energy ax, 2) rating feeling healthy, energy, and control, and 3) using images.

B. General State

During the second workshop, the *recording of the general state* was one of several functionalities further explored. In a collaborative prototyping session, three design proposals (Figure 3) were presented in the form of both paper-based and digital prototypes. Collaborative prototyping enables the translation of values and needs into design requirements [48][49]. The three proposals reflected different ways of mapping the patients' energy levels and mood. The recording of the general state through images was perceived as more creative and personal. In the discussion that followed, the difference between taking your own photos and finding images on the net was explored, with one participant expressing the concern that finding and uploading images from the net needed focus and energy, which was not always available. Another participant mentioned:

> *When you are really down, we all have our ups and downs, when you are in a bad period, you can go back and see, 'OK, I had a bad January but see how good my February was'. And to see different photos and that there is one, for example, that makes you happy. For example, when you are admitted to the hospital, you can go back and look for what gives you energy, and look at the photos* [46].

C. Mood

The discussions of the three prototypes evolved around the use of photos, colors, and mood. The next iteration of the function for mapping the user's general state focused on these three aspects and consisted of three low-fidelity digital prototypes, which were also produced as plasticized paper printouts. In the ensuing discussions, a new iteration emerged, consisting of a photo tagged with a colored frame, which would be an expression of the mood associated with the photo. Inspired by Snapchat, the popular image messaging and multimedia mobile application, the snapshots take within the KOOL app were named *MoodSnaps*. In order to enable the user to "go back" in time, we used the concept of the *timeline* as an organizing principle for the photos: each photo would be tagged with a date, creating a *MoodLine* (see Figures 4 and 5). During the third workshop the different prototypes were explored and discussed (Figure 4). The participants preferred the option to scroll up and down through the list of photos. Secondly, they preferred photos of the same size to the option to have different sizes, because this gave a better overview of the photos in the timeline. The timeline itself should depend on the date, not on photos, so it would be clear to them on which days they were too tired or sick to add a photo to the timeline.

Figure 4. Prototypes of the *MoodLine* explored in the 3rd workshop.

The timeline of the *MoodSnaps*, photos with different color-tags, inspired a discussion of what they could do with the colors. One participant proposed to add a new option to the mood tracker, namely the possibility to see only photos tagged with one color, similar to Instagram. For example, on a difficult day, the user could scroll through photos tagged with the color-tag *happy* (e.g., yellow), in order to get through the day and inspire or motivate oneself with photos that presented better times or moods. We also explored different options for personalization through colors [47]. The option to allow the user to configure the colors' associated mood meanings was chosen over option to use colors with a default set of moods (See Figure 6). The combination of images and colors enabled a focus on tracking their mood, not on taking pretty pictures. This option also expresses the wide variety of color associations found among the participants, which were the result of age, gender, and personal preferences [47].

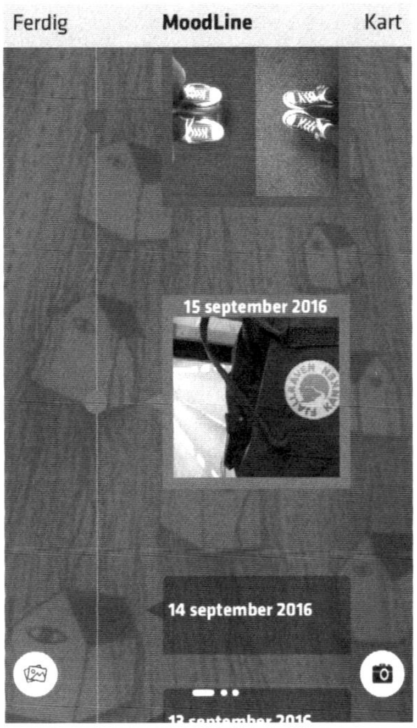

Figure 5. The *MoodLine* (KOOLO app)

D. *Final iteration*

The final iteration of the mood function was produced in InVision, an online prototyping software for clickable, high-resolution prototypes. During the last workshop, our co-designers were invited to access what was now named the KOOLO app in Invision, in order to click through the different options, such tagging colors with a mood, adding a photo, color-tagging the photo, scrolling through photos, and accessing the mood map to select a collection of photos tagged with the same color. All the participants received information on how to access the online prototype and an invitation to use and evaluate the prototype.

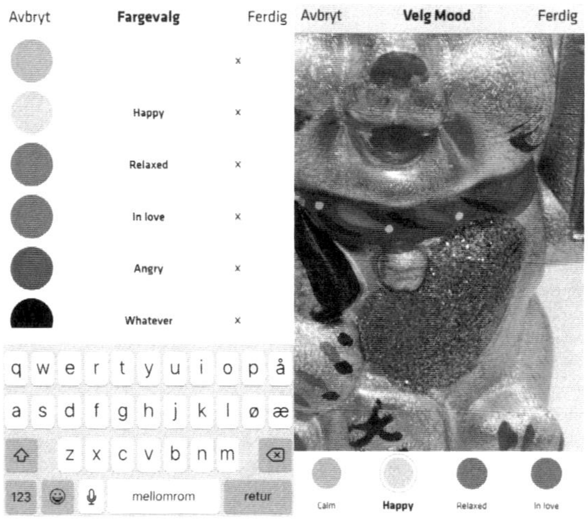

Figure 6. Changing the tags associated with the colors (left) and tagging a *MoodSnap* with a color (KOOLO app).

V. Discussion

"Lived experience is coloured by mood" [39]

A systematic review of apps supporting adolescents' personal management of chronic and long-term physical conditions [50] shows that the lack of large-scale studies makes it difficult to find empirical evidence of their benefit, but that engaging the adolescents contributes to changes in the mobile intervention's design. The use of the KOOLO app hasn't been studied yet, but we did find that the engagement of young patients as co-designers did have a tremendous effect on the design of the KOOLO app in terms of it functionality and the particular design aspects within each functionality.

The KOOLO app now has three main functionalities: i) mood tracking, ii) a calendar to keep track of health-related appointments and events the users wish to keep separated from the native calendar app of the phone, and iii) interactive transition checklists, which are based on the paper-based checklists developed and implemented by the Royal Children's Hospital Melbourne [3], the MYHealth Three Sentences Summary of Sick Kids Toronto[4], and Akershus University Hospital[5]. In particular in the mood tracker, the co-designers' preferences and needs form the core of the design (see summary in Table I).

[3] http://www.rch.org.au/transition/factsheets_and_tools/transition_checklists/
[4] http://www.sickkids.ca/Good2Go/For-Youth-and-Families/Transition-Tools/MyHealth-3-Sentence-Summary/Index.html
[5] http://www.ungdomsmedisin.no/resources/

TABLE I. IMPLEMENTATION OF DESIGN SPECIFICATIONS FOR THE MOOD TRACKER

Requirement	Implementation
1. Recording the general state	Photos in an 'Instagram'-like environment, framed by a mood color
2. Time as organizing principle	A*MoodLine* organized by dates, including dates without photos
3. Color as organising principle	No default settings for tags
	Can be used for personalization of the whole app
	The photos can be organized by color via the *MoodMap* option
4. Privacy	Photos are stored in the app, which is password/code protected

A. Recording of the general state

In the discussions on *recording the general state*, the co-designers included their existing experiences with apps, such as that it was easier to take a photo in an app than to find a photo on the web and to import it into the app. They also knew they were often experiencing a lack of energy and had to find the most energy-efficient way to record the state they were in.

Instagram, the popular online photo- and video sharing app, was used by all participants. Their knowledge of how to collect and share data in Instagram, played a central role in how they envisioned the recording of their general state in the app.

The combination of image and color, in the form of a photo framed by a color representing a mood, enables the users to register or track their mood in meaningful way. It enables a bi-directly meaning-making process. The mood color provides context to the image and the image provides context to the color. The fact that the color-framed images are organized by time, enables a third layer of meaning-making, as the date of the color-framed image can be linked to the calendar, another functionality in the transition app (See Figure 7).

B. Time as organizing principle

The concept of the timeline evolved very early in the design process into an image-based mood functionality. The *MoodLine* could use the existing functionality of the mobile phone (the native photo app) as input and the participants perceived this as an intuitive, easy, and personal way to track one's mood. Also, the shape of the images reflected the participants' existing app use: square shape of the images was preferred over round-shaped ones, because of its similarity with square-shaped images of the popular Instagram app (see Figures 4 and 5).

Our co-designers also made clear that they wanted to track both positive and negative moods and did not want to favor one type of mood over the other by presenting them in different formats or styles. As an example they mentioned that a day with a negative mood could be a very important day, but that this could get lost in a design that would present positive mood images larger than negative mood images.

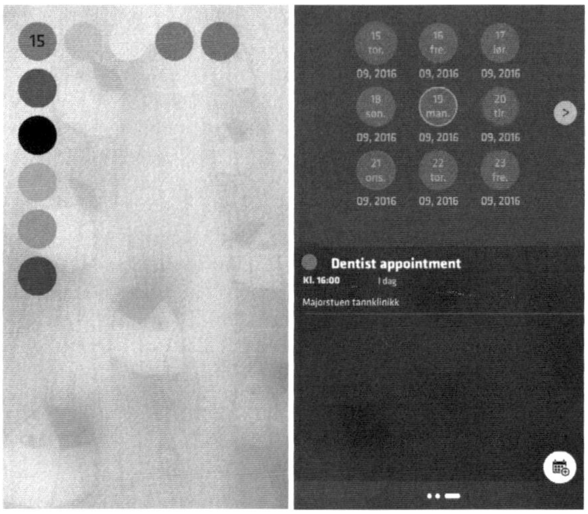

Figure 7. Tagging the date in the calendar with a color (left) and dates tagged with a color in the calendar view (KOOLO app).

This example makes clear that the co-designers were able to find and explore connections between their *lifeworlds* and the specifications of the mood functionality. That they wanted to track their mood in relation to their lived experiences became also clear in the design of the timeline and the application of mood colors to other functionalities in the app. They preferred the *MoodLine* to track all days, not only the days in which a user added a photo. This way, a day without a photo has meaning as well, by evoking reflection on the reason for not adding a *MoodSnap* to the *MoodLine*, such as being too tired or too sick.

Inspired by the color tags of the *MoodLine*, they proposed to use color tags in other functionalities of the app, such as the dates in the calendar functionality of the app. A date tagged with a color thus became a meaningful way to highlight days with doctor appointments or test results (Figure 7).

C. Color as organizing principle

The idea for the *MoodMap* (Figure 8) came up in a discussion about keeping an *overview* of things. The larger the MoodLine would become over time, the more difficult it would be to find patterns that were meaningful in the user's life. The proposal for a *MoodMap* was inspired by the Instagram photomap, which geographically maps where a user has taken a photo and shows all photos taken on that same location. Once proposed by one of the members of the AHUS Youth Council, all participants perceived this as a fun and intuitive way of organizing their mood images. The *MoodMap* gives an indication of how many photos are tagged by a particular color. Selecting one color in the *MoodMap* results in a *MoodLine* with only images tagged with the selected color (see Figure 9).

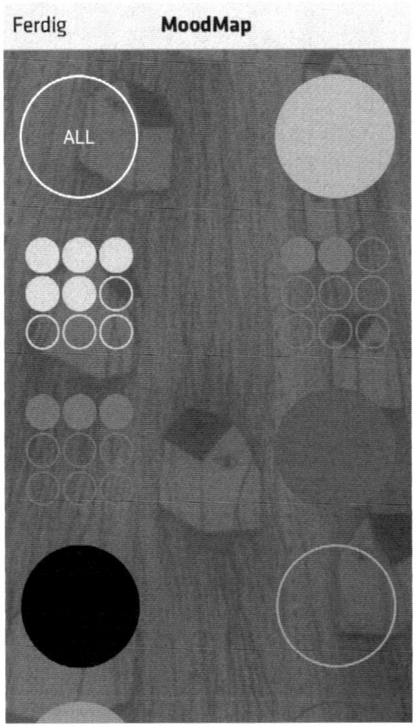

Figure 8. The *MoodMap* (KOOLO app).

The *MoodMap* visualizes the data tracked in the *MoodLine* in the form of an overview of how many times a particular mood has been tracked in the *MoodLine*. This quantification of mood should not be understood as fixing emotions with a symbol systems [51], but rather it provides i) a new level of meaning to the experienced moods, ii) a new way of accessing moods, and iii) a possibility to influence a mood.

The young patients can use the mood functionality to keep an overview of their moods over time as well as per mood. In addition, they can use mood colors in other functionalities of the app, such as calendar and date functionality. This can give them an understanding of the context in which their moods appear. Keeping an overview and looking for meaning are related to mastery, the experience of emerging stronger from a very stressful health condition [52]. The experience of mastery increases when young patients can participate in a meaningful way in decisions that affect their life. The *MoodMap* allows the user to focus on one particular emotional state, which may affect motivation, inspiration, learning, and change.

D. Privacy

Lastly, the *privacy* specification: the co-designers proposed a strict division on their mobile phone between general apps and an app focusing on their diagnosis or health challenges. The design of the mood functionality, and the KOOLO transition app as a whole, are designed according to *Privacy by Design* principles [53]. Privacy is default, as well as integrated to the system, without diminishing functionality. There is very limited communication between this app and the other apps stored on the mobile phone - data produced in the app, calendar events, photos, and checklist entries are stored within the app – and there is no communication with a website or with third parties. The source code is open and available for investigation.

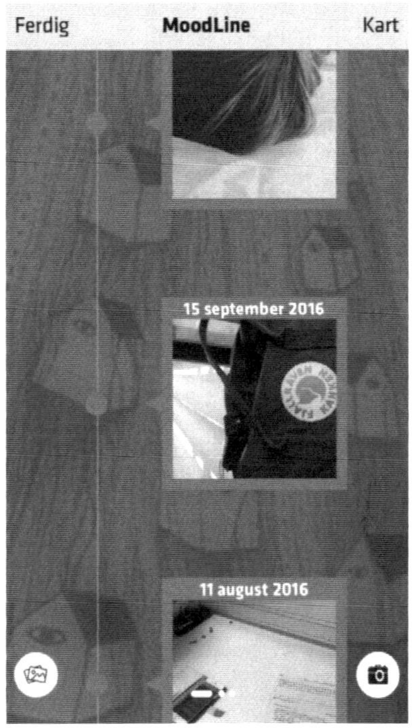

Figure 9. The view of the *MoodLine* when selecting only one color in the *MoodMap* (KOOLO app)

E. Visualization

Ruckenstein [2], reporting from an empirical self-monitoring study of heart-rate variations, discussed how visualizations enable, promote or intensify emotional attachments between people and their data. It became clear that visualizations represent data that are only a partial presentation of the empirical world [p.76-77]. Ruckenstein concludes that self-tracking technologies have the "ability to reimagining the present" [p.81]. It is this reimagining that is enabled in the KOOLO mood-tracking functionality. For example, in the *MoodLine*, dates without data (a date without a color-framed photo), can be made visible. They can be meaningful, in terms of days, or a whole period, in which the user was too tired or ill to take a picture.

This stands in contrast with many other self-tracking apps, which depend on a daily and structured data input to produce meaningful visualizations. In empirical research on the use of one of those apps [54], we found that the push notifications to the users' phones, prompting them to log the status of their health, were experienced as clashing with their lived bodies. The participants in our study did not continue to use the app because it became too intrusive in their symptom-free periods, when they did not identify themselves as patients. This indicated that they only wanted to track their health when they felt like 'patients' (i.e., had symptoms or were involved in activities that brought out their patientness). This provides an important implication for the design of self-tracking devices for young patients.

The *MoodMap*, which visualizes the data of the *MoodLine*, adds another level of meaning. It quantifies the qualitative self-tracking data of the MoodLine, but at the same time offers an esthetical visualization of moods that can be used to *zoom in* into one mood, creating a *MoodLine* of only one mood. The *MoodMap* enables user-initiated ordering and re-ordering of all self-tracked data: mood data as well as non-data, in the form of date tags without mood data (see Figure 5).

F. The SHARM approach

The five principles of the SHARM approach played a central role in creating a *lifeworld-led design process* with the co-designers, the young people with long-term health challenges. The design workshops took place in the hospital, enabling a safe place for reflecting on their experiences and needs as young patients (situation-based action). The iterative approach, in which the design preferences, ideas, and results from the previous workshop were presented in a more developed manner in the following workshop, provided the co-designers the opportunity to see the results of their participation.

The methods we used in the workshops enabled a mutual learning process that was at the one hand explorative and inspiring, and on the other hand based on research and experience. The participants brought in their existing experiences with using apps to discuss options for mood tracking. They were all Instagram users and could bring this experience, in particular the ease of adding a photo and ways of organizing photos, into discussions on the design of the mood tracker.

The SHARM approach extended beyond the design process itself, as the *Adaptability* principle which concerned itself with adapting to the participants' changing physical or emotional state was translated into the MoodLine functionality and availability of visualizing the non-data. Further, the *Adaptability* principle resulted in increased focus on facilitating user appropriation of the features in the KOOLO app. The option to assign moods to colors used in *MoodSnaps* and Calendar allows users to track other values than moods if they choose to do it. In addition, while the design assumes that the main value and information comes from the color tag on the images in the *MoodLine*, we have included a zoom-in functionality in case the users want the images to be the primary source of information.

The KOOLO app has now been fully developed for both the Android and iOS platform. It was launched in a public event with the Youth Council of AHUS, representatives of healthcare organizations, and the design and development team. The Youth Council members expressed their appreciation for being able to participate in a complete design process and to see their ideas and contributions materialized in the application.

VI. CONCLUSIONS

Our study confirms that the participation of young people with health challenges in the design of their own interactive technologies can result in creative and important contributions to the design process. A participatory and *lifeworld*-led design process, based on collaborative methods and an iterative approach, allows young patients to explore mood-related needs and values in a more holistic and relational manner. This resulted in very specific design requirements that were closely related to the young persons' everyday experiences with technology. The popular Instagram app was an important inspiration in the design process. Secondly, it resulted in a more meaningful mood tracking and mapping practice, such as personalizing the use of self-selected colors and self-produced images (*MoodSnaps*); the equal importance of positive and negative moods and days with and without images (*MoodLine*); and the organization of photos by mood (*MoodMap*).

The young patients were met as co-designers and experts of their own life, which enabled them to be heard as well as to have a say in the design process. This allowed them to make important contributions to the design of health IT. In turn, this enabled the researchers to learn more about the young patients' lived bodies, their *lifeworlds*, and the role of technology in their life. SHARM, our design approach, enabled a lifeworld-led design process. As a result, methodology, methods, and design specifications transformed into a holistic process. This became especially clear in the methodological principle of *Adaptability*, which was translated into the design of the mood tracking functionality.

The design of the mood tracking functionality resulted in two new design concepts for organizing mood data, the *MoodLine* and the *MoodMap*. The use of photos, framed with colors representing self-assigned emotional states, enabled a meaningful recording of the young persons' mood in a visually pleasant manner (*MoodLine*) and in a meaningfully organized way (*MoodMap*). The visualization of qualitative self-tracking data is an unexplored topic. In this context, the *MoodMap* provides a simple example of how visualization enables meaning-making as well as providing opportunities for support and change.

The literature mainly discusses self-tracking in the context of quantitative data gathering and the objectification of the human body. We found that it is possible to self-track the lived body, when the self-tracking technology focuses on data that is meaningful to the user and that enables the user to create visualizations.

Future work consists of making the transition app, including the mood functionality, available to a group of test users, with and without a diagnosis, followed by qualitative interviews with the users as well as health personnel. We will also explore what other means of qualitative self-tracking can be added to the mood-tracking functionality of the KOOLO app.

ACKNOWLEDGMENT

We thank the Youth Council of the Akershus University Hospital for sharing their expertise and time. We are grateful to the Hospital's staff for supporting our research. We also acknowledge the contribution of former master student Nora Svarverud Aasen. A special thank you to the reviewers for their insightful and detailed comments.

REFERENCES

[1] M. van der Velden and M. M. Sommervold, "MoodLine and MoodMap: Designing a mood function for a mobile application with and for young patients" The Eighth International Conference on eHealth, Telemedicine, and Social Medicine (eTELEMED 2016), IARIA, April 2016, pp. 214–219.

[2] M. Ruckenstein, "Visualized and interacted life: Personal analytics and engagements with data doubles," Societies, vol. 4, no. 1, pp. 68–84, Feb. 2014.

[3] G. Wolf. *Know thyself: Tracking every facet of life, from sleep to mood to pain, 24/7/365. WIRED*, 2009. [Online]. Available from: http://www.wired.com/2009/06/lbnp-knowthyself/ 2016.12.01

[4] M. Merleau-Ponty, Phenomenology of Perception. Motilal Banarsidass Publishers, 1996.

[5] Akershus universitetssykehus. *Ungdomsrådet på internasjonal HPH-konferanse, juni 2015.* [Online] Available: from: https://www.youtube.com/watch?v=izWTk5lqzbM 2015.11.02

[6] K. Crawford, J. Lingel, and T. Karppi, "Our metrics, ourselves: A hundred years of self-tracking from the weight scale to the wrist wearable device," Eur. J. Cult. Stud., vol. 18, no. 4–5, pp. 479–496, Aug. 2015.

[7] D. Lupton, "Self-tracking modes: Reflexive self-monitoring and data practices," Social Science Research Network, Rochester, NY, SSRN Scholarly Paper ID 2483549, Aug. 2014.

[8] S. M. Pritz, "Making emotions count: The self-tracking of feelings (extended abstract)," in Lifelogging, S. Selke, Ed. Springer Fachmedien Wiesbaden, pp. 179–187, 2016.

[9] L. Wiedemann, "Self-Monitoring," in Lifelogging, S. Selke, Ed. Wiesbaden: Springer Fachmedien Wiesbaden, pp. 207–212, 2016.

[10] K. D. Haggerty and R. V. Ericson, "The surveillant assemblage," Br. J. Sociol., vol. 51, no. 4, pp. 605–622, Dec. 2000.

[11] Quantified Self. *Quantified self - Knowledge through numbers*. [Online]. Available from: http://quantifiedself.com/ 2016.08.31

[12] M. Carrigan. *Qualitative self-tracking and the qualified self.* [Online]. Available from https://markcarrigan.net/2014/07/23/qualitative-self-tracking-and-the-qualified-self/ 2016.12.01

[13] J. Davis, "The qualified self" Cyborgology, 2013. [Online]. Available from: https://thesocietypages.org/cyborgology/2013/03/13/the-qualified-self/ 2016.12.01

[14] E. Boam and J. Webb, "The qualified self: Going beyond quantification," Designmind, 2014. [Online]. Available from: https://designmind.frogdesign.com/2014/05/qualified-self-going-beyond-quantification/ 2016.12.01

[15] D. Huang *et al.*, "Personal visualization and personal visual analytics," IEEE Trans. Vis. Comput. Graph., vol. 21, no. 3, pp. 420–433, Mar. 2015.

[16] M. Ruckenstein, "Visualized and interacted life: Personal analytics and engagements with data doubles," *Societies*, vol. 4, no. 1, pp. 68–84, Feb. 2014.

[17] S. Few, "Data visualization for human perception: The Encyclopedia of Human-Computer Interaction, 2nd Ed.," The Interaction Design Foundation. [Online]. Available from: https://www.interaction-design.org/literature/book/the-encyclopedia-of-human-computer-interaction-2nd-ed/data-visualization-for-human-perception 2016.12.01

[18] M. A. Case, H. A. Burwick, K.G. Volpp, and M.S. Patel, "Accuracy of smartphone applications and wearable devices for tracking physical activity data," JAMA, vol. 313, no. 6, pp. 625–626, Feb. 2015.

[19] J.-M. Lee, Y. Kim, and G. J. Welk, "Validity of consumer-based physical activity monitors," Med. Sci. Sports Exerc., vol. 46, no. 9, pp. 1840–1848, Sep. 2014.

[20] L. Piwek, D. A. Ellis, S. Andrews, and A. Joinson, "The rise of consumer health wearables: Promises and barriers," PLOS Med, vol. 13, no. 2, p. e1001953, Feb. 2016.

[21] D. Nettle and M. Bateson, "The evolutionary origins of mood and its disorders," Curr. Biol., vol. 22, no. 17, pp. R712–R721, Sep. 2012.

[22] P. M. A. Desmet, "Design for mood: Twenty activity-based opportunities to design for mood regulation," Int. J. Des., vol. 9, no. 2, 2015.

[23] J. Alvarez-Lozano *et al.*, "Tell me your apps and I will tell you your mood: Correlation of apps usage with bipolar disorder state" Proceedings of the 7th International Conference on Pervasive Technologies Related to Assistive Environments, New York, NY, USA, 2014, p. 19:1–19:7.

[24] A. Miloff, A. Marklund, and P. Carlbring, "The challenger app for social anxiety disorder: New advances in mobile psychological treatment," Internet Interv., vol. 2, no. 4, pp. 382–391, Nov. 2015.

[25] N. Shen *et al.*, "Finding a depression app: A review and content analysis of the depression app marketplace," JMIR MHealth UHealth, vol. 3, no. 1, Feb. 2015.

[26] J. McNamara. Get Happy iPhone app gets you happy one tip at a time. [Online]. http://www.theappreviewzone.com/education-apps/get-happy-iphone-app/ 2016.12.01

[27] M. Matthews, G. Doherty, J. Sharry, and C. Fitzpatrick, "Mobile phone mood charting for adolescents," Br. J. Guid. Couns., vol. 36, no. 2, pp. 113–129, May 2008.

[28] Y. Seko, S. Kidd, D. Wiljer, and K. McKenzie, "Youth Mental Health Interventions via Mobile Phones: A Scoping Review," Cyberpsychology Behav. Soc. Netw., vol. 17, no. 9, pp. 591–602, Jul. 2014.

[29] Y. Seko, S. Kidd, and D. Wiljer, "Apps for those who help themselves: Mobile self-guided interventions for adolescent mental health," Sel. Pap. Internet Res., vol. 3, 2013.

[30] R. Kenny, B. Dooley, and A. Fitzgerald, "Feasibility of "CopeSmart": A telemental health app for adolescents," JMIR Ment. Health, vol. 2, no. 3, Aug. 2015.

[31] M. S. Klein-Gitelman and M. L. Curran, "The challenges of adolescence, mood disorders, and chronic illness," J. Pediatr., vol. 167, no. 6, pp. 1192–1194, Dec. 2015.

[32] S. Turkel and M. Pao, "Late consequences of pediatric chronic illness," Psychiatr. Clin. North Am., vol. 30, no. 4, pp. 819–835, Dec. 2007.
[33] E. Diener and M. Y. Chan, "Happy people live longer: Subjective well-being contributes to health and longevity," Appl. Psychol. Health Well-Being, vol. 3, no. 1, pp. 1–43, Mar. 2011.
[34] A. M. Kanstrup, P. Bertelsen, and C. Nøhr, "Patient innovation: An analysis of patients' designs of digital technology support for everyday living with diabetes," Health Inf. Manag. J., pp. 1–9, 2014.
[35] L. S. Liu, K. M. Inkpen, and W. Pratt, "'I'm not like my friends': Understanding how children with a chronic illness use technology to maintain normalcy" Proceedings of the 18th ACM Conference on Computer Supported Cooperative Work & Social Computing (CSCW'15) March 2015, pp. 1527–1539.
[36] M. van der Velden and K. E. Emam, "'Not all my friends need to know': A qualitative study of teenage patients, privacy, and social media," J. Am. Med. Inform. Assoc., vol. 20, no. 1, pp. 16–24, Jan. 2013.
[37] M. Larsson, A. J. Sundler, and M. Ekebergh, "Beyond self-rated health the adolescent girl's lived experience of health in Sweden," J. Sch. Nurs., vol. 29, no. 1, pp. 71–79, Feb. 2013.
[38] J. A. Aho and K. Aho, Body Matters: A Phenomenology of Sickness, Disease, and Illness. Lexington Books, 2008.
[39] L. Todres, K. Galvin, and K. Dahlberg, "Lifeworld-led healthcare: Revisiting a humanising philosophy that integrates emerging trends," Med. Health Care Philos., vol. 10, no. 1, pp. 53–63, Jul. 2006.
[40] K. Dahlberg, L. Todres, and K. Galvin, "Lifeworld-led healthcare is more than patient-led care: an existential view of well-being," Med. Health Care Philos., vol. 12, no. 3, pp. 265–271, Aug. 2009.
[41] A. Pulman *et al.*, "Empathy and dignity through technology: Using lifeworld-led multimedia to enhance learning about the head, heart and hand," Electron. J. E-Learn., vol. 10, no. 3, pp. 349–359, 2012.
[42] J. Simonsen and T. Robertson, Routledge International Handbook of Participatory Design. New York: Routledge, 2012.
[43] M. van der Velden and C. Mörtberg, "Participatory design and design for values," in Handbook of Ethics, Values, and Technological Design, J. van den Hoven, P. E. Vermaas, and I. van de Poel, Eds. Netherlands: Springer, pp. 1–22, 2014.
[44] M. van der Velden, M. M. Sommervold, A. Culén, and B. Nakstad, "Designing interactive technologies with teenagers in a hospital setting," in Perspectives on HCI Research with Teenagers, L. Little, D. Fitton, B. T. Bell, and N. Toth, Eds. Springer International Publishing, pp. 103–131, 2016.
[45] V. P. Seidel and S. K. Fixson, "The application and limits of design methods and reflexive practices: Adopting design thinking in novice teams," J. Prod. Innov. Manag., vol. 30, pp. 19–33, Dec. 2013.
[46] N. Aasen, "Transisjonsapp - Ansvar for egen helse", Master Thesis, University of Oslo, Oslo, 2014.
[47] S. Bødker and K. Grønbæk, "Cooperative prototyping: users and designers in mutual activity," Int. J. Man-Mach. Stud., vol. 34, no. 3, pp. 453–478, Mar. 1991.
[48] Y.-K. Lim, E. Stolterman, and J. Tenenberg, "The anatomy of prototypes: Prototypes as filters, prototypes as manifestations of design ideas," ACM Trans Comput-Hum Interact, vol. 15, no. 2, p. 7:1–7:27, Jul. 2008.
[49] M. van der Velden, M. M. Sommervold, and A. L. Culén, "Patient-initiated personalisation: Privacy, moods, and colours," presented at the 7th International Conference e-Health, Las Palmas de Gran Canaria, Spain, 2015.
[50] R. Majeed-Ariss *et al.*, "Apps and adolescents: A systematic review of adolescents' use of mobile phone and tablet apps that support personal management of their chronic or long-term physical conditions," J. Med. Internet Res., vol. 17, no. 12, Dec. 2015.
[51] S. Selke, Ed., Lifelogging. Wiesbaden: Springer Fachmedien, 2016.
[52] J. B. Younger, "A theory of mastery," ANS Adv. Nurs. Sci., vol. 14, no. 1, pp. 76–89, Sep. 1991.
[53] A. Cavoukian and M. Prosch, "The roadmap for privacy by design in mobile communications: A practical tool for developers, service providers, and users," Information Privacy Commissioner of Ontario, Ottawa, 2010.
[54] M. M. Sommervold and M. van der Velden, "Transition cards: Designing a method with and for young patients," IADIS Int. J. Comput. Sci. Inf. Syst., vol. 10, no. 2, pp. 79-94, 2015.

Designing for Capacities Rather Than Disabilities

Investigating the relationship between psychomotor capacities and interaction opportunities

Suhas Govind Joshi
Department of Informatics
Faculty of Mathematics and Natural Sciences, University of Oslo
Oslo, Norway
joshi@ifi.uio.no

Abstract— **This paper explores how designing based on psychomotor capacities instead of disabilities can reconnect old people with technology. We introduce four alternative designs for radios to demonstrate how facilitating a design process that acknowledges psychomotor challenges associated with aging can both help participants rediscover their own psychomotor capacities and simultaneously re-establish meaningful interaction. The paper presents findings from quantitative analysis of performance testing and qualitative analysis from reflection activities involving 65 participants over four years. We use our findings in a discussion of how we can incorporate knowledge about the participants' psychomotor capacities in the design process to help design artifacts that can prolong interaction.**

Keywords — psychomotor abilities; elderly; radio; assistive technology.

I. INTRODUCTION

The radio is an important device to many. This is particularly the case for the oldest generation in Norway where the radio is one of the most appreciated and well-used devices among older adults. In a local care home in Oslo (with the average resident age of 84 years), which was part of our empirical context, we observed that 91% of the 90 elderly residents had a radio device in the home that they would use on an average day. However, most radios are operated by the use of hands and fingers and rely on psychomotor capacities that may decline during old age [1]. Not acknowledging such bodily changes may complicate or prevent interaction with technology. Our prior studies have demonstrated how something seemingly simple as a radio is not considered as simple or functional when aging symptoms appear [2].

This paper aims at investigating how a better understanding of both psychomotor abilities and disabilities can help inform the design process and aid people re-establish and prolong interaction with radios. Our aim is to shift the design process from revolving around disabilities and instead acknowledge that despite declining functional abilities all people still inhabit psychomotor capacities that can be utilized in the design process. By collaborating with participants who are no longer able to operate commercial radios, we have co-designed four radios and used them to explore opportunities for them to re-enable their interaction with radios. We present four different functioning radios that are specifically designed for older people and discuss the psychomotor properties of these interfaces regarding the interaction opportunities they offer. Our study involved 65 participants who contributed to our research between 2013-2016. To anchor our understanding of how these physical changes manifest themselves, we apply Fleishman's taxonomy of psychomotor abilities and skills [3] to identify, measure, and discuss the participants' ability to operate the four different radios. The paper presents two phases of an investigation focusing on a various aspect of the relationship between psychomotor abilities and interaction with radios. The first phase includes a statistical analysis of performance testing of three of the four radios. The results are used to demonstrate how various participants preferred different interfaces based on their psychomotor capacities, and how participants with motor challenges in certain cases were able to match the performance of older adults without these difficulties. The second phase included three activities where participants explored and assessed their own psychomotor capacities – both individually and in groups – and provides insight into how participants experienced interacting with the four radios and what actions and interfaces that proved the most challenging.

The paper is structured as follows. We introduce the motivation for focusing on the radio in Section II. In Section III, related work on psychomotor and age-related studies within HCI is presented, while Section IV covers the taxonomy used to describe and measure psychomotor abilities. The two phases and involved research methods, as well as the four developed radios, are outlined in Section V followed by results and analysis in Section VI. The paper ends with a discussion where we argue that both the design result and the design process can benefit from acknowledging the psychomotor challenges associated with old age.

II. BACKGROUND

According to statistics from Statistics Norway (SSB), the older part of the population (aged 67-79) remains stable in the national average of radio listening in Norway [4]. The red line in Figure 1 shows an overview of the mean percentage of the population who listens to the radio while the blue line shows the corresponding percentage for people aged 67-79.

The number of minutes in average spent listening to the radio is illustrated in Figure 2, and as we can read from the graph, there is only one recorded case in the past 23 years (1997) where the elderly fraction of the population on average would listen less to the radio compared to the general population. We can also read from Figures 1 and 2 that even in years where the number of elderly radio listeners was lower than the national average (i.e., 1994, 1995, 2001, 2009, and 2010), the number of minutes spent in front of the radio was higher for the elderly radio listeners. The difference between the older generation and the rest of the population seems to have diverged over time, and the difference in a ten-year perspective is now greater than ever. The mean difference between the amount of time the elderly used for radio listening compared with the rest of the population in the period from 1991 to 2000 was 7.0 minutes while the corresponding difference in the period from 2005 to 2014 was over four times larger (33.1 minutes). This difference demonstrates an interesting phenomenon, namely that the radio as a piece of technology is not on its way to extinction. Quite the contrary, they are on the rise again regarding both share of the population that listens to the radio (Figure 1), and the number of minutes spent in front of the radio per day (Figure 2).

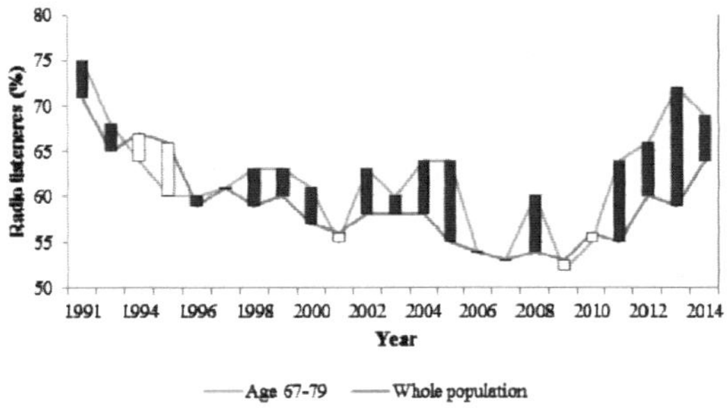

Figure 1. Percentage of population listening to the radio on an average day

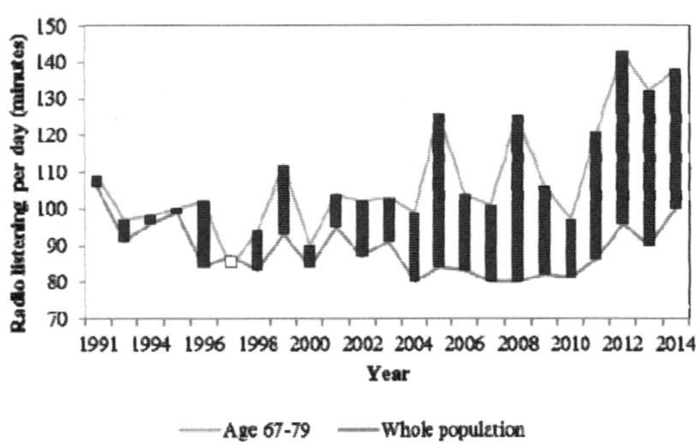

Figure 2. Number of minutes spent listening to the radio on an average day

In our prior research (e.g., [5] and [2]) we have discussed aspects of the role technology has in the lives of older adults. We have touched upon related topics such as the social importance of being able to operate communicative technologies such as radios to stay in touch with the outside world [5]. We also explored deeper issues concerning the ability to operate such devices and the way such devices are presented, e.g., design that is oversimplified or stigmatizing [2]. These studies have concentrated on the experience of interacting with technology and would consequently be better suited to further discuss the social and contextual aspects of interaction with technologies, for instance, loneliness and boredom. However, in this paper, the focus remains on the psychomotor ability to interact with the radio, and more precisely re-establishing a lost relationship between old users and technology.

III. RELATED WORK

A long time has passed since researchers began systematically investigating the relationship between aging-related disabilities such as arthritis and the ability to interact with computers [6]. Morgan et al. [7] described significant differences in the execution of movement when comparing young adults with older adults, and more precisely the speed, sub-movements, and smoothness in movement. Similarly, Riviere & Thakor [8] use a comparative study between young, old, and motor-disabled subjects with regards to performance when operating tracking with a computer mouse. Their study claims that both aging and motor disability affect performance by increasing the inaccuracy and nonlinearity. Age has an apparent impact on our ability to interact and the extent to which we are able to adapt to new interaction mechanisms. This partly manifests itself through changes in psychomotor capacities. A recent study [9] claims the existence of age-related differences in the strategic repertoire, distribution, and execution within the sensorimotor domain. Regardless of the age of the intended user group, fine psychomotor abilities should be included in the determining of successful interactions [10].

One of the very few laws that attempt to descriptively explain the psychomotor role of human-computer interaction through mathematical formulas is Fitts' law. The original model was formulated over six decades ago and attempted described the linear relationship between movement time and index of difficulty. The model is still used today to quantify the difficulty of performing tasks and was in 2002 included in the ISO standard ISO 9241-9, which concerns non-keyboard input devices. However, since its conception, the model has undergone several modifications and refinements and does not pertain a universally accepted formulation today [11]. A shortcoming of Fitts' law is its ability to properly determine and evaluate differently observed result in the psychomotor performance when studying different task types, varying motor skills and differences in motor performance [12]. Others have argued that there are several factors affecting our endpoint performance not adequately captured in the mathematical model [13].

In the context of aging, studies on how psychomotor abilities affect user performance with computer tasks within the field of HCI can also be traced back to at least the early 90s where researchers claimed and studied a relationship between the two [8]. Studies have been conducted within the field of HCI focusing on traditional interfaces, including WIMP and trackpads. For instance, psychomotor skills are an essential part of the ability to operate a computer mouse, and several studies have investigated the relation between psychomotor abilities and use performance operating a mouse or trackpad [6][10][14]-[17]. Common for most of these studies is that they include several components that make up the list of psychomotor abilities described in Fleishman taxonomy, e.g., precision control, arm-hand steadiness, manual dexterity and wrist-finger speed [13].

Previous exploration of various input mechanisms and the physical properties of the design also contributes to our research. For instance, the research of [18] argues that proper understanding of materials used in the design can help support habits and reinforce competences; hence, the exploration of input mechanisms and modes of operation becomes important to the understanding and experience during use. The aging process introduces changes to cognitive and bodily capacities that may complicate or extend the training required to incorporate new interaction mechanisms or patterns [19]. Similarly, the importance of acknowledging the strong relationship between the design and the homely environment has been the emphasis of several studies, e.g., [20, 21], and we have seen similar tendencies in our own prior explorations [2]. Several studies have argued for a strong relationship between material attributes and the perceived experience of digital devices [22]-[24], and that wrongful use of materials can by itself contribute to people withstanding from engaging with technology [20, 25]. We have also conducted exploration of materials in design within our empirical context and investigated the role of materials in perceived familiarity and context-adaptability [21, 26].

IV. PSYCHOMOTOR ABILITIES

People undergo multiple reductions in both cognitive and motor skills as when entering later stages of life. In this study, we have chosen to focus on reduced psychomotor capacities in the hands and fingers, and how these changes affect the likeability to interact with radios. We have chosen not to describe this shift as a limitation in the ability to interact since that would indicate an impossibility in the interaction between these individuals and the radio as technology. Instead, we believe that despite the undeniable changes in bodily capacities, our ability to interact with technology is not deprived, or necessarily not even reduced. We aim to demonstrate how adapting the technology to these changes in physical capacities can prolong and re-establish interaction. Nevertheless, the focus of this study is older people with symptoms, illnesses, and diagnoses associated with reduced capabilities in the hands and fingers. This includes individual types of rheumatic disorders associated with hands and fingers, osteoarthritis, as well as more general motor system disabilities such as Parkinson's disease. Non-diagnosed older adults showing symptoms affecting hands and fingers, such as trembling, involuntary movements, spasms were also included, as fine motor skills tend to decline with age [27]. We expanded our experimental group with elderly people claiming inability to operate radios, despite not being able to provide a medical record of a specific disability, as challenges associated with aging like inadequate blood flow and circulation to the muscles, injuries, stress, fatigue may also produce spasm in muscles that would reduce the psychomotor capacities. Several residents in our empirical context also reported similar symptoms of cramps from medical side effects, in particular from medication related to Parkinson's disease and Osteoporosis. Other types of developmental or genetic disorders that may have an impact on psychomotor capabilities, but that are not particularly prominent symptoms among the older adults, were not included in this study (e.g., Down's syndrome, cerebral palsy and dystonia).

A. *Fleishman's taxonomy*

Based on cognitive, sensory, physical, and psychomotor factors, Fleishman derived 52 skills and abilities describing human performance. Although this model was initially developed for a job-related environment, the taxonomy of Fleishman describes abilities and skills that can be associated with performance in everyday tasks [28]. The taxonomy separates abilities from skills; abilities are defined as characteristics and traits shaped throughout the first phase of our lives while skills describe the degree to which we can effectively carry out an action directly related to a given task. Common for the two is that both skills and abilities related to psychomotor capacities involve complex movement patterns and require practice and maintenance in order to remain intact [29].

As the aging process does not follow a schematic or linear development, it is hard to consider any abilities or skills as less relevant than others. For instance, the cognitive factor constitutes the biggest share of skills and abilities and is obviously relevant also in the discussion of aging-related reduction of interaction capacities. It is further apparent that some of the motoric challenges stem from changes in the cognitive capacities, e.g., ideomotor apraxia where changes in semantic memory capacity reduce the ability to plan or complete motor actions. Studying this category involves abilities and skills that fuse cognitive, perceptual and physical abilities [30].

Studies that focus on older adults with motor challenges in their hands tend to carry an increased attention towards the abilities and skills that fall under the taxonomic category of physical factors. This is because the muscular restrictions and reduced bodily capabilities in the hands mainly tend to affect the abilities and skills covered by this category. Examples of abilities and skills included in this category are stamina, physical strength and flexibility, balance, and coordination. In previous studies of digital devices in the context of older adults, we have been concerned with both stamina and physical strength (e.g., in [2]), but in this paper, we mainly focus on psychomotor factors. This is because most of the actions associated with the operation of a radio and other similar digital devices require movement and a configuration of hands and body that relies on the ability to combine physical movement with cognitive functions. Thus, psychomotor factors constitute our main interest, as this organically includes physical skills such as coordination, dexterity, reaction and manipulation. Unlike physical factors, psychomotor factors are also subjected to the influence of reduction in skills and abilities associated with secondary categories; psychomotor capacities often depend on a supportive capacity in addition to the physical. A reduction in other seemingly unrelated features (e.g., visual impairment) may, as Jacko & Vitense [30] point out, have an impact on psychomotor skills.

B. *Scope*

Our study is limited to psychomotor challenges of hands and fingers. Due to inadequate access to fully medically-assessed participants, as well as claimed expertise, we do not address the impact of the decline in cognitive abilities and skills in this paper (e.g., dementia, depression, and forgetfulness). Our scope does not allow us to identify the best interfaces for a given disease but instead let us study the relationship and possible correlation between motor challenges and performance when interacting with radio interfaces. Nor do we want to identify all skills and abilities that are included in the performance of work-related tasks;

Figure 3. The four radios included in the study

we aim to identify the specific abilities and skills that are involved in the operation of radios, and affected by reduced capacity in the hands and fingers. Abilities and skills in the taxonomy of Fleishmann are described as independent of each other [13], and it should consequently be possible only to study a selection of these. A similar approach has been conducted in prior research, more specifically in the research of [13, 15, 16, 17]. Table I gives an overview of the psychomotor abilities included in our study. A description is provided for each ability based on the original taxonomy of Fleishman [3] in the right column of the table.

TABLE I. OVERVIEW OF PSYCHOMOTOR ABILITIES

Psychomotor ability	Description
Precision control	Ability to move control and the degree to which they can be moved quickly and repeatedly to exact positions.
Arm-hand steadiness	Ability to keep the hand and arm steady, both when suspended in air and while moving. Independent of strength and speed.
Manual dexterity	Ability to make quick and skillful coordinated movements with arms and one or both hands, as well as the ability to assemble, grab and move objects.
Finger dexterity	Ability to make quick, skillful, and coordinated movements with fingers of one or both hands.
Wrist-finger speed	Ability to repeat fast movements with wrist and fingers.
Multi-limb coordination	Ability to use two or more limbs simultaneously to coordinate movements when the body is not in motion.

While all the abilities and skills described in the psychomotor category of the taxonomy are relevant in a broader scope, we have excluded certain abilities and skills from our test. These are abilities that are not relevant for our purposes, and the decision is taken by both the physical challenges we are focusing on, and the digital components and interfaces included in the study. Not all abilities are relevant for the operation of our radios; hence, measuring these abilities would be difficult with the radios. More precisely, rate control, reaction time, speed of limb movement, and response orientation have been excluded. The reason is that these four abilities are not directly determining the capacity to interact with our four radios, but instead, describe the degree to which we can interact with them, as well as the performance during use. Rate control is not appropriate in situations where speed and direction of an object are perfectly predictable [30] while the other three (reaction time, speed of limb movement, and orientation response) mainly concern efficiency of performance, rather than the distinctive ability to perform them. Also, both reaction time and response orientation are intended to capture our reaction to a given signal and our ability to quickly initiate the response routine, something which would be unnatural in a context where our participants are testing our radios. Thus, these four abilities have not been included in our tests.

V. RESEARCH METHOD

A. *Radio #1*

The first radio is the top-left radio in Figure 3, and it was developed in 2013. The focus of the radio is to provide an interface that provides users with similar experiences and interaction mechanisms as they are used to from their traditional radios. The feedback one gets from operating radio is reminiscent of interaction found in traditional radios with a distinct response to actions. The focus has also been on finding the materials that provide the best grip and resistance during the interaction. We have explored the properties of various materials (wood, steel, plastic) to find the best functioning design for the knobs. The main interaction takes place by turning on a coarse switch that clearly snaps in place when selecting the channel. A second switch is used to adjust the volume.

B. *Radio #2*

The second radio is the top-right radio from Figure 3, and was developed in 2014. This radio depends on physical interaction and does not use traditional switches or buttons. As with the other two radios, this radio is also screenless. The user operates the radio with the use of wooden cubes with built-in Near Field Communication (NFC) chips. The NFC chips are preconfigured with a given radio channel, and by placing these physical cubes on top of the radio, one interacts with the interface. By placing a piece with a given channel on top of the radio starts playing. Removing the cube ends the playback. The focus has been on designing a radio that does not require fine motor skills in fingers. During the design process, material, weight, size and shape were explored in consultation with users to find the best objects for physical operation of the radio.

C. *Radio #3*

The third radio is the bottom-left radio in Figure 3, and was developed in 2015. The purpose of this radio was to allow users with tremors, involuntary twitching, and reduced fine motor skills to operate it. The radio is made of oak and has an aluminum cylinder with a wooden knob that automatically snaps to predefined positions using magnets. One operates the radio by positioning the wooden knob at a predefined position. A secondary exploratory feature is that the wooden knob swivels around the cylinder. The design of the radio offers deliberate constraints that prevent users from making mistakes during the interaction. The wooden knob is locked to the pole and the magnet in the cylinder both guides and limits the positioning. This allows involuntary actions to have less impact on the accuracy.

D. *Radio #4*

The fourth radio is the bottom-right radio in Figure 3, and was developed in 2016. The radio is made of wood and covered with pearl gray oak to blend into homely environments. A simple slider allows adjustment of volume while the pods represent radio channels or podcasts similar to Radio #2. Circular pods are placed in a hollowed and lowered circle to initiate the radio and removing the pods ends the operation. RFID tags are used to communicate between pods and the radio. The pods are coated with soft felt fabrics with strong colors and contrast to help guide the channel selection. The design of the pods is meant to be strong, durable, and easily graspable for people with a reduction in dexterity and motor challenges.

E. *Research design*

This study was divided into two phases. Our two phases included 65 participants in total, with 52 participating during the first phase and 13 participating during the second phase. The requirement for participation during both phases was that the participant suffered from reduced ability or no ability to operate a store-bought radio and thus needed a more customized interface. The three store-bought radios used for participant selection were Pinell Supersound DAB, Pop DAB Radio and Argon DAB Radio, three highly popular brands in Norway. The data for this study was collected in the period 2013-2016. The four radios used in this study were also built during the same period.

The first phase emphasized statistical analysis of psychomotor performance tied to the three first radios, i.e., Radio #1-3. The goal was to explore whether participants were able to interact with our alternative radio designs and how their performance scored compared to an independent control group. The second phase revolved around three activities, and we relied on qualitative methods to get the participants to reflect upon their own psychomotor capacities. This phase introduced Radio #4 as both a fourth alternative design and a thinking tool to help participants explore, assess, and discuss their psychomotor interaction challenges and opportunities.

This study was conducted at three local care facilities in Oslo. Each care facility consists of a set of apartments, with the largest holding 90 apartments. The care facilities consist of senior residents residing in independent apartments, but with shared access to a range of facilities, e.g., cafeteria, lounge, fitness center, and 24-hour staffed reception. The limited access to participants with motor challenges in hands and fingers led to four years of data gathering in order to yield an appropriate set of data.

F. *Phase 1: Performance testing of psychomotor abilities*

39 participants (M = 82.1 years, SD = 6.31) participated in six tests of Radio #1-3. For each test, we recruited an independent control group consisting of 13 older adults with no apparent motor disabilities (M = 80.4 years, SD = 5.29) who were asked to perform the same tasks as the experimental group. The testing in the first phase involved 52 participants in total. Most people had medical documentation to assess their motor disabilities. The documentation was provided to us by themselves or by the local care home administration with their consent. A few participants unable to operate store-bought radios and in the lack of proper medical documentation of disability were also invited to participate in the experimental group as they showed symptoms similar to those with proper diagnoses. Table II gives an overview of the participants and the documented or self-assessed disability or illness.

TABLE II. OVERVIEW OF PARTICIPANT GROUPS IN PHASE 1

Disability or illness	**N**
Cramps	8
Muscle stiffness	3
Osteoarthritis	8
Parkinson's disease	4
Rheumatoid arthritis	3
Tremor	13
Control group	13
Total	**52**

The participants in both groups were asked to interact with the three radios Radio #1-3 through a series of repeated tasks to measure their psychomotor performance. Three different tables and eight chairs were used to provide all participants with a setup that supported their preferred bodily configuration. Some participants were also sitting in their wheelchairs during the test, specifically three participants from the experimental group and one participant from the control group. For each of the radios, the participants were given a set of tasks that mimicked the context applicable parts of assignments given in standardized tests of psychomotor abilities, e.g., rotary pursuit test, steadiness tester, Minnesota manual dexterity test, Purdue pegboard, tapping board (as seen in [13], as well as O'Connor finger dexterity test, box and block test, Jebsen hand function test, and Moberg pick-up test. We also took into consideration the values embedded into psychomotor abilities defined in prior research, e.g. some of the skills defined by [29] such as timing, response ability, and speed, as well as the tasks presented in [12], most notably steadiness and aim.

As we used our own set of tasks, the results are not meant to demonstrate the external validity and be directly comparable to other test results, but instead provide a set of tasks applicable to the four radios, thereby providing us with a measurement comparable within the study. To eliminate learning effects and bias due to unfamiliarity with novel interaction mechanisms, each participant was given a demonstration of the intended interaction of each radio, and each participant conducted ten trials for each radio (similar to [6]). The task order was randomized for each participant. We relied on randomized repeated measures to minimize bias due to interpersonal variations between tests. The task set consisted of 12 tasks: gripping, turning, positioning, re-positioning, and resetting the main and secondary interaction element, as well as lifting and moving the radio. Time (seconds), error (count) and precision (position and distance) were observed and measured for each task, and the performance was graded on a normalized scale from 1-10 to make the performance metrics comparable. The computationally-generated normalized score used the four metrics above (seconds, count, position, and distance) to calculate the final score. Thus, the performance scores are not intended to be comparable beyond the scope of our research. In Figure 4, we see two participants from the experimental group testing the positioning and re-positioning of the main interaction element for Radio #2.

Figure 4. Two residents participating in psychomotor measurements

G. *Phase 2: Reflection on psychomotor abilities*

The second phase continued the exploration of how 13 participants (M = 81.1 years, SD = 5.5) – who were recruited following the exact same participation requirements as during the first phase – experienced the radios. Table III provides an overview of the participants who contributed to the second phase. The goal of this phase was to facilitate environments for participants to both individually and collectively explore, assess, and discuss their own psychomotor capacities. This was achieved by investigating how different modes of input affected the operating of the three radios introduced during the first phase, as well as through an exploration of a newly introduced fourth radio (Radio #4). Four participants in the second phase had previously been part of the experimental group of the first phase, and to allow them to continue their exploration we introduced a fourth radio as a new alternative. The second phase consisted of three main activities; (1) think-aloud testing of Radio #4, (2) semi-structured demonstrative interview, and (3) input device workshop. All 13 participants took part in all three activities. All three activities yielded qualitative feedback that supplemented the quantitative results from the previous phase.

TABLE III. OVERVIEW OF PARTICIPANT GROUPS IN PHASE 2

Disability or illness	**N**
Cramps	3
Muscle stiffness	2
Rheumatoid arthritis	4
Tremor	4
Total	**13**

The first activity was the think-aloud testing of the fourth radio. This radio was new to all participants, including those who had participated previously. The participants were asked to follow the same 12 randomly-ordered tasks as those used during the first phase where Radio #1-3 were evaluated. Rather than measuring time, error, or precision like we emphasized during the first phase, we gave the participants space to explain the details they perceived as most important as we moved along the tasks. Our experience from the former phase suggested that not all tasks were seen as equally difficult or interesting; we expected the distribution of time and attention to not be portioned equally across the 12 tasks amongst the participants. The testing was conducted in 13 single-sessions.

Following the think-aloud testing, we conducted a semi-structured demonstrative interview with where we asked all 13 participants to demonstrate challenges with the four radios and elaborate on the main difficulties during the interaction. We also structured parts of the interview to concentrate on those tasks and interaction forms that the participants mastered. We did not provide any tasks or present the radios in a particular order; the participants were free to use any radio or any task to demonstrate their experienced challenges and mastery. As we had previously seen wide ranges of physical and cognitive endurance in participation during similar activities [31] we did not enforce any time limits; the participants were free to participate for as long as they desired themselves. Due to these practical limitations with participation, these interviews were held in single sessions or with small groups.

The final activity was a workshop conducted in two sessions with five and eight participants respectively and gave the participants an opportunity to explore various input mechanisms for the four radios. To accommodate the workshop, we brought various elements that were compatible with the four radios such as different types of knobs, wheels, blocks and rings. The different components were of different shapes, sizes, textures, and materials and represented the variety of physical options. We organized this exploration as a workshop to help the participants learn about their own psychomotor capacities before making any comments or self-assessments as purely interview-based exploration might have yielded gender-based biases as found by [28] who suggested a tendency of men estimating their own capacities higher than their female counterparts. The workshop followed a similar structure as we had previously facilitated in [21, 26] where we focused on the exploration of various material components. Participants were asked to first freely explore and discuss the various components before presenting their favorites to the rest of the group. A selection of the components is depicted in Figure 5.

Figure 5: A selection of components used during the input device workshop

VI. RESULTS AND ANALYSIS

A. *Phase 1: Performance testing of psychomotor abilities*

The means and standard deviations for the psychomotor performance on a normalized scale from 1-10 across both groups are shown in Table IV. As expected, the control group had a better performance relatively compared to the experimental group across all three radios. The variation was larger for the control group, and we can read from the table that both groups demonstrated a similar within-group performance for each of the three radios. The average performance score was 7.43 (SD = 0.32) for the control group while it was 4.60 (SD = 0.22) for the experimental group. In Figure 6, we present the estimated marginal means for the control group vs. the regular group for all three radios.

TABLE IV. PSYCHOMOTOR PERFORMANCE SCORE

Radio #	Group	Mean	Std. Deviation	Lower Bound	Upper Bound	N
1	Control	7.385	.7372	6.730	8.039	13
	Experimental	4.517	1.2824	6.471	7.658	39
2	Control	7.064	.5755	7.156	8.536	13
	Experimental	4.389	1.1787	4.139	4.895	39
3	Control	7.846	.4328	4.046	4.732	13
	Experimental	4.897	1.4000	4.499	5.296	39

A 2 (group: selection or control) x 3 (radio: #1, #2 or #3) between-subjects analysis of variance (ANOVA) was conducted to study the psychomotor performance between the three radios as a function of the performance. We registered significant main effects of group, $F(1,150) = 173.6$, $p < .005$, $n = .536$, and radio, $F(2,150) = 3.1$, $p = .048$, $n = .040$. The main effects were not qualified by an interaction between group and radio, $F(2,150) = 0.142$, $p = 0.867$, $\eta p^2 = .002$. The participants in the selection group (M = 4.601, SD = .107) had significantly lower performance than the participants in the control group (M = 7.432, SD = .186). The analysis also revealed a slightly lower performance difference between the three radios: (M = 5.951, SD = .186), (M = 5.726, SD = .186), and (M = 6.372, SD = .186). Levene's test for equality of variances was found to be violated for the present analysis (p = .001), and Bonferroni post-hoc analysis for the radios showed that Radio #2 had significantly lower performance than Radio #3 at the .05 level, while differences between Radios #1 and #2 and Radios #1 and #3 were not significant.

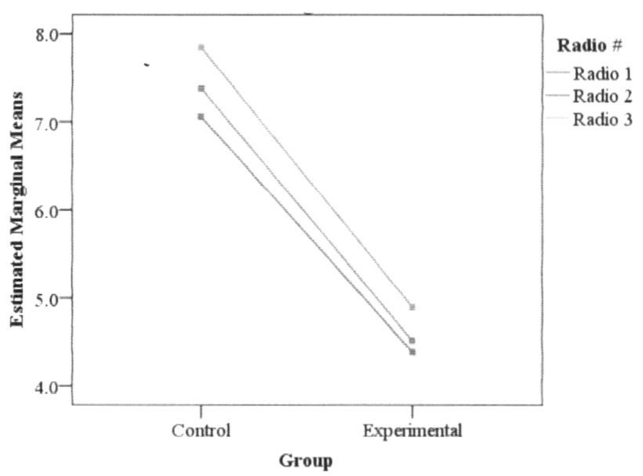

Figure 6. Estimated marginal means of performance for both groups

The results from Figure 6 only demonstrated how the estimated marginal means of the overall performance for all participants in the treatment group compared to the control group. For a post hoc evaluation of the performance within the experimental group, we performed a separate repeated measure analyses for each level within the grouping factor to study the relationship between performance and psychomotor disability.

We analyzed the data with mixed-design ANOVA using a within-subjects factor of disability (cramp, muscle, osteoarthritis, Parkinson's disease, Rheumatoid Arthritis, Tremor) and a between-subject factor of radio (Radio #1, Radio #2, and Radio #3). Mauchly's test indicated that the assumption of sphericity had been violated ($\chi^2(2) = 2.681$, $p = .026$). Degrees of freedom were corrected using Huynh-Feldt estimates of sphericity ($\varepsilon = 1.000$) as Greenhouse-Geisser estimates reported an epsilon value above 0.75 ($\varepsilon = .926$) [32]. There were non-significant main effects of disability, $F(2, 66) = 5.566$, $p = .006$ and radio, $F = (1, 33) = 8.129$, $p = .007$. However, the main effects were qualified by a significant interaction between disability and radio, $F(10, 66) = 17.011$, $p < .001$. In Figure 7, we demonstrate how the interaction between disability and radio yielded a significant variation in the estimated marginal means of performance.

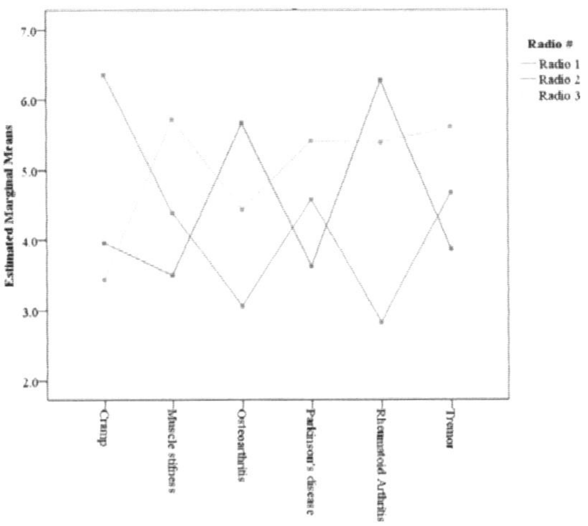

Figure 7. Performance for each disability group across Radio #1-3

Again, the statistical results of this study do not attempt to provide a medical explanation for the performance but instead demonstrates a significant correlation in order to exemplify the need for various interfaces when addressing older adults with psychomotor disabilities. The study only claims the presence of a significant difference in performance but does not provide any solutions.

B. Phase 2: Reflection on psychomotor abilities

The qualitative results generated in the second phase complements the statistical analysis from the first phase by providing additional positive and negative perspectives on the interaction with radios. The qualitative data from the three activities (think-aloud testing of Radio #4, semi-structured demonstrative interview, and input device workshop) were clustered in order to support a holistic analysis of the relationship between psychomotor abilities and challenges that arose during use of the radios. In general, the feedback from the participants provided more depth to our understanding, but also contributed to increasing both the individual and general knowledge amongst the participants. For instance, we clearly saw how the co-exploration with other participants during the input device workshop and demonstrative interviews had an impact on the participants' own self-assessment. 11 out of the 13 participants expressed a positive attitude towards more than one radio as it was usually a minor issue with the design that prevented the interaction. One participant (female, 81) said that there were very small and precise details that prevented her from using the less-favored radios and that she thought she was alone in caring about those details. However, through the three activities of the second phase, participants were exposed to the challenges of other people as well as design alternatives that contributed to learning about alternative interfaces and interaction mechanisms. This mutual learning amongst the participants positively affected their self-esteem and self-assessment as well as the general level of knowledge about the relationship between psychomotor difficulties and their impact on opportunities for interaction.

Since the statistical analysis from the first phase revealed that all participants found purpose with at least one radio, we wanted to further analyze the relationship between psychomotor abilities and concrete tasks. We did not look for a correlation between specific psychomotor disabilities and tasks during this phase, but rather which tasks that introduced the most challenging interaction for our participant group as a whole. From the list of 12 tasks, only two proved to be consistently perceived as challenging. The first common challenging task was the turning of knobs and wheels. Regardless of material, the double-action interaction, i.e., retaining a grip and simultaneously turning the hand, was the most eminent challenge. The following input device workshop confirmed that coarse and jagged knobs and wheels significantly helped on both the grip and resistance. According to the participants, the main challenge was both retaining a firm grip on the knob and simultaneously turning and twisting the knob back and forth. The coarse and jagged input devices helped to interlock the fingers to the knob or wheel and thereby required less pressure on retaining the grip as the hand turned the knob. One participant (male, 78) said that his grip would slip once he started turning his hand as he could not concentrate on maneuvering the fingers and the wrist simultaneously and that the resistance of the jagged edges of the knob supported his concentration. Another important way of counteracting the challenges of turning knobs was to relieve the demand for precision by applying steps with automatic snapping (such as with Radio #1). This helped participants rely less on accuracy and put less pressure on precise movements, something that proved particularly difficult for those experiencing tremor or cramps. Nine participants expressed concerns with turning in general, but with the snapping gesture of Radio #1 only three retained their attitude towards knobs as challenging interfaces.

The second-most challenging tasks was positioning and re-positioning. During the think-aloud testing of Radio #4 similar patterns as seen during the testing of Radio #2 in the first phase emerged. Participants struggled with precise movement of the pods in the air when there were no embodied constraints to restrict involuntary movements and help maneuver or pace the motion. The results from the think-aloud testing of Radio #4 revealed similar issues as with Radio #2 where participants would struggle with the operation due to the raising of the pods midair to initiate the interaction; lifting, suspending, and moving the pods through the air required both jerking and stretching of the arm. Several participants said they were dependent on physical constraints to prevent involuntary movements even during the short duration of the input interaction. Radio #1 and Radio #3 were particularly favored by these participants as the design prevented adverse effects such as dropping pieces or undoing past actions. Even with unintended actions such as sudden spasms or cramps, the design would prevent disruptive consequences. Both Radio #2 and Radio #4 depended on solid cubes or pods to control the radio, and they were partially inoperable to certain participants. These constraints were of particular importance to one female participant (81): *"The sturdiness of the metal bar on Radio #3 neutralizes any involuntary movements I make with its weight and texture, and the friction prevents the wooden ring from sliding away from where I left it"*. Still, there were no significant correlations between the type of psychomotor disability and the degree of need for such physical constraints, but the sample size of 13 participants may not be large enough to identify such patterns. When combined with having to precisely place the pods in a designated area, the combination of strength, flexibility, and accuracy made this task troublesome for many participants. One participant (male, 84) expressed a desire for a snapping mechanisms that would allow the placement or drop to depend less on accuracy similar to the snapping of the knob in Radio #1: *"If it had snapping properties such as found in magnets, it would put less effort on the placement and allow for more concentration of moving the object through the air"*. If we analyze the data from all three activities of the second phase, this issue of positioning was reported by eight participants. However, simple constraints such as the slightly elevated borders encircling the placement zone on Radio #2 made a decisive difference for four of the participants.

The demonstrative interviews also revealed that the participants were highly concerned with progress during the interaction. Most participants stated that they were not directly bothered by using a few attempts to start the radio. The most important factor was whether the failed attempt would reset their progress or not. For instance, turning the knob on Radio #1 in the right direction, even if not reaching the desired channel, would still get the user closer to the goal. A half-finished attempt would allow the user to continue the operation in the next attempt. On the other hand, Radio #2 used cubes that when used unsuccessfully would reset the interaction. We expected participants to be able to hit the top surface at least when not dropping the cube within the designated square, yet only one participant was able to do so. The struggle was tied to the raising of the cube and all incomplete attempts at interaction ended mid-air, and in the best-case scenario, the cube would drop on the table next to the radio. Several participants commented that the limited surface area outside the square area was too narrow to have the cube land on top of the radio in case of missing the square. Thus, it was not failed attempts that would eventually lead to demotivation and frustration; it was not experiencing a sense of progress during the failed attempts. One participant (male, 80) summarized this issue by saying that he did not mind having to repeat gestures to get it right – that was how he already dealt with various equipment in his home – but the moment he felt no progress, he lost interest.

VII. DISCUSSION

A. *Psychomotor disabilities as a shift rather than a loss*

The analysis from the first phase presented in the previous section demonstrates some significant findings. First and foremost, we see that grouping all older adults in one common category cannot be considered scientifically justifiable when their needs, capacities, and performances are so different. To group the participants in one common category is both stigmatizing and improper design practice as it neglects individual needs. Also, we have presented empirical data suggesting that even the specific group of older people suffering from motor deficits in the hands and fingers would highly benefit from designs that paid individual attention to their needs.

At first glance, it might look like Figure 6 illustrates a steady and consistent difference between the control group and the experimental group. However, this was not the case. Irregularities in performance resulted in statistically counteracting mean values, and glancing at Figure 6 one may wrongfully conclude that the older participants yielded a seemingly equal performance score for each radio regardless of their motor capacities. However, as presented in the secondary analysis of the relationship between disease and performance (illustrated in Figure 7), we see performance scores with high fluctuation within each group. We can confirm this by looking at the statistical analysis which indicated a significant interaction between disability and radio ($p < .001$).

One way of understanding this phenomenon is to look at average performance score for each group. The participants who suffered from trembling serve as a good illustration. This group, which accounted for a third of the participants in the experimental group, had the lowest performance score on Radio #2 ($M = 4.19$, $SD = 0.40$), an intermediate performance score on Radio #1 ($M = 05.07$, $SD = 1.57$), and the highest on Radio #3 ($M = 6.08$, $SD = 0.98$). These results can be explained by the different types and various symptoms of tremor. Participants reported issues with intention tremor that could affect their aim, specific tremor which influenced goal-oriented action), as well as general stressing tremor. As Radio #2 required participants to raise a cube in midair and place it within a designated area, it was difficult for several participants to operate this radio. With more degrees of freedom compared with the other two radios, there was more room for both intentional and deliberate errors. This group performed best on Radio # 3 as involuntary movements would not give adverse effect or hinder progress in solving the task.

A similar pattern can be seen in the group of participants who suffered from Rheumatoid Arthritis. They reported challenges with swelling, decreased sensitivity and reduced mobility, which resulted in problems with the interface of Radio# 1 ($M = 2.83$, $SD = 0.99$). The reduction in sensitivity, in particular, would mean that they struggled more with sensing moving, clicking, and snapping feedback from the radio. However, they delivered a good average performance score for Radio # 2 ($M = 6.28$, $SD = 1.74$), suggesting that they still had the capacity for interaction.

Thus, loss or reduction in motor capacities does not an automatically reduce or deprive our interaction opportunities; it mainly shifts them. All four of our radios were developed to allow people with motor impairments in their hands and fingers to still use these limbs for interaction. Moreover, our results suggest that they are highly capable of doing so if presented the right interface. In their studies of differences in pointing movements between older and younger users, [17] argues that older people maintain the use of residual sensory information (vision and proprioception) and can achieve similar precision levels as younger users. However, the radios in our study do not need to be operated by hands and fingers. There are also opportunities that explore new bodily uses and configurations. In certain context, radios are naturally operated through different interaction mechanisms, e.g., in cars. Prior studies have also demonstrated interaction opportunities for people with motor disabilities by the use of other bodily capacities. For instance, [33] uses head gesture recognition for wheelchair control for older adults who have Parkinson's disease and other restrictions in limb movement. The authors of [34] study wrist rotation as input mechanisms for mobile devices, and suggest that both hands-free and eyes-free interaction techniques would be feasible with further research. The research of [35] uses a voice-driven drawing application to include users with motor impairments.

We should never exclude any people as potential users just because their capacities prevent them from using a given interface. Incompetence or inability in use should not be tied to technologies, but instead, be a use dimension related to the specific interaction mechanisms that the technology provides. Radio might be considered one piece of technology, but there are limitless opportunities when it comes to the way it is presented to the user. The results in this paper have demonstrated that people can re-establish meaningful relationships with technology by shifting the way of presentation.

B. *Designing with psychomotor abilities in mind*

The second phase provided insight into how we should address the matter of psychomotor challenges both during the design process and in the design artifact. The self-assessment amongst the participants strongly depended on how the participants were given an opportunity to explore and reflect upon their own capacities; experiencing design alternatives as simple or demanding helped participants express and explain their perspectives during all three activities. Presenting participants with a wide selection of alternatives has previously helped us to support decision-making and mutual learning the during design processes [31]. The input device workshop clearly helped participants obtain an insight into own capacities and preferences that would not have been possible without actually interacting with physical prototypes and objects. Some aspects of psychomotor abilities, e.g., tactics or response-ability [29], are hard for participants to imagine and reflecting upon these capacities supported by physical props to enhance the exploration clearly contributed to a more insightful and honest feedback. During the input device workshop, the participants in both groups unanimously agreed that amongst the alternatives they were exploring they could all find several components that they would be able to operate. The different components exploited material properties such as texture, size, shape, and color to provide various ways of providing input. It was important for the participants' self-esteem to revisit various modes of input and thereby reminding themselves of their capacities despite their psychomotor challenges. This also motivated the participants to talk more positively about their own bodily capacities and reflect about their psychomotor challenges with a more optimistic and salutogenic outlook. While we did not investigate gender-based differences with regards to self-assessment of psychomotor abilities – something [28] argued could yield differences between genders – we believe the input device workshop helped participants realize both own capacities and limitations and adjust their self-estimates accordingly. In future studies, it would be interesting to further investigate the correlation between participants' self-assessment own psychomotor abilities and their performance by the use of standardized models such as those presented in [28].

We also registered how participants would successfully perform tasks that required a single type of psychomotor ability, but would struggle when the tasks introduced multiple actions depending on several types of abilities. The trouble of performing simultaneous actions has been previously addressed by [6], and the issue became particularly evident during the second phase where participants explained how both turning and positioning required simultaneous rather than sequential actions and put more pressure on their abilities. The results from the second phase suggest that constraining design, e.g., the aluminum bar in Radio #3 or the volume slider in Radio #4, helps reduce the number of simultaneous actions required to perform a task. While several participants favored radio #2 and #4, the elevated position of the placement area on top of both radios became a challenge when the placement also required accuracy. This issue was further enhanced by the level of difficulty of the individual tasks, in particular, accuracy. Preciseness in gestures and movements was considered one of the most isolated challenging issues as the tension, flexibility, and endurance required for precise maneuvering usually involved a high level of physical effort and concentration. This observation is supported by the registered patterns presented in [12], where it is claimed that accuracy levels are only kept constant when contributing more time. Thus, we clearly saw value in understanding and addressing the psychomotor capacities, both individually and combined, when shaping the interface of the radio. In particular, physical and embodied constraint as well as guides for movement reduced the simultaneous actions required from the participants and eased the physical demand from the user.

Another way of reducing the tension from simultaneous actions was to support psychomotor capacities with cues. In particular, participants suffering from reduced mobility and sensitivity emphasized the importance of visual cues to support tactile or haptic feedback. Radio #4 did not provide as clear borders for the placement zone as Radio #2 and certain participants were insecure about their own precision once the pod was placed as they could not feel the pod dropping into the shallow circular pit. One participant said that just increasing the depth of the circular area of Radio #4 would have provided better feedback from him as the physical constraints would be enforced as well as help provide visual feedback of correct placement. In our empirical context, we have previously seen how material characteristics can not only influence how the participant understand the interaction but by its properties, e.g., surface, shape, and color, provide cues on how to properly interact with technology [21, 26].

C. Extending and re-establishing purposeful interactions

It is important to note that none of the three radios used in the first phase were perceived as uniformly better than the rest. Each radio would yield good scores with one or more groups, but there was always another group that would struggle with the same interface. This supports our claim that radios designed for a specific group of people, and with features that may even fully compensate for the motor deficit, will still not necessarily work for everyone. Hence, the results of this study demonstrate not only the need but also the possibility, to make individual adjustments in the design of interfaces. Even though we developed four radios, they all utilized nearly identical hardware, and the basic electronic components are the same in all four radios. The back of the three radios Radio #1-3 and how their hardware is enclosed in similar casement taking up roughly the same size is demonstrated in Figure 8. They were developed in four independent processes focusing on various psychomotor challenges, yet we see that only the packaging, i.e., the "outer shell" enclosing technology, is changed. By designing four different interfaces, we have shown that it is possible to re-enable an entire group of older adults who would otherwise have to abandon interaction with radios. We achieved this while letting them continue to use their hands and fingers, something which is not a requirement for successful interaction. If we expand the design area to include all other bodily capacities, the potential to re-establish purposeful interaction would be even greater, and the chance is simultaneously greater for technology to remain meaningful longer, even when living through a decline in psychomotor capacities. To offer users a variety of interfaces on top of the technology also provides users the ability to customize the interaction to their capacity levels, even if they were to discover at some point that some of their motor skills develop in a positive sense. Adapting to skill levels is encouraged by [29]. It would also open up more room to address changes in movements, actions and bodily configurations as psychomotor skills among user group changed. The authors of [7] suggest that there is a natural discontinuation in slow movements among older people. This is also supported by [6] who suggest that older participants depend on interfaces that allow for more sub-movements in interaction. In general, it is considered reasonable to spend more time on interface adaptations since the majority of prior research only studied two-factor analysis of the interaction and psychomotor capacity in a context where other conditions such as frequency of use and expertise could have had an impact on the interaction [10].

Figure 8. The back of the three radios Radio #1-3

In our empirical context, this idea of introducing multiple interfaces is of particular importance as Norway is facing an infrastructural change where all radios are switching from FM broadcasting to digital audio broadcasting (DAB). This will render all current FM radios unusable as of 2017. People with older radios are forced to buy new devices where the interaction may depend on users properly learning and understanding new interfaces, new terminologies, new frequencies and new mechanisms. However, prior research simultaneously suggests that elderly people are less willing to modify current strategies or adapt new strategies [6, 36]. This forced transition gives us a golden opportunity to introduce a variety of interaction mechanisms that can be incorporated into routines and habits while people are relatively able-bodied and only shows early symptoms. By doing so, the technology could potentially remain with them even if they were to enter a downward phase with reduction of capacities. If someone should not develop symptoms consistent with the expectations, having incorporated these new interaction mechanisms may still have a positive effect as it is often the underlying factors that are to be blamed for reduction of psychomotor skills, e.g., in the performance of tasks aiming [13].

Another important factor is the degree of stigmatization associated with use. Technology tailor-made for a particular group of people often succumbs to design choices so distinctive that other people can interpret the intended users their weaknesses just from the design itself. Our participants claimed that all four radios, but, in particular, Radio #3 and Radio #4, had an appealingly aesthetic look that did not suggest being specifically designed for the target audience. The design did not emit the stigmatizing radiance often found in technology tailored for the elderly [5]. Early exposure to interfaces that can have a secondary function later will also allow older users to make acquaintances with interaction mechanisms that have not yet become vital for their use. This would mean fewer chances of experiencing the design and interface as stigmatizing, even though it sometime in the future may become the very interaction mechanism allowing interaction; the interaction is associated with routines and habits rather than to imposed solutions.

This discussion of avoiding stigmatizing design further aligns with the idea of universal design. Design tailored for specific disabilities or illnesses does not exclude people without disabilities from using them. On the contrary, we found that the design of our four radios, and, in particular, Radio #3, appealed to participants and stakeholders that were not in the user group such as family members, employees at the care home, and even our self as designers. In future research, it would be interesting to investigate this aspect of the design further. While our results does not provide any significant evidence of one radio fully re-establishing interaction for all types of psychomotor disabilities, we did see examples of radios elevating the interaction performance to the level of the control group for multiple types of disabilities and illness (as demonstrated with Radio #1 and Radio #2 in Figure 7). It is therefore not unreasonable for further research on this topic to generate designs that can reach even more people and help users achieve even better performance scores. Nevertheless, the aesthetics of the four radios demonstrate the important underlying idea that design tailored for a specific user group can very well be fully usable and appealing to everyone. There is no reason that design for older adults cannot be design for all.

VIII. Conclusion

This paper has attempted to bring attention to the richness of psychomotor capacities that still inhabits aging bodies. Despite certain capacities declining or disappearing, a better understanding of both the psychomotor abilities and disabilities of the participants can help inform the design and thereby re-establish and prolong interaction. We have used four radios co-developed with old people to demonstrate how people unable to operate commercial radios have not only rediscovered interaction opportunities but simultaneously achieved levels of performance comparable to people operating commercial radios. We have also facelifted activities that has generated important knowledge about what types of interfaces and interaction mechanisms that proved the most difficult and how we can address those issues in the design of radios. A total of 65 participants were involved over four years in two phases to help gather the data used in this paper. Our findings are limited to our empirical context but still demonstrate on a broader scale how the body inhabits capacities that when understood and acknowledged properly can help users continue to interact with technology despite experiencing psychomotor disabilities.

References

[1] S. G. Joshi, "Re-establishing Interaction Through Design of Alternative Interfaces," in eTELEMED 2016, The Eighth International Conference on eHealth, Telemedicine, and Social Medicine. Venice, Italy: IARIA, pp. 220-229, 2016.

[2] S. G. Joshi, "Designing for Experienced Simplicity. Why Analytic and Imagined Simplicity Fail in Design of Assistive Technology," The International Journal on Advances in Intelligent Systems, 8(3&4): pp. 324-338, 2015.

[3] E. A. Fleishman and M. E. Reilly, "Handbook of human abilities: Definitions, measurements, and job task requirements," Consulting Psychologists Press, 1992.

[4] S. Norway, "Norwegian Media Barometer, 2014," SSB, 2014.

[5] S. G. Joshi, "Emerging ethical considerations from the perspectives of the elderly," in Ninth International Conference on Cultural Attitudes in computer-Human Interactions, M. Strano, H. Hrachovec, and S. Fragos, pp. 1-15, 2014.

[6] M. W. Smith, J. Sharit, and S. J. Czaja, "Aging, motor control, and the performance of computer mouse tasks," Human Factors: The Journal of the Human Factors and Ergonomics Society, 41(3): pp. 389-396, 1999.

[7] M. Morgan, et al., "Age-related motor slowness: simply strategic?," Journal of gerontology, 49(3): pp. M133-M139, 1994.

[8] C. N. Riviere and N. V. Thakor, "Effects of age and disability on tracking tasks with a computer mouse: Accuracy and linearity," Journal of Rehabilitation Research and Development, 33: pp. 6-15, 1996.

[9] C. Poletti, R. Sleimen-Malkoun, J.-J. Temprado, and P. Lemaire, "Older and younger adults' strategies in sensorimotor tasks: Insights from Fitts' pointing task," Journal of Experimental Psychology: Human Perception and Performance, 41(2): p. 542, 2015.

[10] C. Sutter and M. Ziefle, "Psychomotor user characteristics as predictors for a successful usage of small input devices," in Proceedings of the HCI International 2005.

[11] R. W. Soukoreff and I. S. Mackenzie, "Towards a standard for pointing device evaluation, perspectives on 27 years of Fitts' law research in HCI," International journal of human-computer studies, 61(6): pp. 751-789, 2004.

[12] C. Sutter and M. Ziefle. "Psychomotor performance of input device users and optimized cursor control," in Proceedings of the Human Factors and Ergonomics Society Annual Meeting. SAGE Publications. pp. 742-746, 2006.

[13] Y. Cheong, R. L. Shehab, and C. Ling, "Effects of age and psychomotor ability on kinematics of mouse-mediated aiming movement," Ergonomics, 56(6): pp. 1006-1020, 2013.

[14] Y.-K. Cheong, "Performance and movement kinematics of mouse pointing task: Perspectives from age, psychomotor ability, and visual ability," University of Oklahoma, 2007.

[15] N. Đorđević, D. Rančić, and A. Dimitrijević. "Evaluation of User Cognitive Abilities for HCI," in Proceedings of the 11th WSEAS International Conference on COMPUTERS, Agios Nikolaos, Crete Island, Greece, Citeseer, pp. 468-473, 2007.

[16] J. Knight and G. Salvendy, "Psychomotor work capabilities." Handbook of industrial engineering, 2nd edition, Wiley-Interscience, New York, pp. 978-989, 1992.

[17] L. Zhang, J. Yang, Y. Inai, Q. Huang, and J. Wu, "Effects of aging on pointing movements under restricted visual feedback conditions," Human movement science, 40: pp. 1-13, 2015.

[18] J. Krasner, "Accumulated lives: Metaphor, materiality, and the homes of the elderly," Literature and Medicine, 24(2): pp. 209-230, 2006.

[19] W. Spreicer, "Tangible interfaces as a chance for higher technology acceptance by the elderly," in Proceedings of the 12th International Conference on Computer Systems and Technologies, ACM, pp. 311-316, 2011.

[20] T. Hirsch, et al. "The ELDer project: social, emotional, and environmental factors in the design of eldercare technologies," in Proceedings on the 2000 conference on Universal Usability, ACM, pp. 72-79, 2000.

[21] S. G. Joshi and H. Bråthen, "Lowering the Threshold: Reconnecting Elderly Users with Assistive Technology Through Tangible Interfaces," in International Conference on Human Aspects of IT for the Aged Population, Springer, pp. 52-63, 2016.

[22] Y. Fernaeus and P. Sundström, "The material move how materials matter in interaction design research," in Proceedings of the Designing Interactive Systems Conference, ACM: Newcastle Upon Tyne, United Kingdom, pp. 486-495, 2012.

[23] A. Vallgårda and J. Redström, "Computational composites," in Proceedings of the SIGCHI conference on Human factors in computing systems. ACM, pp. 513-522, 2007.

[24] M. Wiberg, "Methodology for materiality: interaction design research through a material lens," Personal and Ubiquitous Computing, 18(3): pp. 625-636, 2014.

[25] T. Greenhalgh, et al., "What matters to older people with assisted living needs? A phenomenological analysis of the use and non-use of telehealth and telecare," Social Science & Medicine, 93: pp. 86-94, 2013.

[26] S. G. Joshi and H. Bråthen, "The Role of Materials in Design of Familiar and Contextual Assistive Technologies," in International Conference on Interfaces and Human Computer Interaction 2016, IADIS Press, pp. 101-109, 2016.

[27] B. Makofske, "Manual Dexterity," in Encyclopedia of Clinical Neuropsychology, Springer, pp. 1522-1523, 2011.

[28] A. Furnham, S. Von Stumm, A. Makendrayogam, and T. Chamorro-Premuzic, "A Taxonomy of Self-Estimated Human Performance: The General Factor," Journal of Individual Differences, 30(4): pp. 188-193, 2009.

[29] M. H. Fogtmann, "Kinesthetic empathy interaction–exploring the possibilities of psychomotor abilities in interaction design," in Second International Workshop on Physicality, p. 37, 2007.

[30] J. A. Jacko and H. S. Vitense, "A review and reappraisal of information technologies within a conceptual framework for individuals with disabilities," Universal Access in the Information Society, 1(1): pp. 56-76, 2001.

[31] S. G. Joshi and T. Bratteteig, "Designing for Prolonged Mastery. On involving old people in Participatory Design," Scandinavian Journal of Information Systems, 28(1): pp. 3-36, 2016.

[32] A. Field and G. Hole, "How to design and report experiments," Sage, 2002.

[33] J. Gray, P. Jia, H. H. Hu, T. Lu, and K. Yuan, "Head gesture recognition for hands-free control of an intelligent wheelchair," Industrial Robot: An International Journal, 34(1): pp. 60-68, 2007.

[34] A. Crossan, J. Williamson, S. Brewster, and R. Murray-Smith, "Wrist rotation for interaction in mobile contexts," in Proceedings of the 10th international conference on Human computer interaction with mobile devices and services, ACM, pp. 435-438, 2008.

[35] S. Harada, J. O. Wobbrock, and J. A. Landay, "Voicedraw: a hands-free voice-driven drawing application for people with motor impairments," in Proceedings of the 9th international ACM SIGACCESS conference on Computers and accessibility, ACM, pp. 27-34, 2007.

[36] N. Walker, D. A. Philbin, and A. D. Fisk, "Age-related differences in movement control: Adjusting submovement structure to optimize performance," The Journals of Gerontology Series B: Psychological Sciences and Social Sciences, 52(1): pp. 40-53, 1997.

Smart Cities: Challenges and a Sensor-based Solution

A research design for sensor-based smart city projects

Lasse Berntzen, Marius Rhode Johannessen
School of Business
University College of Southeast Norway
Norway
{lasse.berntzen, marius.johannessen}@hbv.no

Adrian Florea
Faculty of Engineering
"Lucian Blaga" University of Sibiu
Sibiu, Romania
adrian.florea@ulbsibiu.ro

Abstract - **In this article, we present a research design for smart city initiatives, based on the argument that there is a connection between smart cities and the concepts of "smart buildings" and "smart users". Smart cities refer to "places where information technology is combined with infrastructure, architecture, everyday objects, and even our bodies to address social, economic, and environmental problems". Smart buildings refer to ICT-enabled and networked constructions such as traffic cameras and lights, buildings and other man-made structures. With inexpensive hardware such as the Raspberry Pi, Intel Edison, Arduino, NodeMCU and their ecosystems of sensors, we can equip these structures with sensors. Smart users refer to the high level of education in developed societies, allowing us to utilize technology such as smart phones to create better cities. Citizens can provide data through their smart phones, and these data can, together with sensor data from buildings, be used to analyze and visualize a range of different variables aimed at creating smarter cities. We propose that a first step of smart city research should be a thorough process of identifying and collecting input from relevant stakeholders in order to find the most relevant objectives for research. Finally, we present case evidence from a pilot study that has followed our approach, which has now received funding for further development.**

Keywords - smart cities; smart buildings; sensors; sustainability; research design.

I. INTRODUCTION

This paper extends the previous work that was presented at the Fifth International Conference on Smart Systems, Devices and Technology (SMART 2016) [1], by presenting evidence from a pilot study of developing an environmental monitoring unit. Starting from a research design for smart city that identifies and collects first the inputs from relevant stakeholders in order to find the most relevant objectives for research, we then present our experiences from a pilot project for environmental monitoring using an integrated hardware-software system, sensors-based. This represents an important contribution to the field of environmental monitoring using the idea of the car as a sensory device and generating some profile indicators for cities per certain periods of time through the project platform.

As of 2009, more than 50 percent of the world's population lives in urban areas [2], and this number is forecasted to increase in the coming years. Cities occupy only 2 percent of the planet, but account for 60-80 percent of energy consumption [3]. As the sizes of cities grow, so do the challenges facing cities [4]. These challenges include issues related to public health and socio-economic factors [5], energy consumption, transport planning and environmental issues [6]. Air pollution caused by traffic jams is but one concrete example of the many challenges facing growing cities [7]. In order to reduce traffic and environmental impact it is necessary to implement safe, reliable, rapid and inexpensive public transport. Therefore, itis an obvious need for cities to be smart. Dameri and Coccia [8] summarize the major objectives of smart cities:

- Improve environmental quality in urban space, reducing CO_2 emissions, traffic and waste;
- Optimize energy consumption, by making buildings, household appliances and electronic devices more energy efficient, supplemented by recycling energy and use of renewable energy;
- Increase quality of life, delivering better public and private services, such as local public transport, health services, and so on.

In this paper, we argue for the application of sensors and data analytics for resolving some of the challenges facing cities. There is a connection between smart cities and the concepts of smart buildings and smart users. Smart cities refer to places where information technology is combined with infrastructure, architecture, everyday objects, and even our bodies to address social, economic, and environmental problems [9]. Examining how to achieve this connection between ICTs and the world around us is the focus of our paper.

Smart buildings and *smart homes* refer to the use of built-in infrastructure to provide safety and security, entertainment, improved energy management, and health monitoring [10]. A smart building or a smart home relies on the use of sensor technologies to achieve this. The data collected by such sensors can also be aggregated and used by the city for various purposes. Sensors can provide information to law enforcement, emergency response, power management, home care services, environmental protection, city planning, and intelligent transport systems.

The concept of *Internet-of-Things* (IoT) is characterized by devices connected to the Internet that can exchange data with external computerized systems. In the context of smart cities, such devices can monitor traffic, pollution, noise level, use of electrical power, etc. [11].

Inexpensive hardware such as the Raspberry Pi, Intel Edison, Arduino, NodeMCU and their ecosystems of sensors, enables us to deploy sensor technology on a large scale. Such low cost devices can provide valuable information for optimizing energy use, infrastructure and public transport planning, as well as emergency response and other vital services. Applying sensors is just the first step towards smarter cities.

The next step involves smart users. *Smart users* refer to the high level of education in developed societies, allowing us to utilize technology such as smart phones to create better cities. Cities in and of themselves are not smart, nor is a smart phone or computer smart unless the person using it does so with a specific purpose in mind. Actually, the apparent intelligence of the computing systems comes from the amount of human intelligence that was invested in it.

Citizen participation is seen as an important element in smart cities [12]. Studies show a causal relation between high levels of education and growth in the number of available jobs [13]. In our context, we see citizens both as providing input through traditional participation projects, but also as providers of data for analysis. Citizens can provide data through their smart phones, either actively or passively (with consent), and these data can, together with sensor data from buildings, be used to analyze and visualize traffic patterns, movement through the city and between cities, environmental factors etc.

We apply these concepts to the framework for smart city planning [12], in order to present a research design for the application of sensors and analytics in Smart City planning. This approach is in part the result of an ongoing collaboration with regional analytics businesses.

The rest of the paper is structured as follows: Section II discusses the use of sensors for data collection. Section III discusses how analytics can be applied as input for participatory planning, and Section IV presents the outline of a research design, using the Smart City framework of [12]. Section V presents the results of a pilot study applying our research design. The pilot study led to a successful application for funding to take the research further. In Section VI, we present our final research design, based on the Chourabi et al. framework [12], experiences from the case, and user centered design principles. Finally, we provide implications and conclusions in Section VII.

II. A WORLD OF SENSORS

A sensor is a component able to detect a change in its environment and convert this change into an electrical signal. The signal returned by a sensor may be binary (on/off), a value within a range, e.g., temperature, light, wind, humidity, precipitation, position, and acceleration. Camera sensors return images or even image streams. Since sensors are operating in real time, they can produce large amounts of information. Therefore, sensors are normally connected to some kind of unit that monitors changes, and forwards information at regular intervals, or when the change is big enough. The left part of Fig. 1 shows how sensors are connected to an aggregation and preprocessing unit.

Many mobile devices have built in sensors, e.g., a GPS sensor, camera or accelerometer. The number of built-in sensors is expected to increase with new versions. Newer cars also have built-in computers handling sensor input, local processing and communications [14]. According to Abdelhamid et al. [15] a 2013 model car has on average 70 sensors, while luxury models may have more than 100 sensors. The number of sensors is expected to grow.

Typical applications for hand-held or car mounted devices are traffic monitoring and prediction. The devices send their coordinates, and the server software receiving this information decides if a specific traffic route is clogged or not.

Another application is environmental monitoring. One example is the Green Watch project [16]. The project distributed 200 smart devices to citizens of Paris. The devices sensed ozone and noise levels as the citizens lived their normal lives, and the results where shared through a mapping engine. The project showed how a grassroot sensing network could reduce costs dramatically, and also engage citizens in environmental monitoring and regulation. Bröring et al. [17] used the built-in diagnostic interface of cars (OBD-II) to obtain sensor data used to estimate current fuel consumption, CO_2 emission, noise, standing time and slow moving traffic.

Citizens can also act as sensors themselves, by reporting what they observe. One example is FixMyStreet.com, a web application that enables citizens to report problems with roads and other types of infrastructure. Today, low cost devices (e.g., Raspberry Pi, Intel Edison, Arduino and NodeMCU), have both processing and communication capabilities. Such devices can easily be connected to different types of sensors [18] [19], and can do local processing of data, before packing the results and sending it to a central processing facility for further processing, analytics and visualization. Raspberry Pi 3 and Intel Edison have built-in wireless communication capabilities, which make connection to citywide Wi-Fi networks even easier. Separate components are available to connect such devices to mobile networks.

The most obvious examples can be found within the following fields:

- Safety and security
- Energy monitoring and control: Smart power meters
- Environmental protection
- Health

A. *Safety and security*

An important aspect of smart cities and smart buildings is to make people feel safe and secure. Sensors can be used for a multitude of application, both to secure property and to keep citizens safe. This includes intrusion alarms, surveillance cameras, fire detection and flood alarms. Such alarms can connect to law enforcement and emergency response, but also to private operators and trusted neighbors. The Norwegian company Lyse, originally an electrical utility company, has developed *Smartly* (http://www.smartly.no), an integrated solution for controlling temperature and lighting, house alarms and surveillance, in-house entertainment and fire detection. Fire and house alarms are connected to operators who will check what happens in case of an alarm.

B. Energy monitoring and control

Sensors can be used to monitor temperature and lights. Detection of movements can turn lights on, and heating and air-conditioning can be optimized to not spill unnecessary energy. Smart meters can provide information useful for energy planning, and prevent blackouts and brownouts by adjusting the price of electrical power. Fregonara and Curto [20] suggests developing a tool that incorporates data from real estate, environmental technology, architecture and materials science, which would make new buildings a lot more energy efficient than they currently are. Other researchers have developed frameworks for comprehensive monitoring aimed at increased energy efficiency. Most of the needed data is available through various sources, but is not yet linked so that it provides a holistic picture [21].

C. Environmental monitoring and protection

By collecting environmental data, the building itself and the city can get early warnings on pollution levels and other environmental problems, and initiate necessary actions. While it may be necessary to build new and expanded infrastructures (i.e., In public transport), much can be done by increased information and access to information about what choice to make. This could lead to citizens being more aware of their environmental footprint, and thus to citizens making better choices [22]. In Stockholm, a pilot study of «smart urban metabolism» applied data from various sources to analyze relevant data and intervene where necessary. As with [21], this study also found that much of the data was already available, but not yet linked and utilized for environmental purposes [23].

D. Health

Older citizens want to live in their homes as long as they feel safe. Sensors can be used for daily health monitoring, where data are sent to medical professionals, but also detect medical emergencies, like fall detection. Boulos and Al-Shorbaji [24] discuss how IoT sensors coupled with data analytics can contribute to a healthier population, and point to the World Health Organization's (WHO) healthy cities project, and the UK's objective to spend £45 million on IoT and related technologies. Another study discusses how technology can be used to alleviate the consequences of flu outbreaks, by spreading information to people in infected areas [25].

E. Privacy issues

Deploying large networks of sensors (proximity sensors, presence sensors, surveillance cameras, gas and smoke sensors), and in particular the data collection from personal devices raise some concerns related to privacy of the individual. Therefore, it is necessary to implement legal mechanisms to regulate how information can be obtained, what information can be obtained, and for what purpose the information can be used. The public must be informed and give their consent of use of the information. Legal and privacy issues will of course vary between different countries, but most countries will have laws governing what we can and cannot do.

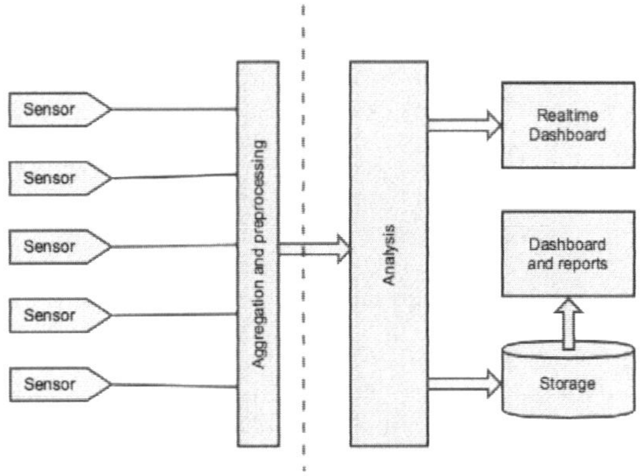

Figure 1. Sensor network, analyzing and visualization architecture

III. APPLYING ANALYTICS AND VISUALISATION IN PARTICIPATORY PLANNING

Mining and analyzing data has been on the agenda of researchers since the 1960's. However, the period from ca. 2000 to present is the most interesting one in the history of data mining, because of the emergence of the world wide web and the large amounts of data generated from the web [26].

A review of data mining literature between 2000 and 2011 reveals that a number of different areas have been developed, which can all be used for various types of analysis [26]:

- Neural Networks - For classification, time series prediction, pattern recognition • Algorithm architecture - For calculation, data processing, clustering
- Dynamic prediction - For prediction, forecasting and tracking
- System architecture - For association, decision making and consumer behavior
- Intelligent agent systems - For autonomous observation and acting on external input
- Data modeling - For representation or acquisition of expert knowledge
- Knowledge-based systems - For knowledge discovery and representation

Most of these can be applied in collecting data from sensors, and there are many examples from literature. One study shows how data mining and predictive analytical techniques can be applied to predict the number of vacant properties in a city [27]. Geographic information can be combined with a plethora of different data to provide valuable information for decision makers. Massa and Campagna show how geographic data extracted from social media can improve urban planning in a smart city context, and present a methodology for social media geographic information analytics [28]. A similar study mines data from the location-based social network FourSquare to identify under-developed neighborhoods [29].

De Amicis et al. [30] have developed a geo-visual analytics platform for land planning and urban design, and argue for the importance of visual, 3D analytics. Another system, STAR CITY, uses sensor data from both machine and human-operated sensors to analyze traffic patterns in cities. The prototype has been tested in Dublin, Bologna, Miami and Rio de Janeiro [31]. Another study uses sensor data to model traffic noise and predict the areas that were most likely to experience noise on a given day [32].

Energy monitoring for the purpose of reducing the city's carbon footprint is another area made possible by analytics. Researchers are working on a framework, which would allow for integration of energy monitoring in entire neighborhoods [33].

Visualization of the results produced by the analytics, can help decision-making. Information can be presented real time through the use of dashboards, using different types of graphical visualizations show issues that need to be dealt with. The combination of analytics and visualization is shown in the right portion of Fig. 1.

This Section has provided a brief overview of analytics and its coupling to visualization, and also given examples of existing systems that at various levels and from several perspectives provide decision makers with important input. The combination of sensors, geographic information and user-generated data can, especially when coupled with some form of visualization, be a powerful instrument for decision makers. Coupled with citizen participation [34] projects, this can be a great resource for the development of smart cities. In the next Section we provide a brief outline of a possible research design for participatory- and sensor-based smart city projects.

IV. TOWARDS A RESEARCH DESIGN FOR PARTICIPATORY PLANNING OF SMART CITIES

Chourabi et al. [12] presents a framework for smart city initiatives, which is separated into internal and external factors (Fig. 2). These factors influence each other, and depending on the type of project, some are more important than others. The framework can be applied as a tool for planning smart city initiatives, and we will in this Section discuss how it can be applied as the foundation for a research design.

Our objective is to create a research project where environmental sensor data from buildings, cars and people are collected, analyzed and visualized, so that decision makers have access to data about issues related to transport and movement, pollution and city planning. We have already made a mobile platform for environmental monitoring, and the first step will be to use this platform to help decision makers make better decisions on restricting car use when pollution levels are high. With this in mind, the framework of Chourabi et al. [12] can be used for the initial project planning:

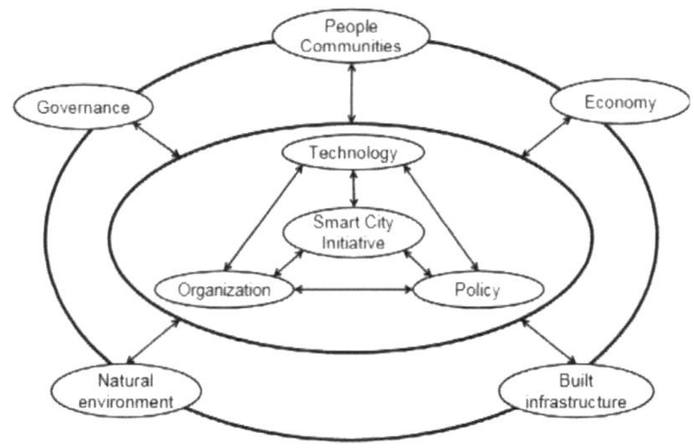

Figure 2. The Smart City Initiatives framework [12].

The Smart City Initiative is as described above. In our home regions, there are several smaller cities in close distance to each other, and we are working to set up a case study of how sensor technologies can help these cities become even more integrated as one single job and housing region. Further, it is a political goal that even if the region becomes more integrated, emissions from transport should not increase. Thus, smart solutions for transport planning and environmental monitoring will be an essential part of the project. The approach may be influenced by urban congestion and by city topographic classes: compact, river and seaside.

The Technology consists of sensors, software and hardware for data mining and analytics. Using existing technologies such as Raspberry Pi, Intel Edison, Arduino, NodeMCU and smart phones would be a natural first step of such projects. A second step could be to evaluate the use of existing technology in order to examine if there is a need for further custom development.

Technological challenges include IT skills of the end users, and issues related to organizational culture [35]. In Norway the population generally has good IT skills, so this challenge is not a major one. Setting up and creating the sensor platforms is another challenge. The project partner from Romania (LBUS) has long experience with embedded systems design, and is responsible for creating the sensor systems. The project partner from Norway (USN) has done several technology projects in collaboration with local cities and municipalities, and has focus on collecting, analyzing and visualizing data.

The bigger challenge would be to overcome organizational barriers. We propose that the cities involved in the project be responsible for setting goals and objectives, recruiting participants and for procurement of necessary hardware and software, as well as placement of sensor platforms. Local media could also be a partner in recruiting "human sensors" to collect information.

For the *Organization and Policy* factors, there are some challenges to be addressed. Organizational issues include alignment of goals and turf wars, and both formal (legal) and informal (normative) challenges as issues to consider when making new policy [12]. The region where our project will take place already has a formalized collaboration on a range of different issues. This means that most of the factors related to governance and policy have already been addressed in previous collaborations. The major challenge will be to get the different cities to agree on a set of goals, as well as what these goals mean in practice.

The external factors of our projects will also have implications. The framework lists collaboration, leadership, participation, communication, data-exchange, integration, accountability and transparency as typical governance issues. Again, the established collaboration between the project partners should help alleviate these challenges.

The *People and Communities* factor involves issues such as accessibility, quality of life, education, communication and participation. Citizen participation through the use of smart phone sensors will be a key factor in our project, so recruiting participants is a major issue. As the objective of the project ultimately is to create regions that are better to live and work in, and to travel between, we will need to be very clear about the potential benefits of participation. Communicating these through traditional and new media will most likely be essential. We address this factor in more detail below.

Economy and Built infrastructure: Smart city initiatives are easier to implement in areas with high levels of education, entrepreneurial businesses and a good ICT infrastructure [12]. The cities we are trying to set up our project with have challenges related to growth, but there are several innovative businesses and industries in the region. A challenge often facing these businesses is how to attract the right employees, so it is likely that they will be positive towards any initiative where this could be an outcome. The IT infrastructure in the region is good, but there will likely be some challenges in more remote parts. For example, there are still areas without 3G or 4G mobile data coverage, and some of these areas could be in places where it would be useful to place sensors.

The final factor, *Natural environment*, addresses the need for more sustainable and greener cities. Therefore, placing sensors that monitor traffic patterns and pollution, building usage and learning more about how and where the people in the region travel, are objectives in our proposed study. Knowing more about travel patterns allows for optimal use of available public transport, and could also facilitate the creation of apps for carpooling. Another use of sensors could be to scan cars passing tollbooths, and to impose higher tolls on vehicles with higher CO_2 and NO_X emissions.

A. Recruitment and participation

We would argue that the people and communities factor is essential in our proposed project. Close collaboration with the people who would be affected by any policy changes that might come from the project might help alleviate some of the resistance that could otherwise arise. As the brief overview of sensor technology and existing research projects show, there are so many possibilities that some kind of process is needed to narrow the scope of the project. Because cities and regions have different challenges, we propose to gather relevant stakeholders in a planning workshop, where the objective is a) to identify the most pressing objectives for the region in question, and b) to figure out the technical, legal and organizational challenges facing each individual objective. Identifying relevant stakeholders can be done for example through the stakeholder framework of Podnar and Jancic [36].

Participation and collaboration between government, citizens and organizations is seen as essential in the development of smart communities [37]. Many of the activities (parks and recreation, planning and community development) typically involved in smart city projects can benefit greatly from citizen participation [38], and there is a clear correlation between cities' adoption and implementation of sustainability policies and public participation in policy formulation [38].

In addition to smart city benefits, many researchers and political theorists see political participation as essential for democracy [39]. By engaging more citizens in political processes, they will take more responsibility for their own situation, and contribute more to society. Simultaneously, other research [40] has shown that citizens are not that interested in participating. Their main interest is that government provides services in a good way.

This latter view finds support in evaluations of participation studies. There have been many initiatives to utilize electronic communication to improve participation. However, citizens tend to remain passive [41]. Those who report to be active participants in democratic processes only make up a small percentage of the population [42]. Thus, Hibbing and Theiss-Morse [40] argue for so-called "stealth democracy", where citizen input is collected in other ways than through direct and active participation.

While active participation is difficult, people can be willing to contribute in other ways. Decision-makers can implement passive crowdsourcing, which requires less commitment and time than other forms of participation [43]. This can be done by using sensors and smartphones, coupled with analytics software that provides important data for decision-makers as outlined in the previous Sections. Passive crowdsourcing is an important part of the project we report on in Section V.

However, active participation is also necessary in order to create useable applications that will encourage people to become "passive participants". The EU-supported NET-EUCEN thematic network has proposed a framework for measuring user involvement, with indicators for how well users are involved in defining, developing and assessing digital government [44]. While this framework was developed for eGovernment in general, the principles of involvement can be transferred to the smart city context. The individual indicators for the three dimensions are presented in Table I.

Our goal is to involve users and stakeholders in all phases of the project. In the definition phase, the users and stakeholders will discuss and decide on issues where senor input, analytics and visualization will be of most value. In the development phase, the users and stakeholders will be involved in the design and development process to make sure that both technology and visual output is useful to handle the issues found during the definition phase. In the assessment phase, the users and stakeholders will be asked to provide feedback on possible modification or extensions.

Table I. Dimensions and indicators of user involvement

Dimension 1: Definition		**Dimension 2: Development**		**Dimension 3: Assessment**	
Engagement of citizens/users in elicitation of needs	Yes:0.25 No : 0.00	Involvement of users/testers in common shared environment	Yes: 0.20 No: 0.00	Involvement of ALL user categories in the assessment	Yes: 0.33 No: 0.00
Involvement of users in the service definition	Yes:0.25 No : 0.00	Involvement of user in interface test and refining	Yes: 0.20 No: 0.00	Instrument used gather the users' feedback: phone calls	Yes: 0.0825 No: 0.00
Involvement of users in functionalities definition	Yes:0.25 No: 0.00	Involvement of user in functionalities test and refining	Yes: 0.20 No: 0.00	Instrument used gather the users' feedback: web modules	Yes: 0.0825 No: 0.00
Involvement of users in the complete interaction definition	Yes:0.25 No : 0.00	Involvement of user in check of documentation / guidelines	Yes: 0.20 No: 0.00	Instrument used gather the users' feedback: consultations	Yes: 0.0825 No: 0.00
		Involvement of ALL user categories in the tests	Yes: 0.20 No: 0.00	Instrument used gather the users' feedback: workshops	Yes: 0.0825 No: 0.00
				Scope: improvement of the service usability	Yes: 0.165 No: 0.00
				Scope: definition of new features	Yes: 0.165 No: 0.00
I1	**Max score 1.0**	**I2**	**Max score 1.0**	**I3**	**Max score1.0**
Total score: I1/3 + I2/3 + I3/3					

V. Experiences from a Pilot Project: A Mobile Platform for Environmental Monitoring

In this section, we present experiences from our pilot project to design and develop a mobile platform for environmental monitoring. Many cities have problems related to air quality. In discussions with city administrators and politicians, we found that environmental monitoring is high on their agendas.

The Norwegian cities of Oslo and Bergen experience severe problems with air quality, especially during the winter season. The two cities have implemented regulatory measures to reduce the emission of pollutants. When pollution levels are high, the City of Bergen restricts the use of cars based on the last digit of the number plates. In Oslo, the city will be closed for cars with diesel engines on days with high pollution levels. Romanian cities, in particular Bucharest, experience high pollution levels due to heavy traffic. The problem is global, with most big cities reporting environmental problems.

Air quality is commonly monitored by use of stationary units. Such stationary units are expensive, and provide data with low granularity. The stationary units are located throughout the city, but the number of units is small (e.g., the City of Oslo has 12 such stationary units). This low granularity has led to criticism from motorists, who claim that air quality measurements are not reflecting the actual level of pollution, only the level of pollution in a few selected areas. Thus, having more measurements from more locations can help justify policy measures to reduce emissions on days with high pollution. In addition, people who experience health problems due to pollution can use these numbers to avoid staying in, or travelling to, high pollution areas.

A. *The Pilot Project*

The main objective of the pilot project was to design and develop an inexpensive environmental monitoring unit using off-the-shelf components to be deployed in cars. The cities own a lot of cars, and they are regularly parked throughout the city. One example is the cars used by the home care service. The caregivers park their cars when visiting patients, and moves from one location to the next at regular intervals.

In the pilot project we built a prototype of the environmental monitoring platform, and secured funding for production of twenty units to be deployed in cars. These twenty units will allow us to demonstrate the practical usefulness of our mobile platform, and also provide a platform for further research and additional funding.

B. *Project Partners and their Expertise*

"Lucian Blaga" University of Sibiu (LBUS) has been working on embedded systems for many years, developing an application that keeps track of people inside a building based on collecting data from sensors [45] and using artificial intelligence tools to model energy consumption in buildings based on alternative data sources, such as the number of vehicles in a parking lot. LBUS experience related to smart buildings concept was materialized in development of a PLC-based embedded system that aims to automate processes and reducing the house energy consumption by optimizing the entire hardware assembly and software algorithms [46].

University College of Southeast Norway (USN) has a research group focusing on "smart cities". Smart cities use technology to improve services and the quality of life for citizens. The smart cities research is well aligned with the embedded systems expertise of LBUS. USN has also collaborated with cities and municipalities on many technology related projects.

C. *Related Work*

The pilot project included a literature search to find related projects and developments. We found examples of mobile environmental monitoring units, and a couple projects related to monitoring by cars:

The Green Watch project [16] distributed 200 smart devices to citizens of Paris. The devices sensed ozone and noise levels as the participants walked the streets of Paris.

CITI-SENSE, a project funded by the European Union, developed LEO (Little Environmental Observatory), a hand-held environmental monitoring unit [48]. This unit monitors three gases (nitrogen dioxide, nitrogen monoxide and ozone), as well as temperature and humidity. CITI-SENSE targeted people living in nine participating cities – Barcelona (Spain), Belgrade (Serbia), Edinburgh (UK), Haifa (Israel), Ljubljana (Slovenia), Ostrava (Czech Republic), Oslo (Norway), Vienna (Austria) and Vitoria (Spain).

A research team from South Korea used a dedicated van containing environmental measurement equipment [47]. The van can be driven to locations where measurements are wanted.

As mentioned before, Bröring et al. demonstrated the use of the OBD-II [17] interface connector to collect information from the car itself (velocity, fuel consumption).

We have not found anyone pursuing the idea of using parked cars as sensor platforms. Such solution will provide more data and better granularity than existing solutions. Further, the similar projects we have identified are all large, well-funded and to varying degrees relying on expensive production processes. We demonstrate that projects such as these can be done in a low-cost way, using off the shelf hardware and a bit of creativity.

D. *The Prototype*

Our prototype used Intel Edison combined with sensors (air quality, temperature, humidity barometric pressure, noise) and a GPS receiver. The communication with the server was done through an Android phone. The Intel Edison used the built-in Bluetooth to communicate with the phone.

The prototype was tested and evaluated. The feedback made us reconsider the use of an Android phone for communication. It requires the phone owner to install and configure an app, and also pay for the data traffic. A dedicated phone would be expensive, and many city employees would object to use their own mobile phones. It would also exclude iPhone owners. The noise sensor did not provide useful information when sampled at intervals. Noise is contextual. A large truck passing the sensor at the right moment may give a very high reading. The Intel Edison processor is also quite expensive compared to alternatives.

Based on our experiences with the prototype, we have redesigned our environmental monitoring unit. The new version uses a LinkIt Smart 7688 Duo with two processors. The main processor is running the OpenWrt Linux distribution and will handle communication and location data from the GPS receiver. The second processor is compatible with Arduino, and handles the sensors. We also decided to include a GSM mobile data unit to avoid the use of an Android phone. A dust particle sensor replaced the noise sensor. Fig. 3 shows the architecture of the environmental monitoring unit. A total of sixteen units have been produced for field testing.

Whenever the car is parked the environmental monitoring unit will start sending environmental data to a server at regular intervals. This allows us to collect information from many different locations, and thus provide a much better granularity than existing solutions.

E. *Platform Design*

After launching the software (at boot-up), the platform needs about three minutes for heating and calibrating the air quality sensor. The Arduino compatible processor will then start collecting information from the sensors (air quality, dust particles, temperature, humidity and barometric pressure). The other processor, running Linux, will collect location and time from the GPS, and connect to the server. The Linux application will then collect data from the Arduino part, and send the data to the server.

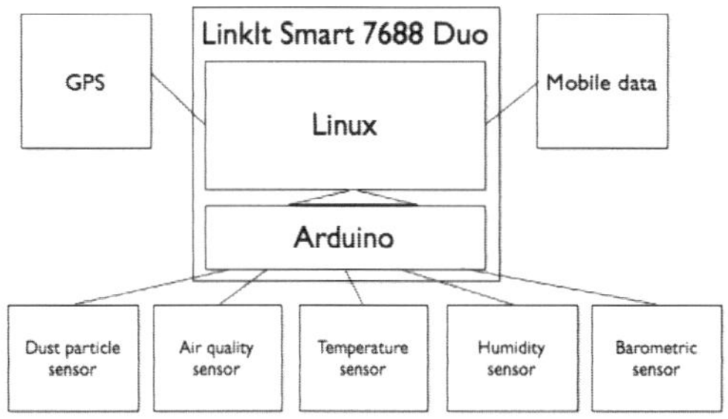

Figure 3. Environmental Monitoring Unit Architecture.

F. *The results and project impact*

The pilot shows the possibility of making affordable units based on off-the-shelf technology. Twenty units will be enough to show the feasibility of our proposed solution. The increased granularity of measurements will help decision makers making better decisions, and will be important to identify specific locations with air quality problems.

The "proof of concept" prototypes will be used for experiments, but more important to pave the road for a larger joint project on data analytics and visualization of collected environmental data.

The results will be available on a web site, and citizens can use the results to avoid exposure to high levels of pollution. This is of particular value to citizens suffering medical conditions like asthma. Citizen can put pressure on politicians to reduce pollution levels. Politicians and city administration can use the results to explain the necessity of using regulatory measures to reduce traffic when environmental conditions are bad. The results may also be an instrument to make citizens aware of the need to cut down the car energy consumption and reduce their carbon footprint.

The platform can be used for other purposes. It can be used as an inexpensive stationary unit attached to buildings and other structures. By changing the sensors, it can also be used to measure water pollution, to monitor patients in their homes or to make buildings and houses more safe and secure. In such cases most of the software can be reused. It is our hope that this demonstration and platform can motivate others to follow their own ideas for how sensors can be applied.

VI. DISCUSSION – A USER CENTERED RESEARCH DESIGN

In Section IV, we presented the Chourabi et al. [12] framework for smart cities, and applied it to our project in order to identify challenges that will have to be addressed. Analyzing these challenges, it became apparent that all of them were related to user involvement and stakeholder management in one way or another.

The technologies we use demand a certain set of skills that can be met by involving our project partners from analytics and engineering.

Organizing the project across different municipalities is another challenge, and again user involvement/stakeholders are important for resolving the challenge, as there is an existing partnership between the municipalities, where we have access to key stakeholders.

Addressing the people and communities factors requires citizens who are willing the act as human sensors, by installing the sensor pack in their cars and contributing to a cleaner environment.

Finally, economy and infrastructure challenges include the region's slow growth, and the scattered knowledge hubs located in different cities in the region. Local knowledge about where to find the skills is necessary and it is also essential to set up a regional network of partners in order to fulfil the overall project goal of creating a more integrated and green region.

VII. CONCLUSION AND IMPLICATIONS

In this paper, we propose a research design for smart city projects using sensors to collect data on a range of variables related to transport, energy use, safety, health and the environment. The sensors may be stationary (fixed to buildings), mobile (e.g., mounted in cars) or part of smartphones and their ecosystem (e.g., smart watches containing sensors).

The collected data can be analyzed and visualized so that decision makers are able to make better informed decisions related to day to day management of cities. The collected data can also be used for prediction of what will happen in the future.

We apply the smart city framework of Chourabi et al. [12] to address the potential issues involved in such projects. In addition, we argue that it is essential for smart city projects to find ways of involving key stakeholders, as different cities and regions are faced with different challenges. Key stakeholders should be involved in both project definition, project development and project assessment.

Finally, we present findings from a pilot project that has followed our approach, in order to demonstrate its relevance.

Implications for research: we contribute towards testing the Chourabi et al. framework [12] in a real life setting, verifying that the framework is useful for analyzing smart city projects, and uncovering challenges and obstacles that needs to be overcome in order to create successful smart city projects. Further, we show the need for user involvement in these projects, and present an example of a research design that might be useful for other research projects in the future.

Implications for practice: we show that the factors put forth by Chourabi et al. [12] are indeed important to address, and suggest that the best way of addressing them is by involving key stakeholders, and by utilizing the power of the crowd by having citizens act as "human sensors". Further, we address issues related to the granularity of existing air quality measurements. Current sensors for measuring air quality are few and far between. Most Norwegian cities only have one or two locations. Pollution can be a very localized phenomenon, restricted to certain areas because of buildings, winds, density of traffic and many other reasons. By fitting cars with sensors we are able to get measurements from many different areas, and can therefore create real time pollution maps with a much higher level of detail than those currently being made. This can be of great help to population groups such as parents with small children, asthmatics and people with allergies, as they can access data about polluted areas and make plans to avoid these if necessary.

Finally, and most importantly, we show that sensors can be deployed at low cost. There are other projects similar to ours that use sensors to measure pollution and other variables (see for example the citi-sense project, http://www.citi-sense.eu/), but those are large, EU-funded projects. We demonstrate that by using off-the-shelf technology and some creative assembly, it is possible to reach the same results with fewer resources. For low- and middle-income countries, cost is an important issue.

Limitations and further research: First, while we have finished part of the project and report on this here, this is still but a small piece of the entire project proposal. We need to conduct further research in order to address the entire scope of the project (creating a more integrated and greener region). In the next phase of the project, which is currently underway, we will build and deploy the 20 sensor sets we have received funding to build. After having been deployed for some time, we can experiment with the proper tools and techniques for analyzing the data. Later research articles will present the findings from these phases of the project.

Despite these limitations, our current progress is promising, and demonstrates how smart technology can contribute towards a better future for cities and their inhabitants, in an inexpensive way.

ACKNOWLEDGMENTS

This work was partially supported by a grant from Iceland, Liechtenstein and Norway, contract type "small size bilateral cooperation projects", "Scholarships and inter-institutional cooperation" program - RO15, EEA Financial Mechanism 2009-2014, the Romanian National Agency for Community Programs in the Field of Education and Vocational Training, Contract Nos. 3/07.07.2016, COD: 16-SEE-PCB-RO SIBIU01 / 01.

REFERENCES

[1] L. Berntzen, M. Rohde Johannesen, and A. Florea, "Sensors and the Smart City," in Proceedings of SMART 2016, The Fifth International Conference on Smart Cities, Systems, Devices and Technologies (IARIA), May 2016, pp. 31-36, ISSN: 2308-3727, ISBN: 978-1-61208-4763.

[2] S. Dirk and M. Keeling. "A Vision of Smarter Cities: How Cities Can Lead the Way into a Prosperous and Sustainable Future," IBM Global Business Services: New York: Somers, 2009.

[3] J.M. Barrionuevo, P. Berrone, and J.E. Ricart. "Smart cities, sustainable projects," IESE Insight, Vol. 14, pp. 50-57, 2012.

[4] B. Johnson, "Cities, systems of innovation and economic development," Innovation Management Practice and Policy, 10(2-3), pp. 146-155, 2008.

[5] B.A. Israel, J. Krieger, D. Vlahov, S. Ciske, M. Foley, P. Fortin, R. Guzman, R. Lichtenstein, R. Granaghan, A.G. Palermo, and G. Tang, "Challenges and Facilitating Factors in Sustaining Community-Based Participatory Research Partnerships: Lessons Learned from the Detroit, New York City and Seattle Urban Research Centers," Journal of Urban Health. 83(6): pp. 1022-1040, 2006.

[6] E. Holden and I.T. Norland, "Three Challenges for the Compact City as a Sustainable Urban Form: Household Consumption of Energy and Transport in Eight Residential Areas in the Greater Oslo Region," Urban Studies, 42(12): pp. 2145-2166, 2005.

[7] P. Sanders, "How Traffic Jams Affect Air Quality," [Online] Available from: http://www.environmentalleader.com/ 2012/01/05/how-traffic-jams-affect-air-quality/, 2012.

[8] R.P. Dameri and A. Cocchia, "Smart city and digital city: twenty years of terminology evolution," in Proceedings of ITAIS - 10th Conference of the Italian Chapter of AIS, 2013, pp. 1-8.

[9] A.M. Townsend, "Smart Cities: Big Data, Civic Hackers, and the Quest for a New Utopia," New York: W.W Norton & Company, 2014.

[10] BIT, "Smart Living with Automation," in Proceedings of World Congress of U-homes,. Nov. 2011.

[11] G. Kortuem, F. Kawsar, D. Fitton, and V. Sundramoorthy, "Smart objects as building blocks for the internet of things," IEEE Internet Computing, 14(1): pp. 44-51, 2010.

[12] H. Chourabi, T. Nam, S. Walker, J.R. Gil-Garcia, K. Nahon, S. Mellouli, T.A. Pardo, and H.J. Scholl, "Understanding Smart City Initiatives: An Integrative and Comprehensive Theoretical Framework," in Proceedings of the 45th Hawaii International Conference on System Sciences, 2289-2297, 2012.

[13] J.M. Shapiro, "Smart Cities: Quality of Life, Productivity, and the Growth Effects of Human Capital," Review of Economics and Statistics, 88(2), pp. 324-335, 2006.

[14] R. Newman, "The next groundbreaking mobile device: your car," [Online] Available from: https:// ca.finance.yahoo.com/news/the-next-groundbreaking-mobile-device--your-car-191728738.html, 2015.

[15] S. Abdelhamid, H.S. Hassanein, and G. Takahara, "Vehicle as a Mobile Sensor," Procedia Computer Science, vol. 34, pp. 286-295, 2014.

[16] C. Ratti and A. Townsend, "Smarter Cities - The Social Nexus," Scientific American, 305(3): pp. 42-48, 2011.

[17] A. Bröring, A. Remke, C. Stasch, A. Autermann, M. Rieke, and J. Möllers, "enviroCar: A Citizen Science Platform for Analyzing and Mapping Crowd-Sourced Car Sensor Data," Transactions in GIS, 19(3): pp. 362-376, 2015.

[18] K. Karvinen, T. Karvinen, and V. Valtokari, "Make: Sensors, A Hands-On Primer for Monitoring the Real World with Arduino and Raspberry Pi," Maker media, 2014.

[19] E. Gertz and P.D. Justo, "Environmental Monitoring with Arduino - Watching our World with Sensors," Maker media, 2012

[20] E. Fregonara, R. Curto, M. Grosso, P. Mellano, D. Rolando, and J.-M. Tulliani, "Environmental Technology, Materials Science, Architectural Design, and Real Estate Market Evaluation: A Multidisciplinary Approach for Energy-Efficient Buildings," Journal of Urban Technology, 20(4): pp. 57-80, 2013.

[21] U. Sivarajah, H. Lee, Z. Irani, and V. Weerakkody, "Fostering smart cities through ICT driven policy-making: Expected outcomes and impacts of DAREED project," International Journal of Electronic Government Research, 10(3), pp. 1-18, 2014.

[22] M. Tomitsch and M.H. Haeusler, "Infostructures: Towards a Complementary Approach for Solving Urban Challenges through Digital Technologies," Journal of Urban Technology, 22(3): pp. 37-53, 2015.

[23] H. Shahrokni, L. Årman, D. Lazarevic, A. Nilsson, and N. Brandt, "Implementing smart urban metabolism in the Stockholm Royal Seaport: Smart city SRS," Journal of Industrial Ecology, 19(5): pp. 917-929, 2015.

[24] M.N.K. Boulos and N.M. Al-Shorbaji, "On the Internet of Things, smart cities and the WHO Healthy Cities," International Journal of Health Geographics, 13(1): pp. 10-15, 2014.

[25] I. Kickbusch and C. Sakellarides, "Flu City-Smart City: applying health promotion principles to a pandemic threat," Health Promotion International, 21(2), pp. 85-87, 2006.

[26] S.-H. Liao, P.-H. Chu, and P.-Y. Hsiao, "Data mining techniques and applications –

A decade review from 2000 to 2011," Expert Systems with Applications, 39(12), pp. 11303-11311, 2012.

[27] S.U. Appel, D. Botti, J. Jamison, L. Plant, J.Y. Shyr, and L.R. Varshney, "Predictive analytics can facilitate proactive property vacancy policies for cities," Technological Forecasting and Social Change, (89), pp. 161-173, 2014.

[28] P. Massa and M. Campagna, "Social Media Geographic Information: Recent Findings and Opportunities for Smart Spatial Planning," TeMA Journal of Land Use, Mobility and Environment. Special issue, June 2014, pp. 645-658, 2014.

[29] D. Quercia, and D. Saez, "Mining Urban Deprivation from Foursquare: Implicit Crowdsourcing of City Land Use," Pervasive Computing, IEEE, 13(2): pp. 30-36, 2014.

[30] R. de Amicis, G. Conti, B. Simões, R. Lattuca, N. Tosi, S. Piffer, and G. Pellitteri, "Geo-visual analytics for urban design in the context of future internet," International Journal on Interactive Design and Manufacturing (IJIDeM), 3(2): pp. 55-63, 2009.

[31] F. Lécué, S. Tallevi-Diotallevi, J. Hayes, R. Tucker, V. Bicer, M. Sbodio, and P. Tommasi, "Smart traffic analytics in the semantic web with STAR-CITY: Scenarios system and lessons learned in Dublin City," Web Semantics: Science, Services and Agents on the World Wide Web, (27-28): pp. 26-33, 2014

[32] E.Y.W. Seto, A. Holt, T. Rivard, and R. Bhatia, "Spatial distribution of traffic induced noise exposures in a US city: an analytic tool for assessing the health impacts of urban planning decisions," International Journal of Health Geographics, 6(24), 2007

[33] O. Pol, P. Palensky, C. Kuh, K. Leutgöb, J. Page, and G. Zucker, "Integration of centralized energy monitoring specifications into the planning process of a new urban development area: a step towards smart cities," e & i Elektrotechnik und Informationstechnik. 129(4), pp. 258-264, 2012.

[34] K. Yang and S.K. Pandey, "Further Dissecting the Black Box of Citizen Participation: When Does Citizen Involvement Lead to Good Outcomes"? Public Administration Review, 71(6), pp. 880-892, 2011.

[35] Z. Ebrahim and Z. Irani, "E-government adoption: architecture and barriers," Business Process Management Journal, 11(5), pp. 589-611, 2005.

[36] K. Podnar and Z. Jancic, "Towards a Categorization of Stakeholder Groups: An Empirical Verification of a Three-Level Model," Journal of Marketing Communications, 12(4), pp. 297-308, 2006

[37] A. Coe, G. Paquet, and J. Roy, "E-Governance and Smart Communities: A Social Learning Challenge," Social Science Computer Review, 19(1), pp. 80-93, 2001.

[38] K.E. Portney and J.M. Berry, "Participation and the Pursuit of Sustainability in U.S. Cities," Urban Affairs Review, 46(1): pp. 119-139, 2010.

[39] Ø. Sæbø, J. Rose, and L. Skiftenes Flak, "The shape of eParticipation: Characterizing an emerging research area," Government Information Quarterly, 25(3), pp. 400-428, 2008.

[40] J.R. Hibbing and E. Theiss-Morse,"Stealth Democracy: Americans' Beliefs About How Government Should Work," Cambridge Studies in Public Opinion and Political Psychology. Cambridge University Press, 2002.

[41] A. Kolsaker and L.L. Kelly, "Citizens' attitudes towards e-government and e-governance: a UK study," International Journal of Public Sector Management, 21(7), pp. 723 - 738, 2008.

[42] E. Amnå and J. Ekman, "Standby citizens: diverse faces of political passivity," European Political Science Review, (2), pp. 261-281, 2014

[43] Y. Charalabidis, E.N. Louikis, A. Androutsopoulou, V. Karkaletsis, and A. Triantafillou, "Passive crowdsourcing in government using social media," Transforming Government: People, Process and Policy, 8(2): pp. 283-308, 2014

[44] L. Berntzen, "Citizen-centric eGovernment Services: Use of indicators to measure degree of user involvement in eGovernment service development," in Proceedings of CENTRIC 2013, The Sixth International Conference on Advances in Human-oriented and Personalized Mechanisms, Technologies, and Services (IARIA) Oct. 2013, pp. 132-136, ISSN: 2308-3492, ISBN: 978-1-61208-3063.

[45] J.A. Oliveira-Lima, R. Morais, J.F. Martins, A. Florea, and C. Lima, "Load forecast on intelligent buildings based on temporary occupancy monitoring," Energy and Buildings, Volume 116, pp. 512–521, Elsevier, 2016.

[46] A. Florea and I. Băncioiu "Future House Automation," in Proceedings of the 19th International Conference on System Theory, Control and Computing, Oct. 14-16, pp. 699-704, 2015

[47] C.-M. Li, B. Liu, R.-F. Qin, and N. Yang, "An urban mobile monitoring system integrating remote sensing and environmental sensors," in Design, manufacturing and mechatronics: Proceedings of the 2015 International Conference on Design, Manufacturing and Mechatronics (ICDMM2015)., pp. 510-519, 2015.

[48] A. Bartonova and the CITI-SENSE team, "CITI-SENSE Citizens´ observatories and what they can do for you," [Online] Available from: http://www.citi-sense.eu/Portals/106/Documents/Dissemination%20material/CITI-SENSE%20selected%20products%20information%20material_15032016.pdf, 2016.

Proof-of-concept Evaluation of the Mobile and Personal Speech Assistant for the Recognition of Disordered Speech

Agnieszka Bętkowska Cavalcante

Gido Labs sp. z o.o.
ul. Romana Maya 1
60-133 Poznan, Poland
Email: a.b.cavalcante@gidolabs.eu

Monika Grajzer

Gido Labs sp. z o.o.
ul. Romana Maya 1
60-133 Poznan, Poland
Email: m.grajzer@gidolabs.eu

Abstract—**Recently, Assistive Technologies tend to exploit speech-based interfaces as a means of communication between humans and machines. While they perform very well for normal speech, their efficacy is very limited for people suffering from a variety of speech disorders, especially in the presence of environmental factors related to the disease. To overcome these issues, we have proposed a Mobile and Personal Speech Assistant (mPASS) – a platform providing the users with a set of tools, which enable to intuitively create their own automatic speech recognition system (ASR) corresponding to their needs and capabilities. The system can be designed at users' home and tailored to the domain, vocabulary, and language they find most useful. The personalized speech recognizer can be used with diversified speech-based applications. The initial results depict the baseline performance of ASR systems created with the mPASS platform and help to identify the most accurate system set-up. Moreover, a proof-of-concept field trial shows that the mPASS speech recognition system was successfully used in the voice-controlled application, achieved high recognition accuracy and was identified by the user as better than the traditional touch input.**

Keywords–dysarthric speech recognition; personal speech assistant; speech recognition for assistive technologies; mPASS platform evaluation.

I. Introduction

The ability to speak, communicate and exchange thoughts is one of the fundamental needs of human beings. Unfortunately, it cannot be sufficiently satisfied in case of people suffering from a variety of speech disorders. As a result, communication situations, which are natural part of everyday activities, can become a formidable obstacle requiring help of an accompanying person. In addition, current technological achievements in the fields of ambient and assisted living, control of smart devices, smart homes, etc. tend to exploit speech-based interfaces as a core means of communication between humans and machines. Moreover, motor functions impairments, which call for the use of Assistive Technologies, are very often associated with speech production problems. Standard automatic speech recognition (ASR) systems, targeted for regular speakers, perform very poorly for people with speech disorders [1]–[4]. Hence, a significant group of people is not able to use many voice-controlled state-of-the-art technology advances, which could support their independence in handling daily activities [1].

It is estimated that 1.3% of the population encounters significant difficulties in speech-based communication [5]. The ability to use speech-based interfaces would significantly improve the lives of people suffering from speech impediments, in particular those with accompanying motor skills disorders. However, there are many diversified speech disorders and it is very challenging to design a single ASR system, which could recognize the impaired speech in each particular case [4]. Traditional methods of constructing ASR systems, used with success for normal speakers, fail in such a task – they require large-scale databases, which are not feasible to be created for disordered speech. Adaptation of standard ASR systems to the disordered speech led to the very limited system performance [4][6][7]. There have been several attempts to design a speaker-dependent dysarthric speech recognition systems [2]–[10], but they were trained mainly in the laboratory environments. Only a few of them were created and tested in real usage scenarios [3][5] with the limited achieved performance, which was not sufficient for the practical implementation [5]. Moreover, speech recognition systems usually require a lot of recordings to initially train the classifier, while collection of even a few speech samples may be very challenging in case of people with severe speech disorders and accompanying other diseases [1][3][4][6][7].

The design of a disordered speech recognition system with a good recognition performance for diversified speech impediments is very challenging. In order to increase the practical application of disordered speech recognizers in Assistive Technologies, we present a concept of a mobile and Personal Speech Assistant (mPASS) – a platform providing the users with a set of tools for building an ASR system, which is tailored to their speech disorders, needs, and capabilities. The mPASS toolchain is designed for non-technical user – the expert knowledge, in particular the knowledge about speech recognition, is not required. One of our key goals is a user-centric interface design allowing to use the platform by people with motor functions impairments and other disabilities. The user can choose the scope, in which he/she wishes to use the system, record training samples, and create personalized speech recognizer, which can be later used as a core engine for different speech-based endpoint applications. In case of people with severe motor disorders and/or accompanied intellectual disabilities the help of a user's carer or other person can be mandatory to operate the system, however, the technical background of such a person is not required [1].

The mPASS platform is to be exploited at users' home.

Therefore, the users are not obligated to attend long recording sessions at a remote location, which is a significant obstacle for the people with disabilities. By maximizing their comfort, more speech samples can be collected and, at the same time, users' motivation to work with the system is improved. In addition, the samples are recorded in the environment in which the ASR system will be later used – this should increase the recognition performance. Such an approach was never practised for a disordered speech thus far. By realizing this idea, we envision that we will be able to engage in our study many users, who will create different types of ASR systems, addressing diversified needs and being successfully used in many practical deployments [1].

In this paper we will also present the initial results depicting the baseline performance of ASR systems created with the mPASS platform for the group of 8 users with diversified speech impairments. They provide meaningful information, which will help to improve the design and accuracy of future disordered speech recognition systems. Moreover, we will present the results of a proof-of-concept field trial where an ASR system created with the mPASS platform was successfully used in the voice-controlled application.

This paper is organized as follows: Section II provides a brief overview of related work, Section III depicts lessons learned from the analysis of these approaches, which helped to come up with the user and system requirements for the mPASS platform, while Section IV presents the summary of identified design challenges. Sections V and VI present the mPASS solution and its architecture. The preliminary results are discussed in Section VII and Section VIII concludes the paper.

II. RELATED WORK

In the recent years, an increased attention has been put towards the design of disordered, in particular dysarthric, speech recognition systems (dysarthria is the key group of speech disorders) [2]–[12]. Two key initiatives in this field are the STARDUST project with its continuations (SPECS and VIVOCA) [3][5][13]–[17] and the Universal Access project [8][18]. The STARDUST system is based on the recognition of selected commands and, in latter versions, also phrases being a chains of words from the trained vocabulary. The system was developed mainly for the environmental control systems. Interestingly, the objectives were to teach users how to better articulate words towards increased speech recognition performance. Thus, the methodology here is opposite to the common ASR systems adaptation, where the recognizer tries to adjust itself to the particular user articulation and its variability. The most recent investigations revealed, however, that the system performance in realistic usage conditions have not met user requirements and therefore was not perceived as practically applicable [5]. This suggests that the proposed methodology was not sufficiently effective.

The second key initiative is the Universal Access project. It is the only system we have approached that was investigating also a possibility of more complex, phoneme-based, recognition, which is more challenging than word-based recognition. The project was focused particularly on the design of new speech recognition techniques, allowing for good performance with dysarthric speakers in large-vocabulary ASR systems. Nevertheless, the final performance results were often far from the levels achieved for normal speakers, especially in case of severe dysarthria. However, the recognition by the ASR system was still able to outperformed human listeners. This suggests that well designed systems for people with dysarthria can bring a significant improvement in the communication with others. Universal Access system was developed in a laboratory environment.

In general, the investigated related works [2]–[10] were mainly targeting the limited-vocabulary, discrete speech recognition systems focused on the command and control target applications. The final dysarthric speech recognition system was task specific and could have been used only with one, selected, speech-based application. This assumption was driving the methodology selection and ASR system set-up. A common practice was also to use the speech recognizers designed for natural speakers and adapt them to dysarthric speech (e.g., Dragon Dictate, Swedish solution Infovox or traditional models based on the Hidden Markov Model (HMM) solutions) [2][6][7]. The performance of these recognizers was limited, especially in case of severe speech impairments. Although, in general, the top performing systems presented 80-90% of accuracy, those results were obtained in the laboratory conditions. The trials conducted in more realistic environment revealed that the external factors (such as background noises) significantly degraded the investigated systems to unacceptable levels [5][6]. Substantially, the diminished performance did not allow for practical exploitation, as concluded from the year-long project VIVOCA [1][5][19].

III. LESSONS LEARNED AND USER REQUIREMENTS

Based on the detailed analysis of the related works, we have identified a list of user-related factors that the authors of other solutions perceived as important. They are particularly significant in case of disordered speech recognition systems, where user-related factors highly influence the achievable performance. The lessons learned during the analysis of the available literature helped to improve the mPASS system design. Hence, our observations constitute a set of tips and user requirements that the mPASS system should fulfill in order to increase its practical usage potential:

1) **The process of training, testing and using the system:** The speech recognition system should be trained and tested in the environment similar to the targeted environment of final speech-based application in which the recognizer will be used. This allows to catch and model the factors related to background noise, microphone type, sounds produced by the access technology interface and a person himself/herself, which were identified as very important [5]–[7]. Moreover, only those interfaces should be used, which are known to the users (e.g., a mouse dedicated for the people with motor skills disorders). This eliminates possible errors and frustration, which could result from using new, unknown access technology [6]. Additionally, it was also depicted, that although combined audio-visual interface is beneficial, the users encountered problems when both audio and visual information was available simultaneously [13]. Furthermore, gamification and similar technologies can positively influence user motivation and commitment [6]. From this perspective also the ability to train, test and use the system at user's home or school is of primary importance, since the need

for travelling to the training sessions can be a significant obstacle [6]. As reported in the literature, most participants of the system trials encountered problems with long training sessions. Hence, the system should use short training sessions and allow users to take breaks whenever necessary. Good and stable results were observed after longer work with the system – the process could have been spanned across the period of several days or weeks, but longer breaks (e.g., related to serious health issues) had negative impact on the performance [6]. Thus, systematic work with the system is important.

2) **Speech recognition techniques and system features:** The core speech recognizer technologies as well as other supporting techniques should be diversified and aligned to the severity of speech disorder, existing motor skill impairments (if any) and user needs. In particular, from the articulation perspective, the system should offer solutions capable of dealing with [4][7]: decreased intelligibility, limited articulation of some (or many) phonemes, explosive speech, slow speech, presence of additional sounds other than speech (loud, involuntary pause sounds, loud breathing, etc.) and unnaturally long pauses between words (disfluencies). Professional dysarthria assessment tests can be helpful in identifying particular problem a user encounters. Feedback information given to the user about the appropriateness of a produced sound volume, quality of recordings, background noises disturbing the system, speech recognition performance, etc., is meaningful.
3) **Problems encountered by the people with dysarthria:** The work with an ASR system was a new experience to the users – they had to get familiar with the technology and the interface. Hence, often the first training sessions were very fluctuating and some time was required to achieve a stable state [3][4][6][20]. Moreover, motor skill disorders are often associated with speech disorders. This influences mainly the interface design, but also the microphone usage – there were several problems reported with headsets and, thus, it is recommended to use stationary microphone [5][7]. In general, for people with motor skills impairments, the need for interaction with the system should be kept minimal (button pressing actions and similar). In spite of the interface improvements towards enhancing user comfort, in many cases the help of accompanying person can be necessary, at least during training phase.
4) **Selection of training material:** Selection of a text material, which should be recorded, can be challenging. It should be aligned uniquely to each user's needs, since predefined training sets can be difficult to pronounce for many users due to their particular speech impairment. In many studies (e.g., [3][6]) the users were allowed to change frequently misclassified or unrecognized words (in command-based systems) to different ones. Moreover, it should be allowed for the users to articulate their "version" of a given command, even if it is pronounced significantly different than by natural speakers (however, the "own" version has to be always the same). Considering the above findings, the selection of training words and/or sequences should be combined with the creation of language model and dictionary for the ASR system.

IV. Design Challenges

The analysis of related works led to the conclusion that the system performance in normal, practical usage situations is influenced by the degree of speech disorder and motor functions impairments, environmental factors (e.g., noises), system access technology design, etc. User motivation was also thoroughly depicted by other researchers as a crucial element of a successful system usage. From the performance perspective, it was assessed as even more important than a degree of speech impairment – better motivated users with severe disorder can train the system better than less motivated ones with milder disorder [6]. These factors have significant impact on the design of an ASR system as a whole [1].

Taking into consideration the outcomes of the related works, it turns out that the challenges in the design of such a system for the disordered speech focus on two factors [1]:

1) the core speech recognition technology, which calls for the development of new techniques targeting disordered speech, especially with regard to acoustic modelling
2) disability-oriented, user-centric system design, taking into account the user needs, which allows for a comfortable usage in the presence of accompanying difficulties

Usually, the second factor is perceived as much less important, especially at the research stage of product development, and it does not influence performance. However, when designing the system for the demanding and diversified group of people with disabilities, its importance becomes equally relevant as the technical excellence of the core speech recognition technology. Hence, our goal is to address both these challenges and come up with a solution, which would conveniently combine novel research outcomes with the user-centric design. Substantially, we also perceive a positive practical verification of a solution as a key challenge and an important success measure [1].

V. mPASS Approach – Mobile and Personal Speech Assistant

To address the above challenges, we propose a platform, which allows *non-technical users* to build their own speech recognition systems, tailored to their particular needs and speech disorders. Our vision is that disabled users, without computer science and artificial intelligence knowledge, will use the mPASS platform to define the domain, vocabulary, and language that is most useful for them in order to communicate effectively with the outside world. They will then train their own ASR system and adapt it to their individual way of speaking. The mPASS system allows to create different types of speech recognizers, at different levels of complexity, ranging from small-vocabulary, command-based systems, to dictation-based systems with different vocabulary sizes for the recognition of sentences and phrases. More complex systems are envisioned for people with mild and moderate speech disorders, since the users with severe speech disorders usually do not use speech in such broad contexts [1].

The personalized speech recognizer can be used later on with many diversified speech-based applications. The proposed mPASS platform is available on a desktop computer as a web-based application providing tools for creating user- and task-dependent speech recognition systems. The models created and trained with this application can be than ported to a mobile device and used in the final speech-based application of interest (where the models for the disordered speech need to substitute or complement the ASR models for the natural speech). Hence, the speech recognizer built by using the mPASS toolchain *can be used with many different speech-based applications*, which were thus far not available to the users with speech disorders. Those applications are widely exploited in the environmental control systems, command-and-control systems (e.g., to steer some home appliances with voice commands), control of mobile device functions, converters transforming (possibly disordered) speech to text or to a synthesized speech, and many more [1]. Some examples of such end-point applications, currently being developed by us to showcase the capabilities of the mPASS technology, are [1]:

1) dictation-based, task-specific application allowing to "translate" impaired speech during a conversation in a restaurant, bank, at the doctor's office, etc.
2) educational game, targeted for autistic users, aiming at helping them in speech therapy classes
3) mobile communication application for users with very severe speech disorders and motor skills impairment (the user exploits a few sounds he/she can produce to control an image-based "communication book")

Having in mind the identified challenges, we present below the key objectives the mPASS system aims to accomplish. They also constitute the differences between our approach and the related works [1].

In contrary to other approaches, the process of building a disordered speech recognizer with mPASS should be *automated* and should limit the need for external help to minimum. Since the influence of practical usage constraints is tremendous, they should drive the system set-up [1].

The ASR system should be created *at user's home* and a training process can span across longer period of time, if necessary. Thus, the time spent on training the recognizer can be adjusted to the user's health condition, motivation and other factors. In addition, such an approach also minimizes the problem of reduced performance in case of systems trained in the silence conditions, which are used in the environment with existing background noise [1]. With the mPASS platform the recordings are to be made in the environment in which the system is then to be used. As a result, it is possible catch and model the factors related to background noise, microphone type, sounds produced by the access technology interface and a person himself/herself. This enables to create ASR systems, which will better deal with such environmental conditions.

Finally, the mPASS toolchain is intended to allow for the *exploitation of existing resources*, which are proved to be good for creating speech recognition systems. *Novel approaches* are to be provided only where necessary, e.g., while building acoustic models for dysarthric speech, where we are developing a new method of the dysarthric speech recognition based on the modified speech classification methods [1].

At this stage the targeted language is polish, however the platform by design is language-agnostic and could be used for building speech recognizers for other languages as well [1].

VI. System Architecture

The mPASS platform guides the user through the steps required to build the speech recognition system (Figure 1). During the process, the user follows on-screen instructions. The core part of the platform is a web-based application – a client side is implemented by using *AngularJS* framework and the server side is based on the *Node.js* framework. The voice is captured by the HTML5 function *getUserMedia*. The client and the server exchange data in the JSON format. The speech recognition system trained with this application is then incorporated with a target speech-based application, on a mobile or embedded device [1]. The below steps present how the process is organized and which consecutive actions are expected to be executed by the user:

1) The user has to create a *profile*, which is strictly related to the level and scope of the envisioned system usage (e.g., command-based, recognition of sentences, continuous speech). There can be different profiles created for the same user, each targeting different kind of speech recognizer for different tasks (e.g., containing vocabulary/training sets for controlling TV, going to doctor's office, restaurant, etc.). Based on the selected system level, the baseline speech unit is automatically defined as word, syllable or phoneme [1].
2) **Creating texts to be recorded, dictionary and language model**: These elements are usually combined and they influence each other. For instance, in command-based ASR systems it could be most convenient to start with a vocabulary, while for the other ones it could be better to start with a set of texts for recording. The mPASS toolchain further guides through the next steps, including support for intuitive creation of language model and dictionary. The final relation between text selection, dictionary and language model is proposed automatically [1].
   a) **Text selection tool**: it is equipped with several phonetically balanced and phonetically rich texts for polish language. They have been created by us based on a well-known poems and short stories for children in order to make them easy to pronounce by the users with disordered speech. The phonetic balance of the recorded text should be duly considered, especially while building more sophisticated systems [13]. It is also possible to create the text automatically based on the existing dictionary and language model [1].
   b) **Dictionary tool**: Dictionary contains the list of words that the system will be able to recognize. It can be created either manually or by extracting words from the texts selected previously for recording or from the language models defined by the user. It is also envisioned that the dictionary tool will automatically suggest additional entries that could maximize ASR performance. For that purpose the dictionary will be analyzed by the mPASS platform in terms of length of the words, phonetic differences between them, and others. There is also an option to substitute frequently unrecognized words with their synonyms based on the user input or automatic suggestion from the mPASS system [1].
   c) **Language model tool**: The purpose of this tool is to create grammar or statistical *n*-gram language models.
   In the first case the user is supported to manually create grammar rules via dedicated interactive graphical interface (technical knowledge is not necessary at this step). Grammar consists of a set of rules that define the possible combination of words in the dictionary. The related mPASS tool enables to create such rules –

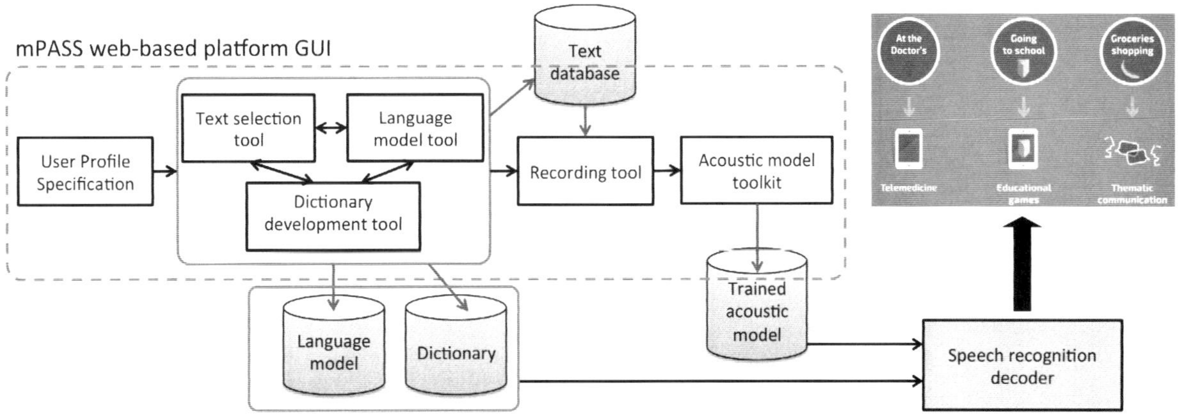

Figure 1. Mobile and Personal Speech Assistant architecture – an overview [1].

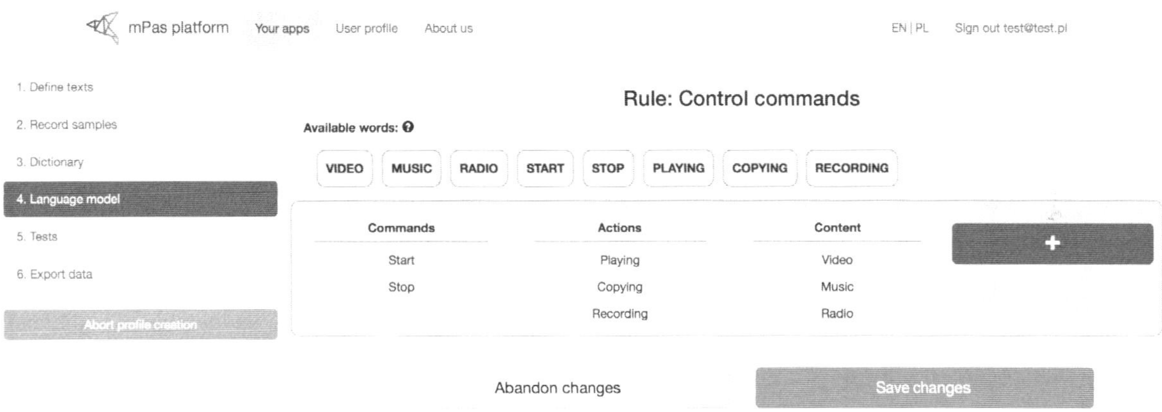

Figure 2. The screen from the mPASS web-based application [22].

the first example is created automatically based on the training texts or by using some predefined examples. The user is then allowed to extend or modify it. The user does not need to understand the methods and formats of grammars, but can intuitively follow the tool's suggestion. mPASS will also automatically verify and, if necessary, correct the convergence between dictionary and language model, so that the latter does not contain words that are not present in the dictionary and vice versa. Figure 2 depicts an exemplary screen from the grammar-based language model creation in the mPASS web-based application.

Alternatively, the mPASS system can automatically modify the pre-loaded generic statistical n-gram model for a given language, in order to align it to the scope of the desired ASR system. The statistical n-gram model specifies the probability of particular n-gram sequences.

3) **Recordings**: The user records selected texts and/or word lists. There is a minimal suggested number of recordings specified. In addition, the system gives a possibility to add new recordings at a later time, pause and resume the recording sessions. The tool also allows to play additional audio information on the attached headphones. The supplementary audio-visual information is supposed to help people with intellectual disabilities, visual impairments, children, etc. We also aim to supply the tool with mechanisms allowing for monitoring and potential correction of wrong recordings [1] – the user will be given a real-time feedback information presenting the recorded waveform and whether the required volume is achieved. Hence, feedback information will refer to the appropriateness of a produced sound volume, quality of recordings, background noises disturbing the system, speech recognition performance, etc.
4) **Training the acoustic model**: This step is an automated background process. Only experienced (developer-type) users are allowed to change some of the parameters, e.g., choose different methodologies/techniques, such as HMMs or Support Vector Machines (SVMs). We are also developing our novel acoustic modelling methods, which will be included in the mPASS system [1].
5) The obtained acoustic model, dictionary and language model are then *exported* to be used in the desired target speech-based application. Optionally, the initially created acoustic model can be later on extended based on additional recordings collected while creating other user profiles for different contexts [1].

TABLE I. DESCRIPTION OF USERS, WHO PROVIDED VOICE SAMPLES COLLECTED WITH THE MPASS PLATFORM

User	Speech disorder	Severity of disorder	Age	No. of sessions
User 01	dyslalia	low	child	10
User 02	sigmatism, devoicing of phones	moderate	youth	27
User 03	dysarthria	moderate	youth	20
User 04	dysarthria	severe	youth	22
User 05	dysarthria	low-moderate	adult	30
User 07	dysarthria, praxic functions disorders	low	youth	12
User 12	dyslalia	low-moderate	child	10
User 13	dysarthria, prosodic disorders	low	youth	21

All recordings, recorded texts, dictionaries and language models are stored in a database. The user may wish to share them with others (if agreed) in order to help develop better ASR systems for the other users in the future [1].

From the user perspective, the recording tool functionality is the most important part of the mPASS platform. It is, however, also the most vulnerable to possible errors – wrong recordings, additional background noise and other factors affecting the recorded material will directly influence the acoustic model and its performance. Hence, in order to tune our interface design and system features to real user needs, we have performed initial recording sessions with several users having diversified speech disorders: one adult with explosive speech and associated motor impairments, 4 teenagers presenting variable levels of dysarthria and 4 healthy children 3-6 years old with impaired speech typical to their age. Those trials helped to improve the system design and obtain an initial database used by us for the evaluation of acoustic modelling techniques. Currently, the key components of the mPASS platform are implemented and it can be used for further evaluation [1].

VII. PRELIMINARY RESULTS

A set of initial experiments has been conducted with the use of voice samples recorded with the mPASS platform. The goal was to:

1) evaluate the recognition accuracy with regard to the selection of the basic recognition unit as either phoneme, word or syllable
2) evaluate 3 acoustic modelling methods based on Hidden Markov Models (HMMs), Support Vector Machines (SVMs) and Structured SVMs
3) perform an initial field trial conducted by a single user, who was using the voice-controlled application for sending SMS-es and e-mails

This initial evaluation constitutes a proof-of-concept evaluation of the mPASS approach, provide important insights towards the most accurate set-up of speech recognition systems for the disordered speech and present the borderline of the achievable performance. During the course of further research we will investigate further improvements of the mPASS platform, especially with regard to acoustic modelling, which should further improve the recognition accuracy.

A. System performance for diversified recognition units

In each speech recognition system the recognizer is trained with regard to particular recognition unit, which can be specified as either phoneme, word or syllable. The aim of experiments reported in this section was to verify, which recognition unit would be the most suitable in case of the disordered speech recognition.

We have investigated 4 different variants of basic recognition units:

- word: each word is represented by an HMM model with particular number of states equal for each word, e.g., the word "nine" is represented with a single HMM model with n states and the word "ten" is represented with another HMM model with n states, where n is an arbitrary selected value adjusted experimentally (i.e., *nine* $\rightarrow$ *nine*, *ten* $\rightarrow$ *ten*).
- phoneme: each phoneme is represented by a single HMM with 3 states; each word in a dictionary is represented as a sequence of phonemes, however, different words can include the same phoneme (i.e., *nine* $\rightarrow$ *n a y n*, *ten* $\rightarrow$ *t E n*) (phonemes are represented in SAMPA notation).
- phoneme/word: each phoneme is represented by a single HMM with 3 states; each word in a dictionary is represented as a sequence of phonemes, however, each phoneme can be present only once, e.g., *nine* $\rightarrow$ *n_1 a_1 y_1 n_11* (HMM for a word with 12 states), *ten* $\rightarrow$ *t_2 E_2 n_2* (HMM for a word with 9 states). This system can be envisioned as a word-based system, where HMM for each word is represented with different number of states.
- syllable: each syllable is represented by a single HMM with particular number of states equal for each syllable and each word is represented as a sequence of syllables; different words can have the same set of syllables (i.e., *nine* $\rightarrow$ *nine*, *eleven* $\rightarrow$ *e lev en*).

For the needs of initial experiments, the recordings database was collected by means of the mPASS platform. It contains the speech samples of 8 users with diversified speech disorders. The group consists of 2 pre-school children with impaired speech typical to their age and 6 persons with variable speech disorders and other dysfunctions. Their speech impairments were described and characterized by the language therapist. The short characteristic of each user is presented in Table I. All users were recording the training sessions containing numbers from 1 to 10. The speech samples were recorded at users home. The sessions were then divided into 3 sets: training set, development set and test set. Hence, each set was containing several sessions with 10 samples each

TABLE II. PERFORMANCE COMPARISON OF HMM- AND SVM-BASED DISORDERED ASR SYSTEMS CREATED WITH THE MPASS PLATFORM

User	word	phoneme	phoneme/word	syllable
User 01	97.38% (26 states)	94.92%	**98.19%**	94.98% (11 states)
User 02	90.25% (7 states)	**94.58%**	94.33%	93.00% (8 states)
User 03	89.50% (6 states)	91.41%	**93.24%**	90.46% (10 states)
User 04	62.25% (28 states)	54.94%	62.84%	**65.85% (21 states)**
User 05	91.37% (13 states)	94.10%	**96.47%**	91.81% (12 states)
User 12	66.96% (19 states)	75.41%	**79.45%**	69.65% (16 states)
User 13	84.98% (19 states)	90.07%	**92.45%**	81.09% (15 states)

(numbers 1-10).

The HMM-based ASR systems were created for the users identified in Table I. In case the basic recognition unit was set to word or syllable, it was necessary to define the most suitable number of HMM states, which would be allocated per recognition unit. It was done experimentally by evaluating the recognition performance for HMM models containing 3 to 27 states, and for different number of mixtures – 1, 2, 4 or 8 per state. The best results were selected for the comparison and are depicted in Table II. For the other 2 cases (i.e., phoneme and phoneme/word), the number of HMM states was variable, depending on the length of a particular word.

Evaluation of the obtained recognition results reveals that the phoneme/word basic recognition unit provides the best outcome for most of the users. For User 02 better values were obtained for a phoneme-based system, however the differences in comparison to the phoneme/word version are negligible. In case of User 04, the best performance was obtained for a syllable-based system – most likely phoneme as a basic unit is too small to properly reflect variability of different units in case of severe speech disorders (more specifically, the syllable is not only longer, but it also always has a vowel, which makes recognition easier). Nevertheless, for both User 04 and User 02 the word/phoneme-based system performs still relatively well. Hence, this recognition unit should be recommended for the small-size ASR systems. Additionally, such a recognition unit is also used in the popular, open-source CMU Sphinx speech recognition software [21]. In case of more complex speech recognition system the word/phoneme-based model could be substituted with a phoneme-based systems in order to reduce system complexity.

Following the results presented in Table II, the mPASS platform will select the default recognition unit as phoneme/word, however will also automatically evaluate other options in case the recognition accuracy will not be satisfactory. In such a case the platform will also automatically specify the most accurate number of HMM states, where necessary.

B. System performance for diversified acoustic modelling techniques

The key acoustic modelling techniques were selected for the initial performance evaluation of disordered speech recognizers created with mPASS platform, namely HMMs and SVMs. HMM method is traditionally used in many ASR systems – it aims to model the speech recognition process as a sequence of most probable states of the hidden Markov process. The SVM method is a promising solution, which exploits discriminative supervised machine learning technique to classify observed speech samples into the most probable classes (labels) representing the final output. One of the variants of this technique, using the additionally structured label space, is a Structured SVM methodology. It will also be evaluated in the performed study. The SVM-based techniques were not widely exploited for the speech recognition thus far. Hence, their comparison to traditional HMM-based methodologies will provide meaningful insights into the future development of improved acoustic modelling techniques.

The experiments were performed for the database of recordings presented in Section VII-B. The speech recognition system was created and trained on the sessions from both – the training set and development set (this is driven by the objective to properly compare results between the HMM- and SVM-based systems, which will be described later on in this section). In case of HMM-based acoustic models, the basic recognition unit was phoneme/word, where each phoneme was represented by a 3-state HMM model with 1, 2, 4 or 8 mixtures – the particular value for each case was selected experimentally, depending on the size of the training material. For the training and recognition process the Mel-Frequency Cepstral Coefficients (MFCC) acoustic feature were used. The trained ASR system was then evaluated based on the recognition of samples from the test set.

For the speech recognition based on the SVM and Structured SVM acoustic models, the system is trained in the 2-step process. Firstly, the HMM-based model is trained, similarly as in the previous case, on the training set only. Secondly, this model is used for the recognition of samples from the development set, which allows for the computation of features from the log-likelihood feature space for these recordings. This input is then used to train the SVM or Structured SVM model. Finally, the acoustic model trained in this 2-stage process is used for the recognition of samples from the test set.

For both HMM- and SVM-based ASR systems, the above procedure was repeated 5 times, each time using different selections of sessions for training, test and development sets. The average recognition performance obtained in this experiment is presented in Table III. The Structured SVM model achieved the best performance in most cases or performed comparable to the reference HMM-based solution in the remaining cases. Hence, it can be perceived as the best solution among the 3 investigated ones. Interestingly, the pure SVM model performed poorly, often worse than the traditional HMM-based method. The advantages of the Structured SVMs over HMMs are particularly visible for the least-performing users, with the most severe speech disorders. This feature makes this technology an interesting alternative to HMM-based models in

TABLE III. PERFORMANCE COMPARISON OF HMM- AND SVM-BASED DISORDERED ASR SYSTEMS CREATED WITH THE MPASS PLATFORM

User	Training set size	Development set size	HMM	SVM	Structured SVM
User 01	4	2	86.68%	85.31%	**93.02%**
User 02	11	3	**93.10%**	89.36%	92.83%
User 03	10	3	**88.73%**	84.50%	88.61%
User 04	10	5	47.94%	47.21%	**49.51%**
User 05	15	5	98.33%	98.07%	**98.48%**
User 07	8	2	70.13%	68.06%	**74.53%**
User 12	6	2	66.59%	62.3%	**72.29%**
User 13	11	3	87.07%	79.31%	**89.41%**

TABLE V. RECOGNITION PERFORMANCE IN A MOBILE APPLICATION FOR THE SPEECH RECOGNITION SYSTEM CREATED WITH THE MPASS PLATFORM – COMPARISON BETWEEN A USER WITH DISORDERED SPEECH AND A HEALTHY SUBJECT

Action	User with disordered speech	User with normal speech
Action commands recognition	81%	100%
List control commands recognition	88%	89%
Pre-defined messages recognition	80%	96%
Average	84%	94%

the context of disordered speech recognition. Hence, as a part of future work we will be proposing a modification to the Structured SVM methodology in order to further increase the recognition accuracy.

System performance observed for User 01, 02, 03, 05 and 13 was high, exceeding 88% for all cases. The best result was as high as 98.48% for User 5. This is a very good outcome for disordered speech recognition. The worst performance was achieved for User 04, who has the most severe level of disarthria among all investigated cases. Lower accuracy was also observed for two cases – User 07 for who praxic functions disorder accompanies dysarthria making the speech disorder more complex and User 12 being a child with dyslalia. The low result of User 12, who has relatively low speech disorder, can be explained by the problems encountered during recording sessions, related to the age of the user – the recordings are of diversified sound volumes, the user was moving, etc. In general, however, the results present that the recognition performance is highly dependent on the severity of speech disorder of particular users, which confirms observations from the previous studies, e.g., [7]. In practice, the users with the most severe speech disorders would usually train the system with very limited, self-selected vocabulary, which would allow to introduce several control commands. The recognition accuracy in such set-up would likely be improved (in this trial we have pre-selected the vocabulary, so the user had to align to this selection, even if it was difficult for him/her to pronounce particular words). Nevertheless, our further works on this topic will focus on the new acoustic modelling techniques, which could improve recgnition performance for the most challenging group of users.

C. Proof-of-concept field trial

The initial proof-of-concept field trial was executed by the adult with explosive speech and cerebral palsy. With the mPASS platform, he created an ASR system for the exemplary voice-controlled mobile application, which allows to send an SMS or e-mail with one of predefined messages to a recipient from a phone contact list [22]. User-defined voice commands are exploited to control the application. Some of its screenshots are presented in Figure 3. The user recorded 8 messages of his own choice (e.g., "I will be back in 1 hour"), as depicted in Table IV, several action commands ("send", "SMS to", etc.) and list control commands ("up", "down", "OK", etc.) – all together 21 phrases, 30 times each [1].

The ASR system was using the HMM-based acoustic model. The 3-state HMM model was used to represent each phoneme and the MFCC-based acoustic features were exploited. The basic system performance, with regard to accuracy of the recognition of the selected phrases and commands, was tested in a laboratory environment with the pocketsphinx speech recognition toolkit [21] (please note that the recordings were made at user's home). For this purpose, the speech recognizer was trained with 2, 4, 6, 8 and 10 recording sessions selected randomly for each phrase. The remaining sessions (out of 30 collected) were used for testing. Each experiment was repeated 20 times and the results were averaged [22]. In case the training was performed for 10 recordings of each phrase, the recognition performance was 99%. It dropped to 82% when training on the smallest set of 2 sessions. Hence, for further

TABLE IV. MESSAGES SELECTED BY THE MOBILE APPLICATION USER, WHICH CAN BE SENT OVER SMS OR E-MAIL

No.	Message
1	I am in the park
2	I will be back in 1 hour
3	Just arrived
4	Are you at home?
5	Please, help me
6	Empty battery
7	I will be back later
8	I am going to the park

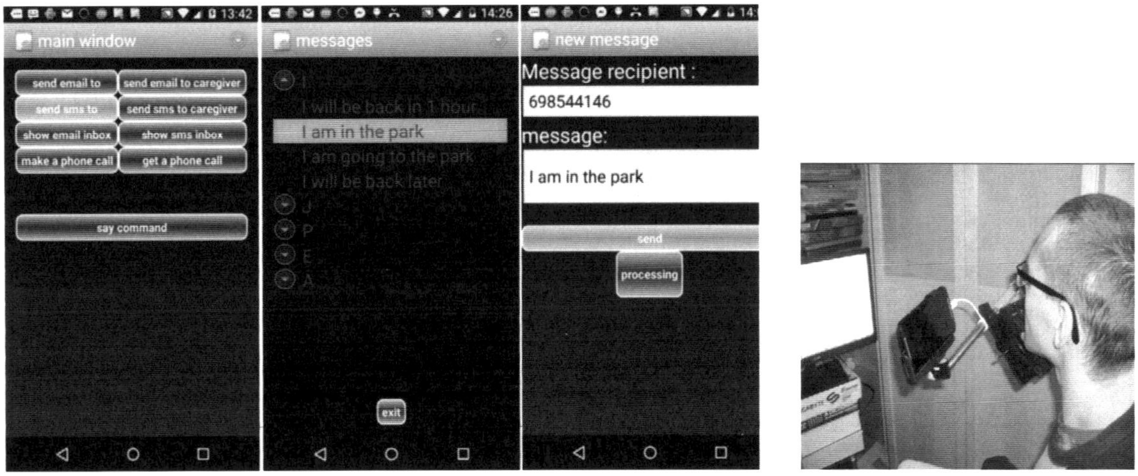

(a) The set of selected screensshots

(b) User controlling the computer and the application on a mobile device with his chin

Figure 3. An exemplary application using mPASS platform to dictate and send SMS-es and e-mails.

evaluation we have used an ASR system trained on randomly selected 10 recordings of each phrase/command.

The recognition performance under the real-usage conditions was evaluated with a disordered-speech user and a healthy user as a reference [22]. Such methodology is widely used for results comparison in case of speaker-dependent ASR systems, which are highly correlated with the context and vocabulary they are trained on. During the field trials both users were performing a given task with the dedicated application – they were sending an SMS and e-mail with a self-selected message. During the entire trial, the disordered-speech user spoke all together 82 commands (words or phrases), while the reference subject spoke 72 commands. The number of all spoken commands is smaller in case of healthy person, since less repetitions were necessary to complete a task. The overall recognition performance was evaluated based on the number of correctly recognized commands in relation to the total number of spoken commands.

The comparative results are presented in Table V. The disordered-speech subject was using the system in a home-office environment. Under such conditions, healthy subject achieved the accuracy close to 100%. Therefore, the experiment with a healthy person was also repeated in more demanding conditions – outdoors with relatively strong wind. These results are presented in Table V. The recognition accuracy in case of the user with disordered speech was on average 84%. It increased to 94% in case of normal speech, even though the user with unimpaired speech was testing the

TABLE VI. Comparison of the time required to complete an action with a voice-controlled and manual entry [1]

Action	Voice input	Manual input	Gain
Send SMS to caregiver	31s	56s	45%
Send e-mail to caregiver	33s	65s	49%

application in more demanding outdoor environment. Although the performance was lower in case of disordered speech, the achieved levels enabled to successfully control and use the application.

Additionally, we investigated performance measures related to the person's judgement of system's applicability and usability. We compared the time required to complete particular actions when using the dedicated voice-controlled application and the regular touch input (the person controls mobile phone installed on a wheelchair with his chin). In this measure we have also included the time lost for necessary repetitions when speech recognition errors occurred. The results were averaged over 20 trials and are given in Table VI. It can be observed that the voice-controlled version outperformed the manual entry for up to 49% – considering the time gain, which was observed with the voice input in comparison to manual input. Substantially, the user assessed a voice-controlled mobile speech assistant as the preferred option, which is the most important success measure [1].

D. Discussion

The initial trial presented above constitutes a first proof-of-concept evaluation. At this stage, the obtained results cannot be directly compared to the ones presented in the related works, since they were gathered for different usage scenarios and with different ASR systems, especially with regard to the selected vocabulary. However, we have also made an attempt to compare the proposed system with standard state-of-the-art speaker-independent speech recognition solution provided by Google (using the Google Speech API [23]). For this purpose, the disordered-speech user spoke several commands used during the proof-of-concept trial to the Google ASR system – 3 times each. Although this system is a top-performing speech recognition solution for normal speech, it was unable to recognize the disordered speech – in each single executed trial the Google system response was incorrect, leading to recognition performance of 0%. This constitutes a confirmation that traditional ASR systems fail for disordered speech and further comaprisons with them cannot bring any additional information during the evaluation of disordered-speech recognition systems created with mPASS. Therefore, we have decided to compare the field trial results obtained for disordered speech with a healthy subject using the ASR system trained with the same methodology.

In general, the recognition performance of ASR systems created with mPASS reached very high levels for the laboratory environments. This finding is a consequence of the proposed mPASS system design, which allows to 1) create ASR systems with a scope corresponding to user expectations and capabilities, 2) collect speech samples in the environment in which the system is later used, 3) easily record the necessary number of speech samples in a convenient manner (the system automatically verifies, if it is necessary to collect additional samples in order to obtain the required recognition accuracy) and 4) use new SVM-based techniques for acoustic modelling. Substantially, the proposed ASR system also performed very well in real usage environment of home/small office – the proof-of-concept trials were concluded with a very promising outcome, which was rarely achieved before. However, we could also observe the drop of recognition accuracy in case of people with severe dysarthria. This effect was also widely observed in other trials reported in the literature and suggests that the scope of their ASR systems should be carefully adjusted to the sound pronunciation capabilities of these users. More detailed performance evaluation, including more complex ASR systems created with the mPASS platform, is a part of the future work. It is envisioned to be executed based on the database of recordings collected from another 7-10 users.

In addition, based on our observations, we have identified voice activity detection (VAD) functionality of the recording tool as one of the key challenges. In the trials performed to date the standard VAD techniques based on the analysis of the differences in volume level and signal to noise ratio often failed in case of disordered speech users. The level of additional involuntary sounds such as loud breathing, grunts, etc. and the noise occurring during recordings (e.g., sounds given by the computer access technology or a wheelchair) is frequently of significant volume. Hence, more sophisticated VAD techniques should be used to overcome such issues. Potential techniques can use machine learning technologies and reasoning based on the pre-recorded "silence patterns" for a given person. Such solutions are within a scope of our future research.

VIII. Conclusion

The mPASS system proposes a unique combination of an intuitive, user-centric system design with the top performing ASR tools. It provides an automated toolchain, which enables to easily follow the process of creating a speech recognition decoder. We believe that by using this technology the wide variety of users, with different speech impairments, will be able to build disordered speech recognition systems – tailored to their needs and achieving high recognition performance. Substantially, the users will be allowed to create and train the system at home environment. The initial results are very promising, especially taking into account a positive users' feedback.

In the initial experiments we have investigated two types of acoustic models for the needs of disordered speech recognition. Our findings revealed that the Structured SVM method outperformed the traditional HMMs for the vast majority of cases. The performance of ASR systems created with the mPASS platform for 8 users allowed to reach high levels – often close to or higher then 90%. This is a very good result for disartric speech. Additionally, the comparison with HMMs shows that SVM-based techniques are an interesting methodology, which will be further investigated by us in the future. However, it was also observed that the achieved performance drops with the increase of speech disorder, which suggests that users with more severe speech impairments should align the complexity of their ASR systems to their capabilities. The mPASS platform, due to its flexibility, should allow to address this challenge accordingly. Moreover, the performance trials executed with the collected database of recordings allowed to investigate the most applicable system set-up with regard to the basic recogition unit selection. The results present that the recognition using a combination of phoneme and word would address well the variety of cases and speech disorders.

Additionally, the proof-of-concept field trial, with a dedicated voice-controlled mobile application, revealed a promising outcome. The speech-based input was assessed as up to 49% faster than the traditional manual input by a person with severe speech impediments and motor skills disorder. In the future, we plan to evaluate the mPASS platform with more users in several scenarios related to different mobile applications, which will be based on the ASR systems trained with mPASS. By using the proposed toolchain, we hope to achieve disordered speech recognition systems ready to be used in practical conditions with a variety of endpoint speech-based applications. Hence, our solution could be effectively exploited by people with speech impairments and assist them in their daily activities.

Acknowledgements

The presented work is financed by the National Centre for Research and Development in Poland under the grant no. LIDER/032/637/l-4/12/NCBR/2013. The authors would like to thank Michał Koziuk for his help with the system implementation and Leszek Lorens for his help with mobile application development and field trial organization.

References

[1] A. B. Cavalcante and M. Grajzer, "Mobile and Personal Speech Assistant for the Recognition of Disordered Speech," in Proceedings of the Second International Conference on Smart Portable, Wearable, Implantable and Disability-oriented Devices and Systems (SPWID 2016), May 22-26, 2016, Valencia, Spain, 2016, pp. 6–10.

[2] S. K. Fager, D. R. Beukelman, T. Jakobs, and J.-P. Hosom, "Evaluation of a speech recognition prototype for speakers with moderate and severe dysarthria: A preliminary report," Augmentative and Alternative Communication, vol. 26, no. 4, 2010, pp. 267–277.

[3] M. S. Hawley, P. Enderby, P. Green, S. Cunningham, S. Brownsell, J. Carmichael, M. Parker, A. Hatzis, P. O'Neill, and R. Palmer, "A speech-controlled environmental control system for people with severe dysarthria," Medical Engineering & Physics, vol. 29, no. 5, 2007, pp. 586–593.

[4] K. Rosen and S. Yampolsky, "Automatic speech recognition and a review of its functioning with dysarthric speech," Augmentative and Alternative Communication, vol. 16, no. 1, 2000, pp. 48–60.

[5] M. S. Hawley, S. P. Cunningham, P. D. Green, P. Enderby, R. Palmer, S. Sehgal, and P. O'Neill, "A voice-input voice-output communication aid for people with severe speech impairment," Neural Systems and Rehabilitation Engineering, IEEE Transactions on, vol. 21, no. 1, 2013, pp. 23–31.

[6] C. Havstam, M. Buchholz, and L. Hartelius, "Speech recognition and dysarthria: a single subject study of two individuals with profound impairment of speech and motor control," Logopedics Phonatrics Vocology, vol. 28, no. 2, 2003, pp. 81–90.

[7] P. Raghavendra, E. Rosengren, and S. Hunnicutt, "An investigation of different degrees of dysarthric speech as input to speaker-adaptive and speaker-dependent recognition systems," Augmentative and Alternative Communication, vol. 17, no. 4, 2001, pp. 265–275.

[8] H. V. Sharma, M. Hasegawa-Johnson, J. Gunderson, and A. Perlman, "Universal Access: Preliminary experiments in dysarthric speech recognition," in Proc. 10th Annual Conf. of the Internat. Speech Communication Association, 2009, p. 4.

[9] K. Caves, S. Boemler, and B. Cope, "Development of an automatic recognizer for dysarthric speech," in Proceedings of the RESNA Annual Conference, Phoenix, AZ., 2007, p. n/a.

[10] E. Rosengren, "Perceptual analysis of dysarthric speech in the ENABL project," TMHQPSR, KTH, vol. 1, no. 2000, 2000, pp. 13–18.

[11] AAC-RERC Project D2-B: Recognition of Dysarthric Speech. [Acccessed: 28 November 2016]. [Online]. Available: http://aac-rerc.psu.edu/index-28962.php.html

[12] ENAbler for computer-Based vocational tasks with Language and speech (ENABL). [Acccessed: 28 November 2016]. [Online]. Available: http://cordis.europa.eu/project/rcn/35115_en.html

[13] M. Parker, S. Cunningham, P. Enderby, M. Hawley, and P. Green, "Automatic speech recognition and training for severely dysarthric users of assistive technology: The STARDUST project," Clinical linguistics & phonetics, vol. 20, no. 2-3, 2006, pp. 149–156.

[14] STARDUST Project. [Acccessed: 28 November 2016]. [Online]. Available: http://spandh.dcs.shef.ac.uk/projects/stardust/

[15] Speech Technology Applications Toolkit - STAPTK. [Acccessed: 20 April 2015]. [Online]. Available: http://spandh.dcs.shef.ac.uk/projects/staptk/

[16] S. Judge and Z. Robertson, "Speech Driven Environmental Control System (SPECS): From Specification to Prototype," in Recent Advances in Assistive Technology and Engineering (RAATE) 2009, 2009, [Acccessed: 28 November 2016]. [Online]. Available: http://eprints.whiterose.ac.uk/10330/

[17] Speech-driven Environmental Control Systems (SPECS). [Acccessed: 28 November 2016]. [Online]. Available: http://www.sheffield.ac.uk/cast/projects/specs

[18] Universal Access Project. [Accessed: 28 November 2016]. [Online]. Available: http://www.isle.illinois.edu/sst/research/ua/

[19] VIVOCA Project. [Acccessed: 28 November 2016]. [Online]. Available: http://www.sheffield.ac.uk/cast/projects/vivoca

[20] A. Hatzis, P. Green, J. Carmichael, S. Cunningham, R. Palmer, M. Parker, and P. O'Neill, "An integrated toolkit deploying speech technology for computer based speech training with application to dysarthric speakers," in INTERSPEECH, 2003.

[21] CMU Sphinx - Open source speech recognition toolkit. [Accessed: 28 November 2016]. [Online]. Available: http://cmusphinx.sourceforge.net

[22] A. B. Cavalcante and L. Lorens, "Use case: a mobile speech assistant for people with speech disorders," in Proceedings of the 7th Language & Technology Conference, November 27-29, 2015, Poznan, Poland, 2015, pp. 192–197.

[23] Google Cloud Speech API. [Accessed: 29 November 2016]. [Online]. Available: https://cloud.google.com/speech/

The implementation of ERP systems in Iranian manufacturing SMEs

Maryam Rezaeian
The Business School
University of Gloucestershire
Cheltenham, UK
MaryamRezaeian@connect.glos.ac.uk

Martin Wynn
The Business School
University of Gloucestershire
Cheltenham, UK
MWynn@glos.ac.uk

Abstract **– The quest to implement Enterprise Resource Planning (ERP) software to support all main business functions has been actively pursued by in-house IT departments, software vendors and third party consultancies for over three decades. It remains a key element of many companies' information systems strategy in the developed world, and increasingly, in the developing world. In the specific context of Iranian SMEs, there has been relatively little research on information systems in general, and very little specifically on ERP systems projects. This paper attempts to help address this dearth in the existing literature by examining three case studies of ERP systems deployment in Iranian manufacturing SMEs. It investigates the underlying information systems strategies and examines how this has been implemented in the core process areas of these companies. The analysis is based on a conceptual model that combines defined implementation phases with change dimensions and elements, which provide the basis for the development of an implementation framework for subsequent ERP projects in this business and technology environment.**

Keywords – Enterprise Resource Planning; Total Systems; Iranian SMEs; information systems; ERP; process change; IS strategy; implementation framework.

I. Introduction

Enterprise Resource Planning (ERP) software packages first appeared on the market in the late 1970s and early 1980s, since when they have been widely deployed in the developed world, particularly by large corporations. Since the turn of the century, there has been an increase in the use of these integrated software systems by small to medium sized enterprises (SMEs) in the developed world. This has been paralleled – part cause, part effect – by an increase in the number of ERP vendors specifically geared to the requirements and budgets of SMEs. In the developing world, the uptake of these new systems has been slower, for a number of reasons, including the lack of the human and financial resources needed for such projects, and the non-availability of sales and support offices for many of the main ERP vendors operating in the developed world. Nevertheless, the use of ERP packages in developing world countries has accelerated in recent years, as evidenced by recent case study research [1], but the current literature suggests that there have been both significant failures [2] as well as some qualified successes [3][4].

One interesting development in Iran has been the emergence of integrated software solutions developed in the country, by and large for the home business market (Table I). These are sometimes called "Total Systems," being produced and sold by Iranian software companies. The term "ERP" is also used, but these products are usually more customizable than western based ERP products to specific user requirements, and are also available in both the Parsi language, as well as English. Although the sanctions on trade with the West have now been eased, Iranian companies tended to look within Iran for software solutions when these restrictions on trade were in place. This article examines the implementation of such packages in three Iranian SMEs and identifies the key factors involved in determining project

TABLE I. HOME GROWN ERP SYSTEMS PACKAGES IN IRAN (INDICATING VENDOR WEB ADDRESSES)

BEHKO	http://www.behko.com/?page_id=96
GREEN/ GALAX	http://www.greendataware.com/about/history/
PARS ROYAL	http://parsroyal.net/products
MEDAR GOSTARESH	http://www.itorbit.net/
HAMKARAN SYSTEM	http://www.systemgroup.net/products/%D8%B1%D8%A7%D9%87%DA%A9%D8%A7%D8%B1-%D8%AF%D9%88%D9%84%D8%AA
RAYDANA SYSTEM	http://www.danabarcode.com/
EADEGOSTAR	http://ideagostarco.net/Page/About
EADEPARDA ZAN	http://www.eadepardazan.com/pages/ltr/LTRDefault.aspx?pid=2&lang=2
RAYVARZ	https://rayvarz.com/about-us
FARAGOSTAR	http://www.faragostar.net/automation/
PARNIAN PARDAZESH PARS	http://www.parnianportal.com/OA/Pages/Home.aspx
BARID SAMANEYE NOVIN	http://www.baridsoft.ir/products/integrated-approach/office-automation

outcomes. This analysis provides the basis for the development of a framework for successful ERP project implementation in similar business contexts. This introductory section is followed in Section II by a discussion of the relevant background literature. In Section III, a description of the case study methodology used in this research is given. Sections IV then reports in some detail on the case study findings, and Section V focuses on implementation issues and what can be learned from the case examples. Finally, Section VI makes some concluding remarks that pull together a number of themes discussed in the paper.

II. Literature Review

ERP is a modular but integrated software system which automates business processes, shares common data, and produces and accesses information in a real time environment. ERP software can be implemented in stages, module by module, and therefore be used to integrate previously isolated IT systems and functional departments within a company. ERP is also viewed by some researchers [5] [6] as a fundamental method for achieving best practice within business operations – the implementation of an ERP package requiring the application of certain disciplines within main business processes. As Koch has noted; "ERP attempts to integrate all departments and functions across a company on to a single computer system that can serve all those departments' particular needs" [5]. According to Turban *et al.* [7], ERP not only provides business discipline, it also allows the alignment of IT deployment with overall business strategy and business goals. Implementing ERP thus may also require change in core processes, often termed business process reengineering or "BPR" [8].

There remain divergences of opinion regarding the suitability of systems developed in the Western world in a developing world context. When discussing IS in the developing world, Gomez and Pather [9] observe that there is a lack of literature and evaluation studies, and the World Bank view that "analysts and decision makers are still struggling to make sense of the mixed experience of information technologies in developing countries" is highlighted by other authors [10]. In spite of some evidence of failure in the adoption of information systems (IS), the overall deployment of ERP and IS in general is increasing in the developing world.

Increasing professional skills and training is viewed as a key element for successful IS project delivery by Noudoosbeni *et al.* [11], who argue that lack of planning and management as well as inadequate training led to IS project failure in Malaysian companies. Research of companies in Iran [12] [13] [14] highlight a range of issues that have hampered IS deployment in general in the country - lack of managerial skills, low IT maturity, poor training, poor internet access, governmental policies, and poor business planning; but there is very little literature on the more specific issues faced by SMEs attempting to implement ERP software. Other researchers [15] [16] suggest that the lack of human capability and economic conditions in developing countries lead to IS failure and prevent overall economic growth. There nevertheless appears to be a significant market for ERP software in SMEs in the developing world. The studies of Dezar and Ainin [17] and Arabi *et al.* [18] indicate that 90% of businesses in developing countries are SMEs; but adoption of ERP systems by SMEs in developing countries is a relatively recent undertaking, in part due to the high expense and technical complexity of such systems.

Iran is an interesting example of the potential of ERP systems in a developing world country. Talebi [19] reports that the great majority of businesses in Iran are micro, small and medium-sized enterprises. According to Molanezhad [20], the majority of SMEs in Iran are in the manufacturing sector. He also suggests that due to the location of Iran in the Middle East, its access to Russia, Europe and Asia, and its considerable market size, ERP systems have significant potential in supporting Iranian SMEs grow their business and increase their employment. This potential has been reinforced by the recent international agreement on nuclear development in Iran, and the subsequent opening up of trading with the West. Hakim and Hakim [21] assert that "IT, as a new industry in Iran, has not found its rightful place within organizations, as the managers are still adamant and adhere to the traditional management systems, and show resistance to the required organizational and infrastructural changes".

Research by Heeks [22] suggests there are several main elements of change that are important in implementing new IS in developing world environments. He identified people, process, structure and technology as key dimensions of what he termed the "design-actuality gap". Heeks' model can be used in various business change contexts, and in this paper it is used to support the analysis of the implementation of the integrated software systems in the case study companies. Other authors [6] have adopted a similar approach in looking at structures that are embedded in both packages and organisations in trying to assess the reasons for misalignments between IS strategy and the overarching business strategy of the organisation.

The process mapping technique can help assess systems deployment at process level. It generates a sequence of maps that are used in identifying the information systems that are used in defined business areas. While process mapping is used as a framework to identify the business processes and sub-processes, it can also be used as a point of reference for assessing the functionality of the information systems themselves. This "systems profiling" encompasses a review and assessment of functionality, reporting capabilities, user interface and soundness of the underlying technology [23].

There are a number of ERP and IS implementation models in the literature such as Saunders and Jones [24] Bancroft *et al.* [25], Ross [26], Markus and Tanis [27], Parr and Shanks [28] and Esteves and Pastor [29]. Most of these models identify and define a series of stages in the overall implementation process. For example, the model put forward by Markus and Tanis [27] has four stages: charter, project, shakedown and onward and outward. The Process Phase Model (PPM) developed by Parr and Shanks [28] consists of three phases planning, project and enhancement, each with its own critical success factors. The planning phase refers to activities such as package selection, appointment of a steering committee and project team members, defining project scope, determining the implementation approach and allocating resources. The project phase encompasses a range of activities from module selection to package deployment and 'go live'. The model identifies five sub-phases including set-up, re-engineering, design, configuration, and testing and installation. The enhancement phase covers system repair and maintenance, and business improvement and transformation. Ross's [26] five-phase implementation model is similar, including design, implementation, stabilization, continuous improvement, and transformation phases. The ERP life cycle model of Esteves and Pastor [29] has six phases and four dimensions. The dimensions are the different elements of change by which the phases can be analysed. The ERP life cycle model phases are: adoption decision, acquisition, implementation, use and maintenance, evolution, and retirement. The dimensions in the model refer to process, people, product and change management.

Within this context, the study addresses the following research questions (RQs):

RQ1. What has been the nature of ERP systems projects in SMEs Iran, and what has been the underlying information systems strategy?

RQ2. What lessons can be learnt from the implementation process to help guide future projects to achieve successful outcomes?

III. Research Method

The case study is a widely used research method within business research. Bryman and Bell [30] argue that the case study is particularly appropriate to be used in combination with a qualitative research method, allowing detailed and intensive research activity, usually in combination with an inductive approach as regards the relationship between theory and research. The case study is also appropriate for a combination of qualitative methods, which is of particular relevance to this study of information systems in three SMEs, where mapping and profiling techniques are combined with questionnaire and interview material. Saunders, Lewis and Thornhill [31] argue that case studies are of particular value for explanatory or exploratory investigation, such as that pursued in this research.

The case studies under investigation are manufacturing SMEs in Iran. This article reports on the findings from three case studies, for which aliases are used because of confidentiality issues. The first case study is the Isfahan Bus Company, which was founded in 1985 as a family business in Najafabad in Isfahan province. The company designs, manufactures and sells a range of buses, vans and spare parts and currently employs 350 staff. The second case study is Electronic Transmission Systems, a company employing 160 staff which was founded in 1978, and is another family business in the Isfahan province. The company designs, manufactures and distributes electronic vehicles, E-bikes, differential transmission systems (for Pride, Nissan Jounior and Tiba engines), and pinion and gear differential systems and parts. The third case study is the Spare Parts Company, which was founded in 1998 as a family business in Tehran province. The company designs, manufactures and sells spare parts for commercial vehicles (trucks, buses, minibuses and vans) and currently employs 250 staff.

Data collection was undertaken through questionnaires, interviews, and documentary evidence. Yin [32] suggests that the utilisation of multiple sources of evidence is one way of increasing the construct validity of case studies. A detailed structured questionnaire was filled in by three respondents in the first case study, two in the second and five in the third company and follow-up interviews were conducted with the questionnaire respondents. The job roles of these respondents were:

Isfahan Bus Company

Head of IT: he was heavily involved in supporting the company's main departments in specifying their requirements and in the package selection process. In the implementation phase, he had regular meetings with department heads to monitor progress and make sure they understood the implementation process.

Head of quality control and engineering: he was on the project steering group (PSG) that was responsible for selecting and implementing the ERP solution. As main user and responsible for overall project quality, he represented individual departmental needs, and met with the head of IT regularly.

Head of commercial department: he worked closely with the head of IT in the selection and implementation processes, identifying and planning training for most of the staff.

Electronic Transmission Systems

Head of IT: he was involved in selecting the ERP package, but the final decision was made by the company director, based on the recommendation of the head of IT.

Head of human resources: he was not involved in the software selection process but played an important role in post implementation, in reviewing and proposing training needs for new systems users.

Spare Parts Company

Head of IT: he was heavily involved in supporting the main departments in specifying their requirements and was in overall charge of the project team. He was involved in package selection and all implementation phases.

Head of finance: he was on the PSG and was responsible for overall financial management of the project, and more specifically for implementing the financial module of the selected ERP solution.

Head of quality control: he was on the PSG that was responsible for selecting and implementing the ERP package.

Head of sales and marketing: he worked closely with the Head of IT in the selection and implementation processes, identifying and planning training for most of the staff.

Head of production: he was not involved in the software selection process but played an important role in post implementation, in reviewing and proposing training needs for new systems users.

The questionnaire responses and follow-up interviews clarified the processes and sub-processes that are central to the companies' business operations, and allowed a mapping of current technology deployment in each process area. More specifically, the topics included in the questionnaire can be categorised as follows:

a) Company information: basic company data, company profile, size, operations and other general information.
b) Company processes: the company's main business processes and also the secondary processes (sub-processes within each main process area).
c) Information systems: the deployment of systems modules and any remaining legacy systems, and the underpinning technical architecture.
d) Current systems status: the functionality of the main information systems and general satisfaction levels in different departments that use them.
e) Problems and challenges: key problems or issues, both from a technical perspective and from the point of view of the end user; integration and interfacing of systems, report quality, systems performance.

Questionnaires and interviews were conducted in Parsi and have been translated into English.

IV. ERP Deployment and IS Strategy

This section will apply process mapping and systems profiling to the three manufacturing SMEs in Iran, with the objective of establishing the current use and functionality of ERP modules and other systems, and assessing the underpinning IS strategy.

Case Study 1: The Isfahan Bus Company (IBC)

IBC has six major top level business processes and a number of sub-processes. These are briefly outlined below, along with the information systems which currently support them (Figure 1).

The *manufacturing process* comprises three sub-processes: production planning and production, quality control, and engineering. Production planning is automated via the materials requirements planning (MRP) module of the BEHKO system. This systems module assesses the requirements for production against current company stock and suggests replenishment works orders for the appropriate dates and quantities to meet production requirements. The system takes account of current stock levels, outstanding orders, and minimum purchase order quantities. It will suggest a schedule of what should be made and when, what should be purchased and when, and current and future loading of production lines, by resource by week. This sub-process includes the bill of materials (BOM) function. When the MRP module receives an order, it will also create a list of required components to make that order. The MRP module also has additional forward planning functionality. It has the capability to plan requirements for meeting new orders and rescheduling existing orders.

In contrast, the quality control and engineering sub-processes are only partly automated. These sub-processes are supported by Microsoft Excel spreadsheets and an Access database to monitor, store and report upon key events and stock transactions. These include inspection and testing records, and inventory transactions for engineering parts.

The *sales and marketing process* is also supported by the BEHKO system. There are two sub-processes – sales management and marketing management, supported, respectively, by the BEHKO sales management module (that encompasses customer records, sales orders, price lists and quotation functions) and the BEHKO customer relationship management (CRM) module. A customer record includes customer details, customer status, and customer discounts, and is linked to the sales ledger which shows outstanding invoices and displays these along with other real time data from BEHKO so that sales and purchasing staff have a total up-to-date view of pertinent financial data for each customer. The sales order function allows the entry and editing of sales order information and the generation of sales reports. The quotation function allows the processing of requested quotes for business and the generation of quotation reports to send to customers. The BEHKO CRM module provides the systems functionality to manage and report upon sales contacts, prospects, existing customers and suppliers, in support of improved customer service and better information availability across the internal customer facing processes.

The *purchasing and procurement process* centres on purchasing management and related operations. Purchasing management is supported by the BEHKO purchasing module, which provides a full range of purchasing functions. After the MRP module calculates requirements to fulfil a works order, a purchase requisition is generated electronically to be accessed by the purchasing department and processed as a purchase order on the system; copies are also made available electronically to the finance department and processed as a purchase order on the system; copies are also made available electronically to the finance department. The BEHKO purchasing module generates unique supplier reference codes and provides purchase reports for each supplier. It also has the capability to assess suppliers' credit worthiness and overall supply performance, and also attach picture, voice or any other document to supplier files.

The BEHKO finance and accounting module supports the *financial management* process, recording and reporting the current sales order book (accounts receivable), purchase order book (accounts payable), outstanding purchase invoices and staff payments, alongside the company general ledger and cash management transactions. This system assesses current outstanding sales orders to raise sales invoice to customers, and matches goods received notes against purchase orders and purchase invoices. The module defines the financial period start and end dates and can accommodate a variety of foreign currencies and exchange rates.

The *logistics and distribution* process has three sub-processes - inventory management, primary distribution and aftersales services, and agency distribution. Inventory management is automated via the BEHKO stock control module. The primary distribution and aftersales services sub-process manages customers' orders to ensure customer delivery and post sales service. It is supported by an off-the-shelf after sales information systems package called SEVEN.

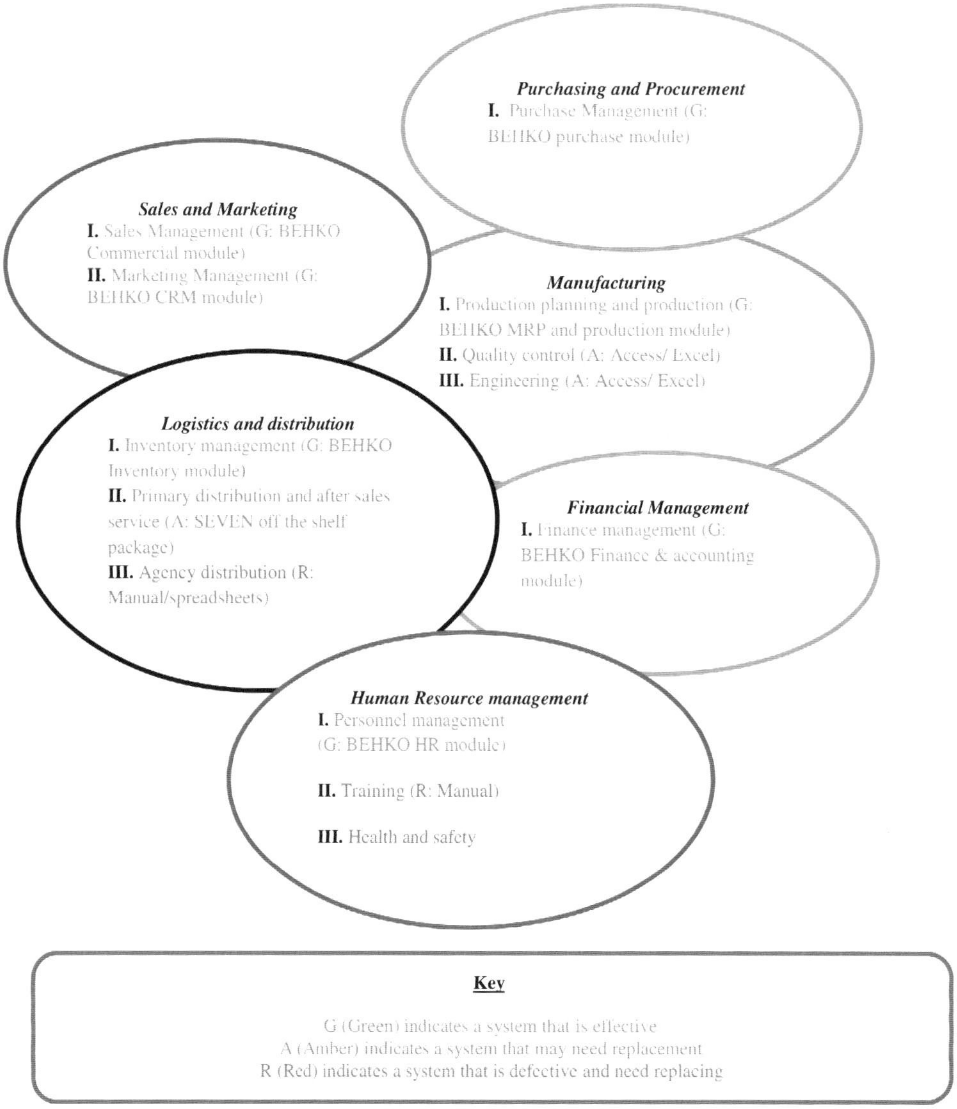

Figure 1. Main Business Processes and IS profiling at IBC

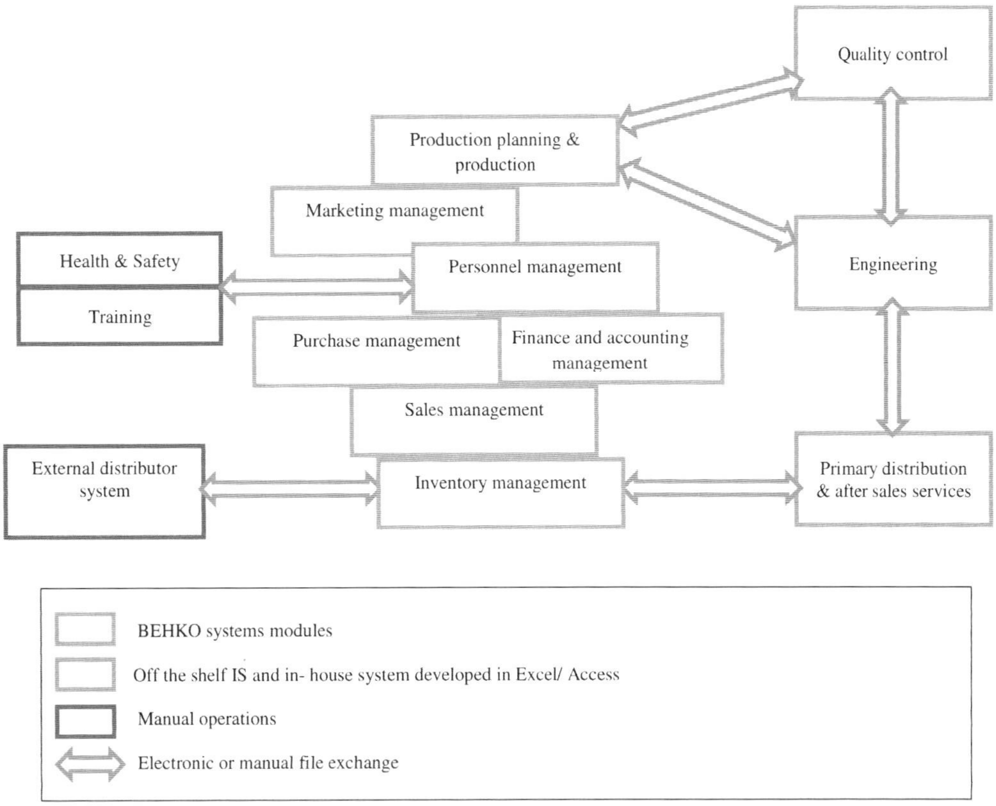

Figure 2. Systems Interfaces at IBC

The agency distribution sub-process involves the sale of spare parts for buses and other vehicles via company agencies located in different cities in Iran. This process is partly manual and partly automated by use of spreadsheets.

The *human resource (HR) management* process can be subdivided into three main sub-processes: personnel management handles employee records (including payment, staff absence and leave, and timesheet recording) and this is centrally managed and automated using the BEHKO HR systems module. There are also the staff training and health and safety sub- processes, which are mainly manual.

The information system strategy adopted at IBC has been to implement modules of the BEHKO total system in the core process areas of the business, some of which have been customized to meet the specific requirements of the company. BEHKO is an Iranian software company, and its selection was based on functionality, language – it uses both Parsi and English – and easy access for systems support and upgrade. IBC pursued a phased implementation to enable a careful phasing out of previous systems and a managed exchange of data between old and new systems. In addition, it allowed staff to adapt to the changes in systems and procedures in an orderly and controlled manner.

Many modules were customised based on requested requirements specified by senior management in each process area. In all, it took three years to implement the system, but even now some sub-processes are still manual or are supported by using spreadsheets and semi-automated file exchanges (Figure 2). Although the BEHKO system modules are well integrated, there is no effective integration with the stand alone SEVEN system, nor with the MS Excel and MS Access applications. The BEHKO system is developed in C++ and uses the SQL database and is administered by senior managers who have access to all system generated reports and invoices. These reports include key business performance information, providing an overview of all sales, purchases, stock levels, and financial data and staff reports.

IBC has five servers comprising a database server, software server, backup server, webserver (mainly for email), and antivirus server. Windows 2012 R2 is installed on all the servers as the operating system. Microsoft SQL 2008 was installed on the database server, whilst the BEHKO modules run on the software server. Database backup and vital files archiving are done on the backup server every day. In addition, IBC has installed the McAfee antivirus software on all desktop computers and all software updates are managed by the antivirus server. The Internet connection installed in IBC is both wired and wireless. All departments are connected via an intranet that is controlled by privilege policy that manages the workflow. They follow a single sign-on technique; therefore, they have 100 desktops that are available to 100 or more users. IBC have also provided twenty portable devices (laptops) if needed by staff members for off-site working, or presentations and meetings. All PCs run under the Windows 10 operating system and have MS Office available. IBC uses a private VLAN and cisco switch to separate each server for higher security and privacy. The company uses firewall network security, located in three different physical areas, to prevent unauthorised access from other networks.

The current IS strategy at IBC was adopted in 2008 in support of the company's business strategy to expand production and drive up bottom-line company profit. The strategy was a formal decision made by a committee comprising selected managers from across all departments - commercial, finance, production, engineering, quality control, and the IT manager. Previous systems were a mix of off the shelf packages and end-user applications. The initial focus was in the logistics and distribution process area, to establish consistent inventory product codes and simplify and standardise product information for both internal processes and also for customer facing sales and marketing departments. After a successful six month parallel run of old and new systems in this area in 2008, the BEHKO systems modules were introduced in stages, completing in 2012. The software vendor continues to provide support and upgrades, and IBC is now planning a major upgrade to the BEHKO ERP product in 2017. This package includes improved functionality which should allow the replacement of the SEVEN package and other standalone applications.

Case Study 2: Electronic Transmission Systems (ETS)

Initial process mapping suggests there are six top level business processes, and each process has several sub-processes. The processes are depicted in Figure 3, along with the information systems which currently support these business processes.

The *manufacturing process* comprises three sub-processes: quality control, production planning, and production and assembly. The quality control sub-process encompasses the inspection of both purchased and manufactured parts and products, and the recording and monitoring of test results. The GREEN/GALAX quality control module records and manages all data associated with product sampling, testing and results recording and reporting. Security aspects are supported by systems controls on access, allowing only staff with the required skills and competence levels to undertake inspection testing.

The production planning sub-process is automated with the GREEN/GALAX materials requirements planning (MRP) module, which determines the quantity and timing of component purchases. MRP stores the bills of materials and explodes these into requirements, based on received orders, and will then compare the demands to available company stock to generate necessary procurement requirements. The production and assembly sub-process encompasses production control and final inspection operations. The GREEN/GALAX production module also provides time estimates for parts delivery at production line and for final inspection of finished products. The production team can attach drawings of product designs and technical specifications to job sheet records.

The *inventory management* process covers stock control and is partly automated with MS Excel spreadsheets monitoring manufactured and component products in and out of the stockrooms. The *product design* process is automated with a range of off-the-shelf design and planning software packages, including Catia V5R18, MSC Super Forge, Master CAM 9.0, Autodesk Mechanical desktop 2007, Power Mill 6.0, Primavera Project planner, MS Project 2007, and Minitab 13.0. This process encompasses the design and drawing of company products based on received orders and customer specifications.

The *commercial management* process has two sub-processes - customer management and supplier management – and both are supported by the GREEN/GALAX commercial management module. This module supports the categorization and management of both customers and suppliers, and recording of relevant details. The *financial management* process is similarly supported by a GREEN/GALAX module. There are two sub-processes: accounts management, and general ledger/asset management. The system manages financial activities, financial figures and reports and invoices; it contains the ledgers for sales and purchase transactions, and records company assets, liabilities, owners' equity, revenue, and expenses.

The *human resource management* process covers personnel management, including employee records, staff absence and leave, and timesheets. The process is mainly manual. Employees have their own identity and attendance card, which are checked and monitored by security guards at the company entrance. Annual leave is also authorised and recorded by a manual, paper-based system.

The information system strategy adopted at ETS is based on the GREEN/GALAX ERP package, combined with point solutions developed in MS Excel. The choice of the main software system again was influenced by the fact that it was available in the Parsi language and there was easy access to software support and technical advisors.

The current IS strategy was adopted in 2014 and was a formal decision made by the IT manager in conjunction with the company director. Modules of the GREEN/GALAX ERP were implemented simultaneously in core business functions in the period October to December 2014. The company has two servers - a database server and a webserver, the Windows 2012 R2 operating system having been installed on both of these. Microsoft SQL 2008 was installed on the database server, on which database back up is scheduled daily, in addition to offsite back up. GREEN/GALAX modules, website and email run on the webserver. Wired and wireless Internet access is installed. They have 25 desktop computers that are available to 27 or more users. ETS provides three portable devices (laptops) if needed by staff for off-site working, presentations or meetings. All PCs run under the Windows 10 operating system and MS Office is used for personal productivity tools and email. The GREEN/GALAX system was developed in C++ and uses the Microsoft SQL 2008 database. The GREEN/GALAX system has a drop list that enables the user to choose which subsystem they wish to access based on their department and login. All users log onto the system with personalised user IDs and passwords allowing different accesses and privileges. This is controlled by thee head of each department who can grant users with additional or restricted access and permissions.

Unfortunately, training was poor and insufficient and there have been significant user issues with some departments reverting to previous semi-manual processes. There also remain a number of file exchange operations whereby data is extracted from the GREEN/GALAX system and input into standalone applications for inventory management and product design (see Figure 4). In 2015, external consultants were engaged to review the status of the ERP project and specifically to provide training and user support. Despite this initiative, there remain significant issues to address. The implementation of new modules has not been adequately coordinated with changes in people capability. The HR system needs to be automated and integrated with finance and the accounting department to prevent duplication and data inconsistencies in payroll. Similarly, the inventory management module of the GREEN/GALAX system needs to be ushered in to provide consistent product codes and enhance the capability and functionality of company business activities. The company needs to address the training issue to encourage and support staff in using all of the available functions in the new system.

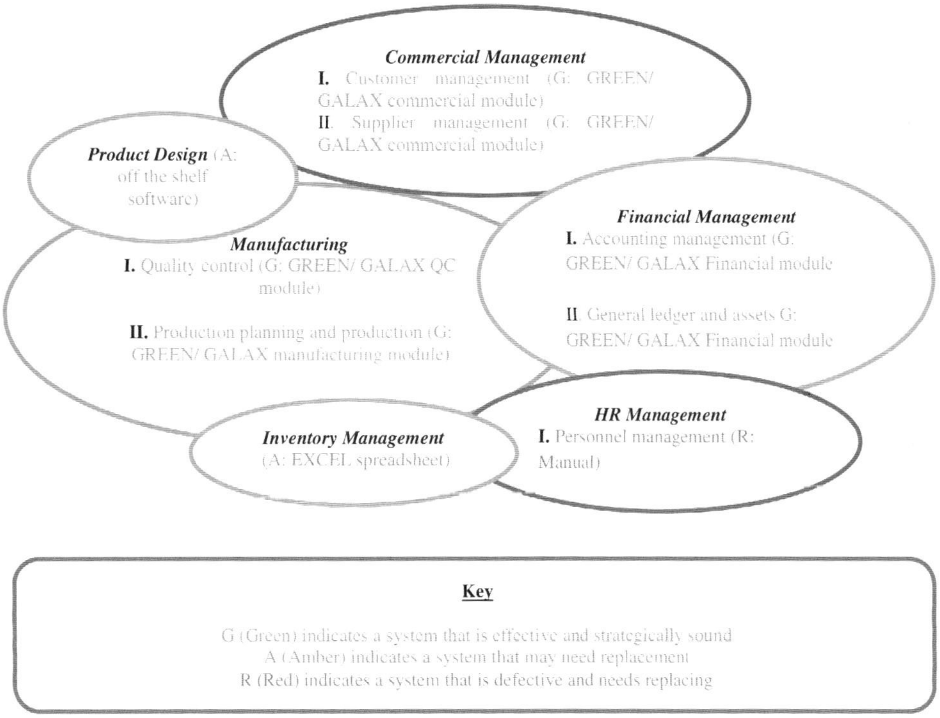

Figure 3. Main Business Processes and IS profiling at ETS

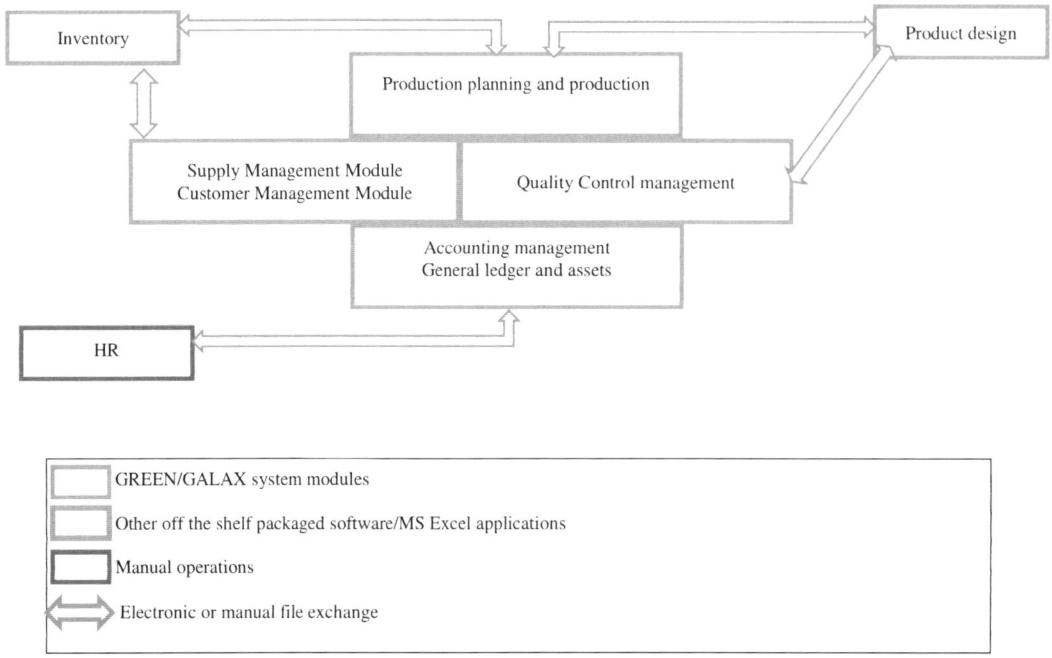

Figure 4. Systems Interfaces at ETS

Case Study 3: Spare Parts Company (SPC)

Initial process mapping suggests there are five top level business processes, and each process has several sub-processes. The processes are depicted in Figure 5, along with the information systems which currently support these business processes.

The *manufacturing process* in this company comprises two sub-processes: production/production planning, and maintenance/engineering. Production and production planning are supported by HAMKARAN manufacturing and operations module. The production/production planning sub- process reacts to forecast demand to generate works orders and procurement requirements to meet those orders. Users are also able to specify cumulative lead times they want to allow for order fulfilment, and also record human resource availability patterns for production. Users also record quality inspection details and outcomes across the internal supply chain from component parts to finished products. The maintenance and engineering sub-process, however, is only partly automated with Microsoft Excel spreadsheets.

The *sales and marketing process* is automated and supported by the HAMKARAN sales and marketing modules. This allows data entry and recording of relevant details for prospects and customers, price lists, and quotations, and reporting and tracking of sales orders, despatches and outstanding invoices, and the monitoring of credit control status of customers and sales performance. The sales team can change product prices and apply discount for specific customers or products.

The *financial management* process is automated using the HAMKARAN finance and accounting module, which is closely integrated with the other HAMKARAN modules. The finance and accounting module is used to prepare financial reports in compliance with Iranian accounting standards and international financial regulations. Standard reports are available from the general ledger, accounts payable, and accounts receivable, including evaluation of payment and cash discount histories.

Figure 5. Main Business Processes and IS profiling at SPC

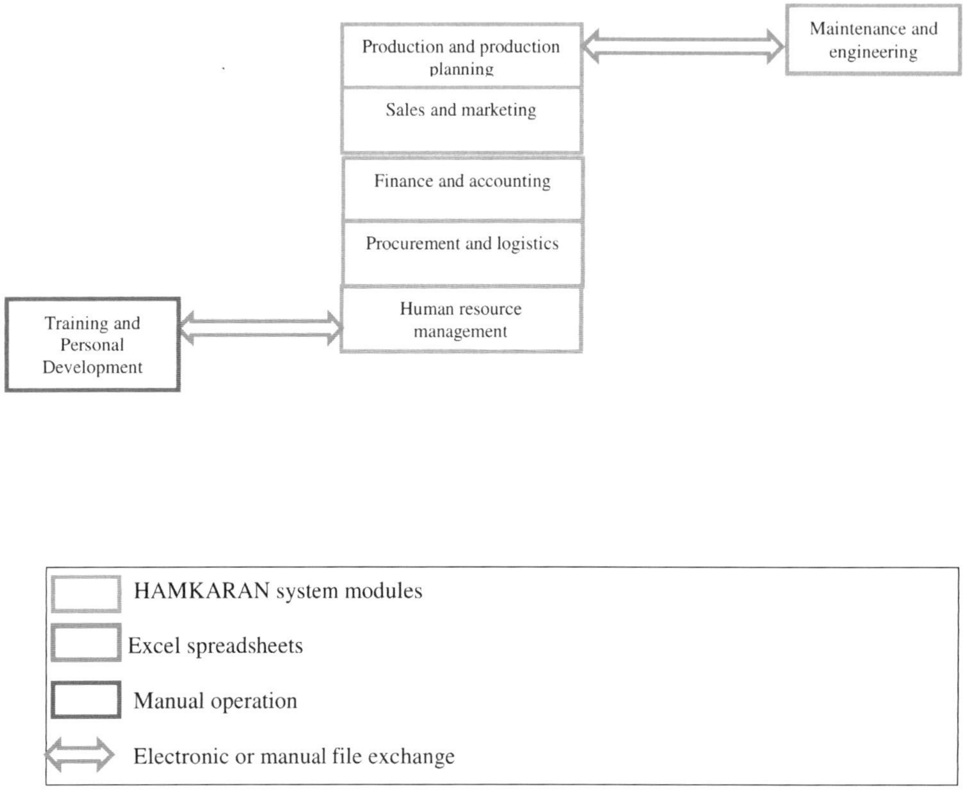

Figure 6. Systems Interfaces at SPC

The *human resources process* has two sub-processes - employee administration, which is automated with the HAMKARAN HR module, and training and personal development, which remains a manually recorded operation. The HR module includes full employee records, payment details, holiday and absence recording and payslip generation. It also has a full payroll function that integrates with production time records.

The *procurement and logistics process* encompasses inventory, purchasing and distribution management which are integrated and automated via the HAMKARAN procurement and logistics module. Once a works order is raised and MRP has calculated requirements based on available stock, a procurement request is processed through the HAMKARAN procurement and logistics module to produce purchase requisitions and purchase orders. This module also has functionality to support both inward and outward distribution, generating reports of expected deliveries against customer orders, and also reporting on finished product distribution.

The information system strategy adopted at SPC has been based around the phased introduction of the HAMKARAN ERP system. HAMKARAN is an Iranian product and the selection was again influenced by language (it uses Parsi), and availability of the Parsi calendar within the system. It also uses mainstream technologies, having been developed in C++ and Asp.Net (3.5/4.0) and runs on the Microsoft SQL server data base. SPC has four servers consisting of a database server running Microsoft SQL, a software server (on which are installed modules of HAMKARAN system), a web and email server, and a backup server. The Windows 2012 R2 operating system is installed on all servers, and the IT manager backs up the data from various servers on a weekly basis. Network connections installed in SPC are both wireless and cable, and all departments are connected via a local area network (LAN). All users have their own specific privileges which are determined by heads of department, and the privileges and accesses of heads of department are authorised by the company director. There are 50 desktop computers for 50 users, besides three portable devices (two laptops and an IPad) for off-site undertakings. All desktop computers run under the windows 10 operating system and have MS Office installed.

Another factor that influenced software selection was ease of access to the software company for software maintenance or upgrades. SPC elected to pursue a phased implementation to allow employees to adapt gradually to changes in their systems and ways of working. All modules were installed simultaneously in 2011 on a few desktop computers and the database server, and some key users were trained up in the use of the system. Systems modules were then installed on other desktops and users trained accordingly. Only then were some users put live, but this was done in phases and followed the order of the training programme. The financial systems users were first to use the new system, followed by manufacturing process users, sales and marketing, procurement and logistics and finally human resources users. Overall this roll-out and move to 'go live' took 4 months in the period November 2011 to February 2012. The project as a whole – encompassing the three phases as depicted Figures 5 and 6 – took an elapsed time of about 18 months spanning 2011-12. The HAMKARAN systems modules are integrated, but links with the Excel spreadsheet in the maintenance and engineering process is still done by file exchange. Nevertheless, the new ERP is now bedding in reasonably well, with the efficiency benefits of automating former manual processes now being delivered.

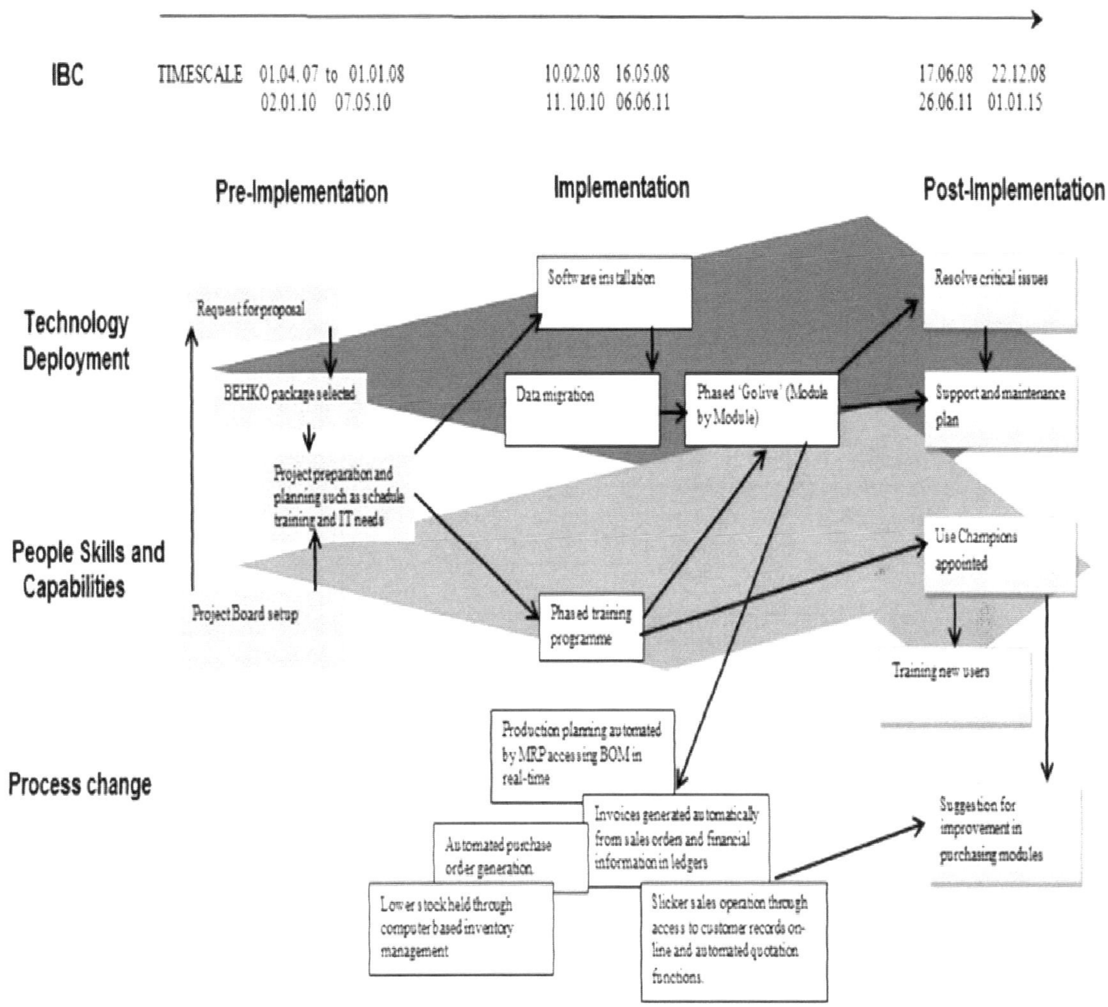

Figure 7. ERP Implementation at IBC

V. Implementation Issues

The current information system strategies at all three companies have some similarities. They all elected to adopt an ERP package from Iranian based software suppliers, to provide the benefits of integrated systems and consistent management information to support company growth aspirations. In all three companies, however, some of the old legacy systems remain in some core process areas, and these are likely to be replaced in the near future with appropriate ERP systems modules.

There were significant differences between the three companies' strategy implementation approaches. At IBC, the strategy development and its implementation was agreed to, and guided by, a cross-departmental steering group that carefully managed a phased implementation of the BEHKO ERP product, providing the necessary training and support for end-users. At ETS, the GREEN/GALAX ERP package was selected as a result of discussions between the IT manager and the company director, and lacked cross-company involvement and support. Implementation was simultaneous in most process areas, increasing the risk of systems problems and data issues. This was compounded by the absence of adequate training and support for end-users, which left the project in a parlous state. Only recently has the engagement of third party support helped to provide much needed training and bed in the new systems modules. At SPC, a phased implementation of the HAMKARAN ERP was successfully undertaken, the project spanning 2011-12

This analysis reinforces the findings of Heeks [22] and other recent studies [33][34][35] that suggest large scale technology implementation, even in SMEs, must be accompanied by appropriate process improvement and an upgrade in people skills to accommodate the new ways of working that are often introduced with new systems modules. There are a some elements of people change that affect ERP implementation throughout the project duration - employee skills (IT and computer literacy), awareness of goals and objectives, appropriate selection of project team and project board, identification of main users (including system champions) and clarity on their responsibilities and roles, planning and training, and having an effective project manager. The people change dimension had a very significant impact on the other dimensions of change (process and technology) in all three cases. Project team and project board decisions at IBC and SPC regarding package and module selection, customisation (at IBC), implementation strategy, and the organisation of the training programme impacted the project positively. The influence of competent project manager(s) is equally important. At IBC and SPC, project managers worked closely with the companies' IT managers - a combination of internal managers who knew the business and external managers who were expert in ERP positively affected project outcomes in a number of ways (such as technology decisions regarding IT infrastructure, implementation strategy, package selection).

Awareness of goals and objectives of the project and a willingness to broadcast them to users to involve them in all stages of the ERP project influenced the implementation process at IBC and SPC. By involving users throughout the project, they were motivated to work as a team. Involving users and sharing the goals and objectives developed a shared perspective with management and fully engaged them in the ERP project. By contrast, at ETS, the gap between top managers and the main users was detrimental to the whole project. The management style was in many ways typical of the Iranian private organisation culture, and put the project at risk. The majority of SMEs in Iran are private family businesses, managed by the owners, who make most of the decisions regarding such projects. This can act against the likelihood of overall project success which requires that all employees buy into the chosen solution and the implementation process.

Manufacturing SMEs in Iran need to be prepared for the process change challenges that are inevitable during a successful ERP project. Businesses should be prepared to modify their processes to fit the ERP system if necessary. The potential misalignment of current business processes with the business model underpinning the ERP system can increase the need for customisation, which negatively affects other project factors, resulting in potential budget cost overruns and exceeding the project timeline. It is important for SMEs in Iran to define their business processes clearly before selecting their package. The case studies also highlight the importance of communication across various stages of implementation. Communicating and sharing goals, objectives and process change plans encourages users to accept these changes and reduces resistance.

This is best illustrated at IBC (Figure 7), where a carefully managed implementation was done department by department, in parallel with a phased training programme for managers and key users. The role of the cross-departmental steering group was critical in guiding the project through a number of key activities, from the request for proposal from ERP suppliers, to the selection process itself, through the phased implementation, the conduct of the training programme and to the final agreement of a support and maintenance plan. It is the project at IBC that perhaps best illustrates a model for future ERP projects in similar companies in Iran.

VI. Concluding Remarks

The case studies of the implementation of three home grown ERP products in Iranian SMEs revealed some interesting results. These ERP products are structured in a similar manner to their western counterparts, albeit they appear to allow greater flexibility in customisation to specific users' needs. The projects were generally successful, being the product of a fairly straightforward IS strategy of replacing old manual and legacy systems with new ERP modules. At ETS, however, there is still a need for more training to ensure the system is used effectively and owned by the users themselves. The implementation process was a little different in the three cases, and the successful outcome at IBC suggests a phased approach is likely to be most successful in which people change elements (steering group, project leadership, training and skills upgrade) are put in place in parallel with technology implementation.

The case studies also provide some interesting insights into the ERP market in Iran, where, with international sanctions now lifted, the opportunities for western based ERP vendors are likely to be enhanced. However, the home-grown ERP (Total Systems) packages have an established user base which is likely to grow, in the short-term at least, given the benefits of customisation and operation in the Parsi language that most of these packages offer.

REFERENCES

[1] M. Rezaeian and M. Wynn, "Implementing Integrated Software Solutions in Iranian SMEs," eKNOW 2016 : The Eighth International Conference on Information, Process, and Knowledge Management, Venice, ThinkMind, pp. 76-84, ISBN: 978-1-61208-472-5

[2] A. Hawari and R. Heeks, "Explaining ERP failure in a developing country: a Jordanian case study," Journal of Enterprise Information Management, Vol. 23 (2), pp. 135-160, 2010.

[3] H. Akeel and M. Wynn, "ERP Implementation in a Developing World Context: a Case Study of the Waha Oil Company, Libya," eKNOW 2015, The Seventh International Conference on Information, Process and Knowledge Management, Lisbon., Feb 22nd – Feb 27th. ThinkMind, ISBN: 978-1-61208-386-5; ISSN: 2308-4375

[4] M. Moohebat, M. Jazi and A. Aseni, "Evaluation of ERP implementation at the Esfahan Steele Company," International Journal of Business and Management, Vol. 6 (5), pp. 236-250, 2011.

[5] C. Koch, "The ABCs of ERP," CIO Magazine, Dec 1999.

[6] C. Soh and S. Sia, "An institutional perspective on sources of ERP package organization misalignments," Journal of Strategic Information Systems, Vol.13 (4), pp. 375-397, 2004.

[7] E. Turban, E. McLean, J. Wetherbe, N. Bolloju and R. Davison, Information Technology for Management – Transforming Business in the Digital Economy, 3rd ed., John Wiley & Sons, New York, 2002.

[8] M. Hammer and J. Champny, Re-engineering the Corporation: A Manifesto for Business Revolution, Harper Business, New York, 1993.

[9] R. Gomez and S. Pather, "ICT evaluation: are we asking the right questions?" Electronic Journal of Information Systems in Developing Countries (EJISDC), Vol. 50 (5), pp. 1-14, 2012.

[10] S. Batchelor, S. Evangelista, S. Hearn, M. Pierce, S. Sugden and M. Webb, ICT for Development: Contributing to the Millenium Development Goals – Lessons Learnt from Seventeen infoDev projects, Wasington DC: World Bank, 2003.

[11] A. Noudoosbeni, N. Ismail and H. Jenatabadi, "An effective end-user knowledge concern training method in enterprise resource planning (ERP) based on critical factors (CFS) in Malaysian SMEs," International Journal of Production Economics, Vol. 115 (2), pp. 72-85, 2010.

[12] A. Shahin, S. Sadri and R. Gazor, "Evaluating the Application of Learning Requirements Planning Model in the ERP project of Esfahan Steel Company," International Journal of Business Management, Vol. 5 (2), pp. 33-43, 2010.

[13] P. Hanifzade and M. Nikabadi, "Framework for Selection of an Appropriate e- Business Model in Managerial Holding Companies: case study: Iran Khodro," Journal of Enterprise Information Management, Vol. 24 (3), pp. 237-267, 2010.

[14] A. Amid, M. Moalagh and A. Ravasan, "Identification and classification of ERP critical factors in Iranian industries," Journal of Information Systems, Vol. 37, pp. 227-237, 2011.

[15] M. Warschauer, "Dissecting the Digital Devide: A case study in Egypt," The Information Society, Vol.19 (4), pp. 7-24, 2003.

[16] R. Wade, "Bridging the Digital Divide: New Route to Development or New Form of Dependency?," Journal of Global Governance, Vol. 8 (4), pp. 443- 466, 2002.

[17] S. Dezar and S. Ainin, "ERP implementation success in Iran: examining the role of systems environment factors," World Academy of Science, Engineering and Technology, Vol. 42, pp. 449-455, 2010.

[18] M. Arabi, M. Zameri, K. Wong, H. Beheshti and N. Zakuan, "Critical Success Factors of Enterprise Resource Planning Implementation in Small and Medium Enterprises in Developing Countries: A Review and Research Direction," Proceedings of Industrial Engineering and Service Science, 2011,http://www.academia.edu/1083186/Critical_Success_Factors_of_Enterprise_ResourcePlanning_Implementation_in_small_and_medium_enterprises_in_developing_countries:_a_Review_and_Research_Direction/ [Retrieved: March, 2016]

[19] K. Talebi, "How should the entrepreneurs of SMEs in Iran change their style in a business life cycle?" Iranian Journal of Management Studies (IJMS), Vol. 1 (1), pp. 10-17, 2007.

[20] M. Molanezhad, "A Brief Review of Science and Technology and SMEs Development in Iran," The inter-sessional panel of the United Nations commission on science and technology for development, 2010.

[21] A. Hakim and H. Hakim, "A practical model on controlling ERP implementation risks," Journal of Information Systems, Vol. 35, pp. 204-214, 2012.

[22] R. Heeks, "Information Systems and Developing Countries: Failure, Success, and Local Improvisations," Journal of Information Society, Vol.18 (2), pp. 101-112, 2002.

[23] M. Wynn and O. Olubanjo, "Demand-supply chain management: systems implications in an SME packaging business in the UK," International Journal of Manufacturing Research, Vol 7 (2), pp. 198-212, 2012.

[24] C.S. Saunders and J.W. Jones, "Measuring performance of the information systems function," Journal of Management Information Systems, Vol.8(4), 63-82. 1992.

[25] N. Bancroft, H. Seip and A Sprengel, Implementing SAP R/3. 2nd ed., 1998 Greenwich: Manning Publications

[26] J.W. Ross "Surprising facts about implementing ERP," IT professional, Vol. 1(4), pp.65-68, 1999.

[27] M. L. Markus and C. Tanis, "The enterprise systems experience-from adoption to success," Framing the domains of IT research: Glimpsing the future through the past, pp. 173-207, 2000.

[28] A. Parr and G. Shanks, "A model of ERP project implementation," Journal of Information Technology, 15(4), pp. 289–304, 2000.

[29] J. Esteves and J. Pastor, "An ERP life-cycle-bnased research agenda," 1st International Workshop in Enterprise Management and Resource Planning: Methods, Tools and Architectures, Venice, 1999.

[30] A. Bryman and E. Bell, Business Research Methods, 3rd edition, Oxford: Oxford University Press, 2011.

[31] M. Saunders, P. Lewis and A. Thornhill, Research methods for business students, 5th ed., 2009, England: Pearson Education Limited.

[32] R. K. Yin, Applications of Case Study Research. 3rd ed., 2012, London: SAGE Publications, Inc

[33] M. Wynn, P. Turner, A. Banik, and A. G. Duckworth, "The impact of customer relationship management systems in small businesses," Strategic Change, Vol 25 Issue 6, pp. 655–670, 2016. Published online in Wiley Online Library (wileyonlinelibrary.com) DOI: 10.1002/jsc.2100.

[34] M. Wynn and M. Rezaeian, "ERP implementation in manufacturing SMEs: Lessons from the Knowledge Transfer Partnership scheme," InImpact: The Journal of Innovation Impact, Vol. 8 No. 1, 2015: Innovation through Knowledge Transfer 2015, pp. 75-92. Online Edition - ISSN: 2051-6002. Print Edition - ISBN: 978-1-911108-03-0

[35] P. Mangin, V. Hovelaque, and L. Bironneau, "Enterprise Resource Planning contribution to firm performance: A literature review over the last 15 years," 11th Congrés International de Genie Industrial - CIGI2015, Québec, Canada, 26-28 October 2015.